Contemporary Human Sexuality

Jeffrey S. Turner
Mitchell College

Laurna Rubinson
University of Illinois/Urbana-Champaign

PRENTICE HALL
Englewood Cliffs, New Jersey 07632

Library of Congress Cataloging-in-Publication Data

TURNER, JEFFREY S.
　　Contemporary human sexuality/Jeffrey S. Turner, Laurna Rubinson.
　　　　p.　　　　cm.

　　Includes bibliographical references and index.
　　ISBN 0-13-175282-0
　　　　1. Sex instruction for youth.　2. Sex.　3. Hygiene, Sexual.
　　4. Sexual ethics.　I. Rubinson, Laurna.　II. Title.
　　HQ35.2.T87　1993
　　306.7—dc20　　　　　　　　　　　　　　　　　　　92-30706
　　　　　　　　　　　　　　　　　　　　　　　　　　　　CIP

Acquisitions Editor: Susan Finnemore Brennan
Editor-in-Chief: Charlyce Jones Owen
Development Editor: Virginia Otis Locke
Production Editor: Mary Anne Shahidi
Copy Editor: Carole Freddo
Cover, Interior Design, and Page Layout: Lorraine Mullaney
Art Director: Florence Dara Silverman/Anne T. Bonanno
Supplements Editor: Sharon Chambliss
Prepress Buyer: Kelly Behr
Manufacturing Buyer: Mary Ann Gloriande
Editorial Assistants: Jennie Katsaros, Asha Rohra
Photo Researcher: Ilene Cherna Bellovin
Photo Editor: Lorinda Morris-Nantz
Marketing Manager: Tracey Masella McPeake
Cover Art: "Picture from a Larger Cycle," by Jan Preisler, 1902.
　　　　National Gallery, Prague/Art Resource.

Dedicated with special appreciation to

My treasured friend and respected colleague,
Donald B. Helms (JST)

My mother, and in loving memory of my father,
and to my friends and colleagues
who supported me
throughout this project (LR)

Printed in the United States of America
10　9　8　7　6　5　4　3　2　1

ISBN 0-13-175282-0

Prentice-Hall International (UK) Limited, *London*
Prentice-Hall of Australia Pty. Limited, *Sydney*
Prentice-Hall Canada Inc., *Toronto*
Prentice-Hall Hispanoamericana, S.A., *Mexico*
Prentice-Hall of India Private Limited, *New Delhi*
Prentice-Hall of Japan, Inc., *Tokyo*
Simon & Schuster Asia Pte. Ltd., *Singapore*
Editora Prentice-Hall do Brasil, Ltda., *Rio de Janeiro*

Contents

9 Sexual Orientation 250

PART FOUR: SEXUALITY AND REPRODUCTION

10 Conception and Pregnancy 285

PART SIX: PROBLEMS IN HUMAN SEXUALITY

16   Sexual Dysfunctions   474

17   Sexual Health and Disease   502

18 The Acquired Immune Deficiency Syndrome (AIDS)   538

19 Exploitive and Atypical Sexual Behaviors   566

20 Sexual Coercion: Rape   594

PART SEVEN: SEX AND THE LAW

21   Legal Issues and Concerns   621

Preface

Knowledge is power only when it is properly used. Young people today know a great deal more than their elders did about such topics as contraception and sexually transmitted diseases, but they often do not apply what they know. Much has been said about the sense of invulnerability that allows the young to engage in risk-taking behaviors. Perhaps they need this seemingly impenetrable armor as they try to meet the many challenges that growing and maturing present. But perhaps, too, we can lessen this need. As teachers of human sexuality for a combined total of nearly forty years, we have both become convinced that the more we help students apply the information we share with them the closer we come to bridging the gap between knowledge and action.

Thus our first and basic goal in writing this textbook has been to give the reader a balanced presentation of theory and data, on the one hand, and of practical application, on the other. Throughout the text we use everyday examples to show students how the information we discuss can be useful to them. And in our boxed inserts and discussion questions we provide further illustrations of how to make practical use of the scholarly and up-to-date information that we provide and to think critically about issues such as the prevention of sexually transmitted diseases, and the control of rape and other violent and abusive sexually related behaviors.

Our second and equally important goal is to engage students in exploring their attitudes, beliefs, and feelings about the many topics discussed and in developing greater sensitivity to the attitudes, beliefs, and feelings of others. We hope students will use our examination of different value systems in choosing their own values and in making responsible decisions about their sexual lives. We hope that an understanding not only of specifically sexual needs but of needs for love, intimacy, and sharing will help readers to create and maintain healthy and fulfilling relationships with others.

The 1990s have seen many issues revolving around human sexuality come to the forefront of our attention. HIV infection and the acquired immune deficiency syndrome, as well as other sexually transmitted diseases; rising teenage pregnancy rates; the increasing incidence of reported rape and other exploitive, abusive, and violent behaviors—sexual harassment, child sexual abuse, incest—demand that we acquire a better understanding of the causes of such behaviors, more effective ways of preventing their occurrence, and better ways of treating their victims.

Contemporary Human Sexuality provides in-depth, scholarly coverage of these and other topics in the spotlight today. It addresses these issues thoughtfully and sensitively, examining the importance and relevance of each to the student's life. Designed primarily for a one-semester, undergraduate human sexuality course, our book cuts across disciplines, blending biological, psychological, and cultural aspects of human sexuality.

A Contemporary Focus

Every chapter of this book discusses material that has significance for young people today. A few topics, however, are particularly crucial for the 1990s: AIDS, sexual communication, and sexual values.

Preface

ACQUIRED IMMUNE DEFICIENCY SYNDROME. Probably nothing in recent history has had such grave implications for our sexual behavior as the advent of HIV infection and AIDS-related illnesses. In our chapter on AIDS we include the latest information on progress in the prevention and treatment of this major health problem. We examine modes of transmission, symptoms, and the various opportunistic infections to which a person living with AIDS is prone. We also explore public response to AIDS and AIDS patients and the legal ramifications of living with the illness.

SEXUAL COMMUNICATION. Clear sexual communication is indispensable to responsible sexual behavior. In our chapter on communication we examine the importance of the honest expression of thoughts and feelings about sexual matters, not only between sexual partners but between parents and children, teachers and students. We feel strongly that effective communication is the foundation for lasting and satisfying intimate human relationships, and we underscore the importance of communication throughout the entire book. Whether the topic is understanding another's values, making responsible sexual choices, talking with a child or adolescent about sexual behavior, or working through a sexual problem with a partner, we stress the importance of intelligent, sensitive, skilled, and caring communication.

SEXUAL VALUES. Like communication, the issue of values is threaded throughout the text. Thus in different chapters we discuss the ethical and moral implications of such matters as premarital sex; assisted reproductive techniques; high-risk sexual behaviors such as unprotected sex and sex with persons at risk for STDs; both the pro-choice and pro-life positions on abortion; and pornography. As a foundation for these discussions, we devote a full section of Chapter 6 to examining different value orientations and exploring the development of value systems.

Focus on Applying Knowledge

Each of our five series of boxes is designed, in a specific way, to help readers apply what they have learned. Together, these series supplement and amplify the practical examples given throughout the text.

"MAKING USE OF WHAT WE KNOW." Many of these boxes offer practical suggestions for everyday life, such as how to do breast and testicular self-examinations and how to talk with a partner about responsible lovemaking. In other boxes readers are offered self-tests that enable them to measure such things as their present sexual values and their capacity for intimacy.

"A WORLD OF DIFFERENCES." In these boxes, which highlight multicultural differences and similarities, we promote students' sensitivity and tolerance for the beliefs and practices of others. Increasing our understanding of other peoples and of the infinite variety of human behavior can be an effective tool in learning to make our own decisions about sexual behavior.

"MYTHS AND MISCONCEPTIONS." False beliefs and ideas about human sexuality may not only reflect lack of knowledge but may prevent one from applying the knowledge one has. In this series of boxes we try to dispel many misconceptions that help to perpetuate unsatisfying and risky sexual behaviors.

"SEXUALITY IN THE NEWS." In these boxes, which appear at the end of every chapter, students see the real-life application of many important topics discussed in the text. Some boxes overview videos from the Prentice Hall–ABC Video Library (see "Supplements"). Others reprint timely and relevant articles from *The New York Times*. All of these boxes include discussion questions that encourage students to relate the material to the text and to think critically about the issues raised.

Pedagogy

Again with the intent of bridging the gap between knowledge and its application, we have adopted a pedagogical structure that emphasizes reference to questions of everyday life.

CHAPTER ORGANIZATION. Each chapter opens with a "Looking Ahead" section that alerts students to important topics covered and closes with a linked, "Looking Back" section that summarizes the crucial points made in the chapter. "Thinking Things Over" questions require students to consider issues covered in the chapter and to apply their knowledge to real-life situations. Some questions suggest practical exercises for students alone or in groups. "Discover for Yourself" sections list and annotate additional readings that we think the student will find useful.

QUESTIONS MOST COMMONLY ASKED BY STUDENTS. Drawing on our teaching careers, we have assembled some of the questions about human sexuality that students most often ask. These real-life questions appear in the margins next to the passages that address them.

QUOTATIONS FROM THE AUTHORS' FILES. Throughout the textbook actual quotations from the authors' students and others illustrate and expand on significant ideas. These quotations are indented and appear in color.

MARGIN GLOSSARY. A formal definition of each key term that is boldfaced in the text appears next to that term, in the margin. All definitions also appear in an alphabetized glossary at the back of the book.

ILLUSTRATIONS. Our book includes approximately 100 figures and other line drawings, as well as a number of useful tables. Two full-color inserts use drawings of medical quality to illuminate reproductive physiology (Chapter 3) and remarkable close-up photographs to display the conception and development of the embryo and fetus (Chapter 10). The text is further enhanced by over 150 photographs with captions that expand on text discussions.

INFORMATION RESOURCES. Many chapters include lists of organizations, hotlines, and other resources for practical information and help. These boxed lists appear at the end of relevant sections.

To the Student

We hope you will read this preface, for although it is addressed to the instructor, it is written as much for you. Having taught human sexuality for two decades, we are keenly aware of how rapidly technological change has added to the burden of what you need to learn about such complex topics as contraception, reproduction, and sexually transmitted diseases. We have tried to ease your task by focusing on the most important facets of human sexuality and by writing this book as if we were talking with you. We hope you will find our book interesting and useful and that the supplements designed for your use (starred in the following section's list) will prove helpful for years to come.

Supplements to this Text

An excellent teaching and learning package is available to instructors who adopt this text and to their students.

INSTRUCTOR'S RESOURCE AND TESTING MANUAL. This manual presents chapter by chapter suggestions for classroom activities and for integrating video and film resources into lectures. It offers chapter overviews and objectives, lecture tips, and additional discussion questions. Its bank of some 1500 multiple choice, true-false, and essay questions offers instructors a well-balanced resource for test administration.

DATAMANAGER AND MACINTOSH TESTMANAGER. These software programs, for both IBM-compatible and Macintosh computers, make flexible test administration possible.

PRENTICE HALL/ABC VIDEO LIBRARY ON HUMAN SEXUALITY.* This library offers feature and documentary-style videos on concepts and topics covered in our book. The video segments, carefully selected to illustrate and expand on text discussions, are taken from a number of award-winning ABC Network television programs—*Nightline, 20/20,* and *World News Tonight,* among them—that present substantial content and are hosted by well-versed and recognized anchors.

STUDY GUIDE.* The Study Guide offers the student self-tests for each chapter of the book. It also includes chapter objectives and overviews as well as lists of key terms and definitions.

THE PRENTICE HALL/NEW YORK TIMES CONTEMPORARY VIEW PROGRAM FOR HUMAN SEXUALITY.* This mini-newspaper, which contains timely *New York Times* articles that are keyed to discussions in the text, further underscores the real-life application of formal knowledge.

AIDS AND STDs SLIDES. This set of 50 slides illustrates the signs and symptoms of the acquired immune deficiency syndrome and other sexually transmitted diseases.

PRENTICE HALL COLOR TRANSPARENCIES FOR HUMAN SEXUALITY. A set of 50 full-color acetates expands our text's illustration program and serves as a valuable classroom visual aid.

YOUR SEXUALITY: A PERSONAL EXPERIENCE WORKBOOK.* This workbook, which the professor can copy and hand out, enables students to record their thoughts and experiences in the realm of sexuality. Designed as a diary, the book makes it possible for students to monitor changes in their attitudes, beliefs, and behaviors.

Acknowledgments

Although writing this book was our responsibility, many people helped in its development, preparation, and publication. A number of our teaching colleagues and professional associates have our deepest gratitude for stimulating our thinking, offering useful suggestions, and providing resources for our book: David Brailey, David Corsini, Susan Hellen, Donald Helms, Frederick Humphrey, Lyn Lawrance, Velma Murry, Janet Reis, Ronald Sabatelli, Cynthia Secor, Monica Uhl, Micki Warner, Charles Whittingstall, Catherine Wright, and Linda Zaloudek. To our students we owe special thanks, for it was their interest and their curiosity that stimulated us to write this book.

Many people reviewed portions of this manuscript and offered us their ideas and suggestions for improving it. We are grateful to the following people:

Jerry L. Ainsworth, Department of Health Education, Southern Connecticut State University

Wayne Anderson, Department of Psychology, University of Missouri at Columbia

Sally Baum, Department of Physical Education, Goucher College

Mary Kay Biaggio, Graduate School of Professional Psychology, Pacific University

Jean Byrne, Department of Health Education, Kent State University

Dennis Cannon, Department of Psychological Sciences, Indiana University-Purdue University at Fort Wayne

Joan DiGiovanni, Department of Human Studies, Western New England College

John DeLamater, Department of Sociology, University of Wisconsin at Madison

Beverly Drinnin, Department of Psychology, Des Moines Area Community College

Karen Duffy, Department of Psychology, State University of New York at Geneseo

Beverly I. Fagot, Department of Psychology, University of Oregon

Kenneth D. George, Department of Graduate Education, University of Pennsylvania

Brian A. Gladue, Department of Psychology, North Dakota State University

Sandy Marie Harvey, Department of School and Community Health, University of Oregon

Dickie Hill, Department of Health Education, Abilene Christian University

Barbara C. Ilardi, Department of Psychology, University of Rochester

Donald Johnson, Department of Counseling and Career Services, University of Colorado

Seth C. Kalichman, Department of Psychology, Loyola University of Chicago

Molly Laflin, Department of Health, Physical Education, and Recreation, Bowling Green State University

Barry W. McCarthy, Department of Psychology, American University

Michael E. Mills, Department of Psychology, Loyola Marymount University of Los Angeles

Roberta Mitzenmacher, Department of Health Sciences, California State University

Ken Murdoff, Department of Social Sciences, Lane Community College

Barbara A. Rienzo, Department of Health Science Education, University of Florida

Janet A. Simons, Central Iowa Psychological Services

David S. Smith, Department of Biological Sciences, San Antonio College

S. Lee Spencer, Department of Psychology, Arizona State University.

We have forged many new friendships at Prentice Hall and want to thank a truly outstanding team of publishing professionals. Susan Finnemore Brennan saw the potential of this project early on and provided many helpful suggestions as she oversaw the entire preparation process. She was a constant source of inspiration and support. Virginia Otis Locke was a splendid editor who proved invaluable with her knowledge, advice, enthusiasm, and dedication. Ginny is responsible for a number of additions, improvements, and refinements, and without her energy and ideas this book would not exist. Mary Anne Shahidi directed the transition from manuscript to book with consummate skill and was a joy to work with throughout the production process. Lorraine Mullaney created the book's outstanding cover and interior design. Anne Bonanno supervised the art program with great expertise, and Lori Morris-Nantz and Ilene Cherna Bellovin assembled the excellent photographs that illuminate the text. Kelly Behr and Mary Ann Gloriande arranged for the typesetting and printing of the book, and Linda Spillane kept everyone on schedule. Sharon Chambliss managed to supervise the production of our fine package of supplements and to have a new son at the same time. Tracey McPeake offered marketing wisdom throughout the process. And Charlyce Jones Owen, Editor in Chief, Social Sciences, Raymond Mullaney, Vice President and Editor in Chief, College Book Editorial Development, and Stephen Deitmer, Managing Editor, College Book Editorial Development, contributed their supervisory expertise to the entire project.

We want to offer special thanks to Philip A. Belcastro, Professor of Health Education, Borough of Manhattan Community College, City University of New York, for his detailed and thoughtful review of our manuscript as well as for his work on the supplements for our book.

We want also to thank our fine team of typists: Jill Baez, Linda Brailey, Anne Marie Deluca, Kathy Lynn, and Sherri Shortt. Each undertook her duties with enthusiasm, professionalism, and creative dispatch.

Finally, to our loved ones goes our deepest appreciation. Writing requires personal and family sacrifice, and the patient understanding of our loved ones enabled us to devote the long hours necessary to complete this project successfully. Because of them, *Contemporary Human Sexuality* has become a reality.

Jeffrey S. Turner   *Laurna Rubinson*
Mitchell College   University of Illinois
Urbana-Champaign

About the Authors

JEFFREY SCOTT TURNER is Professor of Psychology at Mitchell College in New London, Connecticut. Turner, the recipient of many teaching awards, has taught human sexuality and other courses for over 20 years. He is the author of many articles as well as of a number of college textbooks used around the world, including *Marriage and Family: Traditions and Transitions, Lifespan Development, Contemporary Adulthood, Exploring Child Behavior,* and *Basic Principles of Child Development*. A member of the American Association of Sex Educators, Counselors, and Therapists, the National Council on Family Relations, and the New England Psychological Association, Turner lives with his wife, a public health nurse, and their three sons, in Connecticut.

LAURNA RUBINSON is Associate Professor and Graduate Studies Director, Department of Community Health, University of Illinois, where she teaches and coordinates one of the largest U.S. human sexuality courses, educating well over 14,000 students. Rubinson, whose research focuses on contraceptive and AIDS-related behaviors in adolescents and young adults, has published widely on sexual attitudes and behaviors among college-age students. Her books are *Research Techniques for the Health Sciences* and *Health Education: Foundations for the Future*. A Fellow of the American School Health Association and the recipient of honors for research and teaching, she is an editor of the *Journal of School Health,* the *Journal of Sex Education and Therapy* and the *Journal of Sex Research*.

The New York Times and Prentice Hall are sponsoring *A Contemporary View,* a program designed to enhance student access to current information of relevance in the classroom.

Through this program, the core subject matter presented in the Turner/Rubinson text is supplemented by a collection of time-sensitive articles from one of the world's most distinguished newspapers, *The New York Times*. These articles are gathered into newspaper format to demonstrate the vital, ongoing connection between what is learned in the classroom and what is happening in the world around us. To enjoy the wealth of information in *The New York Times* daily, a reduced subscription rate is available in deliverable areas. For information, call toll-free: 1-800-631-1222.

Prentice Hall and *The New York Times* are proud to co-sponsor *A Contemporary View*. We hope it will make the reading of both textbooks and newspapers a more dynamic, involving process.

1 Introduction to Human Sexuality

History is the ship carrying living memories to the future

—Stephen Spender

Since Christianity upped the ante and concentrated on sexual behavior as the root of virtue, everything pertaining to sex has a "special case" in our culture, evoking peculiarly inconsistent attitudes

—Susan Sontag

Maria and Joe live in a rural town and have been dating for over two years. They recently rented an apartment together, and hope to marry sometime within the next year. They engage in sexual relations often, and both strongly believe that sharing love means sharing responsibility for contraception and family planning. Because they are not yet ready to have a child, they realize that they must find a satisfactory form of birth control. Although they initially used the condom, they were generally dissatisfied with it and wanted to consider alternatives. Because they were unsure of the choices available, they turned to a local health services program for help in making a decision. At the health center a trained counselor described the various available methods, demonstrated how to use them, and explored their relative advantages and disadvantages including their health risks.

Nine-year-old Derek is rapidly learning traditional gender-role behaviors. Derek is bright, energetic, and well liked by his teachers. Out of school, he leads a very active life and often engages in rough-and-tough play with his friends. When he isn't on the Little League baseball diamond or Pee Wee football field, Derek enjoys a mixture of activities, from collecting baseball cards and building tree forts to riding his bicycle around the neighborhood.

Nancy is a 20-year-old junior at a university in New England. Throughout high school and college Nancy has been popular and well liked by her many friends. She has always dated the "most eligible" men: her high school's star quarterback and the "big men on campus" at her college. Men seem to be drawn to her, as she is very pretty and has a pleasantly assertive personality. But Nancy has always been somewhat aloof with men, never getting seriously involved.

Recently, Nancy has become close friends with three or four women classmates with whom she enjoys spending a lot of time. Not long ago one of these friends invited her to join in a gay rights rally on campus, and Nancy unhesitatingly said yes. She was a little surprised, though, when one of the other women participants asked her if she was a lesbian. Her immediate reaction was to say no, of course not. But later, when she began to think about the incident and about her feelings for the friend whose interests she had so wholeheartedly supported, she became increasingly uncertain. Exploring her feelings and then talking openly with others about the lesbian life style was stressful at first, but with the support of a campus lesbian-gay group, Nancy has been able to accept a part of herself that she had feared to recognize and to build a comfortable new life style.

Welcome to the study of human sexuality. As these introductory examples illustrate, human sexuality weaves itself into our lives in many different ways. How do our notions of human sexuality affect our decisions about family planning? What are the birth control options that Maria and Joe are learning about? What role does human sexuality play in human development? What forces shaped the very traditional gender-role behaviors that Derek demonstrates? And how can the study of human sexuality help us understand variations in sexual behavior? What do we know about the lesbian-gay life style that Nancy has adopted?

These are just a few of the issues that human sexuality researchers explore. How do they go about studying such topics? Are some areas of human sexuality easier to investigate than others? What kinds of questions do sexuality investigators ask? Is sexuality inborn or learned from the environment? Do childhood experiences provide the foundation for later sexual expression? What social and cultural forces influence the course of human sexuality? Answering such questions lies at the heart of this textbook.

In this chapter you'll discover:

☐ **How studying human sexuality can help you both in your personal life and in further academic pursuits.**

☐ **How the major theoretical frameworks on which the study of human sexuality is based complement one another.**

☐ **How sexuality has been viewed across cultures and over centuries, and how these views affect our modern-day attitudes and beliefs.**

THE SCOPE OF HUMAN SEXUALITY

human sexuality A field of study that encompasses all aspects of human beings that affect their gender-specific and sexual behaviors: their anatomy, physiology, thoughts, attitudes, beliefs, emotions, and social roles. Some of its many topics of study are sexual maturation and reproduction, gender identity, sexual drives and response cycles, sexual life styles, and sexual health and disease.

The concept of **human sexuality** is a broad one, embracing all aspects of human beings that affect their gender-specific and specifically sexual behavior. Not only human beings' anatomy and physiology, but their thoughts, feelings, attitudes, and behaviors are of interest to the sexuality researcher, who may study such topics as sexual maturation and reproduction, sexual identities, sexual drives and response cycles, relationship dynamics, sexual life styles, sexual health and disease, and sexual dysfunctions. The scientific discipline of human sexuality is interdisciplinary in nature, with roots in psychology, sociology, education, anthropology, biology, medical science, health education, and counseling.

There are a number of potential benefits from taking a course in human sexuality. First and foremost, this course should help you to understand your own sexuality and that of others. Second, the course serves as a foundation for advanced courses in the field. Topics covered in single chapters in this book are offered as entire advanced courses in many colleges. Such courses might focus on gender issues, sexual health, or sex therapy. Some of the other benefits of studying human sexuality are:

- Obtaining a clearer picture of the discipline of human sexuality, including its topics of study.
- Learning how to describe human sexuality in precise and objective language.
- Satisfying your intellectual curiosity about human sexuality.
- Enhancing your understanding of sexual intimacy, including ways of improving sexual satisfaction.
- Understanding the concept of safer sex; learning to make responsible sexual decisions; becoming aware of sexual health and hygiene issues, including the prevention of sexually transmitted diseases and unwanted pregnancies.

Students enrolling in a human sexuality course usually have a host of questions, not only about the course content, but also about their own sexuality. While some students are reasonably comfortable with their command of the subject, many are not. Many are also embarrassed by what they perceive as their excessive ignorance, and some feel they will be ridiculed if they openly ask for the information they want. It is not uncommon to feel this way, even at the college level. College students are sensitive about their need for adequate information and their newly achieved status as young adults (Caron & Bertran, 1988).

Over the years we have found not only that students have many questions about human sexuality but that some questions recur again and again. To help you relate the material of this book and course to your own needs, interests, and life style, we've reprinted many of the most commonly asked questions in the margins of the book, next to the paragraphs that answer them. We hope that you'll find this a useful aid to studying the material and also that it will reassure you that every question you have is legitimate and natural.

PERSPECTIVES ON HUMAN SEXUALITY

Human sexuality is not a unitary concept. There is no one way to study it. Rather, as you will see throughout this book, there are many different paths to interpreting data and analyzing events within this broad area of study. From all of these perspectives arise theoretical frameworks that help us to organize our knowledge systematically and to see how concepts are related to one another. The major frameworks of human

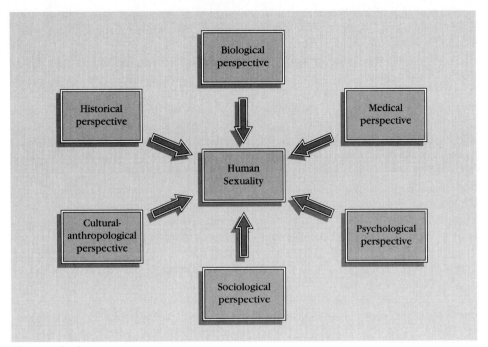

FIGURE 1–1

The study of human sexuality encompasses several different perspectives.

sexuality are the biological, medical, psychological, sociological, cultural anthropological, and historical perspectives (see Figure 1–1).

These perspectives and others have provided us with many answers about the nature of human sexuality. Moreover, because they are not mutually exclusive, they tend to blend together and contribute to our total picture of human sexuality. For example, physiological aspects of sexual functioning influence psychological feelings of self-worth, including those related to sexual performance. And sex-role behaviors typical of a particular contemporary society are often rooted in antiquity or are shown by cultural anthropologists to be common in other modern-day societies.

The Biological Perspective

Taking the **biological perspective,** we study the physical aspects of sexuality—the structure (or anatomy) and function (or physiology) of the body's sexual systems, as well as their development and maturation. Thus in Chapter 3 we will focus on sexual anatomy—both external and internal sexual organs—and the general processes by which reproduction takes place. In Chapter 4 we will explore the functioning of the sexual systems in sexual arousal and sexual response and the way this functioning is influenced by the body's hormones. In Chapter 5 we will see how hormones direct the prenatal development of the sexual systems. And in Chapter 14 we will discuss the further development of these systems that leads to sexual maturation at puberty.

biological perspective on human sexuality A model of sexuality that focuses on its physical aspects: the anatomy and physiology of the body's sexual and reproductive systems, as well as their development and maturation.

The Medical Perspective

The **medical perspective** emphasizes the importance of sexual health and how to maintain it. Many of the topics we will discuss are studied largely from the medical perspective; for example, proper prenatal care (Chapter 10), childbirth and postpartum care (Chapter 11) and effective use of birth control methods (Chapter 12). Other areas of concern to medical specialists are general sexual hygiene and the

medical perspective on human sexuality A model of sexuality that focuses on sexual health and its maintenance.

prevention and treatment of sexually transmitted diseases as well as illnesses or diseases that may interfere with sexual functioning. We will have more to say about sexual health and disease in Chapters 17 and 18.

In general, this perspective is concerned with all factors that either enhance or detract from a state of sexual well-being. We may, for example, look at the special needs of the physically challenged (Chapter 8) from a medical point of view. According to medical specialists, maintaining optimal sexual health means acquiring a base of fundamental knowledge and then applying that information conscientiously. Thus many medical practitioners stress the need for formal instruction about sexual health in the school system, a topic we will consider in Chapter 13.

Within the medical framework the clinical perspective centers most of its attention on specific problems of sexual functioning. As we'll see in Chapter 16, the treatment of sexual dysfunctions, known as sex therapy, is a rapidly expanding field. The primary goal of sex therapy, which encompasses an assortment of treatment approaches and methods, is the resolution of problems that prevent normal sexual functioning. Clinicians also direct their energies toward understanding and treating people whose sexual behaviors vary considerably from the behaviors common to most people in a given society, as well as the individuals who are often the victims of such behaviors. We discuss incest, child sexual abuse, rape, exhibitionism, sadomasochism, and other atypical sexual behaviors in Chapters 19 and 20.

The Psychological Perspective

psychological perspective on human sexuality A model of sexuality that examines the ways sexuality is shaped by personality dynamics, motivation, emotions, attitudes, beliefs, and interpersonal behavior.

The **psychological perspective** explores the ways in which sexuality is shaped by such factors as personality dynamics, motivation, emotions, attitudes, beliefs, and interpersonal behaviors. Emerging from this perspective are a number of psychological theories that have been enlisted to explain certain aspects of human sexuality. For example, the psychoanalytic theory of Sigmund Freud (Chapters 2 and 13) proposes that childhood sexual experiences are influential in shaping sexual behavior in the adult. As we will see later on, Freud also maintained that the sex drive was primarily responsible for behaviors we do not ordinarily associate with sexuality, such as artistic creativity.

Sex education is offered today in schools around the world. Some people think that parents should teach their children about sex. Others think that schools are the logical place for such instruction. Still others think teachers and parents should cooperate in helping young people learn to make responsible decisions about their sexual lives. What do you think?

Psychological theories can be useful in explaining the development of intimacy among people (Chapter 6) and the ways in which people communicate—or don't communicate—their sexual needs and wishes to each other (Chapter 7). Psychology can also help us understand what motivates people to seek sexual relationships outside of marriage and to divorce (Chapter 15).

Theories of learning can help explain particular sexual behaviors. For example, reinforcement learning theory suggests that people tend to repeat behaviors that are reinforced by positive responses and to discontinue those that are followed by negative reactions. For example, a child may learn to greet people with hugs and kisses if she is praised for this behavior. She may also learn not to masturbate—or at least not to do it openly—if she is punished for doing this. Observational learning theory suggests that people learn certain behaviors by watching others' behavior and then modeling the behaviors that appear successful. For example, a little boy may become interested in fixing electrical appliances because he sees his father do this work around the house and receive his mother's praise for it.

The Sociological Perspective

The **sociological perspective** underscores how sexuality is shaped by the society in which a person lives. A basic tenet of this perspective is that private sexual behavior does not take place in a vacuum but instead affects the lives of many people. Thus sociologists study human sexuality against the backdrop of society, exploring such issues as the ways in which people are socialized, or taught the customs of a particular society, the influence of membership in a particular subgroup such as gays or lesbians (Chapter 9), and specific social problems such as sex discrimination and other forms of inequality. The study of human sexuality from a sociological perspective has opened up a rich vein of research activity, including such topics as gender-role learning, cultural expectations for sexual behavior, and the regulation of reproduction.

Sociobiology offers a unique combination of the sociological and biological perspectives. In his theory of **sociobiology** E. O. Wilson (1975) blended population genetics and ethology (the study of animal behavior), claiming that any human behavior that has a genetic component is adaptive. That is, characteristics are selected and inherited because they serve a function. Sociobiologists explore how social behavior, including sexuality, is shaped by evolutionary factors. They propose that not only behaviors such as male dominance but also basic needs, like the sex drive, are inherited and serve to help preserve the nuclear family, "the building block of nearly all human species" (Wilson, 1975, p. 553). Because they hold that there are fundamental differences between men and women that serve the purpose of survival (Eysenck & Wilson, 1979), sociobiologists have incurred the wrath of feminists and others, who argue that this view of sexuality and gender roles perpetuates the notion of male superiority and denies the possibility of loving sexual relationships between people of the same sex.

The Cultural Anthropological Perspective

The **cultural anthropological perspective** analyzes the sexual lives of different groups of people in an effort to discover cross-cultural variations and similarities. Within this perspective are the two subfields of ethnography and ethnology. **Ethnography** is the description of the lives and culture of people in particular social groups, and **ethnology** is the study of the social patterns and cultural practices revealed by such description. Together these areas of study enable researchers to develop cross-cultural comparisons of sexual behavior in different societies.

sociological perspective on human sexuality A model that focuses on the shaping of sexuality by the society in which one lives.

sociobiology A science that combines the sociological and biological perspectives. Sociobiologists explore how social behavior, including sexuality, is shaped by evolutionary forces.

cultural anthropological perspective on human sexuality A model that explores the sexual behavior of different ethnic groups in order to discover cross-cultural similarities and differences.

ethnography A subfield of cultural anthropology that describes the lives and culture of people in particular social groups.

ethnology A subfield of cultural anthropology that develops generalizations about the social patterns and cultural practices of social groups.

Special garments are worn by a young couple of the Banjara tribe for their traditional wedding ceremony in a new housing settlement near Hyderabad, India.

Why is it important to recognize cross-cultural variations and similarities in human sexual and gender-related behaviors? Because we live in a world of many cultures, and we need to realize that a given culture's expression of sexuality is not the only proper or acceptable expression. Your ultimate decisions and choices will be your own and may be different from those of many others. But making effective decisions and choices requires knowledge of options. Moreover, living comfortably with others in a world where diversity is no longer the exotic behavior of people living on the other side of the world but the customary behavior of people living right next door requires tolerance of beliefs and life styles different from those you have chosen for yourself. In an effort to help you acquire the knowledge you need to understand such diverse ways, we have included a series of boxes called "A World of Differences" in this book. Starting with the box in this chapter, these discussions will introduce you to the beliefs and practices of many different ethnic groups and societies, both past and present.

The Historical Perspective

historical perspective on human sexuality A model that examines the way the past has influenced present-day sexual attitudes and behaviors.

The foundation of the **historical perspective** is the notion that the past has played an important role in shaping present-day human sexuality. Thus any comprehensive effort to examine human sexuality must take historical forces into account, as we will do shortly. Historians suggest that expressions of sexuality, including attitudes as well as behaviors, evolve over time.

Finally, the legal perspective on human sexuality deserves our attention. Although the law does not seek to explain sexual behavior, the legal perspective is an important one because societies have used laws to regulate and control sexual behavior. For example, most states in the United States have laws prohibiting what is considered indecent behavior in public, such as appearing nude or engaging in sexual intercourse. Most states forbid people to force others to engage in sexual acts against their will, such as rape and other forms of sexual abuse (Chapters 19 and 20). And most states attempt to regulate the distribution of pornographic material and the business of prostitution. Some laws attempt to regulate contraception and procreation. Other laws, such as those requiring that outbreaks of sexually transmitted diseases be reported to public health authorities, seek to protect public health. Over the years many people have questioned the appropriateness of certain laws designed to regulate sexual behavior, particularly those that appear to threaten the civil rights of the person

*T*heoretical perspectives like those we've reviewed in this chapter should not be viewed as speculative ideas with no practical application. On the contrary, theories serve a heuristic purpose in that they can guide behavior and sharpen observational skills. Theoretical perspectives can clarify your own thoughts and viewpoints on human sexuality by helping you to organize more effectively what you already know about human sexuality through your own personal experiences. As you acquaint yourself with the research investigations discussed in later chapters, knowledge of theoretical perspectives will help you to see which frameworks guided a particular researcher. Thus you may want to refer back to this chapter when framing theoretical questions about the material you read.

None of the theoretical viewpoints should be understood from an either-or perspective. Indeed, it is our recommendation that you become eclectic, picking and choosing those bits of viewpoints that you can accept and then developing your own theories and ideas about human sexuality. Think of your own ideas as a lens and the various perspectives as filters. The views that you select will filter out some facts and impose a pattern on those they admit. It might be interesting to see how your own theoretical perspective of human sexuality changes as you read this book and attend class. By the end of the semester, the chances are that you'll have a clearer idea of your own viewpoints as well as a unified portrait of the field of human sexuality.

MAKING USE OF WHAT WE KNOW

Developing Your Own Perspective of Human Sexuality

---

or persons involved. We'll explore these and other topics related to the legal perspective in Chapter 21.

Now that we have outlined the major perspectives on human sexuality, you may be wondering how you can best apply this knowledge to your course on sexuality and to your life. To help you answer this question and others like it that will undoubtedly arise as you study each chapter in this book, we have created a series of boxes called "Making Use of What We Know." In this chapter the first of these boxes gives you some guidelines for getting the most out of what you've learned about theories of human sexuality.

HUMAN SEXUALITY THROUGHOUT HISTORY

In order to fully comprehend the nature of human sexuality in the modern world, it is important to examine how present-day thinking evolved. The study of human sexuality throughout history is a relatively new field of interest and poses special problems to researchers. Although some ancient accounts have been found, many cultures did not keep written records. Moreover, there was often a conspiracy of silence about this topic. In addition, many historians trying to reconstruct the past have tended to treat sexual matters within a vacuum, independent of social and historical trends.

One of the results of the historical reluctance to deal with the topic of human sexuality forthrightly has been the evolution of many inaccurate ideas about sexual matters. To bring a few of these ideas to your attention we have created a third series of boxed inserts called "Myths and Misconceptions." The box in this chapter dispels several mistaken ideas about sexual attitudes and behaviors in past times.

Over the last 50 years or so, investigators have taken a broader approach to the subject and, as a result, we now have a comprehensive and multidisciplinary body of knowledge. Space precludes offering a worldwide historical survey, but we will touch on a few variations in sexual attitudes and behaviors: gender roles, sexual activity within and outside of marriage, homosexuality and bisexuality, contraception, abortion, and prostitution. We will discover that while some sexual attitudes and behaviors have remained fairly constant over time, other forms of sexual expression have changed considerably. Let's look back through history and examine some representative civilizations.

Mesopotamia

The Mesopotamian civilization was founded before 3500 B.C. in the region now known as Iraq. The people who migrated to the valley formed by the Tigris and Euphrates rivers probably came from the highlands of present-day Turkey or Iran. The culture they built included at one time or another the Sumerians, Persians, Assyrians, and Babylonians. Because Mesopotamia had a great influence on the cultures of the ancient world—notably the Greek and Roman civilizations—and these in turn influenced European culture and society, it is generally considered the cradle of Western civilization.

MYTHS AND MISCONCEPTIONS

Sex Throughout History

Throughout history, emphasis was always placed on the enjoyment and pleasure that sexual activity brought.

*I*n reality, for numerous civilizations, such as that of the ancient Hebrews, procreation was the *only* justification for sex. The early Christians, too, stressed the procreative nature of intercourse and condemned any pleasure or sexual fulfillment that might result in the process. During the Middle Ages St. Thomas Aquinas argued that any kind of sexual activity not leading to procreation was unproductive and could be classified as deviant. Today intercourse has become an end in itself for most people rather than a means to a procreative end.

Sexual "revolutions" were rare events in history.

The truth is that sexual revolutions were fairly common throughout history. Views on sexual behavior have changed drastically since the beginning of time. For example, the Romans were well known for their sexual freedom, the early Christians for their celibacy, the Puritans for their moral strictness, and the Victorians for their sexual repression (Brehm, 1985).

Prostitution was rare in most past societies.

Prostitution was common in most historical eras. Sometimes it was disguised, and sometimes it took an institutionalized form. In ancient Greece prostitution was characterized by a social hierarchy and those prostitutes occupying the upper brackets were well educated, socially refined, and often sought for their intellectual companionship. For the most part, though, prostitutes have been outcasts of society, a trend still apparent today. In the 1990s prostitution is a thriving business despite the fact that it is illegal everywhere in the United States except in Nevada. The passage of time has not lessened the demand for prostitution.

Most sexually transmitted diseases are the product of modern times.

Although this is true of the acquired immune deficiency syndrome (AIDS), which according to present information first appeared in the 1970s, sexually transmitted diseases have plagued humanity for centuries. For example, the Greek physician Galen described some of the symptoms of gonorrhea as early as A.D. 130, and a widespread outbreak of syphilis was reported in France in 1494. Throughout history many superstitions and misconceptions surrounded sexually transmitted diseases, a trend still apparent today among the uninformed. Medical and health officials expend considerable energy dispelling myths and providing accurate knowledge, particularly in regard to AIDS (see Chapter 18).

Not much is known about sexual life in Mesopotamia. Like many other peoples, the Mesopotamians saw the primary purpose of sex as procreation and strongly encouraged marriage. Again, like many other cultures in the past, this society accorded men a dominant cultural role. Public affairs were clearly in the hands of men, while women were expected to bear children, tend to the household, and minister to their husbands' needs.

Among the Sumerians, who ruled Mesopotamia in 3000 B.C., **monogamy** (the marriage of one man to one woman) rather than **polygamy** (having multiple marriage partners) was the law of the land, but interesting variations of the former were practiced. For instance, if a man's wife was sick or infertile, he sometimes kept one or more concubines. A concubine was a woman who was not legally married to a man but who could live with him and bear his children. Under certain conditions a husband could sell his wife, and he was also permitted to hand her over to someone else as a slave for years at a time in payment for a debt.

monogamy The marriage of one man to one woman.

polygamy The marriage of one man to several women or of one woman to several men.

In most instances promiscuous sexual relations were frowned upon in Mesopotamia. A young man who had seduced an innocent girl was legally required to ask her parents for her hand in marriage; to refuse to do so could cost him his life. The Sumerians also disapproved of **adultery,** sexual intercourse with a person other than one's spouse. However, the response to this offense was clearly stamped with sex discrimination. The unfaithful husband was not usually punished, although he was sometimes required to compensate his wife in some way. Adultery by a wife, however, was regarded as an extremely serious offense and during certain periods in Sumerian civilization was punishable with death by drowning. Sometimes both the wife and her lover were bound and thrown into the water to drown together. On other occasions unfaithful wives had their nose or ears cut off and their lovers were castrated.

adultery Sexual intercourse with a person other than one's spouse.

Under the reign of Hammurabi (1704–1662 B.C.), sexual freedom increased and premarital sexual relations were more widely tolerated. Efforts were also made to improve the status of women, particularly within the institution of marriage. For example, once married, a woman assumed possession of the betrothal payment and added to it the dowry, or gifts given the couple by the bride's relatives. These two assets became the bride's inalienable property, which she could bequeath to her children if she wished. If a woman's husband died, she inherited the same share of his property as did each of his children. A widow could marry again, taking with her her original dowry, but relinquishing her share of her late husband's estate. And although it was difficult, a woman could divorce her husband, particularly if he neglected his conjugal duties.

Mesopotamia had the distinction of being one of the first civilizations to offer sacred sexual rituals in its temples. Religious rites and acts symbolizing fertility were encouraged by the priests in an effort to ensure the fertility of both the people and their fields. For example, in Mesopotamian temples young women were often ritually deflowered, or deprived of their virginity.

Religiously sanctioned prostitution, supervised by the temples, was also common in Mesopotamia. The Sumerians established the first of such temples in the sanctuary of Anu, their supreme deity, at Uruk. The prostitutes dedicated themselves to the cult of Anu's lustful daughter, Ishtar. Living in a special house, these "daughters of the temple" practiced their profession under the constant scrutiny of a priestess-manageress. In some of the larger temples, such as those in Babylon, male prostitutes also occupied a special brothel, or house of prostitution. A senior priest was placed in charge of this facility and its occupants.

Female temple prostitutes, particularly a category known as the *harimata*, were generally considered outcasts in Mesopotamia. They were usually viewed with mistrust and suspicion, and men were discouraged from marrying them. The *harimata* were not allowed to bring up their own children but had to surrender them to foster parents. Children of the harimata were forbidden to inquire about their biological fathers.

Egypt

Like the Mesopotamians, the Egyptians were primarily farmers. Both peoples farmed the rich soils of river valleys. Most Egyptians lived in or near the fertile valley of the Nile River.

The Egyptians were apparently a sexually tolerant people, as suggested by the many explicit drawings and paintings that appear on temple and tomb walls depicting men and women with clearly defined sex organs engaging in numerous forms of sexual activity. As in Mesopotamia, temple prostitution and religious fertility rituals were encouraged by the high priests and were an accepted part of Egyptian life.

Although men were dominant in Egyptian society, women were held in high regard. Some of Egyptian women's social and legal privileges were the right to own property and to bring court suits.

Egyptian men and women married early—the average age for men was 15 and that for women, 13. Although monogamy was the rule in Egypt, a husband could take more than one wife; indeed, he could keep a harem if he was wealthy enough. Most Egyptian men expected their brides to be virgins, and sometimes proof of virginity was exacted. It was not uncommon for the bridegroom to cover the index finger of his right hand with a piece of fine muslin and insert it into the vagina of his bride-to-be. Presumably, if the muslin was stained with blood, the bridegroom had his proof. As we will see in Chapter 3, however, evidence of virginity is not so easy to obtain.

matrilineal descent
Inheritance through the female side of the family.

patrilineal descent
Inheritance through the male side of the family.

Interestingly, although the husband and father ruled the family, Egyptians held to the principle of **matrilineal descent.** According to this rule, all property descended in the female line, from mother to daughter. In **patrilineal descent,** of course, all property descends in the male line, from father to son. Thus in ancient Egypt, when a man married an heiress, he enjoyed her property only as long as his wife lived. On her death her property passed to her daughter or daughters and their husbands.

incest Sexual relations or intercourse between close blood relatives such as father and daughter, mother and son, or brother and sister.

The principle of matrilineal descent helps to explain why the Egyptians sanctioned marriages between close relatives, particularly between brothers and sisters. Such incestuous marriages—**incest** means sexual intercourse or other sexual relations between close blood relatives such as father and daughter, mother and son, or brother and sister—are not condoned in many societies today (see Chapter 19). In the United States both incest and incestuous marriage are forbidden by law.

Incestuous marriages were very common in the Egyptian royal family. Many pharaohs (rulers of ancient Egypt) married their sisters or even their infant daughters. The marriages of Cleopatra (see Figure 1–2) illustrate the interweaving of matrilineal descent and incestuous marriage. Cleopatra (69–30 B.C.) was queen of Egypt in 51 B.C. She first married her eldest brother, thus establishing his right to the throne. When he died, she married her younger brother, who also ruled by right of marriage. When the Roman Emperor Julius Caesar conquered Egypt in 48 B.C., he married Cleopatra to make his accession to the throne legal in the eyes of the Egyptian people. After Caesar's death Marc Antony secured the throne of Egypt by also marrying Cleopatra. When Antony fell from power and Octavius arrived, he too was ready to espouse the much-married queen.

Ancient Hebrews

In about 1900 B.C. the ancient Hebrews were a nomadic desert people initially led by Abraham, his son Isaac, and Isaac's son Jacob. Jacob, who was also called Israel, had 12 sons and these 12 sons founded the 12 tribes that later made up the Jewish people. The Jews thus came to be known as the children of Israel, or Israelites.

The ancient Hebrew civilization was a male-dominated society. Women played a subservient role, although they were respected for the work they performed.

Introduction to Human Sexuality

FIGURE 1–2

When Julius Caesar arrived in Egypt, Cleopatra set out to captivate him and to use his position to recover the power she had lost in civil wars. A probably fictitious story has it that in order to escape detection by rival factions she concealed herself in an ornamental rug that was then delivered to Caesar's headquarters.

Polygyny, the marriage of one man to more than one woman, was recognized in Hebrew law, and its practice extended into the Middle Ages. Virginity in a bride was highly valued, and infidelity was not tolerated. With sufficient evidence, a husband could have his wife put to death for adultery. Within this patriarchal society, men held all the power. They could sell their children or divorce their wives without much reason if they wanted to.

polygyny The marriage of one man to more than one woman.

The Hebrew Bible provided directives for everyday life, including sexual conduct. Paramount among these guidelines was God's directive to "be fruitful and multiply." Choosing not to marry was regarded as unnatural and viewed with suspicion. Procreation was extremely important so that family lineage could be maintained and the tribes of Israel could be perpetuated. Indeed, procreation was the only justification for sex. Homosexuality and masturbation were both denounced since neither served to propagate the race.

The Old Testament's account of Onan and Tamar (Genesis 38:8–10) reveals the emphasis placed on productive sexual activity. Many ancient Hebrews practiced the custom of *levirate*. This meant that if an elder brother died without fathering male children, it was the obligation of his younger brother to marry the widow and ensure that procreative sexual activity would continue. Onan, whose brother Er died, knew that he had to marry Er's wife Tamar, but he was reluctant to father a child that would be considered his brother's rather than his own, so he dishonored himself and his family by "spilling his semen upon the ground." Onan died when the anger of the Lord descended upon him for his iniquity. The Old Testament is unclear as to whether Onan's offense was masturbation or coitus interruptus, but historians have leaned toward the former interpretation. Our word *onanism* now means masturbation.

Prostitution was accepted by the ancient Hebrews without moral condemnation, at least early in their history. Female and male prostitutes were attached to the temple in Jerusalem as well as in other locations, and prostitution was sanctioned in most communities. Even after sacred prostitution was banned, the edict was often ignored. However, the Old Testament does contain certain injunctions; for example, fathers were forbidden to prostitute their daughters (Leviticus, 19:29) and priests were forbidden to marry prostitutes (Leviticus, 21:7).

Greece

Although the Greeks of 2000 years ago did not form a unified nation, the city-states in which they lived were bound together by culture, religion, and language. Greek society was divided into three classes—citizens, slaves, and resident aliens—and men were clearly dominant.

Politics in ancient Greece were the exclusive domain of men, and women played a minimal role in public life. With few exceptions, Greek women were viewed as inferior to men and were expected to be subservient. The perceived inferiority of women was a persistent theme in Greek literature.

Marriage in ancient Greece was regarded as a means of producing legitimate children and perpetuating the civilization. As in earlier civilizations, sex served a procreative function. Many marriages were arranged by the fathers of the bride and groom with little regard for the inclinations of the young people. Greek brides were expected to be virgins, but bridegrooms were not. Marriages were officially monogamous, but a man could keep concubines if he wished.

The Greeks placed a great deal of emphasis on physical beauty and wellness. Their gods—led by Zeus and including such deities as Athena, goddess of wisdom, Apollo, god of the sun, and Aphrodite, goddess of love—were physically beautiful, and the Greeks believed that through the care of their bodies they could resemble the gods. Furthermore, good health was inextricably connected with a beautiful body, the pinnacle of which was the body in sexual maturity. The glorification of beauty in Greek sculpture bears witness to this view.

The Greeks' view of health and beauty was an essential part of their religion. Thus physical well-being and beauty were considered the necessary accompaniments of a good soul. The gods were believed to guide and guard the development of human beings' souls as well as their bodies, helping them thus to achieve balance with the universe.

The Greeks' fascination with the body heralded a new era of human sexuality. Greek sexuality was characterized by open eroticism and a tolerance for alternative forms of sexual expression, themes that wove themselves into many aspects of everyday life. Sculptures and paintings of nudes captured this heightened sensitivity to human sexuality as well as the manner in which the Greeks idealized erotic activity. Sensual portrayals of love and loving also emerged in Greek literature. For example, Sophocles wrote that "love keeps watch in the soft cheeks of the maiden," and Aeschylus spoke of the "gentle arrow of love, which beams from the eyes, the heart-gnawing crown of bodily charm."

The pleasures that sex brought were also enjoyed by the gods. Zeus, the supreme god of the Greek religion, was the suitor not only of goddesses but of many mortal women. Zeus also abducted Ganymede, the son of the king of Troy, formally sanctioning homosexual love in the airy heights of Mt. Olympus (the home of the gods). Selene, the moon goddess, regularly visited Endymion, a handsome youth who slept at night in the wooded hills of Latmos. According to Greek mythology, Selene awakened Endymion each night and blessed him with her love. Apollo, the god of sun and light, was sexually attracted to young boys. Aurora, the goddess of dawn, loved everything that was beautiful, especially young men, and she forcibly seized anyone who filled her heart with passion.

Unlike the Hebrews, the Greeks did not regard masturbation as a vice. On the contrary, unless it was practiced in excess (in which case it was believed to have an injurious effect), the Greeks viewed it as an acceptable alternative to sexual intercourse. Vases and terracottas often depicted both male and female masturbation. Greek women were said to stimulate themselves during masturbation with specially crafted instruments called *baubon* or *olisbos*.

Prostitution was common among the ancient Greeks, and a unique social hierarchy characterized the profession. The *dicteriades*, or "whores of the brothel," represented the lowest rank of prostitute. They were similar in status to the harimata of Mesopotamia. The dicteriades lived in an official house of prostitution, where they served the sexual needs of the lower classes. These houses were under the supervision of city officials whose duties included maintaining public decency. Managers of the brothels paid a yearly tax to the state.

The *auletrides*, socially elevated above the dicteriades, included flute players, acrobats, and other entertainers. During the course of their performances, in which they appeared thinly clad, the auletrides made suggestive gestures to the audience and openly encouraged sexual advances. Following the entertainment, or sometimes during the actual performance, the auletrides offered their sexual expertise. This class of prostitute was well paid for her services and often entertained at private banquets and other functions.

At the top of the hierarchy were the *hetaerae*, a class of women who occupied a very special position in the world of ancient Greece. As the "World of Differences" box indicates, rather like the Japanese *geisha*, the hetaerae were educated, talented, and highly respected members of society.

Bisexuality and homosexuality were prevalent among the Greeks. Neither was regarded as a perversion. Rather, both were viewed as alternative sources of sexual pleasuring. Female homosexuality was especially common on the island of Lesbos,

A WORLD OF DIFFERENCES

The *Hetaerae* of Ancient Greece and the Japanese *Geisha*

*T*he *hetaerae* of ancient Greece occupied an important position in Greek life. Not to be confused with common prostitutes, they were given considerable social respect. Beyond the sensual pleasures they might offer, the hetaerae were well educated, mentally stimulating, and socially refined. They were in great demand, and the majority of Greeks paid homage to their special charm, companionship, and social graces. Portrait statues of the hetaerae adorned temples and public buildings, and Greek literature is filled with accounts of how these women charmed statesmen, artists, and generals alike.

An interesting parallel can be drawn between the hetaerae of ancient Greece and the Japanese *geisha*. The eighteenth century saw the rise of the geisha, women who had special skills in dancing and singing as well as refined social graces. Although geisha granted sexual favors to regular clients, they were not common prostitutes. Like the hetaerae, the geisha were stimulating companions because of their training in music, dance, and other artistic media as well as in the art of conversation. Not uncommonly, a geisha's wealthy patron would set her up in her own business. As the head of her own house, she would cease to entertain guests and often would become her patron's mistress. In this position she commanded considerable social respect.

During the mid-1800s there was some confusion in the public mind between geisha and prostitutes, for the latter often tried to imitate the geisha's accomplishments. In 1872 the Japanese government enacted legislation to ensure that only true geisha were employed in geisha houses (Gregersen, 1983).

from which the term *lesbian* is derived. The Greek poet Sappho, who was born on Lesbos, filled her poetry with descriptions of love and sexual pleasuring between women.

Rome

At its height in A.D. 117, the Roman empire included about a fourth of Europe, much of the Middle East, and the entire northern coastal area of Africa. Although the empire's millions of people spoke many languages and worshipped many different gods, Romans were united by the empire's government and military power. Roman society had two main divisions: citizens and noncitizens. Citizens included the ruling aristocracy, wealthy businessmen, and the plebeians, or lower class. Noncitizens included aliens and slaves.

Like earlier societies, the Romans practiced monogamy. The Roman father chose a wife for his son, and the marriage was viewed as an arrangement between families. The concepts of courtship and romantic love had little to do with Roman marriage. The marital structure was patriarchal, but children were brought up chiefly under the mother's care.

In ancient Rome, men could divorce their wives but it was quite unusual for a wife to divorce her husband. Of the grounds for divorce, adultery was the most common. Initially, there were no statutory penalties for adultery. When a wife was the culprit, the husband usually took the matter into his own hands or called on a family council to inflict punishment. Often the wife was flogged and her suitor castrated.

The success of a Roman marriage was often judged by the number of children brought into the world, and boys were much preferred over girls. This was because of the need for civilian manpower or service in the army. Under the rule of Augustus Caesar, material rewards were offered to parents who could conceive three healthy male children. If this goal was attained, the mother was given full legal independence, while the father usually received some form of promotion in his career. As women in Rome had extremely limited political rights, full legal independence was considered a major life accomplishment.

The Romans enjoyed a number of different sexual activities. Homosexuality was viewed with suspicion, however, and was called "the Greek practice." Most Romans also frowned on public nudity; indeed, our words *naked* and *nude* come from the Latin word *nudus*, meaning "rough" or "uncouth." Unlike the Greeks, who enjoyed the sight of the naked human body and the sensuality it represented, the Romans equated nudity with indecency and impropriety.

Prostitution in Rome was a trade and a recognized custom. The philosopher Seneca remarked, "He has done no wrong, he who loves a prostitute—a usual thing—he is young; wait, he will improve, and marry a wife." Other philosophers such as Cicero and Cato perceived prostitution as an activity that protected the institution of marriage because it kept men from breaking up the marriages of others. Still others thought that prostitution was acceptable because people had so little choice in marriage partners.

Roman prostitution was characterized by a social hierarchy that resembled that of ancient Greece, except that there was no class analogous to the hetaerae. At the top of the Roman hierarchy were actresses and dancers, and sometimes harp players and other musicians. At the bottom were the prostitutes of the brothels, who more often than not were slaves. The brothels were dirty and dim little cubicles that often had obscene pictures painted over their entrances.

Early Christianity

Although the Romans persecuted the Christians for many years, Christianity spread rapidly because of the work of St. Paul and other apostles. In the Edict of Milan in A.D. 313, Emperor Constantine granted Christians the freedom of religion. By the late 300s, Christianity was the official religion of the Roman empire.

Christianity did little to reduce the inequality between men and women that had persisted for centuries. Women continued to be treated as second-class citizens in the Christian world. They could not hold public office, and they played a subservient role to men. They were reared to be passive, tranquil, and silent. Indeed, the Bible (1 Corinthians 11:8–9) actually says that women were created for the benefit of men.

The Church would come to affect many facets of sexual behavior. Sexual pleasure was not condoned, and marital sex was viewed as a necessary evil, tolerated only because of the procreative function that it served. All nonprocreative sexual activities, including masturbation and homosexual acts, were condemned, and the Church rejected any attempts at contraception. It forbade engaging in "suggestive" dances, wearing improper or revealing clothing, and singing "wanton" songs. And although kisses were often a form of salutation among early Christians, kissing more than once, for the purpose of pleasure, was considered sinful and warned against.

There were numerous architects of the Church's position on sexual morality, but St. Paul and St. Augustine were two of the more vocal proponents of sexual repression. Both firmly believed that men and women must learn to control their sexual impulses in order to achieve inner spiritual peace. As St. Paul stated (1 Corinthians 7:1–2, 7–9, 25, 28):

> It is good for a man not to touch a woman. Nevertheless, to avoid fornication, let every man have his own wife, and let every woman have her own husband. . . . For I would that all men were even as myself. But every man hath his proper gift of God, one after this manner, and another after that. I say therefore to the unmarried and widows, it is good for them if they abide even as I. But if they cannot contain, let them marry: for it is better to marry than to burn. . . . Now concerning virgins I have no commandment of the Lord: yet I give my judgment. . . . If thou marry, thou has not sinned; and if a virgin marry, she hath not sinned.

Many other Christian leaders besides Paul and Augustine encouraged **celibacy,** the abstention from sexual activity. They viewed sexual urges as the work of the devil and thought that only the cultivation of inner fortitude could protect the soul from these evil forces. They regarded celibacy as one of the highest virtues and evidence that willpower can overcome lust and sin. Moreover, they believed that celibacy helped men to execute their duties as Christians and missionaries of the faith.

celibacy Abstention from sexual activity.

The Church made its presence known within the framework of the marriage structure. For example, it ruled on the degree of kinship allowed between bride and groom, it decreed that a bride must be a virgin, and it even determined that the only acceptable position for sexual intercourse was man above, woman below. Adultery, as one might expect, was a punishable offense. The Church also generally condemned divorce, although it vacillated on this issue for some time.

The ban on divorce meant that couples could not separate even when one spouse was sterile. As a result, more marriages were childless, and the natural population increase among the Christians was retarded. But the Church's condemnation of divorce also helped to strengthen many marriages, increasing the solidarity between husband and wife as well as between parents and children. It would be wrong to assume that unhappy marriages were unknown among Christians, but it is reasonable to conclude that many partners reaffirmed their commitment to one another in the wake of the Church's ban on divorce.

Ancient India and the Far East

Hinduism, the major religion of India, developed over thousands of years. Many cultures, races, and religions helped to shape Hinduism, which includes beliefs about divinities, how followers should conduct their lives, and life after death. Hinduism has many sacred writings, including the *Vedas*, the *Puranas*, and the *Manu Smriti*.

Like most other civilizations, Hindu society was characterized by traditional gender roles. Women were subservient to men, and children were taught at early ages to conform to these societal expectations. Premarital sex was frowned upon, and marriages were arranged by parents with careful attention to similarity of backgrounds. Adultery was condemned in Hindu India.

Hindu society regarded sex as an important component of life. Hindus were taught that sex was an activity to be enjoyed, as evidenced in the *Kama Sutra*, a sex manual written for women and men in the second century. The *Kama Sutra* (meaning "precepts of pleasure") was considered to be a revelation of the gods and contained detailed descriptions of the male and female sexual organs as well as coital positions and pleasuring techniques.

In ancient China and Japan positive attitudes toward sex were also apparent. Both societies regarded sex as an important expression of human functioning, and encouraged men and women to maximize its enjoyment. As in India, in Japan and

*She goes to him, her loveliness self-concealed/ In front of others, devising such artful ways;/She must ward him off, all at the proper time,/Only to finally pretend she can resist no longer—Chang Wen-Ch'eng, c. 657–730 (*Erotic Art of China: A Unique Collection of Chinese Prints and Poems Devoted to the Art of Love. *Crown, 1977.)*

Introduction to Human Sexuality

China sex manuals offered readers glorified accounts of sexual pleasures. In ancient China, for example, "pillow books" provided newly married couples with narratives of sexual pleasuring techniques. Erotic art was also popular in both China and Japan, and artistic representations of couples engaging in sexual intercourse were not uncommon.

The Middle Ages

Historians chart the Middle Ages as lying between the end of the Roman empire in A.D. 400 and the sixteenth century. Also known as the medieval period, the Middle Ages were characterized by a blend of Germanic and Roman life styles as the Germanic tribes moved into the land in central Europe previously occupied by the Romans. Medieval civilization was also influenced by the Moslems in Spain and the Middle East, and by the Byzantine empire in Southeastern Europe.

Marriage remained important throughout the Middle Ages and was therefore strongly encouraged. In medieval England marriages were arranged by the couple's parents, and in many instances the arrangements made between the two families resembled a shrewd business transaction. Concern was often expressed over the worth of the bridal partners' property and the size of the dowry. Although monogamy was the preferred marital arrangement, polygamy and concubinage were not uncommon during this period.

During the eleventh and twelfth centuries relationships between men and women acquired a new dimension as so-called courtly love came into prominence. In courtly love a man and a woman adored one another in a relationship that idealized both the woman's feminine qualities and the man's chivalrous behavior. Chivalry was a code of behavior applied to men of the upper classes—usually knights—in which the qualities of courageousness, honor, and the protection of the weak and of women were required. Courtly love prompted the lover to demonstrate his bravery and to compete for the hand of his beloved. Knights often displayed their courage and skill, fighting with their rivals in tournaments in the service of their ladies. Typically, they wore their ladies' favors pinned to their clothing; gloves, veils, flowers, and kerchiefs were used for this purpose. Courtly love also found its way into the poetry and songs of the minstrels who wandered throughout the countryside, making a living by entertaining others.

Whether married or single, women during the Middle Ages led controlled and restricted lives and were regarded as intellectually inferior to males. As in earlier societies, they were viewed as the property of either their fathers or their husbands. Largely on the basis of Church teachings, women were often perceived mainly as a source of sexual temptation that was to be avoided whenever possible. This was especially true among the Saxons, a Germanic people who, along with the Angles and the Jutes, conquered England in the fifth century A.D. The Saxons tended to view women as a necessary evil.

Medieval women learned at an early age to subjugate themselves to male wishes and demands. Consider the situation of women in the region known today as France. A Frankish woman could never escape male domination, for if her husband died before her, she was obliged to submit to the control of her eldest son. Some Frankish women were not allowed to inherit. Moreover, whatever property and possessions a woman brought into a marriage—including her dowry—became her husband's.

Christianity, which had become the official religion of the Roman empire, remained dominant within the remnants of the empire during the Middle Ages. The Church's efforts to overcome what it saw as sexual pollution continued to exert a forceful influence on sexual behavior. It continued to advocate celibacy and banned all forms of sexual activity other than intercourse between married persons. In time, the Church would make even procreative sexual activity illegal on Sundays, Wednesdays, and Fridays, for three days before attending communion, and for a period of 40 days prior to Easter and 40 days before Christmas. In addition, intercourse was forbidden from the time of conception to 40 days after childbirth.

The repression of sexuality took many other forms. For example, church authorities like St. Thomas Aquinas (1225–1274) perceived masturbation as a greater sin than fornication and denounced its practice. Abortion was also condemned by the Church and laws were devised to prevent it—something that neither the Jews nor. the Greeks nor the Romans had done earlier. Finally, no Christian could marry a Jew or the follower of any other religion.

Prostitution was quite widespread in the Middle Ages, particularly during the Crusades. Some Christian authorities regarded it as an inevitable evil; for instance, Aquinas remarked that it was a "necessary condition of social morality, just as a cesspool is necessary to a palace, if the whole palace is not to smell." In many instances rulers passed laws designed to regulate and control prostitution. In the French city of Avignon, Queen Joanna established a town brothel rather than have prostitution run rampant in the streets. In other cities, such as Paris, prostitutes were kept under the watchful eye of city officials and were prohibited from entering certain city districts. As time wore on, prostitutes were subjected to a wide range of rules and regulations. For instance, in various English cities and towns they were required to dress in a certain way so that they could be distinguished from other women.

Public baths became popular during the Middle Ages and often served as centers for prostitution. Originally designed so that the poor could bathe more frequently, the bathhouses, or "stews," were usually located on side streets. Thinly attired prostitutes often welcomed visitors to the establishment and led them to a tub that had enough room for five or six people. Following the bath, customers usually adjourned to separate rooms for more intimate sexual activity. Figure 1–3 displays a public bath of the Middle Ages.

FIGURE 1–3

Apparently in some bathhouses of the Middle Ages, not only was bathing mixed but the event could be quite a party, offering food, drink, music, and an occasional sexual encounter.

Introduction to Human Sexuality

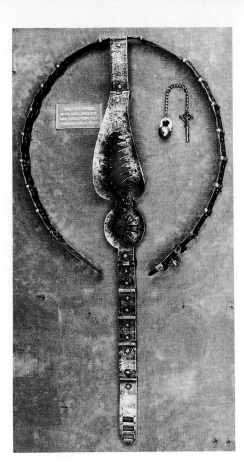

FIGURE 1–4

A wrought iron chastity belt like this one (probably Italian, from about 1700) not only must have been painful to wear but must have posed major problems of personal hygiene.

It has often been said that the Crusades brought about an increase in prostitution during the Middle Ages. The Crusades, which began about A.D. 1100 and ended about 1300, were military expeditions by the Christian powers of Western Europe to recapture the Holy Land from the Muslim forces that had taken over that area. Crusaders not only suffered the hardships and dangers of battle, but also had to spend long periods of time away from their wives or lovers. In acknowledgment of the frustrations of abstinence, leaders of the Crusades often made prostitutes available to the men who served under them.

During the Middle Ages sexual promiscuity and the absence of effective contraception produced many illegitimate births. Interestingly, though, illegitimacy often did not carry a social stigma, at least for males. Indeed, to be called a bastard during the Middle Ages could be a mark of distinction if one's natural father was a knight or a nobleman. Many notable figures, including the emperor Charlemagne and the semilegendary King Arthur, are thought to have been bastards, and William the Conqueror signed his letters "William the Bastard."

The **chastity belt,** a device designed to ensure the fidelity of wives as well as the virginity of young women, was used during the Middle Ages, although it may have been introduced centuries earlier in ancient Greece. The Greek poet Homer, for example, wrote about a chastity belt in the *Odyssey* in 750 B.C. In that epic Aphrodite or Venus, the goddess of love, betrays her husband, Hephaistos, with his brother Ares. In an act of revenge, Hephaistos creates a girdle (the "girdle of Venus") to prevent Aphrodite from further sexual betrayals.

The chastity belt was usually made of metal and locked around the waist (see Figure 1–4). A connected and curved center piece covered the vaginal and anal areas, with small openings left for body elimination processes. Sharp spikes often covered the narrow vaginal opening. Velvet was sometimes used to cover the metal and offer

Were chastity belts really used in past historical times?

chastity belt A device used during the Middle Ages to ensure the fidelity of wives as well as the virginity of unmarried women. Usually made of metal, the belt covered the vaginal and anal areas, leaving a small opening for the passage of urine and menstrual blood.

the wearer some degree of comfort. Wealthy men sometimes had their wives' belts studded with diamonds or other precious stones or inlaid with gold or ivory.

The chastity belt provides an interesting commentary on the sexual lives of medieval people. Such an extreme measure reflected the concept of ownership—women were regarded as the sexual property of men. Interestingly, historians tell us that many women found ways to rid themselves of the chastity belt while their husbands or lovers were elsewhere. Spare keys were sometimes kept hidden by ingenious women.

How widespread the use of chastity belts was is not known, although it is believed that they were used throughout Europe and particularly in Italy and France. The fourteenth-century ruler of Padua, Francesco da Carrara, instructed his wives to wear chastity belts. And in the sixteenth century King Henry II of France had a chastity belt designed for Catherine de Medici. Not only the socially elite, but the working classes as well used them. Merchants and soldiers, for example, were especially likely to fit their wives with chastity belts. In Spain the chastity belt was used up to the nineteenth century.

The Renaissance and Reformation

During the periods known as the Renaissance and the Reformation (the fourteenth to the seventeenth centuries), people and institutions underwent significant religious, moral, and social changes. Indeed, customs and institutions that had dominated European societies for almost a thousand years were swept away during these periods. Among the many important developments of the Renaissance and Reformation were vast increases in commerce and wealth, great intellectual advances, and the establishment of Protestant Christianity.

New attitudes about human sexuality were promoted during the Renaissance, including an appreciation of the human body. There was a rebirth of the Greek love of physical beauty. Artists sensuously portrayed nude men and women in such paintings as Signorelli's *School of Pan*, Giorgione's *Recumbent Venus*, and Cranach's *Gabrielle d'Estrées and Her Sister in the Bath*. Unlike the nudes in medieval art, which were often distorted and associated in some way with sin, Renaissance nudes were beautiful and harmonious. The sex lives of men and women also became popular themes for Renaissance writers and poets.

During the Reformation sexual attitudes and behavior were affected by the weakening of the Catholic Church. The Church's efforts to regulate sexual behavior began to be questioned, as was its insistence on associating sexual pleasure with evil. Gradually, the notion of individual freedom was introduced by Protestant thinkers.

The Catholic Church's promotion of celibacy, in particular, was attacked by many Protestant reformers. Both Martin Luther (1483–1546) and John Calvin (1509–1564) believed that celibacy was contrary to human nature and was endangering Christianity. But there were differences between the two on this issue. While Luther maintained that sex within the institution of marriage was an acceptable and necessary activity, he continued to view the act of intercourse as unclean. Calvin did not view intercourse as unclean, provided it was practiced beneath the holy veil of marriage vows. Both Luther and Calvin felt there was a need to control and moderate carnal desires, and neither man sanctioned masturbation, sex between unmarried persons, or adultery.

Marriage was strongly encouraged during these historical periods, being perceived by most people as a desirable union. Indeed, Luther remarked that marriage was "God's gift to man, a heavenly and spiritual state, a school of faith in love in which every menial task, every trouble and hardship, is a means of religious education." Luther, however, did not believe in the indissolubility of marriage. Unlike the Catholic Church, he permitted divorce, though he conceded authority in this area to the state.

Introduction to Human Sexuality

Although there was an increase in clandestine, or secret, marriages, prearranged marriages continued to be much more common. Women remained subordinate to men during the Renaissance and Reformation, particularly within the marriage relationship. They were expected to be virgins when they married, although this expectation was not as great among Protestants as it was among Catholics. The primary responsibilities of married women were to bear and care for children and to tend to domestic chores.

Prostitution came under severe attack during the Renaissance and Reformation. Many brothels were closed and those that remained open were carefully supervised by public officials. Another reason for the decline in prostitution during this time was the appearance of syphilis, a highly infectious and potentially fatal sexually transmitted disease (see Chapter 17). The disease was believed to have been brought back from the lands of the western hemisphere to Portugal by Columbus's sailors in 1494. Over the next few years it spread throughout Europe, and by 1500, the "bad pox," as it was called, had reached such faraway locations as Russia and China.

Thought to be transmitted exclusively by prostitutes and called a typical soldier's disease, syphilis took a heavy toll on the civilian population. Poor medical knowledge of the disease, questionable cures (treatment with mercury, a poison, was the standard medical regimen), and unsanitary living conditions no doubt hastened the spread of this disease. Government officials issued numerous proclamations to alert and inform the general public about syphilis. For example, in 1495 the German emperor Maximilian instructed men to avoid prostitutes, whom he held responsible for spreading the disease. Some protection against infection was afforded in 1560 when Fallopius invented the first condom, then a linen sheath to be worn under the prepuce. Interestingly, the condom was first used as a disease-prevention measure rather than a contraceptive device.

Colonial America

People who voyaged to America during these periods were searching for a better life in the New World. The early English colonies were divided into three geographical groups: the northern colonies, now the several states of New England; the middle colonies, consisting of New York, New Jersey, Delaware, and Pennsylvania; and the southern colonies, stretching from Maryland to Georgia. The colonial period began with the settlement of Jamestown, Virginia, in 1607 and ended with the start of the Revolutionary War in 1775. During this relatively short era a wilderness was conquered and a new nation was established.

The Puritans, a group of Protestants who broke away from the Church of England because they wanted to purify churches by eliminating priestly vestments and elaborate ceremonies, were guided by the thinking of John Calvin. Subjected to religious persecution in England, they journeyed to America in order to practice their beliefs in freedom.

The Puritans were governed by strong clerical leadership and driven by a compelling work ethic. They brought a number of European customs and beliefs to the New World. For example, they encouraged early marriage and large families out of the European belief that the family should function as an economic unit. Single status was viewed as impractical, since it resulted in a failure to cultivate important farmland. Several colonies imposed special taxes on single men. In Hartford, Connecticut, for example, the penalty for remaining single was 20 shillings a week.

In contrast to Old World custom, most Puritan marriages were not arranged by a couple's parents, though the prospective bridegroom was expected to secure the father's permission for the bride's hand in marriage. The courtship period was generally short and romance was seldom a part of the bonding process.

One of the more unusual and interesting courtship behaviors in colonial North America was known as *bundling*. In bundling two unmarried persons of the opposite sex shared the same bed but remained fully clothed. A center board was placed between them to discourage sexual intimacy. Whether or not the board remained in place was secondary to the fact that parents knew where their daughter was, and with whom.

No one knows exactly how this custom came about, although the English and Dutch are often mentioned as the originators of the practice and the reason behind it is sometimes said to be the cold, stormy winter nights in colonial America. While lovers could walk off into the woods or other locations to be alone during warm months, cold nights forced them (and everyone else) inside. Because there was no such thing as central heating in those days, the fireplace became a crowded location in most colonial homes. Simple hospitality, as well as a parental desire to hasten the courtship process, often prompted an invitation for the suitor to stay and share the young woman's bed.

The Puritan marriage structure was patriarchal, with the husband controlling all domestic matters. Men were expected to provide for their families and to be faithful to their wives. Puritan women occupied a clearly subordinate position to men. Their place was in the home, tending to household responsibilities and caring for children. A woman's property belonged to her husband, and she did not have the right to vote. Men were permitted to punish their wives and children physically if they wished.

The Puritans practiced considerable sexual restraint and the prevailing moral code was quite strict. Even clothing reflected sexual repression. Because they believed that bright colors incited lust, Puritans wore only black, gray, and white. Deriving pleasure from sex was frowned upon. Sex was strictly for the purpose of procreation, and only married partners could lawfully engage in it. Even marital sex was forbidden on the Sabbath, a day devoted to religious activities. Premarital sex, viewed as succumbing to the temptations of the flesh, was not tolerated, and *both* women and men were expected to be chaste before marriage.

Adultery was a serious offense, legally punishable by death. However, adulterers more often than not received lesser penalties such as imprisonment, whipping, banishment from the community, or the stigma of having to wear the letter "A" on their clothing (as Hester Prynne did in Hawthorne's *The Scarlet Letter*). Some adulterers were even branded on the forehead with the letter "A." As far as other sexual behaviors

In Hawthorne's The Scarlet Letter, *Hester Prynne's crime of adultery brought about both social isolation and the ignominious scarlet "A" that she was forced to embroider on her clothing. Sharing a tiny cottage on the outskirts of town with her illegitimate daughter, Pearl, she lived on whatever food and necessities the townsfolk were willing to provide.*

Introduction to Human Sexuality

were concerned, masturbation and oral-genital and anal-genital sex were viewed as sinful and were prohibited.

The Victorian Era

It is important to take our historical narrative back across the Atlantic, for a new European morality would strongly impact on sexual morality in the United States. The Victorian era was a period in British history named for Queen Victoria, who ascended to the throne in 1837, a time when the English neither liked nor respected their rulers. Victoria proved to be a leader of considerable virtue and diligence, and under her rule Great Britain's territorial and economic powers soared.

By living above reproach, Queen Victoria raised the throne to a position of veneration. Her strong moral character and lack of self-indulgence soon became standards of conduct for influential English citizens. Many began to lead more austere lives in which high-mindedness, modesty, and self-righteousness figured as prime virtues.

The Victorian era, then, was a time of heightened morality, a morality that included a very repressive attitude toward sexuality. Interestingly, although both the upper and middle classes espoused these values, it was primarily the middle classes who lived them, modeling themselves on what they perceived to be upper-class behavior. In fact, though, upper-class people enjoyed considerable sexual freedom during the Victorian era.

Among the general population the topic of sex became shrouded in silence, with many almost pretending that sexual desire did not exist. This battle against nature, underlain as it was by an intense preoccupation with sex, was doomed to fail eventually. In the meantime anxiety, guilt, shame, and confusion compounded as Victorians struggled to achieve the high moral standards they had set for themselves.

Victorian sexual repression took many forms. For example, art was censored and often altered to suit the purist attitude. Fig leaves and other adornments were strategically placed over the genitals in museum sculptures. Any work of literature that contained sexual themes or language was attacked. Shakespeare was perceived as a corrupter of morals, as were many other great English poets. Novels in general were condemned; the editors of the English *Evangelical Magazine* wrote that "all novels, generally speaking, are instruments of abomination and ruin." Many publications went underground, and pornographic material flourished secretly.

Profanity became taboo. Even words used in the Bible, such as *fornication* and *whore*, were forbidden. Anything sexual was often referred to in euphemisms. For instance, the word *pregnant* was replaced with the expression "with child," and the French *accouchement* was deemed much more acceptable than the English phrase "delivering a child." Coyness and diminutives, not to mention ambiguity, characterized most euphemisms, such as "sit-me-down" and "botty" for buttocks, "John Thomas" for penis, "Lady Jane" for vulva, and "glue" for venereal disease. Sexual intercourse was referred to by some as a "four-legged frolic," "doing the naughty," or "giving the old man his supper." Even nonsexual words that seemed a bit crude were replaced; for example, the words *perspire* (for men) and *glow* (for women) replaced *sweat*.

Most Victorians believed that masturbation was a pathological habit and ascribed many dire consequences to it, including lowered intelligence, nocturnal hallucinations, and suicidal tendencies. Victorians invented special devices to prevent boys from masturbating or from having nocturnal emissions, including a cagelike shield that could be fastened over the genital area to prevent self-stimulation and a metal ring with spikes protruding inward that could be slipped on the flaccid penis so that if the boy had an erection, the spikes would cause him excruciating pain. William Acton, a noted physician of the day, described the symptoms of masturbation:

The [boy's] frame is stunted and weak, the muscles undeveloped, the eye is sunken and heavy, the complexion is sallow, pasty, or covered with spots of acne, the hands are damp and cold, and the skin moist. The boy shuns the society of others, creeps about alone, joins with repugnance in the amusements of his schoolfellows. He cannot look anyone in the face, and becomes careless in dress and uncleanly in person. His intellect has become sluggish and enfeebled, and if his evil habits are persisted in, he may end in becoming a driveling idiot. (Acton, 1857, p. 57.)

Prostitution, although condemned as immoral by the Victorians, was a thriving business. By the late 1800s, there were over 120,000 prostitutes in the city of London alone, and they catered to all social classes of men. Three types of prostitutes were noted: the well-dressed ones of the brothels, those walking the streets, and the prostitutes of the slums, or "motts." The persistence of widespread prostitution throughout this period is evidence that behind Victorian self-righteousness and prudery there was a strong interest in sex. Thus, although the official attitude toward sex was one of repression, realists considered prostitution a necessary outlet for male sexual desire and a lesser evil than adultery with women of the man's own social class.

The gender roles assigned to Victorian men and women reflected the prudery of the times. Men were taught to be assertive, dominant, and in control. They were expected to postpone marriage until they had established themselves in the vocational world, and commitment to this idea probably helped to sublimate the sexual drive. Women, on the other hand, were brought up to be subservient, dependent, and fragile. They were taught to be sexually submissive to their husbands, but not to enjoy sex. Indeed, female sexuality was viewed with some repulsion. A decent woman did not have sexual feelings of any kind, and her modest clothing reflected her asexual image. Acton wrote that "the best mothers, wives, and managers of households know little or nothing about sexual indulgences. Love of home, children, and domestic duties, are the only passions they feel" (1857, p. 31).

The Industrial Revolution

Those living in late-nineteenth-century North America witnessed the beginnings of a great transformation. The Industrial Revolution, as it came to be known, changed the predominantly agrarian society of America into an urban and industrialized one. This transformation had many direct and indirect effects on human sexuality.

One of the most striking changes was a new alignment of the family with regard to work and the economic support of family members. Where previously families had functioned as a productive agrarian unit, in the growing number of nonfarm families the husband went off to work in an industrial setting, while the wife and children remained at home.

The Industrial Revolution brought about an important shift in gender-role behaviors. Women, once partners in labor in farming families, were exclusively assigned to preserving home and hearth. Employment outside the home and away from the family became the province of men. It can be said, then, that as the Industrial Revolution brought about significant technological changes, it also introduced new gender-role behaviors and expectations.

In time, the need for female workers drew large numbers of women into the labor force, despite resistance to this development. Gender-role stereotyping caused women who worked outside the home to be regarded as unfeminine or negligent of their wifely and maternal responsibilities. Eventually, however, as more and more women joined the paid labor force these attitudes changed. This, in turn, encouraged even more women to seek employment outside the home.

Introduction to Human Sexuality

The frequent need to search for employment prospects during the Industrial Revolution made the family unit more mobile and also more isolated from relatives. Children, who in a more agrarian age had been regarded as needed hands on the farm, now became economic liabilities. Instead of making a productive contribution to the family, they became extra mouths to feed in their parents' daily struggle to carve out an existence in this new state of American history. Work and family life thus became separate enterprises; families still consumed as a unit, but they no longer produced as one.

For these reasons, smaller families became a desirable goal and birth control an important concern. During the 1920s and 1930s Margaret Sanger led the birth control movement in the United States. A nurse, Sanger wrote and distributed booklets on birth control and opened clinics to advise people on methods and techniques. Because it was illegal to distribute birth control information, Sanger, who founded the Planned Parenthood Federation of America, was arrested many times. (More information on Sanger can be found in Chapter 12.)

Abstinence, withdrawal, douching, and abortion were the most widely used methods of birth control at the turn of the century, though a wide range of better contraceptive measures were under development. One of the major goals of the contraceptive movement was to create methods that would be minimally intrusive during moments of sexual intimacy. The oral contraceptive pill, introduced in 1960, was one such method. Although health-related concerns about the pill persist (see Chapter 12), it is a relatively inexpensive, reliable, and simple form of birth control.

Fertility rates in North America declined significantly both during and after the Industrial Revolution. The percentage of families with six or more members was 51.8 in 1790, 32.8 in 1900, and 20.1 in 1930. Meanwhile, the percentage of childless marriages increased. This trend provides an interesting contrast to the high premium placed on having many children during earlier historical periods.

The path to marriage also changed, including new patterns of courtship. The "Roaring Twenties" brought new levels of autonomy and freedom as America experienced a wave of prosperity and self-indulgence. Daring young "flappers" shocked their elders by wearing short skirts and freely using cosmetics and cigarettes; many drank illegal liquor in clubs called "speakeasies." The invention of the automobile made it possible for young couples to be alone together and to engage in much more sexual activity than was possible within the home. The sexual needs and sexual rights of women were increasingly recognized and the notion of the shy, passive female was eroded.

Parental control over courtship lessened considerably, and arranged marriages became a thing of the past for the majority of couples. Women experienced much more freedom in selecting a mate, and for most partners of both sexes love and affection became pivotal features of the relationship. The concept of romantic love was reborn and became increasingly popular.

The Sexual Revolution

Any effort to explore contemporary human sexuality must take into account how sexual attitudes and behaviors have changed over the years. Our sexual attitudes and values have been influenced by many different cultures. For example, we have seen how a double standard for men and women existed from the earliest times, how marriage was regarded as the only proper place for sex, and how sex was justified by its procreative function. While the Industrial Revolution introduced some changes in these attitudes, far more sweeping changes in gender roles, gender-role behavior, and sexual activity occurred in North America in the latter part of the twentieth century.

sexual revolution Changes in thinking about human sexuality that occurred during the 1960s and 1970s and that focused on gender roles as well as specifically sexual behavior.

What happened during the so-called sexual revolution?

National Organization for Women (NOW) The chief organization of the women's movement, NOW has been particularly active in implementing reforms in education and in the workplace.

Many writers have referred to these changes, which began in the 1960s, as a **sexual revolution.** Others, who feel the changes have been less dramatic and far-reaching than the word *revolution* suggests, prefer terms such as the "permissive movement" (Weeks, 1985). Whatever the term of choice, it is indisputable that these changes helped shape society's present sexual attitudes and behaviors. We have seen a shift in relations between men and women, a continuing and accentuated commercialization of sex, changes in the ways sexual behavior is regulated, the emergence of new social antagonisms, and the appearance of new political movements.

The controversy surrounding the sexual revolution has produced conflicting interpretations of the era and the phenomena that have characterized it. Some writers suggest that the sexual revolution brought about more relaxed and tolerant attitudes and a more flexible morality. Some hold that it produced greater equality, both general and sexual, between men and women. Others argue, however, that the only freedom women gained was to be more sexually active and responsive to the desires of men (Weeks, 1985). As far as equality in other aspects of life is concerned, they maintain that the liberated woman is largely a myth. Although many women today hold managerial and leadership positions, most remain trapped in low-paying jobs, have few career opportunities, and shoulder most of the burdens of child care and household work.

In retrospect, the conservatism of the 1950s appears to have been the springboard for many of the changes that occurred during the latter half of the twentieth century (Alston & Tucker, 1973). Vivid eruptions of sexual display characterized the sexual revolution. For example, many rock stars began to present themselves in highly erotic fashion through their dress and movements onstage and in the lyrics of their songs.

In major cities commercialized sex grew rapidly, and there is some evidence that attitudes toward birth control, divorce, abortion, premarital and extramarital sex, cohabitation, and lesbian and gay life styles relaxed somewhat (Granberg & Granberg, 1982). The 1960s also saw a great change in the openness with which sexual matters are discussed. Today sex is spoken about, written about, and visually represented in ways society could never have imagined 30 years ago (Weeks, 1985).

The media played a significant role in the movement away from traditional morality. Bans on books such as *Lady Chatterly's Lover* were removed and Hollywood movies incorporated more sexually suggestive themes. A number of Supreme Court decisions of the 1960s and 1970s (see Chapter 21) were influential in promoting more liberal sexual attitudes; for example, the Court ruled that both graphic discussion and depiction of sexual acts were protected by the constitutional right of free speech. Although standards of enforcement varied from state to state, sexually explicit books, magazines, and films became widely available in the United States. Complete frontal nudity of both men and women was no longer restricted to hard-core pornography but began to appear in such over-the-counter magazines as *Playboy* and *Cosmopolitan.* Sex manuals such as *The Joy of Lesbian/Gay Sex* and *The Sensual Couple* also found their way onto bookstore shelves, offering readers an assortment of sexual pleasuring techniques. In the world of advertising sex was used in more direct ways to promote a diversity of products from blue jeans to sports cars.

Gender-role attitudes and behaviors also began to change. During the 1960s the women's liberation movement worked for the enforcement of laws and regulations promoting the equality of women in the workplace and in other areas of life, as well as greater rights for many other groups. Although this movement was prominent in North American society from the 1840s until the achievement of women's suffrage in 1920, public interest in it declined until the 1960s. Then, spurred by such books as Betty Friedan's *Feminine Mystique* (1963) and Kate Millett's *Sexual Politics* (1969), the women's movement began once again to protest women's second-class treatment. The **National Organization for Women (NOW),** founded in 1966 by Friedan and

Introduction to Human Sexuality

others, is the largest formal organization in the women's movement and has been especially active in implementing reform in the educational and vocational arenas. NOW, for example, was instrumental in framing the Equal Rights Amendment to the Constitution. This amendment states in essence that gender shall have no effect on equality of rights under the law. The ERA passed both houses of Congress in 1972. The fact that at this writing three of the thirty-eight states required to ratify the amendment have yet to do so is an indication of how painfully slow progress in this area has been.

Still, the work of NOW and other similar organizations has raised the level of social consciousness on this issue enough so that the belief in male superiority has dimmed. Some relationships between women and men have become more egalitarian. Espousing the notion of **androgyny,** some couples share domestic chores, avoiding traditional gender-role stereotyping. Their relationship dynamics are based on mutuality and reciprocity. We also find many more dual-career households—that is, households in which both husbands and wives are employed outside the home.

The sexual revolution did not alter the popularity of marriage. Indeed, marriage continues to be the chosen life style for a very high proportion of the population—about 90 percent of Americans still opt to get married at some point during their lives (National Center for Health Statistics, 1990). A growing number, however, are choosing to delay the trip to the altar. In 1976 the median age for marriage was 23.8 for men and 21.3 for women; today it has risen to 25.8 and 23.6, respectively (U.S. Bureau of the Census, 1990). As we'll discover in Chapter 15, there are many reasons to postpone marriage today. For one thing, many men and women are placing their careers ahead of marriage, and more people are enrolling in colleges and in graduate and professional schools.

Other life styles besides marriage are being chosen by growing numbers of Americans. For example, **cohabitation,** or the sharing of a residence by an unmarried man and woman who are sexually intimate, became more common and more socially acceptable in the 1990s. Cohabitation first became popular in the 1960s, when college administrators began to permit other-sex visitors in campus residence halls. Students, who had pressed for more liberal regulations, began to take advantage of new options to rent off-campus apartments. Meanwhile, the liberalization of sexual attitudes and behaviors among young adults made premarital sex more openly acceptable. In the 1990s cohabitation continues to be a popular life style among college students, but as we'll learn later, it also appeals to older adults. Most couples see cohabitation as

androgyny The quality of having both masculine and feminine characteristics. Considered by some to be a desirable quality, inasmuch as both male and female traits and skills are useful and beneficial.

cohabitation The sharing of a residence by an unmarried woman and man who are sexually intimate.

"I hunt and she gathers—otherwise, we couldn't make ends meet."

Introduction to Human Sexuality

27

an additional stage of courtship, not a permanent alternative to marriage. Today there are about 2.6 million unmarried couples living together in the United States (U.S. Bureau of the Census, 1990; Atwater, 1985).

Singlehood has also become a viable alternative for some people. Once considered evidence that a person could not attract mates, singlehood is now thought of as an acceptable life style. Many single people believe they can lead happy, productive lives without becoming part of a "couple." Today some single people adopt and raise children without help from a partner, and some single women choose to give birth to and raise children alone.

Although marital disharmony and collapse did occur in the past, divorce was not widespread until this century. Since the late 1950s, the proportion of first marriages ending in divorce has risen sharply. The granting of approximately one million divorces in 1974 marked the first time in American history that more marriages were ended by divorce than by death. Between 1970 and 1980 the number of divorces increased almost 70 percent. In 1990, 1,172,000 divorces were granted, involving nearly two and a half million adults and over one million children. The United States has the distinction of having the highest divorce rate of any Western nation (U.S. Bureau of the Census, 1990; National Center for Health Statistics, 1990).

Why did couples remain together in the past despite disharmony? Many— perhaps most—stayed together for economic reasons. The family produced and consumed as a unit, and a divorce would cripple the household's operation and finances. Thus it made poor economic sense to divorce. Many other couples stayed together "for the sake of the children," believing that offering their children the advantages of a two-parent home was more important than seeking personal fulfillment. People also remained married for fear of jeopardizing their standing in the community or because obtaining a divorce was expensive, tedious, and time-consuming.

These reasons still hold true for some couples, but for most Americans they have lost their force. Most households no longer produce as a working unit, and growing numbers of women are no longer economically dependent on their husbands. Divorces have become easier to obtain, and although divorced people do experience role readjustment, their sheer numbers have lessened negative community reaction.

Certain societal values have changed along with the divorce rate. Many people place a higher premium on individual choice and personal fulfillment than their ancestors did, and the rising divorce rate may reflect this attitude. Today divorce is often viewed not as a sign of personal disorganization, but rather as a way to improve one's life. As we'll see, the growing emphasis on personal satisfaction and fulfillment has affected many other aspects of sexual behavior.

The first in our series of boxed inserts called "Sexuality in the News" focuses on some issues raised by the changing status of the family in American society. This "News" box, like similar boxes in other chapters, appears just before the chapter summary. Note that it is based on a tape segment from the video library that accompanies your instructor's copy of this book. Some "News" boxes highlight other video clips in that library. Others present *New York Times* articles relevant to chapter topics.

Greater tolerance of sexual experimentation and alternative sexual life styles such as gay and lesbian and bisexuality has also become apparent since the sexual revolution. Although a few organizations, such as the Mattachine Society and the Daughters of Bilitis, had provided support to gay men and lesbians for some years, it was only in 1969, when the patrons of a New York City gay bar called the Stonewall Inn fought off a police raid, that the gay rights movement was born. The Stonewall incident was the catalyst for the formation of the National Gay and Lesbian Task Force, established to reduce discrimination and ensure the civil rights of gay men and lesbians. A host of regional and state organizations now deal with gay and lesbian issues and Gay Pride Week is celebrated annually. Public attitudes have become

Before the 1970s, simply walking with a lover in public was often fraught with anxiety for gays and lesbians. Homosexual bashing, both verbal and physical, was not uncommon, and those who insulted or attacked gays or lesbians were rarely if ever punished.

somewhat more tolerant of living arrangements that were once taboo, and lesbian and gay couples living together openly have become part of the sociocultural scene in the 1990s. We will have more to say about gay, lesbian, and bisexual life styles and issues in Chapter 9.

To sum up, greater sexual freedom and some positive life-style options and changes have been brought about by the so-called sexual revolution of the 1960s and 1970s. But these changes have created a new set of problems. The climate of sexual freedom often pushes young people into relationships that they are emotionally unprepared to handle. Moreover, our relaxed sexual behavior has contributed to sharp increases in such sexually transmitted diseases as gonorrhea and syphilis. Most disturbing of all, medical research has not been able to find a cure for the fatal acquired immune deficiency syndrome (AIDS). We will discuss these issues in greater detail in Chapters 14, 17, and 18.

We hope that our historical narrative has shed some light on present-day conceptions of human sexuality. We trust that you now realize that contemporary attitudes and behaviors did not spring up overnight. As our discussion has shown, people have tried to regulate sexuality for centuries on the basis of either unwritten or written laws of sexual morality. The socialization of both women and men in traditional gender roles and the restriction of sex to a procreative function within the institution of marriage are also themes deeply rooted in antiquity. Our beliefs about prostitution, infidelity, and gays and lesbians also share a long and complex history.

In some ways, though, the civilizations we have examined differed significantly from one another. For instance, the ancient Greeks and Romans tolerated most sexual activities, while medieval Roman Catholic opinion was ascetic and essentially antisexual. And the wide latitude of individual sexual expression ushered in by the sexual revolution of our own century offers a stark contrast to Victorian sexual repression in the last century.

Every interpretation of history is selective and prone to oversimplification. Nevertheless, tracing the roots of human sexual behavior as we have done in this chapter should enable you to see how today's sexual attitudes and sexual expression reflect a convergence of past influences. Indeed, as customs and conventions change or shift and as civilizations advance, sexual expression is also modified. Contemporary society is no exception, and the remaining chapters of this textbook are designed to explore the changes evident in today's sexual attitudes and behavior. By exploring the past, we hope that we've piqued your curiosity about human sexuality in the 1990s and about what the future may have in store for all of us.

SEXUALITY IN THE NEWS

Family: Old Perceptions, New Realities

*T*his ABC News Special report, aired June 9, 1985, explores the status of the American family with such notable public figures as T. Berry Brazelton, M.D., pediatrician and author; Betty Friedan, writer and co-founder of the National Organization for Women (NOW); Senator Daniel Patrick Moynihan, Democrat of New York; and Eleanor Holmes Norton, professor of law at Georgetown University. Moderated by ABC anchor Carole Simpson, the discussions revolve around changes in the structure of the American family and in the roles of its members. Participants engage in an often brisk debate on such issues as how to ensure the well-being and future success of children who either return from school to empty homes or spend long hours in supervised care because both of their parents work outside the home. (52:34 minutes)

DISCUSSION QUESTIONS

1. If the single-parent family is indeed on the rise, many children may grow up lacking appropriate role models. Should we do something to provide children such models? What do you suggest?

2. What is the gist of the argument among Geneva Johnson, president of Family Service America; Connie Marshner, chairman of the Family and Child Protection Institute; and Betty Friedan? Is Marshner arguing against women having professional careers outside the home? Against assistance to families in need? If so, why? If not, what is her point?

3. How would you reconcile Marshner's claim that we have lost values and other things that hold families together with Friedan's arguments that the two-paycheck, equal-opportunity family puts a higher value on the family?

LOOKING BACK

■ Taking a course in human sexuality can help you understand your own sexuality and clarify your sexual beliefs and attitudes. It can also help you understand others' sexual attitudes and behaviors. And it can help you make responsible decisions about sexual behaviors that affect not only your own well-being but that of others as well.

■ Human sexuality focuses on a wide range of sexual behaviors, attitudes, values, thoughts, emotions, and roles. It encompasses such topics as sexual maturation and reproduction, sex-role development, sexual drives

and response cycles, relationship dynamics, sexual life styles, sexual health and disease, and sexual dysfunctions. An interdisciplinary field of study, human sexuality embraces such fields as psychology, sociology, education, anthropology, biology, medical science, health education, and counseling.

■ There are many ways to study human sexuality and to analyze its different aspects. The primary perspectives from which useful theoretical approaches derive are the biological, medical, psychological, sociological, cultural anthropological, and historical perspectives.

■   By examining past civilizations, we find a number of recurrent historical trends. Until the twentieth century sexual activity was generally regarded as having a solely procreative purpose. Most societies placed a high premium on virginity in a bride (though not in a groom) and encouraged marriage at an early age. Infidelity in married partners was generally not tolerated, although punishment for adulterous wives was generally far more severe than that for errant husbands. A similar double standard has characterized divorce; in many societies only men could sue for divorce. Prostitution has been prevalent in most societies. And most societies have attempted to regulate sexual behavior, whether by written or unwritten law. Traditional gender-role behaviors have endured throughout recorded history and only began to change in the late nineteenth century.

■   The Industrial Revolution changed the complexion of the United States, including its sexual attitudes and behavior. Most families experienced an economic realignment, and gender-role behaviors and expectations changed. Smaller families became a desirable goal, making birth control an important concern. As the notion that people could engage in sexual activity for reasons other than procreation became accepted, fertility rates declined significantly. The "Roaring Twenties" heralded new patterns of courtship, including less parental control, more sexual experimentation, and new levels of freedom for women to choose their own mates.

■   Despite conflicting interpretations of the so-called sexual revolution, it is generally acknowledged that the 1960s and 1970s inaugurated many changes that helped shape society's present sexual attitudes and behaviors: the continuing and accentuated commercialization of sex; the continuing push toward male-female equality in all spheres of life; and new efforts to control reproduction—such as contraception and abortion—that have given rise to opposing special interest groups and political movements.

THINKING THINGS OVER

1.   Although some past societies, such as ancient Egypt, were headed by women, such women were often the pawns of powerful men and had little effect on the people they supposedly ruled. Consider the alliance of Cleopatra and Caesar. Can you think of a similar present-day example? Why has it been so difficult for women to exercise real governing power?

2.   Throughout recorded history societies have generally sanctioned the sale of sexual pleasures by women to men, and often by men to men. Consider and discuss in class the reasons for sanctioning prostitution, then and now. Why is the business of prostitution sanctioned while the profession of prostitute is not? Why is the sale of sex by men to women not sanctioned?

3.   We've seen that the Roman Catholic Church tried many efforts to control its followers' sexual behavior: sexual intercourse was valid only for procreation; a married couple could have intercourse only on prescribed days of the week and at certain times of the year. How do you think such rules affected the societies that attempted to abide by them?

4.   The United States has been affected by many social and economic revolutions. One of the most important of these was the Industrial Revolution. What effect did that revolution have on the sexual mores of the population?

5.   What do you think have been the chief effects on North American society of the so-called sexual revolution that began in the 1960s? Did it bring about equality between the sexes? How or how not?

DISCOVER FOR YOURSELF

D'Emilio, J., & Freedman, E. B. (1988). *Intimate matters: A history of sexuality in America*. New York: Harper and Row. A comprehensive but very readable account of sexuality in America. Readers will enjoy the authors' treatment of sexual politics and sexual revolutions.

Duberman, M. B. (1986). *About time: Exploring the gay past*. New York: Gay Presses of New York. A sensitive and thought-provoking historical narrative of the gay life style.

Rosen, R. (1982). *The lost sisterhood: Prostitution in America, 1900–1919*. Baltimore: Johns Hopkins University Press. A good account of prostitution in the United States.

Rothman, E. K. (1984). *Hands and hearts: A history of courtship in America*. New York: Basic Books. Rothman provides a thorough account of dating behaviors and the path to marriage.

Weeks, J. (1981). *Sex, politics, and society: The regulation of sexuality since 1800*. London: Longman. A noted contributor to the field provides excellent insights into political crusades for sexual order.

2 Research on Human Sexuality

It takes a lot of knowledge to know how little we know

—Dagobert D. Runes

Whatever else it may be, science is a way of generating and testing the truth of statements about events in the world of human experience

—Walter E. Wallace

mericans are a very curious people, as the opinion polls, surveys, and studies that the media continually bombard us with suggest. The fact that so many of these studies are concerned with sexuality is understandable if we look closely at our culture. As we saw in Chapter 1, only a few decades ago sex was a hidden part of our lives, but today it is openly acknowledged that sex is an integral and necessary part of our personalities and thus of our humanity. Certainly sexuality is a part of our nature, from birth until death, so the more we learn about our sexual selves, the better we will understand our entire selves.

To learn about something we must have valid and reliable information. That is the goal of human sexuality research: to provide accurate, reliable information to the general public as well as to others who are engaged in research, therapy, or education. Sex research can help us make informed decisions about our behavior, allow us to compare our attitudes with other people's, and enable us to be better lovers and parents.

Research on human sexuality is a relatively new field of endeavor. As you might guess from what you learned in Chapter 1, religious views and teachings in the West tended to stifle any effort at scientific investigation of this topic for a very long time. Nothing much happened in this area until the latter part of the nineteenth century, when Henry Havelock Ellis published his ground-breaking *Studies in the Psychology of Sex*. As we will see, Ellis, Sigmund Freud, and Magnus Hirschfeld were the first investigators to give serious attention to the topic of human sexuality.

The names of Alfred Kinsey and Masters and Johnson may be familiar to you. It was Kinsey (1948) who undertook the first really comprehensive survey of sexual behavior among North Americans. As we will see, the publication of his results in the late 1940s had an enormous impact both on other researchers and on the general public. When 20 years later the team of Masters and Johnson published the findings of their laboratory research on sexual arousal and response, modern interest in sexuality research was firmly established.

After acquainting you with the work of these early investigators, we will consider some basic principles of scientific research before exploring just how sexuality researchers go about collecting and analyzing their data. As we'll discover, there are several ways to collect appropriate data:

1. Surveys that ask for self-reported information.
2. Interviews of subjects by an investigator.
3. Observation of sexual behaviors by researchers.
4. In-depth case studies of single subjects.
5. Experimental research that tries to establish a cause-and-effect relationship between two or more phenomena.

These methods of gathering information will be more fully described later on in the chapter. It is hoped that as you read the following material you will gain some insight into how sexuality research should be conducted and how the findings of the many studies that you read or hear about can be interpreted.

In this chapter you'll discover:

☐ *How pioneers in human sexuality research paved the way for modern scientific inquiry.*

☐ *What the status of modern research on human sexuality is, including how contemporary investigators have enhanced our knowledge of sexual attitudes and behaviors.*

☐ *How the discipline of human sexuality qualifies as a scientific endeavor, and what principles it shares with other sciences.*

☐ *What is meant by the scientific method and what steps make up this important research plan.*

☐ *What major research methodologies are employed by human sexuality researchers.*

☐ *Why ethical research standards are important.*

PIONEERS IN HUMAN SEXUALITY RESEARCH

Around the turn of the century several important people began to contribute to the study of human sexuality. Their thinking was influential in establishing the conceptual horizons of this new field. These historical pioneers stimulated vast amounts of research around the world and provided a foundation for others to generate their own thoughts and ideas.

Henry Havelock Ellis

The British physician and author Henry Havelock Ellis (1859–1939) was something of a rebel, for he persisted in studying human sexuality during the Victorian era, when, as we've seen, the subject was taboo. In his studies Ellis sought to determine not only what sexual behavior fell within the normal range but also how and to what extent individuals' sexual behavior might vary.

In 1896 Ellis published his now-classic *Studies in the Psychology of Sex*, a seven-volume work that presented the results of his findings over a period of 32 years. Because of the repressive nature of Victorian society, some of the books in this series were labeled obscene, and although they were made available to the medical profession, they were kept from the public eye until 1935.

Ellis provided his readers with an objective and systematic account of human sexual behavior, documenting his work with many case studies. Throughout his books he emphasized that sex was a natural instinct and a healthy form of expression. Ellis's research established the interdisciplinary nature of this new area of study, drawing as it did on many fields, including biology, psychology, sociology, history, and anthropology.

Victorians found Havelock Ellis's forward-looking books on sexual behavior shocking, and only physicians were allowed to read them.

Ellis's emphasis on the naturalness of sexual expression differed considerably from the view offered by Richard von Krafft-Ebing (1840–1902), an Austrian psychiatrist and leading exponent of the Victorian approach to sexuality. Like Ellis, Krafft-Ebing analyzed sexual behavior in a systematic manner. Unlike Ellis, however, he focused his attention on sexual pathology, and his major work, *Psychopathia Sexualia* (1886), included detailed and explicit case studies of very disturbed people. This emphasis on pathology set the tone for Krafft-Ebing's overall analysis of sexual variation. A recurrent theme in his book was that virtually all sexual behavior outside of male-female penile-vaginal intercourse was atypical and practiced only by the mentally unbalanced. He considered homosexuality to be a functional sign of degeneracy and maintained that masturbation led people into such sexual deviations as sexual bondage and rape and ultimately caused insanity.

Ellis challenged the notion that sex was a pathological force. He denounced Krafft-Ebing's negative views of homosexuality and suggested that masturbation was a common sexual outlet, not only for men, but also for women (the latter really came as a shock to the Victorians). He also discussed male and female sexual arousal processes, including the importance of foreplay.

Ellis helped to transform people's thinking about human sexuality. He succeeded in establishing an objective body of knowledge about variations in sexual behavior, a collection of research that reflected tolerance and nonjudgmental observations and discussion. The concepts that he proposed set the stage for more modern views of sexuality.

Although some feel that Sigmund Freud's theories of human sexuality were bound to middle-class Austrian society of the late 1800s, Freud swung wide the door that Ellis had opened.

Sigmund Freud

Sigmund Freud (1856–1939) was an Austrian physician who forged a revolutionary theory of personality in which sexual motivation played a dominant role. Born in what is now Czechoslovakia, Freud received a medical degree from the University of Vienna in 1881. While practicing medicine in clinics, he became interested in neurophysiology, especially the functions of the brain. He spent considerable time seeking to understand abnormal brain functions and mental disorders, a pursuit that would eventually bring him to the fields of psychiatry and psychology.

Gradually, through treating neurotic patients with such techniques as hypnosis and free association (asking the patient to say spontaneously whatever comes into his or her head), Freud became convinced that sexual conflict was the cause of most

neuroses. He traced such conflict to sexual and aggressive urges and the clashes of these urges with the codes of conduct required by society.

Eventually Freud developed the theory of **psychoanalysis,** which proposes, among other things, that our past plays an important role in determining our present behavior. Fundamental to Freud's theory are the notions that behavior is unconsciously motivated and that neuroses often originate in early childhood experiences that have subsequently been repressed. Freud also suggested that sexual urges were responsible for most human motivation. He held that because sexual thoughts and needs were often repressed, they were likely to provide unconscious motivation.

We will explore some of the complexities of Freud's theory of psychoanalysis in Chapter 13. Although many of Freud's views remain controversial, many researchers in the field have been influenced by his theory of psychosexual development. According to this theory, the development and maturation of sexual and other body parts has great impact on early life experiences.

Critics of psychoanalytic theory claim that many of Freud's concepts cannot be scientifically measured and are based on poor methodology. Some argue that his theories were bound to the culture of nineteenth-century Vienna and, furthermore, that he downplayed female sexuality.

Nevertheless, Freud's theory has lost none of its luster over the years. Proponents point out that Freud's ideas have extended into many disciplines, including history, literature, philosophy, and the arts. However we view Freud's specific theories, we cannot deny the power of his intellect and the strength of his motivation to discover new dimensions of human behavior.

Magnus Hirschfeld

Magnus Hirschfeld (1868–1935), who founded the Institute of Sexual Science in Berlin, was a German physician best remembered for his progressive and outspoken views on human sexuality. After graduating from medical school in 1894, Hirschfeld

psychoanalysis A school of psychology developed by Sigmund Freud, psychoanalysis suggests that one's past exerts an important role in determining one's present behavior.

Magnus Hirschfeld was the first prominent researcher to propose that homosexual behavior might be an acceptable alternative way of life.

devoted much of his attention to studying problems in sexual functioning, particularly sexual deviations and their etiology.

Homosexuality was of particular interest to Hirschfeld, and he wrote several books on the topic. In a departure from the thinking of the day, Hirschfeld maintained that homosexuality was biologically determined and neither a disease nor a crime. He felt strongly that homosexuals should be protected by law rather than prosecuted and that therapy should aim at helping them accept themselves as members of what he called "the third sex" and at assisting them to be useful citizens.

During the 1920s Hirschfeld was instrumental in organizing the World League for Sexual Reform. This organization brought together professionals in the field of human sexuality and promoted such causes as sexual equality, sex education, and the prevention of sexually transmitted diseases. Hirschfeld's many professional contributions and innovative ideas helped to construct a foundation for the infant field of human sexuality research.

MODERN RESEARCH ON HUMAN SEXUALITY

Spurred on by the research of Ellis, Freud, and Hirschfeld, other investigators began to address a wide range of topics related to sexual attitudes and behavior. In contrast to researchers in some countries (see "A World of Differences" box), U.S. scientists have long made their findings available to the general public, who became increasingly interested in this new avenue of scientific investigation. In this section we will discuss some of the more important contemporary research contributions.

Alfred C. Kinsey

No one before Alfred Kinsey had dared to ask so many people so many direct and detailed questions about their most intimate sexual behaviors. The complete confidentiality Kinsey offered and his sincerity of approach encouraged people's candid response.

As a young biology instructor at Indiana University, Alfred C. Kinsey (1894–1956) was astounded at the barrage of questions about sex aimed at him almost daily by his students. When he tried to find answers to these questions, he was struck by the inadequacy of the research literature. The samples on which many sexuality studies were based were small, and the researchers' generalizations on the basis of these samples seemed to him unfounded.

Kinsey's work in taxonomy (the science of identifying, naming, and classifying living organisms) may have been instrumental in his ability to recognize the inadequacy of existing sex research and also in his decision to launch his own detailed investigation of human sexual behavior. Beginning in 1938, Kinsey and his staff interviewed over 11,000 people (about 5300 men and 5900 women), using a questionnaire that contained 521 items probing such areas as premarital coitus, masturbation, infidelity, and homosexuality. The subjects of Kinsey's study represented a cross-section of geographical residence, education, occupation, socioeconomic level, age, and religion in the United States. However, because Kinsey deemed the population sample of black respondents too small for meaningful analysis, only white respondents were included in his published findings.

Almost all of the 11,000 interviews were handled by Kinsey and his associates: Wardell Pomeroy, Clyde Martin, and Paul Gebhard. Kinsey himself conducted 7,000 of them. This is a staggering total when you realize that each interview required as much as two hours to complete.

Kinsey insisted on the strictest rules of confidentiality in this research. Subjects' responses were recorded by means of a special code; none of the raw data were ever translated into words; and no individual interview record was ever published. The coded materials were kept in locked files in Indiana University's laboratories.

When, in 1948, Kinsey and his associates published *Sexual Behavior in the Human Male* and, five years later, *Sexual Behavior in the Human Female*, the public

A WORLD OF DIFFERENCES

Sexuality Research in China

*U*nlike the United States, where sexuality research results are shared with the general public on a regular basis in a wide variety of media sources, the Chinese Republic for years permitted virtually no information about sexual behavior to reach its people. No publications or any other sources of information, such as classroom sex education for children and adolescents, were made available. Traditionally, Chinese parents did not explain the facts of life to their children until just before they married. Because marriage between 1949 and 1980 was not officially sanctioned until couples reached their mid-20s, sexual ignorance was widespread. Contributing to the veil of secrecy was the Chinese emphasis on propriety, which made it almost impossible to discuss sex, even in private.

Beginning in 1980, however, government officials allowed health experts and educators to share sexually related materials with the general public. For example, readers of medical columns in newspapers were encouraged to submit questions about sexuality for answers by medical doctors. Most sex-related questions were submitted by male readers. Only rarely did Chinese women inquire about sexual matters, and then the questions usually concerned menstruation or pregnancy.

As the decade progressed, newspapers and magazines began to provide new and valuable sources of research information. For example, information became available on such hidden topics as homosexuality, transsexualism, masturbation, and sexual dysfunctions. In 1985 the Chinese government held a national conference on sex education, and in 1988 the government implemented a formal sexuality program in many of China's schools (Ruan & Bullough, 1989).

response was impressive. Never before had a strictly scientific investigation aroused so much general interest. Even the reactions of fellow researchers were greater than usual. With the publication of Kinsey's findings, prevailing conceptions of many facets of human sexuality were radically altered. Indeed, most readers of the Kinsey studies were astonished to discover how widespread certain sexual activities were in the United States. For example, as Table 2–1 indicates, masturbation was engaged in almost universally by men and by many more women than was generally thought. And although society at that time considered oral sex quite objectionable, Kinsey's studies revealed that many couples engaged in this type of activity.

Why was Kinsey's research considered so important to the field of human sexuality?

TABLE 2–1

Some Revelations from Kinsey's Research

1. Masturbating to orgasm was very common: 92% of men and almost 60% of women reported it.
2. Most men and almost 50% of women said they had engaged in premarital sex.
3. About 50% of married men and 25% of married women had engaged in extramarital sex at least once.
4. At least one homosexual experience leading to orgasm was reported by 37% of men and 13% of women.
5. By the age of 23, only about two-thirds of single women were virgins.
6. Of the women in the survey, 25% had had some kind of sexual contact before the age of 12: 30% with friends, 52% with strangers, 9% with uncles, 4% with fathers, and 3% with brothers.
7. By the age of 15, 95% of all men were sexually active.
8. The average man reported having 3–4 orgasms per week.
9. By the age of 35, almost 70% of all men questioned had had sex with a prostitute.
10. Many couples surveyed reported engaging in sexual practices that society in the 1940s considered objectionable, such as oral sex.

Source: Based on Kinsey, Pomeroy, and Martin (1948) and Kinsey et al. (1953).

Although Kinsey's work marked a major breakthrough in social science research, it's important to note some flaws in these studies. Critics have pointed out that while the total numbers of men and women in the studies were pretty well balanced, other variables were not. Specifically, a disproportionate number of the men were uneducated, whereas a preponderance of the women were college graduates. Critics have also noted that Kinsey and his staff interviewed only those subjects who were willing to disclose details of their sex lives, and wondered if such volunteers really reflected the sexual attitudes and behavior of the average man and woman. If these volunteers were, in fact, more exhibitionistic about their sexual behavior than the people who refused to be interviewed, they would have contaminated the overall research findings. Other critics pointed out that asking subjects to recall sexual experiences, particularly those that occurred long ago, raised the issue of distortion due to imperfect memory. Finally, some critics proposed that Kinsey's background as a taxonomist predisposed him to systematically analyze the biological aspects of sexual behavior and downplay its emotional and interpersonal aspects.

Despite all these criticisms, Kinsey's work had many positive dimensions. In addition to its magnitude and scope, his research was distinguished by an unprecedented sophistication and expertise in the use of the interview technique. Even in the 1990s Kinsey's research remains the most comprehensive and systematic body of information on human sexual behavior ever amassed. Today the Kinsey Institute for Research in Sex, Gender, and Reproduction at Indiana University (founded by Kinsey as the Institute for Sex Research) continues his work. In recent years the Institute has launched other investigations of human sexual behavior, including studies of homosexuality and of sex offenders.

Thanks to Alfred Kinsey and his dedicated team of associates, human sexuality research became a legitimate and respectable branch of social science inquiry. Kinsey showed that, properly designed and executed, research methods such as the survey can reliably measure sexual attitudes and behavior.

William H. Masters and Virginia E. Johnson

William H. Masters (1915—) received his M.D. degree from the Rochester School of Medicine in 1943. At Washington University in St. Louis, Masters began exploring the physiology of sex, as well as the treatment of sexual dysfunction. Spurred on by the generally favorable response to Kinsey's research, he decided to launch a more detailed research project on sexual functioning. He enlisted the services of Virginia E.

Virginia Johnson and William Masters remain the only human sexuality researchers to have studied sexual activity, including sexual intercourse, in the laboratory. Although their work has been criticized on various grounds, few if any have improved upon it.

Johnson (1925——), who had studied psychology and sociology at Missouri University, and together, in 1957, they began a laboratory physiological study of human sexual response. The two founded and continued to co-direct the Masters and Johnson Institute in St. Louis. Married but recently separated, they are the most famous team of investigators in the history of human sexuality research.

Unlike Kinsey, Masters and Johnson directly and systematically observed (and filmed) sexual intercourse and self-stimulation, or masturbation. Whereas Kinsey's research represented a statistical analysis of sexual behavior, Masters and Johnson broke new ground by using sophisticated instrumentation to measure the physiology of sexual response. They recruited a total of 694 female and male volunteers for laboratory study (all were paid for their services), including 276 married couples. The unmarried subjects participated primarily in noncoital research activities, such as studies of ejaculatory processes in males and of the ways in which different contraceptive devices affected female sexual response. Although most subjects were between the ages of 18 and 40, Masters and Johnson included a group of subjects over the age of 50 in order to study the effects of aging on sexual response. A careful screening procedure was designed to weed out exhibitionists and people with emotional disturbances.

Following a tour of Masters and Johnson's laboratory facilities and inspection of the equipment to be used in the studies, each subject was invited to a private practice session. The purpose of this was to accustom people to engaging in sexual activity in a laboratory environment. When actual experimental sessions began, subjects performed acts of masturbation or sexual intercourse while being filmed or wearing devices that recorded physiological response to sexual stimulation. For example, a subject might wear electrode terminals connected to an electrocardiograph that would produce a record of her heart's activity during sexual intercourse. Or a subject might have a band placed around his penis to record size and speed of erection in response to manual stimulation.

In over 10,000 sessions Masters and Johnson recorded subjects' responses to sexual stimulation and discovered striking similarities between the responses of men and women. We will devote considerable attention to their model of the sexual response cycle in Chapter 4. Briefly, however, the model consists of four stages of physiological response during which two basic physiological reactions occur: an increased concentration of blood in bodily tissues in the genitals and female breasts, and increased energy in the nerves and muscles throughout the body. Masters and Johnson described their concept of a sexual response cycle in the book *Human Sexual Response Cycle* (1966), and later used the cycle as a foundation for their analysis of sexual dysfunction and subsequent treatment approaches (see Chapter 16). Their findings on sexual dysfunctions appeared in another book called *Human Sexual Inadequacy*, published in 1970.

As we'll discover in Chapter 4, the Masters and Johnson research model was not without its critics. Many viewed the laboratory setting as dehumanizing and mechanizing sex. Others felt that the emphasis placed on the physiology of sex denigrated its interpersonal and emotional aspects. Some critics objected to the research design on ethical grounds, claiming that the project was an invasion of privacy. Against these criticisms we might point out that for those subjects who were willing and able to perform in the laboratory, the setting may not have been dehumanizing. And all laboratory research can be criticized for isolating factors that interact in reality. Privacy is a semi-issue, inasmuch as subjects knew what they would be asked to do and volunteered to do it. Finally, critics questioned whether Masters and Johnson had selected a truly representative sample of the population. In fact, most of the subjects were well educated and more affluent than the average person. Moreover, their willingness to perform sexually under laboratory conditions suggested that they were not typical.

Overall, though, the research of Masters and Johnson had an enormous impact on the field of human sexuality. For the first time, scientific evidence on the physiology of the orgasmic response was systematically gathered. Because of these researchers' efforts, laboratory studies of sexual arousal achieved a new level of respectability among scientific researchers.

Kinsey and Masters and Johnson established the basic guidelines for the study of human sexuality, formalizing the two major approaches: the survey and the laboratory investigation. Masters and Johnson remain the foremost laboratory experimentalists, but the followers of the survey technique are many. Let's examine just a few of the more noteworthy and reliable surveys that were undertaken in the 1970s and 1980s.

The Hunt Study

The Hunt study has the distinction of being the largest survey of sexual behavior since Kinsey's research. The study itself was named after Morton Hunt, a journalist who compiled the published report of the study (Hunt, 1974). Essentially, the data gathered in this survey were compared with Kinsey's findings to see if sexual behavior had changed over a 30-year span. The study was not a replication of the Kinsey surveys, for the questions were worded differently and the format entailed a self-administered questionnaire. Although this investigation was not conducted by academic investigators and contained some research flaws, the information is worthy of our attention.

With funding from the Playboy Foundation, the Research Guild, a market research organization, chose 24 United States cities and selected subjects randomly from telephone books. Potential subjects were asked to participate in a small panel discussion of sexual behaviors and attitudes. Although a questionnaire containing some 1,200 items had been prepared for subjects to complete after participating in the discussion, investigators did not tell people about this during their initial contacts with them. Nevertheless, all subjects who participated in the panel discussions completed the survey questionnaire. A total of 2,026 subjects (1,044 women and 982 men) were involved in the study. Hunt insisted that the sample closely represented the U.S. population of adults over 18 in that 90 percent were white and 10 percent African-American, 25 percent had never been married, 71 percent were married, and 4 percent had been married before but were single at the time of the project. Factoring in such other demographic variables as education, place of residence, and occupation, the sample does appear to have resembled the U.S. population during the 1970s.

Still, critics found several methodological problems in the conduct of the study. The sampling procedure, in particular, met with considerable disfavor among social scientists. Only people who had telephones were selected for the study, omitting those who were poor, illiterate, and in institutions such as colleges or prisons. Thus the study did *not* truly represent the population. Critics of the telephone approach also argued that the sensitivity of the topic necessitated face-to-face contact with respondents. Furthermore, the respondents did not know if the calls were authentic, and the fact that they were not told they would be asked to complete a questionnaire raised the issue of participant consent. Finally, only 20 percent of the people asked to be a part of the study agreed. Such a high refusal rate once again raised the issue of representativeness.

subject bias In research studies, a phenomenon in which inherent bias in the subject or some feature of the study's design interferes with the subject's response.

Another problem that we will call **subject bias** occurs when subjects have inherent biases with regard to a topic or become influenced by some factor in an experimental design. In this case, the panel discussions might have influenced subjects' answers to the questionnaire items. Finally, critics have pointed out that 1,000–2,000 questions is simply too many; the subjects could not possibly have thought carefully about all the questions and their answers to them.

Research on Human Sexuality

The incidence of sexual activity among adolescents has been rising steadily in recent years, with a concomitant rise in teenage pregnancies and cases of AIDS or other sexually transmitted diseases. Fortunately, some young people are beginning to recognize that there are many satisfying paths to sexual pleasure that do not involve sexual intercourse.

Research on Adolescent Sexuality

In the 1970s the social psychologist Robert Sorenson conducted one of the first large-scale studies of adolescent sexual behavior and published his results in a book entitled *Adolescent Sexuality in Contemporary America* (1973). Sorenson's sampling procedures were an improvement on Hunt's. In 200 urban, rural, and suburban areas of the United States, 2,042 households were randomly selected, yielding 839 potential teenage subjects aged 13 to 19. However, because both the parents and the adolescents had to sign consent forms (40 percent of the parents and 25 percent of the subjects refused), only 411 subjects of the original sample participated in the survey. Here again, we have many potential subjects not agreeing to participate. Although a greater percentage of those approached agreed to participate in the Sorenson research than in the Hunt study, we still have the problem of **self-selection**—that is, we don't know if those who refused were different from those who did participate. Compounding the issue is the question of whether the children of parents who refused to permit their teenagers to cooperate had different attitudes and behaviors than those held by the teenagers who did participate in the survey.

It is important to note that Sorenson, like Hunt, asked respondents to answer an exhaustive number of survey questions. Sorenson's survey was 38 pages long, and you will recall that Hunt's survey contained 1,000 items. Would you be able to give your attention to a survey of this length? Why do you suppose these investigators insisted on creating such lengthy surveys? Could it be that their need to demonstrate the seriousness and scientific legitimacy of their purpose got in the way of their common sense?

Despite its shortcomings, the Sorenson project did provide useful information about patterns of adolescent masturbation, petting, premarital sex, gay/lesbian relationships, and other facets of sexual behavior. Among other findings, Sorenson discovered that 45 percent of females and about 50 percent of males had engaged in premarital intercourse before the age of 19. In Chapter 14 we will compare these

self-selection A threat to the reliability of research studies wherein many members of a sample may choose not to participate, throwing off the balance the research hoped to achieve among various characteristics of subjects such as sex and age.

figures with some more recent investigations of teenage sexual behavior (Brooks-Gunn & Furstenberg, 1989; Kahn et al., 1988; Coles & Stokes, 1985).

With support from the federal government, Melvin Zelnick and John Kantner, of Johns Hopkins University, conducted three nationwide surveys during the 1970s focusing on such issues as teenage pregnancy, use of contraceptives, and premarital sex (Zelnick & Kantner, 1977, 1980). The first two studies were limited to young women (aged 15–19), but the third included young men (aged 17–21).

The sampling techniques these investigators used and the questionnaire they devised were of good quality, so their findings were very useful. For example, if we compare Zelnick and Kantner's 1976 survey findings with Sorenson's 1973 results, we find that in just three years the percentage of unmarried young women engaging in premarital sex rose from 45 percent to 55 percent. And by 1979, the year of Zelnick and Kantner's last survey, this figure had risen to 69 percent. Moreover, between 1971 and 1979 pregnancy rates among the unmarried rose from 9 percent to 16 percent.

Studies of Sexual Orientation

From gay bars, public baths, and other gathering places for homosexuals in San Francisco in the late 1970s, Alan Bell, Martin Weinberg, and Sue Kiefer Hammersmith (1981) gathered subjects for face-to-face interviews about gay and lesbian sexual practices.

With sponsorship from the National Institute of Mental Health (NIMH), Bell and his associates trained graduate students to undertake the rather lengthy (almost four-hour) interviews that provided the data for their 1981 book, *Sexual Preference: Its Development in Men and Women*. A total of 1456 subjects—979 gays and lesbians and 477 heterosexual men and women—responded to questions designed to identify the causes of homosexuality. Heterosexuals were used for comparison purposes and were matched to the homosexual respondents in terms of sex, race, age, education, and occupation. To the researchers' surprise, the answers to their questions failed to support any of the hypotheses they had formed based on prevailing thought. Neither parenting practices nor identification with the opposite-sex parent nor any other psychosocial influence could be seen as propelling people into homosexual life styles.

Sexuality in the Aging

Until the research of Linda George and Stephen Weiler appeared in print (1981), many people thought that older people did not engage in sexual activity. In fact, Kinsey's data indicated that the frequency of sexual activity declined among older people. George and Weiler, researchers from Duke University, surveyed 278 married men and women recruited from a health insurance program roster. Over a period of six years (from 1969 to 1975) each of these subjects, who ranged in age from 45 to 71, completed a questionnaire at the beginning of the study and every two years thereafter.

The importance of this research lies in the nature of its design. The so-called longitudinal design, in which subjects are repeatedly queried over a long period, is very useful in determining changes in behavior over time. We will discuss the longitudinal design further a little later in the chapter.

George and Weiler found that, contrary to popular thought, there was not an automatic, sudden decline in the amount or frequency of sexual activity among the group of older people they studied. Although we need further study of sexual behavior patterns among older unmarried people, this research has given us some valuable information. Moreover, as we will discover in Chapter 15, it has provided a springboard for other researchers (e.g., Bretschneider & McCoy, 1988; Turner & Adams, 1988; Starr & Weiner, 1981).

American Couples

American Couples, published in 1983 by Phillip Blumstein and Pepper Schwartz of the University of Washington, was the result of distributing 11,000 questionnaires to couples identified through print or radio and television media. Almost 55 percent of the 11,000 surveys were completed by 4314 heterosexual couples, 969 gay couples, and 788 lesbian couples. The investigators also interviewed 93 lesbian couples, 98 gay couples, and 129 heterosexual couples face to face. This extensive national survey was flawed only by its underrepresentation of minorities and people from lower socioeconomic levels.

The questionnaire was designed to elicit information about both sexual and nonsexual aspects of a relationship. Among the issues explored were sexual satisfaction and emotional intimacy, infidelity, power dynamics in relationships, and career issues. In their analysis the investigators compared the different types of couples: married, cohabiting, lesbian, gay, and heterosexual. It was discovered that those couples who cohabit (both heterosexual and homosexual) had fewer relationship problems than married couples. Can you think of any reasons why this might be?

Blumstein and Schwartz also found that although married couples fought about money management more than all other kinds of couples, harmony in all relationships studied was heavily influenced by control over how money was spent. They also found that whether couples were married or cohabiting, working female spouses or partners performed more housework than did the males.

THE SCIENTIFIC STUDY OF HUMAN SEXUALITY

Students often ask, "Is human sexuality really a science?" Many have difficulty seeing this field of study (as well as such related disciplines as psychology and sociology) as fitting in with the physical sciences like biology, chemistry, and physics. This is probably because the latter "hard" sciences tend to be more precise and lend themselves more readily to controlled analysis than the somewhat "soft" sciences like human sexuality. However, a science doesn't have to involve looking at organisms under microscopes, putting things in centrifuges, or examining beakers of altered substances to be a legitimate way of studying an important aspect of our lives. It should be clear from the research investigations we have just described that knowledge about human sexuality can be obtained from the application of scientific methodology. Researchers in this discipline systematically collect and analyze data in an effort to describe, understand, and predict various aspects of human sexuality.

Is research in human sexuality a truly scientific pursuit?

We must admit that in the literature on human sexuality you will find some ideas that do not seem to be supported by scientific evidence. As we saw in Chapter 1, for a long time the subject of sexuality was considered a forbidden area of exploration. But that taboo didn't keep people from thinking—and sometimes talking—about something that was so inextricably interwoven with other aspects of their lives. As a result, they developed all sorts of common-sense ideas and based their theories on these. Unfortunately, just because something sounds right or makes sense to one person doesn't guarantee that it is accurate. And when you have any number of individuals coming up with any number of ideas, you can expect to find flagrant inconsistencies among these ideas. Thus human sexuality had to come out of the closet before scientists could take its many myths and misconceptions (see the box on "Myths and Misconceptions" in this chapter) and distill out the truths they contained in order to begin to build a true scientific discipline.

MYTHS AND MISCONCEPTIONS

What Research Is and Is Not

All research in human sexuality is of the hypothesis-testing kind.

*I*n some cases so little is known about an issue in human sexuality that the investigator chooses to do an exploratory study rather than test relationships between variables that are only slightly understood. When little is understood about an issue, researchers can hardly expect to state informed hypotheses. Even when hypotheses cannot be stated it is still possible to frame objectives for the research to be undertaken. Specifically stated objectives or hypotheses will direct the research toward achieving what the human sexuality researcher wants to and will prevent aimless wandering (B. C. Miller, 1986).

Because facts are the building blocks of a science, they can "prove" theories.

Although facts are important to the human sexuality researcher, they do not "prove" a theory. Instead, a theory may be supported by additional data or not supported because of conflicting data. Theories are characterized by their tentative nature and are always being tested and refined. As new facts emerge, theories are questioned, challenged, revised, and even rejected.

Correlational data establish cause-and-effect relationships.

When interpreting correlations in human sexuality or any other discipline, it is important to remember that a high correlation does not necessarily indicate that a causal relationship exists between two variables. For example, a high positive correlation between attendance at sex education programs and contraceptive usage does not prove that sex education classes will cause better use of contraceptives. The correlation might be due to other factors—perhaps intelligence, motivation, or a person's ability to see another's point of view. Even when correlations are very strong, they do not provide sufficient information to infer causality.

The discipline of human sexuality adheres to scientific procedures and steers clear of gossip, mythology, and other nonlogical methods of explanation. Scientific procedures enable researchers to explain the events with which human sexuality deals. Moreover, human sexuality researchers critically evaluate experimental research and systematically test their findings. Most researchers are very careful to do this before publishing results of their findings. However, investigators can sometimes become so enthused about their findings that they neglect to review and reflect on their work. Even William Masters and Virginia Johnson fell into that trap when they stated in *Crisis: Heterosexual Behavior in the Age of AIDS* (1988) that the human immunodeficiency virus could be transmitted by a toilet seat. Although at the time they wrote it had not been definitively established that this was not true—and it is *not* true—there was enough doubt that they should have said the matter was still under investigation.

With the use of scientific principles and methods of study, researchers have provided answers to many questions and have established a good foundation for discovering answers to many more. In the next section we will explore how scientific principles can be applied to the study of human sexuality.

Fundamental Scientific Principles

Although the field of human sexuality has carved out some unique ways of gathering data, all scientific research shares some similar goals and basic principles (Miller, 1986). Let's look at the principles of description, explanation, prediction, and control.

DESCRIPTION. Description, the most common denominator of science, is the systematic collection of available information about a phenomenon or an event. Description is a largely empirical process that often relies on counting, frequencies, percentages, and descriptive statistics. Suppose we wanted to explore the topic of mate selection. Description might entail asking people to list all the factors that entered into their choice of a mate and then analyzing all the responses to see which factors appear to be most important, which least important, and so on.

description In scientific research, the empirical process that often relies on counting, frequencies, percentages, and descriptive statistics.

EXPLANATION. An **explanation** attempts to provide reasons for why something happens or is the way it is. Human sexuality researchers seek to identify antecedents and consequences of the behaviors of interest. Explaining mate selection might involve forming hypotheses as to what underlies the factors found to be most significant. For example, we might need to look at such things as similarities in personal goals and in the ways people conceptualize male and female roles in our society.

explanation In scientific research, the process by which one attempts to derive reasons for why something happens or is the way it is.

PREDICTION. A **prediction** tells in advance that something is going to occur. Prediction rests on the same empirical and theoretical underpinnings as explanation. That is, the same ideas and relationships must be grasped in order to explain what has occurred and to predict what is likely to happen. We might want to test our ideas about mate selection in another study in order to discover if what we've hypothesized is valid.

prediction In scientific endeavor, the process of telling in advance that something is going to occur or how it will occur.

CONTROL. When we understand a phenomenon and can explain and predict it, we may be able to **control** it. That is, we can try to promote it if we judge it to be good, useful, and worthwhile; or we can try to prevent it or to intervene and change it if we judge it to be useless or harmful. For instance, we might want to promote such useful activities as dating long enough to get to know a prospective partner well and meeting members of his or her family. We might also want to develop ways of intervening in troubled partnerships or of helping people to anticipate and resolve problems in relationships.

control The stage in scientific research when the ability to explain and predict a phenomenon makes it possible to change or modify that phenomenon.

Facts and Theories

As investigators in the field of human sexuality collect research findings, they must integrate the new data with existing data. This is a difficult organizational chore, but it is essential for any science that continually seeks to refine and heighten its knowledge. Human sexuality researchers are committed to making such crucial knowledge available. **Facts** are collected data, and represent statements of observation. Facts are extremely important to any scientist and form the foundation of all intelligent analysis. The task of the human sexuality researcher is to collect data by making observations and then try to relate these observations to one another.

facts In science, collected data that represent the findings of systematic observation or of experimental manipulations.

With a collection of facts we may be able to formulate a **hypothesis,** or a reasonable guess as to an answer to a problem. Note, however, that in research one often forms tentative hypotheses before collecting data (e.g., a hypothesis can be based on an earlier study's findings).

hypothesis An educated guess as to the nature of some phenomenon or event and its relationship to other phenomena and events.

A **theory** can unify a set of facts or hypotheses and thus help us to gain an understanding of the topic at hand. Theories also often suggest the next steps in scientific inquiry. That is, an explanation may trigger new questions, spurring the scientist on to pursue the topic in greater detail. Theories whet the researcher's appetite for quest of the unknown or uncertain. Thus, they enable researchers to conceptualize, organize, integrate, and classify the facts that they accumulate (Rubinson & Neutens, 1987).

theory An explanation that unifies a set of facts or hypotheses, enabling us to understand their interrelationships.

When conclusions are drawn from any data, special attention must be directed toward the validity of the findings. Two types of validity related to the clarity of research

internal validity The degree to which observed change can be attributed to an experimental treatment and not to some other, extraneous variable.

external validity The degree to which conclusions drawn from one set of observations can be generalized to other sets of observations.

scientific method An organized series of steps designed to promote maximum objectivity and consistency in gathering and interpreting observable evidence.

findings have been identified. A set of observations has **internal validity** when the observed change or difference can be attributed confidently to the experimental treatment and not to some other extraneous variable. Observations have **external validity** when conclusions drawn from them can be generalized to other situations.

Frequently, different theories explain the same phenomenon. For example, we may discover that several theories of mate selection purport to explain how and why individuals are attracted to one another. Different theories of sex therapy have been designed to address sexual dysfunctions, and different theories have been proposed to explain the sexual response cycles of men and women. As you study these and other theories throughout this book, keep in mind that most modern researchers are eclectic—they pick and choose from the available viewpoints and develop a systematic and unified view of the topic under study. Finally, we should point out that making the connection between theory and practice is no easy task. Perhaps the most difficult obstacle researchers face is the search for the vital link between a theory and the way in which it can be successfully implemented. In short, it is far easier to understand a problem than it is to solve it.

The Scientific Method

Any scientific investigation must begin with a plan or structure. Broadly defined, the **scientific method** is an organized series of steps designed to promote maximum objectivity in gathering and interpreting observable evidence. It is the use of the scientific method and related activities that qualifies human sexuality as a science. The several steps in the scientific method can be viewed as a circular process (see Figure 2–1). The scientific method often begins and ends with researchable questions because new hypotheses are frequently generated by a particular research study. Most of these steps come under the scientific principles of description and explanation. The degree to which each of the four scientific principles we've discussed is involved in the steps we describe next will vary according to the purpose of the study, its size,

FIGURE 2–1
The Cyclical Stages of the Research Process.

(Source: Rubinson & Neutens, 1987, p. 10)

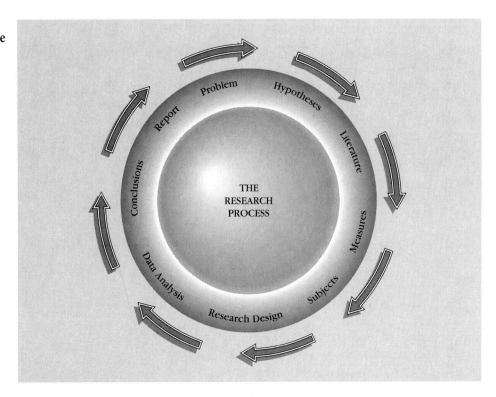

Research on Human Sexuality

and whether the researcher is primarily interested in describing, explaining, predicting, or testing. Also, action taken in one stage has a direct influence on other stages, providing a special need for understanding the entire process. Let's look now at the typical stages in the research process.

SELECTION OF THE PROBLEM. During this initial phase the investigator decides on an area of interest. In selecting a problem, the researcher might draw on what has been learned from earlier studies or from literature read in connection with other studies. For example, a researcher might be interested in exploring what factors affect the use of condoms among college-age men.

FORMULATING THE HYPOTHESIS. Here a tentative explanation that will predict the results of the study is developed. The hypothesis is tentative at this point because it may be revised (or even abandoned) after a formal review of the literature has been conducted. For instance, the researcher might hypothesize that many males do not use condoms for contraceptive purposes.

REVIEWING THE LITERATURE. Now the researcher reviews the relevant literature in order to define the problem more clearly and to state the appropriate hypotheses. It is important at this point to discover if the specific study in mind has been done, and if so, what its parameters were. For example, was it definitive enough that it's not worth replicating at this point? Or did it leave important questions unanswered? Were there specific research flaws that can be remedied?

LISTING THE MEASURES. The investigator now identifies all available measures to help gather the data. These might include questionnaires, observations, and case studies. The research instruments best suited for assessing how widespread condom use is among college-age men must be studied.

DESCRIBING THE SUBJECTS. Now the researcher very carefully describes the subjects to be included in the study. An important goal of this step is to balance subjects so that a representative sample of the population under investigation is obtained. For example, age, gender, and socioeconomic level are factors that can often influence research findings unless evenly distributed among subjects. In studying condom use among college-age men, then, we might want to equate subjects on religious preference, something that might well influence their attitudes and behaviors with respect to the use of contraceptive devices.

CONSTRUCTING A RESEARCH DESIGN AND MEASUREMENT DEVICES. In this step the investigator completely explains the procedures for carrying out the study so that the hypothesis can be tested. The variable being investigated will be measured by the appropriate research instruments. For example, a researcher might use an existing survey to discover rates of contraceptive use among college-age men or he might have to construct a new measurement device.

ANALYSIS OF THE DATA. When measurements have been completed, the researcher must analyze the collected data. For example, a researcher might compare two group scores on a questionnaire scale of contraceptive use.

GENERATING CONCLUSIONS. The researcher then has to carefully study the gathered data and his analyses, and relate the results to the original hypotheses. Sometimes the results will confirm the hypothesis and sometimes they will not. Results that refute a hypothesis may send us back to the beginning of the research process.

WRITING THE RESEARCH REPORT. In this last step a description of the entire study is written and disseminated to interested people. Successful research investigations often enable investigators to turn their attention to the issue of control. That is, when a phenomenon is understood and we can explain and predict it, we may be able to exert some control over it. If we found, for example, that college-age men do not tend to use condoms because they think that they make sex less enjoyable, we might try to devise an intervention plan that would refute this notion. In this way, we would forge a link between data, theory, and the practical application of knowledge (Rubinson & Neutens, 1987).

RESEARCH METHODS AND TECHNIQUES

Although the scientific method offers overall guiding principles, there are many different ways of gathering data. Among human sexuality researchers, surveys and observations are popular modes of data collection. Experimental studies are also a very important means of acquiring scientific information about human sexuality.

Surveys

survey A technique of gathering information from people, a survey generally takes the form of a questionnaire or an interview.

sample A group of people considered to be representative of a larger population.

questionnaire A type of survey that requires respondents to mark their own answers.

A **survey** is a technique of gathering information from people that is generally carried out by means of a questionnaire or a face-to-face interview. A survey is conducted among a **sample,** or a group of people deemed representative of a larger population.

Questionnaires require that respondents write down or mark their own answers. Questionnaires are relatively simple, fast, and inexpensive, and can be administered so that respondents remain anonymous. The last is an important advantage in sexuality research because subjects often do not want to be identified with their answers on this sensitive topic. Another plus for the questionnaire is that because it is self-administered, it does not require the recruitment and training of interviewers. This makes the questionnaire method much less costly than the interviewing technique (B. C. Miller, 1986).

To see how such questionnaires work, try answering the questions from a recent Kinsey Institute survey in the "Making Use of What We Know" box. Because this survey was designed to find out what people know about human sexuality, you can also test your own present knowledge.

Researchers must take great care in writing the instructions for a questionnaire as well as its actual items. The wording of both must be concise so that respondents do not experience confusion or frustration, either of which can cause them to supply inaccurate information or even to give up. Surveys can supply valuable information, but only if they are properly designed.

Interviews

Unlike questionnaires, interviews require a face-to-face encounter between investigator and respondent. In the typical format a trained interviewer asks questions and then records the person's responses. Although the interview technique is more expensive than the questionnaire, it is generally recognized that interviews yield more accurate data and are more flexible. A properly executed interview has the potential

How knowledgeable is the American public about human sexuality? The topic apparently remains clouded by myth and ignorance, at least according to a recent national survey conducted by The Kinsey Institute (Reinisch with Beasley, 1990). More than half of respondents failed a survey commissioned by the Institute to gauge their knowledge of sex and reproduction. Only 5 out of the 1,974 people surveyed got an "A," meaning that they correctly answered at least 16 out of 18 questions.

The survey was conducted by professional interviewers from the Roper Organization. The participants were from all parts of the nation and ranged in age from 18 to 60+. The questions covered such topics as contraception, sexual stereotypes, personal sexual health, and AIDS. Overall, respondents who were younger, more highly educated, and who had higher incomes tended to score best. Generally, respondents over 60 did worse than young people. Men tended to know more about sexual behavior, and women tended to know more about sexual health and contraception. Respondents in the Midwest scored the highest: 55 percent passed the test. The West was second, with 47 percent. Only 40 percent of the respondents in the Northeast and the South passed.

How do you compare with the respondents of this survey? To find out, here are the multiple choice and true-false survey questions posed by The Kinsey Institute. At the end of the box you'll find a scoring guide and the percentage of this national sample of people who got each "grade" on the test.

MAKING USE OF WHAT WE KNOW

Surveys in Action: Measuring Knowledge About Human Sexuality

INSTRUCTIONS: CIRCLE ONE ANSWER AFTER READING EACH QUESTION CAREFULLY

1. Nowadays, what do you think is the age at which the *average* or *typical* American *first* has sexual intercourse?

    a. 11 or younger
    b. 12
    c. 13
    d. 14
    e. 15
    f. 16
    g. 17
    h. 18
    i. 19
    j. 20
    k. 21 or older
    l. Don't know

2. Out of every ten married American men, how many would you estimate have had an extramarital affair—that is, have been sexually unfaithful to their wives?

    a. Less than one out of ten
    b. One out of ten (10%)
    c. Two out of ten (20%)
    d. Three out of ten (30%)
    e. Four out of ten (40%)
    f. Five out of ten (50%)
    g. Six out of ten (60%)
    h. Seven out of ten (70%)
    i. Eight out of ten (80%)
    j. Nine out of ten (90%)
    k. More than nine out of ten
    l. Don't know

3. Out of every ten American women, how many would you estimate have had anal (rectal) intercourse?

    a. Less than one out of ten
    b. One out of ten (10%)
    c. Two out of ten (20%)
    d. Three out of ten (30%)
    e. Four out of ten (40%)
    f. Five out of ten (50%)
    g. Six out of ten (60%)
    h. Seven out of ten (70%)
    i. Eight out of ten (80%)
    j. Nine out of ten (90%)
    k. More than nine out of ten
    l. Don't know

4. A person can get AIDS by having anal (rectal) intercourse even if neither partner is infected with the AIDS virus.

    True   False   Don't know

5. There are over-the-counter spermicides people can buy at the drugstore that will kill the AIDS virus.

    True   False   Don't know

continued

6. Petroleum jelly, Vaseline Intensive Care, baby oil, and Nivea are *not* good lubricants to use with a condom or diaphragm.

       True   False   Don't know

7. More than one out of four (25 percent) of American men have had a sexual experience with another male during either their teens or adult years.

       True   False   Don't know

8. It is usually difficult to tell whether people *are* or are *not* homosexual just by their appearance or gestures.

       True   False   Don't know

9. A woman or teenage girl can get pregnant during her menstrual flow (her "period").

       True   False   Don't know

10. A woman or teenage girl can get pregnant even if the man withdraws his penis before he ejaculates (before he "comes").

       True   False   Don't know

11. Unless they are having sex, women do not need to have regular gynecological examinations.

       True   False   Don't know

12. Teenage boys should examine their testicles ("balls") regularly just as women self-examine their breasts for lumps.

       True   False   Don't know

13. Problems with erection are most often started by a physical problem.

       True   False   Don't know

14. Almost all erection problems can be successfully treated.

       True   False   Don't know

15. Menopause, or change of life as it is often called, does *not* cause most women to lose interest in having sex.

       True   False   Don't know

16. Out of every ten American women, how many would you estimate have masturbated either as children or after they were grown up?

a. Less than one out of ten	g. Six out of ten (60%)
b. One out of ten (10%)	h. Seven out of ten (70%)
c. Two out of ten (20%)	i. Eight out of ten (80%)
d. Three out of ten (30%)	j. Nine out of ten (90%)
e. Four out of ten (40%)	k. More than nine out of ten
f. Five out of ten (50%)	l. Don't know

17. What do you think is the length of the average man's *erect* penis?

a. 2 inches	g. 8 inches
b. 3 inches	h. 9 inches
c. 4 inches	i. 10 inches
d. 5 inches	j. 11 inches
e. 6 inches	k. 12 inches
f. 7 inches	l. Don't know

18. Most women prefer a sexual partner with a larger-than-average penis.

       True   False   Don't know

Scoring the Test

Each question is worth one point, so the total possible number of points you can get is 18. Using this chart, score each item and then add up your total number of points. When a range of possible answers is correct, according to currently available research data, all respondents choosing one of the answers in the correct range are given a point.

continued

Research on Human Sexuality

Question number	Give yourself a point if you circled any of the following answers	Circle the number of points you received
1	f,g	0 1
2	d,e	0 1
3	d,e	0 1
4	False	0 1
5	*	1
6	True	0 1
7	True	0 1
8	True	0 1
9	True	0 1
10	True	0 1
11	False	0 1
12	True	0 1
13	True	0 1
14	True	0 1
15	True	0 1
16	g,h,i	0 1
17	d,e,f	0 1
18	False	0 1

Total Number of Points: _____

*The correct answer is "true," but you get the point for this question no matter what you answered. Respondents may have misunderstood the question to mean there is a "cure" for AIDS which can be purchased at the drugstore, so rather than alter the scoring, the test makers decided to give everyone the point.

Now look up the grade you received.

If you got this number of points	You receive this grade	Percent of national sample that received this grade
16–18	A	<1
14–15	B	4
12–13	C	14
10–11	D	27
1–9	F	55

to be an extremely sensitive device for the acquisition of reliable data. Here are some of the interview's advantages (Adams & Schvaneveldt, 1985):

1. The interviewer can explain the purpose of the study, establish rapport, discuss the interview, and respond to questions at any time. All of this tends to enhance cooperation.

2. The interview has a high participation rate; relatively few subjects refuse or fail to complete it.

3. An interviewer can observe body language, mood, and facial expressions, which are often valuable for understanding the totality of the interview.

4. A skilled interviewer can assess a respondent's mood and rephrase an unsuccessful question later in the interview when an accurate response may be more likely.

5. The interview method is especially valuable for gathering information about personal matters or matters respondents perceive as unusual. Once trust has

been established, respondents usually disclose such information to skilled practitioners.

6. Face-to-face interaction can build rapport, which often increases a respondent's motivation. Motivated people are more likely to respond freely and usefully than those who are participating in a study out of obligation or pressure.

7. People generally like to talk, which is a definite plus for this data-gathering device. Skilled interviewers can guide the conversation so as to attain the goals of scientific understanding.

Interviews do have some drawbacks. While items on questionnaires are uniform and consistent, a staff of interviewers can ask the same question in several different ways and therefore may get answers that differ to some degree. Another disadvantage is that interviewers may not record responses clearly and concisely. Some may even be uncertain as to which responses to record. Finally, as we've said, the interview approach is much more expensive than the questionnaire survey.

Observation

Another technique for gathering data is by means of live action, videotapes, audiotapes, and the like. As you might guess, it is impossible to amass information on as large a sample of people if one chooses to use observation rather than a questionnaire. Even face-to-face interviewers can probably gather data faster than observer-investigators. And the scientific method is based on the idea that only many observations of the phenomenon under study can yield reliable data.

There are some circumstances, however, in which investigators can efficiently make many observations that together will provide sufficient data for a meaningful analysis. For example, in our study of condom use among college students, observers could record the numbers of requests for condoms at local drugstores or at the campus health center over a stated period of time.

ethnomethodology The study of methods people use to communicate in everyday, routine activities.

Ethnomethodology is the study of both verbal and nonverbal methods that people use to communicate in everyday, routine activities. This methodology focuses on the process rather than on the outcome of an activity. For example, in our condom study observers might be asked to sit in on classes in human sexuality in which the use of condoms is discussed. In this part of our study the observers would be asked to pay more attention to the students' expressions of their feelings and attitudes and to the interaction among students and instructor than to any conclusions drawn from the discussions or to any consensus opinion reached.

Theoretically, the advantage of the observation method is that it enables the investigator to observe behavior as it occurs more or less naturally. But the phrase "more or less" tells the story. No observed behavior is completely natural unless those observed are totally unaware that they are being watched. Unfortunately, if we rely on chance opportunities to observe events as they occur naturally, our study could take forever. As soon as we begin to structure our observations, though, we begin to intrude ourselves as researchers into the situation, and thus to influence the behavior of the people we are trying to study. No matter how comfortable a subject is made to feel about having her physiological response to sexual stimulation studied in a lab, that response is very likely to be affected by the knowledge that she is being observed and recorded. And the more measurements and conditions we place on our subjects and studies, the closer we move to experimental research, which we will explore shortly.

Research on Human Sexuality

The Case Study

Another research methodology is the **case study,** in which extensive information is gathered about a single person rather than a group of people. Interviews are usually the primary source of data, and information is often gathered about family dynamics, significant life events, vocational and educational history, and socioeconomic status. Studying a single subject over an extended time period yields a great deal of information on that individual. But while this method is very useful in such areas as the clinical treatment of sexually maladjusted individuals, we can't be sure that what we learn about the sex lives of specific individuals will apply to people in general. And because the case study usually involves a single researcher and only a few cases, its reliability must be supported by testing the hypotheses generated by means of more systematic research techniques, such as a survey or an experimental study.

case study A type of research methodology in which extensive information is gathered about one person only.

Experimental Research

In **experimental research** a series of steps is designed so that relationships between differing phenomena can be determined. This is done either to discover principles underlying behavior or to find cause-effect relationships.

experimental research Research designed to facilitate the determination of relationships between differing phenomena.

There are a great many different experimental designs because each experiment must be tailored to the phenomenon being investigated. If we wanted to know how partners choose contraceptive methods, we would probably rely heavily on questionnaires and interviews. If we wanted to study the influence of alcohol on sexual arousal, we would need to measure and administer precise doses of the drug and to devise or obtain equipment to measure physiological changes in the functioning of the sexual organs. However, the basic principles of experimental design remain the same regardless of specific experimental differences. Certain terms, definitions, and formats are universal.

To take a little closer look at the experimental method of scientific investigation, we need to go back to the steps we outlined in the section on the scientific method. In step 6 we have to decide on a research design. Suppose that we want to find out whether students will know more about human sexuality after studying a course in this subject for a semester than they did before they enrolled in the course. We start by creating two groups, an experimental group and a control group, and we manipulate one factor, or **independent variable,** so that it affects the two groups differently. Thus our **experimental group** will consist of students enrolled in the sexuality course and our **control group** will consist of students not enrolled in the course. Our independent variable will be the instruction offered by the professor to the members of the experimental group. As you can see, the control group is created for purposes of comparison. When the course is completed and we test students' knowledge, their performance on the test will be the **dependent variable**—changes in this variable depend on changes in the independent variable.

independent variable The special treatment given to an experimental group.

experimental group A group of subjects in a research experiment who receive a special stimulus, or treatment.

control group In a research study, a group of subjects used primarily for comparison purposes.

dependent variable In an experiment, the behavior affected by the independent variable.

Our hypothesis, of course, is that our treatment, or instruction in human sexuality, will improve students' knowledge about this topic. To find out whether our hypothesis is supported, we will probably administer a **pre-test** and a **post-test** to both the experimental and control groups. That is, we will give a test on sexuality to both groups *before* the course begins and *after* it is completed. If our hypothesis is correct, the experimental group will score significantly higher on the post-test than on the pre-test, whereas the control group's scores on both pre- and post-tests should be substantially the same.

pre-test A test given before an experimental procedure to establish a baseline for comparative purposes.

post-test A test given after the experimental treatment to both the experimental and control groups to determine whether the treatment given the experimental group has had a significant effect.

In the final phase of experimental research, investigators seek to draw conclusions and make interpretations. Unlike correlational studies, which simply attempt to establish correlations, or relationships, between or among two or more variables,

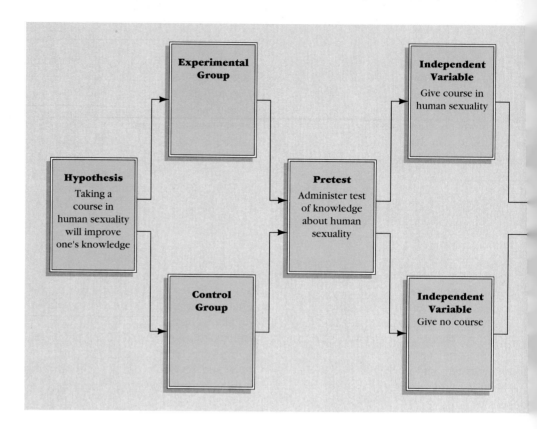

experimental research attempts to establish causality. That is, experimental research tries to establish that one phenomenon, or variable, actually causes another. A well-executed experiment may provide insight into a hypothesis, but the results of an experiment may also raise many new questions and lead the researcher into other avenues of experimentation. Figure 2-2 illustrates the different parts of the experimental method.

Longitudinal and Cross-Sectional Research Designs

The dynamics of human sexuality can be studied by employing either a longitudinal or a cross-sectional research design. In a **longitudinal study** the researcher collects data on the same group of individuals at intervals over a considerable period—years, sometimes even decades. Let's suppose someone wanted to study rates of coital activity among people who cohabit. The researcher employing the longitudinal method might begin by studying a particular group of partners at age 20. Follow-up studies of these same people would be made at fairly regular intervals until the subjects reached a particular age. At each follow-up session, new data would be recorded that ultimately would be included in the final research analysis.

In a **cross-sectional study** researchers obtain comparative data from different groups of subjects at roughly the same point in time. Here the investigator would select several groups of partners—one group about 20 years old, one about 30, one 40, 50, and so on—recording the differences among the various age groups. The differences would then be analyzed.

Each method has its advantages and disadvantages. Although the cross-sectional approach is relatively inexpensive and fairly easy to carry out, it doesn't pick up changes in behavior over time and it is contaminated by generational differences. That is, people who are 20 today may, when they are 50, behave differently from

longitudinal study A research design in which data are collected on the same group of individuals at intervals over an extended period of time.

cross-sectional study A research design in which comparative data are gathered from different groups of subjects at more or less the same point in time.

Research on Human Sexuality

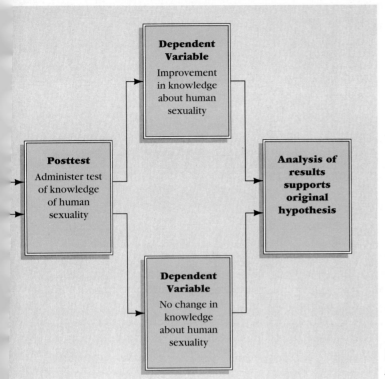

FIGURE 2–2
A Hypothetical Ex-
perimental Design.

today's 50-year-olds. The longitudinal method can provide a fairly accurate picture of developmental changes within subjects, but this research design takes a long time to carry out, is generally expensive, and frequently suffers from subject attrition (for one reason or another, subjects drop out of the study over time).

A recent variation on the longitudinal design is the **short-term longitudinal method,** which lasts a maximum of five years and investigates fewer behavioral phenomena. Because this design takes less time to implement, it loses fewer subjects and it is more likely that the original staff of investigators will be available to carry out the entire project.

short-term longitudinal method A variation of the longitudinal research design that reduces the amount of time subjects are studied and investigates fewer behavioral phenomena.

ETHICAL RESEARCH STANDARDS

Before closing this chapter, we need to emphasize the importance of ethical standards in the conduct of human sexuality research. As in other fields of study, investigators are bound to adhere to certain ethical principles.

The following principles have been formulated by the American Psychological Association (1990) to safeguard the rights of subjects in experimental research:

- Ethical practice requires the investigator to inform the participant of all features of the research that reasonably might be expected to influence willingness to participate and to explain all other aspects of the research about which the participant inquires.
- Ethical research practice requires the investigator to respect the individual's freedom to decline to participate in research or to discontinue participation at any time.

- Ethically acceptable research begins with the establishment of a clear and fair agreement between the investigator and research participant that clarifies the responsibilities of each. The investigator has the obligation to honor all promises and commitments included in that agreement.

- The ethical investigator protects participants from physical and mental discomfort, harm, and danger. If the risk of such consequences exists, the investigator is required to inform the participant of that fact, secure consent before proceeding, and take all possible measures to minimize distress. A research procedure may not be used if it is likely to cause serious and lasting harm to participants.

- Where research procedures may result in undesirable consequences for the participant, the investigator has the responsibility to detect and remove or correct those consequences, including, where relevant, long-term aftereffects.

- Information obtained about the research participants during the course of an investigation is confidential.

When investigators conduct research on human sexuality, they must be especially careful to respect their subjects' rights of privacy. Sexual behaviors and attitudes are personal, private, and sensitive matters, and it is often difficult and embarrassing, sometimes even painful, for subjects to reveal their thoughts, feelings, and actions to an investigator. It is imperative that the researcher gain the confidence and trust of her subjects, for only people who have confidence in and trust a researcher will provide her with truthful information.

Not only the American Psychological Association but the American Public Health Association, the American Association of Sex Educators, Counselors, and Therapists, and other professional organizations have formulated codes of ethics to which their members must adhere. The next time you are asked by a researcher or other investigator to reveal information, think about the ethics involved. Before agreeing to participate, ask whether your information will be held confidential, how the results will be reported, and whether you must complete the survey or interview or can withdraw from the study whenever you wish. And if you conduct research on your own, be sure to obtain formal ethical guidelines from the organization of which you are a member and follow these guidelines in your work.

SEXUALITY IN THE NEWS

Women Still Behind in Medicine
By Philip J. Hilts

Although women are making progress in entering medicine, a new report says that at all levels above medical student, women still have disproportionately low status and pay.

The report, released [in 1991] by the Feminist Majority Foundation and the American Medical Women's Association, said that not a single dean of an American medical school is a woman, that 98 percent of department chairmen are men, and that medical school faculties are still 79 percent men, despite the fact that 36 percent of all medical students are women.

"The health care profession, to this date, is essentially sex-segregated, as 84 percent of physicians are male and 97 percent of nurses are female," the report said. "Women in national organizations fare no better. The American College of Obstetricians and Gynecologists, whose sole mission is to provide health care to women, has never had more than two women in its top 17 offices at any one time in its 41-year history."

No Women as A.M.A. Chiefs

The American Medical Association, the largest organization of doctors in the world, has never had a woman as chief executive officer in its 144-year history, the report said.

continued

The report also noted that women who are doctors made 63.2 cents for each dollar men who are doctors earned in 1982 and that by 1988 women who are doctors made only 62.8 cents per dollar of their male counterparts' salary.

According to figures from the American Medical Association, the gap in pay is not directly linked with experience. The average net income of men with one to four years' experience in 1987 was $110,600, while women with the same experience made only $74,000 on average. Men with 10 to 20 years' experience made $158,800 to women's $99,400.

"People think that it's just a matter of time before women will move up, but it isn't," said Eleanor Smeal, president of the Feminist Majority. "There have been a larger number of women in medical school from the mid-70s through the 1980s. Women have been out there, and we should have seen a change, but we haven't. We had to break down barriers to get into medical schools. Now the barriers are more subtle, but unless we have an organized fight, we won't break down those barriers either."

A spokes[person] for the American College of Obstetricians and Gynecologists, Morris Lebo, said that its 31,000 members now include 20 percent women and that the number has increased steadily since 1978, when 7 percent of the members were women.

As women's numbers in the college have increased, the number in positions of authority has also increased, Mr. Lebo said. Now, from 10 to 20 percent of the members of policy-making committees and commissions in the college are women.

"Women are catching up and catching up fairly fast," he said. "A lot of women are new in the field and haven't had a chance to establish themselves."

Half of all resident medical students in obstetrics and gynecology are now women.

Underrepresented at Upper Levels

Dr. Susan Dooley of Northwestern University, an officer of the College of Obstetricians, said, "Women are underrepresented at the upper levels of medicine, absolutely, and I don't think it will change as quickly as we would like. It will take 10 more years before we will be able to tell if the women now coming up will be well represented at the upper levels."

She said there were a number of reasons for the imbalance. A major one is that women often decide not to enter academic medicine, the field from which the leaders of the profession come, because it is so difficult to raise children and have a demanding academic career as well, she said.

But, she said, there is also some subtle, perhaps unconscious, but direct discrimination against women within the medical hierarchy.

On salaries, Dr. Dooley said that some of the gap between men and women comes because a larger proportion of women have taken up practices in which they work fewer hours. But again, she said, there is some discrimination, and women have not been as active in demanding greater pay as men. (*The New York Times*, September 10, 1991. Copyright © 1991 by The New York Times Company. Reprinted by permission.)

DISCUSSION QUESTIONS

1. What seem to you to be the most important revelations of this study by the Feminist Majority Foundation and the American Medical Women's Association?

2. How would you go about increasing the number of women doctors in positions of authority in their profession and professional organizations, if you agree this should be done? How can men and women's pay for the same expertise and level of experience be equalized?

3. The study reported not only a substantial discrepancy between male and female doctors' incomes, but a widening of this discrepancy between 1982 and 1988. How would you account for this apparent worsening of the inequity?

LOOKING BACK

■　Among the pioneers who have contributed to human sexuality research are Henry Havelock Ellis, Sigmund Freud, and Magnus Hirschfeld. The two major methods in this field—the survey and the laboratory experiment—were established by Alfred Kinsey and William Masters and Virginia Johnson. Other survey researchers often studied the sexual attitudes and behaviors of particular groups, such as adolescents, the aging, and gays and lesbians.

■　As a scientific field of exploration, human sexuality makes use of the scientific principles of description, explanation, prediction, and control. Researchers seek to gather data, formulate hypotheses, and test these hypotheses in order to build useful theories of sexual behavior. Researchers also examine their findings for internal validity and external validity.

■　Human sexuality researchers subscribe to the scientific method, which comprises an organized series of steps designed to promote maximum objectivity and consistency in gathering and interpreting observable evidence. The research steps of the scientific method are: selection of the problem; formulating the hypothesis; reviewing the literature; listing the measures; describing the subjects; constructing a research design and measurement devices; analyzing the data; generating conclusions; and writing the research report.

■　Among the data-gathering techniques used by human sexuality researchers are surveys (including questionnaires and interviews), observation, case studies, and experimental research, including longitudinal and cross-sectional research designs. In all research activities ethical research standards must be followed.

THINKING THINGS OVER

1. Although the pioneers of our field, Havelock Ellis, Sigmund Freud, and Magnus Hirschfeld, all had rather similar goals, each took a different approach to research. How did their approaches differ, and how have they affected present-day methodologies, if you think they have?

2. College students have many questions about human sexuality. List two of your own questions in this area, and for each prepare a hypothesis and a plan to conduct a study to test the hypothesis.

3. The federal government's Department of Health and Human Services recently refused to fund research projects dealing with adolescent and adult sexual behavior, projects the department had approved earlier. What reason might the government have had for failing to authorize funding for

studies it had approved in principle? How would you justify this action?

4. Many of us have answered telephone surveys about issues ranging from which supermarket we use to which candidate we will vote into office. Conducting a sexuality survey by telephone is very difficult because of the sensitivity of the questions asked. Is such a survey appropriate? If so, how would you introduce yourself and the survey if you were conducting a telephone interview? If you think such surveys are not appropriate, why not?

5. It is generally accepted that scientific investigators must adhere to ethical standards when conducting *any* type of research. What standards can you think of that would be specific to sexuality research?

DISCOVER FOR YOURSELF

Drew, C. J. & Hardman, M. L. (1985). *Designing and conducting behavioral research*. Elmsford, NY: Pergamon Press. Students of human sexuality will discover in this book how behavioral scientists design and carry out research investigations.

Fink, A., & Kosecoff, J. (1985). *How to conduct surveys*. Beverly Hills, CA: Sage. A readable and practical account of how to organize a survey and how to evaluate the credibility of others.

Howard, G. (1985). *Basic research methods in the social sciences*. Glenview, IL: Scott, Foresman. A broadly based perspective on research methodology. The author presents the logic, strength, and weakness of major research methods.

Journal of Sex Research, Vol. 22 (February), 1986. This entire issue is devoted to sex research methodology. It is must reading for students of human sexuality.

Kimmel, A. J. (1988). *Ethics and values in applied social research*. Beverly Hills, CA: Sage. Kimmel provides an interesting commentary on the role of ethics in research investigations.

Rubinson, L., & Neutens, J. (1987). *Research techniques in the health sciences*. New York: Macmillan. A comprehensive and informative account of research techniques and methodology.

Yin, R. K. (1989). *Case study research: Design and methods*. Beverly Hills, CA: Sage. Another good reference source for those conducting human sexuality research.

3

Sexual Anatomy and Physiology

I would not have such a heart in my bosom but for the dignity of the whole body

—William Shakespeare

The topics of anatomy and physiology tend to frighten many students. Our purpose in this chapter is not to inundate you with heavy-duty scientific-medical terminology and concepts. Rather, we're going to share with you a foundation of basic knowledge that we think you'll find interesting. Indeed, it is our hope that you'll learn things about your body that you do not already know, and that as you explore what your body looks like and how it functions, you'll develop a more complete appreciation of human sexuality.

This chapter will reveal that the human reproductive system is a complex network of organs and tissues. Understanding what each part does and how the reproductive system functions as a whole provides an essential foundation for the succeeding chapters of this book. This understanding will also help to dispel the mysteries that often surround the subject of human sexuality, such as the kinds of stimulation most likely to produce arousal and orgasm.

In this part of our book we will explore the ways biological forces blend with psychological and sociological aspects of human sexuality. This chapter will examine the basic sexual anatomy and physiology of our sexual and reproductive systems. In Chapter 4 we'll explore the way these systems influence sexual arousal and response. Chapter 5, the final chapter in this part, will look at the way sexual identities are formed. As Chapter 5 will reveal, although a person is born male or female, this is not the complete picture as far as concepts of masculinity and femininity are concerned. Rather, many forces besides biology interact to create our sexual identities.

UNDERSTANDING YOUR OWN BODY

Most of us were taught as children that the sexual parts of our bodies were somehow "not nice"—that they should be hidden, not looked at, not talked about. Yet every time we took a bath, used the toilet, or got dressed or undressed, there those parts were. Some people do examine themselves and get comfortable with their bodies. Some don't, but are untroubled by their lack of knowledge about their own anatomy. Still others continue to feel funny about themselves "down there."

The exercise we discuss next, developed by Maurice Yaffe and Elizabeth Fenwick (1988a, b), is intended to help those of you who would like more direct knowledge of your sexual anatomy. The goal is to accept all of your body as part of yourself and as good, useful, and attractive. To feel relaxed performing this exercise you need privacy and plenty of time.

First, undress completely and study your body in a full-length mirror. Closely examine your face and head first. Examine your eyes, nose, mouth, and hair. Then let your eyes travel down your body to your toes. Imagine that you are looking at yourself for the very first time. Try to see yourself from every angle, and watch yourself as you bend, kneel, sit, or move around. Look over each shoulder to examine the back of your body as well.

Pay attention to what is special about you. You have characteristics or features that make you unique—not perfect, of course, but special. Remember that everyone has a mixture of good and not-so-good features. Look at your body again. Now examine your best characteristics closely. You can note the features you dislike, but simply regard them as parts of your total physical self, not as parts that matter all that much.

Next, study your genitals. Look at them from every angle and enjoy the pleasure their appearance brings you. Women should relax in a comfortable position and use a hand-mirror and a good light. Keep in mind that there is considerable variation in genital size, color, shape, and configuration from woman to woman. Now explore your genital area slowly. To see the clitoris properly, you will need to gently pull back the hood of skin that covers it. A small knob of flesh, the clitoris is extremely sensitive. Next, run your fingers along the inner and outer vaginal lips and back along the perineum. Notice the varying degrees of sensitivity in these parts. Finally, explore the entrance to your vagina. Separate the inner lips to expose the opening. If you wish, you can insert a finger into your vagina. You will probably find the area just around the entrance as well as the outermost third of the vaginal passage itself the most sensitive to touch.

Men do not need mirrors to see their genitals, of course, but they should take a comfortable position to examine them. Begin by feeling your testicles, which are smooth, oval-shaped organs. They should be somewhat firm to the touch. Keep in mind that one testicle or one side of the scrotum—usually the left—hangs slightly below the other. Now look at your penis. Let your fingers move over its surface to discover changes in skin sensitivity. You will probably find that the most sensitive areas are the glans, or head of the penis, and the frenulum, the ridge on the underside where the glans joins the shaft.

When the penis is not erect, it is probably between two and four inches long. As you know, it lengthens considerably when erect. This is because its three cylinders of spongy tissue become engorged with blood when you are sexually aroused. These cylinders are enclosed in a fibrous sheath, and as the spongy tissues fill and press against the sheath, the penis hardens.

Finish the exercise by taking a warm bath. Soap your hands and explore your whole body again. Pay attention to the different sensations you experience by varying your touch and pressure, and identify the changes in skin sensitivity from area to area. When you dry yourself, again focus on sensations. You might want to try using a body lotion and enjoy the feeling as you rub it into your skin.

Female Reproductive System

The female reproductive system consists of the external genitals, or vulva, the internal genitals, and the breasts. The internal genitals include the vagina, uterus, fallopian (uterine) tubes, and ovaries.

External Genitals: The Vulva

The **vulva** (Latin for "covering"), also called the pudendum, consists of everything that is externally visible, from the mons pubis to the perineum. Included in the vulva are the mons pubis, labia majora and minora, clitoris, urethral orifice, vaginal vestibule, and perineal body (see color plate, Figure 3–1).

vulva The female external genitalia, including the mons pubis, labia majora, labia minora, clitoris, urethral and vaginal openings, and perineum.

Mons Pubis. The **mons pubis,** or mons veneris, is a mound of nerve and fatty tissue that covers the symphysis pubis, or the point at which the pelvic bones join. Covered with coarse hair after puberty, the mons serves primarily to protect the pelvic bones, especially during coitus.

mons pubis The mound of fatty tissue over the pubic bone.

Labia Majora. The **labia majora** ("large lips") are two large fatty folds of skin and tissue that originate at the mons pubis and extend down toward the perineum. The outer portions of the labia majora are covered with hair. The pigmentation of the labia tends to be dark, rather like that of the male scrotum. The inner surfaces of the labia majora are smooth, moist, and without hair. The labia majora have an extensive network of nerve endings that makes them very sensitive to touch, pain, and extremes of temperature. In women who have not had children, the labia majora may actually touch one another. Following childbirth, they are often slightly separated, exposing the area in between.

labia majora Outer folds of skin and tissue that originate at the mons pubis and extend backward toward the perineum. The labia majora surround the labia minora.

labia minora Inner folds of skin and erectile tissue that enclose the vaginal and urethral openings.

LABIA MINORA. The **labia minora** ("small lips") are soft folds of skin and tissue within the labia majora. Labia minora tissue is erectile and contains loose connective tissue, nerve tissue, blood vessels, and large venous spaces. During sexual arousal the labia minora, which are usually paler in color than the labia majora, swell and often darken in color.

The labia minora, whose outer surfaces are in contact with the inner surfaces of the labia majora, extend from the clitoris down and back on either side of the vaginal opening. The labia minora vary in size, shape, and color from woman to woman, as Figure 3–2 (see color plate) indicates.

Women report a wide range of attitudes toward the appearance of their external genitals:

> I've always found my genitals beautiful. The lips are especially beautiful and delicate.
>
> I love everything about my genitals, including the lips, pubic hair, and odor of the secretions.
>
> I don't find myself attractive "down there." I'm particularly self-conscious about the odor. (Authors' files)

It is our feeling that no one—female or male—should be embarrassed or ashamed about any part of their bodies. Strangely, however, negative attitudes toward the vulva have existed for a long time. In fact, the Latin word *pudendum* translates into "thing of shame," which pretty much summarizes a centuries-old view of female sexuality.

clitoris A small, highly sensitive organ located at the anterior juncture of the labia minora.

glans The tip of the clitoris.

prepuce Loose-fitting fold of skin that covers the clitoral glans. Also called the clitoral hood.

CLITORIS. The **clitoris** is a small, highly sensitive organ located just below the mons pubis, at the top of the labia minora. The term is derived from the Greek word *kleitoris*, meaning "hill" or "slope." The Greeks regarded the clitoris as the key to female sexual pleasure.

The clitoris is generally homologous to the penis; in fact, both organs develop from the same embryonic tissues (see Chapter 5 for a discussion of hormonal influences on prenatal sexual development). Unlike the penis, however, the clitoris has no known reproductive function. Its sole purpose is to mediate sexual stimulation and pleasure. Composed of erectile tissue, blood vessels, and more nerve endings than the penis, the clitoris fills with blood and swells during sexual arousal. Like the penis, the clitoris has both a shaft and a **glans,** or head. Unless circumcision or other genital alterations are performed (see the box on "Genital Modification or Mutilation" on page 82), the shaft and glans of both clitoris and penis are covered by a **prepuce,** or foreskin. In women this prepuce is often called the "clitoral hood."

vaginal vestibule The cleft, below the clitoris and between the labia, that contains the vaginal and urethral openings.

Skene's glands A group of small mucous glands that open into the vaginal vestibule near the urethral orifice.

Bartholin's glands Two glands that open into the vaginal vestibule on either side of the vaginal opening and that are thought to provide some lubrication during sexual arousal.

hymen A thin mucous membrane that partially covers the vaginal opening.

VAGINAL VESTIBULE. Located between the clitoris and the perineum is the **vaginal vestibule.** The vestibule contains four openings: the vaginal opening, the urethral opening, the ducts of Skene's glands, and the ducts of Bartholin's glands. **Skene's glands** are a group of small mucous glands that open into the vestibule near the urethral orifice by way of two small ducts. **Bartholin's glands** are two bean-shaped glands located beneath the vestibule on either side of the vaginal opening. The precise function of these glands is not clear. We do know that they provide some lubrication during sexual excitement and create a distinctive scent.

The opening to the vagina may be partially covered by a thin mucous membrane called the **hymen.** The hymen varies in thickness and typically has a center of circular perforation. It is through this perforation that the menstrual flow leaves the vagina. Rarely, the hymen completely covers the vagina, a condition called imperforate hymen. This is usually discovered in mid-puberty when no menstrual flow has appeared.

Sexual Anatomy and Physiology

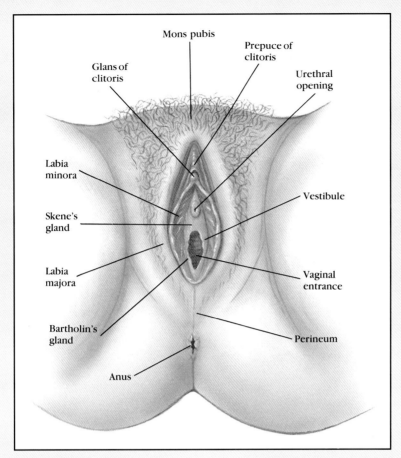

Mons pubis

Prepuce of
clitoris

Glans of
clitoris

Urethral
opening

Labia
minora

Vestibule

Skene's
gland

Labia
majora

Vaginal
entrance

Bartholin's
gland

Perineum

Anus

FIGURE 3–1
External Female Genitalia.

 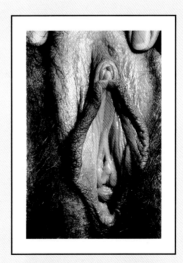

FIGURE 3–2
Variations in Female Genitalia.

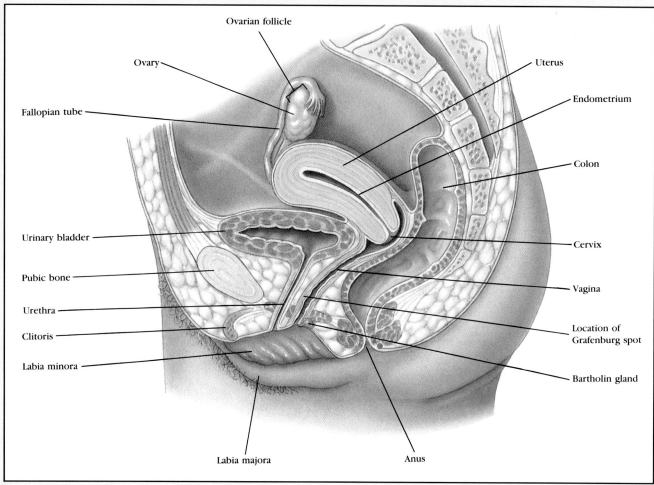

FIGURE 3–3
Female Reproductive System.

Because the exact structure of the Grafenberg spot has not yet been determined, we have simply indicated the spot's presumed location.

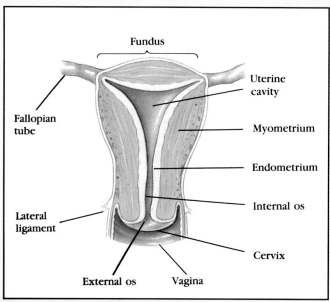

FIGURE 3–4
Major Structures of the Uterus.

Perforation of this type of hymen must be performed surgically so that the menstrual flow can escape.

There are many misconceptions about the hymen, the most common being that a virgin must have an intact hymen. Blood on the sheets of a newly married couple after their first night together was once considered proof that the bride's hymen had been broken during her first experience of sexual intercourse. In fact, the hymen may remain intact after repeated intercourse. Moreover, the hymen may be ruptured by menstruation, the use of tampons, strenuous physical activity, or sometimes masturbation. Finally, hymens vary in size, shape, and strength, and some women are born without them.

PERINEUM. The **perineum** (or perineal body) consists of muscle tissue located between the lower part of the vagina and the anal canal. The perineum is sensitive to touch because of an abundance of nerve endings. It also contains numerous elastic fibers and connective tissue that allow it to stretch considerably. As we'll see in Chapter 11, however, sometimes during childbirth an incision may be made in the perineum to prevent lacerations and tears and to facilitate delivery.

perineum In both men and women, muscle tissue located between the genital area and the anal canal.

Internal Genitals

VAGINA. The **vagina**, or vaginal cavity, is a tubular organ situated between the bladder and the rectum. The vagina serves three important functions. One, it receives the male's penis during sexual intercourse. Two, it provides a pathway for the secretions of the uterus and the menstrual flow. Three, it serves as part of the birth canal during labor.

The vagina is capable of great expansion and can accommodate itself relatively rapidly to objects of different size. During labor and delivery the vagina must expand to four or five times its normal size to allow the baby to pass through. The outer portion of the vagina is more sensitive to touch and pain than its inner portions.

vagina A tubular organ that connects the external genitals with the uterus.

THE GRAFENBERG SPOT. One of the more heated medical controversies is whether or not significant numbers of women have a Grafenberg spot. The **Grafenberg spot**, also known as the G-spot, may be an area of sensitivity in the vagina midway between the cervix and the top of the pubic bone (see color plate, Figure 3–3). Many maintain that the Grafenberg spot exists, although they disagree on its exact anatomical structure. Others remain skeptical. The sparks of controversy have launched many investigations designed to explore the existence of the G-spot and the extent of its occurrence in the population (see, e.g., Heath, 1984; Perry & Whipple, 1981; Ladas, Whipple, & Perry, 1982).

The Grafenberg spot was first described in the 1950s by Ernst Grafenberg, who labeled it an "erotic zone." It is believed to be a mass of erectile tissue that surrounds the urethra just below the neck of the bladder. Normally about the size of a dime, the G-spot can double its size when a woman is sexually aroused. It is especially swollen at and immediately after orgasm. The sensitivity of the G-spot varies from woman to woman, but usually firm pressure is needed to stimulate it.

The G-spot also may consist of glandular tissue that secretes a prostatic-like fluid into the urethra during sexual stimulation. There is some speculation that this fluid might represent the female "ejaculate" reported to occur in some women during orgasm. Figure 3–3 indicates the presumed location of the G-spot.

Grafenberg spot A mass of erectile and glandular tissue that may surround the urethra just below the neck of the bladder. Some women report sexual arousal and orgasm when the G-spot is stimulated.

UTERUS. Situated in the pelvis, the uterus and the associated structures of the fallopian tubes and ovaries are the woman's principal organs of reproduction. They are responsible for the monthly preparation of ova and menstrual flow and for the nur-

uterus A hollow, muscular organ located above the vagina whose primary function is to protect and nurture the developing fetus.

cervix The small, lower portion of the uterus that projects into the vagina.

myometrium The layers of smooth muscle that make up most of the body of the uterus.

endometrium The innermost lining of the uterus that builds up a rich blood supply during ovulation in preparation for a fertilized egg and sloughs off this material each month as the menstrual flow if fertilization does not take place.

ovaries The female gonads, located in the upper portion of the pelvic cavity, one on either side of the uterus.

ovum The female reproductive cell.

primary follicles Podlike structures that contain immature ova.

turance of a fertilized egg. It is within the uterus that the egg attaches itself and prenatal development takes place.

The **uterus** is a hollow, muscular organ. It is thick-walled and pear-shaped, located between the base of the bladder and the rectum, and above the vagina. It is suspended in the pelvic cavity by six ligaments. The uterus has two major parts: an upper, triangular portion, and a lower narrower portion named the **cervix.** As you can see in Figure 3–4 (see color plate), the cervix projects into the vagina. The two fallopian tubes extend from the uterus at the upper outer margin on either side. The upper rounded portion of the uterus between the points of juncture with the fallopian tubes is called the fundus.

Because of its muscular composition, the uterus is capable of expanding during pregnancy. Muscle fibers are arranged in all directions, making possible enough expansion to accommodate the growing fetus. Since its upper portion is freely movable, the position of the uterus may be influenced by a full bladder or rectum, which pushes it forward or backward. The uterus can also change its position when a woman stands, lies flat, or turns on her side.

The outermost layer of the uterus consists of fibrous connective tissues. Most of the uterus is composed of layers of smooth muscle called the **myometrium.** The muscles of the myometrium interweave and give the uterus its flexibility, strength, and potential for the movements necessary to move a fetus down and out of the uterus during labor and delivery. The innermost lining of the uterus, called the **endometrium,** consists of numerous blood and lymph vessels. After puberty, the endometrium exhibits monthly cyclical changes in structure. More specifically, it builds up a rich blood supply during ovulation and sloughs off this lining during menstruation if fertilization does not take place. A detailed discussion of menstruation will be presented later in this chapter.

The cervix is the small end of the uterus, measuring about one to two inches in diameter. Seen through a vaginal speculum (see the following discussion on the pelvic examination), it looks like a raised knoblike projection. Its muscular wall is not as thick as the rest of the uterus. The firmness or softness of the cervix will be influenced by phases of the menstrual cycle.

The cervix has an upper opening called the internal os, which leads from the cavity of the uterine body into the cervical canal. The external os is a lower opening that leads into the vagina. In nonpregnant women the cervix is quite small. During labor the cervix dilates to a size large enough to permit the passage of the fetus (see Chapter 11).

OVARIES. The **ovaries** (from the Latin *ovari,* meaning "place of eggs") are the female gonads (sex glands) and are homologous with the testes in the male. They are two small almond-shaped organs located in the upper portion of the pelvic cavity, one on either side of the uterus. An ovarian ligament anchors each ovary to the uterus (see color plate, Figure 3–5).

During prenatal development the ovaries develop in the abdominal cavity and then descend to the brim of the pelvis. The eventual size and shape of the ovaries varies from woman to woman. They are small in childhood and have a smooth, pink surface. After puberty they increase in size and acquire a gray, puckered appearance.

The primary function of the ovary is to develop and expel an **ovum,** the female reproductive cell, each month and to secrete the two female hormones, estrogen and progesterone. Each ovary contains at birth a large number of immature **primary follicles,** perhaps as many as 400,000. The primary follicles, podlike in structure, contain immature ova. No more follicles will be formed throughout a woman's life, and many of the original follicles will degenerate between birth and puberty. By the time puberty is reached, the original number of follicles will decrease to about 20,000. Over the course of a woman's sexual maturity, it is estimated that only about 400 of the primary follicles will develop enough to expel ova.

Sexual Anatomy and Physiology

Beginning at puberty, one of the ovarian follicles enlarges each month, approaches the surface of the ovary, and bursts. This causes the release of a mature ovum from the ovarian follicle, a process termed **ovulation.** The ovum and the fluid content of the follicle enter the fallopian tube and eventually pass into the uterus. This regular development and maturation of the ovarian follicles continues from puberty to menopause. We will return to the process of ovulation a little bit later when we discuss hormonal influences on the menstrual cycle.

FALLOPIAN TUBES. The **fallopian tubes,** also called the uterine tubes, are two thin, flexible muscular structures attached to the uterus in the upper portion of the uterus. Trumpet-shaped in appearance, the tubes extend upward and outward toward the sides of the pelvis and then curve downward and backward (see color plate, Figure 3–5).

Fertilization of the ovum by the male sperm occurs in one of the fallopian tubes. The primary function of the fallopian tube is to transport the fertilized egg along the canal until it reaches the uterus. **Cilia,** tiny hairlike projections, assist in the process by creating movement and currents within the tube.

Each fallopian tube consists of three major parts. The portion closest to the uterus, called the **isthmus,** is narrow, straight, and has a thick muscular wall. The **ampulla** is adjacent to the isthmus and comprises the outer two-thirds of the tube. It is in the ampulla that fertilization of the ovum by a spermatozoon typically takes place. The muscular wall of the ampulla is thin and distensible. The ampulla terminates in the **infundibulum,** which opens directly into the peritoneal cavity. The infundibulum resembles a funnel and has many moving fringelike projections called **fimbriae** (Latin for "fingers") that reach out to the ovary. When the ovum is released, the fimbriae will draw it into the fallopian tube.

The wall of the fallopian tube has three distinct layers. An outer coat of connective tissue covers the tube. A middle, muscular layer contains both longitudinal and circular smooth muscle and provides the tube with peristaltic movement. Finally, the fallopian tube has an inner mucous layer. Some of the cells within this layer help transport the ovum to the uterus.

The Pelvic Examination

A pelvic examination is designed to check the female reproductive system for any abnormalities of the vulva, urethra, vagina, uterus, fallopian tubes, cervix, or ovaries. Women should have a physician—preferably a gynecologist, a specialist in diseases peculiar to women—perform this examination at least once a year, beginning at age 16 or 18 or at the onset of sexual activity, whichever comes first. The pelvic examination is usually part of an overall gynecological checkup, which typically includes a gynecological history, weight and blood pressure measurements, urinalysis, and an examination of the breasts and abdomen.

The pelvic examination is performed while the woman is lying on her back, usually with her knees bent and her lower legs resting in stirrups that extend from either side of the examining table. The physician usually begins by inspecting the external genitalia for signs of inflammation, bleeding, discharge, swelling, or other local skin changes. The physician then examines the interior of the vagina and the cervix by inserting a small metal or plastic instrument called a speculum, which the physician should first warm (see color plate, Figure 3–6). The speculum expands, enabling the physician to note any unusual signs, such as alteration in the normal size or color of the vaginal interior, erosion of the tissue, or bleeding. The insertion of the speculum is not normally painful, although it may be mildly uncomfortable.

With the speculum in place, smears from various sites in the vagina, cervix, or uterus can be taken. This procedure, known as the Papanicolaou (Pap) smear, is

ovulation The release of a mature ovum from the ovarian follicle.

fallopian tubes Two thin, flexible, muscular structures that connect the uterus with the ovaries, providing a passageway for the ovum to travel toward the uterus.

cilia Tiny hairlike projections that line the fallopian tubes and propel the ovum toward the uterus.

isthmus The portion of the fallopian tube nearest to the uterus.

ampulla In the female, the outer two-thirds of the fallopian tube; the portion of the tube in which fertilization of the ovum by a spermatozoon typically takes place.

infundibulum The part of the fallopian tube that, opening into the peritoneal cavity, draws the ovum released by the ovary into the tube.

fimbriae Fringelike projections of the infundibulum that reach out to the ovary to draw a released ovum into the fallopian tube.

widely used to screen for cervical cancer. The physician lightly scrapes cells from the cervix, places them on slides, and has them analyzed to determine whether any of the cells are abnormal (see Chapter 17 for details).

Removing the speculum, the physician then inserts one or two gloved fingers (covered with a lubricating jelly) into the vagina and palpates the abdomen with the other hand. This is done to feel for enlargements or abnormalities in the shape and contour of the pelvic organs. By pressing with the examining finger on the right and left inner aspects of the vagina while examining both sides of the abdomen with the other hand, the physician hopes to detect any pain or tenderness, or any structural abnormalities in the fallopian tubes and ovaries.

A rectal examination usually concludes the pelvic examination. The physician usually inserts one index finger into the vagina and another finger into the rectum. With the other hand, the physician palpates the lower abdomen to detect abnormalities in the placement, contour, motility, and tissue consistency of the base of the bladder, the uterus, the ovaries, the fallopian tubes, and the rectum.

Breasts

breasts In the female, accessory organs of reproduction, composed of glandular tissue and fat, that are designed to suckle the newborn and that also play a role in female sexual arousal.

nipple The protuberance in the breast through which, in the female, the lactiferous ducts discharge milk.

lactiferous ducts Tubes that drain the lobes, or alveoli, of the breast, which produce milk. Each lobe has its own duct, and all ducts lead into the nipple.

alveoli Milk-producing lobes in the breast that are separated from each other by fibrous and fatty walls and drained by the lactiferous ducts.

areola A pigmented area of skin around the central portion of the nipple.

My left breast is larger than my right one. Is that normal?

A woman's **breasts** are a very important part of her sexuality and her self-image. They are highly sensitive organs that for many women play as important a part in lovemaking as they do in nurturing the newborn. Because the breasts are not directly involved in conception and childbirth, they are considered accessory organs of reproduction. Also known as mammary glands, the breasts are composed of glandular tissue and fat and lie over the pectoral muscles. They are placed symmetrically on the sides of the chest between the second and sixth ribs, and are attached to the pectoral muscles by connective fibrous tissue and to the overlying skin by ligaments. Both men and women have breasts, but development and enlargement of the breasts take place only in the presence of the ovarian hormones estrogen and progesterone.

Each breast has a **nipple,** which is composed largely of erectile tissue and becomes more prominent during the menstrual cycle, sexual excitement, pregnancy, and lactation. In the center of each nipple is an opening that connects to the **lactiferous ducts** (see color plate, Figure 3–7). The lactiferous ducts originate from the 15 or 20 lobes called **alveoli** that are located in deeper tissue and are part of the glandular structures that produce milk.

Around the central portion of the nipple is a pigmented area of skin called the **areola.** The areola varies in diameter from woman to woman and contains numerous glands that appear as small nodules. These elevations, called Montgomery's tubercles, release an oily secretion that protects the surface of the nipple during nursing. The color of the areola varies from light pink to dark brown, depending on the woman's general complexion. During pregnancy the areola usually darkens in color.

The breasts also contain nerves, arteries, veins, and lymph nodes. The breasts' lymph nodes are part of the body's immunological disease-fighting system. They act as sieves and filter bacteria, cast-off cells, and other substances from the lymph fluid.

The appearance of the breasts varies among women (see color plate, Figure 3–8). Some females are large-breasted, others are small-breasted. Breast size is determined by the amount of fat and gland tissue that the breasts contain. Women with large breasts usually have an abundance of both. The size of the breasts has little to do with their ability to produce milk or with their sensitivity.

Some women are high-breasted and others are low-breasted. Contrary to what magazines like *Playboy* or *Penthouse* would like us to believe, the breasts are usually not perfectly matched. Generally one breast (often the left) is slightly larger. There are wide variations in the appearance of nipples, too. For example, nipples can be large and protruding or small and receding. Nipple placement can also vary. Some

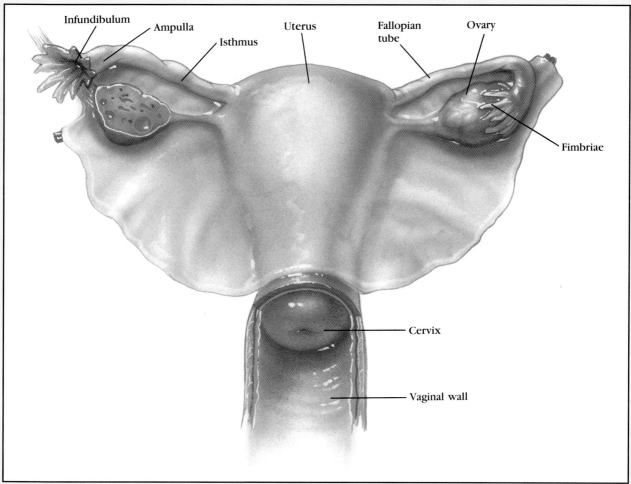

FIGURE 3–5
The Ovaries and Fallopian Tubes.

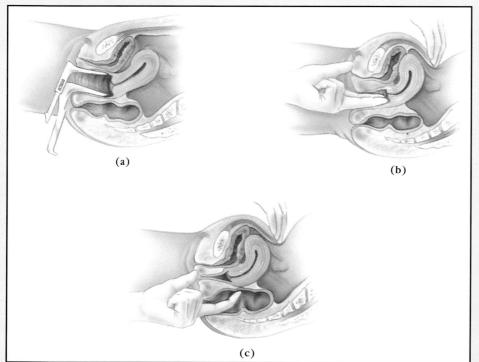

(a)

(b)

(c)

FIGURE 3–6
The Pelvic Examination.

(a) Examination of the vagina and cervix by means of a vaginal speculum. (b) Manual examination with palpation of the abdomen. (c) Manual examination of the rectum with abdominal palpation.

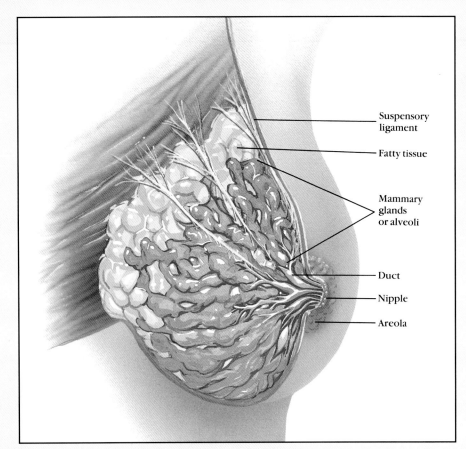

FIGURE 3–7
Structure of the Female Breasts.

Suspensory ligament

Fatty tissue

Mammary glands or alveoli

Duct

Nipple

Areola

FIGURE 3–8
Variations in the Female Breast.

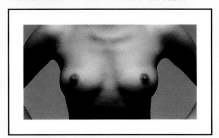

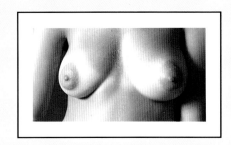

FIGURE 3–9
Hormonal Influences on the Menstrual Cycle.

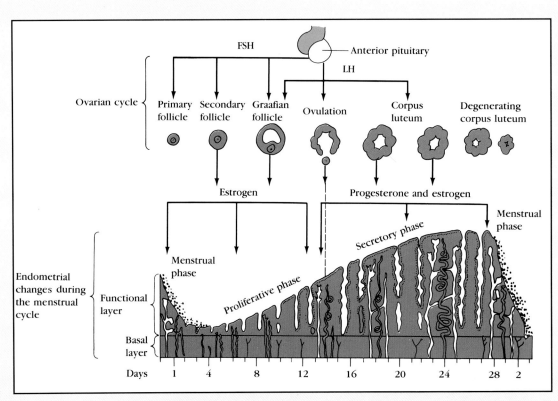

women's nipples are located directly in the middle of their breasts, while in others the nipples occupy a lower position.

We live in a breast-obsessed society. Breasts are perceived as being highly erotic and a symbol of sexuality, and many women are taught that their breasts are a critical part of their anatomy. Many men spend an endless stream of money to view breasts being bared in such places as topless bars, X-rated movies, and adult magazines. Images of cleavage and bulging bustlines are transmitted to us from billboards and video rock music, advertisements, and afternoon soap operas. Interestingly, despite their own interest in breasts, many men need to be reminded (or taught) that women derive pleasure from having their breasts caressed (see Chapter 8).

Women are sometimes preoccupied with the size and shape of their breasts, wondering if their contours are attractive and appealing:

> I am small-breasted and can remember growing up hoping they were going to get bigger. A lot of my friends had big breasts and I couldn't help but compare mine to theirs. I was envious, especially when everyone had a bra but me.

> I don't know what all the fuss is about regarding breast size. I don't believe that bigger is better. My partner loves my breasts just the way they are, just as I love all of his sexual parts. (Authors' files)

Women who find their breasts unappealing sometimes look for ways to improve them. Small-breasted women may turn to lotions, tablets, bust development exercises, or mechanical devices to enlarge their breasts. Unfortunately, none of these methods work.

For some women plastic surgery is an alternative. In recent years plastic surgery has become a thriving business for those wanting to enlarge their breasts as well as for those seeking breast reduction. Like all surgical procedures, breast reduction or enlargement embodies certain risks, including infection, excessive bleeding, and adverse reactions to an anesthetic or medication. Breast reduction entails the surgical removal of excess breast tissue. In breast enlargement or augmentation a silicone pouch containing a silicone gel is implanted into the breast tissue. (Free silicone is no longer injected into the breast, as was done years ago.) The implants have a normal feel and do not usually get hard or lumpy, although the healing breast tissue surrounding the implant can become hard. However, problems have been reported with implants, including silicone leakage (which disrupts the body's immune system), excessive scarring, and infections. More information on the health risks posed by breast implantation can be found in Chapter 17.

BREAST CANCER. Although most breast lumps are benign, breast cancer is a leading cause of death among women and the primary cause of death among women 40 to 44 years of age. In the United States, in 1989, an estimated 130,000 new cases were reported, and over 41,000 women died of the disease. The American Cancer Society (1990) has estimated that one in ten women will develop breast cancer during her lifetime.

Most cancers of the breast are first detected by women themselves or by their sexual partners. The growing practice of breast self-examination (see box on "How to Do a Breast Self-Examination") may be responsible for a recent increase in early detection, which, coupled with prompt diagnosis and treatment, enhances the probability of cure. For 90 percent of those with localized breast cancer, cure is now possible.

Those at particular risk for breast cancer are women over the age of 35, women who have never had children or who have had a child for the first time after the age of 30, and women who began menstruating early or who experienced late menopause. Breast cancer also occurs more frequently in women with a family history of this

Making Use of What We Know

How to Do a Breast Self-Examination (BSE)

Women should perform a breast self-examination (BSE) every month. The best time to do a BSE is two or three days after the end of your period, when the breasts are least likely to be tender or swollen. As you go through the following steps, keep in mind that you are looking for a change in the size, shape, or color of the breast or nipples, puckering of the skin, lumps, alterations in outline, and any bleeding or unusual discharge from the nipple.

1. Stand before a mirror and inspect your breasts, first with your arms at your sides and then with your arms raised above your head.

2. Now press your hands firmly on your hips and bow slightly toward the mirror. As you do this, pull your shoulders and elbows forward.

3. Raise your left arm. Use three or four fingers of your right hand to explore your left breast firmly, carefully, and thoroughly. (You might want to do this part of the exam in the shower because fingers glide over soapy skin, making it easier to concentrate on the texture underneath.) Beginning at the outer edge (the point at which the breast meets the chest), press your fingers against the breast and, keeping your fingers together, make small circles, moving the circles slowly around the breast. Gradually work toward the nipple. Be sure to cover the entire breast. Pay special attention to the area between the breast and the armpit, including the armpit itself. Feel for any unusual lump or mass under the skin. Repeat the exam on your right breast.

4. Gently squeeze the nipple and look for a discharge. Repeat the exam on your other breast.

5. Steps 3 and 4 should be repeated lying down. Lie flat on your back, left arm over your head and a pillow or folded towel under your left shoulder. This position flattens the breast and makes it easier to examine. Use the same circular motion just described. Repeat on your right breast.

If you discover anything unusual, make an appointment with your physician right away. Remember, most breast lumps are not cancerous, and there are other causes for a change in breast appearance. However, only a physician can tell the difference. And if you *have* detected cancer, early diagnosis may mean less surgery and a better outlook for cure.

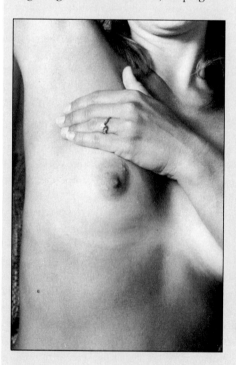

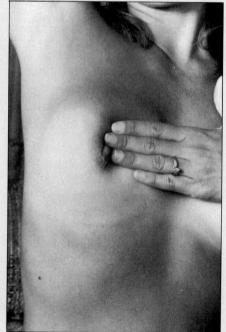

Sexual Anatomy and Physiology

disease and in those who have already had breast cancer. This form of cancer is more common among white women than black women, but its incidence is rising among African-Americans. Asians, especially Japanese women, have low rates of breast cancer.

Breast cancer has numerous warning signals. Among these are persistent changes in the breast, such as a lump, thickening, swelling, dimpling, skin irritation, distortion, retraction or scaliness of the nipple, nipple discharge, pain, or tenderness. It is important to note that most breast lumps are *not* cancerous, but only a physician can make a diagnosis.

In addition to regular self-examination, mammography offers women a valuable early detection technique. **Mammography** is a low-dose X-ray examination designed to reveal breast tumors too small to be felt by the fingers. Mammography uses radiation to create an image of the breast on film or paper called a mammogram. In addition to revealing actual tumors, the mammogram shows changes in the structure of the breast that may point to early cancer. A mammographic examination usually consists of two X-rays of each breast, one taken from the top and one from the side.

mammography Low-dose X-ray examination designed to reveal breast tumors too small to be felt by palpation.

The National Cancer Institute recommends differing early detection methods for women at different ages. Beginning at the age of 20, all women should have their breasts examined by a physician every three years, and women over 40 should have this examination every year. Women should have a first, baseline mammogram (to compare with successive mammograms) anywhere between the ages of 35 and 39. From 40 to 49, women who are not at particular risk should have mammography every one or two years, and women in this category who are over 50 should have the exam every year. Women who have had breast cancer should have yearly mammograms regardless of their ages.

If self-examination or mammography reveals a growth that turns out to be cancerous, a woman has several treatment options, ranging from local removal of the tumor, called a **lumpectomy,** to a **mastectomy,** the surgical removal of all or part of the breast. Other treatments are radiation therapy, chemotherapy, and hormone manipulation. Often two or more of these methods are used in combination. Chapter 17 offers in-depth coverage of these treatment procedures.

lumpectomy Surgery that removes a breast tumor along with some of the surrounding breast tissue.

mastectomy The surgical removal of a breast or part of it.

Menstruation

Menstruation refers to the monthly shedding of endometrial tissue, blood, and other secretions from the uterus that occurs when the ovum is not fertilized by the sperm. **Menarche,** the onset of menstruation, occurs at approximately 12 to 13 years of age (see Chapter 14). Once menarche occurs, the menstrual cycle repeats itself year after year until the woman reaches **menopause,** the cessation of the cycle.

As the box on "The Taboo of Menstruation" suggests, some societies view menstruation as something unpleasant or even dangerous. We will see in Chapter 14, however, that in some other cultures menarche is a rite of passage to be celebrated.

menstruation The monthly shedding of endometrial tissue, blood, and other secretions from the uterus that occurs when the ovum is not fertilized by a sperm.

menarche The onset of menstruation.

menopause The normal cessation of the menstrual cycle.

THE MENSTRUAL CYCLE. The average menstrual cycle (from the beginning of one period to the onset of the next) is 28 days. However, the cycle may vary widely even in the same woman. Few women menstruate exactly every 28 or 30 days. Also, the menstrual cycle tends to be irregular in frequency, duration, and amount of menstrual flow for the first year or so after menarche. After that, a regular menstrual cycle is typically established.

Menses, or the discharge of blood from the uterus, lasts from two to eight days. The total blood loss each month is about 50–60 milliliters. Besides blood, the menstrual discharge is composed of cervical and vaginal secretions, bacteria, and mucous. The discharge is dark red and has a distinctive odor. For reasons that are not clearly understood, menstrual blood does not clot.

menses The discharge of blood from the uterus during menstruation.

*M*any societies have considered menstrual blood evil and dangerous. Some, like the Bakairi of Brazil, the Veddas of Ceylon, and the Arapesh of New Guinea, isolate their women in small "menstrual huts." The menstruating woman often must remain in a crouched position and is not allowed to eat, sleep, or even touch her own body. Men keep their distance from these huts for fear of dying. Many societies prohibit menstruating women from attending religious ceremonies or engaging in sexual intercourse.

In Uganda any cooking utensil a woman touches during her menstrual period must be destroyed. In Costa Rica menstruating women of the Brirbri Indian tribe must use banana leaves for plates. When meals are finished, these leaves must be buried, for death awaits any human being or animal that touches them. Among certain tribes in Australia menstruating women are not allowed to harvest food.

The Doga of East Africa believe that a menstruating woman brings misfortune to everything she touches. As in other societies, such a woman is segregated in a special hut and provided with special eating utensils. If she is seen passing through the village, a general purification must take place.

The menstrual taboo is rooted in antiquity. The Bible states: "And if a woman have an issue, and her issue in her flesh be blood, she shall be put apart seven days: and whosoever toucheth her shall be unclean until the even" (Leviticus 15:19).

The Code of Manu (Hindu law) prescribed: "A woman during her menstrual period shall retire for three days to a place apart. During this time, she shall not look at anybody, not even her own children, or at the sight of the sun. On the fourth day, she shall bathe."

Finally, the Koran tells us: "They will ask Thee also concerning the courses of women; answer, They are pollution; therefore separate yourselves from women in their courses, and go not near them until they be cleansed."

---

proliferative phase A period of time between the 6th and 13th day of the menstrual cycle; also called the follicular phase.

follicle-stimulating hormone (FSH) A hormone released by the anterior lobe of the pituitary gland, FSH is necessary for the growth and maturation of the primary ovarian follicles. It also stimulates follicular cells to secrete estrogen.

graafian follicle A mature ovarian follicle.

estrogens Hormones produced primarily by follicle cells of the ovaries and in the testes in men. There are a number of different types of estrogens, including estradiol, estriol, and estrone.

luteinizing hormone (LH) A hormone secreted by the anterior lobe of the pituitary gland, LH is important in the later stages of maturation of the ovarian follicle. It is also important for ovulation and for the transformation of the emptied follicle into a corpus luteum.

STAGES OF THE MENSTRUAL CYCLE. The menstrual cycle, a sequence of closely integrated processes, occurs as a result of the interaction of hormones that are secreted by the brain's hypothalamus and pituitary gland and the ovaries. While the menstrual cycle exists as a continuum, it can be broken down into three fairly distinct phases: proliferative, secretory, and menstrual. You may find it useful to follow Figure 3–9 (see color plate) as we describe these phases.

Proliferative Phase. The **proliferative phase** (also called the follicular phase) occurs between the 6th and 13th day of the menstrual cycle (the first five days are called the resting or postmenstrual phase from the previous month's cycle). During this time the hypothalamus, a walnut-sized collection of highly specialized brain cells, sends a chemical message to the pituitary gland, which is located just below the hypothalamus. The pituitary gland, in turn, secretes the hormones that regulate the reproductive system. More specifically, a **follicle-stimulating hormone (FSH)** is necessary for the growth and maturation of the primary ovarian follicles. One of these follicles—called the **graafian follicle**—reaches full maturity.

The follicular cells manufacture **estrogen,** a hormone that, among other things, causes the cells of the endometrium to proliferate. The cells on the surface become taller while the glands that extend into the endometrium increase in width and length. These changes increase the thickness of the endometrium six- or eightfold.

When secreted by the follicular cells, estrogen travels through the blood and eventually reaches the pituitary gland. Once a certain level of estrogen in the blood is reached, the pituitary gland decreases its production of FSH and begins to manufacture a **luteinizing hormone (LH).** As we'll see, LH is important in the later stages of maturation of the ovarian follicles.

Ovulation occurs 14 days *before* the start of a woman's next menstrual cycle. (If the cycle were always 28 days in length, ovulation would also occur 14 days *after* its start, but cycle length varies among women.) Induced by LH (see Figure 3–9) to burst from the graafian follicle, the ovum is drawn into the fallopian tube.

Ordinarily, a woman is unable to feel ovulation. However, some women experience abdominal pain at the time of ovulation. This pain, called *mittelschmerz* (German for "middle pain"), can range from mild to acute lower abdominal discomfort, and may last for an hour or more. Reasons for the pain are unclear, although many believe that it is due to the irritation (slight blood and fluid loss) caused by the ruptured follicle.

Secretory Phase. The **secretory phase** (also called the luteal phase) occupies the 15th day to the 25th day of the menstrual cycle. After the ovum leaves the ovary, the empty follicle remains. Under the influence of LH it changes its structure and becomes the **corpus luteum.** The corpus luteum (Latin for "yellow body"), a follicle cell cluster that forms on the surface of the ovary at the site of ovulation, manufactures and secretes the hormone progesterone.

Progesterone supplements the action of estrogen on the endometrium, particularly in stimulating the engorgement and dilation of its glands. The production of progesterone continues until a certain level is signaled to the pituitary gland. When this happens, the pituitary gland stops producing LH. As LH production diminishes, the corpus luteum begins to degenerate and stops manufacturing progesterone. The corpus luteum eventually disappears. If conception occurs, however, it continues to manufacture progesterone and sustains early prenatal development until the placenta takes over (see Chapter 11).

Menstrual Phase. The **menstrual phase** refers to the last three days or so of the menstrual cycle. The cessation of corpus luteum activity leads to a sharp decline in the levels of hormones responsible for building up the endometrium. Consequently, the endometrium degenerates, and it is this breakdown of tissue that creates the menstrual flow.

During menstruation countless small blood vessels rupture in the endometrium and innumerable minute hemorrhages occur. Fragments of the endometrium combine with blood and other substances to create the menstrual discharge. During the first day or two of menstruation, the hormone system is relatively quiet. However, the pituitary gland begins to respond to the absence of estrogen by manufacturing and sending out FSH. Thus the early phase of the next menstrual cycle has begun while menstrual blood is still flowing.

PROBLEMS WITH MENSTRUATION. Normal menstruation should not be accompanied by severe pain and discomfort, though women often experience mood swings, gain weight, and have a feeling of discomfort in the pelvis. They may also have lower abdominal cramping, fatigue, backache, headache, and breast sensitivity. For some women, however, menstruation brings more serious problems. Among these are bleeding irregularities, premenstrual syndrome, and toxic shock syndrome.

Bleeding Irregularities. As we said earlier, menstruation normally occurs first between the ages of 12 and 13. When a female reaches the age of 18 and still has not begun to menstruate, **primary amenorrhea** is often diagnosed. The causes of this condition include emotional stress, malnutrition, debilitating disease, genetic abnormality, or a form of hermaphroditism (see Chapter 5).

Secondary amenorrhea is the cessation of menstruation in a female who has already experienced menstruation. This condition can occur anytime between menarche and menopause, except during pregnancy. Among the causes of secondary

secretory phase The 15th to the 25th day of the menstrual cycle during which the corpus luteum develops, begins to secrete progesterone, and then, unless conception occurs, fades away.

corpus luteum A small body that develops within a ruptured ovarian follicle after the ovum is released; secretes the hormone progesterone, which helps regulate the menstrual cycle.

progesterone A hormone manufactured by the corpus luteum, progesterone is most abundant during the secretory phase of the menstrual cycle. Small amounts of progesterone are also found in the male.

menstrual phase The last three days or so of the menstrual cycle.

primary amenorrhea The absence of menstruation.

secondary amenorrhea The cessation of menstruation in a female who has previously experienced menstruation.

dysmenorrhea Painful menstruation.

premenstrual syndrome (PMS) The cyclic occurrence, between ovulation and the onset of menstruation, of symptoms that interfere substantially with some aspect of a woman's life.

amenorrhea are malfunctions of the pituitary or thyroid glands, disorders of the ovaries or of the nervous system, psychological disturbances, the use of oral contraceptive pills, or continued and intensive athletic training.

Dysmenorrhea, or painful menstruation, can occur in women of any age, although it is very common among those between the ages of 14 and 25. In primary dysmenorrhea there is no physical abnormality, but the condition produces cramping and general discomfort. Pain and discomfort are more severe in secondary dysmenorrhea, and are caused by such conditions as uterine fibroid tumors (noncancerous tumors of the uterus), endometriosis (in which endometrial cells grow outside of the uterus), or pelvic inflammatory disease (infection of the pelvic organs). These and other diseases of the reproductive system are discussed in Chapter 17.

Premenstrual Syndrome (PMS). **Premenstrual syndrome (PMS),** as its name implies, takes place between ovulation and the onset of the menstrual period. PMS is broadly defined as the cyclical occurrence, 7–10 days before each menstrual period, of physical and psychological symptoms that are of sufficient severity to interfere with some aspects of a woman's life (Rubinow & Roy-Byrne, 1984).

Many women—about 30 percent—experience mild symptoms that are akin to PMS just before their periods. However, only about 12 percent are in sufficient distress to require a physician's help and only 3 percent are unfortunate enough to be seriously incapacitated by premenstrual syndrome.

There are over 150 symptoms associated with PMS, and there is wide individual variation from woman to woman (see Table 3–1). Although some symptoms overlap, others are quite distinct. The frequency of their occurrence and their severity are also highly variable. Finally, the same woman may experience a different set of symptoms each month. Consider some of the concerns that women with PMS experience:

It's so difficult to describe—I guess I'm just overwhelmed with everything. I get tense and on edge sometimes; other times I just lose all of my concentration. I can't even think straight. It hits me in waves and I feel like I'm in a daze.

For me, it's depression and overwhelming fatigue. I can't function and can barely manage to make it through the day. I'm lethargic and always tired.

TABLE 3–1

Some Symptoms of Premenstrual Syndrome

Physical	*Psychological*
Bloated feeling	Irritability
Weight gain	Anger, aggression
Breast tenderness	Anxiety
Dizziness	Tension
Acne	Lethargy
Migraine headaches	Depression
Backaches	Fatigue
Food cravings	Loss of concentration
Constipation	Insomnia
Diarrhea	Withdrawal
Nausea/vomiting	Changes in sex drive
Pelvic pain	Confusion
Joint and muscle pain	Suicidal thoughts
Hot flushes	Loss of control

Sexual Anatomy and Physiology

I totally lose control. Worse, I take it out on those around me—my husband and children in particular. One minute I'm fine, the next I'm in a blind rage.

It seems as though I cry for hours on end, usually at nothing. PMS for me is rock bottom—a sadness that completely engulfs me.

It's tough to get through, and I've noticed that I'm drinking more and more to escape from it. When I get aches and pains, I use alcohol to numb me. (Authors' files)

The exact cause of premenstrual syndrome is unknown. Researchers have looked at a number of possible factors, but so far none has been shown to play a clear role in this condition. Among the possible causes are poor diet, lack of adequate exercise, excess estrogen, a deficiency of progesterone, vitamin deficiencies, hypoglycemia (low blood sugar), allergy to hormones, and fluid retention. Alterations in brain chemicals and their effects on the reproductive organs have also been implicated in causing PMS (Covington & McClendon, 1987; Bender & Kelleher, 1986).

Certain risk factors for PMS have also been identified, although conclusive findings on each have yet to be made. For example, women in their 30s are thought to be more vulnerable to PMS, as are long-term users of birth control pills. There is a high incidence of PMS symptoms following pregnancy, abortion, childbirth, and the cessation of nursing. Symptoms also tend to appear after a tubal ligation (a form of sterilization in which the fallopian tubes are cut and tied) or a hysterectomy (the surgical removal of all or part of the uterus).

Currently, there is no cure for premenstrual syndrome nor is there a universally agreed-upon treatment procedure. This is because PMS remains a poorly understood medical disorder as well as because of the wide variations in symptom frequency and severity. However, most treatment plans focus on four main areas: education, diet, exercise, and drug therapy.

Education is the most important treatment of PMS. At the very least, it is reassuring to know that the cyclical symptoms are part of the body's chemical change and that they're shared by millions of women. Loved ones often benefit from understanding the symptoms of PMS, too, since they can provide a valuable support network.

Dietary adjustments can be quite helpful. Reducing salt intake for the two weeks prior to menstruation can help prevent fluid retention and weight gain. Vitamin and mineral supplements may offer some relief for PMS symptoms; you may want to consult some of the books listed at the end of the section for more information. The following general guidelines have been proposed:

- Eliminate or reduce intake of simple sugar, such as candy, baked goods, and sweetened cereals.
- Consume foods rich in complex carbohydrates, which are readily converted into blood sugar. These include whole-grain breads and cereals, fresh vegetables, and beans.
- Consume low-fat sources of protein, such as poultry and fish. Also, reduce the intake of red meat.
- Eliminate or reduce daily intake of coffee, tea, and soft drinks.
- Eliminate or reduce alcohol intake. Women with PMS often have a reduced tolerance to alcohol.
- Maintain a normal caloric intake, but eat six small meals a day rather than three larger ones.

Daily exercise is strongly recommended to help relieve the symptoms of PMS. Among other benefits, exercise has been shown to reduce anxiety and depression. Exercise also helps to reduce excess body fluid and abdominal cramping. The exercise need not be strenuous. Indeed, many experts (e.g., Bender & Kelleher, 1986) feel that milder forms such as swimming or biking are preferable to vigorous forms such as aerobics.

If all these measures fail, a physician may prescribe some form of drug therapy. Tranquilizers, for example, may relieve anxiety and tension. For some women oral contraceptives relieve the discomfort associated with PMS, although this is regarded as short-term drug therapy. Diuretics, drugs that help rid the body of excess fluid, are sometimes used to reduce feelings of distention and bloating.

One of the more controversial treatment approaches for PMS is progesterone therapy. Proponents of this approach maintain that PMS symptoms often become worse in the days just prior to menses, when the body's natural progesterone level declines. Progesterone does appear to reduce depression, irritability, and anxiety. However, the drug has not been approved by the Food and Drug Administration for use in PMS treatment. The potential risks associated with its use include increased probability of developing breast cancer, early or late menstrual periods, weight gain or loss, change in sex drive, and increased menstrual cramps.

WHERE TO FIND MORE ON PREMENSTRUAL SYNDROME

Bender, S. D., & Kelleher, K. (1986). *PMS: A positive program to gain control*. Los Angeles, CA: The Body Press.

Harrison, M. (1985). *Self-help for premenstrual syndrome*. New York: Random House.

Hasselbring, B., Greenwood, S., & Castleman, M. (1987). *The medical self-care book of women's health*. Garden City, NY: Doubleday.

Kass-Annese, B., & Danzer, H. C. (1987). *Say good-bye to PMS*. New York: Warner Books.

---

toxic shock syndrome (TSS) A rare and sometimes fatal disease that develops rapidly when a bacterium called staphylococcus aureus enters the bloodstream. The bacterium manufactures a toxin that causes a breakdown of cell walls.

Toxic Shock Syndrome (TSS). **Toxic shock syndrome (TSS)** is a rare but sometimes fatal disease that develops very rapidly when a bacterium called *staphylococcus aureus* enters the bloodstream. First reported in 1978, toxic shock syndrome tends to strike menstruating women under 30 years of age who use tampons. About 4 percent of victims die.

Staphylococcus aureus manufactures a toxin, or poison, that causes a breakdown of cell walls. This allows blood to seep into the tissues, creating a form of blood poisoning. The onset of TSS is very sudden, causing fever, rash, a decrease in blood pressure, shock, and sometimes even death. In serious cases the low blood pressure and weakened cell walls (which allow foreign bodies to enter) can leave the woman susceptible to further complications, such as liver and heart damage. Moreover, because the body often does not produce enough antibodies to combat this invasion, TSS can recur.

Although tampons are not the primary cause for increased toxin production, their use appears to increase the chances of developing TSS significantly. Particularly risky are superabsorbent tampons, which tend to fill the vagina, blocking the menstrual flow and creating a breeding ground for infection (many bacteria thrive in a warm, moist environment). In addition, women tend to leave superabsorbent tampons in the vagina much longer than the less absorbent varieties, increasing the risk of infection.

Sexual Anatomy and Physiology

Other factors associated with tampon use have been identified. For example, tampon applicators may scratch the walls of the vagina, allowing bacteria to enter the bloodstream. And the tampon may carry bacteria from the hands, the vulva, or the anus into the vagina. One theory being explored is that tampons soak up significant amounts of magnesium, normally present in vaginal tissue and fluid. Many experts maintain that the removal of magnesium enables the TSS bacterium to create deadly levels of toxins.

There are many symptoms of toxic shock syndrome. Typically, a high fever (102°F or higher) develops suddenly. Chills are also common, along with heavy vomiting and diarrhea. A rash usually appears on the soles of the feet and the palms of the hands and may also develop on the face and trunk. Within two or three days after the first symptoms appear, the victim often feels dizzy or faint, particularly when changing body position, such as from sitting to standing. This is a symptom of low blood pressure. Other common symptoms include blurred vision, disorientation, and muscle aches.

The symptoms of toxic shock syndrome require immediate medical attention. Typically, patients are hospitalized and given treatment similar to that given to victims of blood poisoning. Fluids or whole blood transfusions are administered to raise blood pressure, and antibiotics are given to combat infection. When properly treated, most of the symptoms of TSS subside in 7 to 10 days. It may take several weeks, though, for patients to regain their normal energy levels.

Can you protect yourself from toxic shock syndrome? The best precaution is to not use tampons. The Food and Drug Administration requires that warnings to users of tampons be placed on either the tampon package or in an informational leaflet inside the package. If you choose to use tampons, the following precautions may prove helpful:

- If you have any of the early warning signs of TSS—high fever, nausea, vomiting, diarrhea, a rash that looks like a sunburn, dizziness, and/or fainting—remove the tampon immediately and contact a physician.
- Discuss tampon use with your physician if you've had any of the warning signs in the past.

In 1983, Nan Robertson, a New York Times *staff writer, came close to death as she battled an extremely severe case of TSS. Although gangrene forced the amputation of the tips of eight of her fingers, eventually she returned to work, where the first story she wrote at her terminal told of her experience with TSS. She won a Pulitzer Prize for the story.*

- Change tampons relatively frequently (every six to eight hours) and consider using a sanitary napkin or minipad at night. This will help to retard the growth of bacteria.
- Use tampons with the lowest absorbency that are still effective. Evidence indicates that these tampons are less risky.
- Do not use tampons for at least six to eight weeks after giving birth.
- Remember that TSS can recur. If you have had the disease once, you are likely to have it again. Relapse rates may be as high as 30 percent if antibiotics were not used properly or if tampon use is resumed too soon. Talk with your physician before using tampons again (Covington & McClendon, 1987).

MALE REPRODUCTIVE SYSTEM

The male reproductive system consists of the external genitals, internal genitals, and accessory glands. The external genitals consist of the penis and the scrotum. The internal genitals include the testes, epididymis, vas deferens, ejaculatory ducts, and the urethra. Accessory glands include the seminal vesicles, prostate gland, and Cowper's glands.

External Genitals

As we mentioned, many of the male and female genitals develop from the same embryonic tissue—for example, the clitoris and the penis. However, as sexual development takes place, the male genitalia become more visible to the eye. Males usually have a better understanding of what their genitals look like than females do since they touch and hold their genitals when urinating. As with the vulva, there are wide variations in the appearance of male genitalia.

penis The male organ of copulation. The urethra, which passes through the penis, provides a passageway for both semen and urine.

Penis. The **penis** is the male organ of copulation as well as a passageway from the bladder to eliminate urine. As indicated earlier, the penis is generally homologous to the clitoris in the female. It is an elongated pendant structure that consists of a body, called a shaft, and an enlarged conic structure, called the glans (see color plate, Figure 3–10). The penis is attached to the pubic bone, just in front of the scrotum, or testicles.

In a flaccid (unaroused) state the penis measures about 3 to 4 inches. When erect, the average penis measures 6 inches in length. The average diameter of the flaccid penis is 1.25 inches, while an erect penis increases this figure by one-quarter of an inch. The size and shape of the penis varies among men, as illustrated in Figure 3–11 (see color plate). Many males often express concern about the size of their penis, wishing that it could be longer:

Is a large penis necessary for adequate sexual functioning?

Ever since I was a teenager, I felt "the bigger the better." I have this insecurity that women will not find my penis large enough, and this bothers me. I realize that penis size has little to do with sexual pleasuring, but that doesn't make any difference. Maybe I'm just fearful of rejection or ridicule, I don't know. I guess that I'll always be dissatisfied and want an extra inch or so. (Authors' files)

Other men, though, feel that their penis size is just right:

I'm perfectly content with the size of my penis. I've accepted it along with the rest of my body. Even if I had the opportunity, I don't think that I'd change it. (Authors' files)

MOTHER AND I FEEL IT'S TIME WE TELL YOU WHERE YOUR GENITALS ARE.

Many men believe that a large penis is necessary for adequate sexual functioning, thinking that a larger penis will be more likely than a smaller one to bring about orgasm in a woman during intercourse. The truth is that penis length does not play a major role in female sexual arousal. Furthermore, the female vagina stretches to accommodate a wide range of penis sizes.

One source (McCarthy, 1988) notes that it is very misleading to judge the size of a penis when it is in the flaccid state, for generally, the larger a man's penis when limp, the less it will increase in size when erect. Penises that are smaller in the flaccid state have a greater erectile potential. Thus there is an equalizing factor, and the variations in size among erect penises are minimally important.

Unlike the penis of many animal species, the human penis does not have a bone. Rather, it is composed of three cylindrical masses of cavernous tissue enclosed in separate fibrous coverings and held together by a covering of skin. As Figure 3–10 shows, the **corpora cavernosa** are the two larger and uppermost of these cylindrical masses, and lie side by side. The lower, smaller one is called the **corpus spongiosum.** The urethra is contained within the corpus spongiosum.

The three cylindrical masses have an abundant supply of blood vessels and nerves. When the penis is flaccid, the cavities contain little blood. During sexual arousal, however, when these spaces fill with blood, the penis becomes erect.

The shaft of the penis begins where the penis is joined to the body. The shaft itself is relatively insensitive. The **frenulum,** however, located on the underside of the penis between the shaft and the glans, is very sensitive to touch.

At the tip of the smooth, rounded **glans,** which forms the end of the penis, is the external urinary meatus, or opening of the urethra. The penile glans, like the clitoral glans, has an abundance of nerve endings and is highly sensitive, as is the **corona,** or raised ridge of tissue that separates the glans from the penile shaft.

Over the glans is a loose-fitting, retractable layer of skin called the **prepuce,** or foreskin. This foreskin (the clitoral hood in women) contains glands that discharge oily, lubricating secretions onto the penile (or clitoral) glans. The accumulation of these secretions, called **smegma,** should be removed by regular washing, as it can become a breeding ground for infection. When a **circumcision** is performed (see the box on page 82 and Chapter 11), all or part of the foreskin is surgically removed. The external urinary meatus is the opening of the urethra at the tip of the glans.

At the base of the penis the two corpora cavernosa diverge into two tapering parts called the **crura,** which form the actual connection to the pubic bones. At its point of attachment the crura expands into a circular structure called the bulb. Together, the crura and the bulb form the root of the penis.

corpora cavernosa The two larger and uppermost cylindrical masses of penile tissue that lie side by side and are enclosed in separate fibrous coverings.

corpus spongiosum The lower, smaller cylindrical mass of tissue in the penis that contains the urethra.

frenulum The underside of the penis, between the shaft and the glans.

glans The enlarged conic structure at the tip of the penis.

corona A raised rim or ridge of tissue that separates the penile glans from the shaft.

prepuce A loose-fitting, retractable casing of skin that forms over the penile glans. Also called the foreskin.

smegma Accumulation of secretions on the penile (or clitoral) glans from the glands of the foreskin (or clitoral hood).

circumcision A surgical procedure in which all or part of the prepuce, or foreskin, of the penis or clitoris is removed.

crura Tapering parts of the corpora cavernosa that help connect the penis to the pubic bone.

scrotum A skin-covered pouch suspended from the perineal area that contains the testes.

SCROTUM. The **scrotum** is a skin-covered pouch suspended from the perineum, as in females, the area between the genitals and the anal canal. Thin-walled and lying at the base of the penis, the scrotum is homologous to the labia majora of the female. It has many sensory nerves and is quite sensitive.

Internally, the scrotum is divided into two sacs. Each sac contains a testis, epididymis, and part of the vas deferens and spermatic cord (see color plate, Figures 3–12 and 3–13).

The scrotum's outermost layer of skin is generally darker than the rest of the body. The scrotum also has scattered hairs and a somewhat rough, wrinkled surface. The degree of wrinkling is greatest in young men and at colder temperatures. The scrotum also has many sweat glands, appearing as a network of bumps. These sweat glands open directly on the scrotal surface.

The scrotum is at a lower temperature than the rest of the body, which is necessary for the manufacture of sperm (sperm are most effectively produced when the temperature in the testes is 1.5°–2°C below body temperature). It is also sensitive to touch, pain, and temperature changes, thus serving to protect the testes from potential harm. When the temperature is cold, the cremasteric muscles (located beneath the scrotal surface) contract and draw the testicles close to the body. These same muscles relax in warm temperatures, allowing the testicles to move away from the body.

The cremasteric muscles are also in operation during sexual excitement. When a man is aroused, his testicles rise in the scrotum and increase in size. If his arousal does not culminate in ejaculation, the swelling often remains, creating an uncomfortable condition popularly known as "blue balls." This is temporary, though, and causes no permanent damage (McCarthy, 1988).

Internal Genitals

testes A pair of bilateral, oval, glandular organs contained in the scrotum. The testes produce sperm and secrete male sex hormones.

spermatic cord The cord that suspends the testis in the scrotum. It contains arteries, nerves, veins, and the vas deferens.

inguinal canal A tunnel-like passage in the abdominal cavity through which the testes descend during fetal development.

TESTES. The **testes** produce sperm and secrete male sex hormones. You'll recall that the testes are homologous with the ovaries in the female. They are a pair of oval glandular organs contained in the scrotum (see Figure 3–12). Each testis is about 1¾ inches long and a little less than an inch wide, and weighs about a half ounce. For reasons not known, the left testis hangs about a half inch lower in the scrotum than the right. Both testes are suspended in the scrotal sac by attachment to scrotal tissue and spermatic cords. Each **spermatic cord** contains arteries, nerves, vas deferens, and veins.

Early in fetal life the testes develop in the abdominal cavity. By the eighth month of prenatal development, the testes leave this position and begin to move downward through a tunnel-like passage called the **inguinal canal.** Eventually, the testes descend into the scrotal sac and the inguinal canal closes, thus preventing any other tissues from entering into the scrotum. Occasionally, the testicles fail to descend, leading to a condition called cryptorchidism. Measures must then be taken to bring the testes down into the scrotum, for if the testicles remain in the abdominal cavity too long, body heat may harm some testicular processes.

If the inguinal canal fails to close, a loop of intestine can descend, creating an inguinal hernia. This is a condition requiring surgical attention because strangulation of the blood supply to the intestine is possible (see Chapter 17). An unclosed inguinal canal can also lead to the return of one or both testes to the abdominal cavity.

tunica albuginea A fibrous substance covering each testis.

seminiferous tubules Tightly packed, convoluted structures located in the testicles, that produce sperm.

sperm Reproductive cells produced in the testes.

Each testis is covered by a serous membrane called the **tunica albuginea,** a fibrous white substance that also divides the testis into 200 to 300 cone-shaped lobules. Each of these lobules contains up to three tightly packed, convoluted **seminiferous tubules,** the site of sperm production (see color plate, Figure 3–13). **Sperm** are reproductive cells; in fertilization one sperm unites with the female egg, or ovum. If each seminiferous tubule were unraveled, it would measure between one and three

Sexual Anatomy and Physiology

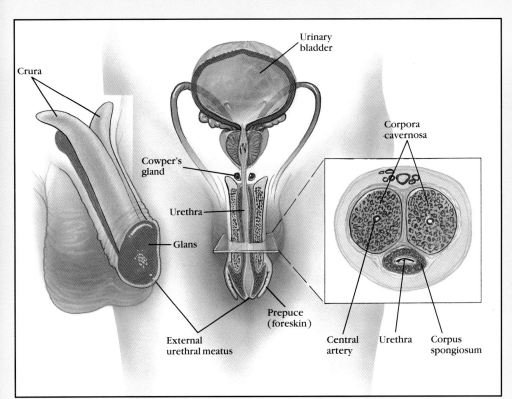

FIGURE 3–10
Anatomy of the Penis.

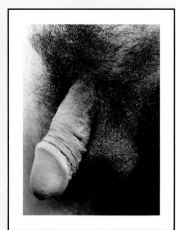

FIGURE 3–11
Variations in the Penis.

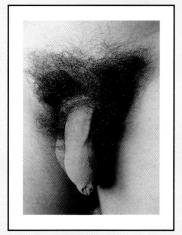

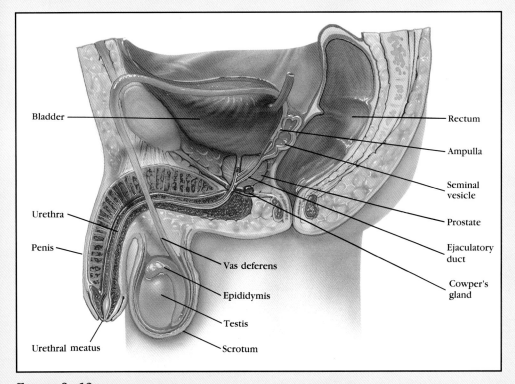

FIGURE 3–12
Male Reproductive System and Structure of the Scrotum.

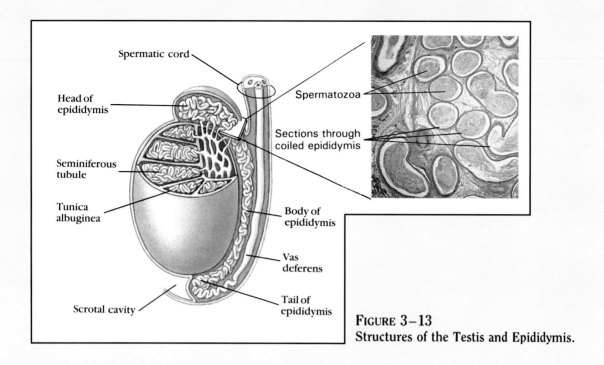

FIGURE 3–13
Structures of the Testis and Epididymis.

FIGURE 3–14
Structure of the Mature Spermatozoon.

The microtubules, mitochondria, and dense fibers of the sperm's middle portion provide the energy to move the tail. This tail, or flagellum, is a unique structure in the human body, able to move a cell from one place to another.

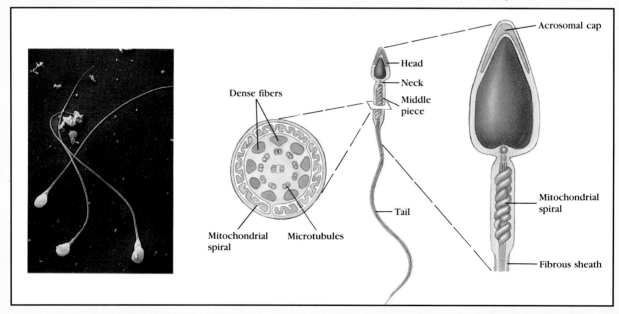

feet in length. It is in the seminiferous tubules that sperm cells (in all stages of development) are arranged in layers.

It is estimated that a mature male has about 1,000 seminiferous tubules, which all together produce millions of spermatozoa each day. The production of mature spermatozoa takes place through a process called **spermatogenesis.** Sperm production varies among and within the tubules, with cells in different areas of the same tubule undergoing different stages of spermatogenesis. Sperm will eventually ripen and mature in the epididymis, which we will presently discuss. The entire process of sperm maturation takes between 65 and 75 days.

A **spermatozoon** (*spermatozoon* is the term used for referring to a single sperm; *spermatozoa* is the plural designation) consists of a head and neck, a middle piece, and an elongated lashlike tail, or end piece (see color plate, Figure 3–14). The head of a spermatozoon carries the genetic message from the male (23 chromosomes), and is covered by an **acrosomal cap.** The acrosomal cap contains a special enzyme, called hyaluronidase, designed to penetrate the outer structure of the ovum. The cylindrical middle piece of the spermatozoon provides energy for sperm locomotion. The tail, or flagellum, consists of a principal structure and a short end piece, and provides motility (movement).

A mature spermatozoon is an extremely small structure. In fact, millions can be placed inside the hull of a grain of rice with room to spare. The head is about 5 microns long, the middle piece about 5 microns, and the tail 40 to 50 microns (one microns = .001 millimeters). In contrast, the ovum is about 130 to 140 microns in diameter.

Located between the seminiferous tubules are the **interstitial** (or **Leydig's**) **cells,** which manufacture the male sex hormones called **androgens.** The most potent male sex hormone is **testosterone.** Following puberty, testosterone production is fairly regular. Testosterone is important not only for spermatogenesis but also for the growth and development of the male sex organs and the other tissues that provide the male with his secondary sex characteristics (see Chapter 14). Testosterone also influences sexual arousal and response, a topic we will explore in detail in Chapter 4.

Before ending our discussion of the testes, we need to say a few words about testicular cancer. Though testicular cancer is rare in middle-aged men, it is one of the most common forms of cancer in men between the ages of 15 and 34. There are 5,000 new cases in this age group each year. Testicular cancer is 40 times more likely to occur in men whose testes never descended to the scrotum or descended after the age of six. (Parents should have their male infants and young boys examined by a doctor to be sure that their testicles have properly descended. If they have not, this condition can be corrected with surgery.) It occurs only one-fourth as often in black men as in white men. The rate among Hispanic men lies between the rates for blacks and whites.

The first sign of testicular cancer is usually a slight enlargement of one of the testes. With continued growth, a sensation of heaviness or general discomfort may be experienced in the scrotal area. One testicle is usually firmer and harder to the touch than the other, or it may have a definite lump. Sometimes there is a sudden accumulation of blood or fluid in the scrotum.

At one time testicular cancer often proved fatal because it spread rapidly to vital organs, particularly the lungs. Recent advances in treatment, though, have made cancer of the testes one of the most curable of all cancers, especially if detected and treated promptly (see box on "How to Do a Testicular Self-Examination"). When discovered early, the cure rate approaches 96 percent; even when the cancer has advanced, survival rates up to 70 percent can be achieved.

When there is no evidence that the cancer has spread to other locations, an **orchiectomy,** or the surgical removal of a testis, is the treatment of choice. Typically, this surgery is followed by postoperative radiation therapy directed at the lymph nodes in the back. Even when the disease has spread beyond the affected testis,

spermatogenesis The process of sperm production.

spermatozoon The male reproductive cell.

acrosomal cap The covering of the head of the spermatozoon that contains a special enzyme designed to penetrate the outer structure of the ovum.

interstitial (Leydig's) cells Cells, located between the seminiferous tubules, that manufacture androgens.

androgens Hormones produced primarily by the interstitial (Leydig's) cells of the testes, and to a lesser extent by the adrenal glands of both males and females.

testosterone A male hormone produced by the testes. Testosterone is essential for the production of sperm, for the growth and development of male sex organs, and for the development of male secondary sex characteristics.

orchiectomy The surgical removal of a testis.

MAKING USE OF WHAT WE KNOW

How to Do a Testicular Self-Examination (TSE)

*I*t is important to examine the testicles on a monthly basis. The best time is following a hot shower or bath when the scrotal skin covering the testes is relaxed and the testes have freely descended to escape the body heat. Each testicle should be gently examined by rolling it between the thumb and fingers of both hands. Normal testes are about 1¾ inches in length and should be spongy to the touch. You should also be able to find the epididymis, a cordlike structure that can be felt at the back of each testis. The epididymis should not be confused with an abnormal lump.

Careful attention should be directed to the size, shape, and consistency of each testis. Any deviation from the normal anatomy, such as a small lump or nodule about the size of a pea, should be promptly reported to a physician. While it may not be malignant, it could be the first sign of a true cancer. Only a doctor can make that diagnosis.

Testicular self-examination performed regularly is an important health habit, but it cannot substitute for a physician's examination. Your doctor should examine your testicles when you have a physical examination. You can also ask your doctor to check the way you do TSE.

radiation therapy (most testicular tumors are very sensitive to radiation), sometimes combined with chemotherapy, can be very effective.

Many young men fail to seek help at the appearance of symptoms because they fear that treatment will cause sterility or impotence. This fear is unfounded, for early removal of a diseased testis does not result in either impotence or sterility. On the contrary, full sexual and reproductive functioning are quite possible with one testis alone.

epididymis A single, tightly coiled tube, lying along the top and behind each testis, that stores spermatozoa.

EPIDIDYMIS. The seminiferous tubules of the testes converge into a single tightly coiled tube called the **epididymis** (see Figure 3–13). The epididymis serves three important functions. First, it provides the first of several ducts through which spermatozoa pass from the testes to the exterior of the body. Second, as we will see, it contributes to the maturation of sperm. Third, the epididymis secretes a very small part of the semen, or seminal fluid.

The epididymis is enclosed in a fibrous casing and lies on top of and behind each testis. It is a curved structure and consists of three parts: a head, body, and tail (see Figure 3–13). Although the epididymis has a very small diameter, if uncoiled, it would measure approximately 20 feet in length.

In many respects, the epididymis is a storage and refinement center for sperm. During the approximate two weeks that it takes sperm to pass through the epididymis,

Sexual Anatomy and Physiology

they are nourished by a fluid. This process develops the motility of the sperm and their capacity to fertilize an ovum.

VAS DEFERENS. The **vas deferens** are paired structures that are continuations of the epididymis. Tubelike and about 15½ inches long, the vas deferens connect each epididymis to the ejaculatory ducts. They have thick, muscular walls that help to propel spermatozoa through the duct system. The transportation of sperm is the only known function of the vas deferens. In Chapter 12 we will discuss the birth control method of vasectomy, in which the vas deferens are severed in order to prevent sperm from reaching the body's exterior.

As you can see in Figure 3–12, the vas deferens ascend from the testes out of the scrotum and, enclosed in the spermatic cord, pass through the inguinal canal into the abdominal cavity. At this point the vas leave the cords and continue alone over the top and down the back surface of the bladder. Just before reaching the prostate gland, each vas becomes enlarged, forming the ampulla. The two **ampulla** join with the seminal vesicles to form the ejaculatory ducts.

EJACULATORY DUCTS. The two short (about an inch each in length) **ejaculatory ducts** pass through the prostate gland and empty into the urethra. The ejaculatory ducts serve as passageways for semen and the fluid secreted by the seminal vesicles.

URETHRA. The **urethra** (see Figure 3–12) is a relatively narrow tube that serves to transport both urine and seminal fluid. The urethra leaves the bladder, passes through the prostate gland, travels through two layers of tissue that connect the pubic bones, and passes through the corpus spongiosum of the penis to the urethral opening, or meatus. The entire urethra is almost 8 inches long and is lined with a mucous membrane. As we'll discover in Chapter 17, glands within the urethra are a major site of infection in sexually transmitted diseases.

ACCESSORY GLANDS. The remaining internal sex organs, referred to as the accessory reproductive glands, are the seminal vesicles, the prostate gland, and Cowper's glands. The primary function of the accessory reproductive glands, secreting essential components of semen, is controlled by the endocrine and nervous systems, which we discuss in Chapter 4.

Seminal Vesicles. The **seminal vesicles** are a pair of secretory glands that lie close to the bladder and in front of the rectum (see Figure 3–12). The seminal vesicles secrete a viscous liquid component of semen that is somewhat alkaline and rich in fructose. Fructose is a simple sugar that serves as an energy source for sperm motility after ejaculation.

Prostate Gland. The **prostate gland** lies just below the bladder, where it surrounds the upper portion of the urethra. It is made up of both muscular and glandular tissue. The function of the prostate gland is to secrete a thin, milky, slightly alkaline fluid that is rich in nutrients into the seminal fluid. The prostate secretion protects spermatozoa from the acidic environment they encounter both in the male urethra and in the female vagina. Unlike the fluid released by the seminal vesicles, prostatic fluid does not contain fructose.

The fact that the urethra passes through the prostate gland can cause problems. Many older men suffer from enlargement of the prostate gland. As it enlarges, the prostate squeezes the urethra, often closing it and creating urination difficulties. If this constriction is great enough to prevent a man from urinating, the result may be a serious condition that must be corrected quickly because retention of urine means retention of toxic matter.

vas deferens Paired structures that serve to transport spermatozoa from the testes to the urethra.

ampulla In the female, the outer two-thirds of the fallopian tube; the portion of the tube in which fertilization of the ovum by a spermatozoon typically takes place.

ejaculatory ducts Two short tubes that pass through the prostate gland and terminate in the urethra. The ejaculatory ducts serve as passageways for semen and fluid secreted by the seminal vesicles.

urethra A small tube that serves to transport both urine from the bladder and semen and seminal fluid from the reproductive system.

seminal vesicles A pair of secretory glands that lie close to the bladder and in front of the rectum.

prostate gland A large structure that surrounds the portion of the urethra that is just below the bladder.

People in many different societies have felt that the genitals should be modified by cutting, piercing, or some other means. Variations of such practices have been observed for centuries and even today represent important rituals and customs around the world.

Female circumcision, usually the cutting off of the prepuce, or clitoral hood, is especially widespread in East, West, and Central Africa, the Middle East, and Southeastern Asia. More extreme is the practice of clitoridectomy, the removal of the clitoris. The Falashas of Ethiopia practice clitoridectomy, as do certain Islamic, Indonesian, and Malaysian peoples. Societies offer different reasons for such genital modifications. Some of these are a desire to link sex with procreation rather than enjoyment, proof of sexual maturity or virginity, treatment for nymphomania or lesbianism, or punishment for masturbation.

Infibulation, the removal of the labia as well as the clitoris, is practiced in East Africa, particularly among the Galla and Somali peoples. In one variety of infibulation, perhaps the most common, the clitoris and labia majora are removed and the vaginal opening is sewed up almost entirely. A very small opening is left to allow both urine and menstrual blood to pass through.

Modification of the male genitals is also widespread. The most common modification is circumcision, the removal of the foreskin, which we discuss later in the book (Chapter 11). Egyptian representations of circumcised men (and even the act of circumcision) date back beyond 2000 B.C. Circumcision is practiced for hygienic, medical, or religious reasons. Circumcision is a religious rite among the Jews, and it is customary among Muslims (although not specifically recommended in the Koran). It is common throughout most of the Middle East and Africa, but there are several areas where it is not practiced, most notably among the southern Bantu, such as the Zulu, and among Nilotic groups of East Africa. Hunting and gathering groups such as the Bushmen do not practice it either.

In many societies of the Pacific the foreskin is not totally removed. Rather, it is slit lengthwise and folded back in what is called supercision. Certain Polynesian groups practice supercision because of the cleanliness that it promotes. The Marquesans stretch the foreskin tightly over a piece of bamboo and then make the inci-

---

transurethral resection (TUR) A surgical procedure used to treat benign prostate enlargement, in which the surgeon inserts an instrument through the urethra and scrapes out some or all of the tissue of the prostate gland.

Enlargement of the prostate may be due to a benign or malignant condition (next to lung cancer, cancer of the prostate is the most common type of cancer in men). Should the enlargement be benign, a **transurethral resection (TUR)** is usually performed. In this procedure excess tissue is removed to clear the urinary tract.

Prostatic cancer is the third most common cause of cancer deaths in men, claiming over 30,000 lives each year (Silverberg, Boring, & Squires, 1990; American Cancer Society, 1990). The incidence of this disease has risen over 20 percent in recent years.

It is estimated that one of every 11 men will develop prostate cancer at some point in his life. African-Americans develop this disorder twice as often as whites, and it is more common among older men. About 80 percent of all prostate cancers are diagnosed in men over the age of 65.

The symptoms of prostate cancer—some of which may also be experienced in benign prostatic diseases—include weak or interrupted flow of urine, the need to urinate frequently, blood in the urine, painful or burning sensations when urinating, and pain in the lower back, pelvis, or upper thighs. Because prostate cancer tends to spread to the bones, patients in whom the disease has progressed may complain of bone pain before any other symptoms.

To help prevent prostate cancer men over the age of 40 should have a rectal examination as part of their annual physical checkup. About 63 percent of all prostate cancers are discovered while still localized within the general region of the prostate,

testes, is also an ancient custom. The Roman priests of the goddess Cybele were eunuchs (castrated men) dressed as women. Although the Koran forbids castration, Islamic societies have made use of eunuchs castrated by Christians: the keepers of harems have invariably been castrated slaves. During the Middle Ages boy sopranos were sometimes castrated so that their voices would not change at puberty.

There are many health risks associated with genital modifications, particularly when unsterilized instruments or tools are used. Infections are not uncommon in both sexes, and scar tissue may interfere with later sexual arousal and reproductive capacities. Many women whose genitals have been modified suffer from urinary tract infections and menstrual complications. Some experience problems in labor and delivery. Because of these health risks, a growing number of African and other women are trying to eliminate what they call female genital mutilation. Physicians and public health officials, especially, are speaking out against such practices and telling people of the medical and health risks involved. (Lightfoot-Klein, 1990; Gregersen, 1983; Pugh, 1983; Taylor, 1985).

A Masai man whose daughter is being circumcised wears charms for the occasion and drinks ritual honey wine from a gourd said to bring good fortune.

sion along the foreskin. Traditionally in almost all cultures, circumcision is performed without an anesthetic.

Castration, the removal of the

---

and 83 percent of all patients whose tumors are diagnosed at this stage are alive five years after treatment. Survival rates for all stages of prostate cancer have improved more than 20 percent in recent years.

The treatment for prostate cancer is usually surgery combined with radiation and chemotherapy or hormone therapy. The surgery, called a **prostatectomy,** typically removes the prostate gland.

Cowper's Glands. **Cowper's glands,** also called the bulbourethral glands, are a pair of small, pea-size structures located below the prostate gland and behind the urethra. Like the prostate gland, Cowper's glands secrete a clear alkaline fluid that becomes part of the semen. This fluid provides additional protection for sperm against the acidic environment of the urethra and the vagina. Moreover, this fluid helps lubricate the lower portion of the urethra during sexual excitement. Sometimes called precoital fluid, this secretion may contain spermatozoa. Thus, although it is rare, a woman can become pregnant as a result of intercourse even if the man withdraws his penis before ejaculation.

Semen

Semen, the male ejaculate, consists of spermatozoa and **seminal fluid** (plasma). As we've indicated, seminal fluid consists of secretions from the seminal vesicles, prostate gland, Cowper's glands, and epididymis. Secretions from the seminal vesicles and the

prostatectomy Surgical removal of part or all of the prostate gland.

Cowper's glands A pair of small pea-shaped structures, located below the prostate gland, that contribute an alkaline fluid to the semen.

semen The male ejaculate, which consists of spermatozoa and seminal fluid.

seminal fluid Fluid made up of secretions from the seminal vesicles, prostate gland, Cowper's glands, and the epididymis.

prostate gland make up the bulk of the volume of the seminal fluid; much smaller contributions are made by the Cowper's glands and the epididymis.

The average amount of seminal fluid per ejaculate is about 2.5–5 ml. (about 1 to 1⅓ teaspoons). Each milliliter contains between 70 million and 100 million viable spermatozoa. This seemingly incredible total makes up only a small proportion of the total volume of semen. The amount and consistency of seminal fluid varies among men, depending on such factors as recency of the last ejaculation.

When a couple is having difficulty conceiving a child, the reproductive systems and functioning of each must be examined. We will discuss this situation in more detail in Chapter 10. Here, however, it is interesting to note that for semen to be considered adequate for impregnation, a sample should contain a ratio of 20 million to 120 million sperm to one cubic centimeter of volume. In severe **oligospermia** there are fewer than 5 million sperm per sample. In other forms of this disorder there may be no sperm in the ejaculate or seminal fluid itself may be absent.

A number of medications can cause temporary reductions in sperm count. Examples are tranquilizers, antibiotics for certain infections, and blood pressure medications. Raising the temperature of the body—including the scrotum—for considerable lengths of time may also inhibit sperm production. For example, hot tubs have been known to lower sperm levels. The ability to produce sperm may also be lessened by high fever or infection of the testes that causes severe inflammation. As an illustration, mumps in postpubertal males may cause orchitis (inflammation of the testes), which may cause permanent sterility. Finally, the problem of cryptorchidism (undescended testicles), which we've already discussed, may account for lowered levels of sperm production.

After the man has ejaculated into the female vagina, sperm have an effective life of about 72 hours. Because the female ovum has an even shorter life than the sperm, the union of the two must occur within 24 to 36 hours of ovulation or the egg will lose its capacity to be fertilized and will be absorbed into the body.

In general, sperm do not move well in the vagina's acidic environment, and many are killed by hostile fluids. A number of sperm also die because of defects in their structure. Many, for example, lack the proper tail structure and never demonstrate the necessary motility. Some travel along the wrong fallopian tube (remember that only one egg is expelled each month) and degenerate without ever reaching their proper destination.

Surviving sperm will travel a little less than a half inch every five minutes. About 300 from the original millions that started the journey will travel along the correct fallopian tube and reach the female ovum. Usually, this happens between 45 and 90 minutes after ejaculation. A detailed description of fertilization is presented in Chapter 10.

oligospermia A condition in which there are very few or no sperm in a man's ejaculate or in which seminal fluid itself is absent.

SEXUALITY IN THE NEWS

Every Woman for Herself

*I*n this segment from ABC's "20/20" show, aired on December 7, 1990, ABC's Barbara Walters and Dr. Timothy Johnson explore what they deem a disturbing state of affairs for women in America. The video takes us through the misreading of a mammogram and the ensuing development of an incurable cancer in the woman whose test was misinterpreted. It shows how such an error can be made and points out that mammograms do not detect all cancers. The show also accuses U.S. physicians of not following through on patients' diagnoses and conferring with other specialists on patients' behalf. The program compares the quality of breast disease care in the United States with the care offered in some countries abroad where, we are told, there is "total commitment, screening units, team diagnoses." (17:38 minutes)

1. Why are some authorities calling the prevention and treatment of breast cancer in the United States a scandal? Inasmuch as the United States has the most expensive health-care system in the world, why do you think this situation exists?

2. According to "20/20," in comparison to some other countries, the United States has few organized breast cancer centers where physicians in different specialties work together as a team to diagnose and care for each patient. When women in Sweden demanded nationwide screening for breast cancer, the Swedish government responded by setting up a major comprehensive breast-care center. Should U.S. women make the same demand on their government? If they did, how would you expect the U.S. government to respond?

3. Are there differences between the U.S. and Swedish health-care systems that might dictate a different response in each country? Should the U.S. health-care system be changed? Why or why not? If you think it should be changed, what changes would you make?

LOOKING BACK

■ The female external genitals, or vulva, are the mons pubis, the labia majora, the labia minora, the clitoris, the vaginal vestibule, which contains the vaginal and urethral openings, and the perineum. The internal genital organs are the vagina, uterus, fallopian tubes, and ovaries.

■ The female external organs play a particularly important role in female sexual arousal and response, as does the vagina. As a group, the internal organs are primarily responsible for the regular cycle of ovulation and menstruation. When an egg is fertilized, the uterus holds, protects, and nurtures the developing fetus. The breasts, accessory organs of reproduction, help nurture the newborn.

■ When a young woman reaches the age of 16–18 or begins to engage in sexual activity—whichever comes first—she should have a pelvic examination as part of an annual gynecological checkup. Such an examination can reveal any abnormalities in the sexual and reproductive organs that might cause irregularities in the menstrual cycle or other problems. The examination also permits the physician to test for the possibility of cervical or uterine cancer. Menstrual difficulties include primary and secondary amenorrhea, dysmenorrhea, and premenstrual syndrome. A rare but sometimes fatal disorder that occurs primarily in women who use tampons is toxic shock syndrome.

■ Women should examine their breasts regularly for possible signs of cancer and should also have their breasts checked annually by a physician. Men should examine their testicles on a regular basis for signs of testicular cancer and should have them examined by a physician during an annual physical checkup.

■ The male external genitals consist of the penis, the male organ of copulation, and the scrotum, the pouch that contains the testes. The primary male internal organs are the testes, epididymis, vas deferens, ejaculatory ducts, and urethra. The testes produce spermatozoa as well as sex hormones. The epididymis helps to mature the sperm and secretes some seminal fluid in which the sperm are carried. The two vas deferens connect each epididymis to the ejaculatory ducts and transport sperm through the system. The urethra is the final common pathway for both urine and seminal fluid. Accessory organs that contribute to the seminal fluid are the seminal vesicles, the prostate gland, and Cowper's glands.

■ Several conditions, such as inflammation of the testes, can result in low sperm production. Sometimes medications such as antibiotics and tranquilizers can lower sperm production, as can excessive heat.

THINKING THINGS OVER

1.   Many college students believe they know the anatomy of both the male and female reproductive systems, but surveys have shown that they are more ignorant than they think. Do you think it's important to understand reproductive anatomy? Why or why not?

2.   Whatever your answer to question 1 was, let's see if you yourself know reproductive anatomy. Without looking back at the illustrations in this chapter, draw and label the external and internal female genitalia and the external and internal male genitalia. Then check your drawings and labels against those in this textbook.

3.   Breast and testicular cancer, if detected early, are not usually fatal. If you were going to present to your friends an explanation of the self-examinations for both of these types of cancer, what would you tell them? Prepare an outline of the procedures you would want your friends to follow.

4.   As you've learned, one of the menstrual problems that women experience is premenstrual syndrome, or PMS. Why do you believe it took so long for PMS to be recognized as a real problem for some women?

DISCOVER FOR YOURSELF

Dalton, K. (1983). *Once a month*. Claremont, CA: Hunter House. An interesting and informative look at many aspects of menstruation.

Martini, F. (1992). *Fundamentals of anatomy and physiology*. (2nd ed.). Englewood Cliffs, NJ: Prentice Hall. Good coverage of the male and female reproductive systems is contained in Chapter 28 of this lavishly illustrated text.

Metz, C. B., & Monroy, A. (1985). *Biology of fertilization*. Orlando, FL: Academic Press. This text is an excellent resource for the student wanting more information on the biological mechanisms of fertilization. Not a book for the beach, though.

Smith, A. (1986). *The body*. New York: Viking. Chapters 5 and 6 present the topics of male and female sexuality in a clear and concise fashion.

Taylor, D. (1988). *Red flower: Rethinking menstruation*. Freedom, CA: Crossing Press. Chapter 1 of this paperback contains some interesting cross-cultural views on menstruation.

4

Sexual
Arousal
and
Response

We reaffirm that the most important organ in humans is located between the ears

—Carol S. Vance

We human beings are complex organisms, and this complexity extends to our sexual responses. In this chapter we will show you that sexual response involves many body parts, from the toes to the genitals, and actually begins in the brain. Referred to by some as the master sex organ, the brain has the capacity to organize a multitude of conscious and unconscious forces and coordinate the perceived sensations of sexual response. A person's overall sexual response thus involves complex interactions of physical, psychological, and social forces (Sizer & Whitney, 1988).

Because the sexual response is not only physical and physiological but emotional as well, it is difficult to define. Investigators have traditionally encountered problems in defining emotions and feeling states like love, fear, and anger (Rosen & Beck, 1988).

The average sixth-grader knows what sexual arousal is, but scientific definitions seldom encompass the complexity of this fundamental emotional experience. Even the most sophisticated conceptions of sexual arousal tend to fragment the phenomenon, focusing on such things as sexual appetite and central versus genital responses. Somehow they fail to specify the necessary conditions for labeling a response "sexual." For instance, would "feeling sexy" in the absence of vaginal lubrication or penile erection qualify as a sexual response? As you will see, although William Masters and Virginia Johnson's model of the sexual response cycle does not deal with nonphysiological arousal and response, Helen Singer Kaplan's model provides specifically for it.

Looking at this question from another point of view, as you will learn in Chapter 15, lubrication and erection occur more slowly as people get older. An older couple may be just as psychologically turned on as a younger couple, but they will take a little longer to show the physical evidence. On the other hand, our genitals often respond in the context of nonsexual situations; for example, erections commonly accompany a particular phase of the sleep cycle called rapid eye movement, or REM.

All of this suggests that the study of human sexual response is a highly complicated undertaking. To unravel some of the mysteries of sexual response, we will begin by exploring those parts of the brain and nervous system that coordinate sexual arousal. Next we'll examine the ways hormones affect sexual response, which is often mediated by actions of the nervous system. Then we will look at two models of sexual response—the four-stage model proposed by William Masters and Virginia Johnson and the three-stage model offered by Helen Singer Kaplan. Finally, we will explore the manner in which drugs of various sorts affect overall sexual functioning.

THE BIOLOGY OF SEXUAL RESPONSE

nervous system A highly complex network of specialized tissue that regulates emotions, thoughts, sensations, behaviors, and bodily functions. The nervous system is subdivided into the central and peripheral systems, and the peripheral system is further divided into the autonomic and somatic systems.

Sexual arousal (excitement and stimulation) and response (physiological changes in response to excitement and stimulation) originate in the nervous system, the most complex and efficient of all bodily systems. The **nervous system** is a network of specialized tissues that regulate emotions, thoughts, sensations, behaviors, and basic bodily functions. As we will see, the brain is the control center of the nervous system; it receives input from the rest of the body through the spinal cord and peripheral nerves. Acting on electrical and chemical impulses it receives from these body parts, the brain enables us to take in and process information, as well as to guide our actions. To understand how the nervous system coordinates sexual arousal and response, we need to explore its different parts.

The Nervous System

The nervous system has two major divisions: the central and peripheral systems. The brain and spinal cord constitute the **central nervous system.** The **peripheral nervous system** is a network of neural tissues that connect the brain and spinal cord with other parts of the body. Together, the central and peripheral nervous systems integrate the body into a unified system under the direct control of the brain.

The peripheral nervous system has two subdivisions: the somatic and autonomic branches. A network of sensory neurons, the **somatic nervous system** controls all of the body's skeletal muscles, such as those that we contract when we move our arms or legs. Thus it connects the central nervous system to the body's voluntary muscles. The muscular tensions that are experienced during sexual activity are controlled by the somatic nervous system.

The **autonomic nervous system,** on the other hand, consists of a set of regulatory centers that, through a network of nerve fibers, control the operation of many of the internal organs and glands of the body. The autonomic nervous system regulates internal functioning that we do not seem able to control voluntarily, such as our digestive processes. And as we'll see, the autonomic nervous system plays a major role in sexual arousal and response.

One of the two subdivisions of the autonomic nervous system, the **sympathetic nervous system,** prepares the body to expend energy, increasing overall activity levels. This system is responsible for increasing heartbeat, raising blood pressure, releasing sugar (for energy), slowing digestion, and increasing the flow of blood to the muscles. The **parasympathetic nervous system,** on the other hand, decreases heart rate and blood pressure, while it increases activity of the digestive tract and other processes that restore or conserve the body's energy. Figure 4–1 displays both branches of the autonomic nervous system and indicates the organs that each affects.

Female and male sexual arousal and response are coordinated by both the sympathetic and parasympathetic nervous systems. The two nervous systems mediate a complex interplay of neural impulses, and the precise role that each plays is not completely understood. In women we know that sexual arousal triggers parasympathetic activity. Parasympathetic impulses are sent from the sacral, or lower, spinal cord to the external genitalia, especially the clitoris. Smooth muscle fibers relax and the erectile tissues become engorged. In addition, the vagina becomes lubricated and some mucus is produced by Bartholin's glands. Orgasm, however, seems to be under the control of the sympathetic nervous system; typically, it is accompanied by such physiological changes as rapid heartbeat and a rise in blood pressure.

Similarly, male sexual arousal activates the parasympathetic system. Parasympathetic impulses pass from the lower spinal cord to the penis and enable the smooth muscle fibers of the erectile tissue to relax. Blood then fills the spongy bodies of the penis, causing the penis to erect. Parasympathetic impulses from the spinal cord also cause the bulbourethral or Cowper's glands to secrete mucus, which provides some lubrication for intercourse. Ejaculation appears to be under sympathetic control, being accompanied, like female orgasm, by rapid heartbeat, increases in blood pressure and respiration, and muscle contractions.

central nervous system
The branch of the nervous system that consists of the brain, the spinal cord, and the nerves that extend out from both.

peripheral nervous system A network of neural tissue that connects the brain and spinal cord, or central nervous system, with other parts of the body.

somatic nervous system A system of sensory neurons that connects the central nervous system to voluntary muscles throughout the body.

autonomic nervous system A set of regulatory centers that control the operation of many of the internal organs and glands of the body.

sympathetic nervous system A subdivision of the autonomic nervous system that prepares the body to use its energy and serves to increase activity levels such as heart rate and blood pressure.

parasympathetic nervous system A subdivision of the autonomic nervous system that stimulates processes that restore or conserve the body's energy.

Sex and the Brain

Now let's see how the brain is involved in sexual response. Although a number of areas in the brain are thought to influence sexual arousal and response, we will focus on just two: the cerebral cortex and the limbic system.

What role does the brain play in sexual response?

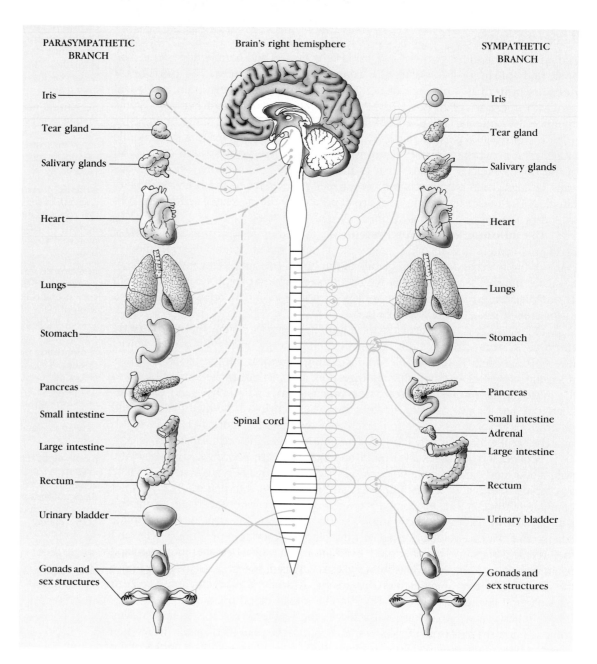

PARASYMPATHETIC BRANCH

Iris

Tear gland

Salivary glands

Heart

Lungs

Stomach

Pancreas

Small intestine

Large intestine

Rectum

Urinary bladder

Gonads and sex structures

Brain's right hemisphere

Spinal cord

SYMPATHETIC BRANCH

Iris

Tear gland

Salivary glands

Heart

Lungs

Stomach

Pancreas

Small intestine

Adrenal

Large intestine

Rectum

Urinary bladder

Gonads and sex structures

FIGURE 4–1
The Autonomic Nervous System (ANS).

cerebral cortex The outer covering of the cerebral hemispheres.

limbic system An integrated network of brain structures that includes the cingulate gyrus, the hippocampus, the septal area, the amygdala, portions of the reticular activating system, and the hypothalamus.

The **cerebral cortex,** the outer covering of the two cerebral hemispheres, sets human beings apart from other animals in that it mediates our unique abilities to think, to speak, and to process information. Whereas infrahuman species are limited to certain stereotyped sexual signals to potential mates, human beings' brains equip them to respond in an infinite number of ways to an infinite number of sexual stimuli. For example, for some people, at least some of the time, simply imagining or fantasizing about a sexual encounter can bring about sexual arousal to the point of orgasm. And we can send sexual signals to each other by writing love poems, driving fast sports cars, excelling in athletic endeavors, holding long philosophical conversations, or gazing into each other's eyes (Bloom & Lazerson, 1988).

Also affecting sexual response is the limbic system, which lies beneath the cerebral cortex. The **limbic system** is an integrated network of structures consisting

90   **Sexual Arousal and Response**

Understanding the complex dynamics of human sexual response has intrigued many researchers.

of the cingulate gyrus, hippocampus, septal area, amygdala, hypothalamus, and portions of the reticular activating system (see Figure 4–2). The reticular activating system, or RAS, is part of a neural network known as the reticular formation, a network that extends throughout the brain stem and influences other parts of the brain. In particular, the RAS helps regulate arousal, attention, and the awake-sleep cycle. The limbic system contains neural mechanisms that generate and regulate a wide range of emotions, such as affection, anger, fear, sorrow, and pain. For this reason, the limbic system is sometimes called the "visceral" or "emotional brain."

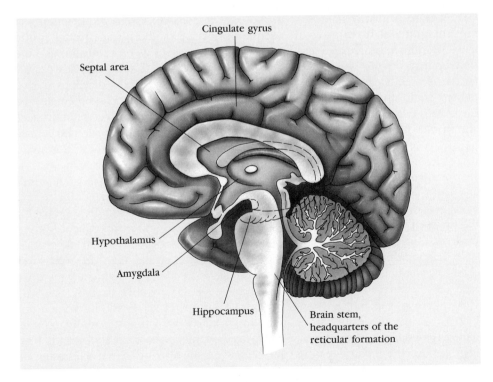

FIGURE 4–2
The Limbic System.

Cingulate gyrus

Septal area

Hypothalamus

Amygdala

Hippocampus

Brain stem, headquarters of the reticular formation

Within the limbic system, the hypothalamus appears to play a particularly important role in sexual functioning. Located deep within the brain, the hypothalamus is instrumental in regulating the autonomic nervous system and several important forms of behavior, including sexual activity, eating, and drinking. The role of the hypothalamus in sexual behavior has been the focus of considerable animal research. Experiments with male rats have revealed that electrical stimulation of the lateral hypothalamus can induce both erection and ejaculation (MacLean, 1976). In one classic investigation a rat received electrical stimulation of the hypothalamus 5 minutes on and 5 minutes off for a 7.5-hour period. Within this period of time the rat mounted a female 155 times. Intromission (insertion of the penis into the vagina) occurred 81 times (Vaudeville & Fisher, 1962). Other research (Caggiula & Hoebel, 1966) suggests that stimulation of a formation that carries fibers from parts of the hypothalamus to other brain locations also creates intense sexual behavior in male rats.

For obvious ethical reasons, research involving electrical stimulation of the human brain is scarce. However, the findings that do exist provide evidence that the hypothalamus plays an equally important role in human sexual functioning. Electrical stimulation of the hypothalamus in human subjects has been shown to produce feelings of sexual pleasure and, in some cases, ejaculation (Sem-Jacobsen, 1968).

We are beginning to understand the complex role that the brain plays in sexual functioning. Research has established the limbic system as the biologic substrate of our emotional and sexual experiences, and has suggested that the system has extensive neural connections with other parts of the brain. The precise location of these pathways, however, and the many functions they serve have not yet been identified.

Hormones and Sexual Response

The nervous system, endocrine system, and gonadal hormones function as a closely integrated network shaping sexual arousal and response. The **endocrine system** (see Figure 4–3) is a group of glands that release specific hormones into the bloodstream. A **hormone,** from the Greek *hormon,* meaning "messenger," is a chemical substance that is secreted by the cells of a particular organ and carried by the blood to other organs or tissues, whose structure or function it regulates.

We are primarily interested in the sex, or gonadal hormones. Beginning at puberty, **gonadal hormones** are secreted primarily by the gonads (testes in the male, ovaries in the female) and influence such processes as reproduction and the development of what we call secondary sex characteristics. A secondary sex characteristic is a bodily feature, like breasts or chest hair, that usually develops during puberty and distinguishes a sexually mature male from a sexually mature female (see Chapter 14). As you will recall from Chapter 3, cells in the testes secrete androgens and in the ovaries secrete estrogens and progesterone, but both male and female hormones are present to some extent in both sexes. Let's look at these hormones more closely.

Androgens are hormones produced primarily by the Leydig cells of the testes and, to a lesser extent, by the adrenal glands in both men and women. Of the several types of androgens, **testosterone** is the most common. Testosterone is essential for the production of sperm and is required for the growth and development both of male sex organs and of the tissues that give rise to male secondary sex characteristics.

Testosterone affects the sex drive of both women and men. In both sexes excessive amounts of testosterone have been associated with a heightened sex drive (see, e.g., Segraves, 1988a; Davidson & Myers, 1988; O'Carroll et al., 1985; Sherwin, 1986; Sherwin, Gelfand, & Brender, 1985; de Kretser et al., 1983). In women this increase in sexual desire can result from treatment with testosterone for certain medical conditions. The opposite is also true: women whose adrenal glands have been removed for medical reasons (the adrenals are the primary source of testosterone

endocrine system A group of glands that release specific hormones into the bloodstream.

hormones Chemical substances that are secreted by internal organs and carried in the blood stream to other organs or tissues whose structure or function they control.

gonadal hormones Hormones secreted primarily by the gonads (testes in the male, ovaries in the female) beginning at puberty and involved in such processes as reproduction and the development of secondary sex characteristics.

androgens Hormones produced by the Leydig cells of the testes and, to a lesser extent, by the adrenal glands in both males and females. Testosterone is the most common type of androgen.

testosterone A hormone produced by the testes. Testosterone is essential for the production of sperm and is also required for the growth and development in males of the sex organs and of secondary sex characteristics.

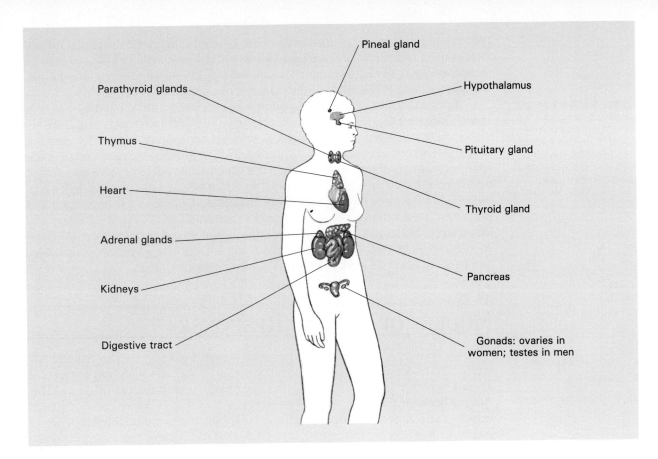

FIGURE 4–3
The Endocrine System.

(Source: Adapted from Martini, 1992, p. 568.)

in women) often experience a lessening of sexual desire (Segraves, 1988a). Men who have low levels of testosterone typically have a lower sex drive and may have difficulty in attaining and maintaining erections (Bancroft, 1985).

Estrogens, hormones produced primarily by follicle cells of the female ovaries but also by the male testes, include estradiol, estriol, estrone, and estetrol; of these, **estradiol** is the most common. Estradiol influences the development and maintenance of the female reproductive organs as well as all female secondary sex characteristics. Estrogens have no known functions in men. Unlike testosterone, estrogens are not critical determinants of sex drive; removal of the ovaries in women does not lessen sexual desire.

As we learned in the last chapter, **progesterone** is a hormone manufactured by the corpus luteum in females and is found in greatest amounts during the secretory phase of the menstrual cycle. Small amounts of progesterone are also found in males. Progesterone interacts with estrogens to prepare the uterus for implantation of a fertilized egg and stimulates growth of the lactiferous ducts of the mammary glands. The role of progesterone in sexual behavior is unclear (see Sanders et al., 1983; Bancroft et al., 1983; Backstrom et al., 1983).

The way the endocrine system regulates gonadal hormones is extremely complicated, and we do not fully understand the process. However, we do know that at puberty gonadal hormones become active in both sexes. At that time the hypothalamus begins to manufacture a substance called **gonadotrophin releasing hormone** (GnRH), which stimulates the pituitary gland to secrete two **gonadotrophins,** or gonad-stimulating hormones. These hormones, as we learned in Chapter 3, are a luteinizing hormone (LH) and a follicle-stimulating hormone (FSH). You'll recall that

estrogens Hormones produced primarily by follicle cells in the ovaries and by the testes in men. Several types of estrogens are estradiol, esteriol, and estrone.

estradiol An estrogen that affects the development and maintenance of the female reproductive organs as well as all female secondary sex characteristics.

progesterone A hormone manufactured by the corpus luteum of the ovary and most abundant during the secretory phase of the menstrual cycle. Small amounts of progesterone are also present in males.

gonadotrophin releasing hormone A substance manufactured by the hypothalamus that stimulates the pituitary gland to secrete gonadotrophins.

gonadotrophins Gonad-stimulating hormones secreted by the pituitary gland.

in women LH assists in the maturation of the ovarian follicles. FSH is critical for the development of the primary ovarian follicles, and it also stimulates follicular cells to secrete estrogen. In males LH stimulates the Leydig cells in the testes to manufacture testosterone, and FHS stimulates the manufacture of sperm cells.

The production of gonadal hormones is coordinated by a regulatory system called a **negative feedback loop.** In males, if the hypothalamus detects an excessively high level of testosterone in the blood, it ceases production of GnRH. This causes a drop in LH secretion by the pituitary gland, which, in turn, leads to a decrease in the testes' production of testosterone. When the hypothalamus detects reduced levels of testosterone, it increases its secretion of GnRh, which begins the cycle again. In females the negative feedback loop is similar but complicated by the fact that estrogen and progesterone secretion vary according to the menstrual cycle. In general, though, as blood levels of estrogen rise, GnRH production is inhibited, which, in turn, leads to reduced levels of FSH. Thus for both males and females, the gonads, hypothalamus, and pituitary gland all work together to regulate hormone levels.

MODELS OF SEXUAL RESPONSE

We have seen how the brain and endocrine system work together to regulate the levels of hormones circulating in the bloodstream. We've also seen how higher and lower levels of hormones influence the intensity of sexual interest or desire. This alliance between the brain and the endocrine system has prompted researchers to explore the concept of a sexual response cycle—that is, a predictable sequence of events marked by a cyclical pattern of physiological responding. Since the turn of the century, a number of researchers have constructed theoretical models of such a cycle. Here we will explore two of these—the Masters and Johnson and the Kaplan models—in some depth.

Havelock Ellis was one of the first researchers to describe a sexual response cycle. In 1906 he proposed a two-stage model of "tumescence" and "detumescence": tumescence was the buildup of sexual energy, and detumescence was the release of such energy. In 1948 Albert Kinsey and his colleagues noted that sexual response consisted of a buildup period, followed by orgasm and its aftereffects. Kinsey was among the first to detail the physiological changes that accompany sexual arousal:

> Erotic stimulation, whatever its source, effects a series of physiologic changes which, as far as we yet know, appear to involve adrenal secretion, typically autonomic reactions, increased pulse rate, increased blood pressure, an increase in peripheral circulation and a consequent rise in the surface temperature of the body; a flow of blood into such distensible organs as the eyes, the lips, the lobes of the ears, the nipples of the breast, the penis of the male, and the clitoris, and the genital labia and the vaginal walls of the female; a partial but often considerable loss of perceptive capacity (sight, hearing, touch, taste, smell); an increase in so-called nervous tension, some degree of rigidity of some part or the whole of the body at the moment of maximum tension; and then a sudden release which produces local spasms or more extensive or all-consuming convulsions. The moment of sudden release is the point commonly recognized among biologists as orgasm. (Kinsey et al., 1948, p. 158)

Other conceptions of a sexual response cycle have emerged since, but none is more prominent than the four-stage model proposed by William Masters and Virginia Johnson in their ground-breaking book *Human Sexual Response* (1966). Masters and Johnson's investigations are considered the most detailed to date, and we will take some time to explore their model. To give you a chance to compare and contrast

The bigger a penis is when at rest, the bigger it is when erect. In their research Masters and Johnson (1966) refuted this particular myth by evaluating a group of men selected from their overall subject population. Forty men whose penises measured 3 to 3.5 inches in length in the flaccid state were compared to forty other men whose penises in the flaccid state measured 4 to 4.5 inches. The length of the smaller penises increased by an average of 3 inches at full erection. Thus the smaller organs about doubled in length in full erection. In contrast, among organs that were significantly larger at rest, penile length increased by only about 2.8 to 3 inches at full erection.

The bigger a man is in muscular and skeletal development, the bigger his penis is in both the flaccid and erect states. Detailed examination of the male subjects in the Masters and Johnson sample revealed that there is no relation between overall body size and the size of external genitalia. The largest penis among the subjects, measuring about 5.5 inches

long in the flaccid state, was in a man 5 feet, 7 inches tall who weighed 152 pounds. The smallest penis, measuring just under 2.5 inches in the flaccid state, was in a man 5 feet, 11 inches tall, weighing 178 pounds.

The vagina is an inflexible organ. As we pointed out in Chapter 3, the vagina is very distensible and can accommodate a wide range of penile sizes. Occasionally, there are women with exceptionally large or small vaginas, just as there are occasional men with exceptionally large or small penises. However, Masters and Johnson identified only one woman with a very large vagina among their 382 female subjects. In tests with an artificial penis, this woman's vagina expanded and contracted like any other to accommodate varying penile sizes, although with smaller sizes, she did experience lessening of vaginal stimulation. In contrast, two women with exceptionally small vaginas, although able to accommodate either a small or a large penis, experienced pain and difficulty with any size penis unless their sexual tension had reached a very high level.

theoretical perspectives, we will then examine the three-stage model developed by Helen Singer Kaplan.

The Masters and Johnson Four-Stage Model

As we discovered in Chapter 2, Masters and Johnson began their research in 1957 at the Washington University School of Medicine in St. Louis. The population they studied—382 women and 312 men—consisted of both married and unmarried subjects and ranged in age from 18 to 89, though most subjects were between 18 and 40.

Masters and Johnson recorded over 10,000 episodes of sexual activity in their work. In the process of describing the sexual response cycle, Masters and Johnson also debunked some long-held beliefs about penile and vaginal functioning (see "Myths and Misconceptions" box). Although these researchers acknowledge that there is wide individual variation in the duration and intensity of physiological responses to sexual stimulation, the foundation of their research has been the concept of a typical sexual response cycle. They have proposed four phases of such a cycle: excitement, plateau, orgasm, and resolution (see Figure 4–4). These phases are successive and exist along a continuum. Together, they provide a framework for describing the physiological variants in sexual reaction, some of which are frequently so transient in nature as to appear in only one phase of the total sexual response cycle. As we will see, phases of the sexual response cycle are essentially the same for women and men, and both sexes often show similar patterns of sexual response

Is the sexual response cycle different for men and women?

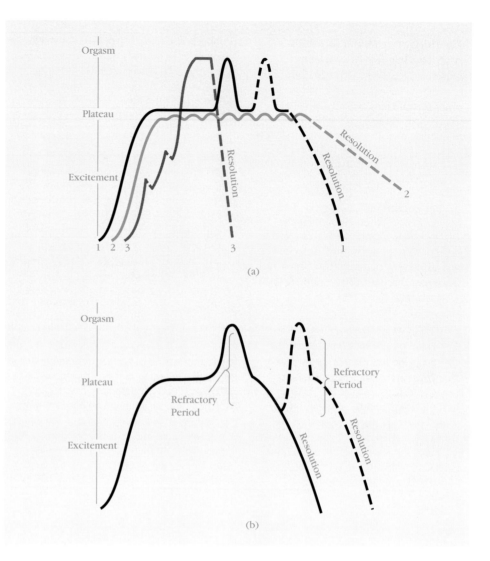

FIGURE 4–4
Sexual Response in Women and Men: The Masters and Johnson Model.

In (a) three variations of female sexual response are identified. Pattern 1 illustrates multiple orgasm; pattern 2 shows an extended plateau phase with no orgasm, along with a slow resolution phase; and pattern 3 depicts brief declines in the excitement phase, no definitive orgasmic phase, and an abrupt resolution phase. In (b) the most typical pattern of male sexual response is depicted. However, the dotted line indicates variation in the response pattern; that is, a second orgasm can occur following the refractory period.
(Source: Masters & Johnson, 1966)

vasocongestion An increased amount of blood in body tissues that causes swelling and, in some cases erection, as in the penis and nipples.

myotonia A generalized increase in muscle tension.

within these phases. However, we will also be looking at some very important differences in the sexual responding of men and women.

There are two basic physiological responses to sexual stimulation. The first is widespread **vasocongestion,** the engorgement with blood of body organs and tissues that respond to sexual stimulation. The second is **myotonia,** or a generalized increase in muscle tension. When sexual excitement occurs, vasocongestion takes place in both surface and deep tissues (producing most notably the erection of the penis and vaginal lubrication). Myotonia may involve voluntary or involuntary muscle contractions (facial grimaces or muscular spasms accompanying orgasm). The more intense vasocongestive and myotonic reactions typically occur in the plateau and orgasmic stages of the sexual response cycle.

excitement phase The first stage of Masters and Johnson's sexual response cycle. It develops from any source of somatogenic or psychogenic sexual stimulation.

EXCITEMENT PHASE. During the **excitement phase** sexual arousal begins. It can originate from a wide range of stimuli—a look or touch, for example—and builds as attention is focused on the particular sexual activity. Sometimes partners are aroused simultaneously, but at other times one person becomes aroused first and foreplay then becomes a way of both arousing the other person and of heightening both partners' excitement and tension. As sexual stimulation continues, the intensity of

Sexual Arousal and Response

sexual response tends to escalate. The excitement phase and the resolution phase consume most of the time expended in the overall cycle of human sexual response.

Foreplay, or activity in which partners arouse each other or intensify their arousal, is the substantive portion of this phase (you'll find a more detailed discussion of foreplay in Chapter 8). Kissing on the mouth, kissing other parts of the body, stroking and caressing any body part, are all part of foreplay. As partners get to know each other, both emotionally and sexually, they learn what activities each enjoys most.

The duration of foreplay is a very individual matter, and it may also vary with each sexual encounter. Sometimes we need or want a longer period of noncoital sexual activity than at other times. As we will see in Chapter 7, communication with our partners about what turns us on and is pleasurable is crucial to satisfying sexual relations.

Female Responses. The first evidence of a woman's sexual response is generally vaginal lubrication. Within 10 to 30 seconds after the initiation of effective stimulation, lubricating material appears on the walls of the vagina, and as sexual tension increases, this material coalesces to form a smooth, glistening coating on the vaginal walls. Then the inner two-thirds of the vagina lengthens and expands. Figure 4–5 shows this enlargement of the vagina.

During the latter stages of the excitement phase, the vaginal walls may alternately expand and contract. In addition, the color of the vaginal walls changes. Vaginal color differs among women, but in general it tends to darken with the accumulation of blood in the tissues caused by vasocongestion. In the early stages of this phase, the heightened coloration may be patchy, but by the time the plateau phase is reached, the entire vagina has darkened perceptibly.

As sexual tension increases, the cervix and the uterus begin to elevate. In general, the clitoris increases in size, although Masters and Johnson noted wide variations in

A WORLD OF DIFFERENCES

Ancient Thoughts on the Sexual Response Cycle

We tend to think of research on the sexual response cycle as a product of modern scientific inquiry, but thoughts on it are rooted in antiquity. For example, in an ancient Chinese sex manual, *Yu Fang Pi-Cheuh* ("Secret Instructions Concerning the Jade Chamber"), a character known as the Yellow Emperor asks the question: "How can I become aware of a woman's sexual arousal?" Another character called the Plain Girl responds: "There are five signs, five desires, and ten movements. By looking at these changes you will become aware of what is happening to the woman's body." The Plain Girl goes on to identify the five signs as: flushing of the woman's face, hardening of her breasts, a growing dryness of her throat, a moist vagina, and finally a transmission of fluid through the vagina. She adds that sexual activity should begin during the second phase; after the fifth phase, a man should slowly withdraw his penis from the woman.

The Plain Girl also describes other cues and signals that indicate a woman's sexual arousal: "If her breath seems taken away, it means that she wants to have sex with you. If her nose and mouth are dilated, she wants to begin sexual activity, and if she embraces you tightly, you will know that the woman is sexually excited and aroused. If she perspires, it means that she is nearing orgasm. Finally, if her body straightens out and her eyes close, it means that she has been sexually satisfied."

This narrative of sexual arousal and response provides interesting parallels to contemporary theoretical models, as well as insights into ancient Chinese sexual customs. As evidenced by this manual, the ancient Chinese attached great importance to paying attention to a partner's sexual responses. In so doing, they believed that sexual partners would attain mutually satisfying sexual encounters. (Adapted from Ruan & Bullough, 1989)

FIGURE 4–5
Changes in the Sexual Organs during the Sexual Response Cycle.

(Source: Adapted from King, Camp, & Downey, 1991, p. 64.)

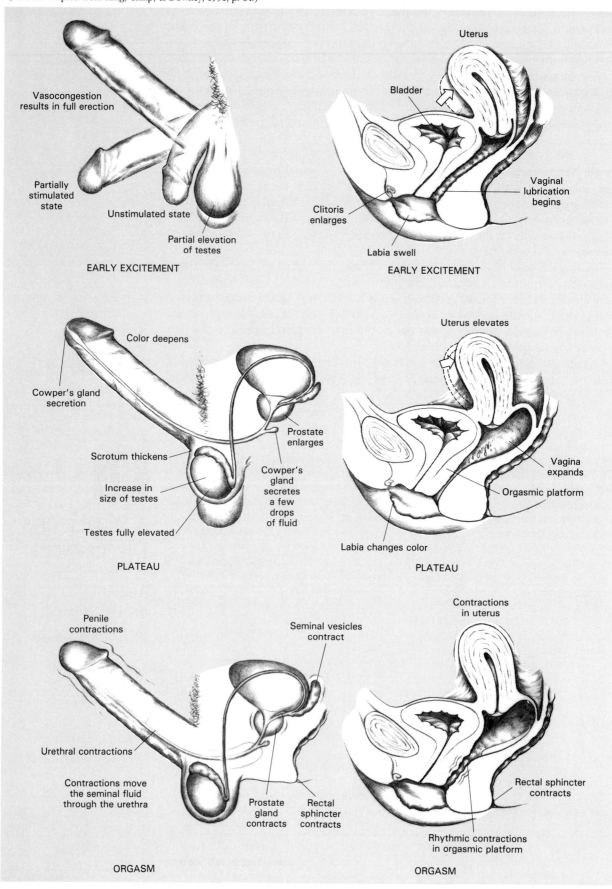

the women they studied. In about half of these subjects the clitoral glans doubled in diameter, but in other subjects the glans did not appear to change in size. In some women the shaft of the clitoris also increased in length.

The labia majora and labia minor also undergo changes during the excitement phase. For women who have never borne a child, the labia majora thin out and flatten against the perineum as sexual tension increases. There is also a slight elevation of the labia in an upward and outward direction away from the vaginal outlet. In women who have given birth, the labia majora tend to become markedly distended and swollen with blood. In all women, the labia minora become swollen and darker in color.

Contrary to what one might think, physical evidence of sexual tension develops throughout the entire body, not just in the genital region. As the "World of Differences" box reveals, the ancient Chinese knew this—and, interestingly, offered what is probably the first account of the sexual response cycle.

The first evidence of the breasts' response to sexual excitement is nipple erection (the nipple swells and becomes firm, seeming to "stand up"). This erection is caused by muscle tension in the fibers surrounding the nipples. During the later stages of the excitement phase, vasocongestion causes the veins in the breasts to become more noticeable (usually in the lower portion of the breast), and there may be a small increase in breast size. Figure 4–6 shows these changes in the breast during the female sexual response cycle.

Many women experience what is called a sex flush late in the excitement phase. The **sex flush**, a darkening of the skin, occurs in both females and males, although it is more common among women and more obvious in fair-skinned people. The sex flush, which varies in intensity and distribution pattern, usually begins on the upper part of the woman's abdomen and spreads over her breasts and up to her throat, neck, and face. As orgasm nears, the sex flush may spread to her lower abdomen, thighs, buttocks, and entire back.

Women experience increased muscle tension in the arms and legs, and their muscles may contract with regularity or in spasm in an involuntary manner. Heart rate and blood pressure also increase as sexual tension mounts.

sex flush A superficial vaso-congestive skin response to increasing sexual tension.

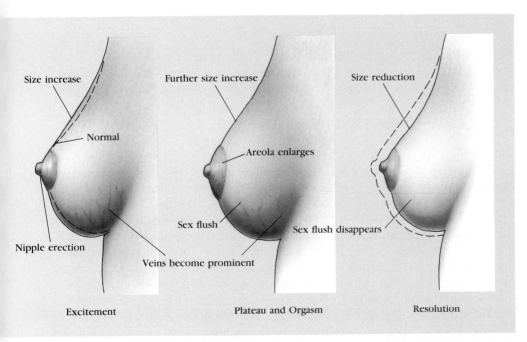

FIGURE 4–6
Changes in the Breasts during the Female Sexual Response Cycle.

(Source: Adapted from Masters, Johnson, & Kolodny, 1988.)

Size increase

Normal

Nipple erection

Excitement

Further size increase

Areola enlarges

Sex flush

Veins become prominent

Plateau and Orgasm

Size reduction

Sex flush disappears

Resolution

Sexual Arousal and Response

99

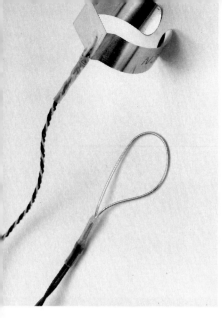

Two types of penile plethysmograph. This instrument assesses vasocongestion by measuring the circumference or volume of the penis. The tracing produced as a man stimulates himself to orgasm generally follows the Masters-Johnson response cycle model.

erection The process by which body tissues like the penis or clitoris become engorged with blood and increase markedly in size and firmness.

plateau phase The second phase of Masters and Johnson's sexual response cycle. It is reached if effective sexual stimulation continues, and it is characterized by increases in sexual tension.

orgasmic platform Swelling of the walls of the outer portion of the vagina as a result of increased vasocongestion during the plateau phase of the sexual response cycle.

Male Responses. Penile erection is a man's first physiological response to effective sexual stimulation. As Figure 4–5 indicates, **erection** is caused by the engorgement of the penis with blood. As we noted earlier, erection is a complex reflex in which both sympathetic and parasympathetic nervous systems play roles that as yet are not entirely clear, but that are initiated by certain tactile, visual, and mental stimuli. The brain's limbic system also influences sexual response by sending nerve impulses to the lower portion of the spinal cord. These impulses are then transmitted to the penis, where they cause rapid (in 5–10 seconds) dilation of the blood vessels of the penile spongy bodies. When this happens, the flow of blood into the penis is increased, filling these bodies, and erection results. An erect penis returns to a flaccid state when constriction of the blood vessels forces the trapped blood out of the penile tissues.

Masters and Johnson note that after full penile erection has been attained, the excitement phase may extend for a brief interval or for many minutes, depending on the intensity and effectiveness of sexual stimulation. Erection can be partially lost and regained many times during an excitement phase that is prolonged intentionally. And penile erection can be impaired by the introduction of asexual stimuli (such as a sudden loud noise or a noticeable change in lighting or temperature), even though sexual stimulation continues.

During the excitement phase the scrotum tenses and thickens. This is caused by both localized vasocongestion and contraction of the scrotum's smooth-muscle fibers. As excitement increases, the unstimulated scrotal patterns of multiple folding and free movement are lost. In addition, scrotal constriction significantly decreases the internal diameter of the scrotal sac and restricts testicular movement.

Another noticeable change is that the testes move up toward the perineum. This is accomplished by a shortening of the spermatic cords. Toward the end of the excitement phase, there will also be an increase in testicular size, which will become more pronounced during the next, plateau, phase.

Many men experience nipple erection and additional nipple tumescence during the latter part of the excitement phase. In addition, muscles throughout the body may begin to contract regularly or in spasm, often as a result of coital positioning (see also Chapter 8). During this phase there is also a moderate increase in blood pressure and heart rate.

Table 4–1 summarizes female and male responses, as well as those responses that are shared by both men and women, during all four of Masters and Johnson's phases. You may find it helpful to refer to this table as you read through the sections that follow.

PLATEAU PHASE. During the **plateau phase** of the sexual response cycle, there is both an increase and a leveling off of sexual tension. In essence, this phase represents a continuation of the excitement phase and moves the person toward possible orgasm. The length of this phase depends on whether sexual stimulation is maintained; if it slows or stops, orgasmic release will not be achieved.

Female Responses. As sexual tension increases, the outer third of the vagina becomes engorged with blood. This vasocongestion creates swelling and distention of the walls of the outer portion of the vagina, known as the **orgasmic platform.** Increasing vasocongestion also expands the size of the uterus and elevates it more fully into the abdominal cavity. By the end of the plateau phase, full uterine elevation has taken place and a "tenting" or ballooning of the inner two-thirds of the vagina has occurred. In addition, uterine muscle contractions often start late in this phase.

The entire clitoral body (shaft and glans) retracts from its normal position. Any portion of the clitoral glans that normally projects from under the clitoral hood when a woman is not sexually stimulated is withdrawn deeply beneath the protective foreskin

Sexual Arousal and Response

TABLE 4–1

Phases of Masters and Johnson's Sexual Response Cycle

Male Responses	Female Responses	Shared Responses
EXCITEMENT		
Penis becomes erect. Erection may be partially lost and regained during a prolonged phase. **Testes** enlarge and elevate. **Scrotum** tenses and skin thickens. Scrotum flattens and is elevated.	**Clitoris** swells; glans becomes tumescent and shaft increases in diameter and length. **Vagina** lubricates rapidly and expands. Color of vaginal walls darkens. **Uterus** elevates and **breasts** enlarge.	**Myotonia** spreads; some evidence of involuntary muscular activity (e.g., partial elevation of testes in men; vaginal wall expansion in women). Heart rate increases in direct proportion to rising tension. **Sex flush** may start in some women. Nipple erection.
PLATEAU		
Increase in penile circumference at **coronal ridge.** Full testicular elevation; enlargement of testes reaches 50 percent increase over unstimulated size. Secretions from **Cowper's glands.**	Continued vaginal expansion; uterine and cervical elevation. Development of **orgasmic platform.** Retraction of clitoris. Secretions from **Bartholin's gland.** Further enlargement of breasts.	Increased muscle tension; superficial and deep **vasocongestion.** Rapid respiration and increase in heart rate and blood pressure; **hyperventilation** may be present. Sex flush starts in some men, becomes more pronounced in women.
ORGASM		
Contraction of accessory organs of reproduction (**vas deferens, seminal vesicles, prostate gland); ejaculation;** contraction of penile **urethra.**	Contractions of orgasmic platform. Contractions of uterus (from fundus toward lower uterine segment).	Loss of voluntary muscle control. Hyperventilation and increased heart rate and blood pressure. Continuation of sex flush.
RESOLUTION		
Loss of penile erection; presence of **refractory period.** Decrease in testicular size; testes descend into relaxed scrotum.	Loss of vaginal vasocongestion and orgasmic platform. Loss of clitoral tumescence; clitoris returns to prestimulated position.	Loss of muscle tension; sex flush disappears. Loss of vasocongestion may cause perspiration after orgasm. Loss of nipple erection. Heart rate, breathing, and blood pressure return to normal.

*Boldface terms appear in the glossary.

as this retraction process takes place. As a result , the clitoral body is extremely difficult to see prior to orgasm. Often the entire body of the clitoris reduces to half its normal length—but it is still responsive to stimulation. This retraction of the clitoral body is a reversible reaction; that is, if stimulation stops, the retracted shaft and glans will return to their normal position. When stimulation resumes, retraction recurs. There are no changes in the anatomy of the labia majora in the plateau phase. However, the labia minora exhibit more color darkening as the orgasm phase nears.

By this time, a woman's breasts have often increased in size by as much as a fourth of their unstimulated, baseline measurement. During this phase the areolae often become so engorged with blood that they overshadow the erect nipples, giving the false impression that nipple erection has been lost.

If present, the sex flush reaches a peak of color concentration and its widest distribution late in the plateau phase and during the orgasm phase. Both voluntary and involuntary muscles tighten, and heart rate and blood pressure also rise. By the end of the plateau phase, there is a marked increase in respiratory rate.

Male Responses. During the plateau phase the penis undergoes a minor vaso-congestive increase in diameter, but one that is confined to the corona of the glans penis. Color may also deepen in the glans penis late in the plateau phase, a development analogous to the darkening of the labia minora in women. However, the darkening of the corona does not always occur nor is it as well defined a change as the color change of the labia. Some men may develop a coronal color change during one sexual response cycle and not during a subsequent one. Also during this phase pre-ejaculatory fluid from the Cowper's glands lubricates the penile urethra.

Testicular elevation continues during the plateau phase until the final pre-ejaculatory positioning, close to the perineum, is reached. If the testes do not undergo at least partial elevation, a man will not experience a full ejaculatory sequence. Instead, there will be a marked reduction in ejaculatory pressure.

At this point an observable increase in testicular size takes place. Before the orgasmic phase is reached, the testes become almost half again as large as they are in their sexually unstimulated state. Some men's testicles actually double in size, especially if the sexual response cycle is of long duration. Generally speaking, the longer a man continues to maintain a plateau-phase level of sexual tension without orgasm, the greater the deep vasocongestion of the testes and the greater the increase in testicular size.

Men often experience a sex flush during the plateau phase. This darkening of the skin usually begins below the breastbone and spreads over the chest, and sometimes includes the back, neck, buttocks, legs, and face.

Among men and women who experience a sex flush, rapidly mounting sexual tension and movement toward orgasm cause the flush to spread quickly. At the same

"Simultaneous orgasms!"

Sexual Arousal and Response

time, muscle tension continues to increase throughout the body, and people may experience involuntary muscle contractions of the arms and legs. It is not uncommon for both men and women to look as if they are in pain or distress, as their facial muscles contract involuntarily in apparent frowns or grimaces. Late in the plateau phase and during the orgasm phase, breathing becomes faster and both blood pressure and heart rate continue to rise.

ORGASM PHASE. In the **orgasm phase** the vasocongestion and myotonia that have developed through the excitement and plateau phases are released. The orgasm phase is the shortest phase of the sexual response cycle, lasting only a few seconds. This involuntary climax and release of sexual tension is reached at whatever point represents maximum tension for the individual in that particular sexual experience. Although we can define orgasm in physiological terms, the experience can only be described subjectively, on the basis of individual reaction patterns. As we will see, although there is great variation in both the duration and the intensity of the female orgasmic experience, the male experience tends to fit a fairly standard pattern.

Female Responses. The primary component of the female orgasm is a series of rhythmic, rapidly occurring contractions of the orgasmic platform, the outer third of the vagina and the engorged tissues surrounding it. A mild orgasm may be accompanied by 3 to 5 contractions, intense orgasm by as many as 12. The intervals between contractions lengthen in duration after the first few and their intensity diminishes progressively. The intensity and the duration of contractions vary from woman to woman, and within the same woman from one orgasmic experience to another.

Not all physiological mechanisms responsible for female orgasm are clearly understood. However, it has been suggested that the onset of orgasm is signaled by an initial spasm of the outer portion of the vagina. A series of vaginal contractions then follows, along with rhythmic contraction of the uterus. Uterine contractions begin in the upper portions of the uterus and work through the middle portion of this organ down to the lower portion and the cervix. More intense orgasms trigger more severe uterine contractions. In many respects, the downward, wavelike movement of uterine contractions resembles the contractions experienced in the initial stages of labor, although they are not nearly as intense.

Masters and Johnson maintain that, physiologically, all female orgasms follow this pattern, regardless of the source of sexual stimulation. An orgasm that comes from intercourse or from breast stimulation alone cannot be physiologically distinguished, they claim, from one that comes from stimulating the clitoris. We will discuss other views shortly.

There are no further noticeable changes in the breasts during the orgasm phase. Involuntary muscle spasms occur throughout the body; for example, the muscles of the abdomen and buttocks often contract, as well as the long muscles of the arms and legs. Often a woman—or a man—may grasp a partner during orgasm and clench vigorously with the hand muscles. Sometimes both hands and feet contract, so that fingers and toes curl under tightly. Sexual partners are often unaware of these extreme muscular exertions during the orgasm phase and may be surprised to experience muscle aches in the lower abdomen, back, legs, or other parts of the body later.

During orgasm the rate of respiration may climb to over 40 breaths a minute and **hyperventilation** (excessive rate of respiration) may continue throughout the entire orgasmic experience. In addition, heart rates may range from 110 to 180 or more beats per minute, and blood pressure readings may rise by as much as 50 points. For example, a person with normal blood pressure of 120/80 might experience a rise to as high as 170/100, a reading that under ordinary circumstances would indicate moderately high blood pressure.

Every woman has her own orgasmic pattern, although it may vary depending on the degree and kind of sexual stimulation she experiences. The notion that all

When inserted in the vagina, the photo-plethysmograph measures vasocongestion in the walls of the vagina. Again, the recording that is made by the device as a woman stimulates herself to orgasm closely follows the response cycle described by Masters and Johnson.

orgasm phase The third phase of Masters and Johnson's sexual response cycles, in which the vasoconstriction and myotonia developed from sexual stimuli are released.

hyperventilation A greatly accelerated rate of respiration, sometimes occurring during orgasm.

What does female orgasm feel like? Are all orgasms the same?

S here Hite (1976) surveyed over 3,000 women between the ages of 14 and 78 from all over the United States for her report on female sexuality. Part of Hite's research focused on orgasmic expression. The following are some of her respondents' descriptions of what the arousal process and actual orgasm feel like (Hite, 1976, pp. 139–143, 149–150, 185–190).

"A heightened sensitivity all over, a vaguely burning sensation in the clitoral area, and a sort of yearning to be touched on my breasts, stomach, ass, and vagina—great!"

"Sometimes I feel aroused generally, without having been touched—it feels like a kind of tension, a sweet tension, and there is a dreaminess in the desire to touch and be touched. Then again, arousal from touching and being touched can be more acute, a kind of pang in my vagina; nerves stand up under my skin. Being too aroused is painful."

"There are a few faint sparks, coming up to orgasm, and then I suddenly realize that it is going to catch fire, and then I concentrate all my energies, both physical and mental, to quickly bring on the climax—which turns out to be a mo-

ment suspended in time, a hot rush—a sudden breath-taking dousing of all the nerves of my body in pleasure—I try to make the moment last—disappointment when it doesn't."

"The physical sensation of orgasm is beautifully excruciating. It begins in the clitoris, and also surges into my whole vaginal area."

Hite also reported that some women differentiated between what they referred to as clitoral and vaginal orgasms:

"Clitoral is stronger and more localized. Intercourse is more total body."

"Clitoral are sharper, but lonelier."

"Masturbatory orgasms are stronger, but I prefer the diffusion and variety of intercourse and the warmth and pressure of a man's body and the sounds and smells of two people."

"Intercourse is better, because the pressure of the penis adds to the pleasure, also the weight of the body, the caresses, etc."

"During intercourse, it goes through my entire body; during clitoral orgasm, it is an outer body sensation."

---

multiple orgasms More than one orgasmic experience within a relatively short period of time.

coitus Penile-vaginal intercourse.

vaginal orgasm A term used to refer to an orgasm that derives from coital activity alone, without further stimulation.

clitoral orgasm A term used to refer to an orgasm that derives from stimulation of the clitoris or other non-coital activity.

orgasms are intense or explosive is simply not true. As Ethel Sloane (1985) sees it, women place a huge burden on themselves and on their sexual partners by expecting the "Big O" to happen every time, on schedule, with the same intensity, from the same formula.

Some women may have one very intense orgasm or one orgasm of a milder nature. Others may experience **multiple orgasms,** defined as more than one orgasmic experience within a short period of time. There are even variations in multiple orgasmic experiences. For example, there may be a series of intense orgasms, or one intense orgasm followed by a few mild ones, or a few mild ones ended by a more intense one. Moreover, each woman's experience of orgasm is likely to differ from situation to situation, whether it be with her partner or during masturbation. Feelings about a partner, degree of relaxation, time of day, and preoccupation with other matters will all influence the orgasmic response (Barbach, 1984).

There are also different paths to orgasm. Coital activity, or **coitus**—penile-vaginal intercourse—is said to lead to a **vaginal orgasm,** whereas noncoital activity, such as manual stimulation by a woman's partner or self-stimulation, is thought to lead to a **clitoral orgasm.** However, manual stimulation in which fingers are inserted into the vagina can bring about a vaginal orgasm, and women have been known to experience clitoral orgasm during sexual intercourse when the coital position chosen allows for sufficient stimulation of the clitoris by the man's thrusting movements.

Over the years much has been written about clitoral versus vaginal orgasms. It is said that Freud began this discourse when he stated that there were indeed two types of female orgasm. In his studies Kinsey (1953) refuted the notion of a vaginal orgasm and, as we have noted, Masters and Johnson claim that no matter what the source of stimulation (vaginal walls, clitoris, breasts), an orgasm is physiologically the same.

To add fuel to the fire, in *The G-Spot* (1982) Alice Ladas, Beverly Whipple, and John Perry suggested that there might be a physiological basis for a vaginal orgasm as differentiated from a clitoral orgasm. Recall from Chapter 3 that the gynecologist Ernest Grafenberg had earlier described a very sensitive area located on the front wall of the vagina almost halfway between the front of the cervix and the back of the pubic bone. Grafenberg proposed that when this spot is stimulated, it swells and the woman feels a brief urge to urinate. According to Ladas and her colleagues (1982), when an orgasm occurs from stimulation of the G-spot, the uterus pushes down instead of up (unlike the changes described by Masters and Johnson). In addition, in the G-spot orgasm the muscular contractions are proposed to occur in the deeper muscles of the vagina rather than in its outer portion. Despite all this theorizing, only 10 percent of women studied seemed to have a G-spot, which does not provide an enormous amount of evidence for the (exclusively) vaginal orgasm (Alzate & London, 1984; Masters, Johnson, & Kolodny, 1985).

Why all this discussion about the female orgasm? No one seems concerned to study the male orgasm with the same intensity; we do not read, for example, about a controversy over a glans- versus a perineum-centered orgasm. Although men's descriptions of orgasm are quite similar to women's descriptions of orgasmic experience, we believe that women have different experiences during orgasm with varying degrees of intensity and agree with Barbara Seaman (1972), who writes, "the liberated orgasm is any orgasm a woman likes."

A persistent theme in the literature is that orgasms resulting from vaginal stimulation (mostly penile-vaginal intercourse) are the exception rather than the norm. For example, Shere Hite (1976) found that only 30 percent of her respondents regularly achieved vaginal orgasm. Seymour Fisher's (1972, 1973) survey of 300 women shows that only about 40 percent experience vaginal orgasm on a regular basis. Helen Singer Kaplan (1979, 1974) estimates that among women who normally do experience vaginal orgasm, only 50 percent or fewer experience it without some clitoral stimulation.

Some researchers have proposed other models of orgasmic expression. Josephine and Irving Singer (1972), who object to the value-laden connotations of "vaginal" and "clitoral" orgasms, have proposed three different models of female orgasm. According to these researchers, a **vulval orgasm** parallels the orgasmic response described by Masters and Johnson, and consists basically of contractions of the outer third of the vagina. The vulval orgasm can occur either as a result of stimulation of the clitoris or during intercourse. A **uterine orgasm** is caused by deep intravaginal stimulation. The thrusting of the penis stimulates the uterus, and as orgasm approaches, Singer and Singer claim, the woman typically holds her breath. Orgasm coincides with the forceful exhalation of breath, followed by feelings of satiation and sexual fulfillment. A **blended orgasm** is a combination of the vulval and uterine types.

What does orgasm feel like to a woman? As the box on "The Experience of Female Orgasm" indicates, there is wide variation in the way women experience orgasm. Many women report a building of pleasurable sensations that usually begin at the clitoris and spread throughout the pelvis. The genitals are often described as pulsating, throbbing, or tingling, and such feelings tend to spread throughout the body. When actual orgasm occurs, many women report a sensation of warmth and, afterwards, a feeling of relaxation as muscle tension dissipates.

Some researchers, such as Wiest (1977) and Vance and Wagner (1976), suggest that men and women have many similar subjective experiences during the orgasm

vulval orgasm According to Singer and Singer, an orgasm that involves contractions of the outer third of the vagina and that can result either from stimulation of the clitoris or from penile-vaginal intercourse.

uterine orgasm According to Singer and Singer, an orgasm caused by deep intravaginal stimulation.

blended orgasm A type of female orgasm proposed by Singer and Singer that consists of a combination of vulval and uterine orgasms.

phase of the sexual response cycle. When male and female subjects from these researchers' studies were asked to detail orgasmic experiences, their descriptions were often indistinguishable. Other researchers, such as Sheila Kitzinger (1983), feel that the female orgasmic experience differs from that of males in that it is more diffuse and does not have the sudden and dramatic ending that a man experiences in ejaculation. Rather, Kitzinger claims, it is more of a sensation of flowing and flooding.

It is often difficult for women to interpret and describe their sexual feelings. Our society has traditionally frowned on the notion of young or adolescent girls masturbating, although it takes for granted that young and adolescent boys engage in self-stimulation. As a result, women who have not masturbated may be unfamiliar with orgasm and its potential. Some females may even have orgasms without being aware that what they are experiencing *is* an orgasm. The notion that "If you don't know whether you've had an orgasm, then you haven't!" is not necessarily true. Some women who believe that they've never had an orgasm may recall having pulsations and pleasurable feelings, and then a sense of relaxation afterwards, but never labeled their sensations as orgasm. Because of their socialization, such women may simply be too inhibited to permit themselves to recognize something they think they're not supposed to feel. Others may fail to realize they've had an orgasm because the culture has led them to believe every orgasm is of seismic strength.

What is male orgasm like? Is it better sometimes than others?

ejaculation The process by which semen is expelled through the penis.

Male Responses. **Ejaculation,** the most obvious manifestation of orgasm in a man, is the process by which semem is expelled from the body through the penis. Before ejaculation, the internal and external urinary sphincters seal off both ends of the prostatic urethra. Compression by the external sphincter muscle helps propel fluid from the Cowper's glands into the prostatic urethra. Meanwhile, spermatozoa and secretions from the genital ducts and accessory reproductive glands are deposited into the posterior urethra. When ejaculation occurs, the bladder neck closes, the external sphincter relaxes, and the perineal and bulbourethral muscles contract, propelling the ejaculate through the urethra and out through the urethral opening. Like women, men report a wide range of subjective feelings when they experience orgasm (see the box on "The Experience of Male Orgasm").

After her study of female sexuality, Shere Hite (1981) surveyed over 7,000 U.S. men between the ages of 13 and 97. Contrary to popular wisdom, Hite found that men's strongest orgasms were not during intercourse. Although the majority of men she surveyed reported enjoying coital orgasms, most usually had their strongest orgasms during masturbation. Still, as the following reflections suggest, coital orgasms may be more satisfying overall even though self-stimulation may bring about more intense sensations (Hite, 1981, pp. 438–441):

"The most fantastic orgasms of all, which combine the psychological excitement and overall release of intercourse with the genital awareness of masturbation, are when I remain motionless and my wife sort of massages my penis with contractions of her muscles in the vaginal area."

"I have my best orgasms by intercourse with a woman, of course. The activity I find most enjoyable is my female mate and I are in a dark room, with a soft bed, exploring each other's bodies, doing everything from oral sex to finger sex, and ending up in intercourse in either dog fashion or me on top of her."

"My best orgasms have been from masturbation, with intercourse a close second. This is due to the refined techniques I need for which most women do not have patience, skill, or interest."

"My most intense orgasms have been from masturbation because I can effect stimulation with greater intensity on a specific area (the one that responds the best on that occasion). However, the most satisfying orgasms are those shared with my lover after I have brought her to satiation."

Like the woman's vaginal contractions during orgasm, expulsive penile contractions are very rapid as orgasm begins, occurring every 0.8 seconds. After the first three or four major expulsive efforts, the penile contractions quickly lessen in frequency and in expulsive force. Minor contractions continue for several seconds in an irregular fashion, but they project only a small amount of seminal fluid under minimal expulsive force.

During the orgasm phase there are usually involuntary muscle spasms throughout the body. Hyperventilation during the orgasmic phase is considered normal for men just as it is for women; Masters and Johnson regularly noted respiration that peaked at over 40 breaths per minute. They also recorded increasing heart rates, with a range from 110 to 180+ beats per minute.

After I've ejaculated, it takes a while for me to achieve another erection. Is there something wrong with me?

RESOLUTION PHASE. In the **resolution phase,** the last stage of the sexual response cycle, vasocongestion and myotonia rapidly dissipate and the person returns to an unstimulated state. Women have the potential of returning to the plateau phase and of having additional orgasmic experiences from any point in the resolution phase if they are stimulated sufficiently. For men, however, immediately following orgasm, a **refractory period** ensues during which they are unresponsive to sexual stimulation. The duration of the refractory period is highly variable; it may last for a few minutes or for several hours or longer. Generally, the refractory period lengthens as a man grows older. Effective restimulation to higher levels of sexual tension is possible only after termination of this refractory period.

Female Responses. Following orgasm, the blood rapidly drains out of the engorged vaginal tissues, and both the outer third and inner two-thirds of the vagina slowly shrink back to their unstimulated state. The vagina loses its deep coloration and regains its normal appearance about 10 to 15 minutes after an orgasm.

resolution phase The fourth stage of Masters and Johnson's sexual response cycle, when vasocongestion and myotonia rapidly dissipate and the person returns to an unstimulated state.

refractory period A period of time after orgasm when a man is unresponsive to sexual stimulation. It is highly variable and may last for minutes or for hours.

The elevated uterus begins its return to the unstimulated resting position in the pelvis. The cervix descends into its normal position, and the passageway through the cervix enlarges. After the last vaginal contraction, the clitoris rapidly returns to its normal position, though it takes a longer period of time for it to shrink to its normal size.

The labia majora return to their normal thickness and positioning; this occurs faster if the woman has had an orgasm. If only plateau-phase levels of sexual tension are attained, an extended resolution phase typically is experienced, and the separated and engorged labia majora may be slow to revert to their normal state. The labia minora return to their normal coloration and size within 10 to 15 seconds after orgasm.

The swelling of the areolae of the breasts rapidly disappears, with the result that the nipples appear to regain full erection. This is an illusion, however, caused by the fact that the engorged areolae overshadowed nipple erection. The breasts themselves usually remain swollen for five or ten minutes after the orgasmic phase has been completed, and superficial venous patterns on the breast surfaces may persist even longer. Generally, women who have not breastfed lose their deep vasocongestion more slowly than those who have.

Muscle tension, heart rate, blood pressure, and respiration rate all return to normal during the resolution phase. Many women perspire on the back, thighs, and chest (this perspiratory reaction may have begun during the orgasm phase). In some women perspiration is limited to the soles of the feet and the palms of the hands, but in others perspiration may cover the entire body.

Male Responses. The shaft of the penis diminishes in size in two stages of the resolution phase. Initially, and rather quickly, the penis decreases to about half of its size at orgasm. Then, as this phase continues, the penis slowly returns to its normal, unstimulated size.

When the excitement or plateau phases have been purposely extended, it usually takes longer for the penis to return to its unstimulated state. When an erection is maintained for many minutes (particularly when the penis remains inside the vagina), vasocongestion may not dissipate immediately after ejaculation. The entire process of detumescence may simply take longer.

In general, the scrotum responds in one of two ways to the loss of sexual tension, and men tend to exhibit one or the other of these patterns consistently. Most common is a rapid loss of the congested, tense appearance of the scrotum and an early reappearance of the folded or creased skin patterns that are characteristic of the sexually unstimulated male. The second, less common, reaction is a slow loss of scrotal congestion and constriction.

Changes in the testicles parallel those in the scrotum itself. The testes may decrease in size and descend into the scrotal sac rapidly or slowly. As with the penis, the return of the testicles to an unstimulated state depends on the duration of plateau-phase levels of sexual tension. The longer tension was maintained, the slower is full testicular detumescence during the resolution period.

In both men and women the sex flush disappears rapidly during the resolution phase. Initially, it disappears from the shoulders and extremities, then from the chest, and last from the neck, face, and forehead. If a man's nipples have become erect, they will slowly relax. Minutes or even an hour may pass, though, before full nipple retraction has taken place.

During this phase muscle tension decreases, and blood pressure, heart rate, and respiration rate rapidly return to normal. Like women, men may experience perspiration during this phase (or even earlier, during the orgasm phase). In men this reaction is usually confined to the soles of the feet and the palms of the hands, but sweat may also appear on the trunk and sometimes the face and neck.

MASTERS AND JOHNSON IN PERSPECTIVE. As we said in Chapter 2, Masters and Johnson were the first investigators to study the physiology of sexual behavior in the laboratory. In the 35 years of their joint endeavors, they have supplied the field with an impressive body of knowledge about sexual arousal and response. To this date, Masters and Johnson's research is the most extensive ever conducted on human sexuality.

Of particular value has been their analysis of the internal genital responses that accompany female sexual arousal. Before their findings were made public, little was known about these responses, partly at least because of their hidden nature. Male erection and ejaculation were more easily observed and studied by researchers. And as we will discover in Chapter 16, the Masters and Johnson sexual response cycle has unique application to the treatment of sexual dysfunctions. Perhaps most important has been Masters and Johnson's proposal that both men and women not only progress through the same four phases of a sexual response cycle, but also have similar responses. This notion has enhanced the groundbreaking nature of their studies.

At the same time, the manner in which Masters and Johnson gathered their research data has sparked considerable controversy over the years. Some critics maintain that their research procedures created a sterile, artificial setting, and that the two researchers mechanized and dehumanized sex, deemphasizing its emotional qualities. Others question their four-phase model of sexual arousal and response, suggesting that it oversimplifies sexual response processes. On the other hand, some discern little or no distinction between the excitement and plateau phases proposed by the two researchers. Finally, some critics maintain that the effort to equate male and female sexual responses overlooks sex differences.

It is important to note that at present there is no consensus about the number of phases in the sexual response cycle and about the order and sequencing of such phases. Note too, that sexual response is a highly individual matter. Models of sexual response may mask important variations in response patterns and in sequencing from one person to another (Rosen & Beck, 1988).

The Kaplan Three-Stage Model

An alternative model of sexual response has been developed by Helen Singer Kaplan (1983, 1979, 1974). Kaplan, who is the founding director of the Human Sexuality Program at New York Hospital-Cornell Medical Center in New York City, proposes that human sexual response in both men and women comprises three separate but interlocking phases: desire, excitement, and orgasm.

DESIRE PHASE. Unlike Masters and Johnson, Kaplan includes a **desire phase** in her model of the response cycle. Maintaining that desire is a critical feature of sexual response, Kaplan refers to sexual desire as an appetite or drive that is produced by the activation of a specific neural system in the brain.

Kaplan acknowledges that the neurophysiologic and neuroanatomic bases for sexual desire are not as clearly understood as are the underpinnings of other drives, such as hunger and thirst. She maintains, however, that sexual desire shares at least four commonalities with other drives.

1. Sexual desire depends on the activity of a specific anatomical structure in the brain.
2. The brain's centers that enhance the drive balance those that inhibit it.
3. Desire is served by two specialized neurotransmitters, an inhibitory one and an excitatory one.

desire phase The first phase of Kaplan's sexual response cycle in which a specific neural system in the brain produces sexual desire, or libido, which leads a person to seek out or become responsive to sexual experiences.

....

Helen Singer Kaplan's desire phase of the sexual response cycle highlights characteristics of human beings that differentiate us from other animals.

Sexual Arousal and Response

4. The brain centers that regulate the sex drive have extensive connections with other parts of the brain that make it possible for sexual desire to be influenced by and integrated into the person's total life experience.

libido Sexual desire. In Freudian psychoanalytic theory, the driving force of the id.

According to Kaplan, sexual desire, or **libido,** is experienced as specific sensations. These sensations motivate the person to seek out, or become receptive to, sexual experiences. When the neural system of the brain that produces these sensations is active, a person becomes sexually excited. However, there is a wide range of arousal patterns. Kaplan notes that a man or woman may feel "horny," may feel genital sensations, may become vaguely sexy, interested in sex, open to sex, or even just restless. Following sexual gratification, these sensations cease. When the neural system is inactive or under the influence of inhibitory forces, she says, an individual has no interest in erotic matters—that is, he or she "loses the appetite" for sex.

excitement phase The second phase in Kaplan's model of sexual response, characterized primarily by genital vasocongestion.

EXCITEMENT PHASE. Kaplan's **excitement phase** is characterized chiefly by reflex genital vasocongestion in both sexes. During sexual arousal specialized areas in the spinal cord become activated and cause the blood vessels in the genitals to dilate. Dilation causes the genital organs to fill with blood and to become swollen and distended, changing their overall shape. Because of anatomic differences in the female and male organs, swelling takes different forms and creates changes that are different but complementary. The vagina balloons and becomes wet, and the penis becomes hard and enlarged.

orgasm phase The third phase of Kaplan's sexual response cycle, in which the vasoconstriction and myotonia developed from sexual stimuli are released.

ORGASM PHASE. Like the excitement phase, the **orgasm phase** is a genital reflex that is governed by specialized spinal nerve centers. These centers are near those that coordinate bladder and anal control. (Because of this, in people who have suffered injuries to the lower spinal cord, orgasm, urinary, and defecatory control may all be impaired.) Unlike the excitement phase, orgasm does not entail a vascular reflex. Rather, it consists of reflex pelvic muscle contractions in both women and men.

KAPLAN IN PERSPECTIVE. The Kaplan model is a welcome addition to the field of human sexuality and offers an interesting alternative to the sexual response model of Masters and Johnson. Kaplan's incorporation of a desire phase into her model emphasizes the importance of subjective psychological and motivational components of sexual response. Her model has also assisted those in clinical practice to obtain a better understanding of sexual dysfunctions and of how to approach them in the therapeutic setting.

Specifically, Kaplan maintains that sexual dysfunctions should usually be analyzed as pertaining to one of the three phases. To illustrate, dysfunction of the orgasm phase results in the clinical syndromes of premature and retarded ejaculation in men and inhibited orgasm in women. When sexual dysfunction is severe, however, all three phases of response become impaired and the person may become totally asexual. However inhibition of only one of the phases, with a sparing of the others, is more prevalent. Thus, a man may be very interested in sex and have no erectile difficulties, but experience an orgasm phase dysfunction. Or a woman may have no desire for sex but be able to lubricate and even have an orgasm on stimulation. In such instances effective therapy requires intervening at the problematic point in the triphasic model.

Critics of Kaplan maintain that her research is not nearly as extensive as that of Masters and Johnson. Since she has not done the meticulous kind of laboratory studies those researchers did to support their physiological propositions, many feel that her physiological analyses of excitement and orgasm oversimplify the processes involved.

EFFECTS OF DRUGS ON SEXUAL RESPONSE

The quest for a perfect **aphrodisiac,** a drug that will heighten sexual desire, pleasure, or performance, is rooted in antiquity. Substances such as belladonna and henbane were key ingredients in the sexual orgies of ancient fertility cults. In Africa yohimbine has reportedly been used to increase sexual prowess, and the mandrake plant was used for the same purpose in medieval Europe. Ginseng, oysters, and vitamin E have all been recommended at various times and in various places for their supposed aphrodisiac powers. However, as we will see in this portion of the chapter, there are few, if any, drug substances that have a direct and positive effect on any aspect of sexual response. Indeed, much contemporary research has revealed the **anaphrodisiac** effects of various drugs. That is, many drugs have the capacity to actually diminish or inhibit sexual arousal, desire, and satisfaction (Rosen & Beck, 1988).

The impact that drugs have on sexual function hinges on many factors. Dosage level and duration of use are of primary significance. The general physical health of the individual is also important, as is the simultaneous use of other drugs and the presence of an underlying medical disorder. In the case of psychoactive drugs such as alcohol and tranquilizers, the expectations of the user must also be considered. Finally, whether or not drug tolerance has been established is important. **Tolerance** means that, with extended use, greater and greater dosages of a particular drug are needed to produce that drug's effects. The pertinence of drug tolerance for sexual functioning is that as the individual needs to take higher dosages of a certain drug to experience a desired effect on sexual response, the likelihood for more detrimental effects increases. Moreover, heavy drug users often experience **withdrawal**—that is, physical pain and intense cravings for the drug when it is unavailable. Withdrawal indicates that **physical dependence** (a physiological need for a drug) has been established and, quite possibly, **psychological dependence** (a psychological need for a drug) as well. Keeping these concepts in mind, let's explore how sexual functioning is affected by drugs used for recreational purposes, as well as by prescription and over-the-counter drugs.

Drugs Used for Recreational Purposes

So-called recreational drugs are often taken in a sexual context because people believe they enhance sexual pleasure. There is an irony here, however, because these drugs often *hinder* sexual enjoyment. The drugs we will consider in this section are alcohol, nicotine, amphetamines, barbiturates and narcotics, marijuana, and LSD and other hallucinogens.

ALCOHOL. Because consumption of alcohol is accepted in most societies, this familiar substance is often not regarded as a drug. It *is* a drug, however, because it affects the central nervous system. Acting as a depressant, alcohol numbs the higher brain centers. As the concentration of blood alcohol increases, there is a progressive impairment or reduction of normal brain function. Gradually, the individual's awareness of and response to stimuli from the outside are diminished. Of all the drugs we discuss, alcohol may be the most dangerous, leading, when abused, to many physical illnesses and disabilities and producing symptoms so serious as to cause death in some cases (Steele & Josephs, 1990; Carrol, 1989; Baker, 1988).

Many people believe that alcohol is an aphrodisiac, that it increases sexual arousability, activity, and enjoyment. However, research reveals that these effects are due primarily to social expectations rather than to the pharmacological action of alcohol. Although alcohol may serve initially to lower sexual inhibitions, ultimately

aphrodisiac A substance that is supposed to heighten sexual desire, pleasure, or performance.

anaphrodisiac A substance that has the capacity to diminish or inhibit sexual arousal, desire, and satisfaction.

tolerance A condition that results when greater dosages of a drug are needed to achieve the effects of that drug.

withdrawal The intense craving and physical pain that results in a heavy drug user when the drug becomes unavailable or the person decides to quit. Withdrawal is a sign of physical, and possibly psychological, dependence on a drug.

physical dependence A physiological need for a drug.

psychological dependence A psychological need for a drug.

Do alcohol or other drugs enhance sexual desire?

it works as a physiological depressant and thus retards and dulls sexual arousal and orgasm. While having a few drinks may make a person more willing to attend to sexual stimuli or to engage in sexual activities, when it comes to actual performance, alcohol is a suppressant (Crowe & George, 1989; Pinhas, 1988; Abel, 1985).

In both sexes sexual dysfunction is far more prevalent among people who are chronic alcohol abusers. Sexual dysfunction in male alcoholics partly is due to organic factors. For example, advanced alcoholic liver disease, which causes an increased reabsorption of estrogens into the blood, may well help to suppress male libido, or sexual desire. Moreover, alcohol abuse also tends to suppress androgen production in men. The effects of chronic alcohol abuse are more difficult to assess in women. For both sexes, sexual arousal in response to erotic stimuli is diminished by alcohol, and it has been shown that alcohol consumption increases the time it takes to masturbate to orgasm (Segraves, 1988b).

NICOTINE. The effects of **nicotine** are often ignored in discussions of the impact of drugs on sexual functioning, partly because many people do not regard nicotine as a drug. In fact, nicotine is a drug that has multiple effects on many bodily systems, including the nervous, endocrine, circulatory, and digestive systems. Nicotine can inhibit the production of testosterone and interfere with erection. Among pregnant women who smoke, there is a greater risk for miscarriages, premature births, and infants with lowered birth weights. Moreover, combining the use of oral contraceptives with smoking increases a woman's risk of heart attack and stroke (Chasnoff, 1991; Fried & O'Connell, 1991).

AMPHETAMINES AND COCAINE. Amphetamines, such as benzedrine and dexedrine, act as stimulants on the central nervous system. Amphetamines constrict peripheral blood vessels, increase blood pressure and heart rate, shrink mucous membranes, and suppress appetite. Also called "uppers" or "speed," amphetamines are often abused by people who want to lose weight, stay awake, or get "high." Overdoses of amphetamines have been known to produce extremely elevated blood pressure, unclear and rapid speech, confusion, and enlarged pupils. When the effects of amphetamines wear off, people frequently "crash," sleeping for long periods of time. Afterward, they are often highly irritable, suspicious, and impulsive (Goode, 1989; Carrol, 1989).

Cocaine, which has increased greatly in popularity in recent years, is an alkaloid that produces similar effects. In mild doses cocaine heightens alertness and makes the user feel greatly energized. Initially, it produces a sense of euphoria and well-being, and users tend to feel that they are smarter and more competent than other people. (In reality, of course, they aren't any smarter or more competent—they just think they are.) The effects of cocaine are temporary and tolerance for the drug sets in rapidly, so that higher and higher dosages are needed to obtain the initial effect. Unfortunately, heavier doses and prolonged use can induce hostility, withdrawal, paranoia, and even death. "Crack," or cocaine that has been converted to a smokable form (smoking crack is called "free-basing"), tends to produce hallucinations, depression, and hostile behavior (Siegel, 1990; Brower & Anglin, 1987; Honer, Gewirtz, & Turey, 1987).

Amphetamines and cocaine are often the drugs of choice for sexual enhancement. They produce a wide variation of sexual reactions both among users in general and within the same person from one episode to another. Users report that, in low doses, cocaine and many amphetamines often increase erotic desire and sexual responsiveness. Some women say that low doses contribute to a more intense and satisfying orgasm, and some men claim that sniffing low doses of cocaine helps them sustain an erection. More frequent use of cocaine, though, tends to result in impaired sexual functioning, including problems achieving erection in men and reduced sexual desire in both sexes (Siegel, 1982).

Alcohol only seems to enhance sexual activity. Alcohol depresses the central nervous system, making it less, not more responsive. And like many other drugs, alcohol blurs the mind, making it less perceptive of sensation, not more.

nicotine A toxic alkaloid found in all parts of tobacco plants but especially the leaves.

amphetamines Drugs that act as central nervous system stimulants, generally causing accelerated bodily functions as well as energy and mood changes.

cocaine An alkaloid that acts as a central nervous system stimulant.

Sexual Arousal and Response

Some researchers (Pinhas, 1988; Resnick & Resnick, 1984) report that applying cocaine directly to the genitals of either men or women acts as an anesthetic, delaying orgasm and thus prolonging sexual excitement. Male users who have a problem with premature ejaculation sometimes resort to this method to "cure" their dysfunction. However, although cocaine used externally diminishes sensations in the genital membranes, the penis becomes engorged with blood because cocaine also has a vaso-constrictive action. In some cases, ejaculation does not occur because of the numbing, but the man is left with a prolonged erection (called "priapism") that causes intense pain lasting up to 24 hours.

BARBITURATES AND NARCOTICS. Barbiturates are drugs that depress the functioning of the central nervous system and are designed primarily to induce relaxation and sleep. Barbiturates—examples are pentobarbital (Nembutal) and secobarbital (Seconal)—are physiologically addictive. (In this section of the text we'll supply the generic name of the drug first and then one of its brand names in parentheses.) Hard-core users often take them to supplement other drugs—for example, to moderate the stimulating actions of amphetamines or accentuate the actions of narcotics. Habitual use of sedative/hypnotic drugs produces drowsiness, mental confusion, and the loss of muscular coordination. As with alcohol, the withdrawal symptoms may be particularly severe, often resulting in delusions and hallucinations, and sometimes even coma (Carrol, 1989).

Like alcohol, barbiturates tend to overcome sexual inhibitions and to create a relaxed sense of well-being. For these reasons, they are often the drug of choice for people with sexual anxieties. Methaqualone (Quaalude), for example, has a street reputation for creating these effects and for being an aphrodisiac. (We discuss methaqualone here because it is a central nervous system depressant. Technically speaking, however, this drug is not a barbiturate.) Prolonged use of barbiturates or methaqualone tends to reduce sexual desire. At high doses, barbiturates have also been associated with erectile dysfunction and difficulty in reaching orgasm.

Narcotics are central nervous system depressants such as morphine, heroin, and methadone. Of all of the narcotics, heroin is the most popular because of its potency and ability to produce euphoric effects. Users report that heroin initially causes intensely pleasurable sensations, often called a "rush." The next several hours are referred to by addicts as a "high," although in this reportedly euphoric state the user is lethargic and usually withdrawn. Then comes a negative phase in which the user has a strong desire for more of the drug. When deprived of the narcotic, heavy users begin to experience withdrawal symptoms, whose severity increases until the drug is taken again. Restlessness, excessive sweating, nausea, severe abdominal cramps, vomiting, and delirium are the most common withdrawal symptoms (Goode, 1989).

Chronic narcotic use often causes the loss of sexual desire and impaired sexual functioning. Both men and women may experience delayed orgasm. In addition, men often have problems achieving an erection as well as reduced testosterone levels and semen volume and impaired movement of sperm. Many men also exhibit a marked delay in ejaculation. Chronic narcotic use among females may cause amenorrhea, or cessation of menstruation (Julien, 1988; Siegel, 1990).

MARIJUANA. Marijuana, made from the leaves and flowers of the hemp plant, is classified as a **hallucinogen**—that is, a drug capable of producing a hallucination, or false sensory experience. The active ingredient of marijuana is THC, a compound known more precisely as delta-9-tetrahydrocannabinol. When marijuana is smoked or eaten (in such foods as brownies), the average person experiences a sense of relaxed well-being or exhilaration and an increased sensitivity to sounds and sights. Time, distance, attention span, vision, hearing, hand-leg reactions, and body balance may be slowed or distorted. Some people become drowsy. Others feel they have greater physical and mental capacities than they actually possess. In general, the

barbiturates Sedative drugs that often induce relaxation and sleep.

narcotic A drug that in moderate doses depresses the central nervous system. Examples are morphine, heroin, and methadone.

marijuana A hallucinogenic drug derived from the leaves of the hemp plant.

hallucinogen A drug capable of producing a hallucination.

marijuana user's experience reflects the situation in which she takes the drug. If she is anxious, taking the drug may heighten that feeling; if she is depressed, she may become more depressed (Goode, 1989; Gieringer, 1988).

Marijuana increases heart rate somewhat but does not seem to affect respiratory rate, blood sugar levels, or pupil size. It also has a tendency to cause bloodshot and itchy eyes and a dry mouth and to increase appetite. When severely abused, marijuana produces lethargy and passivity; excessive use may also result in high blood pressure and even lung cancer (Fligiel et al., 1988).

Research findings on marijuana's effects on sexual functioning are mixed. In some studies (e.g., Weller & Halikas, 1982) subjects report that moderate marijuana use enhances sexual responsiveness and pleasure. Some users report that marijuana alters the perception of the sexual experience, while others claim that it helps them overcome sexual inhibitions. Some report a heightening of sensual and erotic pleasure. However, heavy long-term use tends to decrease sexual desire and excitement as well as the recall of experiences. Among men who are chronic users, marijuana may also reduce overall testosterone levels.

LSD A potent synthetic hallucinogen (known technically as lysergic acid diethylamide) capable of changing the user's perception and creating extreme sensory distortions.

LSD AND OTHER HALLUCINOGENS. Marijuana is considered a mild hallucinogen. Much stronger drugs in this category include LSD, mescaline, and PCP (phencyclidine or "angel dust"). **LSD** (lysergic acid diethylamide, also known as "acid," is a synthetic drug that can change perceptions and create extreme sensory distortions. Affecting cells, tissues, and organs, and changing the transmission of neural impulses in the lower brain centers, drugs such as LSD produce profound physiological and psychological reactions. LSD's effects, like marijuana's, depend on the drug's potency, or dosage, as well as on the social and psychological context in which it is taken (Goode, 1989; Baker, 1988).

It is difficult to assess the sexual effects of LSD and other hallucinogens because of polydrug usage. That is, people who use one drug are likely to use others and often at the same time. Temporal and visual distortions brought on by these drugs tend to detract from the user's ability to concentrate on sexual feelings (Pinhas, 1988). Since hallucinogens can cause sudden shifts in mood and general detachment, use more often disrupts sexual arousal than enhances it.

Although users' expectations of "a good trip" on these drugs can lead them to perceive a glorious sexual encounter, just as often the encounter turns into a terrifying nightmare. Hallucinogens do have mild stimulant properties, which can lead users to feel intensified sexual arousal. Some users claim they are not sexually impaired, but rather have stronger orgasms, but others—those who report the most vivid hallucinations—often experience erectile inhibition and orgasmic dysfunction.

The bottom line is that any substance that changes your mind's functioning and alters your mood is bound to interfere with your ability to truly perceive what is going on, both within and outside your body. Why would anyone not want to perceive clearly what is happening during a sexual encounter?

Prescription and Over-the-Counter Drugs

Many prescription drugs as well as drugs that are sold off the shelves—called "over-the-counter" drugs—affect sexual functioning. It would be impossible in this chapter to examine all such drugs that influence sexual functioning, so we will confine our discussion to some medications that are used very commonly.

As we've already pointed out, the side effects of a drug depend in part on how long one uses it and how much one takes. Side effects are also influenced by interactions with other drugs that the person may be taking simultaneously, as well as by age, sex, and general health of the person. And again, as noted for recreational drugs, the attitudes and expectations of the individual exert a significant influence on the drug's ultimate effect (Baker, 1988; Rosen & Beck, 1988).

ANTIHYPERTENSIVE DRUGS. **Hypertension,** or high blood pressure, is a condition characterized by a persistently elevated pressure of blood within and against the walls of the arteries, which carry blood from the heart throughout the body. The **antihypertensive drugs** known as vasodilators open narrowed blood vessels that contribute to hypertension by increasing resistance to flow. Examples of antihypertensive medication are prazosin (Minipres), hydralazine (Apresoline), and diazoxide (Hyperstat). These drugs often cause a number of sexual side effects in men; for example, they can interfere with desire, erection, ejaculation, and orgasm. In women antihypertensive medication has been most commonly linked to reduced sexual desire (Segraves, 1988b).

A vasodilator receiving widespread publicity in recent years as a sexual stimulant is **amyl nitrite,** known on the streets as "poppers" or "Amy." Amyl nitrite, which is also a smooth muscle relaxant, is used in the treatment of angina pectoris, a painful heart condition that results from blocked coronary arteries. Amyl nitrite increases the diameter of the arteries and lowers peripheral blood pressure. This highly volatile drug is contained in ampules, which are crushed, or "popped," by the patient and held near the nose and mouth so that the contents can be inhaled.

Amyl nitrite has the reputation among recreational drug users of intensifying orgasmic pleasure when it is inhaled just before orgasm (if inhaled too soon, an erection may be lost). Once inhaled, the drug enters the bloodstream from the lungs. It is the vasodilating effects of the drug, particularly the increased blood flow to the genitals, that are supposedly responsible for its sex-enhancing properties. Many users report a "high" during orgasm that prolongs overall sexual satisfaction.

Unfortunately, amyl nitrite is medically dangerous. The drug causes a number of very unpleasant side effects in some people, including headaches, dizziness, and fainting. Other users experience nausea and vomiting. In more serious instances cardiovascular problems and even death have been reported.

PSYCHIATRIC DRUGS. **Psychiatric drugs,** which are used to treat behavioral disturbances, may have sexual side effects. **Antipsychotic drugs** act to calm the activity of certain areas of the brain while allowing the rest of the brain to function normally. Psychotic disturbances, such as schizophrenia, often entail a loss of contact with reality or an inability to function on a daily basis. Examples of antipsychotic drugs are chloropromazine (Thorazine), thioridazine (Mellaril), and haloperidol (Haldol). Many antipsychotic drugs cause reduced sexual desire in both men and women, and in some men, erection problems.

Antidepressants are drugs used to relieve depression, a mood disorder often characterized by hopelessness and lethargy. Examples of antidepressants are imipramine (Tofranil) and amitriptyline (Elavil). People taking antidepressants often show a marked reduction in sexual desire. Imipramine has also been associated with erectile dysfunction and ejaculatory problems in men, and with failure to achieve orgasm in women.

Antianxiety drugs are often used to treat disorders in which anxiety is the primary symptom; they reduce anxiety and induce relaxation and sometimes sleep. Antianxiety drugs are usually categorized as barbiturates, which, as we learned earlier, depress the central nervous system. Examples of antianxiety drugs are hydroxyzine hydrochloride (Atarax), meprobamate (Equanil), diazepam (Valium), and chlordiazepoxide (Librium); common sleep-inducing drugs are flurazepam hydrochloride (Dalmane) and secobarbital sodium (Seconal). For many users, antianxiety drugs reduce sexual inhibitions because they relieve anxiety. For others, these medications may reduce sexual desire.

hypertension A condition characterized by persistently elevated pressure of blood within and against the walls of the arteries, which carry blood from the heart throughout the body. Also known as *high blood pressure*.

antihypertensive drugs Drugs used to treat hypertension (high blood pressure). One class of these drugs is the vasodilators, which open narrow blood vessels that contribute to hypertension by increasing resistance to flow.

amyl nitrite A vasodilator prescription drug used in the treatment of angina pectoris. As a recreational drug, it is used as a sexual stimulant.

psychiatric drugs Drugs used to treat behavioral disturbances. Examples are the antipsychotic, antidepressant, and antianxiety drugs.

antipsychotic drugs Substances that calm the activity of certain areas of the brain but allow the rest of the brain to function normally.

antidepressants Drugs used to elevate mood and relieve depression.

antianxiety drugs Drugs used to reduce anxiety and induce relaxation and sometimes sleep.

ANTIHISTAMINES AND APPETITE SUPPRESSANTS. Antihistamines are commonly prescribed to relieve the symptoms of allergies and colds. Some antihistamines are cyproheptadine hydrochloride (Vimicon), diphenhydramine hydrochloride (Allerdryl), and trimeprazine tartrate (Temaril). Almost all these drugs produce some degree of drowsiness, which may reduce sexual desire, and some antihistamines cause problems with erection in men. Moreover, because continuous use of antihistamines dries all mucous membranes, sexual activity may be uncomfortable or even painful, particularly for a woman.

Appetite suppressants on the market, including diethylpropion hydrochloride (Tenuate) and phentermine hydrochloride (Fastin), are taken by dieters to reduce their cravings for food. They sometimes cause erection difficulties in men, and may reduce sexual desire in both sexes.

DEALING WITH THE SEXUAL SIDE EFFECTS OF DRUGS

When sexual impairment is due to a drug, the problem can usually be reversed by adjusting the dosage, finding a substitute medication, or discontinuing the drug altogether. Too often, though, the failure of patient and doctor to discuss the problem openly keeps them from solving it. Most people hesitate to discuss their sexual problems with their physicians. They may feel comfortable reporting that a drug is causing drowsiness or upsetting their stomachs, but will shy away from reporting an adverse sexual reaction.

It is important to educate yourself about any medication you are taking. Always ask your doctor for the following information:

- The name of the medication prescribed for you, whether generic or brand name. (Generic drugs are less expensive, but sometimes a doctor will specify a brandname drug. It's a good idea to get both names.)
- The exact dosage schedule: how much you should take and at what intervals; how you should take the medication (e.g., with water, after meals, at bedtime); and for how long a period of time you should take it.
- The most common side effects of the drug and which ones are within the normal range—that is, expected in most people and not worrisome.
- What side effects are signals that you should consult your doctor and have your medication adjusted in some way.
- How the drug prescribed interacts with other drugs. It is important to learn if the prescribed medication might interact negatively with other drugs you are taking (even nonprescription drugs such as aspirin, cold pills, or vitamins), alcohol, and caffeine. If you are a woman taking oral contraceptives, you should know that the pill interacts adversely with a number of other drugs (e.g., blood pressure medicines, oral blood thinners, barbiturates). Such drugs may be taken together, but dosages often have to be adjusted to minimize adverse effects from the combination.
- What are the specifically sexual side effects of the drug, if any, and what can be done to prevent or minimize them.

Clearly, you can avoid the sexual side effects of the so-called recreational drugs simply by shunning them altogether or by carefully restricting your use of them. When drugs have been prescribed to treat a specific medical or psychological problem, of course, you have less choice in the matter. However, you should not underestimate the many ways that drug therapies can be manipulated to minimize or avoid sexual impairment. If you talk honestly with your doctor about any problem you are experiencing, you will undoubtedly be able to reach a solution to it.

SEXUALITY IN THE NEWS

In Fish, Social Status Goes Right to the Brain
By Natalie Angier

A mong males of many species, from elephant seals to human beings, the struggle to prevail over competing males often seems to dwarf all other tasks—and perhaps with good reason.

A scientist has discovered that how a male fish interacts with other males and whether it is socially dominant or a tremulous wimp has such a profound effect on the creature that it changes the brain cells in charge of the fish's capacity to breed.

Studying the African cichlid fish, Dr. Russell Fernald, a neurobiologist at Stanford University, has discovered that in aggressive males that command large territories and keep contending males at bay, brain cells in the hypothalamus that allow the fish to mate are six to eight times larger than are equivalent cells in mild-mannered males with no social clout.

What is more, Dr. Fernald has found that the dimensions of those cells are extremely plastic. Should the domineering male be confronted by a larger male able to bully it, the neurons of the defeated fish will rapidly shrink. And after the hypothalamic cells have shrunk, the male's testes follow suit, eventually robbing the fish of its desire and ability to breed.

The discovery is the first persuasive evidence of how social behavior can help sculpt the structure of the brain, and how the altered brain, in turn, influences animal behavior....

"A Marvelous Example" ...

Laboratory ... results provide powerful evidence that the old nature-nurture argument, pitting the influence of biology on behavior against that of the environment, is far too simplistic.

Instead, researchers said, an animal's body, its behavior, and its social milieu very likely represent interdependent points on a giant feedback loop, with one alternately affecting the other.

"This is a marvelous example of how the social environment influences animal biology," said Dr. Darcy B. Kelly, a biologist at Columbia University. "... This goes a long way toward solving the nature-nurture debate, which was a false debate to begin with."

The findings may also have implications for a few finless creatures, including people. Because the brain molecules under study are highly conserved across the evolutionary spectrum, Dr. Fernald suggests that the architecture of the human brain may also be affected by a person's behavior.

Indeed, Dr. Simon LeVay of the Salk Institute of La Jolla, Calif., who stirred an acrimonious debate recently when he said he had detected a difference in the hypothalamus between homosexual and heterosexual men, has expressed great interest in Dr. Fernald's new study.

But researchers concur that it will be far more difficult to decipher the meaning of brain differences in people than it is to investigate the neurobiology of fish....

Dominant males are larger and more brilliantly colored, with bold orange stripes and fins that gleam like rainbows, and they are extremely aggressive. By contrast, both females and subordinate males have cryptic, sand-colored scales and are unlikely to pick a fight.

The Price of Glory

But it turns out that the flamboyance of machismo has its price. The colorful fish are easily seen and predated upon, and once a dominant male disappears, a remarkable event occurs. All the meek males in the neighborhood rush over seeking to fill the vacancy, and a series of violent battles commences....

continued

Eventually, a winner emerges and promptly begins flaunting his success through telltale displays of dominance and territoriality. At that point a welter of physical changes begins. The male grows bigger and gains a bright coat; its gonads swell, and it starts making sperm.

Taking the fish back to his laboratory, Dr. Fernald traced the molecular sequence of events from newfound social dominance to full-fledged sexual prowess. He found that the behavioral changes occur first, and that they in turn spur dramatic growth in brain cells responsible for producing a compound called gonadotropin-releasing hormone. That substance tweaks the pituitary gland to produce hormones that in turn stimulate the fish's testes and switch on sperm production.

Conversely, in experiments where a dominant male is stripped of its preeminence by the introduction of a bigger, nastier male, the chastened fish stops making dominant display and slinks off, and the brain changes follow. Within days, its bright colors have disappeared and its testicles have withered.

"The behavior is what's driving it," said Dr. Fernald. "The failure to play a socially dominant role is the key, which ultimately down-regulates testes size.

That may seem a sad fate for a male who has savored the spoils of power. But then again, said Dr. Fernald, the fish regain their cryptic coloring and hence a potentially longer lease on life. (*The New York Times*, November 12, 1991. Copyright © 1991 by The New York Times Company. Reprinted by permission.)

DISCUSSION QUESTIONS

1. This research confirms the role of the hypothalamus in sexual behavior. But it goes further in suggesting that a creature's behavior can actually change its brain's functioning. If this were true for human beings, how do you think it might affect our sexual behavior and functioning?

2. As we will see in Chapter 9, it is Simon LeVay's contention that the differences he has found in the hypothalamuses of homosexual and heterosexual men indicate a possible genetic basis for homosexuality. What do you think the author of the present article is implying about the relevance of Russell Fernald's research to LeVay's work?

3. Do you think scientists should draw inferences about human functioning and behavior from experiments with infrahuman species? Why or why not?

LOOKING BACK

■   Sexual response originates in the nervous system and depends on the body's integrating mechanisms. Of particular importance is the interplay between the sympathetic and parasympathetic nervous systems. Various aspects of the brain influence sexual response, including the cerebral cortex and the limbic system. The limbic system is an integrated network of structures consisting of the cingulate gyrus, the hippocampus, the septal area, the amygdala, portions of the reticular activating system, and the hypothalamus.

■   The endrocrine system also influences sexual arousal and response. Of particular importance are the gonadal hormones. Androgens are produced primarily by the Leydig cells of the testes and, to a lesser extent, by the adrenal glands of both males and females. Of all androgens, testosterone exerts the most influence on the sexual drive. Estrogens are produced by follicle cells of the ovaries as well as by the testes in men. Progesterone is a hormone manufactured by the corpus luteum in females and is found in greatest amounts during the secretory phase of the menstrual cycle. For both females and males, the gonads, hypothalamus, and pituitary gland work together to coordinate and control the levels of sex hormones in the body.

■   William Masters and Virginia Johnson have proposed a sexual response cycle consisting of four phases: excitement, plateau, orgasm, and resolution. These phases, which are successive, are essentially the same for women and men; indeed, both sexes often exhibit similar patterns of sexual response within these phases. Masters and Johnson's work has been criticized on several grounds, but primarily for treating sex mechanically and failing to account for the emotional and psychological aspects of sexual behavior.

■ Helen Singer Kaplan's model of sexual response proposes that sexual responses can be broken down into three separate but interlocking phases: desire, excitement, and orgasm. Kaplan's theory, while not nearly as extensive as Masters and Johnson's, has supplied insights into the motivational component of sexual response. It has also given clinicians a better understanding of sexual dysfunctions and how to treat them.

■ The impact that drugs have on sexual function depends on many factors: dosage level, duration of use, physical health of the user, simultaneous use of other drugs, the presence of underlying medical disorders, expectations of the user, and whether or not physical or psychological dependence to the drug has been established. Drugs used for recreational purposes that can affect sexual response include alcohol, nicotine, amphetamines, barbiturates and narcotics, marijuana, and LSD and other hallucinogens. Also affecting sexual response are some widely used prescription medications such as antihypertensive drugs, psychiatric drugs, and antihistamines and appetite suppressants.

THINKING THINGS OVER

1. Prepare a diagram that depicts the biology of the sexual response in men and women. Use arrows, labels, and rough sketches of areas like the brain and hormones to track sexual response.

2. Based on what you know, critique both the Masters and Johnson and the Kaplan models in terms of their applicability to real-life situations. If you were to teach a course on sexual arousal and response to your peers, which model would you choose? Explain your choice, and plan how you would teach that model.

3. According to the Masters and Johnson model, women and men have sexual responses unique to their sex but they also share many responses. Do you think it would be helpful to discuss these similarities and differences with a sexual partner? Why or why not? Would you feel comfortable doing so? Why or why not?

4. Describe the differences between male and female orgasms and relate these differences to the differing responses of women and men throughout the response cycle. Take the vaginal-clitoral orgasm controversy into account in your answer.

5. How would you counsel a friend who told you that she or he was using cocaine to enhance sexual pleasure? Alcohol? "Poppers"? Would you use these or any of the other drugs we've discussed for this purpose? Why or why not?

DISCOVER FOR YOURSELF

Abel, E. L. (1985). *Psychoactive drugs and sex.* New York: Plenum Press. Students wanting more information on how drugs affect sexual desire and performance can find it in this excellent resource book.

Kaplan, H. S. (1979). *Disorders of sexual desire.* New York: Brunner/Mazel. Kaplan's triphasic concept of sexual response is explained in Chapter 1 of this useful book.

Karacan, I., Aslan, C., & Hirshkhowitz, M. (1983). Erectile mechanisms in man. *Science, 220,* 1080–1082.

Levin, R. J. (1981). The female orgasm—current appraisal. *Journal of Psychosomatic Research,* 51, 119–133. The author sheds light on the topic of female orgasm, including directions for future research.

Masters, W. H., & Johnson, V. E. (1966). *Human sexual response.* Boston: Little Brown. Masters and Johnson's now-classic account of the sexual response cycle.

Rosen, R. C., & Beck, J. G. (1988). *Patterns of sexual arousal.* New York: Guilford Press. Virtually every aspect of sexual arousal is covered in this comprehensive book. Readers will find the sections on the psychophysiology of orgasm and endrocrine factors in sexual arousal particularly enlightening.

5
Sex and Gender Issues

*Treat people as if
they were what they
ought to be and you
help them become
what they are capable
of being*

—Johann Wolfgang von Goethe

There are many questions we can ask about the differences in behavior between men and women. For example, are men more physically active and aggressive than women? Are women more nurturant and emotionally sensitive than men? Are there differences in the ways men and women approach romantic attachment or sexual pleasuring in the context of an intimate relationship?

Beneath such questions are more basic issues. If women and men do differ in such ways, what are the factors that create those differences? Are they biological? Social? Environmental? Or do they result from the interaction of all three types of factors?

The search for answers to such questions lies at the heart of this chapter. Although most of us are born clearly male or female (as we'll see, there are occasional exceptions to this rule), just knowing what sex we are doesn't necessarily establish how "feminine" or "masculine" we feel or how we conceptualize the roles we will play in society. The culture into which we're born teaches us what attitudes and behaviors are appropriate to our sex, and gradually we develop an identity, a sense of self, that incorporates these teachings—or sometimes rebels against them. How we come to see ourselves functioning as men or women in society has important implications not only for our individual growth but also for the way we interact with others in intimate relationships.

In the first part of this chapter we'll introduce some important terminology designed to enhance your understanding of the material on sex and gender that follows. We will then spend some time examining biological distinctions between the sexes, including how chromosomes and hormones create physiological differences. Next, we'll show how the socialization process influences gender-role development and forges a person's sense of masculinity and femininity. Finally, we'll look at the notion of androgyny and its meaning for intimate relationships.

SEX AND GENDER: SOME DEFINITIONS AND GUIDELINES

The science of human sexuality employs rather specific terminology when describing how human beings develop into men and women. At the most fundamental level, **sex** refers to a person's biological status of being a male or female. This biological status can be broken down into **genetic sex,** which is determined by our chromosomal makeup, and **anatomical sex,** the physical characteristics and features that distinguish females from males. Thus **sexual identity** is one's identity as either female or male based on biological characteristics, both genetic and anatomical.

Gender, on the other hand, refers to the social meanings attached to being a female or a male. Gender can be thought of as encompassing the social dimensions of masculinity or femininity. To proceed a step further, **gender identity** is the psychological awareness or sense of being either a male or a female. It is generally accepted that gender identity occurs by age three. A **gender role** refers to a set of expectations that prescribes how females and males should behave. Understanding the concept of gender roles is very important, for gender roles determine hundreds of things we do every day. They prescribe the way we sit, the way we stand, the kinds of jobs we take, and the kinds of people we choose as mates. They also account for a host of other expectations, ranging from who washes the dishes to who stays home with the children.

A **gender-role stereotype** is a generalization that reflects our beliefs about females and males. Gender-role stereotypes embody expected characteristics or behaviors, attributes or actions, that men and women actually possess or exhibit, or want to possess or exhibit. As the "Myths and Misconceptions" box indicates, ster-

sex A person's biological status as either a male or a female.

genetic sex Biological maleness or femaleness as determined by our chromosomal makeup.

anatomical sex The physical characteristics and features that distinguish females from males.

sexual identity One's identity as either female or male based on biological characteristics, both genetic and anatomical.

*H*ow much of what we hear about gender-role stereotypes is true? Are boys better at mathematics than girls? Is there really a difference between the sexes in displays of aggression? The majority of gender-role stereotypes are untrue; indeed, researchers have discovered that women and men are more psychologically *similar* than different. Here are some of the more popular gender-role stereotypes:

Men are superior to women in analytical reasoning and mathematical ability.

Men and women do not differ on tests of analytic cognitive style or logical reasoning. Neither sex has an edge in concept formation or higher-level cognitive processing. Some researchers (e.g., Maccoby, 1987) maintain that men have better mathematical skills, but others (e.g., Hyde, Fennema, & Lamon, 1990) feel that these differences have been exaggerated. For example, one recent study (Linn & Hyde, 1991) notes that males do outperform females in math—but only in the gifted population.

Men and women experience different emotions.

On the contrary, both sexes experience the same emotions. Where they differ is in how they *express* their emotions. For example, boys are often taught at an early age not to cry or show fear, and girls are often taught to be affectionate and nurturant. As this chapter makes clear, such gender-role programming in childhood has important consequences for the formation and maintenance of intimate relationships.

Women are more "social" than men.

Men and women are equally interested in social stimuli. Both sexes are equally responsive to social reinforcement, and equally proficient at learning from social models. During early childhood neither sex is more willing than the other to play alone (Maccoby, 1990; Maccoby & Jacklin, 1974).

Men have higher self-esteem than women.

The sexes are very similar in their levels of self-confidence and self-satisfaction throughout childhood and adolescence. But men and women do differ in the areas in which they feel most self-confident: women rate themselves higher on social competence, while men perceive themselves as dominant or powerful (Maccoby & Jacklin, 1974).

---

eotypes ascribe certain characteristics or behaviors to *all* representatives of a group despite the evidence that some members of that group do not possess them. For example, you have surely heard people say things like "girls are emotional and dependent," and "boys are aggressive and competent." Such stereotypes abound in our society, and in this chapter we will explore their impact on overall sexual and gender-specific behavior.

THE BIOLOGY OF SEXUAL DEVELOPMENT

The biological status of human beings begins with the fertilization of the female ovum by the male sperm. All fertilized eggs are not alike. On the contrary, they carry different chromosomes and hormones that will create variations in biological development. Let's peer inside the cell to discover more about these differences.

Chromosomes and Genes

A cell is a living unit of organized material that contains a nucleus and is enclosed in a membrane. The nucleus, located in or near the center of the cell, is the control center for the cell's activity. Inside the nucleus are **chromosomes,** thin rodlike structures that occur in pairs. Chromosomes contain **genes,** structures composed of deoxyribonucleic acid, or DNA, that carry the instructions that determine the inheritance of characteristics.

Most of the cells in the human body are **somatic cells** (somatic comes from the Greek word for "body"). The genes contained in these cells control many different characteristics of human beings, such as eye color, height, and a predisposition to disease (e.g., sickle-cell anemia or diabetes mellitus). The remaining cells in the body are **germ cells,** also referred to as *sex cells* or *cells of reproduction*. Male germ cells are the spermatozoa (produced in the testes) and female germ cells are the ova (produced in the ovaries).

Each cell of the human body contains 46 chromosomes, occurring in pairs (see Figure 5–1). Thus there are 23 pairs of chromosomes, and in 22 of these pairs each member is identical to its mate. That is, each resembles the other and the two have the same function—for example, to determine hair color. The 23rd pair of chromosomes are sometimes called the *sex chromosomes*, for they determine the sex of the child. As Figure 5–1 shows, in female cells the 23rd pair consists of two X

chromosomes Thin rodlike structures located inside the cell's nucleus that contain the directions for the cell's activity.

genes Structures composed of deoxyribonucleic acid (DNA) that carry the instructions that determine the inheritance of characteristics.

somatic cells The majority of the cells of an organism, which control all characteristics except those that are sexual.

germ cells An organism's reproductive cells; the female ovum and the male sperm.

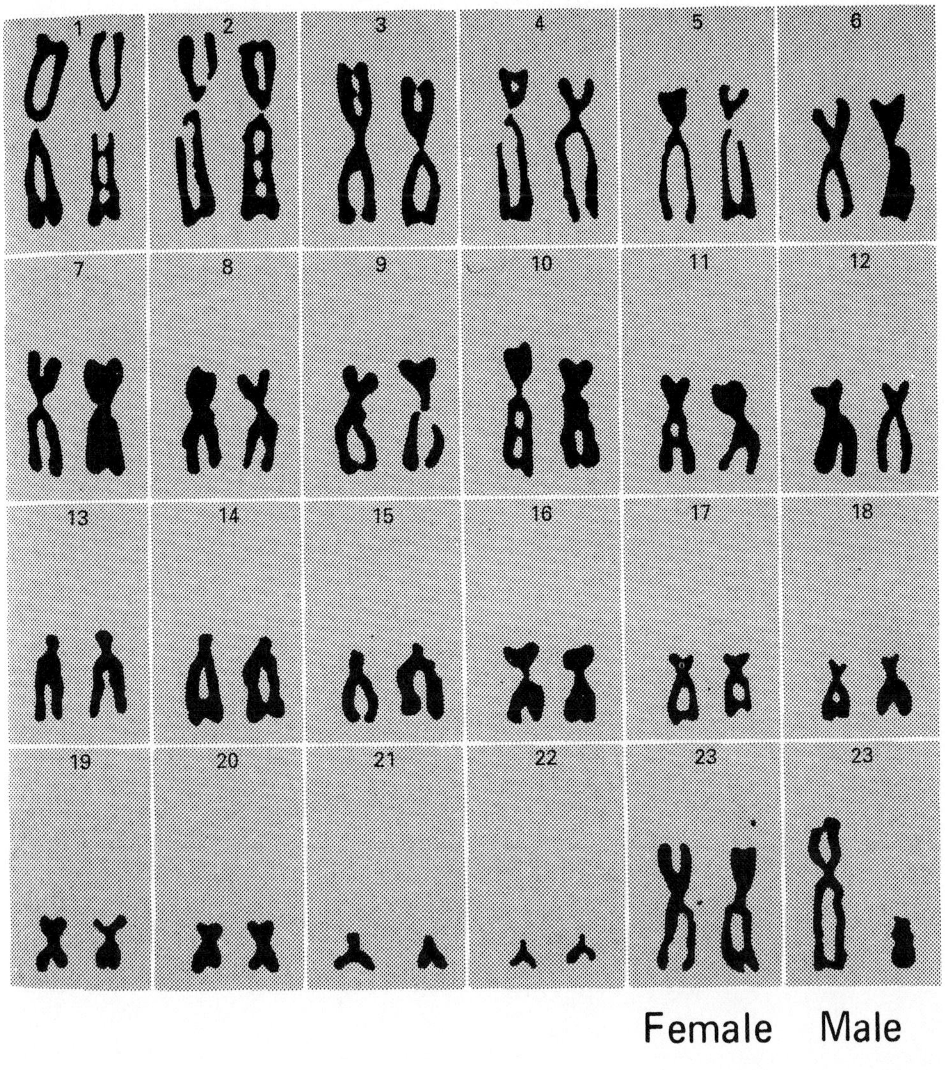

FIGURE 5–1
Human Chromosomes.

In this photomicrograph, the chromosomes are arranged to show matched pairs. Ordinarily they are randomly scattered within a cell. Note that two sets of the 23rd pair of chromosomes are included in order to show the contrast between the XX pair normally found in the female and the XY pair found in the male.

Female   Male

chromosomes, but in male cells the chromosomes in position 23 are mismatched: one is an X, the other a Y.

As you undoubtedly learned in history courses, over the centuries many queens lost their thrones—and sometimes their lives—because they failed to produce a male heir. But it is not the female who determines the sex of the child—it is the male. The female ovum always—and only—contains an X chromosome. The male sperm cell, however, may have either an X or a Y chromosome. If the X-carrying sperm penetrates the ovum, the offspring will be female; if the Y-carrying sperm does, the child will be male (see Figure 5–2). So it would appear that the nations over which these unhappy women ruled should have replaced their kings, not their queens.

There is speculation (Page et al., 1987) that it is only one gene, ordinarily found on the Y chromosome, that determines a person's sex. The testis-determining factor, or TDF, is associated with that gene. Supposedly, this gene launches a sequence of events that leads to male sexual development. If the gene that contains the TDF is absent, the person will be female.

Normal Prenatal Development

Although there are genetic differences between males and females from the moment of conception, there is no way to tell males and females apart for the first six weeks or so (see Figure 5–3). This is because the testes and ovaries—you'll recall from Chapter 3 that these sex glands are called the *gonads*—have not yet developed.

By approximately the eighth week of prenatal life, tissues begin forming that will differentiate the two sexes. The embryo's undifferentiated sex glands will develop into testes, if the embryo's 23rd chromosomal pair is an XY, or ovaries, if the pair is an XX. (The developing organism is referred to as an *embryo* for about the first eight weeks and thereafter as a *fetus*.) Once the sex glands develop, they begin to secrete hormones that direct both external (Figure 5–3) and internal (Figure 5–4) sexual differentiation.

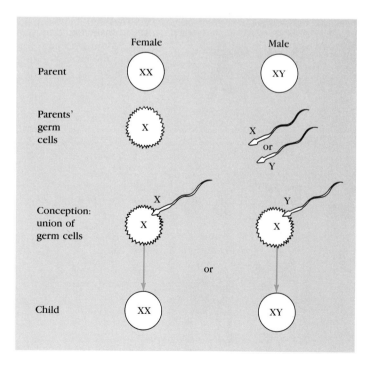

FIGURE 5–2
Determining the Sex of Offspring.

When a man and woman conceive a child together, the union of their germ cells produces either a girl (XX) or a boy (XY), depending on whether the sperm that succeeds in fertilizing the ovum carries an X or a Y chromosome.

Sex and Gender Issues

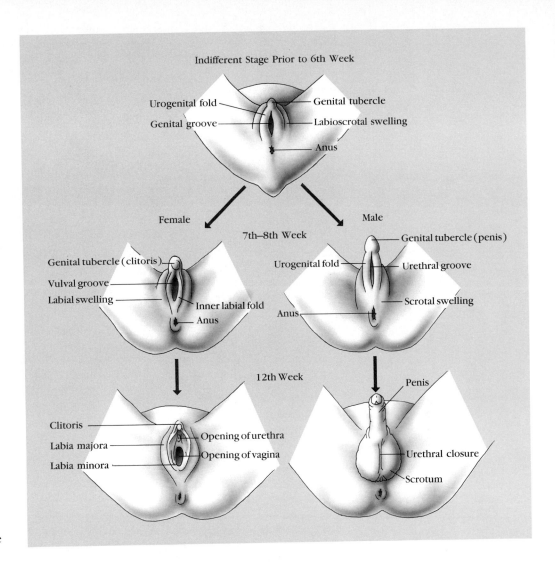

FIGURE 5–3

Prenatal development of the external genitals in females and males, from the undifferentiated to the fully developed stage.

Hormonal Influences

The development of female and male sex organs is quite a complex process. To understand it we must examine some specific developments during fetal life. At about eight weeks, two paired internal duct systems begin forming in both male and female embryos: the **Mullerian ducts,** the potential female structures of the fallopian tubes, uterus, and inner parts of the vagina; and the **Wolffian ducts,** the potential male structures of the epididymis, vas deferens, and seminal vesicles. In the case of male embryos, the testes begin secreting testosterone as well as a **Mullerian-inhibiting hormone (MIH),** a chemical that inhibits the further development of the Mullerian ducts. When this occurs, the Wolffian ducts begin developing into the epididymus, vas deferens, and seminal ducts, while the Mullerian ducts shrink and eventually degenerate. Thus it takes the presence and action of two hormones—testosterone and MIH—to begin the course of male development.

For females, a different scenario takes place. Hormones do not play a role in their sexual differentiation. The absence of testicular hormones causes the Wolffian ducts to degenerate, and the Mullerian ducts begin developing into the fallopian tubes, uterus, and inner parts of the vagina.

Mullerian ducts One of two paired internal duct systems in the embryo that develop into the fallopian tubes, uterus, and inner parts of the vagina in the female.

Wolffian ducts One of two paired internal duct systems in the embryo that develop into the epididymis, vas deferens, and seminal vesicles in the male.

Mullerian-inhibiting hormone (MIH) During prenatal life, a chemical secreted by the testes that inhibits the further development of the Mullerian ducts in the male embryo.

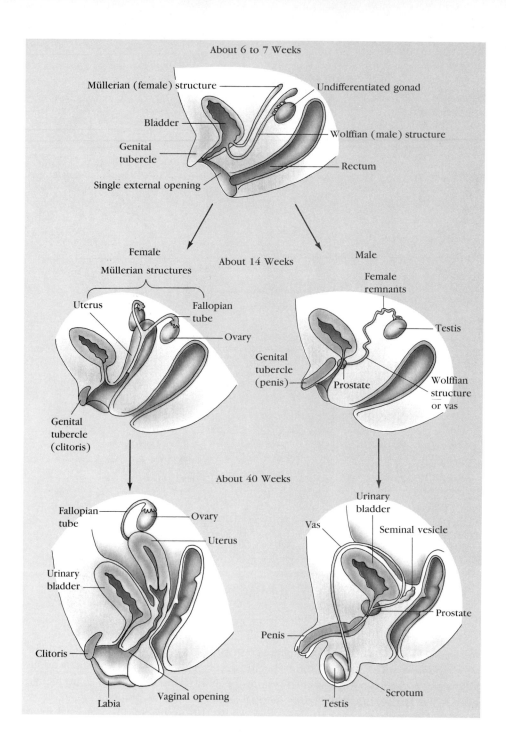

About 6 to 7 Weeks

Müllerian (female) structure

Bladder

Genital tubercle

Single external opening

Undifferentiated gonad

Wolffian (male) structure

Rectum

About 14 Weeks

Female

Müllerian structures

Uterus

Fallopian tube

Ovary

Genital tubercle (clitoris)

Male

Female remnants

Testis

Genital tubercle (penis)

Prostate

Wolffian structure or vas

About 40 Weeks

Fallopian tube

Ovary

Uterus

Urinary bladder

Clitoris

Labia

Vaginal opening

Urinary bladder

Vas

Seminal vesicle

Prostate

Penis

Scrotum

Testis

FIGURE 5–4

Prenatal sexual differentiation of the internal reproductive organs, from the undifferentiated state to fully developed male and female systems.

Fetal Brain Development

Do male and female brains differ?

At one time it was believed that there were no structural or functional differences between the brains of males and females. Little was known about the effects of hormones on brain development until research with lower animal species provided some fascinating insights into the matter (see, e.g., Nottebohm & Arnold, 1976; Young, 1961). For example, it appears that during prenatal development, when the male gonads of many mammals begin to manufacture testosterone, they secrete it directly into the blood so that it reaches the brain. According to Floyd Bloom and Arlyne Lazerson (1988), certain target cells in the brains of many animals are able to distinguish this hormone and to absorb it into their nuclei, where it regulates genetic mechanisms.

We have also learned that the number and location of nerve synapses (connections) in the hypothalamuses of human male and female brains are influenced by the presence or absence of circulating testosterone during fetal life. As you learned in the last chapter, the hypothalamus is a small structure in the limbic system that serves a number of important purposes, including the regulation of sex hormones released by the pituitary gland. The presence of testosterone in males during prenatal development appears to affect cells of the hypothalamus and to create, among other changes, an insensitivity to estrogen in the bloodstream. In females the absence of testosterone during fetal life promotes estrogen sensitivity. Eventually, female differentiation in the hypothalmus will enable sex hormones to coordinate the menstrual cycle, while male differentiation will orchestrate the manufacture of acyclic sex hormones (Levinthal, 1990; Kolb & Wishaw, 1988; Cowan, 1986).

Other differences due to the presence or absence of circulating testosterone have been found in the left and right cerebral hemispheres of female and male brains (Rubin, Reinisch, & Haskett, 1981). The brain is divided into left and right hemispheres that look very much alike but differ greatly in function. Researchers have identified the left hemisphere as the site of language ability, writing, and logical thought (as used in mathematics and science), among other specializations. The right hemisphere appears to control primarily nonverbal functions, such as imagination, the expression of emotion, and artistic and musical endeavors (Springer & Deutsch, 1985; Sperry, 1982).

For some time researchers have explored the question of whether demonstrated sex differences in certain skill areas reflect differences in brain structure or function. For example, women often have superior verbal skills, whereas men tend to have an advantage in visual-spatial reasoning. This has led to speculation that the cerebral hemispheres are organized differently in the sexes, with verbal and spatial functions more widely distributed in both hemispheres in females, and the male brain more specialized bilaterally. However, not all researchers agree with this line of thinking. Indeed, some even downplay the sex differences that exist in these skill areas (see, e.g., Kimball, 1989; Kalichman, 1989; Feingold, 1988).

Are there actual differences in human male and female brains? One study (Geschwind & Bahan, 1982) suggests that testosterone retards the growth of the left hemisphere in males but not in females. As a result, the researchers suggest, the right hemisphere is more developed in males. There is some support for this notion in the fact that left-handedness, which is associated with right-brain dominance, is much more common among males.

According to another study of male and female brains, a difference in the corpus callosum appears as early as the 26th week of prenatal life (Lacoste-Utamsing & Holloway, 1982). In women, these investigators claim, a portion of this band of nerve fibers is much wider and larger. Some writers have speculated that this greater size permits more interhemispheric communication in women (see, e.g., Bloom & Lazerson, 1988). Figure 5–5 shows the location of the corpus callosum and its relation to the two brain hemispheres.

To sum up, there seems to be a fair amount of evidence that during fetal development circulatory hormones create sex differences in certain parts of the brain. However, we don't know what the impact of such differences may be on later behavior. As yet, we have no clear evidence of a correlation between sex differences in the brain and differences in the ways men and women behave. Probably physiological factors and psychosocial forces combine to create these differences in behavior. John Money (1987a) suggests that in all likelihood overall behavior is shaped by a convergence of biological, psychological, and environmental forces. This interactionist point of view emphasizes that although biological differences separate the two sexes,

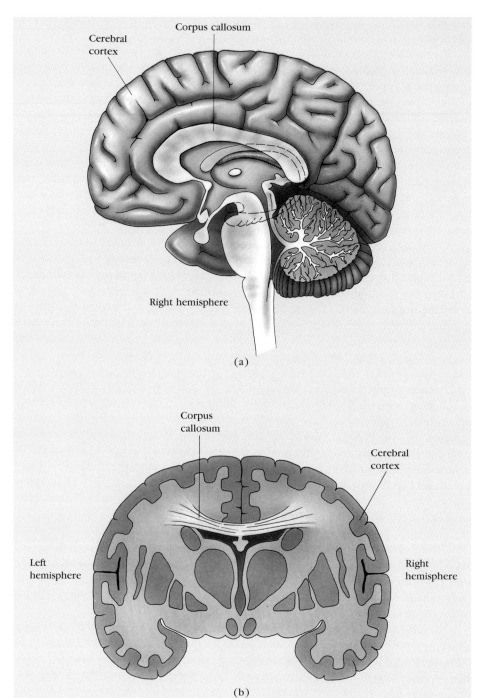

FIGURE 5–5
The Cerebral Hemispheres and the Corpus Callosum.

(a) The right hemisphere of the brain, showing the central position of the corpus callosum. (b) A cross-section, showing how the corpus callosum connects the right and left hemispheres.

society and culture are also influential in molding one's sense of masculinity and femininity (see also Jacklin, 1989; Maccoby, 1987; Cargan, 1985).

Abnormal Prenatal Development

Sometimes the union of the female egg and the male sperm does not result in the normal complement of 46 chromosomes. When the chromosomal makeup of the sex cell is not the ordinary XX or XY, various forms of abnormal sexual development result. We will look at some of the more common of these chromosomal abnor-

Sex and Gender Issues

malities—the Turner, triple X, Klinefelter, and XYY syndromes—as well as at the condition of hermaphroditism, which results from a hormonal error.

TURNER SYNDROME. Turner syndrome is a genetic disorder in which females are missing an X chromosome, making them XO instead of XX. It is a relatively rare disorder, occurring in approximately one out of every 2500 live female births. Girls born with this syndrome appear normal at birth, but signs of the disorder appear at puberty, when they fail to develop breasts. They do not menstruate because their ovaries develop incompletely or not at all, and other internal organs of reproduction do not develop normally. Turner's syndrome women are therefore sterile. Nonetheless, researchers like John Money and Anke Ehrhardt (1972) have found that the interests and behavior of Turner's syndrome women are not distinguishable from those of biologically normal women.

TRIPLE X SYNDROME. The **triple X syndrome** is a genetic disorder in which females have an extra X chromosome, making them XXX instead of XX. Women with this disorder are physically normal except for menstrual irregularities and premature menopause. Among these women, however, mental retardation is common. Moreover, some women have three, four, and five X chromosomes in the 23rd location, and usually the more X chromosomes, the greater the level of retardation.

KLINEFELTER SYNDROME. Klinefelter syndrome is a genetic disorder in which males have an extra X chromosome, making them XXY instead of XY. This syndrome occurs in about one in every 3000 live male births. Men with Klinefelter syndrome have small external male sex organs but the general body contour of a woman, including enlarged breasts. They are also sterile and often below average in intelligence. Research conducted by John Money also shows that these men tend to have low sex drives or to lack interest in sex altogether.

XYY SYNDROME. The **XYY syndrome** is a genetic disorder in which males have an extra Y chromosome. The XYY syndrome came to the attention of the general public in the 1970s, when Richard Speck brutally murdered eight women in Chicago. Physicians and others associated with the case revealed that Speck had this syndrome, and it was speculated that the extra Y chromosome produced an aggressive, violent streak in men. However, subsequent research (e.g., Witkin et al., 1976) has found that XYY men are no more likely to commit crimes than XY men are. However, XYY individuals do tend to be tall, have below average intelligence, and suffer from severe acne.

HERMAPHRODITISM. Hormonal errors can affect the course of sexual development. For example, **hermaphroditism** is a condition in which a person has both ovarian and testicular tissue, and thus has genital features of both sexes. The word *hermaphroditism* comes from the Greek mythical character Hermaphroditus, the son of the gods Hermes and Aphrodite who became joined in one body with a nymph while bathing. The condition is thought to result from faulty sexual differentiation during the early phases of prenatal development, with the result that both ovaries and testes develop independently within the same person.

There are two subdivisions of hermaphroditism: true hermaphroditism and pseudo-hermaphroditism. Both conditions are rare, but pseudo-hermaphroditism occurs more frequently than true hermaphroditism (Imperato-McGinley, 1985). **True hermaphroditism** refers to the possession of characteristics of the sexual anatomy of both sexes. The person is typically a genetic female (XX), but has external genitals that appear male or female or that combine characteristics of both sexes. For example, a true hermaphrodite may have one ovary and one testis, and a vaginal opening may be evident beneath the penis.

Turner syndrome A genetic disorder in which females are missing an X chromosome, making them XO instead of XX.

triple X syndrome A genetic disorder in which females have an extra X chromosome, making them XXX instead of XX.

Klinefelter syndrome A genetic disorder in which males have an extra X chromosome, making them XXY instead of XY.

XYY syndrome A genetic disorder in which males have an extra Y chromosome.

hermaphroditism A condition in which a person has both ovarian and testicular tissue, and thus genital features of both sexes. See *true hermaphroditism* and *pseudo-hermaphroditism*.

true hermaphroditism The possession of characteristics of the sexual anatomy of both sexes.

pseudo-hermaphroditism
A condition that occurs when the person has either ovaries or testes (not both), but external genitals that are characteristic of the opposite sex.

Pseudo-hermaphroditism occurs when the person has either ovaries or testes (not both), but the external genitals are characteristic of the opposite sex. Thus a female pseudo-hermaphrodite will have female sex chromosomes (XX), a uterus, fallopian tubes, and ovaries, but external male genitals. Conversely, a male pseudo-hermaphrodite possesses male sex chromosomes (XY), testes, and other male structures, but external female genitals. Pseudo-hermaphroditism seems to be an inherited disorder caused by androgen imbalances. In female pseudo-hermaphroditism excessive amounts of androgen are created during fetal life (a condition known as *adrenogenital syndrome*), which interfere with the course of early sex differentiation. In male pseudo-hermaphroditism testosterone and other androgens appear to have no effect on body tissues responsible for sex differentiation (a condition called *testicular feminization syndrome*).

The medical management of female hermaphroditism, which is begun in early childhood, usually entails plastic surgery to correct the appearance of the genitals and hormonal therapy. The latter often includes synthetic cortisone to counteract the effects of androgen and female hormones to promote breast development. Given such treatment, these individuals usually experience normal biological development and become reproductively functional females. Male hermaphroditism, on the other hand, is usually not diagnosed until midadolescence, at which time the lack of menstrual periods is noted (menstruation is not possible because of the lack of a uterus). Sometimes surgery is undertaken to remove the testes and increase the depth of the vagina. Because most male hermaphrodites have been brought up as girls, they have female gender identities.

SOCIALIZATION AND GENDER-ROLE DEVELOPMENT

Some writers argue that society is much more influential than biology in creating sex differences. The gender roles promoted by society confront us daily. In some situations, such as dating, one's sex is highly relevant to the interaction. In most situations

Socialization experiences in school are among the most important in the shaping of gender role behavior.

130

in life, however, our sex is essentially irrelevant to what we are doing—for example, being a student, a mechanic, or a checkout clerk in a supermarket. Yet others react to us as a male or female student, mechanic, or checkout clerk, and we ourselves fulfill such specific roles within the broader context of our gender roles. Thus we never stop being masculine or feminine, even when we are doing something that in and of itself is neither masculine nor feminine (Henslin, 1985).

The course of gender-role development is shaped by one's culture. Our culture is competitive, hierarchical, and achievement-oriented and measures success in terms of power, prestige, and the accumulation of material wealth. Conventional masculinity embraces such qualities as independence, competitiveness, aggression, leadership, confidence, and self-control. Conventional femininity, on the other hand, emphasizes dependency, passivity, nonaggression, sensitivity, nurturance, and noncompetitiveness. One woman vividly remembers how she was taught to behave:

> **I was brought up in a very traditional home setting. As a child, I can remember always hearing about how "good" girls behaved or acted. My mother would constantly remind me about staying neat and tidy, and how important it was to always be compliant. I couldn't climb trees and dirty clothes were always frowned upon. In time, I "graduated" to other traditional expectations: avoiding competition, letting men be the decision makers, and placing my needs secondary to those around me. Even at an early age this bothered me, but I put on this front of acceptance and passivity. (Authors' files)**

A man shares how being dominant, competitive, and emotionally detached became part of his personality:

> **My father always told me that a successful man was always in control, always striving to reach the top. He made it a point to emphasize com-**

"No, Mr. Kurlander, I don't have, nor have I ever had, a recipe for cranberry muffins."

Sex and Gender Issues   131

petition and how I would have to compete with other men to prove my worth. Even as a kid playing sports, he drilled into me the importance of finishing first and never letting up on an opponent. He felt that emotions always got in the way and therefore encouraged me to develop this tough outer shell. Whenever I showed the "wrong" emotions, like crying, he would get angry with me and call me a "sissy" or "wimp." (Authors' files)

Note, however, that ideas about gender roles differ from society to society. Consider Margaret Mead's (1950) observations of three primitive New Guinea tribes. She reported that among the Arapesh both men and women behaved in what our culture would call a feminine fashion. In the Mundugumer tribe both women and men possessed such "masculine" traits as assertiveness and competitiveness. And among the Tchambuli, women were independent, dominant, and managerial, whereas men were emotional, submissive, and dependent. Research like this underlines the point we want to make in this chapter: *People are born with a sexual identity, but gender identity and gender role are more apt to be a function of their society and culture.*

Theories of Gender-Role Development

How do we acquire gender roles? Is gender-role learning an active or a passive process? What forces shape gender-appropriate behaviors? A number of different theoretical approaches to the study of these and other questions have been proposed. We will review four of these approaches: cognitive-developmental, behavioral, social-learning, and identification theories.

cognitive-developmental theory of gender-role development A theory proposing that gender-role development emerges through children's growing cognitive awareness of their identity.

COGNITIVE-DEVELOPMENTAL THEORY. Cognitive-developmental theory suggests that gender roles emerge through children's growing cognitive awareness of their sexual identity. Once youngsters are able to consistently conceive of themselves as male or female, they realize that specific roles, activities, and behaviors are gender-appropriate and organize their world on the basis of gender. Thus a young boy decides, "I am a boy; I like to do the things boys do; the chance to do these things is rewarding."

Cognitive-developmental theory emphasizes that children are active rather than passive forces in their own gender-role formation and that the reinforcement for imitating sex-typed behaviors originates from *within* children rather than from external socializers such as parents or siblings. Thus, rather than simply imitating behavior, the child reasons first and then imitates. Cognitive-developmental theory fails to address several important issues. For example, if gender identity is linked to the cognitive development of the youngster, why do children acquire gender identity at the surprisingly early age of three? For that matter, it does not tell us why children aged one to two years, who have not acquired gender identity, nonetheless display sex-typed play activities (Etaugh, Collins, & Gerson, 1975).

behavioral theory of gender-role development A theory proposing that gender-role behaviors are conditioned by the environment.

BEHAVIORAL THEORY. Behavioral theory proposes that gender-role behaviors are conditioned by the environment through the mechanisms of reinforcement and punishment (reinforcement serves to strengthen a desired response, while punishment serves to weaken an undesirable response). Children typically receive parental rewards for behaviors consistent with their gender role and punishment for behaviors contrary to it. To illustrate, a young girl rewarded (e.g., given praise or approval) for her involvement in stereotypically feminine activities (washing the dishes, cleaning the house) is likely to repeat such behavior in the future. A young boy who is punished, ridiculed, or scolded for engaging in feminine activities ("that's a sissy game") or being overly sensitive ("big boys don't cry") will be unlikely to repeat such behaviors in the future.

In contrast to cognitive-developmental theory, which emphasizes children's active construction and regulation of their gender development, behavioral theory views children as passive beings who are shaped and molded by environmental influences. Proponents of behavioral theory maintain that children are exposed to an unending flow of environmental situations in the home, neighborhood, school, and media that ultimately condition their behavior. Critics counter that behavioral theory oversimplifies human behavior and downplays the free will of the child. Indeed, critics argue that gender development is more active than this theory suggests and entails considerably more cognitive involvement.

SOCIAL LEARNING THEORY. The **social learning theory** of gender-role development, like behavioral theory, suggests that individuals are shaped by their environment. However, this approach emphasizes the way boys and girls specifically imitate the gender-typed behaviors they observe. Some of the models children use are their parents, peers, and teachers, and the people they see on television. Thus when a boy sees TV actors or men in real life handling mechanical repairs around the house, he learns that such chores are appropriate for him to engage in. Traditional social learning theorists argue that such observational learning need not involve tangible reinforcements because observation and imitation are intrinsically gratifying.

> **social learning theory of gender-role development**
> A theory suggesting that gender roles are learned through imitation of sex-typed behaviors.

Social learning theory has been criticized for failing to clearly address the cognitive aspects of imitation processes. In recent years a revised social learning theory has proposed that people are shaped by a blend of internal cognitive states and social behavior, but the revision, too, has been criticized for not paying enough attention to cognition.

IDENTIFICATION THEORY. **Identification theory** proposes that a child develops a gender role by interacting closely with the parent of the same sex and imitating that parent's behavior. Proposed by Sigmund Freud, this theory holds that a boy assumes his father's sex-typed behaviors because of the Oedipus complex, or the boy's romantic attachment to his mother (see Chapter 13). Since he perceives that his father's attributes are what captured the love of his mother, the boy decides to emulate those attributes. For girls, the Electra complex creates a similar situation: the daughter becomes romantically attached to her father and imitates her mother's behaviors because she thinks those are what won her father's love. Freud did offer one perspective on identification beyond the Oedipus and Electra complexes—that children develop strong emotional attachment to and dependence on nurturant parents and the closeness offered by such parents leads to childhood identification and emulation.

> **identification theory of gender-role development**
> A psychoanalytic theory that suggests a child develops a gender role by interacting closely with and emulating the behavior of the parent of the same sex.

Unlike the previous frameworks, identification theory proposes that imitation is largely an unconscious effort, that children are not aware of taking on the characteristics they see in others. Today few human sexuality researchers believe that identification theory based on childhood sexual attraction adequately explains the course of gender development. However, we offer it here as food for thought (other Freudian viewpoints appear in Chapters 2, 9, and 13) and encourage you to compare and contrast it with the book's other theoretical perspectives.

The Development of Gender-Role Behaviors

Now that we have explored some of the major theories of gender-role development, let's focus on specific socialization agents responsible for shaping gender-role behaviors. Gender-role development has its beginnings early in life and originates from a variety of different sources. Among the more influential sources are parents, play activities, peers, teachers and schools, and the media.

PARENTS.   Parents exert a significant influence on a child's gender-role development. If they hold traditional or stereotyped views of gender roles, they will teach girls to be affectionate, gentle, and quiet and boys to be aggressive, independent, and active. In time a boy will be taught that holding a job and supporting a wife and children will be his primary adult tasks, and girls will be trained to handle most of the responsibilities associated with child rearing and maintaining a home for their husbands and children.

Today, however, many parents are attempting to ensure that both girls and boys have the same professional opportunities and that they learn to share the responsibilities of family life. Such liberated households are still in the minority, however, for as we learned in Chapter 1, traditional gender roles are rooted in antiquity. And those parents who are not aware of holding differential attitudes succeed in teaching many sex-typed standards through their own behaviors. Thus traditional mothers are usually more nurturant and emotional, while traditional fathers are generally more dominant, competitive, and unemotional (Lewis, 1987; Plomin & Foch, 1981, Honig, 1983; Scanzoni & Fox, 1980). Again, enlightened mothers and fathers tend to exhibit a mixture of these behaviors.

The way parents talk to their children when the children are interacting with their peers may promote particular gender-role behaviors. For example, Barry McLaughlin and his colleagues (1983) recorded the speech of parents as they interacted with their children during free-play situations. Mothers tended to provide more linguistic support for their children, tuning their language to the youngster's needs. Fathers put more demands on their children during the play situations, raising their performance levels. In another study (Bright & Stickdale, 1984) fathers were found to make more demands and exercise more control over their children in structured play sessions as well. Again, mothers played a less active and demanding role. These findings show that mothers and fathers supply sex-typed verbal reinforcement to their children.

Interestingly, fathers seem to be more concerned than mothers about transmitting traditional gender-role behaviors to their offspring. Moreover, fathers usually take active steps to discourage cross-sex behavior in their children, especially in their sons (Richardson, 1988; Langlois & Down, 1980; Zuckerman & Sayre, 1982). Why do you suppose many men behave this way? Is it because they are afraid of losing their dominant role in society, not realizing that sharing power would relieve them of some of the burden of responsibility? Or are they more aware than women of the strong social disapproval that awaits a male who displays "feminine" qualities? Or do some men (and women) sincerely believe that a sex-based division of labor is necessary to a healthy society? What do you think?

PLAY ACTIVITIES.   Stereotypes abound in children's play. Girls are often given dolls, and are encouraged to play house. Boys are given guns and trucks, and are taught to play aggressive games and to avoid "sissy" play activities. Research has shown that by the preschool years children prefer toys that are stereotypically appropriate for their gender (see Lawson, 1989; O'Brien & Huston, 1985). Jill Bardwell and her colleagues (1986) found that even kindergartners can label chores and tasks as more appropriate for either a boy or a girl.

In general, girls' play behavior is more dependent (that is, girls tend to rely on playmates), quieter, and less exploratory (Richardson, 1988). Boys often play with toys that require more gross motor activity, and are more vigorous and independent. Parents frequently support and reinforce such sex-typed play behavior in both sexes (Zheng & Colombo, 1989; DiPietro, 1981; Fagot & Kronsberg, 1982; Muller & Goldberg, 1980).

Again, it is fathers who take the lead in selecting sex-appropriate toys and play behaviors (Huston, 1983). Further pressure to engage in sex-typed play is exerted by the peer group, an increasingly important source of social approval and reinforcement

Girls' competitive sports teams are increasingly common today.

Sex and Gender Issues

as children grow older (Howes, 1988; Pitcher & Schultz, 1983; Maccoby, 1980; Langlois & Down, 1980; Lamb, Easterbrooks, & Holden, 1980).

In what is perhaps evidence of social learning, boys seem to be more aware of sex differences than girls. They avoid playing with objects that might be labeled feminine or "sissy," whereas girls seem to be willing to engage in traditionally male activities. Although both sexes congregate in sex-typed play groups, boys seem to hold more rigid stereotyped beliefs than girls (Richardson, 1988; DiPietro, 1981; Fagot & Kronsberg, 1982). Why do you think this is so? Are girls more secure in their gender identity and therefore more willing to be flexible in their behavior? Do you suppose this has always been so? Or might it reflect a new kind of socialization born out of the feminist revolution? Will such behaviors persist throughout the life cycle?

Today there is some evidence that the traditional view of "masculine" and "feminine" forms of play is changing, though so far the changes are mostly a one-way street. That is, girls are now permitted to enjoy types of play once considered "masculine," such as track and field competition and other organized sports, but boys are still often discouraged from engaging in traditional feminine play activities, such as imaginative story-acting and free-form physical play. Perhaps this is because the traditionally masculine activities are more highly valued in our society simply because they have always been masculine, and in an age of nominal egalitarianism girls are being allowed to "graduate up" to these more prestigious types of play. Still, far fewer activities are banned for either sex today than just a generation ago, and it is our hope that before long an activity considered appropriate for one sex will be considered appropriate for the other, and that girls and boys will be equally rewarded for their accomplishments.

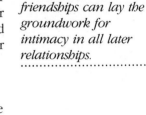

Close same-sex friendships can lay the groundwork for intimacy in all later relationships.

PEERS. As children become more socialized, they learn more about gender-role standards and behaviors from their peer group. And the child who chooses to flout these standards risks peer group rejection. The reinforcement of gender-appropriate behaviors within the peer group also helps to explain the early sex-typed differences apparent in children's play (Howes, 1988; Hayden-Thomson, Rubin, & Hymel, 1987; Lamb, Easterbrooks, & Holden, 1980; Harris & Satter, 1981; Reis & Wright, 1982).

It is during the preschool years that children start to prefer same-sex peer groups and to choose same-sex "best friends." This tendency persists and intensifies throughout the years of middle childhood, although it is more pronounced in boys than in girls (Berndt & Ladd, 1989; Fu & Leach, 1980; Reis & Wright, 1982). Often same-sex play groups openly torment one another, strengthening gender boundaries. As Evelyn Pitcher and Lynn Schultz (1983) observe, when boys taunt and tease girls, they are practicing for future catcalls and whistles.

Although in adolescence the sexes begin to intermingle, sex differences persist, particularly in regard to friendships. The most striking of these differences is the emotional intimacy of female friendships. Adolescent girls tend to have more intimate and exclusive friendships than boys, a trend that will persist throughout adulthood. Moreover, the closer the friendship, the more self-disclosure it will entail. This is often true in female-male friendships as well. Adolescent boys, on the other hand, tend to downplay self-disclosure and emotional closeness in a relationship, preferring to emphasize such things as engaging in common activities (Parker & Gottman, 1989; Kelly & de Armas, 1989; O'Brien & Bierman, 1988; Maccorquodale, 1989; Reis, 1986; Berndt, 1982; Wheeler, Reis, & Nezlek, 1983). The "World of Differences" box suggests that children and adolescents from other nations exhibit similar gender differences in their relationships.

It is our view that boys should be encouraged from an early age to form close same-sex relationships. We believe that this would make it easier for them to develop intimate relationships with women and men in adulthood. Communication between the sexes would improve, making sexual relationships more rewarding and fulfilling.

A WORLD OF
DIFFERENCES

Gender
Differences
in Children's
Friendships

Do children's friendships in other countries show the same dynamics as American children's friendships? Ann Tietjen's (1982) study of Swedish children contains some interesting answers to this question. Tietjen interviewed and observed 72 second- and third-graders and found that boys had larger groups of friends than girls, but girls spent more time in close-knit friendship dyads and with their families. As children grew older, there was a movement toward fewer and more intense friendships, although, as in the United States, this was more true for girls. Both boys and girls also began to pull away from family members as they grew older. This desire to spend more time away from the family also parallels the social dynamics of American children. Another finding was that children in homes where the father was absent had more limited peer networks than youngsters from intact families and also spent less time with their families.

Ruth Sharabany and her associates (1981) explored the nature of Israeli children's friendships. In this research, which studied boys and girls in the fifth, seventh, ninth, and eleventh grades, children were asked to rate their friendships with a same- or opposite-sex best friend. The researchers found that there was a significant age difference in overall intimacy with same-sex friends. Frankness and spontaneity, knowing and sensitivity, attachment, exclusiveness, and giving and sharing were factors that changed with age; while trust and loyalty, and taking and imposing, did not. Opposite-sex friendships increased significantly with age. Boys and girls did not differ in their reported opposite-sex friendships in the fifth and seventh grades, but in the ninth and eleventh grades girls reported higher intimacy than boys did. Like American girls, Israeli girls were higher than boys in sensitivity, giving, and sharing.

Thus we believe that parents have an obligation to teach children of both sexes about intimate emotional friendships.

A middle aged man describes the kinds of friendships he remembers as a boy:

In our neighborhood we had the original "rat pack." Four or five of us would do everything together. We were really close-knit. From dawn to dusk we were always hanging out, particularly during the summer months. Most of the time we centered our interests on a common activity, like stickball, other times we would just hang out together. One of my fondest memories about growing up is that I was always with my friends, always doing something. (Authors' files)

But not all male relationships have been of the "rat pack" variety. Listen to another man speak:

One of life's greatest treasures is having a best friend, and I consider myself a lucky person to have one. My best friend and I have known each other for 12 years. We've shared just about everything, and I feel that I know him better than anyone. I know that he feels the same way about me. When we're together, we always enjoy each other's company and there are never any facades. (Authors' files)

This woman emphasizes the importance of intimacy in her female friendships:

I have a number of close female friendships and regard them to be an important part of my life. I need to share myself with others and have learned to value honesty and sincerity in close relationships. I would be lost without my friends, particularly the intimacy we share. (Authors' files)

Another woman stresses the value of a long, deep friendship:

I have known my best friend since childhood. We were inseparable growing up and stayed that way throughout our school days. We shared everything, and I can remember telling her things that no one else in the world knew about. We helped each other out during difficult times, and shared incredible happiness. As kids we forged a special bond, one that still exists today. (Authors' files)

A number of researchers have investigated self-disclosure within friendships. In one study (Grigsby & Weatherley, 1983) adolescent girls and boys were led to believe that they were sharing self-disclosures with a stranger of the same sex whom they would later meet. Their recorded comments revealed clear-cut gender differences in the tendency to self-disclose: the girls were much more likely to reveal intimate information about themselves during the acquaintanceship process. In another study (Blythe & Foster-Clark, 1987) adolescent girls were also shown to engage in greater degrees of intimacy than adolescent boys. Interestingly, while the girls in this study reported that they were most intimate with a same-sex friend, the boys said they were more intimate with their parents than with same-sex friends.

Sharon Brehm (1985) maintains that despite these demonstrated differences in self-disclosure, the sexes are more alike than not in their desire for intimacy. She claims that *both* men and women need warm relationships and self-disclosure in order to avoid loneliness, but traditional gender-role learning makes it difficult for men to achieve such emotional intimacy.

There are other notable differences between female and male friendships. For example, Thomas Berndt (1982) observes that girls and women *expect* to share thoughts and feelings with their friends more than boys and men do, and perhaps as a result are also more sensitive about rejection. Carol Gilligan (1982) adds that girls and women are also more selective and exclusive about their friendships, maybe because they are more apt to invest emotional resources and to offer strong psychological commitment to a friend. Boys' and men's commitment to a friendship is generally not as great and is often more objective and rational than emotional (see Reis & Shaver, 1988; Snell et al., 1988; Reis, Senchak, & Solomon, 1985; Burda, Vaux, & Schill, 1984; Wheeler, Reis, & Nezlek, 1983; Petty & Mirels, 1981; Hacker, 1981).

As you might have guessed by now, there are also gender differences in communication styles, something we'll explore later in this chapter as well as in Chapter 7. For the moment, consider just one aspect of communication: listening. One study (Booth-Gutterfield, 1984) has suggested that as boys and girls grow up, they are taught and reinforced in different styles of listening. In general, according to this research, boys are taught to listen for facts and girls to listen for the mood of the communication. As a result, men often have trouble picking up nonverbal cues, whereas women are quite good at picking them up. In a related vein, research also indicates that women are more questioning in their conversation style and employ more qualifiers and intensifiers than men (e.g., Kohn, 1988). They use such words and phrases as "perhaps," "quite," "you know," and "it seems to me" to serve as hints to the listener as to how to react.

TEACHERS AND SCHOOLS. Teachers are highly significant in the lives of youngsters and their behaviors and attitudes are very influential. Some teachers deliberately, others unwittingly, contribute to gender-role stereotypes (Sadker & Sadker, 1986; Sadker, Sadker, & Klein, 1986). For instance, some teachers tend to ask girls to water the plants and boys to empty the wastebaskets. Others reward girls only when they are passive, well-behaved, and well-mannered, but reinforce boys for being assertive and asking questions (Morrison, 1988; Eccles & Midgley, 1990).

As boys and girls progress through school, teachers and the educational system exert other influences. Some teachers perpetuate stereotypes by advising students that certain professions are appropriate for women and not for men, and vice versa. Often a school's curriculum stamps a course as masculine or feminine by requiring girls to take, say home economics and boys to take automobile mechanics. Fortunately, many schools in this country are now recommending that all students enroll in a mixture of such courses (Klein, 1988; Ryan & Cooper, 1980).

According to Lucille Lindberg and Rita Swedlow (1985), it is important that from earliest schooling to the end of formal education children and adolescents receive instruction in an objective and sexually unbiased fashion. To reach such a goal, teacher behaviors must be carefully examined and the curriculum objectively assessed, and school districts need to take an active role in training or retraining teachers. And since school boards are locally run and are often composed of parents, it is up to parents to take the lead in this area.

CHILDREN'S LITERATURE. Children's literature also transmits gender-role behaviors early in life. Stereotyping is quite evident within the pages of children's books: girls are often portrayed as passive and domestic, boys as active and adventurous. Boys also outnumber girls in many stories, and careers are often cast in exclusively masculine or feminine terms. Evelyn Pitcher and her colleagues (1984) note that all too often books portray "ferocious" daddy tigers and "gentle" mommy pussycats, and that books about cars, trucks, and trains show only men at the wheels.

Today, efforts are being made to eliminate gender stereotyping from children's books. Books that have sexist themes are being identified and revised. For example, women are being portrayed as confident and independent and as working in occupations traditionally reserved for males. Placing women in business, industry, and other male-dominated areas of life helps to destroy female stereotypes. Male stereotypes are also being reexamined. Instead of always portraying boys as cool, competent, and fearless, more books are making an effort to show that boys can be sensitive, loving, emotional—even scared sometimes. Some stories have male protagonists who go against the stereotype of the ever-competent "superior" male, but who are nonetheless secure in themselves and unashamed of their emotions (Williams et al., 1987).

One hard problem in this area is that many classic works of children's literature do reinforce gender stereotypes. Few people would suggest either rewriting the classics or discarding them. But parents and teachers can use some of the old stories to explain to children how gender roles have changed. And, of course, some of the greatest children's books such as *Alice in Wonderland* and *Huckleberry Finn* feature intelligent, adventurous girls and morally sensitive boys.

There are indications that nonsexist literature can change children's stereotyped images of the sexes. However, because sexist attitudes are woven through the whole fabric of society, we can hardly expect that books alone will produce children who are unbiased and independent in their attitudes.

THE MEDIA. Gender-role stereotyping is particularly devastating in television and the other modern media. Men are usually the leaders, while women characters are often passive, submissive, and defenseless (Condry, 1989). Also, actors generally outnumber actresses on TV (Huston & Alvarez, 1990). In fact, many popular programs lack a regular female character. The same male-female imbalances are evident in television commercials (Wroblewski & Huston, 1987; Durkin, 1985; Downs, 1981; Feldstein & Feldstein, 1982; Williams, LaRose, & Frost, 1981).

One study (Stewart, 1983) that examined 551 major speaking characters in 191 programs found that males clearly outnumbered females in all program types. When family themes were portrayed, most men were employed in white-collar jobs, while women were typically full-time homemakers. In an investigation of how older persons are portrayed on television (Cassata, Anderson, & Skill, 1983), men were found to outnumber women in professional or managerial positions by a ratio of four to one. *All* the homemaker, service, and clerical positions were held by women characters.

Television producers have attempted to change this picture in recent years, and today there are more programs featuring women protagonists. Commercials have also gotten more egalitarian: one study (Bretl & Cantrol, 1988) revealed that men and women appeared equally often as the leading characters in prime-time commercials. Still, about 90 percent of all narrators of commercials were men.

One study showed that even very young children understand the gender-role stereotypes portrayed in television programming (Durkin, 1984). When 17 children 4½ and 9½ years old were interviewed individually and asked to discuss a series of highly stereotyped male and female behaviors shown on television, the children displayed considerable knowledge of gender-role conventions and were able to relate this to their accounts of the televised excerpts. That is, they could infer appropriate feelings and motives and offer plausible accounts of portrayed stereotypes by using their existent gender-role knowledge.

Research also shows that popular music portrays men and women in predictable ways. This was evident in a study (Hyden & McCandless, 1983) that focused on how men and women were portrayed in the lyrics of 110 popular songs. Overall, 72 (68 percent) of the songs were sung by men and only 27 (26 percent) were sung by women. Interestingly, although men were pictured as possessing both masculine and feminine characteristics in these songs, women largely conformed to traditional feminine attributes. Thus while men as well as women could be loving, faithful, and gentle in song, only women were celebrated as young, childlike, and passive. It seems that although song lyrics break down some gender-role stereotypes, they promote others.

A Gender-Identity Disorder: Transsexualism

We have seen that children develop a gender identity at an early age. Gender identity is primarily a psychological process that results in awareness of oneself as either male or female. All the socialization factors we have discussed help to shape gender roles consistent with gender identity. Thus while gender identity is the sense of knowing which sex one belongs to, gender roles are the public expression of this psychological awareness.

Sometimes something goes wrong in the formation of gender identity. In a **gender-identity disorder** there is an incongruence between one's sex and one's gender identity. Usually the disorder is mild and people simply feel some discomfort with their sexual identity. In more severe cases, people firmly believe that they really belong to the other sex. In **transsexualism,** a severe gender-identity disorder, there is a persistent discomfort and a strong sense of inappropriateness about one's sexual identity. In general, the problem does not become acute until these people reach puberty. Eventually, they become preoccupied with getting rid of their primary and secondary sex characteristics and acquiring the sex characteristics of the other sex. Transsexuals invariably want to live as a member of the other sex. They typically complain that they are uncomfortable wearing the clothes suited to their sexual identity and consequently dress in clothes of the other sex (American Psychiatric Association, 1987). This is referred to as *cross-dressing*.

In a variation of transsexualism known as **nontranssexual gender-identity disorder,** people feel discomfort about their sexual identity and cross-dress (American Psychiatric Association, 1987). However, they have no urge to acquire the sex

gender-identity disorder A disorder characterized by an incongruence between one's sexual identity and one's gender identity.

transsexualism A severe gender-identity disorder in which people experience persistent discomfort and a sense of inappropriateness about their sexual identity and often seek sex reassignment surgery.

nontranssexual gender-identity disorder A disorder in which people feel some discomfort about their sexual identity and cross-dress but do not feel compelled to alter their physical sex.

Doris Richards (top) taught high school physical education in Emeryville, California, where students named her teacher of the year. When Richards changed her gender identity to become Steve Dain (bottom), the teaching position melted away. After working for a while in construction, Dain enrolled at San Francisco's Institute for Advanced Study of Human Sexuality to prepare for a new career as a counselor and researcher in the field of gender identity.

sex reassignment surgery Surgery that alters the genitals and sometimes the secondary sex characteristics in order to conform to a person's felt, though not actual, sexual identity.

characteristics of the other sex. This disorder also differs from transvestism, which we will discuss in Chapter 19, because cross-dressing is not done for the purpose of sexual excitement.

Transsexualism is quite rare in both sexes, but even rarer among women. The causes of transsexualism are obscure (Lothstein, 1984). Hormonal imbalances do not appear to play a role, and the impact of psychosocial influences remains uncertain (e.g, Hoenig, 1985). Many people who develop this disorder report having had a gender-identity problem during childhood, but as we've said, the problem generally surfaces during puberty. Extensive childhood femininity in a boy or masculinity in a girl seems to increase the likelihood of transsexualism. This disorder may also develop within the context of a disturbed relationship with one or both parents (Meyer & Dupkin, 1985). Men seek treatment for transsexualism more commonly than women (American Psychiatric Association, 1987). On the whole, efforts to alter gender identity through psychological means have not been successful, and as a result many transsexuals have sought sex reassignment surgery—that is, a physical change consonant with their cross-sexual identity.

Sex Reassignment. Sex reassignment surgery for men starts with removing the external genitals and creating an artificial vagina. Female hormones are administered to stimulate breast development, lessen beard growth, and provide a more feminine texture to the skin. Sex reassignment surgery for women usually removes the breasts, uterus, and ovaries, and seals off the vagina. Many female-to-male transsexuals choose such surgical procedures, along with hormone therapy, but do not opt for an artificial penis. For those who do, a penis can be constructed from abdominal tissue or tissue from the perineum. Such a reconstruction functions normally in the process of urination, but is not capable of an erection. However, it may be possible to simulate an erection with an implant such as that used in the treatment of male erectile dysfunction (see Chapter 16).

Sex reassignment surgery is a controversial area and many physicians are opposed to it. To date, surgical results have been mixed. While some studies report satisfactory outcomes, many find such problems as dissatisfaction with the surgery, inability to perform sexually, and postoperative depression (see, e.g., Satterfield, 1988; Beatrice, 1985; Lindemalm et al., 1986). For these reasons, clinicians stress the importance of carefully screening each candidate for surgery. Candidates must be emotionally stable and usually must undergo a trial period during which they receive hormone therapy, live in the new role, and acquire an understanding of the psychological adjustments they will need to make if they have the surgery.

A Case of Female Transsexualism. Charles, 25 years old, consulted a physician, seeking a "sex change operation." Biologically a woman, Charles had for three years lived socially and been employed as a man. For the last two of these years he had been the housemate, economic provider, and husband-equivalent of a bisexual woman who had fled from a bad marriage. Her two children regarded Charles as their stepfather, and there was a strong affectionate bond between them and Charles.

Charles looked like a not-overly-masculine man. His voice was pitched low, but not baritone. His shirt and jacket were bulky and successfully camouflaged tightly bound, flattened breasts. A strapped-on penis produced a masculine-looking bulge in his pants and was so constructed that, in case of social necessity, it could be used as a urinary conduit in the standing position. Charles had tried without success to obtain a mastectomy so that in summer he could wear only a T-shirt while working outdoors as a heavy construction machine operator. He had also been unable to get a prescription for testosterone, to produce male secondary sex characteristics and suppress menstruation.

Charles had been a tomboy in childhood, and realized when he was an adolescent that he could fall in love only with a woman. He had normal female anatomy, which he found personally repulsive, incongruous, and a source of continual distress, yet laboratory tests of hormone levels were within normal limits for a female (Spitzer, et. al. 1981, pp. 63–64).

We have no further information on Charles, but on the basis of this account, do you think he was successful in obtaining the sex change operation he wanted? Why or why not?

GENDER-ROLE DEVELOPMENT AND INTIMATE RELATIONSHIPS

Up to this point we've focused on early gender-role development and how it affects the growing child. Now we want to explore how the gender roles that men and women have adopted influence their intimate relationships with one another. In the first part of this section of the chapter, we will explore gender patterns in traditional relationships. Then we will examine how cultural role scripts shape intimate relationships. The section concludes with a discussion of how couples might break down traditional gender-role barriers in their relationships.

Traditional Male-Female Relationships

How do traditional gender roles shape male-female relationships? What types of gender differences become apparent? According to Letitia Peplau (1983), gender-role differences are particularly influential in the following areas: language and nonverbal communication, self-disclosure, falling in love, performance of daily tasks, decision-making and influence strategies, conflict and aggression, personal attitudes and values, and reaction to the ending of a relationship.

LANGUAGE AND NONVERBAL COMMUNICATION. We suggested earlier that men and women have different styles of communicating, both verbally and nonverbally. In a later chapter (Chapter 7) we will focus exclusively on the topic of communication, but here we will make a few comments about relationship factors that directly reflect gender-role attitudes and behaviors. Men, in a dominant-style role, tend to do more verbal interrupting, to claim greater personal space when communicating with a woman, and to initiate more touching. They are poorer at decoding nonverbal communications than women are (Jose & McCarthy, 1988; Drass, 1986). Women appear to be better at initiating and maintaining conversations (Kohn, 1988). They also seem to be more supportive of men than men are of them. Moreover, women tend to be better than men at delivering nonverbal messages—at least between husbands and wives. Women apparently make more eye contact than men, particularly when they are sitting close to a partner (Kahn, 1984). Men tend to make eye contact only when their partners are farther away.

Sandra Metts and William Cupach (1989) add that differences in the meanings men and women attach to sexual behavior are also reflected in the manner in which partners communicate sexual interest. Men usually do less kissing, holding, and touching, and women often prefer more conversation, playfulness, and slower courting in bed. Men are often reluctant to verbalize appreciation of a spouse, to talk about their fantasies during love play, or to tell women their feelings after coitus (Brown & Auerback, 1981).

SELF-DISCLOSURE. We noted earlier that women tend to disclose personal information more easily in friendships than men do. In dating relationships and marriage we need to distinguish *preferences* for disclosure from what actually occurs. In an actual re-

....
Women and men may be able to lessen their differences in communicative style by focussing on such things as asserting one's own views and making eye contact.

lationship the amount of reciprocal self-disclosure generally represents a compromise between the preferences of both partners. When one partner discloses more than the other, however, it is usually the woman (Snell, Miller, & Belk, 1988).

Even when men and women disclose things about themselves in equal amounts, there are often differences in the *content* of their self-disclosures. For instance, men are more likely than women to reveal their strengths and conceal their weaknesses. For traditional men, this often means hiding feelings:

> I was always taught to conceal my emotions and not let people get too close.
>
> For years I have played down my inner feelings. Sometimes I play games with emotions and display only those that I consider appropriate. Other times I emotionally shut down and do not give anyone a hint of what I'm feeling.
>
> I keep cool and emotionally detached. Emotions tend to get in the way anyway. (Authors' files)

FALLING IN LOVE. Does it surprise you to read that men are more likely than women to endorse such "romantic" beliefs as: Love comes but once; Love lasts forever; and Love conquers barriers of social class or custom? Men also tend to fall in love more quickly than women. Women are more likely to be pragmatists, saying that they can love many different men, that some disillusionment often accompanies long-term relationships, and that economic security is as important as passion in a relationship (Rubin, Peplau, & Hill, 1981).

Both men and women seem to love their partners equally, though women are more apt to report emotional signs of love (Cancian, 1985). These signs include feeling euphoric and having trouble concentrating on work and other activities because of an obsession with the loved person.

TASK PERFORMANCE. The evidence indicates that husbands and wives perform different types and amounts of family tasks. It's long been the custom in American marriages for women and men to divide up the domestic labor according to how much physical strength tasks require and whether they are performed inside or outside the home. Traditionally, women have done the cooking and cleaning and baby-tending, whereas men have washed the family car, done the yardwork, and carried out the garbage (see, e.g., Werner & LaRussa, 1985; Lewin & Tragos, 1987).

A man explains the division of labor in his home this way:

> We're very traditional about who does what. Lori has always done cooking, laundering, and the like. Why rock the boat? She seems to enjoy what she does and is very good at it. For me, there's a certain satisfaction with what I do around the house. I've always tended to the mechanical chores and taking care of the lawn and garden. Lori has never expressed an interest in these chores nor tried to wrestle them from me. I have a hard time thinking what it would be like any other way. (Authors' files)

A woman looks at her domestic chores this way:

> I guess I'm doing everything that my mother did. I grew up in a traditional home, one that clearly taught sex-typed domestic responsibilities. I was taught to take care of my husband and children. My husband and I agreed that the home was my full-time job while he would hold down a job on the outside. There are times when I get

frustrated with the way things are, but for the most part I'm satisfied. (Authors' files)

Decision-Making and Influence Strategies. Women and men in a close relationship tend to specialize in different areas of decision making. To illustrate, Judith Howard and her associates (1986) found that the traditional woman is less likely to influence and more apt to be influenced by the traditional man. Traditional husbands are likely to make major financial decisions for the family, whereas traditional wives are likely to make domestic decisions, such as those related to meals and home decorating. One woman views traditional decision-making patterns in this fashion:

> **Justin is responsible for the major financial decisions. While he does ask for my input and we openly discuss money matters, he always has the final say. For the most part, this has not led to any big altercations, largely because he is honest and always has our best interests in mind. I'll usually make the decisions about the everyday operations of the household, or matters related to the children. He's pretty good about listening when I need his opinion about something. (Authors' files)**

Today many American couples perceive their relationship as egalitarian and share all decision making equally. When a relationship is not egalitarian, however, the dominant partner is much more often the man than the woman. A woman describes her relationship of two years this way:

> **I've always been the passive one while Tom is outspoken and dominant. He enjoys having the upper hand and always seems to have the last word. While I tried to speak up or assert myself early on in our relationship, I realized that it didn't do any good. He would go out of his way to win every argument or to show that he was right. Being in charge or control is a major part of his makeup and he's not going to change. (Authors' files)**

Men and women tend to use different tactics to try to influence each other. For example, men are more prone than women to use direct means of influencing their wives—for example, logical argument. In contrast, women are more likely to report using indirect strategies, such as withholding speech or affection (see, e.g., Fitzpatrick, 1988; Howard, Blumstein, & Schwartz, 1986).

Conflict and Aggression. Women and men react differently to conflict situations. Men are often motivated to resolve conflict and restore harmony, while women are often rejecting and cold or use appeals to fairness and guilt (Peplau, 1983). Studies of couples (i.e., Pearson, 1985) have found that both sexes expect women to react to conflict by crying, sulking, and criticizing their partner's insensitivity. Often both sexes expect men to show anger, reject the woman's tears, call for a logical approach to the problem, or sometimes try to delay the discussion. Men are more likely to use physical force to resolve conflicts, and women are more apt to be the victims of physical abuse (Gelles & Cornell, 1990; Gelles & Straus, 1988).

Personal Attitudes and Values. Most men and women express a desire for a permanent relationship with someone. Both sexes value companionship and affection over social status in a relationship. In actual relationships similarity is usually further enhanced by the selection of a partner whose attitudes are compatible with one's own and who has a similar background and values. Not surprisingly, marital discord may be at its greatest when a husband is more traditional and a wife more modern in gender-role orientations (Bowen, 1987).

Men and women do seem to value somewhat different qualities in an ideal love partner, although findings are mixed on this topic. Some studies have found, for example, that women value such dimensions as intelligence and occupational achievement in their partners, while men prize such characteristics as youth and sexual attractiveness (Peplau, 1983). However, other research (Daniel et al., 1985) suggests that men and women value similar qualities in a partner: intelligence, sensitivity, physical attractiveness, a sense of humor, and ambition. Interestingly, one study (Buss & Barnes, 1986) showed that the qualities sought in a partner differed for married and unmarried subjects. Among the married, the desired qualities included good companionship, consideration, honesty, affection, and dependability. Unmarried people looked for kindness, an exciting personality, intelligence, physical attractiveness, and good health.

REACTIONS TO RELATIONSHIP DISSOLUTION. The evidence suggests that men tend to react more negatively to relationship breakups than women do. (Peplau, 1983). The association between marital disruption and a variety of illnesses and disorders is stronger for men than for women. And, contrary to what many people suppose, there is also some evidence (Beck, 1988; Peplau, 1983) that men react more severely than women to the end of a dating relationship. This may be partly because, as the research suggests, men are less sensitive to problems in their dating relationships and less likely either to foresee or to initiate a breakup.

Cultural Role Scripts and Intimate Relationships

cultural role scripts
Preconceptions of how one should behave within a relationship setting, including expectations for one's partner.

How might we account for the gender differences in intimate relationships just described? What factors shape such traditional gender-role behaviors? According to Lonnie Barbach (1984), at least part of the answer lies in **cultural role scripts,** preconceptions of how one should behave within the relationship setting, including expectations for one's partner. Some of these scripts are deeply rooted in gender-role tradition and have remained relatively unaltered over the years. In this section we will explore a few of the cultural role scripts that Barbach feels are the most common.

THE "SEX IS GOOD—SEX IS BAD" SCRIPT. The Sex Is Good—Sex Is Bad script gives women a double message. They have been told repeatedly throughout history (see Chapter 1) that sex is dirty, but that they must save it for someone they love. They have been taught that being a virgin is virtuous and that keeping their genitalia pure and untouched is the greatest gift they can give their husbands on their wedding night. (Never mind that their husbands' genitalia might not be equally pure.)

These women remember vividly how they were taught to be "good girls":

> My mother was especially adept at telling me that "nice girls" don't have sex until they're married. If you did have sex, you were a tramp.

> I'll never forget when my mother and father found out that I was sleeping with my boyfriend. They called me every rotten name in the book and told me that they could never respect anyone who had so little respect for herself. I cried for days and will always remember the hurt. (Authors' files)

THE "FANTASY MODEL OF SEX" SCRIPT. The Fantasy Model of Sex script, promoted by popular novels, pictures sexual activity as filled with unrelenting excitement, continuing arousal, and unparalleled satisfaction. Couples learn from this script that a sexual experience is totally pleasurable, without any problems, and that the intensity of the experience builds inexorably to an incredible peak and then explodes in simultaneous orgasms. Since the typical person's sexual experience includes occasional setbacks, does not always result in the most fantastic pleasure imaginable, and only sometimes culminates in simultaneous orgasms, a script like this one can lead to a great deal of frustration.

Several women comment on the perceived importance of having an orgasm and the pressures that believing they must have one puts on them:

> All of my friends talked about orgasms and their supposed importance. I was led to believe that "real" women have orgasms, inadequate ones don't.

> For years I believed that all women have orgasms. In fact, I feared not having one and disappointing my partner.

> I joined the legions of women who bought into the myth of the "big O." I thought everyone had them. (Authors' files)

The Fantasy Model of Sex puts special pressures on men, too:

> Guys face tremendous performance pressure. I mean it's all out front, so to speak, and there's only so much faking you can do.

> While I really enjoy sex, I don't like the anxieties it often brings. Sometimes I wonder if I was good enough or if she was dissatisfied with any part of my lovemaking. (Authors' files)

THE "MEN SHOULD KNOW" SCRIPT. The man is seen as the sexual expert in the Men Should Know script. He must be in total control of the sexual activity. He is responsible for sweeping the woman off her feet, against her better judgment, and then thoroughly satisfying her sexually. This script portrays women as trying to remain pure, innocent, and unknowledgeable, while men are totally knowledgeable, talented lovers.

A man objects to this view of his role:

> I don't like the expectation that men are the sex experts. This creates performance anxieties for me, particularly if something goes wrong. (Authors' files)

THE "WOMEN CAN'T TALK" SCRIPT. In the Women Can't Talk script women are seen as embarrassed to talk about sex, and rightly so, because they shouldn't talk about it. According to this script, it is unladylike to use words that describe sexual activities and sexual organs. This script inhibits many women from communicating their sexual preferences to their partners.

THE "MEDIA" SCRIPT. The Media script often gives men and women an unrealistic set of standards. For example, magazine covers and movies dictate what is attractive and what is not. Many people worry about not being sexually desirable because they don't have these glamorized physical qualities. Cultural pressures like these often make both men and women self-conscious and cause them to forget that real beauty and appeal lie in a person's uniqueness, not in a stereotyped image.

THE "SEX EQUALS INTERCOURSE" SCRIPT. When people talk about *sex*, they rarely have kissing, holding, or touching in mind. According to the Sex Equals Intercourse script, the "real thing" is penile-vaginal intercourse and nothing else. For younger people especially, expectations of intercourse can be unrealistically high, and once they have begun to have intercourse, other activities are often abbreviated, if not omitted entirely. There are many, many sexual activities other than intercourse that give both partners great pleasure and satisfaction. Women may be more aware than men of the benefits that physical and emotional closeness can bring to a relationship:

> The best part of our lovemaking is when we touch and explore each other's bodies. I like it when he's slow and tender.

> Who says that sex always has to be intercourse? There is so much more to lovemaking than this. I derive considerable pleasure just from being physically close to my lover. Touching has always turned me on and I just love feeling his body. In fact, sometimes I prefer slow moments of touching and embracing to racing for intercourse. (Authors' files)

Scripts in Perspective

As you can see, most of Barbach's scripts apply to women. This is because although both sexes have been modeled by stereotypical notions of what is appropriate sexual behavior, women have been particularly ill-served by this socialization process. Led at times to deny their sexuality, at other times to expect multiple orgasms in every sexual encounter (see Chapter 4), it is no wonder that many women are confused about how to express their sexuality. Men, in contrast, have always been given a pretty free rein in expressing their sexuality. As we will see in Chapter 8, however, it appears that men can learn not only how to pleasure a woman in sexual activities other than intercourse, but also how to experience pleasure themselves from those activities. Honestly exploring their biases about gender-role stereotyping can help both women and men to achieve satisfying, intimate sexual relationships.

Sandra Metts and William Cupach (1989) have offered another perspective on sexual scripts. These authors point out that among partners who subscribe to stereotypical, traditional scripts, the man is perceived as having the prerogative to initiate sex and the woman the right to refuse. If both partners are satisfied with this script, there is usually no difficulty. However, problems arise when one partner chooses not to adhere to the traditional script but fails to renegotiate a new script. For instance, if a woman decides she wants to initiate sexual activity on occasion with a man who subscribes to the traditional cultural script, the man may resent her behavior. Or a woman may subscribe to the traditional script, while her partner is frustrated at always having the responsibility for initiating sex and wishes that she would be more sexually assertive.

There's nothing wrong with having a sexual script, provided it satisfies both partners. Negotiation of a script that both partners can be comfortable with is essential for relationship satisfaction.

Breaking Down Traditional Gender-Role Barriers

While breaking down traditional gender-role barriers is difficult, it is not impossible. First, partners need to be open-minded and sincerely interested in releasing themselves from stereotypical roles. Gerald Corey (1990) feels that men and women need to recognize that they're both after the same thing: a loosening of the gender-role rigidity that has trapped them. Many men feel a need to broaden their view of themselves to include capacities that have been traditionally branded feminine and that they have consequently denied in themselves. And many women are seeking to give expression to qualities and characteristics that have been associated with masculinity. As both sexes pay closer attention to attitudes that are deeply ingrained in themselves, they may discover that their emotions haven't caught up with their minds. Couples may well be "liberated" intellectually and *know* what they want, yet they may have difficulty feeling comfortable about what they want. The challenge is wedding knowledge to emotions!

Goldberg (1983) writes that traditional partners who want to change their ways may find that progress is slow because gender-role attitudes and behaviors ingrained since toddlerhood have created a worldview to which they are deeply committed emotionally. Altering a long-held worldview shakes a person's most stable frame of reference. Arriving at a new worldview requires a slow, methodical, trial-and-error approach. According to Goldberg, partners go through a multiphase transition process as they seek to implement changes and integrate them into their personalities and their relationship. Let's look at some of these phases.

My boyfriend and I want to free ourselves from the stereotyped expectations we often hold for each other. How can we do this?

Partners should decide what they really want, rather than what they believe they want, before they try to change. An honest appraisal here can avoid problems down the road. For example, many people desire more closeness or more autonomy in a relationship, but they want these changes to occur without jeopardizing their familiar security. A man may think that he desires more sexual assertiveness or independence from his partner, and a woman may believe that she wants a greater expression of emotion, vulnerability, and need, with less success drive, from hers. However, what each really wants is often an idealized new person who retains all the safe, known qualities of the old person. This combination is often psychologically impossible.

Trying to change one's partner as a way of improving the relationship is not the best way to start. The best and perhaps only effective way to create change in a relationship is to change things about oneself that permit and reinforce the partner's undesirable behavior. The person who tries to modify her partner's behavior rather than work on her own is playing a psychological game. This game allows her to maintain that she wants change, but at the same time to avoid the risks actual change would entail. Why is this so? Because no one can change another's behavior. One can only change one's own behavior and hope that that will lead the other person to change his.

Changing one's own behavior may create a temporary crisis in a relationship. However, this will be overcome when a new understanding is achieved. During disharmonious times blaming, provoking guilt, and threats are common maneuvers designed to push the other person back to a formerly established position and to avoid change.

Traditional polarized relationships look okay on the surface. Maybe, but what looks good and always remains the same can eventually contaminate a relationship. Those couples trying to change may have a relationship that appears to be full of disequilibrium and conflict. However, the transitional relationship is characterized by effort to achieve a satisfying, dynamic balance—as opposed to the pseudo-peace of traditional relationships, where the emphasis is on being "nice" and understanding while suppressing the negative. The new relationship necessarily involves a struggle between partners involved in setting boundaries, retaining their individuality along with the relationship, and sharing responsibility, decision making, control, and power. Conflict rather than peace, therefore, becomes the norm, particularly in the initial stages of transition.

A balanced relationship is much less a matter of who does what than of neither partner being defensive and of balanced interaction in all kinds of human expressiveness. In this sense, a man can be the primary breadwinner while the woman mainly stays at home, and the relationship can still be liberated in its process or essence. A woman can be a corporation president and a man a house-husband, and their relationship can be very traditional or sexist in its moment-to-moment interactions. In general, a persistent pattern of blaming and feeling guilty signifies a polarized sexist relationship, no matter what the external role and chore division. If the moment-to-moment process of being together is genuinely balanced, it will not matter what functions or tasks either partner fulfills.

A relationship cannot be improved simply by good communication. The greatest intellectual awareness and most skillful communication cannot overcome the bad effects of a relationship imbalance. Good communication must be coupled with balanced interaction to attain the best possible relationship.

Honest, nonsexist interaction is the key to balanced relationships. Nonsexist interaction means that the partners are responding to and satisfying each other's real needs, rather than assumed needs. In addressing assumed needs, you are really only validating yourself, with the illusion of satisfying your partner's needs.

In summary, Goldberg (1983), sees the liberation of a relationship from traditional gender-role barriers as producing numerous rewards. As new attitudes and behaviors diminish sexism, the psychological health of the partners will prosper. The resulting balance creates a foundation for a new male-female relationship, one that is characterized by a fluid interaction between two people, each capable of a full range of human responses.

ANDROGYNY AND INTIMATE RELATIONSHIPS

What does androgyny mean?

We close this chapter with a word about androgyny and its impact on intimate relationships. You will recall from Chapter 1 that androgyny means having both female and male characteristics. Androgynous people see themselves as full human beings, not as typecast men or women. Because they do not view personality traits as compartmentalized by sex, androgynous people feel free to be nurturant and assertive, sensitive, and dominant, affectionate and self-sufficient in turn.

Androgyny appears to have beneficial effects. Compared to people who exhibit traditional gender-role behaviors, androgynous men and women seem more competent and demonstrate higher levels of self-esteem. In addition, they are better at maintaining good interpersonal relationships and tend to deal more effectively with their surroundings, including situations involving stress. Androgynous people also tend to be more secure with themselves, more flexible in their behavior, and less anxious (Solie & Fielder, 1988; Stoppard & Paisley, 1987; Payne, 1987; Ganoung & Coleman, 1987; Cooper, Chassin, & Zeiss, 1985; Wiggins & Holzmuller, 1981).

Still, some researchers (e.g., Downs & Langlois, 1988; Gill et al., 1987; Blitchington, 1984; Baumrind, 1982) have complained that the concept of androgyny is too vague, trendy, and difficult to measure. Others (i.e., Werner & LaRussa, 1985) argue that many gender-role behaviors such as male assertiveness and female nurturance have been in existence for millennia and will not vanish under androgynous pressures.

Some critics (e.g., Sampson, 1985) contend that androgyny is a questionable model of psychological adaptation because by insisting that a person can be ideally feminine and masculine at the same time, it suggests that a person can be totally self-sufficient. Others (e.g., Hare-Mustin & Maracek, 1988) maintain that focusing on androgyny draws attention away from women's real needs in society, which depend on righting the present power imbalance between women and men. Taking a similar stance, Sandra Bem (1981) says that instead of encouraging androgyny, we should

Have you ever wondered how androgynous you are? If so, take the following quiz, adapted from the Bem Sex-Role Inventory. Read through the items below and rate yourself on each with a score from 1 (never or almost never true) to 7 (always or almost always true):

____ 1. Self-reliant
____ 2. Yielding
____ 3. Helpful
____ 4. Defends own beliefs
____ 5. Cheerful
____ 6. Moody
____ 7. Independent
____ 8. Shy
____ 9. Conscientious
____ 10. Athletic
____ 11. Affectionate
____ 12. Theatrical
____ 13. Assertive
____ 14. Flatterable
____ 15. Happy
____ 16. Strong personality
____ 17. Loyal
____ 18. Unpredictable
____ 19. Forceful
____ 20. Feminine
____ 21. Reliable
____ 22. Analytical
____ 23. Sympathetic
____ 24. Jealous
____ 25. Has leadership abilities
____ 26. Sensitive to the needs of others
____ 27. Truthful
____ 28. Willing to take risks
____ 29. Understanding
____ 30. Secretive

____ 31. Makes decisions easily
____ 32. Compassionate
____ 33. Sincere
____ 34. Self-sufficient
____ 35. Eager to soothe hurt feelings
____ 36. Conceited
____ 37. Dominant
____ 38. Soft-spoken
____ 39. Likable
____ 40. Masculine
____ 41. Warm
____ 42. Solemn
____ 43. Willing to take a stand
____ 44. Tender
____ 45. Friendly
____ 46. Aggressive
____ 47. Gullible
____ 48. Inefficient
____ 49. Acts as a leader
____ 50. Childlike
____ 51. Adaptable
____ 52. Individualistic
____ 53. Does not use harsh language
____ 54. Unsystematic
____ 55. Competitive
____ 56. Loves children
____ 57. Tactful
____ 58. Ambitious
____ 59. Gentle
____ 60. Conventional

MAKING USE OF WHAT WE KNOW

How Androgynous Are You?

Scoring

a. Add up your ratings for items 1, 4, 7, 10, 13, 16, 19, 22, 25, 28, 31, 34, 37, 40, 43, 46, 49, 52, 55, and 58. Divide the total by 20. This is your masculinity score.

b. Add up your ratings for items 2, 5, 8, 11, 14, 17, 20, 23, 26, 29, 32, 35, 38, 41, 44, 47, 50, 53, 56, and 59. Divide the total by 20. This is your femininity score.

c. If your masculinity score is above 4.9 (the approximate median for the masculinity scale) and your femininity scale is above 4.9 (the approximate femininity median), you would be classified as androgynous on Bem's scale.

Source: From Janet S. Hyde, *Half the Human Experience: The Psychology of Women*, 4th ed. copyright 1991 D. C. Heath and Company, Lexington, MA. Reprinted by permission.

realize that "human behavior and personality attributes should cease to have gender, and society should stop projecting gender into situations irrelevant to genitalia" (p. 363).

Against these criticisms proponents of androgyny maintain that the removal of gender-typed behavioral constraints would allow men and women to demonstrate the best qualities of both sexes. We agree, feeling that children especially would benefit from a more tolerant acceptance of their total selves, rather than being continually told how society expects them to behave. Within the context of intimate relationships, androgynous couples seek to transcend traditional gender-role boundaries, boundaries that, as Judy Long (1984) notes, support the expectation that the female partner is to be directed by the male and that his wishes take priority.

The androgynous relationship does seem to be what today's young adults want. Long's review of the research indicates that women and men admire the same kinds of qualities. The kind of person they want to be and the kind of person they want to spend their lives with are both competent and tender, strong and confident, and capable of both independence and intimacy. To get an idea of how androgynous you are, take the quiz in the "Making Use of What We Know" box.

SEXUALITY IN THE NEWS

Why the Fear of Feminism?

by Susan Jane Gilman

ANN ARBOR, MICHIGAN—I cannot tell you how many times I've heard women preface their opinions with, "Well, I'm not a feminist or anything, but we do deserve equal rights." Or, "I don't think it's fair that women earn only 69 cents to the men's dollar, but it's not as if I'm a feminist or anything. . . ."

Although feminism is, by definition, the theory of the political, economic, and social equality of the sexes, the word has become abused and distorted. Fearing that feminism means being unfeminine, anti-men, and ultimately alone, many women have distanced themselves from it.

Feminism seems to present a social equivalent of Sophie's choice: Which of our children will we let die—our heart or our mind, our attractiveness or our independence? No other oppressed group experiences such a fundamental dilemma, where they feel compelled to choose between fair treatment in society and basic emotional needs. We want self-determination but also love and intimacy. None of this is unreasonable.

For this reason it does not surprise me that women are still reluctant to see themselves as a political force. More of us are of voting age than men, but we have yet to exercise this power in a national election. We have the numbers to make employment opportunity or child care the primary issues in a campaign by threatening not to vote for the candidate who does not support them.

And yet we don't carry out this threat. Millions of women voted for Ronald Reagan and George Bush and for countless other politicians and laws dedicated to restricting our freedoms. Only the threat to abortion has seemed to galvanize some of us—and this on both sides of the issue.

Women have argued time and again, "Why should we regard ourselves on the basis of our gender, as women first, when as human beings so many other issues concern us?"

Because, as much as we insist that we are more than wombs and homemakers, we are still regarded primarily as such by politicians and lawmakers. We can delude ourselves, but one look at recent legislation—the Louisiana abortion bill, the President's veto of the Family Leave Act—confirms our status. If we allow such policies to stand, we will have even less power to influence the things that concern us beyond "women's issues."

We would benefit by looking to the National Rifle Association. Though the N.R.A. supports unpopular ideas—that there should be absolutely no restrictions on semiautomatic weapons, for example—it gets plenty of political backing. How? It has a clear view of what is important to its members. It then singles out those issues for unwavering attention and money. If a politician believes in gun control, the N.R.A. will throw all its power behind the opponent who does not.

N.R.A. members don't get caught up in trying to prove to the world that they're not just gun nuts. And despite this, they've still managed to become one of the most powerful American interest groups.

Women have got to follow suit in three areas: equal pay and opportunity, control over our own bodies, and child care. These issues cut across race and class, which often divide the women's movement. Anyone can become pregnant. Everyone wants equal pay. Most mothers are worried about securing adequate child care and parental leave.

continued

Moreover, we need to improve the way we communicate. Today, universities are the hotbed for feminist discourse. Yet much of this discourse is irrelevant to everyday life: try telling a welfare mother or a harried secretary that they should worry about being a victim of the unconscious processes of phallocentric language.

If women are uncomfortable with the connotations of feminism, it is up to us to stop perpetuating the stereotypes. In the 1988 Olympics, Florence Griffith Joyner dressed in lace running tights. At the time, I remember thinking that this was pathetic. Why couldn't she just run?

In an ideal world, Ms. Griffith Joyner wouldn't be judged on anything but athletic ability. But until this world is created, what a women looks like is still of major importance. And given this, it occurred to me that perhaps she decided to prove that the incongruous was not the irreconcilable, that power could be combined with femininity. At any rate, her style clearly did not compromise her running. She won. (*The New York Times*, September 1, 1991. Copyright © 1991 by The New York Times Company. Reprinted by permission.)

DISCUSSION QUESTIONS

1. Do you agree that women have not exercised their political potential? If you do, why do you think this is so?
2. How do race and class divide the women's movement? Do stereotypes play a major role here? How?
3. Why do you think Florence Griffith Joyner wore lace tights to run the 1988 Olympics race? Do you agree with this reasoning? Why or why not?

LOOKING BACK

■ Sex refers to a person's biological status as male or female, and can be subdivided into genetic sex (determined by chromosomal makeup) and anatomical sex (physical features that distinguish females from males). Sexual identity refers to one's identity as either female or male based on these biological characteristics. Gender refers to the social meanings attached to being a female or a male. Gender identity is the psychological awareness of being either a female or a male, and a gender role is a set of expectations that prescribe how women and men should act. A gender-role stereotype is a generalization that reflects our beliefs about the differences in behavior between men and women.

■ While men and women have an identical number of chromosomes, it is the 23rd pair that differentiates a male from a female. As the sex glands develop during the early phases of prenatal life, they begin to secrete hormones that direct both internal and external sexual differentiation. Fetal hormones also create structural and functional differences in the brain.

■ Chromosomal abnormalities occur when the union between the female ovum and the male sperm does not result in the normal quota of 46 chromosomes, including the two sex cells. Examples of these chromosomal abnormalities are the Turner, triple X, Klinefelter, and XYY syndromes. Hormonal errors can also affect the course of sexual development. For example, hermaphroditism is a condition in which a person has both ovarian and testicular tissue. The subdivisions of hermaphroditism are true hermaphroditism and pseudo-hermaphroditism.

■ Four prominent theories of gender-role development are the cognitive-developmental, behavioral, social-learning, and identification perspectives. Beyond these theoretical perspectives, it is possible to isolate certain socialization agents and assess their influence on gender-role learning: parents, play activities, peers, teachers and schools, children's literature, and the media.

■ A gender-identity disorder is an incongruence between one's assigned sex and one's gender identity. Transsexuals, for example, feel so uncomfortable about their biologically assigned sex that they often seek to have that identity altered by surgical means (sex reassignment surgery).

■ Traditional gender roles impact on intimate relationships in many ways. Men and women differ in their degree of self-disclosure and in the ways in which they express conflict and aggression. Cultural role scripts create preconceptions of how people should behave within an intimate male-female relationship, including expectations for one's partner. Many couples today are choosing to break down traditional gender-role barriers in order to establish a balanced relationship. Such relationships are characterized by androgyny, a concept suggesting that both female and male traits are important and beneficial to possess.

THINKING THINGS OVER

1. Differentiate between gender and sex, giving examples. What part does biology play in gender roles?

2. The socialization of infants and children tends to have a strong influence on later gender adaptability. If you were raising a child today, what guidelines would you follow in gender-socializing that child?

3. Think about your most recent classroom experiences. Have you personally experienced gender-role stereotyping? Did anyone else in your class have such an experience? Describe these situations.

4. How have the gender roles you have assumed affected your intimate relationships?

5. Do you think that the concept of androgyny is a beneficial one in male-female relationships? Why or why not?

DISCOVER FOR YOURSELF

Cassell, C. (1984). *Swept away*. New York: Bantam Books. Cassell takes a probing look at how women perceive the dynamics of relationships, including the impact of romance and sexual intimacy.

Doyle, J. A., & Paludi, M. A. (1984). *Sex and gender*, 2nd ed. Dubuque, IA: William C. Brown. One of the better introductory texts on sex and gender.

Lengermann, P. M., & Wallace, R. A. (1985). *Gender in America: Social control and social change*. Englewood Cliffs, NJ: Prentice Hall. Among the topics considered are sociological theories and the study of gender, the learning of gender roles in childhood, and social structures promoting gender equity.

Maccorquodale, P. (1989). Gender and sexual behavior. In K. McKinney & S. Sprecher (eds.), *Human sexuality: The societal and interpersonal context*. Norwood, NJ: Ablex. Among the topics Maccorquodale discusses in this very informative article are sexual and gender scripts.

Richardson, L. (1988). *The dynamics of sex and gender: A sociological approach*, 3rd ed. New York: Harper & Row. Richardson explores gender-role behaviors within intimate relationships in Chapter 13 of this paperback.

Shaver, P., & Hendrick, C. (eds.) (1987). *Sex and gender*. Beverly Hills, CA: Sage, 1987. Many controversies in the field of gender-role development are discussed in this collection of articles.

6

Intimacy, Love, Sex, and Values

They do not love that do not show their love

—William Shakespeare

In this chapter you'll discover:

☐ *The role that maturity plays in shaping the formation and maintenance of intimate relationships.*

☐ *How the theories of Gordon Allport, Erik Erikson, and Abraham Maslow can be applied to the study of intimate relationships.*

☐ *What qualities are necessary to the development and maintenance of intimate relationships.*

☐ *How intimate relationships develop over time.*

☐ *How love can be expressed and received and the role it plays in intimate relationships.*

☐ *How values shape a person's sexual life.*

Few adults can thrive in isolation. On the contrary, most search for a partner with whom to share life's experiences. The desired outcome of this search is usually twofold: to know and better understand oneself and to construct a worthwhile and satisfying relationship with another person (Pocs & Walsh, 1985). Dating and maintaining a meaningful relationship require that people share intimacy, a state that involves mutual support and feelings of closeness. Getting to know people enables us to develop intimate, satisfying, long-lasting friendships as well as relationships that combine love, intimacy, and the expression of sexuality and that are based on a clear set of values.

In the United States, heterosexual dating begins at an early age, encouraged by school and other social functions such as dances and rock concerts and by the portrayal of dating and love and sexual relationships in the media. Lesbians and gays begin dating at about the same time as heterosexuals, but because their life style is frowned upon by many in our society, dating is more difficult. Many lesbians and gays hide their sexual preferences, even from each other.

Dating provides an opportunity to meet a number of people and serves as a vehicle for recreation, companionship, and socialization. It provides people with opportunities to learn about roles, values, and norms. Some women comment:

> I enjoy the companionship and I've gotten to know myself better.

> Dating is a lot of fun. While I've had my ups and downs with men, for the most part I've enjoyed my dates.

> Dating has given me the chance to meet many different people. It has also taught me the importance of mutuality. (Authors' files)

Men make similar observations:

> I've learned what I want in a partner and a lot about myself.

> Dating has opened up my eyes to relationships.

> Dating is a great way to get to know another person. It gives two people the opportunity to share common interests and to discover if they were really meant for each other. (Authors' files)

Dating has purposes beyond the functions just mentioned. George Dickinson and Michael Leming (1990) describe how it allows participants to gain insight into their own identities. Being in the company of a partner who offers meaningful feedback and support enables people to confirm their identities as well as to explore (and often dismiss) their self-doubts. Finally, dating brings status. Since dating is a positively evaluated social activity, the more one dates, the more one's status is likely to rise in one's social group. However, dating also has the potential to create problems and pressures. As these women observe:

> I've always been frustrated in dating because deep down inside I'm looking for "Mr. Right." I have fairly high expectations for men. As a result, the men in my life always seem to fall short. Because of this, dating often leaves me with an empty feeling.

> Dating is fun, but I'm growing tired of men who don't want to make any kind of commitment.

> Most men have one thing on their mind—sex. I'm tired of the guys who try to talk you into bed after only one or two dates. Some feel that since they've taken you to dinner or to a movie that you owe them sexual favors. (Authors' files)

Dating helps young people define themselves. It can also teach them how people of the other sex think and feel about many important issues.

Men offer these thoughts:

> It can be a rat race. I get tired of the phoniness and the fakery more than anything.

> It's fun, but it's also expensive. All of the women I date expect me to pay for everything. I hear all this stuff about women demanding equality but there aren't any in my life who offer to pick up the tab. (Authors' files)

According to Maxine Zinn and Stanley Eitzen (1990), the courtship process can be conceptualized as a continuum. It begins with casual dating of many partners and progresses to relationships of a more serious, steady nature until gradually, the choice is narrowed down to one partner toward whom the person feels more and more emotionally committed. Through continuous interaction during the courtship process, partners come to understand each other more deeply and to develop feelings of mutuality and reciprocity. These pivotal features of intimate relationships engender' exchanges of intimacy and caring and often determine whether or not the two people are compatible.

MATURITY AND INTIMATE RELATIONSHIPS

Most people will have one or more serious, intimate relationships over the course of their lives. An **intimate relationship** is one in which we come to know the innermost, subjective aspects of another person and to be known by the other in a like manner. It involves the mutual exchange of experiences in such a way that a further understanding of oneself and one's partner is achieved. Intimate relationships do not have to be sexual; one can be intimate with a friend, a relative, or a teacher (Chelune, Robison, & Kommor, 1984).

True intimacy requires **self-disclosure,** the process by which people let themselves be known by others. Self-disclosure involves making decisions about how far to go in revealing one's thoughts, feelings, and past experiences to another person,

intimate relationship
A relationship in which two people come to know the innermost, subjective aspects of each other.

self-disclosure The process of letting oneself be known by another.

Intimacy, Love, Sex, and Values

as well as the appropriate time and place for such disclosure. As a relationship progresses to more intimate levels, partners generally disclose more information about themselves and at a more personal level (Derlega, 1984).

People disclose themselves through a number of different channels. In verbal self-disclosure, you use words to tell others about yourself. Self-disclosure can also take place through body language or one's tone of voice. The manner in which you gesture or emphasize words also says something about you. Finally, people disclose themselves through their actions (Corey, 1990).

maturity A state of psychological well-being that is instrumental in shaping psychological adjustment and competence.

Intimate partners need to possess a considerable degree of maturity for their relationship to flourish. Broadly defined, **maturity** is a state of well-being that is instrumental in shaping psychological adjustment and competence. The mature person typically has an accurate self-concept, satisfying social relationships, stable emotional behavior, a well-developed value system, and intellectual insight. Mature people are also realistic in their assessment of future goals, appreciate and respect others, and possess effective problem resolution skills. All of these characteristics are vital to the establishment and maintenance of satisfying intimate relationships.

Maturity enables partners in intimate relationships to sort out and accept or change gender roles and responsibilities, to understand the importance of commitment and intimacy, to love and be loved, and to communicate honestly and accurately. Maturity also has an important influence on sexual interactions. As we'll see in Chapters 12, 17, and 18, maturity enables people to understand and appreciate the importance of responsible, safer sex and of maintaining their own sexual health. The mature person is knowledgeable or motivated to learn about contraceptive choices, the importance of avoiding unwanted pregnancies, and ways to avoid sexually transmitted diseases.

Maturity is achieved gradually; it is not a sudden giant leap forward. Nor is it a state that necessarily embraces all aspects of oneself—for example, someone may be intellectually mature but lack social maturity. And maturity does not come automatically with adulthood. As we'll see, people must work to achieve maturity, and the failure to do so can result in relationships that are shallow and unsatisfying.

In this section, we will explore some theoretical approaches to the study of maturity, namely, the research of Gordon Allport, Erik Erikson, and Abraham Maslow. As we'll discover, these three theorists offer different but complementary points of view on maturity. Understanding these three theories should enable you to better comprehend why maturity is essential to flourishing intimate relationships.

Gordon Allport's Theory

Gordon Allport (1961) proposes that maturity is an ongoing process involving a series of attainments. Each period of life has its share of obstacles that must be overcome—roadblocks that require the development of goal-formulating and decision-making abilities. Methods for dealing with life's failures and frustrations—as well as its triumphs and victories—have to be devised if full maturity is to be attained.

Allport has identified seven specific dimensions or criteria of maturity that manifest themselves during adulthood: self-extension, warm relations with others, emotional security, realistic perception, skills and competencies, self-knowledge, and a unifying philosophy of life.

SELF-EXTENSION. This first criterion of maturity requires gradually extending one's comprehension to encompass multiple facets of one's environment. The young child's sphere is primarily the family, but over time the child becomes involved in various peer groups, school activities, and clubs. Eventually, the young person develops strong bonds with others and assumes vocational, moral, and civic responsibilities. Each new outlet provides the opportunity to become involved in more meaningful personal

An important component of maturity, self-extension includes the ability to enjoy a wide range of activities and to identify oneself and one's interests with others and their interests.

relationships and to fulfill the need of sharing new feelings and experiences with others.

Of course, merely being involved in something does not imply satisfaction or happiness. Maturity is measured by one's active participation in an activity. It implies movement away from the childish state in which interests are casual, brief, and unconcerned with the intrinsic worth of the activity. True self-extension is a state in which a sense of reward comes from doing something for its own sake. In other words, a person moves toward maturity when she undertakes activities that have true significance for her.

WARM RELATIONS WITH OTHERS. Allport's second criterion of maturity is the ability to relate warmly to others. By this he means the capacity to be intimate with, as well as compassionate toward, other people.

Allport views intimacy as understanding, accepting, and feeling empathy for others. Intimacy implies the ability to overcome interpersonal boundaries. The fully mature person places a high premium on brotherly and sisterly love and a sense of oneness with others.

Intimacy also involves a tolerance of others' weaknesses and shortcomings. Mature people are capable of accepting people's limitations, perhaps because they have recognized and accepted similar weaknesses in themselves.

EMOTIONAL SECURITY. Numerous dimensions of maturity can be grouped under "emotional security," but Allport maintains that four qualities are particularly important: self-acceptance, emotional acceptance, frustration tolerance, and confidence in self-expression.

Self-acceptance is the ability to acknowledge one's self fully, including one's imperfections. Mature people realize that they will never be perfect in every respect, yet they nevertheless seek to fulfill their potential.

People who display *emotional acceptance* acknowledge emotions as part of the normal self. They do not allow emotions to rule their lives, but neither do they reject them as alien and undesirable.

Frustration tolerance is the capacity to continue functioning even during times of stress. To be able to handle frustrations and setbacks while still meeting life's responsibilities is a formidable accomplishment. Mature people have learned how to deal with life's frustrations and maintain a healthy life style.

The final dimension of emotional maturity is *confidence in self-expression*. Mature people are aware of their emotions and are not afraid of them, but exercise control over their expression.

REALISTIC PERCEPTION. Allport's fourth criterion of maturity is realistic perception. Maturity in this sense means staying in touch with reality, not distorting the environment to suit one's own needs and purposes. Sometimes complex events and situations, combined with unrealistic efforts to handle the attendant frustrations and anxieties, lead to an inaccurate interpretation of the environment. The mature mind is able to perceive surroundings accurately.

SKILLS AND COMPETENCIES. The possession of particular skills or competencies is Allport's fifth dimension of maturity. Unless people have some basic skills, they will find it virtually impossible to nurture the kind of security necessary to the development of maturity. While immature adolescents may feel they're "no good at anything," mature adults strive to develop whatever skills they possess.

Furthermore, people with skills are driven to express their competence through some type of activity. They identify with their work and display pride in the skills needed to produce the finished product. Task absorption and personally meaningful activities are important to psychological well-being.

SELF-KNOWLEDGE. Knowledge of the self, or self-objectification, is criterion number six. Most mature people possess a great deal of self-insight. In contrast, many immature people have little knowledge of themselves. According to Allport, knowledge of the self involves three capacities: knowing what one can do, knowing what one cannot do, and knowing what one ought to do. Coming to know oneself is one of the most important growth processes and it is based to a great extent on those enduring roles that are characteristic of adult life. As young adults modify their behavior in order to fulfill their roles as workers, partners, and parents, their knowledge of themselves and others expands.

A UNIFYING PHILOSOPHY OF LIFE. The final criterion or dimension of maturity outlined by Allport is the development of a unifying philosophy of life that embodies a guiding purpose and accompanying needs, goals, ideals, and values. Since mature human beings seek goals, such a synthesis enables them to develop an intelligent theory of life and to work toward implementing it. Mature people tend to view their goals from a balanced perspective and are able to cope with failure when they do not meet their goals.

To summarize, the seven dimensions proposed by Allport are important factors in the development of maturity and instrumental in the initiation and maintenance of intimate relationships. Each of these factors helps prepare a person to contribute successfully to the richness of intimate relationships. Mature people can extend themselves toward one another and share intimacy over time because they bring recognized skills and competencies to a relationship, including self-insight and understanding. They find it easier to accept their partners' shortcomings and weaknesses because they have learned to accept themselves. Moreover, their interactions are characterized by empathy, confident self-expression, and a realistic appraisal of their own and their partners' needs and purposes. A person possessing all of these dimensions is likely to have a relationship guided by a common purpose and by shared goals and values.

Erik Erikson's Theory

Another theory that can be applied to the study of intimate relationships is that of Erik Erikson (see also Chapter 13). Erikson (1982, 1963; Erikson, Erikson, & Kivnick,

1986) has proposed that personality is shaped by social contacts with others through a sequence of eight specific life stages. The achievement of maturity, he stresses, depends on whether or not the person is able to resolve the crisis inherent in each of these stages.

During adolescence, the person is in the midst of resolving the crisis of *identity versus role confusion*. Erikson suggests that adolescents confront not only issues related to their personal identities but also, as Allport indicates, an assortment of adult roles and responsibilities. How one grapples with these interacting forces will influence the course of psychosocial development in adulthood, most notably one's interactions with others. Elsewhere in the literature, the importance of identity formation and its impact on social relationships is a recurrent theme (see, e.g., Allan & Hauser, 1989; Archer, 1989; Powers et al., 1989; Cooper & Grotevant, 1989; Papini et al., 1989).

Once this identity crisis is resolved during the teenage years, Erikson proposes, young adults are motivated to fuse their newly established identity with that of others. This is the stage of *intimacy versus isolation*. Although most young adults seek to gratify their need for intimacy through marriage or a long-term committed relationship, nonsexual intimate relationships are also possible. People may develop strong bonds of intimacy in friendships that offer, among other features, mutuality, empathy, equity, and reciprocity (Hendrick & Hendrick, 1992; Roscoe, Kennedy, & Pope, 1987; White et al., 1986).

Erikson's life stages of identity versus role confusion and intimacy versus insolation, then, are important to our study of maturity and intimate relationships. From an Eriksonian perspective, maturity is likely among those who have achieved a sense of identity and are motivated to sincerely share themselves with others. Mature partners demonstrate comfort with who they are, as well as a capacity to share and understand. They are able to effectively communicate with each other and are sensitive to and tolerant of each other's needs. Erikson, like Allport, recognizes that the growth of commitment, love, and devotion is much more prominent among highly mature people than among the immature.

Abraham Maslow's Theory

Attaining a self-actualizing state also has implications for maturity and the ability to share oneself with others in meaningful relationships. **Self-actualization** is a harmonious integration of the personality enabling people to make full use of their potential. Those who reach self-actualization attain a highly refined state of being, one that is characterized by autonomy, individuation, and authenticity. Abraham Maslow (1968, 1970) has provided an extensive description of self-actualization. He proposes that human needs (and consequently motivations) operate in a hierarchical fashion so that the most basic needs must be satisfied before the person can attend to higher-order needs.

As Figure 6–1 shows, the first set of needs in the hierarchy are *physiological* in nature, embracing adequate nourishment, rest, and the like. At the second level are the *safety* needs, which motivate the person to achieve a sense of security. Next is *belongingness and love*. Belongingness may be defined as the need to be involved in a meaningful relationship or the need to be part of a group and experience sharing. It is from belongingness that love emerges and eventually blossoms. *Esteem* is the fourth need—people require respect and assurance from others in order to realize that they are worthwhile and competent. The fifth need, *self-actualization*, lies at the zenith of Maslow's hierarchy. Before it can be reached, all previous needs have to be adequately met.

Maslow's concept of self-actualization enriches our analysis of maturity and intimate relationships. Self-actualized partners make full use of their talents and abilities in life and are able to engage in relationships that are authentic and meaningful.

self-actualization A harmonious integration of the personality enabling people to make full use of their potentialities, capabilities, and talents.

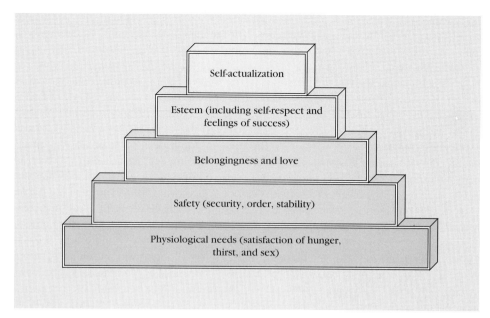

FIGURE 6–1
Maslow's Hierarchy of Needs.

Adapted from A. Maslow *Toward a Psychology of Being* (2nd ed.). (Princeton, NJ: Van Nostrand Reinhold, 1968).

The relationship itself offers a climate of comfort and security, as well as a vehicle for the exchange of belongingness and love. Moreover, the respect and assurance partners receive from each other create an atmosphere of trust and authenticity, important ingredients of self-actualization.

As you have probably realized, the three theoretical positions explored in this section are more similar than different. The components of maturity that Allport, Erikson, and Maslow discuss all contribute to shaping satisfaction and fulfillment within intimate relationships. People who have successfully resolved the challenges posed by each theory are likely to bring considerable maturity, insight, and stablity to their relationships with others. And, as we'll discuss later, the resolution of these challenges creates other relational dividends: sensible and sensitive styles of loving, sound values, ethics, and responsible sexual decision making.

DYNAMICS OF INTIMATE RELATIONSHIPS

Having explored the concept of maturity and its importance to intimate relationships, let's now turn our attention to some of the dynamics of intimate relationshps. In the first portion of this discussion, we'll explore some of the pivotal features of intimate relationships. Then we will take up some of the advantages and disadvantages of having intimate relationships.

Components of Intimate Relationships

Certain qualities are necessary to the development and maintenance of intimate relationships. According to Gordon Chelune and associates (1984), these qualities include partners' knowledge of each other's innermost being, mutuality, interdependence, trust, commitment, and caring. These dimensions are all quite different, but they are interdependent and they overlap.

Intimacy, Love, Sex, and Values

KNOWLEDGE. As intimate relationships develop, mutual self-disclosure of increasingly personal information unfolds. Apparently, it is of central importance to people to be able to share with others all aspects of themselves and to feel understood and accepted as the people they are. According to Chelune, it is also important to know, understand, and accept other people thoroughly. In an intimate relationship, these processes occur simultaneously and reciprocally. They appear to represent a single process characteristic of the relationship as a whole rather than descriptions of the needs and actions of two separate people. A 24-year-old woman looks at partner knowledge this way:

> We've been going together for almost three years, and I feel as though I've known him for my entire life. We have the ability to tune into each other's feelings, and we usually can "read" each other's moods. For example, I know when he's had a bad day, or he knows when I need to get out of the house. Our knowledge and sensitivity toward one another give our relationship a special gift. There are no masks or facades with Robert and me, and none of the other games that I see other couples playing. I know him and he knows me and that's the way we always want it to be. (Authors' files)

MUTUALITY. At the foundation of an intimate relationship is the assumption that the partners are engaged in a joint venture. With the passage of time, they come to know each other in greater depth. Intimate relationships are grounded in a process of sharing such things as interests and goals (Perlman & Fehr, 1986; Roscoe, Kennedy, & Pope, 1987). One woman reflects on the sharing that takes place in her relationship:

Among other things, mutuality in a relationship is based on the partners' sense of fairness—their belief that decisions affecting both should be shared and that each person should guard the other's rights and needs as closely as his or her own.

> We've always enjoyed doing things together, ever since I can remember. Paul is just great company, and even in college, I used to look forward to doing things together on the weekend. Even when we just spend quiet time together, I feel really close to him. If I had to name the best part of our relationship, it would easily be our ability to share our lives and the happiness that such sharing brings. (Authors' files)

Another woman's observation:

> In the last five years, Deborah and I have grown enormously. We have accomplished this growth by a mutual sharing of the intimate parts of our lives. The best part of our relationship has always been the sharing of those intimate details, and with that sharing a growing respect for each other. (Authors' files)

It is important to mention that while mutuality embodies shared interaction, it does not require highly similar or identical interaction patterns. Intimate relationships seem to involve both reciprocal interactions, with the partners showing similar behavior either simultaneously or alternatively, and complementary interactions, in which the behavior of each partner differs from, but complements, that of the other. Reciprocal interactions allow partners to interact as equals and to select life goals and directions satisfactory to them both. Complementary interactions allow partners to help and support each other.

Another feature of mutuality is the concept of "fairness" in rewards and costs within the relationship. Intimate relationships are often characterized by a sense of fairness, shared by both partners, relating to their needs, inputs, and outcomes. This concept of fairness is important to the mutuality of the overall relationship (Hendrick & Hendrick, 1992; Rook, 1987; Sprecher, 1986; McElfresh, 1982; Hatfield et al., 1985).

INTERDEPENDENCE. Adults within intimate relationships learn in what ways they can depend on each other for support, resources, understanding, and action. Partners also share knowledge and goals, increase some interactions with one another while limiting others, pool resources, and slowly intertwine their lives in a variety of ways. However, as intimate relationships grow and develop, partners are increasingly likely to form relationships with other people and to engage in activities outside the relationship. This is probably because they have come to trust each other and to recognize each other's need for private "space."

Unbalanced relationships are characterized by extreme dependency, with little or no scope for outside involvement. Partners in these types of relationships are sometimes referred to as "joined at the hip." They are always a duo and never comfortable in social situations without each other. Often it's impossible to pry such a couple apart in order to spend time with only one partner. However, a more flexible interdependence structure can intertwine two lives for the greater satisfaction of each. A 30-year-old woman reflects on the importance of interdependence this way:

> Jim and I are very much involved with each other, and enjoy the time we spend together. I love his company and look forward to the special moments we share. It's hard to imagine not sharing special time with him. However, we both respect each other's individuality and never want our relationshp to put a stranglehold on our identities. He needs time and space to pursue his own independent activities, while I need my space as well. We think it's healthy, and it doesn't threaten either one of us. On the contrary, it makes the time that we spend together even more special. We've seen too many partners psychologically suffocate each other by not allowing private space. (Authors' files)

It should also be noted that interdependence creates considerable mutual power. As people become dependent on each other, they gain a kind of power—the power to grant or withhold things from each other. Where dependence is mutual, this power is also mutual, and thus something that is shared rather than held over one partner's head by the other. One thing that makes real interdependence possible is trust.

TRUST. As partners share intimacy and increasing amounts of self-disclosure, they become psychologically vulnerable. Thus an intimate relationship requires trust, a sense of confidence in the integrity, truthfulness, and fairness of the partner. In a general sense, trust ensures that neither partner will be unduly harmed by the relationship. More specifically, partners trust each other to be accepting, to avoid purposeful hurt of the other, to keep the best interests of the other and of the relationship in mind, to feel warmth and caring for the other, to need the other and respond to the other's needs, to share, and to continue the relationship. One 21-year-old man had this to say about the trust he feels in his partner:

> I think trust is the most important feature of any honest relationship. When Cari and I entered into this relationship, we agreed that we would always be open and honest with each other. We don't believe in hiding things from each other, and if something bothers either one of us, we constructively confront the issue. Sure, this has led to some uncomfortable moments, but an honest dialogue always seems to help us weather the storm. Mutual respect has a lot to do with our happiness, too, and the trust that we give each other. I respect her as a person and know that she is caring, sincere, and genuine. If anything over the last five years, these feelings have grown since we first got serious (Authors' files)

The love and commitment that go with intimacy characterize many kinds of relationships. During Terry Anderson's long years as a hostage, his sister, Peggy Say, worked tirelessly, day after day, to win his freedom.

COMMITMENT. Intimates continually assess their own and their partner's desires for commitment. The other qualities of intimate relationships seem to be influenced by the extent of this mutual commitment. It has been found, for example, that people will disclose easily and at great depth if they expect a relationship to be short-term. Conversely, if they see the possibility of commitment to a long-term relationship, they tend to disclose themselves more slowly and deliberately, depending on the degree of partner reciprocity. Partners may also be committed to the relationship in varying ways. For example, friends may realize that eventually circumstances will separate them geographically and in time, but nevertheless be committed to continuing the relationship through long-distance caring. Or partners may express their commitment to remain together emotionally and physically through engagement, a commitment ceremony, or the ceremony of marriage. The type of commitment is not as crucial as the mutuality of understanding and agreement on the terms of commitment.

CARING. The last characteristic of intimate relationships outlined by Chelune and colleagues is caring. Intimate relationships are formed for many reasons, but at least one reason will always be a strong sense of caring and affection between partners. Often, particularly in long-term relationships, caring takes the form of fulfilling a partner's needs. This is perceived as rewarding, even when it entails considerable "costs" (see, e.g., Clark & Reis, 1988). A 32-year-old woman expresses caring for her partner this way:

> Susan and I love each other, but we care about each other, too. We both know that we're special in each other's eyes. She's my best friend and I've shared more with her than anyone else in my entire life. She's done the same with me. We have a special bond and I hope we'll always stay close. We care about each other's happiness, and do little things every now and then to show our affection for each other. (Authors' files)

Intimacy, Love, Sex, and Values

163

A 44-year-old man talks about caring in this fashion:

> Pat had major surgery and took a while to recover from it. It gave me a great deal of pleasure to know that I could be there for her, preparing meals, changing her dressings, and just making sure that she was okay. It was a lot of work, but it was something that I wanted to do. Besides, I know that she would do the same for me. (Authors' files)

Advantages of Intimate Relationships

Numerous benefits are attached to intimate relationships. An intimate relationship enables people to gain insight into themselves and how they are perceived by others, including their strengths as well as their weaknesses. An intimate relationship also teaches the importance of being sensitive to another's attitudes, beliefs, and needs and of establishing a framework within which each person can be comfortable in expressing both love and sexual intimacy. (We will have more to say about sexual intimacy a little later.)

There are other benefits. Intimate relationships provide people with a sense of security and attachment. Partners typically give each other reassurance of worth and competence. Also, an intimate relationship often provides commitment and a common purpose. Intimacy may enable a couple to create a warm and secure environment for their children. Or it may enable two friends to collaborate in developing a business or playing a sport.

It has also been found that a connection exists between intimacy and healthy adjustment (see Duck, 1989; Cunningham & Strassberg, 1981; Waring et al., 1981; Waring & Russell, 1980). Some researchers (e.g., Douglas & Atwell, 1988; Berscheid & Peplau, 1983; Fisher & Stricker, 1982) go so far as to say that intimate relationships are one of life's most rewarding and important activities. A review of the literature by Sadell Sloan and Luciano L'Abate (1985) indicates other positive features. For example, intimacy is a major source of comfort and defense in the presence of crisis throughout the life cycle. Indeed, the inability to be intimate with others may trigger depression (see, e.g., Murphy, 1987; Rich & Scovel, 1987; Levin & Stokes, 1986; Waring & Chelune, 1983). To get an idea of your own present capacity for intimacy, take the quiz in the box on "Measuring Your Intimacy Quotient."

Barriers to Intimate Relationships

A friend of mine always seems to hold back when we start talking about our personal lives. Why do some people avoid self-disclosure?

Why, if intimate relationships offer so many advantages, do some people choose to avoid them? According to Valerian Derlega (1984), the need to disclose personal information in an intimate relationship makes people psychologically vulnerable. Derlega points to five potential risks that people incur when they self-disclose.

Discovering that one's partner is not interested in having an intimate relationship. A man may disclose intimate information to his partner, with the intention of developing a serious relationship. She, however, may not be interested in further intimacy and may terminate the relationship.

Being rejected by one's partner. People may find that others don't like them after they disclose certain things. For example, after a woman tells her boyfriend that she is an alcoholic, he may stop seeing her because the disclosed information makes the relationship unacceptable to him.

Having one's partner use disclosed information to gain control or power in the relationship. The person who receives the disclosure may use it to gain

Do you consider yourself a person capable of intimacy? Have you ever thought about the way you share intimacies with others? The following quiz is designed to provide you with some answers. In the space provided, place an **N** (never), **S** (sometimes), or **O** (often) as each item applies to you.

_____ 1. I like to touch and be touched in affectionate ways.

_____ 2. Sexual intimacy for me is a way of expressing and sharing my feelings of closeness to another.

_____ 3. I spend time and energy cultivating and tending my friendships.

_____ 4. I maintain friendships with members of the opposite sex with whom I am not romantically involved.

_____ 5. I feel accepted, valued, cherished, and understood by my family and friends.

_____ 6. I feel naturally high either alone or in the company of others without needing the help of alcohol or drugs.

_____ 7. I enjoy listening to other people's life stories and philosophies and trying to figure out what makes them tick.

_____ 8. I express feelings of tenderness as well as anger, and displaying grief as well as joy with those people I am closest to.

_____ 9. Other people seem friendly and respond generously when I make an effort to show them I care.

_____ 10. I can often tell what other people are feeling and empathize with them.

_____ 11. I share my secret dreams and shames, my self-doubts, and my cherished hopes with people I feel close to.

_____ 12. I enjoy solitude at times without feeling lonely and am comfortable with my different moods and feelings.

Scoring Key: Give yourself a score of 1 for every **N**, a 2 for every **S**, and a 3 for every **O**. Your intimacy quotient, or ability to share yourself with others, is low if you score 12; medium you score 24, and high if you score in the neighborhood of 36. To get another perspective, ask the person with whom you are most intimate to score you on this quiz, then compare the totals (adapted from Keen, 1985).

some advantage over the other. For example, a man may give his partner sensitive and potentially embarrassing information about himself only to have her use it against him—perhaps by taunting him—in order to establish dominance in the relationship.

Being betrayed by one's partner to others, so that the relationship boundary is broken. Here again, a partner uses sensitive information against the discloser, but this time the information is given to others outside the relationship, breaking confidentiality and destroying trust. This leakage of information erodes the boundary between the couple as a unit and others. For example, a woman might tell her best friend about her husband's infidelities and shortly after discover that her friend has told a neighbor.

Putting more into a relationship than one's partner, with resultant feelings of inequity. Someone who consistently reveals more than his partner or gives more to the relationship than his partner may feel hurt and resentful and come to view the relationship as unfair and unrewarding. For instance, a man may feel exploited because his partner refuses to invest himself in the relationship, never revealing his true feelings when sensitive topics arise.

Elaine Hatfield (1984) believes that risks such as these do exist in relationships, as does the potential for the psychological pain of disappointment and rejection. However, as we'll discover in the next section, rejecting intimacy is not the way to avoid pain. Perhaps the first step toward surmounting the barriers we've described is to establish our independence and to accept ourselves as entitled to be who we are, to have the ideas we have and the feelings we feel, and to do the best that we can.

The next step is to establish these entitlements for the partner. People need to recognize their intimates for who *they* are. Though we are often hard on ourselves, we are generally harder on our partners. To enjoy intimate relationships, we must learn to enjoy others as they are, without hoping to "fix them up." Finally, we have to learn to be more comfortable about self-disclosure. To be intimate, partners have to push toward a more honest, trusting, complete, and patient communication process. Such mutuality can reduce many, if not all, of the risks we have described.

STAGES OF INTIMATE RELATIONSHIPS

The manner in which intimate relationships begin, continue, intensify, or decline and terminate has attracted considerable research attention (see Hendrick, 1989; Douglas & Atwell, 1988; Murstein, 1986; Perlman & Fehr, 1986; Snyder & Simpson, 1986; Surra & Huston, 1986; Perlman & Duck, 1986). George Levinger (1983) has proposed one of the most extensive and comprehensive models of relationship development. The strength of Levinger's theory is that it embraces the broad, often diffuse, changes that emerge over time in a relationship from personal, environmental, and relational factors. Let's examine each of the stages in Levinger's theory.

Acquaintance Stage

This stage begins when one person tries to meet another, either directly or through mutual friends or other people. Whom we become acquainted with is influenced by physical, social, and psychological dimensions. The physical envinroment—for example, an urban or rural setting or the density and size of a community—may largely determine whom we encounter and continue to see. Our social environment, or culture, shapes our mate selection process through its values, beliefs, and norms. And our personalities and those of the people we meet affect the way we initiate and maintain relationships.

Initial impressions often govern subsequent interaction (Buss & Barnes, 1986; Howard, Blumstein, & Schwartz, 1986; Snyder, Berscheid, & Glick, 1985). As we'll soon see, a person's first impressions are based both on the potential partner's obvious characteristics, such as physical appearance and perceived competence, and on one's own values, goals, or moods.

Deciding how to approach another person and what to say is usually challenging, particularly if one is shy (Sprecher, 1989; Sprecher & McKinney, 1987; Shaver, Furman, & Buhrmester, 1985). Sandra Metts and William Cupach (1989) point out that, as a general rule, the woman covertly initiates the courtship sequence by sending nonverbal signals of availability and interest to the man; the man then opens dialogue in a presumably promising atmosphere. One source (Moore, 1985) discloses that women employ a variety of nonverbal behaviors to show their interest in potential partners: smiling, short and long gazes, hair flipping, downward glances. When her interest intensifies, the woman tends to rely on such behaviors as leaning close, nodding, smiling, and laughing.

In an interesting study, Chris Kleinke and associates (1986) examined the impact of opening lines used by men and women to meet potential dating partners. The opening lines were placed into three categories: direct approaches ("Hi. I like you."); innocuous approaches ("Are you from around here?"); and cute-flippant approaches ("I'm easy. Are you?"). Overall, the cute-flippant approaches were seen as least desirable, particularly by women. Men tended to favor direct approaches, while women preferred innocuous approaches.

Initial interactions enable two people to explore the possibilities for mutual enjoyment. If either finds the time spent together unrewarding, that person will probably break off the relationship, but if things go well, the two will continue to see each other (Duck, 1989). As time goes on, their interactions will undergo transformations. For example, Jana and Craig met as members of the same psychology class, and their first coffee dates were confined pretty much to talking about the course, exams, and term papers. But as their relationship grew and deepened, and they began to see each other in the evenings and double-date with friends, their conversation broadened to include a diversity of topics, including their personal backgrounds, interests, likes and dislikes, and goals in life. Thus Jana and Craig moved from being acquaintances to close friends, which, in turn, will create new behaviors and standards of interpersonal evaluation.

The Buildup Stage

During this stage, Levinger (1983) suggests, partners move from merely knowing each other to caring for each other. In the buildup stage, the couple test their compatibility. Usually, they find it easy to further each other's goals, and they look forward to rewarding future interactions. The couple's interdependence grows, not only from increased dating frequency, but also from the emotional connectedness that such dating brings.

What is it that attracts one person to another? What forces operate in the selection of a mate? These are difficult questions to answer since attraction and mate selection are highly complex processes. However, certain factors have been identified.

Interaction tends to be enhanced when people are in frequent contact with each other, either at home or at work. This nearness in place is referred to as **propinquity.** In its broadest sense, propinquity means that two people need to have continual contact if their relationship is to endure. Susan Sprecher (1989) adds that the institutional structure of our society provides numerous opportunities for people to interact, allowing potential partners to meet casually. For instance, churches, synagogues, temples, and other places of worship provide settings where potential partners can meet in an organized and legitimate fashion. Schools, colleges, and universities are ideal places for young people to meet others because their homogeneous groupings offer a large number of potential partners. Potential partners also encounter each other in the workplace.

propinquity An element of attraction suggesting that people need to have continual contact with each other if their relationship is to endure.

Another element of interpersonal attraction is physical appearance. In virtually all societies, physical appearance is an important factor in the overall dynamics of interpersonal attraction (see the "World of Differences" box). Indeed, Alan Feingold (1988) discovered that people tend to select partners whose physical attractiveness roughly matches their own. At the same time, as you'll recall from Chapter 5, most research suggests that it is men who are more preoccupied with physical traits, while women tend to focus on psychosocial factors such as ambition, industriousness, intelligence, education, and occupation (Simpson, 1990; Deaux & Hanna, 1984; Riggio & Woll, 1984; Green, Buchanan, & Heuer, 1984; Bolig, Stein, & McKenry, 1984).

What specific elements of physical attractiveness do women and men deem important? Jacqueline Simenauer and David Carroll's (1982) study of single heterosexual adults showed that an important prerequisite for most women was that a man

A WORLD OF DIFFERENCES

Is Beauty Only Skin Deep? Unraveling the Powers of Physical Attraction

*B*eauty rests in the eye of the beholder, and as Edgar Gregersen (1983) points out, the beholder is culturally conditioned. Thus there will always be variations in ideal types across cultures. Physical traits regarded as attractive in one culture may be considered unattractive in others. For example, physical attractiveness may include flattened heads (Kwakiutl), black teeth (Yapese), fat calves (Tiv), joined eyebrows (Syrians), absence of eyebrows and eyelashes (Mongo), enormously protruding navels (Ila), pendulous breasts (Ganda), and crossed eyes (Mayans).

Still, many societies share certain ideas as far as physical attractiveness is concerned. For example, in virtually every society, some form of good grooming is admired and the person who does not follow this convention is considered unattractive. A poor complexion and excessive acne are almost always considered negative qualities, whereas good teeth, clear eyes, and a firm gait appear to have cross-cultural appeal.

In some societies, Gregersen found that men prefer women with a broad pelvis and wide hips. Mangaian men, for example, consider fat desirable, particularly in the breasts, hips, buttocks, and legs. A slender waist, on the other hand, is preferred by men in other cultures. The Dobuans and the Tongans, especially, consider obesity in either sex to be disgusting. For women the world over, male attractiveness is often associated with social status, skills, bravery, prowess, and similar qualities. Among the Toda of India, women reportedly find especially attractive men who are good at catching buffalo at funerals, a prestigious ritual act. Among women of ancient Oriental high cultures, dignity and wealth in a man were usually preferred to strength and athletic ability.

Many societies have altered the body some way to make it conform to aesthetic or erotic ideals. The piercing or perforation of ears, noses, and lips is quite common. Many women in the Ubanqui-Chari region of Africa, particularly the Sara, once inserted large plates or discs inside the lower lip. Neck stretching has been practiced by Padaung women of Burma with the aid of coiled brass neck rings. In other cultures, teeth have been blackened, reddened, knocked out, dug out, filed, chipped, and drilled and filled in with decorative objects. Foot-binding was practiced by upper-class Chinese women from the eleventh century A.D. until the twentieth century. Decorating the skin in some way also knows wide cross-cultural variation, including tattooing, painting, cutting, and, less fre-

be neat, clean, and well-groomed. While many women were drawn to handsome men, many were also attracted to men who were "different" or "individual looking." Women offer the following comments on physical attraction:

> My attention is always drawn to those who take pride in their appearance. It always tells me that they care how they look to others.

> I love a well-groomed man, but I get turned on by the "scruffy" look, too. A day or two of beard growth is sexy.

> A nice smile, including straight, white teeth. Dimples are frosting on the cake.

> I like men in body shirts and stylish suits.

> I enjoy seeing a handsome man in tight-fitting jeans and a bulky sweater. (Authors' files)

Simenauer and Carroll found that men cared more about specific body and facial features than women. When asked about elements of physical attraction, men often noted such features as large breasts and good legs. Do you think men are socialized into looking for these features? Many men preferred that women have

quently, burning. Finally, as we learned in Chapter 3, the modification of both male and female genitals has been practiced for some time.

Diane Ackerman (1990) tells us that efforts to enhance physical attractiveness are rooted in antiquity. Archaeologists have found evidence of Egyptian perfumeries and beauty parlors dating to 4000 B.C. and makeup paraphernalia going back to 6000 B.C. The ancient Egyptians preferred green eye shadow, which was topped with a glitter made from crushing the iridescent carapaces of certain beetles, kohl eyeliner and mascara, black lipstick, red rouge, and fingers and feet stained red with henna. Many Egyptian women shaved their eyebrows and drew in false ones.

Roman men liked cosmetics, and military commanders often had their hair coiffed and perfumed and their nails lacquered before they went into battle. A second-century Roman physician invented cold cream, whose formula has changed little since then. It may also be remembered from the Old Testament that Queen Jezebel "painted her face" before embarking on her wicked ways, a fashion she learned from the high-toned Phoenicians around 850 B.C. In the eighteenth century, some women were willing to eat "arsenic complexion wafers" to make

A young woman of the Padawn hill tribe of northwestern Thailand.

their skin whiter, which worked by poisoning the hemoglobin in the blood so that they developed a fragile, lunar whiteness.

delicate features, full hips, and long hair. Conversely, most men were not attracted to women too "done up," too skinny, or too fat. Men had this to say about the powers of physical attraction:

I love the natural look—no makeup, perfume and definitely no hairspray. The true beauty of a woman should not be disguised.

A nice figure is important to me. I like medium-sized breasts, fairly wide hips, and long legs.

The first thing I look at are a person's eyes. The color is not important, but the sparkle is.

I get turned on by those who have taken care of their bodies and are not overweight.

Nice clothes, a touch of makeup, and tasteful jewelry are elements of attraction for me.

A nice smile goes a long way for me. I usually look at that first, followed by the eyes and then the hair. (Authors' files)

Do men more than women tend to be interested in the physical attractiveness of a partner?

Intimacy, Love, Sex, and Values

Being physically attractive seems to have numerous benefits. Beginning early in life, parents, teachers, and other adults tend to pay more attention and give more praise to children who are good-looking than to plainer children, a bias that continues into adulthood (Berscheid, 1985). Also, physical attractiveness is often correlated with heightened levels of self-confidence and good mental health (Eagly et al., 1991; Dion, 1986; Adams, 1981). Research also indicates (see, e.g., Berscheid, 1985; Cash & Janda, 1984) that attractive people are perceived to be more sensitive, more interesting, kinder, and happier than unattractive people.

The buildup stage enables partners to get to know each other better. People usually tend to associate with those they have someting in common with. This tendency, known as **homogamy,** is based on such factors as similar education, age, and physical appearance. Traditional social pressures long encouraged people to marry within their own religious, ethnic, or national groups. Today, however, some people do marry outside of their particular groups: Catholics marry Protestants, African-Americans marry Caucasians, and German-Americans marry Italian-Americans.

People may also seek partners who complement their own personalities or needs. To illustrate, Gregg, who is outgoing and a good conversationalist, is attracted to Nancy, who is quiet and contemplative. Carla, who hates to cook, is drawn to Marsha, who enjoys preparing meals. In such pairs, mutual needs are fulfilled.

Parental influences may also shape interpersonal attraction. According to Freudian thought, people seek in a mate the image of the parent for whom they nurtured a deep affection during childhood. Although the similarity may be based on physical qualities, usually it involves values or personality traits. Thus a woman may look for a man who is as nurturant as her father was, or a man may seek a woman who appreciates fine art as his mother did.

Exchange and equity are two additional forces influencing attraction. **Exchange** is the principle by which people are attracted to those who provide the greatest relational rewards and require the fewest number of trade-offs or sacrifices. For example, Bill is attracted to Joseph because the perceived rewards that Joseph brings to the relationship (physical attractiveness and career status) are greater than his perceived drawbacks (irritability and geographical distance).

Equity embodies the notion that between two persons there is stability and "fairness" in roles and responsibilities. That is, the set of roles one brings into a relationship and the role expectations one has for the partner are mutually agreeable. For instance, Stan and Kathleen enjoy their relationship because they share their possessions, give and receive emotional support, and promote and care about one another's welfare.

Continuation Stage

According to Levinger (1983), the continuation stage follows a mutual commitment to a long-term relationship. Partners have removed themselves from the interpersonal marketplace and have agreed to restrict their closest intimacies to each other. This stage is characterized by the consolidation of the relationship in a relatively durable midstage, marked in many couples by marriage.

During earlier stages, the relationship was characterized by the couple's experience of ambiguity, novelty, and arousal. Here the relationship reflects familiarity, predictability, and the reduction of emotional and cognitive tension. The more stable a relationship is, the lower will be the partners' ambivalence and self-consciousness.

Mutual trust is essential to the continuation of a healthy relationship. Theodore Issac Rubin (1983) writes that trust embodies confidence in one's mate, including a realization that the partner will not hurt or manipulate one within the relationship. Furthermore, it is characteristic of relationships of high trust that there is no concern whatsoever about equality, about sharing material goods, services, or responsibilities.

homogamy Element of attraction suggesting that people are drawn to partners of similar age, education, and physical appearance.

exchange An element of attraction proposing that people are drawn to those who provide the greatest relational rewards and require the fewest number of sacrifices.

equity Element of attraction stressing the importance of role stability and fairness in relation to responsibilities and expectations.

Intimacy, Love, Sex, and Values

Partners simply take what they need spontaneously, knowing that they will not in any way be exploited by a greedy mate. It is characteristic of relationships of low trust that there is preoccupation with sharing equally. In fact, getting a "fair share" or equal share takes precedence over needs and desires.

An important feature of trust is openness. Openness mainly involves discussion of the emotionally laden "private" areas of a person's life. This may be very threatening indeed. Openness precludes pretense and the constrictive, censoring effects of affection and lack of communication.

Openness also involves nonjudgmental receiving and giving of information, opinions, and the like. Openness is perhaps the most potent form of human interaction. Giving is a crucial part of it, since the privilege of giving is so therapeutic to the person doing the extending. But openness also means being in a condition to receive the other's messages and to respond to them. These messages convey ideas, thoughts, opinions, values, and, above all, moods and feelings without pride or prejudice of any kind. When this happens, there is no pretense between partners (Duck, 1989; Hendrick, 1989; Douglas & Atwell, 1988; Archer & Cook 1986; Falk & Wagner, 1985; Berg & McQuinn, 1986).

Deterioration Stage

Not all relationships deteriorate, of course, but in those that do, Levinger (1983) notes that there are many signals of impending collapse. For example, feelings of discontent and dissatisfaction begin to surface and partners feel rejected and misunderstood. Usually, dissatisfied partners avoid self-disclosure of their feelings or problems. Partners no longer reinforce and support one another, but rather undermine each other's self-esteem through betrayals. A partner's actions—or even mere presence—may interfere with the other's personal plans or activities. As the downward spiral continues, partners inevitably experience a loss of affection, openness, trust, enjoyment, and vitality in their relationship.

Consider the deterioration of Carlo and Sharane's two-year relationship. As their dissatisfaction with each other escalated, they made fewer pleasant remarks (such as compliments) and more unpleasant ones (such as criticisms). As Carlo began to psychologically pull away from the relationship, he engaged in few pleasing acts, such as being helpful around the apartment or hugging and kissing Sharane as he once did. Sharane on her side began to attack Carlo on a regular basis with displeasing remarks, such as accusing him of being lazy and untidy. This only fueled Carlo's anger, and he reciprocated with an onslaught of unkind remarks. When not engaged in verbal battle, Carlo and Sharane were often unresponsive, usually ignoring each other.

A man remembers moving away from his partner this way:

It didn't happen overnight, I know that much. At first we stopped doing little things together, like going out on the weekends or sharing hobbies or interests. Routines dictated our life together and our sex life became nonexistent. In time, we were like two strangers living under the same roof. (Authors' files)

A woman had these recollections:

After a while, I just didn't want to be in his company. I looked for things to divert my attention while at home, and deliberately involved myself in a number of outside activities. I always felt a wave of relief when he went away on business or worked late. (Authors' files)

MAKING USE
OF WHAT
WE KNOW

Severed
Relationships:
Mending a
Broken Heart

The broken relationship, including the assortment of reactions that go with it, is something that many of us have experienced. For some people, separation brings bouts of loneliness, sadness, and varying degrees of remorse. For others, there is anger, resentment, and hostility. Some separated parties feel guilty, incapacitated, or depressed. But for others, separation may bring welcome relief and newfound freedom.

According to Anthony Grasha and David Kirschenbaum (1986), many separated parties believe that they have been failures as partners, and some even question their ability to engage in future relationships. For this reason, forging new relationships and strengthening existing ones are important tasks in the aftermath of separation. This is initially difficult to do if the broken relationship was a long-term one. Then the separated person may not feel like spending time with others. Compounding the problem may be a lack of single friends.

Despite such common problems, Grasha and Kirschenbaum maintain that most people can rebound from a severed relationship. Indeed, many are able to use the experience to strengthen their inner resources and future coping abilities. Grasha and Kirschenbaum offer the following tips on bouncing back.

To begin with, try to follow a role model. If someone you like and respect has adjusted to the breakup of a relationship, talk with that person and borrow whatever useful ideas are offered. This person may also bring objectivity and sensitive guidance to your situation.

Also try to locate a support group. You are not the only person who has ever broken up with someone, and the opportunity to talk with others who have had the same experience is helpful. The lessons they have learned from working through a separation may be just what you need. In most cities, there are organized groups to help people deal with specific problems such as interpersonal communication, personal adjustment, and coping skills for daily living. Along similar lines, college courses on these topics often give people a chance to share experiences, to work on the issues troubling them, and, not incidentally, to meet new people. Support groups, college courses, seminars, or workshops on the topic can help you to expand your horizons and strengthen your inner resources.

Separated people also need to stop putting themselves down. Self-deprecation is a common reaction to loss of a partner. Many people become depressed, pity themselves, or blame themselves for what has happened. Thinking the worst of yourself will get you nowhere. Remember that guilt is self-imposed.

There are ways to counter self-defeating thoughts and self-administered putdowns and techniques to help you gain a balanced perspective of your situation. For example, "Sandi broke off our relationship because of my anger" can be countered with "I did get angry, but she did, too. Whenever I tried to smooth the waters, she wanted too many things her way." Such thinking can give you a more balanced view of the broken relationship. More importantly, it can bring you out of the misery triggered by negative thinking and lingering self-deprecation.

Termination Stage

This stage is marked by the ending of the relationship. At this time, ties to one's partner are severed and wounds need to be healed. Also, new relationships are needed to replace old ones. See the box on "Severed Relationships: Mending a Broken Heart" for some ideas on how people can get their lives back together after a separation.

The emotional impact of terminating a relationship varies widely, but one important determinant is the degree to which the person's plans and behaviors involved the partner. Two people share their feelings about separating from a partner:

When we separated, I wasn't prepared for the emotional aftermath. I thought I could handle it okay, but in reality I had a very difficult time.

I was very angry and depressed. I retreated into my own shell and didn't see anyone. To ease the hurt, I thought it would be best to avoid people. Most of the time I didn't feel like eating and I slept poorly. I felt very empty and alone. (Authors' files)

When Jayne and I split, I felt relief more than anything. This was probably because we had fallen out of love long before and separating was the best thing for us to do. I was neither happy nor sad, and didn't feel any anger toward her. Rather, I was left with an emotionless void, an empty pit. (Authors' files)

LOVE AND INTIMATE RELATIONSHIPS

Love is a complex and multifaceted human emotion that rests at the heart of the intimate relationship. Love can be expressed and received in many different ways. Love relationships are often the central theme of movies, plays, and popular songs. Descriptions, accounts, and narratives of love can be found in virtually all forms of the media, from movies and television to paperback books and supermarket tabloids. The study of love has also produced a wide variety of thoughts and opinions (see, e.g., Hendrick & Hendrick, 1992; Noller, 1990; Sarnoff & Sarnoff, 1989; Douglas & Atwell, 1988; Rubenstein, 1983; Loudin, 1981; Branden, 1981; Money, 1980).

From childhood on, most of us learn the romantic ideal of love. From many different agents of socialization we are taught to expect to "fall" in love at some point in our lives. Moreover, we are taught that love is the eventual outcome of dating and the appropriate basis for marrying and having children. Because of this programming, we come to expect the experience of love (Henslin, 1985).

Gender differences exist in styles of love and loving (see, e.g., Hendrick & Hendrick, 1992; Peplau, 1983). Within loving relationships, traditional women tend to express their feelings and to become emotionally attached to their partners. Most traditional men are cautious about falling in love and tend to de-emphasize love's

Romantic lovers like Romeo and Juliet often came to tragic ends.

emotional components. While men's first feelings on falling in love are usually as ecstatic as women's, many men back off in time. These men speak about holding back from falling in love:

> **For me, falling in love is a bit risky, probably because I've been burned in the past. I don't like feeling so vulnerable.**

> **Falling in love means making a commitment. I'm not sure I can handle the sacrifices that go along with that. I guess I'm afraid of losing my freedom.**

> **I've always been an emotionally cautious person, and falling in love somewhat threatens me. (Authors' files)**

Components of Love

The research of Robert Sternberg (1987, 1985) indicates that although love may be subjectively experienced as a single emotion, it actually consists of a set of feelings, cognitions, and motivations that contribute to communication, sharing, and support. Love includes the following characteristics:

- Promoting the welfare of the loved one.
- Experiencing happiness with the loved one.
- Having a high regard for the loved one.
- Being able to count on the loved one in times of need.
- Mutual understanding.
- Sharing oneself and one's things with the loved one.
- Receiving emotional support from the loved one.
- Giving emotional support to the loved one.
- Intimate communication with the loved one.
- Valuing the loved one in one's own life.

Clifford Swensen (1985) writes that the main content of a love relationship between two adults is communication and that the main method for mutual reward is verbal. For partners who are in love and who plan to have a committed relationship, love is expressed through mutual statements of love and affection, self-disclosure, interest in each other's activities, encouragement and moral support, and toleration of each other's less desirable characteristics. The amount of self-disclosure that furthers the relationship depends upon the degree to which the partners accept themselves and each other (Reiss & Lee, 1988).

All of this means that as love develops, deeper areas of personal life are touched. Such deeper involvement has the potential of creating greater intimacy and interpersonal rewards, and relies considerably on the personality dynamics discussed earlier in the chapter. As you will recall, the capacity to reveal increasingly intimate details about oneself in a love relationship is enhanced by maturity, authenticity, comfort with one's identity, and the willingness to share oneself with an intimate partner. The security and trust offered by meaningful loving relationships help partners to fulfill their needs for belongingness, self-esteem, and self-actualization.

Infatuation, Love, and Friendship

Infatuation and love can feel identical in the early stages. For example, both initially produce strong feelings of pleasurable excitement as well as a powerful desire to be with a particular person. The primary difference is that with love, the feelings not only last, but can deepen (Bessell, 1984).

Probably the most significant sign that one is experiencing a "crush" rather than love is the absence of real caring for the other person. Crushes are based on images rather than on real people. People often develop crushes on those who reflect culturally desirable—and often rather superficial—qualities such as wealth, notoriety, and good looks (Rubin, 1983).

The more you are with someone and get to know that person, the better able you are to judge whether you are enamored of a fantasy or a real person. If your feeling is infatuation, time with the person will usually dampen fantasies and bring the romance to a halt. But if your feelings do not weaken, you may be in love. Table 6–1 displays some of the differences between infatuation and romantic love.

What are the differences between friendship and love? Although we readily distinguish between friends and lovers in everyday life and value each differently, there has been relatively little research on how these two types of relationships differ. Keith Davis and Michael Todd (1984), however, have identified three clusters of qualities and characteristics that they feel distinguish love from friendship. Let's begin with the friendship cluster, which, as you can see from Figure 6–2, is the most extensive of the three. Beyond the fact that two people participate in a relationship as equals, friendships envelop the following characteristics:

- *Enjoyment.* Friends enjoy each other's company most of the time, although there may be temporary states of anger, disappointment, or mutual annoyance.
- *Acceptance.* Friends accept each other as they are, without trying to change or make the other into a new or different person.
- *Trust.* Friends have mutual trust in the sense that each assumes that the other will act in his or her friend's best interest.
- *Respect.* Friends respect each other in the sense of assuming that each exercises good judgment in making life choices.

TABLE 6–1

Differences Between Infatuation and Romantic Love

INFATUATION	ROMANTIC LOVE
Based on limited time with person.	Lasts more than three or four months, usually indefinitely.
A fantasy trip—based on your wishes.	Reality—based on genuine attraction and long-continuing satisfaction with the companionship of this person.
The sexual interest weakens.	The sexual interest persists.
Real and frequent contact breaks the spell.	Real and frequent contact reinforces the attraction.
When the relationship ends, it is over forever, and you feel enlightened and relieved.	The attraction of the other person's personality usually lasts indefinitely.
The desire for association ends with the realization that this has been a case of "mistaken identity."	The desire for association remains indefinitely.
Strong emotion triggered by wish-fulfilling fantasy.	Strong emotion not based upon or continued by fantasy.
Almost always starts quickly and ends rapidly.	Though often starts immediately, it grows and blossoms with more frequent contact.
Feelings die.	Feelings persist.

Source: Adapted from H. Bessell, *The Love Test* (New York: Warner Books, 1984), pp. 7–8.

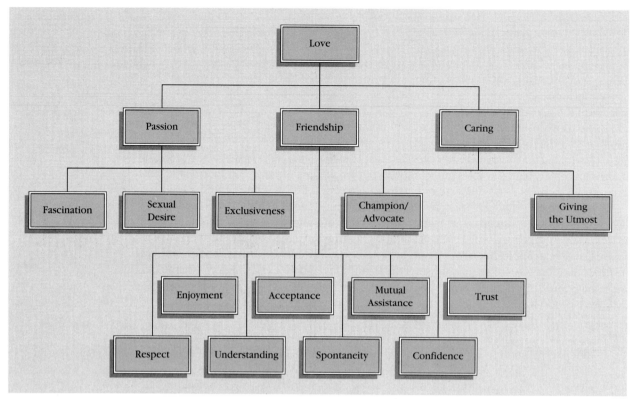

FIGURE 6–2
Love As Friendship Plus Passion and Caring.

From K. E. Davis, "Near and Dear: Friendship and Love Compared," *Psychology Today*, February 1985, pp. 22–30. Reprinted with permission from *Psychology Today* magazine. Copyright © 1985 (Sussex Publishers).

- *Mutual Assistance.* Friends are inclined to assist and support one another. Specifically, they can count on each other in times of need, trouble, and personal distress.
- *Confiding.* Friends share experiences and feelings with each other that they don't share with other people.
- *Understanding.* Friends have a sense of what is important to each and why each does what he or she does. Friends are not routinely puzzled or mystified by each other's behavior.
- *Spontaneity.* Each feels free to be himself or herself in the relationship rather than feeling required to play a role, wear a mask, or inhibit revealing personal traits.

All of the characteristics of friendship are found also in love relationships. However, Davis and Todd say, love includes two other groups of characteristics: the passion and caring clusters. The passion cluster consists of the following:

- *Fascination.* Lovers tend to pay attention to the other person even when they should be involved in other activities. They are preoccupied with the other and tend to think about, look at, want to talk to, or merely be with the other. Fascination can lead to idealization of the loved one or devotion.
- *Exclusiveness.* Lovers have a special relationship that precludes having the same relationship with a third party. Thus a romantic love relationship is given priority over other relationships in one's life.

Intimacy, Love, Sex, and Values

- *Sexual Desire.* Lovers want physical intimacy with the partner, desiring to touch and be touched and to engage in sexual activities. They may not always act on the desire, even when both members of the couple share it, since it may be overriden by moral, religious, or practical considerations. A little bit later on in the chapter we will discuss other elements of sexual involvement in relationships.

Davis and Todd's caring cluster incorporates just two components: "giving the utmost" and "being a champion/advocate":

- *Giving the Utmost.* Lovers care enough to give the utmost when the other is in need, sometimes to the point of extreme sacrifice.
- *Being a Champion/Advocate.* The depth of lovers' caring shows up also in an active championing of each other's interests and in a positive attempt to make sure that the partner succeeds.

Davis and Todd tested their models of love and friendship against the experiences and expectations of approximately 250 college students and community members, both single and married. They discovered, as expected, that the best friendships shared many characteristics with spouse/lover relationships. For example, levels of trust, respect, and acceptance were almost identical, and levels of understanding, mutual assistance, and spontaneity were very similar. Also as expected, the passion cluster differentiated lovers and spouses from best friends. Levels of fascination and exclusiveness were much higher among lovers and spouses.

Surprisingly, however, although it was expected that lovers and spouses would be more willing than best friends to give the utmost when needed and to be an advocate of their partner's interests, only "giving the utmost" showed the anticipated difference, and it was a much smaller difference than those found for components of the passion cluster. The researchers were also interested to find that although lovers were more likely than friends to prefer doing things with each other to doing them with other people, friends were more likely than lovers to view their relationships as stable.

To summarize this section, although infatuation may initially feel like love, over time the differences become quite apparent. Unlike infatuation, love promotes commitment, intimacy, and the growth of the persons involved. Friendship and love are linked in many ways, and friends as well as lovers enhance personal well-being by providing such important psychological vitamins as trust, respect, and understanding.

Of the differences that do exist between friends and lovers, qualities attached to caring and passion seem to be the most important.

Conceptual Models of Love

Just as there are many different ways to experience and express love, there is a plethora of models to describe it. One such model, called the wheel theory, was developed by Ira Reiss (1960, 1980). He suggests that love consists of four components: rapport (feeling at ease with each other), self-revelation (disclosing personal details to each other), mutual dependency (developing a reliance on each other and establishing interdependence), and personality and need fulfillment (satisfying each other's emotional needs).

In a serious, long-lasting intimate relationship, the wheel (see Figure 6–3) will turn indefinitely; in a short-lived romance, it may turn only a few times. Also, the weight of each component will cause the wheel to move forward or backward. To see how the wheel can reverse itself, consider that the self-revelation component has been reduced because of some type of relationship disharmony. This reduction would affect the dependency and personality need fulfillment processes, which would weaken rapport, which would, in turn, lower the revelation level even further.

Another conceptual model of love has been proposed by John Lee (1988, 1976, 1974). Lee developed a typology of love that consists of six main types—eros, ludus, storge, mania, agape, and pragma love. The following is a description of each type.

eros love Love characterized by the desire for sexual intimacy.

Eros love. **Eros love** is characterized by the desire for sexual intimacy and a preoccupation with the physical aspects of the relationship. Erotic lovers usually report a powerful mutual attraction, as well as intense feelings of excitement and anticipation.

FIGURE 6–3
The Wheel Model of Love.

From *Family Systems in America* Third Edition by Ira L. Reiss, copyright © 1980 by Holt, Rinehart, & Winston. Reprinted by permission of the publisher.

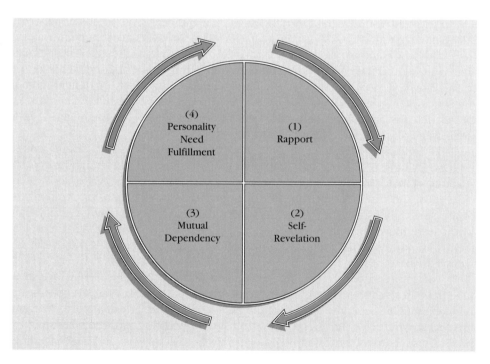

Intimacy, Love, Sex, and Values

Ludus love. Derived from the word *ludicrous*, **ludus love** is playful, flirtatious, and often self-centered. Ludic lovers do not want long-range attachments with their partners. Most also do not want their partners to be dependent on them. Ludus love has often been described as a style that regards love as a game.

Storge love. **Storge love** (pronounced "stor-gay") is a Greek term in origin and means calm, affectionate love. Unlike eros love, storge love has no sudden, dramatic beginning. Rather, it is characterized by quiet commitment. It embodies companionship and the enjoyment of doing things together. Intense emotional involvement is usually avoided.

Manic love. **Manic love** is intense and obsessive. Many manic lovers are overwhelmed by thoughts of their partners, so much so that they're always in a state of anxiety. They need continual affection and attention from their partners, as well as constant reassurance about the other's sincerity and commitment.

Agape love. **Agape love** is also a Greek term in origin and means altruistic love. Agape lovers care deeply about their partners and seek to satisfy their well-being in a warm and kind fashion. This gentle style of loving asks nothing in return.

Pragma love. Pragma is from the Greek word *pragmatikos*, meaning "practical" and "realistic." **Pragma love** is characterized by sensibleness and logic. Pragma lovers are realistic in that they seek to match themselves with a partner whose background is compatible with their own.

ludus love Love that is playful, flirtatious, and often self-centered.

storge love Calm and affectionate love that embodies companionship and the enjoyment of doing things with one's partner.

manic love Love that is intense and obsessive.

agape love A gentle, altruistic form of love.

pragma love Love that is practical and realistic.

Lee believes that many combinations of love are possible. For example, storgic-eros lovers are not possessive of their partners and avoid intense emotional commitment. However, they also tend to emphasize the sexual intimacy and physical closeness that their relationship offers. Although in one person a particular style usually dominates, we are all capable of experiencing each type. Different relationships may elicit different styles.

Research suggests that women tend to be more pragmatic, manic, and storgic in their styles of loving, while men often demonstrate erotic and ludic styles (Dion, 1985). It has also been suggested that people in love demonstrate more erotic and agape love than those who are not in love (Hendrick & Hendrick, 1988).

Another thought-provoking model of love was developed by Robert Sternberg (1988, 1986). Sternberg maintains that love is based on three components: passion (an intense physical attraction and desire for someone), intimacy (feelings of closeness and concern for a partner's well-being), and commitment (recognition of the fact one is in love and a willingness to maintain the relationship). Sternberg conceptualizes these components as a triangle (see Figure 6–4).

Like Lee's model, Sternberg's love triangle enables us to see how three components can exist in different patterns and different degrees. Based on different combinations of passion, intimacy, and commitment, Sternberg identifies seven forms of love:

- *Liking:* Intimacy, but no commitment or passion.
- *Infatuation:* Passion without commitment or intimacy.
- *Empty Love:* Commitment without passion or intimacy.
- *Romantic Love:* Intimacy and passion, but no commitment.
- *Fatuous Love:* Commitment and passion but no intimacy.
- *Companionate Love:* Commitment and intimacy, but no passion.
- *Consummate Love:* Commitment, intimacy, and passion.

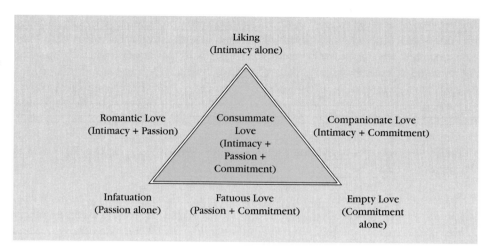

FIGURE 6–4
Sternberg's Triangular Model of Love.

The three basic components of intimacy, passion, and commitment combine to explain all the positive feelings that people can have for each other. From R. J. Sternberg, "Triangulating Love," in R. J. Sternberg & M. L. Barnes (eds.), *The Psychology of Love* (New Haven, CT: Yale University Press, 1988).

Sternberg maintains that these combinations of love can help explain different interpersonal relationships. Liking, for example, is characteristic of friendships, while companionate love is common in long-term relationships. Empty love can probably be applied to those relationships that have become devoid of meaning. Sternberg feels that consummate love is the most rewarding of all love experiences and embraces all three components. It is the ideal, complete form of love.

PUTTING THE MODELS INTO PERSPECTIVE. These three conceptualizations of love are useful in understanding the different experiences of love, including its many complexities. For example, Reiss's wheel theory sheds light on how a love relationship can be conceptualized as an ongoing cycle. The typologies offered by Lee and Sternberg illustrate how love can reflect different feelings, thoughts, and actions. Better yet, they show how in real life a loving relationship rarely consists of a unitary style. Instead, love relationships are often characterized by the *interaction* of several styles. Integrating this chapter's focus on maturity and intimacy with such conceptual models may help readers gain a better understanding of their own friendships and love relationships, including the styles inherent in each.

SEXUAL INVOLVEMENT IN INTIMATE RELATIONSHIPS

Sexual involvement is one way to fulfill intimacy needs within a relationship. Indeed, sexual involvement is often a manifestation of the love, emotional support, companionship, and caring that two people share. But what factors determine whether and how soon in a relationship partners will engage in sexual activity? In an exhaustive review of the literature, Susan Sprecher (1989) answers these questions by analyzing three types of causal factors: individual, relationship, and environmental factors.

Individual Factors

People vary in the degree to which they are willing to engage in sexual activity early in a relationship. Several background, social-demographic, and personality variables are thought to be related to the extent of a couple's sexual behavior.

PREVIOUS SEXUAL EXPERIENCE. It appears that greater lifetime sexual experience is positively associated with more intimate current sexual behavior. Partners who abstain from sex usually have had less prior sexual experience than sexually active partners.

SEXUAL ATTITUDES. Partners abstaining from sex often have less permissive attitudes about sex than do sexually active partners. Sexual attitudes have become increasingly permissive, and most people today approve of premarital sexual intercourse in relationships that are characterized by intimacy and affection (Reiss, 1989; Walsh, 1989). But some people still feel hesitant about engaging in sex until they feel deeply committed to the other person.

DESIRABLE CHARACTERISTICS. There is speculation (Snyder, Simpson, & Gangestad, 1986) that people who have desirable characteristics (at least as perceived by themselves) are more likely to engage in sex in a relationship. For example, men who rate themselves high in social desirability and physical attractiveness tend to engage in more intimate sexual behavior than men who rate themselves lower. Women who engage in early sexual intimacy have been found to have higher self-ratings on desirability as a date, intelligence, creativity, and self-confidence than women who delay sex in a relationship.

PERSONALITY CHARACTERISTICS. Self-monitoring appears to be related to a tendency toward unrestricted casual sex. (Self-monitoring refers to how closely we watch our own actions and adapt our behavior to the situation.) For instance, high self-monitors tend to be more willing than low self-monitors to engage in sex with partners without emotional attachment. Also, sex guilt seems to be negatively related and sensation-seeking positively related to the extent of sexual behavior in a relationship.

INFLUENCE OF GENDER. Women have traditionally been socialized to exhibit less interest in sex than men. Men tend to accept sex in casual relationships and to emphasize sexual over emotional interaction. Women also expect greater commitment from a partner before they find sexual intercourse acceptable (Sprecher et al., 1988; Roche, 1986; Denney, Field, & Quadagno, 1984).

Relationship Factors

Just as partners vary in their desire to share sexual intimacy, so do relationships vary in the degree to which they are conducive to sexual activity.

GENERAL LEVEL OF INTIMACY. Two major factors determining whether a relationship will involve sexual activity are the level of emotional intimacy and the duration of the relationship. The more emotional and/or the longer the partners have been together, the more likely they are to share sexual intimacy (Walsh, 1989; Christopher & Cate, 1985; McCabe, 1987). With greater emotional intimacy and/or length of time in the relationship, even partners who have less permissive sexual attitutdes often feel that it is appropriate to engage in sexual activity.

MORE SPECIFIC FEELINGS AND BEHAVIORS. Research has also examined how specific feelings and behaviors are related to sexual activity in the relationship. For instance, the type of love one feels for a partner may affect the sexual experience. Passionate lovers may feel a need to engage in greater amounts of sexual intimacy than companionate lovers. And, related to our earlier discussion of styles of loving, sexual permissiveness may be positively associated with ludic love but negatively associated with agapic love (Hendrick & Hendrick, 1986).

Individual, relationship, and environmental factors combine to determine when and how sexuality will be expressed in a particular intimate relationship.

EQUITY. As we've seen, an equitable relationship is one based on mutuality and reciprocity. Those partners who claim their relationship is equitable are often sexually intimate and are more likely to say that they had engaged in sexual activity because both partners wanted it. Equity also tends to promote general relationship satisfaction, including sexual satisfaction (Traupmann, Hatfield, & Wexler, 1983).

Environmental Factors

Finally, partners' sexual involvement can be affected by their social and physical environment. To illustrate, partners vary in the degree to which they are given opportunities—by parents, friends, and even the structure of societal institutions— to have private time for sex. Sprecher cites two other ways the environment may affect the couple's sexual activities:

SOCIAL NETWORK AND CULTURAL FACTORS. The individual factors presented thus far are often influenced by the social environment. For instance, sexual standards are shaped by parental standards (especially those of the same-gender parent), peer standards, and standards of one's culture or subculture. Moreover, the more friends one has who are engaging in sex, the more apt one is to engage in sex with one's partner.

PHYSICAL ENVIRONMENT AS FACILITATOR OF SEXUAL EXCITEMENT. While most of what we've said so far concerns the cognitive, decision-making aspects of sexual involvement, it is a fact that sex often occurs in response to spontaneous sexual arousal. Some environmental factors that contribute to sexual arousal are music, lighting, scents, and closeness to others (e.g., in a crowded disco). It has been suggested (e.g., White & Knight, 1984) that before people can feel the intense emotion of sexual excitement or passionate love, they must experience physiological arousal as well as external cues appropriate for the label of *sexual excitement.*

SEXUAL VALUES AND INTIMATE RELATIONSHIPS

sexual value A conceptual structure representing a person's *beliefs* about what is appropriate or inappropriate, desirable or desirable, in sexual behavior.

moral value A type of value representing a person's ethical standards of right and wrong.

sexual value system A framework of values or set of assumptions that shapes a person's sexual life.

Sexual values are important integrating forces of men and women's sexuality and influential in shaping the course of their intimate relationships. Broadly defined, a **sexual value** is a conceptual structure of a prescriptive nature. Sexual values represent a person's *beliefs* about what is appropriate or inappropriate, desirable or undesirable, in sexual behavior. Important determinants of one's sexual values are **moral values,** ethical standards of right and wrong that guide decision making and overall standards of conduct. Sexual and moral values combine to produce a **sexual value system,** a framework that enables people to appraise, explain, and integrate sex-related situations. In a broad sense, a sexual value system is a set of assumptions that shapes a person's sexual life.

We can relate the development of a stable and adequate value system to many of the topics presented in this chapter. You will recall that sound values are an integral part of Gordon Allport's concept of maturity. And people who successfully resolve the Eriksonian psychosocial stages of identity versus role confusion and intimacy versus isolation are likely to become aware of the *personal* significance of the values they hold (as opposed to their absolute meaning). In this way, young adults integrate their own life experiences and motives into a value system that has personal relevance. Reflecting on Abraham Maslow's theory, it is more than likely that sound values help guide a person in the quest for self-actualization. Finally, the development of mature and sensible values aids in the formation and maintenance of intimate relationships. Indeed, a realistic and sound value system may help anchor partners in a responsible, rewarding, and lasting union.

We feel that the selection of values to guide one's sexual life is a multifaceted process, one that follows a sequential pattern. Initially, a person may be confronted with an issue that stimulates her to form an opinion of what is good and bad, right and wrong. Some such issues are the acceptability of premarital intercourse, the notion of shared contraceptive responsibility, the "fairness" of traditional gender-role behaviors, and the desirability of same-sex relationships. When a person confronts such an issue, she usually recognizes the need to establish some type of sexual value. Beyond consulting one's existing sexual value system (which consists, at this point, of values that one has been taught), one may solicit input from family, friends, teachers, or other sources of socialization. The values gathered are then compared and contrasted, and one is ultimately chosen. The choice reflects the most suitable standard for that person for the time being, and usually reflects the following dimensions or characteristics (Fogel, 1990):

- The value has been chosen from the available alternatives.
- The value has been selected with knowledge of the consequences involved.
- The value has been chosen freely, without coercion.
- The value is prized and cherished by the person.
- The value will be publicly affirmed when appropriate.
- The value will be acted upon and become a consistent behavior pattern.

Our discussion has implied that values may be extrinsic or intrinsic. *Extrinsic values* are derived from society's standards of right or wrong and are usually grounded in intellectual conviction. Because extrinsic values typically are a conception of the ideal, they are sometimes limited in their practical application. *Intrinsic values*, on the other hand, derive from personal experience and are the beliefs that govern a person's everyday behavior. Because there may be a gap between people's extrinsic and intrinsic values, it is important to examine both what a person says and how that person actually behaves. The husband who extols agape love outside of the family but batters his wife, and the woman who promotes the value of self-disclosure but always keeps her problems to herself, reflect discrepancies between their conceived and their operative values.

Sexual Value Orientations

As we learned in Chapter 1, every society has sought to regulate and control human sexuality. According to John DeLameter (1989), the social controls of sexual expression are intertwined with the basic institutions of society, such as religion and the family. Religion offers a set of shared values and rituals that reinforce social solidarity, while the family fills society's need to regulate sexual behavior and reproduction and ensure that young children are cared for and socialized properly. To these two ancient institutions we can add the more modern educational institution, which is charged with socializing young people with regard to sexuality, and the medical institution, which evelutes sexual behavior on a healthy-unhealthy dimension. Finally, more informal socialization agents, such as peers and the media, are also instrumental in shaping people's sexual values.

It is from socialization frameworks such as these that sexual value orientations or ideologies emerge: sets of assumptions about the purpose(s) of sexual activity and its place in human life. Such orientations represent the basis for norms that specify

What kinds of sexual values do people hold? What purpose do they serve?

MAKING USE OF WHAT WE KNOW

Surveying Your Sexual Values

*I*t is important to gain knowledge about your sexual values in order to understand and act on your beliefs about sexual matters. Such an exploration may also make you more comfortable with your attitudes and beliefs and assist you in becoming more tolerant of others' values and feelings. The exercise that follows is *not* a test; rather, it is a measure of how you feel about certain sexual behaviors. There are no right or wrong answers. In the space provided beside each item, circle the number that best reflects your attitude. Use the following scale for your responses:

1 Strongly disagree
2 Disagree
3 Neither agree nor disagree
4 Agree
5 Strongly agree

1. I think there is too much freedom given to adults these days.   1 2 3 4 5
2. I think that the increased sexual freedom seen in the past several years has done much to undermine the American family.   1 2 3 4 5
3. I think that young people have been given too much information about sex.   1 2 3 4 5
4. Sex education should be restricted to the home.   1 2 3 4 5
5. Older people do not need to have sex.   1 2 3 4 5
6. Sex education should be given only when people are ready for marriage.   1 2 3 4 5

7. Premarital sex may be a sign of a decaying social order.   1 2 3 4 5
8. Extramarital sex is never excusable.   1 2 3 4 5
9. I think there is too much sexual freedom given to teenagers these days.   1 2 3 4 5
10. I think there is not enough sexual restraint among young people.   1 2 3 4 5
11. I think people engage in sex too much.   1 2 3 4 5
12. I think the only proper way to have sex is through intercourse.   1 2 3 4 5
13. I think sex should be reserved for marriage.   1 2 3 4 5

what types of activity are appropriate and inappropriate, and what types of persons are appropriate partners for sexual activity (DeLameter, 1989; Walsh, 1989). The following are some of the more common sexual value orientations or ideologies that may offer guidelines for people making decisions about their sexuality.

ASCETIC ORIENTATION. The roots of the ascetic orientation in the West can be traced back to early Christianity and the teachings of St. Paul and St. Augustine (see Chapter 1). Essentially, the **ascetic orientation,** also known as *celibacy,* advocates sexual self-denial, the avoidance of all sexual activity, and the implementation of spiritual self-discipline. Rather than sexual involvement, emphasis is placed on developing the romantic and spiritual facets of a relationship.

ascetic orientation A value orientation advocating sexual self-denial, the avoidance of all sexual activity, and the implementation of spiritual self-discipline.

Intimacy, Love, Sex, and Values

14. Sex should be only for the young.   1 2 3 4 5

15. Too much social approval has been given to gays and lesbians.   1 2 3 4 5

16. Sex should be devoted to the business of pro-creation.   1 2 3 4 5

17. People should not masturbate.   1 2 3 4 5

18. Heavy sexual pet-ting should be discouraged.   1 2 3 4 5

19. People should not discuss their sexual affairs or business with others.   1 2 3 4 5

20. Severely handi-capped (physi-cally and men-tally) people should not have sex.   1 2 3 4 5

21. There should be no laws prohibit-ing sexual acts between consent-ing adults.   1 2 3 4 5

22. What two con-senting adult do together sexually is their own busi-ness.   1 2 3 4 5

23. There is too much sex on tele-vision.   1 2 3 4 5

24. Movies today are too sexually ex-plicit.   1 2 3 4 5

25. Pornography should be totally banned from our bookstores.   1 2 3 4 5

Scoring: Reverse the scores for state-ments 21 and 22 in the following way: 1 = 5, 2 = 4, 4 = 2, 5 = 1. For exam-ple, if you wrote 1 for statement 21 ("There should be no laws prohibiting sexual acts between consenting adults"), change that number to 5 for scoring purposes. Reverse score statement 22 similarly.

Add the numbers you assigned to each of the 25 statements. Your score may range from a low of 25 (strongly dis-agreed with all items: 1 × 25 = 25) to a high of 125 (strongly agreed with all items: 5 × 25 = 125). If you scored be-tween 25 and 50, you might be regarded as a high-grade liberal, between 50 and 75, a low-grade liberal. If you scored between 100 and 125, you might be re-garded as a high-grade conservative; between 75 and 100, a low-grade conservative.

Source: W. W. Hudson, G. J. Murphy, & P. S. Nurius, "A Short-Form Scale to Mea-sure Liberal vs. Conservative Orientations Toward Sexual Expression," *Journal of Sex Research 19* (1983): 258–272. A pub-lication of the Society for the Scientific Study of Sex. Reprinted by permission.

PROCREATIONAL ORIENTATION. The **procreational orientation,** another Christian ideology, emphasizes that coital activity is acceptable only within marriage and pri-marily for the purpose of having children. This orientation also views any behavior other than vaginal intercourse as undesirable. Most religions in the United States espouse a procreational, somewhat ascetic, sexual value orientation.

procreational orientation
A value orientation empha-sizing that coital activity is acceptable only within mar-riage and primarily for the purpose of having children.

RELATIONAL ORIENTATION. The **relational orientation,** also called "person-centered" sexuality or "permissiveness with affection," views sexual activity as a natural extension of intimate relationships. While coital activity within casual relationships is considered wrong, sexual intercourse is acceptable if accompanied by love and emotional at-

relational orientation
A value orientation that views sexual intercourse as accept-able if accompanied by love and emotional attachment between partners.

tachment between partners. Indeed, sexual intimacy within a committed relationship is perceived as enhancing emotional attachment.

situational orientation A value orientation suggesting that sexual decision making should take place in the context of the particular situation and people involved.

SITUATIONAL ORIENTATION. The **situational orientation,** made popular by humanist Joseph Fletcher in his book *Situation Ethics* (1966), suggests that sexual decision making should take place in the context of the particular situation and people involved. Rather than making decisions about sexual matters solely on the basis of rules, this case-by-case orientation carefully examines motivations and consequences. Thus the acceptability or unacceptability of a sexual act depends on what it is intended to accomplish and its foreseeable consequences.

hedonistic orientation A value orientation emphasizing the importance of sexual pleasure and satisfaction rather than moral constraint.

HEDONISTIC ORIENTATION. The **hedonistic orientation,** sometimes called the *recreational sexual standard*, emphasizes the importance of sexual pleasure and satisfaction rather than moral constraint (readers may recognize elements of ludic styles of loving within this standard). Sexual desire is seen as a legitimate and appropriate appetite to be satisfied with maximum gratification and enjoyment. Unlike the relational standard, which views coital activity as acceptable provided there is attachment between partners, the hedonistic orientation views sexual gratification in intercourse as an end in itself. While the hedonistic orientation received considerable attention in the 1960s, probably only a small number of men and women cling to this standard today. Fear of contracting HIV-AIDS and other sexually transmitted diseases has created a shift toward more conservative sexual value orientations.

Obviously, then, our complex and changing society offers divergent sexual value orientations, from celibacy to casual sex. Since people are usually exposed to several different orientations throughout the course of their lives, making value choices is difficult. We should point out, though, that these orientations are not entirely separate; rather, many people incorporate portions of all these sexual ideologies into their sexual value systems.

Putting Sexual Values into Perspective

The task of selecting suitable sexual values involves examining extrinsic values, such as those just discussed, and adopting those values that have intrinsic worth and validity. As we've indicated, this is no easy chore since people must strike some kind of balance between the values they have been taught while growing up and those that have become personally meaningful. While it is not our purpose to promote any one sexual value or orientation, we do endorse throughout this book the concept of responsible sexual decision making. To this end, we offer the following thoughts on developing an adequate and sound value system.

To begin with, you do not arrive at a sound value system overnight; on the contrary, it is a process that takes time, dedication, and considerable deliberation (Breckler & Wiggins, 1989; Feather, 1984). You should avoid making snap judgments or gravitating toward values just because they are popular or trendy. In the box on "Surveying Your Sexual Values" you will find an exercise that should help you to become more aware of your present sexual values.

Once you have examined and weighed different sexual values, you should have faith and confidence in the ones you choose as your own. The overall system selected should be consistent with your personality and everyday behavior; there should not be a gap between what you say and what you do.

People with sound value systems also hold accurate assumptions about reality. Thus they tend to be fully informed and up-to-date in their knowledge about human sexuality. Those with healthy value systems often recheck their values, testing them against their feelings and life experiences. Moreover, they are tolerant of the value systems of others. They are usually able to accept other people's sexual orientations and activities without feeling personally threatened and without moralizing or judging. Sound and healthy values are also flexible ones, open to new ideas and fluid enough to allow for adjustment or correction. Finally, people with healthy systems derive satisfaction from living by their chosen values—these values provide meaning to their sexuality and a sense of purpose to their overall life (Reiss & Reiss, 1990; Fogel, 1990; Darling & Mabe, 1989).

SEXUALITY IN THE NEWS

For Lovers, No. 1 Activity These Days Is Worrying
By Jon Nordheimer

*I*f the billion Valentine's Day cards that are expected to be sold this week are any measure, love in the United States is robust and healthy. But Cupid might throw away his arrows if love were measured by the highly publicized cases that have pitted men against women in recent months.

A kiss may still be a kiss, a sigh a sigh, but the fundamental thing that applies today when two lovers woo is, "Can I trust you?" . . .

"People today are much more cautious about making a commitment, perhaps so cautious they just can't sit back and let romance take over," said Paula Kamen, the author of *Feminists Fatale: Voices from the Twentysomething Generation* (Donald I. Fine, 1991). "There are too many things that can go wrong and maybe destroy your whole future or kill you."

While millions of American men and women thrive in relationships rooted in mutual respect and understanding, the William Kennedy Smith and Mike Tyson trials, the Clarence Thomas hearings, and the accusations against Gov. Bill Clinton of Arkansas have ignited a prairie fire of discussion about relationships between the sexes. . . .

"We've thrown out the old values that inhibited sexuality, and we can't agree on the new ones," said Dr. Richard J. Cross, professor emeritus of environmental and community medicine at the Rutgers University School of Medicine, who has taught medical students about sexuality. "The task now is to try and agree on what constitutes mutual responsibility in a relationship." . . .

Stressful and Confusing

Virtually free of old taboos, people of all ages have been left to find a personal comfort zone. . . . Many have found this to be stressful and confusing. And all the while, the shadow of AIDS and other sexually transmitted diseases falls across their lives.

"There's a great sense of chaos now when young people consider sexual activity," said Dr. Richard Keeling of the University of Virginia, chairman of the American College Health Task Force on AIDS. "Students frequently tell you in confidential interviews that the risks they perceive far outweigh the pleasures of sex."

Dr. Ira Reiss, a sociologist at the University of Minnesota, senses a hunger for a new sexual ethic that offers guidance.

But at the same time, there is evidence that many young people still partake in casual sex. "There's still the same pattern of one-night stands and numerous partners," reported Dr. June Reinisch, director of the Kinsey Institute for Sex Research, which has surveyed college students.

Other researchers showed that 90 percent of young women today had intercourse before marriage, she added, compared to 50 percent or so 40 years ago. "A significant difference was that women who did it in the 1940s did it with the man they later married," Dr. Reinisch said. "Today's woman has sex with a number of partners."

Naomi Wolf, author of *The Beauty Myth* (Barrow, 1991), also notes that . . . "for the first time in history, women have money and can support themselves [and are] therefore free to be the sexual selectors on the basis of how gratifying men are as partners."

But others point out that women, more than men, still seek emotional security and commitment in combination with sex.

Ms. Kamen said more young women now insist that there be mutual respect between them and a man before they have sex.

continued

Quality, Not Quantity

"That's the sexual revolution of this generation in their 20s: quality relationships instead of quantity," Ms. Kamen said. "We're taking the first steps, and it's painful and causing a lot of confusion along the way."

For some people the perception of trust may be based on little more than intuition and the circumstances under which they meet. They may be more comfortable establishing a relationship if they meet at work or through family and friends. . . .

A 28-year-old sales representative in Chicago who, like others interviewed insisted on anonymity, lamented the lack of romance and courtship.

"Guys still figure if you don't come across, someone else will," she said. "It's like there's no incentive to wait until you get to know each other better." . . .

Reinforcing Behavior

Images in popular culture reinforce such noncommittal behavior, many believe.

"There's nothing that promotes satisfying long-term relationships or health," said Dr. Reinisch of the Kinsey Institute.

Research by Lou Harris & Associates found that a typical American adolescent viewed nearly 14,000 instances of sexual material on television during the 1987–88 season but only 165 references dealt with sexually transmitted disease, birth control, or abortion.

"The media are not responding to our need for more authentic plots," said Mandy Aftel, a California psychotherapist who is writing a book on how mass culture affects individual behavior. . . .

One popular television program that occasionally touches on complex sexual issues is "Beverly Hills 90210," which . . . has dealt with premarital sex, sex education, and condom distribution in schools.

"Our show may be about an affluent Southern California high school, but the issues crisscross the country and transcend liberal-conservative labels," said Charles Rosin, executive producer of the program.

"Love is not a public health issue to 15-year-olds, and they need support to express their feelings at a time when sex is getting very scary," he said. "Our core audience is teenage girls, and we try to address their point of view. . . . A teen character on our show can advocate abstinence and not be uncool about it.

"Our view is, if we can entertain an audience and get them to think for five seconds before the commercial comes on, we've attained our goal." (*The New York Times*, February 12, 1992. Copyright © 1992 by The New York Times Company. Reprinted by permission.)

DISCUSSION QUESTIONS

1. If you have not yet scored yourself on the statements in this chapter's box, "Surveying Your Sexual Values," do so now. Then try to formulate the new concept of mutual responsibility in a sexual relationship that Richard Cross says we need to agree on. Compare your ideas with those of some friends (or, if your instructor discusses this box in class, with your classmates). What similarities do you find? What differences?

2. How many people do you know who, like the students Richard Keeling refers to, see the risks of sexual activity as greater than its pleasures? What is your own view of the dangers posed by the rising incidence of sexually transmitted diseases and AIDS? You may want to come back to this question after you've read Chapters 17 and 18.

3. What do you think Paula Kamen is talking about when she describes a new sexual revolution: quality relationships rather than quantity of relationships? Explain your answer in terms of the concepts we've discussed in this chapter: intimacy, love, sexuality, and values.

4. Do you think the various forms of the media—television, newspapers, magazines, etc.—have a responsibility to explore ethical and moral issues with regard to sexual relationships? Why or why not?

5. Could you advocate sexual abstinence among your peer group and feel "cool" about it? Why or why not?

LOOKING BACK

■ In an intimate relationship, people come to understand themselves and each other better through the mutual exchange of experiences. In mutual self-disclosure, people let themselves be known by others. Self-disclosure can take the form of verbal expression, body language, tone of voice, or actions. As people move into adulthood and mature, they become increasingly capable of mutuality and reciprocity in intimate relationships.

■ The theories of Gordon Allport, Erik Erikson, and Abraham Maslow can help us study intimate relationships. Allport's conception of maturity explores qualities necessary to establish rewarding intimate relationships. Erikson's stages of identity versus role confusion and intimacy versus isolation illuminate the interaction between personal identity and interpersonal sharing. Maslow's theory shows how belongingness, love, self-esteem, and self-actualization needs affect fulfillment within intimate relationships.

■ Some qualities of intimate relationships are knowing oneself and one's partner, interdependence, trust, commitment, and caring. Barriers to forming intimate relationships include a partner's lack of interest or outright rejection; a partner's use of disclosed information to control a relationship or to betray the other

partner; and unequal contributions by partners in a relationship.

■ The primary stages in a relationship are acquaintance, buildup, continuation, deterioration, and termination. Some dynamics of interpersonal attraction are propinquity, physical appearance, homogamy, parental influences, exchange, and equity.

■ Love is a set of feelings, thoughts, and motives that contribute to communication, sharing, and support. Models of love and its expression include Reiss's wheel theory, Lee's typology, and Sternberg's love triangle.

■ Individual, relationship, and environmental factors combine to determine partners' sexual involvement.

■ Sexual values are people's beliefs about what sorts of sexual behaviors are appropriate to engage in and under what circumstances. One's sexual value system provides a frame of reference for appraising and making decisions about sexual situations. Extrinsic sexual values derive from societal standards of right and wrong. Intrinsic values are based on one's own experiences. Sexual value orientations include the ascetic, procreational, relational, situational, and hedonistic.

THINKING THINGS OVER

1. Draw a diagram to compare and contrast the maturity theories of Allport, Erikson, and Maslow. Which theory seems particularly useful to you? Why?

2. Describe your ideal intimate relationship. What components of that relationship are you willing to negotiate or adjust? How would you make those adjustments?

3. Think of some barriers to establishing an intimate relationship. How would you try to overcome those barriers?

4. Imagine that you have just ended an intimate relationship. What are some of the more constructive things that you could do to get your life back in order?

DISCOVER FOR YOURSELF

Darling, C. A., & Mabe, A. R. (1989). Analyzing ethical issues in sexual relationships. *Journal of Sex Education and Therapy, 15,* 126–144. How sexual values and moral principles shape the dynamics of intimate relationships.

Douglas, J. D., & Atwell, F. C. (1988). *Love, intimacy, and sex.* Beverly Hills, CA: Sage. Readers will especially enjoy the chapters on the development of love and falling out of love.

Duck, S. (1989). *Relating to others.* Chicago: Dorsey Press. An examination of the dynamics of interpersonal relationships.

Laner, M. R. (1989). *Dating: Delights and dilemmas.* Salem, WI: Sheffield Publishing Co. See Chapter 3 for a good discussion of intimacy.

Perlman, D., & Duck, S. (1987). *Intimate relationships: Development, dynamics, and deterioration.* Beverly Hills, CA: Sage. See Part One of this book for a discussion of the development of relationships.

Sprecher, S. (1989). Influences on choice of a partner and sexual decision making in the relationship. In K. McKinney & S. Sprecher (eds.), *Human sexuality: The societal and interpersonal context.* Norwood, NJ: Ablex. A good account of the dynamics that lead to sexual relationships and determine sexual involvement.

7
Sexual Communication and Conflict

Communication is to a relationship what breathing is to maintaining life

—Virginia Satir

Effective communication is crucial to the development, understanding, and expression of human sexuality. While we are growing up, we use communication to learn about sex and to explore our sexual identity. In the development of intimate relationships, we employ communication to signal sexual interest and to give meaning to our sexual encounters. In developed sexual relationships, couples both talk about their sexual relationships and communicate their feelings about it through their actions during sexual encounters (Metts & Cupach, 1989).

There are many advantages to good communication about sexual matters. For example, it has been shown that talking about sex enhances a couple's acquisition of sexual knowledge and promotes overall sexual satisfaction (Gordon & Snyder, 1986; Perlman & Abramson, 1982). An investigation of sexually intimate college students (Wheeless, Wheeless, & Blaus, 1984) revealed that couples whose sexual communication was good had deeper, closer, more satisfying relationships than others. Another source (Yelsma, 1986) notes that the frequency of good sexual communication was positively related to a couple's adjustment and satisfaction. Still other researchers (e.g. Baus, 1987; Cupach & Comstock, 1988; Banmen & Vogel, 1985; Yelsma & Athappily, 1986) have uncovered a similar link between effective sexual communication and relationship satisfaction.

Yet for all these advantages, many people find it difficult to talk about sex with their partners. Discussing sex in a general way interests nearly everybody, but far fewer find it easy to reveal their personal reactions and sexual preferences. Indeed, most couples are poorly prepared to share their sexual selves in an open and frank manner. Many have inhibitions about speaking out, don't know how or where to begin, or are reluctant to speak candidly for fear of hurting their partner's feelings (Yaffee & Fenwick, 1988b).

Sandra Metts and William Cupach (1989) observe that perhaps the most obvious reason people are inhibited from talking about sex with their partners is that it makes them vulnerable. To reveal one's sexual needs or desires, as well as knowledge and attitudes, is to make an intensely personal self-disclosure. As we learned in the last chapter, people often feel at risk in exposing private aspects of their identity. Moreover, they fear that talking about sex with their partner may result in embarrassment or shame.

There are other barriers to sex talk. Partners may feel that they do not need to discuss the sexual aspect of their relationships, or they may perceive the topic as a threat to the relationship (see the "Myths and Misconceptions" box for more detail on this point). For example, Brian decided to approach his wife, Martha, about their less-than-adequate sex life. When he tried to talk about ways to increase the frequency of their sexual relations, Martha refused to discuss the subject, feeling that their sex life would "work itself out" and that Brian shouldn't "rock the boat." A major reason people believe that talking about sex with a partner is risky is that such talk can reveal discrepant preferences in a domain that is central to the relationship and integral to the partners' identities. A man might fear, for instance, that his partner will think he's gay if he wants her to perform fellatio. Or a woman might fear that her partner will be turned off by vaginal scent if she enjoys cunnilingus.

Differences between men and women in how they think and talk about sexual interaction is another obstacle for couples (Metts & Cupach, 1989). Men and women often use different vocabularies in referring to male and female genitalia and the act of copulation, even when communicating with their intimate sexual partners. This use of different terminology is not inherently problematic, but it definitely has the potential for creating communication difficulties—less because it creates misunderstandings than because it affects feelings. To illustrate, a man may find the use of slang such as "pussy" to be arousing, while his partner finds it vulgar. A woman may find a euphemism such as "making love" romantic, while her male partner finds it prudish. One way couples can overcome these different feelings about sex talk is to

In this chapter you'll discover:

☐ *Why it is important to develop good communication about sexual matters.*

☐ *The different stages that make up the communication process, and how feelings, attitudes, and the personalities of sexual partners affect this process.*

☐ *What nonverbal communication is, and how it can serve to transmit important sexual messages.*

☐ *The role that listening plays in the communication process and what couples can do to enhance their skills in this area.*

☐ *How partners can learn to deal constructively with sexual conflict and anger.*

Why is it difficult to talk about sexual matters with my partner?

MYTHS AND MISCONCEPTIONS

Myths About Sexual Communication

*I*t is important for couples to keep the communication lines open regarding their sexual behaviors, ideas, feelings, and wishes (Metts & Cupach, 1989; Simon & Gagnon, 1987). Indeed, many researchers have concluded that effective communication between partners is essential to a healthy and satisfying sexual relationship (see, e.g., Cupach & Comstock, 1988; Baus, 1987; Gordon & Snyder, 1986; Yelsma, 1986; Banmen & Vogel, 1985; Zimmer, 1983). According to Matthew McKay and associates (1983), three myths about sexual communication tend to hinder interaction between partners.

Myth: Lovers shouldn't have to talk about sex because sex will naturally take care of itself.

Because sex is a natural biological process, some people think that it should occur spontaneously. Others go a step further and insist that "good sex" automatically comes with romance and love. Sex thus acquires a mysterious, intuitive quality. When it is going well, it's great. But when difficulties arise, a couple is often at a loss about what to do. The notion that spontaneous sexuality is the only or the best kind gets much of its support from the early part of a relationship, when two people are just getting to know each other and typically, focus only on the positive. Their heightened need to approve and be approved and their desire to please makes this a time when sexual needs are easily gratified, almost magically.

Sooner or later, however, individual differences in sexual preferences are going to surface. Should sexual difficulties appear, there is a tendency to think, "This just isn't right." Instead of considering the possibility that there is a communication problem, many couples throw in the towel. Others simply remark, "The honeymoon is over," and resign themselves to a mediocre sex life.

Couples have to realize that human sexuality is far more than a naturally occurring biological process. As we will see throughout this book, it is sensitive to such psychological and interpersonal factors as roles learned in childhood, past sexual experiences, and current stresses such as career or financial worries, health status, relationship conflicts, and losses. These and other forces affect both sexual desire and performance. When such interference develops, it is important for couples to tune into what they are thinking, feeling, and wanting. The more open partners are with each other, the more likely they are to offer each other support, consideration, and sensitivity.

develop their own personal idioms for referring to body parts, sexual activities, and behaviors. Such idioms not only facilitate communication but also reinforce the uniqueness of the couple's relationship.

Some readers may want to try the following exercise (McKay et al., 1983), which was designed to assess how comfortable partners are with their sexual vocabulary. A couple should first make a list of sexual anatomical parts such as penis and vagina (you might want to consult the terminology covered in Chapter 3) and sexual practices like fellatio and cunnilingus (see Chapter 8 for more ideas). Alongside each term, each partner should list favorite synonyms. Then they should compare their lists and let each other know what terms or phrases are acceptable turn-ons and which they find distasteful. They may ask each other: Are there certain words or phrases that you would like me to say to you while we are making love? Are there words you would like me to use when we are discussing sex away from lovemaking?

The fact that men and women communicate in different ways about their sexual relationships reflects the fact that they think differently about sex and its relational implications. Research (e.g., Wheeless, Zakahi, & Chan, 1988; Stephen & Harrison, 1985; Sollie & Fisher, 1985) suggests that sexual fulfillment and overall relationship intimacy are closely connected for women. And women are generally more ready to

Myth: Your partner should be sensitive enough to know how to sexually satisfy you and considerate enough to do so.

This myth rests on two false assumptions. First, it assumes that a partner is capable of knowing what would sexually satisfy you without being told. Unless your partner is a mind reader, it is highly unlikely that this is going to happen. Second, it assumes that if a partner does not satisfy your sexual needs, it's an indication of lack of consideration. Many people so firmly believe this that they balk at asking for what they want sexually.

People may also hesitate to express their desires because there is risk in asking for what one wants. By conveying our wishes we become vulnerable to rejection. On the other hand, if we fail to state our needs we greatly increase our chances of sexual unhappiness. Whether we choose to be silent or to confide our sexual needs, some risk is inevitable.

Myth: Conflict should be avoided at all costs.

People are often so afraid of turning their partner off or making a bad situation worse that they hold back feelings or wishes they think their partner won't agree with. While some feelings and wishes may kindle conflict, the real prob-lem is refusing to engage in meaningful conflict resolution.

People deal with unresolved sexual problems in many different ways. Some try to talk to their partner about what bothers them sexually, and immediately receive such a negative reaction that they never finish explaining what it was they had in mind. Others repeatedly ask for something and find that their partner incorrectly interprets the request or proves generally unreceptive. Still others fear to say anything because it might turn off the partner or create an unpleasant, awkward situation.

A primary reason people do not insist on what they want is guilt. They feel unentitled to have their sexual feelings and wishes fulfilled. In these cases, the feelings and wishes may be indirectly expressed as accusations or passively expressed by withholding sex or pouting. Conversely, when people feel entitled to their feelings and wishes, no matter how bizarre they may be, they are more likely to express them fully and directly. The partner is then free to deal with an honest request. Even if the partner's response is a direct refusal, it is better than repeating the same old frustrating patterns. Again, *not* communicating is in the long run more destructive than communicating because it not only cripples sexual intimacy but also fuels unhappiness, anger, and resentment.

---

talk about their feelings. Men, conversely, tend to view their sexual relationships primarily in physical terms, are more guarded with their emotions, and often seem inclined to separate sexual intimacy from other aspects of relational intimacy. In short, a man and woman may have difficulty in discussing sex in their relationship because each has a different sexual script (Metts & Cupach, 1989).

DIMENSIONS OF COMMUNICATION

You cannot fully understand the dynamics of sexual communication without gaining a basic appreciation of what the process of communication entails. Communication is affected by a number of factors, including feelings, attitudes, and the personalities of the communicators. In a broad sense, **communication** embraces the exchange of information, signals, and messages. Each of these three dimensions entails a different style of expression and, in many instances, a very different vocabulary. We rely here on the work of Matthew McKay and colleagues (1983) to explain these dimensions of communication.

communication The exchange of information, signals, and messages between people.

The ability to talk honestly about sexual matters is crucial to an intimate relationship.

observations Reports of perceived stimuli, without speculations, inferences, or conclusions.

thoughts Inferences drawn from what a person has observed, heard, or read.

feelings Emotions. The expression of feelings usually reflects neither observations, value judgments, nor opinions.

needs Things that a person feels would help him or her. Statements of need are usually not judgmental or pejorative and, in themselves, do not blame or assign fault.

paralanguage The vocal component of speech, considered separate from its verbal content. Paralanguage includes volume, pitch, articulation, resonance, tempo, and rhythm.

metamessage An intentional alteration of speech rhythm or pitch for emphasis, or the use of special verbal modifiers or body language. Metamessages add another level of meaning to a sentence, often an incongruent one.

Informational Expressions

Informational expressions consist of observations, thoughts, feelings, and needs. An **observation** is a report of what your senses tell you. This kind of communication contains no speculations, inferences, or conclusions. It can best be described as factual communication. The statements "We made love three times last week" and "We went dancing on Saturday night" are examples of observations.

Thoughts are inferences drawn from or conclusions based on what a person has observed, heard, or read. Thoughts are attempts to synthesize observations so that people can perceive what's taking place and understand why and how events occur. Thoughts may also incorporate value judgments in which a person decides that something is good or bad ("Oral sex turns me on"), wrong or right ("Premarital sex is morally wrong"). Beliefs, opinions, and theories are all varieties of thoughts.

The communication of **feelings** involves the expression of emotion ("I love you") and, for the most part, reflects neither observations, value judgments, nor opinions. The expression of feelings is probably the most difficult part of communication. As we've said, many partners have difficulty communicating their sexual feelings and desires, and some don't want to hear what the other feels or wishes.

When people express their **needs,** they are stating what would help or please them ("I need you to be more affectionate"). Statements of need are usually not judgmental or pejorative and, in themselves, do not blame or assign fault. Relationships change, accommodate, and grow when partners can clearly and supportively express what they need from each other.

Signals and Messages

Signals and messages consist of the communication components known as paralanguage and metamessages (McKay et al., 1983). Both work together in creating communication complexities, including contradictory messages. **Paralanguage** is the vocal component of speech, considered separate from its verbal content. Paralanguage includes volume, pitch, articulation, resonance, tempo, and rhythm. It serves to convey moods and attitudes as we speak. The sound of how we say something reveals a great deal about who we are and what we are feeling.

Consider volume as an illustration of paralanguage. A soft voice is often heard as a sign of caring, understanding, and trustworthiness, but it can also indicate a feeling of inferiority, lack of confidence, or a sense that the message is unimportant. Relatedly, a whisper can signify special intimacy and closeness, but it can also convey sadness or fear.

Metamessages are intentional alterations of speech rhythm or pitch for emphasis, special verbal modifiers, or the use of body language. Metamessages add another level of meaning to a sentence, often an incongruent one. We commonly refer to such contradictory styles of communication as *mixed messages, double messages,* or *double talk*. For example, a partner insists "Of course I love you" while gazing out the window in a gesture of boredom and indifference. The classic silent treatment is another example of a metamessage. When one partner asks the other "What's wrong?" the answer is often "Nothing is wrong," accompanied by a tone of voice, deep sighs, and a posture that say "Plenty is wrong."

So you can see how many of the sentences we use have two levels of meaning. One level is the basic information being communicated by the series of words spoken, while the second level is the underlying message being conveyed by paralanguage and metamessages. While these two components of communication need not be incongruent, they often are. Consider the sentence "You're really cute." Taken straightforwardly, it conveys amusement and affection. Analyzing its metamessage potential, however, shows how this sentence could be negative. For example, should the word *you're* be emphasized with a slightly rising inflection, the sentence could communicate irritation and even blame. Should the word *cute* be emphasized, the sentence could convey sarcasm and ridicule.

Metamessages are often at the center of interpersonal conflict. At the surface level, a statement may seem reasonable and straightforward. At its second level, though, the metamessage may communicate blame and hostility. Consider the statement "I'm trying to help." If the verbal modifier "only" is inserted and given a rising inflection, then the metamessage becomes very different. "I'm only trying to help" communicates hurt feelings and defensiveness. The message has now been transformed into what we might call a sneak attack. It is hard to defend oneself against the kind of disapproval expressed in negative metamessages. Often the attack is so subtle that people don't even realize they've been hurt.

Since speakers use metamessages to say something covertly that they're reluctant to say directly, the recipient of the message has little chance for overt retaliation. When a metamessage is heard, though, it can be repeated in the recipient's mind and analyzed for rhythm, pitch, and verbal modifiers. More importantly, a person can say what a metamessage is thought to be out loud, asking the speaker if that was the intention of the message. Unless an interpretation is examined, the recipient will believe, and behave, as if the assumed metamessage is true. Openly examining metamessages is also a good way of teaching people who use this kind of communication to talk more honestly and directly. The thoughts and feelings hidden in the metamessage can then be looked at openly and sincerely.

Couples can become better communicators by expanding their awareness of paralanguage and metamessages. By paying more attention to how they communicate, people can discover whether their voice reflects what they want to say, if their voice is congruent with the words they are speaking, and if there is something about their voice that is irritating and needs to be changed. This is as true for sexual communication as it is for all facets of expression.

My boyfriend sometimes sends mixed messages—he says one thing but often means something else. Why does this happen and how can we address this problem?

STAGES OF COMMUNICATION

Now that we have discussed some of the important dimensions of communication, let's turn our attention to the actual process of communicating. The communication that evolves between two people in an intimate relationship is complex and multifaceted and must be understood if the partners are to enjoy effective, meaningful interaction. This is as true for sexual communication as it is for all the other ways people communicate with each other. Before you read on, if you are currently involved in a sexual relationship, rate your communication skills by taking the quiz in the box on "Rating Your Sexual Communication Style."

Any attempt to chart the flow of communication between two people is necessarily an oversimplification. As you can see from Figure 7–1, for example, feedback, or communicating one's understanding of a message, usually occurs in the seventh and last stage of the model but it can occur at other points in the receiving process. Nevertheless, we can improve our understanding of the communication process by breaking it down into seven stages: ideation, encoding, transmission, reception, decoding, understanding, and feedback (Bedeian, 1986). All messages go through the same basic stages, though these stages constantly overlap.

Stage One: Ideation. In this initial stage, the sender has information for, or needs information from, another person. The information can consist of observations, thoughts, feelings, or needs. Whatever the content, the sender makes a decision to communicate.

Communicating one's thoughts and feelings is often difficult. Sometimes a person is reluctant to say what's on her mind. As a result, her partner may misunderstand the message being communicated and become frustrated.

Sexual Communication and Conflict

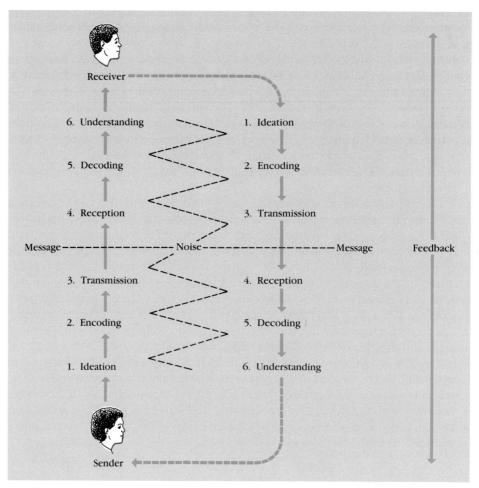

FIGURE 7–1
Stages in the Communication Process.

According to the model, a message is what is transmitted after the sender has thought of what she wants to communicate, translated her thoughts into appropriate symbols, and expressed these symbols verbally or nonverbally, orally or in writing. The receiver may give the sender feedback—confirmation of his understanding of her message—after he has received, decoded, and understood the message. If a message is not clear as the sender receives it, however, he may decide to feed back his impression in order to clarify the message as he processes it. The receiver may then send a message of his own to the sender of the first message, and the process continues. (Source: Adapted from Bedeian, 1986.)

Stage Two: Encoding. In this stage, the sender translates the message to be conveyed into a set of symbols, which she believes the intended receiver will understand. Words are the most obvious symbols, and this step is characterized by the sender selecting the appropriate words to convey her intended message. Encoding is thus a mental operation; it is not oral speech.

Stage Three: Transmission. This stage entails the actual transmission of the message as encoded. Messages can be transmitted in a number of different forms—for example, verbally or nonverbally, orally or in written form. Nonverbal messages may be communicated through body movements such as gestures, facial expressions, and posture. For example, a woman can say "I love you" to her partner, and accompany these words with a hug or kiss. We'll have more to say about such nonverbal messages a bit later.

Sexual Communication and Conflict

How well do you communicate—both verbally and nonverbally—with your partner? To find out, you might want to take the following communication quiz. For each question, circle the appropriate score. Compare your total score with the ratings following the questionnaire.

	YES	NO
1. Do you ever ask your sexual partner if there is anything he or she particularly likes or dislikes when you make love?	1	0
2. Do you find it hard to tell your partner that she or he does something you particularly like or dislike during lovemaking?	0	1
3. Are you able to tell your partner you are not in the mood for sex without making him or her feel rejected?	1	0
4. If you do not want to make love because you are hurt or upset about something, can you explain that you find it impossible to get in the mood for sex when you are upset?	1	0
5. Do you often fake orgasm or pleasure rather than tell your partner that he is not giving you the right kind of sexual stimulation?	0	1
6. Are you comfortable about making the first move when you want to make love?	1	0
7. If you had an erotic dream about your partner, could you describe it to him or her without feeling embarrassed?	1	0
8. Would you be embarrassed to tell a	0	1

	YES	NO
new partner that you wish to use a condom to reduce the risk of STDs or HIV-AIDS?		
9. Are you afraid to get angry or to be critical of your partner because you believe that doing so would destroy the relationship?	0	1
10. When you do get angry, do your quarrels take a long time to resolve and leave you both feeling bitter?	0	1

Scoring

High Rating (8–10)

You communicate well with your partner and are able to make your needs felt and to understand his or hers.

Medium Rating (5–7)

Your score indicates that you may find it hard to talk with your partner about sexual issues without becoming embarrassed. Consequently, when sexual difficulties arise, your inhibition may lead you to ignore them, so that they become more entrenched.

Low Rating (0–4)

Your sexual communication skills are in need of some attention. You are likely to find it hard to express your sexual needs, and should develop new communication skills and strategies. In addition to the material covered in this chapter, you might want to consult some of the suggested readings in this chapter's "Discover for Yourself" section. (From *Sexual Happiness: A Practical Approach* by Maurice Yaffee and Elizabeth Fenwick. Copyright © 1986 by Dorling Kindersley Ltd. Copyright © 1988 by Maurice Yaffee and Elizabeth Fenwick. Reprinted by permission of Henry Holt and Company, Inc.)

Stage Four: Reception. Here the intended receiver receives the message. Obviously, successful communication depends on accurate perception of the sender's message. If the message is verbal, for example, the receiver must be listening and paying attention to the different components of communication discussed earlier or the message will be lost.

Stage Five: Decoding. During this stage, the receiver interprets the message—that is, perceives certain words or sees certain actions and construes them as having a particular meaning. Whether the perceived meaning matches the intended meaning depends on both the skills of the sender in encoding and transmitting and the skills of the receiver in receiving and decoding.

Stage Six: Understanding. Understanding the message is, obviously, critical to the communication process. A message accurately conveyed and successfully decoded should be comprehended. However, as our discussion of paralanguage and meta-messages showed, contradictory messages often result in distorted comprehension.

Stage Seven: Feedback. In this stage, the sender can determine whether or not the intended message has been accurately received. Sometimes a message is not accurately received because of "noise" that exists when it is sent. Noise is any factor that disturbs or distorts a message, ranging from actual noise that makes a message difficult to hear to inattention on the part of the receiver. Feedback recognizes that communication involves a two-way flow of information.

NONVERBAL COMMUNICATION

nonverbal communication
Communication without words, in forms such as facial expressions, gestures, and posture.

As we've learned, not all human communication is verbal. **Nonverbal communication** is communication without words. Its forms include body posture and movement, gestures, eye contact, and the like. Because people continually convey messages through their body language, it is important to analyze the impact of such communications on intimate relationships (Metts & Cupach, 1989; Abbey et al., 1987; Brown, 1986; Abbey & Melby, 1986).

The best way to be sure one has understood something is to ask the person directly whether one's understanding is correct. Conversely, a good way to get one's own message across is to ask for feedback.

Nonverbal communication can be especially effective at conveying feelings and attitudes, but it is not necessarily superior or better adapted to the expression of feelings than verbal communication. Both are important components of the total communication process, and their effectiveness or ineffectiveness rests with the individual communicator. Consider these observations about nonverbal communication:

> I can always tell when Cynthia is preparing for us to have a serious talk: her eyes get somewhat shaded and her upper body becomes a bit rigid.

> Whoever coined the expression "cold shoulder" must have had my husband in mind. Whenever he's uptight, he has a habit of keeping his distance and he avoids any kind of physical closeness.

> The tension always shows in his face, and when it's really bad, he looks off into space or nervously fidgets with objects.

> I can tell when Jill is glad to see me. Her eyes get wide and really sparkle. Her face just fills with happiness. (Authors' files)

Sarah Cirese (1985) proposes that nonverbal communication transmits a unique flow of steady messages. Our movements and actions as well as our facial expressions and silences all say something about us. Cirese estimates that from 65 to 93 percent of the social meaning in face-to-face communication is carried by nonverbal messages. However, she points out that nonverbal communication poses at least three special problems.

First, nonverbal messages are highly ambiguous. They are difficult for others to interpret accurately because they are only implicit indicators. For instance, a frown may signal displeasure, resentment, concentration, or disagreement. Nonverbal messages are revealing, but they have many possible meanings.

Second, compared to verbal messages, nonverbal forms of communication are very limited in what they can express. We must use words to clearly express most of our thoughts, plans, and needs.

Third, as we pointed out earlier in the chapter, verbal and nonverbal messages are sometimes contradictory. We may say one thing through our words ("Yes, I enjoyed it") and quite another through our actions (bored expression). This double-talk creates confusion ("Did she really enjoy it?").

There are some interesting gender differences in nonverbal communication (Pearson, 1985). To begin with, women appear to be more sensitive to nonverbal cues than men are. Women also tend to use more eye contact than men do. Facial expression also varies between women and men; women tend to use far more facial expressions than men do and also to smile more often. Men touch others more than women do, and women are the recipients of more touching than men are.

One of our most important conversational skills resides, not in the tongue, but in the body. Most poor conversationalists do not realize that their body language (poor eye contact, bored expression, and so on) gives the impression that they are unreceptive to communication. We are judged quickly by the first signals we give off—which are usually nonverbal—and if the first impressions we make are not positive, we are likely to experience short-lived conversations (Gabor, 1983).

According to anthropologist David Givens (1983), potential partners show nonverbal attractions and interest in each other in certain ways. While no single recognition sign is 100 percent universal, he discovered that a number of signals are surprisingly uniform across cultures, including pupil size in the eye. People are generally aware that the pupil constricts and dilates in reaction to light and dark. However, there's a psychological component to pupil size, too. For example, a man's pupils will enlarge when he looks at photos of nude women. A woman's pupils will

In a scene from Gone With the Wind, *Scarlett, dimpling and with eyes sparkling, is eager to greet Rhett the morning after a night of passionate lovemaking. But Rhett, unaware that Scarlett has at last begun to love him more than Ashley, misses her nonverbal cues completely and tells her he is leaving.*

dilate when she views attractive-looking men in bathing suits, but interestingly, they will constrict when she sees nude men.

According to Givens, eye contact provides another clue to interest. One telltale signal of attraction is when a stranger looks at another person for longer than two seconds. This is not the "bold stare" that is universally threatening and hard to take. Rather, it is a slightly lingering look that typically ends with a shy glance downward.

Another positive sign of attraction is mirroring. In mirroring, one imitates the posture or gestures of another during a conversation. Crossing the legs or leaning back when a partner does reveals a mutual fondness, such as when friends act alike or move in unison. Generally, the listener mirrors the speaker.

Synchrony provides yet another signal. During friendly conversations, listeners move their heads, shoulders, arms, and hands in time with the speaker's words. It's almost as if speaker and listener are dancing to the same beat. Synchrony springs from overall sensory awareness, and the more a person "feels" the presence of a partner, the greater the visible synchrony.

Other potentially positive forms of nonverbal communication are what Givens has called the forward lean and body alignment. The forward lean connotes interest, and people tend to regard the interest as warm and friendly. But the alignment of the upper body before talking may be the clearest signal of all. In this maneuver, two people demonstrate a readiness or willingness to talk before actually doing so by "aiming" themselves, or squaring up chest-to-chest. A little nod or friendly smile will then signal the beginning of a conversation.

Just as there are positive nonverbal signals that partners give one another, so too are there negative ones. Classic among these is the cold shoulder, the body's automatic reaction of turning away when threatened. Both the head and the body instinctively avert to the side away from danger. Known as a "cutoff," this gesture is partly protective and partly an "ignore it till it goes away" or an "out of sight out of mind" response.

Tensed lips and arm crossing are other negative signals. People can hide many feelings, but they can't keep tension from showing in their lips. Even tiny distresses can trigger tightness and strain in the intricate musculature around the mouth. A person's lips will thin and roll inward as they contract. The greater the anxiety, the greater the tenseness, until the lips actually curl in and almost disappear. (This can

What kinds of messages can nonverbal communication convey?

Sexual Communication and Conflict

also reflect other emotions; e.g., people can press their lips in anger.) People often cross their arms when they feel anxious. While this is sometimes a barrier gesture, more often than not it is used to console and comfort oneself. It is a sign that a person is definitely affected by another party.

What if the person you're speaking to shows no nonverbal sign of response whatsoever? People who choose to exhibit no outward form of expression communicate a loud and clear message: indifference. A blank face, expressionless eyes, and the barest notice signal a bland, matter-of-fact attitude. This posture is characteristic of the typical waiting-line, bus depot, and airport "nonperson" treatment.

LISTENING AND EFFECTIVE COMMUNICATION

The effectiveness of the communication process hinges on good listening skills. Peak communication is a two-way street that requires both clear talking and talented listening. Effective listening is not merely a matter of being passive and quiet while the other is talking; listening is an active skill, and it is hard work. It involves communicating empathy, confirmation, clarification, and attention (Holland, 1985).

Unfortunately, many people are poor listeners. Some lack the motivation to listen, others are inaccurate in decoding messages, and still others have never learned the importance of using this skill. Other reasons for poor listening range from distractions to self-defensive tuning out. People often rely on selective listening; that is, they pick out bits and pieces of conversations that interest them and turn a deaf ear to the rest. One man shares these thoughts about his partner:

> When Tom finds a topic boring or uninteresting, he just tunes me out. I can see the disinterest in his face, and I just know he isn't listening. Sometimes he'll pretend that he's listening by giving me a head nod or some other technique, but I know he's just pretending. (Authors' files)

As you will recall from the last chapter, women appear to be better listeners than men. Research (e.g., Booth-Butterfield, 1984) shows that as boys and girls grow up, they are taught and reinforced in different styles of listening skills. For instance, boys are often taught to listen for facts, while girls are often taught to listen for the mood of the communication. Therefore, men often have difficulty picking up nonverbal cues, while women, used to listening for the mood of the communication, tend to pick them up more readily.

Listening Skills

Sherod Miller and associates (1988) write that if partners want to deal effectively with each other and the issues they face together, each must understand and be understood. John Zehring (1986) concurs. He has found that good listeners distinguish themselves by using a variety of skills that enhance a conversation and forge a bridge of understanding between speaker and listener. We discuss some of the things that couples can do to enhance their listening skills in this section.

Clarifying. Clarification is asking the other person to explain something just said. For example, "I'm not sure I fully understand what you mean. Could you say a little more about . . ." Clarification is critical to the accurate transmission of messages because it prevents distortion.

Confronting. Here a partner is asked to explain inconsistent remarks. "I'm a little confused. You said before that you liked firm pressure on your penis, but now it seems to turn you off. Can you tell me why?" When using confrontation, it is important to be nonthreatening and gentle since otherwise this technique might prompt a defensive reaction.

Probing. Probing is used to acquire more information and perhaps to uncover deeper feelings. When using this technique, listeners pay attention to who, what, when, where, why, and how. For example, "What things do you like best about our lovemaking?" or "How can I be more gentle with you?"

Supporting. Supporting a partner is important, particularly when discussing sensitive issues. A caring partner with good listening skills offers a climate of trust and support. For instance, "I know that was hard for you to say and I appreciate your honesty."

Affirming. An affirming statement or nonverbal gesture is a positive indication of approval or understanding. Affirming is often conveyed by nodding or interjecting short comments—for example, "I love it when you touch me like that."

Restating. This technique involves repeating back what the other has just said. Restating gives the other person a chance to correct your understanding and to expand on the issue if necessary. For example, Todd says to Nora, "You're saying that you like it if I stimulate your clitoris?" Nora, in turn, replies, "Yes, but through the hood, not right on the tip."

Reflecting. Reflecting is looking back on and analyzing what has been said. Rather than repeating what the other has just conveyed, reflecting involves paraphrasing it. When properly used, reflection adds insight and fruitful speculation to communication. To illustrate: "I get the sense that you think our lovemaking would be more exciting and interesting if we tried something different."

Bouncing Back. In this technique, one partner makes a statement and asks the other to react to it. Partners should avoid using close-ended leads—that is, statements or questions that can be answered with a simple "yes" or "no." Open-ended leads require a more expanded answer and hence encourage greater disclosure. To illustrate, rather than saying "That was fantastic . . . was it good for you?" an open-ended lead would be "That was fantastic . . . tell me what it was like for you."

Summarizing. Summarizing serves to crystallize your understanding of what the other has said. Should one partner's summary be inaccurate, the other partner has the opportunity to correct the information. For instance, "So what we've learned is that you would like more foreplay and for me to place less emphasis on my performance."

The Use of Silence

Finally, we should acknowledge the role that silence plays in the listening process. Silence is an important element of conversations that is very often misinterpreted, neglected, or even ignored. For many people, according to Howard Waters (1980), it's the hardest part of communication. You may find our statement that silence is important in a relationship odd because our society places so much emphasis on "polite conversation" and discourages thoughtful silence. Most of us have learned to feel uncomfortable with silences and to regard long pauses in conversation as impolite or as a sign of disinterest. But talking isn't the only way to communicate, and often it isn't even the best way.

Silence can be a powerful form of communication—either negative or positive. People often use the "silent treatment" to reject, defy, or condemn another. Fortunately, there are many ways to use silence as a positive force. For example, when silence is used constructively, a partner can be "drawn out" and encouraged to be more communicative. At other times, silence can be a special form of nonverbal communication. One woman shares how she and her husband use silence following lovemaking:

> **After we've made love, we curl up next to one another and just enjoy the feel of each other's body. Neither one of us says anything and it's just the most peaceful feeling in the world. The quiet is the best part. (Authors' files)**

A man had these thoughts about his partner:

> **When we talk, Frank always needs time to gather his thoughts. He's a very deliberate person and very methodical. At first, I used to talk all the time and only later did I realize that I was interrupting his chain of thinking. I guess that I was threatened by the silence. Now, I just sit back and wait for him to respond. (Authors' files)**

Silence may also help the less articulate partner feel comfortable and accepted. A shy and quiet person may then become more self-accepting and, as a result, more confident and direct in communication. Another value of silence in a close relationship is that remaining silent after a partner's serious expression of feelings often allows that person to think further and to come up with new insight into those feelings. In this way, silence can encourage deeper thought about one's affective side.

Finally, silence can slow down a conversation. Many times, a quick pace is directly related to the anxiety being felt by both people. Silence can help to eliminate some of that tension.

Above all, it is important to be sensitive to what the other person is communicating to you through silence. For example, is your partner merely wondering what to say next? Or is the person feeling something that is difficult to express? Is he pausing in expectation of hearing something from you? Or is she collecting her thoughts and contemplating what was just said? These are but a few of the many reasons for silence. Skilled listeners within intimate relationships are adept at pinpointing their partner's motive for silence and are aware of the many messages that

Poor communication skills usually underlie interpersonal conflict. To ignore or rebuff a partner is especially destructive to a relationship.

MAKING USE OF WHAT WE KNOW

Communicating About Sex: Techniques and Strategies

*C*ommunicating about sex is a skill that couples can always improve. With a little practice, partners can sharpen their ability to talk with each other about their sex life and, in the process, enhance their overall intimate relationship. Here are some ideas:

- *Organize your thoughts.* Don't launch into the topic without some mental preparation. Be clear about what you think, feel, and want regarding your sexual relationship. You may want to think of your partner when you do this and how she or he may respond to what you plan to say.

- *See if your partner is in the mood to communicate with you on this topic.* Talking about sex requires the right time, as well as tact, understanding, and patience. If it's not the right time to talk because there are distractions or you're both too tired, reschedule the discussion for another time.

- *Don't interrupt.* Nothing is accomplished when two people talk at the same time. Moreover, occasional silence can tell your partner that you are taking the time to think about what he or she has said—that you are taking him or her seriously. Also be careful of premature comments, reactions, or observations.

- *Pay attention to nonverbal communication.* Listen with your eyes as well as your ears. Body language can help you to better understand a person and a situation. Also, examine your own body language. Good eye contact and posture indicate that a person is receptive to communication.

- *Try to emphasize the positive side.* Point out to your partner what you like about your sex life and your relationship in general. Also, try to phrase what you don't like in positive terms. For instance, instead of saying, "Don't rub me so hard," say "I'd enjoy it much more if you stroked me more gently."

- *Use "I messages."* Learn to take responsibility for your feelings and wishes. You can reduce confusion greatly by clearly stating your position on a topic and declaring ownership of your feelings ("I feel used when you only satisfy your own needs"). Also, state your own position before asking your partner for his or hers. This way, your partner can see your openness and willingness to be honest and needn't feel threatened by asking for disclosures.

- *Avoid "you messages."* "You messages" attach blame to your partner and do little to facilitate effective communication ("You wouldn't do that if you really cared about me"). Accusing your partner of failing to meet your sexual needs or calling your partner names only creates defensiveness and is more likely to lead to a "win-lose" argument than to an honest dialogue.

- *Be as specific as possible.* You are more likely to get the response you want if you let your partner know exactly what you think, feel, and want. For instance, instead of saying "I wish you would be more affectionate with me," say "I would really enjoy your greeting me at the door when I come home at night with a hug and kiss. I'd also like a hug and kiss before we go to sleep."

- *Be an active listener.* Make sure that your partner has understood what you have said. Don't rely exclusively on nonverbal communication or the statement "Yes, I understand." Ask for a paraphrase of what your partner thinks you said, and if the paraphrase is inaccurate, constructively correct the misinterpretation in a sensitive and caring fashion.

- *Agree on a plan of action and be open to experimentation.* Once you have stated your position on a sexual problem or need and your partner has stated hers or his, try together to devise a tentative solution that is mutually acceptable. Agree to implement it for a specified period of time before you talk about it again and review how effective it's been. If it proves unsatisfactory, negotiate another approach and test it out. (Adapted from McKay, Davis, & Fanning, 1983.)

this behavior can communicate. Other tips on communication are contained in the box on "Communicating About Sex: Techniques and Strategies."

CONFLICT AND COMMUNICATION

It is a myth that most couples do not engage in conflict. Indeed, conflict is inevitable over the many changes and transitions that characterize the intimate relationship, including those of a sexual nature. Marie Kargan (1985) believes that these conflicts can be constructive challenges to the couple because they present opportunities to strengthen a relationship.

Joanna Cole and Holly Laibson (1983) agree, and even claim that not fighting at all is destructive to a relationship, since utter tranquility can promote boredom and even depression. In this sense, conflict helps a couple to grow together—provided they learn to overcome conflict as caring and giving partners, not as opposing armies on a battlefield.

Broadly defined, a **conflict** is an interpersonal process that occurs whenever the actions of one person interfere with the actions of another. While partners can conflict over practically any kind of issue, not all clash in the same areas and at the same levels of intensity. In seeking to analyze the dynamics of conflict, Donald Peterson (1983) has identified three phases of conflict: the initiation of conflict by some precipitating event; the beginning of negotiations, or the intensification of conflict; and the resolution of conflict by either constructive or destructive means.

conflict An interpersonal process that occurs whenever the actions of one person interfere with the actions of another.

How Conflict Starts

Conflict is triggered by some event. The precipitating event is usually criticism, an illegitimate demand, a rebuff, or cumulative annoyance.

CRITICISM. Conflicts occur when verbal or nonverbal acts on the part of one partner are regarded as demeaning or unfavorable by the other. For example, one partner may accuse the other of being a lousy lover or selfish about her sexual needs. The criticized party feels offended and is likely to retaliate with aggression or withdrawal.

ILLEGITIMATE DEMANDS. A demand of any kind by one person upon another is likely to be perceived as interfering. However, the demands most apt to produce the most serious conflict are those beyond the normative expectations that each person has of the other: "Nowadays he demands that we make love whenever he wants it . . . he doesn't care about my needs or whether I'm in the mood." The demand is thus perceived as being unfair.

REBUFF. A rebuff occurs when one party appeals to the other for a desired reaction and the other fails to respond as expected. For example, a woman may feel rebuffed by her partner when she fails to turn him on sexually. The person experiencing the rebuff usually feels devalued and angry with the other. A common reaction to feeling rebuffed is withdrawal: "When he shows sexual disinterest in me, I feel unwanted and unloved. I don't want to be near him."

CUMULATIVE ANNOYANCE. This is a buildup of annoyances until some threshold is exceeded. A first act may go unnoticed, and the next few may be ignored. When the offended person reaches his limit, though, he will tolerate no further acts and the conflict will explode. Consider the cumulative annoyance experienced by Kevin during

his year-long relationship with Victor. For several months, he had been trying to overcome his lack of sexual desire, but whenever they discussed the topic, Victor became angry, hurt, and resentful. To avoid such unpleasant episodes, Kevin decided to leave things alone, hoping that their sex life would get better on its own. However, it did not and the unresolved issues began to combine with a growing list of other annoyances. Finally, his threshold of tolerance exceeded, Kevin ended the relationship.

After the initiating event takes place, the couple may decide either to avoid the conflict or to engage each other. Should avoidance be chosen, it must be mutual. This usually occurs when the issue is seen either as too unimportant to outweigh the distress conflict brings or as intractable, at least for the moment. The couple regards the risk of open conflict as greater than the uncertain gains of an active dispute.

If the couple decides to verbally spar, it is probable that at least one partner sees the issue as threatening enough to require action and believes that a favorable outcome can be gained. Generally speaking, the powerful partner (in terms of resources controlled in the relationship, available alternatives, and so forth) is more likely than the less powerful partner to engage in conflict. By fighting, the powerful partner may reestablish the superiority that the conflict threatened to upset and acquire greater influence over future interactions. But if successive confrontations become intolerable, even a dependent partner may be unwilling to endure the punishment the conflict entails. Once the weaker partner decides to "stand up and fight," the dominant one must deal with the costs of active conflict in pursuing personal aims at the expense of the other.

Conciliation or Escalation

Once activated, a conflict can move in either of two directions: toward direct negotiation and resolution or toward escalation and intensification. When partners choose to negotiate directly, each states his or her position and a straightforward problem-solving exchange follows. Information relative to the conflict is expressed and received without distortion. Both parties work toward a solution until some acceptable outcome is attained. (The major conflict resolution strategies used by couples will be presented a bit later in the chapter.)

Escalation of the conflict often brings intensely angry fighting. Usually, biased perceptions and hostilities based on invalidated beliefs about the other intensify the conflict. The parties invoke strategies of power, along with tactics of threat, coercion, and deception. Manipulation techniques also emerge; the attribution of blame to the other rather than to oneself and name-calling are popular forms. Sexual withdrawal is also a common technique, as shared by this man:

> **When we have a big fight, the first thing to go is our sex life. Marsha will always say something like, "That's it, you're cut off" or "No more for you." She means it, too. When Marsha's steaming, I can't even stand next to her, let alone be intimate with her. The cold shoulder can go on for days. (Authors' files)**

A woman had these thoughts:

> **When we're fighting, sex is the last thing on my mind and I know it's the same for my husband. It's difficult even being civil towards one another, let alone affectionate. Once the dust settles and we've cleared the air about something, we have sex again. It's weird, though, how sex always seems to be better after a good fight. For us, that's one of the few bright spots about quarreling. (Authors' files)**

A heated conflict rarely proceeds to a rational problem-solving stage, particularly if insulting remarks have been exchanged or if there has been physical abuse. Rather, an intermediate step is needed before negotiation can begin. This step takes the form of a conciliatory act that is intended to reduce negative feelings and express a willingness to work toward a remedy. A conciliatory gesture may be saying, "This problem has gotten out of hand; let's get it back in perspective," or "This problem is at least partly my fault; I'll do what I can to solve it."

Sometimes the conciliatory gesture is followed by a reciprocal conciliation from the other. When this happens, anger tends to dissipate on both sides and the combatants are able to move rationally and cooperatively toward resolution of the issue. In other conflict scenarios, there is a reversal of the escalation. Personal attacks are stopped and coercion, as well as the threat of it, is withdrawn. Concern that had been generalized across a range of issues is redirected toward more specific issues. Then the couple can attend to solving the problem rather than injuring each other, and chances for a satisfactory outcome are improved.

Is fighting always bad for a relationship? Doesn't it sometimes help to clear the air?

Conflict Resolution

Conflicts end either constructively or destructively. Let's look at five forms of conflict resolution, ranging from those that lead to the most positive outcomes to those that are the most destructive of relationships.

STRUCTURAL IMPROVEMENT. Partners within healthy relationships may discover that conflict can move them toward new levels of intimacy and actually strengthen their relationship (Stinnett & DeFrain, 1985). Mutual affection grows stronger and mutual understanding deepens in the process of constructively resolving the conflict. Another benefit of conflict is that it can release pent-up tension, resentment, and hostility (Julius, 1986).

INTEGRATIVE AGREEMENTS. When the goals and aspirations of both partners are simultaneously met, the result is an integrative agreement. Purely integrative agreements are rare because it is difficult to reconcile genuinely divergent interests. Most agreements involve the creation of an alternative that satisfies somewhat modified goals and aspirations for one or both partners. Consider the following:

> I'm not crazy about giving or receiving oral sex, but Paul really likes it. In the past, we've had some disagreements over it—I think it's so animal-like and he sees it as completely natural. He's aware of my discomfort and never pushes me when I don't feel like doing it. When I look at it this way, it's kind of like a trade-off. (Authors' files)

COMPROMISE. This approach is marked by both partners reducing their aspirations until they discover a mutually acceptable alternative. In this type of trade-off, interests are diluted rather than reconciled. A 25-year-old married man offers these thoughts on a compromise he achieved with his wife:

> After we had children, we used to fight a lot about not being able to make love like we used to. We both wanted to have sex, but it seemed like we were always tired from our jobs or involved in some aspect of child care. Finally, we realized that some kind of compromise was needed, particularly in terms of our professional lives. We both decided that we needed to trim our careers a bit to restore harmony. We made it a point to deliberately schedule private time together, and even got

Sexual Communication and Conflict

When a couple experiences conflict, one person has to take the initiative of opening up the matter for discussion.

to bed earlier so that there would be time for the two of us. And we made a rule that no office work would be brought home on certain nights. (Authors' files)

DOMINATION. Some conflicts are terminated in conquest. One partner gives way and the other continues to pursue the line of action leading to personal goals. Chronic domination is destructive for the winner as well as for the loser, for in ignoring the partner's wishes in order to gain victory at any cost, the winner has failed to take advantage of the opportunities that conflict offers for positive and constructive change. The domineering "winner" seldom changes habitual responses, nor is he or she able to consider what the most frequent and intense confrontations are all about. By domineering, the "winner" thrives on destructive arguments rather than solving conflicts with sensitivity and compromise. A middle-aged woman describes conflict with her husband:

> After a disagreement, Brian tells me that things will be better, but I know that it's only a matter of time before he slips back into his old ways. He'll begin to get bossy again, and blame me for all of our problems. He likes to dominate everything and be in constant control, and nothing I do makes him want to change. (Authors' files)

SEPARATION. Sometimes one or both parties withdraw without resolving the conflict. Temporary separations can be useful if the time spent apart is used as a cooling-off period in which to search for more creative solutions to the problem. However, more often than not, withdrawal has damaging consequences—especially if it is accompanied by a "parting shot" or aggressive gesture that leaves partners feeling worse about each other and their whole relationship.

Strategies for Resolving Conflicts

As you can see, the way partners deal with conflict influences the overall stability of their relationship. The inability to deal with conflict constructively is a potent dampener of marital satisfaction. Moreover, once conflict occurs, it tends to be repeated. Thus it is important to learn how to handle conflict appropriately. Don Dinkmeyer and Jon Carlson (1984) suggest ways of resolving conflict within a relationship.

DEMONSTRATING MUTUAL RESPECT. Often it is the attitude of one or both of the partners that is at the center of the conflict rather than the immediate issue they are fighting about. In a relationship with mutual respect, each partner seeks to understand and respect the other's point of view.

Yaffe and Fenwick (1988b) believe that it is important for any couple, but particularly for those with sexual problems, to fight fair and deal with conflict and anger constructively. Occasional episodes of unpleasantness arise in nearly every relationship, but they can be resolved without lasting bitterness if the partners are able to talk over without delay the real cause of the conflict. Here are some guidelines for a sensible and realistic approach to such situations:

- Tell your partner exactly what has upset you, and do it at the time, not days or weeks later. This means encoding your concern accurately rather than distorting it with paralanguage and metamessages.
- Deal with the problem in terms of your own feelings rather than by criticizing your partner's behavior. Say, "Perhaps I shouldn't get angry when . . . but I do,"

rather than "You're so selfish, you don't ever . . ." This underlines the importance of using "I messages," that is, of speaking for ourselves, not others.

- Stick to the particular issue and resolve it. Do not use the present argument as an opportunity to get past resentments off your chest. Also, avoid words like *always* and *never* ("You're always inhibited" or "You never want to try anything different").
- Exercise self-control, no matter how irritated you are. Arguments should not be damaging or destructive. So if you are so angry that you feel like shouting at your partner, wait until your rage cools down before tackling the issue.
- Remember the concept of mutual respect and be accepting of the other person's feelings. Also, do not make wounding attacks on the other's shortcomings, since these are not easily forgotten or forgiven. Be assertive and express your anger directly instead of using sarcasm, abuse, blame, or hostile comments.
- The moment an argument seems to be degenerating into a destructive fight, give it up and suggest that you would rather resolve it later when you both feel calmer.

Dealing constructively with conflict means actively listening to each other's views and demonstrating respect for those views.

CLARIFYING THE PROBLEM. Dinkmeyer and Carlson believe that most couples find it hard to identify the central problem or issue that is troubling their relationship. Thus, whether or not to make love or who does what around the house may not be the central conflict, but rather the surface disagreement. Couples need to identify the central problem before they can really resolve the surface disagreements. Often the central problem centers around one or more of the following issues:

- A partner feels a threat to his status or prestige ("Why should I always give in to her demands?").
- One senses one's superiority is being challenged ("If I'm not in control, I feel inadequate").
- One's need to control or one's right to decide is at stake ("Why should I let him decide for me?").
- One feels one's judgment is not being considered or that one is being treated unfairly ("Whose way is the best way?").
- One feels hurt and needs to retaliate ("I'll get even this time").

Once the central problem has been identified, partners can discuss alternative ways to behave and can reach a new agreement. Considering the following questions might help a couple identify their central problem: What are some of the problems that might be causing the conflict? What do I think is wrong? How might my values be contributing to the way I see the problem? Is there something external to our relationship that might be the underlying source of tension and strain?

AGREEING TO COOPERATE. When a conflict takes place, the easiest solution that often comes to mind is to suggest how one's partner could change to alleviate the problem. This may not be the best route, though. A more effective approach is to ask, "What can *I* do to change our relationship?" By focusing on what you are willing to do and by not demanding that your partner change, you are demonstrating *your* willingness to change and you generate an atmosphere in which it may be possible to reach agreement. While the ultimate solution to conflict involves *mutual* changes of behavior, the desire to change is the responsibility of each person.

AGREEING TO DISAGREE. Some conflicts cannot be resolved because they involve behavioral changes that neither partner is willing or able to accomplish. In these cases, the partners may wish to simply agree that they disagree concerning that specific area of conflict. For example, Peggy and Trevor do not see eye to eye on all the issues surrounding Peggy's extramarital affair of four years ago. However, they recognize that searching for concrete answers to why it happened will only lead to a stalemate, so they have come to an agreement to let it alone.

MUTUAL DECISION MAKING. Once the problem is confronted and the issues become clear, either partner may propose a tentative solution. The other may respond by accepting the proposed solution, modifying it, or making a countersuggestion. An attitude of give-and-take and compromise is most effective here. Once an agreement is reached, the role of each partner in executing the decision should be clarified, along with what should be done if either partner doesn't follow through. When two partners participate in conflict resolution and develop creative agreements that are acceptable to them both, power and responsibility are shared equally and cooperation replaces resistance within the relationship.

SEXUALITY IN THE NEWS

Nonverbal Cues Are Easy to Misinterpret
by Daniel Goleman

"*I*f his lips are silent, he chatters with his fingertips; betrayal oozes out of him at every pore," Freud wrote, commenting on the clues to character that can be read in movements and gestures.

Recent studies are lending scientific precision to Freud's observation, pinpointing which patterns of movements during a conversation reveal what personality traits. But they are also confirming something that Freud did not observe: people's confidence in their ability to read character through such cues very often exceeds their actual skill, particularly in some crucial situations.

For example, one recent study found that few people recognize the nonverbal cues that reveal whether someone is lying, though most people believe they can usually catch a liar in the act. . . .

The new research is pointing to areas where people's confidence in reading nonverbal cues outstrips their accuracy. Earlier this month Dr. Robert Gifford reported finding specific nonverbal clues to such traits as aloofness, gregariousness and submissiveness. . . .

While people are right about their reading of character some of the time, especially for more obvious traits like gregariousness, the problem, Dr. Gifford said, is that they are overly confident and assume that they are equally adept at reading more subtle aspects of character when they are actually misjudging. . . .

Misleading Eye Contact

A similar pattern of partial error holds for people's reading of personality traits, Dr. Gifford found in a series of studies, some published this month and some yet to be published. In these, 60 people were evaluated on a range of traits, such as being cold or warm, arrogant or unassuming, socially dominant or submissive.

Systematic analysis of videotapes of their gestures and movements while talking in pairs for 15 minutes yielded dozens of patterns associated with the traits, such as slouching or keeping one's legs under the chair.

But when 21 volunteer judges were asked to evaluate the videotapes, minus the soundtrack, for the personality traits of the subjects, and to name the nonverbal clues to those traits, their showing was poor.

For example, "people who gesture a lot and look you in the eye are perceived to be dominant," said Dr. Gifford. "But that is not the case. A more accurate cue is usually missed: during conversations like these, dominant people fiddle with things much less than do less dominant people." . . .

The nonverbal portrait of the submissive person, on the other hand, is someone who fiddles with objects, gestures little, keeps his legs folded under the chair and slouches slightly, Dr. Gifford found. The most common mistakes here, the study showed, were in judging people to be submissive when they held their heads down and kept their arms folded, instead of on the basis of the true cues.

A Question of Musculature

People were judged to be arrogant "when they did not smile and faced their conversational partners did not look them in the eye, as though checking them out," said Dr. Gifford. "But none of these turned out to be valid clues to arrogance." . . .

A parallel kind of misreading is common with people whose facial musculature happens to emphasize certain expressions, said Dr. Maureen O'Sullivan, a psychologist at the University of San Francisco.

"My husband carries his eyebrows high, with a big space between the eye and the eyebrow," Dr. O'Sullivan said. "It makes him seem perpetually surprised or interested, but that's just the natural lay of his facial muscles."

A similar misreading of sadness commonly occurs with people who, in the natural course of aging, find that gravity pulls the sides of the eyes . . . down.

While such misreadings are benign, other evidence suggests that even experts fare poorly when it comes to some crucial judgments. "Surprisingly, professionals like detectives and judges, who have a lot at stake, are no better than anyone else at catching lies," said Dr. [Paul] Ekman [of the University of California at San Francisco].

Secret Service Expertise

Dr. Ekman tested 509 men and women on their ability to assess which of 10 videotapes showed someone lying or telling the truth about whether or not they liked a film they had just watched. Those tested included 34 Secret Service officers, 60 Federal polygraphers, 126 police detectives, 110 court judges and 67 psychiatrists. . . .

It was Dr. [Bella] DePaulo [at the University of Virginia] who discovered that one cue commonly thought to give away lying, "shifty eyes," is faulty. A review of studies showed that people who were lying actually looked the other person in the eye every bit as much as truthful people.

"The best way to tell if someone is lying is to look for discrepancies, such as between a person's tone of voice and his gestures," said Dr. [Miles] Patterson [of the University of Missouri at St. Louis]. . . .

Dr. Ekman, however, said that training people in specific skills for reading nonverbal cues does seem to improve their accuracy. He has so trained judges, Secret Service officers, and the others in his study.

Another factor that makes it difficult to detect lies is that "the fear of being disbelieved looks the same as the fear of being caught lying," he said.

Dr. Ekman also trains people to read rapidly shifting facial expressions that indicate someone is trying to conceal an emotion and to look for discrepancies between the content of a person's words and his voice, body or facial expression. Other indications of lying are a sudden change in several channels of expression, such as when a person stumbles over his words as his voice gets higher, swallowing several times. . . . (*The New York Times*, September 17, 1991. Copyright © 1991 by The New York Times Company. Reprinted by permission.)

DISCUSSION QUESTIONS

1. How would you go about observing nonverbal communication in order to judge personality traits? Think up a scenario in a social setting in which you meet someone you want to date. Then make a list of some nonverbal behaviors you would look for and the ways in which you would translate these into personality traits.

2. If your instructor has you discuss Goleman's article in class, compare your scenario and list with those of your classmates. Discuss the points on which you differ and try to discover why.

3. How would you convince someone to attend training sessions in interpreting nonverbal behavior? What arguments would you use with a marriage counselor? A corporate executive? A friend?

■ Good communication is important for sexual satisfaction in intimate relationships. Although honest self-disclosure makes people more vulnerable, it also heightens relationship satisfaction. Some myths about sexual communication are that two people shouldn't have to talk about their sexual relationship because it will naturally take care of itself; your partner should be sensitive enough to know how to sexually satisfy you; and conflict should be avoided at all costs.

■ The process of communication is affected by a number of factors, including feelings, attitudes, and the personalities of the communicators. Communication can be broken down into informational expressions such as observations, thoughts, feelings, and needs. Each of these types of expression entails a different style of expression and, many times, a very different vocabulary. Signals and messages consist of paralanguage—the vocal component of speech that includes volume, pitch, articulation, resonance, tempo, and rhythm—and metamessages—intentional alterations of speech rhythm or pitch or the use of special verbal modifiers to get particular messages across. Paralanguage and metamessages add another level of meaning to a sentence, often an incongruent one.

■ The communication that evolves between two people in an intimate relationship is successful only when mutual understanding results—that is, when one partner transmits information that is understood by the other. The process of communication is best understood through analysis of the seven stages of the communication process: ideation, encoding, transmission, reception, decoding, understanding, and feedback. All of these stages overlap and interact as messages are transmitted and received.

■ Not all forms of human communication are linguistic. Nonverbal communication, which includes gestures, mannerisms, eye contact, and body language, is especially effective for conveying feelings and attitudes.

■ Effective communication between partners requires good listening skills. Broadly defined, listening is the psychological procedure of understanding and interpreting sensory experience. Listening skills can be improved by learning such techniques as clarifying, confronting, probing, supporting, affirming, restating reflecting, bouncing back, and summarizing.

■ Conflicts in relationships begin when a precipitating event triggers one or more of four possible conditions: criticism, illegitimate demand, rebuff, or cumulative annoyance. A conciliatory act is usually needed before the couple can start to resolve the problem. There are five possible forms of conflict resolution: separation, domination, compromise, integrative agreements, and structural improvement. Some important communication skills that are helpful in dealing with conflict are demonstration of mutual respect, problem clarification, agreeing to cooperate or to disagree, and mutual decision-making.

THINKING THINGS OVER

1. Explain why good communication is important to a satisfying sexual relationship.

2. Prepare a scenario is which two lovers are having difficulty communicating about their sexual relationship. Describe a problem and develop some possible solutions.

3. Speculate as to why women and men communicate differently about the same things. How might you make yourself more aware of gender differences when you communicate?

4. Three factors that affect the process of communication are feelings, attitudes, and the personalities of the communicators. Which of these factors most affects you in communicating? Why?

5. Nonverbal communication can be as important as verbal communication. Describe nonverbal cues you exhibit when you communicate with others. Do you tend to rely on some cues more than others? Why do you think this is the case?

6. Conflict is almost inevitable in a relationship. Discuss some of the more constructive ways to resolve conflict.

Hall, J. A. (1984). *Nonverbal sex differences: Communication accuracy and expressive style*. Baltimore, MD: The Johns Hopkins University Press. A documentation of gender differences in the sphere of nonverbal communication.

Metts, S., & Cupach, W. R. (1989). The role of communication in human sexuality. In K. McKinney & S. Sprecher (eds.), *Human sexuality: The societal and interpersonal context*. Norwood, NJ: Ablex Publishing Corporation.

Miller, S., Wackman, D., Nunnally, E., & Miller, P. (1988). *Connecting with self and others*. Littleton, CO: Interpersonal Communication Publishers. A particular strength of this paperback is its advice on how to send and receive messages more accurately.

Pearson, J. C. (1985). *Gender and communication*. Dubuque, IA: Wm. C. Brown. An excellent analysis of gender differences in communicating.

Tannen, D. (1986). *That's not what I meant: How conversational style makes or breaks relationships*. New York: Ballentine. A fascinating examination of conversational styles and how we can learn to communicate more effectively with others.

8

Sexual Techniques and Pleasuring

There isn't any formula. . . . You learn to love by loving

—Aldous Huxley

They separated gently, but the movements both used . . . were more like a fitting together

—Doris Lessing

Minutes pass in silence, mysteriously. It is those few minutes that pass after we make love that are most mysterious to me, uncanny

—Joyce Carol Oates

We have a tendency to think of sexual pleasuring and techniques designed to enhance lovemaking as relatively modern areas of interest. But thoughts on how sexual intimacy can be cultivated and enjoyed have been around for some time. For example, the Roman poet Ovid (43 B.C.–A.D. 17) offered many thoughts on erotic pleasuring in *The Art of Love*. Recall from Chapter 1 that in India during the eighth century, Vaatsaayana penned the *Kama Sutra (The Precepts of Love)*, a love manual that includes elaborate descriptions and illustrations of coital activity. This was followed in India by similar publications, including the *Koka Shastra* by Koka Pandit in the twelfth century and the *Anangga Rangga* by Kalyaanamalla in the fifteenth century. In the sixteenth century, the Arabian Nefzawi wrote *The Perfumed Garden*, a detailed narrative of lovemaking, including how to maximize sexual satisfaction. The Italian artist Giulio Romano released a series of paintings depicting 16 coital positions in 1524, and the Japanese artist Hokusai painted the highly erotic series *Loving Couples* in the late 1700s.

Human beings have always had considerable interest in sexual pleasuring. In our times, the intense motivation to learn more about sexual techniques has prompted a flurry of publications on the topic (see, e.g., Stanway, 1989; McCarthy & McCarthy, 1989; Yaffee & Fenwick, 1988a & b; Butler & Lewis, 1988; Harris, 1988; Masters, Johnson, & Kolodny, 1988; Comfort, 1986). It now seems that everything you've always wanted to know about sexual pleasuring is available at the local bookstore.

Our culture traditionally taught that every sexual encounter should lead to penile-vaginal intercourse and orgasm. Because this rather narrow view overlooked many pleasurable sexual activities, and because it was often gender biased (men have orgasms, women just submit to sex), and heterosexist as well, a newer, more liberated view began to affect our sexual mores in the 1960s and 1970s. For many people, the goal became not just intercourse, but orgasm for both partners—simultaneous, if possible–and multiple orgasms for women. In our achievement-oriented society, these demanding goals have often made people feel as if they are running a sexual race.

If partners concentrate on enjoying each other and appreciating their own and the other's feelings and senses, they will likely have a more satisfying relationship than if they act as if they are competing in a marathon. They will understand that sexual intimacy and pleasuring need not always be synonymous with intercourse. Rather, sexuality can be expressed in many different and rewarding ways. As we explore some of these possibilities, keep in mind the importance of having a healthy self-concept, of being willing to experiment, and of demonstrating sensitivity and understanding in sexual relationships.

We begin this chapter with a discussion of sexual fantasies. We then consider masturbation, in both men and women, as well as mutual forms of masturbation. Following a discussion of foreplay techniques, we turn our attention to coitus and coital positions. The chapter concludes with a discussion of the sexual needs and sexual functioning of the physically challenged.

LOOKING AHEAD

....

In this chapter you'll discover:

☐ *What sexual fantasies are and what purposes they serve.*

☐ *How widespread masturbation is and how it is expressed over the course of the life cycle.*

☐ *How sexual pleasuring serves to heighten sexual arousal.*

☐ *The six basic sexual intercourse positions, some of their variations, and the advantages and disadvantages of each.*

☐ *What adjustments the physically disabled and chronically ill must make in view of the special factors that affect their sexual functioning.*

SEXUAL FANTASY

Many women and men regard fantasy as an important part of their sexual lives. A **sexual fantasy** is a mental image or series of images centering around erotic thoughts and desires. Fantasies typically occur during daydreams, masturbation, foreplay, or other sexual activity. They often play a significant role in sexual arousal, and almost everybody has them, if only from time to time. Sometimes fantasies are enhanced by watching an erotic movie, reading an erotic book or magazine, or viewing a real-life erotic encounter. Erotic materials can serve positive functions during fantasizing. On

sexual fantasy A mental image or series of images centering around erotic thoughts and desires.

215

The woman's position in this erotic painting from India looks faintly uncomfortable, but she doesn't seem unhappy. Or is that why she's reaching for the sword?

I sometimes fantasize when I have sex with my boyfriend. Do other people do this?

occasion, fantasies take the place of reality when an activity would be unacceptable or impossible in real life (Stanway, 1989; Lentz & Zeiss, 1984; Stock & Geer, 1982).

A glance at the literature reveals how widespread sexual fantasies are. In Kinsey's research (1948, 1953), about 85 percent of the men queried and almost 70 percent of the women reported having sexual fantasies at one time or another. In another study (Davidson, 1982), about 95 percent of unmarried college men and women said they had experienced a sexual fantasy. In another investigation of college-age students (Sue, 1979), approximately 60 percent of men and women reported fantasizing during intercourse. Sometimes when making love, one or both parties may fantasize about other people (Cado & Leitenbert, 1990). Thus people imagine themselves making love to a friend, a roommate, a relative, a rock star, or some other celebrity.

Sexual fantasies serve a number of purposes. They give sexual pleasure and fulfillment, and for many people, they provide an escape from boredom and routine. Sexual fantasy can bring variety into the love life of an individual or couple or relief from a negative sexual situation. Sexual fantasies can also give people a feeling of control by allowing them to imagine all sorts of desirable scenarios. Fantasies have the potential to heighten sexual arousal during masturbation and coitus. They may also serve as a rehearsal for a new sexual experience such as a novel lovemaking technique. Finally, sexual fantasies may elevate a person's self-worth, especially if they make the person feel more attractive and sexually irresistible.

Sexual fantasies are quite diverse. They can take the form of repeated erotic thoughts, fleeting images, or memories of previous sexual encounters. Some people construct elaborate fantasies about making love in romantic settings, while others have fantasies related to masturbation, mate-swapping, or same-sex erotic encounters.

Sexual Techniques and Pleasuring

Some people like to fantasize about watching others engaging in sex, while others envision being watched.

Two women describe their favorite fantasies:

> I fantasize that I'm in my bed late at night and my partner brings home another woman. We are all sexually attracted to one another. She and I first make love to each other and then we turn our attention to my partner. It's a wild sexual frolic that leaves us all exhausted. (Authors' files)

> I imagine that I'm naked and in a men's locker room. A group of men have just finished showering and I perform oral sex on each of them. When I have finished, they each take turns making love to me. (Authors' files)

Men, too, have preferred sexual fantasies, particularly when they masturbate:

> One of my favorite fantasies involves me right smack in the middle of an orgy. Naked bodies are everywhere, and everyone is moaning with sexual pleasure. I go from woman to woman, enjoying both intercourse and oral sex with the many willing participants. (Authors' files)

> My best friend and I pick up this gorgeous woman and take her back to our apartment. She's very sexually experienced and offers to make love to us at the same time. While she performs oral sex on my friend, I insert my penis into her vagina from behind. Once we've climaxed, we switch positions and start all over again. (Authors' files)

Morton Hunt's (1974) research indicates that favorite male sexual fantasies during masturbation are intercourse with a loved one, intercourse with strangers, and sex with more than one person. Popular female sexual fantasies during masturbation are, in order, intercourse with a loved one, sexual acts that could not really take place and intercourse with strangers. A study of college students' fantasies during intercourse (Sue, 1979) yielded somewhat different themes. Among men the most popular were oral-genital sex, being found sexually irresistible by others, and having sex with an imaginary lover. Women reported, in order of frequency, being found sexually irresistible by others, oral-genital sex, and having sex with a former lover. Both researchers discovered that more women than men fantasized about being forced to have sex, while more men than women fantasized about forcing someone to have sex. Fantasizing forced sex does not mean that the fantasizer really wants to assault someone or be assaulted. Instead, it may reflect the person's need for control or power.

Most researchers believe that sexual fantasies are normal and not a symptom of relationship problems. One study (Zimmer, Borchardt, & Fischle, 1983) found a positive link between couples' sexual fantasies and a satisfying sex life. Many sex therapists (i.e., Stanway, 1989; McCarthy, 1988; Britton, 1982; Barbach & Levine, 1981) recommend sexual fantasy as a technique to enhance sexual arousal. The important thing is to be able to separate sexual fantasies from real life and to banish the guilt that often accompanies them. The healthiest and most rewarding practice may be to cultivate a number of different fantasies, enjoy them all, and not feel guilty about fantasizing. In this fashion, sexual fantasies can become a help to us by acting as a mental bridge to arousal and excitement in actual sexual encounters (McCarthy, 1988).

Some people have sexual fantasies about people in the public eye, like the rock star Madonna.

Sexual Techniques and Pleasuring

MASTURBATION

Does masturbation have any negative side effects?

Masturbation refers to self-stimulation of the genitals or other parts of the body for sexual arousal and pleasure. Masturbation is usually the first sexual experience for both men and women, and it is the most common form of sexual expression other than heterosexual coitus. Readers will recall from Chapter 1 that masturbation has historically been regarded as evil and perverse for its allegedly harmful physiological and psychological effects. Contemporary physicians and psychologists, though, agree that masturbation is a matter of self-pleasuring rather than self-abuse. Nor is it regarded exclusively as a means of relieving sexual tension for the person without a partner. Rather it is viewed as an acceptable way for men and women to learn how best to satisfy their sexual needs and cultivate their sexual responses. Masturbation is a means for discovering the best kinds of sexual stimulation for oneself and a reliable way to learn how to reach orgasm. For many men and women, masturbation allows a freedom not enjoyed when they are with a partner because they feel under no pressure to please anyone but themselves and can take as much time as they need (Stanway, 1989; Yaffe & Fenwick, 1988a, b; Barbach & Levine, 1981).

A Developmental View

As we will discover later on (Chapter 13), sexual self-pleasuring begins at a surprisingly early age. Indeed, many sources (e.g., Martinson, 1981; Gordon & Gordon, 1983) point out that infants and toddlers periodically engage in self-stimulation, indicating that they have discovered some aspects of sexual responsiveness. This early self-stimulation is usually a rehearsal for what is to come. Lessons learned even as early as infancy about what we find exciting and pleasurable endure an entire lifetime and shape our sexual lives with our partners (Stanway, 1989).

Memories are usually vivid regarding masturbation during the early years:

> **I first masturbated when I was 11. I was in bed one night and had been moving my body up and down against the mattress. I enjoyed the sensation and my penis got very hard. Before long, I ejaculated. I distinctly remember how warm and good everything felt, although I was confused about the ejaculation part. I didn't really know what it was or where it came from. (Authors' files)**

> **I was nine at the time. I had been touching myself under my underwear, and really liked stroking my lips and clitoris. Soon I masturbated to orgasm. (Authors' files)**

During adolescence, masturbation becomes very common and both sexes develop an array of self-stimulation techniques:

> **While I masturbated a few times as a child, I began doing it on a fairly regular basis as a teenager and taught myself different techniques. Masturbating became more natural and satisfying, probably because I no longer felt ashamed about what I was doing. Becoming more relaxed heightened the pleasure and enjoyment. (Authors' files)**

A glance at the research reveals how prevalent masturbation is during the teenage years. For example, Alfred Kinsey and associates (1948, 1953) discovered that approximately 21 percent of the men they studied had masturbated by age 12, 82 percent by age 15, and 92 percent by their 20th birthday. By comparison, 17 percent of the women queried had engaged in masturbation at age 15 and about 30 percent by age 20. The percentages for women escalate after 20, though, until about age 45. One source (Wolfe, 1982) estimates that between 70 and 85 percent of adult women have masturbated at some point in their lives. According to another source (Atwood & Gagnon, 1987), nine out of ten college men and eight of ten college women masturbate.

Is masturbation widespread among married adults?

It is incorrect to assume that married adults do not masturbate. In one study (Petersen et al., 1983), 43 percent of the husbands surveyed and 22 percent of the wives reported masturbating more than once a week. Another investigation (Hunt, 1974) revealed that over 70 percent of young adult husbands and wives masturbated once or twice or month. Most people in an intimate relationship are usually unaware that their partners masturbate because many men and women do not disclose this information for a variety of reasons:

Even though my partner and I have an active sex life, I masturbate alone on a fairly regular basis. I have always enjoyed self-pleasuring and consider it an important part of my sex life. It's also very private and secret. Maybe it's the "forbidden" nature of the solitary act that makes me so guarded. I haven't shared this with my partner and feel reluctant to do so. I guess there's a part of me that feels guilty about what I'm doing. Someday I want her to know, but I'm not sure at this point how to broach the subject. (Authors' files)

A woman speaks:

My partner is often away for professional travel. During these times, I miss her and our wonderful sex life. Therefore, I masturbate, usually immediately after we speak over the telephone. I have told her that I infrequently masturbate, but have not revealed the actual frequency. I think she might feel guilty about her travels. (Authors' files)

Many sex therapists recommend masturbation to clients as a way to find out what types of stimulation please them so they can later communicate this to their partners. Some people find it helpful to practice masturbating to orgasm because the orgasmic response becomes easier with practice. For many people, in fact, masturbation provides a different kind of orgasm than those they enjoy with a partner during coitus. Finally, inasmuch as intercourse and other shared sexual activities continue into late adulthood (see Chapter 15), it is not surprising that masturbation does also (Butler & Lewis, 1988).

Techniques of Masturbation

Women give themselves sexual pleasure by touching themselves or moving their bodies in special ways. Shere Hite's (1976) survey of over 3,000 women between the ages of 14 and 78 showed that there are a number of different types of female masturbation. The most common (73 percent) involves manual stimulation of the clitoris and vulva with the hand while lying on one's back (Figure 8–1). Most women stimulate the clitoral area with circular or up-and-down movements of the fingers, usually with increasing amounts of pressure. Many use the other hand to stimulate their breasts.

Variations of this technique involve inserting a finger or object such as a vibrator into the vagina while continuing clitoral stimulation. Some women use insertion during masturbation, while others delay insertion until the moment of orgasm. Still others place their palm on the clitoral area while reaching around with their fingers into the vaginal entrance, making a kind of semicircular shape of the hand. Finally,

FIGURE 8–1
Female Masturbation.

some women momentarily insert their fingers into the vagina for the purpose of increasing lubrication.

Other women prefer to masturbate while lying on their stomachs. Most of the women who employ this technique use their hand or a vibrator and employ the variations just mentioned. However, the pressure of the body appears to make an important difference; some women feel that this increases their stimulation, while others report that they cannot reach orgasm at all on their stomach, or can only with difficulty. Some women move their bodies against their hands, while others move only their hands and not their bodies.

Another masturbation technique involves thrusting against a pillow or other soft object. It typically includes grinding or thrusting the pelvis, especially the pubic areas, against the bed, some pillows, or other objects. The legs are usually held together, and often a pillow or towel or some clothing is folded up and held between the legs. Other women masturbate by crossing their legs very tightly and squeezing rhythmically. This technique can be performed sitting, lying down, or on one's side. Usually the legs are strongly tensed and untensed, particularly the upper thigh muscles.

Some women direct running water over their genitals until they reach orgasm. The most common method is to turn on the faucet with a strong flow and then lie on one's back with legs up on the wall and clitoris positioned under the rushing water. Most women using this technique direct the water massage to the clitoral-vulval area with their legs apart. Finally, some women masturbate to orgasm by inserting a finger or object into the vagina. Although there is a widespread male notion that most women masturbate this way, only a small percentage do so, at least according to Hite's study. Women using this technique manually stimulate their clitoral areas before vaginal insertion.

Statistics cited earlier showed that nearly all men masturbate, at least occasionally. While masturbation is most frequent during adolescence and among men without steady partners, men in steady relationships also practice it. Many men (like women) feel uncomfortable about masturbating and want to get it over with quickly. Even though they know it is not harmful, they cannot escape feeling guilty about it. Part of the problem is that traditional men (and women) have been erroneously taught that the "real thing" is intercourse, not self-pleasuring (Yaffee & Fenwick, 1988b; Barbach, 1984).

Shere Hite's (1981) survey of over 7,000 men between the ages of 13 and 97 revealed a number of male masturbatory techniques. The most popular (82 percent) was direct stimulation of the penis by hand (see Figure 8–2). Hite's research—admittedly criticized for being based on a potentially biased sample—also suggested that most men preferred to stimulate the top of the penis, or glans, but that for some the frenulum or area around the urethral meatus was most sensitive. For still others stimulating the base of the penis prolonged the buildup of sensation before orgasm.

Some men enjoy massaging the testicles and entire genital area in addition to the penis while masturbating. The area between the scrotum and the anus may also be particularly sensitive to stimulation. Others enjoy anal penetration or exterior anal stimulation. Many men like to hold off orgasms during masturbation, increasing their pleasure by stopping and starting stimulation.

Men masturbate in a variety of positions, including standing, sitting, and lying down. Some masturbate by lying on their stomachs and rubbing themselves against a bed. Other men use thigh pressure to masturbate, and some use a vibrator. Lubrication is often applied to the genitals while masturbating, and a few men use water massage to achieve orgasm.

Hite also reported that many of her respondents indicated a real liking for their own semen. Some said they enjoyed rubbing it into their skin, and some even expressed a liking for its taste. Some respondents said they considered their ejaculate proof of their manhood. Others expressed reservations about their semen and found its wetness, its stickiness, and its odor quite unappealing.

Sexual Aids

People use several types of sexual aids both during masturbating and during shared sexual activity. Artificial vaginas and penises—the latter are called *dildos*—can be bought at adult bookstores or sexual supply stores and through catalogues, as can life-size female and male bodies. Dildos are usually made of firm latex, come in many sizes, and, unlike vibrators, are usually not battery powered or electrically driven.

What's the difference between a dildo and a vibrator?

FIGURE 8–2
Male Masturbation.

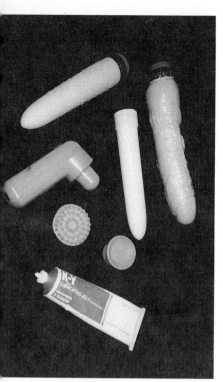

FIGURE 8–3
Vibrators of Various Sorts.

Some women use dildos in masturbating, but they are not commonly used by either heterosexual couples or by gay men or lesbians.

A *vibrator* is a sexual aid designed to enhance arousal. While vibrators are used by both men and women, women tend to use them with greater frequency. One survey of over 15,000 women (Lowe et al., 1983) indicated that 50 percent of the respondents had used some type of vibrator to help them reach orgasm. Some vibrators are penis-shaped and can be inserted into the vagina, but the more popular types are those that can be applied to the vulva or clitoris. Some are plastic and battery powered or electrically driven. Most are either hand held or fitted with straps for the back of the hand. Many can change speeds and come with several attachments. Figure 8–3 illustrates several types of vibrators.

Vibrators that fit over the hand often fail to provide adequate stimulation and can be tiring to use. Most experts recommend an electrically powered machine (never to be used around water) with interchangeable heads that can be used to massage the whole body as well as to stimulate the genital areas.

When using a vibrator, a lubricant such as K-Y jelly should be first applied to the clitoral area. To avoid the risk of contracting either HIV-AIDS or other sexually transmitted diseases and infections, vibrators and other sex devices should never be shared unless they are cleaned thoroughly after use. Also, if the vibrator or other sexual device is used to provide anal stimulation, it should be cleaned thoroughly before attempting vaginal stimulation or insertion (Yaffee & Fenwick, 1988a, b; Stanway, 1989).

A sexual aid that you may already own is the detachable hand-held pulsating shower head. Hot tubs can also be a sexual aid, if you sit near or on the stream of water coming into the unit. Finally, we would be remiss not to mention body oils as a sexual aid. Body oils are used during massage, masturbation, or while having a sexual encounter with another person. Their sensual quality may have to do with the oil itself, the touch of the other person, or a combination of both. Oils can be found in adult bookstores or you can use any commercially prepared baby oil found in drugstores.

MUTUAL CARESSING AND STIMULATION

Mutual caressing and stimulation, or mutual pleasuring, refers to behaviors used to heighten sexual arousal. Our discussion will focus on mutual pleasuring between heterosexual partners, although, as you will discover in Chapter 9, most of the activities we describe are engaged in by both heterosexuals and lesbians and gay men. Since all people use essentially the same mutual pleasuring techniques, some of the quotations from the authors' files are from gays and lesbians and some are from heterosexuals.

erogenous zones Those parts of the body particularly sensitive to erotic stimulation.

Mutual pleasuring includes a wide range of sexual techniques, most of which are directed toward **erogenous zones,** parts of the body that are particularly sensitive to erotic stimulation. The lips, breasts, and genitals are the most intensely erogenous areas, but many other parts of the body, such as the buttocks, the thighs, the back of the neck—even the ears, hands, feet, and toes—are sensitive to stimulation. Stimulating the erogenous zones usually produces sexual arousal, although there are individual variations and many factors such as mood and type of touching affect arousal. The exercises described in the box on "Sexual Sharing: Understanding Your Partner's Needs" are designed to help people learn to enhance each other's sexual pleasure. Many couples enjoy touching or caressing sensitive body parts and consider it an essential part of their lovemaking:

Both my lover and I like a lot of sexual arousal and pleasuring. We usually begin by gently touching and caressing each other. It's best when we take our time and slowly build up the sexual excitement. I love kissing her all over and feeling her body respond to my touch. She likes it when I gently knead her muscles or let my hair brush against her body. I particularly enjoy it when she strokes my back and buttocks, and then turns me over and concentrates on my abdomen, breasts, and legs. When she gently nibbles on the inside of my thighs, I'm usually close to going right through the ceiling with ecstasy. It's difficult hanging on because we're both so aroused from body stimulation. (Authors' files)

MAKING USE OF WHAT WE KNOW

Sexual Sharing: Understanding Your Partner's Needs

An important aspect of sexual intimacy is openness and honesty regarding sexual needs. According to Matthew McKay and colleagues (1983), learning more about your own and your partner's body is critical to sexual sharing. The following exercises suggest ways of enhancing your sexual knowledge of one another.

Seek to develop an accurate understanding of each other's sexual anatomy.

Use this book (particularly Chapters 3 and 4) and related titles as guides to explore your own and your partner's body. Learn to identify by sight and touch the various sexual parts of yourself and your partner. This is the first step toward awareness of the body as a source of sexual pleasure.

Engage in the pleasures of sensual touching.

In a room at a comfortable temperature, have your partner lie naked on his or her stomach on the bed. For fifteen minutes or so, gently massage your partner, using your fingertips to explore his or her body. Do not speak to each other; rely on subtle nonverbal communication to discover what is pleasurable for your partner and what is not. After the allotted time, discuss the experience. How accurate were your perceptions of your partner's nonverbal cues? Reverse roles and repeat the exercise.

Teach each other the concept of sexual pleasuring.

Inform your partner exactly what you want him or her to do to give you pleasure, step by step. This can be kept at the level of a massage or extended to include more sexual activities. Share with your partner how you would like sexual pleasuring to occur: how long, how hard, how fast, and so on. You might want to demonstrate for your partner or guide his or her hand if necessary.

Discuss sexual turn-ons and turn-offs.

Share with your partner what you find to be most pleasurable. Be sure to give your partner validation when he or she does something that sexually stimulates you. Conversely, tell your partner what you don't find pleasurable. Also, try to convey sexual turn-offs in a positive fashion. For instance, instead of saying "Hey, not so fast!" say something like "I'd really enjoy it if we went more slowly."

After a sexual experience, talk about it.

Tell your partner what you liked about the experience and what you would have preferred to have done differently. Such instant replays give you both an opportunity to reinforce the pleasurable aspects of your sexual relationship and provide your partner with immediate feedback.

Kissing can be a source of erotic stimulation.

I love it when we both take our time and we don't rush things. I enjoy a slow buildup with a lot of touching, and not just focused on the genital areas. I like my whole body to tingle. (Authors' files)

Kissing

Since the lips are very sensitive, kissing provides considerable erotic stimulation. There are different types of kisses, from simple lip-to-lip forms of contact to deep, passionate, open-mouthed kissing. In the latter, also known as "french kissing" or "soul kissing," the tongue of one partner probes the open mouth of the other; many partners also nibble the lips and tongue of the other. Kissing can also be directed to other sensitive parts of the body. A woman shares these preferences:

I enjoy the erotic stimulation that kissing brings. I like to be kissed all over, starting with the mouth and neck and then the rest of my body. The slow, lingering kisses are the best. I get really turned on when my partner kisses my breasts and slowly licks and sucks the nipples. The pleasure is heightened when my partner kisses my stomach and inner thighs. (Authors' files)

Although kissing is an important part of lovemaking in most Western cultures, in some parts of the world it is frowned on. The "World of Differences" box describes attitudes and practices in various countries.

A WORLD OF DIFFERENCES

Kissing Customs: Recurrent Themes and Curious Practices

The practice of kissing has been around for many centuries, and has long been an expression of friendliness, respect, and love in the Western world. However, not all peoples use this form of expression; in fact, some societies find the very thought of kissing disgusting. The Thonga of South Africa consider all mouth-to-mouth contact revolting because of the possibility of getting the other person's saliva into one's mouth. The Hindus of India are also not keen on kissing and practice it only very cautiously, since they believe that contact with saliva renders the sexual act ritually contaminating.

Kissing is not very widespread among the Japanese and Chinese, although there are generational differences in its practice. For example, older Okinawan men and women do not really care for kissing and tend to avoid it in public. However, younger couples are more apt to display their affection through kissing and to include it in their sexual activities. Kissing is frowned upon by the Ainu of northern Japan and by the Miao of Asia.

An interesting type of erotic kiss has been labeled the "smell kiss" or "olfactory kiss." It is practiced by placing one's nose near or against the partner's face and inhaling. The ancient Egyptians probably knew this practice because their words for "kiss" and "smell" are the same. Some Samoans also express their affection by sniffing. Nose rubbing may be a variant of the smell kiss or simply an inaccurate label. Nose rubbing has been reported among the Eskimo, Tamil, Ulithi, and Trobriand Islanders. An interesting evolutionary interpretation of the smell and nose kiss has been offered by some anthropologists. They claim that such behavior may be leftover from a long-ago habit of sniffing prey, food, or a potential mate before making a commitment to action (Gregersen, 1983; Chalmers, 1988).

Sexual Techniques and Pleasuring

"Why won't you cuddle?"

Breast Stimulation

The breasts are also very sensitive to stimulation. As we learned in Chapters 3 and 4, the nipples usually respond to the touch of the fingers, tongue, or other objects by becoming erect. While people most often use fingers and mouth to stimulate their partners' breasts, imaginative couples use fabric of different textures (velvet, silk, satin), feathers or hair, or warmed oil, gel, or lotion. Research indicates (James 1984; Masters & Johnson, 1966) that some women are capable of achieving orgasm through breast stimulation alone.

Once again, it should be realized that there are wide individual variations and preferences in arousal patterns. Some women have very sensitive breasts and prefer a gentle touch. Others enjoy a more forceful approach, while still others may not find breast stimulation all that enjoyable. Also, a woman's breasts often become sensitive and tender during certain times in her menstrual cycle, a factor that affects her level of arousal. Men also enjoy having their breasts and nipples stimulated. Women and men who stimulate a man's nipples use the same approaches partners use to stimulate a woman's breasts. Obviously, with all this variation in response, it is important for partners to openly communicate their sexual needs and preferences and demonstrate sensitivity.

Manual Genital Stimulation

Manual genital stimulation is a popular form of mutual pleasuring. Here again, we must stress that there are wide variations in arousal patterns. What feels good to one person may be a turn-off to another. Learning how to touch a sex partner's genitals as well as the rest of the body are lovemaking skills that develop through open discussion and experience.

MANUAL STIMULATION OF THE FEMALE GENITALS. Manual stimulation of the female genitals may lead directly to orgasm or it can lead to oral-genital stimulation, coitus, or both. Many women enjoy having their inner thighs gently stroked as well as the perineum (the area between the vagina and anus) in the initial stages of lovemaking. Before actual clitoral stimulation begins—particularly if the women has not begun to lubricate—spreading the lubrication from the vagina to the clitoris can be helpful. Saliva can also provide enough lubrication to make stimulation comfortable. A lubricant such as K-Y jelly applied to the fingers and vulva may also be used.

The style of stimulation applied to the genitals depends greatly on the woman. Some women like direct clitoral pressure, while others prefer indirect pressure, such as along the sides of the clitoris. Some enjoy slow movement of the fingers, while others like a faster tempo. The simultaneous stimulation of the clitoris with one hand and the breasts with the other is enjoyed by many. Some women like having a finger inserted into the vagina; for others, anal stimulation heightens arousal. Here is how three women prefer manual stimulation of their genitals:

> I like slow circular movements. My excitement builds when the pressure is gradually increased.

> The best is when the clitoral shaft is stroked gently at first and then pressure is increased. This allows my sexual intensity to build.

> I like it when my clitoris is rubbed rhythmically while my anal area is being stimulated at the same time. (Authors' files)

MANUAL STIMULATION OF THE MALE GENITALS. Manual stimulation of the male genitals may lead to ejaculation, or it can lead to oral-genital stimulation, or coitus, or both. The most sensitive areas of the penis are the glans, corona, and the frenulum. Many men enjoy having their inner thighs caressed and their testes gently squeezed. Running the fingers up and down the length of the penis also produces pleasurable feelings. Grasping the penis and stroking it are common forms of stimulation, and some men enjoy anal stimulation. Sexual pleasuring can be enhanced if the man tells his partner where he would like to be touched and how gently or firmly, as well as the desired tempo of stroking:

> The best stimulation is when the shaft of my penis and my scrotum are played with at the same time.

> I like a gentle grip around the shaft of my penis, but I also enjoy alternating pressure.

> I get highly aroused when my lover directs stimulation to the tip of my penis. (Authors' files)

Oral-Genital Stimulation

oral-genital stimulation
Stimulation of the genitals with the mouth, including kissing, licking, and sucking. Commonly referred to as *oral sex*.

Is oral sex a widespread sexual activity?

Oral-genital stimulation, commonly referred to as *oral sex*, means stimulation of the genitals with the mouth, including kissing, licking, and sucking. Oral-genital stimulation can be used as a form of mutual pleasuring or as an alternative means of achieving orgasm. It can be performed individually (one partner to another) or simultaneously (in what is often called the "69" position because the head-to-toe body alignment of the couple suggests that number). Because it leaves the hands free, oral sex can be combined with tactile forms of stimulation. Figures 8–4 and 8–5 illustrate oral-genital stimulation.

Research indicates that most couples have either experimented with oral sex or practice it fairly regularly (Herold & Way, 1983; Kahn, 1983; Petersen et al., 1983). A more recent source (Gagnon & Simon, 1987) states that almost 90 percent of young married couples engage in oral-genital sex, and this form of sexual activity has increased more than any other since Kinsey's surveys in the 1950s. Half of all sexually

Sexual Techniques and Pleasuring

FIGURE 8–4
Oral-Genital Stimulation: Fellatio.

active adolescents report engaging in oral-genital activity, and some women prefer oral sex to intercourse (Newcomer & Udry, 1985).

Many couples regard oral sex as one of their most pleasurable and enjoyable sexual activities. They feel that it is the most intimate of sex acts, an extremely satisfying activity for both giver and receiver. However, some people dislike genital odors and secretions, and others object to oral sex because they find the genitals unattractive. There are those, too, who dislike oral sex because they feel that it is shameful, unnatural, or unhygienic:

> I've never been able to accept the idea of oral sex. It seems unnatural and unsanitary.

> I think oral sex is disgusting. I don't know how people can do such shameful things to the genitals.

> It's perverted and dirty. (Authors' files)

FELLATIO. **Fellatio** is from the Latin word *fellare*, meaning "to suck," and refers to the oral stimulation of the male genitals. A number of fellatio techniques can be employed, including licking the penis as well as the scrotum. Some partners hold the shaft of the penis in one hand while swirling the tongue along the shaft, glans, and frenulum. Others stimulate the anal area while performing fellatio.

Once the penis is in the mouth, many stroke the shaft and scrotum with their hand. The mouth is often moved up and down the penis with as long a stroke as the partner feels comfortable with. The teeth need to be kept away from the particularly sensitive head of the penis. To avoid gagging, those performing fellatio often encircle the penis with one or more fingers, a technique that limits oral penetration. Some partners withdraw their mouths as ejaculation occurs, while others like to swallow the semen.

fellatio Oral stimulation of the male genitals.

Sexual Techniques and Pleasuring

Most men have positive reactions to fellatio:

> I love fellatio and the physical sensations that it brings. I'm in ecstasy when a woman is doing it to me.

> I actually prefer fellatio to intercourse. It's more erotic and arousing.

> I love the feeling of my partner's mouth wrapped around my penis. (Authors' files)

Some men, though, harbor negative feelings toward fellatio:

> It's a degrading act. I wouldn't think of asking a woman to do it to me.

> I personally don't like it. Maybe it's because I've never felt "clean" down there or comfortable with my genitals. (Authors' files)

Women offered the following thoughts on fellatio:

> I enjoy doing it, and I know that he enjoys performing oral sex on me. It's an important part of our foreplay.

> I like performing fellatio because it's sexually arousing for both of us. I love the taste of his penis and really get off watching him enjoy it.

> I'll do it only because he likes it. It isn't my favorite part of lovemaking. (Authors' files)

cunnilingus Oral stimulation of the female genitals.

CUNNILINGUS. **Cunnilingus,** which originates from the Latin words *cunnus,* "vulva," and *lingere,* "to lick," refers to oral stimulation of the female genitals. Many partners use their tongue to kiss, lick, or suck the outer and inner lips of the vagina as well as the shaft and tip of the clitoris. Many women enjoy having their partner slowly penetrate and probe the vagina with the tongue and then swirl or flick the clitoris. As pleasure increases, more rapid and intense licking and sucking is enjoyed. Women remark on favorite cunnilingus techniques by their partners:

> I get really turned on with oral sex. I love it when he kisses and sucks my clitoris and my vagina.

> The best part is when she gently nibbles my clitoris.

> My lover is at his best when he slowly moves his tongue in and out of my vagina. I like when he is also stimulating my anal area with his fingers.

> I like my partner to eat me while I play with my breasts. (Authors' files)

Not all women are enthusiastic about cunnilingus. Many feel embarrassed and self-conscious:

> I guess I'm afraid that I won't taste right.

> I don't think I'm attractive down there.

> Cunnilingus is gross and I would never let a man do it to me.

> I worry about the odor and whether or not it's "ladylike." (Authors' files)

Sexual Techniques and Pleasuring

FIGURE 8–5
Oral-Genital Stimulation: Cunnilingus.

Men had the following thoughts about cunnilingus:

It's a turn-on and I love doing it. I really enjoy the way most women taste.

I enjoy cunnilingus and the way a woman responds to it. I especially like the feel and taste.

I've tried cunnilingus a few times and just don't feel comfortable doing it.

I've never done it and don't intend to. I get turned off by the very thought of it. (Authors' files)

Several considerations should be kept in mind when practicing cunnilingus or fellatio. To begin with, it has now been proved (see Spitzer & Winer, 1989; Staver, 1989) that the human immunodeficiency virus can be transmitted by oral-genital sex (see Chapter 18). This is possible because there is an exchange of bodily fluids. If this virus is present in semen or vaginal fluids, it can enter the partner's bloodstream via cuts or sores in the lips or inside of the mouth. To help prevent the transmission of this virus, a condom should be worn during fellatio and a rubber dam (the kind used in dental work) placed over the vulva during cunnilingus. Only if you and your partner are HIV-negative and monogamous can you engage in this activity with relatively little risk.

Also, the genital area should always be kept clean (many partners wash their genitals immediately before having sex). Oral-genital sex should not be practiced if a partner has any kind of sexually transmitted disease or infection. And a partner should never blow into the vagina because this forces air into the uterus and up into the fallopian tubes, which can cause an embolism (obstruction of a blood vessel by an air bubble). For pregnant women, the forced air can cause placental damage. The genitals should also not be bitten (gentle nibbling is an exception).

Finally, couples need to openly communicate their likes and dislikes about oral sex. For instance, some people may be willing to caress the penis by mouth, but be quite unwilling to have it pushed deep into the back of the mouth or to have a partner ejaculate into the mouth. As Andrew Stanway (1989) puts it, personal rules about oral sex should be understood in advance so that there is no unpleasantness at the last moment.

Anal Stimulation

Anal stimulation is another form of mutual pleasuring. Many heterosexual and gay/ lesbian partners have experimented with some form of anal stimulation (see, e.g., Petersen et al., 1983; Morin, 1981; Barbach & Levine, 1981). While some people consider it a turn-off, others find it quite pleasurable.

The most common form of anal stimulation is manually stimulating a partner's anus during intercourse or oral sex. While some partners gently stimulate the outer anal area, others penetrate the rectum with the finger or some other object.

anal intercourse The insertion of the penis into a partner's rectum.

Some partners practice **anal intercourse,** the insertion of the penis into the partner's rectum. Should anal sex be attempted, there are several important considerations to keep in mind. To begin with, unprotected anal sex is a high-risk sexual practice. The lining of the rectum is thin and delicate and can easily be ruptured. Thus HIV is more easily transmitted in anal intercourse than in any other form of sexual activity. A latex condom should be worn and coated with spermicide or a lubricant containing nonoxynol-9. Most experts warn against anal intercourse because of the danger of HIV transmission (Fogel, 1990; Heyward & Curran, 1988).

As far as other considerations are concerned, since the rectum does not have any natural lubricant, sufficient sterile lubrication such as K-Y jelly (*not* Vaseline, which weakens rubber condoms and causes tearing) is needed. Because penetration can be painful, the penis must be inserted in a slow and gentle fashion. Many heterosexual couples find it easier for the woman to be on top so she can control penile entry. Finally, couples should never engage in vaginal intercourse after anal intercourse because to do so puts both at risk of genital infection. To safeguard against this, the penis should always be washed with soap and water following anal sex.

SEXUAL INTERCOURSE

coitus Sexual intercourse.

Coitus, or sexual intercourse, is from the Latin *coire* meaning to "come together." It conventionally means the full insertion of the man's penis into the woman's vagina, and is one of the most common sexual techniques among heterosexuals. A variety of coital positions can be used to enhance the pleasure of sexual intercourse. We describe here the six basic positions, each of which has numerous variations. Note that different combinations of body rhythm can also be employed.

Man-on-Top, Face-to-Face Position

The man-on-top, face-to-face coital position—often called "missionary position"—is the most commonly used position in the United States. In the basic position, the woman lies on her back, with the man on top (see Figure 8–6). Usually the man

FIGURE 8–6
Man-on-Top, Face-to-Face Coital Position.

supports his upper body with his arms while the woman keeps her legs apart and one or both knees flexed. The man or the woman can guide the penis into the vagina.

There are many variations of the man-on-top position. For example, the woman may curl one leg around her partner, or she may wrap both legs around her partner and cross her ankles together. One or both legs may also be lifted and pointed upward, positions that facilitate deeper penile penetration. Or the man may lean on his hands while the woman places her ankles and legs on his shoulders and holds her thighs for support. Other variations include the man kneeling and supporting the woman's raised body with his hands, or the man kneeling with his legs outside the woman's, which remain straight.

There are several advantages and disadvantages to the man-on-top position. On the plus side, it promotes relatively easy **intromission,** or insertion of the penis into the vagina. Penetration is usually deep in this position. The fact that it is face-to-face allows for eye contact, kissing, and caressing. Should pregnancy be desired, this position more than others increases the chances for conception—especially if the woman keeps her legs raised after ejaculation to enable the semen to flow toward the cervix.

intromission Insertion of the penis into the vagina.

As far as disadvantages are concerned, this position often creates muscle strain for the man, who has to distribute his weight on his knees and elbows. It is also not the best position for a man who is overweight or for a woman who is in late pregnancy. Some women experience discomfort from the deep penetration and desire more freedom to move than this position allows. Since men tend to reach a climax more quickly in this position, it is unfavorable for premature ejaculators (see Chapter 16).

Woman-on-Top, Face-to-Face Position

In this position, the partners are face-to-face with the woman on top. The man typically lies on his back, while the woman is either prone or kneeling upright. If she lies lengthwise, the woman's legs are typically positioned inside the man's, which supplies friction between the vagina and penis. Should a kneeling position be desired, the woman's knees are usually on either side of the man (see Figure 8–7).

Sexual Techniques and Pleasuring   231

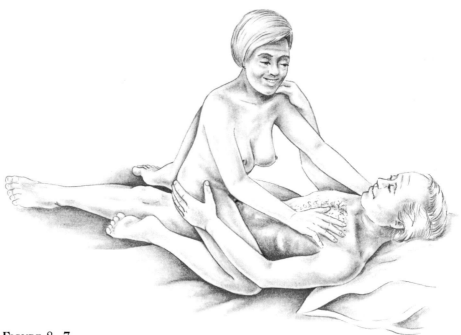

FIGURE 8-7
Woman-on-Top, Face-to-Face Coital Position.

There are many variations to the female-on-top position. For instance, the woman can lean forward or back, supporting her weight on her hands. The woman can lean back while the man sits up, both partners using their hands to support themselves. The woman can sit with her legs wrapped around her partner's back. She can also lean back and support her weight on her hands while he sits in a cross-legged position, or, in a related variation, she can lean back with her legs on his shoulders.

Many women enjoy the female-on-top position because it gives them maximum freedom of movement and allows them to determine the depth of penetration. Many couples are able to start from a kneeling position and shift to a prone position or other variation without losing much or any contact. Since the hands of both partners are usually free in this position, there is scope for considerable touching and caressing. Another advantage to the woman-on-top position is that it enables either partner to stimulate the clitoris during coitus, including with a vibrator if desired. Finally, this may be a desirable position for pregnant women (primarily because it allows the woman to control the depth of penile penetration and because it puts no weight on her abdomen) and for small women whose partners are big or heavy.

There are some disadvantages to the woman-on-top position, though. Some women are shy about taking the more active role it demands of them, and some men dislike their passive role. Other men report that the penis does not receive as much stimulation in this position as it does in the missionary position, and that this delays ejaculation. Precisely because of this, many sex therapists recommend the female-on-top position as one technique to deal with premature ejaculation and other sexual dysfunctions (see Chapter 16). Another disadvantage is that inexperienced couples may find that the penis keeps falling out of the vagina during pelvic thrusts. Finally, the woman-on-top position is a poor one for achieving pregnancy.

Side-by-Side, Face-to-Face Position

The side-by-side position is characterized by partners lying on their sides facing each other, with their legs intertwined in some fashion. For instance, both partners may lie on their sides with the woman's legs apart, outside of the man's. Or the woman may turn slightly on her side while the man lies partly on top of her, with one of his legs between hers (see Figure 8–8). The woman may also lie on her back while the man lies on his side with one leg over her.

Side-by-side positions give sexual partners considerable freedom of movement, and neither has to support the weight of the other. They each have some control over lovemaking so that neither has to do all of the "work." Moreover, such positions give partners the opportunity to engage in mutual caressing and embracing. Many people enjoy these positions because of the leisurely quality they bring to sex, making them favorable for a prolonged encounter. Side-by-side positions are often recommended during pregnancy because they exert minimal abdominal pressure on the woman. They also allow for shallow penile penetration, which is especially important for some women during the last month of pregnancy, when the cervix is sensitive and deep thrusting may cause pain (see Chapter 10). However, the fact that deep penetration is difficult in these positions may loom as a disadvantage. Another disadvantage is that intromission may be difficult.

Rear-Entry Position

There are a number of variations of the rear-entry position, in which the male enters the female's vagina from the rear. For example, the man may kneel upright with legs together while the woman kneels with her head down and legs apart. Or the woman may kneel forward and support her upper body on a bed. Another variation is having the woman lie on her side with her back to her partner, often called the "spoon" position (see Figure 8–9). This is particularly comfortable when a woman is pregnant. For a rear-entry standing position, the man stands upright as the woman leans forward with her hands on a low piece of furniture or other object.

Rear-entry positions offer the advantage of deep penetration as well as numerous lying, kneeling, sitting, and standing variations. Many women enjoy rear-entry positions because the penis stimulates the front vaginal wall, where the G-spot is thought to be located (see Chapter 3). Also, these positions enable the man or the woman herself to stimulate the clitoris during coitus if desired. The man also has the ability to caress his partner's breasts, legs, or buttocks, and the woman can stimulate his scrotum. Many couples enjoy the buttock-body contact that these positions offer.

There are several disadvantages to rear-entry positions. For one, while they offer deep penetration, hard thrusting can cause women pain and discomfort. Some men and women find the angle of penile insertion awkward, and there may be a tendency for the penis to slip out. The absence of face-to-face contact makes this position too impersonal for some couples, while others find it too primitive or "animalistic."

FIGURE 8–8
Side-by-Side, Face-to-Face Coital Position.

FIGURE 8–9
Rear-Entry Coital Position.

Standing Position

Standing positions are novel and not widely practiced. In one variation of this position, the couple stands face to face while the man lifts one of the woman's legs around him. In another variation, the man lifts the woman off the ground while she wraps her legs around him (see Figure 8–10). As the woman wraps her arms around the man's neck, the couple may choose close upper body contact or arch themselves away from each other. And as we indicated, rear entry can also be accomplished from a standing position.

FIGURE 8–10
Standing Coital Position.

Because standing positions require considerable agility and strength, they tend to be tiring and uncomfortable. Obviously, then, they are not recommended for prolonged coitus. Another disadvantage is that intromission is often difficult in standing positions, particularly when men are much taller than their partners. Penile penetration also tends to be shallow in standing positions. Finally, the rear-entry standing position sometimes poses a physical comfort problem when the man has to crouch in order to enter the woman.

Sitting Position

Sitting positions are another novel approach to lovemaking. Usually the man sits on a bed or a chair and the woman sits astride him (see Figure 8–11). In one variation, the man holds the woman as she leans back and places her legs on his shoulders. The woman may also sit with her back to the man.

Many couples find sitting positions erotic and enjoy the physical intimacy they provide. Considerable touching and caressing are possible for both partners. Sitting positions also tend to be restful positions for intercourse. However, they do not allow for much movement and orgasm may be difficult for both partners to reach.

Given the great variety of possible coital positions, couples should experiment until they find the ones that suit them best. They need not go entirely by the book when trying new variations, but should use their imaginations. If a position feels awkward, they should make adjustments until it is right for both of them.

No matter how many positions they try, though, most couples will discover that they keep coming back to the few that give them the most mutual pleasure. This is not being unadventurous, for they have experimented enough to know what they like. Many couples experiment at the beginning of a new relationship, a time when each partner wants to explore the other's body and search out sexual likes and dislikes.

FIGURE 8–11
Sitting Coital Position.

Long-time partners often experiment, too, because they want to enliven their love-making by trying something different. And for some couples, experimentation continues for as long as the relationship endures.

Whatever the reason for experimentation, couples should realize certain fundamentals about sexual positions. First, some positions are especially appropriate for particular situations, such as pregnancy. Second, penetration is easiest when the woman's thighs are widely spread. Putting a pillow beneath the woman's hips is another way to make entry easier. Also, positions in which the woman's knees are bent up to her chest allow for the deepest penetration. Third, positions in which the woman's legs are closed or held together give maximum stimulation to the penis. To postpone a man's orgasm, couples might want to change to a woman-on-top position. Finally, remember that the man-on-top position more than any other increases a couple's chances for conception (Yaffee & Fenwick, 1988a, b).

SEXUAL EXPRESSION IN THE PHYSICALLY CHALLENGED

Although most of us are aware that people with a physical disability such as cerebral palsy or some degree of paralysis have special needs, we rarely think about their sexual needs. Neither do we often consider what adjustments a person with a chronic illness like diabetes or arthritis may need to make in order to enjoy sexual pleasures. In this section, we'll explore the special sexual needs of people who suffer from physical impairments and disabilities that are not reversible or curable.

A physical disability, such as cerebral palsy or a spinal cord injury, is an impairment of body structure or function, including mobility impairments, amputations, skeletal deformities, and disfigurements. A chronic illness, such as diabetes or arthritis, is a progressive disorder caused by a nonreverisible condition that often leaves the person with some type of disability.

The sexual needs of the disabled and the chronically ill are more like those of the healthy population than unlike them. According to Jean Stoklosa (1984), the meaning of sexuality for persons who are disabled or ill varies according to their own unique sexual makeup and experiences, just as it does for healthy people. Although being born with a lifelong disability such as cerebral palsy forces people to focus a great deal of attention on their other basic needs, this does not obliterate sexual desire. And when serious medical illness strikes people later in life, it may actually bring them closer to their partner, increasing their intimacy.

Still, a physical disability or chronic illness often affects sexual expression and fills people with concerns and anxieties about their sexuality. For some disabled or chronically ill people, of course, sexual activity is not an important facet of life—but then, this is true for some perfectly healthy people as well.

Attitudes Toward Disability and Chronic Illness

Simi Linton and Harilyn Rousso's (1988) survey of attitudes toward the disabled reveals an assortment of negative myths. For instance, even in this day and age, many people believe that a disability is punishment for a sin or wrongdoing. Others fear that a disability is contagious and can be spread through tactile contact. Many people see the disabled as dependent, helpless, and childlike. And although using one's own experience as a guide is often helpful in an unfamiliar situation, nondisabled people really can't extrapolate from their experiences with temporary disability or illness to the condition of the permanently disabled. For instance, if a broken arm or a virus immobilizes them and renders them miserable, they conclude that permanent impairments of movement or coordination must be impossible to overcome. In fact, as the disabled know, the processes of adjustment and adaptation that take place over time, plus some creative problem solving, often makes it possible to live quite normally with a disability.

Misconceptions about the chronically ill are equally widespread. Like the physically disabled, the chronically ill are often viewed as asexual. Betti Krukofsky (1988) believes that sick people are frequently forced to deny and repress their sexuality for two primary reasons. First, many chronically ill people are elderly, and society prefers to believe that the aged have no sexual needs. As we will discover in Chapter 15, however, sexual pleasuring is a lifelong activity, and many elderly people enjoy sex on a regular basis. Second, many people assume that sexual activity is the sole domain of those who are in perfect physical condition. Even health professionals tend to ignore the sexuality of the chronically ill, partly because they do not view sex as vital to recovery or optimal functioning, but also because they are uncomfortable dealing with sexual issues.

The many inaccurate beliefs about disability and chronic illness—for a few examples, see the "Myths and Misconceptions" box—need to be replaced with accurate facts. A disability or chronic illness may affect a person's sex life, but so may a lot of other factors. We all face challenges in life that prompt us to look at things from a different perspective and channel our energies into adjustment and adaptation. The biggest barrier faced by people with disabilities or chronic illnesses is the negative attitudes of society. Pervasive prejudice denies them their sexuality and access to sexual health-care services. These societal prejudices must be overcome and sexual health-care services extended to physically disabled and chronically ill men and women because they are entitled to sexually fulfilling lives (Carter, 1990; Linton & Russo, 1988; Krukofsky, 1988; Schover & Jensen, 1988).

Biological, Psychological, and Social Stressors

The biological conditions underlying disability and illness, as well as the medical treatments prescribed for these conditions, often affect sexual functioning and sexual desire. For example, bladder and bowel incontinence (the inability to retain urine or feces) is often experienced by people with spinal cord injury or neurological

*T*here is no scientific evidence for a number of false beliefs about illness and sexuality, yet we often hear them expressed by both patients and clinicians. If patients incorporate such myths into their thinking, they can interfere with motivation to adapt sexually by mastering new skills or even trying old tricks. Here are a few harmful misconceptions:

- Sex saps one's strength and thus is harmful to anyone not in the best of health.
- Having sex weakens the potency of medical treatments like chemotherapy or radiation therapy.

- Too much sex is unhealthy and causes illness.
- Aged people should not be sexually active or even feel sexual desire.
- Heart attacks and strokes happen very commonly during sexual intercourse.
- Cancer is contagious through sexual activity.

Every one of these statements is either totally wrong or has only the tiniest grain of truth. Sexual activity has in general a far more positive effect on the disabled and ill than forced abstinence (Schover & Jensen, 1988).

MYTHS AND MISCONCEPTIONS

Physical Disability, Not Sexual Disability

disease. Positive feelings about oneself and one's sexuality are understandably threatened by incontinence (Sackett, 1990). Some medical conditions, such as paralysis, create anatomical difficulties, interfere with genital sensations, or make it impossible to have intercourse. Fatigue and/or pain that is secondary to a disease, medical treatment, prolonged hospitalization, and impaired mobility are other biological stressors that affect a person's sexuality.

David Bullard (1988) points out that there are also a number of psychological and social factors that affect the sexual lives of patients. Let's look at some of the major psychological and social stressors that Bullard has identified. As you may imagine, the intensity with which sick and disabled people experience these stressors varies greatly.

ADOPTION OF THE "PATIENT ROLE." Many people feel compelled to adopt the "patient role" and to comply with societal and institutional beliefs that anyone with a serious medical condition is "asexual." To counter such negative perceptions, people need validation that their sexuality is a part of who they are, rather than just a reflection of what they do and how often they do it. Medical and paramedical personnel need to be taught—and reminded—that patients have sexual needs and that both the physical and psychological aspects of love promote well-being. For many women and men, sex is part of love, and love cries out for expression no matter how ill or disabled the person is.

ALTERED BODY IMAGE. The powerful effects of disfigurement or radical body changes cannot be denied. Disturbing self-image issues may surface in a person who is devastated, for example, by the loss of a breast through mastectomy (see Chapters 3 and 17), by having a colostomy (a surgical procedure done in some people who have cancer of the colon or rectum, that creates a special opening for the elimination of solid wastes, bypassing the rectum and anus), or by loss of hair as a result of chemotherapy. Some sexual partners also find it hard to recover their sexual desire for someone who has experienced a major debilitating or disfiguring medical condition. A certain amount of time and effort must be given over to grieving for body losses and learning to accept an altered body image, not only by the patient, but also by that patient's lover.

ANXIETY, DEPRESSION, AND ANGER. These emotional states may be related to the illness or disability or may stem from problems with sexual arousal, physiological readiness, orgasm, or sexual satisfaction. Someone with a disability or chronic illness may experience one or all of these emotions—starting when physical symptoms first surface and continuing through diagnosis, treatment, the uncertainty of cure, improvement, and possibly relapse.

FEAR OF DEATH, REJECTION BY A PARTNER, OR LOSS OF CONTROL. These feelings are common in people who suffer serious medical problems. The fear of death resulting from sexual activity is especially prominent in people with cardiac disease, hypertension, and stroke. Sexual partners may also have fears about the fragility of the disabled or chronically ill. Supportive individual psychotherapy and therapy for couples can diminish such feelings and help the ill person to re-experience sexual desire.

SELF-MONITORING. Disabled and ill people often go through a period of hyperawareness of their body's sensations and functioning that diminishes their sexual feelings. For example, a man who has had a prostatectomy (excision of part or all of the prostate gland) may be so obsessed with monitoring his erection that he fails to perceive pleasurable sensations during sex. Usually it takes some time for those who

Sexual Techniques and Pleasuring

have experienced serious medical conditions to recover a sense of themselves as sexual beings.

STRESS. Disability and chronic illness can result in job loss, financial difficulties, and role changes that detract from interest in sex. For most people these issues take precedence over sexual concerns. The struggle to survive, emotionally and financially, often leaves little room for sexual interest.

COMMUNICATION DIFFICULTIES REGARDING FEELINGS OF SEXUALITY. As we have seen, becoming more comfortable in expressing oneself is a significant factor in relationship and sexual satisfaction for everyone. The disabled and the ill, however, face negative social attitudes and a dearth of positive information regarding their sexuality. Empathic discussions with an informed source about their sexuality can greatly enhance these people's self-esteem and comfort level with the topic.

DIFFICULTY INITIATING SEX AFTER A PERIOD OF ABSTINENCE. It is often hard to resume sexual activity after a period of abstinence dictated by a medical condition and its treatment. Talking with a therapist can encourage a couple to try making love, however awkward they may feel. They may also be encouraged to rewrite their sexual scripts to accommodate physical changes and to focus initially on the behaviors most comfortable to them.

LACK OF PRIVACY FOR PEOPLE INSTITUTIONALIZED OR OTHERWISE DEPENDENT ON CARETAKERS. The sexual rights of people who are confined to institutions or otherwise physically dependent is an area receiving increasing attention today. It is ironic that we provide for "conjugal visits" for prisoners, yet deny sexual opportunities to many people institutionalized for illness. Advocates of the sexual rights of the latter are hopeful of making some legal headway in this area in the near future.

Types of Physical Disability and Chronic Illness

Exploring all the physical disabilities and chronic illnesses that may affect sexual expression is beyond the scope of this chapter. What we will do is briefly examine some of the more common types in each category and the special sexual needs that they present. The physical disabilities we explore here are cerebral palsy, blindness and deafness, developmental disabilities, and spinal cord injuries. Then we conclude the chapter with brief discussions of arthritis, cardiovascular disease, cerebrovascular accident or stroke, diabetes mellitus, and multiple sclerosis.

CEREBRAL PALSY. Cerebral palsy (CP) is a physical disability in which a defect in motor control and coordination is caused by brain or nerve damage usually before or around the time of birth. The damage may result when brain tissue becomes starved for oxygen for whatever reason—for example, separation and bleeding of the placenta in late pregnancy or diabetes in the mother.

cerebral palsy A disability characterized by defects in motor control and coordination.

Characteristically, the muscles of people afflicted with cerebral palsy function in uncoordinated patterns, so that they find it very difficult to walk, talk, and execute fine-motor movements. People with cerebral palsy may involuntarily grimace a great deal, and they often make many superfluous movements, sometimes in fixed, repetitive patterns.

Approximately half of all those with cerebral palsy are intellectually limited (Shea, 1990), but others are talented and creative people who must work against great odds to achieve career success and comfortable life styles. Sometimes the brain damage that causes cerebral palsy results in other deficiencies, such as hearing and visual defects, epilepsy, and learning disorders, but this is by no means inevitable.

Cerebral palsy does not affect genital sensations nor does it diminish sexual arousal. However, superfluous movements and uncoordinated muscle patterns often make masturbation, intercourse, and other forms of sexual activity difficult without assistance. Muscle spasms or deformity of the legs, pelvic joints, and other body parts may also make certain coital positions painful. For example, a woman with CP may find it difficult to part her legs when on her back; a man may encounter trouble supporting his body with his arms. Cushions of different sizes and shapes can help these people get into comfortable positions. Often the side-by-side or sitting coital positions are most comfortable.

BLINDNESS AND DEAFNESS. The body's sexual responsiveness is not affected by either blindness or deafness. However, people severely impaired in these areas tend to lead more isolated lives, have difficulty establishing a sense of self-worth, and lack confidence in relating to others. Many blind and deaf persons also have distorted body images—those blind from birth especially, since they've never had the opportunity to see their own bodies or the bodies of other people. Also, many blind and deaf people have been deliberately denied the opportunity to learn about sex.

The causes of blindness include congenital and infantile cataracts, prenatal infections such as rubella and syphilis, drugs and radiation taken by the mother during pregnancy, accidents, infections, inflammations of the eye, tumors, and vascular disease. The causes of deafness are also quite varied, including hereditary defects, congenital malformations, injury, chronic infection, skull fractures, exposure to loud noises, and viral diseases such as rubella contracted by the mother during pregnancy.

Special intervention is needed to help the blind and the deaf feel more comfortable about their sexual selves, including their relationships with others. For example, the blind need the opportunity to touch and handle sex-related items like condoms, diaphragms, tampons, and sex toys. Perhaps we can learn a lesson or two about sex education for exceptional people from the Europeans. In special classes in Sweden and other parts of Europe, blind persons learn about anatomy by touching live nude models (see Helsinga, 1974). The deaf are taught about sexuality through sign language and special visual materials. Both the blind and the deaf can be taught to compensate for their impairment by amplifying other body senses.

developmental disability
Significantly below-average intellectual functioning, along with difficulty in adapting to everyday life.

DEVELOPMENTAL DISABILITY. A **developmental disability,** or mental retardation, refers to significantly below-average intellectual functioning, along with difficulty in adapting to everyday life. Mild retardation is defined today as having an IQ between 53 and 69, moderate retardation as having an IQ between 36 and 52, severe retardation as having an IQ ranging from 20 to 35, and profound retardation as having an IQ below 20. Of primary importance in any classification attempt are the person's degree of retardation, educability or trainability, capability for adaptive behavior, and the amount of supervision the person needs (ranging from little to total).

There are many causes of developmental disabilities. For example, at conception a defective gene may be transmitted from either parent to the offspring. Down syndrome is an example of a chromosomal abnormality. This disorder is characterized by an extra chromosome at the twenty-first position, so that there are 47 chromosomes instead of the normal 46. To date, it is not clearly known why this extra chromosome is present, but the health of the female ovum or male sperm may be involved. Maternal age is also an important consideration. Women between the ages of 18 and 38 are less likely to give birth to a Down syndrome child than are younger or older women (Landesman & Ramey, 1989).

Other causes of mental retardation include the pregnant mother's exposure to certain drugs, radiation, and viruses and infections such as rubella and syphilis. Maternal thyroid disease, diabetes, and ingestion of toxic agents may also adversely affect the fetus. Postnatally, injuries to the brain inflicted through trauma, infection, or anoxia (lack of oxygen at birth) are considered causes. Mental retardation can also result from cultural, sensory, or maternal deprivation.

Bernard Suran and Joseph Rizzo (1983) note that there are many popular misconceptions about the developmentally disabled. A lot of people are under the impression that all the developmentally disabled are institutionalized and incapable of leading normal lives. In fact, many mildly retarded persons hold jobs, marry, own their own homes, and raise children. Another popular area of ignorance is the sexual behavior of the mentally retarded. Retarded men are often suspected of being sexually hyperactive and potentially assaultive, and retarded women are believed to be naively promiscuous. Actually, the developmentally disabled are rarely sexually assaultive and are no more likely to be sexually exploited than nondisabled people.

The answer to the sexual needs of the developmentally disabled is not sexual segregation in institutions or sterilization. Rather, developmentally disabled people need structured learning opportunities to better understand their sexuality. To this end, sex education needs to be incorporated into the exceptional class curriculum, so that topics such as menstruation, sexual hygiene, masturbation, intercourse, sexually transmitted diseases, and contraception are understood as fully as possible. Parents should be educated, too, so they can better understand the sexual needs of their developmentally disabled children.

The issue of privacy for the developmentally disabled also needs to be addressed. Mentally retarded persons have the right to sexual expression, but need to learn when and where such expression is appropriate. To that end, they should be taught that sex is a private matter that is to be practiced discreetly (Shea, 1990).

The selection of appropriate contraception for the developmentally disabled depends on the retarded person's level of understanding. For example, proper use of a condom or diaphragm is too difficult for many developmentally disabled people to learn, which is why some authorities think that oral contraceptives are a more appropriate choice. The Norplant contraceptive implant (see Chapter 12) is an especially promising alternative. Finally, of course, the prevention of sexually transmitted diseases must be made a part of sex education for the developmentally disabled.

SPINAL CORD INJURIES. You will recall from Chapter 4 that the spinal cord, which is located within the vertebral column, relays sensory messages between the brain and the peripheral nerve system. The spinal cord has four segments: cervical, thoracic, lumbar, and sacral (see Figure 8–12). The cervical and lumbar segments are the most vulnerable to injury. About 80 percent of spinal cord–injured adults are men. Compression can be caused in many ways, such as by an accident involving the spine or by a tumor.

Spinal cord injuries often cause paralysis, the loss of the ability to move a part of the body. Paralysis can vary in severity and degree, from affecting a few small muscles to immobilizing almost the entire body. For example, serious injury to the lower spinal cord can paralyze the lower part of the body, resulting in a condition called **paraplegia,** in which movement of the legs and control over bowel and bladder functions are impossible. Serious injury to the upper spinal cord can paralyze all four limbs—a condition known as **quadriplegia.**

paraplegia Paralysis of the legs and lower part of the body, including bowel and bladder tone loss.

quadriplegia Paralysis of all four body limbs.

The degree to which sexual functioning is affected depends on the extent of the spinal cord injury. Not all spinal cord–injured women and men experience impaired arousal and orgasm abilities. However, more serious injuries present special problems. For example, men with injuries to the lower portion of the spinal cord often lose the ability to achieve erections from physical stimulation, although they may experience them from psychological stimulation. Conversely, upper spinal cord injuries may prevent erections from psychological stimulation, but they may be possible from physical stimulation of the genital area. In some cases, anal stimulation causes erection (Sackett, 1990; Boller & Frank, 1982).

For both men and women, the loss of sensation in the genitals, bladder control difficulties, and restricted physical movement pose special sexual challenges. New

How does a spinal cord injury affect a person's sexual functioning?

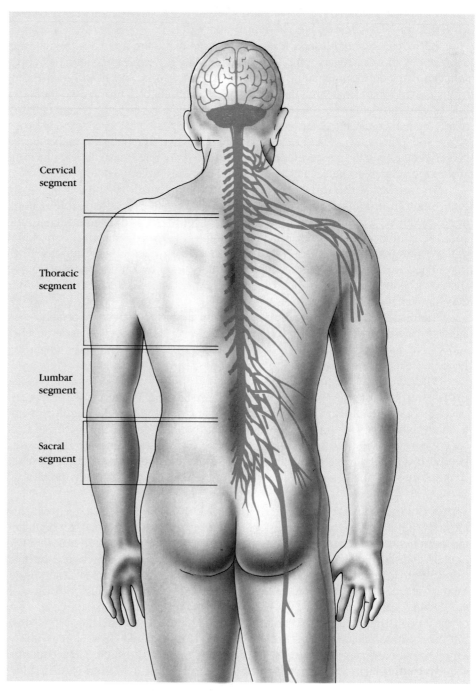

Cervical
segment

Thoracic
segment

Lumbar
segment

Sacral
segment

FIGURE 8–12
The Spinal Cord and Its Four Segments.
Note that all major nerves in the body have their origin in the spinal cord.

routes to sexual and sensual pleasure often need to be discovered. For example, amplifying the intensity of sensation in parts of the body that remain sensitive to tactile stimulation may enable those with spinal cord injuries to relearn the experiences of arousal and orgasm. This process of heightening sensation may be facilitated by the use of relaxation and self-hypnotic techniques, which may also decrease anxiety and performance pressure. If coital activity is no longer possible, alternative forms

of sexual intimacy can be substituted, including manual genital and oral-genital stimulation and body massage (Schover & Jensen, 1988; Levin & Wagner, 1987; Stoklosa, 1984).

ARTHRITIS. Arthritis is broadly defined as inflammation of a joint. There are two main types. The most common kind, called **osteoarthritis,** is characterized by the gradual wearing away of cartilage in the joints. It often involves large weight-bearing joints such as the knees or hips. Usually, the cartilage degeneration causes pain and swelling and stiff joints. Joint stiffness can be brief and is often relieved by activity, but it may recur upon rest.

    Rheumatoid arthritis affects all of the connective tissues in the body. Onset is usually before late adulthood and development is typically slow. Rheumatoid arthritis is much more common in women than in men. In its most severe form, this arthritic condition inflames the membranes lining and lubricating the joints. Pain and swelling, as well as fatigue and fever, are common reactions. Eventually, the cartilage will be destroyed and gradually replaced by scar tissue, which makes the joints rigid and misshapen (Dalton, 1990).

    Simple medications such as aspirin are often used to reduce the pain of arthritis. Most of these drugs (corticosteroids are an exception) do not interfere with either sexual desire or sexual performance. Authorities such as Robert Butler and Myrna Lewis (1988) advocate experimenting with new sexual positions that do not aggravate pain in sensitive joints. Slowed or painful hip action during sex is one of the most frequent arthritic problems. Many couples find that sexual activity in the side-by-side position (either face-to-face or back-to-front) is preferable, particularly when there are tender areas and pain trigger points. Couples need to experiment with coital positions, though, until they find the ones that work best.

    Heat relaxes muscle spasms and tends to reduce arthritic discomfort. Thus the application of heating pads, warm compresses, or heat lamps or taking a bath or hot shower before sex is often beneficial. The timing of sexual activities can also be

arthritis Inflammation of a joint.

osteoarthritis A type of arthritis characterized by the gradual wearing away of cartilage in the joints.

rheumatoid arthritis A type of arthritis that inflames the membranes lining and lubricating the joints.

important. If pain and stiffness diminish or disappear completely at certain times of the day, sexual activity might be planned for those times. Some couples ask their doctor to time pain or anti-inflammatory medications so they will be most effective when sexual activity is likely to occur. A condition called Sjogren's syndrome that results in reduced bodily secretions accompanies some arthritic conditions. A lubricant such as K-Y jelly will compensate for inadequate vaginal secretions.

cardiovascular disease Disorders that involve the heart and blood vessels.

coronary artery disease A condition in which the accumulation of fatty deposits in the coronary arteries lessens the flow of blood to the heart.

congestive heart failure A condition that interferes with the heart's ability to pump blood.

angina pectoris A cardiac condition that occurs when the supply of blood to a part of the heart muscle is not enough to meet its needs, as during exercise.

CARDIOVASCULAR DISEASE. In most cases, cardiovascular disease does not preclude sexual activity, although certain precautions need to be taken. There are many different types of **cardiovascular disease,** disorders that involve the heart and blood vessels. Among the major kinds are coronary artery disease, congestive heart failure, and angina pectoris. **Coronary artery disease** (CAD) is the presence of atherosclerosis (fatty deposits) in the coronary arteries, which narrows the arteries so that less blood flows to the heart muscle. Coronary artery disease is serious and can cause heart attacks. Indeed, it is the most common cause of cardiac disease in adults and the leading cause of death in this country.

Most heart attacks occur when a poor blood supply causes a portion of the heart muscle to die. Atherosclerosis can precipitate this in one of three ways. First, it can completely block a coronary artery. Second, the rough surface of the atherosclerosis can provide a location for a blood clot to form, and if the clot gets big enough, it can close off an artery. Third, coronary arteries narrowed by atherosclerosis may be too constricted to pump enough blood into the heart muscle during times of extreme physical exertion or emotional excitement. Without enough oxygen-rich blood, the heart may stop beating rhythmically.

Another kind of cardiovascular disease is **congestive heart failure,** a condition that interferes with the heart's ability to pump blood. Damage to the heart muscle reduces its contracting power, resulting in a less efficient blood flow into the arteries. The blood then tends to back up into the lungs, where it causes congestion.

Angina pectoris is a cardiac condition that occurs when the supply of blood to a part of the heart muscle is not enough to meet its needs, such as during exercise. Because of this inadequate blood supply, the person experiences a recurring, distressing discomfort, typically in the chest area. Like heart attacks, most angina attacks are caused by atherosclerosis. The difference is that the heart muscle does not suffer damage due to blood deprivation and scar tissue does not form. Some people who have recovered from a heart attack develop angina, but many do not. Conversely, many people have angina without ever experiencing a heart attack.

There is considerable variation in the effects of cardiovascular disease on sexual functioning. We do know, though, that a number of sexual difficulties for both men and women can result. One review of the literature (Schover & Jensen, 1988) reveals that the frequency of sexual activity decreases in 40 to 70 percent of cardiovascular patients, and sexual dysfunction increases, especially loss of sexual desire in both sexes and erectile dysfunction and difficulty in reaching orgasm in men.

Unfortunately, many physicians do not address the sexual concerns of patients and their spouses, although this would greatly reduce the anxiety that often precipitates sexual dysfunction. Many patients avoid sex because they are afraid that sexual activity will overtax their hearts and trigger further cardiovascular problems. Spouses and partners often have similar anxieties and avoid sexual intimacy to protect the patient from any danger (McCann, 1989; Sikorski, 1985; Bedsworth & Molen, 1982).

The belief that sex is "out" after a heart attack is generally incorrect. For most heart attack victims, there are no physical reasons why sexual activity cannot be ultimately resumed under appropriate conditions (see the box on "Sexual Guidelines for Cardiovascular Patients"). The physical energy expended during coitus is equiv-

- The safety of sexual activity for you hinges on your own particular condition. Your physician can provide guidelines based on your medical history, exercise testing, or a home EKG.
- Some medications for cardiac problems and hypertension can interfere with sexual function. If you have a sexual problem, discuss it with your physician. Do not stop taking your medication or change the dosage without consulting with your physician.
- An aerobic exercise program can help your sex life by building up your strength and making your heart more capable of exertion. If you have had a stroke, working on regaining as much independence and mobility as possible is also part of sexual rehabilitation.
- For men with erectile dysfunction, reducing smoking and limiting drinking to small amounts of alcohol often improve sexual function.
- When you plan to engage in sexual activity, avoid heavy meals or too much alcohol. Also make sure the room is at a comfortable temperature.

- If you have not had sexual activity in some time, resume it in a gradual, non pressured fashion. Using self-stimulation to orgasm or asking your partner to help you reach orgasm manually or orally can be a good preparation for intercourse.
- Most women and men can use any position they prefer for caressing or intercourse. If you are using one that makes you tired or short of breath, try another position that gives your partner more of the responsibility for movement.
- It is perfectly normal to experience a more rapid heart beat and to breathe heavily when you are sexually aroused or excited. However, if you get chest pains during lovemaking, consult your physician.
- At the foundation of a harmonious sex life is effective communication. If you or your partner is worried about sex, talk with each other and with your physician. If you need to make changes in your sex life because of your illness, your willingness to share your feelings with each other is important. (Schover & Jensen, 1988)

MAKING USE OF WHAT WE KNOW

Sexual Guidelines for Cardiovascular Patients

---

alent to that used in climbing a few flights of stairs or scrubbing a floor. During average sexual activity, the heart rate ranges from 90 to 160 beats per minute—the level for light to moderate physical activity. Most experts recommend waiting 8 to 14 weeks before resuming coital activity, depending on the patient's interest, general fitness, and conditioning (being able to exercise at a certain level without adverse blood pressure, pulse, or cardiogram measurements). Self-stimulation or mutual masturbation can usually be started earlier than sexual intercourse (Burke, 1990; Covington & McClendon, 1987; Butler & Lewis, 1988; Cooper, 1985).

CEREBROVASCULAR ACCIDENT. A **cerebrovascular accident,** or stroke, is any interruption of the brain's arterial flow that results in a loss of body functions. When such an interruption occurs, the brain is deprived of its supply of oxygen and nutrients. Depending on which side of the brain is affected (damage to cells on the right side of the brain will impair function on the left side of the body, and vice versa), a stroke has the potential for creating numerous impairments, among them loss of vision, paralysis, speech difficulties, memory loss, and coma. Death can result if the brain's vital centers, such as those controlling circulation or breathing, are destroyed.

Most cerebrovascular accidents are caused by the narrowing of a brain artery and/or by a blood clot. Others occur when a blood clot formed in another part of

cerebrovascular accident
Any interruption of the brain's arterial flow that results in a loss of body functions. Also called a *stroke.*

the body finds its way to an artery leading to or within the brain. Strokes may also result from hemorrhage, or bleeding, into the brain after damage to a blood vessel.

Unless a stroke causes severe trauma to the brain, sexual desire often remains undamaged. Sexual performance, though, is more likely to be affected. But this does not mean that sexual activities need to be discontinued. If there is paralysis, appropriate sexual positions can be chosen to compensate for it. Sexual activity is not known to be a precipitating factor in cerebrovascular accident, nor does it cause more damage in those who have already had a stroke (Butler & Lewis, 1988).

diabetes mellitus A chronic metabolic disease in which the body is unable to properly process carbohydrates.

DIABETES MELLITUS. Diabetes mellitus, often called *sugar diabetes,* is a chronic metabolic disease in which the body is unable to properly process carbohydrates (sugars and starches). Disturbances in the production, action, or metabolic rate of insulin—a hormone secreted by the pancreas—is involved in the disease. In diabetes mellitus, there is almost always insufficient insulin available for use in carbohydrate metabolism. The precise causes of diabetes are elusive, but the disorder seems to be genetically transmitted. Diabetes is more common among women, and most diabetics have a history of obesity. Diabetes can lead to eye disorders, such as retinopathy, poor blood circulation, and nerve damage.

It is estimated that as many as 50 percent of men who have had diabetes for more than five years will develop erection problems. Older men especially are vulnerable to erectile difficulties. Damage to the nerves mediating erections is the probable cause (Leiblum & Segraves, 1989). Low sexual desire is also a commonly reported problem, and some men experience retrograde ejaculation (of sperm back into the bladder). Among women, diabetes has been linked to the inability to sustain a pregnancy and reduced vaginal lubrication (Manley, 1990; Newman & Bertelson, 1986; Jensen, 1985). Some research (e.g., Schreiner-Engel et al., 1987) indicates that women who have the adult-onset form of the disease and who do not take insulin treatment may also experience diminished sexual desire. Intervention for diabetics might include sex therapy to deal with low sexual desire. Penile implants (see Chapter 16) are also a possibility for diabetic men with erectile dysfunction.

multiple sclerosis A chronic, progressive disease of the central nervous system.

MULTIPLE SCLEROSIS. Multiple sclerosis is a chronic, progressive disease of the central nervous system. It is characterized by patchy, irregular areas of degeneration that appear in the white matter of the brain and in the outer part of the spinal cord. As the degeneration progresses, the nerve fibers are destroyed, eventually causing such symptoms as weakness and fatigue, general incoordination, and impaired speech. More extensive nerve damage may result in loss of muscle control and confinement to a wheelchair. The cause of multiple sclerosis is unknown, and it affects men and women about equally.

Multiple sclerosis in women may result in difficulty in achieving orgasm and diminished levels of sexual arousal. It may also cause reduced genital sensations. For men, advanced stages of multiple sclerosis often create erection problems and, sometimes, the loss of ejaculation capacities. However, since the course of the disease is marked by remissions, these problems may come and go. Paradoxically, a few men with multiple sclerosis report increased genital sensitivity, a condition that often makes manual stimulation and orgasm painful and unpleasant (Hill & Kassam, 1984; Stoklosa, 1984).

As with the other disorders discussed in this chapter, multiple sclerosis patients need advice on coping with their physical limitations. They can be taught to time sex to avoid periods of fatigue or pain, and to use positions that are less strenuous, pillows to support a body part that is painful or weak, or a vibrator to compensate for decreased genital sensations (Schover, 1989).

Sexual Techniques and Pleasuring

SEXUALITY IN THE NEWS

Birds Do It, Bees Do It, So Does TV
by John J. O'Connor

urphy's preggers, Doogie's no longer a virgin. Roseanne's teen-age daughter is on the pill. Perfume ads are pushing the equivalent of soft porn. Even up in the northern exposure of Alaska, Chris the poetic D.J. is emitting a body scent that reduces women to eager slaves. There's hardly an hour on network entertainment schedules these days without sexual reverberations. Sex is on a rampage, promising the ultimate in quick-fix escapism, with perhaps a cuddly doll-like baby down the line to make studio audiences go "aaahhh" in soundtrack unison.

Much of this whoopee-making might well be cause for celebration. This country tends to be prudish, sometimes ridiculously so. Assorted television watchdogs get far more upset about a glimpse of nudity than about a steady stream of blood-curdling violence. Healthy, uninhibited attitudes toward sex certainly deserve encouragement. . . .

There is a hitch. In television's sexual sweepstakes, as in life's, getting there can be more than half the fun. The question of will they or won't they keeps plots perking. When they finally do, interest can begin to wane, as Maddie and Dave discovered in "Moonlighting." If everyone just starts hopping into bed on automatic pilot, television loses an invaluable titillation tool. . . .

The sexual act itself remains a relatively modest affair on network television. HBO series like "Dream On" and "Sessions" are far more frank about very personal details, and their exhibitions of bare female breasts border on fetishism. (Complete nudity is still rare, and the penis remains strictly off limits, perhaps because selectively demure males dominate most productions.) Network television, restrained from such permissiveness, is stuck with clichéed shots of carefully lighted limbs, artfully intertwined.

Levels of sensitivity vary. The deflowering of Doogie of ABC's "Doogie Howser, M.D." on his 18th birthday was handled with obvious care. Afterward, Doogie concluded that being a man was less contingent on having sex than on being professional and compassionate with a patient. The episode was a rare instance of television deciding not to substitute short-lived pleasure for more lasting fulfillment. The injection of perspective seemed almost radical.

More typical is Fox's "Beverly Hills 90210," now perhaps the most popular series among young viewers. When not sizing each other up for possible sex, at times evidently "unprotected," the students at West Beverly Hills High are preoccupied with fashion statements and constantly commenting on each other's wardrobes. The series provides the perfect illustration for an observation made by Herbert T. Schiller in his 1989 book "Culture Inc.": "The near-total utilization of television for corporate marketing represents at the same time the daily ideological instruction of the viewers." Watch for a line of series-related products.

The result is a cascade of mixed messages in everything from sitcoms to beer ads. Sexual abstinence is virtually ignored. Casual sex is steadily promoted—even as the networks refuse to accept condom commercials—while the country reels from the specter not only of AIDS but also of younger and younger mothers giving birth to children often damaged in the womb by drug use. Schools complain of staggering increases in learning-disabled children.

Yes, of course, Murphy Brown is a self-sufficient, sophisticated woman capable of raising a child on her own. And the students on "Beverly Hills 90210" are old enough, presumably, to make responsible decisions. But their behavior is being watched and absorbed by highly impressionable youngsters who haven't even reached their teens. Something is dangerously out of kilter. "Wouldn't it be great," a letter writer asks me, "to see a program depict what it's really like to be an unmarried, pregnant adolescent?"

A Delaware-based citizens' group, Message to the Media, finds "mounting evidence that socially insensitive mass media are contributing heavily to our societal crises," and it appeals to the broadcast industry to institute "a voluntary code of socially responsible practice standards." Members cite a comment made by George Gerbner of the Annenberg School for Communication: "Learning about the world is increasingly a by-product of mass marketing. Most of the stories about life and values are told not by parents, grandparents, teachers, clergy and others with stories to tell but by a handful of distant conglomerates with something to sell."

continued

DISCUSSION QUESTIONS

1. Do you agree or disagree with Vice President Dan Quayle's statement that the pregnancy of Murphy Brown, unmarried news anchorwoman of the TV show "Murphy Brown," sent a negative message about "family values"? Support your view.
2. Do you agree with the letter writer quoted here that it would be great "to see a program depict what it's really like to be an unmarried, pregnant adolescent"? Explain your answer.
3. Do you think the media send mixed messages about sex and drugs? If so, describe some of these messages. What, if anything, should we do about this situation?

LOOKING BACK

■ Sexual fantasies play an important role in the sex lives of both men and women. Fantasies may occur in daydreams, or during masturbation, mutual caressing and stimulation, or in the midst of intercourse. Sexual fantasies serve a number of purposes, and many different types are reported. Most researchers feel that sexual fantasies are normal and not necessarily a sign of problems in a relationship. What appears to be important is being able to separate sexual fantasies from real-life sexual encounters and rejecting the guilt that often surrounds them. They are healthy as long as they remain fantasies, don't become obsessive, and are not acted out in compulsive ways that could harm the person or others.

■ Masturbation is the self-stimulation of the genitals or other parts of the body for sexual arousal and pleasure. Masturbation is usually the first sexual experience for both men and women and the most common form of sexual expression other than heterosexual intercourse. Masturbation begins at an early age and continues throughout the life cycle. There are various styles of masturbation among men and women, with some using vibrators and other sexual aids to enhance self-stimulation.

■ Mutual pleasuring refers to behaviors used to heighten sexual arousal. Mutual pleasuring includes a wide range of sexual activities, most of which are directed toward parts of the body that are sensitive to stimulation (the erogenous zones). Kissing, breast stimulation, manual genital stimulation, anal stimulation, and oral-genital stimulation—both fellatio and cunnilingus—are common forms of mutual pleasuring.

■ Sexual intercourse conventionally means full insertion of the man's penis into the woman's vagina. A variety of coital positions can be used to enhance the pleasure of sexual intercourse. Each of the basic positions—man-on-top, face-to-face; female-on-top, face-to-face; side-by-side, face-to-face; rear-entry; standing; and sitting—can be varied to suit individual needs and preferences.

■ A physical disability is an impairment of body structure and function. A chronic illness is a progressive disorder caused by a nonreversible condition that often leaves the person with some type of disability. The sexual needs of the disabled and the chronically ill are more similar to than different from those of healthy people. However, people with physical disabilities and chronic illness do have to make special adjustments. In addition to the biological stressors of the disability or illness, psychological and social stressors also affect the physically challenged.

THINKING THINGS OVER

1. Do you think it's okay to fantasize about a former sexual partner during a sexual encounter? A current friend or acquaintance? A rock star? Why or why not?

2. What advice would you give a friend who had never had a satisfying sexual experience and was too embarrassed to tell her or his partner? Would you suggest masturbation? Why or why not?

3. Mutual masturbation is a technique that is sometimes suggested to couples who do not wish to engage in sexual intercourse. How do you feel about this? Do you think mutual masturbation could be a satisfying alternative to intercourse?

4. Sexual pleasuring was long referred to as "foreplay," based on the notion that all noncoital sexual activity led ultimately to sexual intercourse. Do you agree or disagree with that idea? Why or why not? What might "afterplay" consist of?

5. If you have ever had a serious physical injury—for example, a broken leg—you can perhaps imagine some of the difficulties that confront a physically challenged person in lovemaking. Try to imagine how being blind or deaf might affect a person's lovemaking. How might the blind and deaf compensate for their disabilities?

DISCOVER FOR YOURSELF

Schover, L. R., & Jensen, S. B. (1988). *Sexuality and chronic illness*. New York: Guilford Press. Part II of this text deals with specific chronic illnesses and how they affect sexual functioning.

Silverstein, C. (1977). *The joy of gay sex*. New York: Crown. The author presents a wide range of topics related to gay sex.

Sisley, E. (1977). *The joy of lesbian sex*. New York: Crown. An interesting and insightful analysis of lesbian lovemaking.

Stanway, A. (1989). *The art of sensual loving*. New York: Carroll & Graf. Topics include enhancing your sexual body, sensual communication, erotic massage, and lovemaking positions.

Yaffee, M., & Fenwick, E. (1988). *Sexual happiness for men: A practical approach*. New York: Henry Holt. A practical guide to male sexual behavior and fulfillment, illustrated throughout.

Yaffee, M., & Fenwick, E. (1988). *Sexual happiness for women: A practical approach*. New York: Henry Holt. A companion to the previous book, aimed at enhancing female sexual satisfaction.

9
Sexual Orientation

People who are targets of any particular form of oppression have resisted and attempted to resist their oppression in any way they could. The fact that their resistance is not generally recognized is itself a feature of the oppression

—Ricky Sherover-Marcuse

I am a child of every
Mother
Mother of each
daughter
Sister of every
woman
And lover of whom I
choose or chooses me

—Elsa Gidlow

Some people are attracted to members of the other sex, some are attracted to members of their own sex, and some are attracted to members of both sexes. The direction of our preferences for partners, including sexual as well as affectional attraction, is known as **sexual orientation.** Sexual orientation has long been a puzzle to human sexuality researchers, who have made many efforts over the years to unravel the mysteries attached to heterosexual, homosexual, and bisexual preferences. In this chapter, we explore such research endeavors to enhance your awareness and understanding of sexual orientation.

To the best of our knowledge, virtually all past and present cultures have been predominantly heterosexual, but attitudes toward homosexuality have varied immensely (Bullough, 1990). Some societies have condemned and punished homosexuals, while others have viewed homosexuality as an acceptable life style. In the United States, homosexuality was labeled a disorder by the American Psychiatric Association until 1973. Books on the topic treated homosexuality as a pathological problem to be solved, and people with same-sex orientations were viewed with a mixture of discomfort, fear, and disgust. As long as homosexuality was seen as a sickness, the homosexual person was usually regarded as perverted, unhappy, and desperately lonely.

In 1973, the American Psychiatric Association removed homosexuality from its list of mental disorders. This classification change was largely the result of efforts by leaders of the gay liberation movement and their supporters, some of whom were prominent psychiatrists and clinical psychologists. Since this took place during a period of general liberalization of sexual attitudes, the public's perceptions of homosexuality began to slowly change. Homosexuals banded together to assert their human rights, demanding the respect and equality they had long been denied. Many openly declared their homosexuality and phrases such as "gay pride" were heard more and more often. Meanwhile, researchers stepped up the pace of their scientific inquiries into the complexities of sexual orientation, with the result that homosexuality began to be better understood.

Contrary to what was once thought, most gays and lesbians are well-adjusted and emotionally stable. While some may exhibit anxiety or depression, so do some heterosexuals. When maladaptive behavior does occur in lesbians and gays, some clinicians propose that it is often attributable to the social stigma attached to homosexuality instead of to something pathological in the nature of homosexuality itself (Sarason & Sarason, 1989; Ross, Paulsen, & Stalstrom, 1988; Stein, 1988).

LOOKING AHEAD

In this chapter you'll discover:

☐ *What lesbian, gay, and bisexuality are and how widespread these life styles are.*

☐ *What we know about the origins of sexual orientation.*

☐ *What "coming out" and "outing" mean.*

☐ *How relationships of gays and lesbians and heterosexuals compare.*

☐ *What homophobia and heterosexism are.*

☐ *What gay liberation is and how it has emerged as a political movement promoting the civil rights of gays and lesbians.*

THE CONCEPT OF SEXUAL ORIENTATION

As we noted at the outset, a person's sexual orientation can be heterosexual, homosexual, or bisexual. While heterosexuality involves attraction to members of the other sex, **homosexuality** refers to sexual attraction and emotional attachment to persons of the same gender. Today there is a move away from using the term *homosexual* to describe same-sex attraction because of the exclusively sexual connotation of the word. While sexual interaction is shared by many partners, it is not the primary focus of all relationships. The terms **gay** and **lesbian** are preferred because they seek to take into account nonsexual aspects of a person's life. The word *gay* is a term sometimes applied to both men and women, while *lesbian* is applied exclusively to women. Finally, **bisexuality** refers to sexual attraction and emotional attachment to both women and men.

Contrary to popular notions, gays and lesbians are not confused about their gender identity. Readers will recall from Chapter 5 that gender identity is the psy-

sexual orientation A person's preference for sexual and affectional relationships with persons of the other sex, of the same sex, or of both sexes.

homosexuality Sexual attraction and emotional attachment to persons of the same gender as oneself.

gay A term preferred by male, and some female homosexuals to describe themselves, though *lesbian* is preferred for gay women.

lesbian A woman who is attracted sexually and emotionally to other women.

bisexuality Sexual attraction and emotional attachment to both women and men.

251

MYTHS AND MISCONCEPTIONS

Some Stereotypes About Homosexuality and Bisexuality

It's easy to spot a gay or lesbian in a crowd.

*M*any people incorrectly think that most gay men are effeminate and most lesbians are masculine or "butch." According to these stereotypes, gay men walk, talk, and dress in feminine ways, while lesbian women look rugged, wear their hair short, and have deep voices. Although these stereotypes apply to some, they do not describe the behavior of most gay men and women.

Within a relationship setting, gays and lesbians mimic traditional heterosexual patterns.

This myth suggests that one gay partner assumes the traditional masculine role and the other the traditional feminine role. While this occurs in some gay relationships, such role playing is the exception rather than the norm. Many gay couples share roles and do not restrict themselves to one or another.

Lesbians and gays are always trying to seduce heterosexuals.

This myth suggests that gay men often make passes at attractive straight men and, especially, at straight male teenagers and children. Lesbians are often seen as "coming on" to attractive straight women and female children. The reality is that gay and lesbian people are attracted to other gay and lesbian people, not to heterosexuals. Moreover, heterosexuals are far more likely than gays to seduce children.

Gays and lesbians are oversexed.

Actually, the sexual behavior of gays is more like than unlike that of heterosexuals. Lesbians and gays do not have a stronger sex drive than heterosexuals, nor do they engage in sexual activity more often than straight persons.

Bisexuals have the best of both worlds.

On the contrary, many bisexuals find themselves in a "double closet." That is, they hide their heterosexual activities from their gay peers and their gay activities from their straight peers. To avoid embarrassment or ostracism, many bisexuals feel compelled to switch back and forth between giving a gay/lesbian appearance and giving a heterosexual appearance, depending on the social context (Zinik, 1985).

chological awareness of being either male or female. Lesbian women are not different from heterosexual women in their sureness of being female, nor do gay men differ from heterosexual men on this dimension (Silberman & Hawkins, 1988; Peplau & Gordon, 1983). Some other mistaken ideas about gays, lesbians, and bisexuals are discussed in the "Myths and Misconceptions" box.

Prevalence Data

How widespread is the gay or lesbian life style?

How many people are straight, lesbian, gay, and bi? According to Alfred Kinsey and associates (1948, 1953), precise distinctions among the three sexual orientations are not possible. Rather, heterosexuality and homosexuality represent extreme poles on a continuum, and in between we find many people whose experiences and behaviors combine both components. In his classification attempts, Kinsey devised a heterosexual-homosexual rating scale to illustrate the continuum of sexual orientations (see Figure 9–1). As you can see, the scale ranges from 0 to 6, with 0 representing an exclusively heterosexual orientation and 6 an exclusively homosexual orientation. Someone whose overt experience and psychological reactions were more or less equally heterosexual and homosexual would be rated a 3 on this scale.

Using this classification system, Kinsey found that about 75–85 percent of men and 80–90 percent of women were exclusively heterosexual, 4 percent of men and

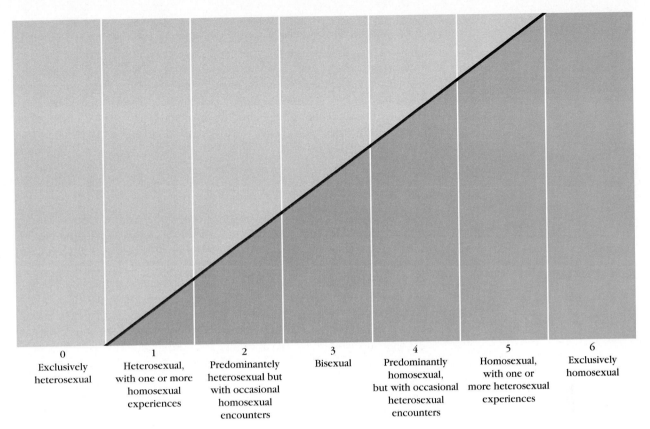

0	1	2	3	4	5	6
Exclusively heterosexual	Heterosexual, with one or more homosexual experiences	Predominantely heterosexual but with occasional homosexual encounters	Bisexual	Predominantly homosexual, but with occasional heterosexual encounters	Homosexual, with one or more heterosexual experiences	Exclusively homosexual

FIGURE 9–1
Kinsey's Heterosexuality-Homosexuality Continuum. (Adapted from *Sexual behavior in the human male*, by Kinsey et al., the Kinsey Institute. Reprinted by permission of The Kinsey Institute for Research in Sex, Gender, and Reproduction, Inc.)

2 percent of women were exclusively homosexual, and 10–15 percent of men and 8–10 percent of women had bisexual preferences. About 37 percent of men and 13 percent of women reported at least one overt homosexual experience to the point of orgasm sometime between adolescence and late adulthood. Overall, Kinsey found that homosexual responses had occurred in about half as many women as men, and contacts that had proceeded to orgasm had occurred in about one-third as many women as men. Moreover, compared with men, only about one-half to one-third as many women were, at any age, primarily or exclusively lesbian.

When we compare Kinsey's data with the findings of other researchers, we see similar patterns of prevalence. For example, one source (Ellis & Ames, 1987) pointed out that in both Europe and the United States, the figures for exclusive homosexuality are about 4 percent of men and 1 percent of women. One survey (Harry, 1990) involving a random sample of men indicated that about 2.5 percent of the respondents were gay. John Gagnon (1977) estimated that exclusive male homosexuals represented about 2 to 3 percent of the population. Morton Hunt (1974) maintained that about 2 percent of men and 1 percent of women were exclusively homosexual. Finally, in a study involving college students (Knox & Wilson, 1981), approximately 3 percent of men and less than 1 percent of women reported that they were gay.

What of the much higher prevalence rates Kinsey found for people who have experienced at least one overt homosexual experience to orgasm in their lives? While other researchers did not find prevalence rates as high as Kinsey's they did find significantly higher rates than they did for exclusive homosexuality. For example, one source (Fay et al., 1989) reanalyzed a 1970 sample of men and concluded that a minimum of 20 percent of the respondents had had sexual contact to orgasm with another male at some time during their lives. Hunt's (1974) earlier mentioned research reported that about 23 percent of the men studied and 14 percent of the women had had at least some gay or lesbian experiences.

Research such as this shows that the percentages of gay men and lesbians in our society have remained fairly constant since the time of Kinsey's investigations, though percentages do vary according to locale of the study, the respondents' age, and their propensity to conceal aspects of their sexual behavior. Since social pressure still prompts many respondents who are gay, lesbian, or bisexual to shield their sexual orientation, we have no way of knowing exactly what percentage of people are heterosexual, homosexual, and bisexual.

Historical and Legal Perspectives

Homosexuality has existed since the beginning of time and was practiced and tacitly approved in a number of societies. For example, it was evident in ancient Greece as well as among the Tanalans of Madagascar, the Siwamis of Africa, and the Keraki of New Guinea. As we've noted, however, for just as long homosexuality has been viewed with mistrust and suspicion. Gays and lesbians have often been a stigmatized minority group and the object of considerable fear, dread, and hostility. In Judaism, and later in Christianity, the wickedness that caused God to destroy the ancient cities of Sodom and Gomorrah was the practice of homosexuality (the word *sodomy*, meaning anal intercourse, originates from this biblical event). Homosexuality was viewed as sinful since any sex other than that between a man and a woman was considered naturally wrong. Many early Christian leaders believed that gays should be put to death by burning or hanging, though the customary penalties were less severe ("offenders" were usually exiled or administered forms of corporal punishment). During the Middle Ages in England, homosexuality was considered an offense as serious as heresy, blasphemy, and witchcraft, and was punishable by death. Not until 1861 was the maximum penalty for homosexuality in England changed to life imprisonment. For a glimpse at some past and present attitudes toward homosexuality in India, see the "World of Differences" box.

In the United States, laws against gays and lesbians were equally harsh. The Puritans denounced homosexuality, many of them believing it a symptom of the English moral corruption they were looking to escape in the New World. Using English common law as their basis, the early colonists implemented a number of antisodomy statutes that pronounced homosexuality unnatural and a "crime against nature." During the seventeenth and eighteenth centuries, punishment for gays and lesbians in the colonies included whipping, castration, and drowning. Some escaped with such lesser sentences as discharge from work, public ostracism, or imprisonment.

In the late nineteenth century, the medical and academic professions sought to understand homosexuality better and a diverse body of researchers began to contribute their thoughts on the topic. Still, gays remained a persecuted minority whom

The Stonewall incident has come to symbolize gays' and lesbians' assertion of their right to be treated no differently from heterosexuals and to live, love, and work as they choose.

254

A WORLD OF
DIFFERENCES

Homosexuality
in India

*I*n India, Hinduism and, to a lesser extent, Islam have restricted people's sexual behaviors for centuries. Homosexuality was generally frowned upon and considered defiling. The gay life style was viewed as clashing with the central importance of the family to society (Gregersen, 1983).

In the 1990s, however, change is coming to India. In Bombay bars, parks, and train stations, gays gather openly and young men find friends or dates. And a group of Indian gays and lesbians is publishing *Bombay Dost*, the country's first gay magazine. Once an underground publication, the magazine is now registered with the government and can be legally distributed through the mail.

While homosexuality is still illegal because of a holdover law from the British colonial statutes, the new gay assertiveness indicates a willingness to skirt the statutory limits regulating sexual behavior. The public expression of homosexuality mirrors the emerging social and cultural complexity of India's growing middle classes. Most of the gays in Bombay are young professionals who are employed in the city's private sector and whose standard of living is well above the national average.

Interestingly, while homosexuality has long been denounced in India, reference to same-sex preference is evident in Indian mythology. According to Gargan (1991), for example, in the Mahabharata, the Hindu epic poem about good and evil, the god Krishna dresses as a woman and gives himself as the first sexual experience to the first-born son of Arjun—the greatest warrior of the epic. And in Kerala, the god Ayyappa is said to have been born of a homosexual union of the gods Vishnu and Shiva.

Since its inception, *Bombay Dost* has made a concerted effort to raise the consciousness of gays and help them attain a positive identity. Another focal point of the publication has been the lack of legal rights for gays. Recently, *Bombay Dost* received a grant from an international health organization to buy pamphlets on safer sex practices and condoms, which staff members have distributed around Bombay. While AIDS is not widespread in Bombay, or in India as a whole, there is a growing awareness of the need to prevent HIV transmission (Gargan, 1991).

---

society continually sought to control through various antisodomy laws. Most of these statutes were ill-defined and nebulous. For example, North Carolina's original antisodomy statute reads: "Any person who shall commit the abominable and detestable crime against nature, not fit to be named among Christians . . . shall be adjudged guilty of a felony and shall suffer death without the benefit of clergy." Given such antiquated sex laws and pervasive social condemnation, homosexuals remained scorned and oppressed in American society into modern times.

Until the 1960s, gay and lesbian behavior was prohibited throughout the United States through some type of antisodomy statute. Then in 1961, Illinois became the first state to enact the American Law Institute's Model Penal Code provision, which, in essence, decriminalized homosexual acts between consenting adults in private. In support of its position, the American Law Institute (ALI) noted that progressive Western nations like Great Britain, France, Italy, Denmark, and Sweden had all repealed their antisodomy statutes (Sloan, 1987).

You may recall from Chapter 1 that the gay liberation movement was born at a gay bar called the Stonewall in Greenwich Village, New York, in 1969. For decades, gay men had been harassed by the New York police, and in June of that year, they fought back for the first time. For homosexuals simply to be allowed to meet and drink at a bar was inconceivable to U.S. society until June 28, 1969. Today there are many bars, restaurants, and hotels where lesbians and gays can congregate in safety.

The gay liberation movement has helped gays and lesbians to feel less guilty about their life style and has encouraged people to stop concealing their sexual orientation. The movement has had an effect on the ways police deal with gays and lesbians. It has exerted its political strength to win legal changes and to fight job and other forms of discrimination. The National Gay and Lesbian Task Force is a central clearinghouse in Washington, D.C., for many of the gay liberation groups.

As the gay rights movement developed into a strong activist and lobbying force in the 1970s, the ALI provision decriminalizing private consensual homosexual conduct was passed in 20 additional states. At this writing, 26 states have repealed their antisodomy laws (Chapter 21 offers more in-depth coverage of the legal status of homosexuality today). Also as a result of pressure from the movement, many cities have passed bills assuring lesbians and gays equal rights with heterosexuals in housing and jobs. In some cities, gay and lesbian couples have even been granted the same rights married people have with regard to insurance and health benefits. We are convinced that eventually American society will acknowledge gay-lesbian rights as civil rights.

THE ORIGINS OF SEXUAL ORIENTATION

What creates a person's sexual orientation?

Sexual orientation is generally viewed as the result of biological, psychological, and interactionist forces, although a precise and conclusive explanation of the origins of sexual orientation has yet to emerge. The best we can say at this point is that it seems a number of forces blend together to create sexual orientation.

The Biological Perspective

The biological perspective emphasizes biology as the primary determinant of sexual orientation. Two of the more important biological perspectives are the genetic and hormonal imbalance theories.

GENETIC THEORIES. Genetic theories propose that the predisposition to sexual orientation is inherited. To discover whether this explanation is correct, some researchers have studied identical twins who were separated early in life and raised in contrasting environments. These twin studies make it possible to analyze the relative importance of heredity and environment (nature and nurture) in determining sexual orientation. Because identical twins share the same genetic makeup, it is reasoned that any difference in their sexual orientation must be due to environmental influences. (In contrast, it is suggested that differences in sexual orientation between fraternal twins can be due to either hereditary *or* environmental influences.) Substantial similarity in sexual orientation in identical twins raised in different environments would, of course, confirm the importance of the genetic explanation. Those who use twin studies often refer to the concordance rate, or the percentage of cases in which a particular characteristic (e.g., gay/lesbian orientation) is present in both twins when it is present in one twin. The biological perspective would lead us to expect a high concordance rate for sexual orientation for pairs of identical twins and a low concordance rate in pairs of fraternal twins.

An early twin study conducted by Franz Kallman (1952) found a 100 percent concordance rate for homosexuality for pairs of identical twins compared with a 12 percent rate for pairs of fraternal twins. However, there were important research flaws in this study, including the fact that all of the identical twins were raised together, so environmental factors might explain the observed similarities in their sexual orientation. Also, the twins studied were recruited from prisons or psychiatric institutions, which raised the issue of how representative Kallman's subjects were. Other twin studies (e.g., Heston & Shields, 1968) found a much lower concordance rate than Kallman reported.

In 1991, there was a resurgence of interest in the potential role played by genetics in sexual orientation. Michael Bailey and Richard Pillard (1991) studied concordance rates of homosexuality in 56 identical twins, 54 fraternal twins, and 57 adopted brothers of gay men. They discovered that 52 percent of the identical twin brothers of gay men were also gay, compared with only 22 percent of the fraternal twins of gay men and 11 percent of the genetically unrelated brothers. The researchers concluded that the degree of the genetic contribution to homosexuality ranged from 30 percent to 70 percent, depending on how representative their sample of twins was of the general population. Despite the rather strong genetic link they discovered, Bailey and Pillard acknowledged that environmental forces also shape sexual orientation.

Another important study conducted in 1991 by the neurobiologist Simon LeVay also shows that sexual orientation may have biological origins. In this investigation, autopsied brain tissue from an area of the hypothalamus in 19 gays, 16 heterosexual men, and 6 heterosexual women was examined. Readers will recall from Chapter 4 that the hypothalamus is part of the limbic system and plays a role in sexual functioning (see Figure 4–2). It was discovered that in gay men a small segment of the anterior hypothalamus (see Figure 9–2) was only one-quarter to one-half the size of that area in heterosexual men and closer to the size of that area in heterosexual women. This

FIGURE 9–2
Brain Structure and Sexuality.

The area of the brain in which neurobiologist Simon LeVay recently detected a structural difference between heterosexual and homosexual men is located in the anterior, or forward, portion of the hypothalamus.

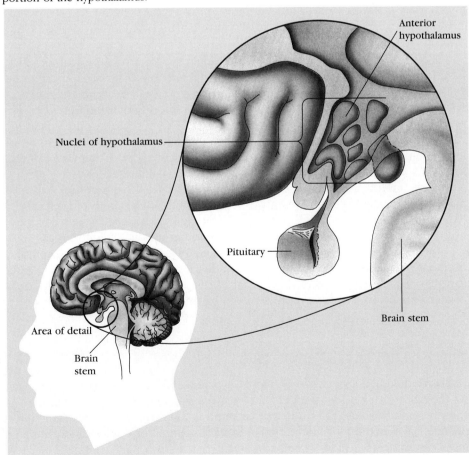

area, in fact, was almost undetectable in gay men, while it is about the size of a large grain of sand in heterosexual men.

It was speculated that the hypothalamic variation arises during fetal development, but whether it is the result of genetics or of hormonal interactions in pregnancy that affect fetal brain development is unclear. In addition, LeVay noted that most of the gay men whose brain tissue was examined had died of AIDS, a factor that could have influenced his findings in some as yet unknown way. He also did not rule out the possibility that sexual orientation could somehow influence neural pathways later in life.

This preliminary but groundbreaking study of gay men has important implications for future research. Indeed, given the spark created by this investigation, follow-up studies on brain structure may shed new light on the biological aspects of sexual orientation. And while LeVay acknowledges that sexual orientation is likely due to a combination of inborn factors and environmental influences, his findings may also affect social attitudes toward gays. If sexual orientation turns out to have a definitive, innate foundation, gays may be more readily accepted by mainstream society. Research (e.g., Whitley, 1990) suggests that people who believe sexual orientation is uncontrollable rather than a willfully chosen life style hold fewer negative attitudes toward gays.

HORMONAL IMBALANCE THEORIES. Another theoretical approach suggests that hormonal imbalances are largely responsible for the development of a lesbian/gay orientation. Some researchers (e.g., Kolodny et al., 1971) maintain that homosexual men have lower testosterone levels than heterosexual men. However, other investigators could not confirm this finding (Gartrell, 1982; Meyer-Bahlburg, 1980, 1977; Tourney, Petrilli, & Hatfield, 1975; Pillard, Rose, & Sherwood, 1974). Against the hormonal imbalance theory is the fact that higher rates of homosexuality have not been found in men with hypogonadism, a condition characterized by a deficiency of sex hormone production. Also, medical treatment with sex hormones to change endocrine imbalance has not been shown to affect the direction of sexual behavior. Finally, people may shift from a gay to a heterosexual sexual orientation without any change taking place in their hormonal balance.

Some researchers (e.g., Money, 1987; Money & Ogunro, 1974; Dorner, 1976) have focused on the impact of prenatal hormonal imbalances on later sexual orientation. You will recall from Chapter 4 that during prenatal life hormones serve to either masculinize or feminize the brain. It has been proposed that male fetuses who receive too little testosterone may be predisposed to homosexuality during later life, while female fetuses exposed to too much testosterone may be predisposed toward lesbianism. These are intriguing propositions and some support for them has emerged in studies with animals (see, e.g., Money, 1987; Meyer-Bahlburg, 1979).

One line of research (Ellis & Ames, 1987) proposes that a critical period of brain development occurs between the second and the fifth month of prenatal life. Exposure at this time to hormone levels typically experienced by females might predispose a person (whether female or male) to become attracted to males.

Some researchers (e.g., Heyl, 1989; Ricketts, 1984; Hoult, 1984) are skeptical of hormonal imbalance theories because no study has as yet produced data that can be shown systematically to connect prenatal hormone functioning with adult sexual orientation. Clearly, we need more research on this issue.

The Psychological Perspective

The psychological perspective examines how parent-child interactions and the overall psychological dynamics of the person affect sexual orientation. One of the earliest contributors to this field of study was Sigmund Freud, whose psychodynamic interpretation of sexual orientation provided interesting food for thought and prompted many researchers to explore family dynamics.

Psychologists view the development of sexual identity and sexual preference from many different perspectives. Although there is some evidence of genetic influence, environmental factors, such as modeling a parent's behavior, probably also play a role.

PSYCHODYNAMIC THEORIES. In his stage theory of psychosexual development, Freud 1948, 1946, 1938) theorized that the third, or phallic, stage was crucial in shaping a person's sexual orientation (see also Chapter 13). Specifically, he proposed that between the ages of four and six a boy develops strong but unconscious romantic feelings for his mother. These feelings lead him to fear that his father—with whom he is in competition for his mother's affection—will castrate him. The boy's castration anxiety can be resolved only if he keeps his desire for his mother under wraps and develops a close bond with his father and seeks to identify with him. According to Freud, this is the normal course of events for every male child.

Some boys, however, become excessively preoccupied with the possibility of being castrated, Freud said, and to counteract this fear, they block out all awareness of female genitalia—their mother's or anyone else's. Freud also suggested that some boys see the female genitalia as capable of tearing off the penis. Either line of thinking could lead to the avoidance of women and, by default, to a sexual interest in other men.

Freud attempted to adapt the psychodynamics of the phallic stage to the lives of females, but he was forced to admit that his efforts were far from satisfactory. His theory goes like this: During the initial phases of the phallic stage, a girl realizes that she and her mother do not have a penis, which she feels symbolizes power (Freud referred to a female's unconscious disappointment over not having a penis as "penis envy"). She blames her own lack of a penis on her mother and turns away from her, in the process becoming romantically attached to her father. However, rejection by the strongly loved father causes the girl to transfer her romantic attachment back to her mother, who then becomes the object of sexual identification. According to Freud, homosexuality results when a girl realizes that she cannot have sexual exclusivity with her mother and chooses not to transfer her affections back to her father, but instead directs her affections and attachments to other women, or "mother figures."

Freud's work spurred considerable research activity into the area of family dynamics and sexual orientation. For example, the psychoanalyst Irving Bieber (1962) studied the family backgrounds of 106 homosexual and 100 heterosexual men and their early interactions with their parents. He reported that homosexuality was encouraged by the presence of a dominating and overprotective mother and a detached, hostile father. Often the mother dominated the father and prevented the son from pursuing masculine interests. Many mothers, unhappy with their marital relationship, also directed their frustrated romantic and seductive desires toward their sons. Meanwhile, the detached and often absent father served as a poor sex-role model. In the midst of such family dynamics, many boys developed an aversion to females and renounced heterosexuality.

Other researchers have also uncovered a link between troubled family relationships and homosexuality. Some (e.g., O'Connor, 1964; Schofield, 1965) have found that many gay males had overpossessive mothers and stormy relationships with their fathers. Charlotte Wolff's (1971) research showed that compared to heterosexual women, many lesbians had rejecting, indifferent mothers and distant fathers. Whether or not a family remains intact may also have implications. For example, Marcel Saghir and Eli Robbins (1973) found that 39 percent of adult lesbian women, compared to 12 percent of a control group of heterosexual women, had lost one or both parents before the age of 15.

Other researchers, though, have failed to find a connection between troubled parent-child relationships and homosexuality. One study (Greenblatt, 1966) concluded that the fathers of gay men were perceived by their sons as generally positive influences, while the mothers did not exert dominance or overprotectiveness. A comparison of the family relationships of gay and heterosexual men (Siegelman, 1974) showed no significant differences. Alan Bell and associates (1981) found no support for Bieber's contention that most homosexual men had overprotective and dominant mothers.

In conclusion, we really don't know whether troubled family relationships are a cause of homosexuality. Human sexuality researchers agree that negative family dynamics are important factors, but there is no firm agreement that rocky parent-child interactions are the primary cause of homosexuality. More study of family dynamics may bear fruit, but at present there is no solid evidence that troubled parent-child interactions cause homosexuality. Furthermore, there appears to be little evidence that gays and lesbians are not well-adjusted. Indeed, with the exception of their sexual preference, most lesbians and gays are remarkably similar to heterosexuals (Browning, 1984).

ENVIRONMENTAL THEORY. Environmental, or behavioral, theory sees sexual orientation as essentially the product of conditioning and learning experiences. Behavioral researchers maintain that it is through interaction with the environment that people develop their sexual orientation. Thus people who experience pleasant or rewarding heterosexual contacts tend to develop a heterosexual sexual orientation, while those who experience positive reinforcement for homosexual behavior, punishment for

Close same-sex relationships are common among preteens and help young people acquire the capacity for intimacy. Such friendships don't necessarily predict what sexual orientation will eventually characterize a person.

heterosexual behavior, or both tend to develop a lesbian/gay orientation. According to this view, homosexual behavior is established when it is followed by pleasurable events such as orgasm or when heterosexual exploration is met with threats or punishment. Parents therefore shape a child's sexual orientation by punishing certain kinds of behavior (Diamant, 1987).

Considerable controversy swirls around environmental explanations of sexual orientation. As we have seen in Chapter 5, "Sex and Gender Issues," according to behavioral, social learning, and other theories of gender-role development, children learn innumerable gender-linked behaviors from their interactions with parents, teachers, peers, and television performers. However, some research (e.g., Green 1987) indicates that signs of sexual orientation appear so early in childhood that it seems unlikely that environmental influences could have exerted much effect as yet. This finding could of course argue for a genetic theory of sexual orientation, as could the fact that societal condemnation does not alter gay and lesbian sexual preference.

The Interactionist Perspective

We pointed out at the beginning of this discussion that no one theory adequately explains the origins of homosexuality. For this reason, many contemporary researchers lean toward an interactionist perspective of sexual orientation, one that acknowledges both biological and environmental forces. Interactionists take into account such factors as heredity, hormonal imbalances, parent-child relationships, and behavioral forces. They believe that no one factor overshadows another, but rather that each interacts and blends to create a person's sexual orientation.

Michael Storms (1981) posits that sexual orientation results from a mixture of sexual maturation and social development during early adolescence. As hormonal activation initiates the sex drive during the teenage years (usually between the ages of 13 and 15), the people who socialize the individual shape the direction of that individual's sexual orientation. An unusually early sex drive (at about age 12) may create a gay/lesbian orientation, since the person's social contacts at that age consist primarily of friends of the same sex. When such a youngster is confined to homosocial groupings, Storms feels, erotic feelings become centered on members of the same sex. The same youngster placed in a primarily heterosexual environment would likely develop a heterosexual orientation.

Certain research supports Storms' theory of sexual orientation. For example, there appears to be a significant difference in the age at which gay and heterosexual men recall becoming aware of their own sexuality, including sexual arousal. Approximately 70 percent of gay men report having had a noticeable sex drive before the age of 13, while only 25 percent of heterosexual men recall having had a sex drive that young. A similar pattern of early sexual awareness and arousal has been reported for lesbians (Saghir & Robins, 1973; Goode & Haber, 1977). We should point out, however, that all these studies are based on retrospective analysis—that is, respondents were asked to recall past sexual feelings and experiences. Such recollections may be inaccurate or subject to distortion as time wears on.

Theories of Sexual Orientation in Perspective

As we conclude this section, we remind the reader once again that there is as yet no single, conclusive explanation of the origins of sexual orientation. The theories we covered suggest that the causes of sexual orientation are complicated. While there is some limited evidence that a person's sexual preference reflects a particular biological predisposition, family history, or set of environmental influences, it seems far more likely that sexual orientation results from a convergence of all these forces. In the years to come, we can expect to see more research efforts aimed at solving this complex puzzle.

GAY AND LESBIAN LIFE STYLES AND RELATIONSHIPS

Morton Hunt (1987) believes that stereotypes and misconceptions have created a limited and imperfect idea of what homosexuality really is. People often think of gays and lesbians as having a single kind of personality pattern and exhibiting a single kind of behavior. Actually, there is no way to describe "the" gay/lesbian life style because there is no monolithic homosexual life style. Gays and lesbians have many different kinds of life styles, just as heterosexual people do.

The Diversity of Gay/Lesbian Life Styles

An extensive study by Alan Bell and Martin Weinberg (1978) involving almost 1,000 gay men and lesbians illustrates how diversified lesbian/gay life styles are. The researchers recruited their subjects from such sources as gay organizations, public advertisements, mailing lists, and recruitment cards distributed in gay bars. After gathering information about their background and behavior, Bell and Weinberg developed a typology of five life styles. About 70 percent of the subjects could be placed into one of these five basic categories, while the remaining 30 percent were too diverse to be grouped. Let's look at Bell and Weinberg's five types.

CLOSE-COUPLED. The people in this group were involved in one-to-one relationships that resembled heterosexual marriages. Partners were closely attached to each other and reported considerable interpersonal satisfaction and sexual fulfillment. Few sought a sex partner outside of the relationship. Close-coupled lesbians/gays had the fewest sex problems of all the categories and the highest levels of happiness and fulfillment. Most did not regret their sexual orientation. Twenty-eight percent of the lesbians and ten percent of the gay men could be placed into this category.

OPEN-COUPLED. Lesbians and gays in this category lived in one-to-one relationships, but sought sexual partners outside the primary relationship. Compared to close-coupled gays and lesbians these lesbians and gays had more sexual problems and were more likely to regret their homosexuality. Seventeen percent of the lesbians and 18 percent of the gay men studied were classified as open-coupled.

FUNCTIONAL. People in this category were uninvolved in a relationship. They had a higher number of sexual partners than members of any other group, reported the most interest in sex, and experienced the fewest sexual problems. Functional gays and lesbians were also least likely to regret their same-sex orientation. About 15 percent of gay men and 10 percent of lesbians fell into this typology.

DYSFUNCTIONAL. Single gays and lesbians who had a high number of sexual partners and a substantial number of sexual problems were categorized as dysfunctional lesbians and gays. They experienced the most sexual problems of any category, most of them expressed regret about their homosexuality, and their overall psychological adjustment was poor. Approximately 12 percent of gay men and 5 percent of lesbians were classified as dysfunctional gays/lesbians.

ASEXUAL. The people in this final category tended to have a low interest in sex and little involvement with others. Compared to people in other categories, asexual gays and lesbians reported more sexual problems and greater difficulty in finding sex partners. They were also more secretive about their homosexuality. About 16 percent of the gay men studied and 11 percent of the lesbian women were placed into this category.

The Bell and Weinberg study provides an interesting typology of gay and lesbian life styles. Its strength lies in its stress on diversity rather than homogeneity. Moreover, Bell and Weinberg enable us to see that certain life styles lend themselves to more satisfactory adjustment than others. That is, close-coupled lesbians and gays tend to be happy and well-adjusted, while dysfunctional and asexual types tend to be unhappy and unstable.

Dynamics of Gay and Lesbian Relationships

Let's examine some of the dynamics of gay and lesbian relationships. Contrary to what many people think, they are more like than unlike the dynamics of heterosexual relationships. Partners are sought so that a rewarding union may be formed, and the maintenance of a relationship hinges on mutual support, caring, love, and understanding. Like straight—that is, heterosexual—relationships, gay and lesbian relationships tend to flourish when partners possess maturity and authenticity, a stable sense of self, and a willingness to share intimacy on a regular basis. All intimate relationships thrive on trust and commitment and offer such important social and psychological vitamins as security, affection, and comfort.

There are, however, some significant differences in lesbian and gay relationships, including a tendency to maintain a more egalitarian relationship. In one study of gay male couples (Tuller, 1988), most were found to be free of the stereotypical role playing or mirroring of heterosexual roles sometimes attributed to gay couples. Most of the couples studied agreed that whenever two people are involved in a relationship, there is usually one personality that is more prominent or outgoing, but that this "dominance" does not necessarily indicate that one partner plays the masculine (sometimes called "butch") role, while the other assumes the submissive ("femme") role. Indeed, many couples in the study believed that there was more equality between partners in gay and lesbian relationships than between partners in heterosexual relationships simply because homosexuals do not feel forced to play the types of roles many heterosexuals feel bound to.

Jeane Maracek and associates (1988) found that lesbian/gay and heterosexual couples experienced similar degrees of satisfaction in their intimate relationships. Moreover, egalitarian relationships provided greater avenues to satisfaction than relationships that are gender-role-typed. They observed that among both same-sex and heterosexual couples, partners' satisfaction decreased as reported amounts of gender-role behavior increased. They also found that being in the feminine role was less satisfying than occupying the masculine role. Partners in the feminine role in highly gender-role-typed relationships were the least satisfied of all.

A body of research launched by Letitia Ann Peplau and her associates (Peplau, 1981; Peplau & Gordon, 1983; Peplau & Cochran, 1980, 1981) sheds considerable light on the relationship dynamics of gay and lesbian partners. Among other findings, the researchers note that most gays and lesbians want to have steady relationships, although this is somewhat more important to women than to men (a finding consistent with Bell and Weinberg's data). Both gay men and lesbians, as well as heterosexual couples, desire certain elements in a close relationship: affection, companionship, and personal development. Concerning qualities sought in partners, gay men, lesbians, and heterosexuals all look for such traits as honesty, affection, and warmth. These findings shatter the myth that sex is the sole basis for gay and lesbian relationships.

In one study (Peplau & Cochran, 1980), matched samples of lesbians, gay men, and heterosexual men and women rated the importance of various features of love relationships, including revealing intimate feelings, spending time together, holding similar attitudes, having an equal power relationship, and practicing sexual exclusivity. There were remarkably few overall group differences between heterosexuals and lesbians/gays. Both groups, for example, put greatest importance on "being able to talk about my most intimate feelings" with a partner.

The one major difference these researchers discovered between lesbians/gays and heterosexuals was that sexual exclusivity in relationships was much more important to heterosexuals. Both gay men and lesbian women gave sexual fidelity an average rating of somewhat more than 5, compared with a rating of just over 7 by heterosexuals (the highest possible importance rating was 9). Gays and lesbians were less likely than heterosexuals to endorse monogamy as an ideal for relationships.

Two interesting gender differences also emerged. Whatever their sexual orientation, women valued emotional expressiveness and the sharing of feelings more than men did. This finding is what we might expect given men's traditional gender-role socialization to conceal their feelings and present a tough exterior. The other gender difference was that both lesbian and heterosexual women cared more than men about having egalitarian relationships. The researchers speculated that the social trend toward female equality had made women more sensitive to the desirability of equal power in love relationships.

These differences notwithstanding, the research has brought out an important point that relates to our entire discussion: Lesbian, gay, and heterosexual couples are more similar than dissimilar in terms of relationship dynamics. Thus, if we want to describe what actually happens in a relationship between two gays or two lesbians— what makes for the success of that relationship and what may create problems—we do not have to use a different language. We can use the same terms we would use to describe a relationship between two heterosexuals. In our intimate relationships, we are all much more alike than we are different (Brehm, 1985).

Developmental Models of Gay and Lesbian Relationships

Just as individuals experience life changes and challenges, so do couples. While every relationship is unique, we learned in Chapter 6 that couples often encounter the same series of stages or transitions, many of which present developmental challenges to be resolved. While a considerable number of researchers have enhanced our knowledge of such transitions for heterosexual couples (see, e.g., Murstein, 1986; Perlman & Duck, 1986; Levinger, 1983), there hasn't been too much research on how gay and lesbian relationships develop. In fact, only recently have investigators explored the stages that gay and lesbian couples go through.

In this portion of our discussion, we will examine two such stage theories. First we will focus on a model of gay male relationships developed by David McWhirter

Relationship dynamics are more similar among gays, lesbians, and heterosexually oriented women and men than they are different. All intimate partners seek mutual love, support, and sharing.

and Andrew Mattison; then we will explore a model of lesbian relationships designed by D. Merilee Clunis and G. Dorsey Green. These two models are not opposed, nor is either opposed to models of heterosexual relationships. Remember, there are more similarities than differences in the overall relationship dynamics of gay men, lesbian women, and heterosexual couples. In fact, the differences between men and women are much greater than the differences between heterosexuals and gays/lesbians.

THE MCWHIRTER AND MATTISON MODEL OF GAY RELATIONSHIPS. David McWhirter and Andrew Mattison (1988, 1984), surveyed 156 gay male couples living in California. The men's ages ranged from 20 to 69 years, the mean age being 37.4. The mean duration of a relationship was 8.7 years, with the median being slightly over 5 years. From the gathered data, the researchers proposed six stages of gay relationships: blending, nesting, maintaining, collaborating, trusting, and repartnering.

McWhirter and Mattison point out that their developmental model is not intended as a new typology for couples, but rather as a broad framework for understanding some of the developmental phases that gay couples experience. While the stages are organized and presented around time periods, there are many variations in duration. As an illustration, stage one may be shorter for those men who have experienced previous relationships. To help bring these stages to life we will weave the relationship of Paul, a 54-year-old history professor, and Stephen, a 49-year-old accountant, into the discussion.

Blending stage. The blending stage, which occurs during the first year of the relationship, is marked by intense romantic involvement. Similarities bind partners together and differences are usually overlooked. For example, Paul and Stephen met at a concert and were immediately attracted to each other. As time progressed, they began to do everything together, until eventually they decided to share an apartment. The romantic aspect of their love was intense and reciprocal. Equality for Paul and Stephen was manifested in shared financial responsibility and the equal distribution of domestic chores. Their sexual relationship was exclusive and was marked by intense feelings and excitement.

Nesting stage. The nesting stage usually occurs between the first and the third year of the relationship. While men generally have limited concerns about their living environment during their first year together, they turn their attention to their surroundings during the nesting stage. During this period, homemaking activities, such as decorating a new home or rearranging an old one, invariably emerge. Partners also become aware of each other's shortcomings as well as the complementarities that enhance compatibility. Romance tends to fade in this stage, a development that often creates concern and worry. The quest for compatibility and the dimming of romantic feelings produces a mixture of positive and negative feelings about the value of the relationship.

For Stephen and Paul, romantic love declined rapidly, and at first both thought their relationship was on the rocks. Instead, they discovered the growth of a different, more mature form of love. Rather than passionate emotion, they began to experience deep sharing, caring, and loyalty toward each other.

Maintaining stage. Sometime between the third and fifth year, partners enter the maintaining stage. They discover that relationship maintenance hinges on the establishment of balances between togetherness and individualization, autonomy and dependence, conflict and its resolution, and confusion and understanding. This individualization in the context of togetherness is often accompanied by greater levels of self-insight and self-disclosure. While couples may once have done everything together, they now afford each other opportunities to pursue individual interests. It's also at this time that family and friends may recognize and begin to support the couple's relationship. Stephen and Paul each found people with whom to share activities in which the other was not interested: Stephen enjoyed sports events, whereas Paul liked to play chess. Neither felt threatened by the other's outside involvement; indeed, both saw it as a means to ensure growth and avoid stagnation. Both men found considerable support among their friends, and Paul's family came to accept Stephen and their relationship, although Stephen's family remained distant.

Building stage. The building stage occurs between the fifth and tenth years of the relationship. Building means working together in a cooperative fashion and becoming increasingly productive. Couples at this stage find that the relationship offers new levels of security and dependability. Collaborative adjustments can produce effective complementarity. Combined with the coping mechanisms for dealing with boredom and conflict, complementarity offers new energy for mutual as well as individual productivity. The individualization of the previous stage can promote independence, sustained by the steady, dependable availability of a partner for guidance and support.

For Stephen and Paul, collaboration emerged out of the familiarity and comfort each derived from the other's company. Not only did they move psychologically closer together over the years, but they each made sure to leave room for an individual self at the same time. Whether doing the dishes together or making a difficult joint decision, their collaboration sustained and increased the strength of their relationship.

Releasing stage. This fifth stage of the McWhirter and Mattison model occurs between the tenth and the twentieth year of the relationship. As time passes, partners build trust in each other, a trust that embodies nonpossessiveness and a strongly positive mutual regard. For Stephen and Paul, trust lessened possessive feelings and jealousy. The gradual merger of money and possessions may also be a manifestation of relational trust. During this stage, Stephen and Paul developed a true sense of "our" money and "our" possessions. Other people going through this stage, however, may withdraw from their partner or come to take the relationship for granted.

Renewing stage. The final stage starts when the relationship is about 20 years old and continues on from there. The researchers found that many couples reported a renewal of their relationship during this stage. Most men's goals include financial security, and the men in the McWhirter and Mattison model had usually accomplished this by 20 years. Most couples assume that they will be together until separated by death. At this stage, many men worry about security and health, loneliness, and the death of their partners or themselves. Most are struck by the passage of time and often reminisce about their years together. Stephen and Paul, for instance, now enjoy looking back at their lives together, sharing anecdote after anecdote. Sometimes they relive the past; other times they muse about what it would be like to be starting again. They find sharing their relationship history pleasurable.

THE CLUNIS AND GREEN MODEL OF LESBIAN RELATIONSHIPS. Merilee Clunis and Dorsey Green (1988) have developed a six-stage model of lesbian relationships. The stages are labeled prerelationship, romance, conflict, acceptance, commitment, and collaboration. In developing their model, the authors blended the ideas of Susan Campbell (1980) about male-female relationships with the just-described McWhirter and Mattison (1988, 1984) model for gay relationships.

Like other theorists, Clunis and Green caution that relationship building is a process in which stages often overlap. They do not offer a timetable; indeed, they point out that it is difficult to say how long a couple will stay in a stage or how often they will repeat a stage. Finally, Clunis and Green note that couples don't always go through the stages in the order they are presented—in fact, some couples never go through all of the stages.

Prerelationship stage. The prerelationship, or "getting to know you," stage is short, lasting only weeks or even days, and usually encompasses a number of choices. One choice after meeting someone is deciding whether to invest time and energy in getting to know her better. Another choice is deciding whether, or when, to include sex. The latter choice may prove troublesome because the available guidelines for women's sexual behavior are based on a heterosexual model that is possibly out of date (e.g., "don't let him kiss you before the third date" or "save yourself for marriage"). Consequently, lesbians often feel confused about what to do in this initial stage.

Consider Janice and Beth, who met at a friend's party. The two women discovered that they had a lot in common. Both worked in the field of hotel administration—Janice as a banquet manager, and Beth as a public relations consultant—and when they began to see each other regularly, they found they enjoyed each other's company and wondered if their friendship could develop into something more. Neither wanted to get her hopes up too high, however, and both pondered who should make the next move. This kind of uncertainty is common during the prerelationship stage.

Romance stage. The merging of two separate identities is the central goal of this stage. As time progresses, sharing and cooperative patterns of interaction bring partners closer together, with the result that their mutual feelings of love, tenderness, and appreciation escalate. It is important during this stage to temper romantic love with a realistic appraisal of the budding relationship. Partners need to clarify their needs and expectations and not fall headfirst into a serious relationship. Moreover, each partner must be honest with the other and not present a false image. Some partners in this stage put their best foot forward to such an extent that they find themselves stuck with maintaining an image, rather than able to relax and be themselves. Janice, for instance, sometimes felt inadequate. She needed to share that with Beth. And Beth needed to share the parts of herself that caused her worry or unhappiness.

The merging and togetherness of the romance stage are typically more intense for lesbians than for heterosexual couples. In heterosexual relationships, the differences between men and women help to establish boundaries on this type of fusion. As Clunis and Green note, just being physically different helps to set boundaries. With lesbian couples, it is easier for the partners to assume that there are no differences between them because both of them are women.

Conflict stage. During this stage, partners begin to see each other's imperfections. After the initial excitement and romanticism of the earlier stages, partners must come down out of the clouds and tend to the business of living together and seeing the

When partners begin to explore their points of agreement and difference and to seek useful compromise, their relationship matures and grows deeper.

267

world in more realistic terms. The discovery that a partner is flawed often creates relational turbulence and requires conflict resolution skills. While some couples may terminate the relationship at this point rather than face the conflict, others effectively negotiate their differences. The basic ground rules and communication patterns for the relationship emerge from the struggles of this stage.

When Janice and Beth arrived at the conflict stage of their relationship, each realized that the other was not the person she thought her to be. Moreover, there were times when neither was getting what she wanted and expected to get from the other. Both women sometimes felt hurt, disappointed, and resentful. For Janice and Beth, the conflict stage meant establishing relationship goals and defining and adjusting the expectations they held for each other.

Acceptance stage. This stage can be likened to the calm after the storm. At this point, partners have accepted that they are separate human beings complete with shortcomings. Instead of accusing and blaming each other during conflict situations, they now look at themselves and try to discover how they are contributing to the disharmony. Janice and Beth, for example, saw their disagreements as opportunities to learn more about each other rather than as contests for which they kept score. Moreover they began to recognize certain patterns: As the same conflicts appeared repeatedly, they learned to resolve the issues faster. The experience of resolving problems built up their confidence in the relationship to the point where they no longer feared that every disagreement or argument risked terminating the relationship.

Commitment stage. According to Clunis and Green, commitment means making choices about the relationship, being responsible for them, and working at maintaining harmony and stability. It requires renunciation of the search for the perfect partner, the guaranteed future, the "happily-ever-after" ending. By this stage, most couples have accepted the necessity for change in their relationship and have come to think of their partners as basically trustworthy. They do not experience differences as threats or changes as losses.

This does not imply that couples never have doubts at this time. Even committed partners may feel uncertainty, doubt, or regret at a particular moment. Many couples also have to work on balancing their opposing needs. For example, Janice and Beth recognized that they each had needs for togetherness as well as for private space, and that their relationship required balancing the two. They mutually decided to seek out and create liberating activities designed to meet their individual needs. For Janice, camping became a liberating activity, while Beth chose a sculpting class at a nearby art school.

Collaboration stage. By this stage, partners have found that they can have conflict without ending the relationship and both have made a solid commitment to the relationship. Some partners now decide to collaborate on creating something beyond the relationship; for example, they might decide to start a business together, to become involved in political action, or to raise a child. Such collaboration often enhances the relationship, and miniversions of the earlier stages often reappear. In a less tangible fashion, collaboration may also include cooperation and compassionate commitment to the relationship. In looking to the future, partners recognize the importance of joining forces and working together. This experience often reignites romance, acceptance, and commitment. Collaboration for Janice and Beth culminated in opening a bed-and-breakfast inn together. The inn was a dream come true for the two of them, and they had spent years planning for it. Best of all, they discovered the inn enhanced their relationship, strengthened their resources for coping with change, and solidified their mutual commitment.

Sexual Techniques and Pleasuring

What do gays and lesbians do in their bedrooms? How do they make love? The specific sexual activities of gays, lesbians, and heterosexuals are very similar, including such techniques as kissing, caressing, hugging, massaging, and manual and oral stimulation. Gays and lesbians use a variety of lovemaking positions: lying down, standing, sitting; different partners on top or bottom; partners facing each other or front to back; both partners engaged in oral-genital contact.

There are some differences in approaches to sexual activity, though. In their extensive research investigations, William Masters and Virginia Johnson (1979) found that among committed gays and lesbians (partners who had lived together for at least one year) there is a greater willingness to experiment and more attention paid to style. When given privacy and environmental comfort, both gay and lesbian partners tend to take a leisurely, relaxed approach to lovemaking and do not rush to achieve orgasm. Masters and Johnson observed that sexual interaction tends to be a matter of mutual agreement and doing what feels good at the moment rather than adhering to a prearranged script. Let's look more closely at the sexual behavior of gays and lesbians.

How do gays or lesbians make love? What kinds of sexual techniques do they use?

SEXUAL PRACTICES AMONG GAY MEN. Research indicates (e.g., Peplau & Gordon, 1983) that gay men report high satisfaction with sex in their relationships. They tend to have sex with their steady partners as often or more often than heterosexual couples do. Committed gay partners usually take their time during sexual interactions. Most move slowly through the excitement and plateau phases of the sexual response cycle and employ a variety of inventive sexual techniques and styles. Most committed gay male couples initiate sexual interactions with hugging, caressing, or kissing. Nipple stimulation (manually or orally) and "teasing" forms of genital play are also common. Initially, stimulation is often directed to the thighs, lower abdomen, perineal area, and anus. Attention is then often directed to the frenulum of the penis. Often a man will bring his partner close to orgasm, allow him to regress to a lower level of excitement, and then restimulate him to orgasm (Masters & Johnson, 1979).

Fellatio is the most common form of gay male sexual activity leading to orgasm. Anal intercourse is another sexual activity, although it is far less common among gays than popularly thought (Bell & Weinberg, 1978). Other gay male stimulation techniques are penile-interfemoral stimulation (penis of one partner between the thighs of the other) and mutual masturbation.

When AIDS was first documented in 1981, it was exclusively linked to gays, bisexuals, and intravenous drug users. However, today it is recognized (see Chapter 18) that AIDS is not restricted to these groups, but rather is largely connected to unsafe sex practices. One such practice is having multiple sex partners. Sexually active nonmonogamous gay and bisexual men run a higher risk of contracting AIDS than heterosexual men do (Zimmerman, 1989; Darrow, Echenberg, & Jaffe, 1987; Chmiel et al., 1987) because they are more likely to come in contact with people who carry HIV. Because of the danger of AIDS and other sexually transmitted diseases, many gay and bisexual men are reducing the number of their sexual partners and choosing to practice so-called safe sex. In general, this means avoiding the exchange of bodily fluids and wastes, using condoms, refraining from deep kissing, avoiding injury to body tissues during sex, and never sharing vibrators, other sexual aids, or intravenous drug needles and other drug paraphernalia. Chapters 17 and 18 discuss AIDS and other sexually transmitted diseases and offer some suggestions on how to avoid these very serious illnesses.

SEXUAL PRACTICES OF LESBIANS Some researchers (e.g., Peplau & Gordon, 1983) suggest that lesbians experience orgasms more regularly during sex than heterosexual women do. This is probably because a majority of women reach orgasm more easily through clitoral stimulation than vaginal penetration and clitoral stimulation is the focus of most lesbian sexual activity. Other researchers (Yaffee & Fenwick, 1988b) have found that sex offers considerable emotional satisfaction to lesbian partners. Tenderness and affection play a vital part in nearly all committed lesbian relationships. Intimate body contact—something heterosexual women also value highly, but frequently fail to find in their lovemaking—is often at the heart of lesbian sex.

Lesbian couples usually share full body contact and engage in considerable holding, kissing, and touching before attempting breast or genital stimulation. The breasts are slowly stimulated both manually and orally, with considerable attention focused on the nipples. During genital stimulation, contrary to the patterns followed by many married heterosexual couples, lesbians rarely approach the clitoral area first, nor do they insert their fingers into their partner's vagina. Instead, they usually direct initial stimulation to the area around the mouth of the vagina in relaxed and deliberate ways. Most also stimulate the labia, mons, and inner thighs. When clitoral contact is initiated, the contact is usually casual, low-key, and nondemanding. Following initial contact with the glans, the clitoral shaft is typically the primary focus of stimulative activity (Masters & Johnson, 1979).

Like gays, lesbians often engage in "teasing" patterns of genital stimulation— that is, a partner is brought to high levels of arousal, allowed to regress, and then brought back to her previously elevated arousal level. Many couples also employ rapidly increasing genital stimulation intensity until orgasm is reached. Compared to heterosexual men, lesbians usually use a lighter touch when stimulating the clitoris. Few lesbians use a dildo during their lovemaking.

Cunnilingus is the most common form of lesbian sexual activity leading to orgasm. Masters and Johnson observed that the lesbian approach to cunnilingus usually starts with the breasts, moves to the lower abdomen and thighs, and, in turn, the labia and often the vaginal outlet before focusing on the clitoris. Clitoral stimulation varies from forceful stroking to a slow, gentle approach. Other lesbian sexual stimulation techniques include rubbing the genitals against a partner's body or genital area (called tribadism), mutual masturbation, and anal stimulation.

Finally, Maurice Yaffee and Elizabeth Fenwick (1988b) found that lesbian women tend to be more sexually honest with each other than heterosexual women are with men, in that they rarely fake orgasm. If one partner experiences difficulty in achieving orgasm, she is likely to say so, and often the couple will try to solve the problem.

Lesbian and Gay Parenting

We have a tendency to think of gay and lesbian relationships strictly in terms of the adult partners. Today, however, many gays and lesbians are choosing to form family units. The couple may adopt children, or they may have youngsters from previous heterosexual relationships. Some lesbians use artificial insemination to have children.

Seeking to become a gay or lesbian parent almost always presents legal problems. Many gays and lesbians have to fight ex-spouses for custody of their biological children. Most child placement agencies are reluctant to give children to known gay men or lesbian women. Some organizations that provide artificial insemination services insist that eligible candidates show evidence of a long-term heterosexual relationship (Blumenfeld & Raymond, 1988).

One lesbian shares her pain at not being granted custody of her son:

Having come out as a lesbian has been real difficult for me because my child was taken away by his father. I was granted visitation rights and because I didn't know to make it specific, I've gone for six months without seeing him. It takes that long sometimes for legal proceedings to work themselves out. It's amazing how the men—the fathers—get such special treatment. I mean, a battering husband is not treated the way a lesbian mother is. At the same time, though, it was being a lesbian and stepping out as a strong woman that made me able to withstand what followed. (Boston Women's Health Book Collective, 1984, p. 158).

It is incorrectly assumed that lesbian and gay parents create severe adjustment problems for their children, including problems of gender identity and gender-role development. Many people believe that exposure to gay and lesbian parents causes children to become gay themselves. Indeed, some people are convinced that homosexual parents try to persuade their children to be gay or lesbian. Research indicates, however, that the incidence of homosexuality among children of lesbians or gays is not above that in the general population, so the great majority of children of gay parents turn out to be heterosexual. And, as we saw earlier, all the evidence suggests that most homosexuals were brought up in exclusively heterosexual households (Robinson et al., 1982).

Neither is there support for the popular notion that lesbian and gay parents are poor role models for children because they themselves were raised in unhappy, unstable homes. Most gay and lesbian parents were brought up in intact heterosexual families and highly value secure and trusting relationships with their children. One investigation (Skeen & Robinson, 1985) showed that most gay fathers were reared in homes with little marital discord and wanted their children to experience a stable and harmonious domestic life. Findings such as this show that the aspirations of gay and lesbian parents do not differ from those of heterosexual parents. Indeed, when the two groups are compared, parenting behaviors, goals, and interests are usually found to be the same (see Kirkpatrick, 1982). Lesbian and gay parents also have the same kinds of problems single heterosexual parents have. For lesbians, who as women still earn significantly less than men, economic survival can be a major struggle.

Both gay/lesbian parents and their children do have to make some special adjustments (see, e.g., Ricketts & Achtenberg, 1990; Pies, 1990; Bigner & Bozett, 1990; Gottman, 1990). Youngsters made the targets of ridicule by peers and others may become uncomfortable with their parents' sexual orientation. For this reason, many gay and lesbian parents inform their children as early as possible about their own sexual orientation. Most children understand and come to accept their parents' homosexuality, and although they may have to defend their parents occasionally, they can usually expect their peers to get accustomed to their parents' life styles.

WHERE TO FIND MORE ON GAY AND LESBIAN PARENTING

Organizations

National Lawyers Guild Gay Caucus
558 Capp St.
San Francisco, CA 94110
(415) 285-5066

Lesbian Rights Project
1370 Mission St., 3rd Floor
San Franciso, CA 94103
(415) 621-0674

Gay and Lesbian Parents
    Coalition International
Box 50360
Washington, DC 20004
(703) 548-3238

Books

Alpert, H. (1988) *We are everything: Writings by and about lesbian parents.* Freedom, CA: The Crossing Press.

continued

Back, G. (1985). *Are you still my mother, are you still my family?* New York: Warner.

Curry, F. H., and Clifford, D. (1981). *A legal guide for lesbian and gay couples.* Reading, MA: Addison-Wesley.

Maddox, B. (1982). *Married and gay.* San Diego, CA: Harcourt, Brace, Jovanovich.

Pies, C. (1985). *Considering parenthood: A workbook for lesbians.* San Francisco, CA: Spinster's Ink.

Schulenburg, J. (1985). *Gay parenting: A complete guide for gay men and lesbians with children.* New York: Anchor Press/Doubleday.

BISEXUALITY

Bisexuality refers to sexual attraction and emotional attachment to both women and men. The desire to have intimate relationships with both sexes may or may not include sexual contact. Most bisexuals usually lean toward one sex or the other in something of a sixty-forty or seventy-thirty ratio; fifty-fifty bisexuals are quite rare. Even though they exhibit a preference for one or the other sex, bisexuals usually continue to eroticize both sexes and remain open to sexual involvement with men and women (Zinik, 1985).

Like homosexuality, bisexuality is not well understood. So strong is the tendency to dichotomize sexual orientation that many people simply do not believe it exists. Indeed, many gays and lesbians view the bisexual as no more than a gay or lesbian person who lacks the courage to fully "come out." And until recently, the only type of bisexual who had been researched was the married man who had furtive, clandestine sexual encounters with other men. Many such "bisexuals" are predominantly or exclusively gay men who use marriage to shroud their preferred sexual orientation, although others are probably genuinely interested and attracted to both sexes (Nichols, 1989).

According to Charles Hansen and Anne Evans (1985), much of the confusion that abounds about bisexuality arises from the insistence on emphasizing genital sexual activity instead of the larger issue of loving. As we've shown throughout this book, genitality is not all there is to sexuality. Sexuality, including bisexuality, encompasses affiliation and affection as well as genital behavior. This simple distinction is critical to an understanding of all sexual orientations.

Today we know that there are different types of bisexuality, including simultaneous, concurrent, and serial forms. **Simultaneous bisexuality** refers to having sex with at least one partner of the same sex and one of the opposite sex at the same time. **Concurrent bisexuality** means having sex with both men and women during the same period of one's life, although not necessarily maintaining *both* types of relationships simultaneously. **Serial bisexuality** refers to alternating female and male sexual partners over time. Serial bisexuals may have monogamous relationships, thus giving the appearance of living a more or less heterosexual or gay/lesbian life style (Zinik, 1985).

Given the research problems presented earlier, it is difficult to determine the prevalence of bisexuality. One estimate is that about 25 million Americans exhibit some combination of heterosexual and lesbian/gay behavior, with more men than women having bisexual histories. Most bisexuals first eroticize the opposite sex and identify as heterosexuals. During their 20s or 30s, though, they discover gay/lesbian interests. Sometimes lifelong gays and lesbians suddenly develop heterosexual interests and become bisexual. In general, bisexuals prefer one sex over the other, although they are attracted to both men and women and remain open to sexual involvement with both sexes (Saliba, 1982; Bell et al., 1981; Zinik, 1985).

simultaneous bisexuality
Having sex with at least one partner of the same sex and one of the opposite sex at the same time.

concurrent bisexuality
Having sex separately with men and women during the same period of one's life.

serial bisexuality
Alternating female and male sexual partners over time.

This 25-year-old female bisexual shares her sexual motivations and attractions:

I enjoy sharing sexual intimacies with both men and women, and get the most satisfaction when there is mutual tenderness and emotional closeness. Before college I was a heterosexual and fully enjoyed my sexual experiences with men. Then I met a woman during my senior year of college and became involved in a very intimate relationship. Although I was reluctant at first, we had sex, and to my pleasant surprise, it was unbelievably exciting and arousing. I never thought that making love to a woman was anything I would ever do, let alone enjoy. We saw each other until the end of the school year, but then drifted apart after graduation. Since that time I have had sex with several different men and women. I am currently seeing a male co-worker who I really care about. (Authors' files)

An interesting comparison of bisexuals, gays/lesbians, and heterosexuals was provided by Gary Zinik (1983). He discovered that male and female bisexuals reported that they experienced similar levels of erotic excitement with female and male sexual partners. However, both men and women experienced more emotional satisfaction with their female partners. Relatedly, both male and female bisexuals reported falling in love with women more often than with men, although a considerable number had fallen in love with individuals of both genders at least once. Why do you think these patterns exist? Can you relate any of these findings to material we covered on gender issues (Chapter 4) and intimate relationships (Chapter 6)? Did you expect the findings to be different in any way?

Zinik also discovered that almost 80 percent of his bisexual subjects had experienced some confusion and conflict because of their bisexuality. Most subjects said that the confusion was usually due to bisexuality's inherent complexity, their need as bisexuals to balance so many variables, and their lack of social support. Many reported that they enjoyed being bisexual in spite of the difficulties, and that bisexuality contributed to their personal happiness and fulfillment.

Bisexuality does present certain problems. Difficulties often arise for couples in which one person is bisexual and the other is either heterosexual or homosexual. If the bisexuality was not acknowledged at the beginning of the relationship, issues of betrayal, hurt, and anger often surface and must be confronted. After learning the truth about a bisexual partner, many partners feel "used," hurt, and shocked. Sometimes the withholding of such information is symptomatic of a basic disharmony between the couple, not the cause of disharmony. In this sense, it can compound other stresses in the couple's life (Lourea, 1985).

On the last point, Jean Gochros (1985) studied wives' reactions to being informed by their husbands that they were bisexual. She found that these women struggled less with the fact of their husband's sexual orientation than with feelings of isolation, stigma, loss, cognitive confusion, and the lack of knowledgeable, empathic support or help in problem solving. Other factors affecting the wife's reaction were her levels of self-esteem, independence, and assertiveness, and her attitude toward bisexuality. If the husband disclosed his bisexuality in a voluntary, sensitive, and honest way, and if a professional support system was immediately available, the wife was generally empathic. Indeed, the immediate consequences for many couples were better communication, a reaffirmation of love, an improvement in their sexual relationship, and a general relief of tension.

Finally, we need to acknowledge the feelings of isolation and alienation that bisexuals often experience. Many people see bisexuality as a chic life style, but David Lourea (1985) contends that those who believe bisexuals have the "best of both worlds" do not realize that "both worlds" are often closets. For instance, a bisexual woman can get recognition and support from lesbians for her feelings toward women only if she is willing to conceal her heterosexual feelings. A bisexual man can obtain affirmation for his heterosexual prowess only if he can keep his homosexual desires secret. Thus, contrary to Woody Allen's jest that "bisexuals double their chances for a date on a Saturday night," the bisexual woman does not have the option of meeting a woman in a straight setting, and the bisexual man knows he will be chastised and maybe rejected by gay friends if he exhibits any interest in women. The lack of a bisexual subculture and social support network often adds to feelings of loneliness and alienation.

SOCIETAL ATTITUDES TOWARD LESBIAN AND GAY LIFE STYLES

We've stated throughout this chapter that even in the 1990s gays and lesbians must contend with considerable prejudice, discrimination, alienation, and ridicule. Unfortunately, the AIDS epidemic fueled these negative attitudes and set back the gay/lesbian community in terms of acceptance. When it was first discovered, AIDS was thought to be a disease of gay men or bisexuals, but as we learn more about this plague, we realize how unwarranted this view is. All one has to do is look around the world—in Africa, Asia, and Europe, high rates of AIDS are found among heterosexuals. To understand more about societal perceptions of gays, let's look at two related concepts: homophobia and heterosexism.

Homophobia and Heterosexism

homophobia A fear and dread of homosexuals as well as a fear of the possibility of homosexuality in oneself.

heterosexism The belief that heterosexuality is the only acceptable and viable life option.

Homophobia, sometimes called "homosexual phobia," is at the root of prejudice and discrimination against homosexuals. The term was coined by sociologist George Weinberg in 1972, who defined it as a fear and dread of gays and lesbians as well as a fear of the possibility of homosexuality in oneself. Homophobia is closely allied with **heterosexism,** the belief that heterosexuality is the only acceptable and viable life option. Heterosexism forces gays, lesbians, and bisexuals to struggle constantly with their self-esteem and makes it much harder for them to integrate a positive sexual identity (Blumenfeld & Raymond, 1988).

Homophobia and heterosexism are widespread in the United States, along with the prejudice and discrimination these attitudes give rise to. In 1983, a Gallup poll found that a majority of Americans felt that homosexuality should not be considered a socially acceptable life style. In the same poll, 59 percent of those surveyed would exclude lesbians and gays from teaching in the public schools and another 51 percent would exclude them from the clergy. A study of almost 2,500 undergraduates (Segal, 1984) revealed that fear of and prejudice toward homosexuals is the norm rather than the exception. Another investigation (Coles & Stokes, 1985) showed that most teenagers have negative impressions of homosexuality and cling to stereotypes about gay men and lesbians. And a survey (Davis & Smith, 1987) comparing attitudes toward gays in 1973 and 1987 revealed that negative opinions remained essentially unchanged.

Certain variables appear to be associated with homophobia. For example, heterosexual men have more hostile feelings toward gays and lesbians than heterosexual women do (Herek, 1988; Larsen, Reed, & Hoffman, 1980). One of the most limiting things about homophobia in men is that their fear of being attracted to other men can prevent them from developing deep same-sex friendships. Many men have friends who are really just buddies to do things with: work, drink, or engage in sports (Nelson, 1985).

Gregory Herek (1988, 1985) argues that people with strong homophobic attitudes have certain characteristics in common. Among other things, according to Herek, such people are likely to:

- Be older and less well educated.
- Express traditional attitudes about gender roles.
- Be authoritarian.
- Have very conservative religious beliefs.
- Feel that their peers hold negative attitudes toward homosexuals.
- Hold relatively less permissive attitudes toward sexuality and sexual expression.
- Have had little personal contact with gays or lesbians.

Clearly, not all people who have the foregoing characteristics are homophobic. And, conversely, not all people who view gay and lesbian lifestyles negatively share these characteristics. Moreover, this is a new area of research in which information is accumulating rather slowly.

Another study (MacLaury, 1982) discovered that people who are religious tend to hold more negative attitudes toward homosexuality than those who are less devout, probably because homosexuality is depicted as sinful and immoral in so many religious

---

MAKING USE OF WHAT WE KNOW

Personal Homophobia Inventory

Do you have homophobic attitudes? If you do, have you ever stopped to think how and why they originated? The following questions may help you to confront your feelings. There is no "score" attached to this inventory; rather, it is designed to encourage you to explore your attitudes toward same-sex preferences.

1. Do you stop yourself from doing or saying certain things because someone might think you're gay or lesbian? If yes, what kinds of things?

2. Do you ever intentionally do or say things so that people will know you're not gay or lesbian? If yes, what kinds of things?

3. Do you believe that gays or lesbians can influence others to become homosexual? Do you think someone could influence you to change your sexual and affectional preferences?

4. If you are a parent, how would you (or do you) feel about having a lesbian daughter or gay son?

5. How do you think you would feel if you discovered that one of your parents or parent figures, or a brother or sister, were gay or lesbian?

6. Are there any jobs, positions, or professions that you think lesbians and gays should be barred from holding or entering? If yes, why?

7. Would you go to a physician whom you knew or believed to be gay or lesbian if that person were of a different gender from you? If that person were of the same gender as you? If not, why not?

8. If someone you care about were to say to you, "I think I'm gay," how would you respond? Would you suggest that the person see a therapist?

9. Have you ever been to a gay or lesbian bar, social club, party, or march? If you have, why did you go? If not, why not?

10. Would you wear a button that says "How dare you assume that I'm heterosexual?" If not, why not?

11. Can you think of three positive aspects of a gay or lesbian life style? Can you think of three negative aspects of a nongay life style?

12. Have you ever laughed at a "queer" joke?

Copyright © 1985 National Association of Social Workers, Inc. *Lesbian and Gay Issues.*

teachings. It is also rejected for its perceived violation of traditional heterosexual norms. Many people thus perceive lesbians and gays as refusing to fulfill societal expectations about marriage and family life.

Homophobic attitudes can be changed, although this is a hard task because homophobia tends to be deeply rooted and fueled by considerable fear and anxiety. Changing such attitudes requires public education in sensitive, extensive, and diverse ways. To become aware of your own attitudes, answer the questions in the box "Personal Homophobic Inventory."

Community outreach programs have been somewhat effective in educating the public about homosexuality, especially in dispelling myths and misconceptions about gays, lesbians, and bisexuals. Speakers' bureaus, newsletters, and support groups have been among the approaches used. At the college level, courses in human sexuality and gay and lesbian life styles tend to alter students' attitudes toward same-sex preferences in a positive fashion. For example, Daniel Watters' (1987) review of the literature indicates that such courses, when effectively taught, often increase students' awareness and tolerance of gay, lesbian, and bisexual life styles. Many students report a decrease in prejudicial feelings after completing such a course.

Prejudice and Discrimination Against Gays and Lesbians

Gays and lesbians are an oppressed group and many kinds of prejudice and discrimination are aimed at them. According to Warren Blumenfeld and Diane Raymond (1988), the prejudice and discrimination are sometimes blatant and deliberate, at other times unintentional and unconscious. Consider for a moment the many prejudicial attitudes and feelings that center on being lesbian or gay:

> Homosexuality has been called many things. Fascists say it's a sign of racial impurity, Communists blame it on Western bourgeois decadence, Westerners say it's a sign of deviance, and parents around the world blame themselves. Religious leaders call it sin and perversion and try to purge it, psychiatrists have called it an illness and disturbance and have tried to cure it. Governments attempt to isolate and sometimes eradicate it, and school children learn from their elders to fear and hate it. (Blumenfeld & Raymond, 1988, p. 267).

Society labels gays and lesbians deviants and punishes them in a variety of ways. The visible sanctions are primarily financial and legal. However, more pervasive and more damaging are the personal attacks and constant harassment homosexuals have to endure, such as malicious mimickry and jokes and raids on gay bars and meeting places. Living under these conditions is a hard and alienating experience. That society tolerates—even encourages—these conditions does little to foster equality (Silberman & Hawkins, 1988).

Andrea Parrot and Michael Ellis (1985) state that discriminatory treatment against lesbians and gays is still the norm. Marriages between lesbians and between gay men are legally prohibited. As we mentioned earlier, most adoption agencies are reluctant to place children with gay men or lesbian women. Gays and lesbians are also officially barred from the armed services as well as from various other organizations and occupations. The educational system has frequently denied them teaching positions because of the public's fear that they will sexually abuse children or recruit them to the so-called lesbian/gay way of life. The media also tend to depict homosexuality in an unfair and/or unrealistic light. But, say Parrot and Ellis, perhaps the worst blow to gays and lesbians is the ignorance and prejudice that causes family members to turn their backs on them. Lesbian and gay children are often rejected by their families because the family is embarrassed by them.

Let's consider two of the forms of discrimination we've mentioned in more detail: the legal prohibition against homosexual marriage and the physical violence against gays and lesbians. The reasons usually given for marriage of heterosexual couples are love, to have children, to attain the right to make important decisions for a spouse when the spouse is incapacitated (e.g., in an intensive care ward), to pass on property, to be able to own things together (such as a house), to support each other financially, to gain cultural recognition as a couple, and to file joint tax returns. Almost all these rights are important to gay and lesbian couples too, but they are denied the legal right to marry and claim them. Tax and insurance regulations also discriminate against same-sex couples (see the "Sexuality in the News" box at the end of this chapter). For instance, if one member of a married couple is working and the other is not, the working spouse's income is taxed based on two deductions rather than one. The tax savings for joint filings are significant (Parrot & Ellis, 1985).

Anti-gay and lesbian violence has risen dramatically in recent years. The National Gay and Lesbian Task Force (1988) reports that there were over 2,000 cases of assault, arson, rape, and murder in 1985 in which lesbians and gays were the victims, and that this figure climbed to 5,000 in 1986. In 1987, the number of cases rose to approximately 7,000. The Task Force also estimates that about 75 percent of the crimes committed against gays and lesbians are never reported.

According to one source (Blumenfeld & Raymond, 1988), assailants tend to be white males in their teens and early 20s who have taken it upon themselves to act out society's prejudices against gays and lesbians. The purpose of these assaults is not theft, although this sometimes occurs. The purpose is to use violence, intimidation, and humiliation to let gays and lesbians know that they and their life styles are despised. Among a growing number of heterosexuals, such expressions of hatred, bias, and bigotry are socially acceptable (Wertheimer, 1989). In the final analysis, a society that condones this sort of violence is brutalizing itself.

Responses to Prejudice and Discrimination

Many gays, lesbians, and other concerned persons actively seek to reduce homophobia, hostility, and the many types of discrimination discussed in this chapter. By the 1950s, homosexuals had begun to organize their own political groups. In 1951, the Mattachine Society was founded in Los Angeles, followed in 1955 by the Daughters of Bilitis in San Francisco. (The Mattachine Society was named after a secret fraternal order of unmarried men who dressed as women and performed in thirteenth-century France. The Daughters of Bilitis were named after the lesbian poet Bilitis, who lived with Sappho on the island of Lesbos in ancient Greece.) During the 1960s, the **gay liberation movement** emerged as a political movement promoting the full civil rights of homosexuals and an end to discriminatory practices. The gay liberation movement embraces many subgroups, the best-known being the Gay Liberation Front and the Gay Activists Alliance.

In 1973, the **National Gay and Lesbian Task Force** was founded in New York City and is now headquartered in Washington, D.C. According to spokesperson Bruce Voeller (1983), the purpose of the NGLTF is to re-educate society, including its gay and lesbian members, to esteem gays and lesbians at their full human worth and to allow them to attain their goals and contribute to society according to their full potential. The organization was instrumental in getting the American Psychiatric Association to declassify homosexuality as an illness and has helped to pass legislation decriminalizing consensual homosexual sex and protecting the civil rights of gays and lesbians in many states and localities. At this writing, the NGLTF is the largest organization in the gay liberation movement.

A number of other organizations have been formed to combat antigay and antilesbian violence and to assist its victims. Among these are the Violence Project of the National Gay and Lesbian Task Force, the Committee on Lesbian and Gay Victims'

gay liberation movement A political movement seeking to reduce discrimination and ensure the civil rights of gay men and lesbians.

National Gay and Lesbian Task Force An organization that promotes the acceptance by society of its homosexual members and that seeks to ensure that gays and lesbians have the same opportunities as heterosexual men and women to achieve and to contribute to society.

Concerns of the National Organization for Victims Assistance, and the Lesbian Caucus of the National Coalition Against Sexual Assault. Besides assisting victims, these organizations seek to implement crime prevention programs, launch community education programs to dispel myths and fears about homosexuality, develop training sessions to sensitize police officers, and promote more accurate reporting.

All of these organizations offer avenues for gays, lesbians, and bisexuals to band together to try to change public attitudes and policy. John D'Emilio (1989) feels that while such organizations have succeeded in making some gains, progress has been slow and many more issues need to be addressed. One gain is indisputable, though, and that is the growth of a sense of community. Because of the gay rights movement, what was once secret, despised identity has become the basis for a community. That community has, in turn, spawned a vigorous politics that has brought it national influence.

WHERE TO FIND MORE on LESBIAN AND GAY RIGHTS

American Civil Liberties Union
132 West 43rd Street
New York, NY 10036
(212) 944-9800

Fund for Human Dignity
National Gay/Lesbian Clearing House
666 Broadway/4th Floor
New York, NY 10012
(212) 529-1600

**Gay and Lesbian Advocates
  and Defenders**
P.O. Box 218
Boston, MA 02112
(617) 426-1350

National Gay Rights Advocates
540 Castro Street
San Francisco, CA 94114
(415) 863-3624

**National Lawyers Guild Gay
  Caucus**
558 Capp Street
San Francisco, CA 94110
(415) 285-5066

**National Gay and Lesbian Task
  Force**
1517 U Street, NW
Washington, DC 20009
(202) 332-6483

COMING OUT

coming out The public self-disclosure by a homosexual of his or her same-sex preferences.

When gays or lesbians acknowledge, accept, and disclose their same-sex preferences to others it is known as **coming out.** Some gay men and lesbians deny to themselves as well as to others that they are attracted to members of their own sex. Others admit their same-sex preferences to themselves, but not to the heterosexuals around them. Such people typically lead double lives, enjoying same-sex contacts in secret but behaving heterosexually in public. Finally, some gays and lesbians choose to fully disclose their homosexual orientation—a decision for which the full term is "coming out of the closet."

Disclosure is a difficult decision (see the box on "Deciding to Come Out"). Indeed, deciding to come out is often one of the most painful, yet important, decisions a gay or lesbian can make. Since most communities are conservative in their attitudes toward gays and lesbians, there is a justifiable fear of repercussions (Rothbaum, 1988; Padesky, 1988).

In recent years, some people have been forced out of the closet by a practice known as outing. **Outing** refers to the public disclosure, by someone else and without the individual's permission, of a public figure's homosexuality. Outing has created a rift in the gay/lesbian community. Some gay and lesbian rights groups, believing that public figures really have no private lives, publicize the sexual orientation of a gay or lesbian person. This procedure can have severe negative consequences. One is that the "outed" person's family might not have known about the life style before the public revelation, and such a shock could cause a permanent rift. Another is the possible jeopardizing of the "outed" person's job. Those who argue in favor of outing claim it is positive for the gay/lesbian community whenever a person the public has come to accept as talented and as a role model is revealed as gay. How do you feel about the practice of outing? What ethical issues does the disclosure of people's sexual orientation, without their knowledge and very possibly against their will, raise?

outing The public disclosure, by someone else and without the individual's permission, of a public figure's homosexuality.

A Model of the Coming Out Process

Most researchers (e.g., Troiden, 1988; Rothbaum, 1988; Sophie, 1986; Gramick, 1984) acknowledge that the coming out process is a multifaceted transformation. The Australian psychologist Vivienne Cass (1979) examines the dynamics of coming out in a stage-oriented framework. According to her model, if accurate identity formation is to be realized and the coming out process is to be successfully completed, a person must move through six interconnected stages: identity confusion, identity comparison, identity tolerance, identity acceptance, identity pride, and identity synthesis.

Cass based her theory on both her clinical observations and her research data involving gay and lesbian subjects. The stages of her theory are relatively sequential, although sometimes they overlap and recur. In general, however, each stage represents a transformation of the one that preceded it and prepares the way for the next one. In the beginning, she suggests, people perceive themselves and their behavior as heterosexual, but at some point these perceptions change in favor of a same-sex orientation. Cass's model is not an age-stage sequence; that is, she does not propose that the coming out process follows a predictable timetable. While most gay people come out during adolescence, it is not uncommon for self-discovery of a gay/lesbian identity to occur during childhood or adulthood. To make this theory concrete, we will share the experiences of Nancy, whom we met in Chapter 1, as she moves toward coming out.

IDENTITY CONFUSION STAGE. In this stage, people begin to realize that they are different from their peers. Many label their behavior or thoughts as possibly gay or lesbian, but usually they seek to maintain a heterosexual self-image and rarely disclose their feelings to others. A growing sense of inconsistency regarding sexuality becomes evident. Some people deny the personal relevance of information regarding homosexuality or disown responsibility for their own same-sex behavior. While Nancy is dating men, she is beginning to feel that her sexual self-portrait is not what she once thought, and this makes her uncertain and confused. She senses a subtle barrier between herself and her boyfriends, but she denies to herself that her growing interest in her women friends has any relevance to this feeling. Even though she knows that some of her new friends are lesbian, she often remarks to herself, "It has nothing to do with me."

IDENTITY COMPARISON STAGE. People enter this stage when they face the possibility that they might be lesbian or gay. The identity comparison stage is characterized by a heightened sense of alienation and the early relinquishment of a heterosexual orientation. Whereas the previous stage centered on the issue of self-alienation, social alienation becomes more apparent at this time. That is, people feel increasingly different

In the mid-1980s, Barney Frank, Democratic congressman from Massachusetts, found himself embroiled in a scandal involving criminal activity by his lover. In order to extricate himself from the situation, in which he said he had no part, Frank was forced to declare publicly that he was gay.

Sexual Orientation

MAKING USE OF WHAT WE KNOW

Deciding to Come Out: Guidelines for Disclosure

*M*aking the coming out decision is usually difficult. There are no rules for coming out, and each person needs to clearly understand why he or she wants to share this information with others. Moreover, people need to assess the possible consequences, both positive and negative, of doing so. It is also important to recognize that for most homosexuals, coming out proves a never-ending process and decisions about disclosure have to be made again and again in different contexts (Silberman & Hawkins, 1988).

Because of the stigma attached to same-sex preference, many gay men and lesbians choose to remain secretive about their sexual orientation. Others, though, find that coming out makes life easier. Obviously, the matter rests on individual choice and the presenting set of circumstances. For those thinking of choosing disclosure, particularly to their families, Betty Berzon (1984) offers the following advice:

■ *Before you disclose, spend some time gathering your thoughts.* You need to examine your attitudes about being gay and clarify why you feel like disclosing at this particular time. If you have mixed feelings, these will probably be conveyed and the disclosure process may turn out to be a negative experience.

■ *Consider when and where to disclose.* If possible, don't make a disclosure when other events are likely to absorb the listener's attention. Choose a quiet, private location where there are no distractions, and budget plenty of time for reactions, questions, and discussions.

■ *Try to accentuate the positive reasons for your disclosure.* Avoid such openers as "I have something terrible to tell you," and "You're not going to like this, but . . ." A better beginning would

be, "There is something about me I want to tell you because I care about you, and I want to be able to share more of myself with you."

■ *Once disclosure occurs, be prepared for questions.* Questions usually abound, although all of them may not be asked right away. Some of the more common ones are: How long have you been gay or lesbian? Are you sure you are gay? Have you tried to change? Are you happy? Do you think you'll always be gay? Have you told anyone else? In preparation for questions such as these, you might read some of the lesbian/gay-affirming books on the market. One of the better ones about disclosure is called *Coming Out to Your Parents*, published by Parents and Friends of Lesbians and Gays (P.O. Box 15711, Philadelphia, PA 19103).

■ *Realize that guilt is a common parental reaction.* No matter how good a job you do with your disclosure, many parents will relate the information to their own homophobic conditioning. You might want to assure them that they did nothing wrong and that it is unnecessarily self-punishing for them to view your homosexuality as a result of bad parenting. It is also inaccurate, since the determinants of sexual orientation are unknown.

■ *Give people time to adjust.* Different people adjust in different ways. While some may be totally accepting from the beginning, others may become sad or angry, and still others may become silent or withdrawn. Some may be hungry for more information, others may not want to hear another word on the subject. You need to provide time and understanding. Be available for follow-up questions and discussions, but don't be pushy. Keep your perspective and try to normalize the topic of your gayness by talking about it naturally, as a part of your life.

from their families, friends, and society as a whole. For Nancy at this stage, giving up a heterosexual orientation is troublesome, particularly because she now lacks behavioral guidelines and expectations for her future. Complicating matters, she keeps her sexual orientation a secret, which adds to her unsettled feelings and emotions.

Three techniques for dealing with alienation are commonly observed during this stage. First, people may react positively to being different and de-emphasize the importance of heterosexuals in their lives. Or they may accept the gay/lesbian definition of their *behavior*, but reject the definition of their total *self* as homosexual. By compartmentalizing their sexuality and keeping it separate from other aspects of their lives, people feel less alienated from the important heterosexuals in their lives. The third way of dealing with the alienation experienced in this stage is for people to accept themselves and their behavior as gay, but inwardly fear negative reactions from others should they find out. To cope with this fear, people will inhibit overtly gay behavior, devalue homosexuality, and give greater emphasis to heterosexuality.

IDENTITY TOLERANCE STAGE. The third stage occurs with the recognition of the sexual, emotional, and social needs that go along with being lesbian or gay. People at this stage are aware that they are probably gay, and many of them seek out other gays to combat their feelings of alienation. At this point, Nancy begins talking with her college friends about her sexual orientation. To her relief, these friends give her considerable support, understanding, and compassion. As a result, her self-concept becomes more positive.

IDENTITY ACCEPTANCE STAGE. Contact with other gays escalates in this stage and new friendships are forged. At this point, people accept rather than tolerate their gay self-image and evaluate other gays more positively. Many deliberately reduce their contacts with heterosexuals, and some make selective disclosures of their sexual orientation to family and friends. Still, many people going through this stage want to fit into society as unobtrusively as possible. This is the case with Nancy, who is now more comfortable with her sexual identity and has developed positive identification with other lesbians, but is determined not to make waves. She feels that being gay is acceptable in private, but thinks that being totally public about it is not for her at this time.

IDENTITY PRIDE STAGE. A "them and us" attitude permeates stage five. People who reach this stage have usually nurtured a full legitimization of the gay/lesbian self and

"HE ASKED ME ABOUT SOME OF MY LOVERS. THAT DIDN'T BOTHER ME, AND I ASKED HIM ABOUT SOME OF HIS LOVERS. WELL, THAT DID BOTHER ME. IT SEEMS SOME OF MY LOVERS WERE SOME OF HIS LOVERS."

intensified their identification with the gay/lesbian community. For Nancy, daily contact with heterosexuals and homophobic attitudes generates feelings of alienation and frustration. She reacts with anger toward heterosexuals, but in the process comes to feel proud of her sexual orientation. She increasingly abandons her earlier strategies to conceal her homosexuality and becomes more deeply involved in the gay and lesbian subculture.

IDENTITY SYNTHESIS STAGE. The homosexual identity is interwoven with all other aspects of the total self in this stage, which marks the completion of the identity formation process. The anger toward heterosexuals prevalent in the previous stage lessens. Nancy recognizes that some heterosexuals can be trusted, but she finds herself devaluing those who are nonsupportive. Finally, she discovers that her sense of pride has grown deeper.

SEXUALITY IN THE NEWS

Insurance for Domestic Partners
by Claudia H. Deutsch

*F*ive years ago, Berkeley, Calif., became the first American municipality to offer medical benefits to the live-in partners—both gay and heterosexual—of unmarried employees. The Bay Area's high incidence of AIDS led many doomsayers to predict that Berkeley's insurance claims, and thus its premium costs, would skyrocket.

Neither has happened. "Our health-care costs haven't gone up any more than anyone else's," said Michael Brown, city manager.

Neither have those at The Village Voice newspaper, which has offered domestic-partner benefits since 1982; or at Ben & Jerry's Homemade Inc., [which offers employees such benefits] after two years; or the American Friends Service Committee, the Quaker group, after five years. Moreover, although most domestic-partner plans are written at the behest of gay employees, they are used more by unmarried heterosexuals.

"Smoking and exercise are better predictors of who will file claims than are sexual orientation or marital status," said Lyn S. Thompson, vice president of the Washington-based Consumers United Insurance Company, the only insurer that routinely includes domestic partners in its policies.

Many nonprofit groups, including Greenpeace, the National Organization for Women, and Planned Parenthood, offer domestic-partner benefits. So do several cities, including Seattle; Santa Cruz, Calif., and Madison, Wis. But in the private sector, benefits for nonspousal partners remain controversial.

Proponents say that companies have no right to discriminate on the basis of marital status—particularly when they are increasing medical benefits to part-time workers, and offering day care and dependent care leave to other employee groups. And they say the payback is immeasurable. "This benefit yielded a lot of good will when the wage package was not good," said Jeff Weinstein, a Village Voice senior editor.

But opponents insist that, with health-care costs skyrocketing, this is no time to consider adding to benefits packages. "Our health-care costs are exorbitant enough," said Mary Gross, a spokeswoman for Levi-Strauss, which has been on the cutting edge of family benefits.

William B. Rubenstein, director of the American Civil Liberties Union's Lesbian and Gay Rights Project, says that attitude is rampant. "The movement to expand benefits to more groups is running smack into programs to cut costs," he said.

Domestic-partner benefits also face huge resistance from the insurance industry. Although the Health Insurance Association of America says its members are rarely asked to write domestic-partner policies, West Hollywood, Calif., and several other employers were forced to self-insure because no company would provide domestic-partner benefits.

Employees of the American Psychological Association can only get domestic-partner coverage through the Insurance Trust, a plan for association members that carries higher premiums and deductibles than the Aetna Life and Casualty plan that most employees use. And Liberty Mutual, which administers the trust, insists on a one-year wait before providing coverage, to guard against pre-existing conditions and against anyone passing off a casual friend as a long-term partner.

"We've been insuring spouse-equivalents since 1983, and they haven't filed higher claims than anyone else, yet that's still the best plan we can get," said Margaret A. Bogie, the trust's executive administrator.

Independence Blue Cross in Philadelphia also remains unconvinced that claims on this type of coverage can stay low. Five years ago it reluctantly agreed to insure domestic partners of American Friends' employees. Bessie L. Williamson, American Friends' assistant treasurer, says that unmarried couples have not filed more claims than married ones. Yet the insurer has turned down requests for similar policies from other clients and insists that the American Friends' policies be written as separate, single contracts.

"Our actuaries are concerned that enrolling domestic partners would increase claims," said David Bongiovanni, the insurer's deputy general counsel.

Employee groups keep pressing for domestic-partner benefits. Kathleen M. Chaplin, Ben & Jerry's personnel operations manager, has had some 35 calls from people asking her for advice on how to get their employers to offer such benefits.

Similarly, consultants report that while their clients would probably like to ignore the issue, their employees simply will not let them. "Pressure is percolating up from the work place," said Frank B. McArdle, a benefits specialist with Hewitt Associates. "It's not a groundswell, but it's there." (*The New York Times*, July 28, 1991. Copyright © 1991 by The New York Times Company. Reprinted by permission.)

DISCUSSION QUESTIONS

1. Why are insurance benefits for nonmarried couples highly controversial in the private sector? How would you counter the argument that such benefits will raise costs for the employers?

2. How can employees who want domestic-partner benefits convince employers to provide appropriate coverage?

3. Why do you suppose the employers mentioned in this article—such as Ben and Jerry's, the American Friends Service Committee, and Greenpeace—have agreed to provide domestic-partner coverage for their employees? (Note that, although a private-sector company, Ben and Jerry's has donated money and staff time to a number of social service efforts.)

LOOKING BACK

- The direction of our preferences for partners, including sexual as well as affectional attraction, is known as sexual orientation. A heterosexual sexual orientation refers to attraction to members of the other sex; a homosexual sexual orientation refers to attraction to members of the same sex; and bisexual sexual orientation refers to sexual attraction and emotional attachment to both women and men.

- It is hard to assess the prevalence of the different sexual orientations. Alfred Kinsey maintained that pure heterosexuality and pure homosexuality are extreme poles on a continuum, and that in between we find many people whose experiences and behaviors combine both. When statistics are analyzed according to Kinsey's classification, about 75–85 percent of men and 80–90 percent of women are exclusively heterosexual, about 4 percent of men and 2 percent of women are exclusively homosexual, and about 15 percent of men and 10 percent of women have bisexual preferences. Since Kinsey's time, these prevalences have remained about the same.

- Throughout history, being lesbian or gay has been both endorsed and denounced. In our society, people have attempted to control homosexuality by creating strong legal and social sanctions against it. Same-sex preference has not been considered a form of abnormal behavior or mental illness by the psychiatric profession since 1973, when it was eliminated as a category of mental disorder from the American Psychiatric Association's classification of mental disorders. There are three principal views on the etiology of sexual orientation: the biological, psychological, and interactionist perspectives.

■ Research illustrates how diversified gay and lesbian life styles are. Models of gay and lesbian relationships tend to show that the differences that exist between men and women are much greater than those that exist between heterosexuals and gays/lesbians, and that the sexual behavior of lesbians/gays and heterosexuals is very similar. Many gays and lesbians today are choosing to raise children in a family unit, which often creates legal problems. However, most research shows that the aspirations of gay and lesbian parents do not differ from those of heterosexual parents, and there is no support for the claim that they serve as poor role models.

■ Bisexuality is not well understood, but most evidence shows that bisexuals tend to prefer one sex over the other. Most bisexuals first eroticize the other sex and identify as heterosexuals. Then, during their 20s or 30s, they discover homosexual interests as well. Sometimes lifelong homosexuals develop a heterosexual interest later in life and become bisexual.

■ Gays and lesbians face considerable prejudice, discrimination, alienation, and ridicule. They often en-counter personal attacks, including jokes about their sexual orientation, harassment in the workplace, and raids on their meeting places. Homophobia, or anti-homosexual feeling, is at the root of prejudice and discrimination against gays. Homophobia is often found in people who also espouse heterosexism, the belief that heterosexuality is the only acceptable and viable life option. Gays, lesbians, and bisexuals have banded together in organizations such as the National Gay and Lesbian Task Force to try to change public attitudes, policy, and law.

■ Coming out is the acknowledgement, acceptance, and disclosure of one's same-sex preferences. Outing is a type of forced coming out in which a public figure's same-sex preference is publicly disclosed by someone else and without the public figure's permission. The Cass model of the coming out process proposes a six-stage evolution: identity confusion, identity comparison, identity tolerance, identity acceptance, identity pride, and identity synthesis.

THINKING THINGS OVER

1. How do you think most lesbians and gays in the United States feel about their role in society and about society's attitudes and behavior toward them? On what do you base your belief?

2. Can you think of three gays and three lesbians who are "out" on your campus? Are these people well-accepted members of your college community? If not, what factors do you believe have impeded their acceptance?

3. How would you explain to your best friend that you are straight? Gay? Lesbian? Bisexual? Do you believe it is nec-essary to explain your sexual preference to others? Why or why not?

4. If there's a gay-lesbian-bisexual student-staff organization on your campus, find out why it was formed. If there is no such organization, try to discover whether there are people who feel such a group would be useful.

5. How do *you* define heterosexism? Is it a valid or invalid concept? Why or why not?

DISCOVER FOR YOURSELF

Blumenfeld, W. J., & Raymond, D. (1988). *Looking at gay and lesbian life*. Boston, MA: Beacon Press. The authors present a well-researched text on virtually every aspect of gay and lesbian life.

Clunis, D. M., & Green, G. D. (1988). *Lesbian couples*. Seattle, WA: Seal Press. An interesting look at lesbian life, including stages of relationships, sexuality, and work and money.

DeCecco, J. (ed.) (1988). *Gay relationships*. New York: Harrington Park Press. Of particular interest are the sections dealing with how to maintain a gay relationship and how to solve relationship problems.

Diamant, L. (ed.) (1987). *Male and female homosexuality: Psychological approaches*. New York: Hemisphere Publishing. Covers theories and research, clinical concerns, and society and the homosexual individual.

Klein, F., & Wolf, T. J. (eds.) (1985). *Two lives to lead: Bisexuality in men and women*. New York: Harrington Park Press. A good collection of research articles on the complexities of bisexuality.

McWhirter, D. P., & Mattison, A. M. (1984). *The male couple: How relationships develop*. Englewood Cliffs, NJ: Prentice Hall. A thorough analysis of the stages in a male homosexual relationship.

10
Conception and Pregnancy

*His own parents,
he that father'd him
and she that had
conceived him in her
womb and birth'd
him. They gave this
child more of
themselves than that,
they gave him
afterward everyday,
they became part
of him*

—Walt Whitman

*Oh, what a power is
motherhood!*

—Euripides

LOOKING AHEAD

In this chapter you'll discover:

☐ *The motivations couples share for having children.*

☐ *How conception occurs and prenatal development unfolds during a woman's pregnancy.*

☐ *What infertility is and what types of medical interventions are available for infertile couples who want children.*

☐ *What kinds of prenatal problems can interfere with labor and delivery.*

☐ *How fetal problems and defects can be detected and treated.*

A child is born—we call it the miracle of life. A single fleck of tissue has transformed itself into a fully developed human being that at birth weighs on the average six to seven pounds and measures between 18 and 21 inches head to toe. The processes and events responsible for intrauterine development are one of nature's astounding accomplishments.

The manner in which conception occurs and prenatal development proceeds has long aroused our interest. The Greek physician Hippocrates (460?–377? B.C.) maintained that both the man's testes and the woman's ovaries produced semen, a substance that somehow triggered the beginning of life. Aristotle downplayed the role of women in conception, though, asserting instead that they were merely passive participants in the whole process whose only function was to provide the shelter of their bodies as unborn children grew. Historians tell us that Aristotle's theory endured for centuries.

Other thoughts and beliefs on how conception occurred would ultimately surface. During the 1600s, many argued that prenatal life began with a completely formed miniature human being. However, no one really knew where this preformed human being originated. One theory proposed that it was contained in the head of the sperm and grew only when it reached the incubatorlike safety of the womb. Another line of thought led to just the opposite conclusion: the preformed fetus was contained within the mother's egg and was activated when sperm made contact.

It wasn't until the 1700s that true scientific reasoning emerged. In 1759 researcher Kaspar Wolff wrote that both parents play equal roles in conception and that the organism gradually grew over nine months' time. In 1827 Karl von Baer further disproved the preformed fetus theory by showing how cell reproduction supplies the true building blocks of life. In 1843 Martin Barrie described with great accuracy the manner in which the sperm and egg combine to create a new organism.

These advances were only the beginning. In time, other important discoveries would be made, scientific explanations that further unraveled the mysteries surrounding the beginnings of life. It was from these efforts that the science of embryology was born. With it came a more exact understanding of reproductive processes and the nature of life in the womb.

Despite our growing knowledge, many people harbor inaccurate beliefs about the way in which life begins. For a few such mistaken notions, see the "Myths and Misconceptions" box.

WHY HAVE CHILDREN?

Couples report many reasons for having children (Turner & Helms, 1988). For many people, children are an extension of the self or a source of personal fulfillment and satisfaction. Some couples want children because they enhance the couple's identity.

One of the most compelling reasons for a couple to have a baby is the desire for something that belongs to both of them. A child is a couple's own, to love and to care for, and represents a part of each of them. The bond that forms between parent and child is one of the strongest human connections.

Due dates can be precisely calculated.

*T*he chances are only 8 percent that a women will give birth on the exact due date calculated (Shapiro, 1983). This is because many physicians calculate the due date from the first day of the woman's last menstrual period rather than from the actual onset of pregnancy, which begins with fertilization just after ovulation. Unless couples know exactly the date of conception, a due date is only an approximation. Even with precise knowledge of the time of conception, the delivery date can vary a great deal, for while the average full-term pregnancy lasts about 266 days from conception to full term, some are as long as 300 days and others as short as 240 days (Shapiro, 1983; Lauersen, 1983).

Small-breasted women should not plan on breast-feeding their baby.

This is a misconception because breast size gives no indication of how much milk breasts can produce. Recall from Chapter 3 that larger breasts are large because they contain more fat, not more milk ducts. Since it is the glandular tissue that produces breast milk, almost every woman can produce milk after her baby is born. And the more a baby nurses, the more milk a mother's body produces.

The pregnant mother and fetus share the same bloodstream.

Although in the placenta blood vessels from the mother and the fetus intermingle, there is no mixing of maternal and fetal bloodstreams. The two bloodstreams are separate, and substances that pass from the mother to the fetus (or vice versa) have to emerge from one bloodstream and cross the placenta before they can enter the other bloodstream.

A pregnant woman should "eat for two."

The generally recommended weight gain during pregnancy is about 25 to 30 pounds. This includes the extra weight of the fetus, placenta, expanded uterus, amniotic fluid, enlarged breasts, and other body changes. If a woman gains more than 30 pounds, she'll have extra pounds to lose even after she's shed her pregnancy-related weight. This extra weight does not enhance the nourishment of the baby and can make the mother feel sluggish during and after her pregnancy. Although she needn't eat for two, the pregnant woman may need extra doses of certain vitamins and minerals to meet her baby's requirements for nourishment (Cherry, 1990).

Infertility and sterility are synonymous.

Sterility is the *permanent* inability to conceive a child. *Infertility* refers to the inability to achieve pregnancy after at least one year of regular, unprotected intercourse, and it is curable for most people. In about 75 percent of infertility cases, conception is possible with the use of drugs and/or microsurgery. Reproductive technologies such as in vitro fertilization and artificial insemination provide hope for the remaining percentage of infertile couples, as we discuss elsewhere in the chapter.

MYTHS AND MISCONCEPTIONS

Misperceptions About Conception and Pregnancy

Other partners desire children because they look forward to the companionship that youngsters will bring. Some become parents because they want to nurture, teach, motivate, and help children become happy and mature beings. Others become parents to give their children what they themselves never had. Still others maintain that children will provide security to them when they're old. Finally, many couples have children because society expects it of them; it is what married people do.

Two fathers reflect on some reasons for having children:

Having children was always something Peggy and I wanted. When we were engaged, we always talked about how we really wanted to be

parents someday. As I think back, it was never a matter of not wanting children, but rather how many.

Would you believe it just happened? We really didn't intend to have a child, but I was out of condoms and we thought it was a safe time for my wife. We took the chance and Sue became pregnant. As it turns out, we're both glad it happened. (Authors' files)

Two mothers had these thoughts:

We both wanted children, but we were also both heavily involved in our careers. We agreed to work for a while in order to establish some financial security. I can remember while we waited, a lot of our married friends were having children. We became a bit envious of their happiness, and it was hard to stick to our career plans. We wanted to be just as happy and fulfilled as parents. When Don and I eventually conceived, it was like a dream come true.

I think in the beginning I wanted to have a child more than Paul. While he wasn't opposed to the idea, I always seemed to be the one who brought up the topic. Part of the reason was that I was an only child and wanted to have a lot of kids when I got older. We talked at length about having a child and finally agreed to give it a try. Four months later I was pregnant. (Authors' files)

Modern contraception methods (see Chapter 12) have brought about a small revolution of choice concerning parenthood. If people conscientiously use an effective means of birth control, parenthood can indeed be an option today. Contemporary Americans subscribe to a different set of values than those prevalent at the beginning or even the middle of this century. Couples can choose to remain childless, have one, two, or more children, or begin having children in their 40s.

Parenthood has also become an option for single people. There are many children available for adoption and just as many qualified single adults who decide they want to raise a child. Furthermore, single women and men are choosing to have their own biological children by artificial insemination or other means.

Some lesbians and gay men also choose to become parents. Many lesbian and gay partners either adopt children or have their own. While society has not embraced this idea, the more lesbian and gay couples who are courageous enough to pursue this option, the easier it may be for those partners to live comfortably in our society.

CONCEPTION AND THE JOURNEY TO THE WOMB

How does conception occur?

You will recall from Chapter 3 that each month, approximately halfway through the 28-day menstrual cycle, one of a woman's ovaries releases a mature egg, or ovum. Gently pushed by cilia, the fine hairlike projectiles that line the fallopian tube, this egg begins about a week's journey to the uterus. The uterine walls have been accumulating a large supply of blood vessels to nourish the egg if it is fertilized in the fallopian tube. If the egg remains unfertilized, it disintegrates and is discharged from the body with the built-up uterine lining as the menstrual flow.

Because sperm only have an effective life of about 72 hours and the egg an even shorter life, conception must occur within 24 to 36 hours of ovulation. Once ejaculation has taken place, sperm do not move well in the vagina's acidic environment, and many are killed by the hostile fluids. A number of sperm also die because of defects in their structure—for example, many lack the proper tail structure and never demonstrate the needed motility to reach a fallopian tube. Some travel along the wrong fallopian tube and degenerate without ever reaching their proper destination. Surviving sperm will travel a little less than half an inch every five minutes. About 300 from the original millions that started the journey will travel along the correct fallopian tube and reach the female ovum. Usually, this happens between 45 and 90 minutes after ejaculation. Once one sperm has penetrated the ovum, the ovum becomes impervious to other sperm.

The fertilized egg, containing its own 23 chromosomes plus the 23 chromosomes from the sperm, is called an **embryo.** The embryonic period lasts roughly eight weeks. The embryo goes through two stages of development. At first, as a *zygote*, it drifts down the four-inch fallopian tube toward the uterus. During its journey, it begins to divide and multiply to form new cells. By the time the zygote reaches the uterus, which takes about three days, the original cell has become a tiny sphere called a *blastocyst*. The blastocyst, which now contains about 60 cells, is filled with fluid and covered by an outer layer of cells called the *trophoblast*. The trophoblast helps the blastocyst implant itself in the uterine wall and eventually gives rise to the placenta. The process of implantation takes between 7 and 10 days. Figure 10–1 illustrates the way conception and implantation take place.

embryo The developing organism during the first eight weeks of prenatal life.

PRENATAL DEVELOPMENT

The duration of pregnancy can be divided into three equal segments called **trimesters** (a trimester is a period of about three months). As one can see, each month within the trimesters reflects a distinct phase of prenatal growth and development (see Table 10–1). Let's examine these three trimesters and the changes that take place during them.

trimester Term referring to the duration of pregnancy. Pregnancy is divided into three trimesters, each lasting about three months.

FIGURE 10–1
Conception and Implantation.

A sperm fertilizes the egg after it is released from the ovary and has begun to travel through the fallopian tube. About 10 days later, the fertilized egg implants itself in the uterine wall.

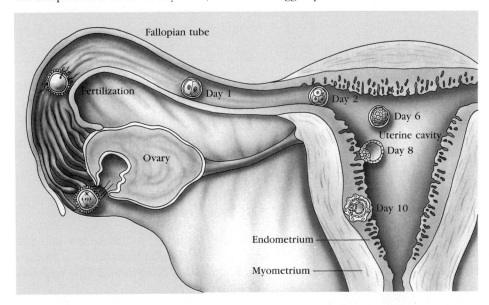

TABLE 10–1

Some Significant Prenatal Developments

Age in Months	Size and Weight	BODY SYSTEM				
		Skin, Nails, Hair, etc.	Skeletal	Muscular	Nervous	Sensory
1	0.2 in. 0.007 oz.				**B:** Neural tube (precursor of system)	**B:** Eyes, ears
2	1.1 in. 0.09 oz.	**B:** Nail beds, hair follicles, sweat glands	**B:** Formation of cartilage		**B:** CNS and PNS organization, growth of cerebrum	**B:** Taste buds, olfactory tissue
3	3.2 in. 1.6 oz.	**B:** Skin layers	**B:** Bone formation from cartiege	**C:** Rudiments of musculature	**C:** Basic spinal cord and brain structure	
4	5.3 in. 5 oz.	**B:** Hair, oil glands **C:** Sweat glands	**B:** Articulation of system; facial and palatal organization	Fetus starts to move	**B:** Rapid expansion of cerebrum	**C:** Eyes, ear structure
5	8 in. 1 lb. 1 oz.	**B:** Nail production				
6	11.2 in. 1 lb. 10 oz.			**C:** Perineal muscles	**B:** CNS tract formation; layering of cortex	
7	14–15 in. 2 lb. 11 oz.	**B:** Nail, hair formation				**C:** Eyelids open; retina sensitive to light
8	15–17 in. 4 lb. 6 oz.					Taste receptors functional
9	19–21 in. 6 lb. 10 oz. to 7 lbs. 15 oz.					
Postnatal development		Hair changes in consistency and distribution	Growth continues	Muscle mass and control increase	CNS tract formation continues	

Source: Adapted from Martini, 1992, Table 29–4, pp. 972–973.

The First Trimester

THE FIRST MONTH. When the blastocyst becomes implanted in the uterine wall, the cells begin to exhibit marked differentiation. On the eighteenth day after conception, the embryo's heart structure begins to appear, and by about three weeks the heart has begun to undergo muscle contractions, although it is not under neural control. The

Conception and Pregnancy

Endocrine	Cardiovascular	Respiratory	Digestive	Urinary	Reproductive
	B: Heartbeat	**B:** Lungs and trachea	**B:** Intestinal tract, liver, pancreas		
B: Thymus, thyroid, glands pituitary, adrenal glands	**C:** Basic heart structure, major blood vessels	**B:** Bronchial branching **C:** Diaphragm	**B:** Intestinal subdivisions, salivary glands	**B:** Kidney formation	**B:** Mammary glands
C: Thymus, thyroid	**B:** Blood formation in bone marrow		**C:** Gall bladder, pancreas		**B:** Gonads, genitalia
	B: Blood formation in spleen				
		C: Nostrils open	**C:** Intestinal subdivisions		
C: Adrenal glands	**C:** Spleen, liver, and bone marrow	**B:** Formation of lung alveoli			
C: Pituitary					**B:** Descent of testes
		C: Pulmonary branching and alveolar formation		**C:** Kidney structure	**C:** Descent complete by delivery
	Immune system becomes operative				

B = Development begins; **C** = development is completed.

heart beats and blood pulsates through a small enclosed bloodstream that is separate from the mother's. By the end of the first month, the central nervous system (brain and spinal cord) begins to develop. Specialized cells form a tubelike structure that eventually develops into the spinal column.

Such internal organs as the lungs, liver, kidneys, and endocrine glands are starting to develop, and the digestive system has begun to form. Small "buds" that

Conception and Pregnancy

will eventually become arms and legs start developing by the end of the first month. Throughout the course of prenatal life, leg development lags behind that of the arms. Four weeks after conception, the embryo measures only 0.2 inch in length but is 10,000 times larger than the zygote.

THE SECOND MONTH. As the embryo enters its second month, rapid cell division and specialization continue. By the end of eight weeks, the embryo is just over an inch long and weighs 0.09 oz. A brain with two recognizable lobes has become apparent at the end of the spinal column. The limbs are also enlongating, showing distinct division of knee and elbow, although they are less than ¼ inch long. More specifically, the shoulders, arms, hands, and fingers rapidly develop during the second month. Underneath the tissue of the arms and legs the bones continue to form and are becoming padded with muscles. The internal organs also continue to develop quite rapidly, not only in form and structure, but also in functional properties. For example, the kidneys are capable of moving uric acid from the bloodstream, and the stomach can manufacture primitive digestive juices. By the sixth week, the ears appear, and by the end of the second month, the embryo's facial features look human. The nose, jaw, and eyebrows become recognizable. Also, the external genitalia are evident.

THE THIRD MONTH. The end of the eighth week and the start of the ninth week mark the end of the embryonic period and the start of the **fetal period** (or the third through the ninth month of prenatal life). From now on, the developing organism is referred to as a **fetus.** During this time, the brain and spinal cord continue to mature. Brain cell development is especially rapid, and the brain's major structures begin to take shape. Also, the progressive maturation of both nerves and muscles, which leads to generalized movements in response to external stimulation, now occurs. The baby will also turn as early as the ninth or tenth week (although the mother will be unaware of all this activity).

By the end of 12 weeks, the fetus can kick, curl the toes and fingers, move the thumb, and even squint in response to external stimulation. The fetus is now just over 3 inches long and weighs 1.6 oz. Arms, hands, fingers, legs, feet, and toes are now fully formed. Even nails are developing on the fingers and toes. Tiny tooth sockets, complete with the "buds" of future teeth, are present in the jawbone. The eyes, almost fully developed, have lids that remain fused.

By the end of the this trimester, a very tiny but highly complex organism is in utero. Other developments reveal how complex the organism has become. For example, the nerves and muscles have tripled in number. The heart can now be heard by use of special instruments, the kidneys are operable, and sexual development has reached the stage where sex can be ascertained. Meanwhile, the soft cartilaginous substance of the ribs and vertebrae have turned to bone.

INTRAUTERINE STRUCTURES AND MECHANISMS. Within the mother's womb, fetal life is sustained by a vital support system consisting of an amniotic sac, placenta, and umbilical cord. Enveloping the fetus is a transparent membrane called the **amniotic sac.** Contained within the sac is **amniotic fluid,** which holds the fetus in suspension and protects it not only from being jarred but also from any pressures exerted by the mother's internal organs. It also serves to provide an even temperature for the fetus.

Attached to the uterine wall is the **placenta,** or afterbirth. This is a membrane that allows nourishment to pass from mother to embryo and for waste products to be channeled from embryo to mother. It should be noted here that there is no direct connection of blood vessels between mother and embryo. Substances are transmitted to and from the mother's and embryo's blood vessels via the placenta. As we'll see shortly, the placenta is not a barrier, and many substances—for example, drugs like aspirin—cross it. Sole source of food, oxygen, and water for the unborn, the placenta

A Close-Up View of Conception and the Developing Fetus.

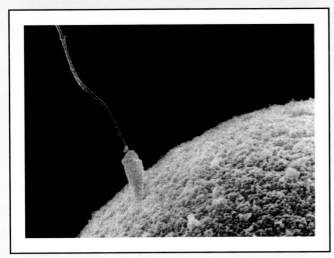

Although several hundred sperm finish the race to the awaiting ovum, only one succeeds in fertilizing the egg. The fertilized egg is called the zygote.

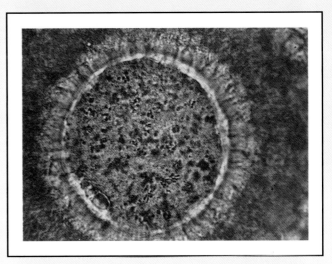

The zygote before it begins a series of many cell divisions.

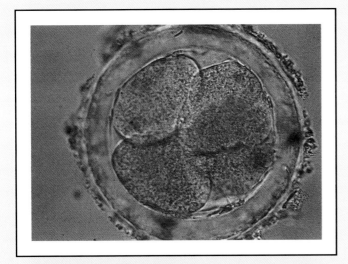

At about the second day after fertilization, the zygote has divided into four distinct cells.

The zygote continues to subdivide, and on the 7th or 8th day it is ready to implant itself in the uterine wall.

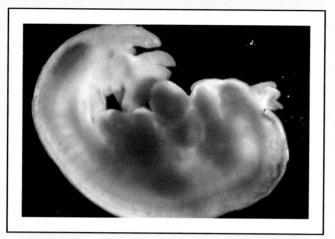

The embryo's heart structure is well underway at 4–5 weeks. One can see the neural tube, stretching from the top of the head to the tail.

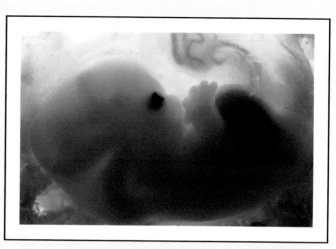

Although barely an inch long, this 7-week embryo clearly has human form. Its head has taken shape, and one can see its eye socket, hand, and fingers.

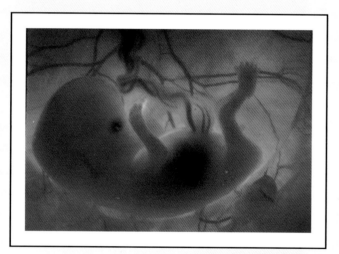

At 11–12 weeks the formation of the fetus's brain and spinal cord is nearly complete, and the skeletal structure and musculature have begun to form; you can see that the arms and legs are clearly defined.

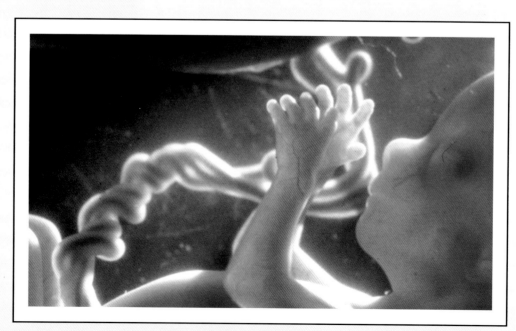

In the fourth month, the fetus's nose and mouth have developed, and its hands and fingers are well formed. The umbilical cord, with its vein and arteries, and the placenta are clearly visible.

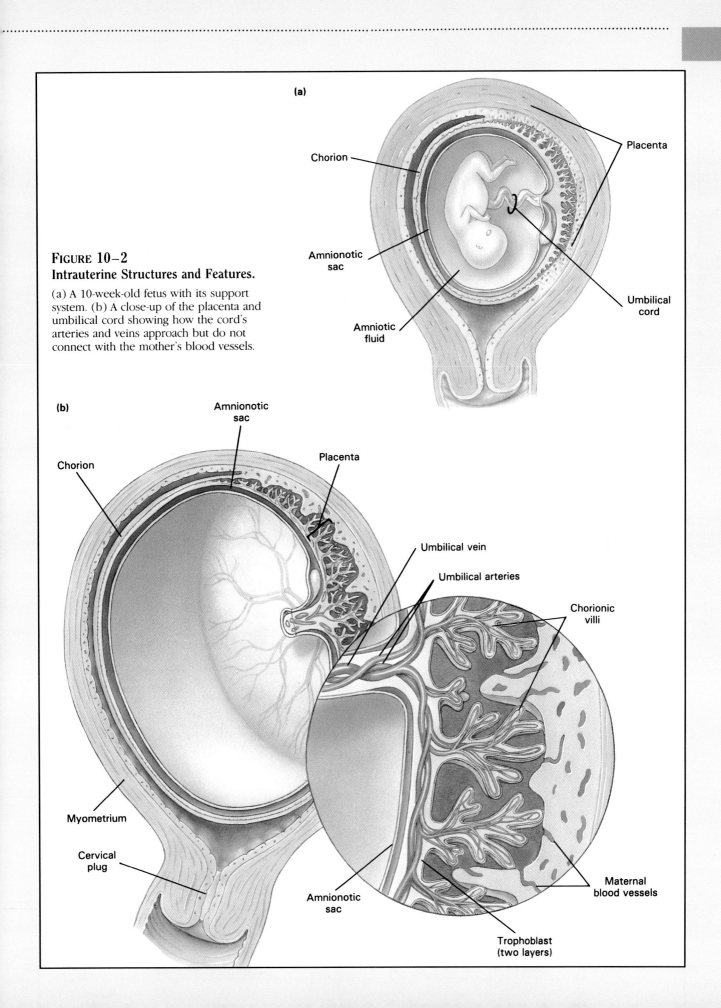

(a)

Chorion

Placenta

Amnionotic
sac

Amniotic
fluid

Umbilical
cord

FIGURE 10–2
Intrauterine Structures and Features.

(a) A 10-week-old fetus with its support
system. (b) A close-up of the placenta and
umbilical cord showing how the cord's
arteries and veins approach but do not
connect with the mother's blood vessels.

(b)

Amnionotic
sac

Chorion

Placenta

Umbilical vein

Umbilical arteries

Chorionic
villi

Myometrium

Cervical
plug

Amnionotic
sac

Trophoblast
(two layers)

Maternal
blood vessels

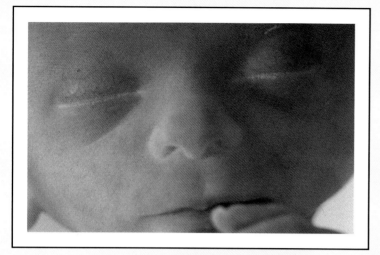

At five months the face is strikingly like that of a newborn, although the eyelids are still fused. The nose is fully developed and the nostrils are open. Note the baby's fingers at its mouth; thumb-sucking begins about this time.

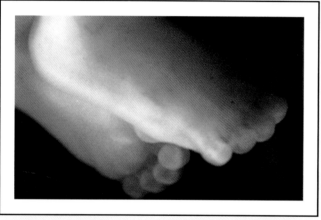

The fetus's feet at five and a half months look much like yours or mine. The heel and metatarsal arch can be seen clearly, and the toes are fully formed.

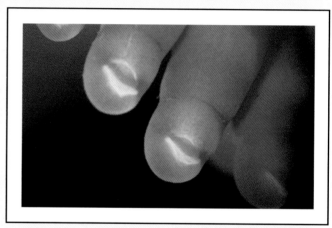

In this close-up of the fetus's fingers you can see the nail beds. Nail production continues throughout the 5th and 6th months.

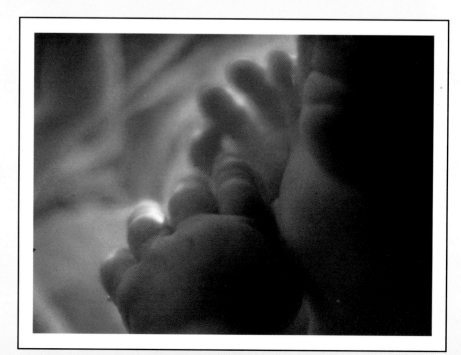

Between the fifth and sixth month the fetus sucks its thumb with gusto. In the background you can see a part of the umbilical cord as well as the filmy amniotic sac that encloses and protects the fetus.

must grow in relation to the organism's needs. Originally microscopic in size, at birth the placenta is about 6 to 8 inches in diameter, a little over an inch in thickness, and weighs about 14 to 21 ounces.

Connecting the placenta to the fetus is the **umbilical cord.** The umbilical cord contains three blood vessels: one a vein carrying oxygenated blood from the placenta to the fetus, and two arteries that carry blood and waste products from the fetus to the placenta. Since the umbilical cord is without nerves, clamping and cutting the "belly button" at delivery is a painless matter. At birth, the umbilical cord averages $^8/_{10}$ inch in diameter and is about 21 inches in length. Figure 10–2 (see color plate) displays these intrauterine features, as well as close-ups of the placenta and umbilical cord.

umbilical cord A cord connecting the placenta to the developing organism. It contains three blood vessels: a vein carrying oxygenated blood from the placenta to the organism, and two arteries that carry blood and waste products from the organism to the placenta.

The Second Trimester

THE FOURTH MONTH. The fetus now approaches over 5 inches in length and weighs approximately 5 ounces. The head is disproportionately large in comparison to the rest of the body, and the brain's major structures resemble those of an adult. A strong heartbeat is present, along with a fairly well-developed digestive system. The eyebrows and genital organs are quite noticeable. Since the fetus is now quite active (its mouth can open and close), there is an increase in the intake of food, oxygen, and water. The placenta has increased from three to four inches in diameter, allowing for a more rapid exchange of nutrients and waste products between mother and fetus. In appearance, the fetal skin is translucent because of the blood flowing through the circulatory vessels and the lack of pigmentation in the skin.

quickening Fetal movements that can be felt by the mother. Quickening usually begins between 16 and 18 weeks.

THE FIFTH MONTH. By the end of 20 weeks, a rapid increase in body size has occurred. The fetus is now 8 inches long and weighs just over 1 pound, a considerable gain from the four ounces of 16 weeks earlier. The eyelids are still fused shut and a fine downy growth of hair termed *lanugo* appears on the entire body. The skin is also usually covered with a waxylike substance called the *vernix caseosa*. Its purpose is to protect the fetus from constant exposure to the amniotic fluid. The internal organs are rapidly maturing with the exception of the lungs, which lag behind in development.

At between 16 and 18 weeks the first fetal movements are usually felt by the mother. This is known technically as **quickening.** As time progresses, the mother will become very much aware of the ripplings and flutterings inside her. The fetus now has both sleeping and waking moments. During wakefulness the fetus cries, sucks its thumb, hiccups, and performs somersaults!

....
The first time an expectant mother feels her baby move can be a joyous event. It's the first tangible and personal proof she has of her baby's existence, and it heightens her feelings of connection with her child.

THE SIXTH MONTH. Just about a foot in length, the six-month-old fetus has started accumulating subcutaneous fat and now weighs up to 1 pound 10 oz. The skin becomes coarser and develops more pigmentation, and hair grows on the head. The eyelids have separated and tiny eyelashes can now be observed. The fingernails extend to the end of the fingers, and the fetus can now make a fist. A hardening of the bones has also begun. Despite all these signs of maturity, the fetus has only a slim chance of survival if it is born at this point in the pregnancy. The primary reason for death in premature infants is immaturity of the lungs and kidneys.

The Third Trimester

The third trimester, consisting of the seventh, eighth, and ninth months of pregnancy, is marked primarily by rapid gains in growth and weight. The fetus grows in length by 50 percent and gains nearly six pounds in the last three months. During the last two months the fetus gains an average of a half-pound a week. The brain's cortical

Conception and Pregnancy

MAKING USE
OF WHAT
WE KNOW

Choosing a
Pediatrician

pediatrician A specialist in
the treatment of children, including hygienic care and
diseases particular to them.

*B*efore the baby is born, it is important for couples to choose a pediatrician. A **pediatrician** is a medical doctor who will provide health-care services
to the baby after it is born. The pediatrician can be in the delivery room as part
of the team that examines and cares for
the newborn. The pediatrician will be
alert for any immediate problems in the
newborn's adjustment to life outside the
womb.

Couples should do research and
decide on a pediatrician as carefully as

- Does the pediatrician have a private
  practice? If so, how can he or she be
  reached when not available at the office? If the pediatrician is a member of
  a group practice, who provides care for
  what and when?

- Is the pediatrician board certified in
  pediatrics? What hospital(s) is the pediatrician affiliated with? Which one(s)
  would you have to take the baby to if
  the need arises?

- Does the pediatrician make house
  calls? If an emergency arises outside
  regular office hours, can you get telephone advice? If yes, how?

possible. Suggestions can be sought from
the woman's obstetrician or other professional providing maternity care, other expectant parents in prenatal classes, or a
childbirth educator. Family care providers, neighbors, relatives and friends are
other possible sources.

Once a couple has narrowed down
the possibilities, they should interview
the few pediatricians they are seriously
considering. Any good professional wel-
comes such an interview. The following
questions are worth asking:

- What does a regular office examination
  of a baby entail?

- What are the fees for starting care of
  the baby (including examination after
  birth)? What are the fees should complications be encountered? What are
  the fees for regular office care, including immunizations? What are the fees
  for special services, such as laboratory
  tests and special examinations?

- Which health-care insurance plans
  does the pediatrician accept for payment? Is payment accepted directly
  from the insurance company? (Adapted
  from Lubvic & Hawes, 1987)

areas for motor and sensory behaviors continue to mature, and there is rapid development of the reflexes that will be seen at birth. The cortex also exhibits pronounced
growth during these final months. During the eighth month, a male fetus's testes
begin their descent toward the scrotum. As growth increases (much of the weight
gain is subcutaneous fat) and the uterus becomes cramped, fetal movements are
curtailed.

An important task for the parents during the last trimester is to select a physician
for their baby—a specialist who will care for their child from birth throughout
childhood. The "Making Use of What We Know" box "Choosing a Pediatrician," offers
some guidelines in this area.

PRENATAL CARE

In nine months' time the fetus must develop from a single cell to a highly complex
being of approximately seven pounds. As this development takes place, the fetus is influenced by its external and internal environment. The external fetal environment is the
amniotic fluid. The internal environment consists not only of the proteins and enzymes
manufactured within the organism but also of a continuous inflow of nutrients, hormones, oxygen, chemicals, and other substances from the mother's bloodstream.

It was noted earlier that there is no direct connection between the blood vessels
of mother and fetus. A mixing of blood in the placental region never occurs. Rather,

molecules of many substances are released by the maternal bloodstream and pass through the placenta. If small enough, these substances are assimilated by the blood vessels within the umbilical cord, making the placenta an area of exchange. The placenta is not a filtration system. What passes through the placenta has an environmental impact on the fetus. Thus it is crucial that a pregnant woman eat right and stay healthy. In addition, she should be regularly seeing a physician—usually a specialist in obstetrics and gynecology—who is qualified to offer prenatal care (Coustan, 1990; Hales, 1989; Henry & Feldhausen, 1989; Krause, 1984; Hamilton & Whitney, 1982).

Eating Right

The ability of the fetus to develop normally depends on nourishment supplied by the mother. Poor maternal nutrition may affect the fetus either directly, by not meeting its nutritional needs, or indirectly, by increasing the mother's susceptibility to disease. Malnutrition can not only cause poor health, rickets, scurvy, physical weakness, miscarriage, and stillbirth (a stillbirth is the birth of a fetus that has died), but possibly mental retardation as well. A seriously malnourished fetus can have as many as 20 percent fewer brain cells than the normal fetus (Chez & Chervenak, 1990).

All of this points to the importance of eating balanced, sensible meals during pregnancy. Paula Hillard and Gideon Panter (1985) add that such meals must supply enough energy and nutrients to satisfy the mother's needs as well as those of her unborn child. Pregnancy is not a time for weight reduction, but neither is it a time for massive weight gain beyond what is necessary for the appropriate growth of fetal and maternal tissues.

Although every woman should work out with her physician a pregnancy diet that is tailored to her particular needs, here are some general guidelines that are often considered in planning such a diet:

- Eat 2½ to 3½ ounces of protein daily.

- Consume 500 calories over your normal diet—that is, a total of about 2,600 per day. Caloric needs will be greater if the mother is underweight, under severe emotional stress, has had a previous miscarriage or stillbirth, or is having another baby within one year of giving birth—and especially if any combination of these factors exists.

- Use salt to season foods during cooking, but avoid adding extra salt at the table. It's also a good idea to avoid high-sodium foods like potato chips, ham, and sausage.

- Toward the end of the pregnancy, eat five or six small meals a day instead of three large ones—for your own comfort and easier digestion.

- Take daily vitamin supplements containing 30 to 60 mg. of elemental iron and 0.2 to 0.4 mg. (400 to 800 micrograms) of folacin.

- Remember that the nearer foods are to their natural state, the higher their food value: fresh is best, frozen next, canned foods last. (Hotchner, 1984)

Avoiding the Use of Drugs

All drugs pose potential problems for the embryo and fetus. The specific effects of drugs varies, depending not only on which drug is involved, but also on the quantity used and the time during pregnancy when it is taken. As far as smoking is concerned,

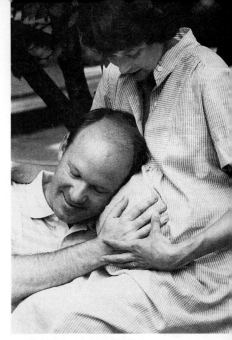

Pregnancy is a shared experience and often draws partners even closer to each other. Hearing and feeling his child move can be just as exciting for an expectant father as it is for the mother.

how much nicotine is needed to produce which prenatal effects is not precisely known. Researchers who have weighed and measured the newborns of smokers and non-smokers have found that the average baby born of a mother who smokes weighs less than the baby born of a nonsmoking woman. While it is not known how or why this phenomenon occurs, an educated guess is that the fetus of a nonsmoker receives its full quota of oxygen, while that of a smoking mother receives various gases, tars, and nicotine through the placenta, possibly at the expense of oxygen and/or of other nutrients (Hillard & Panter, 1985; Behrman & Vaughn, 1987).

Nicotine apparently has other bad effects. Just as adult heavy smokers have an increased heart rate, it has been suggested that the fetuses of women who smoke experience increased heart rates. Smoking may also lead to fetal hyperactivity. In addition, women who are heavy smokers are more apt than nonsmokers to give birth to premature babies. Finally, women who smoke are more likely to give birth to infants with life-threatening complications such as respiratory infections and diseases (Olds, London, & Ladewig, 1992; Khoarg, Gomez-Farias, & Mulinare, 1989; Vorhees & Mollnow, 1987; Moore, 1988; Shiono, Klebanoff, & Rhoads, 1986; Naeye, 1981; Fribourg, 1982).

What about alcohol consumption? Heavy intake of alcohol can lead to what researchers label the **fetal alcohol syndrome.** This is a condition in which infants are often born undersized, mentally deficient, and with several physical deformities, such as abnormal limb development, facial abnormalities, and heart defects. Some children of alcoholic mothers develop complications later in life, including poor attention skills and slow reaction times (Abel, 1990; Brendt & Beckman, 1990; Streissguth et al., 1989; Moore, 1988; Feinbloom & Forman, 1987; Briggs et al., 1986; Streissguth, 1984).

One study (Streissguth, Barr, & Martin, 1983) examined the effects of maternal alcohol use during midpregnancy on infant habituation. Habituation refers to an infant's tendency to get used to and eventually ignore stimuli that it experiences repeatedly. For example, a baby may first pay attention to a novel figure or pattern, but then, over time, pay less attention to it. Habituation is an important aspect of learning because it shows that memory is developing; that is, the baby remembers the stimuli she has been exposed to.

In this study mothers reported the amount of alcohol they consumed during the fifth month of pregnancy, and newborns were evaluated by means of a specialized infancy assessment test. It was found that maternal alcohol consumption was significantly related to poorer habituation and low arousal in newborns, even after the researchers adjusted for smoking by mothers, maternal age, nutrition during pregnancy, sex and age of the infant, and obstetric medication.

Addictive drugs, such as heroin and methadone, pass through the placenta readily, causing mothers who are addicts to give birth to babies who are also addicted (i.e., have developed a physiological dependence upon the drug). An addicted newborn experiences all the symptoms (tremors, fever, convulsions, and breathing difficulties) that adults do when they go through withdrawal from the drug. These babies are generally smaller (heroin babies seldom weigh more than five and a half pounds) than average and exhibit disturbed sleep patterns as well, often as impaired motor control (Hans, 1989). Numerous researchers (e.g., Lynch & McKeon, 1990; Lipsitt, 1989; Behrman & Vaughn, 1987; MacGregor et al., 1987; Weiss & Mirin, 1987; Bartol, 1986; Briggs et al., 1986) have also found that cocaine and its derivatives (such as crack) used by the mother during the second half of pregnancy tend to cause fetal distress, hypertension, premature labor, and even death.

Teratogens also have an impact on prenatal growth and development. A **teratogen** (from the Greek word *tera*, meaning "monster") is any substance that creates a change in normal genetic functioning, which, in turn, produces an abnormality or malformation in the developing organism. Examples of teratogens are radiation (men-

fetal alcohol syndrome
Condition among newborns caused by excessive alcohol consumption by the mother. Affected infants are often born undersized, mentally deficient, and with assorted physical deformities.

teratogen Any substance that creates a change in normal genetic functioning and in turn produces an abnormality or malformation in the developing organism.

tal retardation, eye anomalies), infectious agents such as rubella (mental retardation, deafness, cardiovascular problems), and chemicals such as thalidomide (limb deformities), as well as excessive dosages of vitamin A (cleft palate, facial abnormalities) and vitamin D (heart defects, facial deformities). The development of fetal organs and appendages is especially vulnerable to teratogens. The most dangeous time for the developing organism is the first two or three months after conception, a critical period for these fetal developments (Brendt & Beckman, 1990; Moore, 1988).

As we'll learn in Chapter 18, HIV, or the AIDS virus, may also be transmitted by the mother to her developing fetus. Because AIDS can have an incubation period of up to 10 years, pregnant women are sometimes unaware that they are carrying HIV. An infected woman's child has a 35 to 60 percent chance of contracting HIV either before or during birth. Some researchers think that when the virus is transmitted to the unborn fetus, it happens sometime between the 12th and 16th weeks of pregnancy.

Babies born infected with HIV rarely survive for more than a few years; some never become well enough to leave the hospital. However, there are instances where there is a lag of five years or more between initial infection and the onset of AIDS (Trofatter, 1990; Pizzo, 1990; Landers & Sweet, 1990; Hales, 1989; Seibert & Olson, 1989; Grossman, 1988).

Getting Regular Checkups

From the time that pregnancy is discovered until delivery begins, most women can expect to visit their doctor or practitioner about 12 times. This includes once every month until the 28th week, then every other week, and finally, during the last month, weekly. The initial appointment will include a review of both the mother's and the father's medical histories, along with a thorough examination of the mother. If genetic disorders run in the family, or if the mother will be 35 or older at the projected delivery date, amniocentesis may be recommended. If a woman is unsure when she last started to menstruate, an ultrasound scan may be suggested to pin down the baby's age. Certain blood tests will also be run to supply information about a woman's general health:

- **Blood type.** A woman's blood type is either A, B, AB, or O, and she may or may not have what's called an Rh factor. If a pregnant woman is diagnosed as

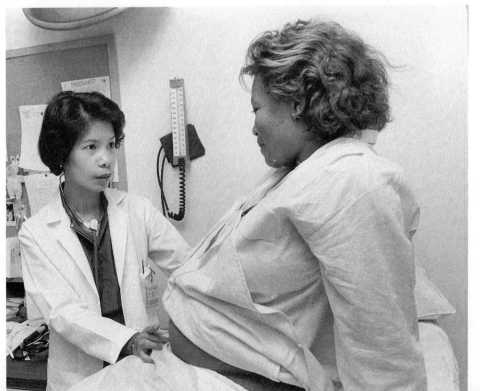

Getting proper medical care throughout the nine months one is expecting a baby is crucial to a safe pregnancy and delivery. Whether one is cared for by a clinic doctor or a private obstetrician-gynecologist, the important thing is to get regular checkups and immediate care if anything seems amiss.

297

Rh negative, she may need special monitoring if her husband is Rh positive. (We discuss this topic later in the chapter.)

- **Complete blood count.** This test counts the number of red and white blood cells in the pregnant woman's body. It also measures the amount of oxygen-carrying hemoglobin, as well as the total volume of cells and plasma. A low red blood count and/or low hemoglobin could mean that a woman is anemic and needs iron supplements.

- **Rubella titre.** This is a test to discover if the pregnant woman has been exposed to rubella (German measles). If she has, chances are she is immune and her blood carries antibodies to the disease. If she has not, she must take care to avoid exposure since getting rubella during the first three months of pregnancy can have serious effects on the developing organism.

- **Toxoplasmosis.** An optional blood test may be performed to see if the pregnant woman has been exposed to this parasitic disease, also called *cat fever*. Toxoplasmosis is contracted either from a cat that is a carrier or by eating raw meat. If a woman has been exposed, antibodies in her blood may indicate that she is now immune.

Each prenatal checkup follows a predictable pattern in certain areas. For example, weight gain and blood pressure are measured, and a urine specimen is taken to check for the presence of protein and sugar. The latter will indicate signs of pregnancy-related illnesses such as toxemia. The growth rate of the uterus and fetus are also recorded, and a fetoscope (similar to a stethoscope) is used to monitor the fetal heartbeat. Finally, the position of the fetus is externally checked by feeling for the location of its head, limbs, and buttocks.

Internal examinations can vary from practitioner to practitioner. In general, though, they are usually performed either at the beginning of the ninth month or a few weeks sooner. By this time, the baby's weight can be estimated fairly accurately, and many practitioners want to recheck a woman's pelvic dimensions to judge whether the birth canal can accommodate the fetus. An internal examination also helps to determine the following signs of readiness for labor (Lesko & Lesko, 1984):

Consistency. The change of the cervix from firm to soft.

Dilation. The widening of the cervix, which gradually opens to about 4 inches just before the baby's head emerges.

Effacement. The thinning out of the cervix as it is drawn up to become part of the lower section of the uterus.

Station. The descent of the baby's head.

Position. The forward movement of the cervix as labor progresses, in contrast to its usual far-back, difficult-to-reach position.

Having a Healthy Pregnancy

Aside from occasional fatigue and some early-stage nausea (called "morning sickness" despite the fact that it can occur at any time of the day or night) women generally feel well during pregnancy. And some, perhaps because of happiness at expecting a child, feel even better than usual. Proper prenatal care, however, is a must for all expectant mothers. To repeat, every pregnant woman should see a qualified medical practitioner on a regular basis. If a woman has risk factors like diabetes or heart disease she should see a specialist in obstetrics and gynecology who is experienced in dealing with her particular condition.

The worst thing is for a woman to try to doctor herself. At the same time, it's important to be a responsible patient. A woman should participate actively in her own care, asking questions of her doctor and reporting symptoms faithfully. The following list summarizes some of the issues we've discussed in this section and offers a helpful guide to ensuring a healthy pregnancy (see also Eisenberg, Murkoff, & Hathaway, 1991):

- **Maintain a balanced diet.** A proper diet gives every woman the chance for a healthy and successful pregnancy. For specific suggestions, look back at the section on "Eating Right."

- **Don't smoke, drink, or take any other drugs.** As we saw in the section on "Avoiding the Use of Drugs," all drugs pose a risk to both mother and baby, and the safest course is simply to avoid them. Remember, too, that if people around a pregnant woman—most important, her partner—smoke, she will become a "passive smoker." Note also that even caffeine and over-the-counter or nonprescription drugs can have negative effects on pregnancy.

- **Try for a sensible weight gain.** Today, doctors recommend no more than a 30-pound gain, on average. We'll explore this issue further in the next section.

- **Try to prevent getting infections.** It's important to prevent all infections, from the simplest cold or flu to sexually transmitted diseases like herpes or genital warts (see Chapter 17). Any such infection should be treated immediately by a doctor who knows the woman is pregnant.

- **Get enough exercise.** It's best to begin a pregnancy with a well-toned, exercised body, but it's never too late to begin. Regular exercise helps avoid constipation and improves respiration, circulation, muscle tone, and skin elasticity. All these qualities contribute to a comfortable pregnancy and a safer, easier delivery.

- **Get adequate rest.** Getting enough rest is far more important than getting everything done, especially for a high-risk pregnant woman. A woman should not wait until her body starts pleading for relief before she slows down. And if her doctor recommends beginning maternity leave earlier than she had planned, she should take her doctor's advice.

CHANGES IN THE MOTHER DURING PREGNANCY

A woman's body undergoes many changes during pregnancy. Some are highly visible, like abdominal swelling and the enlargement of the breasts. Others, like the thickening of the vaginal walls and the softening of the cervix, are detectable only by a physician. Let's explore some of these changes.

Weight Gain

Most pregnant women gain 25 to 30 pounds over nine months' time. This weight gain is gradual and steady, but distributed differently. The first pounds go into building up stores of fat and protein that can be used by the fetus later in the pregnancy. Some of these stores are held in reserve even longer to help meet the mother's nutritional requirements after pregnancy and to help produce breast milk. Nature assumes that human mothers, like other mammals, will breast-feed their young, and wisely stores energy and nutrient supplies in the maternal body.

How much weight does a woman gain during her pregnancy?

Exercise classes for expectant mothers are available in most areas and are an excellent way of keeping fit and preventing muscular aches and pains. Properly supervised exercise can also be a useful accompaniment to Lamaze training (see text discussion).

Other parts of the mother's body also grow during the early months of pregnancy. Blood plasma increases in quantity by almost 50 percent, as do other body fluids. Breasts begin to grow in anticipation of feeding the baby after birth and by midpregnancy weigh about a pound more than before pregnancy. The uterus also becomes bigger.

During the second half of pregnancy, stores of fat decrease as the fetus uses them for growth, but changes in other parts of the mother's body make up for the lost weight. The amniotic sac fills with about two pounds of amniotic fluid. The placenta also grows significantly during the second half of pregnancy. And, of course, the fetus itself gets bigger daily.

Changes in the Reproductive Organs

Of all the changes that take place within the body during pregnancy, the most crucial are in the organs of the reproductive system.

The uterus increases in size dramatically during pregnancy. Before pregnancy the uterus—as we saw in Chapter 3, a small pear-shaped organ located in the pelvic cavity—is about 2½ inches high and about 1½ inches in diameter and weighs about 2 ounces. By the time of delivery, the uterus has grown to about 11 inches high and 8 inches in diameter and weighs about 2.2 pounds. This great increase in size permits the uterus to accommodate the growing fetus, the placenta, and the protective amniotic sac and fluid.

Individual cells of the uterus exhibit significant size increases under the stimulating influence of estrogen and the distention caused by the developing organism. Fibrous tissue between the muscles also increases, forming an important muscle network. During the first few months of pregnancy, the uterine walls grow considerably thicker. This thickening process ceases at about the fifth month, at which time the musculature begins to distend. This results in a thinning of the muscle wall to a thickness of about ⅕ inch or less at term. The circulatory requirements of the uterus also increase as it enlarges and the fetus and placenta develop. By the ninth month of pregnancy, one-sixth of the maternal blood volume is contained within the vascular system of the uterus.

The cervix also undergoes significant changes during pregnancy. One of the earliest physical signs of pregnancy, softening of the cervix, may occur as early as one month after conception. The glandular tissues of the cervix also become active, increasing in number as well as in secretions. Glandular tissues distend and secrete mucus, which eventually thickens and forms a mucous plug that seals the uterus and protects it against invasion by bacteria or other substances in the vagina. The mucous plug will be expelled at the onset of labor when cervical dilation begins.

The ovaries do not produce eggs during pregnancy. Many follicles temporarily develop, but never reach full maturity because the necessary hormonal stimulation is absent.

The vagina and the external genital organs become thick and soft and receive an increased blood supply that gives tissues a darker hue compared to the color found in a nonpregnant woman. There is also a thickening of mucus, a loosening of connective tissue, and an increase in vaginal secretions. Vaginal secretions are considerably greater toward the end of pregnancy, becoming thick, white, and acidic. The acidic quality of these secretions plays an important role in preventing the invasion of bacteria, but also contributes to the growth of yeast organisms that produce a rather common vaginal infection during pregnancy known as *moniliasis*.

After the second month of pregnancy, the breasts become larger, firmer, and more tender. Superficial veins are more obvious and the nipples become more prominent. As pregnancy progresses, the nipples and the areola become darker in color. The areola, in particular, tends to become puffy and its diameter widens to two or three inches. During the last trimester of pregnancy, a yellow secretion known as **colostrum** may be expressed from the breasts. Colostrum is a precursor of breast milk.

colostrum A thin yellowish fluid secreted by the breasts toward the end of pregnancy.

LOVEMAKING DURING PREGNANCY

There is considerable confusion about what effect sexual activity has on prenatal development. For many couples, sexual relations during pregnancy are anxiety-ridden experiences. Traditionally, physicians have advised couples to avoid intercourse during the last month or six weeks of pregnancy as well as during the first six weeks after birth, but this recommendation is based on little factual information.

Although the medical literature contains conflicting reports, we do know that during an uncomplicated pregnancy sex is not harmful. A persistent fear of many couples is that intercourse will cause a miscarriage or harm the fetus, but there is no medical evidence that this is true for normal pregnancies. A physician may advise a woman who has already had a miscarriage to avoid sex, however, because contractions of the uterus during orgasm could cause another miscarriage.

Should a pregnant woman avoid intercourse?

If a woman has experienced spotting (a blood-tinged discharge from the vagina) during early pregnancy or has had a previous miscarriage, she should ask her doctor whether she should avoid intercourse, and if so, for what period of time. Sometimes spotting results from a cervical irritation, and intercourse can aggravate the condition. However, in the absence of bleeding, ruptured membranes, cervical weakness, or threatened premature labor, there is no reason couples should not continue to enjoy normal sexual activity throughout the duration of pregnancy (Hillard & Panter, 1985).

Many writers suggest that changes in coital positions can help to accommodate a woman's increasing abdominal girth in late pregnancy (see, for example, Shapiro, 1983; Samuels & Samuels, 1986). The traditional man-on-top position tends to be the most common coital position prior to pregnancy and during the first two trimesters. During the final trimester of pregnancy, though, the side-by-side position tends to be very popular, as are the rear-entry and woman-on-top positions.

Variations of the side-by-side position allow for shallow penile penetration in late pregnancy and may thus be more comfortable for the woman. Many women also favor the woman-on-top position because it puts no weight on the abdomen and allows them to control the depth of penile penetration. The rear-entry position is often chosen because it enables smooth penile entry and allows women to enjoy breast and clitoral stimulation during intercourse:

> I expected sexual intercourse to be uncomfortable and even painful during my pregnancy, but it wasn't. We often used the rear-entry position to ease penetration and keep my belly from getting in the way. We also discovered new levels of sexual excitement and satisfaction. My breasts were more sensitive to stimulation and we enjoyed touching and fondling more than ever before. (Authors' files)

Michael and Nancy Samuels (1986) write that a decrease in interest in intercourse and orgasm leads to a natural period of abstinence for most couples as the delivery date nears. This does not necessarily mean that partners feel estranged from each other or that sexual tensions increase in uncomfortable ways. Rather, many couples enjoy kissing, massaging each other, lying together, or sharing some other form of physical intimacy that involves considerable touching and skin-to-skin contact. This is usually pleasurable to both mother and father:

> Tim really tuned into my emotional needs during our pregnancy. He went out of his way to cuddle me and was always at my side when I needed him. He would give me backrubs and massages, and often we would stay in bed just to lie in each other's arms. Sharing our pregnancy was an emotional high for both of us and it gave us a sense of intimacy we'll always remember. (Authors' files)

PROBLEMS IN CONCEIVING AND BEARING A CHILD

Most couples have little difficulty conceiving a child. Sometimes, however, partners who have practiced birth control (see Chapter 12) for a considerable period of time are a little slow to conceive, and in still other cases, couples try for years without success. The most important factor in conception is timing intercourse; conception is most likely during ovulation. Most women do not ovulate on the 14th day of a 28-day cycle, primarily because most women do not have a 28-day cycle. To determine the time of ovulation, a couple should use a basal body temperature chart such as the one described in Chapter 12. Once ovulation has been determined, intercourse should take place within two days before or on the day of ovulation. You may recall from Chapter 8 that the man-on-top coital position is the best choice for conception because sperm have a better chance of reaching the cervix through the pull of gravity.

Frequency of intercourse also becomes a consideration when trying to conceive. It may surprise you to learn that having intercourse frequently may *not* improve the chances for conception. A high sperm count is necessary to fertilize an egg, and it takes a man at least 24 hours to produce the 300 million sperm expended in an ejaculation. Thus intercourse should not occur more than once every 24 to 48 hours. We will come back to this topic shortly.

Another consideration when trying to conceive is the pH factor, or the acid-alkaline balance within the vagina. Because acidity kills sperm, the vagina should be kept free of douches that contain vinegarlike solutions, as well as lubricants and suppositories that may also kill the sperm.

When a woman suspects that she is pregnant, she should see a doctor to have the pregnancy confirmed (see the "Making Use of What We Know" box, "Tests for Determining Pregnancy"). But if partners follow all of the guidelines we've just outlined and still haven't conceived after many months, they may need to take further steps to bring about the desired pregnancy.

Infertility

Not all couples can become biological parents. **Infertility,** defined as the inability to achieve a pregnancy after at least one year of regular, unprotected intercourse, poses a special set of problems. It is estimated that about 15 percent of the population—approximately one in seven couples—is infertile at any given time. However, patience is sometimes the answer for many of these couples. Pregnancy statistics tell us that for normal women who aren't using birth control and are sexually active, 25 percent will become pregnant in the first month, 63 percent will in six months, and 80 percent will in one year. An additional 5 to 10 percent will become pregnant the following year (Conkling, 1991; Muasher, 1987; Hotchner, 1984).

About 40 percent of infertility problems can be traced to the man and 40 percent to the woman. About 20 percent of the time couples share the problem of infertility, for reasons that often go unknown (Hatcher et al., 1990; Olds, Ladewig, & London, 1988; Batterman, 1985; Frank, 1984). Among the more common causes of male infertility are poor sperm quality, low sperm count, and poor sperm motility, or movement. One of the causes of decreased sperm number and motility is varicocele, a condition that causes dilation of veins near the testicles (see Chapter 17). Other possible causes of decreased sperm number are chronic fatigue and illness; poor nutrition; excessive use of caffeine, tobacco, or marijuana; too-frequent intercourse; nervous stress; fear of impotence; hormone abnormalities; birth defects; certain medications and treatments such as radiation to the testes; and possibly tight underwear and pants. In addition, an undescended testicle or underdeveloped testes will fail to produce adequate numbers of sperm (Mahlstedt, 1987).

The most common causes of female infertility are the blockage of fallopian tubes and ovulatory defects. A number of causes may account for blockage, including tubal scarring from pelvic infections. As we'll see in Chapter 17, growing numbers of women are developing pelvic inflammatory disease when sexually transmitted diseases such as chlamydia spread into the uterus and fallopian tubes, in the process affecting a woman's ability to conceive. Endometriosis (see Chapter 17), a condition in which uterine tissue migrates to sites outside the uterus, may cause infertility by blocking the fallopian tubes. Ovulatory defects include the inability of an ovary to develop or release an egg or of the hypothalamus, pituitary, or ovaries to produce their hormones in proper amounts or sequence (Chapter 3). Another cause of infertility is the failure of the cervix at midcycle to secrete cervical mucus, which is necessary to sperm survival. Or the cervix may produce abnormal amounts of mucus, which impedes the movement of sperm (Mahlstedt, 1987; Muasher, 1987).

Infertility can be related to aging processes. Women under age 25 have about a 7 percent chance of being infertile, but by the age of 40, one out of every three women is unable to have a child. A woman in her 30s does not have many fertile years left. Male infertility is also partly determined by age; a man of 50 generally has a lower sperm count than a man of 20, although the natural decrease in his sperm count may not prevent him from having children if enough of his remaining sperm are healthy (Lauersen, 1983).

Other causes of infertility include sexual dysfunction, inappropriate timing of intercourse, and immunological factors. The mind/body connection also cannot be overlooked. Stressful life styles, personal problems, vocational pressures, and general

infertility The inability to achieve a pregnancy after at least one year of regular, unprotected intercourse.

What causes infertility? Can it be corrected?

MAKING USE OF WHAT WE KNOW

Tests for Determining Pregnancy

There are several different tests for determining pregnancy, but all of them measure the presence of a pregnancy hormone called *human chorionic gonadotrophin* (HCG). This hormone is detectable in the blood or urine of a pregnant woman eight or nine days after ovulation. A serum pregnancy test run in the laboratory or doctor's office can detect pregnancy with more than 95 percent accuracy as early as 8 to 10 days after conception, and with virtually 100 percent accuracy (barring lab error) six weeks after conception. A laboratory urine pregnancy test can detect HCG with an accuracy of about 95 percent, often as early as 20 days after conception.

Today we also have urine pregnancy tests that a woman herself can administer at home. Less accurate than the laboratory procedure, these tests also determine pregnancy by detecting HCG in urine. They can tell if a woman is pregnant as early as nine days after a missed menstrual period, or about three and a half weeks after conception. If the tests are done correctly, they are almost as accurate as a urine test done in a doctor's office or laboratory. But there are draw-backs to these home tests. For one thing, they can be more expensive than a lab test. For another, the woman is less likely to feel confident of the results and prone to want to confirm them with another test—which adds further to the cost. The major risk with these tests, however, is that an incorrect negative result leads most women to postpone visiting a doctor and taking proper care of herself and her baby. A woman who does decide on a home test should buy it the day before she plans to use it (it requires a first-of-the-morning urine sample), and follow the instructions carefully (Eisenberg, Murkoff, & Hathaway, 1991).

We might add that some signs of pregnancy can be detected even before pregnancy is confirmed by a test. Following a missed period, many pregnant women feel bloated, tired, and experience increased fullness of the breasts. Other changes that often occur over time include darkening of the areola, frequent need to urinate, irregular bowel movements, morning sickness (nausea and vomiting), and an increase in vaginal discharge.

mental health may affect the reproductive systems of both men and women. Environmental conditions such as exposure to pesticides or work hazards are other considerations (Mahlstedt, 1987; Greenfeld et al., 1986; Keye, 1984).

Infertiity brings considerable pressure and distress into the lives of couples. Patricia Mahlstedt (1987) writes that the process of diagnosing and treating infertility has a pervasive impact on those who undergo it, creating friction in the most stable marriage or intensifying existing problems between partners. And though this impact is usually greater when the treatment process is prolonged and/or unsuccessful, psychological pressures begin to develop when a couple first realizes they are not conceiving as planned. Most begin to have doubts, worry, become frustrated, and wonder why they can't do something as natural as conceive a child.

Barbara Higgins (1990) has found that infertile couples often face other consequences, including the loss of sexual pleasure because of the "task" orientation that procreation comes to assume and discomfort from painful procedures and surgery designed to help them conceive. Grief, anger, and guilt are common reactions in infertile spouses. Infertile couples may also alter their social interactions in an attempt to avoid painful reminders of their childlessness.

The support of family and friends can be very beneficial to the infertile couple, as can that of other couples who have experienced infertility. A self-help group called RESOLVE is a national organization that offers counseling, referral, and support services to infertile couples. Through this group, infertile couples can meet and discuss their concerns with others who know the traumatic physical, psychological, social, and relational effects of infertility. RESOLVE encourages interaction between couples who have achieved resolution of their infertility problem and those who are in the process of working it through. The first group of couples, who may have resolved their problem by achieving pregnancy or by adopting a child or even, ultimately, by viewing childlessness as an acceptable life style, can be valuable models for the latter group (Higgins, 1990; Seibel, 1990).

Interventions for Infertility

Initial intervention for infertility usually includes taking a history from and doing a physical examination of both partners. The woman is often asked to chart her basal body temperature (see Chapter 12) so that the physician can assess the regularity of her menstrual cycle, when she is ovulating, and the optimum time for the couple to have intercourse. The man may be instructed to abstain from sexual activity for several days before the woman's fertile period is expected, in the hope that his sperm count will rise. Sometimes the drug clomid (clomiphene citrate) is administered to the woman to induce ovulation. Clomid works by stimulating the pituitary gland to secrete the lutinizing hormone and the follicle stimulating hormone, two hormones that help orchestrate the menstrual cycle (see Chapter 3). In one study (Archer, 1989) clomid induced ovulation in 80 percent of a group of women studied, and 40 percent of these women became pregnant.

Fertility in men is tested with a semen analysis, which assesses the number, quality, and motility of sperm. Should infertility be traced to the man, surgery might be in order to repair blockage in the testicles, such as varicocele or blocked sperm ducts. Other forms of intervention include the medical management of hormonal abnormalities or infections. Hormonal therapy for men has not consistently demonstrated an increase in sperm production and is still considered largely experimental.

For women, blood and urine tests are given to determine estrogen, gonadotrophin, and progesterone levels, and cervical mucus tests are used to assess whether sperm can penetrate and survive within the cervix. A physician might use a laparoscope (a telescopic surgical instrument designed to explore the abdominal area) to assess any disease or blockage in the reproductive system. Microsurgery is sometimes employed to correct blocked fallopian tubes, and laser surgery has recently been used to treat endometriosis. Chapter 17 discusses endometriosis in some detail.

In about 75 percent of infertility cases, these procedures prove successful. If such measures fail, hope lies in several sophisticated reproductive technologies: in vitro fertilization, artificial insemination, surrogate motherhood, and embryo transfer. These technologies are important medical breakthroughs, but as we'll discover in Chapter 21, they have also engendered serious legal and moral controversies. Let's examine each more closely.

IN VITRO FERTILIZATION (IVF). In **in vitro fertilization (IVF)** one or more ova are surgically removed from the mother, combined with the father's sperm, and placed into the uterus. The procedure is usually employed when the woman's fallopian tubes are blocked or diseased. Women with normal menstrual cycles and men with normal sperm counts are considered good candidates for IVF, which is one of the most common forms of reproductive technology. By 1990, an estimated 15,000 children had been conceived this way throughout the world, and more than 200 IVF clinics had opened in the United States.

Although pioneers in vitro fertilizations used the woman's natural menstrual cycle for the procedure, clinics today experience higher success rates by hormonally

in vitro fertilization A procedure in which one or more ova are surgically removed from the mother, fertilized by the father's sperm, and then placed back in the mother's uterus.

stimulating ovulation with fertility drugs and "harvesting" three to five eggs, rather than just one naturally produced egg. To assess the exact time of ovulation, the physician examines the woman's abdomen by ultrasound. When the eggs are mature, they are removed from her body by a surgical technique called laparoscopy. In this technique, under general anesthesia, a small incision is made adjacent to the navel and the earlier-described laparoscope is inserted, enabling the physician to see inside. The eggs are retrieved with a hollow needle and placed in a petri dish, where they are allowed to mature for several hours before they are fertilized with the father's sperm. The fertilized eggs are then placed in an incubator. About 48 hours later, when each egg has gone through the cell divisions necessary to produce a blastocyst, several are implanted in the woman's uterus (Issacs & Holt, 1987; Speroff, Glass, & Case, 1989).

The success rate of in vitro fertilization varies depending on the clinic consulted, and to some extent, on the particular approach to assisted reproduction used. For example, one study (Soules, 1985) found a 10 percent success rate per single embryo transfer, 15 percent per two embryos transferred, and 19 percent per three embryos transferred. Obviously, then, a woman's chances for conception improve when two or three embryos are placed in her uterus. However, when more than three embryos are transferred, the risks of multiple fetuses and miscarriage are thought to outweigh any benefit. As we'll discover in Chapter 21, the fate of the unused embryos has aroused a great deal of debate. They may be discarded, or they may be used for research in order to improve IVF and enhance our understanding of embryonic development. Or—a more recent option—they can be "cryopreserved" (frozen) and then later thawed and implanted again, perhaps as a donation to another woman.

Variations of in vitro fertilization have been developed in recent years, and may be more ethically acceptable because they avoid manipulating the blastocyst. For

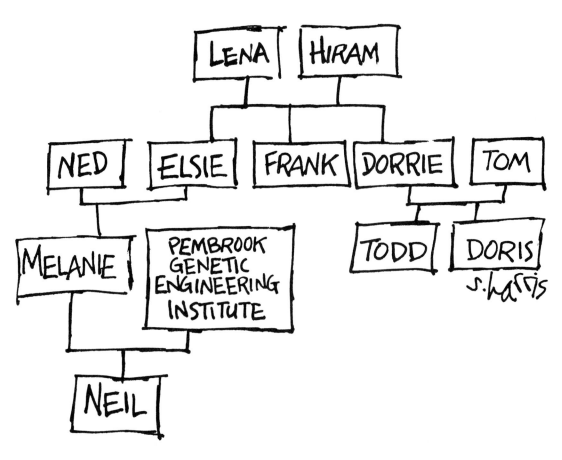

Conception and Pregnancy

example, in gamete intrafallopian transfer (GIFT), ova are gathered in much the same way described above and mixed with the father's sperm. Then both ova and sperm are placed into one or both fallopian tubes, the normal site of fertilization. Should fertilization occur, the zygote then travels to the uterus, where prenatal development proceeds. This approach is particularly effective in dealing with endometriosis (see Chapter 17). Another technique is zygote intrafallopian transfer (ZIFT). Here ova are retrieved from the woman and mixed with the man's sperm, as in in vitro fertilization, but the zygote is transferred back to the woman's body at a much earlier stage of cell division and, as in GIFT, is placed in the fallopian tube rather than in the uterus (Olds, London, Ladewig, 1992; Devroey, 1989). For help in finding good reproductive technology services, see the box on "Guidelines for Selecting an IVF clinic."

ARTIFICIAL INSEMINATION. Artificial insemination involves artificially injecting sperm (fresh or frozen) into a woman's vagina, either on or near the cervix, at the time of ovulation. There are three types of artificial semination. One type uses sperm from the husband (called artificial insemination, homologous, or AIH), often when his sperm count is low or the wife has one of the earlier-mentioned cervical mucus problems. Sometimes a physician injects several of the husband's ejaculations (which are preserved by refrigeration) in an effort to increase sperm count and motility. When the husband's sperm count is too low to use AIH, artificial insemination by donor (artificial insemination, donor, or AID) is practiced, which utilizes sperm from an unrelated, usually anonymous donor (Lasker & Borg, 1987). A third type of artificial insemination combines sperm from a husband who has a low sperm count with sperm from an unrelated donor (artificial insemination, combined, or AIC), so that there is some hope that the resulting child will be the husband's (Issacs & Holt, 1987). Artificial insemination has an overall success rate of between 70 and 80 percent, usually by the third attempt.

Should a sperm donor be used, he is screened and matched as closely to the husband as possible for such characteristics as ethnic background, stature, complexion, and blood type. Special screening is also given to prevent genetic defects, sexually transmitted diseases, and other potential problems.

AID, though practiced for several decades, is quite controversial (see, for example, Moghissi, 1989; Dunn, Ryan, & O'Brien, 1988). Many people consider it unnatural or immoral. Others have expressed concern about the criteria used in selecting and screening donors. We present more information on this issue in Chapter 21.

SURROGATE MOTHERHOOD. Surrogate, or substitute, **motherhood** is used by some couples when the man is fertile but the woman is unable to conceive or carry the child to term. In this technique, which is a variation of artificial insemination, a chosen surrogate mother is artificially inseminated with the husband's sperm. The surrogate mother carries and bears the child, which she then gives back to the couple. About 500 babies have been born in the United States via surrogate motherhood. The cost of this service, usually sponsored by a surrogacy clinic or center, was approximately $20,000 in 1990. Usually a $10,000 fee is paid outright to the surrogate mother, with the rest of the money going to the center. The surrogacy center handles the screening of candidates, arranges medical, legal, and psychological services for the couple and the surrogate mother, and offers a standard contract to govern the transaction.

Surrogate motherhood raises a number of religious, ethical, and legal questions. To date, we have no clear-cut or comprehensive laws covering the arrangement, and only a few states have attempted legislation to settle the complex issues arising from surrogacy. Some who have examined these issues (e.g., Isaacs & Holt, 1987) raise important questions: Should surrogacy be banned as unnatural and immoral, a form of baby selling or a procedure that is inherently exploitative of poor women? Or

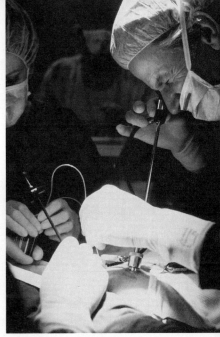

In the technique of in virto fertilization, the first step is to obtain mature eggs from a woman's ovary, using a laparoscope and a hollow needle (see text for further discussion).

artificial insemination A procedure in which sperm (fresh or frozen) are artificially injected into a woman's vagina, either on or near the cervix, at the time of ovulation.

surrogate motherhood A procedure in which a chosen surrogate mother is artificially inseminated with the husband's sperm. The surrogate mother carries and bears the child, which is then given to the couple.

MAKING USE OF WHAT WE KNOW

Guidelines for Selecting an IVF Clinic

*M*ore than 2.5 million American couples have tried unsuccessfully for at least a year to conceive a child. Many who don't succeed with traditional fertility treatments eventually turn to one of the country's more than 200 in vitro fertilization clinics. Winifred Conkling (1991) advises couples who are selecting an IVF clinic to ask the following questions:

■ *What percentage of IVF attempts result in healthy babies?* About one-fourth of all IVF pregnancies end in miscarriage. Some clinics tout their high *pregnancy* rates, but are reticent about their *birth* rates. The average birth rate is about 12 percent, but the best clinics achieve success rates as high as 20 percent.

■ *Are the doctors board certified in reproductive endocrinology?* To find out, consult the *Directory of Medical Specialists* (available in most libraries) or contact the American Fertility Society (2140 11th Ave. S., Suite 200, Birmingham, AL 35205-2800; 205-933-8494).

■ *Does the clinic have facilities available to freeze any unused embryos?* Using frozen embryos on subsequent IVF attempts is much cheaper and easier then repeating the entire egg-retrieval process.

■ *Does the clinic have a financial consultant on staff to help with paperwork and insurance claims?* IVF procedures are expensive: about $5,000 to $10,000 per treatment in 1990 dollars. Most insurance companies won't pay for IVF. However, a few states—Hawaii, Texas, and Maryland—mandate insurance coverage for in vitro fertilization.

For more information on infertility and IVF, contact:

RESOLVE, Incorporated
5 Water Street
Arlington, MA 02174-4814
800-662-1016

This nonprofit nationwide information network serves the needs of infertile couples.

---

should it be permitted as perhaps the only way some infertile couples will be able to have a child genetically related to at least one of them? Linda Whiteford (1989) has raised a number of issues regarding the rights and obligations stemming from surrogate motherhood: Whose rights take precedence—those of the unborn child, the child's biological mother, the child's biological father, the contractual (or social) mother? Is the biological mother to be considered only a "vessel" used to produce a child? We will direct our attention to these complex and multifaceted issues in Chapter 21.

embryo transplant A procedure in which a woman other than the prospective mother is impregnated with the husband's sperm. After several days, the fertilized egg is removed from her womb and placed within the mother's uterus.

EMBRYO TRANSPLANT. Somewhat related to surrogate motherhood is **embryo transplant,** although it is a much more experimental procedure. This technique involves impregnating a woman with the sperm of a man whose wife is infertile. After several days the fertilized ovum is removed from her uterus and placed within the wife's uterus, which has been hormonally prepared to accept it. This is done when the menstrual cycle of the wife indicates that she is prepared to accept a pregnancy. In some instances, the embryo is frozen and implanted at a later time.

Reproductive technologies increase couples' options, but also raise a number of challenging issues. At a minimum, as Sandra Danziger and Dorothy Wertz (1989) note, these procedures radically circumvent the traditional transition to parenthood. They create a wide range of options in fertility and reproduction that beg to be studied. For example, it is now technically possible for a child to have three mothers: a genetic mother, who provides the egg; a bearing mother, who carries the fetus and bears the child; and a rearing mother. How should we weight the genetic contribution, the experience of childbearing, and the years of child rearing? Are we on the verge of redefining motherhood?

Some Problem Pregnancies

Most pregnancies follow a normal course of development. Occasionally, however, development goes awry and serious problems—often signaled by symptoms like those listed in Table 10–2—result. Such conditions as toxemia, Rh factor incompatibility, ectopic pregnancy, and miscarriage require medical intervention.

TOXEMIA. Toxemia is a general term referring to the presence of a toxic substance in the blood. Toxemia takes two distinct forms, preeclampsia and eclampsia. In **pre-eclampsia** the mother's retention of salt and water leads to an increase in weight, swelling, and raised blood pressure. In severe cases, there may also be headaches, vomiting, visual disturbances, and urinary complications. Preeclampsia is potentially dangerous because it may cause the body's blood vessels to become constricted, reducing the flow of blood to the womb by as much as 50 percent and inevitably affecting the placenta and fetus.

Preeclampsia is treated with drugs that reduce blood pressure, bed rest, and, if needed, mild sedatives. Rest tends to stimulate the flow of blood to the kidneys and womb, as well as to increase the amount of urine produced. When left untreated, preeclampsia can lead to **eclampsia,** the more serious toxemia. Eclampsia is a rare disorder, affecting only 1 in 1,000 mothers. It typically begins with muscle spasms and rapid reflex movements, and eventually the woman goes into convulsions and seizures. In its most serious stages, eclampsia can threaten the lives of both fetus and mother. Usually, treatment for eclampsia calls for anticonvulsant drugs, blood pressure medication, and the prompt delivery of the baby (Iams & Zuspan, 1990; Speroff, Glass, & Case, 1989).

RH FACTOR INCOMPATIBILITY. Although a cure has been found, fetuses and newborns continue to die because their blood is Rh positive (Rh+), while their mother's is Rh negative (Rh−). Rh+ is a genetically dominant trait, so the child of two Rh− parents,

toxemia The presence of a toxic substance in the blood.

preeclampsia A type of toxemia characterized by the mother's retention of salt and water, which often leads to weight increases, swelling, and raised blood pressure.

eclampsia A type of toxemia causing muscle spasms, rapid reflex movements, and eventually convulsions and seizures.

TABLE 10–2

Danger Signs in Pregnancy
....

A pregnant woman should consult her physician immediately if any of the following symptoms occur, explaining how long the symptom has been present and how often and with what severity:

- Severe abdominal pain.
- Increased, unusual thirst, with reduced amounts of urine or absence of urination for a day despite normal fluid intake.
- Severe nausea or vomiting.
- Vaginal bleeding or bloody discharge.
- Puffiness of the face, eyes, or fingers, especially if very sudden.
- Persistent, severe headaches, especially in the second half of pregnancy.
- Chills and fever over 100°F not accompanied by a common cold.
- Dimming or blurring of vision.
- Painful urination or burning when urinating.
- From the 30th week on, absence of fetal movement for as along as 24 hours.

Source: Adapted from Hotchner, 1984.

or an Rh− father and Rh+ mother, is not at risk. The Rh factor comes into focus only when the father is Rh+ and the mother Rh−.

Positive and negative blood types are incompatible. It is common during the birth process for fetal blood to enter the maternal bloodstream during hemorrhaging. When a fetus's blood is Rh+, the mother's body reacts by producing antibodies. During a first birth there are few if any antibodies present, so the Rh factor is unimportant. When the woman again becomes pregnant, however, these antibodies pass through the placenta and cause a condition in which the antibodies attack the fetal blood cells, generally causing death.

Today Rh immune globulin can be administered to the mother after the birth of each child to prevent the formation of antibodies and allow an Rh incompatible couple to produce other healthy children.

What is meant by an ectopic pregnancy?

ectopic pregnancy
Pregnancy that results when the fertilized egg becomes lodged somewhere outside the uterus.

ECTOPIC PREGNANCY. On rare occasions (about once in 200 pregnancies) a fertilized egg becomes lodged somewhere outside the uterus. The egg cannot develop and such an **ectopic pregnancy** must be terminated. Most such pregnancies occur in a fallopian tube and are referred to as *tubal pregnancies*. A fertilized egg stuck in a tube will continue to grow for a while, but eventually the tube (unlike the flexible, muscular uterus) will be unable to expand its delicate wall any further and it will burst. This invariably happens sometime during the first three months and will trigger an increasing degree of pain and vaginal bleeding. It will also produce bleeding directly into the abdominal cavity (the result of the fallopian tube bursting), which must be stopped by an abdominal operation to remove the tube (Hall, 1983). Figure 10–3 shows how an ectopic, tubal pregnancy occurs.

FIGURE 10–3
A Tubal Pregnancy.

A fetus that begins to develop within the narrow fallopian tube stretches the walls of the tube far beyond its capacity. A tubal pregnancy poses grave danger to a woman and must be terminated.

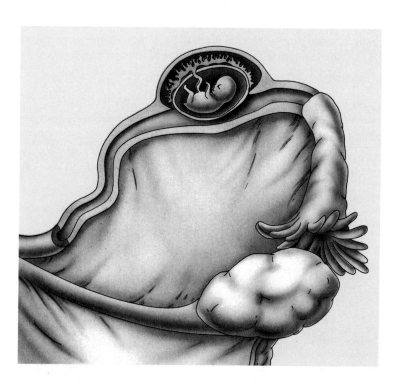

Conception and Pregnancy

MISCARRIAGE. A **miscarriage,** or spontaneous abortion, is the natural termination of a pregnancy before the embryo or fetus has the opportunity to fully develop. It is estimated that 90 percent of all miscarriages occur during the first three months of pregnancy. About one out of ten known pregnancies results in a miscarriage. Probably many more are unknown because some women abort without being aware that they are pregnant during the early weeks of gestation (Olds, London, & Ladewig, 1992; Abbott, 1989).

The cause of many miscarriages is a genetic abnormality that creates a defective embryo that is unable to develop normally. Early miscarriage is viewed by some as a natural selection process in which the defective organism is rejected before it has a chance to fully develop (see, for example, Hales & Creasy, 1982).

Certain factors are believed to increase the risk of miscarriage. Women who have chromosomal abnormalities, smoke, consume large amounts of alcohol, or who are over the age of 35 are more likely to miscarry (Simpson, 1990; Korones, 1986). Other factors suspected of triggering a miscarriage include rubella, X rays, and severe infections such as pneumonia (Anderson, 1989; Eisenberg, Murkoff, & Hathaway, 1991).

Detecting and Treating Fetal Problems and Defects

Thanks to modern-day technology, we have new and different ways to detect and study problems within the prenatal environment. These advances have given us a better understanding of the disorders that can exist early in life, as well as ways to deal with them. Among the new techniques are genetic counseling and amniocentesis, sonography, fetoscopy, and intrauterine fetal surgery.

GENETIC COUNSELING AND AMNIOCENTESIS. While is is true that some genetic defects occur randomly, more often than not there is a pattern to their occurrence. As geneticists have learned more about the way one generation transmits a defect to another, they've been able to counsel parents about potential risks to their unborn children. Today there is a network of genetic counseling centers across the country, staffed by physicians or other specially trained people and equipped with computerized information-retrieval systems that provide immediate access to the facts and statistics about certain problems. Genetic counseling is recommended for certain groups of parents most likely to have children with defects, including:

- Women over the age of 35.

- Parents of a child with a single-gene abnormality (a genetic defect from one parent, rather than both) or another form of physical or mental impairment.

- Women who have had three or more miscarriages.

- Couples with chromosomal abnormalities.

- Women who may be carriers of X-linked disorders. (The most common X-linked problems are hemophilia, the failure of the blood to clot; and Duchenne's muscular dystrophy, an impairment of muscle tissue.)

- Couples whose family members have a high incidence of certain diseases or unusually frequent cases of cancer or heart disease.

- Couples whose ethnic or racial backgrounds increase the likelihood of a particular problem. (Hales & Creasy, 1982)

One of the laboratory techniques employed in genetic research is amniocentesis. **Amniocentesis** allows for the detection of chromosomal abnormalities in the fetus. Amniotic fluid is sampled by inserting a hollow needle through the mother's abdominal wall and into the amniotic sac (see Figure 10–4). A syringe is then attached and amniotic fluid is withdrawn. This fluid contains discarded fetal cells, which can be observed, measured, and analyzed for size, shape, and number.

Amniocentesis has been used since the early 1960s. At present, doctors and scientists can test for more than 50 chromosomal abnormalities. For instance, if an extra chromosome is found at chromosome site number 21, the child will inherit a condition known as Down syndrome and will be mentally retarded. Another condition, found mostly among Jews of northern European origin, is Tay-Sachs disease, which causes blindness, mental retardation, and early childhood death. The disease is caused by an enzyme deficiency that is detectable in fetal amniotic cells.

Because amniocentesis also reveals the sex of the fetus, there has been some concern that people would use it to select the sex of their children, aborting a child if it were not of the desired sex. In fact, this is just what happened in India in the early 1980s, as the "World of Differences" box describes.

For women wishing to undergo amniocentesis, the 14th to the 16th week of pregnancy seems optimal. There are sufficient fetal cells in the amniotic sac, which is also large enough to lessen the likelihood of puncturing the fetus. This also allows time for a safe abortion, if desired (Feinbloom & Forum, 1987; Kaye, 1981).

FIGURE 10–4
Amniocentesis.

The very small amount of amniotic fluid withdrawn from the sac in this process provides a wealth of information about birth defects and genetic conditions that could affect the fetus.

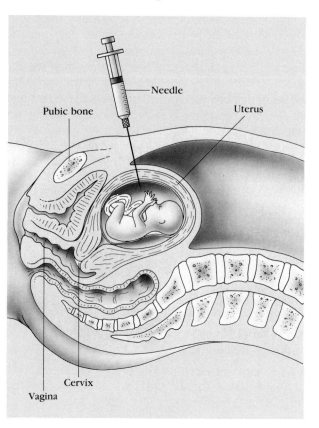

Conception and Pregnancy

A more recent diagnostic procedure for birth defects is called chorionic villi sampling (CVS). The test involves insertion of a thin catheter through the vagina or abdomen into the uterus, where some of the chorionic villi (threadlike protrusions on the membrane surrounding the placenta) are removed and analyzed (see Figure 10–5). This procedure can detect many of the same genetic disorders found by amniocentesis, although it is not considered as precise with more subtle abnormalities. The advantage of CVS over amniocentesis is that it can be done as early as the 7th week rather than the 14th and yields results faster (Olds, London, & Ladewig, 1992; Iams & Zuspan, 1990). However, one of the risks of CVS is spontaneous abortion. One study (Hogge, Schonberg, & Golbus, 1986) revealed a 3.8 percent rate of spontaneous abortion after CVS was performed.

SONOGRAPHY. Sonography (also called *ultrasound*) is used for such purposes as estimating fetal age, detecting the position of the fetus, identifying multiple fetuses, and detecting physical defects. Ultrasonic waves are transmitted to and from the mother's abdomen through a cluster of quartz crystals placed inside a small handheld transducer. When this transducer is moved over the surface of the skin, the ultrasound waves are directed against the placenta and the amniotic sac containing the baby. Once the waves hit a permanent organ, they are deflected outward and picked up by a special receptor, which feeds the transmitted impulses of sound into a scanning machine that prints them out onto the ultrasound screen. A clear picture

sonography Technique used to explore the prenatal environment. Also called *ultrasound*, the technique utilizes sound waves to gather such information as fetal age, position, defects, and the presence of multiple fetuses.

A WORLD OF DIFFERENCES

Amniocentesis Use in India

*I*n the early 1980s, pregnant women in India began using amniocentesis in large numbers to determine the sex of their unborn children so that if a child was female, they could abort it. Male children have long been preferred in India. This tradition dates back centuries, and is especially strong in remote areas, where sons help in the fields, add to the family income, and offer parents security in their old age.

Amniocentesis is used elsewhere in the world chiefly to determine the health of the fetus (Feinblum & Forum, 1987; Olds, London, & Ladewig, 1992). The use of this procedure in India solely to determine the sex of the fetus set off a raging controversy between women's groups and the doctors who administered the test. Women's groups contended that since amniocentesis test results routinely led to abortion of female fetuses, the procedure was an outrage against morality and against females in general. Many doctors countered that in overcrowded India it was a socially desirable alternative to the practice of having six or seven unwanted daughters in an attempt to gain one son.

Amniocentesis was first introduced as a technique for sex determination in 1982, in the northern state of Punjab. Bombay then became the center for the practice. Over 20 clinics specializing in amniocentesis testing are scattered throughout the city, and many more individual physicians also offer it. Most of the clinics are capable of doing more than 1,000 procedures a year, and many also perform abortions. No official figures are available on the sex of aborted fetuses in India, but speculation is that almost all are female. The cost of amniocentesis in 1990 dollar figures ran from $8 to $20. The procedure is widely advertised on trains and buses, often with unabashed praise for male children.

Despite government policies that foster family planning, India's population of about 780 million is expected to grow to one billion shortly after the year 2000. Abortion is not officially part of the country's family planning policy, but it is legal and easily attainable. While a son is a prize for an Indian family, a daughter is viewed as a deficit and female infanticide is still practiced in some tribal areas. Daughters are considered a burden because they usually don't earn money and must be given hefty dowries upon their marriages. (Chhaya, 1986)

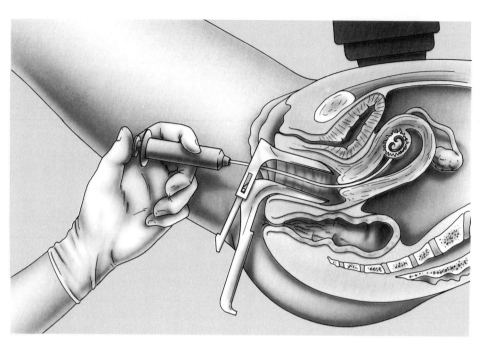

Figure 10–5
Chorionic Villi Sampling.

In this procedure some of the threadlike protrusions on the chorion, the membrane that surrounds the placenta, are removed through the vagina and analyzed for signs of genetic disorders in the developing fetus.

of the various fetal organs can be put together by moving the transducer over different areas of the abdomen. The size, location, and contour of various organs can then be measured and analyzed (Lauersen, 1983). Figure 10–6 depicts the technique of sonography.

fetoscopy Technique that inserts a fetoscope, equipped with a light source and biopsy forceps, into the amniotic cavity to view the fetus directly and take blood and skin samples for chromosomal and biochemical studies.

FETOSCOPY. Fetoscopy enables the physician to view the fetus directly and take blood and skin samples for chromosomal and biochemical studies. Fetoscopy is particularly useful for diagnosing hemoglobin disorders, including sickle cell anemia, hemophilia, and disorders of the white blood cells. A fetoscope, a viewing instrument that has a diameter slightly greater than that of a large needle, is inserted through the abdominal wall into the amniotic cavity in much the same manner as in performing amniocentesis. The fetoscope contains a high-powered fiberoptic light source that enables the physician to view the fetal and placental surfaces, although because of the small diameter of the fetoscope, the area observed at any one moment is quite limited. The fetoscope is also equipped with biopsy forceps, which are used to take samples of tissues from the fetus. The prenatal diagnosis of a variety of congenital skin diseases is also possible with this technique. By inserting a tiny needle into the placenta and umbilical cord, doctors have been able to obtain samples of fetal blood for analysis (Shapiro, 1983; Lauersen, 1983).

intrauterine fetal surgery Microsurgery on the unborn child to correct problems diagnosed during the mother's pregnancy.

INTRAUTERINE FETAL SURGERY. Intrauterine fetal surgery involves microsurgery on the unborn child to correct problems diagnosed during the mother's pregnancy. Such delicate surgical operations, aimed at improving an infant's chance of survival

Conception and Pregnancy

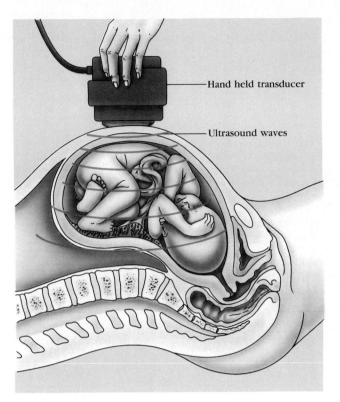

Hand held transducer

Ultrasound waves

FIGURE 10–6
Sonography.

Recording ultrasound waves that bounce back from the fetus and its surrounding structures produces an image on a monitor that can be printed out as a sonogram—a "picture" of the developing fetus.

and preventing permanent damage, might be performed to correct such defects as hydrocephalus (excessive fluid within the skull) or obstruction of the fetal bladder. In addition, if the fetal blood supply is inefficient or the baby's health status is in jeopardy, blood transfusions can be injected into the umbilical cord. Medicines, nutrients, and vitamins can be injected into the amniotic fluid and thus be absorbed by the fetus.

In 1991 a fetus-to-fetus tissue transplant operation added a new dimension to intrauterine fetal surgery (Hilts, 1991). Blood cells from the liver tissue of a fetus aborted in an ectopic pregnancy were injected into the chest cavity of a fetus diagnosed with Hurler's syndrome (Hurler's syndrome is a genetic disorder characterized by the inability of cells to produce an enzyme capable of breaking down sugar in some cells). The transplanted cells reached the fetus's liver and from there traveled to bone marrow, where they manufactured cells that traveled to other parts of the body and created the needed enzyme. Because the transplant was done in the womb, the immature immune system of the fetus did not reject the foreign cells. While intrauterine fetal surgery such as this is still experimental and considered controversial (it is opposed by antiabortionists, and as of our press time, the use of federal money for research involving fetal tissue transplants is still barred), the procedure offers hope for genetic disorders as well as other impairments discovered before delivery. Further research and follow-up studies are needed to fully assess such innovative prenatal surgery.

When Grandmother Is the Mother, Until Birth

by Gina Kolata

*I*n a small Midwestern city, a 42-year-old woman, a school librarian, is pregnant with her own grandchildren.

The woman, Arlette Schweitzer of Aberdeen, S.D., is carrying twins produced from her daughter's eggs, fertilized in a laboratory dish with sperm from her daughter's husband. The embryos that resulted were implanted in Mrs. Schweitzer's womb. The babies are due in November.

Mrs. Schweitzer said she was bearing her 22-year-old daughter's babies as an act of love for her daughter, Christa Uchytil of Sioux City, Iowa, who was born without a uterus and cannot bear children.

Questions Linger on Surrogacy

Doctors and lawyers who specialize in reproductive technology say this would be the first time in the United States that a woman gave birth to her own grandchildren. The only other case they know of is that of a woman in South Africa who gave birth to her daughter's triplets in 1987.

The experts say the story of Mrs. Schweitzer and her daughter brings into sharp focus difficult questions about surrogate motherhood that have never been satisfactorily resolved. For one thing, the financial questions that trouble many ethicists are absent here.

Mrs. Schweitzer took no money from her daughter and says she is horrified at the thought of being paid to carry the babies. So the case makes clear that some ethicists, lawyers and researchers are troubled by the very idea of surrogacy, even when the only motive is love.

Experts say the sort of surrogacy Mrs. Schweitzer entered into, one in which she is only carrying the fetus, providing no eggs of her own, is becoming increasingly common. . . .

The only case that has gone to court was one in California last year, involving a woman who was paid to be a surrogate and refused to relinquish the baby. The court awarded custody to the child's biological parents, who had paid the woman, but the ruling has been appealed. . . .

Admiration and Misgivings

Reactions to Mrs. Schweitzer's decision to carry her own grandchildren include expressions of admiration and feelings that such acts, even though undertaken with the best motives, are a mistake.

Dr. Arthur Caplan, an ethicist at the University of Minnesota, said he had nothing but praise for Mrs. Schweitzer. . . .

But Dr. Jay Katz, a professor of law, medicine, and psychiatry at Yale University, disagreed. He said he thought Mrs. Schweitzer's surrogacy was "a very, very bad idea" and could create problems for the children.

"Is the grandmother the grandmother or the mother?" he asked. "It may ultimately create too many tensions for the child and for the family. I appreciate and I would not dispute the loving intentions of the woman's mother. But sometimes love can create problems of its own. . . ."

Mrs. Schweitzer said she and her daughter had never questioned whether her surrogacy was the right thing to do. Mrs. Uchytil has a brother with three children, but there are no other women in the family to bear her children.

"In our case, it goes beyond ethical questions," Mrs. Schweitzer said. She and her daughter have talked about the surrogacy for six years, coming up with the idea at a time when doctors very rarely offered the procedure, if at all, and have never wavered from their desire to do it.

"It Was Devastating"

Their decision was made shortly after they learned that Mrs. Uchytil had no uterus, a problem that occurs in about one in 5,000 women. . . .

Two years after the diagnosis, Mrs. Schweitzer took her daughter to the Mayo Clinic in Rochester, Minn., for consultation. She said to the doctor who examined Christa, "I wish you could transplant my uterus because I'll never need it again. . . ."

Arlette Schweitzer, awaiting the birth of her daughter's twins.

She and her daughter suddenly realized that maybe there was a way out. She would not have to literally give her uterus to her daughter. But she could, in a sense, lend it to her. . . .

The two were examined by a psychiatrist, to make sure there were no hidden motives or psychiatric difficulties that would argue against the procedure.

Success on First Attempt

Then Dr. [William] Phipps [at the University of Minnesota] went ahead, giving Mrs. Schweitzer hormones to prepare her uterus to receive the embryos and giving Mrs. Uchytil hormones to prompt her ovaries to produce as many eggs as possible.

Mrs. Schweitzer got pregnant in the first attempt at placing the embryos in her uterus, beating the one in three odds that the procedure would work right away.

The total cost was about $7,000, Dr. Phipps said, compared with the more than $10,000 that most clinics charge. . . .

Mrs. Uchytil said that she expected and wanted her mother to have a very close relationship with the twins but that it would always be clear that they were her babies. . . .

Mrs. Schweitzer said she had had no second thoughts about her decision. "You do what you do for your children because you love them," she said. "If you can do something to help your children, you do it." [Ed.: The twins were born on schedule and, as we go to press, are doing well.] (*The New York Times*, August 5, 1991. Copyright © 1991 by The New York Times Company. Reprinted by permission.)

DISCUSSION QUESTIONS

1. Consider the issue of surrogate motherhood. Make two lists, one of arguments for surrogacy, the other of arguments against it. Can you decide to support or oppose surrogacy by weighing your arguments? If your instructor discusses this article in class, compare notes with your classmates.

2. Do you agree or disagree with Dr. Jay Katz that Mrs. Schweitzer's surrogacy was "a very, very bad idea"? Support your position.

3. Suppose a child of yours was born to a surrogate mother. How would you explain this to your child?

■ Couples report many motivations for having children. Some believe children are an extension of the self or a source of personal fulfillment and satisfaction. Children may enhance a couple's identity or provide a source of companionship or security. Some couples have children because they want to nurture, teach, motivate, and help youngsters become happy and mature beings. Others have children so they might give to them what they themselves never had. And many couples are motivated to have children because of social expectations and pressures.

■ Conception occurs when the male sperm penetrates the female egg to create a zygote. As the zygote travels along the fallopian tube, it begins to divide and multiply to form new cells, eventually forming a tiny sphere called a blastocyst. Upon reaching the uterus, the blastocyst attaches itself to the uterine wall. Prenatal development continues for nine months, divided into three equal segments called trimesters. Each trimester of about three months encompasses a distinct phase of prenatal growth and development.

■ The intrauterine mechanisms of the amniotic sac, ambiotic fluid, placenta, and umbilical cord provide the fetus with an ideal environment for its growth and development. By the end of the ninth month, the average fetus weighs six to seven pounds and measures between 18 and 21 inches from head to toe. Internal systems and bodily processes are set to make the necessary adjustments to life outside the womb.

A pregnant woman must take steps to safeguard both the prenatal environment of her fetus and her own well-being. Among other health considerations are those related to nutrition, nicotine, drugs, and teratogens. Seeking a qualified practitioner early in the pregnancy and being alert to the signs of a problem pregnancy are especially important. Most pregnant women gain 25 to 30 pounds, which is gradually and differently distributed as the pregnancy progresses. Of all the changes that take place within her body, the most obvious are in the organs of reproduction.

■ Infertility is defined as the inability to achieve a pregnancy after at least one year of regular, unprotected intercourse. Approximately 40 percent of infertility problems can be traced to the man and 40 percent to the woman; 20 percent of the time, couples share the problem and the reasons often go unknown. In about 75 percent of infertility cases, medication and/or microsurgery proves successful. For the other 25 percent parenthood can sometimes be achieved through such reproductive technologies as in vitro fertilization, artificial insemination, surrogate motherhood, or embryo transfer.

■ Among the complications and problems that can accompany pregnancy and interfere with labor and delivery are toxemia, Rh factor incompatibility, ectopic pregnancy, and miscarriage. Some modern-day techniques to help safeguard prenatal environment are genetic counseling and amniocentesis, sonography (ultrasound), fetoscopy, and intrauterine fetal surgery.

THINKING THINGS OVER

1. Think of three reasons you do or do not want to become a parent. Then reverse your thinking and give three opposite perspectives.

2. If you wanted to become a biological parent and found you could not, which, if any, specialized reproductive technique would you use? Why would you choose this method over the others?

3. A friend of yours has become pregnant and has asked you for advice on maintaining her health during pregnancy. What would you advise her to do?

4. Fetal alcohol syndrome can have devastating effects on children. Devise an awareness program for the students on your campus that will eventually benefit their children.

5. You have learned that miscarriages can and do occur fairly frequently among some segments of the female population. What advice would you offer a woman who has recently miscarried?

DISCOVER FOR YOURSELF

Eisenberg, A., Murkoff, H. E., & Hathaway, S. E. (1991). *What to expect when you're expecting*, rev. ed. New York: Workman. One of the better pregnancy guides for mothers- and fathers-to-be. Loaded with practical suggestions and supportive guidance.

Hales, D. (1989). *Pregnancy and birth*. New York: Chelsea House. See Chapters 4 and 5 for discussions of prenatal care and testing.

Henry, A. K., & Feldhauser, J. (1989). *Drugs, vitamins, and minerals during pregnancy*. Tucson, AZ: Fisher Books. A good look at how medications, vitamins, and other substances affect prenatal growth and development.

Hotchner, T. (1984). *Pregnancy and childbirth*. New York: Avon. An extremely comprehensive account of pregnancy and birth, filled with numerous charts and tables as well as practical advice for expectant couples.

Moore, K. L. (1988). *The developing human*, 4th ed. Philadelphia: W. B. Saunders. A sophisticated look at life's earliest beginnings and the course of prenatal development.

McClure, N., & Bach, J. (1986). *Pregnancy and birth*. Emmaus, PA: Rodale Press. A beautifully illustrated and practical guide to the many challenges of pregnancy.

11
Childbirth and Parenthood

There was a star danced, and under that I was born

—William Shakespeare

Babies are born perfect. That's because parents have yet to make any mistakes

—Steve Martin

Going into labor is the culmination of months of anticipation and waiting. But—invariably—there is a sense of surprise, for this is not an event that a mother schedules like her doctor's appointments. No one—mother, father, or practitioner—can predict what will happen over the next several hours or even days. For most couples, birth is a very unusual situation—exciting, but also a bit scary, a little like embarking on a trip, without plans, to a place you've never been before (Samuels & Samuels, 1986).

Throughout history, childbirth has occasioned very different observations, practices, and customs. For example, the ancient Egyptians held pregnant women in high esteem and paid special attention to their medical needs. Papyrus scrolls dating back to 2200 B.C. give guidelines on how to relieve pain during labor, and scrolls from 1550 B.C. elaborate on health concerns during pregnancy.

Susruta, a Hindu surgeon writing in the seventh century offered many observations on childbirth. Among other topics, he described the use of primitive forceps and the management of both normal and abnormal labor. The ancient Athenians recognized the need for special attendants during the delivery process. In fact, Athenian law required that a pregnant woman be attended by a midwife, usually a woman who had borne children herself but was past the childbearing age.

Superstition, charms, and rituals have surrounded childbirth in many civilizations. Medieval Europeans often placed a fresh egg next to the newborn to symbolize fruitfulness, and a gold coin was often given to the child to ensure ample means in later life. Among many North American Indian tribes, ritual chanting was practiced when women went into labor in an effort to lure the baby out of the womb.

In Arapesh, New Guinea, sanctions were directed at the father. He could not be present during the baby's birth, but following delivery could lie in bed with the newborn. Both father and mother fasted for one day after delivery, then spent five days together in strict seclusion. For months afterward, they observed a strict taboo against intercourse.

Similar practices were observed in Kurtachi, Solomon Islands. There the father was not allowed to enter his home for three days after the birth of his child. Moreover, while labor was in progress, he had to abstain from food of any kind. He also could not carry anything heavy or touch a knife, axe, or any sharp instrument, because it was believed that doing so would injure the baby or cause it to die. On the fourth day the father was permitted to see his child, and on the fifth day he washed with his wife in the sea.

Modern perceptions of childbirth reflect our own attitudes, beliefs, and customs. It is our tendency to view childbirth as a normal, positive event rather than a traumatic, painful necessity. Moreover, childbirth today is very often an event shared by both parents. As we'll see in this chapter, growing numbers of couples not only share the birth experience but also can choose among a variety of delivery alternatives. Contemporary parents thus present an interesting contrast to their counterparts in both the distant and the near past: they no longer have to accept either the pain and isolation in which women typically gave birth in previous centuries (see Figure 11–1) or the regimented hospital rules and procedures that in more recent times separated them during the birth of their child.

Our knowledge of childbirth today is extensive and sophisticated, largely because of advances in **obstetrics,** a branch of medicine concerned with pregnancy, labor, and delivery. Modern obstetrics has helped to diminish many fears about childbirth. In place of the painful trauma suffered by so many mothers years ago, most women today experience safe, natural deliveries with less discomfort.

In this chapter you'll discover:

☐ **The important characteristics of the three stages of labor.**

☐ **The varying ways in which a baby may be delivered.**

☐ **The several alternatives to traditional labor and delivery that many couples are now choosing.**

☐ **The kinds of adjustments that mothers and fathers face during the postpartum period.**

☐ **The special challenges that parenthood presents, and the child-rearing options and strategies that can promote healthy growth and development.**

obstetrics The branch of medicine concerned with pregnancy, labor, and delivery.

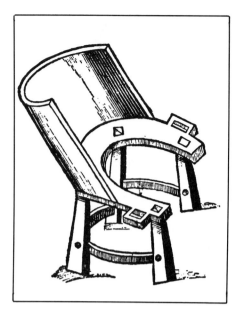

FIGURE 11–1
Childbirth through the Ages.

(a) The birthing chair, referred to as early as in the Old Testament, was designed to allow space for the passage of the baby from the mother's body. The chair's obvious lack of comfort was probably masked by the pain of childbirth itself. (b) A sixteenth-century woman gives birth on such a chair. In use well into the seventeenth century, the chair has reappeared in recent years but in a greatly improved design including the capacity to be tilted, raised, or lowered to suit the circumstances of the delivery and the mother's comfort. One advantage a vertical or near-vertical position has in delivery is that gravity helps the mother push the baby through the birth canal.

WHEN LABOR BEGINS

labor The process of giving birth, including uterine contractions, actual delivery of the baby, and expulsion of the placenta.

Labor, the climax of pregnancy, encompasses the processes involved in giving birth: uterine contractions, delivery of the baby, and expulsion of the placenta. The precise physiological mechanisms that trigger labor are unknown, although it is speculated that the fetus's adrenal glands manufacture hormones that cause the placenta and the uterus to increase the secretion of *prostaglandins* (human hormones). Prostaglandins, in turn, stimulate the muscles of the uterus to contract. These uterine contractions, which are gradual at first and then increase in both regularity and intensity, are the first sign of labor for most women.

lightening Descent of the fetus into the pelvis during the early stages of labor.

Before the onset of labor, most pregnant women experience a phenomenon known as lightening. **Lightening** means that the fetus is beginning to settle into the pelvis, causing a downward movement of the uterus. Lightening can occur at any time during the last month of pregnancy, but usually it happens about 10 days before delivery.

Lightening enables the woman to breathe easier since the fetus is no longer pressing on her diaphragm. She may experience an increased need to urinate, though, since the fetal descent creates greater pressure on her bladder. Many women also report leg pain because of pressure on the sciatic nerve.

What is false labor?

Braxton Hicks contractions Intermittent uterine contractions prior to the onset of actual labor.

Many women experience "false labor," or Braxton Hicks contractions, before the onset of actual labor. **Braxton Hicks contractions** are irregular and painful contractions in the abdomen and groin area that do not affect the cervix. As we'll see shortly, true labor contractions create both size and structural changes in the cervix, and are usually also felt in the lower back and extend to the front of the abdomen.

322   Childbirth and Parenthood

Another sign of impending labor is a pinkish discharge from the vagina referred to as "pink" or "bloody show." However, some women do not experience this until the first stage of labor begins. The pink show is caused by the release of the mucous plug from inside the neck of the cervix. As the fetus descends, minute capillaries in the mucous membrane of the cervix tend to rupture. Usually, this creates a small quantity of blood, similar in amount to the blood loss at the beginning of a menstrual period, mixed with mucus. Sometimes there is an initial discharge of clear watery material instead of the show, which indicates the imminent rupture of the fetal membranes.

Beyond these classic early warnings, women report other signs of impending labor. Some experience a sudden burst of energy (commonly called "nesting behavior"). Others report increased backache and vaginal secretions. Still other women have a fluid loss in the final weeks of pregnancy. Finally, loose bowel movements or diarrhea are often reported.

THE THREE STAGES OF LABOR

Labor is broken down into three stages. The first stage begins with the onset of true labor contractions and ends with the complete dilation of the cervix. The second stage consists of the delivery of the baby. The final stage is the expulsion of the placenta.

My girlfriend was in labor for over 12 hours with her first-born. Is this considered a long labor?

The duration of labor varies from woman to woman, although the average for first labors tends to be about 14 hours. This breaks down to about 12½ hours in the first stage, one hour and 20 minutes in the second stage, and 10 minutes in the third stage. Later labors tend to be about six hours shorter than first labors. This breaks down to an average of 7½ hours in the first stage, a half-hour in the second stage, and 10 minutes in the final stage.

The First Stage

During the early parts of the first stage, uterine contractions are short and about 10 to 15 minutes apart. They produce a feeling of discomfort in the lower back, and gradually spread to the front of the abdomen. Rupture of the amniotic sac often occurs, causing the amniotic fluid to be released (this is commonly referred to as "breaking of the waters"), although this may happen a few days before labor begins. The amniotic fluid can release itself in a sudden gush or in a trickle. Sometimes the amniotic sac does not break on its own, even after labor is under way. In such cases, the obstetrician will rupture it deliberately.

As labor progresses, uterine contractions become more frequent and more painful. At their peak, contractions occur about every 2 to 3 minutes and last approximately 45 to 60 seconds. One sign of possible problems in the delivery of a child is the absence of such strong contractions. Table 11–1 lists this and other signs of abnormal labor.

Uterine contractions may be accompanied by labored breathing, abdominal and leg cramps, excessive perspiration, and nausea. Contractions also increase the amount of pink show since they tend to rupture capillary vessels in the cervix and lower uterine area.

Uterine contractions create effacement and dilation of the cervix. **Effacement** is the shortening and thinning of the cervical canal. As effacement occurs, the cervix changes from a long, thick structure to a structure that is paper-thin. **Dilation** is the enlargement of the cervix so that the fetus can successfully pass through it. From an opening of about 4 centimeters (about 1½ inches) during the first stage of labor, the cervix reaches full dilation with a diameter of 10 cm. (about 4 inches). This is a temporary change. Immediately after childbirth, the cervix begins to contract, and by

effacement The shortening and thinning of the cervical canal during labor.

dilation The enlargement of the cervix during labor.

TABLE 11–1

Signs of Abnormal Labor

- Discontinuance of good strong contractions during first-stage labor.
- Continuous and severe lower abdominal pain, often accompanied by uterine tenderness.
- Abnormally slow dilation of the cervix, a subjective judgment made by attendants based not only on the mother's pain tolerance but also on the strength of the contractions.
- Excessive vaginal bleeding, which could be caused by a cervical laceration or delivery before full cervical dilation is reached.
- Abnormality in the fetal heart rate, in which case the mother is usually moved onto her left side to take the pressure off the major blood vessels on the right.
- Appearance at the cervical opening of the cord, placenta, or one of the fetus's arms or legs.
- Adverse change in the condition of the mother (fever, high blood pressure) or the fetus (fetal heart rate).

Source: Adapted from Hotchner, 1984.

one week postpartum, it has returned to its normal size. Figure 11–2 shows effacement and dilation of the cervix during labor.

The Second Stage

During the second stage of labor, contractions continue to be long and severe. The fetus begins to descend down the vagina, soon revealing its scalp through the vulva. Gradually, the vulva is stretched and eventually encircles the diameter of the baby's head (the head is normally the widest part of the fetus). **Crowning** is the encirclement of the largest diameter of the baby's head by the vulva. As the vulvar opening becomes dilated and distended by the head, the woman's perineal area and anus stretch and protrude.

crowning During childbirth, the encirclement of the largest diameter of the baby's head by the vulva.

FIGURE 11–2
Effacement and Dilation of the Cervix.

(a) At the beginning of labor the cervix, now softened, is more or less its normal size and shape. (b) As the baby's head begins to press harder and harder against it, the cervix appears to reduce in size, becoming thinner and shorter. (c) As labor continues, so does this reduction. The cervical opening begins to dilate, or widen, and the mucous plug that has protected the fetus from external influences is expelled. (d) When the fetus is ready to be delivered, the cervix is fully dilated and its tissues seem almost to have disappeared into the uterine walls. (Source: Adapted from Olds, London, & Ladewig, 1992)

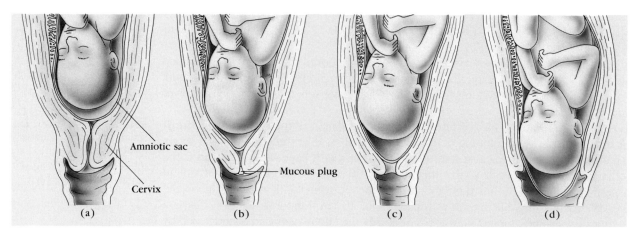

Amniotic sac

Cervix

Mucous plug

(a)　　　(b)　　　(c)　　　(d)

Three women remember this stage of labor:

The urge to push was just overwhelming. I'll never forget how I would catch my breath, push, take another breath, and then push again. I would do this until the contraction passed and then I was overcome by exhaustion. I remember how I would slump back against the pillow and try to relax before the next contraction.

The contractions became very intense at this time—about every two minutes and very strong. I can remember thinking, "This is for real—no pretending." I was frightened that I would lose control and at times I felt helpless and scared. Thank God my husband was there because he calmed me down and gave me verbal and physical support.

It was hard work, to say the least. The thing I remember most was trying to relax and not letting the contractions overwhelm me. My husband helped me to use slow breathing patterns, which we had practiced together beforehand, and he lightly stroked my arms and back to try and relax me. His touch made me less tense and helped me to cope better with the pain. (Authors' files)

A partner reflects:

I had a stopwatch to time Carol's contractions, and that helped us to see the developing patterns. When the contractions got really intense, I squeezed her hand and said "Push, push hard!" I was so proud of her and the way she was working. I really got caught up in the excitement and at times became momentarily overwhelmed. But I managed to regain my composure and supply Carol with encouragement and support. As I look back at the whole experience, I'm glad that we went in as a team. I knew she needed me and I wanted to be there to help. (Authors' files)

....

In the second stage of labor, crowning, or the appearance of the top of the baby's head through the vulvar opening (a), generally indicates that the baby is ready to be born. The baby's head (b) and shoulders are the widest part of its body, so that when they have emerged the rest of the body (c) is delivered rather easily.

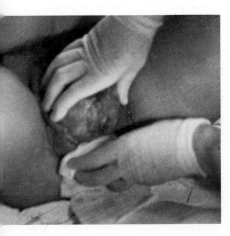 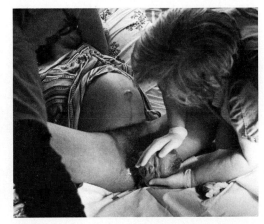 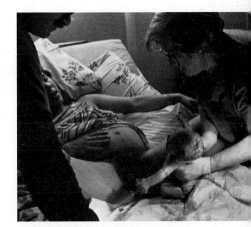

When crowning occurs, the baby is usually ready to be expelled. Delivery generally takes place between contractions and as slowly as possible. This is to help prevent lacerations during extreme vaginal stretching. Recall from Chapter 3 that an incision called an *episiotomy* may be made in the woman's perineum to protect it, the sphincter, and the rectum from laceration and to shorten the second stage of labor (Rockner, Wahlberg, & Olund, 1989; Cunningham, MacDonald, & Gant, 1989).

Research indicates that an episiotomy is one of the most common procedures in childbirth (e.g., see Rockner, Wahlberg, & Olund, 1989). It is estimated that the rate of episiotomies in all births is over 60 percent. However, there has been some opposition to routine episiotomies in recent years (see, for example, Thorp & Bowes, 1989). Critics maintain that this procedure is an unnecessary surgical intrusion that is performed more for the convenience of the doctor than for the sake of the woman. They argue that the vaginal opening can stretch on its own without tearing, and that an episiotomy causes pain and perineal discomfort when healing during the postpartum period. Additional complications associated with episiotomies may be infection and blood loss (Olds, London, & Ladewig, 1992; Borgatta, Piening, & Cohen, 1989).

forceps An obstetrical instrument designed to assist in the delivery of a baby.

It also may be necessary to use **forceps,** an obstetrical instrument designed to assist delivery. Forceps consist of two steel parts that cross each other like a pair of salad tongs and lock at the intersection. They may be used to gently pull or turn the baby, or both.

A forceps delivery may be chosen because the mother is unable to deliver even after complete dilation of the cervix. Or forceps may be necessary to assist the birth because the woman has heart disease and pushing is dangerous for her. Heart disease weakens the heart, making it more difficult for the woman's heart to accommodate the higher workload of labor (Olds, London, & Ladewig, 1992; Cruikshank, 1990). In rare cases, there may be a danger that the uterus will rupture or the placenta will prematurely separate from the uterus. A doctor may also decide to use forceps when labor has been overlong and the mother is exhausted. Finally, a condition known as **fetal distress** may call for the use of forceps. This condition is defined by unusual changes in fetal activity, such as a slow, irregular heartbeat, indicating that the fetus is in jeopardy (Parer & Livingston, 1991; Parer, 1989; Cunningham, MacDonald, & Gant, 1989).

fetal distress Unusual changes in fetal activity, such as a slow, irregular heartbeat, indicating that the fetus is in jeopardy.

The umbilical cord is quite long (15 to 30 inches) to allow free movement of the baby during delivery. Sometimes, however, it becomes looped one or more times around the neck, arm, leg, or other parts of the body. Usually, this does not present a problem, for the cord can be slipped back over the baby's body or brought over its head. If the cord's specific position causes it to be compressed so that the flow of oxygen to the baby is reduced, however, steps must be taken to relieve the compression. Should this prove impossible, an emergency cesarean section may have to be performed.

Most babies present in a head-downward position for delivery (see Figure 11–3). Birth is facilitated by positional changes in the baby, including a rotating movement. This movement tends to accommodate the irregular shape of the pelvic canal by providing the smallest possible diameters of the presenting part. Thus the baby encounters as little resistance as possible. Once the head and shoulders are delivered, the baby's body is quickly expelled because of its smaller size.

One mother remembers the moment of birth:

> I was pushing and pushing and I could see the baby's head in a mirror they had in the delivery room. I remember that she had dark hair, and everyone began telling me how far the head was coming out. My body took over at that point and the rest seemed to happen all at once. I felt warm and tingling and the next thing I knew Sarah was born. It was wonderful. (Authors' files)

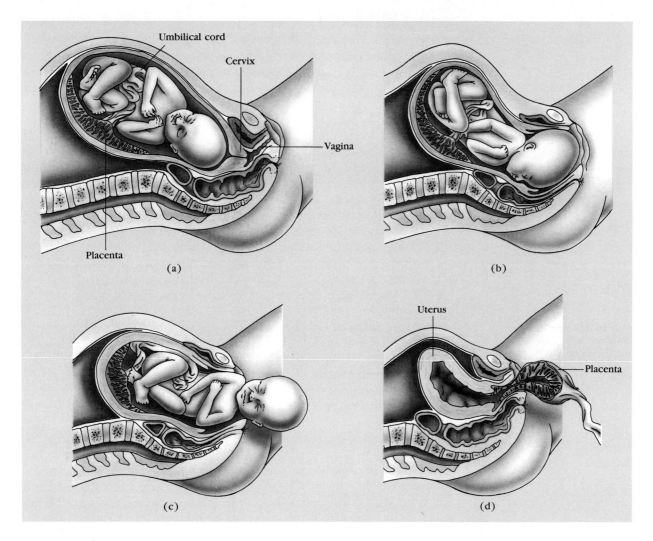

FIGURE 11–3
Labor and Delivery.

(a) The fully developed fetus is ready for birth. (b) Effacement and dilation are almost complete, and the baby's head pushes against the cervical opening. (c) The baby's head, which has the largest diameter of any portion of the baby's body, has passed through the cervical opening, and the rest of its body will follow immediately. (d) In the final stage of labor the placenta is expelled. (Source: Adapted from Martini, 1992, p. 977, Figure 29-14)

A father had these thoughts:

> I thought that I would get squeamish and avoid watching the birth, but that wasn't the case. I didn't miss a beat, and it was a beautiful experience to be right there with my wife. After the baby was born, I remember being in awe of what had happened—like I had been part of something that would never be forgotten. I couldn't stop reliving the whole delivery experience and I talked about it with family and friends for a long time afterwards. (Authors' files)

After the birth, the umbilical cord still connects the baby to the placenta. However, pulsations in the cord soon diminish, indicating a reduced flow of blood to the baby. The cord is then clamped and cut with a pair of sterile surgical scissors about

½ to 1 inch from the abdomen. The clamp is removed in the newborn nursery about 24 hours after the cord has dried. The cord itself typically shrinks and falls off within a few days after birth (Olds, London, & Ladewig, 1992; Iams & Zuspan, 1990).

Not all babies are born in a head-downward position. Rather, about 5 percent engage themselves in what is called a breech presentation. A **breech presentation** means that the lower part of the fetus appears first during delivery. In the *complete breech* the knees of the fetus are flexed and a sitting position appears to have been assumed. In a *frank breech* the legs of the fetus are bent straight up at the hips, with the knees straight. In a *footling breech* one or both feet or knees lie below the buttocks of the fetus. This can be either a single footling or a double footling, depending on whether one or both feet are coming first. Finally, a *kneeling breech* occurs when the legs are bent at the knees and the knees themselves are presented first. Breech presentations may prolong labor because the lower part of the fetus does not exert as much pressure on the cervix as the fetal head. Complicating matters is that the largest part of the fetus (the head) emerges last, which may increase the risks of trauma to the head, malformation, interference with respiration, and maternal infection (Olds, London, & Ladewig, 1992; Cruikshank, 1990; Cunningham, MacDonald, & Gant, 1989). Because of such risks, most obstetricians elect to deliver babies in the breech position by cesarean section.

In **cesarean delivery** (or C-section) the baby is delivered through a surgical incision made in the mother's abdominal and uterine walls. The word "cesarean" comes from the Latin *caedere*, meaning "to cut." Possible reasons for a cesarean section, besides breech presentation, are the mother's failure to progress normally through labor, a disproportion between the size of the fetus and that of the birth canal, fetal distress, abnormalities in the labor process, and a previous cesarean section in the mother.

Cesarean delivery is not a recent innovation. An early Roman law known as *lex regia* required that a baby be removed from the uterus of any woman dying in late pregnancy. This law persisted under Roman rulers, eventually acquiring the name *lex Caesarea* under the rule of the Caesars. Contrary to popular belief, the cesarean procedure is not named after Julius Caesar, nor was he delivered this way. The fact that Caesar's mother lived many years after his birth makes it very unlikely that he was "untimely ripped" from her womb; the mortality rates for abdominal operations in ancient Rome were very high.

Although cesarean deliveries have recently begun a slow decline, they reached a high point in the late 1980s, when some 30 percent of births in U.S. hospitals were performed by this method (Freeman, 1990; Danziger & Wertz, 1989). Among the reasons for the great increase in the number of cesarean sections performed, from only about 4 percent in the 1950s, were the increasing numbers of older women and teenagers giving birth (both groups tend to have more difficulties in childbirth). Some writers (e.g., Freeman, 1990) argue, however, that obstetricians have often performed unnecessary cesareans because they can charge higher fees for this procedure.

Without question, cesarean sections have helped to reduce infant deaths in the recent past. However, critics of the upsurge in cesarean births believe that many of the sections being done today are potentially harmful to both mother and child, posing such risks as postoperative infection (Dunn, 1990). Recovery from a cesarean may also make postpartum adjustment and new-baby care more difficult (Davis & Rosen, 1986; Feinbloom & Forman, 1987; Cohen & Estner, 1983).

When a cesarean section is planned, the operation is done before the onset of labor (the mother is usually admitted 24 hours before surgery) to ensure that the uterine contents will be sterile. Once labor begins, bacteria tend to ascend from the vagina into the uterus and are a potential source of infection.

breech presentation The appearance of the lower part of the fetus first during delivery.

cesarean delivery The baby is delivered through a surgical incision made in the mother's abdominal and uterine walls.

Childbirth and Parenthood

Preparations for a cesarean section are similar to those for any other abdominal operation, except that they include preparation for the care of the baby. The other major difference is that the use of narcotic drugs is avoided because of their depressant effect on the baby. When doctors perform the classic cesarean operation, an incision is made directly into the uterine wall. Once this is accomplished, the baby and the placenta are removed. The incision is then closed with sutures. A more popular technique today is called the *low cervical transverse cesarean section*. Here the incision is made through the tissues of the lower uterine segment and cervix. Compared to the classic cesarean operation, the low cervical transverse section leaves scar tissue that is much less likely to rupture during later labors. This is because most of the force of a uterine contraction comes from the upper, rather than lower, segment of the uterus. Thus many women who have had this type of C-section can deliver vaginally in subsequent pregnancies (Scott, 1990; Pridjian, 1991; Rosen, 1991).

The Third Stage

The third and last stage of labor is the expulsion of the placenta. Once the baby has been delivered, the uterus begins to relax and contract, which reduces the area of placental attachment. This causes the placenta to detach itself and move toward the lower uterus. The actual expulsion of the placenta can generally be accomplished by the bearing-down efforts of the mother. If this is not possible, the clinician applies gentle traction to the cord while exerting pressure on the fundus (the upper, rounded portion of the uterus). This should be done only when the uterus is hard and there is no bleeding.

**MAKING USE
OF WHAT
WE KNOW**

**What a Healthy
Newborn Looks
Like**

*M*any parents are unprepared for the sight of their newborn. Unless well above the average of 8 pounds, the baby looks very tiny. Top-to-toe measurement is only 18 to 21 inches.

The newborn's skin is quite thin, almost translucent. Upon close inspection, veins can be seen through it. The skin may be wrinkled because of its exposure to amniotic fluid. It is also temporarily rosy red. The skin of African-American, Asian, and other nonwhite babies usually has not achieved its full pigmentation at birth.

The head looks too big for the body. It may also be temporarily elongated or lopsided from the pressure exerted on it during labor. Parents will discover when touching the scalp that there are two soft spots, called *fontanels,* one above the brow and the other close to the crown of the head in the back. Both fontanels, which consist of strong bands of connective tissue, will close by the time the baby is 18 months old.

Some babies are born with a full head of hair, while others have hardly any. Hair color typically changes after it grows for a few months. Many newborns have blond hair that eventually turns dark; sometimes the reverse occurs.

Facial features may also be far from what the parents expected. Pudgy cheeks are characteristic of most newborns, along with a broad, flat nose. Typically, the chin recedes and the jaw is undersized. The eyes, usually gray or dark blue, are often crossed. The eyelids themselves are swollen.

A newborn's neck is short, and the trunk has small, sloping shoulders. Often the breasts are swollen and the abdomen is large and rounded. The genitals of both sexes seem large, particularly the male scrotum.

Should the newborn cry, a deep flush spreads over its entire body. Since tear ducts are not yet functioning, there are no tears. Strong crying will cause the veins on the head to throb and swell.

The hands are usually clenched in a fist. If opened, there are finely lined palms, creases at the wrists, and loose-fitting skin. The fingernails are paper-thin. The legs are often drawn up against the abdomen in a prebirth position. The knees are slightly bent and the legs are bowed. (Adapted from Helms & Turner, 1986; American Baby for the Mother-to-Be, 1973)

ASSURING THE NEWBORN'S SURVIVAL AND GOOD HEALTH

As the newborn is adjusting to extrauterine life and parents are admiring their new arrival (see, for example, the box on "What a Newborn Baby Looks Like"), delivery attendants are busy ensuring its survival. Respiration and heartbeat are the first concerns. Measures are taken to assure that respiration occurs as soon as the neonate is fully outside of its mother. Mucus and fluids are removed from the nose and mouth to assure normal respiration. After the delivery is completed, the neonate is held in a head-downward position, which prevents mucus and other matter (amniotic fluid, blood, etc.) from entering the respiratory passage. Gauze or a small suction bulb is generally used to clean out this matter, especially when a newborn has more than the normal amount of liquid present in its respiratory passage.

The birth cry does not always occur simultaneously with birth. Rather, the baby gasps or cries shortly after the mucus has been removed and respiration commences. All that is required to stimulate crying is a gentle rubbing of the baby's back, which also promotes the drainage of liquids from the respiratory passage. The traditional (now obsolete) slap on the buttocks is more than an unnecessary irritation; it can actually be dangerous.

Tests and Preventive Measures

Approximately one minute after birth and again five minutes later, a "score" is given to the newborn based on a "systems check" designed to evaluate critical life signs. The **Apgar test** is a relatively quick, simple, and safe procedure to evaluate the baby's overall condition.

The Apgar test is based on five life signs: heart rate, respiration, muscle tone, reflex irritability, and color. A score of 0, 1, or 2 is given for each sign according to the degree of "life" present. By taking all of the vital life signs into account, the newborn can be given an Apgar score in a surprisingly short time. A total score of 7 to 10 indicates that the baby is in generally good condition. A score from 4 to 6 is considered fair, in which case further clearing of the air passage and immediate administration of oxygen are likely to be done. A score of 0 to 3 indicates that the newborn is in critical condition and requires immediate emergency procedures.

Next the baby's footprints are taken, as well as a fingerprint of the mother. This is required by law and essential for identification purposes in the rare event of a mixup in the hospital nursery. Weight in pounds and ounces (and in grams), head-to-heel length in inches, and the diameter of the largest part of the newborn's head and chest are recorded. The baby's temperature is also taken with a rectal thermometer.

Certain preventive measures are also taken. For example, the baby is given an injection of vitamin K1 to prevent hemorrhaging. In addition, all states require that because the eyes are especially vulnerable to gonococci in the birth canal, eye drops of silver nitrate or, more commonly today, ophthalmic erythromycin, be given to prevent the infant from contracting gonorrhea. This treatment also wards off pneumococcal and chlamydial infections.

Apgar test An assessment of the newborn to check basic life processes. The test evaluates five life signs: heart rate, respiration, muscle tone, reflex irritability, and color.

Circumcision

For many newborn boys, circumcision is another adjustment they must make to extrauterine life. Remember that circumcision is the surgical removal of all or part of the prepuce, or foreskin, of the penis to permit exposure of the glans. About 90 percent of all male babies in the United States were circumcised in the 1950s and 1960s, but this figure dropped to about 70 percent in the latter part of the 1980s.

One of the major reasons for circumcision is that it makes it easier to retract the foreskin for cleansing purposes. However, there are other reasons parents have their newborn boys circumcised: the desire to conform to a dominant cultural practice or religious rite of passage into manhood, the wish that the child resemble his father, and cosmetic appearance (Lund, 1900; Scharli, 1989; King, Caddy, & Cohen, 1989). Further motivating many parents is the fact that rates of cancer of the penis seem to be lower in circumcised men, although there is conflicting evidence on this (see, for example, the American Academy of Pediatrics, 1989; Lund, 1990). Additionally, the incidence of cervical cancer may be lower in women married to circumcised men.

Opponents of routine circumcision of male babies maintain that the surgery is an unnecessary trauma for the newborn. Circumcision also poses certain surgical risks, such as the development of penile ulcerations, adhesions, damage to the urethra, discomfort, and restlessness (Olds, London, & Ladewig, 1992). Opponents also feel that, with good hygiene, uncircumcised males can be just as clean and comfortable as circumcised males.

If parents decide to have their infant circumcised, the surgery is usually scheduled for the day before the baby is due to be discharged from the hospital to ensure that he has become well stabilized. A variety of surgical procedures are possible, all of which produce minimal bleeding. In one of the more common techniques, the prepuce is pulled back and then clamped. Excessive prepuce is then cut off and the prepuce is sutured in place. Figure 11–5 illustrates this circumcision procedure.

Why are circumcisions performed? Are there any advantages to being circumcised?

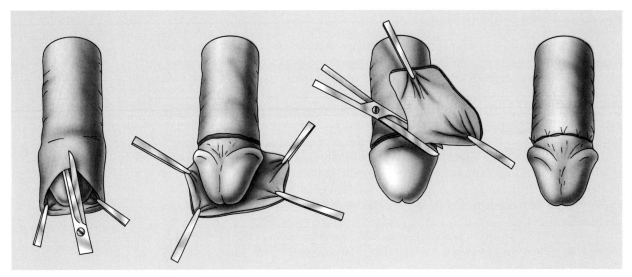

FIGURE 11–4
One Technique of Circumcision.

The prepuce, or foreskin, is slit and excess foreskin is cut off. Then the remaining foreskin is sewn in place behind the corona of the penis.

ALTERNATIVE DELIVERY TECHNIQUES

While large percentages of mothers continue to deliver their babies in conventional medical and hospital settings, growing numbers are pursuing nontraditional alternatives to hospital labor and delivery. Most are doing so because they object to the use of anesthesia during delivery and to other medical intrusions on the mother and baby. Some also object to the de-emphasized role of the partner in the delivery of the baby (Wertz & Wertz, 1989; Danziger & Wertz, 1989; Edwards & Waldorf, 1984).

natural childbirth Method of childbirth that avoids the use of anesthesia and allows both husband and wife to play an active role in the delivery of their baby.

Natural childbirth attempts to avoid the use of anesthesia and to allow both husband and wife to play an active role in the delivery of their baby. A natural childbirth technique was developed as early as 1940 by the English obstetrician Grantley Dick-Read. Couples choosing natural childbirth attend classes that stress special breathing exercises and relaxation responses. This approach assumes that fears of one sort or another cause women to tense their muscles during delivery, a factor that delays the birth process and increases the mother's pain. If women know what to expect and learn how to relax, proponents of natural childbirth say, discomfort can be significantly reduced.

The Lamaze Method

Lamaze method A natural childbirth approach that emphasizes a conditioned learning technique in which the mother replaces one set of learned responses (fear, pain) with another (relaxation, muscle control).

The **Lamaze method** (named after Dr. Fernand Lamaze, a French obstetrician) is one of the most popular alternative approaches to labor and delivery. In Lamaze classes mothers and fathers learn the importance of preparing for childbirth. They are taught breathing techniques and muscular exercises, as well as about prenatal development and the stages of labor. The Lamaze method and others like it are conditioned learning techniques that teach the mother to replace one set of learned responses (fear, pain) with another (concentration on relaxation and muscle control). The partner serves as a "coach" who helps the mother to relax during labor and delivery.

WHERE TO FIND MORE INFORMATION ON NATURAL CHILDBIRTH

American Academy of Husband Coached Childbirth
P.O. Box 5224
Sherman Oaks, CA 91413
This group offers information on natural childbirth classes, including referrals to area programs.

American Society for Psychoprophylaxis in Obstetrics
1840 Wilson Boulevard
Suite 204
Arlington, VA 22201
A national nonprofit association that promotes the Lamaze method of childbirth as well as certain types of maternity care.

Childbirth Without Pain Education Association
20134 Snowden Place
Detroit, MI 48235
This group offers a wide range of information on natural childbirth, pregnancy, and parenting in general.

International Childbirth Education Association
P.O. Box 20048
Minneapolis, MN 55420
A resource center for childbirth and parenting topics.

Maternity Center Association
48 East 92nd Street
New York, NY 10128-1397
A nonprofit health agency that publishes resource material on maternity and infant care.

National Association of Childbirth Education
3940 11th Street
Riverside, CA 92501
Provides referrals to childbirth programs and dispenses information on family-centered child care.

A mother describes how her baby was born with the Lamaze method:

Doug and I took Lamaze classes together and felt really comfortable with our knowledge of natural childbirth. He was great during labor and really helped me to get control of my contractions and to relax. When I was brought into the delivery room, he was right there with me and gave tremendous support. Having Doug there when my baby was delivered was the most special moment of our lives. (Authors' files)

A father had these observations:

I'll be honest—I was hesitant at first about Lamaze and reluctant to go to the classes. But as time wore on, I realized the importance of my role as a "coach" and how much my wife needed me. Seeing our baby Denise born was a fantastic experience, and I'm glad that I played a part. I also got to cut the umbilical cord. Just going through the experience together gave me a special feeling and brought us together. (Authors' files)

The Leboyer Method

The **Leboyer method** stresses the importance of a gentle delivery and minimal trauma for the newborn. Developed by French obstetrician Frederick Leboyer and detailed in his book *Birth Without Violence* (1975), this delivery method is markedly different from conventional childbirth procedures. The baby is born into a dimly lit delivery room that is kept relatively silent. Immediately after birth the infant is placed on the mother's stomach to be gently massaged, in the belief that tactile stimulation and contact soothe the baby and promote bonding. The infant is then further soothed by a warm bath. Only after this is the baby given a routine medical examination.

Leboyer suggests that such steps are transitions that minimize the trauma of birth. His ideas have not gained universal acceptance. Critics maintain that it is dangerous to postpone the examination of the neonate after birth, especially when dim lighting may prevent the accurate detection of vital life signs. Moreover, researchers (e.g., Maziade et al., 1986; Nelson et al., 1980) have not been able to find any long-range benefits among infants delivered by the Leboyer method.

Home Births

More couples today are opting for home births in rebellion against rising hospital costs and impersonal neonatal and postpartum care. Home births are especially popular among women who have some college education (Gilgoff, 1988; Pearse, 1987)

A WORLD OF DIFFERENCES

Home Births in the Netherlands

At the turn of the century in the United States, 95 percent of babies were born at home. Because there were fewer hospitals and physicians in those days, a midwife was typically summoned to deliver the baby. In an effort to combat high infant mortality rates, hospitals began to handle difficult deliveries in the early decades of the century, and home deliveries became less and less common. Today about 99 percent of all births in this country take place in a hospital, and most are supervised by obstetricians (Danziger & Wertz, 1989).

In startling contrast to American practice, about 35 percent of all Dutch women give birth at home. Even though the Netherlands has a highly sophisticated health-care system, it leads the industrialized world in the proportion of home births. Midwives assist at virtually all home and hospital births.

Interestingly, statistics show that the rate of infant mortality within a week of birth is higher in hospitals than at home. However, this is because virtually all problem births are detected in advance and take place in a hospital setting. National health insurance policies cover most Dutch deliveries, and home births are regarded as so safe that the insurance does not pay for a hospital birth unless it is medically indicated.

The popularity of home births in the Netherlands can be traced to the importance of the home in Dutch social life. The small geographical size of the country and its above-average roads make it possible for expectant couples from any location to get to a hospital within half an hour, if necessary. When delivery does take place in a hospital, a "short-stay" policy has most mothers and their newborns in their own homes within five hours after the birth.

Childbirth and Parenthood

and, as you'll discover in the "World of Differences" box, home births are popular in other nations.

Home births are often presided over by certified **nurse-midwives**, trained delivery specialists who provide qualified medical care to expectant mothers. Usually the midwife has earned a bachelor's degree in nursery-midwifery and works on a medical team including a gynecologist and an obstetrician. The nurse-midwife spends considerably more time than physicians do with the mother before, during, and after the delivery and offers close, personal attention in a relaxed and comfortable setting. Some nurse-midwives are in private practice (depending upon state licensing requirements), while others work out of a physician's offices, a birthing clinic, a hospital, or their own homes.

A mother reflects on her home birth:

> **Having Sam at home was the most wondrous, painful, and exciting event of our lives to date. Our two midwives were professional and caring. Would we have another birth at home again? Absolutely! (Authors' files)**

Lay midwives have been trained by other midwives and are not certified. Poor people often seek the services of lay midwives because they charge less than certified nurse-midwives.

For low-risk women, research (e.g., Sullivan & Weitz, 1988; Gilgoff, 1988; Cohen, 1982; Clark & Bennetts, 1982) indicates that home births are as safe as hospital births. Sandra Danziger and Dorothy Wertz (1989) add that women who give birth in familiar surroundings, at their own speed and without medication, often feel a sense of accomplishment and uninhibited family closeness that is difficult to experience in a hospital. However, home birth has often been criticized, especially by medical personnel, because this method cannot provide the security that hospitals offer against unforeseen complications, as well as on the grounds that some midwives lack formal training (Pearse, 1987; Wolfson, 1986).

Rooming-in and Birthing Room Facilities

Rooming-in and birthing room hospital facilities are also increasing in popularity. **Rooming-in hospital facilities** allow the mother to care for the newborn in her own room. The infant is usually brought to the mother's room within the first few hours of birth and remains there (rather than in the nursery) during the duration of

nurse-midwife A trained delivery specialist who provides qualified medical care to expectant mothers. Usually the midwife has earned a bachelor's degree in nurse-midwifery and works on a medical team including a gynecologist and an obstetrician.

rooming-in hospital facilities Facilities that allow the parents of newborns to care for their baby in the mother's hospital room.

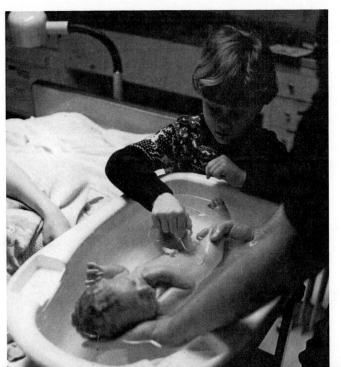

An eight-year-old boy helps give his newborn sister a bath. In some hospitals today, a woman can go through labor and delivery in a special birthing room and have her family about her immediately after her baby is born.

335

TABLE 11–2

Planning the Birth of Your Baby

How do you plan to deliver your baby? The birth of a child should be as comfortable and wonderful an experience as humanly possible. The expectant parents need to decide how and where the mother will deliver the baby and who will assist her. Compatibility with the chosen practitioner is the most important consideration for the mother. She must feel that the practitioner and she have the same values and goals in the delivery process.

One way to choose a practitioner is to ask women who have recently delivered their babies about their experiences. You can also visit all types of practices in your area, and perhaps even attend a birth to gain insight into the procedure. Here are some questions to guide your search for information:

Questions to Ask Yourself

1. Probably 90 percent of births are normal and occur without complications, but childbirth does entail risks no matter where it occurs. Where would you feel most comfortable in the event of a complication? Who would you want to be there?
2. Birth attendants' philosophies vary regarding responsibility for birth procedures. How much control do you want over your labor? How do you want to divide responsibility for what happens?
3. What role do you want technological equipment to play in your labor and birth?
4. The medical establishment considers home births unsafe and often disdains the midwifery profession. How would you feel about going against conventional medical advice?
5. The most thought out plans may have to be altered if labor does not proceed as expected. How flexible are your plans? How would you feel about changing birth environments in midlabor?

Questions to Ask Doctors

1. What are their experiences with and attitudes toward the type of labor and delivery you have chosen? How do they feel about labor-inducing drugs, electronic fetal monitoring, episiotomy, and anything else you would like to include or exclude?
2. What percentage of their deliveries have been made by cesarean section? The national average is in the 10–20% range, but this is considered excessive by some health workers.
3. Who are their backup doctors, and do they share your attitudes toward your birth choices?

Questions to Ask Midwives

1. How broad is the training and experience they have had? Are they certified?
2. How have they handled emergencies in the past?
3. What kind(s) of backup do they have? Some midwives have a specific doctor who will assist or take over if a complication arises; others have informal relations with the staff of a local hospital.
4. How would they handle a transfer to a hospital if it became necessary? Would they stay with you?

(Adapted from Levinson, 1984)

---

birthing room Delivery room offering a homelike, relaxed atmosphere within the hospital's general delivery unit.

birthing chair A special chair that elevates a woman's body so that it is in a near-vertical position during delivery.

hospitalization. A **birthing room** offers a homelike and relaxed atmosphere within the hospital delivery unit. The mother goes through both labor and delivery in this room rather than being rushed to the delivery room prior to birth. Many couples today combine the birthing room with the natural childbirth approach to labor and delivery.

Many hospitals today also offer a **birthing chair,** which elevates a woman's body so that it is in a near-vertical position during delivery. (A medieval version of this chair is shown in Figure 11–1.) The modern version of it usually has a molded seat that is set on a pedestal. A motor allows it to be tilted, elevated, or lowered.

With so many different methods of childbirth available, how can a couple choose the delivery technique that is most suitable for them? Table 11–2 offers you some guidelines in making this choice, including questions to ask of doctors and midwives whom you may interview. In addition, the resources box on page 333 lists agencies that can provide helpful information.

POSTPARTUM ADJUSTMENTS

The **postpartum period** refers to the first month or so after childbirth. It is a period full of adjustments, adaptations, and challenges. For the mother, it is a time when her body readjusts after undergoing the rigors of pregnancy and childbirth. For both parents, it is a time for tending to the needs of the newborn and adjusting to their new roles.

postpartum period The first month or so after childbirth.

The Puerperium

The **puerperium** is the time after childbirth in which the mother's reproductive organs return to their prepregnant condition. For most women, this takes about six weeks, although the method of delivery as well as the circumstances associated with it affect the manner in which the body returns to its normal condition. We discuss here some of the major processes that take place in the reproductive system during the puerperium.

puerperium The time after childbirth in which the mother's reproductive organs return to their prepregnant condition.

UTERUS. Within hours of delivery of the placenta, the uterus contracts to a firm mass of tissue about the size of a grapefruit—less than half its size at delivery. The uterus remains about the same size for the first few days after delivery, but then rapidly shrinks. Within five to six weeks, it returns to its prepregnant size.

The uterus has the ability to rid itself of materials remaining after delivery, something that generally assists the overall healing process. This discharge, called **lochia,** may last for several weeks after childbirth. Lochia is similar to menstrual discharge, and the amount of it varies from woman to woman. It has a musty, stale odor that is not offensive. In fact, a foul odor suggests infection and the need for prompt assessment.

lochia During the puerperium, the discharge of materials remaining after delivery.

CERVIX. Following delivery, the cervix is a soft, open, spongy structure. It begins to retract rapidly until, by the end of the first week, only a fingertip opening into the vagina is visible. However, the shape of the cervix is permanently altered by a woman's first experience of childbirth. The opening into the vagina remains slightly more open than before, although the opening into the uterus is closed. Moreover, if delivery caused any significant cervical lacerations, the cervix may appear somewhat lopsided.

VAGINA. The vagina also needs some time to recover from the distention caused by childbirth. While it will reduce greatly in size, it usually remains a little wider than before pregnancy. The vagina as well as the hymen are also usually bruised and small lacerations may be evident. The labia typically become softer after childbirth. Tightening of the vaginal orifice may require perineal exercises, which for most women can begin soon after delivery. Kegel exercises, which involve contraction and relaxation of the pubococcygeal muscle, have been shown to improve the tone and contractibility of the vaginal opening (see Chapter 15's box on these exercises).

MENSTRUATION. The first menstruation typically occurs within six to eight weeks of delivery. Mothers who breast-feed often do not resume their normal menstruation pattern until weaning occurs, although this is not a certainty.

lactation The secretion of milk in the mother's breasts.

THE BREASTS AND LACTATION. Increased levels of estrogen and progesterone during pregnancy stimulate breast development. This activity plays a major role in **lactation,** the secretion of milk. Lactation generally occurs by the third or fourth day postpartum. Before this point, the breasts secrete small amounts of a thin yellowish fluid called *colostrum* (discussed in Chapter 10).

As stores of milk build, the breasts become larger, firmer, and more tender. Several factors account for these changes. First, childbirth results in a significant reduction of estrogen and progesterone with a concomitant increase in the secretion of prolactin by the anterior pituitary gland. When the infant sucks on the mother's nipple, a hormone called *oxytocin* is released from the posterior pituitary gland. Oxytocin increases the contractibility of cells in the mammary ducts, which results in a flow of milk. Interestingly, oxytocin can also be released when a mother hears her baby cry. As oxytocin helps to stimulate the flow of breast milk, a "letdown" reflex occurs, which women often describe as a prickling or tingling sensation during which they can feel the milk trickling toward the nipple. The letdown reflex can also be initiated by tactile stimulation, such as by the newborn's sucking.

Breast milk, which is normally bluish-white in color, varies in quantity. Generally speaking, though, the amount of breast milk a woman produces increases as her infant's need for it increases. Suckling is the most important factor in maintaining an adequate supply of breast milk. However, other factors, such as the mother's diet,

MAKING USE OF WHAT WE KNOW

The Breast or the Bottle?

*C*hoosing between breast-feeding and formula-feeding is a difficult decision, one that has stimulated debate and aroused controversy for years. Most new mothers encounter numerous opinions on the subject from a multitude of diverse sources, ranging from watchful-eyed grandparents and in-laws to biologists, anthropologists, and psychologists. Infant feeding is a focal chapter in nearly every manual of child rearing. Subjected to so much "authoritative" but conflicting advice, the new mother often has a hard time deciding what to do (Lawrence, 1989).

Until the 1930s, when formula feeding was perfected, there was no really safe and reliable substitute for breast milk, although a woman could hire a wet nurse (a woman who breast-feeds and cares for an infant not her own) rather than nurse the baby herself. Since then, most mothers have had a choice—and a chance to weigh the supporting evidence for each alternative. The proponents of breast-feeding, supported by an international organization called the La Leche League (*leche* is the Spanish work for "milk"), maintain that nursing promotes close physical and psychological bonding between mother and infant. They assert that nursing is the "natural" way to nourish an infant and that it prevents most feeding problems, as well as

constipation and some allergic reactions. They also argue that breast-fed babies have fewer serious illnesses, including respiratory and gastrointestinal illnesses. Moreover, breast milk may contain antibodies to many of the infectious organisms newborns are exposed to (Pipes, 1989; Lawrence, 1989; Worthington-Roberts & Williams, 1989).

Many nursing mothers report experiencing a calm inner peace during feeding times. Sally Olds and colleagues (1992) maintain that breast-feeding en-

rest, and level of contentment, affect the overall supply. One month after delivery, a mother who regularly breast-feeds her baby produces about 20 ounces of breast milk a day. This will increase, on average, to a maximum of about 30 ounces a day if she continues to nurse. Some thoughts on breast-feeding versus formula-feeding can be found in the "Making Use of What We Know" box, "The Breast or the Bottle?"

Postpartum Depression

Many mothers feel an emotional letdown during the first week or two after their baby is born. In its mild form, this affective state is referred to as the *postpartum blues* and often manifests itself in bouts of sadness or crying. The more extreme form, called *postpartum depression*, lasts somewhere between six and eight weeks, and is often characterized by insomnia, pessimism, lethargy, feelings of inadequacy and inability to cope, and fatigue (Dodge, 1990; Fendrich, Warner, & Weissman, 1990; Field et al., 1990; Fleming et al., 1990; Goodman & Brumley, 1990; Hammen, Burge, & Stansbury, 1990; Hock & DeMeis, 1990; Zahn-Waxler et al., 1990).

A number of factors contribute to this emotional letdown. To begin with, there are many psychological and physical changes that accompany pregnancy, childbirth, and early child care. Many new mothers report unsettled feelings about their new parenting role, anxiety about caring for the newborn, and concerns about not getting

Why do many women feel an emotional letdown or the "blues" after childbirth?

hances attachment by providing the opportunity for frequent direct skin contact between the newborn and the mother. It is also generally accepted that breast-feeding inhibits the mother's menstrual cycle, as well as the mood swings associated with menstruation. This may enable nursing mothers to respond to the baby's needs in a more relaxed and calm manner.

Bottle feeding also has its supporters. One advantage is that it allows the father to feed his child. The chief advan-

tages for the mother are greater mobility and freedom. Most mothers cannot go back to work shortly after giving birth unless they can rely on formula feedings for their babies. Bottle feeding also permits the mother to spend more time with her other children, who may resent the continual contact that a breast-fed baby receives. In addition, some mothers find nursing physically annoying or painful, while others simply don't like the practice or are embarrassed by it, particularly in the presence of other people. One study (Ryan, Rush, & Krieger, 1991) notes a steady decline in breast-feeding in recent years. Among the reasons cited by the researchers were that breast-feeding is no longer considered "fashionable," the decline in the promotion of breast-feeding in the popular media, and the aggressive marketing of infant formulas.

Obviously, this issue is still controversial. Both sides of the argument have merit, and this may relieve a mother's sense of guilt for choosing one approach over the other. How a mother interacts with her infant during feeding—her warmth, care, and attention, as well as the trust she stimulates by meeting life's most basic need—is probably the most critical factor for the baby's well-being (Lauwers & Woessner, 1990; Satter, 1990; Renfrew, Fisher, & Arms, 1990; Lawrence, 1989; Sawley, 1989).

enough sleep and support. We must also remember that a woman's body is under a great deal of stress during labor and delivery. Once the placenta is expelled, the estrogen and progesterone it has been generating abruptly cease. Another physical change is in the level of natural painkillers, called beta-endorphins, that are produced during labor. When the mother delivers the baby, she is on a high from these beta-endorphins, but following birth, their level declines abruptly and this may cause depression.

The emotional letdown caused by all these factors is uncomfortable, but usually transitory. It is considered a normal reaction to motherhood's many challenges and responsibilities. Fathers, too, sometimes report "postpartum blues" and depression, especially if they feel overwhelmed by child-care responsibilities or inadequate at helping their wives cope with the baby. It is important for both mothers and fathers to acknowledge any feelings of discouragement, sadness, or perceived helplessness. People vary widely in how they deal with these feelings. Some prefer to talk about them with their mate or a close friend, while others choose to sort out their emotions alone. Once people realize what is happening and discover that they are not the only new parents who feel this way, it usually becomes easier for them to cope with postpartum blues (Lauersen, 1983).

Michael and Nancy Samuels (1986) suggest that situations that are problematic for the new mother or father should be solved one by one. Probably at no other time in life is the resolution of small problems so meaningful. Each solution, however minor, contributes to a parent's sense of well-being, competence, and control. When faced with emotional letdown, the mother especially might also use relaxation techniques, such as those focusing on deep breathing or the reduction of muscle tension (see, for example, Charlesworth & Nathan, 1984; Shaffer, 1982). Relaxation usually lowers a mother's anxiety and helps her to see her problems and concerns in a more optimistic light. A relaxed state is ideal for getting in touch with feelings and for becoming more aware of both the positive and negative elements of parenthood.

Lovemaking After Childbirth

How soon after childbirth can a couple resume intercourse?

At one time it was almost always recommended that couples avoid intercourse until six weeks after the birth of a child. Today many authorities feel that intercourse is safe at two weeks postpartum, provided there were no complications in the delivery, sutured lacerations, or an episiotomy. Most episiotomies heal by the end of the third week. The abdominal incision made in a cesarean section generally takes about two weeks to heal; barring medical complications, intercourse should be safe at this time.

Still, intercourse may be uncomfortable for a few months because vaginal tissues remain delicate and fragile. There also may be residual pain from the episiotomy. Moreover, the vaginal area is often drier than usual, because of lower estrogen levels during breast-feeding. This reduction in vaginal lubrication often creates discomfort during intercourse.

All of this means that a woman needs to feel physically and psychologically comfortable before the couple resumes intercourse. Several things can be done to assist her physical comfort. Couples may use a lubricating jelly, such as K-Y jelly or Surgilube, when they first resume intercourse. The man should enter the vagina very gently in the beginning and should control the intensity of his penile thrusting. The woman may prefer to be on top so that she can control the movement of the penis. Should discomfort persist and waiting become necessary, we remind the reader that there are many ways besides intercourse to share sexual intimacy. Some of these are oral-genital sex, caressing, and mutual masturbation. Partners can create their own unique ways of making love without having intercourse if they communicate and are patient with each other. It is only a matter of time before the vaginal tissues fully heal and hormonal activity returns to normal. The vagina will eventually heal completely, and then sex should be as pleasurable as or more pleasurable than it was before childbirth (Lauresen, 1983).

Some sources (i.e., Shapiro, 1983) recommend that oral-genital sex be undertaken gingerly because the mouth contains potentially harmful bacteria that, when introduced into a vaginal, urethral, or vulvar laceration, can cause an infection. If couples are contemplating oral-genital sex less than three weeks after childbirth, the woman should carefully inspect her vulva and vagina with a hand mirror for evidence of lacerations that have not healed. If she feels uncertain how to do this, she should consult a gynecologist.

Couples may find that they also have to make psychological adjustments in their sexual relations after childbirth. New child-care routines and fatigue have a tendency to disrupt sexual intimacy and "spoil the mood." Some men (and women) may also react negatively to a woman's changed body, such as abdominal stretch marks and breast changes. When the woman is breast-feeding, couples should be forewarned that during orgasm milk may spout from the nipples because sexual activity releases oxytocin. Some couples find this pleasurable or amusing; others choose to have the woman wear a bra during sex. Some women nurse before lovemaking to reduce the chances of milk release (Olds, London, & Ladewig, 1992).

Finally, a few comments regarding postpartum contraception. Although it is rare, a woman can ovulate and become pregnant as early as four to six weeks after birth. Consequently, adequate birth control measures need to be taken before intercourse is resumed. Some people hold that breast-feeding inhibits ovulation, but there is no scientific evidence to support this contention (Mischel, 1989).

Up until a woman's six-week postpartum examination, the most adequate and easy-to-use contraceptives are condoms (lubricated varieties will not irritate sensitive vaginal tissues) and vaginal spermicides in the form of nonprescriptive aerosol foams, jellies, tablets, creams, and suppositories. A woman should not try to use her old diaphragm before her six-week postpartum examination. Because of changing anatomy and the greater sensitivity of vaginal tissues after childbirth, the diaphragm is usually difficult to insert. Also, it may no longer adequately cover the cervix and may need to be replaced with a larger size.

For non-nursing mothers, oral contraceptives are a possible method of birth control. They are not an option for nursing mothers because combination birth control pills contain estrogen and reduce the quantity of breast milk. Progestin-only birth control pills do not seem to affect milk production, but they may affect the composition of the milk by reducing its protein and vitamin content. For these reasons, nursing mothers should choose an alternative form of birth control.

PARENTHOOD

"Just Molly and me, and baby makes three—we're happy in my blue heaven." So go the lyrics to a song from yesteryear, but parenthood is not so simple as the song suggests. In fact, the transition from couple to family is one of the most complex and dramatic changes most people will ever make in their lives. As Lloyd Saxton (1990) sees it, after the birth of a child, a new and irrevocable life phase begins for the couple, for with parenthood, they assume responsibility for a new human being. The couple no longer has the luxury of relating just to each other. Now there is a third person to consider: a new, unique person who initially makes limitless demands.

Unfortunately, as several writers have noted, first-time parents get little formal preparation (Stinnett, Walters, & Stinnett, 1991; Dickinson & Leming, 1990; Zinn & Eitzen, 1990). This is discouraging, for parenthood signifies full entrance into adult society, including assumption of all the responsibilities that such status brings. Both

MYTHS AND MISCONCEPTIONS

Folklore About Parenthood

When deciding whether or not to have children, and also while bringing up children, adults strive to base their judgments on sound, rational principles. According to E. E. LeMasters and John DeFrain (1989), though, some common ideas regarding parenthood are based less on logic than on romantic misconceptions about parenthood. Some of these misconceptions are:

Children will turn out well if they have "good" parents. Almost everyone knows of at least one nice family with a black sheep in the fold. Children are so complex that parents simply do not have the kind of "quality control" found in industrial production. Skillful parents usually turn out a more reliable "product" than those with more modest talents—but even for good parents, there is no such thing as "zero defects."

Today's parents are not as good as those of yesteryear. This belief is impossible to prove or disprove, of course, but it seems quite prevalent. One thing is true, though: higher standards are applied to today's parents, and the modern world in which they have to function is more complex than the world of yesterday.

Child rearing is easier today because of modern medicine, modern appliances, child psychology, and so forth. Although some people claim that modern parents have an easier time of it because they have access to such conveniences as dishwashers and diaper services, the truth is that today's parents, with their busy schedules, are in much more of a rat race than their grandparents ever imagined.

All married couples should have children. This is a dubious proposition and one that few (if any) experts on childhood would support. Many married couples enjoy their own exclusive company and can sustain their marriage without the addition of children. And despite what many people think, the birth of a child does not necessarily improve the marital relationship.

Love is enough to ensure good parental performance. While love is a very important dimension of parenting, it is not enough. It must be accompanied by knowledge and insight, as well as dedication to the parenting role, maturity, flexibility, warmth, and supportive understanding.

partners must integrate the parent role into their other role sets, including spouse and worker. Moreover, parenthood has profound psychological, social, and sexual implications for partners, for their mutual relations, and for their relation to the larger society (Entwisle, 1985).

Besides failing to prepare people for parenthood, society tends to paint an idealistic image of parenthood that veils the reality (the "Myths and Misconceptions" box illustrates some of the more inaccurate notions about having children). Certainly there are many positive aspects to childrearing—nurturing and cuddling your own child, teaching and watching her learn and grow, giving her things you didn't have, loving her and receiving her love. But there are also negative aspects that new parents are seldom prepared for—dealing with a baby's often inexplicable distress and crying, his sicknesses, or his willfulness and oppositional behavior as he becomes more and more independent. Right from the beginning, couples need to accept the realities and realize that while parenthood has its share of triumphs, it also has its share of frustrations and headaches.

Numerous researchers (e.g., Goetting, 1986; Goldberg, Michaels, & Lamb, 1985; Harriman, 1986) have expounded on the joys of raising children. While they acknowledge the demands of parenthood (such as loss of sleep, physical fatigue, financial concerns), they also emphasize the many satisfactions that child care brings. Of course, the stability of the marital relationship is an important consideration. As Linda Harriman (1986) observes, a good marriage tends to maximize the benefits and minimize the liabilities of having children.

Larry Jensen and Merril Kingston (1986) note that most parents steadily grow more satisfied and confident. As they make the necessary adjustments and establish routines, their anxieties about child care usually subside and the pleasure they take in parenting soars. Fears and anxieties also begin to disappear as people learn that they don't have to do everything "by the book." As lessons are learned firsthand, parenthood begins to acquire a more relaxed quality. Consider the positive reflections of this mother:

> I wouldn't trade places for anything in the world. I look forward to spending time with Emily, enjoying each moment. Many times I'll just hold her in my arms and realize how beautiful and perfect she is. She gives me a wave of contentment that I never before experienced in my life. My husband feels the same way. We both work outside the home, so we end up splitting child-care responsibilities. Depending on who stayed home, stories are invariably told about Emily's latest escapades. The other day she took her first step and my husband couldn't wait to tell me all about it. (Authors' files)

Most new mothers and fathers, however, do feel somewhat uneasy about certain aspects of parenthood, particularly unfamiliar child-care routines and demands. Unsureness often increases their anxiety and confusion, and many parents feel added pressure from mounting child-care chores. One father reflects on the care his infant son needed:

> I've got to admit, it's a lot more work than I thought it would be. Maybe it's because I chose to get involved with our son and not be a distant father. Anyway, he keeps my wife and I on our toes. When I get home from work and have had a tough day, it's especially challenging. For example, last week he had a cold and that really made things hectic. It seemed like everything we tried didn't work and we all ended up being angry and frustrated with one another. What a relief when he got better. (Authors' files)

A mother clearly remembers the physical fatigue she and her husband felt from the constant chores of infant care:

> Always feeling tired and losing sleep were the biggest adjustments we had to make. It's funny, I always remember that line, "People who say they slept like a baby usually don't have one." How true! For the first six or eight months, we went to work bleary-eyed and drank what seemed like gallons of coffee to stay awake. (Authors' files)

Life with baby also affects patterns of intimacy and affection between partners. Many couples are surprised by how difficult it can be to enjoy each other's exclusive company after they have a baby. Social life is also affected as interactions and visits with friends become restricted.

The transition from couple to family means that the child's needs often compete with those of the spouse. That is why it is not uncommon for parents to feel angry, jealous, and frustrated during stressful times. A mother shares how parenthood changed her pattern of sexual intimacy with her husband:

> Our sex life really suffered and that bothered both of us. Either we were both too tired, or we were worried that the baby would hear us. When Carl got older, we were always afraid that he would walk in on us during our lovemaking. It's hard to relax in the sack when you constantly have to keep your guard up. (Authors' files)

A father put it this way:

> The biggest sacrifice to be made when Brian was born was the loss of our privacy. No longer did we have the place to ourselves and unlimited access to one another. We managed, though, and ended up spending quality time together in spite of it all. It just took better planning and a little more work. (Authors' files)

Becoming a Mother

It is during the early stages of parenthood that mothers typically discover just how much their lives have been altered by the birth of a child. In traditional homes the mother is thrust almost immediately into her new role and has to make decisions regarding her offspring—for example, whether to breast-feed or bottle-feed the infant. Cooking, cleaning, and other domestic chores also await the traditional mother.

Not too long ago all mothers were expected to remain at home to care for their children. Many felt that to venture away from the family in search of a paycheck, particularly during a child's early years of development, was uncaring and unwise. Today, however, increasing numbers of women are breaking this traditional stereotype and working outside the home. As Lois Hoffman (1989) notes, maternal employment has become a fact of modern life. Moreover, there is a growing social acceptance that a woman can handle the roles of breadwinner and mother simultaneously and that working mothers can have quality time with their children.

While mothers with jobs outside the home reap their share of benefits and satisfactions, such as personal and career fulfillment (see Gilbert & Davidson, 1989; Spitze, 1988; Pietromonaco, Manis, & Markus, 1987; Pleck, 1985; Voydanoff, 1988, 1984), they also commonly make certain sacrifices. Cleaning, cooking, and child care

Becoming parents for the first time is wonderful and exciting, but it also makes many demands on a couple. Every experience is new, and each partner needs to support the other not only in caring physically for the baby but in dealing with the inevitable anxieties about what the baby needs and whether they're doing things right.

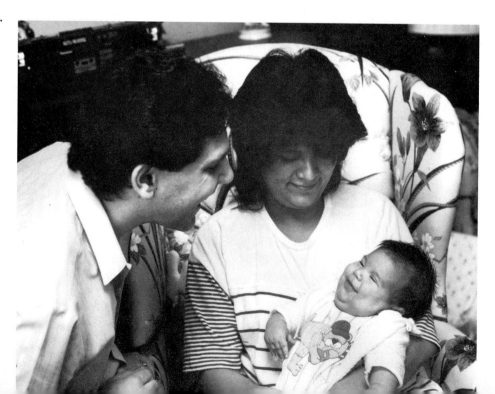

continue to be mainly the mother's responsibilities, for while many fathers say they prefer an equitable domestic arrangement, far fewer actually do their share of the work around the house. Thus most working mothers put in long days and find they have little leisure time (Benin & Agostinelli, 1988; Kamo, 1988).

Many working mothers also report feeling some anxiety about their children's well-being and a nagging doubt about whether they've made the right choice. On the other side, however, many women who are full-time mothers often want to go back into the labor force. One mother talks about this "Catch-22" situation so many women find themselves in:

> **When I made the decision to return to work, I remember that I looked forward to returning to the office. But I was not prepared for the sadness and guilt that would follow. Even though I secured quality child care, the pangs of guilt began when I said goodbye to her in the morning and continued throughout the day. I thought about her constantly at work and felt angry and cheated. In time, I got over the guilt, but those were very trying times. (Authors' files)**

Becoming a Father

Until recently, the father's role in child rearing was largely overlooked. This neglect can be attributed, at least in part, to the fact that American society was long extremely "mother-centered" in its philosophy of child care. With more dual-career households and a declining emphasis on gender-role differences, however, the father's influence on the developing child is now being recognized. In the last decade many researchers have explored the father's role and presented us with a wealth of information (see, for example, Pruett, 1987; Lewis & O'Brien, 1987; Robinson & Barret, 1986; Lewis & Salt, 1986; Hanson & Bozett, 1985; Lamb, 1981; Parke, 1981).

Glen Palm and Rob Palkovitz (1988) note that there are different degrees of paternal involvement and have identified five types of fathers on that basis:

- *Primary Parent Father.* This is the househusband or the single custodial father. He has the primary responsibility for the day-to-day care of his children.
- *Co-Parental Father.* This father represents the ideal in many dual-earner households because of his egalitarian spirit. The co-parental father actively rejects the traditional notion of fatherhood by becoming equally involved with the mother in daily child-care responsibilities.
- *Assistant Parent Father.* This kind of father behaves rather like the traditional father, except that he is a mother's helper who is capable of taking over child care some of the time. However, he does not share equally in child-care tasks and responsibilities.
- *Traditional Father.* The traditional father demonstrates a strong commitment to his family in the primary role of breadwinner. He tends to define his role as one of some interaction with, and responsibility toward, his children.
- *Uninterested and Unavailable Father.* This father exhibits minimal interest in his children and is usually remote, both physically and psychologically, from their upbringing.

Earlier in this chapter we noted that growing numbers of fathers are participating in natural childbirth classes and assisting the mother to deliver their baby. Such involvement appears to have numerous positive consequences that extend beyond the delivery room. Fathers who were involved in the delivery tend to interact more with their newborn children and to participate more in infant care than uninvolved fathers (Jones, 1989; Miller & Bowen, 1982; Cordell, Parke, & Swain, 1980).

We also know that fathers are able to establish strong bonds of attachment to their children and vice versa. Infants regularly turn to their fathers in times of distress. Such father-infant interaction debunks the myth that child attachment is the exclusive domain of the mother. This father shares his feelings of attachment and protection toward his children:

> **I always wanted to be a father. I love my kids and have always felt a special type of attachment toward them. This bond began when they were very young and has strengthened over time. I feel really connected to them and always want to be a provider for them. I don't think that attachment happens just between mothers and children. Fathers play an equally important part in child rearing, and offer their children a different dimension. I want to stay as involved with my children as I can. I need them as much as they need me. (Authors' files)**

Research also discloses that the father has a strong influence on a child's overall development. His presence and attention to his children have both immediate and long-term benefits. The absence of his care also seems to affect the development of the child. For example, the lack of a positive father-child relationship seems to negatively affect academic achievement and IQ levels in children. Fathers also affect children's progress in school, which subjects they prefer, and even the kinds of occupations they eventually choose. Like mothers, fathers serve as role models and influence their children through their mannerisms, interactions, and personalities (Lewis & Salt, 1986; Parke, 1981; Radin, 1981; Lamb, 1982, 1983; Adams, 1984).

While many new fathers look forward to child care, some resist the idea that they should spend much time with their children. Many men feel poorly prepared for the task of parenting. They report considerable anxiety, confusion, and uneasiness about their ability to take care of their children (Spieler, 1982; Nannarone, 1983). But it must be remembered that mothers also feel considerable anxiety and confusion about parenting. Our society does not prepare people for the intense, multiple needs of their offspring. The adaptations, demands, and adjustments required of both fathers and mothers are numerous (Pruett, 1987; Roopnarine & Miller, 1985; Waldron & Routh, 1981; Clark, 1981; Miller & Sollie, 1980).

Parenting by Same-Sex Couples

Couples of the same sex who choose to become parents seem to manage in some areas as well as, if not better than, male-female couples. For example, two women

A baby whose parents are lesbians or gays doesn't necessarily lack nurturing from the other sex. Most gays and lesbians have friends and relatives who provide other-sex models.

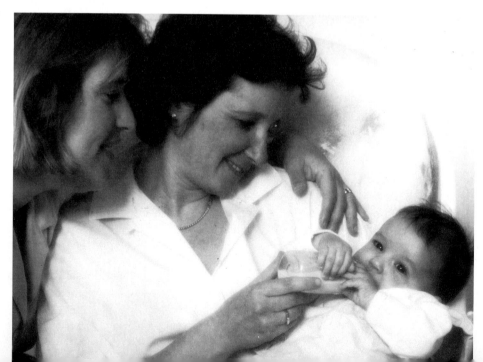

would not necessarily bring to parenting an explicit division of responsibilities, as a man and a woman so often do. Two men may have a more egalitarian philosophy so that it does not matter who feeds, changes, and rocks the baby. Both men might work outside the home and share financial responsibilities *and* caregiving equally. The same might be said of two women parenting a child. More information on same-sex parenting can be found in Chapter 9.

CHILD-REARING OPTIONS AND STRATEGIES

One of the responsibilities of parenthood is to adopt child-rearing standards that promote healthy growth and development. Beginning around the turn of the century, the United States experienced an unprecedented interest in this topic, and ever since, a long line of child-care experts has addressed the practical aspects of rearing children. There is little doubt that the resultant barrage of child-rearing books, articles, seminars, and workshops has helped to better inform parents about children and their needs. But the range of differing opinions and philosophies has also confused parents.

What kinds of child-rearing options do parents have today?

A good example of conflicting child-rearing advice is in the area of freedom. The swing of the pendulum on the issue of how much freedom a child should be given has historically been extreme. A *restrictive* child-rearing approach that emphasized strict parent-child relations was popular at the turn of the century. Experts of that time placed a premium on the development of self-control, respect, and a disciplined character. While parental affection was not discouraged, it was felt that excessive amounts of it would lead to immaturity, impulsiveness, and irresponsibility.

A *permissive* approach to child rearing emerged during the 1940s and proved quite popular with middle-class parents. Parents were advised to generate a loving attitude toward their children and to demonstrate understanding, sensitivity, and affection. The permissive school discouraged parents from using physical punishment, urging them instead to use relaxed, but firm, measures of discipline. They were also exhorted to develop confidence in their roles as parents. The permissive approach is evident in many books, the most notable being Benjamin Spock's *The Common Sense Book of Baby and Child Care*, first published in 1945. This enormously popular book is still used by many parents today.

The following child-rearing approaches are also widely practiced by contemporary parents:

DEVELOPMENTAL-MATURATIONAL APPROACH. This approach was developed by Arnold Gesell (1940) and is best known as an age-stage theory of child rearing. Gesell maintains that most children pass through basic patterns of growth at fairly predictable ages (although there are individual variations). He stresses that parents should be aware of these developmental sequences and should structure their expectations, demands, and child-rearing strategies accordingly.

BEHAVIOR MODIFICATION APPROACH. Borrowing from such learning theory concepts as conditioning and reinforcement (see Chapter 1), experts who take the behavior modification approach emphasize the importance of surroundings in shaping a child's behavior. Specifically, they advocate the use of positive reinforcement for desired behavior (giving children toys to reward good behavior) and negative reinforcement to reduce or eliminate undesirable behavior (sending children to their rooms because of a temper tantrum and then allowing them to return when they calm down). Proponents of the behavior modification approach claim that when consistently adhered to, these principles enable parents to nurture desired behavioral patterns in their children.

HUMANISTIC APPROACH. The focus of the humanistic approach, developed by Haim Ginott (1965), is the development of parental empathy, sensitivity, and insight into the needs of children. Parents are urged to improve their communication abilities so that they can better appreciate their children's feelings and motivations. Ginott suggests that parents precede statements of advice with statements of understanding, resolve conflicts without attacking their children's personalities, and renounce the use of all threats and sarcasm.

PARENT-EFFECTIVENESS APPROACH. Developed by Thomas Gordon (1978), parent-effectiveness training (P.E.T.) seeks to teach parents how to enhance their children's self-image and potential. Gordon's techniques include reflecting positive images back to the child, engaging in mutual negotiation when problems arise, and practicing "active listening" or verbally feeding back to youngsters what the parent thinks they have expressed. The last technique, Gordon believes, will help children to understand what they have said and assist them in solving their own problems. He also advocates the use of "I" rather than "you" messages ("I get upset when you disturb me like that," as opposed to "You're a rude child to bother your father this way") on the grounds that they are more likely to impart facts, while "you" messages tend to blame the child, promote rebellion, and damage the child's self-concept.

DEMOCRATIC APPROACH. The democratic approach is popular in the writings of many child-rearing experts, the most notable being Rudolph Dreikurs (1964). He believes that the family unit is the primary force in shaping children's behavior. Parents should seek to integrate children as fully as possible into the family network so that they can benefit from everyone's observations, feedback, and encouragement. Children should take part in family decision-making processes, including the establishment of rules and expectations, so that they will learn the "logical consequences" of their behavior and those expected behavioral standards that ensure the fair treatment of all family members. Dreikurs believes that a collective and cooperative atmosphere promotes security, trust, and a sense of belonging in the child.

Dreikurs's views have received some support from current research indicating that children from close-knit, nurturing families are more successful in school than children who lack strong parental guidance and support. For instance, a recent study of Indochinese refugee families in the United States found that the children's grade point averages were related positively to the amount of parental and family support they enjoyed (Caplan, Choz, & Whitmore, 1992).

A FINAL WORD ON CHILD-REARING STRATEGIES. The approaches described provide us with a great deal of insight into the nature of child rearing. As we learned in Chapter 1, however, theoretical positions are not mutually exclusive. One of these theories might work best at one time, and another at a different time or under different circumstances. In fact, it is not uncommon for two or more theories to be applicable simultaneously. For example, the fact that a child is at a specific developmental stage according to Gesell's developmental-maturational theory does not mean that principles of reinforcement are not operating or that the youngster's interaction with the family unit becomes nonexistent.

This is the primary reason why many parents today take an eclectic approach to child-rearing theories. They select the parts of theories they find acceptable, and then develop their own strategies. All theories need to be adapted and modified to take account of the individuality of the child—and, for that matter, of the parent. Remember, too, that a child-rearing theory is really a perspective, one possible way to view development. While each of these theories has broadened our understanding, none answers all our questions about child rearing. No approach yet devised can be said unequivocally to offer the "best" way to rear youngsters. We need further investigations in this field, as well as reassessment of the theories and viewpoints generated thus far.

*T*he baby in the plastic case lies swathed in a Mickey Mouse blanket whose cartoon characters dwarf him in size. One month after birth, he has already suffered major bleeding in his head, requiring brain surgery, and still needs a respirator to breathe. Born almost four months prematurely, weighing just over a pound, the baby is sustained by a battery of tubes and machines.

His skin is thin as parchment and his eyes are sealed shut, but he is clearly a human child. A minuscule blue and white stocking cap prevents heat loss through his head.

"Could you turn off the respirator on this baby?" asked Dr. Harry Dweck, director of neonatal intensive care at the Westchester County Medical Center in Valhalla, N.Y. "Could you? I couldn't. If his parents asked me to do it, I'd go to court."

Life at $2,000 a Day

Intensive care for premature infants is now keeping alive more and more infants born very early in pregnancy. But the cost is immense—more than $2,000 a day—and the emotional burden on parents immeasurable. Many surviving infants who weigh less than 750 grams, about 1 pound, 10 ounces, at birth turn out to have physical or mental disabilities, but there is no reliable way at present to predict the outcome. For doctors and parents the treatment of these babies thus creates even more difficult economic and ethical dilemmas.

Dr. Dweck says he has seen infants like his patient become normal children, although he admits the chances that the survivors will be normal are less than 1 in 4.

The remainder suffer brain damage. . . . Although health care economists have recently focused their attention on intensive care for the elderly, in fact most hospitals spend far more treating the very, very young. The stakes are higher, too, since a premature baby who survives intact gains a lifetime, while an infant who survives with terrible damage may require decades' worth of high-cost care. To complicate matters, the most premature infants, the ones who can run up bills close to half a million dollars, are also the least likely to be helped. . . .

Care More Costly Than New Heart

Premature infants stay in high-tech wombs for about the same length of time that they should have remained in their mother's: four months for the most premature, who are born at 24 weeks' gestation and weigh in the neighborhood of 500 grams, or slightly over a pound. . . . Just 10 years ago, it was a rare child born under 1 pound, 8 ounces who even survived, and before the early 1970s, when neonatal intensive care units began operating, few children under 2 pounds survived. But as advances allow medicine to save more and more babies, the demand for neonatal intensive care has risen and existing units are bursting at the seams. Babies born prematurely to women who use crack or have had no prenatal care have swelled the demand. . . .

For Some, Home Will Be Hospital

While pediatricians say that babies in need ultimately find a hospital that can squeeze them in, the crunch has led some to call for more public financing and others for a more "rational" use of existing beds. . . . Some beds are occupied for months or years by the growing number of severely brain-damaged children or children on respirators who, saved from death in the intensive care unit, are too chronically ill to go home or even move to a regular hospital bed.

A 1990 New York State Health Department report on neonatal services in New York City found that in the larger units an average of two beds were occupied by such children, sometimes for years.

Situations like these are leading people to question whether million of dollars should be spent on intensive care to the tiniest infants, who are unlikely to live.

In Oregon, where the Legislature is developing a priority list of various medical treatments to guide Medicaid financing, intensive care services for infants under 500 grams ranked 708 of 709 treatments; meaning it would not be covered. . . .

(continued)

SEXUALITY IN THE NEWS

As More Tiny Infants Live, Choices and Burden Grow

by Elisabeth Rosenthal

Long-Term Ills and Impairment

For doctors and parents, decisions on care of premature infants are inevitably tortured affairs, complicated by the impossibility of determining the ultimate fate of any given infant. While doctors know, for example, that about 40 percent of babies weighing 600 grams at birth, about 1 pound, 5 ounces, will apparently be normal at one year, they have few clues as to which babies will fall into which group. And no one knows if babies who have normal brain examinations at 1 year will be developmentally normal at 6 or 7....

Of Mortality and Legality

Also driving doctors to aggressively save the tiny infants are fears. What if they withdraw treatment and the baby survives—and is left even more damaged? ...

And many worry about legal obligations in the wake of the Baby Doe cases of the mid-1980s when pediatricians were told they could be prosecuted under child abuse and neglect laws for withholding or withdrawing care from sick infants.... (*The New York Times*, September 29, 1991. Copyright © by The New York Times Company. Reprinted by permission.)

DISCUSSION QUESTIONS

1. What are some of the options for a physician who must decide how to treat a tiny premature infant? Should a physician make decisions—including whether to treat an infant at all—in consultation with the parents or without their input? Support your answer.

2. What are some of the long-term and short-term effects of long hospital stays on tiny infants? How might such stays affect members of the infant's family?

3. Many tiny infants are born to teenage mothers or to mothers who have used crack, had poor diets, or lacked proper prenatal care. Compare the long-term costs of preventing such births through better prenatal care and more widespread contraceptive services to teenagers with the costs of treating and caring for such infants on a continuing basis. What do you think we should do about this very serious problem?

LOOKING BACK

■ Labor, the climax of the entire pregnancy cycle, consists of three stages: uterine contractions, delivery of the baby, and expulsion of the placenta. The duration of labor varies from woman to woman. The average for first labors is about 14 hours; later labors tend to be about 6 hours shorter than first labors.

■ The first stage of labor begins with the onset of true labor contractions and ends with the complete dilation of the cervix. The second stage consists of the delivery of the baby. Most babies are born in a head-downward position, but about 5 percent engage in a breech presentation. In a cesarean section the baby is delivered through a surgical incision made in the woman's abdominal and uterine walls. The final stage of labor is the expulsion of the placenta, which occurs when the placenta detaches itself from the uterine wall.

■ While the great majority of mothers deliver their babies in a conventional medical setting, growing numbers of women are pursuing birthing alternatives, mostly because they object to the use of anesthesia during delivery and to other medical intrusions on mother and baby. Among the alternatives to traditional delivery are the Lamaze method, the Leboyer method, home births, and rooming-in and birthing room hospital facilities.

■ The postpartum period encompasses the first month or so after childbirth. For the mother, it is a time when her body readjusts after the process of childbearing; for both fathers and mothers, it is a period of learning to attend to the needs of the newborn and adapt to their new parental roles. The puerperium is the time after childbirth during which the mother's reproductive organs return to their prepregnant condition. Both the method of childbirth and the circumstances associated with delivery affect the manner and length of the puerperium.

■ Parenthood is a complex transition for which most people are poorly prepared. Society tends to paint an idealistic picture of parenthood, one that obscures the reality of bringing up children. Motherhood introduces a special set of challenges. Women today are often overcommitted, having to juggle the roles of wife, mother, community participant, breadwinner, and household decision maker. In recent years, researchers have discovered that fathers have a much greater impact on the development of their children than was traditionally believed. Numerous child-rearing theories have been proposed to help parents nurture the healthy growth and development of children. Among these are the developmental-maturational, behavior modification, humanistic, parent effectiveness, and democratic approaches.

THINKING THINGS OVER

1. Giving birth in a hospital is not the only way to deliver a child safely. If you were having a baby or were the partner of a woman about to give birth, which of the alternatives we've discussed would you choose? Why?

2. What are the factors that contribute to postpartum depression? How can some of these factors be alleviated?

3. Sexual intercourse both immediately before and after the delivery of a baby can be problematic. What precautions would you take if you wanted to engage in intercourse during these times? What alternative sexual activities would you consider?

4. Same-sex parenting has become popular in recent years. Based on the discussions in this chapter and in Chapter 9, what advantages and disadvantages do you see in same-sex parenting?

5. You have been asked to deliver a speech to first-time parents entitled "Child-Rearing in the 1990s: Options and Strategies." Your goal is to make the audience aware that there is no one "right" way to raise a child. Explore the child-rearing options we discussed in this chapter. Do you find yourself leaning toward one or more theories as you prepare your "speech"? Why or why not?

DISCOVER FOR YOURSELF

Jones, C. (1989). *Sharing birth: A father's guide to giving support during labor*. Westport, CT: Greenwood Publishing Company. An excellent description that tells fathers how they can take an active part in childbirth.

Lubic, R. W., & Hawes, G. R. (1987). *Childbearing*. New York: McGraw-Hill. Part Three of this book offers detailed coverage of the childbirth experience.

Mercer, R. T. (1986). *First-time motherhood: Experiences from teens to forties*. New York: Springer. The experience of motherhood, particularly how mothers perceive and manage their children, is the subject of this book.

Michaelson, K. L. (1988). *Childbirth in America: Anthropological perspectives*. Westport, CT: Greenwood Publishing Company. A comprehensive examination of childbirth in America, from pregnancy to early postpartum.

Simkin, P. (1989). *The birth partner: Support in childbirth*. Boston: Harvard Common Press. A good narrative of how fathers and other birth partners can provide support during labor and delivery.

Wertz, R. W., & Wertz, D. C. (1989). *Lying-in: A history of childbirth in America*. New Haven, CT: Yale University Press. The authors provide an interesting historical account of childbirth in America.

12

Contraception and Abortion

The cautious seldom make mistakes

—Confucius

Without the means to prevent and to control the timing of conception, economic and political rights have limited meaning for women

—Alice Rossi

B irth control is hardly a recent phenomenon. On the contrary, it seems to have been attempted throughout most of recorded history. Primitive forms of diaphragms and cervical caps, made from such materials as gold and ivory, date back more than 2,500 years. Cleopatra reportedly experimented with using bits of hardened sea sponge and other materials as primitive intrauterine devices.

Among the Romans, a special charm, often including the liver of a cat placed in a tube or part of a lioness's womb sealed in ivory, was worn in an effort to prevent unwanted pregnancies. The *Kama Sutra* suggested that the blossoms of the palash flower were effective as an oral contraceptive. In the seventeenth century silk and linen condoms were used in the Orient and parts of Europe, primarily to guard against venereal disease. Among certain Indian tribes of North America, a "snake girdle" made of beaded leather and worn around the navel was a popular contraceptive symbol.

In remote corners of the world today, primitive birth control techniques are still practiced. For instance, many women of the Kavivordo people in Africa stand up after intercourse and shake their bodies in a quick jerky rhythm to remove semen from the vagina. Among the Sande of Africa, women repeatedly slap the lower back and abdominal area to achieve the same result. In some primitive societies plant and animal poisons are sometimes used to abort pregnancies. Unfortunately, these toxic substances run the risk of killing the mother, too. Sometimes tight bands are tied around a pregnant belly or sharp sticks are inserted into the vagina in an effort to extract the unwanted fetus.

Today there are many sophisticated measures designed to prevent or space pregnancies, as well as techniques to abort unwanted pregnancies. In general, such birth control methods fall into three main categories. **Contraception** refers to any natural, barrier, chemical, hormonal, or surgical method of preventing conception. In **sterilization,** a permanent method of birth control, a surgical procedure is used to prevent sperm and egg from meeting. Finally, **abortion** is the termination of a pregnancy either naturally or by artificial means.

All of these methods are available to us today because of the pioneering efforts of people like Margaret Sanger (1883–1966), who became interested in women's health issues through her experiences in nursing. Sanger worked among poor women in New York City at a time when both contraception and abortion were illegal. Pregnancy was a "chronic condition" for these women, who often induced their own abortions and frequently died in the process.

Frustrated by her inability to help these women within the confines of the era's medical practice, Sanger left nursing to found the National Birth Control League in 1914. Although the League's magazine, *Woman Rebel*, did not violate the Comstock Act of 1873, which made it illegal to send contraceptive information through the mails, Sanger barely escaped imprisonment by fleeing to Europe, where she visited the world's first birth control clinics.

In 1916 Sanger opened a birth control clinic in Brooklyn where women could obtain diaphragms and birth control information. She was jailed for 30 days and her clinic closed. But ultimately she won the right to keep the clinic open, and shortly after that doctors were legally allowed to dispense contraceptive information.

Sanger also promoted birth control research, fighting for a highly reliable birth control method that could be controlled by women themselves. That method finally materialized in 1960, when birth control pills became available in the United States.

CONTRACEPTION ISSUES

Each year in the United States there are about 6 million unwanted pregnancies. This astonishingly high figure is clear evidence that nature stacks the odds heavily in favor of pregnancy when an effective form of contraception is not used. It is estimated that

- ☐ *What contraceptive methods are available at present.*

- ☐ *What promising contraceptive choices may become available in the near future.*

- ☐ *What factors affect contraceptive use.*

- ☐ *How vasectomies and tubal ligations are performed.*

- ☐ *How a spontaneous abortion differs from an induced abortion.*

contraception Any natural, barrier, chemical, hormonal, or surgical method used to prevent conception.

sterilization A family planning measure that permanently blocks a person's reproductive capacity.

abortion The termination of a pregnancy by natural or artificially induced means.

couples who use no contraceptive have an almost 90 percent chance of achieving pregnancy over the course of a year (Hatcher et al., 1990; Harlap, Kost, & Forrest, 1991).

Is U.S. Research Up to Date?

Some contraceptives are clearly more effective than others, but all of them incur a certain number of failures. However, most unplanned pregnancies occur because of human factors. Correcting mistaken notions about contraception (see the "Myths and Misconceptions" box), choosing the contraceptive with the highest theoretical effectiveness, understanding the method chosen, using it consistently, and being seriously motivated to prevent pregnancy are the keys to successful birth control.

Although numerous birth control choices are available in the United States today, American birth control research has fallen behind that of other nations. In fact, sexually active couples do not have many more choices today than they did 20 years ago. This is in sharp contrast to the situation in many European nations, where birth control research is producing a number of new alternatives. Among these are a two-month

MYTHS AND MISCONCEPTIONS

Mistaken Notions About Contraception

Douching prevents pregnancy. Those who cling to this myth believe that sperm can be washed away after intercourse. The truth is that sperm are generally deposited high in the vagina and move quite rapidly into the uterus. While a douche is effective for cleansing the vagina, it cannot remove sperm from the uterus. Indeed, douche liquid may even push sperm through the cervix into the uterus.

Oral contraceptives make a woman less fertile after she discontinues them. If a woman is fertile before she starts on the pill, taking it should not affect her ability to have children later. Some women experience a short period of adjustment after discontinuing oral contraceptives, but they usually become pregnant soon after.

All condoms act as a protective sheath that helps prevent the transmission of sexually transmitted diseases. Laboratory studies indicate that this is true only for latex condoms. They do indeed provide a barrier against sexually transmitted diseases, provided there are no holes or tears in them and they are used properly. Using a latex condom with a spermicide such as nonoxynol-9 provides extra protection against sexually transmitted diseases (as well as against pregnancy). Lambskin condoms, however, have pores in the membrane that are large enough to allow HIV and the hepatitis and herpes viruses to escape.

All lubricants are the same and can be used with the contraceptive of choice. All lubricants are *not* the same. Some are water-based (e.g., K-Y lubricating jelly, Today Personal lubricant, Surgilube) and others are oil-based (Vaseline, baby oil). Oil-based lubricants weaken latex and cause it to deteriorate; thus they should not be used with condoms and diaphragms. Water-based lubricants are recommended instead.

Following a vasectomy, a man loses his ability to ejaculate. This myth supposes that sterilization destroys a man's sexual arousal and response along with his reproductive capacity. In reality, erection and ejaculation responses remain the same after a vasectomy, the only difference is that a man's semen no longer contains sperm. While sperm is still being manufactured by the body, it is prevented from being ejaculated. Instead, it accumulates in the testes and epididymis, breaks down, and is reabsorbed by the body. Most men cannot detect any change in their ejaculate.

Contraception and Abortion

injectable contraceptive, a male contraceptive pill, and RU-486, a drug that induces menstruation after fertilization takes place.

What factors account for this lag in U.S. research and development? One is that the U.S. Food and Drug Administration has traditionally been slow and cautious in granting approval to new drugs. It sometimes takes as long as 15 years and millions of dollars to move a contraceptive (or any drug, for that matter) from the laboratory to use by the general public. Another factor is the threat of liability suits, which has forced some pharmaceutical companies to take their contraceptive products off the market. This was the case with the now bankrupt A. H. Robins Corporation and its Dalkon shield intrauterine device. A third factor is the resistance by certain religious and political groups to both current contraceptives and future possibilities (Elmer-DeWitt, 1990).

In 1990 the Food and Drug Administration did approve a radically new method of birth control, a long-acting contraceptive implant called Norplant. Norplant gave American women a contraceptive choice already available to women in 16 other countries. First approved in Finland in 1983, the implant has been used by over half a million women in other countries. Before it won FDA approval, over 2,400 women in the United States participated in safety and effectiveness studies.

Factors Affecting Contraceptive Use

Contraceptive use varies according to age and other characteristics. One study (Morrison, 1985) that focused on contraceptive behavior among adolescents and young adults discovered that one-third to two-thirds of teenagers used no contraception at all for their first intercourse, although rates of nonuse tended to be lower among girls than among boys. For both sexes, nonuse of contraceptives declined with age. The reasons respondents gave for failing to use a contraceptive ranged from mistaken notions about fertility to difficult access to contraceptive devices. Although condoms and withdrawal were the most commonly used methods at first intercourse, many adolescents shifted away from these male-dependent methods to oral contraceptives over time.

Research has also shown that contraceptive use is greater among people who feel good about themselves, accept their sexuality (Whitley & Schofield, 1984; Kastner, 1984; Adler 1981), and have a positive self-image (Flick, 1986; Geis & Gerrard, 1984). In contrast, people who feel anxious or guilty about their sexual behavior are less likely to use contraceptives (Mosher & Vonderheide, 1985; Gerrard, 1982; Leary & Dobbins, 1983).

Several researchers (Cvetkovitch & Grote, 1983; Zabin & Clark, 1981) have noted that effective contraception is also more likely to be practiced by partners who are engaged in serious, intimate relationships. Those who begin intercourse early (age 16 or younger) are less likely to use effective contraception than those who start later (Faulkenberry et al., 1987). Such factors as the social support of peers and good communication with one's sexual partner also promote effective contraceptive use (Milan & Kilman, 1987; Sack, Billingham, & Howard, 1985; Herold, 1981; Herold & McNamee, 1982; Jones & Philliber, 1983).

Young people who have higher educational or achievement goals are also more likely to use effective contraception (Furstenberg et al., 1983; Herold & Samson, 1980). Programs that enhance contraceptive knowledge have been found to promote effective contraceptive use (Zabin et al., 1986; Dawson, 1986; Marsiglio & Mott, 1986). Finally, perceptions of the benefits (e.g., pregnancy prevention) and drawbacks (e.g., too difficult to obtain or use) of contraceptives affect overall usage (Condelli, 1986; Pagel & Davidson, 1984; Fisher, 1984; Jorgensen & Sonstegard, 1984; Kastner, 1984; Jorgensen, 1980).

Kathleen McKinney (1989) points out that women in general and both men and women who have a less traditional view of gender roles feel more positive about

Margaret Sanger, who initiated and led the movement to find safe and effective methods of birth control, wrote and lectured widely. She was often heckled, however, and at one meeting, in Boston, was forced to appear with her lips taped. She wrote her message on a blackboard.

"How can we prevent pregnancy. We don't even know what causes it."

contraception. Indeed, one source (Rosen & Ager, 1981) found that nontraditional gender roles are often associated with greater contraceptive use. Another investigation (McKinney & DeLamater, 1982) reported that among college students women had more positive attitudes and perceptions toward contraception than men. Many men today, especially younger single men, believe that birth control is the woman's responsibility. Here are some men's statements on the subject:

> I've always been programmed to view birth control as the woman's job, not mine. Besides, using a condom or withdrawal are the only measures that I could really provide.

> To avoid unintended pregnancy, a woman's task is to protect herself.

> I don't go to bed with unprepared women. It's their responsibility to take care of birth control. (Authors' files)

Many women are unhappy about these male expectations:

> It's just another example of male chauvinism. Most men expect women to fill their every need or desire, even in bed.

> Why is it the female's responsibility for birth control? It bothers me that men always assume a woman is prepared to have sex. Just once I would like to hear a man willing to accept the responsibility for contraception and take my needs into consideration. I'm tired of always sacrificing my body. (Authors' files)

Many married couples and others in long-term relationships do feel that birth control should be a shared decision. A husband offers these thoughts:

> My wife and I have always been open and flexible about the topic of birth control. For years we used condoms but then switched to the pill for greater convenience. Prior to our first child, Cathy changed to a diaphragm. We fully discussed each of these contraceptive choices, weighing the pros and cons and making sure that each other's needs were taken into account. We're doing the same thing now while I'm looking at the possibility of a vasectomy. (Authors' files)

A wife had these reflections:

> It strikes me as unusual that two people can enjoy lovemaking but only one is expected to make the birth control decision. I believe that contraceptive choices must be made by both partners before sexual escapades begin. It is irresponsible for both the man and woman to have unprotected sex or to assume that the other will always handle it. (Authors' files)

It is our feeling that couples should share the responsibility for birth control. As we said in Chapter 6, sexual responsibility and maturity require a well-thought-out sexual value system. Mutual support and open discussion between partners about contraceptive options are also important. Partners should be aware of each other's needs, feelings, and values. They can also share the experience of gathering information about contraceptives from a clinic. For some questions commonly asked by couples making contraceptive choices, see the box on "Choosing a Method of Birth Control."

The responsibility for birth control should rest with *both* the man and the woman. Couples should engage in an open and honest dialogue about their options and select a birth control method that is effective and that both partners feel comfortable with. Answering the following two questions will help couples start their decision making.

1. What type of birth control are you thinking about? _____
2. Have you ever used this method before? _____ If yes, how long did you use it?
_____

Couples can then go on to the remaining 19 questions:

MAKING USE OF WHAT WE KNOW

Choosing a Method of Birth Control

	Yes	No	Don't Know
3. Are you afraid of using this method?	—	—	—
4. Would you rather not use this method?	—	—	—
5. Will you have trouble remembering to use this method?	—	—	—
6. Have you ever become pregnant while using this method?	—	—	—
7. Do you have unanswered questions about this method?	—	—	—
8. Does this method make menstrual periods longer or more painful?	—	—	—
9. Does this method cost more than you can afford?	—	—	—
10. Does this method ever cause serious health problems?	—	—	—
11. Do you object to this method because of your religious beliefs?	—	—	—
12. Have you already had problems using this method?	—	—	—
13. Is your partner opposed to this method?	—	—	—
14. Are you using this method without your partner's knowledge?	—	—	—
15. Will using this method embarrass you or your partner?	—	—	—
16. Will you enjoy intercourse less because of this method?	—	—	—
17. Will this method interrupt lovemaking?	—	—	—
18. If this method interrupts lovemaking, will you avoid using it?	—	—	—
19. Has a doctor or nurse instructed you not to use this method?	—	—	—
20. Is there anything about your personality that could lead you to use this method incorrectly?	—	—	—
21. Are you at any risk of being exposed to HIV or other sexually transmitted infections?	—	—	—

Now examine your total response profile. If you have any "don't know" responses, both of you need to learn more about the method of birth control you've selected. Moreover, the more "yes" answers you've checked off, the more likely it is that you are dissatisfied with the method you've chosen and the more likely it is that you should consider switching to another method. (Adapted from Hatcher et al., 1990)

CONTRACEPTIVE METHODS

In this section we present contraceptive methods now available to sexually active couples, including a description of how they prevent conception or pregnancy, their effectiveness, and some of their advantages and disadvantages. As you'll discover, almost all contraceptive methods (e.g., condoms, oral contraceptives) are *reversible*;

that is, fertility is restored when people stop using them. But sterilization is considered irreversible: although microsurgical techniques are having some success reversing sterilization, any man or woman who opts for this method should be prepared for a permanent end to fertility.

Abstinence

abstinence The avoidance of sexual intercourse.

Abstinence, the avoidance of intercourse, is clearly the surest method of birth control. Used consistently, it is 100 percent effective and has no cost factor (see Table 12–1). Some sex educators advocate abstinence, especially for young teenagers. Adolescent sexuality education programs encouraging abstinence (see, e.g., Christopher & Roosa, 1990; Mast, 1988; Moyse-Steinberg, 1990; Roosa & Christopher, 1990; Shornack & Ahmed, 1989) try to reach teenagers early with information on how and why they should defer sexual activity, clarify their own sexual values, resist social pressures to become sexually active, and build assertiveness skills (Brindis, 1990). Other programs, recognizing that sexual activity among teenagers is not going to go away, focus on teaching them to practice noncoital sexual behavior, such as oral sex, mutual masturbation, and other types of intimacy short of intercourse. These alternatives to intercourse have been termed *outercourse* and have been viewed as a variant of birth control.

TABLE 12–1

Failure Rates of Contraceptive Methods

METHOD	THEORETICAL FAILURE RATE (%)*	TYPICAL FAILURE RATE (%)†
Abstinence	0	0
Oral contraceptives		
Combination	0.1	3.0
Minipill	0.5	2.5
Contraceptive implant	0.5	3.0
Intrauterine device (IUD)	1.0	5.0
Diaphragm (with spermicide)	3.0	18.0
Vaginal spermicide	3.0	21.0
Condom	4.0	12.0
Cervical cap (with spermicide)	5.0	18.0
Basal body temperature technique	2–14.0	20.0
Sympto-thermal technique	2–14.0	20.0
Rhythm method	2–14.0	20.0
Vaginal sponge	10.0	18.0
Withdrawal	16.0	23.0
Male sterilization	0.1	0.3
Female sterilization	0.2	0.4

Source: Adapted from Hatcher et al., 1990; Trussell et al., 1990; Harlap, Kost, & Forrest, 1991; Jones & Forrest, 1989.

*The theoretical failure rate is the rate at which a contraceptive method fails when it is used perfectly (both consistently and correctly) and without mechanical error.

†The typical failure rate is the rate at which a contraceptive method actually fails, taking into account such factors as human error, carelessness, and mechanical failure. The percentages cited are the percentages of times that pregnancy can be expected to occur among 100 couples using a method over a one-year period.

Oral Contraceptive

The **oral contraceptive,** also referred to as the "pill," was the first birth control method to be almost 100 percent effective (see Table 12–1). A hormonal method, the oral contraceptive is today the most popular form of birth control among American women under age 30. It is estimated that about 13 million women in the United States and about 50 million worldwide use oral contraceptives. Over 150 million women throughout the world have used the pill at some time in their lives.

Oral contraceptives, which are available only by prescription, fall into two broad categories: combination pills and minipills. **Combination pills** contain a synthetic estrogen combined with synthetic progesterone derivatives, called *progestogens* or *progestins,* that prevent ovulation (see Table 12–1). Some of the more common brand names of combination pills are Brevicon, Demulen, Modicon, Norinyl, Morlestrin, Ortho-Novum, and Ovral.

When a woman takes a combination pill, it signals her pituitary gland (recall from Chapter 3 that the pituitary gland directs hormonal activity) *not* to release the hormones that would normally stimulate her ovaries to release an egg. If no egg is released, there can be no fertilization no matter how many sperm are released during intercourse. If by chance an egg *is* released and fertilized, however, the combination pill reduces the chance that it will implant in the uterus by decreasing the amount of mucus in the uterine lining. The pill also causes a mucous plug to form at the entrance to the cervix, preventing sperm from entering the uterus. Thus, combination pills both alter the events of the menstrual cycle and render the uterine wall unreceptive to a fertilized egg.

Combination pills are taken daily on a 21-day schedule. The regimen is started on the 5th day after menstruation begins and ended on the 25th day. Following the 21-day regime, the user waits a week before she begins the next pack of pills. Thus there is an interval of 7 days during the 28-day menstrual cycle in which no pills are taken and menstruation takes place. Preferably, the pill is taken at the same time each day. If a woman forgets to take a pill one day, she can make it up the next day.

The **minipill** contains progestin alone and does not always prevent ovulation. Rather, its major contraceptive function is to change the composition of cervical mucus so that no sperm can enter the uterus. Like the combination pill, the minipill makes the lining of the uterus unreceptive to implantation of the fertilized egg. The minipill, which is slightly less effective than the combination pill, must be taken consecutively over a 28-day regimen. It is often prescribed for women who cannot tolerate the estrogen in the combination pill or who are at high risk for estrogen use complications (a subject we will discuss shortly). Some of the more common brands of minipills are Micronor, Nor-Q.D., and Ovrette.

Oral contraceptives are preferred by many people largely because of their convenience, effectiveness, and low cost. If a woman becomes pregnant, it is usually because she has discontinued the pill and failed to begin another method of contraception. One of the major advantages of oral contraceptives is that they do not interrupt lovemaking, as some of the mechanical devices do. Another plus is that the pill seems to have noncontraceptive benefits. Women who use oral contraceptives tend to have lower rates of pelvic inflammatory disease and of breast and ovarian cysts. Users also report less menstrual cramping and more regular periods (Willis, 1985; Cates, 1986).

Most research (e.g., Stone, 1989; Colditz, 1988; Stampfer, 1988) indicates that the best candidates for oral contraceptives are young (under age 35), healthy women who do not smoke. However, even among these women there are potential side effects, most caused by the pill's estrogen component. Some women experience fluid retention, nausea, headaches, weight gain, increased size and tenderness of the breasts, and periodic depression. Oral contraceptives have also been linked to high blood pressure, sugar, and fat levels, as well as to abnormal insulin responses. Finally, it has

oral contraceptive Birth control pill that prevents ovulation. It is a hormonal method of birth control.

combination pills Oral contraceptives that contain a synthetic estrogen combined with chemicals called *progestogens* or *progestins* (synthetic progesterone derivatives).

How does a birth control pill prevent pregnancy?

mini-pill An oral contraceptive that contains progestin and no estrogen.

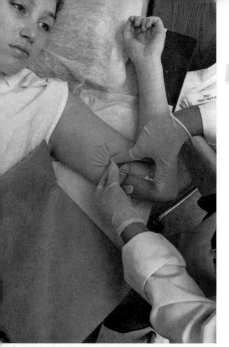

FIGURE 12–1
Norplant: A Contraceptive Implant.

The fact that this implant avoids the preparation required by many other contraceptive methods made its 1990 debut exciting to many. It is too soon to tell, however, whether the implant will have undesirable long-term effects on fertility.

I've been reading a lot about contraceptive implants lately. How do they act as a form of birth control?

contraceptive implant A female birth control device consisting of six small silicone rods implanted under the skin of the inner arm, just above the elbow. The rods contain the hormone levonorgestrel, which is released slowly over five years.

been suggested that birth control pills increase the risk of stroke and cardiovascular disease. However, there does not appear to be a link to breast cancer, as was once thought (Stadel, 1989; Thomas, 1989; Cates, 1986; Sattin et al., 1986).

Thus, while oral contraceptives are the most effective reversible method of birth control, they are not suitable for everyone (Shapiro, 1986). They are not recommended for women with a history of high blood pressure, blood-clotting problems, hepatitis, or cancer of the uterus or breast. A woman over 35 who smokes heavily is advised to stop smoking if she wants to take the pill. Oral contraceptives should not be taken by a woman who suspects she may be pregnant. Finally, women with diabetes, epilepsy, or heart, liver, or thyroid disease may be advised not to take the birth control pill, depending on the nature and severity of the disease.

Because of the potential risks associated with oral contraceptives, women using this method of birth control need to see their gynecologist or doctor for regular examinations. The likelihood of a serious problem is low for most users, but all women who are thinking of using the pill should learn to recognize the danger signs listed in Table 12–2.

Contraceptive Implant

The Food and Drug Administration approved a long-acting **contraceptive implant** called Norplant in 1990. Marketed by Wyeth-Ayerst Laboratories, Norplant consists of six silicone rubber rods about $1\frac{1}{3}$ inches long (see Figure 12–1) that are inserted in a fanlike arrangement under the skin of a woman's inner arm above the elbow. The minor surgical procedure is done under local anesthesia in a doctor's office or a clinic. The implants contain the hormone levonorgestrel, a synthetic progestin also used in oral contraceptives. The hormone is released slowly over five years. The implants can be removed at any time and fertility is usually quickly restored (Hatcher et al., 1990; Trussell et al., 1990).

The contraceptive implant is considered an excellent birth control method (see Table 12–1). Besides its excellent effectiveness, the implant may be chosen because it is convenient and does not interrupt lovemaking. It is popular among women who have had all the children they want, but are not sure if they want to be sterilized. Norplant's major side effect is menstrual irregularities, including prolonged periods and spotting between periods. Other side effects include occasional headaches, mood changes, nausea, and acne. Like oral contraceptives, Norplant should not be used by

TABLE 12–2

Danger Signs in Oral Contraceptive Users

If a woman experiences any of the problems listed below, she should stop taking birth control pills and see her physician immediately. This is important even if a woman is not sure whether the problem is serious. If her physician is unavailable, the woman should not hesitate to go to a hospital emergency room.

Chest pain or shortness of breath	These symptoms could indicate blood clots in the lung or even a heart attack.
Abdominal pain	Chronic abdominal pain could mean a blood clot, pancreatic inflammation, gallbladder disease, or ectopic (tubal) pregnancy.
Visual problems	Severe and chronic headaches, dizziness, and blurred vision may be advance warning signs of dangerously high blood pressure or even a stroke.
Severe leg pain	Persistent pain in the calf or thigh could indicate the presence of blood clots in the leg.

women who have acute liver disease, unexplained vaginal bleeding, breast cancer, or blood-clotting problems.

Intrauterine Device (IUD)

The **intrauterine device (IUD)** is made of plastic, usually coated with copper wire, and designed in a variety of shapes. It is inserted into the uterine cavity by a physician and can remain in place for several years if no difficulties arise. The IUD prevents pregnancy by not allowing a fertilized egg to implant itself in the uterine lining, or endometrium. Exactly how it does this is not known, although it is believed that the IUD acts as a foreign body, stimulating an inflammatory reaction in the endometrium. The addition of copper to the IUD or the slow-releasing progesterone embedded in the plastic tend to increase the inflammatory reaction. While this reaction creates no discomfort to the user, it creates an environment unfavorable to the implantation of the fertilized ovum. It has also been proposed that the presence of an IUD stimulates tubal movement and ovum transport, which inhibit implantation.

The first intrauterine devices were developed during the early part of the century, but concerns about infection and cancer led to their being virtually abandoned soon after. The development of polyethylene, a biologically inert plastic, and advances in antibiotic therapy sparked renewed interest in the IUD. In the 1960s the IUD was manufactured in its new plastic form, and other innovations followed. In the early 1970s, for example, medicated IUDs containing metallic copper or progesterone that had superior anti-implantation properties became available.

The IUD comes in several different sizes and shapes (see Figure 12–2). For example, the Progestasert and Tatum-T are T-shaped, while the Copper-7 resembles the number 7. The Lippes loop has a coiled appearance. All of these IUDs have a tail of plastic string that extends out of the cervix into the vagina (after inserting the IUD, the physician usually cuts the string so that only about two inches of it protrude into the vagina). A woman should feel with her finger for the presence of the string at least once a month. If she cannot find the string, it may have been drawn up into the cervix or uterus or it may have been expelled. In any case, she should consult her physician immediately.

An effective birth control device, the IUD has a low failure rate (see Table 12–1). An estimated 85 million women worldwide use some form of the IUD, including about 40 million in the People's Republic of China. Besides being very effective, the IUD offers ease of use and lack of interference with lovemaking. Once it is inserted, it requires little care and only occasional checking, provided there are no problems.

Unfortunately, there *are* problems with the IUD. It causes spotting, bleeding, and pain in some women. Severe menstrual cramps and increased menstrual bleeding have also been reported, as well as a mucuslike vaginal discharge. The IUD can also cause intestinal obstruction and bowel strangulation. These medical complications have prompted the removal of many IUDs from the market. As of 1990, only two IUDs are marketed in the United States: the hormone-releasing Progestasert-T, manufactured by the Alza Corporation; and the Copper-T 380-A IUD, manufactured by GynoMed Pharmaceutical.

Some of the problems caused by IUDs no longer on the market, like the Dalkon Shield and the Lippes Loop, were even more severe than those we have just described. Both of these two IUDs were linked to a number of serious medical conditions, including pelvic inflammatory disease, miscarriage, infertility, and perforation of the uterus. And it has been alleged that the Dalkon Shield caused the deaths of twenty women.

The IUD is not recommended in certain situations: if a woman suspects she may be pregnant, has pelvic inflammatory disease or a history of PID, has a history of ectopic pregnancy, or has any gynecological bleeding disorder. Women taking

intrauterine device Small, plastic birth control device that is inserted into the uterus so that a fertilized egg cannot implant itself in the uterine lining.

My girlfriend once used an IUD for birth control but was told it posed quite a few health risks. What are some of the problems it can cause?

FIGURE 12–2
The Intrauterine Device (IUD).

The IUD, a semi-permanent device, has one of the lowest failure rates of all contraceptives in preventing pregnancy. Like many other birth control methods, however, the IUD does nothing to prevent the transmission of STDs or AIDS.

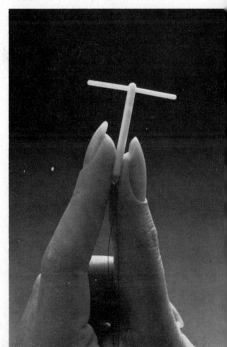

Contraception and Abortion

condom A thin sheath made of latex rubber or processed lamb intestine tissue that is placed over the erect penis before intercourse. The condom is categorized as a barrier method of contraception because it prevents sperm from entering the vagina when ejaculation occurs.

anticoagulants should also avoid the IUD since these drugs in combination with the IUD often prevent normal blood clotting during a heavy menstrual flow. If a woman's uterus is abnormal in size and shape, an IUD will not fit properly.

Condom

The **condom** is a thin sheath made of latex rubber or processed tissue from lamb intestines that is placed over the erect penis before intercourse to prevent sperm

MAKING USE OF WHAT WE KNOW

How to Use a Condom: Some Crucial Do's and Don't's

Sexual abstinence is the only *sure* way to prevent pregnancy and to protect yourself from sexually transmitted diseases like AIDS (see Chapters 17 and 18). But if you do decide to have sex, using a condom correctly will help you protect yourself and your partner against these risks. The following do's and don't's are a guide to the best protection currently available.

How to Buy Condoms

DO buy latex, reservoir- or nipple-end lubricated condoms. They come in different textures, colors, and sometimes sizes. A good-quality condom is the single most important factor in safer sex.

DO check the expiration date on the outer package.

DO check the lubricant. It should contain nonoxynol-9, which provides a chemical barrier against sexually transmitted diseases.

DO store condoms in a cool, dry place.

DON'T buy condoms made of anything other than latex. Only latex prevents passage of harmful germs.

DON'T buy old (outdated) condoms. Condoms deteriorate after about two years.

DON'T store condoms in an automobile glove compartment. Heat damages condoms, as do sunlight and fluorescent light.

DON'T carry condoms in a hip wallet for long periods of time. They can deteriorate and become useless.

How to Put a Condom On

DO remove rolled condom from package.

DO roll condom down on penis *as soon as it is erect*. Don't continue lovemaking until you've done this.

DO leave ¼ to ½ inch space at the tip of the condom to catch the ejaculate in the condom nipple.

DON'T unroll condom; instead, roll it carefully on all the way to the base of the penis (see Figure 12–3).

DON'T put condom on only when ready to enter a partner. This may be too late because drops of semen may escape from the penis *before* ejaculation and may impregnate or infect your partner.

DON'T twist the condom or let it come into contact with sharp objects like fingernails that can puncture or tear it. The tiniest hole can allow semen to leak out, possibly impregnating or infecting your partner.

How to Take a Condom Off

DO hold the condom at the rim. Remove soon after ejaculation.

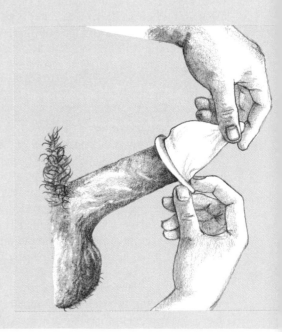

from entering the vagina when ejaculation occurs. Other names for condoms are *rubbers, sheaths, skins, safes*, and *prophylactics*. The condom is categorized as a *barrier* method of contraception because it prevents sperm and egg from joining.

The earliest known use of a penile sheath was in Egypt around 1350 B.C., primarily for decorative purposes. In 1564 Fallopius, an Italian anatomist, described a sheath made of linen. Casanova, a well-known lover who lived from 1729 to 1798, popularized the use of condoms for both contraception and protection from venereal disease. After vulcanized rubber was developed in the 1840s, condoms came into widespread

DO withdraw the penis *before* it becomes soft. If you wait until it is soft, the condom may drop off and protection will be lost. Holding the rim at the base of the penis while withdrawing will help to avoid the spillage of semen into the vagina.

DO examine the used condom for tears. If you find one, the woman should immediately insert contraceptive foam or gel into her vagina.

DO wash your hands or any body part semen comes into contact with.

DO wrap the used condom in tissue and dispose of it safely.

DON'T let the used condom touch your partner's genitals or other body parts.

DON'T tug to pull the condom off. It may tear.

DON'T allow semen to spill on your hands or body.

DON'T allow semen to come into contact with a skin break, cut, or open wound.

Special Points to Remember

- **DO** use another method, such as the vaginal sponge or a spermicide, along with a condom. This will increase the effectiveness of protection against both pregnancy and disease.

- If you buy unlubricated condoms, you may need a lubricant. **DO** use only water-soluble lubricants, such as spermicidal jelly (e.g., K-Y jelly). This will increase your protection at the same time.

- **DON'T** use oil-based lubricants such as petroleum jelly or vegetable oil with latex condoms because they can damage the condoms.

- **NEVER** use a condom more than once.

- When people use condoms correctly, they are more comfortable because they know they are taking responsibility for their behavior and protecting themselves and their partners by having safer sex. For some tips on how to convince a partner to use a condom, see the box on "How to Talk About Condoms with a Resistant Partner" in Chapter 17.

(Adapted from R. Adams, E. Fliegelman, & A. Grieco, "How to Use a Condom," *Medical Aspects of Human Sexuality*, 1987. Copies of the original source can be purchased in bulk; contact G. Philippe, Cahners Publishing Company, 249 West 17th Street, New York, NY 10011.)

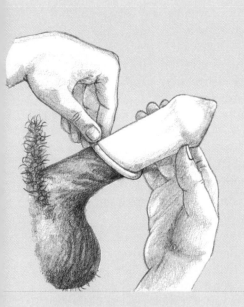

FIGURE 12–3
Putting a Condom on the Penis.

The condom should be unrolled downward onto the erect penis. A reservoir of space should be left at the tip to contain the semen.

Casanova, the famous eighteenth-century Italian lover, is said to have used condoms to prevent both conception and disease. If we are to believe this painting, he was not shy about publicly testing a condom for potential defects.

use. In the century and a half since, improvements in the flexibility and durability of rubber, and the addition of lubrication for increased comfort, have added to their appeal. Condoms have had a resurgence of popularity in recent years because they are believed to protect users against HIV and other sexually transmitted diseases (see Chapters 17 and 18).

The condom is the only temporary and reliable form of contraception directly under the man's control. It is also the major barrier method used around the world. As Table 12–1 shows, the condom is considered a quite effective contraceptive. About 500 million condoms are sold in the United States each year. Condoms can be purchased in packages of 3 or 12 and come with or without a lubricant. All condoms should be used with a lubricant and, in fact, the pre-lubricated condoms are the more popular ones. Condoms may also be straight-sided or tapered, have ribbed or textured surfaces, and are available in different colors. Some have an adhesive inside that is designed to seal the condom to the penis and thus help prevent semen leakage. Generally the fancier the condom the more expensive it is. Some popular brands are Trojans, Sheik, and Fourex.

Spermicidal condoms are also available. These condoms, such as the Ramses Extra, contain 0.5 gram of the spermicide nonoxynol-9 on their inner and outer surfaces. When ejaculation occurs, the spermicide destroys sperm within the condom. Research is inconclusive as to whether the spermicide is effective outside of the condom should it break or tear.

The condom is a safe, effective, and relatively simple method of contraception. The proper use of a condom is detailed in the box on "How to Use a Condom." It is the most widely used reversible method of birth control in the United States after oral contraceptives. Condoms are a relatively inexpensive form of birth control that are widely available. Their use does not require an examination or a prescription. Moreover, they have a number of noncontraceptive benefits:

■ Latex condoms help to prevent the sexual transmission of the human immunodeficiency virus (HIV), the virus that causes AIDS, as well as other sexually transmitted diseases. However, skin condoms are *not* effective in preventing the transmission of HIV and other sexually transmitted diseases (see "Myths and Misconceptions" box). Spermicidal condoms are best for the prevention of sexually transmitted diseases.

■ Condoms may help a pregnant woman to avoid infection with herpes simplex virus, HIV, gonorrhea, trichomonas, hepatitis B, syphilis, and chlamydia, thus preventing these diseases in her baby as well as herself.

■ The use of condoms encourages the man's participation in contraception.

■ Occasionally, men are unable to maintain an erection during intercourse. This problem often occurs in older men and other men who have had certain lower abdominal surgery. The rim of the condom may have a slight tourniquet effect, enabling these men to maintain an erection for longer lengths of time.

■ Lubricated condoms reduce mechanical friction and irritation of the vagina or penis.

■ Rarely, women are allergic to their partner's sperm and/or semen. Condoms make it possible for such couples to have intercourse without problems.

■ Some women do not like the postcoital discharge of semen from the vagina. This is avoided with condoms. (Hatcher et al., 1990)

There are also certain disadvantages to condom use. An interruption in lovemaking is necessary to put on the condom (but many couples include putting the condom on as part of their lovemaking and consider it a very sensual experience). Also, some men feel that the condom diminishes sexual sensations; others claim that they ejaculate prematurely while putting it on. Some men cannot retain an erection

Male condoms, rolled and unrolled to show the reservoir tip.

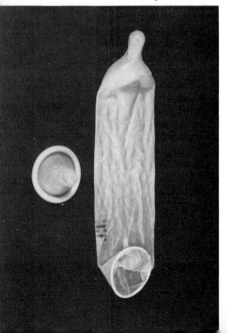

Contraception and Abortion

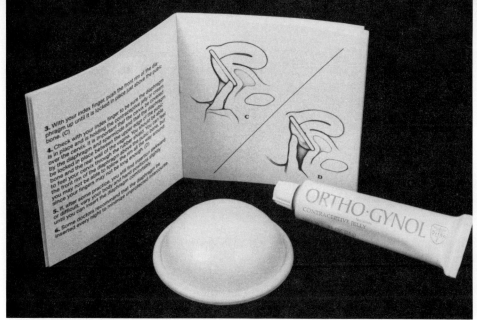

FIGURE 12–4

The diaphragm, used with a spermicide as pictured, is the most effective barrier contraceptive method to date. However, it does not protect a woman from sexually transmitted diseases such as AIDS.

when using a condom. Occasionally, the condom slips off as the man withdraws his penis after ejaculating, so that some semen enters the vagina. Condoms have been known to develop tiny holes, tears, or ruptures, causing leakage of semen. Finally, some users report an objectionable odor, particularly from the lubricated varieties (scented condoms are available).

Diaphragm

The **diaphragm** is another barrier method of contraception. A thin sheet of rubber or latex stretched over a flexible spring rim, the diaphragm is coated with a jelly or cream that kills sperm and then inserted into the vagina so that it covers the cervix, the entrance to the uterus. The diaphragm is considered an effective contraceptive choice (see Table 12–1). Diaphragms vary in terms of the strength or tension of the spring, the firmer springs being designed for women with less muscle tone or structural problems like a tipped uterus. Figure 12–4 displays different types of diaphragms.

The diaphragm must be carefully fitted by a doctor or a clinician during a pelvic examination. Diaphragms come in different sizes to accommodate variations in the size and shape of female internal genitalia. Larger sizes are often prescribed for mothers, since childbirth has a tendency to slightly stretch the vagina and cervix. Childless women and teenagers usually require smaller sizes. A woman should have her diaphragm rechecked for proper size if she gains or loses 20 pounds or more.

The actual fitting of a diaphragm only takes a few minutes. Typically, a series of flexible rings of different sizes is inserted into the vagina and checked for comfort and secure position (a diaphragm that is too small will move around too much, while one that is too large will not fit into place properly and the woman will be conscious of its presence). Once the proper size has been determined, a prescription for the diaphragm, as well as for the spermicidal jelly or cream to be used with it, is filled by a pharmacist. The combination of diaphragm and spermicide gives double protection against pregnancy.

Most women choose to insert the diaphragm manually, although a plastic inserter may be used. Before it is inserted, about a tablespoon of the spermicide is smeared around its inside surface, including the rim. With the diaphragm held in a dome-down position, the opposite sides of its rims are pressed together so that it folds. A woman then uses her other hand to spread apart the lips of her vagina and inserts the diaphragm. It should be pushed downward and along the back wall of the vagina as far as it will go so that the back part of the rim hooks under the cervix. The front

diaphragm A female method of contraception that provides a barrier between the sperm and the egg. It is a thin sheet of rubber or latex stretched over a collapsible spring rim that is inserted into the vagina so that it covers the cervix, the entrance to the uterus.

Are all diaphragms the same size?

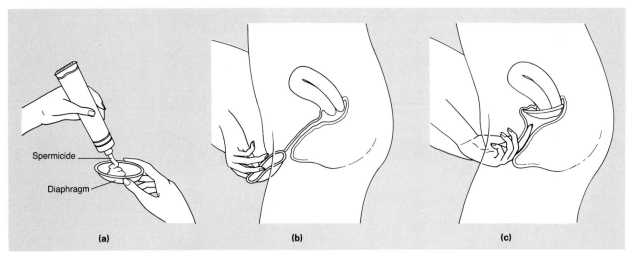

FIGURE 12–5
Using the Diaphragm.

(a) About a tablespoon of spermicide should be applied to the center of the diaphragm and then smeared lightly around the ring. (b) The ring of the diaphragm should be squeezed gently between thumb and fingers so that it can be inserted into the vaginal canal. (c) When the diaphragm is positioned correctly, a woman can feel her cervix through it.

rim should then be tucked upward behind the pubic bone. A woman can check for proper positioning of the diaphragm by feeling the cervix through the diaphragm with her fingers. Figure 12–5 illustrates how to insert a diaphragm.

A well-fitted and properly inserted diaphragm should not be felt by either partner during intercourse. If intercourse is repeated several times during a sexual encounter, more spermicidal jelly or cream should be added prior to each penetration. This can be done with an applicator without disturbing the diaphragm. The diaphragm should remain in place until at least 6 hours after the last act of intercourse, but it should not be left in place for more than 24 hours. The diaphragm can be removed by hooking one finger around the front rim, and then pulling downward and out. Once removed, it should be washed with a mild soap and water, powdered lightly, and returned to its container. Because a diaphragm can develop small holes or tears, a woman should inspect it regularly. A woman who wants more lubrication than the vagina naturally provides or than is provided by the spermicidal jelly or cream should *not* use Vaseline or other petroleum products. Instead, she should use K-Y jelly or Surgilube.

The diaphragm seldom creates serious side effects or major health concerns. Women with vaginal abnormalities or with very poor vaginal muscle tone may have difficulty using it, as may women who are virgins. Both women and men occasionally have an allergic reaction to the rubber or the spermicide. Leaving the diaphragm in place for more than 24 hours may increase the risk of toxic shock syndrome, an infection caused by a buildup of bacteria (see Chapter 3). Other potential risks are urinary tract infections, cramps, pelvic discomfort, and, on rare occasions, the dislodgment of the diaphragm during lovemaking.

vaginal spermicides
Agents that have sperm-killing properties. They come in a wide variety of forms, including aerosol foams, creams, jellies, tablets, and suppositories.

Vaginal Spermicides

Vaginal spermicides are agents that have sperm-killing properties. They are categorized as *chemical* methods of contraception, and come in a wide variety of forms, including aerosol foams, creams, jellies, tablets, and suppositories. Aerosol foams are the most popular. The spermicidal chemical responsible for killing the sperm is usually

Contraception and Abortion

nonoxynol-9 or octoxinol-9. Vaginal spermicides rate as only fair in effectiveness (see Table 12–1).

Vaginal spermicides do not require a doctor's prescription, but can be bought in most drugstores. They should not be confused with lubricating gels and creams often found on the same pharmacy shelves. Foams, creams, and jellies come with easy-to-use plastic applicators. Some of the most common brands are Delfen Contraceptive Foam, Dalkon Foam, Koromex II Contraceptive Cream, and Ortho-Gynol Contraceptive Jelly. The plastic applicator can be used repeatedly and may be purchased with initial starter packs. Refill packs are less expensive because they do not contain the applicators. Some of the more popular suppositories are Encare Oval, Intercept, and Semicid.

Timing is critical to the effectiveness of vaginal spermicides. Before intercourse takes place, the applicator should be filled with a premeasured amount of the desired form. To be effective, the spermicide must be inserted far up into the vagina, as close to the cervix as possible. If tablets or suppositories are used, they must be inserted with the fingers and rested against or near the cervix. Foam, cream, and jelly protection only last about 30 minutes, while tablets and suppositories offer protection for about 90 minutes.

A vaginal spermicide must be used *every* time a couple has intercourse, and it must be in place before the penis enters or comes near the vagina. Of the different forms of vaginal spermicides, foam ranks as the most effective. In addition to its spermicidal effect, its effervescence creates a dense barrier obstructing the entrance to the cervix and the foam usually distributes itself uniformly in the vagina. If the woman uses a spermicide and the man wears a condom, the effectiveness of these combined methods is close to 100 percent.

Among the advantages of spermicides are ease of use, widespread availability, and the fact that there is no need for a medical examination, prescription, and supervision. Besides having only minimal health risks, vaginal spermicides apparently offer some measure of protection against such sexually transmitted diseases as gonorrhea and genital herpes. They may also help to prevent common vaginal infections such as trichomoniasis (see Chapter 17). Special uses of vaginal spermicides are:

- As a contraceptive prior to and during the first month of oral contraceptive use.
- As a backup contraceptive during the first several months after IUD insertion, when expulsion of the IUD is most likely to take place.
- As an emergency method of contraception to have on hand for times when a woman runs out of oral contraceptives or finds that her IUD has been spontaneously expelled.
- As extra protection for a diaphragm user who has intercourse a second time before removing the diaphragm.
- As an immediate emergency measure when a condom tears, leaks, or slips off during intercourse.
- As a sole contraceptive when neither a condom nor a diaphragm is felt to be desirable.
- As a supplemental contraceptive during that part of the menstrual cycle when ovulation is most likely to occur. For instance, a condom and vaginal spermicide might be used together during a woman's most fertile days.
- As a vaginal lubricant by couples who require additional lubrication.
- As a convenience for women who have intercourse only infrequently. (Covington & McClendon, 1987)

Some users of vaginal spermicides are sensitive to the chemicals and develop some itching, swelling, or burning. Other complaints are that some spermicides have

FIGURE 12–6
The Cervical Cap.

Like the diaphragm, the cervical cap is used with a spermicide and covers the cervical opening. The cap is stronger and costs a bit less than the diaphragm, but because it can be left in place longer—and often is—the wearer risks developing infections, toxic shock syndrome, or even cancer.

cervical cap A barrier contraceptive that blocks sperm from passing from the vagina into the uterus. It resembles a miniature diaphragm with a tall dome and must be used with a spermicide.

vaginal sponge A disposable spongelike device made of polyurethene that contains one gram of nonoxynol-9 spermicide.

a chemical odor and that the application procedure is somewhat untidy. Couples engaging in oral sex may find the taste of some spermicides unpleasant.

Cervical Cap

Like the diaphragm, the **cervical cap** is a barrier contraceptive that blocks sperm from passing from the vagina into the uterus. The cervical cap measures about 1½ inches in diameter and is made of soft rubber. It resembles a miniature diaphragm with a tall dome (see Figure 12–6). Like the diaphragm, the cervical cap must be used with a spermicide and is available in different sizes to fit the woman's internal anatomy. The cervical cap has good overall effectiveness (see Table 12–1).

The cervical cap is held in place by suction and surface tension, and is usually more rigid than the diaphragm. Spermicide within the cap is pressed against the cervix to destroy any sperm that traverse the barrier. The cap should be filled about one-third full of spermicide before it is inserted into the vagina and placed on the cervix. Its position can be checked by running a finger around the cap. It is left in place for a minimum of 6 to 12 hours after intercourse.

Like the diaphragm, the cervical cap must be fitted by a doctor during a pelvic examination. It is preferred by many women since it is not as fragile as the diaphragm, nor does it tear or leak as often. It also permits greater sexual spontaneity because women can wear it for up to 48 hours. The cervical cap is less expensive than the diaphragm, and smaller amounts of spermicide are needed. Most experts recommend that a single cap be used no longer than one year (e.g., Powell et al., 1986).

There are some specific health risks associated with the cervical cap. Some tests have shown that users have higher rates of abnormal Pap tests, indicating possible infection and cervical cancer. For this reason, the FDA recommended in 1988 that the cervical cap be prescribed only for those women whose Pap smears are normal. It is also recommended that a Pap test be performed after three months of cap usage. Other potential problems are similar to those diaphragm users risk: toxic shock syndrome, urinary tract infections, and allergic reactions among both women and their male partners to the rubber or the spermicide. Also, an odorous discharge is possible with prolonged cap wear. Some women experience cervical or vaginal lacerations or abrasions caused by excessive rim pressure or prolonged wearing (Cagen, 1986; Powell et al., 1986).

Other potential problems are a poor fit and difficulty in cap insertion and removal. Because of the cap's relatively small size, some women find the diaphragm easier to use. Another disadvantage is that the cap sometimes becomes dislodged during intercourse. Rates of failure go up if the cap is removed too soon after lovemaking or the women does not use a spermicide. Finally, the cervical cap is not an alternative for some women, principally those with an abnormal cervical shape, cervical lacerations or erosion, cervical cysts, or inflammation of the cervix (cervicitis).

Vaginal Sponge

The **vaginal sponge** is essentially a method of delivering a spermicide to the cervix and vagina. This disposable spongelike device (see Figure 12–7) is made of polyurethene and contains one gram of nonoxynol-9 spermicide. It is slightly concave and round, and designed to feel like normal vaginal tissue. The vaginal sponge is fair in terms of overall contraceptive effectiveness (see Table 12–1).

The sponge, which only comes in one size, has a dimple on one side that is intended to fit over the cervix. The sponge is moistened with tap water prior to use, and then inserted deep into the vagina, where it continuously releases spermicide for up to 24 hours. The sponge not only provides a physical barrier between sperm

FIGURE 12-7
The Vaginal Sponge.

The disposable vaginal sponge contains its own supply of spermicide, which it releases continuously for up to 24 hours. The sponge is one of the least effective contraceptive methods, and it offers no protection against disease.

and the cervix, but also traps sperm within itself. Unlike the diaphragm, the sponge does not require additional applications of spermicide even for multiple acts of intercourse. It has a loop designed for easy removal, and is discarded after use.

Unlike a diaphragm, the contraceptive sponge does not have to be fitted. It can be purchased over the counter; a prescription is not necessary. The sponge can be inserted several hours before lovemaking, but must be left in place for at least six hours following intercourse. It does not interfere with lovemaking, since neither partner should be able to detect its presence. The sponge is less messy to use than vaginal spermicides, and can be inserted easily and quickly. There is some evidence that the vaginal sponge offers a degree of protection against such sexually transmitted diseases as chlamydia and gonorrhea.

No major health risks are associated with the vaginal sponge. However, as with vaginal spermicides, sensitivity to spermicide may cause irritation, including vaginal itching. Also, the inserted sponge may become a breeding ground for infection if it is used improperly. Women with a history of toxic shock syndrome, anatomic abnormalities of the vagina or a tipped uterus, or specific allergies to polyurethene or nonoxynol-9 should not use the vaginal sponge.

Rhythm Method

The **rhythm method** of birth control (also called *natural family planning*) requires no mechanical or chemical means. It is considered a poor to fair contraceptive method (see Table 12–1). Couples using the rhythm method refrain from intercourse on days when conception is most likely—that is, during ovulation, which, as we saw in Chapter 3, occurs about once a month throughout a woman's reproductive life. Thus the rhythm method depends on figuring out when ovulation will occur each month and refraining from intercourse during the days of greatest likelihood of conception (interestingly, the same technique is used in a reverse manner by couples who want to conceive). The rhythm method is the only method of birth control approved by the Roman Catholic Church.

The term *rhythm* in the context of this method refers to the cyclical nature of menstruation which, you'll recall, we discussed in Chapter 3. To use this method, a woman must first maintain a menstrual calendar recording the length of each of

rhythm method A type of birth control that involves abstaining from intercourse on days when pregnancy can occur. Also called *natural family planning*.

her menstrual cycles over the most recent eight-month span (the first day of menstrual bleeding or even light spotting is Day 1 of a cycle). Fertile days are then predicted on the basis of these menstrual records. The earliest day on which a woman is likely to be fertile is computed by subtracting 18 days from the length of her shortest cycle; the latest day on which she is likely to be fertile is calculated by subtracting 11 days from the length of her longest cycle (Hatcher et al., 1990).

Based on the rhythm method, the basal body temperature and sympto-thermal techniques have lower theoretical failure rates than the rhythm method (see Table 12–1). The **basal body temperature technique (BBT)** involves predicting ovulation based on the elevation of a woman's temperature after ovulation—the result of progesterone release from the ovary—and its continued elevation until menstruation begins. Couples using this technique keep a record of the woman's basal body temperature (BBT) to identify periods of fertility. The best way to do this is to take

basal body temperature technique (BBT) A birth control technique in which couples compile a record of the woman's basal body temperature to identify her periods of fertility.

MAKING USE OF WHAT WE KNOW

How to Use the Sympto-Thermal Technique

*T*he success of this technique depends heavily on a woman's awareness of mucous secretions during her menstrual cycle. Most fertile women can detect fairly regular changes in the moisture just inside the vagina, which is the result of normal hormonal variations. Here are some guides to learning to make effective use of this contraceptive technique.

- Each time a woman uses the bathroom she should insert a finger into her vagina and note how moist it feels, comparing the moisture detected from one day to the next. She should also note whether she can collect any mucus on her finger and check for a sticky, stretchable quality to the mucus.

- Most women find that the quality of their mucus follows a fairly predictable pattern. During menstruation, of course, the menstrual discharge obscures any other moisture. After menstruation ceases, the vagina may feel moist for a few days, but it is not distinctly wet nor is any mucus present. Within another few days a thick, cloudy, whitish or yellowish sticky mucus may be noticeable. As soon as a woman notices real wetness and/or any mucus at all she should consider herself fertile.

- As ovulation approaches, the vagina feels increasingly wet and mucus becomes more abundant. Now, however, the mucus is clear, slippery, and very stretchable. It's sometimes possible to stretch it three or more inches between the thumb and forefinger. The peak or last day of wetness, combined

with this type of mucus, is assumed to coincide with the time of ovulation. *A woman's fertile period lasts from the first sign of real wetness and/or mucus until the fourth day after this peak, or the last day of wetness and mucus.* Once the clear, slippery mucus is no longer detectable, either the thick, cloudy mucus returns or there is none at all until the time of the next menstrual period.

- The sympto-thermal technique may not give a woman enough advance warning of ovulation to prevent pregnancy. For more effective protection, it is wise to abstain from intercourse or to use an additional birth control method during the first part of a woman's cycle until the fourth day after the peak.

- The menstrual cycle is affected by many factors, including vaginal infections, use of vaginal spermicides or artificial lubricants, douching, medications, and sexual activity itself (both semen and the secretions of sexual arousal).

- A woman should make a habit of keeping accurate records on her cycle, recording her findings on a special chart each day. If she checks her vagina several times in one day, she should record only the *most fertile* observation for that day.

- Most women need to monitor their mucous changes for several menstrual cycles before they understand them clearly. A woman should make sure she fully understands her own personal mucous signs before she relies on this method of birth control.

Contraception and Abortion

the temperature early in the morning after at least six hours of sleep with a basal body thermometer (which is calibrated in units of 0.1 degrees for ease of reading).

The **sympto-thermal technique** combines basal body temperature readings with observation of the woman's bodily symptoms indicative of ovulation. Variation in cervical mucus during the menstrual cycle is the most important symptom. As ovulation nears, the ovaries begin secreting hormones that thicken the mucus and ready it for accepting and transporting the sperm. A few days before ovulation, cervical mucus has a clear, lubricative, raw eggwhite consistency. After ovulation, the mucus become thick and opaque. Couples using this approach learn to read these signs (see the box on "How to Use the Sympto-Thermal Technique") and abstain from intercourse during fertile periods.

In the United States, rhythm, BBT, and the sympto-thermal techniques are losing popularity, but for those who choose natural family planning, the absence of mechanical devices or drugs is considered a big advantage. However, consistent record-keeping and careful calculations are crucial to making this approach work. Moreover, its effectiveness rate is highest for women whose monthly periods are regular. Even then, illness, fatigue, stress, and other factors can throw off the most deliberate and carefully planned calculations.

> **sympto-thermal technique** A birth control technique in which couples combine the woman's basal body temperature readings with observations of changes in the character of the woman's cervical mucus.

Withdrawal

Withdrawal, also called *coitus interruptus*, is perhaps the world's oldest method of birth control. It is also one of the riskiest (see Table 12–1). When the withdrawal technique is used, intercourse proceeds until ejaculation is about to occur, at which time the man withdraws his penis from the vagina and ejaculates away from the woman's external genitalia.

Withdrawal does not require mechanical devices or chemicals, it doesn't have any medical side effects, and it doesn't cost anything. However, this technique does interrupt intercourse at its peak, and all too often the man withdraws too late and semen enters the vagina. Moreover, most of the sperm in one ejaculation are in the first third of the ejaculate. In addition, the pre-ejaculatory fluid often emitted by the penis during intercourse contains sperm. Thus withdrawal of the penis before the moment of orgasm is not a foolproof method of contraception, and if a man has difficulty controlling his ejaculation the method is almost useless. Finally, withdrawal offers no protection whatsoever against the transmission of disease.

> *Is withdrawal a risky form of birth control?*

> **withdrawal** A method of birth control, also called *coitus interruptus*. Intercourse proceeds until the man is at the point of ejaculation, at which time he immediately withdraws his penis from the vagina and ejaculates away from the woman's external genitalia.

Figure 12–8 summarizes the major contraceptive choices we've discussed, emphasizing their effects on a woman's future fertility and health as well as their effectiveness in preventing pregnancy. Note how *inconsistent* use of almost all methods both diminishes their potential benefits and heightens the risk of health problems. The cells colored the darkest shade of blue mark the methods that are most likely to further a specific goal. Used consistently, these methods will greatly improve a woman's chances of attaining a particular goal under the conditions indicated in the lefthand column of the figure. Cells colored the next-darkest shade of blue indicate methods that give a woman a good chance of attaining her particular goal. The middle shade of blue denotes choices that are neutral with respect to particular goals. Finally, the palest blue and white cells mark methods that literally decrease a woman's chances of reaching her goal—be it preventing unwanted pregnancy, ensuring her future fertility, or staying free of life-threatening disorders like cardiovascular disease and cancer (Harlap, Kost, & Forrest, 1991).

We tried to include information on the effectiveness of different contraceptive methods in preventing sexually transmitted disease in Figure 12–8 but found it impossible to do this without making the figure confusing. We will be returning to the subject of disease prevention in Chapters 17 and 18.

Goal	Behaviors and underlying conditions	No method	Periodic abstinence		Withdrawal	
			Consistent User	Inconsistant user	Consistent User	Inconsistant user
Preventing Pregnancy and Its Health Complications						
Preserving Future Fertility	*Mutually monogamous*					
	Not mutually monogamous					
Protecting Current Health— Preventing Cardiovascular Disease	*Nonsmoker without risk factors*					
	Smoker**	Pregnancy may be dangerous		Pregnancy may be dangerous		Pregnancy may be dangerous
	At increased risk for cardiovascular disease***	Pregnancy may increase risk		Pregnancy may increase risk		Pregnancy may increase risk
Protecting Future Health Preventing Ovarian and Endometrial Cancer						
Preventing Breast Cancer				Pregnancy may increase risk temporarily in young women		Pregnancy may increase risk temporarily in young women
Preventing Cervical Cancer				Pregnancy may increase risk	Theoretically improved, no data	Pregnancy may increase risk

* Tubal ligation may cause more complications in heavy smokers than it causes in nonsmokers.

** Light smokers do not necessarily risk pregnancy complications.

*** High blood pressure, high cholesterol, diabetes, previous thrombosis or embolism, family history of heart attack before age 60.

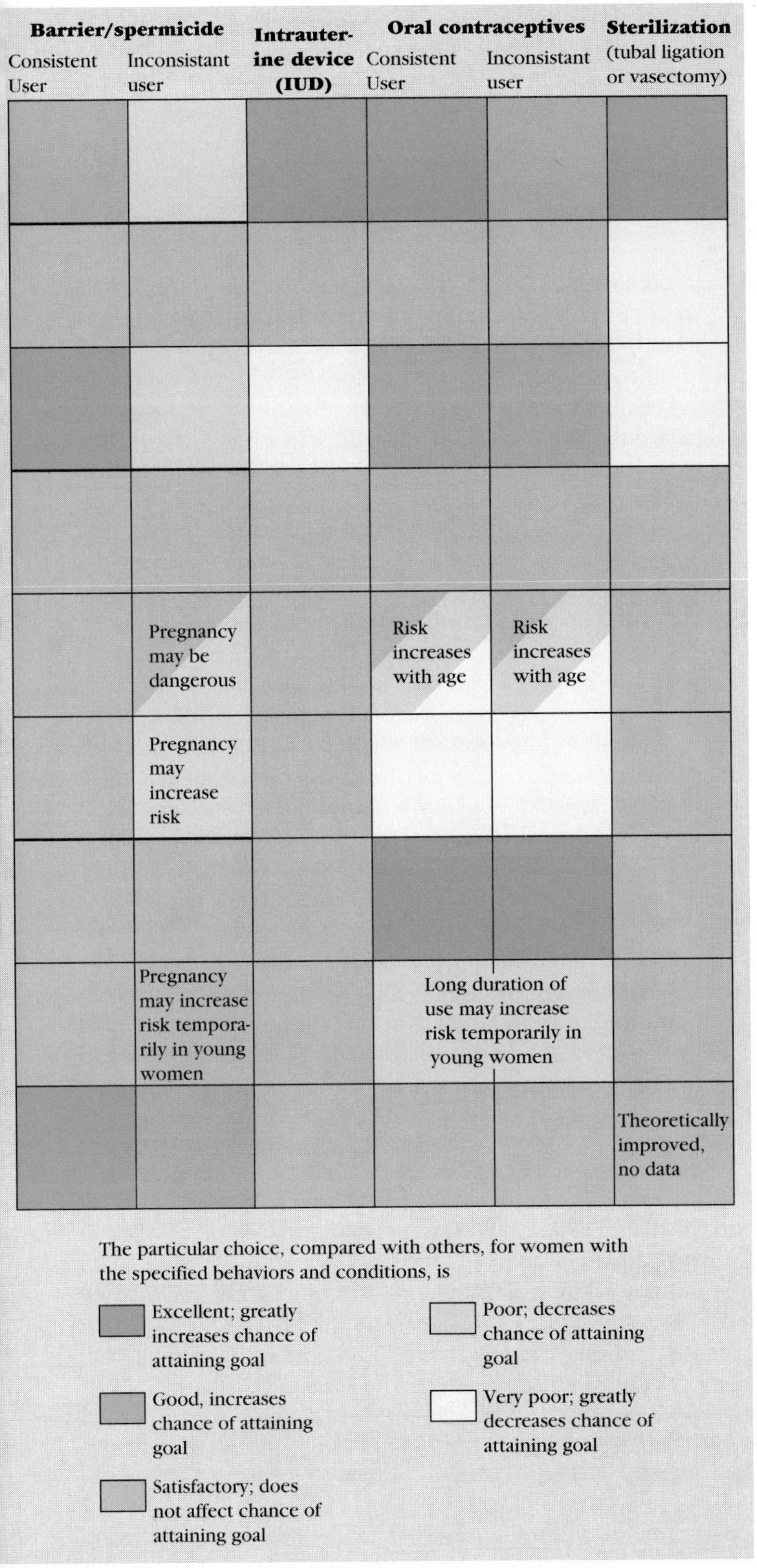

Barrier/spermicide		Intrauter- ine device (IUD)	Oral contraceptives		Sterilization (tubal ligation or vasectomy)
Consistent User	Inconsistant user		Consistent User	Inconsistant user	
	Pregnancy may be dangerous		Risk increases with age	Risk increases with age	
	Pregnancy may increase risk				
	Pregnancy may increase risk temporarily in young women		Long duration of use may increase risk temporarily in young women		
					Theoretically improved, no data

The particular choice, compared with others, for women with the specified behaviors and conditions, is

Excellent; greatly increases chance of attaining goal

Good, increases chance of attaining goal

Satisfactory; does not affect chance of attaining goal

Poor; decreases chance of attaining goal

Very poor; greatly decreases chance of attaining goal

FIGURE 12–8
Effects of Various Contraceptive Methods on Reproductive and General Health Goals.

Using most methods consistently will improve the chances of reaching these goals. (Source: Adapted from Harlap, Kost, & Forrest, 1991)

CONTRACEPTIVES OF THE FUTURE

What is the future of birth control technology? Are we likely to see improved techniques of fertility regulation in years to come? Will some of the methods used today become obsolete tomorrow? As we address these issues, researchers are exploring an assortment of new methods. Their ultimate goal is to provide men and women with a contraceptive device that is very safe, highly effective, and easy to use. Among the more promising approaches, some of which are already being used abroad, are RU 486, "gossypol," nasal sprays, vaccines, a new kind of IUD, a vaginal "ring," and a condom for women.

RU 486. A postcoital birth control method, RU 486 has been used in clinical trials by over 4,000 women in 20 countries. It is an antiprogesterone agent that, when taken after a woman misses a period, induces a miscarriage. RU 486 prevents a fertilized egg from implanting itself in the uterine wall. The procedure calls for the woman to take a single dose (600 mg.) of RU 486 within three weeks of a missed period, then, 48 hours later, to take a small dose of prostaglandin, usually in the form of a vaginal suppository or injection, to assist in emptying the contents of the uterus. The effect is as if she were having a heavy period.

Researchers have uncovered other potential uses for the progesterone-blocking capacities of RU 486. For example, it may prove useful in assisting the delivery of a full-term, normal baby when the cervix doesn't open well, and thus prevent some cesarean sections. It has also been shown to reduce the pain of endometriosis. In trial studies, breast cancer tumors, excessive adrenal function, and glaucoma due to excessive corticosteroids have also responded well to RU 486 therapy.

Originally developed in France by Etienne-Emile Baulieu, RU 486 has stirred considerable controversy. Its critics label it an *abortifacient*—a substance that causes termination of pregnancy—though proponents of the drug prefer to label it a "contragestive"—a substance that blocks gestation. Defenders of RU 486 feel that it is preferable to surgical abortion. One advantage of this drug is that it enables a woman to make the decision to end a pregnancy privately, in consultation with her doctor and without clinical assistance (Couzinet et al., 1986; Shoupe et al., 1986; Cameron, Michie, & Baird, 1986). As we go to press, one or two deaths have been attributed to the use of RU 486, but the evidence for this is not yet clear.

In 1992, the Supreme Court rejected the plea of a California woman attempting to regain possession of RU 486 seized from her by the U.S. Customs Service. Leona Benten purchased RU 486 in England during the early weeks of her pregnancy and had the pills confiscated when she arrived in New York. In its ruling, the Supreme Court refused a request to reverse a Circuit Court of Appeals order blocking the Customs Service from releasing the pills. After the ruling, Benten elected to have a surgical abortion.

MALE ORAL CONTRACEPTIVE. The possibility of a male oral contraceptive may lie in *gossypol*, a cotton-based extract. This substance has been given in pill form to men in China in an effort to curb that nation's overpopulation problem. However, while gossypol has been effective in preventing pregnancy by inhibiting sperm production and mobility, it has produced serious side effects, including infertility after discontinuing the drug and a loss of potassium in the men who have used it.

CONTRACEPTIVE NASAL SPRAYS. Another contraceptive possibility for both women and men is a nasal spray that contains a synthetic hormone similar to luteinizing hormone-releasing hormone (LHRH). In women, the spray is used once each day to inhibit ovulation, which it does by mimicking the natural hormone and thus causing the pituitary gland to stop producing it. Early testing indicates the spray is effective but the correct dosage is difficult to determine. Side effects include some irregular bleed-

Contraception and Abortion

ing and postmenopausal symptoms. The version of the nasal spray developed for men is less promising. In men the synthetic hormone inhibits sperm production, but larger doses and a sustained release appear to be required.

CONTRACEPTIVE VACCINES. This is another possibility for both women and men. Part of the female vaccine is made from the urine of pregnant women. It produces antibodies that neutralize the human chorionic gonadotrophin hormone (HCG) that is needed to support a pregnancy. The vaccine for men originates from a pituitary gland hormone that interferes with the production of sperm, but not of testosterone. The contraceptive vaccine is injectable and lasts for two months.

Interestingly, genetically engineered vaccines are also being developed for controlling populations of animal pests. These vaccines work by immunizing a female against the male's sperm, a concept researchers believe can eventually be applied to human contraception. A single dose of a perfected vaccine could protect the user for a period of years.

PROGESTIN-RELEASING INTRAUTERINE DEVICE. This special IUD is inserted and removed in the same way as IUDs in current use. The difference is that it contains levonorgestrel, a synthetic progestin, that is released into the uterus. It can remain in place for up to five years. In clinical trials users had fewer of the heavy bleeding problems and other risks associated with the present versions of the IUD.

VAGINAL RING. The vaginal ring is shaped like a thin donut and secretes hormones designed to prevent pregnancy. It can be worn in the vagina for 21 days, then removed for 7 days to allow for menstrual bleeding. Rings containing both progestin and estrogen, and those containing progestin alone, are being evaluated. Side effects are minimal, and the pregnancy rate in clinical research is 2 percent, about the same as for the pill.

FEMALE CONDOM. In 1988 a female condom was introduced into the United States. Called a "vaginal pouch" by one of its manufacturers, it is made of two flexible rings that are connected to each other by a tube of thin polyurethane. One of the rings is also covered by a sheet of polyurethane. The female condom is designed to line the vagina. When it is inserted, the ring that is covered by polyurethane is placed over the cervix, just like a diaphragm, and the other ring remains outside the vaginal opening (see Figure 12–9). In addition to its contraceptive purpose, the female condom affords protection from sexually transmitted diseases.

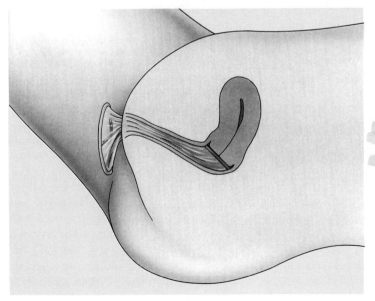

FIGURE 12–9
The Female Condom.

According to Wisconsin Pharmacal Company, the manufacturer of the "Reality" condom, this new female contraceptive device is designed to protect against sexually transmitted diseases and HIV infection (see Chapters 17 and 18) as well as against pregnancy. According to the company, the polyurethane used in this condom is 30 times stronger than the latex rubber used in most male condoms, diaphragms, and cervical caps. As we go to press, the federal Food and Drug Administration is continuing to investigate the quality and safety of this new device, and there are signs that it may be approved by the fall of 1992.

STERILIZATION

Sterilization is a family planning technique that permanently blocks reproductive capacities. Specifically, it is a surgical procedure that interrupts the reproductive tracts of either the man or the woman so that fertilization is prevented. A properly performed sterilization virtually always prevents conception. The theoretical and typical failure rates of male and female sterilization are shown in Table 12–1.

At one time sterilization in the United States was performed primarily on women. Today, though, more than half of all sterilizations are done on men. Among couples married longer than ten years, sterilization is the most popular form of birth control. Some of the reasons for its popularity are the simplicity of the surgical procedures; the fact that, once adopted, this method requires no further attention; and fear of the potential risks of oral contraceptives and the IUD. Moreover, sterilization does not interfere with intercourse (Jarow, 1987; Kendrick & Rubin, 1986).

Over one million sterilization procedures are performed each year in the United States. Sterilization is also a widespread form of family planning in other nations. More than 100 million couples around the globe are currently protected from unwanted pregnancy by voluntary sterilization—a seven-fold increase over the last 20 years (Harlap, Kost, & Forrest, 1991; Hatcher et al., 1990).

People who are considering sterilization should realize that it is almost certainly permanent (at present, reversible methods are not perfect). They should carefully weigh their values, feelings, and particular situations. Some points to question: What are the alternatives to sterilization and are you willing to use those alternatives? Will sterilization affect your relationship with your present and/or future partners? Are you positive that you do not want any (or any more) children? Have you considered the possibility that a living child might die? After you have made the decision to be sterilized, your physician should review the procedure and its consequences with you and answer any questions that you might have.

Male Sterilization

vasectomy A surgical procedure in which the vas deferens are severed, thus preventing sperm from passing from the epididymis into the ejaculate.

The **vasectomy** has become a very popular method of birth control in the United States (Harlap, Kost, & Forrest, 1991; Hatcher et al., 1990; Jarrow, 1987). It is a relatively simple surgical procedure in which the vas deferens are cut to prevent the passage of sperm. A tiny incision is made in the scrotum on either side (or sometimes a small incision is made in the midfrontal area) and each vas deferens is cut and tied. The surgery can be done in 15 or 20 minutes in a doctor's office under local anesthesia. The vasectomy does not interfere with ejaculation, since sperm constitute only a very small portion of the ejaculate. The sperm that are still produced by the testes degenerate and are reabsorbed by the body. Figure 12–10 illustrates the surgical procedures involved in a vasectomy.

After a man has a vasectomy, he is considered sterile when two successive semen examinations are found to be sperm-free. The recovery period from a vasectomy is about two days of relative inactivity. Sexual relations can usually be resumed within a week or so, and the man's sexual desire and response remain normal.

Can a vasectomy be reversed?

Surgical reversal is quite difficult and expensive, and the operation has a poor success rate. It requires that the scarred ends of the vas deferens be removed and the two ends then rejoined. This is a very delicate operation that is performed with microsurgical techniques. Even if the operation is successful, other problems often remain. For example, sperm counts typically remain low following a vasectomy because the body has developed antibodies to destroy sperm. The difficulty in successfully reversing a vasectomy underscores the need for men to be certain about their sterilization decision.

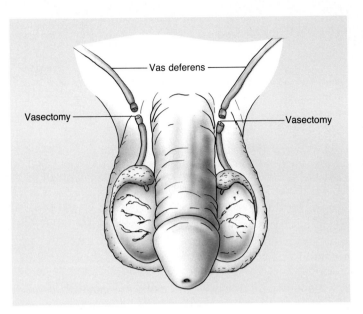

FIGURE 12–10
Vasectomy.

In male sterilization, a simple procedure, both vas deferens are cut and tied to prevent the passage of sperm. (Source: *Medical Aspects of Sexuality*, vol. 13, no. 6, p. 91)

Vasectomies have become more acceptable to men because the once common, erroneous idea that such surgery destroys a man's sexual power has been dispelled (see "Myths and Misconceptions" box). Today most people are aware that a vasectomy in no way changes sexual desire or inhibits a man's capacity to have an erection or to ejaculate.

There are no major postoperative side effects. The most common complaints following surgery are pain and swelling around the incision, as well as some bruising and discoloration. These are considered minor effects that may last from a few days to two weeks. They may be alleviated by mild analgesics, ice packs, scrotal support, and reduced activity. More serious possible complications include a hematoma (mass of clotted blood) due to heavy straining or physical activity, swelling and tenderness of the testicles, hydrocele (collection of fluid around the testes), and infection. Infections usually occur around the site of the incision or sutures. A man should see his physician without delay if he experiences any of these complications.

Female Sterilization

The most common form of female sterilization is a type of surgery called **tubal ligation,** often referred to colloquially as "tying the tubes." By preventing eggs from traveling through the tubes to the uterus, tubal ligation makes fertilization impossible. New instruments and surgical techniques have made it possible to perform this surgery under local or short-acting general anesthesia.

There are two ways to perform a tubal ligation. One involves making an abdominal incision approximately one inch long. Each fallopian tube is then gently pulled to the opening of the incision, blocked by cutting and tying the cut ends or by applying rings or clips, and allowed to slip back into place. The other approach—called a laparotomy—involves inserting a magnifying-like instrument into the abdomen, through which the doctor can see the internal organs and block the tubes by cauterizing them or by applying rings or clips. Either procedure can be performed

tubal ligation A form of sterilization in which the fallopian tubes are cut and tied.

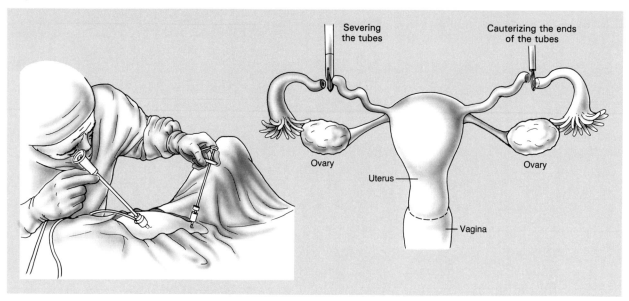

FIGURE 12–11
Tubal Ligation.

In a laparotomy, a woman's fallopian tubes are severed and cauterized with instruments inserted through a very small incision in the abdomen. Like other forms of tubal ligation, this procedure prevents sperm and egg from meeting. (From Kelley/Byrne, *Exploring Human Sexuality*, copyright © 1992, p. 121. Reprinted by permission of Prentice Hall, Englewood Cliffs, New Jersey.)

on most women in about 10 to 20 minutes, usually without an overnight hospital stay. Such "Band-Aid" approaches to surgery have revolutionized the concept of female sterilization. Figure 12–11 illustrates the second type of procedure.

Both of these procedures are highly effective, and a tubal ligation does not decrease sexual feelings. Patients are advised to rest at home for a few days, though, and to refrain from sexual intercourse for about a week. Menstruation continues, but the ovaries' eggs, when released, are trapped in the blocked-off tubes and reabsorbed by the body.

Like a vasectomy, a tubal ligation is difficult and expensive to reverse. Reconnecting the tied or cauterized ends of the fallopian tubes is a delicate procedure and is not often successful. The more damage the tubes have suffered in the original surgery, the higher the failure rate of reversal. In addition, serious complications may follow a tubal ligation if the surgery is not highly skilled. For example, a tube can rupture or another internal structure, such as the urethra, can be damaged. In many cases, however, the woman experiences only mild discomfort from the incision or an easily treated infection.

WHERE TO FIND MORE INFORMATION ON BIRTH CONTROL

Planned Parenthood Federation of America
810 Seventh Avenue
New York, NY 10019
This organization provides medical services, counseling, and a wide range of information on birth control, sexuality, infertility, abortion, and other areas. Services are provided in 735 clinics throughout the United States.

National Family Planning and Reproductive Health Association
122 C Street, N.W.
Suite 380
Washington, D.C. 20402
A national organization offering family planning and reproductive health-care services.

Couple to Couple League
P.O. Box 111184
Cincinnati, OH 45211
A Christian interfaith, nonprofit organization established to teach the techniques of natural family planning.

ABORTION

Abortion is the termination of a pregnancy by natural or artificial means. A natural, or **spontaneous, abortion** is commonly called a *miscarriage*. Spontaneous abortions occur when pregnancy terminates before the developing organism is mature enough to survive outside the womb. Physiologically, this happens when the embryo separates from the uterine wall and is expelled by the uterus. One source estimates that 43 percent of all pregnancies end in spontaneous abortion, usually during the first two or three months (Olds, London, & Ladewig, 1992). Precipitating factors include severe trauma, abnormalities of the reproductive tract, maternal viral and bacterial infections, and defective sperm or eggs (Scott, 1986). An **induced abortion** is the deliberate removal of the organism from the uterus.

The Abortion Debate

Induced abortions were legal in ancient China, and for many centuries in Europe as well. In the thirteenth century the Catholic theologian Thomas Aquinas stated that the male fetus developed a soul 40 days after conception and the female fetus 80–90 days after conception. Aborting a fetus after these times was made a criminal offense (Rodman, 1987). Six hundred years later Pope Pius IX stated that a human being exists from the moment of conception and abortion at any stage is the equivalent of murder. This is still the official view of the Catholic Church.

During the 1860s, abortion became illegal in the United States except to save the mother's life. While the reason often given for passing antiabortion legislation was that the primitive abortion procedures then in use endangered women's lives, some believe (e.g., Shuran, 1987) that the real reason was that a male-dominated society felt threatened by the nineteenth-century movement seeking equality and independence for women (Shuran, 1987). After abortion became generally illegal in this country, women who wanted to end a pregnancy had to seek illegal abortions or attempt to abort themselves. Those who suffered the most from the legal ban were poor women, whose only recourse was to unsafe places and medically incompetent practitioners. In the 1960s some states (e.g., California and New York) began changing their abortion laws, and in 1973, in a decision known as *Roe* v. *Wade*, the Supreme Court legalized a woman's right to have an abortion before the fetus became viable (able to survive outside the mother's body). *Roe* v. *Wade* was decided in the wake of the feminist movement of the 1960s and early 1970s (see Chapter 1), and reflected a growing sentiment that women should have the right to decide whether or not to have children.

What's the difference between a spontaneous abortion and an induced abortion?

spontaneous abortion
Separation of the organism from the uterine wall, followed by expulsion by the uterus. Also referred to as a *miscarriage*.

induced abortion
Deliberate removal of the organism from the uterus.

A WORLD OF DIFFERENCES

Birth Control in Other Nations

*F*amily size has shrunk in many developed nations as a result of the contemporary emphasis on the dangers of overpopulation and the advantages of deliberate family planning. The average American woman gives birth to two children, down from 3.2 in 1960. Should present trends continue, the United States will reach zero population growth by the year 2020. *Zero population growth* means that a given population neither increases nor decreases; rather, it is in equilibrium.

Other developed nations, such as Germany, Austria, Denmark, and Hungary, have already reached zero population growth. In fact, the *fertility rate* (the number of live births occurring each year) in these nations is causing *negative population growth*, or a decrease in overall population. Some countries have sought to reverse the population downswing by implementing pronatalist legislation, under which couples receive government-sponsored rewards for conceiving more than one child. Nations such as Ireland, Poland, and the Commonwealth of Independent States have fertility rates around 2.10 births per woman. This is about the fertility rate needed to balance a nation's births and deaths, and thus to maintain a stable population (van de Kaa, 1987).

As might be expected, the percentages of married women using contraception are highest in the developed nations. Over 70 percent of married couples in the United States, Belgium, Denmark, Hungary, Portugal, and the United Kingdom use some form of birth control. The lowest percentages are found in Africa, where the concept of family planning—at least for limiting fertility—is far from fully accepted. On that continent the percentage of couples using contraception ranges from 3 percent in Cameroon to about 5 percent in Senegal and 7 percent in Kenya. In Asia the figures range from about 7 percent in Nepal to 12 percent in Bangladesh and about 55 percent in Thailand. In Latin America the percentages vary from 34 percent in El Salvador to 61 percent in Panama. In all of these nations the percentages of teenagers using contraception are significantly lower (Donaldson & Tsui, 1990; Senderowitz & Paxman, 1985).

Large families are the rule in many parts of the world that lack adequate birth control methods. Kenyan women, for example, average eight children each, causing the population of that Texas-size country to increase 4.2 percent every year. Kenya's population was estimated to be 21 million in 1988, and if current fertility rates hold, it will quadruple to 83 million by 2025. Haitian and Pakistani women give birth to about six children each. Tunisian women average about five children.

Knowledge of family planning is an obvious prerequisite to lowering the birth rate in overpopulated countries. However, the number of children brought into the world is influenced by many other factors. One of the most important of these is the economic role of children, particularly in developing nations. Large families are typically found in agricultural areas where intensive labor is needed, such as Latin America. In India and Bangladesh large families result from the desire for healthy male children. Boys represent economic security for the mother should she become widowed.

While *Roe* v. *Wade* made it possible for middle- and upper-class women to get abortions fairly easily, low-income women had a much harder time, especially after the Hyde Amendment, passed in 1977, stopped federal funding of Medicaid abortions (a few states—e.g., New York—still pay for Medicaid abortions). Before this amendment was passed, one-third of all abortions were paid for with Medicaid funds. Now, unless low-income women can find a way to have the abortion funded, they have no choice in most states but to give birth to a baby they may neither want nor be able to afford.

Some states—Missouri, North Dakota, and Pennsylvania—have sought to legislatively overturn *Roe* v. *Wade* and put in place major restrictions on legal abortions. In 1989 the U.S. Supreme Court ruled in *Webster* v. *Health Reproductive Services* in favor of three Missouri restrictions: barring public employees from performing abor-

In some nations certain customs and practices contribute to the high fertility rates. In Rwanda in East Africa, for example, contraception has never been popular. Only about 11 percent of married women over the age of 15 use *any* form of family planning, and 80 percent of these women rely on periodic abstinence. The average Rwandan woman is married before she reaches 20 and bears eight children during her lifetime. In other African countries a taboo on postpartum intercourse that can last as long as two years reduces the fertility level.

No discussion of family planning is complete without some reference to the People's Republic of China. Here family planning is not a voluntary decision made by couples. Rather, it is the government that makes birth decisions. In an effort to contain their population, which is now over one billion, Chinese authorities allow couples to have only one child. China is thus the first nation to restrict a couple's right to procreate. To reduce the risk that couples will be tempted to have more than one child, the government has set the minimum age for marriage at 20 for women and 22 for men and encouraged even later marriages.

The Chinese government enforces its one-child-per-couple limit through material incentives, peer pressure, and attempts to persuade newly married couples that practicing restraint in procreation will mean a better future for their own families, their communities, and their nation. The government actively promotes sterilization and abortion, and has experimented with a male oral contraceptive. Other forms of birth control are available through family planning centers situated throughout the nation, as well as through visiting health officials who regularly monitor fertility patterns in towns and villages.

China today contains over one-fifth of all the world's people. If the one-child limit proves successful, it is estimated that the population will stabilize at 1.2 billion early in the next century. By the twenty-second century, government officials hope that the population will have shrunk to 700 million. But if the policy is unsuccessful and the population continues to grow, China's ability to feed its people will be in jeopardy.

Chinese couples who follow the approved policy are entitled to numerous benefits, including more living space, higher pensions, free education, lower-cost health care, and better medical care. The only child receives preferential treatment in the school system as well as in the labor force. Couples who produce a second child forfeit all of these benefits.

Militating against the government's success in this area is the fact that Chinese families have traditionally preferred male children. Should their firstborn child be a girl, many couples try to conceive again in hope of having a son. The government has fought this custom with rather draconian measures. Indeed, in one province of China couples expecting a second child have their wages docked if the woman decides not to have an abortion. In 1988 about one in every four pregnancies in the People's Republic China was aborted.

tions when the mother's life is not in jeopardy; requiring physicians to perform a viability test (measuring the potential of the fetus to survive) if the woman is at least 20 weeks pregnant; and barring the use of public buildings for abortions. In 1992, the Supreme Court upheld most of Pennsylvania's 1989 restrictive abortion law.

The abortion debate will continue because both those in favor of keeping abortion legal (who call themselves "prochoice" advocates) and those opposed to abortion (who call themselves "right-to-life" advocates) have large constituencies and are increasingly active in the political arena. The major distinction between the two forces is that prochoice groups believe that women have the right to control their own bodies and only the individual who is pregnant should be able to decide whether or not to continue that pregnancy, while right-to-life groups believe that a full human being is present at conception and the right of this being to continue to live takes

At this pro-choice demonstration, a pro-life activist joins the march.

precedence over the woman's desire not to continue her pregnancy. This is a highly complex issue on which public opinion is divided, as we shall see when we return to the topic in Chapter 21.

Approximately 1.5 million induced abortions take place annually in the United States, and another 40 to 60 million occur worldwide. In the United States about 50 percent of all abortions are performed by the eighth week of pregnancy, and approximately 90 percent take place within the first trimester of pregnancy. Rates of induced abortions are greater for unmarried women and teenagers than for married adult women. Almost three-quarters of induced abortions are performed on unmarried women, and about half of these women are childless at the time (Henshaw, Forrest, & Van Vort, 1987).

Today about 10 percent of the world's people live in countries that forbid abortion (for example, the Dominican Republic and Indonesia). Almost 40 percent live in nations where abortion on request is allowed, at least in the first trimester of pregnancy. The rest of the world's people live under laws that allow abortions under conditions that range from saving the mother's life to economic hardship. In the past 15 years 17 countries (including Canada, India, Norway, and Great Britain) have liberalized their abortion laws; during that same period seven nations (Bulgaria, Czechoslovakia, Hungary, Romania, Iran, Israel, and New Zealand) have adopted more stringent legislation (Donaldson & Tsui, 1990; Tietze & Henshaw, 1986). For a global view of birth control, attitudes, and practices, see the box on "Birth Control in Other Nations."

Abortion Methods

There are a number of abortion procedures, distinguishable by the extent of medical intrusion involved. In general, the earlier the procedure is performed, the lower the risks for the mother. The five procedures discussed in this section are vacuum aspiration, dilation and curettage, dilation and evacuation, amniotic fluid replacement, and hysterotomy.

vacuum aspiration A form of induced abortion generally used during the first trimester of pregnancy. With this technique, the embryo is suctioned from the uterus.

VACUUM ASPIRATION. Also referred to as *vacuum curettage* or the *suction method*, **vacuum aspiration** is performed during the first three months. The woman lies on her back on a table with her knees up, in a position similar to that assumed for a pelvic examination. Usually a local anesthesia is injected into the cervix and ligaments supporting the uterus. After the cervix is slightly dilated, a small, hollow tube attached to a vacuum machine is inserted through the cervix into the uterus, which is emptied by gentle suction. This procedure generally takes a few minutes and the patient recovers within a few hours. About 90 percent of all abortions performed in the United States employ the vacuum aspiration technique (Henshaw et al., 1985).

dilation and curettage A type of induced abortion used during the first trimester of pregnancy. The organism is removed from the uterus by curettage.

DILATION AND CURETTAGE (D&C). Dilation and curettage (D&C) can also be performed during the first three months. The patient's position is the same as that assumed for a vacuum aspiration, but after local or general anesthesia is administered, the cervix is widened to a greater extent by inserting a series of increasingly larger instruments called *dilators* into it. When the desired width is reached, the contents of the uterus are loosened and removed from the uterine wall with a small spoon-shaped instrument called a *curette*. The procedure does not involve the cutting of any body tissue and takes about 15 minutes.

dilation and evacuation A type of induced abortion employed from the 13th to the 20th week of pregnancy. The technique involves the removal of the organism by an alternation of suction and curettage.

DILATION AND EVACUATION (D&E). Dilation and evacuation (D&E) is a fairly recent medical innovation and can be performed between the 13th and 20th weeks of pregnancy. With the woman under local anesthesia, the cervix is slowly and grad-

Contraception and Abortion

ually dilated and the fetal material is removed by an alternation of suction and curettage. This procedure requires only a few hours' recovery period.

Amniotic Fluid Replacement. **Amniotic fluid replacement,** also called *amniocentesis abortion* or *instillation abortion*, is a procedure usually performed between the 16th and 20th weeks of pregnancy (18 to 22 weeks from the last menstrual period). In this procedure a needle is inserted through the abdominal wall into the uterus. A small amount of amniotic fluid is then withdrawn and replaced, most often, with a solution containing the drug prostaglandin. This injection usually causes fetal death, contractions, and expulsion of fetal tissue within 12 to 24 hours. This procedure usually requires a two- to three-day hospital stay.

amniotic fluid replacement A type of induced abortion usually performed between the 16th and 20th weeks of pregnancy. Most often the drug prostaglandin is used to cause contractions and fetal expulsion.

Hysterotomy. A **hysterotomy,** performed between the 16th and 24th weeks of pregnancy, involves surgery (an operation like a cesarean section). (The 24th week of prenatal life is the commonly accepted standard beyond which induced abortions are no longer performed except to save the life of the mother; beyond this point, fetal survival outside of the womb is possible.) This type of abortion is rare and analogous to a cesarean delivery (see Chapter 11) during the second trimester. Essentially, an incision is made through the abdominal wall and the fetus and placenta are removed. A hysterotomy may require a hospital stay of four to seven days and full recovery may take several weeks.

hysterotomy A type of induced abortion usually performed between the 16th and 24th weeks of pregnancy that involves surgery to remove the fetus.

Postabortion Considerations

The nature of postabortion care depends, of course, on the type of abortion performed. Generally speaking, though, women are encouraged to take showers instead of tub baths, and to use sanitary pads for a few weeks instead of tampons. Some women experience bleeding for several days or weeks. For a few weeks after the abortion, there is also a chance of developing a pelvic infection. For this reason, intercourse should be avoided during this time.

An abortion does not reduce a woman's ability to conceive, although there is some evidence (i.e., Stubblefield, 1984) that women who have had two or more abortions have a higher incidence of miscarriage in their later pregnancies. Regular menstrual periods usually resume a month or two after an abortion. It is a myth that pregnancy cannot occur for an extended length of time after an abortion. Indeed, a woman can get pregnant before her next period if she does not use birth control. If a woman is on the pill, she can generally resume taking it right after the abortion. A diaphragm can be fitted at a woman's follow-up visit, after her uterus has returned to its normal size. The contraceptive sponge can only be used after all bleeding stops, preferably after the first normal menstrual period. Foam and condoms can be used right after the abortion. Rhythm methods may be used beginning with the first normal menstrual period.

Psychological Issues. There are many psychological sides to having an abortion. Some sources (e.g., Holden, 1989) contend that most mentally healthy women do not suffer psychological trauma following an abortion. Indeed, many women feel a sense of relief rather than distress. Having an abortion may also contribute to heightened decision-making abilities, particularly in the area of contraceptive choices (Wolhandler & Weber, 1984).

For some women, though, the termination of a pregnancy can be a negative emotional experience. Uncertainty, anxiety, depression, loneliness, and guilt may be felt before as well as after the operation. This seems to be especially true for women having repeat abortions. One source (Robins & DeLamater, 1985) reports that support from the woman's partner, both before and after the abortion, helps to reduce these feelings. However, it is not uncommon for men whose partners are having an abortion to experience confused feelings themselves, including a sense of loss, powerlessness, guilt, and sadness (Shostak & McLouth, 1984).

While competent medical care is essential, the woman's psychological needs also require attention. There are a number of important factors that a pregnant woman, married or not, should consider before making a decision about abortion. Arlene and Howard Eisenberg (1983) summarize these factors as follows:

- *The health of the woman.* Does her physician feel that pregnancy and a new baby would endanger the mother's physical or psychological health?
- *Condition of the fetus.* Do prenatal tests or prenatal trauma or an illness of the pregnant woman indicate that the fetus may be defective in some way?
- *The present family.* Does the woman already have more children than she and her family can handle, either financially or emotionally?
- *Beliefs and convictions.* Does the woman have a strong religious or ethical conviction that abortion is morally wrong? Does she view it as the equivalent of murder or feel it will bring shame upon her family?
- *Couple agreement.* Do both partners fully accept the idea of abortion? Or is there strong pressure from one upon the other or from outside influences?
- *Future plans.* What will the couple have to sacrifice (in terms of vocation, education, financial security, freedom, etc.) for the baby? Will they resent such sacrifices in the future?

CLINIC SELECTION. Once a woman has decided upon abortion, it is very important that she choose the right clinic and doctor to do the procedure. We should hardly have to say that "do-it-yourself" abortions are out of the question. Women cannot induce an abortion with punches to the stomach, laxatives, handfuls of birth control pills, cola douches, hot baths, or starvation. Much worse is trying to induce an abortion with a coat hanger or other implement. While there is a chance these methods may succeed in ending a pregnancy, they may also end the woman's life. The possibility of locating and dislodging the embryo is actually lower than the risk of puncturing the walls of the uterus, which are soft and have a rich blood supply during pregnancy. *No* form of self-induced abortion is safe.

The first step a woman should take after she has decided to have an abortion is to gather information and decide on a plan of action. All abortion procedures must be performed by a licensed physician. While many doctors do abortions, it is advisable to seek a board-certified obstetrician or gynecologist. Some doctors perform first-trimester abortions in their office. Most large cities and many smaller communities have clinics where abortions are performed. Whatever the abortion facility chosen, it should be within ten minutes' driving time of a hospital where the doctor has operating privileges.

All abortion clinics do not provide the same services or do similar procedures in the same way. Fees are no indication of the range or quality of care. It is therefore essential to learn about proper abortion clinic practices. The following features of abortion clinics are considered important (Planned Parenthood Federation of America, 1987):

- Adequate, private space specifically designated for interviewing, counseling, and pregnancy evaluation.
- Conventional gynecologic examining and operating accessories, drapes, and linen.
- Approved and electrically safe vacuum aspiration equipment, and conventional instruments for cervical dilation and uterine curettage.
- Adequate lighting and ventilation for surgical procedures.

- Facilities for sterilization of all instruments and linen, and for surgical scrub for all personnel; adequate supply of instruments.
- Laboratory equipment and personnel (or immediate access to laboratory facilities) for preoperative and emergency determinations and for tissue diagnosis of uterine contents.
- Postoperative recovery room, properly supervised, staffed, and equipped.
- Adequate supplies of drugs, intravenous solutions, syringes, and needles; four to six units of plasma volume-expander liquids for emergency use (until blood is available).
- Dressing rooms for staff and patients and appropriate lavatory facilities.
- Ancillary equipment and supplies, including stethoscopes, sphygmomanometers (for taking blood pressure), anesthesia equipment—including oxygen and equipment for artificial ventilation and administration of anesthetic gases—and resuscitation equipment and drugs.
- Ability to transfer a patient without delay to a conventional operating theater and a written letter of agreement from a full-service hospital regarding transfer of emergency patients.
- Special arrangements for patient emergency contact (on a 24-hour basis) for evaluation and treatment of complications, for postoperative follow-up and examination, and for family planning services.

SEXUALITY IN THE NEWS

The Politics of Abortion

*T*his segment from ABC's "Nightline," anchored by Ted Koppel, focuses on abortion as a political issue. Aired on October 11, 1989, the show offered several candidates for political office, as well as representatives of the national Right to Life Committee and the National Abortion Rights Action League, the opportunity to exchange views on this critical issue.

DISCUSSION QUESTIONS

1. ABC reporter Jeff Greenfield notes that in July 1989, in *Webster* v. *Reproductive Health Services*, the Supreme Court upheld the right of the state of Missouri to restrict access to public abortion services. The clear implication of this ruling is that other states may follow suit in trying to overturn *Roe* v. *Wade*. Discuss how and why the question of abortion has become a political issue, using the additional material presented in this chapter, under "Abortion," and in Chapter 21, "Abortion and the Law."

2. Do you agree with the statement by Howard Fineman of *Newsweek* that if a political candidate is going to take a stand on abortion, the politically wiser stand to take is prochoice? Why or why not?

3. The present U.S. Supreme Court is considered a conservative Court. The Court is expected to rule on a number of abortion cases in the near future. How will the Court's decisions affect the general U.S. population? Do you think the Supreme Court should have the final say on abortion? Why or why not?

LOOKING BACK

- Modern society offers numerous family planning options, although contraceptive research in the United States lags behind that of other nations. Contraception refers to any natural, barrier, hormonal, or surgical method used to prevent conception. Sterilization permanently blocks reproductive capacities by preventing sperm or egg from being released. Although tubal ligations and vasectomies are technically reversible (at great expense), the success rates are low. Abortion is the termination of a pregnancy by natural or artificial means. Many personal and social factors influence people's attitudes toward contraception, including self-image, communication between partners, and the perceived benefits and drawbacks of contraceptives.

■ The most common birth control alternatives in use today are abstinence, oral contraceptives, intrauterine devices, condoms, diaphragms, vaginal spermicides, withdrawal, cervical caps, rhythm methods, vaginal sponges, and contraceptive implants. Although all birth control methods except abstinence have a certain theoretical failure rate, most unplanned pregnancies occur because of human error. Choosing the contraceptive with the highest theoretical effectiveness, acquiring a thorough knowledge of that particular method, using it consistently, and being strongly motivated to prevent pregnancy are the keys to successful birth control.

■ Future birth control possibilities include RU 486, male oral contraceptives, nasal sprays, contraceptive vaccines, a progestin-releasing intrauterine device, a vaginal ring, and a female condom. Some of these methods are already being used in other nations.

■ Sterilization is a surgical procedure that interrupts the reproductive tracts of either the man or the woman to prevent fertilization. A vasectomy involves cutting and tying the vas deferens to prevent the passage of sperm into the ejaculate. A tubal ligation involves tying each fallopian tube so that sperm cannot reach the ovum. Both of these procedures are fairly common in the United States. Among people married more than ten years, sterilization is the most prevalent form of birth control.

■ An induced abortion is the deliberate removal of the embryo or fetus from the uterus. The five most common induced abortion procedures are vacuum aspiration, dilation and curettage, dilation and evacuation, amniotic fluid replacement, and hysterotomy. In general, the earlier an abortion is performed, the safer it is.

THINKING THINGS OVER

1. If you are sexually active, what is your rationale for using or not using contraceptives? What factors helped you develop that rationale?

2. In your own mind, compare and contrast the contraceptives described in this chapter in terms of ease of use, effectiveness, and other good and bad points. Which would you choose and why?

3. If you were to debate the abortion issue, which side would you choose? Outline the key elements of your position.

4. How would you defend the statement that "contraception is a shared responsibility"?

5. Conduct an informal, brief survey among willing friends to find out whether those who are engaging in intercourse are using contraceptives. Do your respondents' choices reflect the popular notion of "safer sex" (see Chapters 17 and 18 for discussion of this concept)? Why do you think they do, or do not?

DISCOVER FOR YOURSELF

Donaldson, P. J., & Tsui, A. O. (1990). *The intentional family planning movement*. Washington, DC: Population Reference Bureau. A comprehensive examination of birth control from an international perspective. Among the topics covered are behavior and attitudes toward family planning in developing and developed nations.

Hatcher, R., Stewart, F., Trussell, J., Kowal, D., Guest, F., Stewart, G. K., & Cates, W. (1990). *Contraceptive technology 1990–1992*, 15th ed. New York: Irvington Publishers. An excellent sourcebook on contraceptives designed for providers of health services.

Harlap, S., Kost, K., & Forrest, J. D. (1991). *Preventing pregnancy, protecting health: A new look at birth control choices in the United States*. New York: Alan Guttmacher Institute. Up-to-date information on how contraception affects the likelihood of avoiding an unintended pregnancy.

Jones, E., Forrest, J. D., Henshaw, S., & Silverman, J. (1989). *Pregnancy, contraception, and family planning*. New Haven, CT: Yale University Press. An insightful look at family planning and contraception in modern society.

McKinney, K. (1989). Social factors in contraceptive and abortion attitudes and behaviors. In K. McKinney and S. Sprecher (eds.), *Human sexuality: The societal and interpersonal context*. Norwood, NJ: Ablex. An excellent review of sociological and social-psychological empirical research investigating people's attitudes and behavior concerning contraception and abortion.

Tietze, C., & Henshaw, S. K. (1986). *Induced abortion: A world review*, 6th ed. New York: Alan Guttmacher Institute. A scholarly and thorough look at abortion, including worldwide trends on its accessibility and incidence.

13
Childhood Sexuality

Oh, what a tangled web do parents weave when they think their children are naive

—Ogden Nash

The effort to inhibit all sex curiosity and pleasure in the child is quite useless; one succeeds only in creating repression, obsessions, and neuroses

—Simone de Beauvoir

psychosexual development
The Freudian notion that early sexual experiences are important to personality development. The individual must successfully pass through a series of five sequential stages to reach psychosexual maturity.

C ontrary to what many people believe, children are not asexual beings. Sexuality does not suddenly emerge in human beings at puberty. Rather, its development begins early in life and is influenced by numerous physical, emotional, mental, and sociocultural forces—all of which intertwine and shape the course of sexuality throughout the life span (Orbuch, 1989).

A few examples will illustrate how different aspects of sexuality unfold early in life. There is some evidence (e.g., Calderone, 1983) that reflex erections occur in male fetuses several months before birth, and that newborn boys are capable of having erections and newborn girls of having vaginal lubrication within 24 hours of birth. Infants experience pleasure and delight in the sensual body-care experiences of being caressed, comforted, and fed. In the midst of such experiences and later interactions with their parents, children acquire an early awareness of what love is and how it can be shared. As another illustration, both female and male infants can experience sexual arousal—vaginal swelling and penile erection—while they're being bathed or otherwise tended to (Langfeldt, 1981). Both have also been observed making coital-like movements of their pelvic areas (Kinsey et al., 1953, 1948). Finally, recall from Chapter 5 that early in life youngsters have an awareness of which sex they belong to and acquire many of the gender expressions and roles that go along with it.

Our purpose in this chapter is to explore how the foundations of sexuality are established. In the process we set the stage for the next two chapters on adolescent and adult sexuality. We begin our developmental journey by examining the years of infancy and toddlerhood, and then move on to childhood and preadolescence. We conclude the chapter with a discussion of sexuality education.

DEVELOPMENTAL THEORY

Our understanding of how the experiences of childhood and adolescence shape adult sexuality has been greatly influenced by the developmental theories of Sigmund Freud and Erik Erikson. In the pages that follow, we will intersperse their thoughts on development with our discussion of childhood sexuality. To establish a foundation for this framework, let's first examine some of the operating principles of these two theories.

Freud's Psychosexual Theory

Sigmund Freud's theory of **psychosexual development** (1953; 1938) states that everyone passes through a series of stages in developing both sexual maturity and a mature personality. Thus the past plays an important role in determining present behavior. To fully appreciate Freud's contributions to the understanding of human sexuality, we must first see how the three levels of consciousness and the various personality components he identified influence the psychosexual stage sequence.

THEORY OF THE UNCONSCIOUS. One of Freud's major contentions was that people are generally not aware of the underlying reasons for their behavior. He believed that mental activity occurs at three levels. The first is called the *conscious* level. It includes whatever a person is thinking about or experiencing at any given moment. Information and immediate awareness are very fleeting: our conscious thoughts flow by like water in a stream. In fact, this level of mental activity is sometimes called the *stream of consciousness*.

The second level of mental activity, *preconscious*, includes all of a person's stored knowledge and memories that can easily be brought to the conscious level. For example: What is your home telephone number? Even though you were probably not thinking of your phone number a moment ago, right now you could retrieve it from your preconscious.

The third level of mental activity is the *unconscious*, a vast area of primitive urges and irrational wishes. The largest area of the mind, the unconscious contains socially unacceptable sexual desires, fears, aggressive feelings, and anxiety-producing thoughts that have been repressed by the conscious level of the mind. Because these feelings are very threatening to us, we keep them locked up in the unconscious. When we dream, however, these feelings and urges are sometimes released, though generally in so distorted a fashion that we do not recognize them. According to Freud, these beliefs, urges, and desires are all motivators of behavior and influence us in some way.

THE ID, EGO, AND SUPEREGO. Freud proposed that an individual's personality consists of three interrelated parts: the id, ego, and superego. The **id** is the instinctive part of the personality that contains the basic motivational drives for air, food, water, sex, and warmth. All emotions are also housed in the id, which operates at the unconscious level.

id According to Freud, the instinctive aspect of one's personality that contains the basic motivational drives for air, food, water, sex, and warmth.

One of the most powerful dynamic forces of the id is the **libido,** which supplies sexual energy (the term *libido* derives from the Latin for "lust" or "desire"). When this energy builds up, the person feels an increase in tension and unhappiness, which must be released. After release, the person experiences feelings of contentment and pleasure. The id operates on the hedonistic or **pleasure principle,** which is the tendency to seek pleasure and avoid discomfort. The id demands instant gratification of primary biological needs. Since it has no ability to reason, it does not understand denial or deferral of wants, but craves immediate satisfaction.

libido In Freudian psycho-analytic theory, the driving force of the id.

pleasure principle The human tendency to seek pleasure and avoid discomfort. The id operates on this principle.

Freud believed that an infant functions solely at the id level for the first eight months of life, after which the ego commences its slow and gradual development. Until this time, the id is in total control of the child's behavior. Thus when an infant's internal tension level rises because of hunger pangs or soiled or wet diapers or other discomforts, the infant will cry until the tension is changed to an acceptable or pleasurable state.

The **ego** is the partly conscious part of the personality that serves as the individual's contact with the external environment. Its purpose is to figure out how to satisfy the desires or demands of the id without destructive consequences. Later in life it also mediates between the id and the superego. As the ego develops, it learns to operate according to the **reality principle,** which states that there are socially acceptable ways of satisfying needs. Freud viewed the reality principle as the "servant" of the pleasure principle rather than as a separate or sovereign entity. As the ego learns that using socially acceptable behavior to satisfy the id's demands is beneficial to the person, it is more and more able to placate the id without resorting to behavior that produces instant gratification. Because their egos are not developed enough to know this, infants, toddlers, and preschoolers operate at a "gimme, gimme, gimme" level, wanting everything for themselves immediately and exhibiting little tolerance for delayed gratification. Ego maturity consists partly of the ability to restrain the id's demands until they can be met according to the guidelines and values of the culture.

ego According to Freud, the part of the personality that serves as a rational agent and the mediator between the id and the superego.

reality principle The notion that human needs can be fulfilled in socially acceptable ways. The ego operates on this principle.

The third component of the Freudian personality system is the **superego,** which appears when the child is approximately five years old. Like the ego, the superego is partly conscious. It is best thought of as the conscience: the internalization of principles taught by one's family, religion, and society. Like the id, it makes strong but largely unconscious demands on the ego. However, the superego resembles the ego in that it tries to control the id's urges. As the superego begins to form, the child will do something wrong (e.g., stealing) and then feel guilty about it. As this personality component becomes more fully developed, it generally prevents the person from wrongdoing.

superego According to Freud, the part of personality that represents societal expectations and demands.

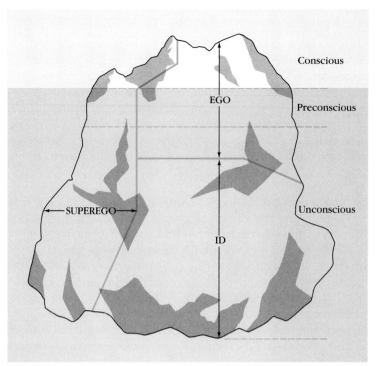

FIGURE 13–1
The Relationship of the Id, Ego, and Superego to Levels of Consciousness.

Freud likened the mind to an iceberg, the great bulk of which lies beneath the water's surface. Most personality processes, he proposed, take place at either the preconscious or the unconscious level; thus the ego and superego are only partly conscious, and the id is wholly unconscious.

In summation, these three personality components constantly interact to influence behavior: the id is the source of psychic energy that insists on immediate fulfillment of desires; the superego is the moral aspect of personality; and the ego is the reality-oriented, rational part of personality that intervenes between the id and the superego to negotiate a settlement between their conflicting demands. To picture the interplay between these three forces (see Figure 13–1), consider how the id becomes activated when a young child naturally touches his genitals and experiences pleasurable sensations. The superego comes into play when parents voice disapproval of this activity, and the ego intervenes when the youngster decides to engage in such behavior only when his parents aren't around.

Erikson's Psychosocial Theory

A person's sexuality is shaped by numerous developmental forces, including social interactions. How children learn to interact and share themselves with others has important implications for later relationship building and sexual expression. Erik Erikson (1982, 1963) proposed that people pass through eight stages of **psychosocial development,** the course of which socializes them into a given culture. Erikson was as concerned as Freud with the development of the individual, but he emphasized the child's interactions with the environment and hence, in contrast to Freud, viewed the ego rather than the id as the major driving force of human behavior.

Erikson also disagreed with Freud's emphasis on infantile sexuality. Because of his anthropological training, Erikson perceived behavior as more influenced by society

psychosocial development
The Eriksonian notion that social interactions are critical to personality development. The individual must successfully resolve eight sequential crises to reach psychosocial maturity.

Childhood Sexuality

than by the sex drive. This emphasis on social interaction had important implications for his descriptions of such interpersonal dynamics as love, caring, trust, and intimacy. Erikson's comprehensive theory of development encompasses the years from infancy through old age. He believed that the course of development is reversible, so that the events of later childhood can undo—for better or for worse—earlier personality foundations. Both Freud and Erikson related stages to ages in the sense that aging leads to movement to a new stage regardless of experience and regardless of reorganizations at previous stages.

Essential to Erikson's theory is the development of the ego and the ego's ability to deal with a series of crises or potential crises throughout the person's life span. Each stage of life presents a crisis that arises primarily out of the person's need to adapt to the social environment. Stable personality development is characterized by the successful resolution of these crises. Thus from the beginning of life to its culmination, people are confronted with a series of psychosocial crises, challenges that continually influence their ego development and shape the course of their sexuality. A comparison of Freud's and Erikson's developmental theories is presented in Figure 13–2.

An infant's earliest interactions with others, particularly its parents, help to form its capacity for relationships of all kinds.
....

Life Stages	Freud	Erikson	Age in Years
Old Age		Integrity vs. Despair (65+)	65
Middle Age	Genital Stage (12+)	Generativity vs. Self-absorption (30-65)	60 / 50 / 40
Young Adulthood		Intimacy vs. Isolation (20-30)	30
Adolescence		Identity vs. Role Confusion (12-20)	20
Preadolescence	Latency (6-12)	Industry vs. Inferiority (6-12)	10
Childhood	Phallic Stage (4-6)	Initiative vs. Guilt (4-6)	
Infancy and Toddlerhood	Anal Stage (2-4)	Autonomy vs. Shame, Doubt (2-4)	
	Oral Stage (0-2)	Trust vs. Mistrust (0-2)	0

FIGURE 13–2
Developmental Stages of Life: Freud and Erikson Compared.

Partly because of his concern with the sexual instinct and its influence on early human development, Freud did not expand on the genital stage—though he saw it as continuing throughout life. Erikson placed less emphasis on the sexual instinct and more on the need of the developing human being to find an identity and a role in society, to relate effectively to others, and to contribute something to the growth and development of humankind (see also Chapters 14 and 15).

Childhood Sexuality   391

INFANCY AND TODDLERHOOD

Psychosexual-Psychosocial Development

oral stage Freud's first stage of psychosexual development, which occurs during the first year of life.

THE ORAL STAGE. In his psychosexual theory of personality development, Freud defined the first year of life as the **oral stage** of development because he believed that the mouth is the primary source of pleasure and satisfaction to the very young child. As he put it, the infant is "pleasure bent on sucking." Anyone who has observed an infant sucking nipples, thumbs, fingers, and pacifiers has little doubt that much of the infant's contact with the environment occurs through the mouth.

If the infant obtains satisfaction during the oral stage, a foundation is laid for the continuation of normal personality development. However, if the infant's needs are not gratified, or if they are gratified excessively, a *fixation* is said to occur. That is, oral needs may continue throughout the person's life and greatly influence behavior. Behavioral examples of an oral fixation are thumb sucking; cigarette, cigar, and pipe smoking; and the manipulation of the lips with the fingers or other objects such as pens or pencils. Other oral personality characteristics are overeating, greediness, gum chewing, and nail biting. Note that a fixation can occur at *any* of the psychosexual stages if the id remains focused on one erogenous zone rather than shifting to the next one.

basic trust versus mistrust The first of eight psychosocial crises proposed by Erik Erikson. It takes place during the first year of life.

BASIC TRUST VERSUS MISTRUST. The two psychosocial crises faced during infancy and toddlerhood are basic trust versus mistrust and autonomy versus shame and doubt. Children confront the **basic trust versus mistrust** crisis in their first year of life when they either experience warmth and security and develop trust or fail to do so and develop mistrust. Trust arises from positive interactions with caregivers, such as during feeding or tactile stimulation (e.g., cuddling or fondling), and promotes feelings of security, comfort, and confidence. Quality affectional relationships thus provide a foundation for the formation of trust.

Mistrust arises when the child experiences negative interactions, such as being emotionally rejected by a mother or father who is tending to the child's physical needs. The more severe the basic mistrust is, the more limited the infant's repertoire of emotions will become. A child who is mistrustful of the environment may exhibit only the negative emotions of anger, fear, distress, and apathy. This child may never learn how to express or respond to positive emotions such as love and warmth. Whereas Freud emphasized in this first stage of life the *quantity* of oral pleasure that the infant experiences, Erikson stressed the *quality* of security and comfort provided by the caregiver.

autonomy versus shame and doubt The second of eight psychosocial crises proposed by Erik Erikson. It takes place between the ages of one and three.

AUTONOMY VERSUS SHAME AND DOUBT. The second psychosocial stage is **autonomy versus shame and doubt.** This stage occurs between the ages of one and three. As infants become increasingly aware of their environment, they begin to explore it and to establish their independence. Walking, for example, enables toddlers to investigate more of their surroundings and to gain a sense of mastery and power. It is important for parents to encourage a toddler's attempts to explore and to provide opportunities for independence (after "baby-proofing" the environment for safety). According to Erikson, when a child is restrained or discouraged from exploring, feelings of shame and doubt surface.

Attachment and Love

Parental behavior and the emotional atmosphere of the home greatly influence a child's sexual and personality development. During the early years especially, parental attitudes are critical. Infants perceive feelings toward them that either foster a sense of love and security or that promote anxiety and mistrust.

Early sexuality in particular is shaped by the infant's contact with someone who is familiar and expected. **Attachment,** or the affectionate bond between infant and caregiver, is a vital prerequisite of healthy sexual, emotional, and social functioning (Thompson, 1991; Bowlby, 1989; Fox et al., 1989; Egeland, 1989). Attachment is the first experience of a close relationship with another person and teaches the infant that other people can be trusted. People's ability to be outgoing and friendly, as well as their degree of social independence and willingness to make emotional investments in others, may be traced to their early attachment experiences. In this sense, infant attachment helps to determine the type of social animal that we become, including the degree of comfort we feel in the presence of others.

Children usually develop strong attachments to both parents. However, it is not uncommon for a child to feel a strong attachment to the mother but not the father, or vice versa. In time, attachments come to mean those special relationships that make some people very important to a person and not readily replaceable by others. As they get older, children become attached to "best friends." Adolescents and adults in love become attached to their loved ones. Most people also become attached to groups, ideals, and even abstract ideas of great importance. Indeed, people seem to develop their sense of self and identity from their attachments as much as from any other single factor (Heins & Seiden, 1987, Hartup, 1989; Bowlby, 1989; Pederson et al., 1989; Etaugh, 1980; Londerville & Main, 1981).

Bem Allen (1990) observes that the dynamics of adult romantic relationships correspond to childhood attachments—that is, there are analogies between how people related to their parents and how they react to their lovers. For instance, the bond between parents and young children hinges in part on the responsiveness and sensitivity of the parents. Whether youngsters in the first few years of life feel more joy or distress depends on parents' sensitivity to their needs and willingness to fulfill those needs. Similarly, in adulthood, people's mood depends considerably on whether their lover is responding to their needs for affection and for reassurance that the relationship will continue.

According to Allen, youngsters whose parents come when beckoned by a cry or gesture and repeatedly demonstrate their love have a number of positive qualities. They tend to be happier than children whose parents are less attentive, are less likely to be distressed, display more willingness to explore their surroundings, and are more eager to interact with strangers. Lovers who feel secure that their partners will be there for them when needed tend to be less defensive and worried and more relaxed, spontaneous, and creative than lovers who feel less secure about their partners.

Note that the behaviors that promote parent-child attachments—holding, touching, smiling, and making eye contact—are the same behaviors that promote attachment between lovers. In addition, both children separated from parents and lovers who are parted commonly feel distress and sadness. Finally, those who are securely attached share an intense desire to share their accomplishments and discoveries. This is as true for children and parents as it is for lovers.

Early Sexual Awareness

The early years are important for the development of healthy sexual attitudes and behavior. During infancy and toddlerhood children explore their bodies, including their genitals, and learn that touching and stroking their bodies is pleasurable. Such early explorations are normal and help youngsters to become aware of themselves as sexual beings.

Sexual pleasure, though, is not confined to stimulation of the genitals, nor is all pleasant physical contact related to sex. Children need to feel good about their

attachment The affectionate bond between infant and caregiver that is a vital prerequisite of healthy sexual, emotional, personality, and social functioning.

How important is attachment between infant and caregiver?

As children begin to become aware of themselves as sexual beings their curiosity sends them looking for answers to their questions about sexuality.

bodies. As Sol and Judith Gordon (1989) observe, even the youngest of babies learn about the pleasures of physical contact through constant loving and fondling. Parents stroke, kiss, and cuddle their babies, and the babies typically respond with affectionate delight. The quality of the physical intimacy reflects the caregiver's feelings about intimacy.

Since early sexual learning experiences shape later sexual feelings and attitudes, these experiences must be handled with patience and understanding. Parents must stop and think before punishing, deciding as honestly as possible whether they are doing so for the child's good or merely for their own convenience or in reaction to their own, possibly unjustified, fears. If parents slap a child's fingers or pull his hand away from his genitals but smile and comment on how cute he looks when playing with his toes, the child will be confused and may come to associate the genitals with feelings of guilt and shame.

Some sources (Kinsey et al., 1953, 1948) contend that infants are capable of masturbating and even orgasm. When infants discover their genital organs and engage in such self-stimulation, they are initiating the active functioning of the sexual response system. Parents can help children accept sexuality as a good and important part of themselves, so that years later, when they are physiologically ready for normal sexual functioning, they will feel competent at sex and capable of taking pleasure in it. Parents are a child's first sex educators, both by their actions and by the verbal and nonverbal messages they give the child (Corbett, 1991; Calderone & Johnson, 1989; Orbuch, 1989).

Gender-Role Development

We learned in Chapter 5 that gender-role development begins very early in life. In fact, this socialization process starts at birth, when the infant is swaddled in a pink or blue hospital blanket. As time goes on, children receive different kinds of attention from their mothers and fathers. In homes where traditional gender roles rule, mothers are typically nurturant and affectionate and indulge in cuddling, kissing, and stroking their children. Fathers display their affection by roughhousing with their children and sharing their hobbies and sports. Many parents are determined that their boys be "masculine" and their girls "feminine," so it is no wonder that very young children have a fairly clear picture of what society thinks is appropriate gender-role behavior (Jacklin, 1989; Maccoby, 1989, 1987; Reinisch, Rosenblum, & Sanders, 1987).

Infant paraphernalia is designed to reflect these different gender expectations. Laurel Richardson (1988) observes that there are different styles and colors for male and female infants in such basics as cribs, potty seats, comforters, changing tables, diaper pins, toys, and—most important—infant clothing. Girls' clothing racks are loaded with dresses, while pants and shorts abound on the boys' racks. Even the popular unisex romper suits are adorned with "masculine" or "feminine" motifs like baseballs and footballs or butterflies and ruffles.

Although Richardson believes that there has been some relaxation of infant dress codes in recent years, major differences persist. Girls are more readily dressed in boys' play clothes than boys are in girls'. When youngsters are "dressed up," the distinctions are even more pronounced. Different clothing styles not only signify to others what sex the child is and therefore how the child is to be treated, but also affect the child's freedom of movement.

A research study conducted by Madeline Shakin and associates (1985) involving 24 infant girls and 24 infant boys found that although almost no parent spontaneously admitted selecting baby clothes on the basis of gender suitability, most dressed their babies in colors and styles that announced the wearer's sex and surrounded them with accessories that advertised gender. Seventy-five percent of the girls in the study wore pink; seventy-nine percent of the boys were dressed in blue; most of the others were dressed in either yellow or white. Blue was seldom seen on girls; red even more rarely. Even when a neutral outfit left a child's sex in question, passers-by were usually tipped off by something like a pink pacifier or a blue carriage blanket. Despite the fact that the oldest infant in the study was only 13 months old, strangers correctly identified the babies' sex 87.5 percent of the time.

Why were parents so reluctant to admit that they chose baby clothes and accessories according to their child's sex? The researchers couldn't determine whether the parents in the study were really unconscious of their strong labeling tendencies or were merely reluctant to own up to them in these "liberal" times.

Reinforcement of gender differences persists throughout toddlerhood. Parents provide different toys and games for boys and girls and have different sets of expectations for them. Both mothers and fathers are more likely to play more vigorously with their sons and to show more apprehension about physical danger to their daughters. Differences in boys' and girls' general patterns of behavior also become apparent at this age. For instance, girls typically stay closer to their mothers while shopping or playing outside. By the end of the first year, boys have usually ventured further into their environment and attained a greater degree of social independence than girls (Maccoby, 1989, 1987; Doyle, 1985; Brody & Steelman, 1985). According to the behavioral and social-learning theories of gender-role development (see Chapter 5), these behavioral differences may reflect either parental reinforcement or children's emulation of adult actions.

Parents must realize that gender identification and gender-related expectations are a crucial part of their child's overall sexuality. Children first become aware of which sex they belong to, the roles that identification brings, and some of the appropriate expressions of those roles during toddlerhood. Toddlers need to know that whichever sex they are, it is worthy. Girls who are rascally and boys who are placid need to feel accepted for themselves, rather than be pushed into a stereotypical mold (Oppenheim, Boegehold, & Breener, 1984).

According to Sally Wendkos Olds (1985), the degree of comfort children feel with their gender identity influences whether they will act in appropriate male or female patterns and how they will feel about their total selves. As we have seen, children learn healthy sexual attitudes by exploring their own bodies and by seeing those of other children and of adults. Combined with healthy gender-role development, this exploration enables youngsters to gain a sense of their sexuality and to learn cultural standards of sexual behavior.

CHILDHOOD

Psychosexual-Psychosocial Development

THE ANAL STAGE. According to psychoanalytic theory, between the first and second years children pass through the **anal stage** of psychosexual development. At this stage they become aware of their body's elimination processes and take pleasure from both the elimination of feces and their retention. Youngsters are often fascinated by their own excretions, even to the point of peering into the toilet bowl and observing or handling fecal matter. This is also a time when many children engage in "toilet talk"—slang expressions for bodily elimination processes. The expressions "poop-head," "do-do on you," "pee-pee," and "crap" are sometimes used by children at this age. And some writers have suggested that the frequent use by adults of words like "shit" and "bullshit" reflect a degree of fixation at the anal stage.

Again, adult reactions during this stage will determine children's later feelings and behavior. Adults who convey the idea that children's bodily elimination processes and products are "dirty," "messy," or "bad" may inadvertently be giving their children the impression that they themselves are bad. Parents who enforce early toilet training may produce children who are obsessively clean and neat, reflecting the adults' own rigid and somewhat Victorian view of the body's natural functions. On the other hand, parents who neglect toilet training may produce children who will later exhibit slovenliness, indifference, and other undesirable traits.

According to Freud, many children in the anal stage resent adult authority and learn that although they can't yell or fight back at their parents, they do have two ways to retaliate—retaining feces or expelling them at inappropriate times. The psychoanalytic interpretation of children who are slow to be toilet trained is that they may not want to be trained because their untrained behavior serves as an outlet for pent-up frustrations and hostilities.

THE PHALLIC STAGE. The **phallic stage,** Freud's third stage of psychosexual development, takes place when children are three to six years old. Now interest and pleasure shift to the genital area. Children not only explore their own genitals but become curious about the anatomical differences between boys and girls and between children and adults. How comfortable parents are with such curiosity helps shape the course of the child's psychosexual development.

As we learned in Chapter 9, Freud believed that a boy of this age develops unconscious romantic feelings toward his mother and competes with his father for her love and affection. This creates what Freud called the *Oedipus conflict*: the boy wants to possess his mother but is unable to do so because of the presence of his powerful father. The Oedipus conflict is resolved when the boy recognizes that his father might punish him for his sexual feelings, represses such feelings, and eventually comes to identify with his father. Girls go through a similar scenario Freud named the *Electra conflict*. The little girl becomes romantically attached to her father, fears her mother's disapproval of that attachment, represses her feelings, and eventually identifies with her mother.

INITIATIVE VERSUS GUILT. **Initiative versus guilt** is the name given by Erik Erikson to the psychosocial crisis of early childhood. Having established a sense of trust and autonomy during the first few years of life, children set out to prove they have a will

anal stage The second stage of Freud's psychosexual development theory. It occurs between the first and second years.

phallic stage The third stage of Freud's psychosexual development theory. It occurs between the ages of three and six.

initiative versus guilt The third of eight psychosocial crises proposed by Erik Erikson. It occurs during the years of early childhood.

of their own. Youngsters at this stage actively explore their surroundings and try to satisfy their curiosity. Characteristic of this age are a high energy level, rapidly developing physical skills, an expanding vocabulary, a desire to be with others, and a new ability to get around and do novel and different things.

Whether children lean toward initiative or guilt once again depends largely on their interactions with their parents. If parents give their youngster enough opportunities to explore their environment, ask questions, exercise their physical skills, and be with others, the child is likely to achieve initiative. Conversely, if they act as if the child's inclinations to interact and explore are annoying or ineffectual, the child is likely to feel guilty and inhibited. Such feelings usually undermine self-assurance or produce a pattern of thoughtless conformity in an effort to achieve belongingness or acceptance.

Parents need to answer children's questions about sexual matters such as pregnancy simply and honestly, but without giving them more information than they can absorb.

Sexual Curiosity

As children grow older, their curiosity about sex increases. Exploration and stimulation of the genitals continues during the preschool years, as does exploration of the entire body. Most children in this age bracket are well aware that their bodies differ from those of their parents and are usually aware of the differences between boys and girls.

Preschoolers ask many questions to satisfy their curiosity. These questions are typically frank, reflecting their general inquisitiveness about themselves and their surroundings. Common at this time are questions related to the origins of babies, sex organs and their functions, and the physical differences between the sexes (Corbett, 1991).

Marilyn Heins and Anne Seiden (1987) believe that parents should welcome these questions, be proud of their children's developing curiosity, and give them simple, straightforward answers. It is not necessary to give preschoolers a full explanation of the processes of birth and intercourse or the moral issues of sexuality. There will be plenty of time to elaborate on these issues as the child matures. But adults should use correct terminology and not cloak their explanations in symbolism so that they don't distort their children's curiosity or plant misconceptions in their minds. Examples of the kinds of questions children ask about sex appear in the box on "Budding Curiosity: Questions Children Often Ask About Sex."

Should adults use correct terms when answering children's questions about sex?

"Of course I need to wear a top. How else do you expect me to keep an aura of mystery?"

Childhood Sexuality

MAKING USE
OF WHAT
WE KNOW

Budding
Curiosity:
Questions
Children Often
Ask About Sex

*T*hroughout childhood, most young-sters ask a multitude of questions about sex. Such questions typically grow more complex as the youngster's body of sexual knowledge increases. Here are some of the more common questions children ask at different ages:

Six Years of Age and Under

- Where did I come from?
- How did I get inside Mommy's body?
- Where was I before I got inside Mommy's body?
- Does it hurt to have a baby?
- Why is Daddy's penis bigger than mine?
- Why don't I have a chest like Mommy?
- Do you love me as much as Daddy?
- What's "privacy"?

Seven, Eight, and Nine Years Old

- Does every woman have a baby?
- What is birth control?
- What is a tampon for?

- Do I have to be married to have babies?
- How does a baby get out of Mommy's belly?
- What if someone wants to touch your private parts?
- What's a prostitute?
- How can a woman know if she's pregnant?
- What's incest?

Preteen Years

- What kind of people are nudists?
- How much blood do girls lose during their periods?
- Can a girl have periods when she's pregnant?
- Do girls have wet dreams?
- Does a guy ever have a "safe" period?
- Can anyone tell by examining me that I masturbate?
- What is orgasm like?

(Adapted from Gordon & Gordon, 1989; Somers & Somers, 1989)

Childhood Masturbation

Because they are aware that stimulating the genitals produces pleasurable sensations, most children engage in masturbation. As we said earlier, masturbation may begin as early as infancy. It typically increases during the preschool years, when children use it to discover how their bodies feel and respond to stimulation.

Most childhood experts, such as Joanne Oppenheim and her associates (1984), maintain that a moderate amount of sexual activity in children is not harmful, that it may even relieve some stress, and that parents should accept it as natural. But if parents are made very uncomfortable by masturbation (or any other sexual explo-rations), they'd do better to ask their child to stop than to attempt to hide their feelings. Children sense parents' true feelings. Thus parents who say one thing and believe another often send mixed messages, confusing their children or making them feel guilty and anxious. Since most parents do feel embarrassed or angry when their child masturbates in public, they should let the child know, as privately as possible, that this kind of behavior is not acceptable in public, that while it may feel good, it is something that people do only in private. The important point is not to punish children or make them feel guilty for their curiosity:

Is childhood mas-turbation common? Is masturbation at an early age harmful?

I was around age eight when I first masturbated. I can remember how good it felt, but I also remember my parents' nervous disapproval.

> I masturbated at about age nine, maybe even earlier. My mother caught me once and really flipped out. She pushed my hand away from my vagina and told me to stop being naughty.

> I can't remember how old I was, but I do remember my parents' reactions. They told me that only bad boys did it. (Authors' files)

Excessive masturbation in children may originate in a guilty desire to overdo something that is disapproved of (Gordon & Gordon, 1989). Remember that masturbation is a normal expression of sexuality at any age. If this idea is conveyed to a child, the child will usually not feel guilty about it and will be less likely to masturbate compulsively.

Gender-Role Development

Earlier we indicated how parents' shape early gender-role development. As children grow more socially independent, however, other influences may counteract parental shaping. So no matter how hard modern parents try to socialize their sons and daughters into believing they have capabilities and opportunities equal to those of children of the other sex, outside influences may undermine their early training. Gender-appropriate behavior is modeled by adults, peers, the media, and sometimes direct admonition, and there is little doubt that preschool children learn these lessons well.

As children drift toward peer groups of the same sex in the preschool and early school years, they often learn traditional gender-role standards and behaviors. In fact, failure to comply with such expectations may be grounds for rejection by the peer group. The reinforcement of gender-appropriate behaviors by the peer group also helps to explain the differences observed in boys' and girls' early play (Block & Pellegrini, 1989; Howes, 1988; Reis & Wright, 1982; Harris & Satter, 1981).

Boys are typically encouraged—or at least permitted—to be quite active, while girls are usually expected to be quieter and calmer. Boys are more often given cars, trucks, and building blocks—toys that encourage activity—while girls receive dolls, books, and other "quiet" toys. It is noteworthy that the sex-related limitations imposed at this age are fewer for girls than boys. If they so choose, girls can ride tricycles, engage in rough-and-tumble play, and wear policeman hats and cowboy boots without much comment from adults. Boys, on the other hand, are likely to be scolded for crying or playing with dolls and to be told that ladies' hats and purses are strictly for girls. If they don't spontaneously gravitate toward active play, they may be pushed into it. In contrast, girls of this age may be learning that since they receive fewer admonitions than boys, they matter less (Lay-Dopyera & Dopyera, 1990).

Most early childhood experts emphasize the importance of treating boys and girls equally. Parents and teachers, book publishers, television producers, and toy manufacturers need to be aware of the limiting effects of many gender-role prohibitions. Setting a broad range of expectations or goals for all children and then allowing for individual differences is the wisest course.

Even as adults encourage children to venture beyond the narrow restrictions of gender roles and stereotypes, however, they must be careful to help them value their basic sexuality as well, since it is an important facet of everyone's personality. If children grow up with the notion that sexuality is trivial—or worse, that reproduction and sexuality are smutty topics to be snickered at in public and investigated in secret—adults will have unwittingly undone much of what they hoped to accomplish by taking a nonsexist approach to children's upbringing (Hendrick, 1992).

PREADOLESCENCE

Psychosexual-Psychosocial Development

latency stage The fourth stage of psychosexual development proposed by Sigmund Freud. It occupies the years of middle childhood.

LATENCY STAGE. Freud labeled the middle years of childhood the **latency stage.** This stage of psychosexual development is characterized by a tapering off of biological and sexual urges. In fact, it is a tranquil period of transition during which children grow and acquire new skills. The latency stage is a time of continued ego identity formation, including ego strengthening and learning of *defense* or *coping mechanisms* for protecting the self against life's failures and frustrations. Primary defense mechanisms are *rationalization* (attempting to prove that one's behavior is justifiable and worthy), *projection* (blaming others for one's difficulties), and repression (pushing painful thoughts out of awareness).

industry versus inferiority The fourth of eight psychosocial crises proposed by Erik Erikson. It takes place during middle childhood.

INDUSTRY VERSUS INFERIORITY. Erikson's psychosocial stage of **industry versus inferiority** occupies all of middle childhood, and therefore corresponds to Freud's latency period. Children at this stage have reached a point in their cognitive development when they can more easily comprehend their surroundings. Strivings for self-worth and dignity become important. Children become industrious in their play, and the product of that play is all-important to their self-esteem. However, children who frequently fail to be productive may feel inferior and even worthless. In their search for positive self-regard and esteem, children at this stage need the support and guidance of adults.

Sex Play and Experimentation

Youngsters remain curious about sex throughout middle childhood, although they acquire information about it differently than they did in early childhood. While parents and teachers continue to supply information on matters related to sex, many children begin to suppress their curiosity in the presence of adults and turn to a friend or classmate for answers. This trend persists throughout middle childhood and adolescence. Indeed, one source (Thornburg, 1981) indicates that most sex information obtained by youngsters comes from their peer group. Another potent source of information about sexuality during the middle years is the media. Contemporary movies, television, musical lyrics, magazines, books, and, particularly, TV soap operas (Hayes, 1987) portray sexual behavior quite explicitly.

Boys have long learned about sex—or at least about women's bodies—from magazines like Playboy. *Girls rarely seek information in this way.*

Masturbation continues during middle childhood, as does heterosexual and same-sex play. Alfred Kinsey and associates (1953, 1948) estimated that about half of all boys and a third of all girls engage in some type of same-sex play by age 12. Other studies (i.e., Kolodny, 1980; Hite, 1981) reveal equally high percentages. Same-sex play usually takes the form of mutual exploration of sex organs and may include the insertion of objects into bodily orifices, attempted intercourse, exhibitionism, and masturbation. Boys may masturbate in a group, in what is sometimes called "a circle jerk." Sexual play takes place between friends as well as between siblings. A man shared these childhood memories:

> **My friend and I used to masturbate behind a shack in his backyard. We were both in the sixth grade at the time, and we often had contests on who could ejaculate first. We did that quite a bit in the summer, but not much after that. (Authors' files)**

Childhood Sexuality

A woman reflected on her childhood sex play with her sister:

> When I was 10, I used to share a bedroom with my 11-year-old sister. Some nights she would come into my bed and fondle me all over. We would take turns stimulating and arousing each other. (Authors' files)

Mary Calderone and Eric Johnson (1989) believe that such sex play and experimentation originate out of natural curiosity. Children want to know about each other's bodies, and unless they are strongly inhibited or explicitly forbidden to do so, they will attempt to see what another child's body looks like. The fact that most youngsters do these things in secret shows that they have already absorbed the lesson that activities connected with the sexual parts of the body are taboo in public. However, these kinds of activities are rarely erotic—that is, arousing or satisfying sexual desire—but rather represent a form of learning.

According to Calderone and Johnson, many adults are alarmed by children's sex play because they tend to project their own adult attitudes and feelings into children's acts. When adults or late adolescents engage in sex play, of course, the activity is highly arousing and closely connected with the urge to have sexual intercourse. However, this is not true of younger children. Nor does sex play in children signify the beginning of sexual promiscuity. When adults misinterpret sex play and get upset, youngsters typically become frightened and miserable since they can't understand why something that was merely cute and funny one minute is bad and dangerous the next. Unfortunately, the fright and misery can stay hidden within them for years.

Interestingly, while sex play and experimentation emerge during middle childhood, modesty does also. Modesty is a sign of sexual self-consciousness. Usually the child becomes shy first with nonfamily members, and then later with family members. Girls typically go through this stage earlier than boys. Even in homes where family nudity is common, children experience this modesty urge. Children who have older siblings or much contact with older children may go through the modesty stage earlier than others. Parents should prepare their children for this stage by discussing privacy with them in a positive fashion. This includes being able to use the bathroom in private, knocking on a family member's bedroom door before entering the room, and learning not to infringe on a sibling's private space. Children need to learn that all family members deserve privacy (Heins & Seiden, 1987).

Why do some children like to engage in sex play?

Love and Loving

Because love has many dimensions and abstract qualities (see Chapter 6), children cannot fully comprehend it until their cognitive facilities mature. Usually, the physical dimensions of loving (kissing, hugging, etc.) are understood before the psychological aspects (mutuality, reciprocity, etc.) are grasped. As we've seen, children learn about love early in life, particularly as they form bonds of attachment with their parents. It is usually from these attachments that youngsters derive their early feelings of security and self-worth. Children who feel securely loved by their parents come to accept themselves as important objects of affection to others and become capable of giving love in return (Corbett, 1991; Allen, 1990; Orbuch, 1989; Douglas & Atwell, 1988; Orthner, 1981).

The manner in which love is expressed changes throughout childhood. Preschoolers usually demonstrate their love physically, through kissing and hugging. This is true of school-age children, too, but they have learned that love can also be expressed through other channels such as sharing and talking. As they leave behind an egocentric

Expressing love for a friend is an important part of learning how to relate warmly to others and a significant psychological vitamin for both children and adults.

point of view and develop sensitivity toward others, children's expression of love gradually matures. They love not only their family and friends but animals as well. Once again, gender often dictates explicit behavior. If boys are taught that it is unmasculine to exhibit tenderness, then tenderness may not become part of their repertoire of love. Thus the gender roles that children acquire are important determinants of their definition and expression of love (Cox, 1984).

Gender-Role Development

By middle childhood, youngsters exhibit a strong preference for associating with groups of their own gender, in the process assuming gender-appropriate mannerisms, recreational patterns, attitudes, and values from the surrounding adult culture. By this stage of life, most children have an extensive knowledge of gender-role stereotypes, and these standards become even more deeply rooted over time (Jacklin, 1989; Maccoby, 1987; Tavris & Wade, 1984; Harris & Satter, 1981).

Parents also continue to influence gender-role development. As we discovered in Chapter 5, traditional parents shape their children by giving predictable messages about the sexes. These women remember the gender-typed lessons of their childhoods:

> **I was taught to always be polite and nice. Being outspoken or assertive was always frowned upon in our house.**

> **Mom told me it was important to always take care of the man of the house and tend to the children.**

> **A great emphasis was placed on prettiness and tidiness. I was also taught to smile a lot and be a "good" girl. (Authors' files)**

Men had these memories of traditional gender-role teachings:

> **No "sissy" stuff was ever allowed, especially crying. My father had this thing about toughness and drilled into me that real men are strong, provide for their families, and never complain.**

> **My father used to tell me that the only men who got ahead in life were those who were aggressive, confident, and independent.**

> **I was always told "big boys don't cry." (Authors' files)**

Children of this age generally perceive gender roles in much the same fashion as adults do. In addition, they understand which stereotyped occupations go with which sex. Children's growing cognitive awareness and expanding social horizons contribute to their gender-role development. Their new cognitive skills enable them to understand which behaviors are appropriate to their sex, while exposure to a growing number of role models in life and in the media reinforces this understanding (Carter, 1989; Martin, 1989; Wehren & DeLisi, 1983; Hess & Grant, 1983; Courtney & Whipple, 1983).

The gender-typed play that began during the preschool years becomes more evident during middle childhood. Elementary school youngsters readily state a preference for play activities that are appropriate to, and characteristic of, their sex. Boys typically involve themselves in physical and independent types of play, while girls are less physically oriented. Many toys for boys this age require more physicality than those intended for girls (Whiting & Edwards, 1988; Howes, 1988; Isenberg & Quisenberry, 1988; Pitcher & Schultz, 1983).

Throughout childhood, youngsters may pose questions about sex that are difficult for adults to answer, be it on gender roles, biological issues, or relationships. Parents who are uncertain how to reply to some of these questions might find suitable answers in books written to help them. Books aimed at children can also be helpful, since they have pictures and text that children can understand. The accompanying box lists books that may make parents feel less anxious about what to say and how to say it.

Where to Find More on the Development of Sexuality

Books for Parents

The Eternal Garden by Sally Wendkos Olds (Times Books, 1985).

Talking with Your Child About Sex by Mary S. Calderone and James W. Ramey (Random House, 1982).

Getting Closer: Discover and Understand Your Child's Secret Feelings About Growing Up by Ellen Rosenberg (Berkley Books, 1985).

How to Talk with Your Child About Sexuality: A Parent's Guide by Faye Wattleton (Doubleday, 1986).

Books for Children

Did the Sun Shine Before You Were Born? by Sol Gordon and Judith Gordon (ED-U Press, 1982).

Making Babies by Sara Bonnett Stein (Walker, 1974).

How Was I Born? by Lennart Nilsson (Delacorte Press, 1975).

How Babies Are Made by Andrew Andry and Steven Schepp (Little Brown, 1984).

Books for Preadolescents

Am I Normal? (for boys) and *Dear Diary: An Illustrated Guide to Your Changing Body* (for girls), both by Jeanne Betancourt (Avon Books, 1983).

Ellen Rosenberg's Growing Up Feeling Good by Ellen Rosenberg (Beaufort Books, 1983).

What's Happening to My Body? A Growing Up Guide for Mothers and Daughters by Lynda Madaras and Area Madaras (Newmarket Press, 1983).

SEXUALITY EDUCATION

sexuality education
Intervention on the part of parents and teachers to provide children with age-appropriate sex-related information.

Throughout this chapter we have stressed how a person's sexual attitudes and responses are established during childhood. Whether or not these attitudes are healthy depends largely on the source of the child's information. Obviously, then, proper guidance and understanding are needed to prevent ignorance and misinformation. In the pages that follow, we will focus on home and school-based **sexuality education,** intervention on the part of parents and teachers to provide children with age-appropriate sex-related information.

Sexuality Education in the Home

The issue of who should provide sex information to children has been controversial and hotly debated for years. Sexuality education is unquestionably an important parental right and responsibility. The home environment, including child-rearing practices and the parent-child relationship, is a vital influence in shaping a child's sexuality and future behavior. However, whether all parents are knowledgeable enough about the topic of sex and comfortable enough with it to discuss it properly with their children is debatable (Boyer, 1987; Walen & Roth, 1987).

Judith Alter's (1989) review of the literature indicates that in homes where sexuality is discussed with children, the discussions tend to be infrequent and restricted to the biological aspects of reproduction. Several factors account for this limited communication. Because many parents come from homes where sex was not discussed, they cannot draw on past experience and adequate adult role models when attempting to discuss sex with their own children. Others feel inadequate, either because they aren't knowledgeable enough, or because they don't know how to explain what they do know. Uncomfortable with the topic, they tend to postpone discussions of sex or avoid them entirely. Some are torn between new and old sexual values and are confused about what they really believe and what they want to convey to their children. Others assume that if their children are interested in the subject, they will ask about it, and are fearful that providing information prematurely will lead to sexual experimentation.

Why are so many parents uncomfortable and nervous about discussing sexual matters?

Susan Jackson (1982) is convinced that too many modern parents have not conquered their inhibitions about sex and that, in their desire to protect their children and safeguard their innocence, they shroud the subject in silence. Assuming that young children cannot cope with sexual knowledge, that it will shock and disturb them, they develop elaborate strategies of concealment. As their children grow older, these parents feel they ought to let them in on the secret, but unfortunately, they don't know where to start. These adult anxieties do not protect children, but rather expose them to danger and inculcate guilt in them. Hiding sex makes children's learning far harder and aggravates the pain and trials of adolescence. In addition, parents who bring up boys and girls to have different aims and different desires promote inequality.

For all these difficulties, most sources indicate that both parents and children think that parents should be responsible for their children's sexuality education (e.g., Corbett, 1991; Orbuch, 1989; Boyer, 1987; Hunter, 1982; Goodman, 1985; Abbey-Harris, 1984; Kirby, Peterson, & Brown, 1982). Moreover, children want *both* mothers and fathers to assume this responsibility (Bennett, 1984). Additionally, both children and parents desire more open communication on the topic. Finally, most parents express a desire to acquire more sex-related information so that they will be better prepared to meet the needs of their children.

On the last point, there are today many structured programs on sexuality education for parents. These programs range from a few hours' duration to courses

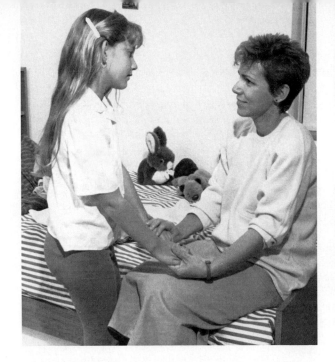

stretching over months, and are offered to parents of various ethnic groups and to those with children ranging in age from infancy to 18 years. Among the sponsors of such programs are federal agencies, private foundations, health clinics, social service organizations, and churches. The objectives of these programs are to help parents become more comfortable with their own sexuality, to teach them communication skills, to provide them with accurate knowledge, to aid them in honestly exploring their attitudes and values, and to encourage them to address sexuality issues with their children (Alter, 1989).

BASICS FOR SEXUALITY EDUCATION IN THE HOME. Most experts agree that teaching children about sex requires both sexual knowledge and communication skills. (Some guidelines for talking to children about sex appear in the box on "Talking to Children About Sex: Guidelines for Consideration.") Most parents also need to learn about normal physical and psychological development throughout childhood so they can anticipate their children's changes and help them through them. In addition, Judith Alter (1989) feels that parents need to be reminded of the following points so they can raise self-confident, responsible youngsters who have a positive sense of their own sexuality.

Children need to nurture positive attitudes about body and gender. Adults must avoid inculcating shame and apprehension about the human body and its functions in their children. Parents also need to convey the message that being a boy or a girl is equally special and that there are experiences and opportunities unique to each sex.

Parents need to set standards of conduct. All children can develop the capacity to make responsible decisions and to set standards for themselves, but this is not an innate process. Rather, it must be modeled and taught. Even though children will inevitably test the limits parents set on them, it is important for parents to set those limits (e.g., dating curfew hours). As children pass through adolescence and show greater maturity, parents should gradually relinquish their control by first setting standards together with their children, and then finally allowing their children to establish their own rules.

In providing sexuality education to children, parents and teachers need to be as relaxed and as open as possible. The more comfortable everybody is, the more likely children are to listen to adults' ideas and suggestions and to ask the questions that concern them.

Childhood Sexuality   405

MAKING USE OF WHAT WE KNOW

Talking to Children About Sex: Guidelines for Consideration

*L*orna and Phillip Sarrel (1984) note that even the most basic facts about sexuality can be confused in children's minds because they are prone to spin their own fantasies about how babies get started, where they grow, and how they are born. Thus they need to learn about sex and reproduction many times, not just once. An open flow of communication—one that permits questions to be asked and asked again—is important.

Parents should introduce the topic of sexuality from time to time, but in a way that is appropriate to the child's level of reasoning. They will be better able to do this effectively if they understand their own views on sexuality and decide ahead of time what they will do and say in certain situations. Calling the parts of the body by their real names is highly recommended.

The Sarrels feel that talk about sex and descriptions of it in books for both adults and children usually suggest the man is the active agent and the woman is the passive recipient. The penis always enters the vagina, and the sperm are pictured as swimming furiously toward and then penetrating the egg. The fact that the egg moves through the woman's genital tract and plays an active role at the moment of fertilization is often omitted. Adults should say, "When the man and woman join together," or "When the egg and sperm come together." Adults should try to avoid describing sex as something a man does to a woman.

Parents need to hone their communication skills before discussing sex with their children. Leon and Barbara Somers (1989) emphasize the importance of being a good listener and building trust between adult and youngster. The following suggestions may enhance such skills:

- *Don't betray confidences.* If a child overhears you jokingly telling another adult how a question was asked, the child's feelings will be hurt and it may be a long time before the child trusts you again.

- *Try to be natural.* Children's sexually oriented questions are often asked out of spontaneous curiosity. If you act flustered and shocked, you will undermine the child's questioning spirit.

- *Don't interrupt and don't be impatient.* Don't try to put words in the youngster's mouth. Don't urge children to hurry up and finish what they are saying. If you are too pressed for time to answer a child's question fully, then set aside another block of time to finish the discussion.

- *Be encouraging.* Positive reinforcement encourages the child's inquisitive spirit. Say such things as "That sounds like an important question—I'm glad you asked me that," or "Good for you."

- *Don't put the child down.* If you do, the child may not ask such questions of you again but go elsewhere for information. Avoid such expressions as "You don't know that?" or "Where did you get a silly idea like that?"

- *Don't get angry with children if they use language that is offensive to you.* They are trying to ask you something that is important to them and they will use whatever words they've heard. Rather than condemn a child's vocabulary and extinguish curiosity, caution the child about where and when such words are inappropriate.

- *If children ask a question at an inappropriate time, tell them you'll be glad to get back to the question later, and then be sure that you do.* For example, if a child points at a woman in a crowd and says loudly, "How come she's got a big tummy?" it's okay to say firmly, "I'll tell you all about it when we get home. Right now, we don't want to make the lady feel uncomfortable." This way, you kill two birds with one stone: you teach both respect for the child's questions and good manners.

Children need evidence of the love and respect their parents feel for them. Youngsters learn to respect and esteem themselves from how they are treated by those around them. They quickly discover which receives more attention—their strengths or their limitations. They thrive when adults enjoy their company and appreciate their thoughts and opinions. Children need affection at all ages, since it nurtures self-esteem and prepares them to share love with others.

Children learn from confronting and overcoming frustrations. Adults who always take over when their youngsters encounter obstacles thwart the development of autonomy, self-esteem, and the ability to handle problems independently. Whatever the issue—friendships, heterosexual interests, social life—children need to experience frustration and failure in order to learn how to overcome obstacles.

Children need privacy. Many parents want their children to be spared the inhibitions common to their own generation, so they attempt to provide a home atmosphere free of hangups about bodies and bodily functions. Without meaning to, they may introduce situations that are overwhelming, confusing, and insensitive to the child's current emotional development. Parents should maintain reasonable standards of modesty and respect their children's need for privacy.

Parents need to reflect on the messages they convey when they react (or don't react) to their children's exploration and discovery of their own sexuality. For example, a parental response to an infant's discovery of her genitals is one of the first sex education lessons the child receives. Parents who ignore or downplay their adolescent's obvious display of promiscuous behavior also convey a strong message.

Children learn about adult relationships through their relationships with each parent and their parents' relationship with each other (or other partners). Children are very observant of parental interactions. Positive, loving relationships during the good times and responsible interactions during the tough times leave a lasting impression.

Children need to realize that parents have private lives from which they are excluded. This can be a particularly difficult issue in single-parent homes. Parents need to insist on the private side of their lives and help their children cultivate interests outside the home.

Sexuality Education in the School

Sexuality education in the school is a specific intervention that provides information and self-assessment opportunities in an age-appropriate manner. School programs seek to give children and adolescents the opportunity to have a serious exchange of ideas, thoughts, and feelings under the guidance of a trained facilitator. They also prepare children for puberty, adolescence, and the stages of adulthood. They tell them that the changes they are experiencing are normal and help them learn to make decisions that take consequences into account. These programs also help children understand the place of sexuality in human life and loving (Tatum, 1989; Orbuch, 1989).

Unfortunately, comprehensive sexuality education is far from the norm in our schools. Our society devotes much time and energy to coping with unwanted pregnancies, sexually transmitted diseases, and related problems, but very little to preventing these problems in the first place. One source (Gordon & Gordon, 1989) estimates that only about 10 percent of our nation's young people receive an adequate sex education in the public schools. The remaining 90 percent are exposed to scattered presentations on basic reproductive facts—the "plumbing" of human sexuality. Since only a small number of parents educate their children about sex, we have a lot of sexually vulnerable citizens.

It is hard to understand why we have fallen so short in this area since for years surveys have indicated that most Americans favor sex education in the public schools (see, for example, Yankelovitch, Clancy, & Schulman, 1986). Perhaps it is because there is so much disagreement about the *content* of sex education, how and by whom it should be taught, and whose values should be conveyed. (As you can see from the "World of Differences" box, there is increasing support worldwide for sexuality education and for broadening the content of instruction beyond the simple anatomy and physiology of sex.) Another reason is that the opponents of sex education tend to be well-organized and determined. Some believe that knowledge is inevitably harmful: "If you tell kids about sex, they'll do it!" Proponents of sex education respond that kids *are* doing it, but without the benefit of responsible knowledge.

Issues such as AIDS, homosexuality, and abortion add to the controversy. Adolescent discussions on AIDS, for example, almost have to include some open dialogue about condoms and other strategies for safer sex. For opponents of sex education, that is anathema because they believe it erodes moral opposition to premarital sex and contraception. Just the impartial listing of homosexuality as an "option" undermines other traditional teachings. Critics fear that the mere mention of abortion in classes will make it seem like an easy solution to an offhand mistake (Leo, 1986).

Those in favor of sexuality education think differently. Andrea Parrot (1984) believes that adolescents who participate in sexuality education programs at home and in school are more likely to postpone sexual experimentation longer than their peers. Furthermore, when they do become sexually active, they are more likely to use contraceptives to prevent pregnancy. In short, adolescents who have accurate, comprehensive information about their sexuality are apt to make decisions that are right for them based on fact, not peer pressure.

Despite all the controversy, concerned educators are continuing to develop and refine sexuality programs for both children and adolescents. The threat of AIDS, as well as the rise in abortion, sexual abuse, and teenage pregnancy, has motivated many school boards to implement new classroom approaches to meeting the needs of today's youngsters (see, for example, Corbett, 1991; Bignell, 1982; Benesch, Kapp, & Peloquin, 1985; Cooperman & Rhoades, 1983; Wilson & Kirby, 1984).

CURRICULUM COMPONENTS. It is difficult to generally prescribe a sexuality education curriculum since the content should be developed by a school's educational staff in cooperation with a broadly based community committee. One general rule is that the curriculum should parallel the youngsters' physical, cognitive, and psychosocial development. Mary Calderone and Eric Johnson (1989) make the following proposals for a comprehensive age-graded sexuality education program:

- It should start with the biological facts of sex and reproduction.
- The basic facts of birth control and family planning should be included. Even people who are for religious reasons opposed to artificial birth control need to know these facts, for if they don't, they will be at the mercy of rumor and half-truths.
- The differences in sexual behavior between other animals and human beings should be stressed. The sexual behavior of animals is largely programmed by instinct and innate physiology, whereas the sexual behavior of human beings is mostly learned. People can make choices about how they will behave sexually, and therefore are directly responsible for the consequences of their choices. (Chapter 6 includes a discussion of sexual values and decision making.) Too many youngsters who have viewed animals copulating in life or on film conclude that human sexuality is the same.

Childhood Sexuality

While prevailing social attitudes bar sexuality education from schools in some countries and significant opposition groups battle its implementation in others, support for such education is growing around the globe. For example, surveys show that over 80 percent of young people in India favor sexuality education courses, though Indian teachers and parents are concerned about what should be taught to children about sexuality and family planning. The same is true in South Korea, Kenya, and the Philippines.

A major trend in sexuality education has been a broadening of the subject matter from a narrow biological focus to teaching about sex in the context of human relationships. Sweden, the acknowledged leader in providing sexuality education, made the transition from biologically oriented courses in the 1930s to mandatory sexuality education in 1956 to the present situation of "instruction in sex and personal relationships." These are some of aspects of sexuality education in the Swedish school system:

- Instruction about sex is combined with teaching about togetherness and respect for the integrity of the other person. This is a central value judgment that sets the tone of sexuality education as a whole.

- An effort is made to apply to sexual relationships the same demands for consideration of others and responsibility for the consequences of one's actions as hold in other areas of life. It is stressed that no one should be regarded exclusively as a means for the satisfaction of another's interests and needs.

- The traditional double standard by which moral sentence is passed upon women for actions that a man can commit with impunity is emphatically rejected. This is but one aspect of teaching designed to combat prejudice about gender roles.

Many nations are still quite hesitant to implement sexuality education. Where it exists, it is typically incorporated into other subjects. In Costa Rica, the Philippines, Hong Kong, and Thailand, for example, "family life education" is incorporated into the science, health, or social studies curriculum. In Japan and China sexuality education has only recently been introduced as a pilot project in selected schools.

Private and voluntary agencies throughout the world have also launched diverse programs. Programming in non-school settings has the advantage of being less formal and more elective. Both the group itself and the activities included in the program are voluntary. Young people can help design and implement the project and parents can also get involved. Such projects gain easier acceptance in the community when they are carried out by traditional and respected organizations.

In Hong Kong a partnership has been forged between a family planning association and the Girl Guides (the British equivalent of Girl Scouts). Courses are provided every Saturday in Girl Guide centers to help participants "understand the physical changes during adolescence, personal hygiene, and to establish a correct concept of dating and marriage."

In the Philippines the Ministry of Social Services and Development created an organization named "Population Awareness and Sex Education for Out-of-School Youth," which is carried out by a national youth agency. The Supreme Council for Youth and Support in Egypt has conducted a similar program through youth centers. And in Grenada a family planning association works with youth organizations to implement a program that includes discussion groups, a publication geared to the topic of sexuality for young people, and contraceptive distribution centers for sexually active teenagers (Senderowitz & Paxman, 1985).

A WORLD OF DIFFERENCES

Support for Sexuality Education Is a Worldwide Trend

- The differences between men and women, including gender role, sexual response, and personality as well as biological differences, should be discussed.

- Children should be given the facts about masturbation and its role throughout the life cycle. Because of students' embarrassment, this subject is unlikely to come up spontaneously in class and therefore needs to be introduced.

- Children should be told the facts about homosexuality, and the rights and special adjustments of people with same-sex preferences should be discussed.
- The facts about sexually transmitted diseases should be imparted—not in a manner that scares young people, but in a realistic way so they can protect themselves against dangers to their health.
- The possible results, both good and bad, of sexual intercourse should be explained, along with the steps that lead up to intercourse.
- The place of sex in family life should be explored.
- The place of sex in the social life of teenagers should be frankly acknowledged and treated.
- Finally, it is important to stress throughout the program that sexual feelings differ from person to person. Young people need to learn consideration for others and to develop empathy and sensitivity.

Experts agree that one of the most important determinants of the success or failure of a sexuality education program is the teacher. A poor teacher can ruin even the best-designed program. The greatest worry parents have in this area is that the teacher will convey either personal values they disapprove of or inappropriate information to their children. However, if they meet a well-trained and qualified teacher, they are usually reassured. It is essential that classroom teachers obtain training in all aspects of sexuality education, feel comfortable with the topic and with their own values, and possess effective communication and group facilitation skills (Tatum, 1989).

Sexuality education should be an integral part of the school curriculum. It should provide vital information, life skills, perspectives, and insights that can make an important difference in how youngsters feel about themselves, relate to others, and approach their day-to-day experiences and decisions. Ellen Rosenberg (1989) writes that thus implemented and taught, sexuality education becomes a gift especially for children and adolescents experiencing significant physical, emotional, social, and sexual changes. Claire Scholz (1989) shares this sentiment and adds that sexuality education helps children develop into all-around healthy, responsible, informed adults.

SEXUALITY IN THE NEWS

Children and Sexually Explicit Material
by Lawrence Kutner

*I*t was the phone bill that tipped off his parents. The charge for one morning's calls amounted to $622, all made to a telephone sex line by their 14-year-old son and three of his friends.

"I'd never had anybody talk to me like some of these girls would," said the boy, who lives in a suburb of Minneapolis and insisted that his name not be used. "It's probably something I won't ever hear again."

The matter of the phone bill was quickly resolved. The telephone company canceled the charges on the condition that the families accept free locks on their phones to prevent additional calls to the 900 exchange.

But the parents faced a bigger issue: What do you do when your child sees sexually explicit material that you feel could be upsetting or could lead the child to behave recklessly?

"A lot of parents are very confused and tongue-tied when this happens," said Ms. Lennie Roseman, a co-author of the sex education curriculum used in New York City public schools.

"Parents don't know if their value system fits in with today's values," added Ms. Roseman, who also offers advice on the videotape "If You Can Talk to Your Kids about Sex, You Can Talk to Them About Anything" (East West Media Productions, available for $24.95 by calling 1-800-645-1100). "But you have to share your values with your children."

Experts on children's sexual development say that isolated incidents, like watching a sexually explicit movie on cable television, buying a pornographic magazine or trying a telephone sex line, are generally nothing to worry about.

"In the vast majority of circumstances, this is part of normal development and will have no long-term negative effects," said Dr. Jordan W. Finkelstein, a professor of pediatrics at Pennsylvania State University who specializes in adolescent behavior.

These situations can, however, provide parents with an opportunity to talk about sexuality and values with their children. In deciding how (and whether) to react, the age and emotional maturity of the child are almost always your guide—even as to whether to react. Less important is the type of sexual material or behavior you discover.

The boys who called the 900 sex line needed one another's encouragement. They were impressed that adult women would talk that way. As early adolescents, they were trying to discover what sexual relationships are all about and to figure out where they might fit. Older teen-age children, who are much more likely to place such calls while alone, know more about sexual relationships and are usually experimenting with eroticism. A parent who responds primarily to the fact that the child placed the call misses this critical difference.

At least as important, but often overlooked, are the repeated messages about sexuality and sexual behavior that children see on television. Teen-age girls who are avid viewers of soap operas, for example, may develop an unrealistic and self-defeating approach to their own sexuality.

"Sit down and talk about the values the soap operas are promoting," said Ms. Roseman. "Many of the young women on those programs aren't worried about AIDS or pregnancy. They're worried about being caught. Teen-age girls tend to mimic that concern."

You might want to discuss the values and assumptions of sexually explicit materials. Ask your child if he has any questions about what he saw or heard.

"You don't have to be comfortable talking about sex," said Debra Haffner, the executive director of the Sex Information and Education Council of the United States, which is based in Manhattan. "You can tell your child that you feel uncomfortable with the topic, but you feel it's very important that you talk about it." (*The New York Times*, October 24, 1991. Copyright © 1991 by The New York Times Company. Reprinted by permission.)

DISCUSSION QUESTIONS

1. How common do you think calls to telephone sex lines are among children who are approaching adolescence?

2. What do you think motivates children to make these calls? Discuss the differentiation this article makes between the motives of younger and older teenagers.

3. Prepare a script of a conversation between a boy who has used a telephone sex line and his parents. You may want to try role-playing such a sketch in the classroom.

LOOKING BACK

■ Sexual development begins early in life, and the theories of Sigmund Freud and Erik Erikson help to chart the course of this development. Freud's psychosexual theory embraces different levels of consciousness and the interplay between the id, ego, and superego. Erikson's psychosocial theory elaborates on how both relationship building and sexual expression are shaped by psychosocial forces.

■ The years of infancy and toddlerhood mark the oral stage of development in Freudian theory, which emphasizes the importance of oral gratification at this stage. Eriksonian theory characterizes this stage of life as one in which the child goes through the psychosocial crises of basic trust versus mistrust and autonomy versus shame and doubt. The foundation of attachment and love is laid at this time. Children explore their bodies and become aware of themselves as sexual beings. Gender-role development also begins at this stage, and often reflects parental gender expectations.

■ The childhood years encompass the Freudian anal and phallic stages as well as the Eriksonian psychosocial crisis of initiative versus guilt. Sexual curiosity increases during the childhood years. Exploration and stimulation of the genitals continue, as does a general exploration of the entire body. Most children are likely to engage in some form of masturbation, which many began during infancy and toddlerhood. Gender-role development is furthered by influences from the peer group, school, and the media.

■ Preadolescence is characterized by Freud as the latency stage of psychosexual development and by Erikson as the psychosocial stage of industry versus inferiority. Children at this stage actively engage in sexual experimentation, including heterosexual and homo-sexual sex play. The expression of love changes as children become older and begin to understand its many dimensions and abstract qualities. Most youngsters this age exhibit a strong preference for sexually separate groups and understand and practice behaviors appropriate to their sex.

■ The greatest influence on youngsters' developing sexuality is the family unit, although many parents have a problem transmitting sex information to their children. Sexuality education in the school is a specific intervention that provides information and self-assessment opportunities in an age-appropriate manner. Comprehensive sexuality education is not widespread in our public schools, despite the evidence that most Americans favor it. One of the most important determinants of the success or failure of a sexuality education program is the teacher.

THINKING THINGS OVER

1. You have learned that attachment is an important component of an infant's developing capacity for loving and sexual relationships with others. As a parent, how might you strengthen the bonds of attachment? Conversely, what kinds of parental behaviors do you think discourage attachment?

2. How do infants and toddlers develop their gender roles? How do parents inadvertently teach gender roles?

3. Critique the Freudian theory of psychosexual development. Is Freud's theory still relevant in the 1990s? Why or why not?

4. Create a scenario in which two sexually curious four-year-olds are engaged in some type of sex play or experi-mentation when, suddenly, the parents enter the room. What kinds of reactions from both parents and children might you expect? How might such a situation be successfully handled?

5. How and when do children learn about love? Can children distinguish among the various types of love? If so, how?

6. You are an elementary school sexuality education teacher in your hometown. Are there topics that you would not be able to discuss in the classroom? If so, why do you think such taboos persist?

DISCOVER FOR YOURSELF

Calderone, M. S., & Johnson, E. W. (1989). *The family book about sexuality*. New York: Harper and Row. Two noted contributors to the field discuss childhood and adolescent sexuality, including how parents can better understand developmental dynamics.

Cassell, C., & Wilson, P. M. (1989). *Sexuality education: A resource book*. New York: Garland. See Part II of this book for a discussion of sexuality education in the schools.

Goldman, R., & Goldman, J. (1982). *Children's sexual thinking*. Boston: Routledge & Kegan Paul. An interesting analysis of how children perceive gender identity, contraception, birth, nudity, and other sex-related topics.

Gordon, S., & Gordon, J. (1989). *Raising a child conservatively in a sexually permissive world*. (Revised edition). New York: Simon & Schuster. The authors provide a sensible and readable account of many topics, including sexual concerns of children and the role of the schools in sexuality education.

Somers, L., & Somers, B. C. (1989). *Talking with your child about love and sex*. New York: Penguin Books. The authors supply excellent suggestions on how to enhance communication skills between parent and child when the topics of love and sex are discussed.

14
Adolescent Sexuality

I think that what is happening to me is so wonderful and not only what can be seen on my body, but all that is taking place inside. I never discuss myself with anybody; that is why I have to talk to myself about them

—Anne Frank

In this chapter you'll discover:

☐ *What puberty is, and how it affects the body's structure and functioning.*

☐ *What primary and secondary sex characteristics are, and how being an early or a late maturer can affect one psychologically.*

☐ *How dating has changed over the years.*

☐ *How widespread adolescent coital activity is in the United States today, and what the health implications of this behavior are.*

☐ *Why sexual experiences in the company of same-sex peers are relatively common during adolescence.*

adolescence The life stage between childhood and adulthood.

Adolescence, from the Latin word *adolescere,* meaning "to grow into maturity," is the life stage between childhood and adulthood. Like other phases of the life cycle, this period is marked by great change. Among the many challenges adolescents face are the need to adjust to pronounced physical and sexual changes, the search for their own identity, and the formation of new interpersonal relationships that include, for the first time, the expression of sexual feelings.

Adolescent sexual development cannot be separated from other developmental forces. For example, how adolescents react to the physical changes that accompany sexual maturation, including whether they and others perceive these changes as attractive or unattractive, will affect how they ultimately perceive themselves. Note the connection here between physical forces and cognitive, personality, sexual, and social forces (Brooks-Gunn & Warren, 1989; Lerner, Lerner, & Tubman, 1989).

Not long ago, many writers focused on the inner turmoil and problems of adjustment faced by the typical adolescent and often borrowed the expression *Sturm und Drang* ("storm and stress") from the eighteenth-century movement in German literature to describe this period of life. Today the problems faced by many teenagers—such as sexually transmitted disease, pregnancy, and abortion—appear to a lot of adults to far exceed the difficulties they themselves confronted in adolescence. Some contemporary researchers feel, however, that most modern teenagers meet the challenges of adolescence with considerable success (Offer & Church, 1991; Petersen, 1988; Offer et al., 1988; Garbarino, 1985).

M. Lee Manning (1983) believes that we should stop viewing adolescence as a time of disruptive and rebellious behavior because this myth distorts our perceptions of actual adolescents. Moreover, as many other researchers (e.g. Spencer, 1991; Brookins, 1991; Gibbs, 1991; Busch-Rossnagel & Zayas, 1991) have reminded us, ethnic, cultural, and class differences affect how the individual young person deals with adolescence, including the course of sexual development.

This chapter investigates the major sexual developments that take place during adolescence. Consistent with the format of the last chapter, we first explore the psychosexual and psychosocial challenges of these years. Then we examine the impact of puberty and the physiological changes that it brings. This is followed by a discussion of the psychological implications of puberty, including adolescents' sexual responsiveness to their changing bodies. We then examine adolescent sexual relationships, and conclude with a discussion of adolescent pregnancy and marriage.

PSYCHOSEXUAL AND PSYCHOSOCIAL DEVELOPMENT

You will recall from the last chapter that Sigmund Freud's psychosexual theory and Erik Erikson's psychosocial theory shed light on the developmental nature of human sexuality. Specifically, Freud identifies the genital stage and Erikson the psychosocial crisis of identity versus role diffusion as the key developments during adolescence.

Genital Stage

The onset of Freud's final, genital stage is a turbulent time for adolescents. The biochemical upheaval associated with sexual maturation makes them acutely aware of the erotic zones of their bodies. After the relative calm of the latency stage, the adolescent experiences the sensual pleasures associated with the genitals and feels strong stirrings of attraction toward the other sex.

Unlike pregenital development, in which each new stage marked the onset of a new conflict, the genital stage revives old conflicts, particularly the Oedipus and

Electra complexes. Freud emphasized the all-important role of experiences during the first few years of life and, to some extent, saw adolescence as a recapitulation of infantile sexuality. Still, he defined adolescence as a distinct era in psychosexual development during which people learn to gratify their sexual needs more maturely and to have a less egocentric perspective on their surroundings. Moreover, the superego becomes more flexible and realistic during this stage. All of these changes enable adolescents to enter into more mature intimate relationships and to begin to function independently as adults.

Identity versus Role Diffusion

Erikson's fifth psychosocial crisis, **identity versus role diffusion,** is often referred to as the *search for identity*. It is perhaps the most famous of his eight stages of development.

    Upon the onset of puberty and genital maturity, young people realize that their childhood has disappeared and adulthood is approaching. Therefore, their egos must re-evaluate reality, and in so doing, teenagers become more conscious of the ideas and opinions of others, paying particular attention to any discrepancies between their self-perception and the perception of themselves by others. The goal of this stage is an integrated ego.

    The passage to an integrated ego is seldom smooth, however. Nearly all adolescents experience a certain amount of role diffusion. Hence the eternal adolescent questions "Who am I?" and "What is my purpose in life?" as young people attempt to integrate their various roles and experiences. The need to refine the sexual self also becomes pressing at this time (in parallel to Freud's genital stage). Adolescents often develop subcultures with which they strongly identify, becoming clannish and accepting very little deviance in dress, thought, or behavior. This intolerance is a temporary defense against role diffusion until the ego can develop a strong sense of identity.

identity versus role diffusion The fifth of eight psychosocial crises proposed by Erik Erikson. It encompasses the years of adolescence.

THE PHYSIOLOGY OF PUBERTY

The stage of physical development during which primary and secondary sex characteristics mature and people become capable of having children is known as **puberty** (from the Latin *pubertas,* meaning "age of adulthood"). While it is difficult to pinpoint its beginning, puberty is a gradual process that transforms the internal and external child's body into that of an adult (Brooks-Gunn, 1991; Brooks-Gunn & Reiter, 1990).

    Many non-Western cultures have elaborate ceremonies at puberty to symbolize a boy or girl's transition to adulthood. Often these ceremonies require a demonstration of such skills as self-defense or hunting; in other instances they entail circumcision or other bodily alterations. In Western cultures there are few formal rites of passage marking the transition from childhood to adulthood and defining adult roles and expectations. Most of those rituals we do have are religious or social in nature, such as bar mitzvahs, confirmations, and "sweet sixteen" parties. But, there are no special customs that accompany puberty, nor any obvious changes in social status that follow it. Moreover, the kind of information on puberty that parents and school systems have tended until recently to provide approaches the topic from a personal hygiene perspective rather than regarding it as a maturational milestone (Dole, 1984; Greif & Ulman, 1982).

    The physical changes that characterize puberty take place along a continuum, or growth sequence. Nearly every part of the muscular and skeletal system exhibits a characteristic pattern of growth. This growth sequence is the same for everyone, although the rates vary from person to person (Brooks-Gunn, 1991; Malina, 1991;

puberty The stage of development during which physiological changes create sexual maturity, including reproductive capability.

Brooks-Gunn & Warren, 1989; Lerner, Lerner, & Tubman, 1989). On average, girls enter puberty about two years earlier than boys do.

Hormones and Puberty

The physiological mechanisms responsible for puberty are not fully understood, though it is known that hormones account for many of the changes that take place (Kulin, 1991; Susman & Dorn, 1991). Prior to puberty, the brain's hypothalamus (discussed in Chapters 4, 5, and 9) stimulates the pituitary gland, which, in turn, stimulates other glands by secreting increased amounts of a growth hormone into the bloodstream. This causes a rapid increase in body development—especially in length of the limbs—signaling the onset of a growth spurt, which we will discuss shortly. The growth hormone affects cell duplication of virtually all body tissue except the central nervous system. The pituitary gland also releases a hormone that stimulates the testes and ovaries. The testes and ovaries, in turn, secrete gonadotrophins, or sex hormones. As you know, the male sex hormone is testosterone, and the female sex hormones are estrogen and progesterone.

Testosterone directs the development of the male genitals, growth of pubic hair, and other features of sexual development. Estrogen controls, among other phases of growth, the development of the uterus, vagina, and breasts. Progesterone aids in the development of the uterine wall, particularly its preparation for implantation of the fertilized ovum and of fetal and placental development after implantation has taken place.

It is unclear how the accelerated processes triggered during puberty slow down again, although it is believed that high levels of sex hormones in the bloodstream are largely responsible (Rabin & Chrousos, 1991). Once a particular phase of physical or sexual development is complete, these high levels of sex hormones signal the pituitary gland and hypothalamus to cease further production of a given hormone.

Puberty and Abnormal Hormonal Functioning

precocious puberty A condition that results when excessive amounts of gonadotrophins are released during the early years of childhood.

When gonadotrophins are secreted either excessively or insufficiently, the result is an atypical pattern of sexual development. For example, **precocious puberty** is caused by the release of excessive amounts of gonadotrophins during the early years of childhood. Puberty is regarded as precocious when primary or secondary sex characteristics mature before the age of 8 in girls and 10 in boys. We do not yet know what causes precocious puberty. We do know that the hypothalamus begins to stimulate the pituitary unusually early, but we can't tell what causes the hypothalamus to do this.

There are different types of precocious puberty. In *true* or *complete precocious puberty,* both the reproductive system and the secondary sex characteristics show full maturation. *Partial* or *incomplete precocious puberty* is characterized by isolated changes such as the growth of pubic hair or the development of the breasts. Precocious puberty is more common in girls than in boys. The clinical course is extremely variable, with some affected children completing sexual maturation rapidly and others slowly. In girls the first sign is usually development of the breasts, followed by the appearance of pubic hair, the development of the external genitalia, axillary hair, and the onset of menstruation. Menarche has been observed as early as the first year of life in girls with precocious puberty. In boys the first signs are often enlargement of the penis and testes, the appearance of pubic hair, and the experience of frequent erections. Spermatogenesis has been observed in boys as young as five years old. In both girls and boys there are early height and weight gains. However, premature bone-hardening processes tend to curtail eventual physical size. Thus about one-third of the children who experience precocious puberty do not achieve a height of five feet as adults.

Adolescent Sexuality

As adolescents' bodies develop during the "growth spurt," they become more aware of each other as sexual beings and they often "horse around," kidding each other about some of these changes.

Inadequate supplies of gonadotrophins can result in **delayed puberty.** This condition can be triggered by disturbances in the endocrine functions of the ovaries or the testes, called *primary hypogonadism.* In *secondary hypogonadism,* defective functioning of the pituitary gland or of its connections with the hypothalamus may result in the production of insufficient levels of gonadotrophins. Both primary and secondary hypogonadism can disrupt the normal course of sexual development. In girls the breasts are usually slow to develop, pubic hair fails to appear, and the genitalia remain infantile. Moreover, menstruation does not occur. In boys some of the symptoms are failure of the genitalia to enlarge, sparse or absent pubic hair, and a childlike voice.

delayed puberty Impeded puberty that results because of inadequate supplies of gonadotrophins.

Adolescent Growth Spurt

An accelerated rate of physical growth that occurs just before puberty and continues at a lesser rate throughout adolescence is one of the most apparent physical changes of the teenage years. This **adolescent growth spurt** involves increases in height, weight, and skeletal growth. It generally begins about two years earlier in girls (10½ years) than in boys (12½ years) (Tanner, 1991; Malina, 1991).

Since girls reach physical maturity earlier than boys, they have a height superiority between the ages of 11 and 13. By the age of 15, however, boys begin a period of rapid development that enables them to surpass girls in height. During their peak years of growth, male adolescents gain from 3 to 5 inches, whereas female adolescents gain only 2 to 4 inches. Because the rate of growth is greater in the legs than in the trunk, many adolescents have a gangling appearance. By the age of 17, most young women have reached their adult height, whereas for young men, this does not occur until age 21 (Malina, 1991; Tanner, 1991; Petersen & Taylor, 1980; Chumlea, 1982).

By age 11, both sexes have started to put on noticeable amounts of weight, averaging between 10 and 14 pounds a year during the peak years of development. Muscles contribute more to body weight in boys and fat contributes more to body weight in girls.

The skeletal structure of both sexes increases in length, weight, proportion, and composition. Girls exhibit more rapid skeletal development than boys; their bone structure reaches mature size by age 17. Boys reach this mature stage of development almost two years later. Skeletal weight for both sexes increases throughout puberty, but appears to be more marked in boys.

adolescent growth spurt The rapid rate of height, weight, and skeletal growth that precedes puberty and continues at a slower rate throughout adolescence.

A World of Differences

The Celebration of Menarche in Other Cultures

*I*n many cultures menarche is an honored rite of passage and an occasion for special ceremony. People in Ceylon have a special ritual celebrating menarche in which the young girl sits on banana leaves, eats raw egg prepared in ginger oil, and is given a milk bath. After the ceremony, her entire family joins her for a special feast in honor of her new status as a mature woman.

To the Pygmies of Central Africa, menstrual blood is a gift joyously received by the entire community. The girl who has reached this milestone enters the home of a female village elder with her closest friends, where she is taught the arts and crafts of motherhood. This is followed by a celebration lasting a month or two, during which friends come from near and far to pay their respects.

A Navajo menarche ceremony called *kinaalda* involves an elaborate five-day-and-night celebration. During it the girl becomes Changing Woman, the Navajos' most important deity, and assumes a position of great respect in the society. Historically, *kinaalda* has been regarded as the most sacred of all Navajo religious rites.

Among the Mescalero Apaches, an annual puberty ceremony pays tribute to all the young women who began menstruating in the past year. An elaborate four-day public ceremony, including

Among the Apache of the United States Southwest, a young woman must perform a special dance during the ceremony that celebrates her attainment of puberty.

feasting, the exchange of gifts, and other festivities, is followed by an additional four days of private observation. Like the Navajos, the Mescalero Apaches regard menarche as an important cultural event, and further believe that it ensures the tribe's survival (adapted from Taylor, 1988).

While height and weight gains are the most obvious changes during the adolescent growth spurt, other bodily changes are also taking place. Growth can be observed in pelvic and shoulder diameters, hand and foot length, and head circumference.

Primary and Secondary Sex Characteristics

A particularly notable development in puberty is the growth of primary and secondary sex characteristics. **Primary sex characteristics** are characteristics of the sexual and reproductive organs—the male penis and testes and the female ovaries, fallopian tubes, uterus, and vagina. **Secondary sex characteristics** are nongenital; they include facial hair in boys and breast development in girls.

FEMALE SEXUAL DEVELOPMENT. The female internal organs develop rapidly during puberty. The vagina increases in length and its lining becomes thicker, while the uterus increases in overall weight and develops the intricate musculature it will need for pregnancy and delivery.

The ovaries also increase in size and weight. As we learned in Chapter 2, each ovary has at birth about 400,000 primary follicles, which contain immature ova. By

primary sex characteristics The fully developed sexual and reproductive organs, including the male penis and testes and the female clitoris and vagina.

secondary sex characteristics Nongenital bodily features that usually develop during puberty and serve to distinguish a sexually mature man from a sexually mature woman.

Adolescent Sexuality

the time a girl reaches puberty, most of these primary follicles have degenerated and only 30,000 remain. Over the course of a woman's mature sexual life, it is estimated that only about 400 of the primary follicles will develop enough to expel ova. At puberty, this development process begins in monthly cycles.

You will recall that menstruation is the last stage of the female monthly cycle in which the uterus prepares to receive and nourish a fertilized egg, and then sloughs off the built-up lining when implantation does not take place. Menarche, which we defined in Chapter 3 as the beginning of menstruation, is experienced by most North American girls by 12 or 13 years of age (the normal age range is 10 to 15½ years). The average age at menarche varies from 12 to 18 throughout the world (Hood, 1991; Paikoff, Buchanan, & Brooks-Gunn, 1991; Brooks-Gunn, 1988, 1987).

When do most girls get their first period?

In some societies, formal ceremonies make the onset of menstruation a happy event. See, for example, the box on "The Celebration of Menarche in Other Cultures." In many western countries, however, menarche can be confusing and frightening:

I didn't like it at all. The biggest problem was that I was not told about it. I was scared.

My mother never told me what was going to happen to my body. When I got my first period, I was confused and afraid.

I'll never forget the day it happened. I was home and my mother was at work. I started getting my period and wasn't sure what to do. I tried putting pads in place but they didn't fit or feel right. I kept locking myself in the bathroom all day and kept changing pads and my underwear. I was nervous and scared. Finally, I called my mother up on the telephone and told her what happened. (Authors' files)

Others remember feeling more positive about menarche:

It made me feel grown-up and not different from my peers. Most of my friends had gotten their periods (or so they said) and I didn't want to be the only one who hadn't.

It was great. I was happy that I had now become a mature woman.

It was a very positive event in my life. I told my mother and she in turn shared the news with my father. (Authors' files)

While menarche is the first definite sign of female sexual maturity, it does not necessarily mean attainment of reproductive capacity. Early menstrual cycles, which for some girls are more irregular than later ones, often occur without ovulation. Thus there is often a period of adolescent sterility after menarche. The average duration of this period is 12 to 18 months, but it is extremely variable (Tanner, 1981).

Breast development begins for most girls between the ages of 10 and 11, although it can start as late as age 14. The breasts develop to mature size over a span of about three years (see Figure 14–1). During the early stages of breast development, there is elevation and enlargement, along with pigmentation of the nipple and the surrounding aureola. This is followed by an increase in underlying fat surrounding the nipple and areola. Finally, there is an increase in mammary gland tissue, accounting for a larger and rounder breast.

Female pubic hair usually starts to appear after the breasts have begun to develop but before the onset of menarche. Appearing first on the outer lips of the vulva, by the end of adolescence pubic hair is dark, curly, and coarse and has formed a triangular pattern over the mons. Hair under the arms usually appears about two years after pubic hair.

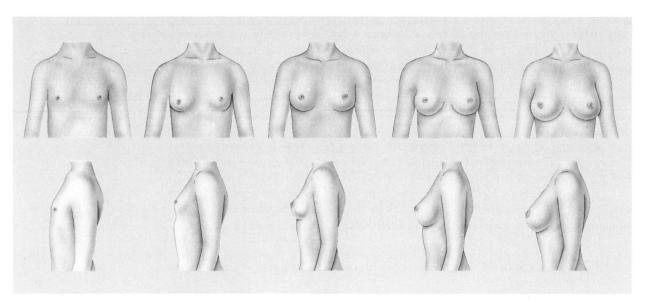

Figure 14-1
Development of the Breasts.

The sex hormones are also mainly responsible for the changes that transform the girl's body from its childhood shape to the contours of womanhood. Early in puberty the pelvis widens, an important change considering that childbirth usually requires the passage of a baby's head through this bony ring. At the same time, the laying down of more subcutaneous fat around the pelvic girdle exaggerates the breadth of the hips. Fat is also deposited in the shoulder girdle, back, abdomen, and legs. As the breasts develop, the apparent depth of the chest increases, enhanced by growth changes in the bony and muscular structures underlying the breasts.

MALE SEXUAL DEVELOPMENT. For most boys, growth of the testes and penis begins to accelerate by approximately age 12 (Tanner, 1991; Malina, 1991). Most of the increase in the size of the testes is due to development of the seminiferous tubules. By age 18, testicular development is fairly complete. During this time the penis increases in length and circumference. In its mature state the average flaccid (unaroused) penis measures about three to four inches in length and its diameter is about 1.25 inches. Figure 14-2 shows several stages in the development of the penis and testes.

Figure 14-2
Development of the Male Genitals.

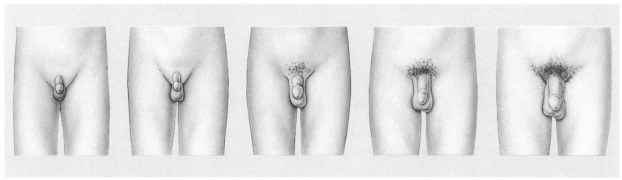

Adolescent Sexuality

Spontaneous erections are now experienced with increasing (and often embarrassing) frequency. The production of seminal fluid and first ejaculation, sometimes referred to as **spermarche,** occurs by about age 15. There are few viable sperm in this first ejaculate; as in girls, there is an initial period of sterility in boys undergoing puberty. When the ejaculation of seminal fluid occurs during sleep, it is known as a **nocturnal emission.** Nocturnal emissions are a normal phase of sexual development, frequently caused by sexual excitation in dreams or by a physical condition such as pressure from pajamas or a full bladder.

The development of male pubic hair begins between the ages of 12 and 14, usually starting at the base of the penis and extending upward toward the abdomen. Two years after pubic hair growth starts, hair on the limbs and the trunk begins to appear and underarm hair develops. Chest hair appears in late adolescence and continues growing throughout young adulthood. Boys often consider chest hair an important sign of virility.

Facial hair develops in a definite sequence. The downy hairs at the corners of the upper lip become noticeable and begin to extend over the entire upper lip. Slowly, the boy acquires a moustache of fine hair, which becomes coarser and more heavily pigmented with age. Later hair appears on the upper part of the cheeks and the midline below the lower lip. Finally, it develops on the sides and border of the chin, as well as on the upper part of the face just in front of the ears.

Other secondary sex characteristics that appear in boys during puberty are increased activity of the sweat glands and marked voice changes. The deepening of the voice, due primarily to a rapid increase in the length of the vocal chords and growth of the larynx, is greater in boys than in girls. With age, there is also an increase in voice volume and tone. Table 14–1 charts the average sequence of primary and secondary sex characteristics in male and female adolescents.

spermarche The first ejaculation of seminal fluid.

nocturnal emission The ejaculation of seminal fluid during sleep.

TABLE 14–1

The Development of Primary and Secondary Sex Characteristics

FEMALES	AVERAGE AGE OF OCCURRENCE	MALES
Onset of growth spurt	10–11	
Increased activity of oil and sweat glands (acne can result from clogged glands)	11	Increased activity of oil and sweat glands (acne can result from clogged glands)
Initial breast development	11–12	Onset of growth spurt
Development of pubic hair	12	**Growth of testes**
Onset of menarche (age range is 10–16)	13–14	Development of pubic hair
Development of underarm hair	13–14	**Growth of penis**
	13–14	Deepening of the voice
Earliest normal pregnancy	14	
Completion of breast development (age range is 13–18)	15–16	**Production of mature spermatozoa**
	15–16	**Nocturnal emissions**
	15–16	Development of underarm and facial hair
Maturation of skeletal system	17–18	Maturation of skeletal system
	17–18	Development of chest hair

Note: Primary sex characteristics are in boldface type.
Source: Adapted from Turner & Helms, 1991.

THE PSYCHOLOGY OF PUBERTY

The pronounced physical developments that take place during puberty affect the way adolescents perceive themselves. Preoccupation with the changing sexual self is common as the primary and secondary sexual characteristics mature. The adolescent also must adjust to the changes brought on by the growth spurt. How teenagers react to this process will greatly affect how they ultimately evaluate themselves (Adams, 1991; Koff & Riordan, 1991; Wright, 1989; Brooks-Gunn & Petersen, 1983; Petersen & Taylor, 1980; Adams, 1980; Higham, 1980).

Certain aspects of the changing body may produce psychological discomfort, particularly for those who have received no advance information about what to expect. Menstruation and seminal emissions may be a source of anxiety, as may the gangling appearance and disproportionately rapid hand and foot development characteristic of the growth spurt. Considering that these developments are often accompanied by acne, physical awkwardness, and voice breaks, it is no wonder that many teenagers feel uncomfortable about their changing physical selves. A male teenager expressed himself this way:

> I have this hangup that I'm not normal. I look around and see all of my friends going through adolescence without any problems. Their bodies have changed and they look a lot older than me. Most of them shave, and one guy even has hair on his chest. I don't have any of these things. When I go to gym class, I'm afraid that the guys will laugh at me when I take off my clothes. My father says to me, "Just wait, you're a late-bloomer." To tell you the truth, I'm getting tired of all this waiting. (Authors' files)

A female teenager shares these anxieties:

> It seems like I'm self-conscious about everything. I look in the mirror and criticize myself almost every day. I think my eyes are too small and my nose is way too big. I can't stand having to wear braces, and the pimples on my face are just plain gross. I'm self-conscious about my boobs because they're so small. (Authors' files)

As the first example suggests, teenagers who are late maturers may feel especially self-conscious. A late maturer is someone who lags behind established developmental norms, while an early maturer is someone who spurts ahead of prescribed developmental timetables. Because physical development is an individual phenomenon, adolescents can differ dramatically in overall rates of growth (see Figure 14–3).

Adolescents generally report higher levels of personal satisfaction when they mature early than when they mature late. Early maturers tend to be more independent, self-confident, and self-reliant, and are more socially adept than late maturers (Petersen, 1987; Gross & Duke, 1980; Wilen & Petersen, 1980). They also seem to be more popular and to have a greater capacity for leadership. Later maturers frequently have poorer self-concepts, are overly concerned about social acceptance, tend to be immature, and frequently resort to attention-seeking behavior.

Early-maturing boys, in particular, tend to have more positive body images than their late-maturing agemates, who often report intense dissatisfaction with their physical selves. Early-maturing boys are often given more responsibilities and privileges by their parents and have fewer conflicts with their mothers and fathers over such things as curfews and choice of friends (Savin-Williams & Small, 1986; Blyth, Simmons, & Zakin, 1985; Brooks-Gunn, 1984; Brooks-Gunn & Ruble, 1983).

FIGURE 14–3
Developmental Differences in Adolescents.
Sometimes the earlier female growth spurt is only too obvious.

Although their overall social adjustment seems to be smoother, early maturers do encounter problems. For one thing, they have to adjust to the physical changes of puberty a lot faster than late maturers. This seems to be especially true for girls experiencing early menarche, who may be confused and anxious about the event. A few studies (see, e.g., Aro & Taipale, 1987; Duncan et al., 1985) have found that some early-maturing girls are somewhat less confident and popular than their late-maturing counterparts. Research on both sexes suggests that the external harmony often exhibited by the early maturer sometimes disguises internal disharmony (Simons & Blyth, 1988; Livson & Peskin, 1980). Indeed, adolescents who mature about on time tend to have the most positive self-images.

Early sexual maturation also has implications for sexual behavior. Although the early maturer is physically capable of engaging in sexual relations, a mature body is no guarantee of a mature mind. Thus many adolescents begin having sexual relations before they are psychologically ready. This is true of both sexes, but the consequences for girls are greater for the obvious reason that they can get pregnant. As we'll see later in this chapter, the rate of teenage pregnancy is escalating in this country, with many mothers under age 15.

This is a good example of how development in one area (physical maturity) may affect development in other areas (sexual behavior), a point we made at the beginning of this chapter. It also underscores the need to teach teenagers what to expect from their developing bodies, which includes giving them information about the psychological and physiological risks of adolescent pregnancy. Such efforts may help to reduce the exploding numbers of ill-prepared teenage parents.

PUBERTY AND SEXUAL RESPONSIVENESS

The onset of sexual maturity heralds new levels of sexual understanding and responsiveness. As primary and secondary sex characteristics mature, the teenager becomes more aware of sexual feelings and desires and more interested in the social processes of dating and mate selection. When boys and girls enter adolescence, society expects them to begin the transition from childhood submissiveness, nonresponsibility and asexuality to adult independence, responsibility, and sexuality. So there are both biological and social pressures toward full sexual development (DeLamater, 1989, 1981).

Unfortunately, society often gives teenagers confusing mixed messages regarding their sexuality. On the one hand, the media promote adolescent sexuality by using young actors and actresses and models dressed in provocative fashions. On the other hand, parents and other social agents try to discourage sexual engagement by imposing curfews and other limitations on teenagers. Adolescents have to evaluate these inconsistent messages against the background of a changing culture (Garbarino, 1985).

These conflicting prescriptions for acceptable sexual attitudes and behaviors are not as extreme as those offered by either of the societies described in the box on

A WORLD OF DIFFERENCES

Learning About Sex in Two Very Different Cultures

*T*he manner in which North American adolescents learn about puberty and their changing sexual selves is particular to our culture. Around the globe there are wide cultural variations in teachings about sex that reflect very different sexual attitudes and behavior. The following two illustrations represent extremes in how adolescents learn about their changing bodies and sex in general.

On the Polynesian island of Mangaia, anthropologist Donald Marshall (1971) observed that sexual permissiveness abounds. From an early age, sexual curiosity and exploratory sex play are encouraged. Both boys and girls are taught to be proud of their bodies, including the pubertal changes that transform them into men and women. Outside the family, children hear stories and jokes about sex, and the language itself is rich in sexual words. At age 12, boys and girls are fully initiated into the world of adult sex. They learn that masturbation is an accepted practice, not an activity they should feel ashamed about. Premarital sex is an accepted practice, and both sexes are instructed in how to satisfy their partners. For example, male adolescents are taught about the pleasures of oral-genital sex, the stimulation of breasts, and techniques to achieve mutual climax. They are also taught how to bring a woman to climax several times before they climax themselves. Female adolescents are often initiated into intercourse by an experienced male relative. Virginity is frowned upon by the islanders since it is felt that virgins deprive others of sexual pleasure and satisfaction.

Now consider the sexual repressiveness that John Messenger (1971) found on Inis Beag, an island off the coast of Ireland. (Inis Beag is a pseudonym chosen to protect the island's inhabitants.) Sex education is virtually nonexistent on Inis Beag. In fact, the topic of sex is entirely avoided in front of children, even in the home. While parents are affectionate toward their children, physical contact such as hugging and kissing is minimal. Breast-feeding among the women of Inis Beag is rare, largely because islanders view the practice as sexually permissive and because it entails indecent exposure. Adolescents learn about puberty and sexuality from their peer group. Premarital sex is forbidden, and dating is considered unnecessary since marriages are prearranged by island elders. There is considerable ignorance about sexuality among both young and old. For example, the islanders know little or nothing about the physiology of menstruation, and maintain that intercourse is physically taxing and takes a toll on one's health.

For this reason, the men of Inis Beag refrain from intercourse on the eve of sporting events or strenuous workdays. When marital sex does take place, the husband always initiates the activity and it is always performed in the male-superior position. Foreplay is limited and the husband does not seek to satisfy his wife, who is taught that marital sex is "her duty." He ejaculates as quickly as possible and then falls asleep. Female orgasm is a relatively unknown experience on Inis Beag.

"Learning About Sex in Two Very Different Cultures." (And, as you can see, both Mangaia and Inis Beag set up their own sexual and gender conflicts.) But at least until the onset of the sexual revolution (see Chapter 1), North American society as a whole tended to promote the notion that sex is shameful—that one should feel guilty about engaging in sex or perhaps even thinking about it (Sarrel & Sarrel, 1984).

The sexual outcome of puberty is based on the individual's reaction to both physiological and psychological changes. Adolescents have to come to grips with the fact that they're now sexually mature, which implies coming to terms with their sexual identity. At this time of life young people consolidate their sexual preferences, think seriously about their sexual values—deciding which of their parents' values they accept and which they want to replace—and often worry about their sexual competence (Olds, 1985).

Masturbation

Much of the guilt and shame adolescents feel about their own changing bodies and about sexuality in general is rooted in harmful ideas about masturbation. Once regarded as sinful and dangerous, masturbation today is widely recognized as a normal form of sexual expression. By age 21, masturbation is quite widespread, especially among male adolescents (Davidson & Darling, 1989; Belcastro, 1985).

Robert Walsh's (1989) review of the literature indicates that while female masturbation is becoming more commonplace, it often begins as an accidental discovery. Young girls are not socialized into the activity the way young boys are. They generally do not discuss it among themselves, and many repress even the thought of it. As we noted earlier, girls in our society were traditionally taught not only that sexual activity was solely for men's pleasure but also that it was a painful and distressing experience to which they had to submit for the sake of having children. It is only recently that women have begun to realize their capacity for sexual pleasure.

Lorna and Phillip Sarrel (1984) point out that we are emerging from a dark age of misbelief about masturbation. Nineteenth-century books on the subject now sound absurd with their dire warnings about "self-pollution" causing everything from sallow complexions to insanity. Nevertheless, such ideas persisted well into the twentieth century. Until about 1920, there were still neuropsychiatric centers in this country where people with nerve-degenerative diseases and other as-yet-unclassified ailments were treated in "masturbation clinics."

Discovering how to masturbate is actually a major sexual turning point in a person's life. If this discovery is accompanied by a sense of shame, an ambivalence about sexuality often arises that can damage the person's life. To prevent this, Sally Wendkos Olds (1985) maintains that people need to learn that masturbation is an acceptable form of sexual expression. It's ironic that while our society endorses giving teenagers information about reproduction, it doesn't approve of telling them anything about self-pleasuring. These men recall how alarmed they were by their first ejaculation:

I was scared when I actually ejaculated. I wasn't sure what was coming out of my penis.

No one really told me about the ejaculation part. I didn't know if I was bleeding or had hurt myself. I was afraid to tell my father.

It felt really good, but I was unsure about the ejaculate. I wondered if I would ever be able to urinate normally again. (Authors' files)

These women remember the guilt that accompanied masturbation when they were teenagers:

> **I started masturbating at age 14, despite the horror stories that my mother told me about self-pleasuring. She used to tell me that only naughty girls masturbated.**

> **It felt good, but I remember how guilty I felt afterwards. I wanted to confess to my mother, but always changed my mind.**

> **When I masturbated as a teenager, I was always worried that I would get caught by my parents. I felt sneaky, like I was doing something that was wrong. (Authors' files)**

A study of 1,067 teenagers (Coles & Stokes, 1985) provides considerable insight into adolescent masturbation. The average age at which masturbation began was about 11 years. Of those who masturbated during adolescence, 90 percent started before they were 15. To no one's surprise, these teenagers felt considerable guilt about their masturbation. Fewer than a third (31 percent) of respondents said they felt no guilt when they masturbated, and one-fifth (20 percent) felt either "a large amount" or a "great deal" of guilt. Many of the respondents believed that masturbation was something that shouldn't be talked about. Even those who agreed intellectually that masturbation was okay felt reticent about it.

What kinds of things do teenagers fantasize about when they masturbate?

The study uncovered some interesting trends about sexual fantasies during masturbation. Fantasies about one's boyfriend or girlfriend were most common (57 percent), followed by fantasies of TV or movie stars (44 percent), acquaintances (41 percent), strangers (36 percent), rock stars (28 percent), and imaginary people (17 percent). Male adolescents (77 percent) were more likely to have fantasies than female adolescents (68 percent). And the objects of their fantasies were noticeably different.

While the sexes were about equally likely to fantasize about current girlfriends or boyfriends, male teenagers were much more likely than female teenagers (52 percent vs. 38 percent) to fantasize about strangers. (Interestingly, the study did not confirm the popular notion that female fantasies frequently revolve around being forced by some mysterious figure to do things they won't allow themselves to admit they want to do.) By a somewhat larger margin (56 percent vs. 38 percent), the male adolescents fantasized about acquaintances. Though the sexes were equally likely to fantasize about rock stars, more male teenagers (52 percent vs. 37 percent of girls) fantasized about TV or movie stars. In fantasizing about imaginary lovers, however, the sexes were approximately equal.

The only fantasies that more than 15 percent of these teenagers reported having more than twice a week involved boyfriends and girlfriends. Here, almost a fifth of the adolescents (19 percent) fantasized at least once a day, and more than a third (36

Rock singers often dress provocatively and draw excited response from their teenage audiences.

426

percent) did so at least twice a week. The sexes did not differ significantly in frequency of these fantasies; they both fantasized about boyfriends and girlfriends more than twice as often as they did about other subjects. The researchers concluded that it appears the chicken-and-egg question can be answered: Having a sex partner was more likely to lead to sex fantasies than having sex fantasies was to having a sex partner.

Patterns of Dating and Courtship

Dating generally begins during the teenage years. American teenagers start to date earlier than teenagers in other countries. As we learned in Chapter 5, dating serves a number of important functions. It is a social vehicle that enables people to learn more about themselves and the way others perceive them, including their strengths as well as their weaknesses. Dating also teaches the importance of sensitivity, mutuality, and reciprocity, and enables the person to experience love and sexual activity within mutually acceptable limits. Finally, dating is the process through which people usually select a marriage partner (Lauer & Lauer, 1991; Dickinson & Leming, 1990; Zinn & Eitzen, 1990; Lloyd, Cate, & Henton, 1984).

The complexion of dating has changed over the years for both adolescents and adults. In the past, dating was a structured and formal affair characterized by traditional gender-role stereotyping. The young man usually took the initiative in asking for a date, provided the transportation, and absorbed the expenses. Dating is a more casual affair today, especially among the teenage population, and many couples share expenses and responsibility for transportation. Some young women even take the initiative in asking a young man out (Turner & Helms, 1989; Stouse, 1987; Bell & Coughey, 1980; Murstein, 1980).

In general, girls start dating earlier than boys. They also have different attitudes toward dating. Although anxious about it during the early stages of adolescence, they tend to exhibit deep understanding, sensitivity, and emotional involvement with their partners by late adolescence. Male adolescents (and adults) tend to de-emphasize the emotional and intimate features of the relationship. As we learned in Chapter 5, this is because of traditional gender-role learning that often teaches them to be emotionally guarded (Berndt & Perry, 1990; Parker & Gottman, 1989; Selman, 1981; Coleman, 1980).

Adolescents look for certain qualities in a date. Physical attractiveness is equally important for both sexes, as are personality and compatibility. How socially prestigious a date is appears to be more important for girls—perhaps because they are more likely to view dating as a way to increase their popularity and status in the peer group. Finally, both sexes value honesty in a partner, as well as the capacity to bring companionship and joy (Duck, 1989; Hansen & Hicks, 1980; Rubin, 1980).

More serious dating may lead to going steady (also called "seeing" or "going with" someone). Although the meaning of this type of relationship varies from couple to couple, going steady generally implies a rather permanent relationship in which both parties refrain from dating others. Going steady is more common today than in the past, and it begins earlier. Many teenagers go steady as early as age 14 or 15.

Compared to the randomness of casual dating, going steady has certain advantages. One practical benefit is that it assures dates, which promotes a sense of security. Another is that it allows adolescents to practice their interpersonal communication skills. Going steady can teach people how to nurture and handle intimacy with another human being. Adolescents who go steady have the opportunity to learn some of the relationship qualities we discussed in Chapter 7, like openness, feedback, and conflict resolution skills—all of which are important prerequisites to marriage.

There are also disadvantages to going steady. An exclusive dating arrangement reduces the adolescent's contacts with other peers of both genders, which may hamper overall social development. The custom also promotes an escalation of physical intimacy, which often leads to sexual intercourse before the partners are ready for it. This, of course, increases the risk of teenage pregnancy and premature marriage.

SEXUAL BEHAVIOR AMONG ADOLESCENTS

Few topics about the development of adolescents arouse more curiosity than their sexual behavior. The most consistent research finding is that teenagers' attitudes toward sex have become more relaxed and tolerant in recent decades. As American society has moved from an antisex to a prosex orientation, that change has become quite obvious in teenage dating patterns.

Still, it is incorrect to assume that because sexual *attitudes* have become more liberal, sexual *behavior* is equally liberal. While there has been some convergence of behavior and attitudes, not all adolescents act as permissively as they think.

Philip Dreyer (1982) believes that the sexual attitudes of adolescents reflect this group's particular moral perspectives. To begin with, most contemporary adolescents cling to the permissiveness-with-affection moral standard—that is, premarital intercourse is acceptable provided there is emotional closeness or attachment between partners. Also, today's teenagers tend to be confused about sexual norms, largely because of the mixed messages society gives them. Whereas some segments of society are liberal about sexual relationships, others are quite conservative. Peers, parents, and the media often offer contrasting messages about appropriate sexual conduct. Thus, deciding what is acceptable and unacceptable is a difficult chore for today's adolescent.

It is interesting to note that the sexual double standard is alive and in full bloom among adolescents. Gender-role stereotypes that have been operating since infancy come to be acted upon during the teenage years. Male adolescents are usually expected to have, and boast about, sexual conquests. Young men who don't "score," or want to, are frowned upon by their peers. To gain approval, the male adolescent must be sexually aggressive. Consider the following comment:

> **It seems like I'm the only one in the neighborhood who hasn't had sex with a girl. All of my friends tell me about their sexual escapades and I can't help but feel inadequate. I think about it all the time, wondering what it will be like. Here I am, 17 years old and still a virgin. Worse, I can't even get to first base with a girl. I've had one date so far in high school and that was a disaster. (Authors' files)**

Very different behavior is expected of female adolescents. While they are supposed to be interested in the other sex, they are also supposed to remain virgins until they get engaged or, at the least, are going steady. It's a no-win situation. The girl who gives in and has sexual intercourse is likely to be labeled "easy," while the one who holds out may be tagged "prudish" and not be asked out again.

Before we turn our attention to premarital intercourse, we want to mention petting as a form of sexual behavior. Petting is physical caressing to cause erotic arousal, but without intercourse. *Light petting* refers to any sexual activity above the waist, such as fondling and/or stimulation of the breasts. *Heavy petting* includes sexual activity below the waist, such as manual or oral stimulation to the point of orgasm. Petting as an alternative to intercourse is one of the more common sexual activities during adolescence. Engaging in petting enables young people to learn about their own sexual responses as well as those of their partners. Intimacy can be developed by using any mutually satisfying technique.

Rates of Sexual Intercourse

Research confirms the widespread suspicion that a greater percentage of adolescents are engaging in sexual intercourse today than in the past. Indeed, a general theme in the literature is that most adolescents in the United States have become sexually active by age 19, although rates of coital activity are usually higher for men, especially among African-Americans (London, Mosher, Pratt, & Williams, 1989; Brooks-Gunn & Furstenberg, 1989; Walsh, 1989; Mott & Haurin, 1988; National Research Council, 1987). One study (Moore & Peterson, 1989) estimates that 80 percent of both white and black women have engaged in coital activity by 19. Another investigation (Sonenstein, Pleck, & Ku, 1989) shows that, among men, 85 percent of whites, 96 percent of African-Americans, and 82 percent of Hispanic-Americans were sexually active by 19.

How widespread is teenage intercourse today?

Most of the increase in female sexual activity in the past decade was among white adolescents and adolescents from higher-income families, which means that previous racial and income differences are narrowing (London et al., 1989; Moore & Peterson, 1989; Hayes, 1987). In reviewing the literature, Patricia Voydanoff and Brenda Donnelly (1990) observe that the percentage of sexually active female adolescents tended to peak among blacks in the 1970s, but that the percentage continued to go up among whites. So although sexual activity is still more common among African-American female teenagers than among whites, recent years have seen a narrowing of the gap between blacks and whites in this respect.

A few representative research studies will illustrate the magnitude of adolescent coital activity. One study (Pratt et al., 1984) of female adolescents between the ages of 15 and 19 revealed that over half the respondents had had sexual intercourse by their nineteenth birthday. The proportion engaging in intercourse rose steadily with age, from 18 percent at age 15, to 29 percent at age 16, to 40 percent at age 17, to 54 percent at age 18, and to 66 percent at age 19. The proportions who engaged in regular sexual relations were lower, but nonetheless substantial. About 25 percent of those aged 15 to 17 engaged in regular sexual intercourse, and this figure escalated to 49 percent among those 18 and 19. Robert Coles and Geoffrey Stokes' (1985) survey of over 1,000 teenagers revealed that rates of premarital intercourse for female and male adolescents were about equal: 53 percent of the young women and 46 percent of the young men reported having had intercourse by age 18.

Many adolescents have their first coital experience in their early teens. Research gathered by the Alan Guttmacher Institute (1991) shows that in 1982, 19 percent of unmarried 15-years-old girls had experienced intercourse; in 1988, this figure had jumped to 27 percent. William Pratt (1990) notes that by age 15, about one-quarter of the girls he surveyed had coital experience; by age 19, the statistic was about four out of five. In another investigation involving 114 black and white adolescents of both sexes (mean age: 13.9 years), 28 percent reported having had sexual intercourse at least once (Scott-Jones & White, 1990).

Melvin Zelnick and colleagues (1981) studied the sexual behavior of female adolescents between 15 and 19 and found that the age at first intercourse was about 16. Partners tended to be about three years older and intercourse took place about three times a month. Approximately four-fifths of those who had been sexually active for four or more years had had more than one partner. Another investigation headed by Zelnick (Zelnick & Shah, 1983) revealed that the average female adolescent had her first coital experience at 16.2 years of age, while the corresponding figure for male adolescents was 15.7 years.

Finally, few adolescents have intercourse only once. Research tells us (i.e., Miller & Moore, 1990; Moore & Peterson, 1989; Sonenstein, Pleck, & Ku, 1989) that over two-thirds of adolescents experience sex again within six months of their first intercourse. One investigation (Alan Guttmacher Institute, 1991) discloses that about 6 out of 10 sexually active female adolescents between 15 and 19 reported having had two or more sexual partners. Another investigation (National Center for Health Statistics, 1991) reports that among those young women who began having sexual intercourse before the age of 18, 75 percent had had two or more partners and 45 percent had had four or more partners. As we'll shortly discover, young people who have more than one sexual partner are at greater risk for unintended pregnancies as well as for sexually transmitted disease (Harlap, Kost, & Forrest, 1991).

What Motivates Adolescent Sexual Behavior?

Many factors are causing these high rates of adolescent sexual involvement. Chief among them are desire for intimacy; feelings of trust, love, and caring; pressure to please a partner; and trying to improve a relationship. Other prominent reasons are the physiological need for a sexual outlet and the desire to test the sexual capacities of a prospective marriage partner.

Roger Rubin (1985) has advanced further motivations: loneliness; relief from tension and frustration; the desire to control and dominate others; getting revenge; escaping oneself; communicating; conveying love. Sex is sometimes used to try to salvage a doomed relationship. Sex may also make a person feel wanted and loved even without a deep commitment. It can serve as an outlet for aggression or as an expression of gratitude. Sexual activity may be used to bolster an ego wounded by failure in school or to flee the ugliness of a family breakup. Finally, it may be a source of power, even for people who are weak and vulnerable.

There are a number of reasons some adolescents do *not* engage in sexual intercourse. For girls, two of the more common ones are fear of pregnancy and guilt over the loss of virginity. Being responsible for a pregnancy is also a source of anxiety for male adolescents. Teenagers of both sexes may fear bringing public disapproval on themselves and contracting a sexually transmitted disease.

Pamela Dole (1984) observes that sexual options without intercourse are not often presented to adolescents. If adults want to guide today's adolescents, they may need to support such alternatives to intercourse as sensual touch, petting, oral-genital sex, and both individual and mutual masturbation. These behaviors do not interfere with normal sexual development and provide reasonable outlets for the insistent hormonal urges of adolescence. Their acceptance would help to curb rising rates of teenage pregnancy. The "Making Use of What We Know" box provides ideas for discussing sexual issues with adolescents.

IMPLICATIONS OF ADOLESCENT SEXUAL ACTIVITY

The widespread coital activity among today's adolescents brings up three areas of concern: pregnancy, abortion, and the risk of disease.

Adolescent Pregnancy

More than one million teenagers get pregnant every year in the United States and about half of them give birth. While the overall birth rate among teenage mothers has stabilized, there has been a rise in births among those aged 15 to 17. Approximately one out of every ten teenagers will become a mother by her nineteenth birthday.

Adolescent Sexuality

_P_uberty provokes numerous questions about sexual functioning. For adults who want to provide guidance and support, this is the time to start discussing social-sexual communication, sexual attitudes, and sexual options. Pamela Dole (1984) offers the following points as guidelines for discussion:

- Consider the adolescent's cognitive and emotional development, and when counseling someone under the age of 15, use concrete rather than abstract terms.

- Is the young person cognitively mature enough to make responsible decisions?

- Why has the adolescent made a certain decision about sexual activity now?

- Evaluate motives for the adolescent's behavior. Do they represent curiosity or acting-out behavior, or have they been logically deduced?

- If the adolescent is ambivalent about starting sexual activity, suggest making a list of the advantages and disadvantages and select one or two to discuss.

- What is the nature of the family constellation? Is the teenager able to communicate with parents? Do the parents have knowledge about their teenager's behaviors? (Remember always to uphold the teenager's right to confidentiality.) Do the parents like their adolescent's boyfriend or girlfriend?

- What is the trust or intimacy level in the teenager's relationship with his or her partner? Are they going steady or dating casually? Is the partner caring and responsible, or exploitative? If the teenager is in an exploitative or high-pressure situation and sexual interaction is not consensual, provide support for saying no. (This may require some role-playing about the situation.) Will the sexual interaction promote the acquisition of skills and sensitivity for mutual sexual satisfaction? (*Note:* First sexual experiences for young women are sometimes unsatisfactory and unrewarding. Young men may report similar dissatisfaction. Counsel the adolescent to regard the first experience as something that should be mutually experimental and satisfying.)

- Stress the importance of communication between partners, but acknowledge that this can be embarrassing at first.

- Is the adolescent concerned or confused about his or her sexual orientation, whether it is to heterosexuality, homosexuality, or bisexuality? Teenagers are commonly confused about their orientation when they begin to interact sexually. It is often helpful to clarify the difference between behavior and fantasy, and to validate different sexual-orientation fantasies and behavior as normal. Statistically, homosexual orientation occurs far more frequently in fantasy than in fact.

- Is the adolescent in a safe and/or protected environment?

- Does the adolescent understand the risks of intercourse, such as pregnancy and sexually transmitted diseases, and how to counteract these risks?

- For the adolescent who is considering heterosexual intercourse, assess his or her knowledge about contraception. What options does the adolescent have in the event of a contraceptive failure and an unwanted pregnancy? Is the adolescent economically well enough off to afford a child or an abortion? Discuss sexual alternatives to intercourse.

- Encourage the adolescent to ask before engaging in sexual activity:
  "Will I be humiliated?"
  "Will I feel guilty"?
  "Will I feel comfortable in my peer group?"
  Adolescents who have already asked themselves these questions should be given approval for having done so.

MAKING USE OF WHAT WE KNOW

Guidelines for Discussing Sex and Sexuality with Adolescents

Many adolescents become pregnant in their early or middle teens, about 30,000 of them under age 15 each year. If present trends continue, it is estimated that 40 percent of all of today's 14-year-old girls will be pregnant at least once before reaching the age of 20. Our adolescents have one of the highest pregnancy rates in the Western world—twice as high as rates found in England and Wales, France, and Canada; three times as high as those in Sweden; and seven times as high as those in the Netherlands

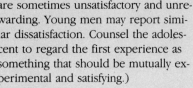

How common is teenage pregnancy in the United States today?

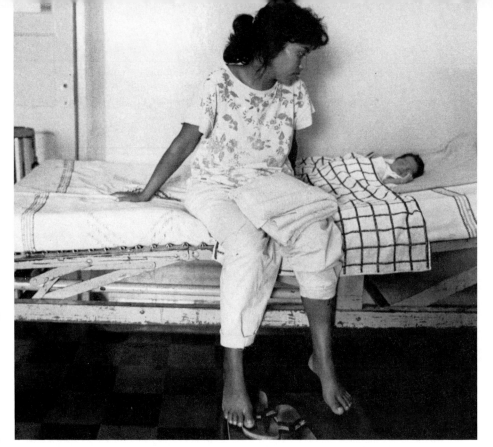

Teenage mothers are faced with a task few are ready for. Although they may love their babies, they may come to resent having to give up the only truly free time they have—their youth—to care for their children.
....

(Alan Guttmacher Institute, 1991, 1989; Roosa, 1991; Henshaw et al., 1989; Rickel, 1989; National Research Council, 1987).

Teenage pregnancy rates are higher for black Americans than for white Americans (Dash, 1989; Franklin, 1988). Approximately half of all African-American female adolescents become pregnant at least once before turning 20 (Hayes, 1987; Forest, 1986). In 1985 the pregnancy rate for 15- to 19-year-old black women was 18.6—twice the rate (9.3 percent) for whites (Henshaw & Van Vort, 1989). Racial differences are even greater for adolescents under age 15: 5.1 percent for blacks versus 0.9 percent for whites. Adolescent pregnancy rates are also disturbingly high among Hispanic Americans (Lopez, 1987).

The children of adolescent mothers suffer many health risks. The younger the mother is, the higher the chance of infant death. Adolescent mothers are more apt to give birth prematurely than older mothers, and are also more likely to experience labor and delivery complications, including toxemia and anemia. The babies born of teenage mothers often have low birth weights and frequently suffer from neurological problems and birth defects. Children of adolescent mothers also tend to have lower IQs and to perform more poorly in school than the children of older mothers (Furstenberg, Brooks-Gunn, & Chase-Lansdale, 1989; Giblin et al., 1989; Franklin, 1988).

Babies often disrupt the lives of adolescent mothers and fathers, *their* parents, and society as a whole. Many adolescent parents lack both a supportive family and parenting skills and have nowhere to turn for child-care assistance (Furstenberg, 1991; Paikoff & Brooks-Gunn, 1991; Treboux & Busch-Rossnagel, 1991; Jones & Battle, 1990; Thomas, Rickel, & Butler, 1990; Davis, 1989). Besides costing the taxpayers excessive sums of money each year, unwed adolescent mothers often face social disapproval and financial hardship. Those who do marry have an exceptionally high divorce rate (Lockhart & Wodarski, 1990; Miller & Moore, 1990; Furstenberg, Brooks-Gunn, & Chase-Lansdale, 1989; Teti & Lamb, 1989).

WHERE TO FIND MORE ON ADOLESCENT PREGNANCY PREVENTION PROGRAMS

Academy for Educational Development
100 Fifth Avenue
New York, NY 10010
(212) 243-1110

The Alan Guttmacher Institute
2010 Massachusetts Avenue NW
Washington, DC 20036
(202) 296-4012

Carnegie Council on Adolescent Development
2400 N Street NE, 6th Floor
Washington, DC 20037
(202) 429-7979

Child Welfare League of America
440 First Street NW, Suite 310
Washington, DC 20001
(202) 638-2952

Center for Population Options
1025 Vermont Avenue NW
Suite 210
Washington, DC 20005
(202) 347-5700

Center for Reproductive Health Policy Research
University of California at San Francisco
1326 Third Avenue
San Francisco, CA 94143
(415) 476-5254

Family Resource Coalition
230 N. Michigan Avenue
Suite 1625
Chicago, IL 60601
(312) 726-4750

Abortion

Of the one million adolescents who become pregnant annually, about 45 percent have abortions. About one-quarter of all abortions in the United States are performed on adolescents—a rate more than double that of any other nation. Among teenagers 15 to 19 years old, African Americans have more abortions than Caucasians, but this is because black teens have higher rates of pregnancy than whites. Thus the proportion of pregnancies ended by abortion does not differ significantly between whites and blacks (Voydanoff & Donnelly, 1990; Henshaw & Van Vort, 1989; Children's Defense Fund, 1988; Hayes, 1987).

Researchers have established a profile of the adolescent who chooses abortion. She is likely to be enrolled in school and doing well, and to be from a middle- or upper-socioeconomic family. Adolescents who use illicit drugs are also more apt to obtain an abortion. Conversely, the adolescent who decides not to abort is usually poor, has friends or relatives who bore children when they were teenagers, and comes from a very religious family (Henshaw & Silverman, 1988; Yamaguchi & Kandell, 1987; Leibowitz, Eisen, & Chow, 1986).

The overall rise in teenage abortion rates in the United States is due to many factors, including the legalization of abortion in the 1970s and its consequent accessibility (Nathanson & Kim, 1989). Adolescents who marry after they get pregnant are less likely to seek an abortion, while teenagers who receive support for abortion from their boyfriends are more likely to elect abortion. People besides boyfriends who are significant in the teenager's life also influence this decision. Family members, especially the adolescent's mother and sister, and close friends, are important influences (Miller & Moore, 1990; Brazzell & Acock, 1988).

Sexually Transmitted Diseases

What kinds of risks do sexually transmitted diseases pose to adolescents?

Increased sexual activity among adolescents has made this group particularly vulnerable to sexually transmitted diseases. A higher incidence of sexually transmitted diseases is found among people who began sexual intercourse at an early age and those who have had many sexual partners, both recently and over the course of their lives. People who have multiple partners over a specified period (e.g., several months) increase their risk of getting gonorrhea, syphilis, chlamydia, and chancroid. Having a large number of sex partners over a lifetime raises one's chances of acquiring viral infections such as hepatitus B, genital herpes, and the human immunodeficiency virus (National Center for Health Statistics, 1991; Centers for Disease Control, 1991; Aral & Holmes, 1990).

Of the more than 12 million cases of sexually transmitted diseases reported each year in the United States, 2.5 million are among adolescents. Adolescents are at a higher risk than adults for all sexually transmitted infections, presumably because they have more partners. For example, adolescents have higher rates of gonorrheal and chlamydial infections than any other age group. Of the one million women who experience pelvic inflammatory disease (PID) each year, 16 to 20 percent are teenagers. Genital warts affect as many as 40 percent of all adolescent girls. Overall, black adolescents have a higher incidence than white teenagers of gonorrhea, chlamydia, syphilis, and pelvic inflammatory disease (Aral & Holmes, 1990; Cates, 1990; Shaffer & Sweet, 1989, Johnson, Nahmias, & Magder, 1989; Mitchell, Drake, & Medley, 1986; Washington, Sweet, & Shaffer, 1985).

Adolescents are also at a particularly high risk for contracting the HIV virus (Boyer & Hein, 1991; Rotheram-Borus & Koopman, 1991; DiClemente, 1990; Hein, 1989a, b; Schinke, Holden, & Moncher, 1989; Guinan, 1986; Koop, 1987). Despite widespread public information campaigns, too many American teenagers remain unclear about the causes of AIDS, the modes of transmission, and effective prevention strategies. Many of them engage in unprotected intercourse and share needles with other intravenous drug users (Broering et al., 1989; Carrera, 1988; DiClemente, Zorn, & Temoshok, 1987). If teenagers had intercourse less often and used condoms whenever they did have it, their chances of contracting HIV would decrease considerably. But studies conducted among high school and college students show that most adolescents believe they are not at risk and thus fail to take the recommended precautions (Becker & Joseph, 1988; Kegeles, Adler, & Irwin, 1988; Strunin & Hingston, 1987; Price, Desmond, & Kukulka, 1985). Chapter 17 explores sexually transmitted diseases in detail, and Chapter 18 is devoted to AIDS.

Reasons for Unsafe Sex Practices

As we'll see in Chapter 17, "safer sex" refers not only to using effective contraceptive methods but to using methods that protect against sexually transmitted diseases. Safer sex also means making informed and rational decisions about sexual activity; thus it requires knowledge about the prevention of both pregnancy and disease and responsibility for acting on that knowledge (Fogel, 1990; Fogel, Forker, & Welch, 1990; Smith, Lauver, & Gray, 1990).

Given the high rates of pregnancy, abortion, and sexually transmitted diseases in their age group, why do so many young people engage in unsafe sex practices? Most sexually active adolescents do not consistently use any type of contraception, and many are misinformed about available birth control methods (Hayes, 1987; Hofferth & Hayes, 1987). The great majority of teenage girls are already sexually active before they use a contraceptive or visit a family planning clinic. One study (Mosher & Horn, 1989) found that only 17 percent of those aged 15 to 24 who were making their first visit to a family planning clinic came before having intercourse. About 10 percent made their first visit the same month they began coital activity. For the remaining 73 percent, the median delay between first coitus and first visit was an astonishing 23 months.

Why do teenagers engage in unsafe sex practices?

Most adolescents of both sexes *say* they believe in responsible use of contraceptives, but few put this belief into practice (Chilman, 1988). This is especially true of male teenagers. Most of them are unwilling to assume any responsibility for contraception, although in recent years there has been some increase in condom use (see, for example, Sonenstein, Pleck, & Ku, 1989). The younger they are, the more likely male adolescents are to view birth control as their partner's "problem." Moreover, many adolescents have a firm prejudice against condoms, even though condoms are a good method of preventing both pregnancy and sexually transmitted diseases, especially the HIV infection (Kegeles, Adler, & Irwin, 1988; Strunin & Hingston, 1987; Hofferth & Hayes, 1987; Pleck, 1989; Jones et al., 1986).

Contraceptive use varies according to age and other characteristics. One study (Morrison, 1985) that focused on contraceptive behavior among adolescents and young adults discovered that one-third to two-thirds of adolescents used no contraception at first intercourse. However, use increased with age and overall rates tended to be higher among young women. The reasons given for not using contraception ranged from erroneous beliefs about fertility, problems getting contraceptive devices, and the feeling that pregnancy wouldn't be such a negative event. Condoms and withdrawal were the most commonly used methods at first intercourse, but with experience, many adolescents shifted to oral contraceptives. Several researchers (i.e., Harlap, Kost, & Forrest, 1991; Jones & Forrest, 1989; Hayes, 1987) note the popularity of the pill among sexually active adolescents.

One study (Sonenstein, Pleck, & Ku, 1989) of 15- to 19-year-old male adolescents found that 55 percent of them used a condom at first intercourse, 7 percent used an effective female method without a condom, and 38 percent used an ineffective method or no contraception at all. African-American male adolescents were less likely to use a condom and more likely to use an ineffective method or none at all at first intercourse than whites or Hispanic Americans. Rates of condom use were lower and rates of ineffective methods or no method were higher for adolescents who started coital activity before the age of 15 than for those who began between 15 and 19.

Many adolescents seem to believe they are invulnerable to the risks of pregnancy and of contracting a sexually transmitted disease. This is the sort of magical thinking in which very young children often engage: "Nothing bad can happen to *me*." Others have difficulty understanding such issues as shared responsibility for contraception,

"I WAS HOPING WE'D GET SOME HANDS-ON EXPERIENCE."

birth control alternatives, and the consequences of unsafe sexual practices. Finally, some are simply too immature to envision the possibility of pregnancy. Debra Gordon's (1990) review of the literature indicates that the same kind of immature thinking that prevents a lot of teenagers from understanding the needs of their sexual partners makes it impossible for them to grasp elementary probability theory. The fact that once a month, month after month, a woman continues to have the same probability of conceiving a child if she has sexual intercourse fails to get through to them. They think if they escaped pregnancy one month, they will be that lucky again and again. The inability to think maturely also prevents these teenagers from realistically weighing the alternatives when they do get pregnant (e.g., adoption, abortion, raising the child with the support of their family, establishing an independent household, marriage).

We believe that adolescent sexuality education programs should take account of these common limitations in thinking skills. Educators need to recognize that while adolescents can usually grasp certain elements of sexuality education, others are more elusive. It is fairly easy, for example, for teenagers to understand the anatomy and physiology of the reproductive systems and facts about sexually transmitted diseases. But personal and shared responsibility for safer sex practices and the psychological, reproductive, and social consequences of having intercourse at an early age are more abstract and not so easily understood.

For these reasons, sexuality education should foster more sophisticated thinking and reasoning in adolescents. Rather than tell teenagers *what* to think, we need to teach them *how* to think. To this end, programs should not only teach adolescents to systematically explore and evaluate alternatives, such as the range of contraceptive choices available, but also to analyze *why* safer sex practices are important. They should show teenagers how to overcome their tendencies to impulsiveness. Research (e.g., Victor, Halverson, & Mongague, 1985) reveals that the ability to use reflective cognitive strategies promotes more deliberate and cautious behavior.

Sexuality educators should also focus on overcoming the teenage myth of invulnerability. As we've noted, many adolescents do not perceive a personal risk in their dangerous behaviors. To take one example, AIDS will not be eliminated merely by providing young people with concrete facts about how the disease is passed on. As Debra Haffner (1989) aptly shows, adolescents tend to take risks even when they are well informed about the theoretical consequences of their behavior. It is better, therefore, to emphasize concrete strategies to alter the motivations and attitudes behind so much adolescent risk taking. Areas that should be covered are chance and probability (e.g., helping adolescents to understand the real chances of becoming pregnant and of getting a sexually transmitted disease when they indulge in unprotected intercourse), sexual decision making (e.g., assertiveness training and learning how to say no), sexual alternatives (e.g., noncoital expressions of sexual intimacy), and negotiation strategies (e.g., how to bring up and effectively discuss safer sex practices with partners).

Adolescents also benefit from learning cognitive skills aimed at relationship building, including the ability to communicate. Recall from Chapter 12 that effective contraceptive use is often linked to good communication between partners (Milan & Kilman, 1987; Cvetkovich & Grote, 1983; Herold & McNamee, 1982). Cognitive enrichment techniques also help adolescents to understand such important abstract qualities of a sexual relationship as reciprocity, mutuality, sensitivity, and empathy. As Catherine Chilman (1990) points out, the typical adolescent finds it hard to form a close, value-compatible egalitarian relationship because these relational qualities require the kind of advanced thinking they have never learned. Learning about such relational qualities provides numerous rewards (Weinstein & Rosen, 1991). For example, maturing adolescents are able to see sexual activity as an expression of closeness, respect, and sensuality, as well as to take responsibility both for themselves and for their partner. This view enriches their intimate relationships.

Advanced cognitive skills make shared contraceptive responsibility possible because they move the adolescent away from an egocentric style of thinking. Interestingly, research (e.g., MacCorquodale, 1984; Rosen & Ager, 1981) shows that nontraditional gender roles are associated with more consistent contraceptive use. Sexuality education should combat the idea that contraception is solely a female responsibility by using role-reversal or perspective-taking exercises. The common male notion that condoms are outmoded or inhibit sexual pleasure should be challenged through concrete reasoning. Both sexes need to be shown that condoms offer excellent protection against both unwanted pregnancies and sexually transmitted diseases (DiClemente, 1990; Kegeles, Adler, & Irwin, 1988; Conant et al., 1986; Goedert, 1987; Reitmeijer et al., 1988).

Sexuality education programs that emphasize abstinence-based prevention (see, for example, Christopher & Roosa, 1990; Moyse-Steinberg, 1990; Roosa & Christopher, 1990; Shornack & Ahmed, 1989) can also benefit from a cognitive enrichment format in such areas as how and why to defer sexual activity, values clarification (including

A high school teacher leads juniors and seniors in a discussion of the problems of early pregnancy.

437

asserting one's beliefs and learning to say no), and problem solving and decision making.

Finally, a cognitive enrichment format is useful in intervention efforts for pregnant teenagers and teenage parents. It has been shown (see, for example, Baranowski, Schilmoeller, & Higgins, 1990; Cervera, 1991; Hanson, 1990; Rubenstein, Panzarine, & Lanning, 1990; Thomas, Rickel, & Butler, 1990) that adolescents benefit from a sophisticated cognitive approach to pregnancy resolution and the development of parenting skills. Pregnant adolescents are taught how to use reflective thinking skills to explore such issues as abortion and adoption. For those adolescents who decide to keep their babies, the cognitive approach emphasizes problem-solving skills (geared to the problems posed by infants and children), perspective-taking capacities (geared to reducing egocentrism and learning how to take the child's point of view), and decision-making abilities (geared to envisioning parenting alternatives).

SAME-SEX SEXUAL ENCOUNTERS

Is same-sex play common during adolescence? What kinds of sexual activities are shared?

Sexual experiences in the company of same-sex peers are relatively common during adolescence, but homosexuality is much less common. Alfred Kinsey's research in the middle of this century (1953, 1948) revealed that more than half of all men and a third of all women had experienced some type of homosexual sex play as children or young adolescents. However, homosexual sex play for most people stops during adolescence. Only a small percentage of people go on to establish a primarily gay/lesbian orientation in adulthood.

Kinsey's research discovered sex and age differences in homosexual sex play. The mean age of first homosexual sex play for the men he studied was about nine years. Exhibition of genitalia was the most common form of homosexual play, followed by manual manipulation of genitalia and oral or anal contacts with genitalia. In adolescence, many of the men had exhibited masturbatory techniques to lone companions or to whole groups of other boys. Sometimes this exhibitionism was a simultaneous group activity.

Exhibitionism occasionally led to each person stimulating the other's genitals. This kind of activity was usually casual among younger adolescents, who did not perceive the emotional possibilities of the experience. Kinsey observed that in only a small percentage of cases did this sort of manipulation cause arousal and/or orgasm in the partner. Manual manipulation was more likely to be arousing and/or orgasmic if the partner was an older adolescent or an adult. Without help from the more experienced, many preadolescents took a good many years to discover masturbatory techniques that were sexually effective.

Anal intercourse was reported by about 17 percent of those who had engaged in homosexual play, although among younger boys actual penetration usually failed. Oral manipulation was reported by nearly 16 percent of those who had homosexual play experiences. For younger adolescents, it was harder to attain erotic arousal by oral contact than by manual manipulation. Anal and oral activities were limited because even at these younger ages there was some knowledge of the social taboos on this kind of sex.

About 15 percent of Kinsey's women respondents reported experiencing some type of same-sex play by age seven. The figure rose to over 30 percent by early adolescence. As with boys, exhibition of the genitalia was the most prevalent form of sex play, and exhibitionism sometimes led to each person stimulating the other's genitals. Eighteen percent reported inserting objects, or at least fingers, into the vagina of other girls, and three percent experienced oral-genital contacts.

Female same-sex play during adolescence was of short duration. Most of Kinsey's subjects reported confining such activity to a single year, and many had had only one or two such experiences. However, 17 percent continued same-sex play for two years, and 8 percent continued it for five years or more.

Another study, by Sorenson (1973), discovered that approximately 11 percent of male adolescents and 6 percent of female adolescents had experienced some type of same-sex play. As in the Kinsey studies, most of these experiences took place between peers and did not influence adult sexual orientation. For a majority of the teenagers in Sorenson's study, sexual experiences in the company of same-sex peers was experimental.

Some adolescents do define themselves as lesbian or gay (Remafedi, 1987). Because of society's disapproval of their sexual preference, these young people do not feel they belong to *any* group and have no friends in whom they can confide. While some colleges and universities have organizations for the assistance and support of lesbian and gay students, high school administrators are afraid to allow such organizations because they could be accused of contributing to the deliquency of minors. We hope that in the 1990s our society will realize that young gays and lesbians are human beings and have the same rights to help as heterosexuals.

Robert Coles and Geoffrey Stokes (1985) found that although approximately 20 percent of the adolescents they studied had participated in some type of same-sex sexual play as children, only 5 percent engaged in homosexual activity as adolescents. These researchers discovered generally negative attitudes toward homosexuality when they explored the issue in depth. While a little more than half (53 percent) of their respondents thought it was okay for women to have sex together if they both wanted to, three-quarters had negative feelings about such actions. Just under half (49 percent) thought it was okay for two men to have sex together, but more than four out of five (84 percent) had negative perceptions of such men. Although young men and women were equally intolerant of male homosexuality, male respondents (68 percent) were significantly less likely than female respondents (84 percent) to react negatively to lesbianism.

In one way, Coles and Stokes' female respondents were more tolerant than their male respondents toward homosexuality. When asked what they would do if a same-sex friend told them he or she was gay or lesbian, only about a third (35 percent) of the young men, but fully one-half (50 percent) of the young women, said they would remain friends with that person. By a margin of 32 percent to 16 percent, male respondents were more likely to say explicitly that they would end such a friendship. The wide gap between the sexes in this area led the researchers to postulate that for young women the bonds of friendship are strong enough to overcome any moral uneasiness they might feel about lesbianism.

Coles and Stokes discovered other factors besides gender that affect perceptions of homosexuality. While urban, suburban, and rural adolescents were about equally likely to say they would remain friends with someone they discovered was gay or lesbian, the higher the income level, the higher was the degree of tolerance. Another finding was that blacks (34 percent) were significantly more likely than whites (22 percent) to say they'd terminate a friendship if they learned a friend was gay or lesbian.

It seems that an adolescent's attitude toward homosexuality in general is strongly influenced by how well that adolescent knows a particular person who is gay. Adolescents who knew homosexuals and those who didn't were about equally ready to call two girls who'd had sex together "disgusting," but those who had gay friends were far more tolerant than the majority.

Though all the adolescents in the Coles and Stokes study tended to be fairly liberal when asked if consensual homosexual activities were morally okay, here again, teenagers who had gay or lesbian friends were more tolerant. When the question was asked about women, the margin of tolerance for those who had a lesbian friend was

79 percent compared to 49 percent for those who did not have a lesbian friend; when the question was asked about men, the margins were 72 percent and 45 percent. Urban adolescents (13 percent) were more than twice as likely to have lesbian or gay friends as were suburban adolescents (6 percent), and more than three times as likely as rural adolescents (4 percent). The finding that suburban young people were somewhat more tolerant than both urban and rural teenagers might be attributed to their generally higher levels of income. Finally, tolerance was closely associated with educational plans. Adolescents who intended to go on to higher education exhibited notably more liberal attitudes than those who did not.

Psychosocial Problems

A. Damien Martin and Emery Hetrick (1988) maintain that the problems of gay or lesbian adolescents do not originate in their sexual orientation per se. Rather, they stem from society's stigmatization of gays and lesbians, a recurrent theme in the literature (see, for example, Savin-Williams, 1990; Hetrick & Martin, 1987; Hunter & Schaecher, 1987; Martin, 1982). Three problems are particularly acute: isolation, family rejection, and violence.

Isolation can be cognitive, social, and/or emotional. Cognitive isolation is created by the kind of information about sexual orientation generally available to gay and lesbian adolescents, which emphasizes the peculiarity, abnormality, and/or immorality of homosexuality. Cognitive isolation creates social isolation because it prevents adolescents from learning how to manage their social identity as lesbians/gays. They often fail to see they belong to a minority group, which keeps them from sharing learning experiences with others like themselves. Having no one to share their feelings with makes many adolescent homosexuals feel lonely and emotionally removed from those around them.

Family rejection is the second problem adolescent lesbians and gays confront. Rejection ranges from the isolation of the homosexual child to outright violence and expulsion from the home. Most lesbian and gay adolescents are terrified of telling their families about their orientation. They experience a painful cognitive dissonance that arises from the contraction between their family's expectations for them and the fact of their homosexuality. The knowledge that what they are is disappointing to their families often leads to guilt, shame, anger, and a fear of rejection. These feelings, in turn, can cause the adolescent to become progressively more alienated, depressed, and isolated (Boxer, 1988; Irvin, 1988; Herdt, 1988).

The third problem for adolescent lesbians and gays is *violence*. Those at highest risk of violence in all situations are adolescents who have been discredited—usually young men who are perceived as effeminate. Family violence is common and usually comes from parents, though sometimes it comes from siblings. Running away or expulsion from the home are often the immediate result of family violence, with prostitution a secondary consequence. When violence is met with at school, dropping out may be the adolescent's only perceived solution because most school authorities refuse even to discuss homosexuality, let alone address the problem of violence against gays or lesbians. Social service agencies, including emergency shelters, admit that they are powerless to protect homosexually identified youngsters in their care. Rape is a prevalent form of violence against gay and lesbian adolescents, especially in institutional settings. Often those who run such institutions feel forced to put lesbian or gay adolescents back on the streets for their own safety.

Health Problems

AIDS and other sexually transmitted diseases are another threat to the sexually active gay or lesbian adolescent. AIDS is neither an exclusively gay or lesbian disease nor

Some communities have established centers where gays and lesbians of all ages can not only socialize with each other but can get counseling on health and other crucial issues.

Adolescent Sexuality

one peculiar to the young. However, adolescent gays are particularly at risk, especially if they are promiscuous. It is crucial that they learn AIDS prevention techniques at this period of their lives, when they are acquiring the behaviors that will influence their later sexual interactions.

What can be done to help adolescent gays and lesbians combat their special problems? Martin and Hetrick (1988) believe that some active measures are needed. One is an effort to reach these youngsters at an early age with programs emphasizing physical, mental, emotional, and social well-being. We also need to train professionals to work with gay and lesbian youths.

Today there are few safe places where gay and lesbian teenagers can interact socially. These adolescents need opportunities for simple socializing, like young people's groups or dances.

Like most teenagers, gay and lesbian youths are convinced they are immortal. They find it nearly impossible to imagine getting a life-threatening disease like AIDS. As with heterosexual adolescents, education and prevention programs must take this age-related type of thinking into consideration. It is important to provide gay and lesbian adolescents with the opportunity to interact with their peers within a setting where accurate health information and counseling are available (Martin & Hetrick, 1988).

SEXUALITY IN THE NEWS

Teen Pregnancy

According to Mississippi governor Ray Mavis, "When our children have children, we all lose." In this four-part video series, originally aired on ABC's "World News Tonight" on June 26–29, 1989, Mavis, ABC anchor Diane Sawyer, and others explore teenage sexual behavior. Topics include the age at which sexual activity begins, the contraceptive practices teenagers use, and the social pressures that lead them into sexual experimentation.

This report acknowledges the epidemic proportions of teenage pregnancy and its enormous costs to society, to young mothers, and to their children. It claims that only about a third of sexually active teenagers use contraceptives. It is peer pressure, this disturbing program suggests, that leads most teenagers into sexual activity. The series also discusses how to teach adolescents to avoid pregnancy and reviews the approach to teenage pregnancy adopted in the Netherlands.

DISCUSSION QUESTIONS

1. It seems pretty clear that the "just say no to sex" campaign of the 1980s has not been effective. Speculate why this is so and how the campaign could be improved upon.

2. Most teenage fathers take neither moral nor financial responsibility for their offspring. What do you think the teenage father's responsibilities are? What are his rights?

3. Of the many teenage pregnancy prevention programs in the United States, New York City's Children's Aid Society has one of the few that seems to work well. What do you think makes this program work? How would you go about implementing a similar program in other U.S. cities?

4. What are the major differences between pregnancy prevention programs for teenagers in the United States and those in the Netherlands? Would the Dutch programs work in the United States?

LOOKING BACK

■ Adolescence is marked by many changes. Freud's genital stage and Erikson's psychosocial crisis of identity versus role diffusion help shed light on the developmental challenges of adolescence. Puberty is the point in development when sexual maturity begins. The growth sequence of puberty is the same for everyone, although rates of growth vary from person to person.

■ The hypothalamus, pituitary gland, and gonads interact to create the many physiological changes associated with puberty. Precocious puberty results when excessive amounts of gonadotrophins are released during the early years of childhood. Inadequate amounts of gonadotrophins can cause delayed puberty, a condition triggered either by primary or secondary hypogonadism.

■ The rapid rate of physical development prior to puberty is referred to as the adolescent growth spurt. This growth spurt involves increases in height, weight, and skeletal growth, as well as in pelvic and shoulder diameters, hand and foot length, and head circumference. The growth spurt begins about two years earlier for girls ($10\frac{1}{2}$ years) than for boys ($12\frac{1}{2}$ years).

■ Primary sex characteristics are the mature genitalia of each sex. Secondary sex characteristics include such developments as female breasts and male-pattern facial hair. Preoccupation with the changing sexual self is common and affects how adolescents perceive themselves. Being an early or a late maturer may produce extreme self-consciousness. Sexual maturity is usually accompanied by heightened levels of sexual responsivity, including masturbation. Discovering how to masturbate marks a major sexual turning point in a person's life.

■ An ever-greater percentage of adolescents are engaging in sexual intercourse. Among the implications of adolescent sexual intercourse are unplanned pregnancy, abortion, and sexually transmitted diseases. Sexual experience in the company of same-sex peers is relatively common during adolescence, but homosexuality is much less common. Problems encountered by gay adolescents include isolation, family rejection, and violence.

THINKING THINGS OVER

1. Many psychological changes occur during puberty. Describe some of these changes and suggest ways that peers can help each other during these trying times.

2. Teenagers often have an unusually high level of sexual responsivity during puberty. What are some positive ways adolescents can deal with their "raging hormones"?

3. Do you think that adolescents are pressured into dating? If so, who do you think is responsible for this pressure? How can teenagers learn to interact with one another, naturally and comfortably, without formal dating?

4. Nonmarital sexual intercourse is becoming increasingly widespread among teenagers. Do you think this is a good or bad thing? Why do you think it is happening? What would you tell your children or nieces or nephews about nonmarital sexual intercourse?

5. Why is same-sex sexual experience common during adolescence? Speculate about the responses of parents when they learn their teenagers are engaging in these behaviors.

6. What do you think accounts for the enormous rise in teenage pregnancy in this country? Can we do something about that rate? What would you suggest?

DISCOVER FOR YOURSELF

Allen-Meares, P., & Shapiro, C. S. (eds.) (1989). *Adolescent sexualities*. New York: Haworth Press. AIDS education, teenage pregnancy, and sexual orientation are among the topics presented.

Bancroft, J., & Reinisch, J. M. (eds.) (1990). *Adolescence and puberty*. New York: Oxford University Press. Among the subjects covered are the biological mechanisms of puberty, sexual behavior, and contraception.

Coles, R., & Stokes, G. (1985). *Sex and the American teenager*. New York: Harper & Row. A thorough and extensive examination of contemporary sexual behavior among adolescents.

Dryfoos, J. G. (1990). *Adolescents at risk: Prevalence and prevention*. New York: Oxford University Press. An excellent review of some of the problems of adolescence, including pregnancy, and intervention efforts.

Rickel, A. U. (1989). *Teen pregnancy and parenting*. New York: Hemisphere. An excellent survey of teenage pregnancy and the problems that adolescent parents face.

15
Adult Sexuality

Aging and the wear of time teach many things

—Sophocles

Grow old along with me!
The best is yet to be,
The last of life,
For which the first was made

—Robert Browning

In this chapter you'll discover:

☐ **Why the single life and cohabitation have become popular in recent years.**

☐ **Why many people today postpone marriage and what couples' reasons for marrying are.**

☐ **The important determinants of sexual satisfaction and contentment within a marriage.**

☐ **What factors account for the increase in extramarital sexual relationships today.**

☐ **How widespread divorce is in modern society and what adjustments divorced people must make.**

☐ **That older men and women can remain sexually active as long as they wish, despite changes in their sexual functioning.**

intimacy versus isolation The sixth of eight psychosocial crises proposed by Erik Erikson. It occupies the young adulthood years.

generativity versus self-absorption The seventh of eight psychosocial crises proposed by Erik Erikson. It occurs during middle adulthood.

integrity versus despair The eighth and final psychosocial crisis theorized by Erikson. It takes place during late adulthood.

single life style A life style in which persons choose not to marry.

Adulthood is the dawning of a new stage of life. The challenges people meet at this point in their life cycle are numerous and diverse. Satisfactory integration into adult society and culture requires acceptance of one's sexual self and of responsibility in sexual interactions. Adulthood heralds new sexual roles and expectations, which for most people include selecting a mate, starting a family, and rearing children.

Adult sexual relationships are likely to be more fulfilling, rewarding, and satisfying than adolescent relationships. Most adults know their goals in life and are mentally, socially, sexually, and emotionally mature. When men and women have established a fairly stable organization within themselves, including a realistic awareness of their overall qualities and capacities, they are in a better position to disclose and share themselves with others. They are also more sensitive to their partners' sexual needs than adolescents are. All of these factors tend to make adult sexual relationships more reciprocal and satisfactory than adolescent relationships.

Erik Erikson (1982, 1963) refers to early adulthood as the life stage in which people confront the psychosocial challenge of **intimacy versus isolation.** Intimacy may mean marriage, the establishment of warm and nurturant friendships, or both. People who are unable or unwilling to share themselves with others suffer a sense of loneliness or isolation. Erikson presents two other psychosocial crises during the adult years. The crises of **generativity versus self-absorption,** which takes place in middle adulthood, challenges people to look beyond themselves and care about future generations, or risk leading impoverished, self-centered lives. In the crisis of **integrity versus despair,** which occurs during late adulthood, people evaluate their lives either with a sense of dignity and satisfaction or with a sense of despair and regret. A summary table of Erikson's eight psychosocial crises can be found in Chapter 13.

Marriage is more popular in the United States today than it was at the turn of the century. In the 1990s the great majority of Americans expect to marry, and despite a high divorce rate, most also expect their marriages to last. But not everyone chooses to exchange traditional wedding vows. On the contrary, growing numbers of adults are choosing to adopt such life styles as single living and cohabitation. Let's examine each of these choices before we turn our attention to marriage.

THE SINGLE LIFE STYLE

Some people choose not to marry and adopt the **single life style.** There are currently over 20 million never-married adults 18 years of age and older in the United States. Moreover, this figure has been steadily rising in recent decades: since 1960, the number of single people living apart from relatives has increased over 100 percent (U.S. Bureau of the Census, 1990). Moreover, the populations of divorced and widowed men and women are also growing. Currently, one out of every three married people can expect to be single within the next five years, and by the end of the 1990s this figure may reach one in every two. There are now 67 million single adults in the United States; most will marry or marry again, but the percentage of those who choose to remain single may be growing (U.S. Bureau of the Census, 1990; Simenauer & Carroll, 1982).

Clearly, people's actual circumstances don't always reflect exactly what they want. For example, people may postpone marriage for career reasons, or they may be caught in a generation decimated by war or other destructive forces. Still, statistics from the U.S. Bureau of the Census (1990) and other writers (Stein, 1989, 1981; Masnick & Bane, 1980) suggest that the numbers of single people are growing:

■ Over the last quarter of a century, there has been a large increase in the percentage of people between the ages of 20 and 29 who are single. Among 20- to 24-year-olds, 55 percent of women and 73 percent of men are single; the cor-

Adult Sexuality

responding figures for the 25- to 29-year-old group are 25 percent for women and 38 percent for men.

- During the last 25 years, the percentage of people between the ages of 25 and 34 who have never married and maintain their own households almost tripled. Over 50 percent of never-married women and about 45 percent of never-married men have their own households.
- Today about 28 percent of all women ages 25 to 29 are unmarried, an increase of 16 percent since 1975. About 46 percent of men between the ages of 25 and 29 are unmarried, an increase of 6 percent since 1975.
- Among 30- to 34-year-olds, about 20 percent of men and 13 percent of women have never married, and among 45- to 54-year-olds, 6 percent of men and 5 percent of women have never married.

There are many reasons why the single life is so popular in the 1990s. One of the most important is the growing educational and career opportunities for women (Houseknecht et al., 1987; Rollins, 1986). Pursuing a degree or a career rather than marrying at an early age is proving attractive to many women. Single women (and men) are able to devote more time and energy to their careers. Another reason for the increase in single living is that there are more women than men of marriageable age. Yet another reason is that more people crave the freedom and autonomy single life allows. Others are wary of marriage because of today's gloomy divorce statistics. Table 15–1 lists the factors that affect people's choice of marriage or the single life. As the table shows, people can be motivated by both positive and negative factors— that is, someone may choose to live alone out of a desire to carve out a significant career (positive) or out of the conviction that it is impossible to find a suitable marriage partner (negative).

The single life style can offer considerable potential for happiness, productivity, and self-actualization. Among its positive features are unfettered opportunities for development and change. The years after school are typically a time when men and women clarify their career goals, life-style preferences, and political, social, and sexual

TABLE 15–1

Factors That Affect the Choice of Marriage or the Single Life

NEGATIVE FACTORS	POSITIVE FACTORS
Marriage	
Pressure from parents	Approval of parents
Desire to leave home	Desire for children and own family
Fear of independence	Example of peers
Feelings of loneliness and isolation	Romanticization of marriage
No knowledge or perception of alternatives	Physical attraction
	Love, emotional attachment
Cultural and social discrimination against single people	Security, social status, and prestige
	Legitimization of sexual experience
	Social policies favoring the married
The Single Life	
Lack of friends, prospective mates	Career opportunities and career development
Restricted availability of new experiences	Availability of sexual experiences
Fear of being trapped in a negative one-to-one relationship	Exciting life style
	Psychological and social autonomy
Boredom, unhappiness, anger	Support structures, sustaining friendships, collegial groups, counseling or therapy groups
Poor communication with other sex	
Sexual frustration	

Source: Adapted from Peter Stein, *Single Life*. Reprinted by permission of Peter Stein.

*"What do you say we call this the end of Date One,
and just start Date Two?"*

identities. Those who remain single during this period enjoy more freedom to reflect, experiment, and make significant changes in their beliefs and values. Of course, the freedom to construct new identities can lead to the confusion of having too many new identities. Yet the friends and other support networks that single people develop can help them through some of those conflicts (Stein, 1989, 1981; Stein & Fingrutd, 1985).

A 34-year-old single man offered these thoughts on his life style:

I presently do not have a desire to be married. I enjoy my freedom and do not feel restricted in any way. While marriage may be a possibility for me some day, I'm currently satisfied pursuing a very exciting and rewarding career. I also like the variety of dating partners that the single life makes possible. While there have been some frustrations and bouts of loneliness, for the most part, being single has been a positive experience. (Authors' files)

A 28-year-old single woman reflects:

I was married for six years before my divorce and probably will not get married again. Being single is a more realistic life style for me. I like the variety that it offers, as well as the challenges that it brings. I'm happier in my line of work and have more friends. Also, the dating scene offers unlimited partner possibilities. (Authors' files)

Two diametrically opposed misconceptions about the single life style are quite popular. One is that single men and women are lonely losers. The other is that they

Adult Sexuality

are "swinging" types who live in a fast-paced way and consume a lot of expensive recreation and entertainment. Neither of these stereotypes fits most single people, and the "swinging" image is largely a creation of the media. Consider what this single man has to say:

> One need only live the single life style for a few months to shatter the myths attached to it. I've been single for most of my adult life and have rarely seen the fast-paced life style that the media love to portray. I'm sure the "swinging single" is out there, but he or she hardly represents the majority of single people. Most of us are average, ordinary people carving our way out of life—no more, no less. (Authors' files)

According to Robert Bell (1983), choosing to marry or remain single has important implications for a person's identity. Often the single person finds the world of married couples quite exclusive and is able to enter it in only a limited way. Marriage forges a strong sense of identity for both partners—not only as a couple, but also as individuals. Single people, on the other hand, construct their identities primarily on their own—unless, of course, they are involved in an intimate relationship.

Finally, the literature indicates that single people are not as lonely as popular opinion suggests (see, for example, Stein, 1989, 1981; Cargan & Melko, 1985, 1982). As Robert and Jeanette Lauer (1991) point out, to be single does not necessarily mean to be alone. This is particularly true of living arrangements; many single adults live with their parents, share an apartment with friends, or cohabit.

Single people usually want to meet other single people to date and for companionship. Where do they meet? Single bars were very popular in the 1980s, but seem to have lost their appeal in the 1990s. Women did not like the "meat market" feeling, and some men did not appreciate having to play "aggressor." Health and fitness clubs, newspaper and magazine ads, and dating services have become popular among single adults. Introductions to other available people by friends and engaging in sports or hobbies are other common ways to meet people.

COHABITATION

Cohabitation refers to the sharing of the same residence by an unmarried woman and man. It is extremely popular in the 1990s. Unmarried couples living together have increased from nearly a million in 1977 to about 2.6 million in 1990. (These statistics do not reflect the lesbian and gay partners engaging in this type of life style.) Moreover, it is projected that during the 1990s about 7 percent of all U.S. households will consist of unmarried couples living together (National Center for Health Statistics, 1990; U.S. Bureau of the Census, 1990; Glick, 1988). Figure 15–1 shows how dramatically cohabitation has increased in the United States since 1960.

My girlfriend and I are thinking of living together before we get married. Do many couples do this today?

There are many reasons behind the growing popularity of cohabitation. As we've seen throughout this book, sexual values are changing—for example, there has been a gradual weakening of the old double standard and an increasing acceptance of the idea that relationships should be judged by their values rather than by their legality (see Chapter 6). Moreover, the widespread availability of contraceptives and the legalization of abortion have reduced the risk of pregnancy among sexually active cohabitants, which gives them less reason to marry. Peer support for cohabitation encourages couples to remain unmarried, and many contemporary men and women don't view marriage as having the social status it once did. Finally, adults who have witnessed the breakdown of their parents' marriage often have little faith in formal marriage as an institution that provides security and happiness (Oliver, 1982).

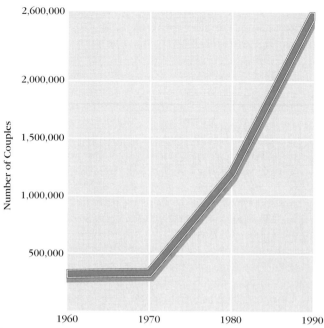

FIGURE 15–1
Growing Number of Unmarried Couples Living Together in the United States.

(Data from U.S. Bureau of the Census, 1990, 1988; National Center for Health Statistics, 1990.)

Most cohabitants are under 35, although one source (Macklin, 1988) reveals that the average cohabiting couple is about six years older than the average couple at first marriage. Often one of the partners has been separated or divorced. Cohabitation is also popular among college students, largely because of the availability of off-campus housing, co-ed dormitories, and liberal student attitudes. In recent years there has been an increase in the number of older cohabitants as well. It is estimated that approximately 350,000 men and women over age 55 live together (U.S. Bureau of the Census, 1990; Glick, 1988; Glick & Spanier, 1980).

Many types of arrangements come under the classification cohabitation. Some couples live together for purely economic reasons or for convenience; they have no intention of becoming involved in a personal intimate relationship. Others cohabit

Money is often one of major reasons people decide to live together. Sharing expenses can be very helpful, and it can also be a good way to learn about a partner's values.

448

precisely to establish a close relationship. The largest category of cohabitants consists of couples who believe marriage is on the horizon. For these couples, living together is a precursor to marriage, not an alternative to it (Bumpass, 1989; Macklin, 1988; Cherlin & Furstenberg, 1983). One study (Bumpass & Sweet, 1988) found that more than half of recently married couples had cohabited first. A woman explains why she lived with her fiancé before they got married:

> **Kevin and I lived together for two years before we were married. We had been going together for about 18 months when we made the decision. I was finishing up my graduate degree and he was working in an accounting firm nearby. It was great for our relationship and economically convenient as well. We never looked at living together as an alternative to marriage. If anything, it was a trial arrangement before the real thing. We learned a lot about each other's personal living habits and picked up on things we wouldn't have seen if we were just dating. (Authors' files)**

Age makes a difference in couples' attitudes toward cohabitation. Older single men and women tend to think of living together as a transitory experience rather than a prologue to wedlock. Young men and women, especially students, consider living together a trial marriage. The younger the partners, the more likely they are to view the arrangement this way. Besides age, a few other characteristics affect attitudes toward cohabitation. College-educated people are somewhat more likely to think of living together as a permanent relationship than people who graduated from high school. Single professionals are less prone to live together than white- and blue-collar people. These characteristics, however, do not have the pronounced effect on attitudes that age has. Younger single people—who are statistically less likely to have been married—see cohabitation as a preliminary part of the marriage process, while older single people—who are statistically more likely to be divorced—view it as an escape from marriage (Simenauer & Carroll, 1982).

Two forms of cohabitation can be distinguished by their duration: courtship and long-term premarital cohabitation. Courtship cohabitation usually occurs between young adults who have never been married. In this type of cohabitation, living together is not expected to be a permanent arrangement, nor is there a desire for children to be part of the relationship. Most of the participants in courtship cohabitation have defined themselves as not yet ready for marriage. Courtship cohabitation typically lasts for only a few months, and is best understood as a variation of steady dating that openly acknowledges sexual intimacy (Atwater, 1985).

Premarital cohabitation can last for years. Some partners enjoy this opportunity to combine love, work, and sex in a setting that is free of parental control yet lacking in the constraints posed by a legal bond. Also, for some it fills the need to test the ability to relate intimately with a partner, a necessary skill for the survival of legal marriage. Cohabitation allows some people to grow and change together without forcing them to make a permanent mutual commitment before they feel ready for this. And it may allow them to separate without the burden of failure and guilt associated with divorce.

At the same time, cohabitation has its negative features, and people considering cohabitation need to consider potential problems (see the box on "Legal Considerations for Cohabitants"). Some partners feel guilty about their living arrangements and may even try to keep these arrangements secret so as not to upset or anger parents, other relatives, or friends. And some partners feel stunted and closed in by this life style; for example, they may want to have their own children or adopt and raise others. Pregnancy often poses complications for those choosing cohabitation over marriage (Macklin, 1988). For example, when cohabitants do have children, separating can be as difficult and distressing as any legal divorce.

MAKING USE
OF WHAT
WE KNOW

Legal
Considerations for
Cohabitants

There are no state laws regulating cohabitation. Consequently, any "rights" concerning property and earnings have been established through court decisions. For example, the California Supreme Court ruled in 1976 that a person has the right to claim a share of a former cohabitant's property and earnings if it can be shown that the couple had such an agreement while they were living together. (The award is called *palimony*, a word play on the traditional alimony awarded to a divorced spouse.) Since 1976, other states have followed California in ruling that cohabitants have a legal obligation to one another. And in a few localities like Berkeley and West Los Angeles, the legal rights of gay and lesbian cohabitants are recognized.

Therefore, if you are contemplating cohabitation—or are already in such a living arrangement—you should consider drafting an agreement that spells out the economic parameters of your relationship. To draft an informal contract, you and your partner should begin *before* the beginning of your relationship— by listing the major items that each of you brought to the partnership. This will make it easier to walk out with them later on. If you decide to make joint purchases, and particularly if you buy a house, you need to spell out your proportionate shares of ownership. Both of your names should be on the deed and mortgage (or rental agreement). You also need to state clearly what you agree is to happen to the property when you split up—for example, whether the house will be sold and the proceeds split evenly. If

you or your partner wants to keep the house, that person should have the option of buying the other out. In that case, you will need a way to put a value on the house. You could average three appraisals, or settle for just one. You should also specify in your contract how the mortgage (or rent) will be paid immediately after one partner moves out and the other is left to deal with the bills.

Your agreement should also clearly state who is responsible for which chores, particularly if one partner is expected to do more to compensate for a lower cash contribution. If one partner promises to support the other in case of separation, the amount of the payment and how long it is to continue should be spelled out.

The easiest and simplest agreement for cohabitants is a waiver of all financial claims on each other. The waiver should clearly state the following:

- Any property acquired while you live together belongs to whoever paid for it.
- Neither person expects compensation for any services rendered the other.
- Neither person has an obligation to support the other.
- Neither person has any intention of sharing earnings or property with the other.
- Any future agreements to share earnings or property must be clearly stated in writing. (Adapted from Macovsky, 1983)

MARRIAGE

As we said at the beginning of the chapter, most people in the United States intend to marry, and despite the rising divorce rate, they expect their marriages to be permanent. Although many lesbian and gay partners consider themselves married, and some have formal ceremonies to celebrate their union, these people are not included in the census count of those married in the United States. If current trends continue, about 93 percent of Americans will exchange marriage vows at one time or another in their lives. However, there have been some notable shifts in marriage trends among young Americans. In 1970 about 45 percent of men and 64 percent of women in their 20s had already married. By 1990, these percentages had dipped to 30 and 50, respectively. Thus, while demographic trends indicate that the overwhelming majority of modern Americans marry, people are postponing this step (National Center for Health Statistics, 1990; U.S. Bureau of Census, 1990; Glick, 1988).

Marriage rates peaked in the United States in 1946 in the surge of weddings that followed World War II. Then the marriage rate was 16.4 per 1,000 people. The rate remained relatively high throughout the 1950s, then started to decline in the 1960s and 1970s. Today the marriage rate per 1,000 persons is about 9.7 (National Center for Health Statistics, 1990; U.S. Bureau of the Census, 1990). However, this rate is still higher than the marriage rate in many other countries (see the box on "Marriage Rates Around the Globe").

In 1990 the total number of weddings in the United States was just over 2,405,000. Such a large number might seem surprising considering the decline in the marriage rate, until we remember that the maturing of the large post–World War II baby boom generation has greatly increased the number of people of prime marriageable age (National Center for Health Statistics, 1990; U.S. Bureau of the Census, 1990).

Age at First Marriage

The timing of marriage in the 1990s is different from past eras. Because of the trend to postpone marriage, the median age at first marriage has increased. A *median* is a statistic that represents the midpoint in a series of numbers, scores, or the like. Thus *median age* here means that one-half of the people marrying for the first time in a given year get married before the given age, and one-half after. As you can see from Figure 15–2, the median age at first marriage has risen pretty steadily over the years.

The reasons already given for choosing the single life (e.g., pursuing a degree or career) also apply to the postponement of marriage. One strictly demographic factor during the last two decades is known as the "marriage squeeze"—a consequence of the upward trend in births during the baby boom (the high birth rate between 1946 and 1964). Women are usually two or three years younger than the men they marry. Thus a woman born in 1947, when the birth rate had risen, would be likely to marry a man born in 1944 or 1945, when the birth rate was still low.

FIGURE 15–2
Rise in Median Age at First Marriage.
(Data from U.S. Bureau of the Census, 1990, 1988.)

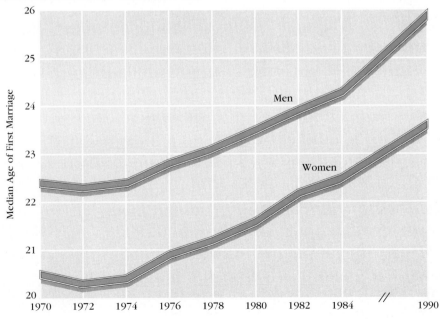

A WORLD OF DIFFERENCES

Marriage Rates Around the Globe

Marriage rates in the United States are statistically high, ranking near the top of the list in comparison with other industrialized nations such as Japan, West Germany, Canada, Israel, and Australia. France, Spain, and Ireland have over twice as many people who have never married as the United States has (Broderick, 1989).

In contrast to the nuptial postponement patterns of the United States, certain countries encourage early marriages. Bangladesh has the highest known proportion of married 15- to 19-year-old women (70 percent) and the lowest mean age at marriage (11.6) in the world. Proportions of 15- to 19-year-old women are also high and age at marriage low in the populous countries of Indonesia (30 percent married, age at marriage 16.4), Nepal (59 percent and 16.0 years), and Pakistan (31 percent and 15.3 years). Collectively, the developed nations of North America (Canada and the United States), Europe, and Australia and New Zealand, along with Japan, have the lowest proportion of never-married women aged 15 to 19. Virtually all are below 10 percent on this measure (Senderowitz & Paxman, 1985).

In parts of Northern and Western Europe marriage rates have been declining since 1970. This is particularly evident in Sweden, Denmark, and Switzerland, nations where cohabitation and marriage postponement are widespread. Should these trends persist, it is predicted that only 60 percent of men and women in Northern and Western European countries will ever marry. Though cohabitation has become a way of life for many of Europe's young adults, it was uncommon until the end of the 1960s. Sweden and Denmark were the first countries to accept this life style. In contrast to the pattern in the United States, cohabitation in European nations is not a prelude to marriage. Rather it is a life style in and of itself. Instead of being a trial marriage, it is regarded by many as a distinct alternative to marriage.

This development has affected the age at which woman first marry, if they marry at all. The mean age at first marriage for Swedish women is 27.3, while for Danish women it is 26.1. In these two nations, as well as in Iceland, where the proportion of out-of-wedlock births is

In India recently a 10-year-old bride was rescued from her new 60-year-old husband. Child marriage, long an accepted practice in India, has at last been outlawed.

well above 40 percent, the mean age of women at first marriage is now higher than the mean age of women at first birth. It is not uncommon for children to be present at their parents' first wedding ceremony.

The decline in the propensity to marry in Northern and Western Europe is paralleled by a general reluctance to remarry. While the number of second marriages has increased in recent years, a good many divorced and widowed men and women opt to remain single rather than enter into a new legal bond. In many cases, this decision is influenced by financial concerns, such as the prospective loss of benefits or pensions derived from the former marriage. But a more basic reason may be the waning of marriage as an institution. With the dramatic improvement in living conditions brought about by the welfare state and the widespread acceptance of cohabitation, marriage is no longer necessary for European young adults. Consequently, never marrying and not remarrying after the dissolution of a marriage are comfortable options. For that matter, divorce is much easier to consider than it was generations ago (van de Kaa, 1987).

A wedding has traditionally been an occasion for joy, with friends and relatives wishing the young couple a long and happy married life. Yet some say that marriage is in danger of losing its status as an institution and of becoming simply another relationship. What do you think?

Consequently, since the late 1960s, there has been a shortage of men, of all races, in the primary ages for marriage. By 1970, the number of white men 20 to 26 years of age was only 93 percent of the number of white women 18 to 24. The corresponding figure for black men was 82 percent (Glick, 1988, 1984). By 1980, this percentage had escalated somewhat, to 98 percent for all races. By 1995, the figure is expected to reach 108 percent, as the declining birth rates of the 1960s and early 1970s create a reversal of the marriage squeeze phenomenon in which there will be an excess of men of prime marriageable age.

Why People Marry

Why do people marry? The motives for entering the married state are many and diverse. The most popular reasons are love, companionship, conformity, legitimization of sex and children, sense of readiness, and legal benefits (Turner & Helms, 1988).

LOVE. Couples choose to marry because they want to share a loving and enduring relationship, one they feel is best secured within the institution of marriage.

COMPANIONSHIP. Sharing one's life with a regular companion tends to generate emotional and psychological well-being, which, in turn, breeds feelings of security and comfort.

CONFORMITY. Getting married is still seen by most people as the final stage of the mate selection process. Contributing to this motive are social pressures, both subtle and direct, from family, friends, and others prompting the couple to marry.

LEGITIMIZATION OF SEX. Married status confers social approval on sexual behavior. Even though many contemporary Americans have a rather tolerant attitude toward premarital and nonmarital sexual relationships, marriage is still seen as the most legitimate relationship.

LEGITIMIZATION OF CHILDREN. Many couples would never consider marriage if they didn't want to have a child. Children born into a marital relationship have a legitimate identity. Moreover, some segments of society feel that bearing a child out of wedlock is immoral.

SENSE OF READINESS. Many couples report that they decided to marry when they felt "ready." They had accomplished what they wanted to accomplish—whether finishing an education, launching a career, or tending to personal or family matters—before they married.

LEGAL BENEFITS. Married status has tax advantages, as well as insurance and certain legal benefits. For couples concerned about the economic stability of their relationship, this motive may be strong.

As we've already pointed out, the motives for *not* marrying include both the belief that one can have love and companionship without a legal contract—which is increasingly true—and the fear of losing one's freedom and independence—which doesn't have to be true. Just as these motives for staying single can be wrong, so can some motives for getting married. As Table 15–1 shows, social pressure and a host of other factors can lead people to marry before they're ready. One divorced man reflects on his early marriage:

> **I was too young at the time to realize that we got married for other people's reasons. Marriage just seemed like the thing to do and our parents were all for it. If I could do it all over, I would have dated more women and made more of an effort to understand relationships in general. I would also have taken more time. My wife and I rushed to get married, and before we knew it, the children were born. While we love the kids, becoming parents put added pressure on us and eventually made things worse. (Authors' files)**

Marital Sexual Adjustments

Does a married couple's sex life tend to fizzle over the years?

The married couple's overall happiness and harmony are determined by the quality of interaction between them. Both partners are responsible for making a marriage work. How committed they are to meeting each other's expectations will ultimately determine whether the marriage is successful (Lauer & Lauer, 1991; Stinnett, Walters, & Stinnett, 1991; Fincham & Bradbury, 1990; Kantor & Okun, 1989; Turner & Helms, 1988; Swenson & Trahaug, 1985).

Interaction is very important to sexual satisfaction. A harmonious, honest, and stable relationship relieves people of sexual anxieties. Mutuality, trust, and understanding are important determinants of sexual fulfillment.

Most married couples regularly engage in sexual intercourse, although the frequency declines with advancing age. Research indicates that married couples in their 20s and 30s have intercourse an average of two or three times per week (Frank & Enos, 1983). One study of over 7,000 married couples (Blumstein & Schwartz, 1983) revealed that after 10 years 63 percent of couples were still having intercourse at least once a week. Rarely does sex become infrequent in a marriage. Only 15 percent of couples married more than 10 years had sex once a month or less often. This study also uncovered a link between frequency of intercourse and a couple's satisfaction with their sex lives.

According to Carl Rubenstein (1988), the arrival of children often causes a decline in the frequency of a couple's sexual relations. Of the approximately 6,000 couples Rubenstein surveyed, about one-fifth reported having sexual relations once a month or less, and one-third said that they had sex between once a week and twice a month. Many of the new mothers surveyed attributed this decline to lack of desire and overall fatigue.

Regardless of how often partners engage in sexual intercourse, the more they enjoy sexual interaction, the happier and better satisfied they tend to be. Sally Wendkos Olds (1985) observes that when partners lose interest in each other sexually, they also tend to lose interest in doing other things together. Thus boredom in bed breeds boredom out of it (and vice versa).

What Is Marital Sexuality Really Like?

Marital sexuality is a dynamic, ongoing process. Although we have learned a great deal in recent years regarding its expression and importance to couples, according to William Talmadge (1985), several inaccurate notions about marital sexual behavior continue to plague us.

THE SEXUAL RELATIONSHIP AND THE MARRIAGE RELATIONSHIP ARE SEPARATE ENTITIES. This myth implies that there is no correspondence between marital sexual fulfillment and other marital factors. The truth is that the sexual and the nonsexual sides of marriage are closely related. Factors that seem to strongly link the two sides are the degree of communication, emotional intimacy, and self-disclosure within the relationship, and prior experiences with premarital sex.

SEX IN MARRIAGE CREATES INTIMACY. According to this myth, sexual expression between partners automatically creates intimacy within the relationship. However, research reveals that effective communication and self-disclosure are more apt to generate intimacy. Equally important is the ability of the couple to *express* their emotional intimacy.

MARITAL SEX IS ALWAYS EXCITING, ROMANTIC, AND ORGASMIC. Particularly among newly married people there is an expectation that sex will always be delightful. This expectation is unrealistic and often leads to harsh disappointment in the marriage. It denies the developmental stresses and strains that all couples go through, and ignores the disruptive influence of health, personal, and career crises.

For many people, one great thing about sex within marriage is that they have the time and opportunity to learn how to please each other and to experiment continually with new and different techniques of lovemaking.

455

SEXUAL FREQUENCY IS THE PRIME INDICATOR OF SEXUAL COMPATIBILITY AND MARITAL HAPPINESS. As we have seen, the rate of intercourse tends to decline after the first year of marriage. But over the duration of the marriage, the frequency of intercourse often goes up and down according to the mood of the relationship. *Frequency* of intercourse is not an indicator of marital happiness. Rather, it is sexual *satisfaction* that is highly correlated with marital happiness. Moreover, mutuality of enjoyment appears to be the key factor in marital sexual compatibility.

POOR SEX LEADS TO UNHAPPY MARRIAGES AND EXTRAMARITAL AFFAIRS. The basis of this misconception is the belief that if partners have sex often, use many varied techniques, and keep each other happy with sex, then their marriage will be happy. As we've already seen, neither high nor low rates of sexual relations create marital happiness or unhappiness. Sexual incompatibility is a symptom of marital unhappiness rather than the cause of it. More often than not, the difficulties within the relationship (poor communication style, an imbalance of power, lack of equity, and so on) are the reasons for the sexual incompatibility as well as for the marital unhappiness. Relatedly, extramarital affairs usually are not caused by poor marital sexual relations, but rather by the poor quality of the whole marital relationship. Later on in the chapter, we will devote more attention to the topic of extramarital sexual affairs.

HAPPILY MARRIED COUPLES DO NOT HAVE SEX PROBLEMS. This misconception overlooks the developmental changes that every marriage goes through. As we mentioned earlier, research tells us that there is a decline in the frequency of intercourse during the first year after a child's birth. Research also shows that some happily married couples experience sexual difficulties. Whether the couple needs therapeutic help for these problems is determined by the quality of their marital relationship. Those couples who communicate well with each other, are emotionally intimate, and have good problem resolution skills, can usually resolve their sexual difficulties without seeking outside help.

IF I AM ONLY ATTRACTIVE ENOUGH AND DO ALL OF THE THINGS THAT MY PARTNER WISHES, THEN WE WILL HAVE A SATISFYING MARITAL SEXUAL RELATIONSHIP. This myth denies the individual. It implies that if one partner will only be and do everything the other partner wants, then the couple will enjoy constant sexual satisfaction. Unfortunately, many people accept this myth, which is a great favorite with the media. Television, popular magazines, and the movies lead them to believe that if they act as romantically as possible—wearing the "right" type of cologne or perfume, drinking the "right" type of beverages, and going to the "right" places—they will enchant their partners and live happily ever after. But people are individuals who have lives outside the marital relationship. No one can exist entirely for another.

Instead of being governed by myth, Talmadge suggests that married couples view their sexual relationship as a complex set of interacting variables—communication, affection, intimacy, problem perception and problem resolution skills, commitment, ability to work and play, and sex drive—operating within their total marriage relationship. It is the total relationship that determines sexual compatibility. In addition, marital sexual compatibility is greatly enhanced by the couple's commitment to engage in a long-term process of interaction in which they express their affection, needs, desires, likes, and dislikes in a trusting, caring atmosphere.

EXTRAMARITAL SEXUAL RELATIONSHIPS

Many married men and women go outside the boundaries of marriage in an attempt to find sexual satisfaction and pleasure. An extramarital sexual relationship can be defined as any sexual activity that occurs with someone other than one's spouse. There are two major categories of extramarital sexual relationships: nonconsensual and consensual.

Nonconsensual Extramarital Relationships

A **nonconsensual extramarital relationship,** commonly referred to as *adultery* (see Chapter 1), is sexual activity with another person without the consent of one's spouse. There are different types of nonconsensual extramarital relationships, depending on the form of involvement and escalation. Of these, the *isolated affair* is the most common. This relationship, often referred to as a "one-night stand," is defined as sexual activity without emotional commitment or future involvement. The less common *intense affair* is characterized not only by regular sexual activity but also by emotional involvement with the partner and the escalation of attachment.

Although estimates vary on how many men and women engage in nonconsensual extramarital relationships, there is fair agreement that at least half of all married men and about a quarter of all married women have affairs at one time or another (see, for example, Moultrup, 1990; Seagraves, 1989; Sponaugle, 1989; Wyatt et al., 1988; Forsyth & Fournet, 1987; Brecher, 1984; Petersen et al., 1983; Wolfe, 1982; Hassitt, 1981). These figures may be too low, though, since some respondents are probably reluctant to admit to such behavior. For this reason, Frederick Humphrey (1987) suggests that nonconsensual extramarital sexual relationships occur in a majority of all marriages.

Why are nonconsensual extramarital sexual relationships so common? To begin with, some segments of our society have adopted a very permissive attitude toward sexual behavior, and the resulting climate of freedom encourages sexual expression that would otherwise be reined in. The constant theme of extramarital sex in the media is certainly an encouragement. Thus some people have affairs simply because they are curious about "what it would be like" with someone else. Others are bored with their marital sexual relationship—quite possibly because of their own inability or unwillingness to experiment with new ways to turn their partners on. Many people say that sexual frustration is their underlying motivation. Others use these relationships for the companionship they offer or for a boost to their egos. A faltering sense of masculinity or femininity within the marital relationship prompts some men and women to turn to an outsider for reinforcement or fulfillment. Finally, common misconceptions about the nature of extramarital affairs (see the "Myths and Misconceptions" box) may account for some of their appeal.

What kinds of people are more likely to become involved in a nonconsensual extramarital relationship? Although most people who have affairs are somewhat dissatisfied, sexually and otherwise, within their marriages, some of those who stray are actually very happy and content with their spouses and their marriage. Still, married people who have affairs have certain predictable qualities: they tend to be liberated and also to have a high need for sexual intimacy and a low level of emotional dependency on their marriage partners. Some use affairs as a form of rebellion or retaliation against their partners—especially to "get even" with a partner who had or is having an extramarital sexual relationship (Sponaugle, 1989; Wyatt et al., 1988; Forsyth & Fournet, 1987; Brecher, 1984; Macklin, 1980).

These married men provide some reasons for having affairs:

I wanted to feel more appreciated.

It didn't start out this way, but one of the primary reasons for continuing my affair was the satisfaction it brought. I got to know new dimensions about myself that I never knew existed.

nonconsensual extramarital relationship Sexual activity with another person without the consent of one's spouse.

How common are extramarital affairs? Why do some marriage partners like to cheat on each other?

MYTHS AND MISCONCEPTIONS

Misconceptions About Infidelity

According to Frank Pittman (1989), people have many faulty ideas about extramarital affairs. Let's look at seven of the most inaccurate notions of what causes infidelity and how to handle it.

Everybody has affairs.

Although many married men and women have affairs, the majority have only one, and much infidelity occurs in the last year of a dying marriage. Most husbands and wives are faithful to each other most of the time. The vast majority of Americans strongly believe in marital fidelity, though they do not always achieve it.

Affairs are good for a marriage.

Many people mistakenly think that infidelity can revive a dull marriage. In reality, an affair is dangerous and can damage or destroy a relationship. Even a little bit of infidelity can set in motion forces that can eventually destroy a marriage.

Affairs prove that love has disappeared from the marriage.

Whether or not the adulterous partner loves the other partner, the adulterer may remain committed to the marriage. From the very beginning of the marriage relationship, the feelings one partner has toward the other are complicated. This complexity cannot be reduced to a simple question about the presence or absence of love.

The lover is sexier than the spouse.

Because an affair involves sex, it is often thought that the object of the affair is a champion sexual athlete. While this is sometimes true, many married people who have affairs acknowledge that sex was actually better at home. Moreover, some affairs do not involve much sexual activity. Often the lover's appeal is based on difference from the spouse rather than superiority to the spouse. Many people who become involved in an extramarital relationship are not seeking an alternative to their marriage, but rather a supplement to it.

The affair is the fault of the person betrayed.

The irresponsible accusation "You drove me to it" is often accepted by both the betrayer and the betrayed. This kind of accusation reflects the defense mechanism known as projection—blaming another person for one's own shortcomings or failures. In reality, one partner cannot "drive" the other into having an affair.

If you ignore a spouse's affair, it will eventually stop.

Ignoring an affair allows one to also ignore problems in the marriage and evade doing anything to solve them. It must be remembered that affairs thrive on secrecy. The conspiracy between the lovers produces an alliance, while the deceit and lies practiced at home create discomfort between the marriage partners. We all tend to feel bound to those who share our secrets and uncomfortable with those to whom we are lying. The greatest power of an extramarital relationship may well be its secrecy. The greatest weakness in a marriage may well be a tendency to avoid the issues.

After an affair, divorce is inevitable.

There is no mistaking the fact that an affair constitutes a crisis for most marriages. However, it is incorrect to assume that an affair automatically dooms a marriage. Although some couples do divorce and others stay together in an increasingly unhappy and loveless arrangement, some couples are capable of using the crisis to improve their marriage and renew their love. Counseling or therapy often helps couples to work through and resolve their marital problems.

Being viewed as attractive or a turn-on to my lover were important reasons to continue the affair.

I became engulfed by the excitement and hidden quality of the affair. Its secretive nature was a turn-on in itself.

I loved the sexual excitement. (Authors' files)

Married women offered these reasons for their infidelity:

I needed to feel needed. My lover was tender and caring, always wanting to fill my every need. He made me feel like a total woman, something my husband couldn't do.

The sexual pleasuring was the underlying motivation. He was a fantastic lover and taught me new and different ways to enjoy sex and love my body.

He truly cared about me. We were lovers as well as intimate friends. We shared everything together.

I chose to be unfaithful because my relationship with my husband was miserable. It had a hollow, empty quality and I saw no hope of it ever improving. (Authors' files)

One source (Atwater, 1982) points out that the opportunities for nonconsensual extramarital relationships are greater in urban societies where people come into contact with so many other people every day. The workplace, especially, requires married men and women to spend considerable time together. In this vein, the growing incidence of nonconsensual extramarital sex among women is probably due, in part, to the influx of married women into the workplace in recent years.

Kathleen Seagraves (1989) agrees that nonconsensual extramarital relationships are more common among working wives than among homemakers. Interestingly, she found in her research that while the frequency of affairs declines with age in men, it goes up with age in women. She also discovered that husbands tend to have their first affair within five years of marriage, while wives have their first affair later on in the marriage. Couples who are married two years or less have fewer affairs than those married ten or more years. Finally, husbands tend to have affairs with women who are roughly the same age as they are, while wives are often drawn to younger as well as to older men.

Robert Bell (1983) writes that deceit and dishonesty are typical of the nonconsensual extramarital sexual relationship. Excuses must be fabricated to make up for absences and time away from home, and sometimes to explain changes in mood or dress. More often than not, lies must be spun to shroud the situation, not only from the partner and other loved ones, but also from work associates and even friends and acquaintances.

These married men share their feelings of guilt about being unfaithful to their wives:

When I was younger, I cheated on my wife more than once. To this day I feel guilty and deceitful.

My wife never knew about my lover. When the affair took place, I'd sneak around, always lying and making excuses about my whereabouts. Deep down inside, I felt cheap and dishonest. (Authors' files)

A married woman puts her negative feelings about affairs this way:

While the affair did wonders for my self-worth, it left me frustrated and, worst of all, heartbroken. (Authors' files)

Extramarital affairs complicate people's lives. The details of where and when to meet have to be carefully and secretly planned to avoid suspicion and discovery.

Under these conditions, the chance of the relationship developing into a deep and meaningful love affair is usually doomed from the start.

Frederick Humphrey (1987) underlines the serious negative consequences of extramarital affairs for the couple's children and family, the extramarital sex partner, and that partner's family. The consequences for the adulterous spouse can be equally serious: the violation of a religious code of behavior; the breaking of trust; guilt, anger, and regret; lost respect and love; the disruption of a career and the loss of reputation; sexually transmitted diseases; sexual conflicts and dysfunctions; and sometimes even suicide or homicide.

Consensual Extramarital Relationships

consensual extramarital relationship Sexual activity with someone other than one's spouse, but with the knowledge of that spouse.

A **consensual extramarital relationship** is sexual activity with someone other than one's spouse, but with the spouse's knowledge. Such extramarital sexual involvement may even be supported and encouraged by the spouse. Many sources note that consensual affairs are far less common than those of a nonconsensual variety (see, for example, Seagraves, 1989). Two types of consensual extramarital sexual relationships that have been much discussed since the 1970s are open marriage and swinging.

open marriage A marriage that is flexible and stresses the importance of continual self-growth for both partners.

OPEN MARRIAGE. In contrast to the traditional marriage, an **open marriage** is flexible and stresses the importance of continual self-growth for both partners. Although we

TABLE 15–2

Traditional and Open Marriages

ISSUE	TRADITIONAL MARRIAGE	OPEN MARRIAGE
Expectations for the future	Believe marriage will last forever	Value change in the marital relationship, even if change results in ending the marriage
Privacy	Don't believe in separate vacations	Feel that it is important to spend some vacation time apart
Communication	Don't share fantasies or dreams that might hurt each other	Share all dreams; believe in self-disclosure
Role flexibility	Have specific roles	Exchange roles to suit convenience
Companionship	Believe that a caring relationship with someone of the other sex is a risk to the marriage	Believe that a caring relationship with someone of the other sex is acceptable
Equality	Allow one partner to have more freedom and responsibility than the other	Grant freedom and responsibility to each spouse equally
Identity	Compromise personal life styles to meet long-term needs of the marriage	Believe each spouse is free to pursue his or her own unique life style
Trust	Worry about what spouse may do when the other is away	Have no qualms about what spouse may do in the other's absence

Source: Adapted from Wachowiak & Bragg, 1980.

Adult Sexuality

might expect this to be true of any marriage, as Table 15–2 shows, partners in open marriages and traditional marriages make quite different assumptions.

The proponents of open marriage believe that marriage should not place partners in bondage to each other, diminishing their individual identity in order to create a "couple image" and enforcing togetherness in the belief that this is the only way to preserve the relationship. They feel that marriage should not impose traditional rules on people, suggesting instead that couples learn to communicate openly so they can arrive at a mutual consensus for living together (Wachowiak & Bragg, 1980).

Open marriage encourages trust, freedom, and full communication, both within and outside the boundaries of marriage. Each partner is free to engage in friendships with the other sex, and even in extramarital sexual relationships—although the latter is a controversial area. All points considered, this nontraditional life style is not practical for most couples since it promotes feelings of insecurity, resentment toward outside parties, and sexual jealousy (Watson, 1981).

SWINGING. Swinging, sometimes called *mate swapping*, is a relationship involving two or more married couples who decide to switch sexual partners or to engage in group sex. Swingers are usually upper-middle-class people who are employed in professional and white-collar occupations. Swinging is rare among people under 30, especially men.

Swingers use a variety of sources to locate partners, including newspaper ads, swinging bars, and socials sponsored by swinging magazines. Swinging takes different forms. *Closed swinging* refers to a situation in which several sets of couples pair off in separate rooms in order to engage in sex. *Open swinging* refers to group sex, or sex engaged in in the presence of others (sometimes called an "orgy"). A wide variety of sexual activities are usually accepted, and the stress is on sex for purely physical pleasure rather than for emotional gratification (Dacey, 1982).

Many couples plunge into swinging in the hope that it will improve a strained relationship. Some regard it as an adventure, a way to act out their fantasies. For those who are so inclined, swinging offers certain sexual satisfactions:

> **Both my wife and I like sexual variety and know a couple who feel the same way. The four of us were drinking pretty heavily one night when the topic of swinging came up. I remember what a turn-on it was just talking about it. Anyway, one thing led to another and we swapped partners. It was incredibly arousing to be in bed with another woman while hearing the sexual moaning of my wife in the next room. It was even more exciting later when we told each other what it was like. (Authors' files)**

Robert Whitehurst (1985) believes that swinging, by its very nature, tends to be short-lived, especially with men. He feels that once a man's fantasy of having the candy-store freedom to grab all the sex he can from anyone nearby is gratified, he is rapidly satiated. Male sexual appetites tend to be large in prospect but small in retrospect (wanting lots before the fact, but becoming sated more easily than imagined). It seems that while women are more reluctant to begin swinging, men are more reluctant to continue it. Swinging has become less intriguing to both men and women under the contemporary threat of AIDS and other sexually transmitted diseases.

swinging A relationship involving two or more married couples who decide to switch sexual partners or to engage in group sex. Also called *mate swapping*.

What is meant by "swinging"?

DIVORCE

The dissolution of a marriage by divorce or death can occur at any stage of adulthood. Although death is the leading cause of family breakup in the United States, our divorce rates are astronomical. In 1990, 1,172,000 divorces were granted in this country, a total involving nearly two and one-half million adults and over one million children (National Center for Health Statistics, 1990). In this section we examine some statistical trends related to divorce, and then discuss the sexual and other adjustments and adaptations divorced people must make.

Divorce Rates and Trends

In the United States in 1990, there were about 4.7 divorces per 1,000 population, a high rate compared with other countries. In Poland, for example, the divorce rate is 1.3 per thousand, and in El Salvador it is only 0.3. Moreover, the U.S. rate in 1990 was almost double the rate recorded for 1965 (National Center for Health Statistics, 1990; U.S. Bureau of the Census, 1990; Population Reference Bureau, 1985).

It is often reported that almost 50 percent of all U.S. marriages end in divorce. This is a specious statistic, as a little analysis will show. The 50 percent figure was arrived at by comparing all the divorces granted in one year with all the marriages performed during the same year. So in 1990, for example, there were about half as many divorces as there were new marriages (National Center for Health Statistics, 1990). But because divorces granted in any year are the result of marriages performed in earlier years, this statistic is greatly misleading. It makes no sense to compare the number of divorces for marriages contracted from one to 50 years ago with the number of the current year's weddings.

Divorce does not affect all social groups equally. Divorce rates are higher among African-Americans than among whites, for example, probably more for economic reasons (African-Americans experience greater job instability, lower income, and higher unemployment) than for racial/cultural reasons. Also, the higher the educational level, the lower the divorce rate—with one rather interesting exception: women with graduate degrees. The disproportionately high divorce rates of these women may be due to their social independence and economic security. Divorce is also related to the marriage cycle. People tend to divorce relatively early in their marriage. Thus divorce rates are at their peak two to five years after marriage, a statistic that has changed little over the years (National Center for Health Statistics, 1990; Booth et al., 1986; Glenn & Supancic, 1984; Spanier & Thompson, 1984).

Adjustments and Adaptations

After going through a divorce, people need to critically examine themselves and consider what they want to do with the rest of their lives. Unfortunately, the immediate aftermath of a divorce is rarely a time when people are able to think clearly and employ good judgment. The legal battle may have been long and tiring. When children are involved, adjustments multiply and become much more complex (see, for example, Hetherington, 1989; Hetherington, Hagan, & Anderson, 1989; Maccoby & Mnookin, 1989; Wallerstein & Blakeslee, 1989; Wilson, 1989).

It is not uncommon to experience a sense of failure, loneliness, sadness, and fear after a divorce. Some people, however, feel relieved to be starting over. One woman remembers the emotions she experienced the day after her divorce was finalized:

> The courtroom proceedings were a blur, but I do remember a sense of relief once things were finalized. The pressure and turmoil began to subside and I felt that a new chapter in my life was beginning. I must say, though, that after the divorce I felt a bit uptight about the great unknown that stretched ahead. The single life was new territory for me, and the prospects of facing life alone created a few sleepless

Adult Sexuality

nights. **I had a great support group, though, and received the guidance of many trusted friends. That helped a lot.** (Authors' files)

As divorced people move from the mutual identity of a marriage toward autonomy, they often find they must redefine themselves. The divorce process is a change in status that is only complete when one defines one's status as "single" rather than "divorced" and attains stability and harmony in this new life style. The time it takes to complete this process varies from person to person. Sometimes it does not happen until one or both of the divorced parties create a mutual identity with another person. With that step, the feeling of tentativeness usually disappears. For some people, though, the process of separation is never completed. They are never able to construct a new harmonious life style (Vaughan, 1986).

Men are more prone than women to deny they need help or support after a divorce, perhaps because they have been socialized to think they must uphold an image of independence at all costs. Nonetheless, they often experience anger, guilt, shame, and fear. When children are involved, their concerns and anxieties mount. Divorced men face a considerable change in their life styles. In addition to bearing child support, alimony, and other court-related expenses, they have the economic burden of setting up a new household by themselves and undertaking often unfamiliar domestic tasks like cooking, laundering, and cleaning (Price & McKenry, 1988; Oakland, 1984; Price-Bonham & Balswick, 1980; Rosenthal & Keshet, 1980).

A special set of adjustments and adaptations awaits the divorced woman, particularly if she has children. In most cases it is the woman who gets custody of the children and thus must bear the brunt of child-care responsibilities. This makes rebuilding a social life especially hard. Divorced women may also encounter difficulty in establishing credit—a factor that hampers their financial independence. Banks, utilities, and stores often treat divorced women differently than divorced men with similar incomes.

Despite all these hurdles, Elizabeth Cauhape (1983) has found that most divorced people successfully adjust to their new lives—though not without costs, trade-offs, and sacrifices. Success seems to depend mostly on the ability to transform problems into opportunities for a new self-definition—something most people are equipped to do.

Divorce, then, can lead to growth. In the process of adapting and adjusting, many people discover strengths and emotional resources they never knew they possessed. They find they can survive loneliness and loss, and they use their new freedom to learn about themselves, seek out new interests, pursue other careers, and find more fulfilling relationships (McKay et al., 1984).

Divorce is tough on everyone. The irritations caused by partners having to assume unfamiliar tasks and children having to put up with changed routines are often only the outward manifestations of inner distress.

Stages of Postmarital Sexual Adjustment

All of what we've said so far suggests that divorced people need to focus considerable energy on life-style adjustments and adaptations. Among these, according to Joan Atwood (1988), are problems related to sexuality. Atwood identifies four stages of postmarital adjustment: denial, conflict, ambivalence, and acceptance.

DENIAL STAGE. Right after the divorce, people may not be interested in sex at all. Many newly divorced men and women repress their feelings of sexuality or deny their sexual fears. Repression and fear are emotional states that may eventually impair healthy sexual expression. Loneliness is common during the denial stage, including empty and sorrowful emotions. Some people report feelings of impending doom when they first face life without an emotional partnership.

CONFLICT STAGE. During this stage people may feel that they want to or should date, but remain unsure of themselves as they reenter the single world. Some may push themselves to date and have sex, only to feel depressed and ashamed afterward. It is important during this time to clarify values about dating, relationships, and sexuality. Sexual needs must be balanced with other personal needs and expectations. This includes choosing whether and when to engage in sex and on what terms.

AMBIVALENCE STAGE. People often experiment sexually during this stage, dating and having sex with several partners in an effort to learn more about their new sexual identity, including their values and needs. Many men and women sense they are not engaging in sex for appropriate reasons, but rather are acting out of curiosity or to affirm their attractiveness to the other sex. During the ambivalence stage people need to further clarify their values regarding sexual motivations. More often than not, those who engage in sex out of curiosity or to prove they are still attractive lack self-esteem, commitment, and intimacy—qualities that are important to good sexual and social relationships.

ACCEPTANCE STAGE. At this point people have a solid awareness of their own needs and desires and are ready to establish and maintain a healthy social and sexual relationship. They can achieve a balance between the self and any relationship they enter into, a blending process that allows intimacy, internal stability, and satisfaction. At last they are comfortable with their sexual selves.

SEXUAL FUNCTIONING IN THE OLDER ADULT

Contrary to what many younger people think, there is no automatic decline with age in the expression of sexual intimacy. Rather, older adults enjoy sexual activity regularly—unless, of course, ill health or the loss of a partner interferes. Decreases in sexual activity may also originate in social and emotional problems or as a side effect of certain medications (Leiblum & Seagraves, 1989; Butler & Lewis, 1988; George & Weiler 1981; Martin, 1981; Weg, 1983).

Is sex really possible among the elderly?

As we will see, sexual functioning and desire are not immune to the aging process. When people understand the changes of aging and how to cope with them, however, they can remain sexually active for as long as they choose. For most, that means for as long as they live (Kart, 1990; Renshaw, 1988; Stone, 1987; Brecher, 1984). When we examine experience in other nations, interesting variations in aging and sexuality emerge (see the box on "Aging and Sexuality Among the Abkhazians").

These older women describe how sex with their partners became better over the years:

> There's such a derogatory image attached to sex during one's later years, especially the idea that the elderly do not have (let alone enjoy) sex. My husband and I have been married 41 years and enjoy sex on a regular basis. In fact, sex is better today than it was when we first got married.
>
> It's better because we know each other's likes and dislikes. Actually, my husband has gotten better with age.
>
> I like it better now because there are no expectations nor any need to rush. We take our time and enjoy it. (Authors' files)

Older men had these thoughts:

> I know myself better now, particularly what I like and don't like.

At age 95, he goes to work every day picking apples while standing on the top of a rickety ladder. At age 93, his wife remains home and tends to domestic chores: preparing the day's meals, tending to the animals, mending, and the like. Happily married, they enjoy each other's company at the end of each day, as well as that of their seven children, who range in age from 31 to 58.

Discussions of aging and sexuality would be incomplete without some reference to the Abkhazians, who live in mountain villages in a land called Abkhazia, tucked between the Black Sea and the Caucasus Mountains in the old Soviet Union. For years reports coming out of Abkhazia have focused on the remarkable longevity of these mountain people and their active life style extending well into their twilight years. Indeed, these rural people are still vigorous and performing everyday chores when most Americans are languishing in nursing homes.

Abkhazia boasts five times the number of centenarians as the United States. In a recent survey, over 500 residents of Abkhazia out of a population of 520,000 were 100 years of age or older. While earlier longevity records were suspect because of poor record keeping and because residents had a tendency to overstate their ages, more sophisticated research confirms these statistics.

What is it about Abkhazians that promotes their longevity and active lives? Blood tests show that Abkhazians are not strikingly different from their geographical neighbors, although they may have a genetic resistance to disease. Their diet is not unusual, although it is wholesome and includes little alcohol. Cancer is also rare among Abkhazians, probably for genetic and dietary reasons as well as because they live in the countryside away from industrial wastes.

The sexual practices of Abkhazians are also thought to affect their overall longevity. Sexual relationships are generally discouraged until about age 30, at which time most people get married. Abkhazians maintain that their sexual practices help to conserve energy, which, in turn, helps to prolong their lives (Kart, 1990).

Gerontologists believe that the Abkhazians' active life style and their reverence for old age also contribute to their lengthy life spans. Abkhazians feel no apprehensiveness about growing older, and elderly villagers are regarded as both attractive and wise. The aged have real power in the family and in the daily life of the rural village. Besides continuing to work, Abkhazians of advanced years participate in a council of elders. They also serve in a number of hospitality roles, an important element of their village culture, and are sought out by the young for advice, including that of a sexual nature. Such practices contribute to a graceful transition to old age and help to preserve the dignity and well-being of the elderly. In contrast to the widespread assumptions in most of the Western world, sex in Abkhazia is not just for the young, nor is it linked to negative humor.

All of these factors create psychological comfort among the aged and may help to explain why people live longer in this remote land of the Caucasus (Turner & Helms, 1991; Sullivan, 1982).

A WORLD OF DIFFERENCES

Aging and Sexuality Among the Abkhazians

The love and respect I have built up over the years toward my wife continue to make sex a great experience. At age 67, I still experiment and discover new ways to gain sexual satisfaction. (Authors' files)

Unfortunately, some members of our society regard older adults as asexual, while others have crude misconceptions about their sex lives. Some maintain that sex is neither necessary nor possible during old age. Old men are often thought of as being either impotent or "dirty old men" overly interested in sex; postmenopausal women are frequently viewed as "frustrated." Those elderly people who claim to be sexually active may be regarded as either morally perverse or boastful and deceitful (Kart, 1990; Leiblum & Segraves, 1989; Aiken, 1982; Ludeman, 1981). In some quarters (Riportella-Muller, 1989) an older person's interest in sex is considered evidence of a vain desire to remain youthful.

George Bernard Shaw is said to have remarked that "Youth is wasted on the young." Maturity and aging, though they may alter some abilities, can heighten knowledge and understanding and deepen caring.

Society makes a number of false assumptions about the sexuality of older adults (Kay & Neely, 1982): One, the elderly do not have sexual desires. Two, the elderly simply cannot make love even if they want to. Three, because the aged are physically fragile, sex is dangerous to their health. Four, the elderly are physically unattractive and consequently sexually undesirable. All of these assumptions are both derogatory and untrue, the product of blatant ageist prejudices that are upheld only by the ignorant. Negative sanctions are particularly strong for older women, single elderly men and women, and older gays and lesbians. In a predominantly heterosexual, paired, and youth-oriented society, the sexual needs of such groups are often disregarded (Solnick & Corby, 1984; Robinson, 1983; Abu-Laban, 1981).

Men and women who have enjoyed long and stable sex lives without lengthy interruptions are likely to remain sexually active longer than those whose history is different. Sex in old age is thus likely to mirror sex in earlier life. Partners who have experienced long-standing conflicts may use age as an excuse to give up sexual relations that were never satisfactory. Rewarding sexual relations in old age do rely heavily on the physical vitality of the couple and each partner's commitment to share and sustain sexual intimacy. A marriage based on mutuality, understanding, and tenderness provides a vital basis for satisfying sexual relations throughout adulthood (Riportella-Muller, 1989; Butler & Lewis, 1988; Stone, 1987; Lauer & Lauer, 1986; George, 1980).

Judy Bretschneider and Norma McCoy (1988) studied the sex lives of over 200 men and women between the ages of 80 and 102. Over 60 percent of the men and about 30 percent of the women reported having sexual activity, ranging from once a day to once a year. The most common activity was caressing and touching a partner, reported by over 80 percent of the men and almost 65 percent of the women. About 70 percent of the men and 40 percent of the women practiced masturbation.

In another study Barbara Turner and Catherine Adams (1988) traced the patterns of sexual activity of 99 heterosexual men and women between the ages of 60 and 85. Almost half of these subjects experienced little, if any, change in patterns of sexual activity over the years. With the others, though, a change was apparent. Some who had preferred petting when they were younger now preferred coital activity. For others, the reverse was true: masturbation and petting were now preferred to intercourse. However, intercourse remained the sexual activity most highly correlated with positive sexual experiences and overall life satisfaction.

An extensive study of sexuality among the heterosexual aged was undertaken by Bernard Starr and Marcella Weiner (1981). These two researchers explored the sexual lives of 800 men and women between the ages of 60 and 91. For most of those surveyed, sexual activity was as good as it ever was—in some instances, even better. More than half of the couples reported having sexual relations twice a week, 18 percent reported having sexual relations five times a week, and 9 percent reported having intercourse daily.

This study, like the other research cited, disproves the myth that sexual activity decreases dramatically after age 60. The average number of sexual relations per week for those in their 60s was 1.5; for those in their 70s it was 1.4. Finally, in a study of 800 heterosexual women (Pearlman, Cohen, & Coburn, 1981), a clear majority of the respondents, who ranged in age from their mid-30s to mid-60s, reported that their sexual desire was as strong as in their youth, if not stronger. Furthermore, most of these women did not regard themselves as past their prime; on the contrary, many felt more sexually desirable with age and viewed physical changes in a positive light.

Most research does conclude that older women are less sexually active than older men, but the reasons are usually unrelated to sexuality. For one thing, women generally live longer than men, so there are many more older women than older men. Thus widowers have a wider choice of suitable partners than widows. For another thing, it is more socially acceptable for an older man to marry a young woman than for an older woman to marry a young man. And then there is the double standard: society frowns on a woman's extramarital sexual activity more than on a man's (Kart, 1990; Riportella-Muller, 1989; Stone, 1987; Aiken, 1982).

Changes in the Female Reproductive System

Aging brings some alterations to a woman's genitalia. Over time, the vagina decreases in both width and length and its walls become thinner. Its expansive capacity is also reduced. The mons, labia majora, and labia minora lose fatty tissue, causing them to shrink and flatten. The folds of the labia majora and labia minora become less pronounced, and the clitoris, ovaries, and uterus get slightly smaller. The loss of fatty tissue leaves the clitoris less protected and more easily irritated, though it still remains a source of sexual pleasure.

With increasing age, the Bartholin glands that lubricate the vagina upon sexual stimulation respond more slowly and provide less lubrication. Consequently, many older women complain that they are never wet enough for comfortable penetration or that intercourse is scratchy and painful (Leiblum & Bachmann, 1988). Poor vaginal lubrication and the less expansive capacity of the vagina can also cause vaginal burning, pelvic aching, and urinary difficulties.

These problems can often be solved with K-Y jelly, baby oil, or other artificial lubricants. However, the best rejuvenator of the vagina is sexual intercourse with orgasm as often as possible. The aphorism "Use or lose it" really applies here. Even women without partners can retain the natural resiliency and lubrication of earlier years by masturbating at least once a week. Moreover, **Kegel exercises** (see the box on these exercises) performed on a regular basis help the vagina remain elastic and well-toned (Henig, 1985).

Kegel exercises A set of exercises designed to restore the tone of the pubococcygeal muscles between the vagina and the anus.

The phases of a woman's sexual response cycle (see Chapter 4) also change with age. For example, the excitement phase is longer. Whereas a young woman's vagina will lubricate within 15 to 30 seconds after stimulation, an older woman's vagina may require 3 to 5 minutes to achieve lubrication. The orgasm phase of the sexual response cycle is also shorter and less intense in older women. Uterine contractions typically diminish from three to five per orgasm to one or two. The resolution phase also becomes shorter.

MENOPAUSE. Menopause generally occurs during the late 40s or early 50s. It is a normal development in a woman's life, but a frequently misinterpreted one. Paramount among the erroneous beliefs about menopause is that is brings a woman's

MAKING USE OF WHAT WE KNOW

Kegel Exercises

*K*egel exercises, devised by surgeon Arnold Kegel in the 1950s, are a simple set of exercises aimed at restoring the tone of the pubococcygeal muscles between the vagina and the anus. This area, commonly referred to as the *pelvic floor*, often slackens and weakens during pregnancy and childbirth, as well as during late adulthood because of the normal aging process.

Kegel exercises consist of about 20 contractions of the muscles of the pelvic floor at least five times a day. These muscles are tightened, held for a count of 10,

and slowly released. They should be pressed together with enough force to stop urine in midstream. The exercises can be performed in either a sitting or a standing position.

When properly done, Kegel exercises strengthen the pelvic floor area and help to improve perineal muscle tone, prevent incontinence (urine loss), and relieve hemorrhoids. Some women also use Kegel movements during sexual intercourse to enhance pleasure for themselves and their partners.

---

sex life to a halt. Let's debunk this and other myths by examining what menopause is and what if isn't.

You'll recall (Chapter 3) that menopause refers to the cessation of menstruation. The period from the onset of irregularity of the menses to their total cessation (menopause) is called the **climacteric.** During the climacteric ovulation, menstruation, and reproductive capacity gradually cease. The female climacteric may last only a few months, or it may extend over several years.

A number of physiological processes cause menopause. After 30 to 40 years of menstrual cycles, a woman has released almost all of her ova, or eggs. Although men continue to produce sperm throughout adulthood, women are born with a fixed number of ovarian follicles (see Chapter 3). By the age of 45 or 50, a woman's supply of follicles is nearly depleted, and only a few remain.

As the number of follicles decreases, there is an accompanying decline in production of the female sex hormone estrogen. One result of this is that menstrual periods become irregular and often unpredictable. When estrogen production declines to a certain point, the climacteric culminates in the complete cessation of cyclic ovarian activity—the menopause.

Because of the rapid decrease in secretion of the female hormones estrogen and progesterone, other physical changes occur: The woman's mammary glands atrophy, as do her uterus and vagina to varying degrees. Some women experience a significant loss of bone density—a condition known as *osteoporosis*.

A woman's body does not stop producing estrogen after menopause (a common misconception), but continues to produce it in areas other than the ovaries. The adrenal glands, fatty tissues in the body, and the brain all increase their levels of estrogen production to compensate somewhat for the lost ovarian production (Millette & Hawkins, 1983).

Women react to menopause in highly individual ways. It is possible, however, to isolate two general periods when some women experience specific psychological effects of these long-term hormonal changes. The first occurs during the climacteric, the other upon reaching menopause.

During the climacteric a woman must readjust her life from one that has been physiologically stimulated by the production of estrogen and progesterone to one that is devoid of these feminizing hormones. Loss of these hormones may cause such symptoms as hot flashes (moments of feeling warm and uncomfortable, often accompanied by perspiration); irritability, frequent mood changes, and even depression; insomnia, fatigue, and anxiety; and, often, sensations of dyspnea (labored or difficult breathing). Dyspareunia (painful intercourse) due to insufficient lubrication is the most common sexual complaint (Bachmann, Leiblum, & Grill, 1989; Leiblum & Se-

climacteric The period of a woman's life from the onset of irregularity of the menses to their total cessation.

What happens when a woman goes through menopause?

468   Adult Sexuality

graves, 1989; Moore, 1984; Millette, 1982; Uphold & Susman, 1981; Gray, 1981; Frey, 1981; Heilman, 1980; Guyton, 1981).

Besides these physiological symptoms, the menopausal woman encounters the normal crises of middle adulthood: anxieties about children entering the adult world, financial worries, health concerns and fears about growing old, and the prospect that life goals set in youth may be unattainable. Women who do not have children or have remained single may regard menopause as signaling the final chapter in their lives. Thus many psychological threads are interwoven with this important physiological event (Millette & Hawkins, 1983).

Millions of women in the United States take estrogen in an effort to deal with menopausal symptoms. In 1989, 31 million estrogen prescriptions were filled, mostly for postmenopausal women, compared to only 14 million in 1980 (Elias, 1990). Estrogen replacement is used to counteract such physiological symptoms as hot flashes, hair loss, atrophy of the breasts and vagina, and loss of skin elasticity. Lifetime estrogen therapy can also help to protect older women from osteoporosis and the risk of stroke and cardiovascular disease (Schover & Jensen, 1988).

Estrogen replacement therapy unfortunately has some negative side effects. For example, the long-term use of high-dose estrogen has been associated with uterine cancer. Some studies (i.e. Bergkrist, 1989) have uncovered a possible link between long-term estrogen therapy and increases in the incidence of breast cancer. Other negative side effects sometimes associated with estrogen therapy are high blood pressure, vaginal infections, and breast discomfort. Because of such problems, many doctors are less than enthusiastic about prescribing estrogen to menopausal women unless their symptoms are severe—and even then, the lowest possible dose is generally prescribed for the shortest possible time (Elias, 1990; Schover & Jensen, 1988; Gastel & Hecht, 1980; Schultz, 1980).

MISCONCEPTIONS ABOUT MENOPAUSE. Now let's turn our attention to the myths and misconceptions that surround menopause. The notion that there is something "wrong" about menopause—that it is somehow "unnatural"—is the primary reason for many of these myths and old wives' tales. They are perpetuated by a lack of free discussion and silently influence the thinking of both women and men of all ages. The following are the most popular myths about menopause:

- *Menopause is a disease.* Both doctors and the general public once regarded menopause as an illness requiring medical treatment. Today menopause is viewed by physicians as a deficiency syndrome, in that a woman's estrogen secretion has diminished. Some degenerative changes usually occur, which may or may not require medical attention.

- *Menopause is always accompanied by depression and mood swings.* There is little evidence linking such psychological turbulence to menopause. Some symptoms attributed to menopause, such as anxiety, are actually caused by other stresses that emerge during middle adulthood and may be only indirectly related to menopause.

- *All menopausal women suffer from severe and incapacitating hot flashes.* Estimates of the percentage of women who have hot flashes vary widely. One source (Sarrel & Sarrel, 1984) claims half to three-quarters of all menopausal women experience hot flashes from time to time. Others put the percentage much lower. Most sources do agree, though, that the percentage of women who have severe and incapacitating flashes is very small. Most hot flashes are mild to moderate and do not disrupt normal activity.

- *After menopause women need full replacement of the hormone estrogen.* As we've already indicated, even though the ovaries stop manufacturing estrogen at menopause, other parts of the body continue to produce this hormone. So while estrogen production diminishes, it does not stop altogether. There is still no clear-cut answer about the desirability of estrogen replacement theory.

- *Women who have had a hysterectomy will not experience natural menopause.* This depends on the extent of the surgery. In a partial hysterectomy only the uterus is removed, while a total hysterectomy means that the cervix and sometimes the ovaries are also removed. A woman who retains one or both ovaries after the operation will experience a natural menopause as her ovarian cycle winds down.

- *Menopause signals the end of sexual desire.* The reality is that many women find themselves enjoying sex more after menopause, particularly since they're no longer worried about birth control and pregnancy. A majority of women report that they feel no different about themselves sexually and can detect no change in their sexual arousal (see, for example, Leiblum & Segraves, 1989; Myers & Morokoff, 1985; Morrell et al., 1984). Some women do report a decrease in sexual desire, but it is hard to say whether this change is due to psychological or physiological factors.

- *A woman becomes less active after menopause.* On the contrary, the reverse is often true. Postmenopausal women may be peppier, healthier, and in better spirits than they were before the change of life. Many report feeling freed from the mood swings that characterize some women's menstrual cycle, as well as from worries about birth control and pregnancy (Stone, 1987; Skalka, 1984; Millette & Hawkins, 1983).

Most menopausal women benefit from a meaningful support system that offers them understanding and sensitivity. In addition, Brenda Millette and Joellen Hawkins (1983) feel that a woman's adjustment to menopause depends, in part, upon the experiences of her mother, her peers, and other significant women in her life. Women (and men) need factual information about what to expect during this important developmental event. A fully prepared woman usually sees menopause as a milestone, not a millstone, in her life.

Changes in the Male Reproductive System

Aging causes certain changes in the male reproduction system as well. The scrotum hangs lower and the testes become smaller and less firm. Sperm production declines, and there is a thickening of the seminiferous tubules as well as a decrease in their diameter. While sperm production diminishes, aging men remain capable of manufacturing mature sperm cells. So, unlike women, men are fertile and able to reproduce throughout adulthood. Testosterone production declines with advancing age, and by age 80 may be only one-sixth the level of that of a young man (Leiblum & Segraves, 1989; Schover, 1984).

While the penis does not generally change in size or shape, it does become less sensitive to stimulation. Erections may not be as firm or full as when the man was young, and their angle also tends to decline with advancing years. One source (Schiavi & Schreiner-Engel, 1988) indicates that nocturnal erections become less frequent in older men. Pubic hair also becomes sparser and finer. For most men, the prostate gland grows larger, a development that may cause medical problems (see Chapter 17).

Like older women, older men experience changes in their sexual responsiveness. Sandra Leiblum and Taylor Seagraves (1989) observe that although the capacity to respond to sexual stimuli remains, a man's drive to seek sexual release diminishes during late adulthood. It also takes longer for older men to achieve an erection and climax. Most men experience a reduction in the force of ejaculation, and the penis usually becomes flaccid immediately after ejaculation. (A younger man's penis typically remains erect for minutes after ejaculation.) The refractory period is also longer, so it takes an older man longer than his younger counterpart to have a second erection and orgasm. While younger men may be able to have several erections and orgasms in one day, most older men have only one orgasm or erection per day or per week.

Because men remain capable of fathering children throughout their lives, they cannot be said to experience a "change of life" analogous to the female menopause. But since hormonal production and the functioning of the male sexual organs do change, some writers have argued that men may have many of the same psychological symptoms as menopausal women, such as mood swings from acute irritability to depression, fatigue, and anxiety (see, for example, Riportella-Muller, 1989; Leiblum & Seagraves, 1989; Stone, 1987; Featherstone & Hepworth, 1985).

The physiological changes of aging, combined with the psychological burdens frequently shouldered during middle adulthood, make some men feel a great sense of urgency to live life to its fullest before it is too late. Taking such a dramatic life perspective puts them under some tension and may create anxiety, stress, and bouts of depression. Notice the similarity with menopausal women. In fact, research indicates that men and women are more alike than different in their middle years.

This is an area worthy of further investigation. Research already conducted suggests that just as some menopausal women are helped by the administration of extra estrogen, some middle-aged men may be assisted by the administration of the hormone testosterone. We also need more information about the psychological changes of midlife so therapeutic interventions can be designed to assist people experiencing acute psychological disruptions.

SEXUALITY IN THE NEWS

There's Life After Menopause

Menopause is a natural life event that needs to be understood by both women and men. In this segment from ABC's "20/20," aired August 10, 1990, Dr. Timothy Johnson leads a discussion of the effects of menopause on women and the advantages and disadvantages of various kinds of medical interventions such as estrogen therapy. The video makes the point that although some women regard menopause as signaling the end of many important activities, many other women go through this change while continuing to lead healthy, happy, and productive lives.

DISCUSSION QUESTIONS

1. What triggers menopause? What are some of its symptoms? Why do some menopausal women become disinterested in vaginal sex?

2. According to one of the physicians interviewed in this video, women are becoming more candid about menopause and more willing to discuss their feelings. Why do you think this may be so?

3. Some women experience emotional difficulties during menopause. What factors are instrumental in producing these problems? How can these women be helped through the changes they're experiencing?

4. As the video indicates, estrogen therapy has been used increasingly in recent years. What are the benefits and risks associated with this type of therapy?

LOOKING BACK

■ The single life style is growing in popularity. There are about 67 million single adults in America, counting those who are divorced and widowed as well as those who never married and those who are postponing marriage. There are many reasons why single living is so popular in the 1990s: career and educational opportunities for women, a greater number of women than men in the prime marriageable age groups, a desire for freedom and autonomy, and an awareness of the specter of divorce.

■ Cohabitation is also extremely popular today. Since 1960, the numbers of people cohabiting have increased dramatically. While most people with this life style are under 35, there has been an increase in older cohabitants in recent years. Often one of the partners is separated or divorced. Cohabitation can be distinguished according to its overall duration: temporary (a prelude to marriage) or permanent (an alternative to marriage). The most important reasons for the popularity of cohabitation are the gradual weakening of the double standard and the growing acceptance of the idea that it is the quality of a relationship that counts rather than its legal status, the widespread availability of contraceptives and the legalization of abortion, peer support for this life style, and the fact that people today are less concerned about achieving the status of marriage.

■ Most people expect to marry at some point in their lives, although many choose to postpone marriage, often for the same reasons that others choose the single life—principally to pursue a degree or a career. From a demographic point of view, the "marriage squeeze" can also be cited as a reason. The principal motives for marriage are love, conformity, companionship, legitimization of sex and children, a sense of readiness, and legal benefits. The transition from single to married life requires many adjustments, including those of a sexual nature.

■ An extramarital sexual relationship is sexual activity with someone other than one's spouse. A nonconsensual extramarital relationship is sexual activity with someone other than one's spouse without the spouse's knowledge. A consensual extramarital relationship refers to sexual activity with someone other than one's spouse, but with the knowledge of that spouse. The latter category includes open marriage and swinging.

■ The loss of a partner through death, divorce, or separation entails many adjustments and adaptations. Divorce is widespread in this country, and rates are highest two to five years after marriage. Following a divorce, it is not uncommon for men and women to feel a sense of failure, loneliness, sadness, and fear. A redefinition of the self often evolves as the divorced person moves from mutual identity to autonomy. The stages of postmarital sexual adjustment are denial, conflict, ambivalence, and acceptance.

■ Menopause, or the cessation of menstruation, is a normal developmental event in the life of a woman, and is often accompanied by greater rather than lesser enjoyment of sex. Some women experience psychological symptoms such as anxiety and depression. Some men experience similar psychological distress as they grow older. Both men and women show a slowing of sexual response and a diminishment in the intensity of desire, though they can continue to enjoy sexual activity as long as they wish.

THINKING THINGS OVER

1. Remaining single into middle age has become more acceptable. Why are more people choosing the single life style? Speculate on why some segments of society have accepted this phenomenon.

2. You are about to enter into a cohabitation arrangement and want to draft an agreement that describes the economic aspects of your relationship. Why is such a document considered important? What kinds of things should it spell out?

3. Young adults cohabit for many reasons. Why do you believe older adults cohabit? Do they have the same motivations as their younger counterparts? What are the benefits of cohabiting?

4. In any long-term relationship sexual satisfaction can decline. What are some of the factors that can cause this decline? What are some of the factors that contribute to sexual sat-

isfaction and fulfillment? Do you believe there is one element of a sexual relationship that is more important than all the others? If so, what is it?

5. Why do you think the U.S. divorce rate is so high? Why do you think the divorce rate is lower in other nations? Compare the reasons given for divorce in this chapter with the reasons given for the dissolution of a relationship in Chapter 6. How do you intend to avoid being another divorce statistic?

6. Why do you think many segments of society have negative stereotypes about sexuality in older adults? How did these myths originate? Do you think other cultures have such a derogatory view of the sexual lives of the elderly? Why or why not?

DISCOVER FOR YOURSELF

Butler, R. N., & Lewis, M. I. (1988). *Love and sex after sixty*. New York: Harper & Row. Two noted contributors to the field explore the social, medical, and psychological aspects of sexuality during late adulthood.

Henig, R. M. (1985). *How a woman ages*. New York: Ballantine Books. Henig explores the sex lives of older women in Chapter 10 of this paperback.

Millette, B., & Hawkins, J. (1983). *The passage through menopause: Women's lives in transition*. Reston, VA: Reston Publishing Co. An excellent examination of menopause and how it affects women's lives.

Pesman, C. (1984). *How a man ages*. New York: Ballantine Books. Chapter 8 explores how aging processes affect a man's sexuality and sex organs.

Pittman, F. (1989). *Private lies: Infidelity and the betrayal of intimacy*. New York: Norton. A probing but captivating look at marital infidelity.

Wallerstein, J. S., & Blakeslee, S. (1989). *Second changes: Men, women, and children a decade after divorce*. New York: Ticknor & Fields. An informative analysis of the long-term effects of divorce on children and their parents.

16
Sexual Dysfunctions

*Nothing is so firmly
believed as that
which is least known*

—Michel de Montaigne

S exual intimacy can be a garden of delight and renewal or an arena of struggle and anxiety. About half the heterosexual couples in the United States experience a sexual dysfunction or impairment at some point in their relationship. For many of these couples, all that's required is a little information and education, or perhaps some help in learning how to communicate better with each other (see Chapter 7). Others need some type of brief therapeutic intervention to alleviate their sexual problem. But some couples require more extensive and prolonged therapy to unravel the causes of the problem and find a solution to it.

Significant advances have been made in the knowledge and treatment of sexual problems in recent years. Our plan in this chapter is to make this information available to you. We begin with an overview of sexual dysfunction. Then we examine the major categories of sexual problems, including their origins. The chapter concludes with an exploration of the major models of sex therapy and how they are applied to the treatment of sexual disorders.

DEFINING AND CHARACTERIZING SEXUAL DYSFUNCTION

Sexual dysfunction is broadly defined as a problem of sexual response during any phase of the sexual response cycle, which, you will recall, we described in Chapter 4. Usually it affects both the person's subjective sense of desire or pleasure and the person's sexual performance. The actual diagnosis of a sexual dysfunction is made by a clinician, who takes into account such factors as how often the problem occurs, the subjective distress it triggers, and its effect on other areas of functioning in the person's life. Persistence and recurrence of the problem are important diagnostic considerations.

All of the sexual problems we discuss in this chapter may be physical only or both physical and psychological. Sexual problems may exist from the beginning of a person's sexual functioning, or they may appear suddenly after a period of normal sexual activity. They may occur in all situations, with all partners, or they may occur only when the person is with a particular partner. While in the majority of cases the dysfunction occurs during sexual activity with another person, sometimes it happens during masturbation. Also, some people may exhibit more than one sexual dysfunction. For instance, a man may have both inhibited sexual desire and the inability to maintain an erection (American Psychiatric Association, 1987).

How Common Is Sexual Dysfunction?

According to the American Psychiatric Association (1987), the exact prevalence of sexual dysfunctions is not known, though the majority of them are believed to be common, especially in their milder forms. Since the statistics we have were gathered from people who sought help and many people do not seek help, the reported statistics may considerably understate the prevalence of sexual dysfunction. At any rate, our best estimates are that about 20 percent of all adults have experienced a sexual desire disorder. About 30 percent of women have an inhibited orgasm disorder, 30 percent of men have experienced premature ejaculation, and 8 percent of young men have experienced an erectile disorder.

Overly high subjective standards of sexual performance, anxiety, and hypersensitivity to real or imagined rejection by a sexual partner may predispose people to develop an acquired sexual dysfunction. For example, as the women's movement has

Do many people have sexual dysfunctions?

sexual dysfunction A problem in sexual responding that may occur at any phase of the sexual response cycle.

encouraged women to become more sexually aggressive, some men have developed "performance anxiety" about being able to please their partners. Women need to take responsibility for their own sexual satisfaction by teaching men how they want to be pleasured. Negative attitudes toward sexuality caused by internal conflicts, adherence to rigid cultural values, and bad experiences in the past may also predispose people to develop sexual problems (American Psychiatric Association, 1987).

A Preview of Some Causal Factors

Early adulthood is the most common age for sexual dysfunctions. Typically, men seek help in their late 20s and early 30s, a few years after they have formed a sustained sexual relationship. A common complaint is premature ejaculation, which usually began with their first sexual encounters. Male erectile disorder, in contrast, often becomes a problem later in life. The sex ratio varies for particular dysfunctions. Inhibited orgasm and sexual aversion disorder, for example, are more common in women. While dyspareunia is possible in men, it is much rarer than it is in women.

The course of development for sexual dysfunctions is variable. Sometimes the dysfunction is experienced only once or for a brief period. Sometimes there is a pattern of episodic dysfunction. In other cases the problem is so major and complicated that it disrupts sexual relationships.

Often the dysfunction is accompanied by no other signs of disturbance. This is especially true of inhibited sexual desire, since it does not necessarily entail impaired sexual performance. In other instances there is a vague sense of being unable to live up to some concept of sexual normality. Or the person may be plagued by an assortment of complaints, such as guilt, shame, frustration, depression, or physical symptoms. Many people with a sexual dysfunction develop a fear of failure and a "spectator" attitude—the habit of monitoring themselves with acute sensitivity to the reaction of their sexual partners. In this type of cognitive interference, people focus more on analyzing their sexual performance than on enjoying the moment. For example, while making love to his partner, a man may constantly ask himself: How am I doing? Will I be able to excite her? Is she as turned on as I am?" The spectator attitude may so erode satisfaction and performance that eventually the person avoids sexual activity altogether (American Psychiatric Association, 1987).

Now that we have given you some idea of sexual dysfunction in general, let's turn our attention to the major categories of sexual dysfunction: disorders of sexual desire, arousal, and orgasm, and pain disorders. Table 16–1 contains a summary classification of these dysfunctions.

TABLE 16–1

Classification of Sexual Dysfunctions

CATEGORY	BRIEF DESCRIPTION
Sexual Desire Disorders	Lack of sexual drive or motivation. Includes Inhibited Sexual Desire and Sexual Aversion Disorder
Sexual Arousal Disorders	Lack of sexual arousal when there is adequate stimulation during sexual activity. Includes Female Sexual Arousal Disorder and Erectile Dysfunction
Orgasm Disorders	Persistent or recurrent delay in, absence of, or rushed orgasm following normal sexual excitement. Includes Inhibited Female Orgasm, Retarded Ejaculation, and Premature Ejaculation
Sexual Pain Disorders	Sexual discomfort. Includes Dyspareunia and Vaginismus

Sexual Dysfunctions

SEXUAL DESIRE DISORDERS

Sexual desire disorders are characterized by a lack of sexual drive or motivation. These disorders can be broken down into two specific types: inhibited sexual desire disorder and sexual aversion disorder. In **inhibited sexual desire** a person has sexual fantasies and desires either rarely or not at all. **Sexual aversion disorder** refers to the persistent avoidance of all or almost all genital sexual contact with a sexual partner (American Psychiatric Association, 1987).

Sexual desire varies widely from person to person, and also fluctuates according to age and situation. There are no norms for frequency of sexual activity, whether solitary or with a partner. For that matter, *frequency* of sex is not identical with *desire* for sex. It may well be that the best criterion for diagnosing a sexual desire disorder is a discrepancy between partners' sexual needs. Acceptable frequency in this respect is whatever keeps partners happy.

Both women and men can experience sexual desire disorders, although research focusing on men is relatively recent. A person with such a disorder typically lacks erotic feelings and is unwilling to either initiate or participate in sexual activity. For those suffering from sexual aversion, even the thought of sexual activity is often disgusting, and most feel anxiety and tension whenever sexual contact is initiated. Some people have such an aversion to sex that they experience panic at the prospect (Kaplan, 1983). In some cases, sexual trauma, such as rape or incest (see, for example, Becker, 1989), triggers the aversion.

Over the last decade sexual desire disorders have become one of the most common sexual dysfunctions (LoPiccolo & Friedman, 1988; Kilmann et al., 1986). They are found in young and old, in people with intact and broken marriages, in traditional and nontraditional couples, and among the healthy as well as the ill and the disabled.

Anxiety about AIDS is noticeably dampening sexual desire among gay men and single heterosexuals. But it is busy two-career couples who represent the largest percentage of the reported cases. Usually they complain of extreme fatigue, the boredom of routine, or the stresses of everyday life. Some sex researchers refer to sexual desire disorders among dual-career couples as the "new Yuppie disease." Many couples are discovering they can't come home at 7 or 8 o'clock, eat dinner, catch up on their work, become aroused and make love, and then go to sleep—to begin the grueling routine all over again the next day (Gelman, 1987).

Other possible causes of sexual desire disorders are fear of pregnancy, depression, hormonal imbalances, and the side effects of certain medications such as antidepressants, sedatives, and antihistamines. Other possible causes are lack of attraction to a partner, relationship conflict, and poor lovemaking skills (LoPiccolo & Friedman, 1988).

inhibited sexual desire
A condition in which the person has sexual fantasies and desire for sexual activity only rarely or never has them at all.

sexual aversion disorder
Persistent or extreme aversion to, and avoidance of, all or almost all genital sexual contact with a sexual partner.

Problems of sexual response are not uncommon in today's two-paycheck families. The stress of long hours combined with household chores and childcare may produce fatigue and anger that cannot easily be willed away.

477

SEXUAL AROUSAL DISORDERS

Sexual arousal disorders are characterized by a general lack of sexual arousal when there is adequate stimulation during sexual activity. There are two main types: female sexual arousal disorder and male erectile disorder.

Female Sexual Arousal Disorder

Do women ever have arousal problems?

female sexual arousal disorder A sexual dysfunction characterized by difficulties in attaining or maintaining the lubrication-swelling response of sexual excitement, as well as a lack of subjective sexual excitement and pleasure.

Either one of two diagnostic criteria is used in identifying a **female sexual arousal disorder.** The first is persistent or recurrent partial or complete failure to attain or maintain the lubrication-swelling response of sexual excitement until completion of the sexual activity. The second is a persistent or recurrent lack of a subjective sense of sexual excitement and pleasure during sexual activity (American Psychiatric Association, 1987).

Arousal disorders overlap with orgasmic disorders. Most women with an arousal disorder do not show the physical signs of sexual responsiveness, such as vaginal lubrication and swelling. Subjectively, they tend not to experience erotic feelings and sensations and may feel little or no arousal from sexual stimulation. However, arousal difficulties sometimes occur when manual stimulation does not create an adequate sexual response or when the woman is insufficiently aware of stimulation to be able to respond sexually (Beck, Rawlins, & Williams, 1984).

This dysfunction is considered to be a *primary arousal disorder* if the woman has never experienced sexual arousal with any partner in any situation. *Secondary arousal disorder* is the term used to describe a woman who was once capable of arousal, but is no longer.

Many psychological causes for female sexual arousal disorder have been cited. Psychoanalysts have suggested that women with this disorder have unresolved conflicts about their sexuality, often stemming from unpleasant childhood experiences and memories such as negative parent-child relations, sexual abuse, and emotional neglect. Other causes that have been proposed are a bad relationship with the sexual partner; stress, fear, and anger; general fatigue; and fear of pregnancy. Arousal disorders can have physical causes as well. For example, lack of vaginal lubrication can be due to estrogen deficiency during menopause. In other instances, arousal disorders are linked to illness and certain drugs, such as tranquilizers and antihistamines (Rosen & Leiblum, 1989; Leiblum & Rosen, 1988; Leiblum & Pervin, 1980).

Erectile Dysfunction

erectile dysfunction The inability to attain or maintain an erection during sexual activity, as well as a subjective lack of sexual excitement and pleasure.

Erectile dysfunction, once referred to as "impotence," is diagnosed by one of two primary criteria. First, there can be persistent or recurrent partial or complete failure to attain or maintain an erection until the sexual activity is completed. Second, there can be a persistent or recurrent lack of a subjective sense of sexual excitement and pleasure during sexual activity (American Psychiatric Association, 1987).

Like female sexual arousal disorder, an erectile dysfunction can be primary or secondary in nature. *Primary erectile dysfunction* refers to a condition in which a man has never been able to experience an erection sufficient for intercourse with a sexual partner. *Secondary erectile dysfunction* is a condition in which a man has experienced erectile adequacy with a sexual partner at some prior point, but is currently unable to do so on a consistent basis.

The chief cause of male erectile disorder can be physical or psychological. However, in determining the origins of erectile dysfunction, Joseph LoPiccolo (1985) believes that it is incorrect to diagnose the patient as having either a physical or a

What's happening to those men who "can't get it up"?

psychologically caused dysfunction, because in perhaps the majority of cases, *both* physical and psychological factors underlie erectile failure.

Secondary erectile disorder is more common than the primary type, and is generally more easily treated (Rosen & Beck, 1988). It has been estimated that almost half of all adult men have occasional episodes of erectile dysfunction (Sharlip, 1984) and that the percentage escalates after age 50 (Tiefer & Melman, 1989). However, an erectile disorder can occur at any time in a man's life from adolescence to old age, and is known in every culture, race, and socioeconomic group (Rosen and Leiblum, 1992).

Some of the physical factors known to cause an erectile dysfunction are alcohol use, smoking, drug abuse, diabetes, barbiturate and amphetamine use, cardiac and respiratory disorders, neurological diseases, and complications after surgery for cancer of the bladder, prostate, or rectum. Arteriosclerosis of the internal pudendal and penile arteries may make the blood supply to the penis inadequate, another physical factor to consider. Other noteworthy physical causes are pituitary gland dysfunctions, chronic kidney failure, and spinal cord injuries (McCarthy, 1992; Rosen & Leiblum, 1992; Tiefer & Melman, 1989; Melman, Tiefer & Pedersen, 1988; Mueller & Lue, 1988; LoPiccolo, 1985; Schiavi & Fisher, 1982).

One source (Beck, Rawlins, & Williams, 1984) identifies five symptoms whose presence indicates a physically based erectile disorder. One, the erectile disorder is present in the same degree in all sexual circumstances. Two, there is an absence of nocturnal erections or they are only partially turgid. Three, significant life events are not associated with the beginning of the dysfunction. Four, normal erectile functioning had occurred in the past. Five, there is an intact sexual desire, interest, or libido.

In recent years several surgical treatments for irremedial organically based erectile dysfunction have been developed (Tiefer & Melman, 1989; Lewis, 1988). *Penile revascularization,* a technique designed to correct penile arterial insufficiency, entails microsurgical revascularization (developing an alternate blood vessel supply) of penile arteries. More common is the **penile implant,** or a prosthesis that is inserted into the penis to achieve erection. There are two primary types of penile implants. The *semirigid penile prosthesis* consists of a pair of silicone rods that are implanted in the corpora cavernosa (see Figure 16–1a). The penis is then semierect at all times, but flexible enough so that it can be bent downward and contained by underwear. A semirigid penile prosthesis is an expensive surgical procedure and has certain possible complications, such as infection of the corpus cavernosum, penile pain, and discomfort from an improperly sized prosthesis. However, the overall surgical success rate is excellent, as is patient and partner acceptance of the implant.

The other surgical approach is the *inflatable penile prosthesis,* expandable silicone cylinders that are implanted in the corpora cavernosa and attached to a container of fluid located near the bladder and to a pump in the scrotal sac (see Figure 16–1b). When the man desires to have an erection, he squeezes the pump and the fluid fills the cylinders in much the same way that blood enlarges the penis during an erection (if penile sensation has been lost because of organic causes, it will not be restored by the penile implant). To end the erection, the man presses a release valve on the side of the pump, and the fluid flows back into its container. This method of treatment is both more expensive and more surgically complicated than the semirigid penile prosthesis. It, too, runs the risk of infection, and poses mechanical complications as well, such as fluid leakage. However, as with the semirigid penile prosthesis, patients and partners report satisfaction (see, for example, Pedersen et al., 1988; Tiefer, Pedersen, & Melman, 1988; Sharlip, 1984).

Vacuum constriction devices are a nonsurgical medical treatment for erectile dysfunction. The man places his penis in a tube in which a vacuum is artificially created, causing blood to rush into the sinusoidal spaces of the penis and producing an erection. Then the man puts a constricting band at the base of his penis to maintain the erection. Problems with vacuum construction devices include numbness caused

Drug abuse often causes sexual dysfunction. Some people take cocaine to enhance sexual pleasure, but over the long haul it can lessen sexual desire and cause erectile dysfunction.

I've heard that a man who can't have an erection can have a special device implanted into his penis to make it erect. Is this true? Does it always stay hard?

penile implant A prosthesis that is inserted into the penis to achieve erection.

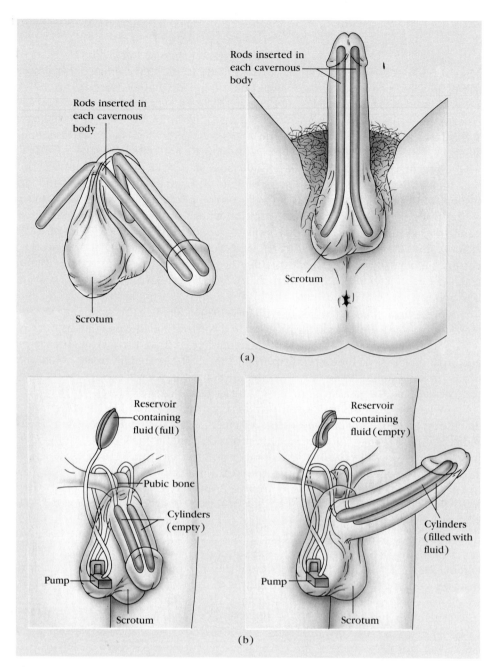

FIGURE 16-1
Two Types of Penile Implants.

A shows the semirigid prosthesis, whose flexible rods allow the penis to be bent down when erection is not desired. The inflatable type of prosthesis shown in *B* makes temporary erection possible by pumping fluid into cylinders in the penis. The fluid can be released at will, returning the penis to a flaccid state.

by the constricting band and the unwieldy and mechanical method of producing the erection (Witherington, 1988; Tiefer & Melman, 1989).

Drug therapy is another option in treating erectile dysfunction. The administration of testosterone is sometimes successful. Also used is papaverine, a muscle relaxant and vasodilator that causes erection when injected into the corpora cavernosa of the penis. The man achieves an erection within five minutes after the injection,

Sexual Dysfunctions

and it lasts about two hours (similar to penile implants, drug therapy of this nature does not restore sensitivity lost to organic causes). However, papaverine produces undesirable side effects in many men, including numbness and difficulty in reaching orgasm, so it (and similar drugs) is not widely used to treat erectile dysfunction (Morales et al., 1988; Althof et al., 1988).

Some of the psychological causes of erectile dysfunction are anxiety about performance and partner satisfaction, depression, tension and pressure, feelings of worthlessness, hostility, fear of rejection, frustration, self-pity, and guilt about the sexual encounter. Ignorance about how to sexually satisfy oneself and one's partner has also been cited as a contributing factor (McCarthy, 1991; Rosen & Leiblum, 1992; Althof, 1989; Marshall, 1989; Kilmann et al., 1987; Gagnon, Rosen, & Leiblum, 1982; Ellis, 1980). The box titled "Benjamin: A Case of Erectile Disfunction" provides a case study of male erectile disorder, including causes and therapeutic intervention.

ORGASM DISORDERS

Orgasm disorders are a category of sexual dysfunction that can be experienced by both women and men. The orgasm disorders are subdivided into three basic types: inhibited female orgasm, retarded ejaculation, premature ejaculation, and faked orgasm.

Are some women incapable of achieving orgasm? What can be done to help them?

Inhibited Female Orgasm

Inhibited female orgasm refers to a persistent or recurrent delay in, or absence of, orgasm following adequate sexual arousal and stimulation. Today it is a common

MAKING USE OF WHAT WE KNOW

Benjamin: A Case of Erectile Dysfunction

*B*enjamin was a successful 49-year-old salesman for a boat-building concern. He had always been a fairly heavy drinker, but during one period in his life when there was an increase of pressure on the job, combined with trouble with his teenage son, he began to consume more liquor than he was able to handle. On one occasion, Benjamin became quite drunk at a party, and when he and his wife arrived home, he tried to make love to her. He was unable to get an erection, and even though his wife understood it was because of the alcohol he had consumed, the episode worried and depressed him. When he attempted to have intercourse with her the next day sober, he initially achieved an erection but was unable to maintain it. This pattern continued. A few times he was able to maintain an erection and function successfully, but most of the time he could not. Eventually he stopped attempting sex with his wife altogether.

Benjamin's initial erectile problem resulted from a combination of alcohol and personal and business pressures, but at the time he was unable to see it from this perspective. The drinking became so out of control that he was forced to admit that he was becoming an alcoholic. With the aid of Alcoholics Anonymous, he managed to give up drinking completely, but his erectile disorder remained. . . .

It was at this point that Benjamin and his wife sought therapy. At first he was quite negative and appeared to have given up hope of ever regaining erectile functioning. Eventually, however, he began to see that erection problems often feed on anxiety. He and his wife began doing nongenital and genital pleasuring exercises for the purpose of increasing comfort and arousal. There was a temporary prohibition on intercourse so as to reduce performance anxiety. Benjamin responded well to this treatment, and in a matter of weeks he was getting more frequent erections. (McCarthy, 1988, pp. 209–210)

sexual complaint of women (Heiman & Grafton-Becker, 1989; Bancroft, 1983; Heiman & LoPiccolo, 1983).

There are three different types of orgasm difficulties. *Primary inhibited orgasm* means that the woman has never had an orgasm, regardless of the type of stimulation experienced. Often the term *preorgasmic* is used to describe this category, since it is believed that these women are capable of learning the orgasmic response. *Secondary inhibited orgasm* is a category used to describe women who once experienced orgasm, but are no longer responsive. *Situational inhibited orgasm* means the woman experiences orgasm, but only under certain circumstances. For example, she may be able to each orgasm through masturbation, but not in the presence of a sexual partner. Or she may be orgasmic only with specific partners or in certain sexual positions.

The causes of inhibited female orgasm disorders are varied, but are mostly psychological in origin. Among the reported causes are depression, fear of losing control, performance anxiety, fear of being abandoned, and a reluctance to assert independence. Some anorgasmic women feel guilty about their sexuality, often because of a strict religious upbringing. As with the other sexual dysfunctions, psychoanalysts emphasize the presence of unresolved, unconscious conflicts and fears rooted in such trauma as sexual abuse or coercion (Kernberg, 1987; Scharff & Scharff, 1987; Jordan, 1985; Surrey, 1983).

Lois Goldsmith (1988) believes that some women at least have inhibited orgasm because they do not receive sufficient clitoral stimulation. This often happens because sexual partners unrealistically expect the woman to reach orgasm merely in response to rapid penile thrusting, without much foreplay and without clitoral contact. To illustrate how erroneous this expectation is, Shere Hite (1976) found that only about 30 percent of the women she studied could attain orgasm regularly merely from intercourse. But even though the vaginal orgasm is the exception rather than the norm, most women feel guilty when it eludes them.

Lonnie Barbach (1980) thinks there is a connection between female orgasm disorders and feminine role scripting. She suggests that low-orgasmic women often have stereotyped "feminine" attitudes toward sex: they do not talk about sexual matters, are basically passive and rarely initiate sex, focus selflessly on their lover during sexual activity in an attempt to please that person, and amiably go along with whatever happens during lovemaking. Many of these women do not have enough accurate anatomical and physiological knowledge to guide their sexual lives. Some feel too insecure and ashamed to let their partners know what kind of sexual stimulation they want. Others are too anxious to be able to "let go" and enjoy orgasmic pleasure. Considering all these factors, it is no surprise to find that many women report faking an orgasm at one time or another.

Orgasm disorders rarely have a physical cause, although physical factors may contribute to the problem. Factors identified include degenerative diseases and tumors that destroy the spinal centers and nerves that mediate the orgasmic reflex, diabetes, and disorders of the endocrine system. Orgasm disorders have also been linked to alcohol use as well as to taking drugs such as psychotropic medications (Nurnberg & Levine, 1987; Riley & Riley, 1986; Segraves, 1985; Jensen, 1985; Pohl, 1983; Aldridge, 1982).

Retarded Ejaculation

retarded ejaculation A persistent or recurrent delay in, or absence of, intravaginal ejaculation following adequate sexual excitement.

Retarded ejaculation is defined as a persistent or recurrent delay in, or absence of, intravaginal ejaculation following adequate sexual excitement. This problem is less common than premature ejaculation, which we will discuss shortly. Men with retarded ejaculation are capable of becoming sexually aroused and of having a full erection, but they cannot climax within their partner's vagina. Orgasm is generally possible with other types of stimulation, such as masturbation.

Sexual Dysfunctions

MAKING USE OF WHAT WE KNOW

Jack: A Case of Inhibited Male Orgasm

*J*ack was a 38-year-old technical writer whose three children from two previous marriages lived with him. Jack was generally well-adjusted, led an active, stimulating life, enjoyed being a single father, and reported that he had good relationships with women. But while he always experienced orgasm when he masturbated, Jack found that he was ejaculating less and less often in his sexual encounters with women. He consoled himself with the "blessing in disguise" theory that even if he was missing out on orgasm, at least he was a good lover, since his partners were nearly always orgasmic.

During therapy, it emerged that Jack felt it unmanly to request stimulation from his partner. Instead, he focused most of his attention and energy on making sure that he was performing well, so his partner could have no cause to complain about his ability to satisfy her. As a result, he never got very excited during sex. As soon as he had an erection he initiated intercourse. Jack felt it "selfish" and "immature" to request additional penile stimulation. He made himself into a kind of "sexual servant" who was not allowed or entitled to enjoy the experience himself.

In therapy, Jack learned to request specific kinds of stimulation from his partner. He found oral stimulation particularly arousing when he was moving rather than remaining passive. He found that it was especially stimulating when his partner moved her pelvis in a circular manner during intercourse and when she stroked and fondled his testicles. As he became more confident about making specific requests and gave himself permission to let go and enjoy the experience, Jack began to experience orgasm more and more regularly. (McCarthy, 1988, pp. 226–227)

The primary causes of retarded ejaculation are psychological. Clinicians cite such factors as guilt, fear of partner rejection, and fear of intimacy. Some men worry so much about not ejaculating as the sensation approaches that they create a level of anxiety that actually checks the ejaculatory mechanisms. Ambivalence or anger toward a partner may also be predisposing factors, as may the opposite: compulsion to please a partner sexually. Disgust at one's ejaculate is often a related causal factor: some men fear "soiling" their partner with ejaculate (Apfelbaum, 1989, 1988). Other men have a dread of being discovered while having sex, often because of a severely traumatic sexual incident in their past.

Certain medications can inhibit male orgasm. For example, phenothiazines and certain antihypertensives may impair the ejaculatory reflex. Other inhibiting drugs are alcohol, barbiturates, and methaqualone (Rosen & Beck, 1988; Kaplan, 1983; Buffum, 1984). For a case study, see the box titled "Jack: A Case of Inhibited Male Orgasm" in this section.

Premature Ejaculation

Premature ejaculation is the term for the persistent occurrence of male orgasm and ejaculation as a result of minimal stimulation or before, on, or shortly after penetration. (Orgasm *can* occur without ejaculation, as in prepubertal boys or after prostate surgery.) It is a specific disorder only when one or both sexual partners are dissatisfied by its occurrence. Most commonly reported by heterosexual couples as an interference in coitus, this disorder can occur in noncoital activity as well as in gay relationships (McCarthy, 1989). In assessing the seriousness of this problem, a therapist must take into account such factors as age of the partners, newness of the sexual relationship, and frequency of sexual activity between the partners (American Psychiatric Association, 1987).

Approximately a quarter of all men experience early orgasm and ejaculation during a first intercourse experience with a new partner. Most often, ejaculation occurs

premature ejaculation
Persistent or recurrent ejaculation with minimal sexual stimulation before, upon, or shortly after penetration and before the couple wish it to happen.

Early sexual experimentation can lead to later problems in sexual functioning. Young people may be hesitant to talk about their feelings and sensations and to say what they want, and female orgasm in particular may often be inhibited. The fear of discovery may compound the problem, leading to erectile and ejaculatory problems.

before the penis has actually penetrated the vagina. Many young men complain of early ejaculation, and a considerable number of adult men report that they reach orgasm and ejaculate more rapidly than they would like (McCarthy, 1989). However, if sexual partners are committed to a loving and intimate relationship (Chapter 6) and are able to communicate clearly and sensitively with each other (Chapter 7) they can usually work through this difficulty on their own.

When true premature ejaculation is diagnosed, a physical cause such as hypersensitivity of the glans should be considered, but by and large the causes of this disorder are psychological. Some writers (e.g., Annon, 1984) have suggested that early learning experiences can condition a man to reach orgasm quickly. For example, sexual activity that is hurried for fear of discovery by parents or others, Annon suggests, may lead to a conditioned response of rapid orgasmic function. It is also possible that a man who is anxious about his ability to perform or to satisfy his partner may be unable to control his excitement. Anxiety can also fuel a sense of insecurity that may lead a man to seek power by denying his partner satisfaction in this way.

Traditionally, premature ejaculation was not recognized as detrimental to a couple's sexual fulfillment. Barry McCarthy (1988) observes that when intercourse was viewed primarily as a man's right and a woman's duty, men had little motivation to prolong sex to ensure their partner's enjoyment. Indeed, since it was believed that "nice" women did not enjoy sex, a man who could get the job done quickly was admired. Women who were conditioned to view intercourse as unpleasant or uncomfortable were inclined to urge their partners to "get it over with." Even today, this kind of thinking lingers to a certain degree, particularly among men who are ignorant of female sexual responses and women who are socialized to the idea that women do not really enjoy sex. But this hurried style and insensitivity are unsatisfying to women who desire more affectionate and elaborate pleasuring as well as prolonged intercourse. The problem can be aggravated if the woman decides to voice her dissatisfaction and the man then becomes overly anxious about his performance.

Faked Orgasm

Why do some women fake orgasm? Do men ever do the same?

Finally, clinicians see faking orgasms as a kind of orgasm disorder. It is women who most often pretend to have orgasms. It's rather difficult for a man to fake orgasm, especially the first one in an encounter (no ejaculate!). One study (Darling & Davidson, 1986), found that 66 percent of women and 33 percent of men had faked an orgasm at least once. This conscious decision to pretend to have an orgasm is usually the result of not wanting to embarrass or disappoint a partner. Here again, performance pressure rears its ugly head. Other, less common reasons for this deception are inability to communicate truthfully about sexual relations, the hope of gaining a partner's approval, the desire to protect a partner's ego, and the attempt to conceal that the relationship is really over (Lauersen & Graves, 1984). Men may also be led to fake orgasm because they feel pressured into having multiple orgasms. Some men who have ejaculatory inhibition pretend to have an orgasm to hide this problem.

Faking orgasms may lead to deeper problems. Because the deceiving partner fails to acknowledge that sexual relations are less than satisfactory, the ignorant partner may believe the relationship is fine as it is and never see any reason to change sexual behavior. This, in turn, may lead to anger, resentment, and hostility on the part of the woman or man who feels obliged to dissemble, and eventually the dissolution of the relationship.

SEXUAL PAIN DISORDERS

So far we have examined sexual desire, sexual arousal, and orgasm disorders. One other major category of sexual dysfunctions remains: coital pain. Two types of sexual pain disorders are dyspareunia and vaginismus.

Dyspareunia

Dyspareunia means "painful intercourse," and it can occur in either a man or a woman before, during, or after sexual intercourse. The pain experienced can include such sensations as tearing , burning, aching, and pressure. The intensity and duration of the pain vary from person to person.

Painful intercourse can have both physical and psychological causes. Physical causes include gynecological and urological disorders, including diseases of the urethra and bladder, and lesions (injuries or wounds) of the genital tract. Some men develop a condition called **Peyronie's disease,** in which hard fibrous plaques form in the sheath of the corpus cavernosum. This causes curvature of the penis when it becomes erect, creating pain and making coitus difficult. Women may suffer from dyspareunia because of clitoral adhesions (the union of adjacent tissues caused by inflammation or injury), inflammations, or allergic reactions to douches and creams, as well as because of surgical damage to the uterus or vagina (Lazarus, 1989, 1980).

The psychological causes of dyspareunia fall into three main categories: developmental, relational, and traumatic. Examples of *developmental* causes are an upbringing that associated sex with shame and guilt, misinformation that engendered tension and anxiety, and religious taboos that sparked confusion and ambivalence about sex. *Relational* causes include such situational events as foreplay inadequate for arousal, anxiety that children may wander into the room during sexual activity, and fears of being overheard. Other relational factors are resentment and antagonism toward one's sexual partner and a partner's clumsiness. *Traumatic* factors are chiefly fears precipitated by earlier painful coital experiences, such as rape or incest (Lazarus, 1989).

Vaginismus

Vaginismus is a female sexual pain disorder characterized by recurrent or persistent involuntary constriction of the musculature surrounding the vaginal opening and the outer third of the vagina (see Figure 16–2). In the most severe form of vaginismus,

dyspareunia Recurrent or persistent genital pain in either a man or a woman before, during, or after sexual intercourse.

Peyronie's disease A condition characterized by the formation of hard, fibrous plaques in the sheath of the corpus cavernosum.

vaginismus A female sexual pain disorder characterized by recurrent or persistent involuntary constriction of the musculature surrounding the vaginal opening and the outer third of the vagina.

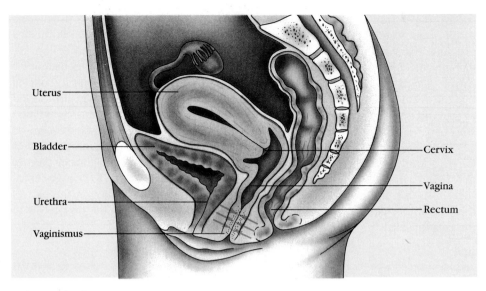

FIGURE 16–2
Vaginismus.

In this condition the musculature surrounding the outer third of the vaginal canal constricts involuntarily so that penetration is impossible.

penetration of the vagina by any object, including a penis, is impossible. In less severe cases, penetration is possible, but painful. Typically, women with vaginismus experience little difficulty with sexual arousal. Lubrication occurs naturally, noncoital sex is often reported as arousing and satisfying, and orgasmic responsiveness is frequently unimpaired (Rosen & Beck, 1988).

Most cases of vaginismus are psychologically based, although endometriosis, pelvic tumors, and surgical injuries to the genitals are physical conditions that can create pain during intercourse. A thorough pelvic examination will disclose the presence of any of these factors. Psychological causes include fear or guilt about intercourse, prior sexual trauma, unconscious conflicts, a learned phobia, concern about a partner's erectile disorder, and a strict religious upbringing (Leiblum, Pervin, & Campbell, 1989; Drenth, 1988).

THERAPY FOR SEXUAL DYSFUNCTIONS

We have seen that the causes of male and female sexual dysfunctions are highly complex and may have a number of precipitating factors. Complicating the situation is the fact that the problem is often of long standing before the person seeks help, creating anxiety, loss of control, rejection, or an immobilizing fear of failure. Sex therapy usually focuses on improving communication between partners and teaching sexual techniques, sensitivity, and skill. Sometimes the severity of the sexual disorder warrants more intensive therapeutic intervention (Beck, Rawlins, & Williams, 1984).

Important advances have been made in the treatment of sexual dysfunctions. Therapeutic strategies originally concentrated on the individual experiencing the dysfunction. Today partner and group treatment approaches are proving successful in treating sexual disorders ranging from the simple to the very complex. Not only are there more therapy models to choose from, but new knowledge and greater clinical sophistication have made interventions much more effective (Goldsmith, 1988).

The PLISSIT Framework for Sex Therapy

In the first part of this section, we will examine a conceptual framework of sex therapy known as the PLISSIT model. This is a flexible and comprehensive scheme that enables clinicians to organize their therapeutic approaches. As we shall see, the PLISSIT framework includes examination (physical and psychological); diagnosis of type and severity of the problem; consideration of options; and implementation of a chosen intervention, if needed.

The primary goal of sex therapy is the resolution of sexual conflicts or any other factors that are impeding normal sexual functioning. To accomplish this, a treatment approach, or framework for therapy, needs to be established. Most treatment approaches have been devised for heterosexuals, but there are therapists trained and experienced in applying these approaches to the treatment of lesbians and gays.

Jack Annon (1984) has identified a conceptual scheme referred to as the **PLISSIT model.** This model of treatment consists of four progressive levels: permission, limited information, specific suggestions, and intensive therapy. The first three levels can be viewed as brief therapy, while the fourth involves intensive therapeutic intervention. The PLISSIT model can be used by a wide variety of therapy professionals because it allows for a range of treatment choices geared to the competency level of the therapist. The model also supplies a framework for discriminating between sexual problems that are responsive to brief therapy and those that require an in-depth approach.

PLISSIT model A framework for the treatment for sexual dysfunctions consisting of four progressive levels: permission, limited information, specific suggestions, and intensive therapy.

LEVEL ONE: PERMISSION. It is important for clients to be reassured that they are normal and that what they're feeling or experiencing is not "deviant" or "perverted." Often people are not bothered so much by the specific behavior in which they are engaging as by the notion that there is something "wrong" or "bad" about it. Thus people who seek professional help are frequently looking for a sounding board so that they can check out areas of covert concern, such as thoughts, fantasies, or dreams. Thus, a therapist might reassure a client that it is not unusual to have sexual fantasies about someone other than one's partner, or that it is not uncommon to feel anxiety about experiencing sexual arousal to what is considered inappropriate stimulation (for example, the father who has an erection when his son is playing on his lap or the mother who feels sexual arousal when breast-feeding her baby).

Permission giving by the therapist is not always appropriate, however. It is the therapist's responsibility to inform the client of the possible adverse consequences of engaging in certain proscribed overt behaviors such as rape or sexual activity with children. Also, the extent to which therapists feel comfortable with the permission-giving approach generally depends on their breadth of sexual knowledge, theoretical orientation, and value system. Finally, there is the issue of self-permission. Therapists should be able to give permission to themselves *not* to be experts. They should not be reluctant to admit that certain answers escape them. Therapists do what they can for their clients based on their knowledge and experience. No therapist is a total expert or has all the answers.

LEVEL TWO: LIMITED INFORMATION. This level entails providing clients with specific factual information relevant to their particular sexual concerns. Armed with this information, people can continue to do what they have been doing or make adjustments in their thinking, feelings, or overt behavior. Providing limited information is an excellent way to dispel harmful sexual myths, whether they be specific ones such as those pertaining to genital size, or more general ones such as those related to masturbation or frequency of intercourse. Limited information is typically provided in conjunction with permission giving. Not only is there an overlap between the two levels, but both can be applied to the two remaining levels of treatment.

"I sense a little anxiety when we approach the subject of sex."

Annon (1984) supplies a common example of the provision of limited information. A young man's major problem was a feeling of inadequacy because he considered his penis "too small." This conviction had depressed him to the point where he had withdrawn from any social contact and was even considering surgery to correct his "deficient" penis. His clinician provided an assortment of information, such as the negative effect of comparing his penis to other men's and the fact that size is usually unrelated to sexual performance and pleasure because the flexibility of the vagina allows it to accommodate a penis of most any size. This relevant information was sufficient to help the young man overcome his negative self-appraisal.

LEVEL THREE: SPECIFIC SUGGESTIONS. Before giving specific suggestions, the therapist needs to take a sexual history from the client. This sexual history includes: (1) a description of the current problem; (2) the onset and course of the problem; (3) the client's concept of the cause and persistence of the problem; (4) past treatment and outcome; and (5) current expectations and goals of treatment.

Specific suggestions are direct attempts to help clients change their behaviors so they can reach their stated goals. Suggestions are given in situations where the therapist is only able to see the client once or for a few sessions. They are often geared to such concerns as performance anxiety, masturbation, and problems of sexual arousal. Clients frequently receive readings or homework assignments that further address the problem. If the suggestions do not prove helpful within a relatively brief period of time, the client is usually advised to undertake more intensive therapy. The efficiency of the specific suggestions of treatment hinges on the therapist's skill, knowledge, experience, and awareness of relevant therapeutic suggestions.

To illustrate the specific suggestion level, consider the man who has difficulty achieving an erection or the woman who experiences inhibited female orgasm. Thoughts such as "Will it happen again?" are common in these instances, and are often incapacitating. Specific suggestion treatment might be helping the person to learn to say, and to believe, "There is always another time" or "There is always another occasion." This belief would relieve the grim, self-defeating determination that many men and women demonstrate when trying to overcome this kind of sexual problem. In addition, the therapist would offer specific suggestions that are relevant to the problem. The most helpful suggestions are usually those that can be made to both sexual partners together.

LEVEL FOUR: INTENSIVE THERAPY. This level consists of a specialized therapeutic effort designed for the particular client, based on a careful assessment of that client's unique situation and experiences. It is intended primarily for sexual problems that cannot

Sexual Dysfunctions

While sex therapy is a relatively recent discipline, speculations about the causes and cures of sexual dysfunctions have been around for millennia. For example, the ancient Mesopotamians had incantations to prevent male erectile dysfunction and ointments for its cure. The potency incantations were typically recited by women to their lovers. The ancient Greeks knew about inhibited sexual desire and arousal, although their explanations for these phenomena sound odd today. The physician Galen maintained that among women such disorders could eventually affect the uterus and create hysteria, a condition producing such symptoms as dizziness, paralysis, and epileptic-like fits. Women who wanted to avoid hysteria were urged to make a conscientious effort with their husbands or lovers to restore their sagging libido to more active levels.

Nonwestern cultures have spun a variety of folk explanations around erectile disorders. For example, the Dogon, Hausa, and Fang of Africa once believed that if milk from a woman's breast dripped onto her infant son's penis while he was nursing, he might grow impotent. Among the Fang, elephant tusks were once associated with impotence, a man who stepped over a tusk would be plagued with this sexual disorder for the rest of his life. The Wolof of Africa once regarded sex on Wednesdays as taboo, and believed that if a boy should be conceived on that day, he would become impotent.

Among the Mangaians of Oceania, there were several degrees of impotence, the most serious being *tiranara*, meaning a "lost" or "hidden" penis. The Mangaians described the penis as withdrawing into the body and believed that this withdrawal could kill the man unless he abstained from sexual intercourse for several months and was treated with smoke therapy. The latter required him to squat over smoldering herbs and allow the smoke seeping through punctured coconut shells to reach his genitals.

Aphrodisiacs—substances supposed to be capable of heightening sexual excitement—have been used in almost all cultures to help restore diminished sexual desire and arousal. The ancient Egyptians concocted one of the earliest aphrodisiacs known; it consisted of a crocodile's penis dried and ground to powder. A Roman aphrodisiac involved rubbing the soles of the feet with pepper and the penis with the urine of a bull that had just copulated. The Greeks consumed seafood, while the Peruvian Indians recommended cocoa and chocolate.

Throughout history, penislike objects such as animal horns were sometimes sought by the sexually troubled because of their supposed powers. The horn of a white rhino was once especially prized in China and Southeast Asia. (Adapted from Gregersen, 1983)

---

be solved with the brief approaches of levels one to three. In the discussion of sex therapy models that follows, we explore a variety of techniques that are applicable to particular needs and circumstances.

Is there one set way to deal with sexual problems, or do therapists have you try different things?

Sex Therapy Models

There are numerous therapeutic approaches to the treatment of sexual dysfunctions. While thoughts on how to treat sexual problems are nothing new (see the accompanying "A World of Differences" box about approaches taken in antiquity), modern-day sex therapists have meshed techniques for changing sexual behavior with approaches to enhance interpersonal relationships. Here we examine both the theoretical underpinnings and the applicability of five influential approaches: the Masters and Johnson, Kaplan, behavioral, cognitive, and group models.

THE MASTERS AND JOHNSON MODEL. This approach to sex therapy evolved from the clinical work of William Masters and Virginia Johnson, whose research on human sexuality we discussed in Chapter 1. The **Masters and Johnson model of sex**

Masters and Johnson model of sex therapy An intensive two-week treatment approach that includes, among other features, treatment of the couple rather than the individual, and use of a male-female co-therapy team.

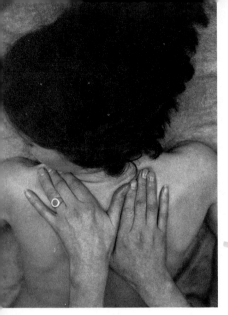

Exchanging back rubs and other forms of body touching and massage can help a couple relax with each other. Becoming comfortable in the enjoyment of pure physical sensation, they can give and receive the specific caresses each one likes.

male nondemand position A position proposed by Masters and Johnson to reduce anxiety related to sexual performance. The man lies on his back while his partner sits between his legs facing him.

therapy emphasizes that in any relationship in which there is some form of sexual inadequacy, both partners are involved in the problem (Masters and Johnson, 1970). Isolating a man or woman in therapy from his or her partner ignores the fact that sexual response represents interaction between people.

The Masters and Johnson model uses teams of male and female cotherapists. This way, each partner has an advocate as well as an interpreter in the therapeutic setting. The Masters and Johnson model is an intensive two-week program. Following history taking and physical examinations, an extensive discussion between the therapists and the patients focuses on the general sexual activity of the couple as well as on the sexual dysfunction being evaluated. Emphasis is placed on sharing factual sexual knowledge, removing negative attitudes about sexuality, reducing anxiety, and enhancing verbal and nonverbal communication between partners.

Throughout the program couples are given exercises that are designed to heighten their awareness of each other's sexual needs and to enhance their sexual pleasure. These exercises are often given as homework assignments to be practiced in the privacy of the couple's motel room during the two-week therapy course or at home after the conclusion of the program. One of the best known of Masters and Johnson's exercises is *sensate focus*. Nude and in bed, partners learn to touch each other in ways that create pleasure. Initially, they do not touch each other's genitals. Rather, the emphasis is on giving and receiving pleasure, tuning into each other's likes and dislikes, and reducing anxiety related to sexual performance. As anxiety diminishes, the exercises gradually lead to genital pleasuring and eventually to intercourse.

Depending on the specific sexual dysfunction, various other techniques are added to sensate focus to accomplish particular goals. For example, as the sensate focus technique is applied to male erectile dysfunction, the woman is first asked to stimulate the man's penis manually or orally while they are in a **male nondemand position.** In this position the man lies on his back while his partner sits between his legs facing him (see Figure 16–3). When an erection occurs, the woman is instructed to stop fondling or stroking the penis and to let the erection subside. This will allow the man to see that losing an erection is not a failure and that it can return with further stimulation. This technique also discourages rushing into intercourse as soon as an erection is achieved—a habit that can create anxiety. Only after a man gains confidence in his erectile capacity is intercourse attempted. The woman is advised to insert the penis herself in order to reduce pressure on the man to decide when the time is right.

Figure 16–3
Male Nondemand Position.

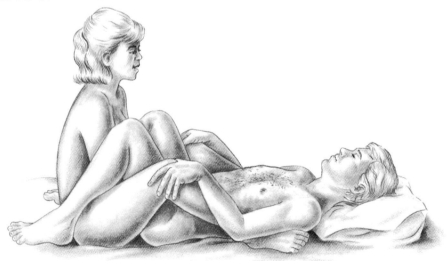

Sexual Dysfunctions

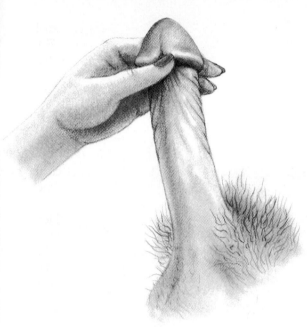

FIGURE 16–4
The Squeeze Technique.

Gently but firmly squeezing the penis, from front to back, just under the corona, can retard male orgasm during lovemaking. Once ejaculation has become inevitable, however, the technique no longer works.

Masters and Johnson also devised the **squeeze technique** for the treatment of premature ejaculation. After a couple has mastered the sensate focus exercise, they are taught to practice this technique, which involves squeezing the penis just below the coronal ridge (see Figure 16–4). Prior to orgasm, firm pressure is applied, front to back, for about five seconds, and then released. This causes a partial loss of erection and delayed orgasm. The squeeze technique is repeated four or five times before ejaculation is allowed to occur.

Inhibited male orgasm is treated with a special sequence of graded sensate focus exercises. First, the man masturbates to ejaculation alone, and then in the presence of his partner. If this is successful, the next step is for the partner to manually stimulate the man's penis to ejaculation. Finally, the partner stimulates the man's penis to the point of excitement and then inserts it into her vagina. Typically, ejaculation is achieved. After a few successes with this sexual sequence, most men lose the fears and inhibitions that characterized their inhibited orgasm disorder.

Masters and Johnson have also treated female arousal and orgasm disorders successfully. After the man and woman do sensate focus exercises, the man strokes all of the sexually stimulating parts of his partner's body. Couples assume a **female nondemand position** so that the man can easily reach and stimulate the woman. This position requires the man to sit behind the woman in a slightly reclining fashion (see Figure 16–5). She then places her hand lightly on his to indicate her preferences for stimulative contact. This "hand-riding" technique allows the woman to convey her desire for a lighter touch, more pressure, or a faster or slower style of stroking. Once the woman is sexually aroused, the couple assumes the female-superior position for intercourse. After the penis is inserted, the woman is instructed to remain still and concentrate on the pleasurable sensations of having her partner's penis inside her vagina. Slow pelvic thrusting is then begun and continues for as long as it is pleasurable to them both. Then follows an interval of rest during which the couple lie in each other's arms. The sequence is repeated several times, and then the couple adopt the lateral coital position for intercourse, which Masters and Johnson feel is the most effective for sexual experimentation and stimulation.

The Masters and Johnson format has also been used successfully to treat vaginismus. The woman is first given a pelvic examination, usually with the man present, and then is taught how to relax the muscles in the vaginal area. Self-awareness exercises as well as relaxation techniques are aimed at reducing the anxiety and tenseness that

squeeze technique A technique developed by Masters and Johnson to treat premature ejaculation and inhibited male orgasm. Pressure is applied to the penis just below the coronal ridge prior to ejaculation to cause a partial loss of erection and delayed orgasm.

female nondemand position A position proposed by Masters and Johnson to reduce anxiety related to sexual performance. The man sits behind the woman in a slightly reclining fashion while she places her hand on his to indicate preferences for stimulative contact.

FIGURE 16-5
Female Nondemand Position.

accompany this condition. The couple then use various-sized plastic dilators to slowly and gradually dilate the vaginal opening and stretch the musculature. The woman keeps the dilator in place for 10 or 15 minutes at a time. In addition to this treatment mode, psychological aspects of vaginismus as well as relationship issues are addressed before intercourse is attempted. The latter typically occurs within five days if treatment has been successful.

THE KAPLAN MODEL. Helen Singer Kaplan (1989, 1983, 1979, 1974) expanded the Masters and Johnson model of sex therapy and combined it with parts of the psychoanalytic school of thought. The **Kaplan model of sex therapy** seeks to explore both immediate and more deeply rooted and hidden causes of sexual dysfunctions. While some couples are treated by a male-female co-therapy team, most are seen by one therapist of either gender. Kaplan uses a psychodynamic approach in which couples receive therapy weekly rather than in the intensive two-week program of the Masters and Johnson model. Because Kaplan's approach is not time-limited, some couples remain in therapy for an extended period.

Kaplan acknowledges that such factors as poor communication, anxiety about sexual performance, and lack of sexual knowledge contribute to sexual difficulties. She also thinks that sexual disorders can result from learned responses. However, her approach emphasizes that many dysfunctions are the product of unconscious motivations and conflicts that must be brought to a conscious level of awareness and put into a proper perspective before sexual harmony and stability can be achieved. Unlike traditional psychoanalysts, who expend considerable energy and time delving into a client's past and unraveling deep-seated conflicts, Kaplan focuses on how the past has created present-day sexual problems. Her plan for therapy therefore leans heavily on a "here and now" approach.

Kaplan proposes a mixture of approaches and techniques to resolve sexual problems. Some things she borrows from the Masters and Johnson model, such as sensate focus exercises. For treatment of premature ejaculation, however, Kaplan proposes the "stop-start" method instead of the squeeze technique. In the "stop-start" technique, first introduced by James Semans in 1956, the partner stimulates the man's penis manually until the man is close to ejaculating. At this point, the partner stops the stimulation, waiting for the urge to ejaculate to diminish. This stop-start cycle is

Kaplan model of sex therapy An approach to the treatment of sexual dysfunctions developed by Helen Singer Kaplan. It seeks to explore both immediate and more deeply rooted and hidden causes of dysfunctions.

repeated several times before ejaculation is allowed to occur. Kaplan has also developed numerous sexual exercises geared specifically to a couple's sexual problem. For inhibited sexual desire, the exercises might range from sharing erotic fantasies to slow and nondemanding penile insertion. Or the couple might be asked to focus on emotional interaction before they start actual lovemaking. Such specific exercises address the particular couple and their unique relational dynamics.

THE BEHAVIORAL MODEL. The **behavioral model of sex therapy** is based on the notion that sexual dysfunctions are conditioned forms of behavior. Just as normal sexual behavior is learned, so, too, are the disorders covered in this chapter. According to behavioral therapists, most sexual dysfunctions are the result of conditioned anxiety responses. Thus the therapeutic goal of this model is to eliminate, or extinguish, undesirable sexual behaviors and replace them with more appropriate ones (e.g., Fichten, Libman, & Brender, 1986; McCarthy, 1989, 1985; Kuriansky, Sharpe, & O'Connor, 1982; Evaraerd & Dekker, 1982).

In most instances, a behavior therapist meets weekly with the couple. The therapist does not explore unconscious conflicts or spend time seeking to understand the clients' past lives. Rather, the first goal is to specify the overt symptoms of the dysfunction and the environmental conditions that sustain it. For example, since behavioral therapists tend to view female orgasm as a learned response, a woman's failure to achieve it is considered to be the result of inadequate learning. To take another example, some women feel intense anxiety about participating in sex because of learned habits (Barbach, 1980; McCarthy, 1989). Once the problematical behaviors and the sustaining conditions have been identified, the therapist arranges learning procedures to eliminate them.

Behavioral sex therapists employ a diversity of techniques and approaches. One common technique is systematic desensitization, developed by Joseph Wolpe. **Systematic desensitization** serves to counteract the anxiety aroused by a sexual situation by interposing and associating a relaxation response with that situation. The client is told to imagine a series of scenes or events that trigger the emotional discomfort. Then these scenes are rank-ordered, from the least to the most disturbing. After being taught relaxation responses (breathing and muscle exercises designed to reduce anxiety and tension), the client is asked to imagine the least threatening situation. When this can be done without arousing anxiety, the next most stressful scene is imagined, and so on, until the client can visualize the most anxiety-producing sexual scene from the series calmly. At that point the client may be ready to try engaging in the actual behavior, as the box on "Systematic Desensitization" illustrates.

behavioral model of sex therapy A therapeutic approach to sexual dysfunctions that emphasizes how disorders are conditioned forms of behavior.

systematic desensitization A therapeutic approach employed by behavioral practitioners. In the treatment of sexual dysfunctions, it is used to counteract the anxiety of a sexual situation by interposing and associating a relaxation response to that situation.

Behavior therapists like Professor Arnold Lazarus can teach people who have sexual and other problems the relaxation response. Once they have learned to relax at will, clients can move on to the next step in systematic desensitization—imagining a series of increasingly anxiety-arousing situations while maintaining their relaxed state.

MAKING USE OF WHAT WE KNOW

Systematic Desensitization

Ms. A., aged 24 years, had been in a monogamous, living together relationship for two and one-half years, during which time she claimed to have had coitus with her partner on less than two dozen occasions. She always experienced violent dyspareunia during intercourse as well as "disgust and anxiety at the whole messy business." She could tolerate casual kissing and caressing without anxiety and at times found these experiences "mildly pleasant." The background to her problem was clearly one of puritanical upbringing, in which much emphasis was placed on the sinfulness of carnal desire. Ms. A.'s partner had endeavored to solve their difficulties by providing her with books on sex techniques and practices. Ms. A. had obligingly read these works, but her emotional reactions remained unchanged. She sought treatment of her own accord when she suspected that her partner was involved with another woman.

After several interviews and tests, the following systematic desensitization hierarchy was constructed for Ms. A. (the most disturbing items are at the top of the list):

1. Having intercourse in the nude while sitting on her partner's lap.
2. Changing positions during intercourse.
3. Having coitus in the nude in a dining room or living room.
4. Having intercourse in the nude on top of a bed.
5. Having intercourse in the nude under the bed covers.
6. Manual stimulation of the clitoris.
7. Partner's fingers being inserted into the vagina during precoital love play.
8. Caressing partner's genitals.
9. Oral stimulation of the breasts.
10. Naked breasts being caressed.
11. Breasts being caressed while fully clothed.
12. Embracing while semiclothed, being aware of partner's erection and his desire for sex.
13. Contact of tongues while kissing.
14. Having buttocks and thighs caressed.
15. Shoulders and back being caressed.
16. Partner caressing hair and face.
17. Partner kissing neck and ears.
18. Siting on partner's lap, both fully dressed.
19. Being kissed on lips.
20. Being kissed on cheeks and forehead.
21. Dancing with and embracing partner while both fully clothed.

Variations in the brightness of lighting played a prominent part in determining Ms. A.'s reactions. After four desensitization sessions, for instance, she was able to visualize item 14 without anxiety but only if this activity were supposed to be occurring in the dark. It required several additional treatments before she was able to tolerate this imagined intimacy under conditions of ordinary lighting.

The therapist asked Ms. A.'s partner to make no sexual overtures to his partner during the period of treatment. Ms. A. was taught how to relax and desensitized three times a week over a period of less than three months.

When item 5 on the hierarchy had been successfully visualized without anxiety, Ms. A. "seduced" her partner one evening and found the entire episode "disgustingly pleasant." Thereafter, progress was extremely rapid, although the first two items remained slightly troublesome, and each required over 20 presentations before Ms. A. could tolerate her visualization. A year later, Ms. A. and her partner both said that the results of therapy had remained "spectacularly effective." (Lazarus, 1989, pp. 109–110)

In another technique called *implosive therapy*, or "flooding," the person with a sexual disorder is asked to imagine being in the dreaded sexual situation. The therapist seeks to keep the anxiety-arousing situation foremost in the person's mind rather than to relax him or her (hence the expression "flooding"). Because no actual harm occurs, these images and thoughts gradually lose their capacity to evoke anxious reactions. If this technique is successful, the person's conditioned sexual anxiety gradually disappears.

Variations of *operant conditioning* may also be employed. This is a process through which people learn to repeat those sexual behaviors that yield positive outcomes and to avoid those with negative outcomes. For example, the man who engages in prolonged intercourse and learns to enjoy the pleasures that that kind of sex brings is likely to continue the behavior in the future. Conversely, the woman who comes to see that faking orgasm ends sexual activity before she is satisfied will avoid that behavior. Within the therapeutic setting, an arrangement of environmental rewards is often established to reinforce desired sexual behaviors.

Another popular behavioral technique is *orgasmic reconditioning*, the use of directed fantasy along with masturbation to modify the kinds of sexual stimuli associated with arousal (Wincze, 1989). For example, a man experiencing an erectile disorder might be encouraged to avoid unpleasant thoughts about performance anxiety and instead think about pleasurable sexual fantasies.

Behavior therapists also use sexual re-education strategies aimed at eliminating sexual myths and misinformation, homework assignments such as couple communication exercises, and imagery techniques designed to assess and rehearse desired sexual responses. Finally, assertiveness training exercises focus on teaching sexually inhibited men and women to express their needs and feelings, such as learning how to say no to an activity they dislike (Leiblum & Pervin, 1980).

THE COGNITIVE MODEL. The **cognitive model of sex therapy** proposes that thinking processes are the driving force behind how people feel and what they do. Cognitive therapists maintain that when thinking is logical and sensible, behavior is stable and harmonious, but when thinking is contaminated by irrational thought processes, maladjustment is likely.

Sexual disorders, then, are the result of faulty or distorted styles of thought. To correct dysfunctional behavior, people must change their unrealistic and irrational perceptions and conditions. Cognitive therapists help clients do this by systematically analyzing and manipulating their thinking and reasoning.

One of the best-known cognitive approaches is **rational-emotive therapy,** developed by Albert Ellis (1989, 1980). Ellis proposes that many psychological disorders, including those of a sexual nature, stem from irrational beliefs that are self-defeating and usually reflect inaccurate assumptions about oneself and others. While irrational beliefs take a variety of forms, almost all reflect the notion that one *must* do something: "I *must* be loved by others," "I *must* be a perfect lover" or "I *must* be in control," for example. Such inflexible and unrealistic expectations are bound to create anxiety, frustration, and disappointment. Worse, they perpetuate the original irrational belief in a vicious, self-defeating cycle.

Cognitive sex therapy is very structured and time-efficient, and focuses directly on specific problems identified by the client. The therapist plays an active role by pointing out the client's illogical thinking and suggesting more realistic ways of handling problems. It is very important for clients to realize that their maladaptive behavior is largely self-inflicted. Through this therapy, the client is helped to act more logically and responsibly.

The rational-emotive approach to sexual disorders embraces a mixture of techniques, including many of the behavioral approaches previously discussed. The therapist also focuses on disputing clients' irrational sex beliefs and attacking myths, and provides accurate sex information, partner education, and imaging methods. Imaging

cognitive model of sex therapy A therapeutic approach that emphasizes how people must change their faulty or distorted styles of thought to overcome their sexual dysfunctions.

rational-emotive therapy A therapeutic approach developed by Albert Ellis. It suggests that many psychological disorders, including those of a sexual nature, originate in irrational beliefs.

methods center on the notion that sexual arousal can be "willed" or unspontaneously incited by thinking highly sexual thoughts. Clients with arousal disorders, therefore, may be asked to imagine erotic sexual acts or fantasies to initiate excitement. Other techniques include the provision of unconditional acceptance, reassurance and support, and shame-attacking exercises. These exercises are designed to show clients, such as men with erectile dysfunction, that no act in itself is "shameful" or "humili-

MAKING USE OF WHAT WE KNOW

How to Select a Qualified Sex Therapist

Choosing a qualified sex therapist can be a confusing chore. As we've learned in this chapter, there are many therapeutic models and a number of different types of professionals in the field. Complicating the search is that, to date, there are very few regulations governing the licensing or practice of sex therapists. The following suggestions may help in the overall selection procedure:

- *Look for a referral from a reliable source.* To find a qualified sex expert in your area, you might want to call a local college or university psychology department, mental health association, or mental health clinic. Other possible sources of referral are a family physician, hospital, or religious figure. Never accept a referral uncritically. Rather, use it as a starting point for your own analysis and appraisal of choices.

- *Use professional organizations to help you with your search.* For example, you can obtain a list of certified sex therapists from the American Association of Sex Educators, Counselors, and Therapists (AASECT). The address is 435 N. Michigan Ave., Suite 1717, Chicago IL 60611.

- *Examine the therapist's credentials.* Don't be afraid to be assertive. Ask about the therapist's degrees (therapists treating sexual dysfunctions typically hold an M.D., Ph.D., or a master's degree), as well as about areas of expertise and affiliation with particular schools of therapy. Qualified therapists should have training in both psychotherapy and sex therapy from a recognized college or university. Many therapists welcome such inquiries and are happy to provide the information.

- *Do not hesitate to talk to two or three therapists before deciding on one with whom to work.* The chemistry between therapist and client is a critical component of the counseling process. Consider your comfort level with the therapist, particularly with how the therapist assesses your difficulty and proposes to treat it. Avoid any therapist who promises a "miracle cure" or instant results, wants full payment in advance, or, above all, makes sexual advances.

- *Carefully investigate the cost of therapy.* Traditionally, therapists with more advanced degrees, such as psychiatrists, charge the most. However, a higher fee does not necessarily ensure better or more efficient treatment. Some sex therapists offer a sliding-fee scale; that is, their fee is based on your ability to pay. Additionally, health insurance sometimes provides coverage for treatment. Finally, don't forget to investigate group therapy. Many times it is cheaper than individual therapy.

- *Give therapy a chance to be successful.* Therapy takes time and effort; change does not happen overnight. Today many therapists draw up a contract with their clients, outlining what they would like to accomplish in therapy as well as the number of proposed sessions. Such an approach helps to clarify expectations and the degree of commitment needed from both parties. If you are dissatisfied with therapy once it is under way, don't be reluctant to discuss your feelings with your therapist. A reputable therapist will help you sort out your feelings about the therapy, and often will refer you to someone else who is better equipped to deal with your particular problem.

ating" and that it is only made so through the individual's self-deprecating attitude (McCarthy, 1989; Barlow, 1986; Gagnon, Rose, & Leiblum, 1982; Ellis, 1989, 1980).

THE GROUP MODEL. The **group model of sex therapy** is a form of sex therapy in which a group of people (usually six to eight) meet at planned times with a qualified therapist to focus on a particular sexual problem. The group approach to sexual issues such as incest, sexual coercion, and various dysfunctions has become increasingly popular. Many of the previously discussed therapeutic models have been adapted for use with groups, most notably the behavioral and cognitive approaches.

The group model has several advantages. One is that some people feel more comfortable in a group setting than in individual therapy. Many men and women benefit from receiving group support and the reassurance that they are not the only ones with their particular sexual problem. Group members also typically learn from one another's experiences. In addition, groups give individuals some understanding of how their behavior affects others through group feedback. The group approach also helps solve the problem of not having enough skilled therapists available to meet everyone's needs. It is economical as well, both in terms of the therapist's time and the client's finances since it is usually less expensive than individual therapy.

The group model has been used successfully with both individuals and couples and for a wide range of sexual problems. It appears to be particularly effective for reducing feelings of inadequacy because group members realize they have a lot of company in their problems and experiences. The group model helps people learn to communicate better about their dysfunctional sexual behavior. It also provides a protected environment where people can experiment with change and test out their newly discovered knowledge and skills. The group approach has been successfully applied to such problems as orgasm disorders, male erectile disorder, and premature ejaculation, as well as to the enhancement of sexual pleasure for both young and old couples (Kilmann et al., 1987; Spence, 1985; Cotten-Huston & Wheeler, 1983; Weis & Meadow, 1983; Mills & Kilmann, 1982; Kuriansky & Sharpe, 1981; Perelman, 1980; Barbach, 1980).

group model of sex therapy An approach to the treatment of sexual dysfunctions that usually involves six to eight people meeting with a qualified therapist to focus on a particular sexual problem.

Putting Sex Therapy Models into Perspective

All of these models give us a great deal of insight into the therapeutic possibilities for sexual dysfunctions. Though each offers a unique perspective on how sexual disorders are acquired and how they can be approached, these theoretical models do not have to be weighed in an either/or fashion. There is considerable overlap among the five theoretical approaches we discussed, and some have proved more effective than others with certain problems and clients.

Many sex therapists today are eclectic with regard to theories, strategies, and approaches. That is, they take bits and pieces of many theories and develop their own basic therapeutic approach. Then, depending on the problem at hand and the individual client or couple, they construct and apply the most effective theoretical framework. But what does this mean for the person in need of sexual counseling? The box on "How to Select a Qualified Sex Therapist" will give you some guidelines.

While all of these theoretical models have broadened our understanding of sexual dysfunctions, we still cannot answer all of our questions about sexual disorders. No theory developed to date can explain exactly how sexual dysfunctions are acquired and specify the "perfect" way to treat them. This underscores the need for further investigations of sexual dysfunctions and continual assessment of the theories and viewpoints generated.

SEXUALITY IN THE NEWS

When Ugliness Is Only in Patient's Eye, Body Image Can Reflect Mental Disorder

by Daniel Goleman

A woman in her 30's, convinced she had excessive facial hair, was so intent on not being seen in public that she sped from place to place on a motorcycle. She would even run red lights, for fear someone would see her as she waited for the light to change.

A man in his 20's felt people stared at what he imagined were his "pointed ears" and "large nostrils." He eventually quit his job and stayed home rather than face the humiliation he was sure awaited him outside.

And a 28-year-old man who was preoccupied with his thinning hair was unconsoled by reassurances from four dermatologists that his hair loss was normal and barely noticeable. He became deeply depressed.

Diagnosis Is Rare

Each of these people was suffering from what psychiatrists call body dysmorphic disorder, or imagined ugliness, a relatively new formal diagnosis. Such cases are being reported with greater and greater frequency.

Though the diagnosis is made comparatively rarely, psychologists studying body image estimate that 2 percent to 10 percent of people are so self-conscious about some aspect of their looks that it constricts their life in some way: keeping them from making love or dating and even rendering them homebound or suicidal. Many make a fruitless round of cosmetic surgeons, never satisfied. . . .

Most keep secret their firm belief that they are deformed. They may spend hours staring in mirrors at the imagined deformities and may go to great lengths to disguise them with clothing or cosmetics. But typically, "they don't tell a soul," said Dr. Katherine Phillips, a psychiatrist at Harvard Medical School. . . .

Frequently such people go into therapy for other problems, particularly depression, but often are so ashamed of their imagined disfigurements that they do not confide their preoccupations even to the therapists, said Dr. Phillips. And because they are more likely to consult cosmetic surgeons or dermatologists than psychotherapists, they typically get no psychological treatment.

Change Their Attitudes . . .

The number of people who say they are unhappy with their physical features, though not necessarily to the extent that therapy is needed, has risen markedly over the last two decades. For example, a 1972 survey by Dr. Cash said that 35 percent of men and 48 percent of women were dissatisfied with their weight; by 1985 the figures had risen to 41 percent for men and 55 percent for women.

Body image researchers are troubled by findings like a 1987 survey of 500 children in elementary school that found more than half the girls thought they were overweight and 31 percent of 10-year-olds said they "felt fat," though only 15 percent were actually heavier than the norm. Researchers say that such distorted thinking plays a large role in the development of eating disorders.

Distorted views of the body are due in part to "an insidious contrast effect," in which people compare themselves with the models in advertisements, said Dr. Rita Freedman, a psychologist in Scarsdale, N.Y. "Carefully contrived advertisements compress standards of attractiveness into a young, idealized extreme that is virtually unattainable," said Dr. Freedman, who has developed treatments for the problem.

Because the psychological pressures of these standards fall more heavily on women than men, women are, on average, more negative about their bodies than are men. For example, in a 1989 study of 80 men and women, volunteers carried a beeper that randomly signaled them to record their circumstances and thoughts about their body. Men reported many more positive thoughts than did women. Women more frequently reported judging some part of their body harshly. . . .

Dr. Kearney-Cook's approach is to help people see the connection between emotional states and feelings about their bodies. "One woman told me she was in a board meeting

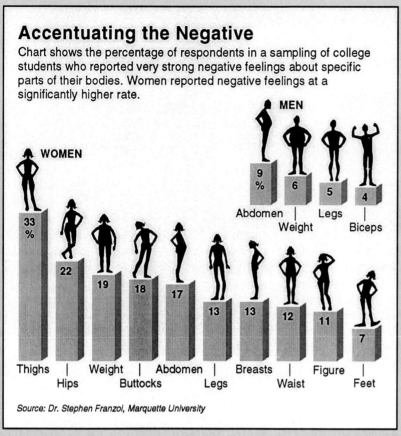

Accentuating the Negative

Chart shows the percentage of respondents in a sampling of college students who reported very strong negative feelings about specific parts of their bodies. Women reported negative feelings at a significantly higher rate.

MEN

9%	6	5	4
Abdomen	Weight	Legs	Biceps

WOMEN

33%	22	19	18	17	13	13	12	11	7
Thighs	Hips	Weight	Buttocks	Abdomen	Legs	Breasts	Waist	Figure	Feet

Source: Dr. Stephen Franzoi, Marquette University

N.Y. Times News Service

when she suddenly got self-conscious that she had acne scars and her nose was too big," said Dr. Kearney-Cooke. "I asked her to recall exactly what was happening at that moment. She had just been challenged to defend her position, which, deep inside, made her feel inadequate and insecure."

In therapy with the woman, Dr. Kearney-Cooke had her relax, then call to mind occasions in her early life when she had felt similar feelings.

"It's often a moment like when parents ignore a child who has come home from school," said Dr. Kearney-Cooke. "The child turns that feeling of being rejected onto something about her own body. But once they see that it's the feeling that's the problem, they can begin to realize that their feelings about their body are a distortion." (*The New York Times*, October 2, 1991. Copyright © 1991 by The New York Times Company. Reprinted with permission.)

DISCUSSION QUESTIONS

1. Were you surprised at the research findings that women are more concerned about their body image than men are? How would you account for this finding?

2. What course of treatment—psychotherapy and/or surgery—would you pursue if you felt you had a physical characteristic that was unattractive? With whom would you first discuss the problem? Support your choice.

3. How might perceived ugliness keep someone from making love, as the article suggests? Might this perception cause feelings of sexual inadequacy or sexual dysfunction?

LOOKING BACK

■ Broadly defined, a sexual dysfunction is a problem in sexual responding that can occur at any phase of the sexual response cycle. Typically, there is a disturbance both in the subjective sense of desire or pleasure and in sexual performance. Sexual dysfunctions may be psychological in origin or they may be caused by both physical and psychological factors. Furthermore, they can be lifelong or acquired, as well as generalized or situational. Moreover, some people exhibit more than one sexual dysfunction.

■ A sexual desire disorder is defined as a lack of sexual drive or motivation and can be broken down into two main types. An inhibited sexual desire disorder is characterized by the absence or near absence of sexual fantasies and desire for sexual activity. A sexual aversion disorder is persistent or extreme aversion to, and avoidance of, all or almost all genital sexual contact with a sexual partner. In addition to fatigue and the boredom of routine, possible causes of sexual desire disorders are fear of pregnancy, depression, hormonal imbalances, medication side effects, lack of attraction to one's partner, relationship conflict, and poor lovemaking skills.

■ Sexual arousal disorders are characterized by a general lack of sexual responsiveness when there is adequate stimulation during sexual activity. Female sexual arousal disorders are said to occur when there is persistent partial or complete failure to attain or maintain the lubrication-swelling response of sexual excitement until completion of the sexual activity. Also, there is a persistent or recurrent lack of a subjective sense of sexual excitement and pleasure during sexual activity. The male counterpart to a female sexual arousal disorder is an erectile dysfunction. Erectile dysfunction refers to persistent or recurrent partial or complete failure to attain or maintain an erection until completion of the sexual activity. Also, there may be a persistent or recurrent lack of a subjective sense of sexual excitement and pleasure during sexual activity.

■ Orgasm disorders are subdivided into three main types: inhibited female orgasm, retarded ejaculation, and premature ejaculation. Inhibited female orgasm refers to a persistent or recurrent delay in, or absence of, orgasm following adequate sexual arousal and stimulation. Retarded ejaculation is defined as a persistent or recurrent delay in, or absence of, intravaginal orgasm following adequate sexual excitement. Premature ejaculation is persistent or recurrent ejaculation with minimal sexual stimulation or before, upon, or shortly after penetration and before the couple wish it to happen. Faked orgasm is also considered to be a kind of orgasm disorder by some clinicians.

■ Dyspareunia and vaginismus are two types of sexual pain disorders. Dyspareunia, which can occur in both men and women, refers to recurrent or persistent genital pain before, during, or after sexual intercourse. Vaginismus is a female sexual pain disorder characterized by recurrent or persistent involuntary constriction of the musculature surrounding the vaginal opening and the outer third of the vagina.

■ Important advances have been made in the therapeutic strategies designed to treat sexual dysfunctions. Annon's PLISSIT model of treatment provides a framework for sex therapy consisting of four progressive levels: permission, limited information, specific suggestions, and intensive therapy. The most widely used sex therapy models are the Masters and Johnson, Kaplan, behavioral, cognitive, and group models. These models need not be weighed in an all-or-none fashion. To date, no one model has exactly explained how all of the sexual dysfunctions originate or how they can be perfectly treated. Therefore, many sex therapists today are eclectic in their strategies and techniques.

THINKING THINGS OVER

1. You have read that many couples encounter some type of sexual dysfunction. Describe one sexual dysfunction and what might cause it. Do you believe this dysfunction might happen to you? Under what circumstances?

2. We know that women and men differ in many significant ways when it comes to sexual dysfunctions. Contrast two sexual disorders, one usually found in women and the other in men, and determine if each disorder is relational or individual in nature.

3. Of the five treatment models you've read about in this chapter, which would you choose if you had a sexual problem? Why?

4. You and your sexual partner have decided to seek guidance from a sex therapist. How would you go about choosing a qualified sex therapist?

Cole, E., & Rothblum, E. D. (eds.) (1989). *Women and sex therapy*. New York: Haworth Press. Part one supplies an interesting feminist critique of the sexual dysfunction nomenclature and the concept of female sexual ecstasy.

Leiblum, S. R., & Rosen, R. C. (eds.) (1989). *Principles and practices of sex therapy*, 2nd ed. New York: Guilford Press. All of the major sexual dysfunctions are featured in this well-written and informative text.

Leiblum, S. R., & Rosen, R. C. (eds.) (1988). *Sexual desire disorders*. New York: Guilford Press. A thorough analysis of sexual desire disorders, including cognitive, biological and medical perspectives.

Masters, W. H., & Johnson, V. E. (1970). *Human sexual inadequacy*. Boston: Little, Brown. A classic text detailing the highly successful Masters and Johnson model of sex therapy.

Rosen, R .C., & Beck, J. G. (1988). *Patterns of sexual arousal*. New York: Guilford Press. Chapters 10 and 11 deal, respectively, with male and female sexual dysfunctions.

Weinstein, E., & Rosen, E. (1988). *Sexuality counseling: Issues and implications*. Monterey, CA: Brooks/Cole. See Chapter 2 of this readable text for a discussion of treatment of sexual dysfunctions.

17
Sexual Health and Disease

The first wealth is health

—Ralph Waldo Emerson

Each contact with a human being is so rare, so precious, one should preserve it

—Anaïs Nin

*T*hroughout this book we have shown how the healthy reproductive system operates in a balanced fashion. When functioning properly, it is a finely tuned network of tissues, ducts, and organs. Each part contributes to the healthy functioning of the larger system and ensures the survival of the individual, not to mention the species.

A smoothly functioning reproductive system also contributes to sexual health. In addition to physiological well-being, the concept of sexual health embraces knowledge of those factors that create optimal sexual functioning, including an awareness of sexually transmitted diseases, infections, and other disorders of the reproductive system, as well as how each can be prevented. Moreover, a sexually healthy person has a well-developed value system that helps guide sound sexual decision making, a topic discussed in Chapter 6.

This chapter is intended to develop your knowledge of sexual health and disease. In the first part of our discussion, we emphasize the sexually transmitted diseases, including their symptoms and treatment. Then we present some of the major non-sexually transmitted diseases that affect the sexual and reproductive organs. Next we explore cancers of the reproductive organs. We include cancers of the reproductive organs in this chapter because of the growing consensus that there is a connection between sexually transmitted diseases and certain forms of cancer (for example, genital herpes has been linked to cervical cancer). Thus you lower your chances of getting certain forms of cancer by making a concerted effort to promote your own sexual health and that of those you love. The concluding section of the chapter, on prevention and safer sex practices, provides a bridge to Chapter 18, which is devoted to the acquired immune deficiency syndrome, or AIDS.

You might think that health—and thus the subject of prevention—should logically precede the section on disease. However, you need to know what sexual diseases are before we can talk sensibly about how to prevent them. So as we go along, keep in mind that we'll explore prevention at the end of the chapter.

In this chapter you'll discover:

☐ *What sexual health is and why it is considered important for optimal sexual functioning.*

☐ *What a sexually transmitted disease is, how widespread such diseases are, and who is at particular risk for contracting them.*

☐ *How sexually transmitted diseases are grouped into viral, bacterial, and parasitic classifications.*

☐ *The nature of nonsexually transmitted diseases of the reproductive system.*

☐ *Some of the major cancers of the reproductive organs.*

☐ *How you can promote your sexual health and prevent disease.*

WHAT ARE STDs AND HOW WIDESPREAD ARE THEY?

A **sexually transmitted disease** is a contagious infection that, for the most part, is passed on by intimate sexual contact with others. The sexual contact can be through French (open-mouthed) kissing, coitus, oral-genital sex, or anal intercourse. Sometimes infections can be transmitted without sexual contact, such as by sharing needles.

Sexually transmitted diseases are quite widespread in modern society and have many sobering consequences. Consider these facts:

- About 10 million people in the United States were newly infected with a sexually transmitted disease in 1990.
- More than half of sexually transmitted disease victims are under the age of 25; almost one-quarter will be infected before they receive their high school diplomas.
- One in four Americans between the ages of 15 and 55 will eventually acquire a sexually transmitted disease.
- Approximately 200 million new cases of gonorrhea occur throughout the world each year.
- About 40 million new cases of syphilis occur annually in the world.
- Cases of genital herpes in the United States have increased tenfold in the last 20 years.

sexually transmitted disease A contagious infection that, for the most part, is passed on by intimate sexual contact with others. The sexual contact can be through open-mouthed kissing, coitus, oral-genital sex, or anal intercourse.

503

- There are approximately 12 million cases of genital warts in the United States today.
- Chlamydial infections have become the most common bacterial STD in the United States.
- Over 100,000 babies born each year in the United States have diseases or malformations associated with sexually transmitted diseases of the mother.
- Pelvic inflammatory disease causes loss of fertility in about 100,000 women annually in the United States.

In presenting these statistics, we must point out that U.S. law requires medical authorities to report only certain sexually transmitted diseases, including AIDS, gonorrhea, syphilis, and hepatitis B. Many others, such as chlamydia and herpes, do not have to be reported, so we can only make an educated guess about their incidence. Complicating matters is the failure of many physicians and clinics to make reports on a regular basis, often out of the desire to protect a long-time patient or family friend from embarrassment. Unfortunately, this usually means there is no adequate follow-up of sexual partners, which makes it hard to break the chain of infection (Boskin, Graf, & Kreisworth, 1990).

Certain population groups are more at risk than others for contracting sexually transmitted diseases. According to Robert Hatcher and associates (1990), these groups include people under 25, minorities, the medically underserved, and gay men. For example, two-thirds of reported cases of gonorrhea occur in those 25 years of age or younger. Rates of syphilis, gonorrhea, and pelvic inflammatory disease serious enough to require hospitalization are highest in adolescents and decline with increasing age.

African-Americans are two to three times more likely than whites to contract a sexually transmitted disease. Low-income people living in urban areas, is also more vulnerable to STDs than people in higher-socioeconomic groups and those living in suburban and rural areas. A number of reasons may explain why these population groups are more vulnerable: inadequate medical services, higher rates of other diseases, unsanitary living conditions, overcrowding, and ignorance about STDs. Other vulnerable groups—such as migrants and immigrants—may also be medically underserved or difficult to reach through traditional health channels. In addition, they may encounter language and cultural barriers to treatment. They may also carry resistant strains of STDs.

Sexually transmitted diseases embody a kind of biological sexism. The signs and symptoms of most STDs are more easily noticed in men, while women frequently have no complaints or clinical signs in the early phases of the disease (particularly gonorrhea and syphilis) and therefore fail to get treatment. Women also suffer more serious long-term consequences from all STDs. Moreover, they are more likely than men to contract a sexually transmitted disease from any single sexual encounter. As an illustration, the risk of acquiring gonorrhea from a single coital encounter in which one partner is infectious is about 25 percent for men and 50 percent for women (Hatcher et al., 1990).

KINDS OF SEXUALLY TRANSMITTED DISEASES

There are different ways to classify sexually transmitted diseases. One approach is to categorize them according to their symptoms, such as skin lesions. Another method is to group them according to their prevalence. Our approach is to categorize STDs according to their etiology, or causes. Even though some STDs are not caused by any

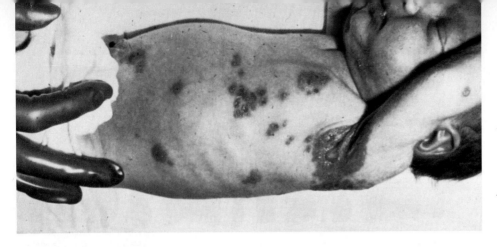

A baby born to a woman with a herpes infection is likely to have any of a number of problems, including skin rashes that can become severely infected.

one agent in particular, we can nonetheless generally distinguish between viral, bacterial, and parasitic diseases.

Viral Diseases

Viral diseases are those caused by a virus. Viruses have no metabolism of their own, so they borrow what they need for growth and reproduction from the cells they invade. They direct cells to produce more virus instead of more cells. Viral STDs include genital herpes, genital warts, and viral hepatitis. The acquired immune deficiency syndrome, or AIDS, which we discuss in the next chapter, is also a viral disease.

GENITAL HERPES. Genital herpes is caused by the herpes simplex virus, also called *Herpes virus hominis,* or HVH. The herpes simplex virus exists in two forms: *herpes simplex I (HSV-I),* which causes cold sores and fever blisters above the waist; and *herpes simplex II (HSV-II),* which causes lesions and infections below the waist on the genitals, anus, buttocks, or thighs. However, the two forms often mix, and either virus type can infect skin or mucous membranes anywhere on the body. Thus genital herpes is an infection of the genital area by either herpes simplex I or herpes simplex II (Corey & Holmes, 1983).

An estimated 10 million Americans currently suffer from genital herpes, with 300,000 new cases being reported every year. Over the past 20 years there has been a tenfold increase in the number of reported cases. Because there is still no cure for genital herpes, the number of cases continues to spiral upward. People between the ages of 15 and 40 are the most frequent victims (Centers for Disease Control, 1991, 1989; Hatcher et al., 1990; Connor-Greene, 1986).

Genital herpes is spread primarily through intimate sexual contact. People who began having sex at an early age and who have multiple partners are at risk for developing the disease. Genital herpes can lead to such complications as meningitis, a narrowing of the urethra, and even blindness. Moreover, a pregnant woman infected with genital herpes can transmit the disease to her child if she delivers vaginally during an active disease stage. Consequences to the child include skin infection, nervous system damage, and even death (Breslin, 1988). Finally, there may be a link between genital herpes and cervical cancer in women.

The herpes virus does not travel from one location to another. After the initial infection, the virus lodges in the center of a specific sensory nerve cell (see Figure 17–1), where it becomes inactive, or latent. However, herpes will "flare up" from time to time in a recurrence of symptomatic disease in which the virus becomes reactivated. It is thought that the virus follows the same nerve, and multiplies on the skin at, or near, the site of the original sore. Sexual contact is not necessary for a recurrence (Lafferty et al., 1987; Judson, 1983).

genital herpes A sexually transmitted disease caused by herpes simplex viruses. The virus itself lodges in the cell center of specific sensory nerves.

Are there different types of herpes, and how is this virus transmitted? Where are the sores most likely to appear?

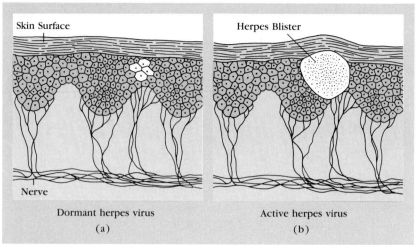

FIGURE 17–1
Herpes Simplex II.

In (a), the virus lies dormant within a nerve cell. In (b), the virus is activated by stress or illness, and herpes blisters result.

The incubation period for genital herpes is between three and seven days, and symptoms recur in over half of those infected (Higgins & Hawkins, 1984). Tingling or burning in the infected area typically accompanies the primary outbreak. Usually, a rash of red patches with white blisterlike sores appears, often in clusters. The infection usually appears on or around the penis in men, and in the vagina in women. Internal sores can also occur in the mouth, vagina, cervix, or anus—anywhere the virus first enters the body. Beyond the rash, one or all of the following symptoms may be present: pain and discomfort in the area of the infection, fever, headache, and a general feeling of ill health. Also common is pain or a burning feeling when urinating. Glands in the groin area may become swollen. Women may notice a vaginal discharge (Stone, Grimes, & Magder, 1986; Freudberg & Emanuel, 1982).

Herpes sores are present for variable amounts of time—some healing in a matter of days, others taking a month or more to heal. Once the sores have disappeared, the person may believe the infection has left the body, but this is not so because the virus remains in the nerve tissue and possibly in the skin. Subsequent eruptions of herpes sores and other symptoms are related to the virus's recurring cycles of infectious activity and inactivity. Each time the virus is reactivated, the person is contagious again (the risk of infection during asymptomatic periods is much lower). Many stimuli can trigger an eruption, including emotional stress, overexposure to the sun, a cold, fever, menstruation, and physical activity. Generally, the symptoms of the first outbreak are more serious than those of recurrent infections.

As we said, there is no cure for genital herpes. However, acute outbreaks can now be treated with either the antiviral drug acyclovir (Zovirax) or laser therapy, both of which heal blisters, reduce pain, and, most important, kill large numbers of the herpes virus. In many people, acyclovir reduces the reproduction of the virus in the initial outbreak, thus possibly lessening the number of subsequent outbreaks (see Wilbanks, 1987; Mertz, 1984). For laser therapy to be effective, it must be started immediately after the first sores appear. Other recommended treatments include the use of aspirin or other pain relievers and the application of ice packs to the affected area (Straus, Seidlin, & Takiff, 1984). Table 17–1 outlines a number of steps that those infected with genital herpes can take to help themselves. (For more information, contact **Herpes Resource Center,** P.O. Box 13827, Research Triangle Park, NC 27709; or the **Herpes Hotline,** 919-361-2120.)

TABLE 17–1

How to Treat Genital Herpes

- See a physician at the first sign of a genital lesion.
- Keep the genital area clean and dry.
- Apply acyclovir ointment or any other medication prescribed by the physician with a finger protector or rubber glove to prevent infecting other parts of the body.
- Avoid sexual contact (including kissing) when lesions are visible. This rule must be followed, especially during the blistering stage, when the disease is most contagious.
- When one or both partners have had a genital herpes infection, barrier contraceptive methods such as latex condoms or spermicides (containing nonoxynol-9) can reduce the risk of transmission during a flare-up of the disease.
- If a woman has had lesions on her cervix, she should use a diaphragm, even if she has no lesions on her external genitals. The use of a vaginal contraceptive sponge impregnated with spermicide (nonoxynol-9) may act as a physical and chemical barrier against cervical herpes lesions.
- Smearing a spermicide on the outer genitalia does not ensure freedom from infection but may offer added protection.
- Wear only 100 percent cotton underwear and loose-fitting clothing during periods when the lesions are visible. Women should avoid pantyhose with nylon crotch inserts.
- Avoid wearing wet clothing (such as bathing suits) for extended periods; wet garments tend to aggravate and spread lesions.
- Sexually active women of childbearing age who have had genital herpes infections should get a Pap smear every six months to improve their chances for early detection of cervical cancer.

Source: Adapted from Covington & McClendon, 1987.

GENITAL WARTS. Genital warts are caused by the human papilloma virus (HPV) and are transmitted almost exclusively by sexual contact. There are many different strains of genital warts, and they are usually found on the penis or vulva or in the vagina or rectum. In rare instances they appear on the mouth, lips, nipple, or umbilicus. Genital warts are a widespread viral condition and tend to afflict men and women who began sexual activity early in life and who have had multiple sexual partners. As many as one in ten Americans may be carrying this virus (Carroll & Miller, 1991).

Genital warts may occur as single or multiple growths (see Figure 17–2). When they develop in clusters, the lesions take on a cauliflower appearance. Some are flat or appear deep within the vagina or on the cervix. The warts range in color from pink to red, and they tend to be moist and soft. They also tend to proliferate with perspiration and poor personal hygiene. People who have once had genital warts are susceptible to getting them again (Becker & Larsen, 1984; Oriel, 1981).

genital warts A sexually transmitted disease originating from the human papilloma virus and usually found on the penis, vulva, vagina, or rectum.

FIGURE 17–2
Genital Warts.

In this case the entire tip of the penis is completely surrounded by the cauliflower-like growths.

The incubation period for genital warts varies from six weeks to eight months. Usually, the person seeks medical care for painless growths in the perineal area, although sometimes the complaint is pain and bleeding. Some people experience occasional itching. If the warts become infected, an odor may develop. Left untreated, genital warts can grow as large as 4 inches (Margolis, 1982).

In recent years genital warts have been linked to cervical cancer. Therefore, any woman with a history of genital warts should have an annual Pap smear. Research (e.g., Richart, 1987) also tells us that the human papilloma virus is one of the major causes of cancers in the lower abdominal organs.

In men genital warts are frequently found in the prepuce or on the urethral meatus or the penile shaft. The damp and warm environment of the prepuce provides an opportune breeding ground for the virus. The vulva and the vaginal and cervical walls are common locations for genital warts in women. For reasons unknown, genital warts proliferate markedly during pregnancy, then regress after delivery.

There are several different modes of treatment for genital warts. A popular approach is the local application of podophyllin, a cytotoxic agent that removes genital warts in two to four days. Podophyllin must be washed off with soap and water four to six hours after it is applied to prevent burns and injuries to normal skin. Podophyllin is not recommended for pregnant women since it may cause fetal mutations. Other treatment approaches include cryotherapy (freezing the warts with liquid nitrogen), electrocautery (using an electric current to burn away the warts), and laser therapy or the local application of such substances as idoxuridine, 5-Fluorouracil, and trichloracetic acid to burn away the warts (Howley, 1986; Ferenczy, 1984).

viral hepatitis An infectious disease that attacks the liver and causes inflammation. The disease is caused by several viruses, including hepatitis A, hepatitis B, and non-A/non-B hepatitis.

VIRAL HEPATITIS. **Viral hepatitis** is an infectious disease that attacks the liver and causes inflammation. It is estimated that almost one million Americans develop viral hepatitis each year. The disease is caused by several viruses, the most common strains being hepatitis A, hepatitis B, and non-A, non-B hepatitis. Let's examine each more closely.

Hepatitis A, also referred to as *infectious hepatitis*, is caused by a virus typically excreted in the feces. Hepatitis A can be contracted by direct contact with fecal matter, as well as through oral-anal contact and anal intercourse. It can also be transmitted by contaminated food, water, or unsanitary living conditions. The latter conditions have been known to cause epidemics of the virus (Francis, 1984).

Hepatitis B, also called *serum hepatitis* because it is found in the body fluids of the infected person, can be contracted through sexual contact, from contaminated blood transfusions, or by using contaminated syringes and needles (including unsanitary instruments used for tattooing, ear piercing, acupuncture, medical or dental work, and the like). Hepatitis B can also be acquired by sharing the razor or toothbrush of an infected person. The virus can live in almost all body fluids, including saliva, semen, urine, and menstrual blood (Lemon, 1984).

Non-A/non-B hepatitis is a more obscure viral strain, and not much is known about it. Its transmission is primarily by blood transfusion from an infected donor. However, it can also be passed by other means, including sexual contact.

The incubation period for viral hepatitis ranges from one to six months. The early symptoms include general fatigue, joint and muscle ache, loss of appetite, fever, and headaches. Because its symptoms are like those of the flu, hepatitis often goes untreated and the virus is allowed to spread. As the disease develops, the liver enlarges and becomes tender. Usually the person experiences weight loss, chills, and a particular distaste for cigarettes, coffee, and tea (Lemon, 1984; Zuckerman, 1982).

In time, other symptoms unique to hepatitis develop. These include darkening of urine color, lightening of stool color, increased liver sensitivity, and jaundice. *Jaundice* is a yellowing of the skin and the whites of the eyes that is caused by an accumulation of yellow pigment in the blood.

Sexual Health and Disease

There is no specific treatment for viral hepatitis. Usually, the body's immune system eventually subdues the disease, which in more severe cases can take several months. The best treatment regimen is avoidance of all strenuous activity, increased fluid intake, and a light, healthy diet. Alcoholic beverages should be avoided since alcohol further strains the liver and can cause serious injury. The person must abstain from sexual contact with others until a blood test indicates that the virus has left the body. In acute cases of viral hepatitis, strict bed rest is usually advised. Some serious cases require blood transfusions to aid recovery.

Viral hepatitis can be prevented or minimized with an injection of antibodies obtained from a donor pool. One such serum is gammaglobulin, which is particularly effective against hepatitis A and offers some protection against hepatitis B. Another serum, hepatitis B immune globulin (HBIG), is effective against the hepatitis B viral strain. A recently developed vaccine against hepatitis B stimulates the production of antibodies to fight the viral infection. In its present state the vaccine is effective at preventing the infection but does not help people who have already become ill (Corey, 1982).

Bacterial Diseases

Bacterial STDs enter the body primarily through sexual contact and cause infection in the genitals as well as in other parts of the body. Unlike viral diseases, bacterial diseases are able to multiply on their own outside a living cell. Among the more common bacterial STDs are gonorrhea, syphilis, and chlamydia.

GONORRHEA. Gonorrhea afflicts more than one million Americans each year. The word *gonorrhea* means "flow of seed" and was first used by the Greek physician Galen in A.D. 130 to describe the typical sign of the disease in men: a discharge from the penis. Gonorrhea is more common in men than in women and is highly contagious. The disease is particularly widespread among people between the ages of 15 and 30 (Peck, 1986; Cates & Holmes, 1986; Barnes & Holmes, 1984; Hansfield, 1984).

Gonorrhea is caused by the bacterium *Neisseria gonorrhoeae*, an organism that can live on any mucous membrane. The bacteria are spread for the most part by direct sexual contact with an infected person. The disease usually affects the penis in men, the vagina in women, and the throat and anus in both sexes. Research indicates (e.g., Platt, Rice, & McCormack, 1983) that women run a greater risk of contracting gonorrhea through a single exposure than men do, probably because the bacteria spread more rapidly in the female vulva. Left untreated in both women and men, gonorrhea can lead to a generalized blood infection, sterility, arthritis, and heart trouble. In men it can spread throughout the prostate gland and the male duct system, causing painful inflammation. In women untreated gonorrhea can lead to pelvic inflammatory disease, tightening of the urethral passage, and infertility. Table 17–2 lists the potential complications of untreated gonorrhea in both sexes.

gonorrhea A sexually transmitted disease caused by a bacterial infection and spread by sexual contact with an infected person. Gonorrhea is much more common in men than in women and is highly contagious.

Will gonorrhea clear up on its own?

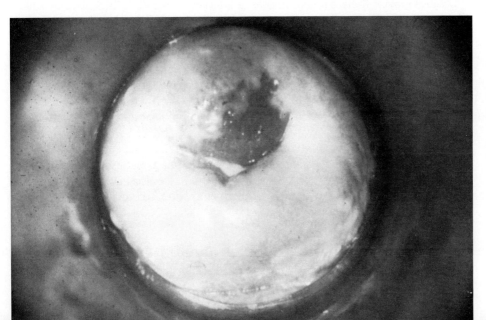

Gonorrhea can attack a woman's cervix—the paler, circular mound in the center of the photo—eroding its surface and providing a breeding ground for pelvic inflammatory disease.

509

TABLE 17-2

Potential Complications of Untreated Gonorrhea

SEX	COMPLICATION
Men	Epididymitis (inflammation of the epididymis)
	Prostatitis (inflammation of the prostate gland)
	Seminal vesiculitis (inflammation of the seminal vesicle)
	Periurethral abscess (a localized pus-containing infection in the area of the urethra)
	Cystitis (inflammation of the bladder)
	Arthritis-dermatitis syndrome (characterized by fever, painful joints, and skin lesions)*
	Sterility (as a result of scarring in the male reproductive tract)
	Endocarditis (inflammation of the membranes that line the heart)*
	Meningitis (inflammation of the membranes of the brain or spinal cord)*
Women	Involvement of Skene's and Bartholin's glands, which may become infected and inflamed
	Parametritis (inflammation of the uterus)
	Cystitis (inflammation of the bladder)
	Proctitis (inflammation of the rectum)
	Pelvic inflammatory disease:
	■ salpingitis (inflammation of the fallopian tube(s)
	■ pelvic abscess (a localized pus-containing infection in the pelvic region)
	■ pyosalpinx (fallopian tube swollen with pus)
	■ adhesions (scar tissue)
	■ peritonitis (inflammation of tissue lining the abdominal cavity)
	Sterility (as a result of scarring in the fallopian tubes)
	Endocarditis*
	Meningitis*

*Occurs only if gonorrhea is disseminated throughout the bloodstream.
Source: Adapted from Covington & McClendon, 1987.

Gonorrhea can also lead to other types of infections if the bacteria come into contact with the eyes. This can happen, for example, when people rub their eyes after having contact with infected genital organs. Also, a baby can contract this disease during the birth process as she/he passes through its mother's infected birth canal. Left untreated in newborns, this infection can cause blindness. Today most states require that a few drops of silver nitrate or penicillin be placed in the eyes of all newborns to prevent gonococcal infection.

The incubation period of gonorrhea is usually three to five days, though it is sometimes longer. In men the symptoms of gonorrhea include a thick, creamy yellow discharge from the penis. Painful and burning urination (dysuria) is also commonly reported. In as many as half of all women infected with gonorrhea, the disease does not cause any observable symptoms in the early stages (Peck, 1986). In time, however, infected women often experience a discharge from the vagina and uretha; frequent, painful urination; cloudy urine, vomiting; and diarrhea. Gonorrhea can also lead to pelvic inflammatory disease, which we will discuss shortly. If the Bartholin's gland becomes infected, the vaginal lips often darken in color and become swollen and tender.

If gonorrhea of the anus is contracted, symptoms often include bloody or mucus-filled discharges from the anus and pain during bowel movements. Gonorrhea of the throat may produce no noticeable symptoms or may reveal itself only by a scratchy, sore throat. As with other infections, gonorrhea is often accompanied by fever and swollen glands (Insel & Roth, 1991).

Uncomplicated gonorrhea can usually be controlled with antibiotics such as penicillin, tetracycline, or the related drug doxycycline (Vibramycin). Other drugs such as ceftriaxone are also treatment possibilities (see, for example, Judson, 1986). People under treatment should abstain from sexual activity until tests have confirmed that gonorrhea is no longer present. These tests are usually done one week after treatment begins, and sometimes again two weeks later. As with all forms of sexually transmitted diseases, every sexual partner of the infected person should be examined and, if necessary, treated (Washington, 1982).

Syphilis. Syphilis is caused by the spirochete *Treponema pallidum*, a thin cork-screwlike bacterium that thrives in warm, moist environments and is highly infectious. It enters the body through any tiny break in the mucous membranes and then burrows into the bloodstream. In most cases, syphilis is transmitted through sexual contact. The disease affects about 50,000–80,000 people each year, particularly those between the ages of 20 and 30 (Centers for Disease Control, 1991, 1989; Fitzgerald, 1984; Sacks, 1983).

Left untreated, syphilis can affect all parts of the body, including the brain, bones, spinal cord, heart, and reproductive organs. Blindness, brain damage, heart disease, and even death can result. Syphilis can also be transmitted from a mother to her unborn baby, causing congenital syphilis in the child. This may eventually result in blindness and deafness, among other serious consequences. Syphilis in a pregnant woman must be treated prior to the eighteenth week of pregnancy in order to prevent infection of the fetus.

The incubation period for syphilis is about 21 days. As a progressive disorder, syphilis passes through four stages: primary, secondary, latent, and late. *Primary syphilis* is marked by a painless open sore called a *chancre* (see Figure 17–3). This appears at the site where the spirochete entered the body, and it is usually the size of a dime or smaller. The chancre typically appears between 10 and 90 days after exposure to the disease, and disappears, with or without treatment, in three to six weeks. However, although the chancre has disappeared, the disease is still active within the body and will enter the second stage if left unchecked.

Secondary syphilis develops within six weeks to six months after initial infection. The symptoms of secondary syphilis may include a skin rash, whitish patches on the mucous membranes of the mouth, temporary baldness, low-grade fever, headache, swollen glands, and large, moist sores around the mouth or genitals. Without treatment, these symptoms typically last from three to six weeks, and the disease then progresses to the third stage.

During the *latent stage of syphilis* all symptoms disappear and the patient appears healthy. However, the spirochetes are still in the bloodstream and are burrowing

How is syphilis spread?

syphilis A highly infectious sexually transmitted disease. The syphilis bacterium can enter the body through any break in the mucous membrane, after which it burrows into the bloodstream.

Figure 17–3
A Chancre in Primary Syphilis.

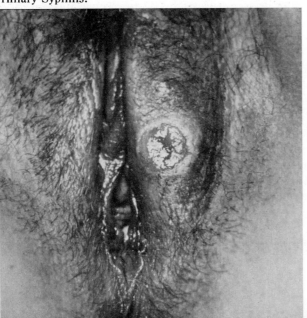

511

their way into the central nervous system and skeletal structure. This stage is a precursor to the highly destructive late stage.

During the *late stage of syphilis,* which may appear up to 15 or 20 years after initial exposure, the symptoms may be lethal. About 10 percent of patients develop *neurosyphilis,* or syphilis of the central nervous system. Neurosyphilis may manifest itself in delusions and hallucinations, seizures, paralysis, and coma that leads to death. In some cases, neurosyphilis causes destruction of nerve cells in the brain, meningitis, and vertigo. Late syphilis can also cause damage to the heart, skin, and bones.

Despite its damaging effects, syphilis is fairly easily treated today. Like gonorrhea, it can be controlled with antibiotics: penicillin, tetracycline, and erythromycin are usually the drugs of choice. Babies with congenital syphilis are usually treated with penicillin. People suffering from the late forms of syphilis usually need more aggressive treatment; often four times the dosage of antibiotics prescribed for early syphilis are required (Hansfield, 1986; Murphy & Patamasucon, 1984).

chlamydia A sexually transmitted disease caused by the parasite *Chlamydia trachomatis.* Chlamydial infections in women often lead to pelvic inflammatory disease and cervicitis; in men the infection often develops into nongonococcal urethritis, epididymitis, and proctitis.

CHLAMYDIA. Although **chlamydia** is one of the lesser known sexually transmitted diseases, it is the most widespread bacterial infection. Chlamydial infections occur in the urethra, cervix, or rectum and can produce serious complications. In recent years chlamydial infections have reached epidemic proportions, affecting 3 to 5 million persons annually. The disease is particularly common among college students (Centers for Disease Control, 1991, 1989; Washington, Johnson, & Sanders, 1987; Sanders, 1986; McCormack et al., 1985; Westrom & Mardh, 1982).

Besides infecting sexually active adults, chlamydia can be transmitted from mother to newborn during delivery. Babies who acquire this infection while passing through the birth canal often develop an eye infection called *chlamydial conjunctivitis,* as well as pneumonia. Pregnant women with chlamydial infections also risk spontaneous abortion, stillbirth, and postpartum fever (Swinkler, 1986, Crum & Ellner, 1985; Stamm & Holmes, 1984).

I've read that chlamydia is fairly common among college students and can lead to some complicated problems. Is this true?

Chlamydial infections are caused by the organism *Chlamydia trachomatis,* which has both bacterial and viral characteristics. Chlamydia is an insidious disease; that is, signs and symptoms of infection may not appear until complications have already set in. The incubation period is typically between one and three weeks. In women chlamydial infections often lead to pelvic inflammatory disease and cervicitis. Chlamydial infections in men often develop into nongonococcal urethritis, epididymitis, and proctitis. Let's examine each of these.

pelvic inflammatory disease (PID) An infection of the pelvic organs in women, particularly the upper genital tract.

PELVIC INFLAMMATORY DISEASE (PID). Pelvic inflammatory disease (PID) is a catch-all phrase that refers to infection of the pelvic organs in women, particularly the upper genital tract. PID strikes over 500,000 women each year, the highest incidence rate being for those between the ages of 15 and 25. *Chlamydia trachomatis* has been isolated in about 60 percent of PID cases. The gonococcus *Neisseria gonorrhoeae* is another leading cause of this disease. Pelvic inflammatory disease is three times more common in women who use IUDs than in women who use some other form of birth control (Centers for Disease Control, 1991, 1989; Washington, Amos, & Brooks, 1986; Bell & Holmes, 1984; McGee, 1984).

Symptoms of pelvic inflammatory disease include severe pain and tenderness in the lower abdominal area, particularly during urination and intercourse. Pain may also be experienced during defecation. Other common symptoms are fever, nausea, and vomiting. Many women also experience disruption of the menstrual cycle in the form of intermenstrual bleeding or prolonged menstruation. Additionally, there is usually a foul-smelling vaginal discharge (Torrington, 1985).

If not diagnosed early, PID can lead to the formation of abscesses in the fallopian tubes and ovaries. *Tubal occlusion,* blockage of the fallopian tubes due to tubal scarring, and sterility can also result. Another complication of PID is ectopic, or tubal, pregnancy (see Chapter 10). Finally, the PID infection can allow bacteria to enter the bloodstream and spread to other parts of the body. For example, PID has been known to lead to peritonitis, which is inflammation of the membrane lining the pelvic and abdominal cavities.

Pelvic inflammatory disease is usually treated with antibiotics such as tetracycline or erythromycin. Aspirin or other painkillers may also be prescribed for pain relief. Bed rest and the application of heat to the lower abdominal area are often recommended, along with abstinence from sexual intercourse until the infection has left the body. IUDs are removed at the first sign of bacterial infection. Sexual partners also need to be examined for infection and, if necessary, treated with antibiotics.

CERVICITIS. Cervicitis refers to a variety of inflammations of the cervix. In most instances, cervicitis is associated with other, more general infections of the genital tract. For example, it often accompanies pelvic inflammatory disease. Cervicitis can be caused by infection from *Chlamydia trachomatis,* gonorrhea or herpes simplex virus, or genital warts. It has also been linked to lacerations or injuries caused during abortion, rape, childbirth, or surgery.

The symptoms of cervicitis vary depending on the cause of infection. Often there is a fever, lower abdominal pain, deep pain during intercourse, and an irregular menstrual flow. In acute cases, there is frequently an abundant pus-filled discharge from the cervix that ranges in color from clear to gray to yellow. In chronic cases the cervix often becomes swollen and red and the top layers of cervical tissue erode because of the irritation of the discharge

As with pelvic inflammatory disease, treatment depends on the specific organism responsible for the infection. Often tetracycline, erythromycin, or one of their derivatives is prescribed. An increased fluid intake is usually advised to help flush the infection from the body. In chronic cases infected tissue is sometimes destroyed by electric cautery or cryosurgery. Care must be taken to keep the infected area clean, and sexual intercourse must be avoided until the infection is cured. In more severe cases bed rest is often recommended.

cervicitis Inflammation of the cervix.

NONGONOCOCCAL URETHRITIS (NGU). Nongonococcal urethritis, also called *nonspecific urethritis,* is an infection of the urethra not caused by gonorrhea. It is transmitted primarily by direct sexual contact with an infected person, and is more common in men than in women. *Chlamydia trachomatis* accounts for about 60 percent of nongonococcal urethritis cases. Other organisms responsible for the condition are *Ureaplasma urealyticum, Trichomonas vaginalis,* and *Candida albicans.* The incubation period for nongonococcal urethritis is between 7 and 21 days (Centers for Disease Control, 1991, 1989; Clark, 1985; Jaffee, 1982).

Because nongonococcal urethritis is not one of the STDs that must be reported by physicians, it is difficult to assess how widespread it is, though it is estimated that as many as two million cases occur annually. The highest incidence rate is for people between the ages of 18 and 25. Left untreated, nongonococcal urethritis can lead to many complications, including prostatitis and epididymitis in men, and pelvic inflammatory disease in women. Pregnant women can pass it on to their babies during delivery, resulting in pneumonia, ear infections, and other disorders in the newborn. It has also been proposed that nongonococcal urethritis increases the risk of stillbirths and sudden infant death syndrome.

Sometimes no symptoms accompany nongonococcal urethritis. In other instances symptoms include painful and burning urination, a frequent need to urinate, and a milky discharge from the penis or vagina. Often there is an itchy feeling in the urethra or around the penis or vagina. Some people experience a feeling of heaviness in the genitalia.

The standard treatment for nongonococcal urethritis is antibiotics; tetracycline and its derivatives are the drugs of choice. Penicillin, which cures gonorrhea, does

nongonococcal urethritis An infection of the urethra not caused by gonorrhea. It is transmitted primarily by direct sexual contact with an infected person, and is more common in men than in women.

not cure NGU. As with all forms of sexually transmitted diseases, it is important that every sexual partner of the infected person be examined and treated, if necessary.

epididymitis An inflammation of the epididymis, causing pain and swelling of the testicle.

EPIDIDYMITIS. Epididymitis is an inflammation of the epididymis, causing pain and swelling of the testicle. It is often a complication of nongonococcal urethritis, and is usually caused by *Chlamydia trachomatis* or *Neisseria gonorrhoeae.* Epididymitis is classified primarily as a sexually transmitted disease, although it can be caused by a urinary tract infection in sexually inactive older men.

You will recall that the epididymis is a coiled tube that runs along the top and side of each testis. Inside the epididymis are several ducts that direct sperm from the testis into the vas deferens. Infection usually reaches the epididymis through the vas deferens from a previously contracted infection of the urethra or bladder.

Epididymitis is usually unilateral—that is, it occurs in only one testicle. Symptoms include fever and scrotal pain, swelling, and tenderness. Usually there is a urethral discharge and discomfort on urination. Many men experience chills, nausea, and vomiting. Left untreated, the condition can lead to epididymal scarring and possible occlusion (blockage) of the epididymis.

The treatment for epididymitis consists of antibiotics, usually tetracycline or related medication. The recommended dosage is typically 500 mg. four times a day for at least 10 days. Other measures include bed rest, ice packs, scrotal support, and analgesics.

proctitis An inflammation of the mucous membranes of the rectum.

PROCTITIS. Proctitis is an inflammation of the mucous membranes of the rectum. Proctitis is often a complication of nongonococcal urethritis, most commonly due to *Chlamydia trachomatis.* The disease is generally restricted to those practicing receptive anal intercourse. Sometimes it is caused by trauma experienced during anal intercourse, usually because of inadequate lubrication or the insertion of foreign objects (Kassler, 1983).

The symptoms of proctitis vary in severity. Often there is rectal pain, bleeding, and painful spasms of the rectal muscles. Many people feel a desire to defecate but are unable to do so. The rectal discharge often contains pus and blood. Other symptoms include diarrhea, lower abdominal pain, and, sometimes, fever.

The cause of proctitis dictates the mode of treatment. Proctitis caused by *chlamydia trachomatis* responds to the treatment regimens used with nongonococcal urethritis, such as tetracycline or erythromycin. If chlamydia is not the cause, more obscure infections must be ruled out and treatment adjusted accordingly. If the proctitis was produced by trauma, the patient is often referred to a proctologist.

Parasitic Diseases

Parasitic diseases live on, in, or at the expense of another viable organism, known as the *host*. These diseases can be spread by sexual contact or through infected objects such as clothes, bed linens, and towels. Scabies and pubic lice are examples of parasitic diseases.

scabies A highly contagious parasitic disease caused by an organism called *Sarcoptes scabei.* The organism is a mite that lives, burrows, and lays eggs in the outer layers of the skin.

SCABIES. Scabies is a highly contagious parasitic disease caused by an organism called *Sarcoptes scabei.* The organism is a mite that lives, burrows, and lays eggs in the outer layers of the skin. Sexual activity plays a major role in the transmission of scabies, but the disease can also be transmitted by other forms of person-to-person contact, such as shaking hands. In addition, scabies can be passed on via infected clothing, bedding, and other materials. The disease is more common in men than in women, and the highest incidence rate is for people between 15 and 40 (Crissey, 1984; Orkin & Maibach, 1984).

The scabies mite is microscopic in size—almost impossible to see with the naked eye. It has a rounded body and four pairs of legs. The female mite is the culprit

Sexual Health and Disease

in human infestation, typically infesting the genital area, buttocks, and armpits. Other common sites of infestation are the finger webs, feet, elbows, wrists, and nipples. As the female mite burrows into the skin, she deposits eggs that hatch within two or three days. New mites then travel to the surface of the skin to begin a new cycle of reproduction. The life cycle of a mite is about 30 days.

Raised reddish tracks develop along the burrowing site. Itching is also a common symptom, usually becoming very intense at night. Intense scratching often causes scabies to spread and usually aggravates the lesions, resulting in further infection.

Scabies is typically treated with lindane (Kwell) lotion or cream. A thin layer of it is applied to the entire body from the neck down, left on for eight hours, and then washed off. Usually one treatment of lindane is sufficient, but some doctors recommend a second application one week later to ensure that all the mite eggs have been killed. Because it is a toxic substance and tends to irritate the skin, pregnant women and nursing mothers should not use lindane, nor should infants or children under 10. Alternative treatments for scabies include crotamiton (Eurax) and sulfur ointments. Recent sexual partners and close personal contacts of the infected person should also be examined and treated. Clothing and bedding should be washed in hot water and machine dried (hot cycle), or dry-cleaned.

What's the difference between scabies and crabs?

PUBIC LICE. Pubic lice, or "crabs," are known in medicine as *Phthirus pubis*. These lice, which feed on human blood, are transmitted primarily by sexual contact and infest the pubic, genital, groin, and anal areas. Pubic lice do not usually infest the scalp because their mating habits require hairs that are relatively far apart from one another. For this reason, they prefer pubic hair, hair on the upper legs and abdomen, underarm hair, and chest hair—sometimes even eyebrows, eyelashes, mustaches, and beards (Billstein, 1984; Crisey, 1984).

Pubic lice are one of three types of lice that infest human beings; the other two are the body louse (*Pediculosis humanus*) and the head louse (*Pediculosis capitis*). The pubic louse is about 4/100th to 8/100th of an inch in length and yellowish-gray in color. It has a wingless body and three pairs of legs, each of which ends with a curved claw that enables the louse to hold firmly onto the hair shaft (see Figure 17–4). It also has a pair of stubby antennae.

FIGURE 17–4
A Pubic Louse.
The louse's pincers, by which it grips a hair shaft, can be seen clearly.

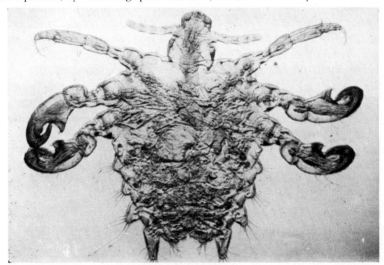

Sexual Health and Disease

Once a person is infested, the female louse begins to deposit eggs at the base of hair shafts. These eggs, called *nits,* attach themselves to the hair shafts with a cementlike substance. Within 10 days or so, young lice begin to emerge from the eggs and, seeking nourishment, pierce the skin and suck blood from the human host. Within two to three weeks the lice reach maturity and are ready to repeat the reproduction cycle. Their average life cycle is about one month.

Sometimes infestation produces no symptoms and people are surprised to learn that they have pubic lice. More usually, intense itching and a rash accompany infestation. Scratching the itches may produce secondary bacterial infections. Other symptoms include mild fever, swollen lymph glands, and muscle aches.

Like scabies, pubic lice infestation is usually treated with lindane, but in shampoo form rather than lotion. The lindane shampoo should be worked into the infected area for five minutes, then rinsed thoroughly. A fine-toothed comb should then be used to remove nits from the hair shafts. Other medications used are malathion (Prioderm) and pyrethrins (A-200 Pyrinate). All sexual and close personal contacts of the infected person should also be treated. Moreover, clothing and bedding should be washed in hot water and machine dried (hot cycle), or dry-cleaned.

Vaginitis

vaginitis Bacterial or fungal infections and inflammations of the vagina that are usually characterized by itching and burning of the external genital organs and a vaginal discharge.

Vaginitis is the name used for any one of a number of bacterial or fungal infections and inflammations of the vagina. It is usually characterized by itching and burning of the external genital organs and a vaginal discharge. Vaginitis can be transmitted through coital as well as noncoital means (Eschenbach, 1986; Lossick, 1984).

The vagina offers a warm and moist environment that is ideal for the growth of certain organisms. Under normal conditions, many bacteria grow in the vagina. These bacteria, called *lactobacilli,* help to maintain a slightly acidic environment, as opposed to an alkaline one. Since most disease-causing organisms (such as those we'll presently discuss) prefer an alkaline environment, these lactobacilli are considered protective.

Certain factors can make the vagina more alkaline and therefore more disease-prone. For example, antibiotics prescribed to combat infections elsewhere in the body may destroy lactobacilli, increasing susceptibility to vaginitis. Birth control pills may also alter the acid-alkaline balance, as can pregnancy, diabetes, and excessive douching. Other factors creating susceptibility to infection are synthetic undergarments, tight-fitting clothes, highly perfumed soaps, and feminine hygiene sprays.

Vaginitis is most commonly caused by one of three microorganisms, each producing a slightly different set of symptoms. *Candida albicans,* a fungal or yeast infection, accounts for most vaginitis cases. Symptoms include swelling and irritation of vaginal tissue, itching and burning during urination, and pain during intercourse. In addition, there is usually a thick white discharge from the vagina resembling cottage cheese in texture and having a "yeasty" odor.

Trichomonas vaginalis is caused by a one-celled protozoan called a *trichomonad.* Commonly called "trich," this form of vaginitis is transmitted most often by sexual contact. Symptoms include vaginal itching and burning, along with a greenish-white discharge and a foul odor. Often the labia become red and tender. These symptoms tend to diminish with menstruation.

Gardnerella vaginalis is caused by hemophilus bacteria. The characteristic symptom is a vaginal discharge that resembles a thin flour paste. It tends to be gray in color and has a foul odor. Many women also report burning and itching of the external genitals.

The treatment of vaginitis depends on which microorganism caused the infection. Proper identification requires that a drop of the vaginal discharge be placed on a slide and examined under a microscope. Fungal infections are usually treated with antifungal drugs, such as miconazole, clotrimazole, or nystatin. Protozoan infections

TABLE 17–3

How to Prevent Vaginitis

■ Take care of yourself and don't get run down. Failure to eat properly, exercise, or get enough sleep will make you more susceptible.

■ Avoid starches and sugars, which create an alkaline vaginal environment. Include yogurt in your diet; this will help to maintain the acidity of the vagina.

■ Avoid excessive douching because it can alter the acid/alkaline balance of the vagina and make you more susceptible to infection.

■ If you use a diaphragm, do not leave it in place longer than necessary.

■ Use latex condoms if you have more than one sexual partner or are starting a sexual relationship with a new partner.

■ After bowel movements, always wipe from front to back to avoid spreading bacteria from the bowel into the vagina.

■ Avoid feminine hygiene sprays, perfumed soaps, and other products that can irritate the vulva and vaginal opening. Such products can also mask odors that are among the signs of vaginitis.

■ Wear cotton underpants. Avoid synthetic undergarments, pantyhose, and tight pants.

Source: Adapted from Madaras & Patterson, 1981.

such as *Trichomonas vaginalis* are usually treated with oral antibiotics such as metronidazole (Flagyl). Metronidazole may cause nausea and vomiting and is not recommended for pregnant women. Bacterial infections are treated with antibiotics such as ampicillin and tetracycline. As with all forms of sexually transmitted diseases, examination and appropriate treatment of sex partners is necessary to prevent reinfection. Nonspecific, noninfectious vaginitis is typically treated by removing or avoiding the irritants causing it, such as chemical sprays, perfumed soaps, or synthetic undergarments (Hasselbring, 1983).

Vaginitis is generally not a serious medical condition. It is often difficult to get rid of, however, and recurrences are common. Table 17–3 gives some tips on the prevention of vaginitis.

NONSEXUALLY TRANSMITTED DISEASES OF THE REPRODUCTIVE SYSTEM

Now that we have examined some of the major types of sexually transmitted diseases, let's direct our energies toward some of the more common nonsexually transmitted diseases of the reproductive system: cystic diseases of the breast, uterine fibroids, ovarian cysts, endometriosis, disorders of the prostate gland, and scrotal and testicular enlargement.

Cystic Disease of the Breast

Cystic disease of the breast is a condition in which noncancerous lumps form in the breast. It is the most common noncancerous disorder of the breast, affecting about one out of every six women between the ages of 35 and 50. It is also referred to as *fibrocystic disease, mammary dysplasia, chronic cystic mastitis,* and *chronic cystic disease*. While the condition is not dangerous in itself, it has been found that women with certain forms of cystic disease are two to four times more likely to develop breast cancer than other women. We'll discuss breast cancer a little later in this chapter.

The exact cause of cystic disease is not known, although it is thought to be hereditary. It is also thought to be linked to female hormone production, since the prime candidates for the disorder are women in their estrogen-producing years. After

cystic disease of the breast
A condition in which noncancerous lumps form in the breast. Also referred to as *fibrocystic disease, mammary dysplasia, chronic cystic mastitis,* and *chronic cystic disease*.

menopause, when the influence of female hormones diminishes, cystic disease tends to subside.

Cystic disease can involve every portion of both breasts or be limited to small areas in one or both breasts. Some women show no symptoms, while others suffer considerable pain in their breasts, especially during their premenstrual period. Other symptoms include swelling, heaviness, and tenderness in the breasts. Often there is a slight discharge from the nipple.

cysts Lumps that are either solid masses or fluid-filled sacs.

The most notable symptom is the appearance of **cysts,** lumps that are solid masses or fluid-filled sacs. The cysts may be singular or multiple, and they may increase in size or remain the same. Large cystic lumps near the surface of the breast may be moved about freely, unlike cancerous lumps, which are usually firmly attached to surrounding tissue. Figure 17–5 illustrates cystic breast disease.

Any woman who discovers a mass or masses in her breast should always seek the advice of her physician to rule out the possibility of cancerous cells. Often cystic disease requires no treatment since some cysts disappear on their own in a few months. Sometimes oral contraceptives help to alleviate the pain, as can drugs such as medroxyprogesterone (Depo-Provera) bromocriptine (Parlodel), and danazol (Danacrine). Large and/or bothersome cysts may be aspirated (drained of their fluid) or surgically removed.

Many medical authorities believe that certain dietary precautions help prevent cystic disease or at least relieve some of the symptoms when the disease does appear. They suggest that women limit their intake of nicotine and a chemical called methylxanthine, commonly found in coffee, tea, cola, and chocolate. Reduced intake of salt, sugar, and alcohol is also recommended. Finally, because they are at greater risk for breast cancer, women with cystic disease should have a physical examination at least twice a year, report any new growths or enlargements of existing lumps, and be sure to perform a breast self-examination each month (see Chapter 3).

Uterine Fibroids

uterine fibroids Solid non-cancerous growths composed of smooth muscle fibers and connective tissue that develop in and on the uterus.

Uterine fibroids are solid noncancerous growths composed of smooth muscle fibers and connective tissue that develop in and on the uterus. They vary in size and shape, and tend to be quite common. Approximately one out of every five women over the

FIGURE 17–5
Cystic Disease of the Breast.

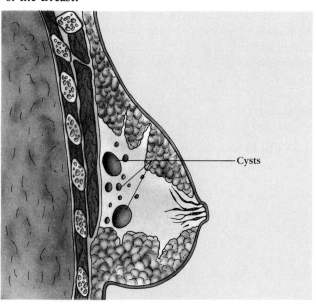

Cysts

Sexual Health and Disease

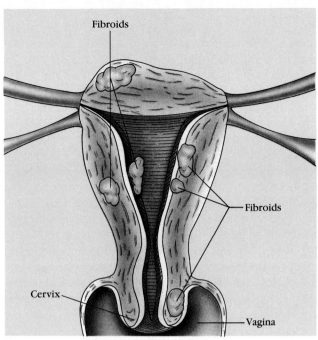

FIGURE 17–6
Uterine Fibroids.

age of 30 has a uterine fibroid. For unknown reasons, they are more common among African-American women.

The cause of uterine fibroids is also unknown, but as with cystic disease of the breast, there appears to be a connection to estrogen production because the fibroids are most prevalent during a woman's reproductive years. Uterine fibroids are seldom seen before puberty and rarely develop after menopause.

Most uterine fibroids stay confined to the thick muscle wall of the uterus and are referred to as *interstitial fibroids. Subserous fibroids* grow large and expand in the direction of the outer surface of the uterus. *Submucous fibroids* grow toward the interior uterine cavity. Finally, *cervical fibroids* appear in the lower, cervical portion of the uterus. Figure 17–6 illustrates the different sites at which fibroids can occur in the uterine area.

Uterine fibroids can develop without bothersome symptoms. Indeed, a woman may not even know that she has a uterine fibroid until it is discovered during a routine pelvic examination. However, often there is pain during menstruation, an excessive menstrual flow, and abdominal pain. If the uterine fibroid is advanced, swelling of the abdomen becomes evident. Should the fibroid grow toward the bladder, pain and discomfort during urination are often reported. Sometimes submucous fibroids produce a vaginal discharge.

Not all uterine fibroids require treatment, other than checkups at specified intervals with a physician. Those producing complications, though, require medical intervention. Moreover, the possibility of uterine cancer needs to be ruled out, particularly with fibroids that steadily increase in size.

Fibroids can be surgically removed with a **myomectomy,** an operation that leaves the muscle walls of the uterus relatively intact. The myomectomy is advised for women who want children, provided the fibroid does not pose severe complications. For women whose fibroids cause severe bleeding, obstruction, or other complications, as well as for older women and women who do not want children, a **hysterectomy**—the surgical removal of the uterus—is often advised. Radiation therapy can be used to shrink uterine fibroids, although this form of treatment is rare today.

myomectomy The surgical removal of uterine fibroids, leaving the muscle walls of the uterus in place.

hysterectomy The surgical removal of the uterus.

Ovarian Cysts

An **ovarian cyst** is an abnormal swelling or sacklike growth on the ovary. The cyst may be fluid-filled, semifluid, solid, or semisolid. Ovarian cysts may be unilateral (affecting only one ovary) or bilateral (involving both ovaries). Most cysts are small in size, measuring less than an inch in diameter. Ovarian cysts are common among women between the ages of 20 and 50. Most are noncancerous.

There are several different categories of ovarian cysts. *Follicular cysts* are fluid-filled growths of the graafian follicle or corpus luteum. *Serous cystadenomas,* also fluid-filled growths, are noted for their unusually large size (some weigh many pounds). *Fibromas* are composed of fibrous connective tissue and are the most common of the solid noncancerous growths. A *dermoid cyst* is a semisolid growth, usually containing an oily fluid along with bits of bone, cartilage, hair, and even teeth (such contents may surprise you, but remember the ovary contains the ova, which have the potential, if fertilized, to produce all of the types of tissue found in humans. Thus, a cyst containing bone, hair, and other tissue growths is not uncommon.)

Depending on the type of growth, the symptoms of ovarian cysts vary. Some present no symptoms and degenerate on their own. Follicular cysts, for example, often rupture spontaneously or are reabsorbed by the body. However, some ovarian cysts cause pain during intercourse, nausea, and fever. Sometimes a cyst twists on the root that carries its blood supply, creating sudden sharp pain and shock. If the cyst presses against the bladder or rectum, it may cause irregularities in urination and defecation. Irregularities in the menstrual cycle are also experienced by some woman.

Determining whether or not a cyst is cancerous is an important first step in treatment and requires the attention of a physician. Even if the cyst proves noncancerous, it needs to be removed. A **cystectomy** is the surgical excision of only the cyst, leaving the ovary intact. If the growth has destroyed a considerable portion of ovarian tissue, the entire ovary must be removed in a surgical procedure known as an **oophorectomy.** When a cyst is malignant, it may be necessary to remove both ovaries, both fallopian tubes, and the uterus because the cancer may have spread to these other structures.

Endometriosis

Endometriosis is a condition in which endometrial cells that normally line the uterus detach themselves and grow elsewhere in the pelvic cavity. Endometrial tissue can grow in many locations, including the outside of the uterus, the ovaries, intestine, bladder, and even on the umbilicus (see Figure 17–7). Endometriosis is a disorder that occurs during a woman's childbearing years and is most common between the ages of 25 and 45. It is rare during pregnancy.

During each menstrual cycle the endometrium normally thickens and swells in preparation for a possible pregnancy. (For a review of the physiological events of the menstrual cycle, see Chapter 3.) When conception does not occur, the excess tissue that has built up breaks down and flows out of the body in menstruation. In a woman who has endometriosis, endometrial tissue that has become displaced outside the uterus is also stimulated at menstruation, so that it swells and bleeds into surrounding areas, causing an inflammation. The body responds to the presence of accumulated blood by building scar tissue around it. Encased blood may lead to palpable growths and masses on the affected organs, called *chocolate cysts* (named for their thick, dark brown texture). Sometimes these cysts rupture and spread endometrial cells still further throughout the pelvis.

No one knows for sure what causes endometriosis. One theory suggests that menstrual blood sometimes flows backward, transporting endometrial tissue through the fallopian tubes into the pelvic cavity. Blockage of the vagina or cervix may also prevent the normal flow of menstrual blood, thus creating a dispersion of endometrial

Sexual Health and Disease

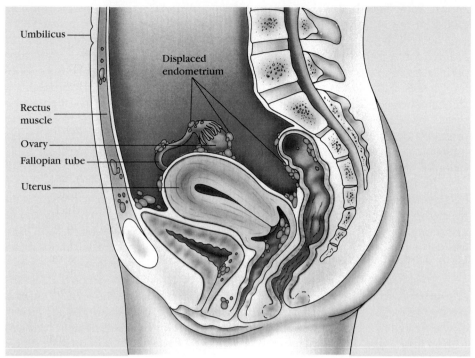

FIGURE 17–7
Endometriosis.

In this condition tissue from the lining of the uterus detaches itself and grows elsewhere in the pelvic cavity.

Labels on figure:
Umbilicus
Displaced endometrium
Rectus muscle
Ovary
Fallopian tube
Uterus

tissue. Surgery could also account for the displacement of endometrial tissue. Finally, endometriosis could be spread through the blood or lymph system.

Usually endometriosis progresses very slowly. The characteristic symptoms are pain and general discomfort accompanying menstruation that become progressively worse. Other symptoms are irregular menstrual flow, blood in the urine, pain during intercourse, and discomfort or a feeling of fullness in the lower abdomen. Symptoms tend to vary widely from woman to woman.

The treatment of endometriosis is highly individualized. Antiovulatory drugs such as danazol (Danocrine) are often given to modify the body's natural hormone secretions so that endometrial tissue will shrink. A woman cannot become pregnant while taking this medication, but she will be able to conceive once the drug regimen is terminated. If drug therapy is unsuccessful, surgery may be necessary. This may entail removal of the scar tissue and endometrial tissue or, in more serious cases, removal of the uterus, fallopian tubes, and ovaries.

Disorders of the Prostate Gland

You will recall from Chapter 3 that the prostate gland is a small doughnut-shaped gland that surrounds both the neck of the bladder and the urethra in men. It is an accessory gland to the male reproductive system, contributing to the overall volume of semen. Besides cancer of the prostate, which we discussed in Chapter 3 and will briefly review toward the end of this chapter, there are two common prostate disorders: prostatitis and benign prostate hypertrophy.

Prostatitis is an infection or inflammation of the prostate gland. The condition can occur at any age and be either acute or chronic, but is rarely a serious disorder if properly treated. Left untreated, though, prostatitis can lead to bladder or kidney damage or obstruction of the urethra or ureter. The exact cause of prostatitis is not

prostatitis An infection or inflammation of the prostate gland.

known. Sometimes bacterial infections are diagnosed, but in other instances no microorganism can be isolated.

One of the primary symptoms of prostatitis is difficulty in urination, including reduced force, increased frequency, and postvoid dribbling. Other symptoms include perineal pain, low backache, lethargy, and general weakness. Many men experience fever, chills, and pain on ejaculation. The usual treatment for bacterial prostatitis is an antibiotic such as erythromycin or ampicillin. Men with acute bacterial prostatitis should remain on antibiotic therapy for a minimum of two weeks. Nonbacterial prostatitis does not respond to antibiotics and is more difficult to cure. Treatment usually includes trimethoprim-sulfamethoxazole, forcing fluids, and the local application of heat.

Benign prostatic hypertrophy is enlargement of the prostate gland. Such enlargement may constrict the urethra and impede the flow of urine. Benign prostatic hypertrophy is common in men over the age of 50. The disorder is characterized by urination that is slow and diminished in force and by postvoid dribbling. Many men feel an increased need to urinate, often at night. Also, some urine is almost always left in the bladder, creating a breeding ground for bacterial infection.

Treatment is not usually necessary for benign prostatic hypertrophy, unless the obstruction becomes severe. Medical intervention usually takes the form of surgical removal of excess glandular tissue. As we saw in Chapter 3, benign prostatic growth can be treated by a transurethral resection, or TUR, in which excess tissue is removed with an instrument inserted through the urethra. In some cases, as in prostate cancer (see Chapter 3), a prostatectomy, or the removal of the entire gland, is performed. Both procedures lead often to **retrograde ejaculation,** in which semen passes back into the bladder rather than out of the body through the urethra. The prostatectomy risks impotence, but new techniques under development may lessen or eliminate this risk.

Scrotal and Testicular Enlargement

There are several medical conditions that create swelling of the scrotum or the testicles within it. Of particular interest to us are inguinal hernias, hydrocele, and testicular torsion.

An **inguinal hernia** occurs when a loop of intestine passes through the abdominal inguinal ring and follows the course of the spermatic cord into the inguinal canal. The descent of the hernia may end in the inguinal canal, or it may proceed into the scrotum. In the latter case, it is said to be a **scrotal hernia.** An inguinal hernia is caused by the intestines being forced by increased intra-abdominal pressure into a congenitally weak inguinal wall. The abdominal pressure can be caused by lifting, coughing, straining, or accidents. While inguinal hernias can occur in women (the hernia sometimes proceeds into the labia), they are much more common in men.

Sometimes herniated abdominal contents in the scrotum can be reduced, or pushed back, into the abdomen; it is largely the size of the defect through which the intestines passes that determines whether or not this can be done. Also, for some men, various supports and trusses offer temporary relief. The only permanent cure for an inguinal hernia, though, is surgery in which the herniating tissues are returned to the abdominal cavity and the defect in the inguinal wall is repaired.

A **hydrocele** is a noncancerous collection of fluid around a testis that leads to swelling of the scrotum (see Figure 17–8). The word *hydrocele* means "sac of water." The cause of hydrocele is unknown, but it can occur in children as well as adults. A small, painless hydrocele usually requires no treatment. However, if the hydrocele becomes large or painful, medical intervention is needed. Bed rest, ice bags, and painkillers can offer temporary relief. The excess fluid can also be aspirated, but this

benign prostatic hypertrophy Enlargement of the prostate gland that constricts the urethra and impedes the flow of urine.

retrograde ejaculation A condition in which semen is passed back into the bladder rather than ejaculated externally through the urethra.

inguinal hernia A hernia that occurs when a loop of intestine passes through the abdominal inguinal ring and follows the course of the spermatic cord into the inguinal canal.

scrotal hernia A hernia that descends into the scrotum.

hydrocele A noncancerous collection of fluid around a testis that leads to swelling of the scrotum.

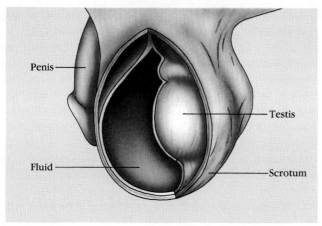

FIGURE 17–8

A hydrocele is a collection of fluid around a testis that causes the scrotum to swell.

is considered to be temporary treatment as well, since fluid may build up again in this area. Surgical excision of the membrane that covers the testis, called a **hydrocelectomy,** is the preferred treatment for a hydrocele.

TESTICULAR TORSION. Testicular torsion is a rotation or kinking of the spermatic artery that causes severe pain, tenderness, and swelling of the testicle. Testicular torsion usually develops suddenly, often when an activity creates abrupt pulling or pressure. When this happens, the blood supply to the testicle is interrupted. To restore the blood supply and prevent permanent damage, immediate medical attention is needed. This usually involves positioning the spermatic cord and testicles correctly by means of surgery.

hydrocelectomy Surgical excision of the membrane covering the testis to treat hydrocele.

testicular torsion A rotation or kinking of the spermatic artery that causes severe pain, tenderness, and swelling of the testicle.

CANCERS OF THE REPRODUCTIVE ORGANS

Throughout the body, cells normally reproduce themselves in an orderly manner so that worn-out tissues are replaced and injuries are repaired. Occasionally, certain cells undergo an abnormal change and begin a process of uncontrolled growth and spread. These abnormal cells grow into masses of tissue called **tumors** (or *neoplasms*). Tumors can impinge on vital organs and block blood vessels, in the process robbing normal cells of needed nutrients.

Tumors can be either benign or malignant. A *benign tumor* typically is harmless and does not invade normal tissue (although if it grows large enough, it can press against organs and cause damage). A *malignant tumor* is cancerous and invades surrounding tissues. It also can spread cancer throughout the body in a process known as **metastasis.** Metastasis can be accomplished either by the direct extension of the original growth or by the detachment of cancerous cells that are then carried through the lymph system (part of the body's infection-fighting mechanism) or blood system to other body parts.

Four types of cancer have been identified. **Carcinomas** arise from *epithelial* cells (skin, mucous membranes, etc.) and tend to be solid tumors. **Sarcomas** develop from muscle, bone, fat, and other connective tissues. **Lymphomas** originate in lymphoid tissues found at various points in the lymph system (e.g., neck, groin, armpit). Finally, **leukemias** are those cancers that develop in the blood system.

No one knows for sure how a normal cell becomes a cancer cell, but it is generally acknowledged that cancer has some hereditary component. Also, cancer

tumor A benign or malignant mass of tissue created by the uncontrolled growth and spread of cells. Also called a *neoplasm.*

metastasis The spread of cancer from an original site to another, new site.

carcinoma Cancer arising from epithelial cells (skin, mucous membranes, etc.). Carcinomas tend to be solid tumors.

sarcoma Cancer developing from muscle, bone, fat, and other connective tissues.

lymphoma Cancer originating in lymphoid tissues.

leukemia Cancer developing in the hematological (blood) system.

can develop through repeated or long-term contact with one or more cancer-causing agents called *carcinogens*. Carcinogens cause body cells to change their structures and grow out of control. Examples of carcinogens are radiation, cigarettes, and industrial agents such as asbestos and polyvinyl chloride.

Cancer specialists have identified seven warning signs associated with cancer: a sore that does not heal; unusual bleeding or discharge; a change in bowel or bladder habits; a nagging cough or hoarseness; indigestion or difficulty in swallowing; a thickening or lump in the breast or elsewhere; and an obvious change in a mole or wart.

Cancer can occur at any point in the life cycle, although more than half of all cancer deaths are of people over 65. Between the ages of 20 and 40, cancer is more common in women than in men, but between 60 and 80, the reverse is true. Overall, more men than women die of cancer. Of the cancers that affect the reproductive organs, the most common are cancers of the breast, ovaries, uterus, vagina, vulva, prostate, testis, and penis.

WHERE TO FIND MORE INFORMATION ON CANCER DETECTION

Cancer Information Service. An organization that answers any cancer-related questions, and sends out free materials on the topic. 1-800-4-CANCER.

American Cancer Society Helpline. Informs cancer patients of local services, including rehabilitation programs. 1-800-ACS-2345.

Y-ME. A 24-hour hotline for women with breast cancer that offers information on surgical options and physician referrals. 312-799-8228.

Cancer Hot Line. Offers supportive counseling and cancer treatment information. 816-932-8453.

Breast Cancer

The breast is the leading site of cancer incidence and mortality in women between the ages of 25 and 75, and breast cancer is the leading cause of death from all causes among women 40 to 44 years of age. Breast cancer is diagnosed in about 175,000 women every year, and 44,500 of them will die from it. When men develop breast cancer, their symptoms are the same as those found in women and recommended treatments are the same. This type of cancer is rare, however, accounting for only about 2 percent of all cancers in men (Silverberg, Boring, & Squires, 1990; American Cancer Society, 1990; Giuliano, 1987).

What is done during a mastectomy? Is the entire breast always removed?

Most breast cancers begin their development from a single area. After an indeterminate amount of time, the cancer spreads to the nearest regional lymph nodes; later it enters the bloodstream to produce distant metastases. Figure 17–9 diagrams the spread of breast cancer through the lymphatic system to the areas of the chest, neck, upper arm, and armpit.

lumpectomy Local excision of a cancerous lump in the breast, along with some of the surrounding breast tissue.

mastectomy The surgical removal of a breast or part of it.

Should a lump in the breast prove to be malignant, several forms of surgical treatment are possible. A **lumpectomy** involves local excision of the cancer, along with some of the surrounding breast tissue. A **mastectomy** is the surgical removal of a breast or part of it. There are different types of mastectomy, each defined by the muscles, gland, tissues, and skin that are removed. A *partial mastectomy* involves the removal of the quadrant of the breast in which the cancer is located. In a *simple mastectomy* the entire breast is removed down to, but not including, the pectoral muscles. Some lymph nodes in the armpit may also be removed. A *modified radical mastectomy* involves removal of the entire breast, some pectoral (chest) muscles, and

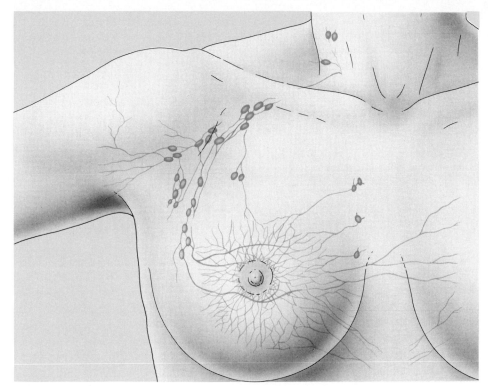

FIGURE 17–9
The Spread of Breast Cancer.

This drawing shows the portion of the body's lymphatic system that is nearest to the breast. Note how a cancer in the breast can spread through the system to many nearby lymph nodes (indicated by dark spots).

more lymph nodes than are excised in the simple mastectomy. In a *radical mastectomy* the entire breast, the major and minor pectoral muscles, the lymph nodes under the arm, and adjacent tissues and fat are removed. Figure 17–10 illustrates the major types of breast surgery.

While the surgical removal of a cancerous breast may save a woman's life, it also often threatens her own appraisal of her femininity and sexual attractiveness. Psychological recovery from a mastectomy can therefore be as important as physical recovery. Following a mastectomy, many women choose to have breast reconstruction, a surgical procedure that involves reshaping a breast from artificial or natural materials. Because of the health risks posed by silicone implants—including a possible link to autoimmune disease, cancer, and neurological disorders—plastic and reconstructive surgeons are changing their surgical procedures. Although the Federal Drug Administration still permits surgeons to do silicone implants in women who have had mastectomies, many surgeons now prefer to use a woman's own tissue, from her abdomen or buttocks, to create a new breast. Others use artificial implants filled with a saline solution. For women who do not choose to have breast reconstruction, a prosthesis, which is often worn in a special pocket sewn into the bra, becomes an important part of rehabilitation. A **prosthesis** is a fabricated substitute for a missing bodily part—in this case, an artificial breast form that simulates normal contours. Breast prostheses have been greatly improved over the years. They come in numerous materials and approach natural breast tissue in weight, contour, and resilience.

In addition to mastectomy, breast cancer may be treated with radiation, chemotherapy, or hormonal therapy. Radiation therapy is usually administered preoperatively to reduce a tumor's size and then postoperatively to lessen the risk that the cancer will recur locally. Radiotherapy may also be used after a lumpectomy, or it may be

prosthesis A fabricated substitute for a missing body part.

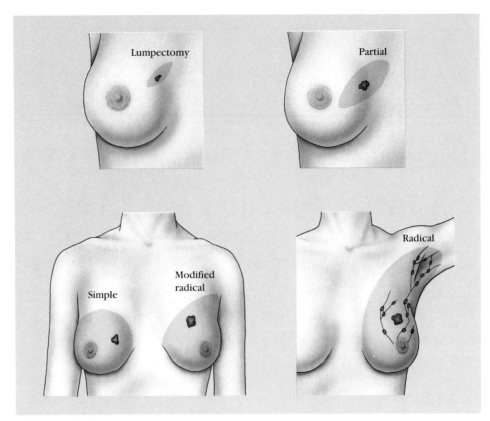

FIGURE 17–10
Major Types of Breast Surgery.

Shaded areas indicate the portions of the breast tissue removed in each type of procedure. The dark spots within these areas are the cancerous lesions. In the radical mastectomy the lymph nodes that extend into the armpit are also removed.

used alone as a primary treatment. In the latter case, the breast and regional lymph nodes may be irradiated over a period of several weeks. Chemotherapy is used as a primary treatment with advanced, recurrent, or metastatic breast cancers, and as supplemental therapy following a mastectomy or radiation therapy.

Hormonal therapy is used mostly for advanced cancer. It is based on the idea that since female breast development is dependent on female hormones, breast cancers may also be hormonally dependent. If tests show the cancer is the hormone-dependent type, removal of glands responsible for female hormone production or administering a male sex hormone to suppress female hormone production may curb

Breast reconstruction (b) after a modified radical mastectomy (a). This woman's new, left breast was reconstructed using muscle, skin, and fat from her abdomen. The nipple was reconstructed with small skin flaps, and the areola was created by tattooing. The right breast was lifted a bit to achieve symmetry. The scars will fade in time.

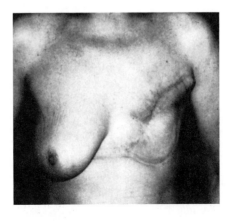
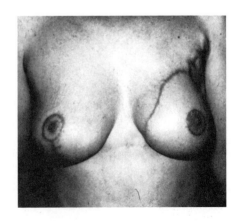

Sexual Health and Disease

tumor growth. However, not all breast tumors are hormone-dependent, and of those that are, only 50 to 60 percent respond to this kind of therapy. Hormonal therapy is usually instituted only after surgery or radiation therapy have been tried and have failed to halt the disease.

We cannot leave the topic of breast cancer without saying something about the importance of prevention. A woman who has had one breast cancer is approximately twice as prone as other women to develop another cancer in the opposite breast. With this knowledge in mind, a woman should take every precaution to detect a tumor as early as possible. Precautions for the postmastectomy patient include check-ups with the surgeon every four months, breast self-examination every month, and a mammography once a year. A physician may also recommend the use of thermography, a technique in which body temperature measurements are used to detect the like-lihood of cancer.

Ovarian Cancer

Ovarian cancer causes over 12,000 deaths annually, the highest incidence rate being for women between the ages of 65 and 84. Women who have had breast cancer are more likely to develop ovarian cancer, and vice versa—which suggests a common etiologic factor, possibly related to abnormal endocrine function. Women who have never had children are twice as likely to develop ovarian cancer as those who are mothers (Silverberg, Boring, & Squires, 1990; American Cancer Society, 1990).

Ovarian cancers usually do not present any symptoms until the disease reaches an advanced stage. Therefore, women over the age of 40 need to get regular pelvic examinations and a cancer-related checkup every year. When the disease has spread, patients typically experience increasing abdominal girth, abdominal pain, weight loss, occasional vaginal bleeding, constipation, and urinary frequency caused by pressure of the tumor on the bladder. If ovarian cancer is diagnosed and treated early, 85 percent of patients live five years or longer. When the disease is diagnosed in an advanced stage, however, the survival rate drops to 22 percent. Treatment often consists of removal of the uterus and both ovaries. Radiation therapy and chemo-therapy are considered beneficial when the cancer is inoperable.

Uterine Cancer

Cancer of the uterus makes up about 14 percent of all cancers in women. Two types of uterine cancer, cervical and endometrial, account for almost 10,000 deaths each year (Silverberg, Boring, & Squires, 1990). Let's look more closely at these two cancers.

CERVICAL CANCER. The symptoms of cervical cancer include unusual bleeding or vaginal discharge between menstrual periods, following intercourse, or after meno-pause. When such symptoms appear, the cancer has usually progressed beyond its early stages. Cervical cancer occurs more frequently in women aged 35 or older who began sexual activity in their early teens and who had multiple partners. Other factors associated with cervical cancer include low socioeconomic status, poor pre- and post-natal care, and in utero exposure to diethylstilbestrol (DES) (American Cancer Society, 1990; Hill, 1987).

Cervical cancer can be detected early through periodic pelvic examinations, including Pap smears (see the box on "Understanding the Papanicolaou [Pap] Smear"). Treatment of cervical cancer depends on how widely the disease has spread. In the early stages changes in the cervix may be treated by cryotherapy (the destruction of cells by extreme cold), by electrocoagulation (the destruction of tissue through intense heat by electric current), or by local surgery. For more advanced cervical cancers, more extensive surgery or radiation may be necessary. In women whose cancer is detected early, the five-year survival rate is 80–90 percent. This figure drops to 60 percent when the disease is diagnosed in advanced stages.

MAKING USE
OF WHAT
WE KNOW

Understanding
the Papanicolaou
(Pap) Smear

Papanicolaou (Pap) smear
A test used primarily to
screen for cervical cancer.

The **Papanicolaou (Pap) smear** is a test used primarily to screen for cervical cancer. This test is based on the fact that tumor cells (as well as normal cells) of such structures as the fallopian tubes, uterus, and vagina are shed regularly and pass into cervical and vaginal secretions. When these secretions are studied, lesions of the cervix and of the lining of the fallopian tubes and the uterus may be detected in their early stages.

The American Cancer Society suggests that women between 20 and 40 who are not in a high-risk category and who have had two previous normal Pap smears should have this test done every three years. Women over 40, those in a high-risk category, and those who have had a recent positive Pap smear should have a Pap smear either yearly or as advised by their doctor.

High risk of cervical cancer appears to be associated with a number of factors: a personal history of cervical or uterine cancer; a previous abnormal Pap test; beginning sexual intercourse at an early age; having multiple sexual partners; and a history of genital herpes infection or genital warts. Women whose mothers took DES (diethylstilbestrol)

during pregnancy are also at high risk for this disorder, as are women who smoke or take birth control pills. The risk is lower in those who use condoms or diaphragms for birth control. Finally, low socioeconomic status and poor pre- and postnatal care are associated with higher rates of cervical cancer.

The procedure for a Pap smear is relatively simple. During a standard pelvic examination (see Chapter 3), with a vaginal speculum holding the vagina open for examination, a cotton swab is inserted into the vagina and several samples of cells and fluid are taken. The samples are placed on a slide, sprayed with a fixative, and then analyzed microscopically. The results are usually reported in numbers from 1 to 5, although some laboratories use slightly different systems. The usual meaning of the test is as follows:

- *Class 1:* The smear is completely normal and no abnormal cells are present. No follow-up is needed, but regular checkups are advised.
- *Class 2:* Some atypical cells are present, but none suggest a malignancy. However, there may be a vaginal or cervical inflammation and/or possible infection.

ENDOMETRIAL CANCER. While endometrial cancer is far less common than cervical cancers in young women, both types occur with approximately equal frequency in postmenopausal women. Factors associated with the development of endometrial cancer include infertility—suggesting a possible link with hormonal imbalances; prolonged estrogen replacement therapy; late-occurring menopause (after age 55); and obesity, diabetes, and hypertension (American Cancer Society, 1990).

Symptoms of endometrial cancer often include intermenstrual or postmenopausal bleeding. Since the Pap test is not effective in screening for endometrial cancer, women at risk for the disease should have an endometrial tissue sample at menopause. Treatment for endometrial cancer includes both surgery and radiation, and the prognosis is most favorable. The five-year survival rate for those diagnosed in all stages of the disease is about 83 percent.

Cancer of the Vulva

Cancer of the vulva is rare, making up less than one percent of all cancers in women. It occurs most frequently in women between the ages of 50 and 70, and is more common in low socioeconomic groups. Symptoms include vaginal discharge, itching, and bleeding.

This cancer is commonly preceded by abnormal thickening and whitening of the vulva, a condition called *leukoplakia*. Leukoplakia can be eliminated with a *simple vulvectomy,* the removal of the skin of the major and minor lips of the vulva and

The Pap test should be repeated between three and six months later.

- *Class 3:* Some abnormal cells are present that suggest, but do not confirm, malignancy (the nuclei are larger than usual and oddly shaped). The degree and kind of abnormality are greater than in the Class 2 result. A Class 3 finding suggests the need to have a follow-up smear and biopsy as soon as possible.

- *Class 4:* The smear contains some malignant cells, and they are more abnormal in appearance than Class 3-type cells, with darker-appearing nuclei. There are signs of early cancer. A follow-up smear and biopsy are needed as soon as possible.

- *Class 5:* The smear contains malignant cells more disorganized than Class 4-type cells. Immediate treatment is necessary.

A Class 3 Pap test result doesn't necessarily mean that a woman has cancer. It does mean, however, that she should have another Pap smear taken very soon. It also suggests that if she has any current vaginal infection, it should be treated before the second Pap smear is done. If the repeat Pap test is also abnormal, or if the first Pap result shows Class 4 or 5 malignant cells, further tests will be needed. Often a colposcopy and a cervical biopsy are used to make a final diagnosis. A *colposcopy* is an examination of the cervix, vulva, and vagina with a magnifying lens. It is not an operation. A *cervical biopsy* is a procedure in which a piece of cervical tissue is surgically obtained and examined under a microscope to determine whether cancer is present.

It is important to realize that a Pap smear does not diagnose cervical cancer; it only *screens* for it. Even when a Pap report indicates that cancer cells are present, there is about a 20 percent chance that a woman does not have cancer. Conversely, about 10 percent of cervical cancers are not detected by this test. The great majority of abnormal Pap smears are due to premalignant changes, which are successfully dealt with by early treatment. Also, a normal Pap smear is not a guarantee that there is no cancer anywhere in the genital tract. Although it occasionally detects cancerous cells from the endometrium, a Pap smear is not an accurate screening test for endometrial or ovarian cancer.

clitoris. New skin will grow in the area to replace the skin removed by this preventive surgery.

In full-fledged cancer of the vulva, invasion of the inguinal lymph nodes and the lower portion of the vagina is common. Surgery is required for cancer of the vulva since radiation therapy is not well tolerated by the tissues of the vulvar and inguinal regions. The surgical approach is usually a *radical vulvectomy,* the removal of the vaginal lips, clitoris, skin surrounding the vulva, and the lymph glands.

Women who have had vulvectomies can become pregnant, although it may be necessary to perform a cesarean delivery (see Chapter 11). However, most women who have vulvectomies are well past their childbearing years. Intercourse is still possible, but depending on the extent of the surgery, sexual responsiveness may be diminished (Madaras & Patterson, 1981).

Vaginal Cancer

Cancer of the vagina is rarely seen as a primary cancer, and when it is, it tends to be in menopausal or postmenopausal women. As with cervical cancer, exposure to diethylstilbestrol while in their mother's wombs has been implicated in vaginal cancer in younger women. Vaginal cancer is rare in African-American women and virtually nonexistent among Jewish women. Major symptoms are vaginal spotting and discharge, pain, groin masses, and urinary symptoms (American Cancer Society, 1990).

Treatment varies greatly. Radiation therapy involves local application of radium in conjunction with total pelvic external radiation. While radiation poses a danger to certain parts of the body such as the bladder and rectum, it generally has a low risk overall. Radical surgery often entails a complete *vaginectomy* (removal of the vagina) and removal of the lymph nodes in the pelvic area.

Prostatic and Testicular Cancers

The most common cancer of the male genital organs is prostate cancer. As we learned in Chapter 3, prostate cancer is the third most common cause of cancer deaths in men (behind lung and colon cancer, respectively) and has risen over 20 percent in the past 25 years. Most cases are detected by rectal examination during a routine physical exam. Ultrasound is often used as a follow-up to determine the size, shape, and properties of the cancer. If the cancer is determined to be malignant by needle biopsy, surgery is performed, either alone or in combination with radiation and/or hormonal treatment.

As we also learned in Chapter 3, cancer of the testis is relatively uncommon, occurring mostly in young men between the ages of 15 and 34. Many testicular cancers metastasize while the primary growth is still quite small, which means that the first manifestation of testicular cancer is usually in the region or organs attacked by the metastatic disease. Treatment of testicular cancers has been improved by advances in radiation therapy combined with chemotherapy. Patients with no clinical evidence of metastases are treated by *orchiectomy,* the surgical excision of one or both testes. This is followed by postoperative radiation therapy to the lumbar lymph nodes.

Cancer of the Penis

Cancer of the penis is rare, especially in men under 40. Penile carcinoma is usually painless in the beginning. It often occurs on the tip of the penis and is found almost

"Remember when the big health hazard was only a cigarette afterwards?"

Sexual Health and Disease

exclusively in uncircumcised men. When it occurs in circumcised men, it is found to be a metastasis from cancers of the bladder, prostate, lung, pancreas, kidney, testicle, or ureter. Urethral obstruction and bleeding are rare symptoms. Treatment usually consists of partial or total amputation of the penis. Radiation therapy and chemotherapy are other forms of treatment (American Cancer Society, 1990).

PROMOTING HEALTH AND PREVENTING DISEASE

Prevention is the best way to minimize the risks of the diseases and disorders we have just discussed. At the outset of this chapter we pointed out that the concept of sexual health refers to a smoothly functioning reproductive system and knowledge of those factors that help ensure optimal sexual functioning. The maintenance of sexual health and well-being is not automatic, but rather a matter of individual responsibility and intelligent and informed decision making. By *intelligent and informed decision making*, we mean building a foundation of knowledge and applying that information on a regular basis. (The most current information regarding STDs is available from the National STD Information Hotline, 1-800-227-8922.) Taking responsibility for your own health will help you to enjoy the pleasures you seek for the rest of your life.

What kinds of things can I be doing to promote my own sexual health?

Sexually healthy adults observe their sexual health on a daily basis and carefully monitor their sexual life styles. They are aware of the importance of cleanliness, sexual self-examination (see Chapter 3 for a review of testicular and breast self-examination), and regular physicals. Sexually healthy people are also knowledgeable about cancer detection guidelines and the importance of cancer-related checkups. And they help their bodies defend against disease by keeping themselves well: exercising, eating a balanced diet, maintaining proper weight, and getting enough sleep so that the body can replenish itself and produce immune-related cells. Table 17–4 offers some guidelines for seeking help for sexual health concerns.

Your campus health service may include, or be able to refer you to, a gynecologist (a physician specializing in women's reproductive health) or a urologist (a physician specializing in men's reproductive health). Contraceptive counseling may be available from physicians, nurse-practitioners specializing in contraception, or peer counselor-students with special training in contraception and other issues related to sexuality. For some situations, psychological counseling may be useful. If you prefer to see someone off campus, consult a family planning clinic in the community (Smith & Smith, 1990).

Safer Sex Practices: Preventing Sexually Transmitted Diseases

A recurrent theme in the literature today is "safer sex" and the prevention of sexually transmitted diseases (see, for example, Fogel, 1990; Bingham, 1989; Whipple & Ogden, 1989; Scotti & Moore, 1987; Covington & McClendon, 1987; Preston & Swann, 1987; Ulene, 1987; Mandel & Mandel, 1986). Donald Kilby (1986) maintains that sexual freedom has become a way of life in modern society, and with it has come a need for people to know how to protect themselves from both unwanted pregnancies and sexually transmitted diseases. Casual sexual relationships have resulted in an increased number of illnesses and infections. Thus learning how to protect oneself and one's partner from STDs is vitally important. So, too, is being aware of erroneous ideas about STDs, several of which are featured in the accompanying "Myths and Misconceptions" box).

TABLE 17–4

When to Seek Help for Sexual Health Concerns

Health-care professionals can help you take care of your sexual health, whether you are suffering from pain or discomfort, evaluating the risks of sexually transmitted diseases, searching for contraceptive options, worried that you might be pregnant, or just have a couple of questions about sexual issues.

Consult a health-care professional when:

- You suspect (or know) that you or a sexual partner has been exposed to an STD.
- You want to be able to discuss sexual issues more clearly with your partner but are unsure of what to say.
- You are sexually active (or are considering becoming sexually active) and are not consistently using effective methods of contraception and STD prevention.
- You are experiencing any of the symptoms of STDs listed earlier in the chapter (including, but not limited to, itching, rash, sores) and have been sexually active.
- You have pain, difficulty, or a burning sensation while urinating.
- You discover any lumps or other unexplained changes in your sexual organs.

If you are a woman, see a health-care provider if:

- Your period is 10 or more days late.
- Your periods are painful or you have premenstrual syndrome that has not responded to self-treatment.
- You do not know how to perform a breast self-exam.
- You have not had a Pap smear in the past year.

If you are a man, see a health-care provider if:

- You do not know how to perform a testicular self-exam.
- You are experiencing sexual functioning problems on a recurring basis (at times other than when you are intoxicated).

Source: Adapted from S. F. Smith and C. M. Smith, *Personal Health Choices*, Copyright © 1990. Boston: Jones and Bartlett Publishers. Reprinted by permission.

Robert Hatcher and colleagues (1990) recommend the following safer sex guidelines to reduce the risks of contracting a sexually transmitted disease:

- Two uninfected, mutually monogamous partners run the least risk of anyone for STDs, but even they can contract infections through such avenues as drug use, poor personal hygiene, or blood transfusions. In any case, it is advisable for each partner to be tested for asymptomatic infection at the beginning of the relationship.
- Unless you and your partner are in a long-term, mutually monogamous relationship and uninfected to the best of your knowledge, always use a latex condom for intercourse—either a condom prelubricated with spermicide or a condom in conjunction with spermicidal cream, jelly, or foam.
- Talk with—and examine—any new or nonmonogamous partner for oral or genital warts, blisters, ulcers, rashes, or discharges. This isn't the most romantic thing in the world to do, but it may help you avoid becoming infected. If you discover any signs of possible infection, avoid sexual intimacy until a clinician has examined and treated the person if necessary. Get into the habit of asking (and disclosing) information about previous partners and infections once it is clear that a new relationship might become sexual.
- Avoid oral-anal and finger-anal contact. If finger-anal or instrument-anal contact occurs, wash the contaminated hand(s) or object(s) with soap and water before having any other oral or genital contact.
- The following sexual activities are low-risk—that is, *reasonably* safe if no lesions are visible: hugging, massage, body contact, dry kissing, and masturbation in

If you have syphilis or gonor-rhea, you will know it. On the contrary, some infected people show no symptoms of syphilis or gonorrhea until many years after they have been infected. In women, for example, gonorrhea is very often asymptomatic.

STD infections in the genitals cannot be transmitted to the mouth, and vice versa. The reality is that transmission of STD infections from mouth to genitals and the reverse do occur.

Birth control pills protect you from STDs. Because birth control pills alter the chemical balance of the vaginal lining, increase the amount of vaginal discharge, and do not offer the barrier protection that a condom does, they may actually *increase* a woman's chances of contracting various STDs.

Once you have been cured of an STD, you cannot get it again. This is a highly dangerous myth. You can get an STD infection any time you come in contact with it, whether you have had it before or not.

Syphilis, gonorrhea, and HIV can be contracted by contact with a toilet seat. This type of transmission is impossible. The germs of these diseases cannot live in the open air.

Source: Adapted from Insel & Roth, 1991.

---

another's presence. But remember, only total abstinence with no body-to-body contact is 100 percent risk-free.

■ The following activities are *possibly* safe if no lesions are visible: vaginal or anal intercourse with a latex condom, fellatio with a latex condom, cunnilingus with a rubber barrier, hand- or finger-to-genital contact (mutual masturbation) with a rubber glove and kissing with an open mouth.

■ The following activity is considered risky: hand- or finger-to-genital contact without a glove.

■ The following sexual activities are definitely high risk for STD transmission unless you are absolutely certain that neither you nor your partner has any infections: vaginal intercourse without a condom, fellatio, cunnilingus, a partner's semen or urine touching a mucous membrane (vagina, rectum, urethra, mouth, or eye), oral-anal contact, blood contact (including menstrual blood or blood transferred by sharing IV needles), and sharing sex toys that have had contact with body fluids without washing them. The highest risk of all is receptive anal intercourse without a latex condom.

Talking with Your Partner About Responsible Lovemaking

The STD epidemic has forced us to rethink and restructure our sex lives. Whether you're married or single, gay, lesbian, or straight, old or young, making love isn't a carefree proposition anymore. Every sexual encounter presents unknown risks, so you need to ask yourself two crucial questions before you engage in lovemaking with a new partner: (1) Do I really want to assume the responsibility for those risks? (2) Do I know my prospective partner well enough to take his or her answers on trust? To answer the first question, you need to know yourself. To answer the second one, you need to know your lover.

According to Marilyn Davis (1988), approaching the topic of safer sex is easier when both you and your prospective partner are equally interested in the subject. However, openly talking about your sexual history before engaging in lovemaking is difficult under any circumstances—and the less familiar you are with your prospective lover, the harder it is. Consequently, the wisest thing to do is to let the relationship

Communicating straightforwardly with a partner about one's health and sexual history is crucial to developing an honest relationship in which safer sex practices are the rule.

MAKING USE OF WHAT WE KNOW

How to Talk About Condoms with a Resistant Partner

*T*he latex condom is not only a very good contraceptive method but is also the single most effective barrier against the spread of disease among sexually active people. For these reasons, it is crucial to get partners to use condoms. (For instructions on how to use the condom properly, see Chapter 12's "Making Use of What We Know" box on "How to Use a Condom: Some Crucial Do's and Don'ts.") At the moment, the traditional male condom is our best bet against STDs, but *both* partners must agree to its use. Believe it or not, women sometimes resist the use of a condom, and if the new female condom (see Chapter 12) proves effective, both men and women may sometimes need to convince one another to use proper protection during lovemaking. Here are some suggestions for how to talk about condoms with a resistant, defensive, or manipulative partner:

If your partner says:	You can say:
"I'm on the pill, you don't need a condom."	"I'd like to use it anyway. We'll both be protected from infections we may not realize we have."
"I *know* I'm clean (disease-free); I haven't had sex with anyone in X months."	"Thanks for telling me. As far as I know, I'm disease-free, too. But I'd still like to use a condom since either of us could have an infection and not know it."
"I'm a virgin."	"I'm not. This way we'll both be protected."
"I can't feel a thing when I wear a condom; it's like wearing a raincoat in the shower."	"Even if you lose some sensation, you'll still have plenty left."
"I'll lose my erection by the time I stop and put it on."	"I'll help you put it on—that'll help you keep it."
"By the time you put it on, I'm out of the mood."	"Maybe so, but we feel strongly enough for each other to stay in the mood."
"It destroys the romantic atmosphere."	"It doesn't have to be that way."
"Condoms are unnatural, fake, a total turnoff."	"Please let's try to work this out—an infection isn't so great either. So let's give the condom a try. Or maybe we can look for alternatives."

develop until you feel reasonably comfortable about revealing the most intimate details of your physical and sexual self. You should then pick a time when both of you are relaxed and at ease. You should also find a location where you won't be distracted or interrupted.

As you broach the subject, realize that honest communication is part of *your* commitment. *Both* of you have the right to know everything before becoming heavily involved. Moreover, the right time is before sex, not after. For most couples, the toughest part is getting started. Here are some possible opening lines:

- "When two people get along as well as we do, I think we owe it to each other to be totally honest. That's why I'd like to share my own sex history with you and would like you to do the same with me."
- "I think we're both responsible adults who want to do what's best for each other and for ourselves."
- "I really like you. Would you be comfortable enough telling me about your recent sex life?"
- "Before we make love, I'd like to tell you how I feel . . ."
- "I love you. Let's talk about real promises about our health."

If your partner says:	**You can say:**
"What kinds of alternatives?"	"Maybe we'll just pet, or postpone sex for a while."
"This is an insult! Do you think I'm some sort of disease-ridden slut (gigolo)?"	"I didn't say or imply that. I care for you, but in my opinion, it's best to use a condom."
"None of my other boyfriends uses a condom. A *real* man isn't afraid."	"Please don't compare me to them. A real man cares about the woman he dates, himself, and about their relationship."
"I love you! Would I give you an infection?"	"Not intentionally. But many people don't know they're infected. That's why this is best for both of us right now."
"Just this once."	"Once is all it takes."
"I don't have a condom with me."	"I do." Or: "Then let's satisfy each other without intercourse."
"You carry a condom around with you? You were planning on seducing me!"	"I always carry one with me because I care about myself. I have one with me tonight because I care about us both."
"I won't have sex with you if you're going to use a condom."	"So let's put if off until we can agree." Or: "Okay, then let's try some other things besides intercourse."

These sample dialogues underscore the importance of sincere and open sexual communication. As we learned in Chapter 7, partners need to nurture a sensitive mutual understanding of their sexual lives, which will, in turn, shape their identity as a couple. By avoiding criticism and threatening postures, communication strategies such as these allow you to structure what you want in ways that make your feelings clearly known.

(*Source*: Adapted from R. Adams, E. Fliegelman, & A. Grieco, "How to Use a Condom," *Medical Aspects of Human Sexuality*, 1987. Copies of the original source can be purchased in bulk; contact G. Philippe, Cahners Publishing Company, 249 West 17th Street, New York, NY 10011.)

Once the ice has been broken, you might consider exchanging such information as when you've each last had a medical checkup (and what it showed); whether either of you has had any recent sexually transmitted diseases; whether previous lovers exhibited any symptoms of STDs or were in a high-risk group; if either of you has a medical condition, and whether it has been treated or cured; and information about any blood transfusions received before 1985 (when effective blood screening for HIV began).

Throughout the entire conversation, it is important for both of you to get all the secrets out and to make your promises genuine. This includes the topic of contraception, especially condom usage and the role condoms play in preventing sexually transmitted diseases as well as pregnancy. The box on "How to Talk About Condoms with a Resistant Partner" offers some realistic suggestions for persuading a potential sexual partner to cooperate with you in practicing safer sex.

Don't let passion cloud your better judgment. Make sure that any risk you take is informed and not under the influence of drugs or alcohol. If you have a sexually transmitted disease, realize that it is your responsibility to make a full and complete disclosure to your partner. Finally, be trustworthy: do not share with friends the information your partner discloses to you (Davis, 1988).

SEXUALITY IN THE NEWS

When Sex Causes Cancer

*I*n this video Barbara Walters, Hugh Downs, and Dr. Timothy Johnson of a "20/20" show aired on April 7, 1989, explore how the human papilloma virus (HPV) is related to almost 7,000 deaths from cervical cancer every year. HPV is transmitted sexually, but few people are aware of this and most do not know how to prevent it. Genital warts are the most common symptom of HPV. We're introduced to Toni and Mike, a young engaged couple who first became aware of HPV when Mike developed a genital wart (14:41 minutes).

DISCUSSION QUESTIONS

1. Physicians encourage couples to have medical examinations for STDs together. Why?
2. Dr. Michael Campion, an Atlanta physician, states that young women are at risk for developing cervical cancer because of HPV. Which screening mechanisms are recommended for HPV, and what steps can you take to avoid contracting HPV?
3. Why do you think HPV has become so widespread in the adolescent population? What advice would you give sexually active teenagers regarding this sexually transmitted virus?

LOOKING BACK

■ The concept of sexual health encompasses physiological well-being, as well as knowledge of those factors that create optimal sexual functioning. This knowledge includes an awareness of sexually transmitted diseases, infections, and other disorders of the reproductive system.

■ A sexually transmitted disease is a contagious infection that for the most part is passed on by intimate sexual contact with others. The sexual contact can be through French kissing, coitus, oral-genital sex, or anal intercourse. Rates of sexually transmitted diseases have rapidly increased in recent years. Especially susceptible are persons under the age of 25, minorities, the medically underserved, and gay men.

■ Viral STDs include genital herpes, genital warts, and viral hepatitis. Genital herpes is caused by the herpes simplex virus (HVH). The herpes simplex virus exists in two forms—(herpes simplex I and II)—and can infect skin or mucous membranes anywhere on the body. Genital warts are caused by the human papilloma virus and are usually found on the penis, vulva, vagina, or rectum. Viral hepatitis is an infectious disease that attacks the liver, causing inflammation. The major types are hepatitis A, hepatitis B, and non-A/non-B hepatitis.

■ Gonorrhea, syphilis, and chlamydia are sexually transmitted diseases passed on by bacterial infection. Gonorrhea is more common in men than in women and is transmitted by bacteria that can live on any mucous membrane. Syphilis is caused by a spirochete bacterium that burrows into the bloodstream. Chlamydia is the most widespread sexually transmitted disease today. Among other complications, it can lead to pelvic inflammatory disease (PID), cervicitis, nongonococcal urethritis (NGU), epididymitis, and proctitis.

■ Parasitic diseases include scabies and pubic lice. Scabies, caused by an organism called *sacroptes scabei*, is highly contagious; it is more common in men than women. Pubic lice, or "crabs," infest the pubic, genital, groin, and anal areas. Vaginitis, which is not caused by any one agent in particular, is usually characterized by burning and itching of the external genital organs and a vaginal discharge.

■ Among nonsexually transmitted diseases of the reproductive system, cystic disease of the breast is a condition in which noncancerous lumps form in the breast. Uterine fibroids are solid noncancerous growths of smooth muscle fibers and connective tissue that develop in and on the uterus. Ovarian cysts are abnormal swellings or saclike growths on the ovary. En-

dometriosis is a condition in which endometrial cells that normally line the uterus detach themselves and grow elsewhere in the pelvic cavity. Disorders of the prostate gland include prostatitis and benign prostatic hypertrophy. Disorders causing scrotal and testicular enlargement include inguinal hernia, hydrocele, and testicular torsion.

■ Tumors can be either benign or malignant (cancerous). The four types of cancerous tumors are carcinomas, sarcomas, lymphomas, and leukemias. Some of the major cancers of the reproductive organs are cancers of the breast, ovaries, uterus (cervical and endometrial cancers), vulva and vagina in women; and cancers of the prostate, testes, and penis in men.

■ Sexual health demands intelligent and informed decision making and proper physical care. Prevention is the best way to minimize the risks of sexual diseases and disorders. Taking responsibility for one's sexual health includes practicing safer sex and insisting on mutual honesty about sexual histories before beginning a sexual relationship.

THINKING THINGS OVER

1. Prepare a chart that depicts the major STDs, their causes, and treatment. Are you at risk for any of these diseases? If so, what steps might you take to eliminate or greatly reduce your risk?

2. You have been asked by 10 of your friends to give them information about safer sex practices. Outline your presentation.

3. Imagine that you have just been told you have a virulent STD. Would you find it difficult to reveal your sexual contacts to the proper authorities? Why or why not? Would you prefer to inform your sexual contacts yourself? Why?

4. You have been dating someone who is defensive about using a condom. You don't want to make this person feel attacked, but you want to make your feelings about the vir-

tues of condom usage known. What kinds of things would you say?

5. You are scheduled to have a complete physical examination in the next month, and this chapter has aroused your interest in your sexual health. Develop a list of questions to ask your doctor about your own personal risk with respect to sexual diseases and disorders.

6. Make a list of positive behaviors that can help protect you against nonsexually transmitted diseases of the reproductive systems, including cancer. How can you strengthen your resolve to practice these preventive behaviors? Now make another list focusing on those behaviors that tend to *increase* your risk of disease. How might you change or avoid these behaviors?

DISCOVER FOR YOURSELF

Covington, T. R., & McClendon, J. F. (1987). *Sex care.* New York: Pocket Books. Part Two of this book covers all of the major sexually transmitted diseases.

Fogel, C. I., & Lauver, D. (1990). *Sexual health promotion.* Philadelphia: W. B. Saunders. An excellent resource book that explores the components of sexual health care.

Kilby, D. (1986). *A manual of safe sex: Intimacy without fear.* Toronto: B. C. Decker. A well-written and concise account of sexually transmitted diseases and how to reduce the risks of contracting them.

Rodway, M., & Wright, M. (1989). *Sociopsychological aspects of sexually transmitted diseases.* New York: Haworth Press. A guide to sexually transmitted diseases.

Scotti, A. T., & Moore, T. A. (1987). *Safe sex.* Toronto: Paperjacks. Covers all major sexually transmitted diseases, including causes, symptoms, and treatments.

Tseng, C. H., Villanueva, T. G., & Powell, A. (1987). *Sexually transmitted diseases.* Saratoga, CA: R & E Publishers. A practical handbook emphasizing protection, prevention, and treatment of sexually transmitted diseases.

18

The Acquired Immune Deficiency Syndrome (AIDS)

The course of an epidemic is shaped not just by the infectious organism and the medical response, but also by the historical setting within which it occurs

—Dennis Altman

Who you are has nothing to do with whether you are in danger of being infected with HIV. What matters is what you do

—C. Everett Koop

Epidemics have long been a curse to humanity and affected the course of history. Plagues contributed to the downfall of ancient Athens and Rome. The bubonic plague caused the deaths of many millions of people during the Middle Ages. An epidemic of typhus and dysentery was partially responsible for Napoleon's defeat by Russia, and the Aztecs of Mexico were conquered by Spanish adventurers after suffering an onslaught of smallpox. During the Civil War more soldiers died of typhoid fever and cholera than were killed on the battlefield. The influenza epidemic of 1918 and 1919 killed more than 20 million men, women, and children around the world.

Today the **acquired immune deficiency syndrome (AIDS)** looms as one of the most serious diseases to confront modern medicine. AIDS is a condition characterized by a breakdown of the body's immune system that makes people vulnerable to a variety of infections, certain forms of cancer, and various neurological disorders. AIDS is caused by a virus named the *human immunodeficiency virus (HIV)*, which lives and reproduces inside human cells and is transmitted by blood and blood products (such as plasma), semen, vaginal secretions, and possibly breast milk. Because there is no cure, AIDS is a fatal condition, although patients are now surviving longer than they did just a few years ago, thanks to new medical treatments. What distinguishes AIDS from many other fatal diseases is that AIDS is preventable.

AIDS was first reported in the United States in the summer of 1981. At that time doctors in New York and California began to see a surprising number of cases of Kaposi's sarcoma, a previously rare form of cancer that produces purple blotches on the skin, and a type of pneumonia called *pnemocystis carinii pneumonia*, an equally rare form of respiratory infection. Both conditions are characterized by depressed immune systems, and both were usually seen in cancer patients who were undergoing chemotherapy and in organ transplant recipients. The cases observed in New York and California, however, were among gay men. As the number of cases mounted, infectious-disease specialists began to investigate this medical puzzle. In 1982 the disease was named the acquired immune deficiency syndrome, and it dawned on medical authorities that a new peril had been unleashed in the world.

Over the past decade AIDS has grown from a rare affliction in gay men to a pandemic disease affecting millions of people worldwide, most of them heterosexuals. In the pages that follow, we show how HIV is spread and how it cripples the body's immune system. We also describe the symptoms and opportunistic infections of AIDS, how HIV infection is diagnosed, and how AIDS is treated. We explore some of the special problems of child victims of the disease. Finally, we conclude the chapter with a look at some of the legal issues that AIDS presents, as well as the public response to the risks of HIV infection and AIDS.

ORIGINS AND CHARACTERISTICS OF AIDS

As we said, AIDS is caused by the human immunodeficiency virus (HIV) and is characterized by a specific defect in the immune system. So far as we know, if a person who is HIV infected lives long enough he or she will eventually develop AIDS and will become susceptible to bacterial, viral, fungal, parasitic, or tumorous disorders that remain dormant in or are fought off by people whose immune systems are normal. Such disorders, often labeled *opportunistic diseases* because they take advantage of the body's crippled immune system, will be discussed shortly. Actually, nobody dies of AIDS. Rather, they die of disorders that are able to thrive in a body whose immune system has been severely weakened. Thus AIDS is a condition in which the body is susceptible to infections, and it is the specific diseases that result from these infections that kill people (Mills & Masur, 1990; DeVita et al., 1988; Leoung & Mills, 1989).

acquired immune deficiency syndrome (AIDS) A collection of diseases caused by the human immunodeficiency virus (HIV). The disorder is characterized by a specific defect in the body's immune system.

539

MYTHS AND MISCONCEPTIONS

Some Myths About the Human Immunodeficiency Virus and AIDS

It is HIV itself that eventually kills the person. Because their immune system has been weakened, people with HIV acquire a variety of diseases that are not usually caught by healthy people. They die from these diseases, not from the HIV infection.

A person carrying HIV cannot pass it on to others unless that person has developed AIDS symptoms. People with HIV *can* transmit the virus to others, even if they do not develop symptoms themselves. Moreover, appearance gives no clue as to whether or not a person is carrying the virus.

Women cannot transmit HIV to their sex partners. Because HIV has been found in vaginal secretions, male partners of infected women have become infected. To date, however, there have been few woman-to-woman transmissions.

HIV can be spread through everyday social contacts, such as touching or being near a person with AIDS. No one should be afraid of getting HIV from casual, social, or family contact. People can, for example, work with HIV-infected people, attend school and public events alongside them, eat at restaurants where they work, and generally be around those with HIV infection without the fear of contracting the virus.

HIV is extremely difficult to kill on surfaces. Soap and water will kill the virus, as will ordinary household bleach, heat (132° F.), and any standard disinfectant like Betadine (available in aerosol spray, antiseptic gel, skin cleanser, and other forms). For body fluid spills like blood, household bleach in a solution made of one part bleach and 10 parts water is recommended.

No one knows for sure where AIDS originated, although the earliest cases have been traced to central Africa in the early 1970s. However, some sources (e.g., Creager et al., 1990) suggest that HIV might have appeared even earlier, perhaps around the turn of the century. There are three possibilities regarding its origins: (1) HIV has always existed but has, for unknown reasons, only recently become harmful to human beings; (2) HIV was originally an animal virus that has only recently infected human beings; and (3) the human immunodeficiency virus is an entirely new organism (Levert, 1987). The "Myths and Misconceptions" box describes some misconceptions about HIV and AIDS.

HOW IS HIV TRANSMITTED?

HIV is extremely fragile outside of human cells. It cannot live in the air and can be killed by such agents as heat, ordinary soap and water, household bleach solutions, and the chlorine used in swimming pools. HIV has been found in blood, semen, vaginal secretions, breast milk, saliva, tears, spinal fluid, amniotic fluid, and urine. Of these, blood, semen, vaginal secretions, and, possibly, breast milk are most likely to transmit the virus from one person to another. Concentrations of HIV in urine, saliva, and tears have not been found to be sufficient for transmission. Table 18–1 charts ways in which HIV can and cannot be transmitted.

HIV cannot pass through unbroken or undamaged skin, the lining of the respiratory tract, or the mucous membranes lining the digestive tract. However, if the skin's protective barrier is broken (by a wound, injury, needle puncture, etc.), fluid containing the virus can enter the body. HIV can enter the body through abrasions in the mucous membranes that line the vagina, endometrium, cervix, penile urethra,

The Acquired Immune Deficiency Syndrome (AIDS)

TABLE 18-1

The Transmission of AIDS

HOW HIV IS TRANSMITTED

Sexual Activity
    Homosexual, between men
    Heterosexual, from men to women and women to men

Blood Inoculation
    Needle sharing among intravenous drug users
    Transfusion of blood and blood products
    Needle stick, open wound, and mucous membrane exposure in health-care workers
    Injection with unsterilized needle (including needles used in acupuncture, medical
        injections, ear piercing, and tattooing)

Childbirth
    Intrauterine (within the uterus)
    Peripartum (during labor and delivery)

HOW HIV IS NOT TRANSMITTED

Food, water	Whirlpools or saunas
Sharing eating and drinking utensils	Coughing or sneezing
Shaking or holding hands	Domestic pets
Using the telephone	Exchanging clothing
Toilet seat	Swimming in a pool
Insects	Bed linens

Source: Adapted from Friedland & Klein (1987) and Hatcher and associates (1990).

rectum, and mouth. For example, because the lining of the rectum is delicate, anal intercourse may cause damage and allow the virus to pass into the body. For this reason, anal intercourse is especially risky for both men and women. Women can also become infected through vaginal sex with a male carrier since penetration can cause tiny abrasions in the vagina. Men having vaginal sex with a female carrier are also at risk because the infection can pass from vaginal secretions to any abrasions on the penis.

HIV is *not* spread by casual contact. In fact, HIV is fairly hard to catch. It cannot be caught by shaking hands, hugging, sneezing, coughing, or social kissing. Although HIV *is* sometimes present in the saliva of people with AIDS, there is little evidence to indicate that it is transmitted by kissing. Still, to be safe, experts advise against deep, prolonged "French kissing" with someone who may be infected with HIV—especially if one has open or bleeding sores in or around the mouth. AIDS also cannot be spread by casual contact in schools, swimming pools, stores, or the workplace. Objects touched or handled by people with AIDS are not contaminated and need not be feared—with the sole exception of objects (e.g., needles) that puncture the skin and contact internal body fluids. For this reason, sharing razors and toothbrushes should be avoided. AIDS is not transmitted through food preparation or food handling. It also cannot be caught from toilet seats, bed linens, insects, or domestic animals (Stine, 1993; Heyward & Curran, 1988; Kurland, 1988). Some self-protective measures that you can take are described in the box on "How to Help Protect Yourself from the Human Immunodeficiency Virus."

How is HIV spread? Can I catch it from a toilet seat or by being around a person with AIDS?

SYMPTOMS AND OPPORTUNISTIC INFECTIONS

People are exposed to HIV infection if blood, semen, vaginal secretions, or possibly breast milk containing infected white blood cells get into their bloodstream. Antibodies usually develop in one to four months—on average, six weeks—after ex-

MAKING USE OF WHAT WE KNOW

How to Help Protect Yourself from the Human Immunodeficiency Virus

*I*t is important to reduce your chances of exposure to HIV by not engaging in high-risk sexual behaviors. Make careful choices about your sexual activities and discuss safer sex practices with your partner. The following guidelines are recommended:

- Don't have sex with multiple partners or with people who have had multiple partners (including prostitutes). The more partners you have, the greater the risk that one of them will transmit HIV to you.

- Do not have sex with people with AIDS, with those at risk for AIDS, or with those who have had a positive result on the HIV antibody test. If you do, avoid contact with their body fluids.

- Know your sexual partners well. Before having sex, ask prospective partners about their health and sexual history and what safety precautions they have used. (For tips on how to approach this topic, see the "Making Use of What We Know" box entitled "How to Talk About Condoms with a Resistant Partner" in Chapter 17.) If you or your partner is at high risk, avoid mouth contact with the vagina, penis, or anus and also take precautions to prevent contact with that person's body fluids.

- Use latex condoms during sex from start to finish. Next to abstinence, a latex condom is the best way to reduce risk during vaginal and anal intercourse. As we pointed out in Chapter 12, condoms made of natural materials, such as lamb's intestines, are not effective in preventing the transmission of HIV. Latex condoms must be used only with a water-soluble lubricant, such as K-Y jelly, or a contraceptive spermicide. Non–water-soluble lubricants such as petroleum jelly weaken condoms and increase the chances that they will tear during use

- Avoid all sexual activities (e.g., sadomasochistic acts designed to give and/or receive pain—see Chapter 19 for examples) that could cause cuts or tears in the linings of the rectum, vagina, or penis.

- Do not use intravenous drugs or share needles if you do. Also avoid mixing alcohol or other drugs with sexual encounters. Drugs cloud your judgment and can lead you to do things you wouldn't do with a clearer head—such as having sex without using a latex condom. Moreover, there is some evidence that alcohol and drugs suppress the immune system.

- Consult with your doctor if you think you may be at increased risk for HIV

---

posure. The average incubation period for AIDS—that is, the time between exposure to the disease and the onset of symptoms—is believed to be between three and five years. However, it can be as short as six months or as long as ten years or more. During the incubation period a person does not have AIDS but rather is said to be HIV positive. Although symptoms may not appear while HIV is dormant, people carrying the virus are infectious to others. This means that while they may appear healthy, they can transmit the HIV infection to a sexual partner or to someone with whom they share a contaminated needle or syringe for drug injection. A pregnant women who carries the HIV infection can pass it on to her baby even if she herself has not developed AIDS.

What's the difference between being HIV positive and having AIDS? What is ARC?

It is estimated that about 20 to 30 percent of people infected with HIV develop AIDS within ten years. Among those whose infection progresses to AIDS, 50 percent die within 18 months and 80 percent within three years. Twenty percent of people who have been infected with HIV will develop a condition called *symptomatic HIV infection* (once referred to as the *AIDS-related complex* [*ARC*]). Symptomatic HIV infection produces many of the symptoms of AIDS, but not the opportunistic infections or malignancies that characterize AIDS. People with symptomatic HIV infection may recover their full health (while remaining infected), or they may continue for an indefinite period with this condition, or they may develop AIDS (Douglas & Pinsky, 1987).

The Acquired Immune Deficiency Syndrome (AIDS)

infection. Consider taking the HIV antibody test, which will enable you to know your health status and take appropriate action.

- Learn about safe and enjoyable alternative sexual activities and use them in lovemaking.

The following list distinguishes safe sexual activities from those that involve some element of risk and those that are clearly unsafe.

SAFE

- Massage
- Hugging
- Body rubbing
- Kissing with closed mouth
- Self-stimulation or masturbation in the presence of a partner
- Erotic books and movies

POSSIBLY SAFE

- Kissing with open mouth
- Vaginal intercourse using a latex condom and spermicide
- Oral sex on a man using a latex condom

- Oral sex on a woman who does not have her period or a vaginal infection with discharge using a latex dam (a piece of latex similar to that used in dental work that covers the vulva and vaginal opening)

UNSAFE

- Any intercourse without using a latex condom
- Oral sex on a man without using a latex condom
- Oral sex on a woman during her period or when she has a vaginal infection with discharge without using a latex dam
- Taking semen into the mouth
- Oral-anal contact
- Sharing sex toys or douching equipment
- Contact of ANY kind with blood (including menstrual blood), sharing needles, and any sexual activity that causes tissue damage or bleeding.

Sources: Stine (1993); Hatcher et al. (1990); Surgeon General's Report on Acquired Immune Deficiency Syndrome, (1987).

The condom is currently the sole device that protects against the transmission of HIV and other sexually transmitted diseases. Only abstinence from sexual intercourse is more effective.

People with AIDS almost uniformly have a reduced number of **lymphocytes**—specialized white blood cells that are critical in combatting infectious diseases such as those caused by viruses. Lymphocytes may also be instrumental in destroying malignancies (cancers) in their early stages. Two types of lymphocytes fight infection: the T-cell and the B-cell. A **T-cell** kills invaders directly, whereas a **B-cell** produces antibodies that fight the infection. In AIDS the number of T-cells are greatly reduced, and the most profound reduction is in a special type of T-cell called the *helper T-cell* (Weber & Weiss, 1988). Figure 18–1 illustrates how HIV enters the body and sabotages its defenses.

According to John Mills and Henry Masur (1990), just how cellular immune function is impaired by HIV is only partly understood. We know that gradually the virus eliminates the helper T-cells, which debilitates the cell-mediated immune response. However, some immune dysfunction is often present even before a decline of helper T-cells becomes evident, which means that the loss of helper T-cells is not the only cause of the impairment. Still, the development of particular opportunistic infections is definitely related to the level of helper T-cells in the blood. Healthy people have about 1,000 such cells in every cubic millimeter of blood. In HIV-infected people, this number declines by an average of about 40 to 80 every year.

When the helper T-cell count diminishes to between 400 and 200 per cubic millimeter, the first symptoms of AIDS usually appear: chronic low-grade fever, swollen

lymphocyte A type of white blood cell, manufactured primarily in the bone marrow, whose primary function is to protect the body from invasive foreign substances.

T-cell Type of lymphocyte that combats infectious diseases. In AIDS victims T-cells are significantly reduced.

B-cell Type of lymphocyte that combats infectious diseases. It produces infection-fighting antibodies when stimulated.

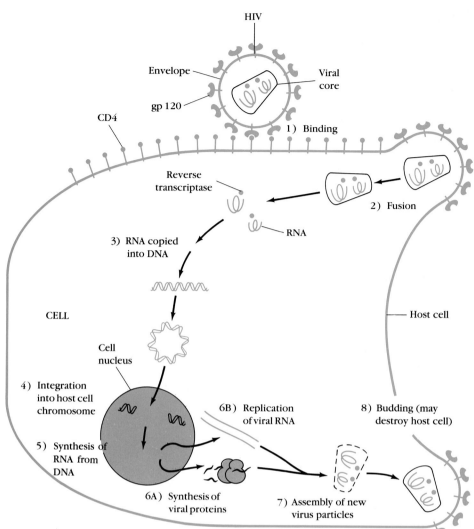

FIGURE 18–1

How HIV enters a host cell, or lymphocyte, replicates within it, and then destroys its host. The process by which HIV reproduces is complex, involving the copying of viral RNA into DNA—which is triggered by an enzyme called *reverse transcriptase*—and then synthesizing RNA from DNA to produce new virus particles. Some researchers have tried to find a way to interfere with some essential step in the replication of the virus. Others have tried to block the binding of the virus's gp120 protein to the cell's CD4 receptors. The budding of many new virus particles from the infected lymphocyte usually kills the host cell. It is suspected that HIV can destroy cells in other ways, too—for example, by provoking an immune response against both infected and uninfected cells. (Source: Adapted from Creager/Black, *Microbiology: Principles and Applications*, Copyright © 1990, p. 525. Adapted by permission of Prentice Hall, Englewood Cliffs, New Jersey.)

lymph glands (in the neck, armpits, and groin), unexplained weight loss, fatigue, night sweats, and recurrent diarrhea. There are also relatively benign but annoying infections of the skin and mucous membranes. Among these may be thrush (painful sores of the mouth caused by the fungus *Candida albicans*), shingles (infection of the nerves and skin by *Herpes virus varicellae*), unusually severe athlete's foot (caused by several types of fungi), and oral hairy leukoplakia (whitish patches on the tongue caused by Epstein-Barr virus). Once such symptoms appear, the person is usually considered to have symptomatic HIV infection (Mills & Masur, 1990; Leoung & Mills, 1989). As immunity wanes still further, serious opportunistic infections usually develop. Many AIDS patients contract one or both of two rare diseases: Kaposi's sarcoma and pneumocystis carinii pneumonia. **Kaposi's sarcoma** is a cancer of the tissues beneath the

Kaposi's sarcoma A type of cancer that often afflicts HIV patients.

The Acquired Immune Deficiency Syndrome (AIDS)

TABLE 18–2

Symptoms and Infections Associated with Symptomatic HIV Infection and AIDS

SYMPTOMS	INFECTIOUS AGENT	TYPE OF INFECTION
Symptomatic HIV Infection		
Night sweats	—	—
Swollen lymph nodes	Lymphoma	Malignancy
Loss of appetite and weight	—	—
Persistent diarrhea	Cryptosporidium	Parasite
White spots in mouth	Candida albicans	Fungus
Painful skin rash	Shingles	Virus
AIDS		
Persistent diarrhea	Cryptosporidium	Parasite
White spots in mouth	Candida albicans	Fungus
Pneumonia, including cough and difficult breathing	Pneumocystis carinii	Parasite
Pneumonia, blindness	Cytomegalovirus	Virus
Oral lesions	Herpes simplex	Virus
Cough	Tuberculosis	Bacteria
Neuromuscular impairments	Mycobacterium	Bacteria
Blindness, mental disorder	Toxoplasmosis	Parasite
Blue or red skin rash	Kaposi's sarcoma	Malignancy

Source: Adapted from *Health Psychology: An Introduction to Behavior and Health*, 2nd Edition by Linda Brannon and Jess Feist. Copyright © 1992 by Wadsworth, Inc. Reprinted by permission of the publisher.

skin and the mucus-secreting surfaces of the digestive tract, the lymph nodes, and the lungs. The lesions characteristic of this disease are often first noticed as bluish to reddish discolorations or raised, firm, purple spots on arms, legs, or feet. These lesions can also appear in the mouth. The lesions neither itch nor are they painful. **Pneumocystis carinii pneumonia** is a parasitic infection of the lungs. It is difficult to treat and may be life-threatening. Some of the symptoms of this type of pneumonia are: fever (often very high, frequently worse in the afternoon and evening); cough (usually without significant sputum); shortness of breath (abnormal breathing sounds); and chest pain. Table 18–2 lists the main symptoms and infections associated with symptomatic HIV infection and AIDS.

pneumocystis carinii pneumonia A parasitic infection of the lungs that often afflicts AIDS patients.

DIAGNOSING HIV INFECTION

There is considerable confusion and legal controversy surrounding "AIDS testing." AIDS cannot be diagnosed simply on the basis of a test. Rather, the diagnosis of AIDS is based on finding evidence of a weakened immune system.

What can be tested for is the presence of antibodies that the body produces in response to HIV infection. The HIV antibody test is called the **ELISA** (enzyme-linked immunosorbent assay) **test.** While the ELISA test can't isolate the human immunodeficiency virus, it can detect whether or not the virus has been present. If a person tests positive, a second ELISA test is typically given. If the second test is also positive, a different test, called the *Western blot assay*, is usually administered for confirmation. If a person does receive two positive readings from a testing center, an experienced counselor on the center's staff will refer him or her to a physician who specializes in HIV-related problems. As we go to press, a third test, known as the single use diagnostic system (SUDS), also became available for diagnostic purposes. Like ELISA and Western blot tests, the single use diagnostic system detects HIV antibodies.

Let's clarify some of the limitations of HIV antibody testing. Some people have a positive test result even though they have never been exposed to HIV. This is referred

ELISA test The enzyme-linked immunosorbent assay test, which can detect whether or not antibodies have been produced by the body in response to HIV.

Can an AIDS test tell me if I have the disease?

When Earvin "Magic" Johnson revealed that he was HIV positive, some people praised him for his honesty and for helping to inform the public about AIDS. Some, however, expressed concern for the many people Johnson admitted he may have infected and felt he should not have received such widespread acclaim.

to as a "false positive" reaction and successive testing should give negative results. Then, too, some people who have been exposed to HIV do not test positive—usually because they have not yet produced enough detectable antibodies. While detectable antibodies may develop within 2 months after infection, it sometimes takes up to 36 months for antibodies to appear in the blood (Creager et al., 1990). If antibody testing is related to a specific exposure, the test should be repeated to take such wide variations into account.

A confirmed positive test result does mean that the person is infected with HIV and can transmit the virus to others. This is true even when that person has no symptoms. Therefore, people who test positive for HIV should take the following steps to protect themselves and others:

- Get a complete medical examination.
- Protect against further infection. It is possible to become infected with another "strain" of HIV, which may accelerate the development of AIDS.
- Either refrain from all sexual activity with others or inform prospective partners that you have had a positive test result, and always use a latex condom to protect partners from coming into contact with your body fluids during sex. Refrain from anal intercourse, oral-genital contact, and open-mouthed kissing.
- Inform any previous sexual partners about the positive test result and urge them to seek medical advice and antibody testing from a doctor or health clinic.
- Refuse to share intravenous drug paraphernalia—needles, syringes, and the like—with anyone. Better still, don't use drugs.
- Do not share toothbrushes, razors, tweezers, or other items that could become contaminated with blood.
- Do not donate blood or plasma, body organs, other body tissue, or sperm.
- Clean spills of blood or other body fluids on household or other surfaces with freshly diluted household bleach—one part bleach to 10 parts water. Do *not* use bleach on wounds.
- When you seek medical help for any complaint, inform all health-care practitioners providing care about your positive test result. This will enable them to protect both you and themselves.

The Acquired Immune Deficiency Syndrome (AIDS)

■ Women who test positive should avoid becoming pregnant until more is known about the risks of transmitting HIV to the fetus (see next section). Because HIV has been found in breast milk, breast-feeding should definitely be avoided. The box titled "AIDS Information Hotline" lists sources of information on AIDS in every state in the United States as well as a number of nationwide resources.

MAKING USE OF WHAT WE KNOW

AIDS Information Hotlines

General Information Hotlines

National AIDS Hotline	1-800-342-AIDS
Spanish AIDS Hotline	1-800-344-7432
Hearing Impaired AIDS Hotline	1-800-243-7889
National AIDS Clearing House	1-800-458-5231
Project Inform (AIDS experimental drug information)	1-800-822-7422
American Foundation for AIDS Research	1-212-719-0033
National AIDS Network	1-202-293-2437
Pediatric and Pregnancy AIDS Hotline	1-212-340-3333

AIDS Hotlines State by State

State	Number	State	Number
Alabama	1-700-228-0469	Missouri	1-800-553-2437
Alaska	1-800-478-2437	Montana	1-800-537-6187
Arizona	1-800-445-7720	Nebraska	1-800-782-2437
Arkansas	1-800-445-7720	Nevada	1-702-885-4800
California (No.)	1-800-367-2437	New Hampshire	1-800-872-8909
California (So.)	1-800-922-2437	New Jersey	1-800-624-2377
Colorado	1-303-331-8320	New Mexico	1-800-545-2437
Connecticut	1-800-342-2437	New York	1-800-541-2437
Delaware	1-800-422-0429	North Carolina	1-800-535-2437
D.C.	1-202-332-2437	North Dakota	1-800-742-2180
Florida	1-800-352-2437	Ohio	1-800-332-2437
Georgia	1-800-551-2728	Oklahoma	1-800-522-9054
Hawaii	1-800-922-1313	Oregon	1-800-777-2437
Idaho	1-208-345-2277	Pennsylvania	1-800-692-7254
Illinois	1-800-243-2437	Rhode Island	1-401-277-6502
Indiana	1-800-848-2437	South Carolina	1-800-322-2437
Iowa	1-800-532-3301	South Dakota	1-800-592-1861
Kansas	1-800-232-0040	Tennessee	1-800-525-2437
Kentucky	1-800-654-2437	Texas	1-800-248-1091
Louisiana	1-800-992-4379	Utah	1-800-537-1046
Maine	1-800-851-2437	Vermont	1-800-882-2437
Maryland	1-800-638-6252	Virginia	1-800-533-4148
Massachusetts	1-800-235-2331	Washington	1-800-272-2437
Michigan	1-800-872-2437	West Virginia	1-800-642-8244
Minnesota	1-800-248-2437	Wisconsin	1-800-334-2437
Mississippi	1-800-826-2961	Wyoming	1-800-327-3577

Recorded Information from the Centers for Disease Control

Statistics on current AIDS cases and deaths	1-404-330-3020
Statistics on the cities and states with the greatest number of AIDS residents	1-404-330-3022
American Red Cross (Washington, DC)	1-202-737-8300
Blacks Educating Blacks About Sexual Health Issues	1-215-546-4140
Drug Abuse Hotline	1-800-662-HELP
National Gay/Lesbian Crisis Line	1-800-767-4297
U.S. Public Health Service	1-202-245-6867

THE TREATMENT OF AIDS

The acquired immune deficiency syndrome is one of the most serious diseases of our century. Since it was first observed, AIDS has generated intense interest among medical researchers, who have expended enormous energy in searching for a cure or vaccine. Although a cure still eludes us, one of the drugs showing promise in the 1990s is the antiviral *zidovudine*, previously known as azidothymidine (AZT). Zidovudine appears to delay the onset of AIDS in people who are HIV positive but have no symptoms, although the evidence is mixed. While white men treated with zidovudine developed such diseases as Kaposi's sarcoma and pneumocystis carinii pneumonia more slowly than those who did not get the drug, among African- and Hispanic-American men early zidovudine use has proved no more effective than later treatment in staving off AIDS. Because zidovudine is highly toxic, about half of all AIDS patients cannot tolerate it (the side effects include various anemias). It is also an expensive medication.

In 1992, a drug called Zalcitabine, or ddC, was approved by the Food and Drug Administration. Marketed under the brand name HIVID, Zalcitabine is used in combination with Zidovudine and tends to cause an increase in white blood cells in the immune systems of people with AIDS. The white blood cell increase is believed to show that the body is maintaining a disease-fighting capability.

In 1991 medical researchers began looking at the effects of experimental drugs such as Septra on pneumocystis carinii pneumonia. Also in 1991 the National Institutes of Health reported that the drug *intravenous immunoglobulin (IVIG)* can suppress serious bacterial infections in HIV-infected children. IVIG doesn't cure the disease, but it does prolong the time between infections in these children.

Some AIDS patients with Kaposi's sarcoma are being treated experimentally with forms of *interferon*, a virus-fighting protein. Although interferon treatment has shown some success against Kaposi's sarcoma, it does not appear to restore immune function. Limited trials of a substance called *interleukin-2*, which scientists believe may help fight the severe deficiencies seen in the immune systems of AIDS patients, have also begun. Preliminary results are promising, but much more work remains to be done before interleukin-2 can be used on a wide scale.

Also being tested are vaccines designed to stimulate human antibody production. One of these, developed in 1987, consists of a substance that has been purified from the protein outer coat of the human immunodeficiency virus. The protein supposedly

The treatment of AIDS requires not only our most advanced medical technologies but the concerned care of medical personnel like Dr. Jordan Glaser of Staten Island Hospital in New York City.

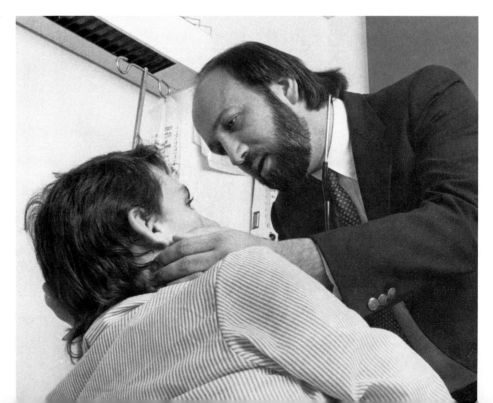

stimulates an immune response but without causing the disease because the components that give HIV its virulence have been eliminated from the vaccine.

Also being investigated are the experimental drugs suramin, ribavirin, dideoxyinosine (DDI), and dideoxycitosine (DDC). All are believed to interfere with a key step in the human immunodeficiency virus's action. Researchers are also exploring how antiherpes medications such as acyclovir, ganciclovir, vidarabine, and foscarnet can be used to interfere with viral replication. In addition, an antifungal drug called fluconazole, developed in 1990, offers promise for restoring weakened immune systems. Other researchers are placing their hopes on the natural properties of egg lecithin, first used in Israel. Also under investigation as a possible treatment approach is a combination of bone marrow transplant and zidovudine. Additionally, in 1990 researchers developed a synthetic protein molecule called CPF that they hope can attach itself to HIV and prevent it from spreading to unaffected cells.

WHERE TO FIND MORE ON AIDS

U.S. Public Health Service, Department of Health and Human Services, Washington, DC 20201.

National AIDS Hotline, Centers for Disease Control, 1600 Clifton Road, Atlanta, GA 30333.

Gay Rights National Lobby, Box 1892, Washington, DC 20013.

KS Research and Education Foundation, 54 Tenth Street, San Francisco, CA 94103.

National Coalition of Gay STD Services, P.O. Box 239, Milwaukee, WI 53201.

National Gay Task Force, 80 Fifth Avenue, Suite 1601, New York, NY 10011.

Minority Task Force on AIDS, 475 Riverside Drive, New York, NY 10115.

AIDS Action Council, 729 8th Street, Washington, DC 20003.

Hispanic AIDS Forum, 853 Broadway, New York, NY 10003.

CHILDREN WITH AIDS

The spread of AIDS to children is a tragic development that affects society in many ways. While the incidence of childhood AIDS is low—approximately 2 to 3 percent of all AIDS cases—it is growing swiftly (Centers for Disease Control, 1992). Let's examine how this segment of the population is affected by AIDS.

Symptoms and Prognosis

Over 80 percent of AIDS children were infected by their mothers during pregnancy, birth, or breast-feeding. During prenatal development HIV may pass through the placenta and mix with fetal blood. The virus can also be contracted during the birth process, and some infants born by cesarean section have also been infected by HIV. More rarely, infants have acquired the virus through ingestion of breast milk (HIV has been shown to be present in the breast milk of infected mothers). Currently, it is not known what percentages of AIDS infants acquired the disease in utero, during birth, and through ingesting infected breast milk (Task Force on Pediatric AIDS, 1989). It is important to point out that not all infants born to HIV-positive mothers contract the virus. It is estimated that 30 to 50 percent of infants born to infected mothers will also be infected (Stine, 1993; Cohen, Sande, & Volberding, 1990).

Can a pregnant woman transmit the HIV infection to an unborn child? What is the prognosis for a child born with AIDS?

Kim and Malcolm Eldredge, of Estella, Pa., whose one-year-old HIV-positive foster baby crawls toward them, hoped to open a shelter for other AIDS babies despite some resistance from township residents.

Infants born with AIDS have certain distiguishing characteristics. Most have a small head, a prominent forehead, protruding lips, a flattened nose bridge, and wide-set eyes. Many also have a bluish tinge to the whites of their eyes. Some infants do not seem sick at birth, but most will develop symptoms within eight or nine months. Infected infants often exhibit retarded motor and language growth and other developmental delays, cognitive deficits, and chronic diarrhea. Many have enlarged lymph nodes, liver, and spleen. And like adult victims of the disease, many children with AIDS are susceptible to bacterial infections such as pneumonia (Task Force on Pediatric AIDS, 1989; Grossman, 1988).

The prognosis for children with AIDS is not favorable. Most succumb to infections that attack their hopelessly weakened immune system before they are three years old. It is rare for these children to live as long as six years. Like adults with AIDS, children with AIDS have no hope at present of effective treatment or cure (Hales, 1989; Seibert & Olson, 1989).

The spread of AIDS to children has given rise to a number of controversial issues (Grossman, 1988). One of these is whether all women who are planning pregnancies should consider HIV antibody testing. Many people believe that at least women who engage in high-risk sexual behaviors should be tested when they become pregnant, and that those who test positive should be informed of the harmful effects of pregnancy on their own immunological status as well as on that of the fetus. For example, one study (Landers & Sweet, 1990) discloses that the progress of clinical symptoms in HIV-positive, asymptomatic women may be accelerated by pregnancy, perhaps because of the immune alterations that naturally occur during any pregnancy. Many authorities (e.g., Olds, London, & Ladewig, 1992) stress that HIV-positive women should be straightforwardly counseled about the implications for themselves and the fetus and that they should be offered therapeutic abortion.

Other concerns focus on the actual delivery of an infant from an HIV-infected mother. The pediatrician and delivery room attendants need to be informed ahead of time that the mother is infected because her body fluids and the placenta will contain HIV and therefore infection-control precautions must be taken.

While many HIV-infected mothers care for their infected children, many others do not because of their medical and social problems. Who, then, is to care for these children? In recent years shelter and foster care programs have been reluctant to accept HIV-infected infants, and putting these children up for adoption isn't a practical answer either, for few people want to adopt an infected baby. Many communities

Some 60 babies lodge on the third floor of the drab, gray Victor Babes Hospital, the only AIDS clinic in Bucharest, Romania. In a few rooms there are two babies to a crib. In one small cubicle four infants close to death lie in a row under a single blanket. Amid the moans and wails of the babies, nurses scurry about carrying syringes, vials, and wet cloths. They often have trouble keeping up with the infants' assortment of medical needs.

Romania has an unusual pediatric epidemic of AIDS, concentrated in crowded orphanages and clinics and spread by the peculiar practice of giving blood transfusions to newborns (World Health Organization, 1991). For many years, in the hope of stimulating early growth in babies, Romanian doctors injected blood into the umbilical cord of newborns. Because each baby was given only a small amount of blood, one pint of HIV-contaminated blood could infect many, many babies.

Of the 2000 Romanian children tested in 1990 in targeted clinics and orphanages, 250 had AIDS and another 200 tested positive for HIV. AIDS among babies is not unique to Romania, of course, but the authorities' willful neglect of the disease allowed it to spread rapidly. The problem was compounded by poverty, poor medical practices, and the large number of children abandoned to institutional care. The epidemic is one of the grim legacies of Nicolae Ceausescu, the former ruler of Romania, who was overthrown in a revolution in December 1989.

Almost two-thirds of the AIDS babies in the clinic were brought there from orphanages. The orphanages, overcrowded, ill-equipped, and underheated, are another Ceausescu legacy, the product of draconian policies against birth control that resulted in thousands of unwanted children.

Prior to the overthrow of Ceausescu, there was no official acknowledgment that AIDS existed in Romania. Thus it is only recently that data about the spread of the disease have become available. *Source*: Bohlen (1990).

---

have had to resort to some form of institutional care for these infants—a sad alternative that is far less likely to meet their developmental and emotional needs than an individual home would (Grossman, 1988; Prothrow-Stith, 1989). The box on "Romania's AIDS Epidemic Among Infants" discusses a special case of AIDS infection in the very young and examines the treatment and care provided for these babies.

Children with AIDS in School

Deciding whether or not to admit a child with AIDS to regular classrooms is not easy. Danek Kaus and Robert Reed (1987) observe that a number of factors should be taken into consideration, not the least of which is the possible emotional trauma for both the child with AIDS and the noninfected children in the class.

So far there have been no reported cases of AIDS transmission in the school setting. The U.S. Public Health Service and the American Academy of Pediatrics have both stated that most children with AIDS should be permitted to attend school. The exceptions are AIDS children who lack control over their bodily functions, have open wounds or cuts, or display behavior such as biting. For these children, individualized instruction outside the classroom is advisable.

Because they have weakened immune systems, children with AIDS or HIV infection who attend school are more likely than others to get such childhood infections as colds, flu, and chicken pox. They also stand a greater chance of developing complications when they do get these routine childhood illnesses. A child with AIDS should be under a doctor's supervision in order to assess periodically whether the child should remain in school (U.S. Department of Education, 1988).

In one of the first court cases concerning the right of a child with AIDS to attend school, Ryan White, a hemophiliac who contracted the disease through blood transfusions, and his mother, Jeanne, accused Kokomo, Indiana, schools of violating Ryan's civil rights and discriminating against him as a handicapped person. Ryan, who died in 1990, is memorialized in the federal Ryan White Comprehensive AIDS Resources Emergency Act of 1990, the purpose of which is to provide financial and other assistance to localities disproportionately affected by AIDS.

To help individual schools and school districts establish rational admission policies, the Centers for Disease Control (1985) developed a number of guidelines. We list the chief points here:

1. Decisions regarding the type of educational and care setting for HIV-infected children should be based on the behavior, neurologic development, and physical condition of the child and the expected type of interaction with others in that setting. In each case, risks and benefits to both the infected child and to others in the setting need to be carefully weighed.

2. For most infected school-age children, the benefits of an unrestricted setting outweigh the risks of their acquiring potentially harmful infections in that setting and the apparently nonexistent risk of transmission of HIV. These children should be allowed to attend school and after-school day care and to be placed in a foster home in an unrestricted setting.

3. A more restricted environment is advised for infected preschool-age children, for neurologically handicapped children who lack control over their body secretions or who display behavior such as biting, and for children who have uncoverable, oozing lesions.

4. Child care involving exposure to the infected child's body fluids and excrement, such as feeding and diaper changing, should be performed only by people who are aware of the child's HIV infection and the modes of possible transmission.

5. Because infections besides HIV can be present in blood or body fluids, all schools and day-care facilities should adopt routine procedures for handling blood and body fluids, whether or not they have children with HIV attending.

6. The hygienic practices of children with HIV infection may improve as they mature. Alternatively, their hygienic practices may deteriorate with age if their condition worsens.

7. Physicians caring for children born to mothers with AIDS or at increased risk of acquiring HIV infection should consider testing the children for evidence of HIV infection for medical reasons.

8. Adoption and foster-care agencies should consider adding HIV screening to their routine medical evaluations of children who are at risk of infection.

9. Mandatory screening of all children before they enter school is not warranted based on available data.

10. People who are caring for and educating HIV-infected children should respect the children's right to privacy and keep their records confidential.

11. All educational and public health departments are strongly encouraged to inform parents, children, and educators about HIV and how it is transmitted. For suggestions on how to talk with young people about HIV infection and AIDS, see the box on "Talking with Younger People About HIV Infection and AIDS."

PUBLIC RESPONSES TO THE RISKS OF HIV INFECTION AND AIDS

Education has played an important part in the battle against HIV transmission and AIDS. The federal government and many state governments and localities have launched AIDS education programs designed to teach people the facts about HIV infection and AIDS, including what kinds of behavior put them at risk and what measures offer false security.

Today's youngsters often face tough decisions about sex and drugs. By providing information about decision making and AIDS prevention, you can help them resist peer pressure and make informed choices that will help protect their health, now and for the rest of their lives. If you feel awkward bringing the topic up, look for cues that will help you. For instance, HIV infection and AIDS receive considerable attention in the media today, and a television or radio program, or a newspaper or magazine article, could provide a natural opening.

To provide meaningful and understandable information about HIV infection and AIDS, you need to consider the child's level of knowledge and experience. For example, how old is she? How much does she already know about HIV infection, AIDS, and other related subjects, such as sex and drug use? Where has she gotten her information? Try also to discover what the child is learning in health, science, or any other class about HIV infection and AIDS.

Talking about HIV infection and AIDS can be difficult. It is not uncommon for people to feel uncomfortable just thinking about the subject. If you are nervous or embarrassed, don't be afraid to admit it. Allowing your feelings to surface may help break the tension. Furthermore, a child or adolescent will sense your uneasiness even if you don't mention it.

The following discussion guidelines may prove useful:

- *Review the Facts*. You don't have to be a human sexuality expert to talk with a youngster about the topic. However, you do need to make a concerted effort to gather basic facts so that you will be able to deliver the right information. Sharing your information with another adult may help you feel more comfortable as you prepare to talk with the child.
- *Use Sensitivity and Empathy*. It is helpful to remember the kinds of things you did when you were the age of the young person with whom you plan to speak. How did you think and perceive your surroundings? The better you understand a young person's point of view, the more effectively you'll be able to communicate. But, remember also that the world you grew up in was considerably different from a child's world today. Being sensitive to this difference can help make your discussion timely and relevant.
- *Talk with children, not to them*. You have to engage in a mutual conversation, not lecture the child. Try for an exchange of ideas and information, and encourage the youngster to ask questions. Involve him by asking about his thoughts, feelings, and activities. This will show that you want to learn from him, just as you hope he will learn from you.
- *Be a Good Listener*. Remember the communication skills discussed in Chapter 7 and practice effective listening. Techniques such as clarifying, probing, reflection, and restatement will indicate to the child that you are attentive and responding to what she is saying. Remember, too, the importance of good body language, including eye contact.
- *Don't Get Discouraged*. It is not uncommon for youngsters—especially adolescents—to challenge what they hear from adults. If a youngster questions what you say, avoid a heated confrontation. Instead, encourage him to check your information with another source, such as the National AIDS Hotline (1-800-342-AIDS). And if your first dialogue is interrupted or cut short, don't give up. Try again at a mutually agreeable time, preferably in a location free from distractions.

Source: Adapted from the U.S. Department of Health and Human Services, (1990).

MAKING USE OF WHAT WE KNOW

Talking with Younger People About HIV Infection and AIDS

Recent surveys show that Americans are becoming more knowledgeable about HIV infection and that some are changing their behavior to reduce their risks of contracting the disease (O'Hare et al., 1991; Zimmerman, 1989; Fineberg, 1988). For example, in one study of sexually active college students (Zimmerman & Olson, 1988),

"I'll show you mine
if you show me yours."

respondents reported that a heightened awareness of AIDS had led them to have sex with fewer partners and with less frequency, and to use condoms when they do have sex.

Other reports, however, reveal that men and women are unwilling to change sexual behaviors they know put them at risk. For example, Bruce Roscoe and Tammy Kruger (1990) examined what information 255 adolescents had about AIDS and whether they had changed their sexual behavior because of it. Although the subjects turned out to be quite knowledgeable about AIDS and its transmission, only 34 percent had altered their sexual behavior as a result of fear of the disease.

A statewide survey (Bowen, 1990) of risk behaviors among female clients of Planned Parenthood clinics in Pennsylvania indicated that a sizable proportion of these women were at high or intermediate risk for exposure to HIV. Nearly 5 percent of the 15,499 women in the sample reported personal behavior, or a partner's behavior, that placed them at high risk, while an additional 20 percent reported behavior that put them at intermediate risk. Specifically, 13 percent of the women surveyed had had three or more partners in the past year, 12 percent had a sexually transmitted disease, 4 percent had partners who were intravenous (IV) drug users, 2 percent were either current or past IV drug users themselves, one percent had bisexual partners, and fewer than one percent had partners who had hemophilia or who were HIV infected.

Finally, a study done in 1990 (DeBuono, 1990) showed that all the publicity about AIDS and other sexually transmitted diseases has not caused college students to make significant changes in their sexual behavior, particularly in their number of lifetime or recent sexual partners. This study compared responses to those from a similar survey conducted in 1975, and found that the percentage of female students who had had only one male sexual partner had dropped from 25 percent in 1975 to just 12 percent in 1989. College health officials found it remarkable that while "public health messages" have helped effect larger changes in the use of tobacco and tampons among female students, they have been quite ineffective in changing sexual attitudes and behavior.

Given the widespread concern about AIDS and HIV infection, why do young people continue to engage in high-risk sexual behaviors? At least part of the problem is the feeling of invulnerability many adolescents have. As we noted in Chapter 14, many teenagers cannot conceive of their own mortality. Researchers such as Linda Brannon and Jess Feist (1992) believe that young people who engage in high-risk sexual behaviors do so as part of an overall pattern of risk taking. Their belief is supported by research (e.g., Biglan et al., 1990) showing that adolescents who engage in one type of high-risk sexual behavior are apt to engage in other high-risk behaviors. For example, those unlikely to use condoms are also more apt to have multiple sex partners and to drink and smoke. This finding suggests that intervention efforts need to focus on the motivations and attitudes behind the overall pattern of risk-taking behaviors in adolescents. Since simply providing young people with concrete facts and informational presentations has not worked, we need to explore and seek to change the complex dynamics behind these adolescents' disregard for their own safety and well-being.

HOW WIDESPREAD IS AIDS?

By 1991, 206,392 cases of AIDS had been reported to the Centers for Disease Control and 133,232 deaths had been associated with the disease. Figure 18–2 illustrates the rapidly increasing magnitude of the HIV epidemic in the United States. *The first 100,000 cases of AIDS were reported during an eight-and-one-half-year period, whereas the second 100,000 cases were reported during a two-and-one-half-year period.* At present, our best estimate is that there are one million HIV-infected persons in the United States and about 20 percent of this total have developed AIDS (Centers for Disease Control, 1992).

At first AIDS was believed to be primarily a disease of gay and bisexual men and intravenous drug users. Before long it became apparent that AIDS could also be transmitted heterosexually, primarily through sexual relations with IV drug users, bisexual men, and prostitutes. In recent years there has been an increase in the heterosexual transmission of HIV. Factors associated with a higher risk for heterosexual transmission include multiple sex partners and the presence of other sexually transmitted diseases. Men and women who have unprotected sexual contact, particularly with partners known to be at risk for HIV infection, are at increased risk for HIV infection themselves. Thus today experts speak not exclusively of *groups* who

Is AIDS primarily restricted to gays and bisexuals?

FIGURE 18–2

The rate at which AIDS cases occur in the United States has tripled over a 10-year period. Notice that the first 100,000 cases of AIDS occurred during a period of eight and a half years, but the second 100,000 took only two and a half years to appear. (*Source*: Centers for Disease Control, *Morbidity and Mortality Weekly Report*, 1992.)

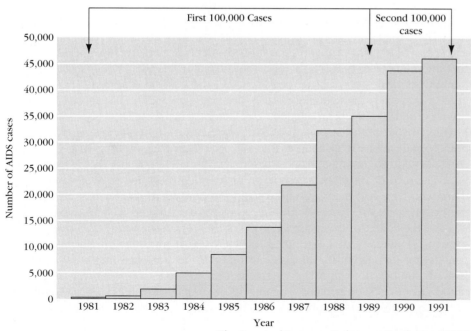

The Acquired Immune Deficiency Syndrome (AIDS)

Making Use of What We Know

Shattered Lives: Profiles of Individuals Stricken with AIDS

Roberta and Her Family

When she was six months old, Roberta, the daughter of a prominent real estate developer and his wife, died of pneumocystis carinii pneumonia due to AIDS. Roberta was a beautiful baby, bright and lively until the illness began. First there was a brief hospitalization for diarrhea, then a longer hospitalization at a large medical center when the diarrhea recurred and didn't respond to conventional treatments. Finally, at the age of five months, Roberta was hospitalized for severe respiratory distress that required mechanical ventilator support to allow her to breathe. Her parents were at her bedside when she died one month later.

Roberta's parents refused to accept the diagnosis of AIDS, and extensive interviews of both parents uncovered no risk factors. The parents themselves were in excellent health when the child died. Two years later, however, Roberta's mother was diagnosed with disseminated tuberculosis. Soon after, she also developed pneumocystis carinii pneumonia and died. Until her death she said it was impossible for her to have AIDS. Again, an investigation revealed no risk factors.

Within six months of his wife's death, Roberta's father was diagnosed with cytomegalovirus infection due to AIDS. Before dying, he finally told doctors that there was, in fact, a risk factor that his wife had not been aware of. Occasionally, on weekends, he had shot heroin with his sister's husband and they had shared needles. Roberta's seven-year-old sister was the only survivor of this family.

A Life Is a Terrible Thing to Waste

Marsha worked hard to escape poverty. She excelled in college and decided to enhance her opportunities for a fulfilling and more prosperous life by enrolling in graduate school. In 1984, as a second-year graduate student, Marsha noticed that she tired easily and felt "run down." She consulted the student health service, which initially attributed her problem to "exam stress." However, Marsha's symptoms persisted, even worsened, after final exams were over.

Within several months Marsha developed pneumocystis carinii pneumonia, and tests confirmed that she had AIDS. Marsha, her family, and her physician were shocked and devastated by the diagnosis. An investigation of potential risk factors in Marsha's life revealed that two

---

are at high risk, but of *behaviors* that heighten the risk of transmission of HIV (Stine, 1993; Centers for Disease Control, 1992; Hatcher at al., 1990; Quinn, 1989; Hein, 1989). The box titled "Shattered Lives: Profiles of Individuals Stricken with AIDS" highlights the differences among persons with AIDS.

The Centers for Disease Control (1992) has analyzed characteristics of the first and second 100,000 persons diagnosed with AIDS (see Figure 18–2). Overall, most reported AIDS cases occurred among homosexual or bisexual men (59 percent) and intravenous drug users (22 percent). Of the first 100,000 reported AIDS cases, 61 percent occurred among homosexual or bisexual men with no history of intravenous drug use, and 20 percent among female or heterosexual male intravenous drug users. In comparison, of the second 100,000 reported cases, 55 percent occurred among homosexual or bisexual men with no history of intravenous drug usage, while 24 percent occurred among female or heterosexual male intravenous drug users.

The second 100,000 cases show an increasing proportion of AIDS cases among those who have had heterosexual exposure to persons at risk for HIV infection. Of the first 100,000 AIDS cases, only 5 percent were attributed to heterosexual transmission; the figure for the second 100,000 cases is 7 percent. Of all AIDS cases among women, 34 percent were attributed to heterosexual transmission, and women accounted for 61 percent for all cases attributed to heterosexual transmission. Of the first 100,000 people with AIDS, 9 percent were women, compared with 12 percent of the second 100,000 persons. The first 100,000 AIDS cases included 1683 children, of whom 81 percent were born to mothers with, or at risk for, HIV infection; the

of her former lovers were in high-risk categories. One man was bisexual, and the other was from a country in central Africa where heterosexually transmitted AIDS rates are much higher than in the United States. Both men had appeared healthy during their involvement with Marsha, and neither was showing any symptoms of AIDS at the time Marsha's diagnosis was confirmed. Marsha's condition worsened at the hospital. She died two weeks after her AIDS diagnosis was confirmed.

No Easy Answers: Coping with the AIDS Diagnosis

Paul, a 34-year-old successful attorney with a prominent Connecticut law firm, was very happy in the relationship he had shared with his lover, Tim, since 1982. In January 1985 he and Tim purchased a 1750 colonial home that they planned to restore. That March Paul noticed that he had swollen glands and a purplish skin lesion on his back, which he initially assumed was just a bruise from the remodeling work. When the bruise failed to heal and he lost 20 pounds in six weeks, he began to worry and decided to see his physician. A blood test ordered by the doctor revealed that Paul was infected with HIV. The doctor diagnosed Paul as having Kaposi's sarcoma and AIDS. Paul and Tim sought counseling from a gay men's counseling service. Although Tim discovered that his blood also carried HIV antibodies, he remained symptom-free.

Four months later, Paul was hospitalized with pneumocystis carinii pneumonia and continued to suffer frequent bouts of illness as his disease progressed. Tim spent much of his time caring for Paul when he was home from the hospital. Paul's family was also very supportive. In December Paul resigned his position at the law firm and committed himself to helping others understand AIDS and the people it affects. Working with a local AIDS counseling program, Paul spoke to a wide range of audiences, explaining how AIDS had affected him and his loved ones and outlining the types of services people with AIDS need. Since Paul's death in 1986, Tim has attempted to continue Paul's work of educating others about AIDS. To date, Tim remains free from any serious symptoms of his HIV infection. *Source:* Adapted from McGarrity (1988).

second 100,000 cases included 1702 children, of whom 87 percent were born to mothers with, or at risk for, HIV infection. Also, the proportion of AIDS cases related to blood transfusions declined in both adults (from 2.5 percent to 1.9 percent) and children (from 11 percent to 5.6 percent) from the first to the second 100,000 cases.

The death rate for women with AIDS quadrupled between 1985 and 1991. Indeed, by 1991, AIDS had become the leading killer of young African-American women in our major cities. It is projected to become the fifth leading cause of death among all American women of childbearing age by the mid-1990s (cancer is the number one killer of women of childbearing age, followed by accidental deaths, heart disease, homicide, and suicide). Worldwide, more than one-third of HIV-infected adults are women, and it is projected that the annual number of AIDS cases in women will begin to equal that of men by the year 2000. Because women who contracted HIV are the major source of infection for infants, this trend predicts disastrous consequences for thousands of children (World Health Organization, 1991; Centers for Disease Control, 1992, 1990).

AIDS strikes African-Americans and Hispanic-Americans disproportionately. Of the first 100,000 reported cases, 27 percent occurred among African-Americans and 15 percent among Hispanic-Americans; of the second 100,000 reported cases, these percentages increased to 31 and 17, respectively. About 80 percent of children with AIDS are African-American or Hispanic-American (Koop & Samuels, 1988; Schinke, Holden, & Moncher, 1989; Marin, 1989). The transmission of HIV among African-Americans and Hispanic-Americans tends to occur more by intravenous drug use and

A WORLD OF DIFFERENCES

AIDS and the African-American Community

AIDS has hit the African-American community hard, and health experts fear that its full impact has yet to be felt. As with so many other health problems, blacks suffer disproportionately from AIDS. While there are more AIDS cases among white gay or bisexual men than among any other single group, HIV spread rapidly among blacks during the late 1980s. Between 1987 and 1989, the number of new AIDS cases among blacks increased by 59 percent, while the number of new cases among white gay or bisexual men increased by only 38 percent. As a result, the African-American share of AIDS victims is growing.

Roughly 50 percent of all AIDS cases among African-Americans—52 percent in 1989 along—resulted directly or indirectly from intravenous drug use. High rates of intravenous drug use, lower educational levels, and reduced access to medical care all favor the continued transmission of the HIV infection among poor blacks. Education about AIDS—in clear, explicit terms—is the single most effective way to curb the spread of the deadly virus. Indeed, an impressive slowdown in AIDS transmission among gay and bisexual men resulted from just such educational strategies.

Recent surveys show that Americans in general are becoming more knowledgeable about HIV infection. In addition, the African-American community has been making a greater effort to respond to the AIDS challenge. For instance, the School of Medicine at Morehouse College in Atlanta manages a health program that includes AIDS education for minority communities in 15 eastern states. Community organizations, government agencies, private foundations, and individuals have tried similar efforts.

But some groups devastated by AIDS are difficult to reach through education alone. Intravenous drug users—who often live outside mainstream society—are a good example. Many researchers feel that checking the spread of AIDS among African-Americans requires an assault on the economic and social conditions that are creating drug abuse—namely, crime, unemployment, homelessness, and school truancy.

Sources: O'Hare et al. (1991); National Center for Health Statistics (1991).

---

heterosexual intercourse than by homosexual activity. As we noted in Chapter 17, a number of factors account for the higher rates of AIDS in these two groups: lack of knowledge concerning AIDS prevention, higher rates of other sexually transmitted diseases, and inadequate medical services. The box on "AIDS and the African-American Community" discusses the effectiveness of efforts to reduce the incidence of AIDS through education.

How widespread is the HIV infection among college students? To estimate the magnitude, Helene Gayle and colleagues (1990) investigated 19 university settings. At each campus blood specimens were tested for HIV antibodies. Of 16,863 specimens in the sample, 30 (0.2 percent) were positive for antibodies to HIV. Positive specimens were found at 9 of the 19 schools. All were from students over 18 years old; 19 (63 percent) were from students over 24. All but 2 of the 30 infected students were men. Thus the prevalence rate for men was 0.5 percent, while that for women was 0.02 percent. Prevalence increased with age—from 0.08 percent for students 18 to 24 years old to 1.0 percent for those 40 or older. The study concluded that the rate of HIV infection on university campuses is far lower than the rates in populations known to be at high risk. Clearly, though, there is a potential for the spread of HIV infection in this population, so preventive measures are essential.

Are other nations experiencing a problem with AIDS?

AIDS is widespread around the globe. It has been reported in more than 125 nations and in the vast majority of cases, transmission occurred through sexual intercourse (Hatcher et al., 1990). It is now estimated that between 5 million and 10 million people throughout the world are infected with HIV, and the figure is expected to mushroom during this decade. One source (Chin, 1991) predicts that 40 million people will be infected with the virus by the year 2000. At present two-thirds of the

The Acquired Immune Deficiency Syndrome (AIDS)

At the Kitovu Hospital, in Uganda, a mother who has AIDS waits with her baby and other family members outside the clinic where the ELISA test for the HIV virus is given.

world's estimated AIDS cases are in the central, eastern, and southern regions of Africa, where researchers believe HIV originated. As many as 5 million Africans may be HIV carriers. The number of women infected roughly equals the number of men, and because many of these infected women are in their prime childbearing years, HIV transmission from mother to child is an increasing problem. In 1990 about 500,000 babies carrying HIV virus were born in Africa (Chin, 1991; World Health Organization, 1991; Palka, 1991; Way & Stanecki, 1991; Edlin & Schanche, 1990).

In some African villages entire adult populations have been destroyed by the disease. Moreover, in many African countries AIDS is the leading cause of death among young adults. In Uganda the number of AIDS cases is doubling every six months. In Rwanda, about 20 percent of the AIDS victims are children. Nations outside of Africa that have been hit especially hard by the AIDS epidemic are Haiti, Bermuda, French Guiana, the Bahamas, and Guadeloupe (Way & Stanecki, 1991; Palca, 1991; Sabatier, 1988; Mann et al., 1988; Chin, 1987; Yarbrough, 1987).

AIDS AND THE LAW

As reported cases of AIDS continue to multiply, a number of complex legal issues have surfaced. While we can't possibly cover all of these matters here, the following discussion explores some of the major legal issues.

Mandatory Blood Testing

You will recall that an HIV antibody test called the ELISA test is used to detect the presence of antibodies produced by the body in response to the human immuno-deficiency virus. While the ELISA test can't isolate HIV, it can detect whether or not it has been present in the person's blood. The test does *not* predict the person will develop AIDS; all it does is reveal that the person has been previously exposed to

HIV. Although it can produce false results—that is, it can fail to detect such exposure—in general the ELISA test has proved valuable in screening blood donations to ensure a safe blood supply for transfusions.

Some people believe that the ELISA and similar tests should be used in a massive screening campaign to help protect the general public from HIV. However, the U.S. Department of Health and Human Services (1986) has stated that such compulsory blood testing is both impractical and unnecessary. One issue raised by mandatory testing is that of civil rights; that is, does the government have the right to impose such testing? Also, as we pointed out earlier, there are certain problems with the ELISA test. Many people who are actually positive test negatively because their exposure to HIV was too recent to be detected in their blood. Conversely, some people who test positively turn out to be negative on further testing. It is not hard to see how massive testing could produce a dangerous sense of security in the first group and a widespread sense of panic in the second. Then, too, a massive screening campaign would probably be unmanageable in a country this size, and the costs would be prohibitive even if such a campaign could be managed. Most experts think that a better alternative to compulsory blood testing is educating people to practice safer sex and making voluntary testing easily available to those who are in the high-risk categories.

Confidentiality of HIV Test Results

Most public health officials favor voluntary HIV antibody testing, with the assurance of absolute confidentiality of test results. The U.S. Department of Health and Human Services (1986) notes that because of the stigma associated with AIDS, many people afflicted with the disease or infected with HIV are reluctant to be identified. In states that require medical authorities to report the names of people infected with HIV to public health authorities so their sexual and intravenous drug contacts can be traced (which is the practice with other sexually transmitted diseases), those infected with HIV often go underground for information and health care. For this reason alone, it is important to protect the privacy of those infected with HIV and to maintain the strictest confidentiality concerning their health records.

There are other reasons to preserve the anonymity of test results. The use of test results to discriminate is already well-documented. Employers have fired staff because of a positive test result, and some insurance companies use the HIV antibody test as a basis for insurability. The military uses test results to screen new recruits. Obviously, then, knowledge of people's test results is a powerful and dangerous weapon (Levi, 1987).

Quarantine

Certain segments of the general public feel that people who test positive for HIV should be quarantined and kept in strict isolation. However, experts such as Jeffrey Levi (1987) disagree. Quarantine is an extreme measure reserved for emergency use with highly contagious diseases transmitted by air or through contaminated water or food. AIDS cannot be transmitted in these ways. Moreover, a quarantine would be impractical for several reasons. For example, who should be quarantined—only those with AIDS, or also the several million people whose blood contains antibodies? Where would we put all these millions? And how would we determine who is infected—by mandatory testing of certain groups, which is bound to raise legal questions of discrimination, or by mandatory testing of all Americans, which, as we have seen, would probably be unmanageable and would certainly be extremely costly.

Furthermore, brandishing quarantine powers before high-risk groups could have a negative effect on prevention efforts that are already showing progress. The threat of quarantine would lead most gay men, intravenous drug users, and prostitutes to avoid participating in important medical research, to evade epidemiological surveillance efforts, and possibly to decide to forgo desperately needed treatment. Most public health officials, recognizing that such punitive action would be counterproductive, advocate less invasive and restrictive alternatives such as sophisticated counseling and education programs.

Discrimination

Discrimination is a pervasive problem for people with AIDS and those considered at risk for getting the disease, according to Abby Rubenfeld (1987). One of the most serious forms of discrimination is in medical care and treatment. Many AIDS victims receive second-class medical care, and some can't find a medical professional to treat them at all. People with AIDS, as well as those perceived to be at risk for AIDS, are often discriminated against in housing. Uninsured people with AIDS or AIDS-related conditions face virtually insurmountable problems in obtaining medical, disability, or life insurance.

Employment discrimination is also prevalent. Many companies do not want to hire, or seek to fire, people with AIDS because they fear the huge insurance costs associated with the disease or because their employees object to working near someone with AIDS. People with AIDS do have some legal protection in this area, however. Several state human rights agencies, including those in California, Florida, and New York, have issued opinions that AIDS is covered by their state "disability" or "handicap" laws. To date, no state has determined that people with AIDS are *not* covered under these kinds of laws. Since nowadays most people with AIDS are not continually incapacitated, and since AIDS is not transmitted by casual contact, AIDS victims are often physically capable of working long after the disease has been diagnosed. Those denied employment because of AIDS can file a discrimination complaint under state and local laws. Moreover, since many state laws also prohibit discrimination based on "perceived handicap," people who are denied job opportunities because they are regarded as being at risk for AIDS or suspected of having the disease can also file a complaint (Rubenfeld, 1987).

To sum up, those who discriminate against AIDS sufferers or HIV-infected people may face penalties and civil damages under state and federal antidiscrimination statutes. There may be additional civil liabilities in jurisdictions that specifically prohibit discrimination on the basis of sexual preference. Finally, disclosure of confidential medical facts, such as a positive diagnosis of AIDS, may make employers vulnerable to legal action for invasion of privacy (Sloan, 1988).

Liability Issues

Liability concerning the transmission of HIV has raised some of the stormiest legal controversies. Under U.S. law people can be liable for damages if they are found to have committed a tort. A **tort** is harm or injury that one person inflicts on another. Most legal experts expect the AIDS epidemic to produce a wide assortment of tort litigation. For example, failure to fully disclose a medical condition that could affect the health and well-being of a sexual partner is grounds for tort action. Recipients of HIV-contaminated blood may also be able to sue under tort law. AIDS-related medical malpractice, including failure to diagnose the disease, misdiagnosis, and failure to inform patients of their diagnosis, is another possible ground for tort liability.

Because AIDS tort is a new area of law, many of the legal issues are still unresolved. It is often difficult to establish causation in suits alleging sexual transmission, and there is some uncertainty regarding which defenses are available. Moreover, there are procedural obstacles, such as the statute of limitations. Nonetheless, growing

tort Harm or injury that one person inflicts on another.

recognition of tort liability for HIV transmission and for AIDS-related medical malpractice has made it possible for some people to obtain compensation and has given others the incentive to alter their behavior to protect themselves against lawsuits (Herman, 1987; Sloan, 1988; Davis, 1988).

By 1990, 22 states had passed laws making it illegal to engage in conduct that could transmit HIV. Still, most cases in the state courts are brought under general criminal laws rather than specific AIDS-related legislation. While the number of AIDS-related prosecutions nationwide is not known, the military seems to have the most success with such cases. It is easier to prosecute under military law because of the more controlled environment and because the defense department and each service branch have regulations governing sexual conduct by service people who know they are infected with HIV.

Caring for People Infected with HIV

Finally we come to the thicket of difficult issues surrounding care for the HIV-infected population. Hospitals and public health facilities in most communities are unprepared to deal with the increased numbers of AIDS patients as the disease spreads from the original risk groups to a wider population. Their funding is often inadequate, as is patients' insurance. One source (Carroll and Miller, 1991) estimates the annual cost of medical care for HIV-infected and AIDS patients at between $5 billion and $13 billion. Political battles involving issues of individual rights often become entwined with public health measures.

Perhaps the most critical issue in this area, though, is the climate of fear surrounding AIDS. Health-care providers often express concerns about their inability to deal with their feelings toward AIDS patients and their difficulty in giving these patients compassionate, nonjudgmental care (see the box on "Providing Support for a Friend Who Has AIDS" for thoughts on helping AIDS patients); their fear of exhausting available resources to deal with the AIDS epidemic; and, most important, their risk of contracting AIDS. Indeed, some health-care providers have refused to treat AIDS patients (Kersey-Cantril & McCarthy, 1987).

For medical personnel working with AIDS patients, special precautions must be taken to avoid contracting HIV. The Centers for Disease Control (1985) has outlined the following procedures to minimize the risk of HIV transmission:

- Consider sharp items (needles, scalpel blades, other sharp instruments) as being potentially infective and handle them with extreme care to prevent accidental injury.
- Place all disposable sharp items in puncture-resistant containers.
- Do not recap, purposefully bend, or otherwise manipulate needles by hand.

The mask and gloves worn by this hospital employee as he cleans Stephen Jenteel's room would be needed only if the employee were handling blood or body fluids or if he were infected himself. Fear of HIV infection is so intense among some health workers, however, that they prefer to protect themselves at all times.

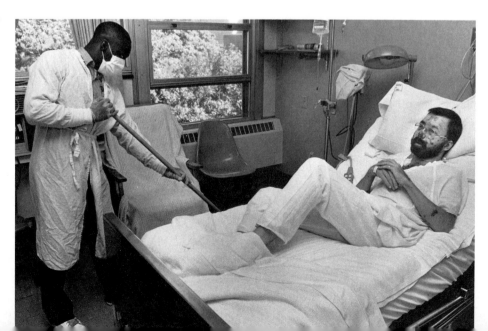

*I*t is not uncommon for people who develop AIDS to feel isolated, unloved, and unwanted. According to Sandra and Christopher Smith (1990), many of us feel uneasy about continuing a relationship with someone who has AIDS. Remember that HIV infection cannot be transmitted by casual contact. In addition, the discovery that one has AIDS is a critical time in one's life, a time when loving and supportive friends are sorely needed. Isolation simply adds another stressor to a person living with HIV infection/AIDS, and stressors damage the immune system even in healthy people.

The Smiths offer the following suggestions for helping a friend or family member who has AIDS:

■ Make it a point to be available. Try not to avoid your friend, but offer the support you've always given. Don't be afraid to touch, hug, or hold hands. This warm and loving behavior will let your friend know nonverbally that you still care and that you aren't disgusted by the disease. One may be disgusted by the disease, but not disgusted with the person with the infection.

■ Give your friend the opportunity to express his emotions. Sympathy is not useful, and sometimes blocks communication. Sharing emotions, on the other hand, allows for the expression of honest feelings and sensitivities.

■ Encourage your friend to make his own decisions. Relinquishing decision making to others lessens one's sense of control and leaves one feeling powerless and insignificant. Do, however, offer to help take care of anything your friend cannot do alone.

■ Offer to accompany your friend to see the doctor.

■ Encourage your friend to take care of her health. Suggest building up the immune system by eating nutritionally balanced meals. Help her explore alternative treatments such as stress reduction or vitamin and mineral supplements. Help your friend comply with the treatment she is now receiving. If medications have been prescribed, support this medical regimen and encourage her to continue to seek medical guidance.

■ Encourage your friend to avoid alcohol and other drugs, which damage the body and the immune system. Join him in exploring other ways to feel good, such as group therapy, counseling, and nonalcoholic social activities.

■ Remember to take care of your own personal health and well-being. Also recognize how you are feeling and find ways of meeting your own needs—to cry, to grieve, to express anger that your friend may be dying.

MAKING USE OF WHAT WE KNOW

Providing Support to a Friend Who Has AIDS

One of the devastating effects of AIDS-related illness is the unsightly physical change it can bring. Having a volunteer help her make her thinning hair look presentable can be a real comfort to an AIDS patient.

■ To minimize the need for emergency mouth-to-mouth resuscitation, keep mouth pieces, resuscitation bags, or other ventilation devices strategically located and available for use in areas where the need for resuscitation is predictable.

■ Use latex gloves when handling items soiled with blood or equipment contaminated with blood or other body fluids.

■ Use gown, mask, and eye covering when performing procedures (e.g., dental, endoscopic, or postmortem examinations) that involve more extensive contact with blood or potentially infective body fluids.

■ Workers with skin lesions should avoid direct patient care and handling of equipment.

■ Dentists and technicians should consider blood, saliva, and gingival fluids of all patients potentially infective and use all of the above precautions to prevent contact with such fluids.

■ Wash hands thoroughly and immediately if they accidentally become contaminated with blood.

Health-care workers justifiably fear getting AIDS from patients, but should patients worry about getting AIDS from health-care providers? This was not a widespread concern until 1991, when transmission of HIV to five patients was traced to Dr. David

Acer, a dentist who died of AIDS in 1990. One of his patients, Kimberly Bergalis, died of AIDS in 1991. This case prompted the Centers for Disease Control to urge all health-care workers infected with HIV to stop performing invasive procedures and to inform their patients of their infection so patients could be tested if they wished. The CDC also stressed the need to use gloves while performing invasive procedures and the importance of careful sterilization of all equipment and instruments. Additionally, the CDC decided to encourage research to identify modifications in medical, surgical, and dental procedures that could reduce the risk of injuries to health-care workers. As we go to press, health-care workers are not required to be tested for HIV.

SEXUALITY IN THE NEWS

AIDS Incidence and Treatment

AIDS and Minorities

*T*he fact that minorities are disproportionately affected by AIDS is pointed out in this video segment from ABC's "Health Show" aired August 20, 1989. While minorities make up only 15 percent of the total U.S. population, 33 percent of all AIDS cases are among minority groups—primarily African-Americans and Hispanic-Americans. Dr. Louis Sullivan, secretary of health and human services, emphasizes that we "must make concerted efforts to reach these communities." According to George Strait, ABC news reporter, AIDS in minority communities is directly related to IV drug use.

AIDS and AZT

In a segment from ABC's "Nightline" aired August 17, 1989, Ted Koppel examines the risk factors for AIDS among different U.S. socioeconomic groups and explores the use of AZT.

DISCUSSION QUESTIONS

1. George Strait suggests that the general public may lose interest in AIDS if it is perceived as a minority disease, affecting only "them," not "us." Do you think this might happen or has happened? Support your view.
2. What are the barriers to the use of AZT or other anti-AIDS medications among African-Americans and Hispanic-Americans? How can some of these barriers be broken down?
3. Earvin "Magic" Johnson received considerable media coverage when he announced that he was HIV positive. Do you think Johnson's announcement has had any effect on attitudes toward AIDS prevention among the general population? Among minorities? How might his disclosure heighten the public's knowledge of AIDS and HIV transmission? Explain your answer.

LOOKING BACK

■ The acquired immune deficiency syndrome (AIDS) is characterized by a breakdown of the body's immune system and consequent vulnerability to infections that healthy people's bodies ordinarily are able to combat. AIDS is caused by a virus named the human immunodeficiency virus (HIV). HIV has been found in blood, semen, vaginal secretions, breast milk, saliva, tears, spinal fluid, amniotic fluid, and urine. Of these, blood, semen, vaginal secretions, and, possibly, breast milk are most likely to transmit HIV from one person to another. People with AIDS are susceptible to a va-

riety of infectious illnesses, often labeled *opportunistic diseases* because they take advantage of the body's crippled immune system. AIDS patients may contract one or both of two rare diseases—Kaposi's sarcoma, a type of cancer; and pneumocystis carinii pneumonia, a parasitic infection of the lungs—as well as other opportunistic infections.

■ AIDS cannot be diagnosed simply on the basis of a test. Rather, the diagnosis of AIDS is based on finding evidence of a weakened immune system. What can be tested is the presence of antibodies produced by the body in response to HIV. This is done with a HIV antibody test known as the ELISA (enzyme-linked immunosorbent assay) test. While the ELISA test can't isolate HIV, it can detect whether or not the virus has been present.

■ There is no cure for AIDS, nor is there a vaccine to prevent it. However, a number of experimental drugs have shown some success in slowing the progression of the disease.

■ Children with AIDS pose many challenges, both medical and social. It is difficult to find foster homes for those who have been deserted or orphaned, and institutional care is often inadequate for their emo-tional and intellectual development. The decision to admit a child with AIDS to a regular public school is often contested. Both the child with AIDS and the non-infected child may experience emotional trauma if this decision is not carefully prepared for.

■ With the rise in the number of AIDS cases over the last decade, society has been forced to confront a number of legal issues: mandatory blood testing, con-fidentiality of HIV test results, quarantine, discrimi-nation, liability, and caring for those infected with HIV. AIDS education programs focus especially on high-risk sexual behaviors. Although Americans today are quite knowledgeable about AIDS, many seem to be unwill-ing to change their high-risk sexual behaviors.

THINKING THINGS OVER

1. Prepare an argument to support either of two positions: "All health-care workers should be tested for the human immunodeficiency virus," or "Health-care workers have the right to insist that all patients be tested for the human im-munodeficiency virus." Discuss your argument informally with other members of your class or, if your instructor wishes, in class.

2. There have been publicized cases of children being excluded from public schools because they have AIDS. What would you do if you discovered your child was in a classroom with a child infected with AIDS?

3. Research the laws with respect to AIDS in your state and in your hometown. Find out what special services and facilities, if any, are available to persons living with AIDS in your hometown. If possible, visit a few such facilities to see what they are like.

4. In the United States AIDS was first viewed as an exclu-sively gay disease. It has since spread to the heterosexual population, however, and in other cultures AIDS is actually more prevalent among heterosexuals than among homo-sexuals. Do you think the same stigma attached to gay AIDS victims will be attached to heterosexual people with AIDS? Why or why not?

DISCOVER FOR YOURSELF

Fogel, C., & Lauver, D. (1991). *Sexual health promotion*. Philadelphia: W. B. Saunders. See Chapter 23 for a good discussion of HIV transmission and AIDS.

Macklin, E. (ed.) (1989). *AIDS and families*. New York: Ha-worth Press. Among the many topics covered are strat-egies for AIDS education and prevention, and the issues confronted by therapists who work with the families of AIDS victims.

Mills, J. & Masur, H. (1990). AIDS-related infections. *Scien-tific American, 263*, 50–57. An excellent account of the available therapies for the opportunistic infections of AIDS.

Norwood, C. (1987). *Advice for life: A woman's guide to AIDS risks and prevention*. New York: Pantheon. The strength of this paperback is its emphasis on personal prevention and continuing education on the topic of AIDS.

Reiss, I. L. (1990). *An end to shame: Shaping our next sexual revolution*. New York: Prometheus Books. A noted so-ciologist offers his thoughts on AIDS and a variety of other issues.

Stine, G. J. (1993). *Acquired immune deficiency syndrome: Biological, medical, social, and legal issues*. Englewood Cliffs, NJ: Prentice Hall. A scholarly account of HIV in-fection and AIDS. Particularly well done are the chapters on prevention and therapeutic intervention.

19

Exploitive and Atypical Sexual Behaviors

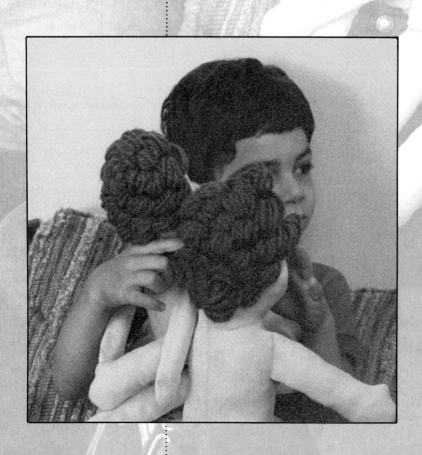

*The fears we know
are of not knowing*

—W. H. Auden

In this chapter you'll discover:

☐ *What distinguishes typical sexual behavior from atypical sexual interests and activities.*

☐ *How incest and child sexual abuse are both different and similar, how each affects the child, and what interventions are available to help victims.*

☐ *The characteristics and dynamics of such atypical behaviors as exhibitionism, fetishism, and transvestism.*

☐ *What distinguishes sexual masochism and sexual sadism from each other and how both can be combined in the same person.*

☐ *What sexual addiction is and how it can be treated.*

Deciding how to present the material in this and the following chapter, on rape, was difficult. All of the behaviors discussed in these two chapters are to some degree atypical, and almost all involve coercion and exploitation. It was largely because of the increasing mass of material on rape—the incidence of which has been rising in recent years—that we chose to give it a chapter of its own.

In this chapter we start out by examining incest and child sexual abuse, which are as exploitive—though not usually as violent—as rape. As we will see, pure sexual pleasure is rarely the motivating force behind these manifestations of *pedophilia*, a term that means (ironically) "love of children." Rather, those who molest children sexually, whether they are related to the child, as in incest, or unrelated, as in child sexual abuse, are motivated by deep-seated insecurities and often by pent-up anger and resentment over their own childhood abuse by family members or other adults.

Similar kinds of emotions and insecurities underlie the so-called *paraphilias* that we discuss next. Many of these behaviors exploit the people at whom they are directed. For example, the exhibitionist often elicits shock and emotional distress from the person to whom he exposes himself. The voyeur, when discovered, may cause the person he has been covertly watching fear and anxiety that he will continue his activity or become more aggressive.

Transvestism, certainly an atypical behavior, is probably the least exploitive of all the behaviors we discuss in this chapter. However, even this behavior can have unhappy repercussions for others; for example, the husband who must dress in women's clothing in order to be sexually aroused can cause his wife considerable emotional distress.

The last category of behaviors we discuss here, sexual addiction, is probably more detrimental to the addicted person than to anyone else. However, as you know from having read Chapters 17 and 18, promiscuous and indiscriminate sexual behavior can cause serious disease and even kill.

SOME BACKGROUND AND DEFINITIONS

All societies in history have attempted to establish a range of sexual behaviors considered acceptable or permissible. You'll recall St. Augustine's dictum that sex should be engaged in only for the purpose of procreation. The Bible (Deuteronomy 22:5) forbids men to wear that which belongs to women and women that which belongs to men. During the Victorian era sexual activities other than intercourse, such as cunnilingus and fellatio, were viewed as deviant and sinful. Early Spanish missionaries condemned polygamy among North American Indian tribes (Bullough, 1988).

Efforts to classify atypical sexual behaviors have also been going on for some time. The German neurologist Richard Freiherr von Krafft-Ebing (see Chapter 2) made one of the first attempts to systematically categorize sexual deviance in his textbook *Psychopathia Sexualis* (1922). He was the first to coin such terms as *sadism* (the enjoyment of inflicting pain on a sexual partner), and *masochism* (the enjoyment of receiving pain). At the turn of the century Magnus Hirschfeld offered diagnostic evaluations of such behaviors as transvestism. Others followed these pioneers, slowly shaping our understanding of the sexually unusual.

Today it is recognized that different societies approve and disapprove of different sexual behaviors. For example, there is considerable disagreement around the globe concerning the practice and legality of prostitution. Furthermore, a behavior once deemed atypical in a society may over the course of time come to be seen as a variation of normal sexuality in that same society. As illustrations, masturbation and homosexuality are no longer considered perverse or abnormal. Recall from earlier chapters that masturbation was once thought to lead to blindness, impotence, and insanity (among other consequences), while homosexuality was classified as a psychiatric disorder until 1973. The latter point shows how official attitudes toward sexual behavior that deviates from the norm can undergo change. Indeed, every time the American Psychiatric Association's guide to the diagnosis of mental disorders, abbreviated as DSM, for *Diagnostic and Statistical Manual of Mental Disorders*, is revised (1968, 1973, 1980, 1987), the classification of sexual disorders is modified.

It is therefore difficult to define what is normal and what is abnormal in sexual behavior. In a broad sense, atypical sexual behavior is that which differs from the sexual behaviors engaged in by most people in a given society. Many atypical sexual behaviors are known as paraphilias. The term **paraphilia** is derived from the Greek word *para*, meaning "beyond the usual," and *philia*, meaning "love." A person who has a paraphilia becomes sexually aroused by objects or situations that do not normally lead to arousal in other people. Important criteria for diagnosing paraphilias include a six-month duration of the disorder, during which time the person has acted on these urges, and being markedly distressed by the paraphilia. To varying degrees, a paraphilia interferes with the capacity for reciprocal, affectionate sexual activity.

The causes of atypical sexual behaviors remain obscure. We do know, however, that they are rare among women. We also know that it is not uncommon for people with paraphilias to have three or four different types (see, for example, Abel, Becker, & Skinner, 1983). Moreover, many of those who exhibit atypical sexuality have other disorders, such as substance abuse or personality disorders. It is important to differentiate between people who occasionally act on an unusual urge and those who repeatedly do so. As we'll see, the person who departs from usual sexual behavior once in a while is quite different from the person who regularly expresses atypical sexual behavior. Finally, unusual behaviors can be distinguished by the harm they inflict on the actor or others. Some unusual behaviors, such as fetishes (the use of an inanimate object for sexual excitement), seldom have a direct negative effect on others, while others, such as incest and sexual abuse of children, inflict immense harm on other people.

THE SEXUAL EXPLOITATION OF CHILDREN

The sexual assault of a child may occur within the family or outside of it. **Incest** means sexual contact between close blood relatives, while **child sexual abuse** means sexual contact between an adult and a child who are in no way related. Both usually refer to interactions between a child and adult in which the youngster is used for the sexual stimulation of that adult or another person. Let's look more closely at both incest and child sexual abuse.

Incest

Virtually every society prohibits sexual relationships between close blood relatives. In fact, the *incest taboo* has been called the *universal taboo* by anthropologists. Incest is a crime in the United States, and although state laws vary regarding the sexual relationships forbidden (see Gordon & O'Keefe, 1984), close blood relatives are always defined to include father, mother, grandfather, grandmother, brother, sister, aunt, uncle, niece, and nephew. Many states also include first cousins. Others expand the definition to take in stepparent-stepchildren, stepsibling, and in-law relationships, although these people are not related by blood (Vander Mey & Nef, 1986).

It is very hard to gauge the prevalence of incest because most victims keep secret. However, it is estimated that as many as 20 million Americans may be victims of incest—almost 10 percent of the population. The first full-scale sexual assault generally occurs when a child is about 11, but it is estimated that most offenders initiate some sort of sexual activity when the child is between 5 and 8. Despite popular

Exploitive and Atypical Sexual Behaviors

belief that incest is mainly a problem among the poor, incestuous families are found in every socioeconomic and educational group (Weinstein & Rosen, 1988b).

Ruth and Henry Kempe (1984) have given us much insight into incestuous child abuse. Their research reveals that father-daughter and stepfather-stepdaughter incest make up approximately three-quarters of reported cases. Girls involved with fathers or stepfathers during preadolescence or very early adolescence are often the oldest daughters in their family. Mother-son, mother-daughter, and brother-sister incest constitute most of the remaining one-quarter of reports. Although sibling incest is rarely reported, it is probably far more common than we know, especially between brothers and sisters before or at puberty. When one sibling is near adulthood and the other a child, the pattern of exploitation resembles parent-child incest. The most prevalent type of sibling incest reported is the abuse of younger sisters and brothers by an older male sibling (Pittman, 1987).

Many cases of incest are never reported to legal authorities, especially in families from upper socioeconomic brackets. These families often seek help through other means, such as private psychiatry, so they are usually not included in the statistical sources. This is particularly true when the incest victim does not seek help until much later, which often happens when the relationship is a more unusual one such as between mother-in-law and son-in-law or father-in-law and daughter-in-law. Reports of father-daughter incest are the most common, because the daughter precipitates a crisis when the situation becomes intolerable to her. In the case of sibling incest, the maturing of the siblings may spontaneously change both partners and, therefore, the nature of their relationship (Kempe & Kempe, 1984).

Many researchers have explored the dynamics of incest (see, for example, Horton et al., 1990; Conte, 1990; Ballard et al., 1990; Gilgun & Connor, 1990; Christiansen & Blake, 1990; Alexander, 1985). One source (Stark, 1984) points out that when the incestuous activity begins, the victims often believe that their silence is necessary to hold the family together, fearing the offending parents will go to jail if the incest is discovered. Some children acquiesce in the relationship because they are desperate for any type of affection. And in many situations the child believes that there is no one to help her. Offenders often convince themselves that there is nothing wrong with what they are doing, but most use either subtle coercion or direct threats to keep their child victims silent.

Unfortunately, in an incestuous relationship the adults with whom the child is most likely to talk are often acquiescent about the exploitation. For example, many father-daughter incestuous relationships exist with the mother's knowledge. It is not uncommon for the mother to remain passive—sometimes because she was a victim of incest herself, sometimes because she is so frightened of her husband or insecure that she is immobilized. Other mothers are absent from the home for extended lengths of time or afflicted with a chronic illness. Finding an available and safe person with whom to communicate is a problem. The child's dilemma is that to expose the secret is to risk being rejected by the family, not being believed, or both (Beck, Rawlins, & Williams, 1984; Lutz & Medway, 1984; Weinstein & Rosen, 1988b).

While "keeping the secret" may cause anxiety in both incest partners, it may also be the source of a strong emotional tie. A combination of secrecy, affection, and sexual pleasure can produce a very powerful bond. If the incest is never discovered, the parties may eventually sort out their conflicting feelings of attraction and avoidance, gain perspective, forgive themselves and, sometimes, the incest partner and the other silent family members who may have known but refused to intervene (Horton et al., 1990; Weinstein & Rosen, 1988b; Russell, 1986; Stark, 1984; Taylor, 1984).

Most incest victims reach adulthood with their abuse a secret. Sometimes they completely repress it or suffer only occasionally from flashbacks. Like other disturbing life events, incest often creates psychological disharmony and turbulence. Judith Becker (1989) writes that it is not uncommon for survivors of incest to experience a wide range of adjustment problems as adults. Incest, like rape, produces both long- and short-term responses, including fear and anxiety, depression, impaired social functioning, sleep disturbances, physiological illnesses, and sexual dysfunctions. And like rape survivors, the adult survivors of incest may experience these problems many years after the event. A little bit later in the chapter we'll look at therapeutic interventions for victims of incest and child sexual abuse.

Child Sexual Abuse

Like incest, the sexual abuse of a young child by an adult is a punishable crime in the United States, and its incidence is not much easier to assess than the incidence of incest. Most researchers (i.e., Faller, 1990; Gomes-Schwartz, Horowitz, & Cardarelli, 1990; Green, 1986; Peters, Wyatt, & Finkelhor, 1986; Browne & Finkelhor, 1986) agree that the problem is occurring at a significant rate, and that reported cases barely scratch the surface. Moreover, Gail Wyatt and Gloria Powell (1988) point out that many reports of child sex abuse are never even passed on to protective agencies, so these children's abuse is not counted in the statistics. Then, too, many sexual abuse cases that are investigated are judged to be too lacking in legal evidence to prosecute. Finally, of course, there are unknown numbers of youngsters who remain silent. The notion that child sexual abuse is not that common, along with other mistaken ideas about this very destructive behavior, is treated in the "Myths and Misconceptions" box.

How common is child sexual abuse?

Some researchers have attempted to estimate the percentage of children victimized by sexual abuse. As far as female victimization is concerned, Diana Russell (1983) found that 38 percent of the women she interviewed reported at least one instance of child sexual abuse. Judith Herman's (1981) detailed analysis of five separate surveys revealed that one-fifth to one-third of all the women queried said they had had some sort of childhood sexual encounter with a male adult. Other reports (most notably Briere & Runtz, 1985; Finkelhor, 1984; Sedney & Brooks, 1984; Bagley, 1985) have estimated that 15 to 20 percent of the women studied experienced some type of sexual abuse during childhood.

Researchers find that boys are abused less frequently than girls. For example, a national survey in Canada (Badgley, 1984) showed that about 6 percent of the men queried had been molested before they reached 15, and almost 10 percent before they were 18. In another investigation (Sorrenti-Little, Bagley, & Robertson, 1984) approximately 10 percent of male respondents experienced some type of childhood sexual abuse. Other studies (e.g., Finkelhor, 1984; Fritz, Stoll, & Wagner, 1981) have placed the figure closer to 5 percent. Note, however, that many researchers (e.g., Condy et al., 1987; Risen & Koss, 1987; Wood & Dean, 1984; Nielsen, 1983) believe sexual abuse of boys is reported or disclosed much less frequently than abuse of girls. Moreover, many experts are convinced it is more prevalent today than assumed (Faller, 1990; Maletzky, 1990; Finkelhor, 1990; Bolton, Morris, & MacEachron, 1990).

The perpetrator of child sexual abuse is referred to as a *pedophile*. Pedophiles have recurrent, intense urges and fantasies involving sexual activity with a child. They are predominantly male, and while they may be either homosexual or heterosexual, most are heterosexual. Many pedophiles are in their late teens or early 20s, but a significant number are in their 30s (see, for example, Salter, 1988; Kempe & Kempe, 1984; Russell, 1986). Pedophiles are usually emotionally dependent men with feelings of inferiority. They tend to come from unstable homes, to harbor poor self-concepts, and to have low levels of self-worth and dignity (Faller, 1990; Salter, 1988; Alexander, 1985; Giarretto, 1982; Lutz & Medway, 1984; Taylor, 1984; Sgroi, 1982; James & Nasjleti, 1983).

One study (Awad & Saunders, 1989) revealed that most pedophiles were socially isolated and maladjusted before they committed their first sexual offense. Generally, their lives have been, and often continue to be, dominated by a significant woman.

Contrary to popular thought, child sexual abusers are more often heterosexual than homosexual. A gay rights demonstration made use of this fact.

The sexual assault of children is a relatively rare phenomenon. Child sexual abuse is three times as common as child battery. An infant girl born in the United States today has a one in four chance of becoming a victim of sexual abuse by the time she reaches age 18. It is estimated that between 50 and 80 percent of sexual assaults on children go unreported.

Child sexual assault is an isolated incident that happens out of the blue and is usually an extreme form of abuse. On the contrary, this kind of abuse develops gradually over a period of time and is generally repeated unless it is stopped. While the forms of abuse may become more serious as time goes on, the overwhelming majority are not of the torture/murder variety sensationalized in the media.

Assailants are strangers. Between 75 and 85 percent of assailants are known to the family.

Children make up stories to get back at someone or to gain attention. Children rarely lie about sexual assault. Younger children do not understand it well enough to lie, and older children are often too embarrassed or frightened to disclose actual assaults, let alone make up false ones.

It will only traumatize children to frankly discuss the possibility of assault with them. Vague warnings like "don't take candy from strangers" can confuse and frighten children. If assault is presented as a safety issue, it is no more frightening than discussing fire or playground safety. Children's fantasies are often worse than the reality; concrete information sensitively presented can empower them and help rid them of fantastic fears.

Children are powerless to protect themselves. Children can be taught to use their own resources to protect themselves: to kick, yell, run, get help, and so forth. What they must know is that there is someone to whom they can turn for immediate and unquestioning help. (Los Angeles Commission on Assaults Against Women, 1983)

Like other abuse offenders, these men often drink heavily. Finally, there is a strong positive correlation between pedophilia and a childhood history of assault inflicted by parents or parent surrogates (Sarason & Sarason, 1989; Ney, 1988; Ginsburg et al., 1989; Hart et al., 1989; Beck, Rawlins, & Williams, 1984).

The pedophile often attempts to fulfill his psychological needs for recognition, acceptance, and mastery by becoming sexually involved with a child. It is not *sexual gratification* that the offender seeks in his sexual contacts with children, but rather evidence of the child's *acceptance* of and *caring* for him. Also, he feels more in control having a sexual relationship with a child because there is less risk of an emotionally devastating rejection than there is with an adult. His sense of competency is not threatened by a child, who is more accepting and less demanding than an adult would be (Groth, Hobson, & Gary, 1982).

As we said, pedophilia in women is rarely reported (Russell, 1986; Finkelhor, 1984). There are several possible reasons for this. To begin with, since women tend to be thought of as nurturant and nonviolent, law enforcement officials may fail to ask victims the right questions—using words like "man" and "he" automatically when trying to elicit from the child the identity of the abuser. Victims, too, may find it difficult to acknowledge or express what a woman has done to them. Female offenders themselves may be more reluctant than men to admit to child abuse, since it is seen in our society as particularly abhorrent and shocking in a woman. Furthermore, child sexual abuse by women tends to be easier to hide than that by men, since children are more frequently left in women's care (Family Sexual Abuse Project, 1987). And finally, it may well be that far fewer women than men commit sexual abuses against children.

Effects of Incest and Child Sexual Abuse

What are some of the effects of incest and child sexual abuse?

In recent years a rich vein of research has focused on the impact of incest and child sexual abuse (e.g., Faller, 1990; Bolton, Morris, & MacEachron, 1990; Gomes-Schwartz, Horowitz, & Cardarelli, 1990; Gelles & Cornell, 1990; Mandell & Damon, 1989; Ginsburg et al., 1989; Paluszny et al., 1989; Ney, 1988). One of the most comprehensive investigations was undertaken by David Finkelhor (1988). Working at the University of New Hampshire's Family Violence Research Program, Finkelhor developed a *model of child sexual abuse* that suggests that sexual victimization in childhood creates four *traumagenic dynamics* that alter the person's cognitive or emotional orientation to the world: traumatic sexualization, betrayal, stigmatization, and powerlessness.

TRAUMATIC SEXUALIZATION. Traumatic sexualization is the shaping of a child's sexuality in developmentally inappropriate and interpersonally dysfunctional ways. Finkelhor believes that several processes converge to create traumatic sexualization:

- Most offenders reward abused children for sexual behavior that is inappropriate for their age and level of development.
- Because of these rewards, sexual abuse victims learn to use both inappropriate and appropriate sexual behavior as a strategy for manipulating others to get their needs met.
- A child's sexuality can become traumatized when sexual activity becomes associated in the youngster's mind with negative memories.
- Children acquire confusing and inaccurate information about sexual behavior and sexual morality because of things that offenders tell them or ways that offenders behave.

Traumatic sexualization in childhood may show itself in victims' later behavior in many ways, including sexual preoccupations, compulsive masturbation and sex play, and sexual knowledge and behaviors that are inappropriate for youngsters their age (August & Forman, 1989; Corwin, 1985; Friedrich, Urquiza, & Beilke, 1986; Tufts New England Medical Center, 1984). Boys, especially, may become sexually aggressive themselves and begin to victimize peers or younger children. Other children become sexually promiscuous. Among the adult symptoms related to traumatic sexualization are an aversion to sex, flashbacks to the childhood trauma during sex, and arousal and orgasm difficulties (Briere, 1984; Langmade, 1983).

BETRAYAL. When children discover that someone on whom they are vitally dependent is causing them, or wishes to cause them harm, they feel betrayed. Sometimes the betrayal is experienced at the time of the initial abuse, as children discover that a person they trusted is treating them with disregard for their well-being. In other instances youngsters experience the betrayal belatedly when they realize they were tricked into doing something bad by the offender's lies or misrepresentations (Peters, 1988; Briere, 1984; Baird, 1982; Cohen, 1983; Steele & Alexander, 1981; Herman, 1981).

Feelings of betrayal extend beyond the offender to other family members. Many sexually abused children experience their greatest sense of betrayal when they discover that their mothers (or other important figures) are unable (or unwilling) to believe and protect them. If a mother fails to protect a child in this sphere—especially if her behavior in all other areas of life has led the child to expect her protection—the effect can be devastating. Most young children believe that their mothers are omnipotent and capable of warding off all harm (Peters, 1988; McCarty, 1986; Briere & Runtz, 1985; Dechesnay, 1983; Collins, 1982; Adams-Tucker, 1981; Herman, 1981).

Betrayal often leads to depression, the result of disenchantment, disillusion, and loss of trust (Peters, 1988; Parker & Parker, 1986; Pelletier & Handy, 1986; Briere & Runtz, 1985; Khan, 1983; Adams-Tucker, 1981). Another symptom may be extreme dependency and clinging behaviors, especially among very young victims. Later in life this same need may manifest itself as a desperate search for a redeeming relationship or as a refusal to believe in the trustworthiness of other people (Summit & Kryso, 1981; Steele & Alexander, 1981).

Some child abuse victims show an opposite cluster of symptoms. In them the sense of betrayal leads to anger, hostility, and an intense distrust of men or intimate relationships in general. As adults, these people generally have a history of failed relationships or marriages. Finkelhor (1988) believes that anger, hostility, and distrust of intimacy are primitive defenses victims use to protect themselves from future betrayals. Antisocial behavior may be a form of retaliation for betrayal (Briere, 1984; Herman, 1981).

The long-term effects of betrayal, as well as of other forms of psychological and social dysfunction originating in incest and child sexual abuse, are well documented in the literature (Hart et al., 1989; Salter, 1988; Peters, 1988; Donaldson, 1983; Silbert, 1984; Finkelhor, 1984; Browne & Finkelhor, 1986; Briere et al., 1988; Fromuth, 1986). For example, John Briere and Marsha Runtz (1988) reported that 44 percent of a random sample of female walk-in clients of a Canadian community health crisis center reported that they were victims of child sexual abuse. As a group, these women had substantially greater psychological symptomatology, were more apt to be using psychoactive medication, and more frequently reported histories of suicide attempts, substance addiction, and battery as adults than did nonabused clients.

STIGMATIZATION. Stigmatization refers to the negative messages of personal worthlessness, shamefulness, and guilt the child receives about the abuse experience. These messages can be communicated in a variety of ways. For example, abusers do it directly when they blame and denigrate the victim, or indirectly when they pressure the child to keep "their" secret. Most of the stigmatization, however, originates in the attitudes or moral judgments victims hear expressed by those around them and the larger society. Thus victims discover that sexual abuse is regarded as deviant and that it's a crime (Weinstein & Rosen, 1988a; Bagley & Ramsay, 1986; Vander Mey & Neff, 1986; Henderson, 1983; Steele & Alexander, 1981; DeYoung, 1982).

Child sexual abuse victims who feel stigmatized often become isolated and resort to self-destructive behavior. Some gravitate to stigmatized societal groups, such as drug abusers, criminals, or prostitutes. Others become depressed, sometimes to the point of attempted suicide. Victims of sexual abuse often harbor low self-esteem and believe that no one else has had similar experiences. Many fear rejection from "normal" people if their "secret" is discovered (Peters, 1988; Kendall-Tackett, 1988; Russell, 1986; Conte & Berliner, 1987; Browne & Finkelhor, 1986; Brett & Ostroff, 1985; Bagley & Ramsay, 1986).

Stigmatization, negative self-perceptions, and other emotional reactions to sexual abuse in childhood have been the subjects of many research studies. One study (Anderson, Bach, & Griffith, 1981) of 155 adolescent girls who were the victims of incest or of sexual abuse outside the family found that 67 percent of the incest victims and 49 percent of the sexually abused subjects experienced some type of negative internalized effects. Feeling stigmatized, fearful, depressed, guilty, shameful, and worthless was common, as were sleep and eating disturbances. Externalized effects, including running away from home and school problems, were noted in 66 percent of the incest victims and 21 percent of the abused subjects.

Researchers at the Tufts New England Medical Center (1984) gathered extensive data on victims of child sexual abuse who ranged from infants to 18-year-olds. The subjects were divided into preschool (4–6), latency (7–13), and adolescence (14–18) age groups. Data were gathered in four areas: overt behavior, physiological reactions, internalized emotional states, and self-esteem. Among the preschool children, 17 percent met the criteria for "clinically significant pathology," exhibiting more overall disturbance than a normal population but less than other youngsters their age who were in psychiatric care. The highest incidence of psychopathology was discovered in the adolescents: about 40 percent scored in the seriously disturbed range. The Tufts study also discovered that stigmatization, depression, shame, fear, anger, and hostility were common emotional reactions in the aftermath of sexual victimization. For example, 13 percent of the preschoolers, 45 percent of the latency age group, and 36 percent of the adolescents were withdrawn and suffered from severe fears of being harmed. About 25 percent of the preschoolers, 45 percent of the latency age group, and 23 percent of the adolescents scored high on tests measuring anger and aggression.

POWERLESSNESS. According to Finkelhor (1988), when a child's will and wishes are repeatedly overruled and frustrated, and when the child is threatened with injury, the child feels powerless. Many features of sexual abuse contribute to this feeling of powerlessness. Perhaps the most basic is the experience of having one's body repeatedly touched or invaded against one's wishes, whether this is done by force or by deceit. The feeling of powerlessness is intensified when children are frustrated in their efforts to end the sexual abuse. This can happen when a child tries to fight back, run away, or outsmart the abuser—but fails to stop the abuse. Ongoing vulnerability, fear, and anxiety compound the sense of powerlessness. Finally, children often experience an overwhelming feeling of powerlessness in the aftermath of abuse, when they find themselves unable to control adult decisions. As the box entitled "Promises, Promises: A Child's View of Incest" makes clear, these decisions may include separation from family, prosecutions, and police investigations (Gomes-Schwartz, Horowitz, & Cardarelli, 1990; Rogers & Terry, 1984; Vander Mey & Neff, 1982; Adams-Tucker, 1981; Herman, 1981).

Powerlessness appears to create three types of effects. First are the anxiety and fear that result from having been unable to control a painful event or events. Symptoms often include nightmares, phobias, physiological complaints, and sleep problems. These symptoms have been noted in both young children and adults. The second type of effect is the impairment of coping skills. Having been frustrated in their efforts to protect themselves, victims often report a low sense of personal efficacy. This frequently contributes to learning problems, difficulties in school and employment, and a generalized feeling of despair and depression. The third type of effect, compensatory reaction, is an unusual need to control or dominate. This is seen particularly in male victims, who often engage in group aggression or become abusers or molesters themselves out of a desire to be powerful enough to compensate for their past powerlessness (Rogers & Terry, 1984; Trainor, 1984; Gelinas, 1983; Goodwin, 1982; Summit & Kryso, 1981; Adams-Tucker, 1981).

Intervention Strategies

Specialized treatment for incest and child sexual abuse victims is a relatively recent undertaking, so therapists don't have much formal knowledge to guide them. Many studies (i.e., McCown, 1981; Blythe & Orr, 1985; Sgroi, Porter, & Blick, 1982) have focused on clients' characteristics and psychological dynamics, producing "laundry lists" of maladaptive behaviors. Theoretical approaches and treatment guidelines tend to be generic. For instance, a conventional therapeutic approach, such as individual or family psychotherapy, is modified by incorporating an emphasis on abuse-related

More than anything else, children need support, comfort, and love when they are sexually abused. Adults need to be especially understanding in their dealings with victims of incest. These children often feel powerless when decisions are being made regarding their safety and well-being, as the following passage illuminates:

I asked you for help and you told me you would if I told you the things my dad did to me. It was really hard for me to say all those things, but you told me to trust you—then you made me repeat them to 14 different strangers.

I asked you for privacy and you sent two policemen to my school in front of everyone, to "go downtown" for a talk in their black-and-white car—like I was the one being busted.

I asked you to believe me, and you said that you did; then you connected me to a lie detector, and took me to court where lawyers put me on trial like I was a liar. I can't help it if I can't remember times or dates or explain why I couldn't tell my mom. Your questions confused me—my confusion got you suspicious.

I asked you for help and you gave me a doctor with cold metal gadgets and cold hands . . . just like my father, who said it wouldn't hurt, just like my father, who said not to cry. He said I look fine—good news for you. You said, bad news for my "case."

I asked you for confidentiality and you let the newspaper get my story. What does it matter that they left out my name when they put in my father's and our home address? Even my best friend's mother won't let her talk to me anymore.

I asked for protection and you gave me a social worker who patted my head and called me "Honey" (mostly because she never remembered my name). She sent me to live with strangers in another place, with a different school.

Do you know what it's like to live where there's a lock on the refrigerator, where you have to ask permission to use the shampoo, and where you can't use the phone to call your friends? You get used to hearing, "Hi, I'm your new social worker, this is your new foster sister, dorm mother, group home." You tiptoe around like a perpetual guest and don't even get to see your own puppy grow up. Do you know what it's like to have more social workers than friends?

Do you know what it feels like to be the one that everyone blames for all the trouble? Even when they were speaking to me, all they talked about was lawyers, shrinks, fees, and whether or not they'll lose the mortgage. Do you know what it's like when your sisters hate you and your brother calls you a liar? It's my word against my own father's. I'm 12 years old and he's the manager of a bank. You say you believe me—who cares, if nobody else does?

I asked you for help and you forced my mom to choose between us— she chose him, of course. She was scared and had a lot to lose. I had a lot to lose, too—the difference was you never told me how much.

I asked you to put an end to the abuse—you put an end to my whole family. You took away my nights of hell and gave me days of hell instead. You've exchanged my private nightmare for a very public one. (MacFarlane, 1989)

MAKING USE OF WHAT WE KNOW

Promises, Promises: A Child's View of Incest

themes. So far, there have been few attempts to evaluate the effectiveness of any set of treatment procedures for victims of incest and child sexual abuse (Wheeler & Berliner, 1988).

Although the pattern of psychological recovery from incest and sexual abuse varies from child to child, the most significant variables in shaping the overall effects of sexual victimization seem to be the following:

- The nature of the abusive act, especially the degree of seduction, coercion, or violence employed.
- Whether the offender is a stranger, belongs to the child's social environment, or is a member of the child's immediate family.

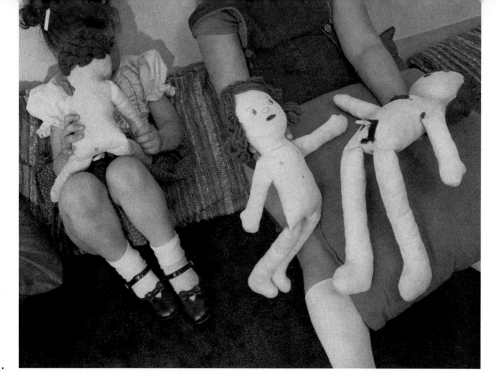

Very young children who are the victims of sexual abuse have difficulty explaining what has happened to them. A therapist can sometimes elicit the truth and help a child to deal with it by the use of anatomically correct dolls.

- The length of time the abuse took place—from a fleeting episode to multiple contacts over months—and the degree of participation by the child.
- The child's age, developmentally and physically, and ability to understand and cope with the sexual event. Symptoms are as likely to relate to youngsters' developmental level and their previous experiences as to the kind of sexual victimization they experienced.
- The reaction of the adults to whom the child confides the abuse.
- The consequences of treatment or legal intervention (Kempe & Kempe, 1984).

Robert Wheeler and Lucy Berliner (1988) maintain that intervention with the parents of sexually abused children is crucial. These parents need to be educated about the effects of sexual victimization and how best to support their youngster. (In fact, *all* parents need to know what steps to take if their child has been sexually assaulted; see the box on "What to Do If Your Child Has Been Sexually Assaulted.") Many parents also need help with their own reactions to the sexual victimization as well as advice on how to overcome the disruptions in their lives that are directly or indirectly associated with the sexual abuse. Parental therapy—individual, family, or group—or participating in a support group is therefore an important adjunct to the child-focused treatment (MacFarlane et al., 1988; Powell, 1988; Alexander, 1985; Lutz & Medway, 1984; Taylor, 1984; Horowitz, 1983; Mayer, 1983; Carozza & Hiersteiner, 1982).

For the child, age and developmental status usually determine the type of therapeutic intervention. Play therapy is often the treatment of choice for a very young child. School-age youngsters usually respond well to a mixture of activities, including therapeutic games and exercises, art therapy, and play-acting (Wheeler & Berliner, 1988). For older children and adolescents, conventional individual or group therapy or both are usually prescribed. Individual therapy gives them the privacy they need during the initial period of shock, and may be prescribed for a longer time for those who require intensive care and close monitoring because of fear or severe depression, or just for the additional support a one-to-one relationship offers (Kempe & Kempe, 1984).

Group therapy, which helps victims to feel less different and alone, has become a popular treatment approach (Mash & Barkley, 1989; Mandell & Damon, 1989; Ber-

*D*iscovering that your child has been victimized can be a devastating experience. More than anything else, your child needs support, comfort, and love. What needs to be done immediately is to reassure your child that you:

- Believe what she has told you.
- Know that it is not her fault.
- Are glad that he has told you about it.
- Are sorry about what happened.
- Will do your best to protect and support him.

Many parents are unsure how to help a youngster. One important way is to quietly encourage your child to talk about the assault. It is important to do this gently and without pressure. If your child doesn't talk about the experience right away, you may want to provide an opportunity. ("If you don't feel like talking about this right now, I understand. But if it begins to trouble you later, or you're thinking about it a lot, it's important that we talk about it.")

While making it clear that the fault lies with the offender, parents need to remember that often the offender is someone known to the child—usually a relative, neighbor, or friend of the family. It is normal to feel angry, but making angry threats against the offender might cause your child to feel guilty about having told. Your response should place the blame and responsibility with the offender in a realistic way: "What he did was wrong. We're going to try to get him some help so he doesn't hurt you or anyone else again."

The decisions that have to be made after a child is sexually assaulted are difficult ones. There are no right answers. Because sexual assault is so disruptive, most experts agree that therapeutic intervention is beneficial for both child and parents. For parents, it is important to openly talk about the victimization in a supportive environment. A counselor trained in child sexual assault can help parents sort out their own feelings, aid them in determining what to do next, make arrangements for follow-up medical care, and assist everyone in the family (especially other children) to deal with the assault. (Los Angeles Commission on Assaults Against Women, 1983)

MAKING USE OF WHAT WE KNOW

What to Do If Your Child Has Been Sexually Assaulted

---

liner & Ernst, 1984; Sturkie, 1983). Groups can draw victims out of their isolation and facilitate peer relationships in a way individual therapy cannot. Group support may also prove useful in alleviating the stigmatization, shame, guilt, worthlessness, and other intense negative emotions often felt by incest and sexual abuse victims. Because anxieties, uncertainties, and sexual inhibitions may endure for years, both group and individual therapy are often productive all through the adolescence and into adulthood.

Anna Salter (1988) points out that youngsters have little information about incest and child sexual abuse and find it hard to comprehend. Victims need to know that they are not alone, that sexual offenses have happened to other children. Abused children also need to know that the adult is the one who committed the offense, not them (Silver, Boon, & Stones, 1983; Taylor, 1983). Additionally, they must be reassured that the sexual victimization did not change their bodies in any way. If there are physical injuries, these must be explained—preferably with drawings—and the children reassured as to the ultimate prognosis.

Abused children often worry that others can tell they have been victimized simply by looking at them. Boys especially worry that others will think they are homosexual or that they actually will become homosexual. Abused youngsters need to be convinced that while sexual victimization may make them *feel* different, it does not make them *look* different, nor does it change their sexual preference (Weinstein & Rosen, 1988b; Bagley & Ramsay, 1986; Henderson, 1983).

An important component of treatment is future prevention. Most researchers (e.g., Wheeler & Berliner, 1988) believe that it is crucial to reduce the victim's sense of vulnerability to subsequent abuse. Indeed, there is some evidence (Russell, 1984;

DeYoung, 1982) that child abuse victims are at increased risk for future sexual victimization. Some investigators (e.g., Fromuth, 1986; Herman, 1981) feel that this vulnerability stems from the powerlessness often experienced by victims of any great wrong or violent crime.

Sexual abuse prevention programs for the larger society did not emerge until the late 1970s, several years after some progress had been made in identifying and treating sexual abuse victims. Federal funds from the National Center for Child Abuse and Neglect became available for prevention work in 1980, but federal funding has remained quite modest. Most prevention programs emerged out of volunteer rape crisis centers, local social service agencies, police departments, or groups of concerned parents and educators. By the mid-1980s, though, prevention programs were a fast-growing component of the movement to deal with incest and child sexual abuse (Finkelhor, 1986).

William Young (1988) believes that properly executed prevention programs reduce the numbers of children victimized by incest and sexual abuse. They thwart offenders by furnishing children, parents, teachers, and other community members with powerful tools: the knowledge necessary to recognize an inappropriate approach by an adult to a child, the understanding that it is always the offender who is responsible for deviant behavior, and the ability to assist youngsters and those who care for them to learn how to respond when approached inappropriately. Effective prevention programs often include such activities as "personal safety" courses in the schools, either free-standing or as part of a broader "family life" program. Other prevention efforts are workshops geared toward teachers, day-care providers, and other professionals who work with children; and workshops for parents aimed at educating them in how to help their youngster avoid being victimized and what to do if it should happen. Numerous publications on the topic of child sexual abuse and its prevention are also available. Finally, an organization called Childhelp USA sponsors a 24-hour-a-day free telephone line (1-800-422-4453) that provides information to callers on any form of child abuse, including sexual victimization.

Salter (1988) stresses the importance of teaching children realistic ways of saying no and being assertive. Assertiveness training programs and personal safety curricula devised for children (e.g., Crisci, 1983; Kent, 1982) are being used in many school systems today. Many therapists use these kinds of training programs in treating abused youngsters to help them cope with their experience by learning how to better protect themselves in the future.

Assertiveness and personal safety programs, particularly those presented within schools, have been evaluated in a number of studies (e.g., Gordon, 1989; Broadhurst, 1986; Nelson & Clark, 1986; Toal, 1985; Conte et al., 1985; Ray, 1984; Plummer, 1984; Gilgun & Gordon, 1984; Koblinsky and Behana, 1984; Riggs, 1982). One such investigation (Wurtele, 1986) compared the effectiveness of various educational approaches designed to teach assertiveness and personal safety skills to children. In the design 71 children from two grade groups (kindergarten and first grade, and fifth and sixth grades) participated in either (1) a filmed program (*Touch*), (2) a behavioral skills training program (BST) designed to teach safety skills, (3) a combination of the two, or (4) a nontreatment control presentation. The BST program, either alone or in combination with the film, proved most effective at both instilling knowledge about child sexual abuse and enhancing personal safety skills. The older children performed significantly better than the younger children did.

Another study (Saslawsky & Wurtele, 1986) explored the effectiveness of a film designed to prevent child sexual abuse. Sixty-seven children from four grade levels (kindergarten, first, fifth, and sixth) were assigned randomly to either a group that viewed the film or a control group. When the children were given a paper-and-pencil questionnaire to gauge their knowledge about sexual abuse and interviewed individually to elicit self-reports of verbal and behavioral responses to potentially abusive encounters, the group that had viewed the film was significantly more aware of sexual abuse and had more effective personal safety skills compared to the control group. Once again, older children scored higher on both assessments. In all age groups, though, the gains were maintained at a three-month follow-up assessment.

WHERE TO FIND MORE ON INCEST AND CHILD SEXUAL ABUSE

Books for Children:

L. Freeman. *It's My Body: A Book to Teach Young Children How to Resist Uncomfortable Touch.* Everett, WA: Planned Parenthood, 1984.

S. Gordon and J. Gordon. *A Better Safe Than Sorry Book.* Fayetteville, NY: Ed-U Press, 1984.

K. McGovern. *Alice Doesn't Babysit Anymore.* Portland, OR: McGovern and Mulbacker Books, 1985.

O. Wachter. *No More Secrets for Me.* Boston: Little, Brown, 1983.

Books for Preadolescents and Adolescents:

C. Adams, J. Fay, and J. L. Martin. *No Is Not Enough.* San Luis Obispo, CA: Impact Publishers, 1984.

E. Bass and L. Thornton. *I Never Told Anyone.* NY: Harper and Row, 1983.

H. Benedict. *Safe, Strong, and Streetwise.* Boston: Little Brown, 1987.

J. Fay and B. J. Flerchinger. *Top Secret: Sexual Assault Information for Teenagers.* Santa Cruz, CA: Network Publications, 1982.

For Adults:

C. Adams and J. Fay. *No More Secrets: Protecting Your Child from Sexual Assault.* Santa Cruz, CA: Network Publications, 1986.

K. Clark. *Sexual Abuse Prevention.* Santa Cruz, CA: Network Publications, 1986.

J. Crewdson. *By Silence Betrayed: Sexual Abuse of Children in America.* Boston: Little, Brown, 1988.

D. Daro. *Confronting Child Abuse.* New York: Free Press, 1988.

B. Dziech and C. Schudson. *On Trial: America's Courts and Their Treatment of Sexually Abused Children.* Boston: Beacon Press, 1989.

R. Helfer and R. Kempe. *The Battered Child*, 4th ed. Chicago: University of Chicago Press, 1987.

ATYPICAL SEXUAL BEHAVIORS THAT MAY EXPLOIT OTHERS

While the atypical forms of sexual expression discussed in this section are nowhere near as prevalent as incest and child sexual abuse, these unusual sexual variations are nonetheless important to identify and understand.

Exhibitionism

exhibitionism The exposure by a man of his genitals to unsuspecting strangers, usually women and children.

Why do flashers enjoy exhibiting themselves to others? Are they considered dangerous?

I used to get obscene phone calls and always wondered about the caller's motives. Why do some people do this?

....
Do you think that the wish to see someone else or to be seen oneself in a sexual context is related to voyeurism or exhibitionism? Why or why not?

In **exhibitionism**, sometimes referred to as "indecent exposure" or "flashing," a man exposes his genitals to an unsuspecting stranger, usually a woman or a child. Typically, the exposure occurs in a public location, such as a park or a street or sometimes a department store or a bus.

Since the exhibitionist usually makes no attempt to molest the involuntary viewer, men with this disorder are not considered dangerous. However, they often use lewd gestures to attract strangers. Some exhibitionists masturbate while exposing themselves; others masturbate later while thinking about the act. According to John Money (1981), some exhibitionists also fantasize about the incident while having intercourse with a partner later. What the exhibitionist desires is to embarrass, frighten, or shock the viewer, prompting speculation that the display is an effort to prove the man's masculinity or demonstrate his power. Therefore, when he is merely ignored, he feels disappointed and frustrated.

We have been able to piece together some characteristics of the exhibitionist. For example, we know that exhibitionistic acts usually occur for the first time before the person is 18. The peak years appear to be the 20s, followed by a decrease in the 30s, with symptoms occurring only rarely in the 40s. Many exhibitionists are socially withdrawn, often battling feelings of inferiority and shyness. As indicated, they also tend to suffer from a faltering sense of masculinity, and many demonstrate psychological immaturity as well. Exhibitionists come from all occupational groups, and many of them are married. Typically, it takes several arrests of an exhibitionist to convince the authorities that he is seriously troubled and needs treatment (Dwyer, 1988; Maletzky & Price, 1984).

Exhibitionism is one of the most common sexual offenses reported to the police. Still, we must point out in our sexually permissive society a certain degree of exhibitionism is tolerated and even encouraged. People appear near-nude at some beaches and swimming pools, and thinly veiled bodies are very chic in certain fashion circles.

The use of indecent language may also be considered a type of exhibitionism, as may graffiti and obscene humor. The latter are sexually provocative and flagrant efforts to elicit a reaction or response.

Making obscene telephone calls is sometimes viewed as a variation of exhibitionism, since the caller is seeking sexual gratification from a nonconsenting person. Like the exhibitionist, the obscene telephone caller is probably out to elicit shock or embarrassment in order to gain a sense of power or proof of his masculinity (most obscene phone callers are male). Most of the time he does not select a specific victim, but rather chooses telephone numbers at random from the phone book or by chance dialing. Sometimes, however, he selects someone he knows is home alone or whose picture he has seen (perhaps a bridal photograph in the newspaper) (Matek, 1988).

Some obscene telephone callers masturbate during the phone call; others masturbate afterward. Some do not speak but emit sounds of sexual pleasure into the phone or breathe heavily. Others utter a steady flow of profanities and obscenities. Some callers bluntly ask for sex or make some other sort of inappropriate overture for meeting the victim. Finally, there are those who present themselves as "taking a survey" and promise to keep the respondent's data confidential as they ask increasingly personal and private details. The case of "Ken, an Exhibitionist by Phone," described in the boxed insert, illustrates the role often played in this behavior by pent-up anger and resentment.

Voyeurism

Voyeurism (from the French word for "to look"), also called "peeping," is an atypical behavior in which the person becomes sexually aroused by looking at unsuspecting people, usually strangers, who are either naked, in the process of disrobing, or

Exploitive and Atypical Sexual Behaviors

Ken, referred for counseling at age 23, began making obscene phone calls at the age of 14. Despite discovery on at least two occasions, followed by personal discussions about this with his minister, he continued in the activity. He feels the urge "to make a call" when he is alone for a long time and "gets to thinking." ... His parents are divorced and were separated when he was eight. He lived alternately with both his mother and father, unhappily in both instances. His father's second wife resented him as an intrusion in their life, and his mother is critical and demanding of him.

Ken has a girlfriend who is outgoing and attractive and quite jealous of the many women who express interest in Ken at his work as a bartender trainee. He is tall, with a muscular build, and rugged good looks and has a somewhat shy interpersonal style. His girlfriend is aware of his behavior problem and puzzled

deeply by it. Ken cannot explain it to her, nor to himself.

In therapy Ken concedes that his obscene telephone calling expresses elements of anger and getting even. When he first began, he would even repeat to himself, "I'll show them" before he made his calls.

On rare occasions, he has masturbated in front of the TV when the program featured closeups of women. He pretends they can see him and cannot do anything about it. He has not engaged in any other exhibitionistic behaviors. The sexual relationship between Ken and his girlfriend seems satisfactory to both. In fact, they are discussing marriage. (From O. Matek, Obscene phone callers, in D. M. Dailey (Ed.), *The sexually unusual: Guide to understanding and helping*. Copyright © 1988 by Harrington Park Press, 10 Alice St., Binghamton, NY.)

MAKING USE OF WHAT WE KNOW

Ken, an Exhibitionist by Phone

engaging in sexual activity. The voyeur's sole purpose in looking is to achieve sexual arousal; he (once again, most offenders are men) doesn't usually seek direct sexual activity with the person or persons he is watching. The voyeur may masturbate to orgasm while watching others, or later on, when recalling the scene (American Psychiatric Association, 1987).

It is perfectly normal for people to want to look at others who are nude. Indeed, looking at one's partner is often a very pleasurable part of sexual activity. And there is abundant evidence that people's interest in the nude body extends beyond the intimate relationship—consider the wide range of formats, including X-rated videocassettes, magazines, and stage presentations, that feature nude bodies. However, the desire to look is considered abnormal when the person observed is unaware that he or she is being watched. Moreover, the voyeur is sexually stimulated by the secretive, illegal nature of his activities. Many times the offender can only be sexually satisfied by this peeping.

How does voyeurism originate? Psychologists feel that it may stem from the danger and excitement experienced while peeping that has become reinforced by sexual stimulation. Thus voyeurism might be explained in behavioristic terms. Voyeurism may also originate in unresolved sexual curiosity or the feeling that secret observation gives the voyeur power or control over the person being watched or bolsters his masculinity.

A profile of the voyeur can be constructed. The onset of voyeuristic behavior usually begins before age 15, and most voyeurs are lonely and insecure. Many of them are so fearful of rejection that they cannot form intimate relationships. And many of these men are sexually inadequate as well. Like exhibitionists, most voyeurs are harmless. The overwhelming majority will flee the scene if they are detected.

Voyeurs resort to a wide range of activities. Some enjoy spying on unsuspecting women through windows, day or night—like the young man described in the box entitled, "A Voyeur from the Executive Suite." Others like to stare at the scantily clad at beauty contests, beaches, fitness centers, or parks—although a public location reduces the "risk" of discovery and hence is less exciting. Then there are the voyeurs

voyeurism A disorder characterized by sexual arousal obtained from looking at unsuspecting people, usually strangers, who are either naked, in the process of disrobing, or engaging in sexual activity. Also called "peeping."

How does a "Peeping Tom" get sexual satisfaction?

MAKING USE OF WHAT WE KNOW

A Voyeur from the Executive Suite

Bob was a 25-year-old articulate, handsome business executive who had no difficulty attracting sexual partners. He dated frequently and had sexual intercourse once or twice a week with a variety of partners. In addition, however, Bob was frequently drawn to certain types of situations he found uniquely arousing. He owned a pair of high-powered binoculars and used these to peep into neighboring apartments. Sometimes he was rewarded for his efforts, but more frequently he was not. Bob would then leave his apartment and go to rooftops of large apartment buildings, where he would search with his binoculars until he found a woman undressing or engaging in sexual activity. He would then masturbate to orgasm while watching, or immediately afterward, and then return home. He experienced the voyeuristic situation, in its entirety, as uniquely pleasureful.

Bob's mother was allegedly warm, expressive, and flirtatious toward men, but not toward the patient. He felt he was his mother's favorite child and wondered whether he would ever fall in love with a woman who measured up to her. By the time of the psychiatric consultation, Bob had never been in love, nor had he experienced a durable, deep attachment to a woman.

Bob's family was sexually puritanical. Family members did not disrobe in front of each other, for example, and the parents avoided open displays of activity that could be interpreted as erotic by the children. Bob recalled, between the ages of seven and ten, watching his mother and sisters undress "as much as possible," but what he saw was within the limits of ordinary family decorum.

Bob had begun "peeping," along with many other boys, at the age of ten, while at summer camp; and he was unable to explain why this particular stimulus subsequently had a unique appeal for him whereas other boys seemed to become progressively interested in sexual intercourse rather than peeping. He had used binoculars to search for erotically stimulating scenes since he was 11, but did not leave his home to do so until age 17. (Spitzer et al., 1981, pp. 44–45)

who visit public restrooms to view the unsuspecting, those who strategically position themselves under stairways to look under women's dresses or skirts, and those who visit movie theaters to watch others view pornographic movies.

Frotteurism

frotteurism Achieving sexual arousal by touching or rubbing against a nonconsenting person, often a stranger.

The American Psychiatric Association (1987) defines **frotteurism** (from the French word meaning "to touch") as recurrent and intense sexual urges to touch and rub against a nonconsenting individual. Usually it is a man who rubs against a woman. It is the touching rather than the coercive nature of the act that is sexually stimulating. As with the other paraphilias, frotteurism is diagnosed when the person has acted on these urges over a period of time or is considerably distressed by them.

The causes of frotteurism are elusive, but we know that the signs of the disorder usually occur by adolescence. Most acts of frottage take place when the person is between the ages of 15 and 25, after which there is a gradual decline. Some people with this disorder report that they initially became interested in touching others while observing others doing the same.

Frotteurism is typically done by men in crowded locations, like shopping malls, busy sidewalks, sporting events, elevators, and buses because in such places the offender can more easily escape arrest. Victims are usually very attractive to the offender, who usually rubs his genitals against the stranger's thighs and buttocks or attempts to fondle her breast or genitalia with his hand. In the process he often fantasizes about an exclusive, caring relationship with his victim. But he also realizes that to avoid possible arrest and prosecution, he must escape detection after touching her. Often the victims do not protest the frottage because they cannot believe that such a provocative act would be committed intentionally in a public arena (American Psychiatric Association, 1987).

Sexual Masochism

Sexual masochism involves achieving sexual pleasure and gratification by being humiliated or made to suffer. The word *masochism* is derived from Austrian novelist Leopold von Sacher-Masoch (1895–1936), who often depicted men subjugated to women. Sacher-Masoch's women characters were often obsessed with the sexual pleasures of inflicting pain and punishment, and he was said to pursue women in real life who were willing to inflict pain on him. Moreover, he reportedly became sexually aroused at the thought of his wife being unfaithful, often begging her to have affairs and then relate to him the most sexually intimate details.

It is unclear how sexual masochism develops, although it has been speculated that it stems from a distortion of the early childhood need to be dependent, the desire to feel secure in the presence of a strong figure. Another possible explanation is that the masochist feels the need to be punished for being "naughty" or "bad." Some masochists report childhood fantasies of being bound, abused, and tortured. Others learned to associate pain with pleasure—for example, a boy or girl being spanked may experience sexual arousal when the genitals rub against the parent's knee. Sexual masochism tends to appear during the early years of adulthood. It occurs in both heterosexual and gay and lesbian relationships.

There are different types of sexual masochists. Some are bothered by their masochistic fantasies, which they invoke during masturbation or sexual intercourse but do not act upon. The masochistic fantasies for these women and men might involve being raped while bound or held by others so that they have no avenue of escape. Other masochists act on their tendencies while alone by, for example, sticking themselves with pins or shocking themselves electrically. Then there are the masochists who find a partner willing to inflict the pain and humiliation they crave. Masochistic acts with a partner might include bondage (restraining parts of the body with, for example, a rope and chains), spanking, whipping, being urinated or defecated upon, and being beaten or cut. Some sexual masochists go along for many years without increasing the potential injuriousness of their acts. Others, though, seek more and more severe masochistic experiences over time (or during periods of stress), which may eventually result in their death (American Psychiatric Association, 1987).

Masochistic acts with a partner may include psychological pain. Charles Moser's review of the literature (1988) reveals that this might involve humiliation, degradation, uncertainty, apprehension, powerlessness, fear, or anxiety. The most commonly sought psychological pain is humiliation, but there is no behavior that is universally humiliating. Psychological and physical pain typically go together. For instance, verbal abuse ("You are a poor excuse for a slave"), demanding that the person do menial or embarrassing things (e.g., cleaning a toilet or kissing a partner's feet), and being left alone in a vulnerable position (i.e., without keys or money) are some acts that illustrate the interplay between psychological and physical humiliation.

Hypoxyphilia is a particularly dangerous form of sexual masochism. **Hypoxyphilia** is sexual arousal by oxygen deprivation. The deprivation may be produced by a noose, plastic bag, mask, chemical, or chest compression. Masochists who practice hypoxyphilia arrange to escape asphyxiation before losing consciousness. They report that the activity is usually accompanied by sexual fantasies in which they asphyxiate or harm others, others asphyxiate or harm them, or they narrowly escape death. Hypoxyphilia may be engaged in alone or with a partner. Sometimes there is an error in judgment (for example, in the placement of the noose or mask) that results in accidental death (American Psychiatric Association, 1987).

Rush-hour subway trains are a favorite spot for frotteurs. The dense crowd often makes it impossible for a victim to tell which person near her is the offender, who may feign indignant surprise if she does identify him.

sexual masochism
Achieving sexual pleasure and gratification by being humiliated or made to suffer.

hypoxyphilia Sexual arousal by means of oxygen deprivation.

Sexual Sadism

Sexual sadism refers to achieving sexual pleasure and gratification by inflicting pain on a sexual partner. The word *sadism* is derived from the Marquis de Sade (1740–1814), a French novelist who often wrote about sexual punishment. Sade engaged in sexual sadism himself—in fact, he was eventually committed to an insane asylum for inflicting cruelty on his sexual partners.

For the behaviorist, childhood conditioning is the probable origin of sexual sadism. Like masochists, sadists may have experienced the pairing of sexual arousal with degradation, shaming, and condemnation. Psychodynamic theorists tend to see sexual sadism as influenced by early insecurities or the need to feel superior. Others view sexual sadism as one extreme on a continuum of aggressive behaviors. At one end of the continuum would be erotic arousal associated with mild pain or discomfort, such as "love bites," "smothering" someone with kisses, "wild" lovemaking, or "crushing" someone in a "lover's grip." Such behaviors, though, do not inflict serious injuries nor do they serve as substitutes for sexual relations. Mildly aggressive behaviors typically serve to increase the emotional excitement of the moment. At the opposite end of the continuum, though, the intention is to inflict pain, and it is from the act of injuring another person that sexual stimulation and gratification are derived.

Like sexual masochism, sexual sadism occurs in both heterosexual and gay and lesbian relationships. It is also not uncommon for sexual sadism and sexual masochism to be present in the same person. This is referred to as **sadomasochism.** The person may shift between these two roles, depending on the sexual situation. In a sadomasochistic relationship both partners are sexually aroused by giving and receiving pain (Weinberg, 1987; Weinberg, Williams, & Moser, 1984; Money, 1984).

According to the American Psychiatric Association (1987), some sexual sadists are troubled by their repeated sadistic fantasies during sexual activity. These people may not act on their fantasies, but unless they seek help or counseling, they will usually continue to experience them. The typical sadistic fantasy involves having complete control over one's partner, who is terrified by anticipation of the impending act. Other sexual sadists, though, act on their urges with a consenting partner who willingly suffers humiliation and pain. Still others act out their sadistic tendencies with nonconsenting victims. In all instances it is the suffering of the victim that is sexually arousing. One analysis of sadomasochism (Moser, 1988) discusses five categories of punishment designed to inflict pain on sexual partners: bondage, physical discipline, intense stimulation, sensory deprivation, and body alteration.

BONDAGE. This category of acts ranges from physically holding someone down to completely immobilizing the person. The sadist might restrain a partner partially by putting a leash around his neck or tying a tight corset on her; or the sadist might use ropes or chains to tie his partner up so that she cannot move.

PHYSICAL DISCIPLINE. This category ranges from slapping to whipping or beating. Physical discipline behaviors can be of low intensity so that no marks are left. However, more intense measures may leave bruising, welts, or lesions that last for days or even weeks. Many times the recipient of physical discipline fails to recognize the level of tissue damage that has been inflicted.

INTENSE STIMULATION. Scratching, biting, and the use of hot wax or ice on the skin are examples of intense stimulation. Such activities produce strong sensations with little or no tissue damage. The range of intense stimulation typically involves duration or manner. As an illustration, scratching someone's back for extended amounts of time can be painful. Also within this category are any behaviors or devices designed to increase sensation. For instance, dropping hot wax from several feet above someone produces a different sensation from dropping it from a few inches above them; a spanking on wet skin is more intense than a spanking on dry skin.

SENSORY DEPRIVATION. This category can also intensify sensations and perceptions as well as heighten feelings of vulnerability. For instance, a blindfold prevents the wearer from knowing where or when the next blow will be struck. Similarly, not being braced for a blow usually heightens sensation and creates anxiety, fear, even panic. It also serves to focus the recipient on the sensations without distraction. Gags, hoods, and earplugs are other methods of achieving sensory deprivation.

BODY ALTERATION. This category includes such behaviors as tattooing, piercing the genitals, burning, or branding the arms, legs, or buttocks. Although many body alterations are designed to be permanent, others are not. Body alterations may be seen as proof of a sadomasochistic commitment, sensory enhancements, or beautifying.

Before leaving the topics of sexual masochism and sexual sadism, we need to point out that some couples use degrees of such behaviors as a form of sexual enhancement. One team of researchers (Breslow, Evans, & Langley, 1986, 1985) found that sadomasochists are often able to sustain long-term relationships. Some partners regard degrees of sadomasochism as part of foreplay, and usually practice it only during sexual interactions. Many practitioners also report that they do not need to engage in sadomasochistic behavior or fantasy to reach orgasm.

Martin Weinberg, Colin Williams, and Charles Moser (1984) report that sadomasochistic behavior is often consensual. Partners typically share an understanding that they are engaging in a sadomasochistic behavior and agree on the limits to such behavior. Also, sadomasochistic partners usually acknowledge who is to be dominant and who is to be submissive. In addition, there is usually a shared awareness that both participants are role playing.

Fetishism

Fetishism involves the use of an inanimate object, or *fetish*, to produce sexual excitement or gratification. Sexual arousal is usually obtained by touching, fondling, or rubbing the object. Kissing, tasting, and smelling the object are also common. Often the person masturbates while touching the fetish or asks a partner to wear the object during their sexual encounters. Shoes, lingerie and stockings, and furs and gloves are common fetishes. When a fetish is an article of female clothing that's used in cross-dressing, the condition is called *transvestic fetishism* (discussed later in the chapter). When the object is designed to be stimulating, such as a vibrator, its use is not considered fetishism (American Psychiatric Association, 1987).

No one knows for sure how fetishism develops. Unconscious motivation, conditioning experiences, and even neural impairments have been suggested (see, for example, Wise, 1985). Sometimes an association formed between the fetish and sexual arousal comes to dominate the person's sexual behaviors. For example, an 11-year-old boy who begins masturbating using a towel may find that he must use a towel from then on while masturbating. Another reason advanced for fetishism is that the fetishist finds some unusual object erotic and is driven toward that object again and again for sexual arousal.

Attachment to a fetish usually begins by adolescence, and once established, the disorder tends to be chronic. It is not uncommon for the fetishist to steal the objects of desire. In fact, a stolen fetish often acquires special powers of sexual excitation. Women's undergarments are frequently stolen by fetishists, who sometimes have collections numbering in the dozens.

No two fetishes are alike. Consider rubber fetishes, which are quite common. According to Thomas Sargent (1988), some fetishists like latex, others prefer real rubber; some like rubber with cloth backing, while others are turned off by the cloth.

fetishism The use of an inanimate object (fetish) to produce sexual excitement or gratification. Sexual arousal is usually obtained by touching, fondling, or rubbing the fetish.

Making Use
of What
We Know

A Rubber
Fetishist
Describes His
Obsession

I go nuts over rubber coats, and will take the time to follow or cross a street just to prolong the delight of sound or vision. Then I will hurry to a place where I can love my rubber while fantasizing about the one I saw. Or I will lay one on top of another, and be very promiscuous by loving the red while fantasizing about the blue, and maybe go to get the blue and become distracted by the black. It's a delight.

One day in a store I watched for a long time as a lady tried on a yellow poncho. She stood and posed in front of a mirror, smoothing the soft rubber over her breasts. I was standing at the rack, touching the same soft rubber. She came over, returning it with a warm smile. Dark hair and brown eyes—the coat was still warm as I scooped it up and bought it. It is still a favorite fantasy.

A small department store . . . always had a supply of various kinds of rubber coats (if I don't have a particular style or color, I must). After years of buying there I was looking for a particular coat in my size. The salesman took me to a private loft upstairs where there were hundreds of rubber coats. I do not know if someone there shared my fetish, but it was my idea of heaven. I took lots of time, so the salesman asked if it was all right if he left me alone. All right? There was a long flight of stairs to the loft, and I could hear clearly, so I went around my heaven with a delightful erection, and sampled the softness of the rubber against my penis. Every coat in the collection. Then I took a few and laid them on a flat surface and made love to them. It was incredible. . . . (From T. O. Sargent, Fetishism, in D. M. Dailey (Ed.), *The sexually unusual: Guide to understanding and helping*. Copyright © 1988 by Harrington Park Press, 10 Alice St., Binghamton, NY.)

There are those who like rubber wet and those who like it dry. Some prefer tight-fitting rubber and some like it loosely caressing. There are fetishists who are stimulated by the odor of urine or sweat on rubber and others who are fastidious. Some like to lie on it, others like to hold it while stimulating themselves. Still others want it to be worn by a sexual partner. Certain types of rubber may be preferred because of the taste, smell, or feel. Among the items preferred by fetishists are rubber baby pants, gloves, bathing caps, condoms, boots, and balloons. One fetishist, featured in the box entitled "A Rubber Fetishist Describes His Obsession," liked rubber coats. All of this means that each person has a fetish unlike any other.

Certain degrees of fetishism seem to be socially acceptable. It is not uncommon for people to collect and become sexually aroused by mementos or seductive clothing. College students, for example, participate in "panty raids" and servicemen stationed overseas request female undergarments sent from home. For the normal person, sexual excitement is derived from thinking of the woman who wore them, particularly if the undergarments have been used. For the fetishist, the undergarments alone elicit excitement.

Transvestism

transvestism Achieving sexual pleasure and gratification by dressing in the clothing of the other sex.

Transvestism refers to achieving sexual pleasure and gratification by cross-dressing—that is, dressing in the clothing of the other sex. Transvestism is not the same as transexualism, which, as we learned in Chapter 5, is a persistent discomfort with, and a strong sense of inappropriateness about, one's sexual identity. Also, contrary to popular thought, most transvestites are heterosexual, not homosexual, and their cross-dressing is really a kind of fetishism. Some clinicians prefer the term *transvestic fetishism* since it emphasizes the act of cross-dressing for fetishistic purposes, not a preset sexual preference (Peo, 1988; American Psychiatric Association, 1987; Wise, 1985).

As with the other paraphilias, transvestism is rare among women. Perhaps the reason transvestism seems almost nonexistent among women is that society allows

"You weren't kidding when you said you'd like to get into my pants."

women to dress in masculine styles and fashions. At any rate, we do not know what motivates the women who dress like men. A man, on the other hand, can hardly go unnoticed in women's apparel. Transvestites usually own a secret collection of women's clothes that they put on whenever the desire to do so overwhelms them. The act of cross-dressing is typically done in private (Krueger, 1982), and when completed, the man usually masturbates, often while looking at himself in a mirror (Croughan et al., 1981). Many of these men also desire to go out in public dressed as a woman. The generally accepted clinical indications of transvestism are as follows:

- Cross-dressing behavior usually begins after five years of age and perhaps not until puberty or later. Early cross-dressing experiences may be linked to sexual or sensual experiences with women's clothing. For example, a boy might become sexually aroused by the soft texture of his mother's lingerie and find that these feelings intensify when he puts such clothing on.
- The transvestite's experience of sexual arousal from dressing in women's clothing may diminish with age or frequency of cross-dressing. As indicated, he may masturbate while wearing the clothing, and this pattern of behavior may continue into adulthood, even when he is in a steady sexual relationship with another person.
- The transvestite's gender identity is typically masculine. Even though he may describe himself as "feeling female" at times, his gender behavior is usually masculine—except when he is fully cross-dressed. Then he will typically emulate feminine behaviors, mannerisms, and voice.
- Sexual preference is usually heterosexual, although some transvestites are bisexual or homosexual (Peo, 1988).

The causes of transvestism remain obscure. Some suggest "petticoat punishment" as a causal factor—that is, punishing and humiliating a boy by dressing him in the clothes of a girl is thought to cause the boy's interest in cross-dressing. If this explanation is valid, it is likely that the forced cross-dressing had some reinforcing

Many transvestites, or cross-dressers, are heterosexual and are happily involved in committed relationships with other-sex partners.

value—perhaps it was the only attention the boy received from his parents. It is more likely, though, that reinforcement of cross-dressing occurred in a more positive fashion—such as a young boy receiving praise or compliments ("how cute") for cross-dressing behavior.

Another explanation of transvestism is that female clothing acquired erotic properties during masturbation or intercourse. Articles of female clothing such as underwear or stockings may have been used for friction during masturbation or the smell of female undergarments may have become paired with orgasm.

Vern Bullough and associates (1983) believe that many boys and men cross-dress in order to escape the pressures placed on them by traditional male gender roles. They feel that when they dress like a female, they do not have to conform to rigid masculine behaviors such as being emotionally reserved, aggressive, rational, and always in control. Another author (Monroe, 1980) maintains that cross-dressing is usually an attempt to temporarily escape male responsibilities. Should this type of explanation be correct, it would be interesting to see what effects, if any, androgyny (see Chapter 5) would have on transvestism.

There are degrees of transvestism, from occasional solitary wearing of female clothes to extensive involvement in a transvestic subculture. Some men wear a single item of women's apparel, such as underwear or hosiery, under their masculine attire. Others wear more than one article or dress entirely as a woman. When fully cross-dressed, they often apply makeup. Some cross-dressers experiment with female hormones, use electrolysis for beard removal, or shave other unwanted body hair (American Psychiatric Association, 1987; Peo, 1988). A case study of a male transvestite is provided in the box entitled "Paul and Susan: A Secret Discovered."

Other Atypical Sexual Behaviors

Now that we have discussed the more common paraphilias, we turn to consider several that are far more rare. In this section we briefly explore necrophilia, zoophilia, coprophilia, and urophilia (American Psychiatric Association, 1987).

necrophilia Sexual pleasure from viewing or having sexual contact with a corpse.

NECROPHILA. Necrophilia is the urge to fantasize about, view, or actually have sexual contact with a corpse. It is considered very rare. In some instances, such as in the 1991 Jeffrey Dahlmer case, necrophiliacs harbor sadistic tendencies and practice murder and mutilation of corpses to obtain sexual gratification. It is not uncommon for those with necrophilia to seek jobs in funeral homes or morgues.

zoophilia The preference for sexual activity with infrahuman animals.

ZOOPHILIA. Zoophilia is the preference for sexual activity with infrahuman animals. The most commonly used animals are sheep, goats, cattle, dogs, horses, burros, and pigs. While men with this disorder tend to engage in coital activity with animals, most female zoophiliacs have animals perform cunnilingus on them. However, some have trained animals such as dogs to mount them and engage in intercourse, and others masturbate the male animal. Many X-rated videocassettes and magazines feature some aspect of bestiality.

Throughout history zoophilia has been written about and depicted in art. Among the ancient Egyptians, women sometimes sexually submitted to male goats. Male warriors of the Crow Indian tribe of North America sometimes had coitus with mares and animals killed during hunts. Special laws against zoophilia were passed in colonial New England. According to one source (D'Emilio & Freedman, 1988), the colonists decreed harsh punishments for those who had sexual relations with animals because they believed the mating of human beings and animals would produce monstrous offspring. Sometimes the animal as well as the sex offender was executed.

Zoophilia is not very widespread and occurs primarily in rural areas. It is usually not a persistent form of sexual activity. Alfred Kinsey and associates (1953, 1948)

Paul is a 29-year-old self-employed carpenter who lives in a small apartment with Susan, a hair stylist from the same town. The two have lived together for three months and hope to marry someday.

Susan did not realize that Paul was a transvestic fetishist until recently, for Paul kept his desire to cross-dress secret. He hid a wardrobe of women's clothing in a special location in the apartment, and when Susan was out of the house or at work, he would often masturbate while wearing such items as nylon stockings and underwear, high-heeled shoes, and short skirts.

Paul became attracted to female clothing when he was 12. When he was alone in his parents' house, he would often take silk or nylon underwear from his mother's bureau and fondle the material. His sexual arousal intensified when he wore such undergarments, as well as when he slipped on a pair of nylons. He liked to masturbate with the panties on, using the sensual fabric to reach orgasm. He also liked to gaze at himself masturbating in a full-length mirror. Paul would pilfer many pairs of underwear and other female attire from his mother and sister and keep them hidden.

With age, Paul's attraction to women's clothing grew more extensive. He began to enjoy full cross-dressing and also purchased several wigs and a collection of makeup to help complete the transformation. While all of his cross-dressing had previously been done in private, he now began to harbor a desire to spend time in public in his special wardrobe. By the time he was 21, he had done this a few times and reached new levels of sexual excitement. While Paul managed to keep his cross-dressing a se-cret during his courtship with Susan, his preoccupation with being discovered took its toll. Shortly after moving in with her, he began to drink excessively and to take sedatives to calm his nerves, using mounting work problems as the excuse for these behaviors. He also experienced bouts of depression.

Susan eventually learned of Paul's inner desires. Already concerned about his anxiety and mood swings, she discovered the hidden wardrobe by accident one day when she was spring cleaning Paul's closet. Much to her surprise, a hidden panel at the rear of the closet revealed an extraordinary discovery: a wardrobe containing dozens of dresses, skirts, and blouses, as well as hundreds of pairs of underwear and nylon stockings, scarfs, and costume jewelry. A separate storage box contained wigs, perfume, and an assortment of makeup.

Later that day Susan confronted Paul with her discovery. Initially, he denied any knowledge of the hidden wardrobe, but then confessed the details of his secret life. Although defensive at first he was largely relieved by these disclosures after the anguish of secrecy and sexual frustration. He was also relieved that Susan did not want out of the relationship, nor did she try to shame and humiliate him. Although initially shocked, Susan desperately wanted to understand Paul's problem. The two agreed that the best approach would be therapy for Paul, something that he had wanted to undertake for years but had continually postponed. To date, counseling has been quite effective, and Paul's desire to cross-dress has declined. He is also less anxious and depressed, and his use of alcohol and sedatives has markedly decreased. (Authors' files)

MAKING USE OF WHAT WE KNOW

Paul and Susan: A Secret Discovered

reported that about 8 percent of men and 3.6 percent of women queried had had at least one sexual experience to the point of orgasm with animals. This figure was a bit higher for boys reared on farms.

COPROPHILIA AND UROPHILIA. These two paraphilias concern sexual arousal related to body elimination processes. **Coprophilia** refers to sexual excitement derived from contact with feces, and **urophilia** entails sexual arousal derived from contact with urine. People with these paraphilias derive satisfaction out of watching others defecate or urinate, with themselves to be defecated or urinated on, or engaging in activities involving their own feces or urine. Both paraphilias appear to reflect a retreat to infantile behaviors.

coprophilia Sexual excitement derived from contact with feces.

urophilia Sexual arousal derived from contact with urine.

Intervention and Treatment

The treatment of atypical sexual behaviors poses two nagging problems. First, people who suffer from these disorders usually do not seek help for their condition unless they have broken the law and are forced to do so or have been discovered by family members or loved ones. Second, current methods of treatment are less than satisfactory. To date, no approach or technique boasts a high recovery rate. The most notable modes of treatment are behavioral, psychodynamic, and biological approaches.

BEHAVIORAL APPROACHES. You will remember from Chapter 16 that behaviorists believe all sexual disorders and problems are learned forms of behavior. Just as normal behavior is acquired through the process of conditioning, so, too, is sexually atypical behavior. The thrust of behavioral therapy is to replace undesirable behaviors with more appropriate ones by employing conditioning techniques.

aversion therapy A behavioral technique designed to reduce or extinguish inappropriate behavior by pairing it with a noxious or unpleasant stimulus.

The three techniques generally used in behavioral therapy are aversion therapy, systematic desensitization, and orgasmic reconditioning. **Aversion therapy** seeks to reduce or extinguish inappropriate behavior by pairing it with a noxious or unpleasant stimulus. Initially, electric shocks were used to try to decondition undesirable behaviors. For example, a person with transvestic fetishism might have been given a series of small but irritating electrical shocks while viewing pictures of himself in female clothing, or the shocks might have been administered at random intervals while he was putting on his favorite female attire (Kilmann et al., 1982).

Contemporary aversion therapy procedures rely on *covert sensitization* and *assisted covert sensitization* (Wincze, 1989). In covert sensitization clients imagine themselves engaging in the sexual behaviors that are to be extinguished. In assisted covert sensitization a foul odor such as valeric acid is presented to clients as they imagine the undesirable behaviors in an effort to heighten the effect of the conditioning procedure.

Systematic desensitization entails the elimination of an undesirable sexual response. In this procedure structured experiences are used to teach people how to relax and reduce the stresses that precipitate the atypical behavior. Suppose, for instance, that an exhibitionist feels a need to expose himself whenever he experiences anxiety or is forced to submit to someone's authority. In the systematic desensitization approach, he might be asked to imagine anxious moments in the presence of authority and at the same time to induce relaxation responses and assertiveness rather than submissive behavior. As he learns to strengthen the relaxation response, his learned response (exhibitionism) and the anxiety surrounding it will diminish.

Finally, *orgasmic reconditioning* is an effort to replace undesirable fantasies with more acceptable ones. For example, a man might be asked to masturbate while thinking about his favorite sadistic fantasy, and then told to switch to a fantasy of nonsadistic intercourse with his wife at the moment of orgasm. The goal of this approach is to develop a bond between sexual arousal and a desirable fantasy (Abel, Mittelman, & Becker, 1985; Quinsey & Marshall, 1983; Schwartz & Masters, 1983).

PSYCHODYNAMIC APPROACHES. Psychodynamic approaches emphasize the importance of past learning and how it affects present behavior. Influenced by the psychoanalytic writings of Sigmund Freud, these approaches assume that repressed childhood experiences are largely responsible for the paraphilias and other forms of atypical sexual behavior. For instance, people suffering from these disorders may have experienced a disturbance at some level of their psychosexual development (e.g., castration anxiety because of a boyhood attachment to the mother). Therapists who subscribe to the psychodynamic approach believe that such sexual turbulence remains active and influences behavior even though it is submerged beneath the person's ordinary level of awareness (Van de Loo, 1987).

Exploitive and Atypical Sexual Behaviors

The therapeutic challenge in a psychodynamic approach is to uncover these influential repressed experiences, bring them to consciousness, and place them in proper perspective. This is often attempted through what is called *free association*, in which the client is asked to verbalize all thoughts, dreams, and fantasies. Sometimes hypnosis is used instead to uncover this material. With either approach, the goal is to make conscious what has been unconscious and, with the help of the therapist, to interpret it so that clients can gain conscious insight into the irrationality of their sexual behavior. When the psychodynamic approach is successful, people are able to redirect their energies away from sexual conflicts into more socially acceptable channels. However, psychodynamic treatment often lasts for years, and overall results have been mixed.

BIOLOGICAL APPROACHES. Drugs have also been used to change undesirable sexual behavior, often in combination with one of the other forms of treatment. **Antiandrogens** are drugs designed to temporarily reduce testosterone levels and thus to moderate sexual aggressiveness. Medroxyprogesterone acetate, sold under the trade name of Depo-Provera, is an antiandrogen that has been used with pedophiles and other paraphiliacs. Although still considered experimental, it seems promising as a treatment option (Wincze, 1989; Wincze, Bansal, & Malamud; 1986; Neumann & Toppert, 1986; Berlin & Meinecke, 1981).

antiandrogens Drugs designed to temporarily reduce testosterone levels and, thus to moderate sexual aggressiveness.

SEXUAL ADDICTION

Sexual addiction (once called *nymphomania* in women and *satyriasis* in men) refers to an excessive or insatiable desire for sexual stimulation and gratification. There is no precise definition of sexual addiction because clinicians cannot agree on its symptoms or on the criteria to be used in making a diagnosis. Some believe that sexual addiction reflects a general pattern of addictive behavior that includes compulsive needs, lack of control, increasing frequency of the behaviors, withdrawal symptoms when the behaviors are stopped, and interference with everyday functioning (Kasl, 1989; Carnes, 1983). Others (e.g., Levine & Troiden, 1988; Coleman, 1987) reject applying the concept of addiction to sexual behaviors because they believe it is too vague and value-laden.

sexual addiction An excessive or insatiable desire for sexual stimulation and gratification.

Sexual addiction is not widespread but is more prevalent among men than women. It is not uncommon for sexual addiction to be combined with other unusual forms of sexual expression, such as paraphilias (Rosen & Leiblum, 1989). Sexual addicts often have sex with total strangers and shun emotional intimacy. Many engage in this behavior to cope with their feelings of fear or sadness; others use it as a means of escaping life's problems or responsibilities. Obtaining reassurance of one's masculinity or femininity and validating one's physical attractiveness or sexual prowess are other possible motivating forces. Some sexual addicts are caught up in the sense of power that compulsive sexual behavior brings; others enjoy the thrill or danger of having sex with strangers (Earle & Crow, 1989; Schwartz & Brasted, 1985).

Having a healthy sexual appetite is not the same thing as being sexually addicted. For instance, the man or woman who wants more coital frequency within a relationship sharply contrasts with the sexual addict who compulsively moves from partner to partner in an uncontrolled fashion. Sexual addicts often seek the illusion of sexual power and intimacy, but their encounters are devoid of fulfillment, satisfaction, and pleasure (Edwards, 1986).

Helen Kaplan (1979) believes that sexual addiction often reflects a compulsive and obsessive sexual *state* rather than excessive sexual *desire*. Sexual addicts tend to be highly anxious people who seek to relieve their discomfort through sexual activity. As in all compulsive states, the anxiety tends to increase when anything prevents the compulsive act. Indeed, sexual addicts typically experience anxiety when they are not engaging in physical stimulation or seduction.

Treatment for sexual addiction varies but often involves modifications of some of the techniques we discussed in Chapter 16. Some treatment plans incorporate parts of the Alcoholic Anonymous recovery program. Sexaholics Anonymous (SA), Sex and Love Addicts Anonymous (SLAA), and Sex Addicts Anonymous (SAA), for instance, insist that people admit they are sexual addicts, recognize that they are powerless to control the addiction and that their lives have become unmanageable, and develop alternative expressions and resources for dealing with their anxiety and frustration.

SEXUALITY IN THE NEWS

A Crime Never Forgotten: Incest

*T*his video was aired on April 21, 1991, on ABC's "20/20." Four sisters tell of their experience of being sexually abused by their father. Each woman takes a different avenue toward healing. The video segment tells us that many incest victims are not aware of the deleterious effects of incestuous acts until adulthood, when their lives begin to unravel. Barbara Walters asks, "Can justice be done once the victims identify the abuser?" Not one of the four women featured in this video ever discussed her abuse with any of her sisters or with their mother. (20:44 minutes)

DISCUSSION QUESTIONS

1. Usually, sexual abusers go unpunished because the victims either do not or cannot report the crime or feel it's too late to do so. How can this situation be changed? What steps did the Rodgers sisters take?

2. Many women who are incest survivors suppress memories and remain numb to their feelings. Why do you believe this happens? What can trigger the awareness for the victims?

3. The Rodgers sisters were determined to confront their father. How did they go about this? Why was it necessary for these women to confront the man who had assaulted them?

LOOKING BACK

■   Exploitive sexual behaviors take advantage of others' vulnerability and cause them some degree of distress. It is often difficult to define what is typical and what is atypical sexual behavior, partly because different societies approve and disapprove of different sexual behaviors. Moreover, behaviors a society once deemed abnormal, like masturbation, may over the course of time be perceived as a variation of normal sexuality in that same society. All exploitive behaviors are atypical, but not all atypical behaviors are exploitive.

■   Two of the most common types of exploitive atypical sexual behavior are incest and child sexual abuse. Incest is sexual contact between close blood relatives. Child sexual abuse is sexual contact between a child and an adult who is not related to that child. In both cases, the child is being used for the sexual pleasure of the adult. Children who are sexually abused by either relatives or others tend to suffer a wide range

of effects, including traumatic sexualization, betrayal, stigmatization, and powerlessness, that may persist for years. Intervention with incest and child sexual abuse victims includes individual, group. and play therapy, as well as efforts aimed at prevention and education.

■   Atypical sexual behavior represents a departure from the norms of a given society and usually harms others psychologically, physically, or both. In the class of disorders referred to as *paraphilias*, sexual arousal occurs in response to objects or situations unrelated to normal arousal-activity patterns.

■   Exhibitionism involves the exposure of the genitals to unsuspecting strangers, usually women and children. In voyeurism a person becomes sexually aroused by looking at unsuspecting people, usually strangers, who are nude or engaging in sexual activity. Frotteurism involves deriving sexual fulfillment from touching and rubbing against a nonconsenting person. In sexual masochism a person derives sexual satisfaction from being made to suffer. In sexual sadism a person is sexually gratified by inflicting pain on a sexual partner. In fetishism objects are used to produce sexual gratification. In transvestism a person experiences a compelling urge to dress in the clothes of the other sex and derives sexual gratification from doing so.

■ A paraphilia may interfere with the capacity for reciprocal, affectionate sexual activity. However, some people are able to maintain satisfying marriages or close relationships despite their atypical behaviors.

■ Some atypical behaviors are obscure and poorly understood. Among these are necrophilia, defined as obtaining sexual excitement from viewing or having sexual contact with a corpse; zoophilia, sexual activities with animals; and coprophilia and urophilia, becoming aroused from having contact with bodily wastes or elimination processes.

■ Treatment options for atypical sexual behaviors are somewhat limited, and no one technique or approach has proved more effective than others. Behavioral approaches seek to replace undesirable sexual behaviors with more socially acceptable ones through conditioning techniques such as aversion therapy, systematic desensitization, and orgasmic reconditioning. Psychodynamic approaches propose that repressed experiences from childhood are largely responsible for atypical sexual behavior and that these experiences must be brought to consciousness and placed in proper perspective so the person can deal with them. One promising biological approach is the use of antiandrogens, drugs designed to temporarily lower testosterone levels in order to moderate sexual aggressiveness. This treatment is typically combined with other therapies.

■ Sexual addiction is an excessive or insatiable desire for sexual stimulation and gratification. Although clinicians do not agree on either the symptoms or the diagnostic criteria for sexual addiction, we do know that it is a relatively rare condition that is more prevalent in men than in women. Sexual addicts tend to be highly anxious people who relieve their anxieties through sexual activity. Their sexual encounters are devoid of fulfillment, satisfaction, and intimacy.

THINKING THINGS OVER

1. We have seen that unusual and exploitive sexual behaviors are distinguishable by the harm they inflict on participants or others. Do you think some of the behaviors we discussed should be against the law? If so, which ones?

2. Incest and the sexual abuse of children are often referred to as "the best-kept secret." Victims tend to lead a life of concealment and isolation; only a minority ever reveal the sexual cruelty they experienced. Prepare a presentation on the effects of incest and child sexual abuse. What kinds of adjustment difficulties do abused children face? What do you think are some of the long-range consequences? Finally, what kinds of treatment do you think are most beneficial for child victims of sexual abuse?

3. React to the statement, "I don't care what anyone does in private, so long as both partners agree to the activity."

4. A friend of yours received an obscene phone call last night and was both alarmed and puzzled by it. She knows that you are taking a course in human sexuality and hopes you can shed some light on her concerns: "What motivates people to make obscene phone calls? Why do they want to shock or embarrass people with their foul language? How do they decide whom to call?" Try to answer her questions.

5. A friend of yours reveals that she has been experiencing some unusual sexual feelings and wants help. What advice would you give to your friend? What kinds of help and treatment are available to her?

DISCOVER FOR YOURSELF

Berrick, J. D., & Gilbert, N. (1991). *With the best intentions: The child sexual abuse prevention movement*. New York: Guilford Press. A detailed analysis of what kinds of prevention programs are available for sexual victimization.

Dailey, D. M. (1988). *The sexually unusual: Guide to understanding and helping*. New York: Harrington Park Press. An excellent resource book for those who desire more information on variations in sexual expression.

Docter, R. F. (1988). *Transvestites and transsexuals*. New York: Plenum. A good account of cross-sex behavior.

Gomes-Schwartz, B., Horowitz, J. M., & Cardarelli, A. P. (1990). *Child sexual abuse: The initial effects*. Newbury Park, CA: Sage. A thorough look at the impact child sexual abuse has on the youngster as well as on family functioning.

Kasl, C. D. (1989). *Women, sex and addiction*. New York: Ticknor & Fields. An interesting look at compulsive sexual behavior.

Wincze, J. P. (1989). Assessment and treatment of atypical sexual behavior. In S. R. Leiblum & R. C. Rosen (eds.), *Principles and practice of sex therapy*, 2nd ed. New York: Guilford Press. A noted contributor to the field provides a clear and concise account of atypical sexual behavior, including definitions and classifications.

20

Sexual Coercion: Rape

What does not destroy me makes me stronger

—Friedrich Nietzsche

We know there is a world without rape, and this world is in our minds

—Susan Griffin

Acts of sexual violence and assault are maladaptive behavioral responses, almost always perpetrated by men against women. Rather than seeking sexual gratification, men who practice sexual coercion seek to control a woman by destroying her self-worth and dignity. At the very least, coercive sex violates the victim's rights. More often it brings about degradation, humiliation, and a host of debilitating psychological and emotional problems.

The study of coercive and exploitive sexual behavior is a relatively recent research pursuit. Until the feminist movement focused attention on women's psychological and emotional victimization, society concentrated almost exclusively on the physical problems sustained by women who were sexually assaulted. We are slowly gaining a better understanding of the total picture, which includes the intrapersonal and interpersonal dynamics of both the victims and the perpetrators of sexual abuse, as well as prevention and treatment strategies. A clearer picture of this massive problem has emerged because of the many women and children who have been courageous enough not only to explore their negative experiences through psychotherapy and counseling but also to confront their violators and to testify against them.

LOOKING AHEAD

In this chapter you'll discover:

☐ *What rape entails and how widespread it is in modern society.*

☐ *Some of the personality characteristics of rapists and what motivates sexual assault.*

☐ *How rape affects its victims, both immediately and over the long term.*

☐ *What acquaintance, marital, and male rape are.*

☐ *What kinds of treatment are available to survivors of sexual assault.*

☐ *How therapists try to treat and rehabilitate rapists.*

THE CRIME OF RAPE

Broadly defined, **rape** is an act of a sexual nature that is forced upon an unwilling person or that an unwilling person is forced to perform on someone else. Most commonly, rape refers to forced sexual intercourse in which a man's penis penetrates a woman's vagina. However, there are other forms of forced sexual violation: a man may have forcible anal intercourse with a woman or with another man; a woman or man may be forced to perform fellatio. The primary motive for rape is rarely sexual. Rather, rape is an act of aggression and violence reflecting a desire to control, degrade, and humiliate another person.

Different types of rape can be distinguished. **Acquaintance rape,** or date rape, is forced sexual intercourse or other forms of sexual activity between people who know each other. **Statutory rape** is intercourse with a female under the age of consent. The age of consent varies from state to state, but usually falls between 12 and 16. **Marital rape** refers to forced sexual intercourse or other forms of sexual activity between married partners.

Incidence and Prevalence

Rape has become increasingly widespread in the United States. Over 100,000 forcible rapes are reported each year. *Forcible rape* involves the use or threat of force, compared to nonconsensual sex, in which the victim is impaired by the use of alcohol or other drugs, developmentally disabled, or otherwise unable to give consent. The 100,000 figure is misleading, however, because rape is one of the most underreported crimes. Evidence indicates that only about 10 to 20 percent of all rapes are reported to authorities. Thus the number of rapes occurring each year is estimated to be considerably higher (U.S. Federal Bureau of Investigation, 1990; 1989; 1988; U.S. Bureau of the Census, 1990; 1989; Riesenberg, 1987).

In relation to the underreported incidence of rape, a 1992 government-financed survey estimated that 683,000 adult women were raped in 1990. The National Women's Study estimated that 12.1 million women have been the victims of rape at least once in their life and that 61 percent of the survivors said they had been raped as minors. The estimate of the number of rapes in 1990 did not include female children and adolescents, or rapes of boys or men. The survey included interviews with over 4,000 women who were chosen to represent a cross-section of all adult women in the United States (Johnston, 1992).

What exactly constitutes rape?

rape An act of a sexual nature that is forced upon an unwilling person or that an unwilling person is forced to perform on someone else.

acquaintance rape Rape that occurs between people who know each other.

statutory rape Sexual assault on a minor.

marital rape Sexual assault in which a wife is forced by her husband to engage in sexual intercourse or other forms of sexual activity against her will.

Rape is essentially a young man's crime. Most men arrested for rape are between 20 and 24. The next largest group is between the ages of 15 to 19. In fact, male adolescents from 12 to 19 commit almost one-quarter of the rapes and attempted rapes against victims of all ages (Davis & Leitenberg, 1987). We list here some other facts about rape gathered from a number of sources (U.S. Federal Bureau of Investigation, 1990; 1989, 1988; U.S. Bureau of the Census, 1990; 1989; Grauerholz & Solomon, 1989; Koss, Gidycz, & Wisniewski, 1987):

- In the United States a rape occurs approximately every six minutes.
- Rape has increased more rapidly in the last decade than any other type of violent crime.
- One out of every four girls born in the United States will be raped at some point in her life.

MYTHS AND MISCONCEPTIONS

Myths About Rape

Many myths about rape create confusion, uncertainty, and erroneous notions about what rape is, who gets raped, who the rapist is, and where the crime is likely to occur. In an effort to dispel some of these myths, the Los Angeles Commission on Assaults Against Women (1983) has supplied the following information:

It could never happen to me. All women are potential rape victims. This means women of any age, race, class, religion, occupation, education, or physical description.

Most rapes are a "spur of the moment" act in a dark alley by a stranger. Rape often occurs in one's home. Very often the offender is a relative, friend, neighbor, or other acquaintance of the victim. Most rapes are carefully planned, and rapists tend to be repeat offenders, generally in the same area of town and in the same manner.

Rape is primarily a sexual crime. Rape is a violent assault that is acted out, in part, sexually. Through psychological and physical abuse, it violates not only the victim's personal integrity but also her sense of safety and control over her life. Many men who rape see sex solely as an act of male domination. They engage in assaultive sex for the sense of power it gives them.

Most rapes are interracial. The overwhelming majority of rapes (more than 9 out of 10) involve persons of the same race or culture.

Rape is a nonviolent crime. Rape is a violent crime. About 87 percent of rapists either carry a weapon or threaten the victim with violence or death. Often the rape is accompanied by a great deal of verbal abuse and other physical abuse.

There is no way to protect oneself against sexual assault. In self-defense classes women can learn to be alert, avoid danger, and use physical skills like karate. But police authorities often warn against taking the offensive lest a failed effort at self-defense further enrage an already angry attacker.

Women are "asking for it" by their dress or actions. Research shows that rapists attack available targets they perceive as vulnerable, not women who dress in a particular way. No woman is asking to be hurt or degraded because of the way she acts or dresses, just as no man is asking to be robbed because he is wearing a good suit and carrying money in his wallet. Rape is the responsibility of the rapist, not the victim.

It is not really possible to rape a nonconsenting adult. It is indeed possible to rape a nonconsenting adult. Fear of death, threat of violence, or physical brutality can immobilize anyone.

Sexual Coercion: Rape

- Twenty-five percent of female undergraduates in the United States have suffered an experience that meets the legal definition of rape. Fifty-four percent of college women have been sexually victimized.
- One out of every seven American women who have ever been married have been raped by a husband or ex-husband.
- In approximately half of all forcible rape cases, the victim is known to the rapist.
- An estimated 250,000 to 500,000 rapes are unreported.
- Most rapes occur between 8 P.M. and 2 A.M.
- The peak months for forcible rape are from May to October.
- About three-quarters of rapists do not leave their own neighborhoods to seek out their victims.

The high-risk ages for rape victims are between 13 and 24. However, rape has been reported in girls as young as 5 months and women as old as 91 years. Black women are much more vulnerable to rape than are white women. The risk of rape is so high for black women that elderly black women (aged 65 to 85) are just as likely to be raped as young white women (aged 16 to 19). Also, married women are about one-quarter less likely to have been raped than never-married or divorced women, and widows are nearly ten times less likely to have experienced rape than women who have never married (Matlin, 1987).

Social and psychological factors undoubtedly contribute to the underreporting of rape. Feminist theory contends that gender-role stereotyping, sexual conservatism, widespread acceptance of myths about rapes, and social acquiescence in sexual violence against women have created an atmosphere that encourages the beliefs that real rape is uncommon, and that when it does happen, it was provoked by the victim (Grauerholz & Solomon, 1989; Check & Malamuth, 1983; Shotland & Goodstein, 1983; Burt, 1980; Clark & Lewis, 1977).

One of the many misconceptions about rape is that a man cannot be raped. (For some other false notions about rape, see the "Myths and Misconceptions" box.) Men and boys *can* be the victims of sexual assault, as we'll see later in the chapter. Reported male victims are usually young children or prison inmates, and the assailant is another male. Male victims are unlikely to report the rape. Older adults are another group who are unlikely to report having been sexually assaulted, probably because of extreme embarrassment and shame. People with physical and mental disabilities make up yet another underreported group (Weinstein & Rosen, 1988a).

Socialization of Victims and Rapists

According to Diana Russell (1975), women have been socialized to become vulnerable to rape. They are seen as physically weak and in need of male assistance to carry heavy packages or open doors. Such a weak person could not possibly fend off a 200-pound attacker. Women are also socialized into a nurturant role; their destiny is supposed to be taking care of others' needs and offering sensitive understanding. How could such a sensitive, caring creature fight off a would-be rapist by kicking him in the groin or gouging his eyes?

The "ladylike" behavior urged upon girls and women perversely works against successful prosecution of rape. Often the first thing a raped woman does is to take a shower so as to appear neat and clean; thus she inadvertently destroys the evidence of her rape. (Hopefully, with more education, women victims will refrain from washing away the evidence.) Fear, a socialized reaction, also contributes to female victimization. Women and girls are so indoctrinated to fear sexual crimes that when one is attempted against them, they often become too paralyzed by fear to try to fight off their attacker (Grauerholz & Solomon, 1989; Weis & Borges, 1973).

On the other hand, traditional male socialization has created a climate in which some men confuse sexuality with aggression (Sanday, 1986; Kanin, 1985; Box, 1983; Russell, 1975). In these men the characteristics traditionally associated with masculinity—dominance, power, aggressiveness, and physical strength—have become linked to the idea that men must dominate in sexual activity and women must be weak, passive, and subservient. Male socialization processes work to pressure men into "proving" their masculinity. For some men, that proof takes the form of raping a woman. Some also feel that such an act establishes their heterosexuality—another important component of traditional manliness.

There is a body of research on the hypersexual socialization to which many groups of male college students subject their peers. College men are often pressured and rewarded for being sexually active. Eugene Kanin (1985), for example, found that 41 percent of acquaintance rapists studied, compared to only 7 percent of a control group, had been involved in a "gang-bang." Also, 67 percent of the date rapists compared to only 13 percent of the control group had participated in intercourse with a woman recommended by friends as sexually willing or easy. Socialization for sexual hyperactivity often sets goals for sexual intercourse at unachievable levels, something that promotes acquaintance rape. In Kanin's research control subjects were satisfied with an average number of 2.8 orgasms per week, but acquaintance rapists set the much higher goal of 4.5.

It would seem that traditional socialization processes often program females to be victims of rape and males to be rapists. This socialization takes place in both subtle and direct ways. We must reshape such socialization processes to make this world a safe place for all of humanity.

PERSONALITY CHARACTERISTICS OF RAPISTS

The defiance and utter lack of remorse shown by this convicted rapist as he is taken off to jail makes this picture especially disturbing.

While no two rapists are alike, it is possible to establish a general personality profile of men who rape. In general, they are not "oversexed, strong, macho men"; rather, they are angry men who cannot handle their hostility effectively. Many rapists are ineffectual in interpersonal relationships. While a small percentage of them would be considered mentally ill because of their other behavior, most of them appear to be basically normal (Ledray, 1986).

Many rapists have a history of violent conduct, often including prior arrests for rape and/or assault and battery. Many were abused as children, either sexually, physically, or emotionally. Rapists also tend to suffer from a sense of worthlessness and low self-esteem. They often lack effective life management skills and consequently do not feel in control of their lives (Benedict, 1985).

The typical rapist is a loner. Lacking inner resources, he places a premium on aggression and sexuality to assert himself. Thus he perceives aggression as necessary to his psychological survival and deploys it in the form of manipulation, intimidation, and domination. Finding normal sexuality psychologically threatening because it creates feelings of vulnerability, he comes to regard sex as a means by which he can aggress against others to achieve control (Groth & Hobson, 1983).

What are some of the motivations behind rape? Do all rapists experience the same emotions? A. Nicholas Groth and William Hobson (1983) have proposed that rapists can be classified according to the motivational intent underlying the assault as well as the dynamics of the offense. On these bases, they identify three types of rapists: the anger, power, and sadistic rapists.

The Anger Rapist

The **anger rapist** typically engages in unpremeditated, savage physical attacks that are prompted by feelings of hatred and resentment and are usually characterized by excessive and uncontrolled violence. The anger rapist is usually not in a state of sexual arousal, has not had rape fantasies, may have difficulties achieving or sustaining an erection, and does not find the rape sexually gratifying. The anger rapist will usually encounter his victim on foot and commit the crime in the general vicinity of his home, place of work, or routine routes of travel (which suggests some degree of premeditation). The location of encounter, assault, and release are usually all the same.

Anger rapes tend to be associated with alcohol abuse. The rape occurs in response to some triggering event, and although the offender is not motivated by sexual desire, he discharges his anger sexually. For example, some form of rejection from another person or failure at work may initiate the anger and prompt the rapist to go out and hurt someone. Thus he uses sex as a weapon, a means of hurting, humiliating, and degrading someone.

anger rapist A rapist who engages in unpremeditated savage attacks that are prompted by feelings of hatred and resentment.

The Power Rapist

The **power rapist** uses intimidation and force to achieve the sexual submission of his victim. The rape is typically preceded by fantasies of sexual domination and activated by some challenge to the rapist's sense of authority or some threat to his feelings of adequacy—perhaps at work or at home. The sexual assault is thus an expression of the power rapist's dominance, mastery, and virility. Prodded by deep-seated feelings of insecurity and vulnerability, he attempts to reverse the situation by placing his victim in a position of helplessness.

To get his victim to submit, the power rapist may use verbal threats, intimidation with a weapon, or physical aggression. The power rapist's intention is not specifically to hurt the victim but to achieve control over her. His mood state is not one of anger, but of anxiety or fear. His offenses are premeditated in that he has rehearsed such crimes in fantasy.

The use of a weapon gives the power rapist a greater feeling of power and control. Because his rapes are preplanned, he often conceals his identity by wearing a disguise or blindfolding the victim. The victim is often raped more than once or forced into a variety of sexual acts. However, the power rapist tends to find the rape sexually unsatisfying, and as a result tends to repeat the offense in a continuing effort to assert himself.

power rapist A rapist who uses intimidation and force as a means of achieving his victim's sexual submission.

The Sadistic Rapist

The **sadistic rapist** uses sexual assault as a preplanned and aggressive ritual, frequently involving torture, bondage, and other forms of sexual abuse. For the sadistic rapist, aggression and sexuality are inseparable, and his violent acts are often directed specifically at the sexual parts of his victim's body. For instance, he may burn his victim's breasts, buttocks, or genitals with cigarettes.

The sadistic rapist seems to be caught up in a kind of compulsive ritual in which the victim symbolizes some person or force that he wishes to control, punish, or destroy. He experiences the rape as the result of inner forces over which he has no control. In some cases, he may kill his victim first, finding his dying exciting and satisfying, and only then commit the rape.

The victims of a particular sadistic rapist often all have similar characteristics. It may be their age, appearance, or profession (prostitutes appear to be at high risk for

sadistic rapist A rapist who uses sexual assault as a preplanned and aggressive ritual, frequently involving torture, bondage, and other forms of sexual abuse.

such victimization). The rapist often employs some instrument of restraint (gag, tape, handcuffs, etc.) and/or abuse, as well as a weapon. He may also render his victim helpless by strangling or suffocating her into unconsciousness.

THE EFFECT OF RAPE ON THE VICTIM

No two rapes are identical and no two people respond to rape in exactly the same way. Most victims report a mixture of fear, terror, panic, and confusion during the actual attack. Some women talk to their attackers during the rape, promising anything, bargaining for freedom, or just trying to make the attacker believe that they should be allowed to live. Some women attempt to focus on a past experience in an effort to mentally block out the trauma. Some women fight. Others attempt to flee. Some focus on their attacker, cataloging every detail that might be helpful to the police. Many victims are physically sickened by rape and respond by vomiting, urinating, or defecating, either during or after the attack (Johnson, 1985; Kilpatrick, Resick, & Veronen, 1981). Some experts advise that any or all of these behaviors may act as a deterrent to rape.

One of the first things a rape victim must do is seek help—certainly a medical examination and treatment and, perhaps, assistance from law officers. The box entitled

MAKING USE OF WHAT WE KNOW

Guidelines for the Person Who Has Been Raped

*I*f you are ever raped, it is important that you get medical attention immediately. The main reason, of course, is to ensure that any injuries caused by the rape are treated—including injuries you may not be aware of. Seek medical help even if you do not plan to report the rape to the police. The following guidelines and suggestions may help you:

- Go to a safe place and try to regain your emotional stability. If possible, call a friend to accompany you to the hospital. You might also want to call the nearest Rape Crisis Center to have a counselor accompany you as well.

- Save all the evidence of the rape, taking special care not to contaminate or alter it until the crime has been reported to a doctor or hospital.

- Do not shower, bathe, wash your hands, brush your teeth, or use the toilet.

- Do not remove semen from the vagina, anal, or oral areas.

- Do not change or destroy your clothing.

- Save any evidence of the rapist's hair, fingernails, clothes, and so forth.

- Most experts recommend reporting a rape to the police. If this is your

choice, be prepared to provide the following information:
—A description of the rapist, including height, age, hair color, eyes, facial and other noticeable features such as accent, speech, and mannerisms.
—The rapist's means of travel.
—How and where the assault took place.

- Undergo an immediate medical examination. This may be done by your personal physician or a physician at the nearest hospital, but it must be performed as soon as possible after the assault. Pregnancy and sexually transmitted disease tests will be conducted during the examination. You may be given penicillin to prevent infection with certain sexually transmitted diseases.

- Submit to a private in-depth interview so you can get all the assistance you need to recall the incident and detail the assailant's appearance, speech, mannerisms, and any visible injuries he may have. These details are essential for identification of the assailant and for the thorough presentation of evidence in court. (Adapted from Johnson, 1985; Sorochan, 1981; Los Angeles Commission on Assaults Against Women, 1983)

Sexual Coercion: Rape

"Guidelines for the Person Who Has Been Raped" offers some suggestions for dealing with the immediate and primarily physical effects of rape.

The more psychological effects of rape have been conceptualized by Ann Burgess and Lynda Holmstrom (1985, 1974) as the **rape trauma syndrome.** This syndrome, which encompasses the many aspects of a victim's life that are affected by the experience of rape—psychological, social, physical, and specifically sexual—is divided into two phases: the acute and the long-term reorganization phases. In examining each of these phases, we will draw also on the American Psychiatric Association's category of *post-traumatic stress disorder* (*Diagnostic and Statistical Manual*, 1987). In this type of disorder a person who has suffered a sudden emotionally distressing and painful event is affected by a number of factors that are clearly present in the rape trauma syndrome.

rape trauma syndrome
The physical, psychological, social, and/or sexual disruption of a victim's life brought about by rape.

The Acute Phase: Stress and Symptoms

The acute phase can last from days to weeks and is characterized by such general response patterns as trembling, shaking, disbelief, and shock. Estelle Weinstein and Efrem Rosen (1988a) note that the degree of trauma experienced during this phase is influenced by the circumstances surrounding the assault, especially such factors as the amount of violence, the length of time over which the assault took place, the type of activities, and the number of attackers. Nancy Cerio's (1988) review of the literature indicates that during the acute phase rape victims often complain of a decrease in or loss of appetite, stomach pains, and nausea. Whether physically or psychologically harmed, victims of sexual violence often react initially with feelings of fear followed by anger. They may also feel embarrassment, shame, and guilt. Many victims initially blame themselves for the rape.

One woman shares her emotional reactions to being raped:

What's it like for a woman recovering from rape? What kinds of adjustment does she face?

> There's no way to describe what was going on inside me. I was losing control and I'd never been so terrified and helpless in my life. I felt as if my whole world had been kicked out from under me and I had been left to drift all alone in the darkness. I had horrible nightmares in which I relived the rape and others which were even worse. I was terrified of being with people and terrified of being alone. I couldn't concentrate on anything and began failing several classes. Deciding what to wear in the morning was enough to make me panic and cry uncontrollably. I was convinced I was going crazy, and I'm still convinced I almost did. (Warshaw, 1988, p. 68).

In this account we can see evidence of all four of the major factors in post-traumatic stress disorder: this woman had experienced a stressful event of significant magnitude; she continued to re-experience the event in nightmares; her interest in normal activities was diminished; and she showed unusual symptoms, such as lack of concentration, inability to make simple decisions, and the feeling that she was losing her mind. Let's look at these factors in a little more depth.

STRESSOR OF SIGNIFICANT MAGNITUDE. Rape victims have experienced an event that is outside the range of usual human experience, one that is markedly distressing and disruptive. As a stressor of significant magnitude, rape encompasses a wide range of stressful states, such as aggression, hatred, and degradation. A rape attack often heightens a woman's sense of helplessness, intensifies her conflicts about dependence and independence, generates self-criticism and guilt that devalue her as an individual, and interferes with her partner relationships. The stress that rape creates seriously erodes the victim's adaptive resources (Burgess & Holmstrom, 1985).

Sexual Coercion: Rape 601

Victims of rape may continue to experience fear, anger, depression, a sense of vulnerability, and many other negative feelings for years after being assaulted. Flashbacks, in which such victims relive their attacks in memory, are not uncommon.

INTRUSIVE IMAGERY. The victim of trauma often re-experiences the event. That is, images of the event intrude into the person's mind repeatedly and without warning, sometimes during waking hours, sometimes in dreams. Some women feel as if the traumatic event were actually recurring, and some report intense psychological distress at exposure to events that symbolize or resemble an aspect of the traumatic event.

NUMBING. Many victims of trauma develop a feeling of numbness or a reduced involvement with their environment. They try to shut out thoughts or feelings associated with the trauma, or to avoid activities or situations that arouse recollections of the trauma. Others are unable to recall an important aspect of the trauma, or feel detached or estranged from other people. Some experience a diminished interest in significant activities, a restricted range of feelings, or a sense of a foreshortened future.

SYMPTOMS. People experiencing post-traumatic stress disorders typically exhibit a range of symptoms not evident before the event. Common among rape victims are difficulty falling or staying asleep, irritability or outbursts of anger, difficulty concentrating, hypervigilance, and an exaggerated response to any sudden stimulus. Many people react physiologically when exposed to events that resemble in some way the traumatic event. For example, a woman who was raped in an elevator might break out in a sweat when entering any elevator.

The Long-Term Phase: Reorganization and Recovery

In the long-term reorganization phase women restore order to their lives and re-establish a sense of control over their world. This phase can last from months to years.

We are only now beginning to get a clearer picture of the long-term effects of rape. In general, research has revealed that stress-induced reactions gradually dissipate for many women. However, it is not uncommon for survivors to remain fearful or to display other adjustment difficulties up to one year after the assault. Indeed, one study (Bateman, 1986) showed that many victims hadn't fully recovered for as long as four to six years after the attack. Another study (Kilpatrick et al., 1985) compared patterns of adjustment among rape victims to those among victims of aggravated assault and other crimes. The rape survivors had more mental health problems, including greater suicidal tendencies.

FAMILY RESPONSE TO RAPE

Just as rape constitutes a crisis in the life of the victim, it often disrupts the equilibrium of a couple or a family. Sandra Burge (1983) observes that the family's response may be influenced by the stigma of rape as well as by the physical harm done to the victim, but that generally the experience of crisis depends on the victim's distress. That is, the more agitated a victim is, the more disruptive the rape will be for the family. The impact of the rape on the family causes family members to move through stages of shock and recovery in a manner similar to the victim's own experience. As a result, they may exhibit certain emotional responses and symptoms. Let's examine some of the more common ones.

ANGER AND REVENGE. The spouse or lover of a woman who has been raped often feels personally wronged and attacked by the defilement of his or her partner. Partners often have thoughts of revenge, thoughts that may serve to protect them from their own painful sense of helplessness. However, the rape victim should not have to bear the extra burden of dealing with her partner's anger and revenge.

GUILT. It is not uncommon for partners or parents of rape victims to experience considerable guilt and a sense of responsibility for the rape. Loved ones may feel that they have failed in their duties as protectors. Just as rape victims experience "if only" feelings ("if only I had stayed home," or "if only that window had been locked"), partners or parents may feel that lack of precautions on their part or a flaw in their behavior helped cause the sexual assault.

HELPLESSNESS. Frustration may mount among family members at not being able to "undo" the effects that the rape has had on the victim and themselves. Loss of control over the events in their lives often creates a feeling of helplessness and vulnerability. This, in turn, leaves the family grasping at random coping strategies in an effort to do something that will ease their frustration.

BLAME. Whenever a crime occurs, too often the victim is blamed. This seems to be especially true in the case of rape. While it can be argued that some rape victims used poor judgment and got themselves into situations where they were at risk, *no one has the right to assault another person sexually or to violate her or him in any other way*. Moreover, most victims of rape have *not* placed themselves in jeopardy, but have been taken by surprise and overwhelmed by superior strength and the threat of serious harm or death. Fortunately, people are becoming increasingly aware that the criminal, not the victim, is responsible for rape (Lawson & Hillix, 1985).

SEXUAL REVULSION. Feelings of revulsion on the part of a husband or lover may have a significant impact on sexual relations after a rape. The woman's partner may be repulsed by her experience for a variety of reasons. Some men feel that their wives have been dirtied or contaminated by the rapist. Others cannot seem to help thinking that the woman in some way desired the encounter. Sexual problems are common among rape victims and their partners. A sexual assault often reduces sexual activity levels. Moreover, it can cause both the woman and her partner to dwell on the event, triggering emotions such as sadness, anger, and depression.

SECRET KEEPING. Sometimes victims of sexual assault choose to keep their attack a secret, usually to protect themselves from the kind of negative feedback we have described. Anticipating the withdrawal of affection by loved ones, many victims not only bypass the legal reporting system but tell no one else of the rape. Or they choose to tell a few persons they believe will be supportive. One or more of these confidants may be family members who agree to keep the rape concealed from the rest of the family or from one particular member.

ACQUAINTANCE RAPE

My roommate was recently raped by a man she knew from work. Does this kind of acquaintance rape take place often, or are most rapists and their victims total strangers?

In acquaintance rape the rapist and victim know each other, at least casually. Often they have met through a common activity or a mutual friend, as neighbors, as students in the same class, at work, or while traveling. Or they may have met at a party or on a blind date. Sometimes they have a closer relationship—as steady dates or former sexual partners. While largely a hidden phenomenon because it's the least reported type of rape (and remember that rape, in general, is the most underreported violent crime), acquaintance rape is the most prevalent type of rape committed today (Parrot, 1988, 1986; Ledray, 1986; Warshaw, 1988; DeMaris, 1987; Yegidis, 1986).

Acquaintance rape can occur in many settings. The excitement of meeting someone for the first time can sometimes loosen normal restraints and lead to a situation in which a woman wants to stop but a man chooses to interpret her clear "no" as "yes."

Like other kinds of rape, acquaintance rape is an act of aggression and violence. Acquaintance rapists are motivated by the same kinds of forces that we discussed in the section on the personality characteristics of rapists. Thus acquaintance rape is often an attempt to assert anger or power. Acquaintance rape occurs more frequently among college students, especially freshmen, than in any other age group. However, it can occur to anyone, anywhere, at any time (Christopher, 1988; Muehlenhard, 1988). A college junior had these unpleasant memories:

> I was in good spirits and had been out to dinner with an old friend. We returned to his college dormitory. There were some seniors on the ground floor, drinking beer, playing bridge. I'm an avid player, so we joined them, and joked around a lot. One of them, John, wasn't playing, but he was interested in the game. I found him attractive. We talked, and it turned out we had a mutual friend, and shared experiences. It was getting late, and my friend had gone up to bed, so John offered to see me safely home. We took our time, sat outside talking for a while. Then he said we could get inside one of the most beautiful campus buildings, which was usually locked at night. I went with him. Once we were inside, he kissed me. I didn't resist, I was excited. He kissed me again. But when he tried for more, I said no. He just grew completely silent. I couldn't get him to talk to me anymore. He pinned me down and ripped off my pants. I couldn't believe it was happening to me. (Sweet, 1985, p. 56)

Studies of Acquaintance Rape Among College Students

One extensive study of over 6,000 college men and women (Warshaw, 1988) revealed that about one-quarter of the women had been the victims of rape or attempted rape and nearly 90 percent of them knew their assailants. Almost 60 percent of the rapes happened on dates. Among the other findings:

- For both men and women, the average age when a rape incident occurred (either as perpetrator or victim) was 18½ years.
- One in 12 of the male students surveyed had committed acts that met the legal definitions of rape or attempted rape.
- More than 80 percent of the rapes occurred off-campus, with more than 50 percent on the man's territory, such as in his home or his car.
- Only 27 percent of the women whose sexual assault met the legal definition of rape thought of themselves as rape victims.
- 42 percent of the rape victims told no one about their assaults.
- Only 5 percent reported their rapes to the police.
- Only 5 percent sought help at rape crisis centers.
- 42 percent of the women who were raped said they had sex again with the men who assaulted them.
- 55 percent of the men who raped said they had sex again with their victims.
- 41 percent of the raped women said they expected to be raped again.

If the sexual assaults reported in this study met the legal definitions of rape, why do you suppose that so many victims didn't think they had been raped, had sex again with the men who had assaulted them, and expected to be raped again? Is the traditional male notion that women "really want to be overpowered" right? Or is it that women—who as we saw in Chapter 1 still have less independence and power in society than men—not only fail to assert their rights, needs, and wishes, but sometimes even fail to recognize them? The box on "How to Prevent Acquaintance

MAKING USE OF WHAT WE KNOW

How to Prevent Acquaintance Rape

*T*here is no foolproof way to prevent acquaintance rape, but the following suggestions can help reduce your risk of being victimized:

For Women:

- *Know your sexual desires and limits.* Believe in your right to set those limits. If you are not sure, stop and talk about it.

- *Communicate your limits clearly.* If someone starts to offend you, tell him so firmly and early. Polite approaches may be misunderstood or ignored. *Say "no" when you mean "no."*

- *Be assertive.* Often men interpret timidity as permission. Be direct and firm with someone who is sexually pressuring you.

- *Be aware that your nonverbal actions send a message.* If you dress in a "sexy" manner and flirt, some men may assume you want to have sex. This does not make your dress or behavior wrong, but it is important to be aware of possible misunderstandings. It's not specifically *wrong* to dress to show off your attractiveness, but you must be aware that it can be *risky*.

- *Pay attention to what is happening around you.* Be alert to nonverbal clues. Do not put yourself in vulnerable situations.

- *Trust your intuitions.* If you feel you are going to be pressured into unwanted sex, you probably are.

- *Avoid excessive use of alcohol and drugs.* Alcohol and drugs interfere with clear thinking and effective communication.

For Men:

- *Being turned down when you ask for sex is not a rejection of you personally.* Women who say "no" to sex are not rejecting the person; they are expressing their desire not to participate in a single act. You may not be able to control your desires, but you *can* control your actions.

- *Accept the woman's decision.* "No" means "no." Don't read other meanings into the answer. Don't continue after "no!"

- *Don't assume that just because a woman dresses in a "sexy" manner and flirts that she wants to have sexual intercourse.* As we've said earlier in the book, nonverbal messages are subject to misinterpretation and misunderstanding.

- *Don't assume that previous permission for sexual contact applies to the current situation.* Sexual intimacy should be a mutually acceptable arrangement that reflects sensitivity toward a partner's desires, wishes, and feelings. Given such guiding principles, sexual intimacy is open to negotiation as the relationship develops.

- *Avoid excessive use of alcohol and drugs.* Alcohol and drugs interfere with clear thinking and effective communication. (American College Health Association, 1987)

Rape" may give you some clues about how women and men can learn to communicate their true wishes more clearly to each other.

Another research study undertaken by Bonnie Yegidis (1986) showed that about 10 percent of the college women studied were at risk of sexual victimization by their dates in a given year. A total of 22 percent of these women reported being subjected to a forced sexual encounter by a date at some point in their lives. The study showed that most of the force took the form of verbal pressure by the man to "go further" because of sexual need, arousal, or love. A small percentage of women reported successfully warding off the assault by saying no or by offering physical resistance. Others did not resist because they "felt intimidated."

Another research study (Koss, Gidycz, & Wisniewski, 1987) supplies us with a comprehensive look at sexual aggression and victimization on college campuses in the United States. A total of 6159 male and female students in 32 colleges and universities were surveyed, and responses showed that: (1) 54 percent of the women had been sexually victimized; (2) one in four of the women had been raped, and 84 percent of those women knew the rapist; (3) only 57 percent of the raped women had reported the incident to the police; (4) one in 12 men (8.5 percent) admitted that they had committed acts that met the legal definition of rape; (5) only one man who admitted such acts realized his behavior constituted rape; and (6) 25 percent of the men admitted to sexually aggressive behavior.

The relationship between alcohol use and acquaintance rape and sexual assault among college students has been noted by several researchers (Martin & Hummer, 1989; Parrot, 1988; Ehrhart & Sandler, 1985; Miller & Marshall, 1987). Jean Hughes and Bernice Sandler (1987) found that many victims said later that they drank too much or took too many drugs to realize what was going on; by the time they recognized their predicament, it was too late.

A recent study (O'Shaughnessey & Palmer, 1990) found that when sexual assaults and criminal sexual abuse occurred, approximately 74 percent of the women and 81 percent of the men had been drinking. Of the women who had been drinking prior to the sexual assault, 63 percent reported that their judgment was either moderately or severely impaired, while 51 percent of the men reported their judgment was moderately or severely impaired prior to their act of sexual assault. The victims of sexual assault who reported drinking before the incident were almost all (94 percent) under the age of 21, and 46 percent were drinking at a bar or in a fraternity house.

Fraternities seem to contribute substantially to sexual assault and sexual abuse. In the O'Shaughnessey and Palmer (1990) study, considered by many to be a landmark investigation regarding fraternity membership and sexual violence, it was discovered that 63 percent of the men who reported having committed a sexual assault were fraternity members, and of the sexual abuse cases, 71 percent involved fraternity members. Add to this finding the number of victims who reported drinking in a fraternity prior to the sexual incident and we have a dismal picture of fraternity life on college campuses. Little is known about the reasons for this overrepresentation of fraternity men among sexual violators, but Martin and Hummer (1989) offer this conclusion:

> An analysis of the norms and dynamics of this social construction of fraternity brotherhood reveals the highly masculinist features of fraternity structure and process, including concern with a narrow, stereotypical conception of masculinity and heterosexuality; a preoccupation with loyalty, protection of a group, ... the use of alcohol as a weapon against women's sexual reluctance; the pervasiveness of violence and physical force; and an obsession with competition, superiority, and dominance. (p. 549)

Other researchers (Hughes & Sandler, 1987) maintain that "mixed signals" are an important element in acquaintance rape. By this they mean the woman acts in a friendly manner, and the man interprets her behavior as an invitation to have sex. "No" is read as "maybe," and even a strong protest is ignored under the delusion that women customarily say "no" when they really mean "yes." Sometimes a woman is not clear in her own mind about what she wants or she may think that she will make up her mind as she goes along. If she changes her mind at some point and decides not to engage in sexual relations, the man may feel rejected and angry. Some men interpret her nonverbal messages, such as her enjoyment of kissing and caressing, as meaning that she automatically wants to have intercourse. At this point the man may decide he has been teased or misled and "deserves" sexual intimacy, regardless of the woman's wishes.

According to Hughes and Sandler (1987), although acquaintance rape is usually a spontaneous act, it is often planned, from hours to even days in advance. Some men definitely intend to have sex with a woman, even if they have to force her. These

606   **Sexual Coercion: Rape**

men have usually forced sex on a woman before and gotten away with it. They typically seek out a woman who is unassertive, perhaps someone who is not very popular and would be flattered to go on a date with them. Most of these men do not see themselves as sexual offenders. On the contrary, they characterize themselves as just "out to have a good time."

Eliminating Sexual Violence on the Campus

Mary Roark (1989) has proposed a set of interventions that colleges and universities might well consider in attempting to end sexual violence among the college population. Borrowing from the field of public health, Roark proposes three levels of prevention. In *primary prevention* the long-term aim is to stop the occurrence of sexual assaults by searching for their causes and attempting to change the attitudes and behaviors that promote sexual violence. The goal of *secondary prevention* is more immediate: to identify existing situations that promote sexual violence and to help potential victims learn ways of avoiding sexual assault. *Tertiary prevention* has even more immediate goals: to alleviate the pain and distress of the person who has already been victimized and to bring the offender to justice.

Table 20–1 outlines some of the major steps proposed by Roark for each of these types of prevention. As you examine this table, ask yourself whether your college

Many women who have been the victims of rape or other physical attack—and many others who have not—study self defense in an effort to protect themselves in the future. For women police such as these New York City officers, karate classes are mandatory.

TABLE 20–1

Dealing with Sexual Violence on College and University Campuses: Three Levels of Prevention

PRIMARY PREVENTION

- Teach campus constituents about various forms of sexual and personal violence and offer frequent public presentations on the topic of sexual violence.
- Increase awareness of the social conditions that promote sexual assault.
- Publish and distribute material on all facets of sexual violence, including acquaintance rape and sexual harassment.
- Encourage faculty to address aspects of sexual violence in their classes.
- Ask the president of the university or college to issue a clear, consistent, and firm statement of policy that establishes the institution's stance as prohibiting all forms of sexual violence.

SECONDARY PREVENTION

- Identify areas of security risks in the environment and take action to remedy them.
- Inform students about campus security risks, about ways to minimize personal danger, and about the instructional measures established for their protection. Encourage them to report attacks of aggression and ensure their confidentiality.
- Make training in self-defense available to women faculty and students.
- Establish a campus-wide task force on issues of personal safety and a formal system of collecting and recording data on incidents of campus violence.
- Create a campus resource center to provide information on sexual violence, including available services and support systems.

TERTIARY PREVENTION

- Offer help to the victims of sexual violence through immediate and long-term medical services, counseling, and support groups.
- Establish procedures for reporting sexual violence that are sensitive and readily available.
- Provide protective security services to stop any repeat of sexual assault.
- Involve civil authorities, when appropriate, with accompanying support from campus personnel.
- Establish and/or cooperate with a rape crisis center or volunteer sexual assault service.
- Create reporting mechanisms that fit local needs.

Source: Adapted from Roark (1989).

or university has established any of the procedures recommended. If you don't know whether it has, find out. And if your school has not already instituted some or all of these measures, consider asking the administrators to begin planning for these strategies.

Acquaintance rape has devastating effects on the victims. In the 1990 O'Shaughnessey and Palmer study it was reported that women who were sexually assaulted by someone they knew were slightly more likely to express shame, guilt, feelings of stupidity, and anger at themselves than they were to express hatred, disgust, or anger at the men who had violated them. They also tended to fear and mistrust men, and even people in general. Many indicated that they had learned a bad lesson the hard way and were smarter and more careful now. They tended to have difficulties in subsequent romantic relationships with other men, and to fear or be repelled by sex. Many tried to block the event out of their minds, to forget what had happened to them.

The long-term consequences for women who have been sexually abused or assaulted by male acquaintances are also serious. When negative attitudes about themselves persist, these women may drop out of school, ruining a potentially rewarding career. Worse, they may face life with reduced self-esteem.

In short, acquaintance rape has devastating effects on women. We must do everything we can to prevent it from happening, to deal with every incident that does occur appropriately, and to provide compassionate support for women who have been victimized. Roark has some good suggestions for what individuals can do to change the present climate in which sexual violence has become so common:

1. Learn to take care of your own safety needs. Clear communication is the best protection. Speak up for what you want and don't want. Identify the behaviors you will accept and those you will not. Clarify what you mean and what you don't mean. Speak up early, clearly, and repeatedly, if necessary.

2. If you must drink, do so judiciously and be alert to the effects of alcohol use and abuse.

3. Relax stereotypes about appropriate gender-role behaviors, both in your own life and in your expectations of others. Gender-role socialization processes promote violence when men are encouraged to be aggressive and women to be submissive.

4. Learn to resist the inappropriate use of personal, physical, or institutional power. Sexual violence is typically more about power than it is about sex.

5. Be aware of prejudice and take steps to counteract it whenever possible.

6. Report sexual offenses immediately.

7. Take a stand against violence whenever it occurs or is portrayed in films or other media.

MARITAL RAPE

Is there such a thing as marital rape? Is it a violation of the law?

A type of rape receiving much attention in recent years is marital rape, a sexual assault in which a woman is forced by her husband to have sexual intercourse or other forms of sexual activity against her will. There are approximately 1.8 million battered wives in the United States and a large percentage of these women are also victims of marital rape. In an investigation conducted by Irene Frieze (1983), 37 percent of the women who had been beaten by their husbands had also been raped by them. Although many of these women did not use the word "rape" to describe what had happened to them in their marriages, they did admit that their husbands had forced sex upon them. A 23-year-old wife recalled how she was sexually assaulted by her husband:

> I wasn't interested in having sex and he wanted to. He said, "This is what we're going to do." I'd say there was some force. He'd had a few drinks or maybe we were fighting.... Another time it was kind of half and half. This second time we were arguing and it wasn't like the first time, but still, I felt he forced himself on me. I guess the difference is sometimes a man wants to have sex and you don't, so he just imposes it on you. But there's not anger or violence or meanness; it's just having his way. In the first instance there was anger there, and a sense of violence and his wanting to degrade me. I felt like I'd really been raped.... My memory of it is that we were arguing about something—I don't know what. I was probably putting him down for something he did, and I probably refused to have sex. Then I remember he said, "Well, I'm gonna have sex, and you are too, whether you like it or not." It's like I couldn't get away—that he'd hit me if I tried to leave.... (Russell, 1982, p. 49).

Many states do not have laws against marital rape, but a growing number of people believe it should be a crime subject to prosecution. At present, in over half of our states it is not legally considered a rape when a husband forces his wife to have intercourse. In several states marital rape is not a crime even when the husband and wife are separated.

Why isn't marital rape a crime in so many states? According to Estelle Weinstein and Efrem Rosen (1988a), implicit in the civil marriage contract is the belief that men have the right to have sex with their wives whenever they so desire. Within marriage women who do not comply can be forced to do so because participating in sexual intercourse and other sexual acts is the woman's duty, with no right of refusal. Such acts may therefore not be viewed as rape by the husband, or even by the wife. The difficulty of specifying what constitutes marital rape has prevented the establishment of a uniform legal code in this area.

When Diane Russell (1982) investigated 930 women in San Francisco, she discovered that one in seven of those who had ever been married had been raped by husbands or ex-husbands. Her analysis distinguished between rape by force, rape by threat of force, and rape because the woman was unable to consent (e.g., because she was drugged). Physical force was employed in 84 percent of the marital rapes; in 9 percent rape occurred by threat of force; and in 5 percent the action was categorized as rape because the woman was unable to consent. Two percent of the rapes did not fit into any of these categories. In one case of anal rape the woman was taken by surprise, and in another case the husband used a combination of force (tying up and slapping the woman), threat of force, and rendering the woman unable to consent (by drugging her). The overwhelming majority of marital rapes involving vaginal penetration—82 percent—were completed as compared with 8 percent that were not completed. Seven percent of all the assaults involved forced oral or anal sex, and two percent were attempted forced oral or anal sex.

Russell found several reasons why some rapes were not completed. Sometimes the husband was unable to obtain or maintain an erection; sometimes he abandoned his aim of using violence to force his wife to have sex and instead used it to punish her for refusing to have sex; and sometimes the woman was able to escape or was successful in overcoming the assault.

In another study (Finkelhor & Yllo, 1988) of 50 women whose husbands or cohabiting partners had forced sex upon them, three categories of rape emerged: battering, nonbattering, and obsessive rapes. Most of the women studied were typical battered women. That is, they had been subjected to a great deal of physical and verbal abuse, most of it unrelated to sex, by men who often had alcohol and other drug problems. The researchers observed that sexual violence was simply another aspect of the general abuse these women endured.

Where rape was considered nonbattering, little physical violence was reported in the marriages. At some point, though, a sexual conflict spilled over into violence. The man decided he was being denied and frustrated and that he was going to get what he wanted by force.

A few women reported that their husbands were obsessed with sex. These men tended to be heavily involved in pornography and were extremely demanding of sex from the start of the marriage. These wives reported having sex several times a day to keep their husbands satisfied. As the marriages progressed, the husband's sexual demands became more and more unusual and sadistic.

Making Use of What We Know

Staying Alert to the Danger Signals of Marital Rape

Signs that a troubled marriage (or relationship) is about to erupt in sexual violence often go unnoticed by the woman. Benedict (1985) has described several ways to recognize the potential in a man for sexual abuse. The key to a nonabusive relationship is equal love and respect between partners. In the descriptions that follow, you will find a lack of both. These signs don't mean that the man is definitely going to resort to beating or raping his partner eventually, but they are clear warning signs.

- Does the man seem to especially like sex when his partner doesn't? Has he ever forced sex on her? If he has raped his partner or forced sexual acts on her in any way in the past, he'll almost certainly do it again. He has shown himself to be a man who doesn't care about his partner's needs and desires, only about his own. He won't improve with time.

- Does a man want his partner to perform sex acts the partner really doesn't like? Is he particularly fond of bondage or violence in sex? His tastes won't change as the relationship progresses, so the woman is well advised to get out of it before his preferences turn to rape or torture. Does the man like violent pornography? This may be a sign that he will want to act out some of these scenes with his partner.

- Is the man overpossessive and extremely jealous? Someone who is obsessed by his partner is probably unstable. It may seem flattering to be needed so much, but obsessive need is almost always unhealthy. Does he have temper tantrums? There are appropriate and inappropriate ways to express anger. If he is angry at someone or something else but is in the habit of taking it out on his partner, this, too, is a danger signal.

- Does the man drink too much and become violent when he's drunk? Drinking and other forms of drug abuse are frequently associated with domestic violence, and a person under the influence of drugs is virtually impossible to reason with.

- Has he been violent toward previous wives or girlfriends? If his current partner knows he has—though he will probably try to hide it—there is little hope that he'll change in his present relationship. Does he attack people physically? It is one thing to fight back in self-defense, but if a man is prone to losing his temper and suddenly lashing out at someone, he is not to be trusted.

- Has he ever hit or beaten his partner? Many women mistakenly believe that once a man has a made a commitment to them, he will change and treat them with more respect. If he has hit a partner before, he will most likely do it again.

- Does he want to control a partner's money? This is a serious factor, because the person who controls the money usually controls the relationship.

- Finally, how do his parents behave? Are they abusive to each other? Also look at how they communicate. If the parents don't get through to each other, the son probably won't know how to communicate either, and a relationship with him is likely to be difficult.

Helen Benedict (1985) acknowledges that all the explanations offered for why men rape their wives are speculative—indeed, there may be as many reasons for marital rape as there are men who do it. However, Benedict suggests the following motivations, many of which are intertwined:

- Some men do not see their wives as people with a right to say no to sex. They hold the traditional idea that a wife belongs to her husband, and that sex can occur whenever the husband wants, regardless of the wife's desires. These kinds of men do not see women as their equals, as people who have as much choice over their sex life as men do. Whether their partners desire them as much as they desire their partners does not seem to matter to them.
- Some men make their wives into symbols of all the people and things they hate and want to get back at.
- Some men are angry at their wives—perhaps at all women—and rape is their revenge.
- Some men feel threatened by their wives—by their intelligence, perhaps, or their independence—and want to gain some superiority by dominating them sexually.
- Some men believe, or fantasize, that their wives are interested in other men, and try to repossess their wives by raping them.
- Some men believe that their wives deny them sex too often and that they therefore have a right to take it by force.
- Some men think that getting sex is proof of their manhood, regardless of how they get it.

The box on "Staying Alert to the Danger Signals of Marital Rape" provides suggestions on how to prevent this type of sexual assault.

Kirsti Yllo and David Finkelhor (1985) label marital rape a vicious and brutal form of abuse. They contend that its victims endure intimate violation and experience trauma much like the victims of other types of sexual assault—yet their suffering remains the most silent because the assaults against them are not legally regarded as a crime in many states. Yllo and Finkelhor also feel that as long as marital rape remains legal, it can only be concluded that society condones it—which must be interpreted as a degradation of all women. They propose that criminalizing marital rape, while by no means a real solution to the problem, would be an important symbolic step toward making this a safe society for women.

MALE RAPE

As indicated earlier, male rape can and does occur, although the incidence is low. The rape of one man by another usually involves anal intercourse and fellatio. Contrary to what many people believe, any man can be raped, regardless of his sexual orientation. And male rapists are not necessarily gay, nor are they raping out of lust. Remember, a rapist's motivation is to humiliate and hurt, not to release a sexual drive.

Although male rape victims are usually younger than female victims, the age range is just as wide. The main difference between male and female rape seems to be in the number of assailants and the amount of force used. Many male rape victims are attacked by groups of men and sustain more physical trauma than female victims. Those who come to the attention of the authorities may be a highly select group, however, since physical trauma is often what precipitates the attention. Many male victims initially go to a hospital emergency room to get treatment for the nongenital trauma and do not report the sexual assault itself, which is usually discovered only later. Male rape is more common in settings where women are absent, such as male prisons. As with men who rape women, men who rape other men are out to punish or control (Ledray, 1986).

Can men be raped by women?

While it is highly unusual, women can rape men. The notion that it is impossible for a man to respond sexually when he does not choose to is wrong. Male sexual responses can occur in a variety of emotional states, including fear and anger. There have been corroborated cases in which men were forced by one woman or a group of women to participate in sexual activity, including intercourse, under threat of physical violence. These men reported being restrained physically, and fearing not only for their safety, but also for their lives. Despite their fear, anxiety, embarrassment, and terror, they reported having had erections with no feeling of sexual desire (Ledray, 1986).

Male victims of rape encounter many of the same problems that female survivors face. Donald Cotton and A. Nicholas Groth's (1982) investigation of inmate rape in male correctional facilities indicates that there are often physical, psychological, social, and sexual consequences. Physical consequences may include injury and disease. Psychological distress may be manifested in anxiety, depression, shame, and anger. The man may experience flashbacks to, or a preoccupation with memories of, the assault, impaired ability to concentrate, and difficulty in attending to tasks. He may also feel vulnerable and inadequate, and his self-esteem may plummet. His relations with other people may be marked by distrust, withdrawal, isolation, or aggressiveness.

Cotton and Groth believe that the trauma of sexual assault may be even more psychologically devastating in some respects for a man than it is for a woman. Since sexual power as well as strength and aggressiveness are traditionally attributed to men in our society, the experience of being physically overpowered and sexually attacked devalues a man sexually. Also, since they have been socialized to believe a real man "fights his own battles," many male victims are unable to bring themselves to seek assistance in the form of rape crisis counseling. To ask for help would be yet another disgrace, so they suffer in terrible silence.

In addition to the usual reactions of self-blame and rage, families of male sexual assault victims, especially when the victims are children, are concerned about the victim's subsequent potential for homoeroticism. Hetero-erotic young men who have experienced "homosexual rape" also have fears about their sexual identity and may believe that they were selected because they were seen as "feminine." This feeling may cause them to become aggressive in an attempt to reassert or reconfirm their masculinity. They need to be reassured and educated about these myths (Weinstein & Rosen, 1988a).

TREATMENT AND THERAPY FOR RAPE VICTIMS

The rape trauma syndrome has many sides and does not disappear suddenly. As we indicated at the outset of this chapter, some facets of the trauma may never go away. For example, fear is a persistent problem for victims of sexual assault, as is depression, achieving satisfaction in sexual interactions, and maintaining stability and harmony in social relationships.

In order to overcome these and other adjustment problems, Linda Ledray (1986) emphasizes the importance of resolution and coping skills. Survivors need to accept the fact that the rape has occurred and that it cannot be undone. To put their lives back in order, victims need to evaluate their resources, choose the coping strategies they feel most comfortable with, and begin the process of resolution. While it is possible to do this on one's own, rape counseling and other therapeutic interventions tend to facilitate the adjustment process.

Burgess and Holmstrom (1985) believe that crisis intervention is the best immediate treatment for a rape victim. The basic assumptions underlying crisis intervention are: (1) rape is a crisis that severely disrupts the victim's life; (2) the victim is regarded as normal, that is, as functioning adequately prior to the rape; (3) the aim of crisis intervention is to return the victim to this normal level of functioning as quickly as possible. Crisis intervention is issue-oriented treatment designed to help rape victims deal with their anxiety, fear, depression, and loss of control and assertiveness.

Unless the issues unique to the crisis are resolved and integrated, the victim will fail to achieve a precrisis level of functioning. *Rape work* addresses these issues. Its aim is to assist the rape survivor to regain a sense of safety and self-worth, and to reestablish sharing, altruistic, mutually satisfying partner relationships in a world where rape remains a threat. The type and severity of rape survivors' responses, particularly the more long-term ones, are related to: (1) their general coping abilities; (2) their stage of psychological development; (3) their vulnerability; (4) their age; (5) the state of their mental health before the trauma; (6) the presence of supportive partners, family, and/or friends; and (7) the circumstances under which the assault occurred (Weinstein & Rosen, 1988).

Burgess and Holmstrom (1985) have proposed four models for counseling victims of rape. The *medical model* involves determining the extent of physical damage inflicted by the rape, making a medical diagnosis and prognosis, seeking criminal evidence, preventing possible disease, and arranging for appropriate follow-up. The *social network model* focuses on using victims' social network to strengthen their self-esteem and to help them return to normal daily routines. The *behavioral model* of counseling concentrates on helping victims to "unlearn" maladaptive behaviors, such as unwarranted fears and stresses, and to relearn self-confidence by dealing assertively with daily tasks and expectations. The *psychological model* seeks to help victims come to psychological terms with the assault, including its impact on their overall personality functioning.

It is important to include a victim's partner in counseling. Male partners of female rape victims usually benefit from therapeutic intervention since it helps them to deal with their anger, anxiety, and guilt (Bateman, 1986). Counselors usually encourage partners to express these and other feelings about the incident, help them to understand the meaning of the incident to the survivor, and educate them about

The New York City Police Department maintains a rape crisis van that brings assistance for the rape victim even closer than the NYPD's rape report line.

613

the violence and the victimization syndrome. They also offer individual counseling when needed (Gilbert & Cunningham, 1986).

Most women college students are away from home when they are raped, so it is very important that they be fully supported by their network of friends. Two-thirds of women tell someone about their assault. One survey (Golding et al., 1989) of 100 women survivors of sexual assault showed that most (59.6 percent) tell a friend or relative; some (16.1 percent) go on to inform mental health professionals, police (10.5 percent), physicians (9.3 percent), clergy (3.9 percent), rape crisis centers (1.9 percent), and legal professionals (1.6 percent). As you can see from these percentages, the only people most survivors of sexual assault turn to for support are family members and friends, so it is critical that these people demonstrate sensitive understanding. One source (Hughes & Sandler, 1987) maintains that survivors share certain common needs:

- *The need to feel safe*. Rape is a traumatic violation of a person. Victims often find it difficult to be alone afterward, especially in the beginning.
- *The need to be believed*. With date rape especially, victims need to be believed.
- *The need to know it was not their fault*. Most rape victims feel guilty and believe that the attack was somehow their fault.
- *The need to regain control of their lives*. When people are being raped, they feel they have lost complete control over what is happening to them. A significant step on the road to recovery is to regain a sense of control in the little, as well as big, things in life.

Family and friends can do a number of things to support a survivor of sexual assault (Hughes & Sandler, 1987):

- *Listen; do not judge*. It is not your place to play prosecutor and make her prove her story. Accept her version of the facts and be supportive. Many rape counseling services can be helpful to friends and relatives of rape victims in this area.
- *Offer shelter*. If it is at all possible, stay with her at her residence or let her spend at least one night at your place. This is not the time for her to be alone.
- *Be available*. She may need to talk at odd hours, or a great deal at the beginning. There may not be many people she *can* talk to, so she may overrely on one

Listening, understanding, and comforting a rape victim and supporting her in her decisions are part of helping her to regain her feeling of personal integrity, her sense of security, and her confidence in her own judgments.

614

person. Be there as much as you can and encourage her to either call a hotline or go for counseling.

- *Give comfort*. She has been badly treated. She needs to be nurtured.
- *Let her know she is not to blame*. This is crucial. Many rape victims blame themselves. She needs to be reassured that the rapist is at fault, not her.
- *Be patient and understanding*. Everyone has her own timetable for recovering from a rape. Do not impose one on the victim.
- *Do not be overly protective, though; encourage her to make her own decisions*. She needs to resume control of her life, and this will not be possible if you do everything for her.
- *Accept her choice of solution to the rape—even if you disagree with it*. It is more important that she make decisions and have them respected than it is for you to talk her into what you think is the "right" decision.
- *Put aside your feelings to deal with at a later time*. Although it is comforting to a rape survivor to know that others are as upset about what happened to her as she is, it does her no good if, on top of her feelings, she also has to deal with yours. If you feel enraged, talk to another friend or call a local hotline.

TREATMENT OF RAPISTS

We know that most rapists are repeat offenders, but despite numerous studies, we still don't know exactly *why* they rape. Thus we haven't been able to devise fully effective methods of treating and rehabilitating offenders. Consequently, they are recycled back into the community with no reduction in, or safeguards against, the risk they pose of repeating their sexual crimes.

One of the more successful and comprehensive treatment programs of sex offenders was developed by A. Nicholas Groth (1983). The program, emphasizing group treatment predicated guided self-help, and mutual assistance, includes reeducation, resocialization, and counseling.

Reeducation

The majority of sex offenders are uninformed or misinformed about human sexuality and tend to hold very conservative attitudes about sexual behavior. The *sex education* component of the program gives them a basic course on human sexuality.

Many sex offenders have stereotyped notions of what constitutes a sexual offender and do not regard themselves as falling into that category. Others are convinced that their sexual offenses were the result of alcohol abuse and that they need to address only their drinking problems in the recovery program. The component of the program called *understanding sexual assault* focuses on the dynamics of rape and child molestation; patterns of assault; the psychology of the offender, including his characteristic traits and behavior patterns; and the state of clinical knowledge about this form of pathological sexual behavior.

The majority of sex offenders have little realization of the consequences of their offenses for the victim. To the rapist, the victim is often an impersonal object he gives no thought to following the assault. He typically fails to realize the harm he did. The *victim personalization* aspect of the program emphasizes the immediate and long-term impact of various types of sexual assault on the victim, whether female or male, adult or child.

One method of showing a convicted rapist the devastating effect of his act is to confront him with those who have been raped by other offenders. This approach can be therapeutic for the victims, also, as they vent their rage and sense of violation on someone guilty of the same crime by which they suffered.

Resocialization

The program acknowledges the personality deficits some offenders develop during their formative years as a result of such adversities as neglect, abuse, and emotional deprivation. These deficits impair their ability to negotiate adult life demands effectively and responsibly.

It is in *interpersonal relationships* that the social deficits of sexual offenders are most pronounced. The resocialization part of the program therefore concentrates on concerns and problems offenders habitually experience in relating to others, both men and women.

Sexual assault is more the sexual expression of aggression than the aggressive expression of sexuality. The *management of aggression* component of the program focuses on helping offenders learn how to be assertive without transgressing against others, to deal with adversity in ways other than through retaliation or withdrawal, and to appreciate the long-term adverse consequences of the misuse of aggression on themselves, even though it may prove temporarily effective.

Finally, because the majority of sex offenders had something short of an adequate upbringing, these men have poor parental skills themselves. A chapter of Parents Anonymous helps offenders to recognize and respond to the needs of their children in a responsible and caring fashion.

Counseling

Group therapy is used to help offenders better control their propensity to assaultive behavior. The aim is to get the offender to discover the dynamics of his offense, to identify the factors that increase the risk of sexual aggression, to recognize early warning signals that are precursors of such behavior, and to find alternative ways of managing the unresolved life issues underlying it.

Since the majority of sexual offenders experienced significant abuse and exploitation during their formative years, the *personal victimization* part of the program focuses on helping the offender come to grips with the impact such victimization has had on his life.

In the *combatting sexual assault* component of the program, emphasis is placed on the help offenders can give those in the community who deal with sexual assault. Regular meetings with law enforcement officers, victim counselors, and child protection workers offer sex offenders the opportunity to provide input, based on their own knowledge and experience, to the effort to combat sexual assault.

Sexual Coercion: Rape

Other Treatment Approaches

There are other forms of treatment designed to reduce or eliminate the risk that the rapist will repeat his crime. *Classical conditioning* procedures have been employed to create aversion to assaultive desires. Other behavioral treatment approaches seek to positively reinforce socially acceptable sexual behaviors. *Chemotherapy* is another treatment option, one that is often used in combination with other therapies. Various antiandrogenic hormones, such as medroxyprogesterone acetate (Depo-Provera), have been shown to have a moderating effect on sexual aggressiveness and to enhance self-regulation of sexual behavior. Although the use of Depo-Provera is still in the experimental stage and controversial (see Berlin & Meinecke, 1981), the drug does offer some promise as a treatment option for sexual offenders (Kilmann et al., 1982; Money & Bennett, 1981). For more information on these and other forms of therapeutic procedures for sex offenders, consult John Wincze's (1989) comprehensive review of the literature.

CAN THERE BE A WORLD WITHOUT RAPE?

This chapter has described the devastating effects of sexual assault. We've emphasized throughout these pages that rape is a forcible, violent act, not a sexual one. It is an act motivated by hostility and the wish to humiliate and degrade, one that violates a person's dignity and humanity. And it leaves not only physical scars, but psychological distress that may last a long time.

It is generally recognized that there are a number of things a woman can do to help avoid or prevent a rape from happening. According to one source, if a woman uses good judgment and takes the following commonsense precautions, she may avoid becoming the victim of sexual assault (Sizer & Whitney, 1988):

At Home or in Your Residence Hall:
- Keep your doors and windows locked. Use a dead-bolt door lock to discourage break-ins and a peephole to check visitors before opening the door. If a window can be opened, use a lock that keeps the opening to a maximum of 5 inches.
- Verify the identity of men who claim to be salespeople, meter readers, and the like. Direct those who ask to use your telephone to the nearest pay phone.
- Let no one in except people you know and trust when you are home alone.
- Keep your shades drawn at night.
- If you suspect that someone has broken in, do not go into the house alone.
- Use only your last name on the mailbox and door.
- List only your first initial(s) in the telephone book.
- Do not hide your key around the outside of your house; leave a copy with a trusted neighbor for emergencies.
- Do not invite a man in, or go home with him, on your first or second date, especially if you or he have been drinking; wait until you know him very well.

In an Elevator:
- If a lone man of whom you are suspicious is in the elevator, do not get on.
- Stand near the buttons, and if someone bothers you, push as many as you can, including the alarm button.

- If you are on your way up, do not ride down to the basement first.

In Your Car:
- Always make sure the car is in good working order and has plenty of gas.
- Glance into the car, checking the seats and floors, before you get in.
- Have your keys ready before you reach the car, get in quickly, and lock the doors.
- Carry a whistle on your key chain.
- If your car breaks down on the road, raise the hood, tie a white rag on the handle or aerial, and then get back into the car and lock the doors. Stay in the car and wait for the police.
- Never pick up hitchhikers.

Outdoors:
- Stay alert to suspicious-looking people.
- Use shopping bags and carts to carry things so your arms will be freer for self-defense.
- Walk only on busy, well-lighted streets, even if the way is longer.
- Make sure the street lamps on your block are working.
- Never hitchhike.
- Have your keys ready before you get to your front door.

Unfortunately, even the most careful person with the strongest self-esteem and sense of self-preservation can be taken by surprise by an attacker. Consider a recent event in a human sexuality class taught by one of your authors. In a lively give-and-take discussion of the issue "Can rape be prevented?" the class, made up about equally of women and men, generally agreed that rape *is* a preventable crime. Virtually everyone thought that education is a powerful weapon against sexual assault and that protective behaviors such as those we've outlined in this section can greatly lessen a person's chance of being raped.

As the students were leaving the class, however, one young woman remained behind and approached the author. Voice quivering and tears welling in her eyes, she said, "I did *all* of the things we're supposed to do. *I tried,* I really did ..."

Although we have learned a lot about steps one can take to avoid situations in which rape can occur, we have a long way to go to learn how to prevent people from becoming rapists. Until we find a way to change this ugly, destructive behavior, we must remember that there will always be those who have tried and failed to prevent it. These people should never be shamed, but instead offered every possible form of assistance and support to recover from this senseless act and to bring their attackers to justice.

SEXUALITY IN THE NEWS

Rape

*A*ccording to this three-part series, shown on ABC's "World News Tonight" on January 7–10, 1991, in the United States a rape is committed every six minutes. In some major cities the incidence of rape has increased by almost 50 percent in recent years. Rape is now the fastest-growing violent crime in America. This video segment discusses congressional efforts to pass comprehensive legislation to help deter rapists. We learn that most rape victims do not report their assaults. Moreover, because women have become more afraid to be alone in vulnerable situations in recent years, they seem to be losing some of their hard-won social freedoms. The video depicts Seattle's rape prevention program and informs us about rehabilitation efforts for rapists. (12:34 minutes)

1. The first segment of this video makes a clear connection between rape and violence, a point we've emphasized throughout this chapter. Do you agree that rape is an act of violence rather than a sexual act? Explain your answer.

2. What is the connection between drugs (alcohol and other substances) and rape?

3. Acquaintance rape is the most prevalent form of rape in the United States. What are some ways to prevent this kind of rape? Would you avail yourself of a program like the one King County has developed in Seattle?

4. The Vermont Treatment Program for Sexual Aggressors began in 1982. Do you agree with the premise that we must "rehabilitate the offenders because they are the individuals who create the victims in the first place"? Explain your answer from the victim's perspective.

LOOKING BACK

■   Broadly defined, rape is an act of a sexual nature that is forced upon an unwilling person or that an unwilling person is forced to perform on someone else. Most commonly, rape refers to *forcible* sexual intercourse, in which a man's penis penetrates a woman's vagina. However, there are other forms of forced sexual violation: forcible anal intercourse with a woman or another man; and forcing a woman or a man to perform fellatio. The primary motive for rape is rarely a sexual one. Rather, rape is an act of aggression and violence reflecting a desire to control, degrade, and humiliate another person.

■   Rape has increased more rapidly in the last decade than any other type of violent crime. Over 100,000 cases are reported each year, but this figure is misleading since rape is one of the most underreported crimes. Men between the ages of 20 and 24 make up the largest percentage of people arrested for rape. The high-risk ages for rape victims are 13 to 24.

■   No two rapists are alike, although general categories of rapists—the anger, power, and sadistic rapist—have been identified. Responses to rape also vary. The rape trauma syndrome and the post-traumatic stress disorder are useful models for exploring the physical, psychological, social, and/or sexual aspects of a victim's life that are disrupted by rape.

■   Acquaintance and marital rape are two widespread forms of sexual assault. In acquaintance rape rapist and victim know each other, though often only casually. Marital rape is defined as the use of force, the threat of force, or incapacitation by a husband to get his wife to have sexual intercourse or other forms of sexual activity against her will. Male rape can and does occur, although the incidence of it is much lower than female rape. The intent, however, is usually exactly the same: to humiliate and hurt. Rape survivors need to learn effective resolution and coping skills in order to overcome their trauma. They also need the support and understanding of loved ones.

■   Survivors of rape face numerous adjustment difficulties, and some elements of the rape trauma syndrome may never go away. Crisis intervention is needed as soon as possible to return the victim to her normal level of functioning, and rape work is aimed at restoring a survivor's sense of safety and self-worth. The medical, social network, behavioral, and psychological models represent therapeutic approaches in counseling victims of rape. It is important to include a victim's partner in therapeutic intervention, since it provides an opportunity for a significant other to express feelings about the incident.

■   Rapists tend to be repeat offenders. Their sexual pathology is still not clearly understood, so we have not made much progress in effectively managing, supervising, and treating sexual offenders. One model treatment program focuses on reeducation, resocialization, and counseling. Other treatment approaches include behavioral therapy and chemotherapy, including antiandrogenic hormones such as medroxyprogesterone acetate (Depo-Provera).

THINKING THINGS OVER

1. We have seen that rape is an act of violence, not an act of sexual gratification. How can you distinguish between these two motivations?

2. Rape and sexual assault have been receiving much attention from the media in the 1990s. What factors have spurred the sudden interest in this violent behavior?

3. A woman you know tells you that last night she was raped by her date. Describe your probable reactions to this revelation. What comfort and advice would you offer this woman?

4. React to the following statement: "Women have become socialized by our society to become victims of rape." What are some steps you can take to help change this situation?

DISCOVER FOR YOURSELF

Benedict, H. (1985). *Recovery*. New York: Doubleday. Benedict offers practical advice on how to deal with the many facets of sexual assault.

Burgess, A. W. (1985). *Rape and sexual assault: A research handbook*. New York: Garland. Part II of this research-based book deals with victims of sexual assault, while Part IV examines the aggressor.

Koss, M. P., & Harvey, M. R. (1991). *The rape victim: Clinical and community interventions*. Newbury Park, CA: Sage. An excellent look at the trauma of rape, its prevention, and what can be done to assist survivors.

Holmes, R. M. (1991). *Sex crimes*. Newbury Park, CA: Sage. Chapter 7 of this book offers a good overview of rape, while Chapter 10 discusses treatment of sexual offenders.

LaFree, G. D. (1989). *Rape and criminal justice*. Belmont, CA: Wadsworth. A good effort to explain the application of law in sexual assault cases.

Warshaw, R. (1988). *I never called it rape*. New York: Harper & Row. An extensive look at date and acquaintance rape, including its prevention.

All's love, yet all's law

—Robert Browning

Nothing could be more grotesquely unjust than a code of morals, reinforced by laws, which relieves men from responsibility for irregular sexual acts, and for the same acts drives women to abortion, infanticide, prostitution, and self-destruction

—Suzanne La Follette

A glance back through history shows that at one time or another all societies have implemented laws and legal sanctions to govern sexual behavior. For example, incest was expressly forbidden under Roman law and offenders faced banishment from Rome or even death. In Spain under the Visigoths homosexual acts were punished with castration and death. The domination of the English parliament by the Puritans led, in 1650, to the Act of May 1, according to which sodomy and adultery were punishable by death and fornication by three months' imprisonment and posting of a bond to guarantee good behavior. In Berlin a law passed in 1792 stated that no one could open a brothel without first receiving permission from the police, nor could any landlord rent a room to a prostitute without permission. In the United States the federal customs law of 1842 prohibited the importation of indecent prints and paintings, and in 1873 Congress forbade the mailing of obscene, lewd, lascivious, and indecent writing or advertisements, including material that helped people practice contraception and abortion (D'Emillio & Freedman, 1988; Gregersen, 1983).

Laws and legal sanctions directed toward sexual behaviors are still very much in evidence today, and this chapter focuses on some important features of our laws regarding sexual behavior. As we'll discover, defining what is legal and determining how to enforce laws regarding sex are not easy tasks. Adding to legal complexities is the fact that laws of this kind constantly change, either through legislative action or by court decisions. Controversy swirls around many such laws, with many segments of the public expressing the need to revamp them.

In this chapter we explore some important legal issues of the 1990s, including how sex statutes affect our personal and private lives. In the first portion of our discussion, we examine the legal status of consensual and nonconsensual sexual behaviors. Then we turn our attention to legal issues surrounding homosexuality, pornography, and prostitution. Finally, we discuss legal questions raised in connection with conception, procreation, and sexual discrimination and harassment.

LAWS GOVERNING SEXUAL BEHAVIORS

Before we launch into the subject of the legality of specific sexual behaviors, it is important to note that in the United States laws exist at three levels. *Federal* laws, at the national level, apply to all states. An example of a federal law is the Mann Act, which forbids the transportation of women across state lines for "immoral" purposes. The Mann Act was passed in 1910 in an effort to prevent the abduction of women for purposes of prostitution. *State* laws are enacted independently by each state government and apply only within the boundaries of that state. In California, for example, rape is punishable by a sentence of three, six, or eight years, depending on the circumstances. *Municipal* laws are designed to regulate sexual behavior and activities within a city's territory. For example, most municipalities have ordinances against nude bathing on public beaches.

Consensual Sexual Behaviors

Consensual sexual behaviors are those sexual activities in which adults agree to participate; fornication and adultery are examples. Some consensual sexual behaviors are designated illegal because they are considered to be immoral in and of themselves, or because they occur outside the institution of marriage.

Public support for laws prohibiting fornication and adultery has declined over the years and these laws are less and less often enforced. Of the two, adultery is considered the more serious act because it threatens the family. Only five states—

Arkansas, Louisiana, Nevada, New Mexico, and Tennessee—fail to prohibit adultery. Twice as many states have no laws forbidding fornication.

State laws also prohibit specific sexual behaviors. For example, many states penalize **sodomy** or "unnatural sexual relations." Sodomy includes such noncoital sexual behaviors as anal-genital and oral-genital sex. Sodomy laws, which we inherited from English common law, reflect the notion that any sexual act not directly promoting procreation is sinful. Such laws have been in existence in England and America since the sixteenth century. Until that time, sodomy was a religious offense punishable in the ecclesiastical courts. Today the legal punishments for sodomy include fines and prison terms ranging from 30 days in Arizona to 20 years in Georgia and Rhode Island.

In theory, sodomy laws apply to heterosexuals, homosexuals, and bisexuals alike. In practice, however, they are most often used to prosecute homosexuals. Sodomy laws incorporate many nonprecise descriptive phrases, including "buggery," "crimes against nature," "perversion," and "lascivious acts." Furthermore, they are often written in such unclear language that they are difficult to interpret and apply. Consider this excerpt from the Arkansas statute:

> (1) A person commits sodomy if such person performs an act of sexual grati-
> fication involving: (a) the penetration, however slight, of the anus or mouth of
> an animal or person by the penis of a person of the same sex or an animal or
> (b) the penetration, however slight, of the vagina or anus of an animal or person
> of the same sex or an animal. (Arkansas 41-1813)

Sodomy laws have been characterized by little or no enforcement efforts or public demand for arrest and prosecution. Only a fractional portion of the gay, heterosexual, and bisexual activity that violates sodomy statutes ever comes to the attention of law enforcement authorities. For the most part, it has been only those gay men who engage in brief, impersonal sex with strangers in public or semipublic places like restrooms or parked cars who have been arrested (Mueller, 1980).

Over the years there has been a growing consensus that sodomy laws are unconstitutional. The fact that in most European countries sodomy involving consenting adults is not illegal may have helped bring about this changing view. In 1961 Illinois became the first state to repeal its sodomy laws, essentially decriminalizing homosexual acts between consenting adults in private. By 1986, 36 states had followed suit, and as of this writing, similar action is being considered in Arizona, Arkansas, Louisiana, Michigan, Minnesota, Nevada, and Texas.

The 1986 Supreme Court decision in *Hardwick* v. *Bowers* may have a dramatic impact on future privacy challenges. In 1982 in Atlanta, Georgia, a police officer arrived at Michael Hardwick's home to serve a citation for failure to pay a municipal ticket. A roommate directed the officer to Hardwick's bedroom, and the officer walked in on Hardwick and a male partner engaged in fellatio. Hardwick was arrested for violating Georgia's sodomy law.

A district attorney declined to prosecute the case, but Hardwick filed suit in federal court anyway, seeking an injunction and declaratory judgment that the law violated his civil rights. A lower court dismissed Hardwick's case, ruling that the Georgia sodomy law was not unconstitutional. The Eleventh Circuit Court of Appeals disagreed, and on Georgia's appeal, the U.S. Supreme Court agreed to hear the case.

In its controversial *Hardwick* v. *Bowers* decision, the Supreme Court upheld states' rights to enact sodomy laws and to impose penalties. It rejected the argument that the U.S. Constitution confers a right of privacy that extends to homosexual sodomy. The Court also rejected the proposition that any kind of private sexual conduct between consenting adults is constitutionally insulated from state prohibition. In short, the Supreme Court held that in constitutional terms there is no such thing as a fundamental right to commit sodomy (Sloan, 1987).

sodomy A broad legal term that refers to "unnatural sexual relations," including such noncoital sexual behaviors as anal-genital and oral-genital sex.

The *Hardwick* decision was widely disputed, and many feel that it will have a profound effect on the future regulation of private sexual conduct between adults. Some people claim that the decision was based on the Court's fear of the spread of AIDS and an interest in controlling gay behavior (it is not known how the Court would have acted had the case involved a heterosexual couple committing the proscribed act). Others contend the impact of the decision will not be so severe for two reasons. First, individual states can rely on their own constitutions to remove laws regulating sexual behavior between consenting adults. Second, the fear that decriminalizing such behavior will make it impossible to bring suits against those who knowingly infect sexual partners with a grave disease like AIDS are fading as courts increasingly take the position that an injured party has the right to recover damages if knowingly infected by an incurable disease during consensual sexual activity (Davis, 1988).

Nonconsensual Sexual Behaviors

Nonconsensual sexual behaviors are those that involve the use or threat of force, violence, or exploitation. Rape serves as an example of a nonconsensual sexual behavior. Remember that *statutory rape* is having sexual relations with a minor, or a person too young to give legal consent (the age of consent ranges from 12 to 16, depending on the state in which the act occurs). Other conditions legally deemed to make it impossible to give consent include impairment by drugs and developmental disability. Finally, *forcible rape* is rape that involves the use or threat of force. The sexual contact that occurs may involve the sex organs of one or both parties, including penetration, however slight, of the vagina or anus.

It may surprise you to learn that for many centuries rape laws were designed to protect a man's property, not a woman's safety. Recall from Chapter 1 that, for long periods of time in many societies, women were considered to be the property of, first, their fathers, and then, their husbands. Western rape laws originated in the Roman law of *raptus*. Raptus was the violent theft of any kind of property that belonged to a man—including his wife, children, and slaves. It referred to abduction and theft, not to sexual violation. If sexual assault did take place, it was still the abduction (raptus) that was charged (Ledray, 1986).

Our legal concept of rape comes specifically from English tradition. In England rape was a criminal act falling under common law. It was viewed as illicit carnal knowledge of a female by force and against her will and was therefore, by definition, an act that could be performed only by a man against a woman. Each of the terms—"illicit," "carnal knowledge," and "force"—acquired specific meaning, and from these meanings came many of today's rape laws. For instance, "carnal knowledge," now called "sexual intercourse," required confirming evidence of penetration of the vagina by the penis. Usually, the evidence of such penetration was restricted to the presence of semen in the vagina (Weinstein & Rosen, 1988a).

In the 1990s rape is a very controversial legal area. For example, the legal definition of rape varies from state to state. Some states include such factors as the degree of force or resistance, while other states include penetration with instruments other than the penis in their legal definitions of rape. Some states will prosecute men who rape their wives, but most will not.

Many observers, such as Jon Shepard (1987), feel that sexism is explicitly woven into the language and application of our rape laws. For example, the assumption of many rape laws is that women lie about rape, so unless corroborating evidence of rape can be produced, there should be no prosecution. For women not raped in front of witnesses, and for women who submit to rape because of the threat of violence—and hence show no evidence of struggle and force, such as bruises or lacerations—there is often no legal protection. Moreover, in those rape cases that actually do come to trial, the victim is often treated more harshly than the defendant.

Because of this, many onlookers describe the conduct of rape cases as a trial of the victim, with evidence of her past sexual activity used to undermine her testimony and acquit the accused.

For many rape victims, bringing legal action against the assailant is time-consuming, expensive, risky, and traumatic. For these and other reasons, only about 10 to 20 percent of rape cases are reported to authorities. Moreover, the legal system doesn't work the same way for everyone. Women of color, poor women, divorced women, and lesbian women, for instance, are believed and respected less in court than white, financially stable, married, heterosexual women. Moreover, white, middle-class, married men are rarely prosecuted (Boston Women's Health Book Collective, 1984).

In the wake of such problems, many groups such as the National Organization of Women (NOW) have lobbied for rape-law reform. Leaders of these groups acknowledge that some beneficial changes in the legal system have been made in recent decades, but they believe that more need to be made. For example, in the mid-1970s many states began to charge separated husbands with rape. Another area of reform has been sentencing. In the states where a rape conviction could result in death or life in prison, women were less willing to report the crime, police and prosecutors were less willing to charge the assailant, and juries were far less likely to convict the accused. Now that sentences are more reasonable, conviction is more likely. Other factors in the more frequent successful prosecution of rape today are the greater numbers of female prosecutors, more enlightened men and women on the bench, and a wider understanding of rape among the general public (Benedict, 1985; Ledray, 1986).

Sex Discrimination and Harassment

Legal efforts have focused on the attempt to eliminate **sex discrimination,** the unfair and unequal treatment of a person on the basis of her or his sex. In 1964 Title VII of the Civil Rights Act prohibited discrimination in private employment on the basis of sex as well as of race, color, religion, and national origin. And in 1971 the Supreme Court ruled that unequal treatment based on sex violated the Fourteenth Amendment to the U.S. Constitution, which mandates equal protection of all citizens.

Unfortunately, the most comprehensive statement of the equality of the sexes before the law, the **Equal Rights Amendment (ERA),** is still far from becoming a part of our Constitution. First introduced into Congress in 1923, this amendment was finally passed by both the Senate and the House of Representatives in 1972 and, with a seven-year deadline for ratification attached to it, was sent to the states for their action. As 1979 approached, an insufficient number of states had ratified the amendment, and an extension of time was granted in response to the lobbying efforts of womens' groups. However, by the extended deadline of June 1982, only 35 of the required 38 states (¾ of all states must ratify a constitutional amendment) had ratified the ERA.

Thus we are back at square one. The ERA has been reintroduced into every session of Congress since 1982, but by early 1992 no body of Congress has passed it for a second time. When both the Senate and the House have again voted in favor of the amendment, each by the required two-thirds majority, it will again go to the states for ratification. To date the ERA has been mired in the legislative process for nearly 70 years. How can this be explained? More important, what do you think we should do about it?

A century and a half ago women were excluded from all paying occupations of any significance. They couldn't vote or hold public office, and married women couldn't make contracts or hold property. Clearly, things have changed for the better, but sex discrimination is clearly alive and well in the 1990s. In general, women who are employed full time earn two-thirds as much as full-time employed men in the same

sex discrimination Unfair and unequal treatment of a person on the basis of his or her sex.

Equal Rights Amendment (ERA) An amendment to the U.S. Constitution that states, in essence, that the sexes have equal rights under the law. The deadline for ratification by the states has been exceeded, and the amendment must again pass both houses of Congress and be ratified by three-quarters of the states before it can become law.

or similar occupations. Moreover, women are underrepresented in virtually every prestigious or well-paying occupation, including government bodies in which significant public policy is made, and they are overrepresented in low-paid, dead-end jobs. This unequal treatment extends even to such areas as access to credit and obtaining insurance at reasonable rates (Shilling, 1985).

Sex Discrimination on the Job

Let's examine sex inequality and discrimination in the work force a bit more closely. Despite the fact that growing numbers of women are entering the labor force, many are still confined to low-status occupations. Women continue to be a minority in professional and skilled careers, especially managerial positions. The majority of women who work in office settings today handle secretarial and clerical chores, while the more prestigious and better-paying executive positions are held mostly by men (Andersen, 1988; Tittle, 1988; Rothenberg, 1988).

Consider some occupational groupings. Most physicians, dentists, and lawyers are men, whereas most secretaries, nurses, schoolteachers, and librarians are women. Few women work in construction or engineering, although their representation in such nontraditional jobs has been increasing from the negligible levels of a decade ago. The number of women holding political office has also gone up in recent years, but remains disappointingly small. For example, only about 5 percent of members of Congress and about 16 percent of state legislators are women (U.S. Bureau of the Census, 1990; Diamond, 1988; Gutek, 1988).

Worse, even when they occupy the same jobs as men, women receive substantially lower salaries. On the average, women earn less than 70 cents for every dollar men are paid. The clustering of women in low-paying jobs is the largest factor accounting for this pay discrepancy, but even women with college degrees tend to earn

A WORLD OF DIFFERENCES

Women and Work: Sex Exploitation in the Labor Force

Around the globe, women make up more than one-third of the total paid labor force. Among all the world's women aged 15 to 64, 47 percent work, although this percentage varies from nation to nation. Russia tops the list, with 71 percent of Russian women employed. In the United States about 60 percent of women are in the paid labor force. In Latin America the figure is only 30 percent.

There is no mistaking the fact that women all around the globe earn less than men. In some nations the situation is better than in the United States. In Italy and Denmark, for example, women earn 86 cents to every dollar earned by men. In Sweden they earn over 81 cents, and in France, 78 cents. The unequal pay is usually accompanied by other negative employment conditions. More often than men, women are trapped in low-paying, unskilled occupations, and their chances for advancement in all vocational areas are fewer.

Let's take this issue a step further and examine women's total work involvement. Although the housework and child care women do is not included in any nation's labor or economic statistics, when the value of the cleaning, cooking, and child care that make up this work is calculated, it turns out to equal half the gross national product in many nations. For example, a woman in rural Pakistan spends 63 hours a week on domestic work, and in the developed world women spend about 56 hours per week on household chores.

All of this means that, worldwide, women spend more hours working and have less free time than men do. Illustrative of this are women in rural Rwanda, who do three times the amount of work Rwandan men do. In Europe a working woman has less than half the free time that her husband has, and in Java women work over 20 percent more than men. (Based on Cancelier & Crews, 1986; Hewlett, 1986)

Legal Issues and Concerns

less than men who have only high school diplomas. Retirement benefits are also far lower for women. In 1989 the average retirement benefit for a woman was barely half that for a retiring man (Helson, Elliot, & Leigh, 1989; Andersen, 1988; Rose & Larwood, 1988; Gutek, Stromberg, & Larwood, 1988). The "World of Differences" box explores sex discrimination in vocations from an international perspective.

As we indicated earlier, Title VII of the Civil Rights Act of 1964 prohibits sex discrimination in the workplace. This is the principal law that protects workers from sexual inequality because it prohibits discrimination in recruitment, testing, referrals, hiring, wages, promotion, and fringe benefits. The Equal Employment Opportunity Commission (EEOC), which has the primary responsibility for enforcing Title VII, has published guidelines on sex discrimination making it a violation of Title VII to refuse to hire any individual on the basis of stereotyped characteristics of the sexes. It is also a violation to base employment decisions on the preferences of co-workers, the employer, clients, or customers. An employer cannot label a job a "man's job" or a "woman's job" or indicate a preference or limitation based on sex in a help-wanted advertisement—unless sex is a bona fide occupational qualification for the job (which it rarely is).

Sexual Harassment

Sexual harassment is defined as any unwanted sexual advance, verbal or physical, that occurs in the workplace or in an academic setting. Sexual harassment is a sexually oriented practice that undermines job performance (including that of a student) and threatens one's economic livelihood. Women are the most frequent targets of sexual harassment. Anytime unwelcome sexual conduct creates an intimidating or hostile environment and an inappropriate use of power, sexual harassment has occurred. In extreme or coercive forms of harassment a person is forced to comply sexually or else lose some occupational or academic benefit. Less obvious harassment takes the form of sexual innuendoes and comments, and sometimes inappropriate touching. All forms of sexual harassment are exploitive and make the work or academic environment either uncomfortable or intolerable (Richardson, 1988). To test your knowledge of sexual harassment, try answering the questions in the box on "How Much Do You Know About Sexual Harassment?"

Sexual harassment is widespread in the workplace. One study (Merit Systems Protection Board, 1981) indicated that 42 percent of female workers queried and 15 percent of male workers had experienced some form of sexual harassment. Another investigation (Martin, 1984) found that between 30 and 50 percent of all female employees had been harassed. Sexual harassment received national attention in 1991 when University of Oklahoma law professor Anita Hill leveled charges against then–U.S. Supreme Court nominee Clarence Thomas during his confirmation hearings. Hill appeared before the Senate Judiciary Committee and maintained that she had been sexually harassed by Thomas when she worked for him a decade earlier at the Education Department and the Equal Employment Opportunity Commission. She claimed that Thomas made unwanted sexual advances to her, as well as obscene and lewd remarks. Thomas, who denied the allegations, was not formally charged with sexual harassment. He was later confirmed to the Supreme Court.

Until ten years ago, sexual harassment in the occupational world was defined narrowly by the courts. To win a case the accuser had to prove that someone in a position to hire, fire, or promote asked for sexual favors as a condition of employment or promotion. It is now recognized, however, that sexual harassment can take many subtle forms and that even mild harassment can seriously jeopardize an employee's position in the workplace (see the "Myths and Misconceptions" box). By the early 1980s, the Equal Employment Opportunity Commission (EEOC) and some federal appellate courts began to recognize these subtler conditions as forms of harassment. In 1986 the U.S. Supreme Court ruled that "a hostile or abusive work environment

What is considered sexual harassment? Does it have to involve touching?

sexual harassment Any unwanted sexual advance, verbal or physical, that occurs in the workplace or in an academic setting.

....

The accusations of sexual harassment leveled by Professor Anita Hill at Supreme Court nominee Clarence Thomas in 1991 were neither substantiated nor disproven, and Thomas's nomination to the Court was confirmed. What had been set in motion could not be stopped, however, and Hill's disclosure and testimony put sexual harassment in the forefront of public attention.

Legal Issues and Concerns

MAKING USE OF WHAT WE KNOW

How Much Do You Know About Sexual Harassment?

violates the law," confirming for the first time that the very atmosphere in some offices may be abusive enough to violate people's civil rights (Eagan, 1989).

Can college students be victims of sexual harassment?

SEXUAL HARASSMENT ON CAMPUS. Sexual harassment is no stranger to college campuses. Like some employers, some professors harass students because of the position of authority they occupy. In a definitive sense, "academic sexual harassment" is the use of authority to emphasize the sexuality or sexual identity of a student in a manner that prevents or impairs that student's full enjoyment of educational benefits, climate, or opportunities. Here's an example of sexual harassment on campus:

> In the lab he would stare at me, rub up against me, make crude remarks. He repeatedly asked me out and would make public comments on how well I looked in a certain blouse, dress, and so forth. He implied that I could get a higher grade if I dated him. I refused to go out with him and I got a lower grade than I deserved. The harassment was so intense that I withdrew from school for one quarter to assess the situation and get counseling. When I returned, I quickly finished the research project and refused to deal with anyone from that laboratory, thereby forfeiting any possibility of publishing my work. (Dziech & Weiner, 1984, p. 101)

There have been many surveys gauging the incidence of sexual harassment on campuses. Reported harassment among undergraduate women by one or more male professors vary from 9 percent in one study (McCormack, 1985), to 2–28 percent according to another investigation (Roscoe et al., 1987). One source (Glasser & Thorpe, 1986) estimates that approximately 50 percent of female undergraduates have experienced some sort of sexual harassment from their professors. While acknowledging

2. An employer is not liable for the sexual harassment of one of its employees unless that employee loses specific job benefits or is fired.

3. A court can require a sexual harasser to pay part of the judgment to the employee he or she has sexually harassed.

4. A supervisor can be liable for sexual harassment committed by one of his or her employees against another.

5. An employer can be liable for the sexually harassing behavior of management personnel even if unaware of that behavior.

6. It is appropriate for a supervisor, when initially receiving a sexual harassment complaint, to determine if the alleged recipient overreacted or misunderstood the alleged harasser.

7. When a supervisor is talking with an employee about an allegation of sexual harassment against that employee, it is best to ease into the allegation instead of being direct.

8. Sexually suggestive visuals or objects in a workplace don't create a liability unless an employee complains about them and management allows them to remain.

9. The lack of sexual harassment complaints is a good indication that sexual harassment is not occurring.

10. It is appropriate for a supervisor to tell an employee to handle unwelcome sexual behavior if the supervisor thinks that the employee is misunderstanding the behavior.

11. The *intent* behind employee A's sexual behavior is more important than the impact of that behavior on employee B when determining if sexual harassment has occurred.

Answers: 1, False; 2, False; 3, True; 4, True; 5, True; 6, False; 7, False; 8, False; 9, False; 10, False; 11, False.

(Adapted from Moskal, 1989)

---

that sexual harassment can be directed toward male college students, most sources point out that their rate of victimization is far lower than women students (see, e.g., Grauerholz & Solomon, 1989; McKinney et al., 1987; Gutek, 1985; Adams, Kottke, & Padgett, 1983).

Five types of activity are described as academic sexual harassment (Till, 1980):

1. *Generalized sexist remarks or behavior.* These types of incidents closely resemble racial harassment. The actions or words are often fiercely antifemale (or antimale), but they are not intended to lead to sexual activity. Instead, they are directed at the victim because of her (or his) gender.

2. *Inappropriate unsolicited and unwanted sexual advances.* This category of complaints is distinguished from the first activity by the introduction of requests for social or sexual encounters, often accompanied by touching. In contrast to the first category of harassment, here sexual activity is clearly desired.

3. *Solicitation of sexual activity or other sex-related behavior by the promise of rewards.* In this category of harassment the target is promised something in exchange for sexual favors. Typically the offender uses institutional authority (e.g., an "A for a lay") to induce compliance.

4. *Coercion of sexual activity by threat of punishments.* In the occupational or academic arena this form of harassment is labeled "put out or get out," and is generally thought of as the essence of sexual harassment. It entails exploitation of a difference in authority to compel a choice between extremely unwelcome alternatives.

5. *Sexual crimes.* This category refers to acts that, if reported to police authorities, would be considered misdemeanors or felonies. They usually go unreported, though, even when they are as extreme as forced sexual intercourse, because

MYTHS AND MISCONCEPTIONS

Myths About Sexual Harassment

Sexual harassment in the workplace has been grossly misunderstood. A number of myths about sexual harassment on the job still find widespread acceptance even though they bear no resemblance to reality. Constance Backhouse and Leah Cohen (1981) summarize some of the more common myths:

People who object to sexual harassment have no sense of humor.

Often women (or men) who speak out are viewed as lacking a sense of humor or overreacting to what is essentially harmless behavior. Sexual harassment, with the prospect of imminent reprisals affecting the target's working conditions and future career plans, is neither humorous nor harmless. It is degrading and humiliating. It threaten's one's economic livelihood and in many cases causes negative physical and psychological reactions.

Middle- and upper-class employees do not suffer from sexual harassment.

Sexual harassment is a problem for women and men of all classes and is as serious a job impediment for managerial and professional workers as it is for lower-echelon employees. Although middle- and upper-class women and men may hold positions of some status in their organizations, their harassers hold power and authority over them. Job-related reprisals can be used as effectively against these workers as against lower-level employees.

People often make false accusations of sexual harassment.

It is not true that many people accuse others of sexual harassment without justification. In fact, legitimate victims of sexual harassment more often than not encounter disbelief, ridicule, and accusations of enticement. Some even lose their jobs when they complain openly, and the complaint becomes public knowledge. Other employers may be reluctant to hire the person in the future. Thus women and men who make unwarranted charges of sexual harassment have little to gain and a great deal to lose.

the victim fears the consequences of reporting the incidents to any authority. Unfortunately, fear often introduces a form of consent into the acts, to the extent that students do not resist strenuously and often continue their association with the perpetrator. This robs the acts, especially those involving force, of their criminality.

Students are extremely vulnerable to sexual harassment for several reasons. They may rely on recommendations for graduate school or future employment from professors. They may be in awe of a professor of high repute. And, of course, they are at the mercy of a teacher for a grade. Some professors take advantage of this imbalance of power. Here are warning signs:

- *Staring, leering, ogling.* Whether surreptitious or obvious, these behaviors are inappropriate in college faculty members.
- *Frequently commenting on the personal appearance of the student.* In the academic setting most professors refrain from discussing the apparel and physical traits of their students.
- *Touching the student.* Every physical gesture should be appropriate to the occasion, setting, and need and character of the individual student. Physically touching a student is rarely necessary or advisable.

- *Excessive flattery and praise of the student.* This behavior, in others' presence, is especially seductive to students with either high aspirations or low self-esteem. By convincing a student that she is intellectually and/or physically exceptional, the lecherous professor may gain psychological access to her.
- *Injecting a "male versus female" tone into discussions with students or colleagues.* A frequent behavior of verbal harassers, this conduct signals a generally disparaging attitude toward women. For example, "Women shouldn't get involved in that kind of research" is a sexist comment and expresses a derogatory attitude toward women. Its initial effect is to make the woman student feel like an outsider in the academic environment, but it may also be an indicator of other potential forms of abuse.
- *Persistently emphasizing sexuality in all contexts.* The faculty member exhibits a pervasive, inordinate emphasis on sex both inside and outside the classroom. In effect, sexuality is the prism through which the professor views all topics.

The first step in combatting all forms of sexual harassment is for targets to realize that they are not to blame for such abuse. If you are a victim of sexual harassment, you should report it immediately to the harasser's immediate superior: the department chairperson, dean, or other supervisor. If the issue is not satisfactorily resolved, you should report the incident to higher authorities on campus or the affirmative action officer on campus. Keep records of all your meetings and letters, and, if necessary, make it clear to the administration that you will "go public" with the complaint. It is

"That's the breaks, Greg. Women bosses just don't sexually harass their workers all that much."

imperative that we all take a proactive stance to stem the tide of unwanted sexual advances, no matter what the form.

Unfortunately, most universities do not have specific policies defining and dealing with sexual harassment, even though laws prohibiting sexual harassment have been on the books for years now. While sexual harassment is a difficult issue for college administrators to come to terms with because of their desire to protect faculty, several universities have adopted clear guidelines and policies. Find out whether your school has such policies and guidelines and whether it acts upon them.

PERPETRATORS OF SEXUAL HARASSMENT. What type of person engages in sexual harassment? What are some of the motivations underlying such behaviors? Society wrongly views sexual harassment as sexually motivated.

One study (Backhouse & Cohen, 1981) found that male harassers appear to fall into two categories: the one-time offender and the relentless repeater. The former is often a man in crisis: a death in the family, approaching middle age, or a divorce often precipitate his behavior. The second category—into which the majority of men studied fell—assess that sex "goes with the territory" and is one of their prerogatives over women subordinates. These offenders use sexual harassment to control and undermine women. Many of the relentless repeaters in the cases uncovered had harassed scores of working women throughout their careers.

Another study (Merit Systems Protection Board, 1981) found that most harassers of women tended to be older than their victims, while harassers of men were often younger than their victims. Both women and men had been harassed by married people, though men more often reported that their harassers were divorced or single. Most victims of harassment reported being harassed by persons of their own race or ethnic background. However, minority women were more likely than nonminority women to be harassed by someone of a different race or ethnicity.

Barbara Gutek and Charles Nakamura (1983) point out that if harassment embodies being the target of obscene jokes or catcalls or being expected by members of a work group to do (or being coerced into doing) demeaning tasks, then people at virtually all levels of an organization can be the initiators of harassment. The legal guidelines, however, state that where a lower-level person is the actual initiator of an objectionable behavior (for example, bombarding a co-worker with obscene pictures and letters), the supervisor is also responsible. This suggests that the atmosphere of the workplace is an important factor in sexual harassment and makes managers responsible for supervising this aspect of work.

REACTIONS TO SEXUAL HARASSMENT. Having to fend off unsolicited and offensive sexual advances on a regular basis often causes anger, guilt, stress, and anxiety. Job performance suffers when people are forced to take time and energy away from their work to deal with sexual harassers. The anger they feel at this unjust treatment is often internalized as a deep sense of guilt (Backhouse & Cohen, 1981).

Work-related reprisals for refusing to comply with the harasser's demands can take the form of poor work assignments; sabotaging of projects; denial of raises, benefits, or promotion; and sometimes the loss of the job with only a poor reference to show for it. The stress and anxiety created by such reprisals can drive women or men out of a particular job or out of the workplace altogether (Boston Women's Health Book Collective, 1984).

No one has to work or study in a hostile environment. No person has to put up with lewd comments or touching that makes her or him uncomfortable, and no one has the right to threaten reprisals for refusal of sexual favors. For some tips on what to do about sexual harassment, see the box on "How to Handle Sexual Harassment at Work or at College."

- If the atmosphere of your job makes you uneasy, there are several steps you can take. First and foremost is speaking up. You need to make it clear to an offender that his behavior is offensive. If the behavior doesn't change, you have good cause to pursue the matter through whatever channels your employer provides. Most often, you'll simply have to follow the chain of command, starting with your supervisor.

- Keep records of every incident, including dates, times, and places, exactly what was said and done by everyone involved, and the names of witnesses.

- Bear in mind that the company should not try to solve the situation by transferring you, unless you want a change. Certainly, you should not be punished for lodging a complaint. If anyone has to be involuntarily removed, it should be the offender, particularly if the offender refuses to change his or her behavior.

- If your company does not have an adequate grievance procedure or has one that is unresponsive to complaints of sexual harassment, remind someone significant that the company can be held liable in cases of sexual harassment. Don't threaten; simply point this out so that your superiors will know that you are serious.

- If you are not satisfied with the company's response, there are several courses open to you. You can file a complaint with the local office of the Federal Equal Employment Opportunity Commission (listed in the phone book under U.S. Government agencies). The EEOC can settle the complaint, and can order direct compensation for lost wages, medical expenses, or any other damages you have suffered. A complaint with the EEOC is also the mandatory first step to suing in federal court.

- You can also pursue your case under state law, beginning with the local Division of Human Rights, or proceeding directly to state court. There is no charge to you for such cases.

- If you sue in federal or state court, you can win damages, which can be considerable—although it usually takes years for a case to be resolved. Here, of course, you will probably want to have a lawyer, preferably one experienced in this area. (Eagan, 1989)

College students should keep the following suggestions in mind:

- Become familiar with your college's policy and grievance procedure for sexual harassment cases.

- Seek to discover if any faculty members should be avoided.

- If a professor's behavior is in question, review the situation objectively with someone you can trust. Make sure that you document all incidents.

- Realize that sexual harassment will often increase if you try to ignore it. If this happens, directly tell the professor that you feel uncomfortable with such behavior. Do not hesitate to report the problem to the appropriate college officials. (Dziech & Weiner, 1984; Alliance Against Sexual Coercion, 1982)

MAKING USE OF WHAT WE KNOW

How to Handle Sexual Harassment at Work or at College

Targets of sexual harassment are not the only ones who suffer. Organizations do, too, because they lose the energy and creativity of capable workers. Harassment may also hamper organizations' affirmative action programs. Women may be hired into traditionally male jobs, but unless the employer sees to it that they work in a harassment-free environment, they may leave.

Now that EEOC regulations make employers responsible for sexual harassment, the number of cases reported is likely to rise dramatically. Thus there are both internal and external pressures on organizations today to try to eliminate it (Gutek & Nakamura, 1983).

HOMOSEXUALITY AND THE LAW

Hostility toward gays and lesbians has been a persistent theme in the United States, and over the years various jurisdictions have passed laws that reflect this negative attitude. No community or other jurisdiction has ever ruled that merely to have same-sex preference is illegal. What many states have done, rather, is to decree that specific sexual practices that are more common among and/or preferred by homosexuals—such as anal sex and fellatio—are illegal. And while some municipalities have enacted laws protecting the civil rights of gays and lesbians, no such national statute exists. We look at homosexuality and the law by exploring several important topics: the family, the armed forces, and employment.

Homosexual Family Law

Can gay and lesbian couples legally marry?

Gay and lesbian couples cannot legally marry—even though no state statute expressly denies them this right. Instead, all courts faced with the gay/lesbian marriage issue have relied on the premise that a lawful marriage, by definition, can be entered into only by a man and a woman. No court thus far has taken the stance that prohibition of gay and lesbian marriage is unconstitutional (Sloan, 1987).

Being unable to marry has many implications for gay and lesbian couples. For example, without the legal rights that come with a marriage license, no matter how many years a couple has been together, the partners do not have the right to make medical or financial decisions for each other if one becomes incapacitated. A person may not even be allowed access to an intensive care unit in which his or her partner is being treated for a life-threatening or terminal illness. Partners cannot automatically inherit each other's property, and if they break up, they are not protected by divorce laws. In an effort to combat such discrimination, many gay and lesbian couples are drafting legal documents designed to approximate or duplicate many of the rights of a marriage license (Marcus, 1988). For example, many utilize the cohabitation contracts discussed in Chapter 6 on wills.

The rights of gay and lesbian parents are also legally limited. Many gay and lesbian couples who have children have brought them from a prior marriage or heterosexual relationship of one or both partners, and child custody cases invariably focus on the sexual orientation of such parents. Adoption is also extremely difficult for openly gay and lesbian couples, Irving Sloan (1987) points out that while society's tolerance for alternative life styles is growing, most courts continue to believe that it is in the best interests of a child to be reared in a traditional heterosexual family. The

Many gay and lesbian couples, although they cannot legally marry, participate in ceremonies of commitment whose rituals may closely resemble those of heterosexual wedding ceremonies—even to cutting a cake topped with the traditional figurines.

courts do not deny parents their right to choose alternative life styles, but they do seek to restrict youngsters' exposure to those life styles. Some factors that the courts consider in determining custody and visitation rights are what peer pressures and social stigma the child would have to bear and how the lack of a same-sex role model could affect the child during the formative years.

Eric Marcus (1988) notes that gay and lesbian couples often face certain problems even if they successfully adopt. One is that, just as with custody of a natural child, their right to custody of an adopted child can be challenged at any time. If couples conceal their relationship during the adoption process, they may have to live afterward in fear of being discovered and losing the child. Also, because only one partner can legally adopt the child, if a couple split up, they could find themselves in untested legal waters and a precedent-setting custody battle.

Homosexuality in the Military

Gays and lesbians are ineligible for service in the armed forces. Regulations specifically prohibit military personnel from engaging in private consensual homosexual relations. Such sexual behavior is regarded as a violation of Article 125 of the Uniform Code of Military Justice (UCMJ), which states:

> (a) Any person . . . who engages in unnatural carnal copulation with another person of the same or opposite sex or with an animal is guilty of sodomy. Penetration, however slight, is sufficient to complete the offense. (b) Sodomy shall be punished as a court-martial offense.

In practice, all branches of the military handle the discovery of gay or lesbian activity as an administrative issue, automatically initiating discharge procedures. An administrative discharge for being gay or lesbian can be stated as "honorable," "general under honorable conditions," or "under other than honorable conditions," depending on the circumstances that surround the sexual activity and the quality of the person's service record. The military's continuing policy of discrimination against gay and lesbian members of the service is constantly under challenge in the courts. In fact, that is one of the most heatedly contested areas of the law involving gay and lesbian rights (Sloan, 1987).

In 1991, for example, a U.S. District Court judge for the District of Columbia ruled that the military's ban on gays and lesbians in the armed forces was justified, in part, to prevent the spread of AIDS. Since 1985, the military has screened prospective recruits for the human immunodeficiency virus (HIV). From that time through 1990, about 3500 persons were found to be infected and were denied entry into the military. Active-duty members who contract HIV are allowed to remain in the service until they are too ill to serve, and then are medically discharged. This ruling contrasts with military regulations in other nations. For example, France has no law barring gays and lesbians from the military, and in 1991 Canada began taking measures to remove its antigay military regulations. Great Britain, however, excludes gays and lesbians from its armed forces (Farnsworth, 1991; Schmitt, 1991).

Employment Discrimination

Title VII of the 1964 Civil Rights Act prohibits discrimination in private employment on the basis of race, color, religion, sex, or national origin. In 1990 the Americans with Disabilities Act added age and physical or mental disability to the list of characteristics that may not disqualify a person for employment. Sexual orientation, however, is *not* protected under either of these acts.

Some states, beginning with Wisconsin in 1982, have passed gay and lesbian rights legislation forbidding discrimination in the vocational arena. However, many such ordinances cover only public-sector employment. On the federal civil service level, employees cannot be found unsuitable for employment because of their sexual orientation unless it affects "efficiency of service." The Civil Service Reform Act of 1978 prohibits discrimination "for or against any employee or applicant for employment on the basis of conduct which does not adversely affect the performance of the employee or applicant or the performances of others." Moreover, the privacy rights and constitutional rights of applicants and employees are protected against inquiries into or actions based on non–job-related conduct such as religious, community, or social affiliation or sexual orientation.

Despite such legislation, discrimination in employment still exists in both the private and the public sector. In locales where equal protection is in effect, other reasons for termination may be given (e.g., unsatisfactory job performance, inability to get along with co-workers) to get around the law. In most instances it is difficult to prove discrimination on the basis of sexual orientation. To reduce the risk of getting fired, losing a promotion, or having to deal with hostile or insensitive co-workers, many gay and lesbian workers choose not to reveal their sexual orientation (Blumenfeld & Raymond, 1988; Marcus, 1988).

CONCEPTION AND PROCREATION ISSUES

There are a number of rather new legal issues concerning conception and procreation. We learned in Chapter 10, for example, that while advances in reproductive technology offer new hope for infertile couples, these same advances have raised unprecedented legal and ethical questions. Laws concerning abortion (see Chapter 12) have also generated intense passions.

Reproductive Technology

Without question, such technologies as in vitro fertilization, artificial insemination by donor, surrogate motherhood, and embryo transfer are important medical breakthroughs. However, along with acclaim has come considerable controversy, particularly with respect to surrogacy. For example, the Catholic Church and other groups oppose these scientific advances for religious reasons. To illustrate, the Vatican in 1987 issued an Instruction that condemned artificial insemination even when the sperm is that of a husband (AIH), because the act involves masturbation and because "in seeking a procreation which is not the fruit of a specific act of conjugal union [AIH] objectively effects an analogous separation between the goals and the meanings of marriage." There are also controversies on the legal front. For instance, only 25 states recognize the legitimacy of artificial-insemination-by-donor offspring. Also, there are no clear-cut, comprehensive laws covering the surrogate motherhood arrangement— which is perhaps the most complex legal problem in this whole area.

The 1986 case of Baby M brought to light a number of complicated issues related to surrogacy. The drama of Baby M played out over a three-month period in the Family Law Court in Hackensack, New Jersey. Mary Beth Whitehead, the surrogate mother who bore the child fathered through artificial insemination by William Stern, changed her mind after she gave birth and refused to accept the $10,000 for which she had contracted. Whitehead, the genetic mother, sued to gain custody of the child rather than give the baby to Stern and his wife. The court upheld the surrogacy contract as legal in New Jersey and awarded custody to the Sterns. However, it granted Whitehead visitation rights.

Four years later, in California, a surrogate mother who was genetically unrelated to the child she bore attempted to gain custody of the test-tube baby boy from his genetic parents. This was the first case in which a genetically unrelated surrogate sought custody. Orange County Superior Court Judge Richard Parslow ruled that the child belonged to his genetic parents rather than to the surrogate mother who had carried him. He rejected surrogate mother Anna Johnson's effort to be recognized as a third parent of the five-week-old boy, saying that a surrogate carrying a genetic child for a couple does not acquire parental rights. In making his decision, Judge Parslow stated that he did not want to split the child emotionally between "a three-parent, two natural-mom situation."

Other controversial questions involving surrogate motherhood have so far been settled out of court. One is: What if the parents seeking to have a child conceal something about themselves that the courts have looked on with disfavor? In 1981 Denise Thrane Bhimani contracted with James Noyes to act as a surrogate mother, with no payment other than for medical and incidental expenses. She was inseminated with Noyes' sperm, but before giving birth decided that she wanted custody. The case was filed in court, but settled before trial when it was discovered that Noyes' "wife" was transsexual. The settlement gave complete custody to the surrogate mother, with no visitation rights for Noyes.

Perhaps the stormiest scenario in the surrogate motherhood area took place in 1983. Judy Stiver entered into a contract with a married man, Alexander Malahoff, to be inseminated with his sperm and turn the child over to him after she delivered it. The child was born with microcephaly, a disorder indicating mental retardation. After the diagnosis was made, neither Stiver nor Malahoff wanted the child. Eventually a blood test for paternity was performed and the baby was determined to be that of Mrs. Stiver and her husband. The Stivers had been instructed to abstain from sexual intercourse before insemination took place.

These are not isolated cases. According to experts, many more such cases will surface in years to come. In the last decade there have been over 2000 births through traditional surrogacy (in which a woman's ovum is fertilized with the sperm of a man whose wife cannot conceive) and 85 births through gestational surrogacy (in which the fertilized ovum from one man and woman is placed in the uterus of another woman). Obviously, such arrangements give rise to difficult questions of law, ethics, and mores. What are the legal implications for a surrogate mother who changes her mind or for a natural father who changes his? What if the surrogate mother, contrary to the contract, drinks, smokes, or takes drugs during pregnancy and delivers a damaged child? What happens if the natural father dies before birth or if amniocentesis reveals a genetic disease? Should surrogate motherhood be banned as unnatural and immoral—a form of baby-selling, so to speak? Or should it continue to be permitted as perhaps the only way some infertile couples will be able to have a child genetically related to at least one of them?

We cannot expect to find morally and socially satisfactory answers to such questions overnight. Nonetheless, we must wrestle with them because the issue will not go away. At the very least, surrogate motherhood ought to be legally regulated to protect the interests of the parties involved—especially the child (Issacs & Holt, 1987).

Advances in reproductive technologies have created a gap between science and public policy. Stephen Issacs and Renee Holt (1987) suggest that to narrow this gap we need to formulate some guiding principles. They have suggested five main principles for consideration: protection of children, respect for the right of privacy, ensurance of informed consent, honoring individuals' intentions, and determining access to reproductive technology.

PROTECTION OF CHILDREN. How can the rights of artificially conceived children be protected? These children need legitimacy. They need names and identities. They

*I*t was the first case of its kind in the United States—a woman fighting for control of seven frozen embryos in a 1989 divorce proceeding. Tennessee's Blount County Circuit Judge W. Dale Young had to decide whether the embryos should go to a husband who didn't want children at the time or to a wife who couldn't conceive naturally. As the case wore on, the seven embryos, no bigger than grains of sand, lay frozen in liquid nitrogen at a fertility center in East Tennessee.

Judge Young ruled in favor of Mary Sue Davis, awarding her temporary custody of the embryos. In making his decision, Young grappled with the issue of whether the embryos deserved consideration as potential children (if they did, he would have to decide who would best serve these children's interests) or if they should be considered property (if they were, the matter could be handled like any property dispute). Young ruled that the embryos were children, not property,

and that life began at conception. He added that it was Mrs. Davis's right to carry the embryos to term.

Junior Lewis Davis, the estranged husband, immediately appealed the decision to the Tennessee Court of Appeals. In 1990 that court granted joint custody of the seven frozen embryos to the couple. Davis had asked during the initial trial that Mrs. Davis be barred from ever using any of the seven fertilized eggs without his consent on the ground that he had a right to control his own reproduction. He claimed that awarding the embryos to his wife would force him to become a father against his wishes.

The Tennessee Court of Appeals, in effect, agreed with Davis. It overturned the 1989 landmark decision, ruling that both biological parents shared an interest in the seven fertilized eggs. Judge Herschel P. Franks said that it would be repugnant and offensive to constitutional principles to order Davis to bear the psychological, if not the legal, consequences

need access to their medical records when necessary. They need people willing to nurture and support them. And they need legal rights.

RESPECT FOR THE RIGHT OF PRIVACY. How can we guarantee people their constitutional right to make decisions about personal matters such as having a baby and keep governmental regulations as narrowly drawn and as unintrusive as possible?

INFORMED CONSENT. How can society ensure that informed consent will govern all reproductive technology, or that participants are aware of the risks, benefits, and costs, both monetary and emotional? This will probably need to involve counseling for all concerned parties.

HONORING THE PARTIES' INTENTIONS. Can reproductive technologies be provided in a manner that honors the intentions of the participants to accept or deny the responsibilities of parenthood, regardless of genetics, unless there are compelling reasons not to do so?

ACCESS TO REPRODUCTIVE TECHNOLOGIES. How can society establish uniform standards of screening for genetic and sexually transmitted diseases for everyone who is conceiving a child? Is it possible to redefine the concept of "family" in terms that more accurately reflect social reality? Can society define "capacity to parent" in ways that do not deny parenthood to people simply because they choose an alternative life style?

As of 1990, 10 states have passed laws governing surrogacy contracts like the one under which Whitehead gave birth to the Sterns' child. However, many issues related to reproductive technology still have to be studied and the problems they present resolved. In the meantime, couples who are unable to conceive a child together must research their options on their own—and think very carefully about

of paternity against his will. Franks added that it would be equally repugnant to order Mrs. Davis to implant these fertilized eggs against her will. In 1992, the Tennessee Supreme Court upheld the 1989 ruling, maintaining that privacy rights extend into the realm of forced parenthood. Privacy rights include the right to procreate as well as the right to avoid procreation.

The genesis of this strange case was as follows: After Mary Sue and Junior Lewis Davis married in 1980, Mrs. Davis had five tubal pregnancies, resulting in the rupture of one fallopian tube and the tying of the other. Hearing about the potential of reproductive technology to give them a child, the couple entered a Tennessee in vitro fertilization program in 1988. However, repeated efforts at retrieving an ovum from Mrs. Davis's ovaries, fertilizing it in a petri dish, and then implanting it in her uterus failed. During the last in vitro fertilization attempt, doctors froze what are technically known as pre-embryos, since they are composed of undifferentiated cells, and stored seven for future use. The Davises were never offered a consent form specifying, for example, what might become of their embryos in the event of death or divorce—an omission that helped pave the way for the conflict.

The initial Davis decision recognizing an embryo as a human being was a landmark ruling, one that has serious implications for abortion policies as well as reproductive technologies. The Davis case brings into sharp focus the legal and ethical problems raised by innovative reproductive technologies. Medical knowledge continues to race forward, while we stumble along behind trying to formulate legal and ethical policies to deal with the implications of this revolutionary knowledge. The Davis case illustrates that the rights—or at least the potential rights—of the embryos deserve consideration. (Klein, 1989)

---

the issues involved in their eventual choice (Issacs, 1986). For another illustrative reproductive technology issue see the box on "The Case of the Frozen Embryos."

Abortion and the Law

The issue of abortion is highly charged, as we saw in Chapter 12, and in recent years it has become something of a political football. Both pro-life and pro-choice factions have been backed by opposing political groups with the unfortunate result of shifting the public's focus from the issue itself to such bogus issues as which political candidate holds true "family values."

Although public opinion polls suggest that most Americans are closer to the pro-choice than the pro-life side of the debate, these polls also indicate that many people want some restrictions on abortion, such as a determination of the viability of the fetus, or its ability to survive outside the womb. The early issue of when the fetus develops a "soul" has been translated into such questions as when the fetus's brain is well enough organized to be considered truly human. Because science has not been able to answer these and related questions for us, our beliefs and choices in such matters as abortion and euthanasia (bringing about a painless death in someone afflicted with an apparently terminal illness) must of necessity be based more on values than on empirical evidence.

Many events (see Table 21–1) have shaped the present legal status of abortion in the United States. You will recall from Chapter 12 that the 1973 *Roe* v. *Wade* Supreme Court decision gave American women the right to choose to have a safe and legal abortion, but that the 1989 *Webster* v. *Health Reproductive Services* ruling in favor of a 1986 Missouri law imposed a number of restrictions on women's ability to terminate their pregnancies. Some authorities hold that by limiting the use of public monies either for abortion counseling or for the actual procedure, *Webster* has again made it easier for the wealthy to obtain abortions than the poor. And the ruling's

What is the legal status of abortion today?

TABLE 21-1

Events Shaping United States Abortion Laws

1915 Margaret Sanger is arrested for protesting the failure to care for indigent New York women dying of self-induced abortions.

1962 Sherri Finkbine is denied a legal abortion in the United States, which she sought because of birth defects induced in her fetus by her ingestion of the tranquilizer thalidomide during her pregnancy. She obtained an abortion abroad.

1970 New York and Hawaii pass legislation placing the decision of whether or not to have an abortion in the hands of the pregnant woman and her doctor.

1971 Medicaid funding for abortion care is instituted in New York State.

1973 The U.S. Supreme Court legalizes abortion throughout the United States in *Roe* v. *Wade* on the grounds that a woman's decision to end a pregnancy is supported by the fundamental constitutional right of privacy.

1976 Congress passes the Hyde Amendment, which restricts the use of Medicaid funds for abortions to cases in which the pregnancy endangers the pregnant woman's life.

1977 The U.S. Supreme Court rules that states may deny Medicaid funds for abortions unrelated to medical emergencies.

1979 In *Belloti* v. *Baird* the U.S. Supreme Court reaffirms that a minor, unmarried female does not need parental consent to obtain an abortion.

1980 The U.S. Supreme Court upholds the Hyde Amendment.

1981 The Human Life (Helms-Hyde) Bill proposes enforcing the obligations of states, under the Fourteenth Amendment, not to deprive persons of life without due process of law. The Bill states that human life, and therefore personhood, exists from the moment of conception.

1985 The Reagan administration asks the U.S. Supreme Court to overturn *Roe* v. *Wade*.

1986 The U.S. Supreme Court overturns a Pennsylvania law designed to discourage women from seeking abortion, thus reaffirming its 1973 *Roe* v. *Wade* decision.

1989 The U.S. Supreme Court upholds several provisions of a Missouri law that imposes abortion restraints in its *Webster* v. *Reproductive Health Services* decision. These include a ban on the use of tax money for "encouraging and counseling" women to have abortions not necessary to save a life; a prohibition against any public employee (doctor, nurse, or other health care provider) performing or assisting in an abortion not necessary to save a woman's life; and a ban on the use of any public hospital or other facility for performing abortions not necessary to save a life. Also, doctors are required to determine, when possible, whether a fetus at least 20 weeks old is capable of surviving outside the womb, by tests of lung capacity and other fetal characteristics.

1992 The U.S. Supreme Court rules that women have a constitutional right to abortion, upholding the core of the *Roe* v. *Wade* ruling. However, the Court also approved most of Pennsylvania's 1989 restrictive abortion law, including the provisions: that women contemplating abortion receive information about fetal development and abortion alternatives, such as adoption; that women wait 24 hours for an abortion; and that minors seeking abortion obtain approval from a parent or a judge. The Court struck down a Pennsylvania provision requiring that wives notify their husbands of an abortion.

Source: Adapted, in part, from Covington & McClendon (1987).

The Supreme Court's deliberations in Webster v. Reproductive Health Services *in 1989, brought many people out in demonstrations that included both prolife and prochoice activists.*

requirement that a doctor determine the viability of any fetus that may be aborted adds many medical and philosophical complexities to the picture.

In 1992, a deeply divided Supreme Court ruled in a 5–4 vote that women have a constitutional right to abortion, upholding the core of the *Roe* v. *Wade* ruling. However, by a 7–2 margin, the Supreme Court also voted to uphold most of Pennsylvania's 1989 restrictive abortion law. More specifically, the 1992 Supreme Court ruled that:

- Women seeking abortion must be informed about fetal development and alternatives to ending their pregnancies.
- Women must wait at least 24 hours after receiving that information.
- Doctors are required to keep detailed records, subject to public disclosure, on each abortion performed.

- Unmarried females under age 18 and not supporting themselves are required to obtain the consent of one of their parents, or the permission of a state judge who has ruled that the female seeking an abortion is mature enough to make the decision on her own.
- Married women are not required to tell their husbands about their plans to abort.

The 1989 and 1992 Supreme Court rulings added new fuel to a long-standing and heated debate. While the 1973 *Roe* v. *Wade* ruling was hailed by those favoring a woman's right to control her own body, the 1989 and 1992 Supreme Court decisions embolden states to enact a wave of new laws sharply restricting abortion. Indeed, these recent rulings were viewed by many anti-abortionists as significantly weakening the landmark *Roe* v. *Wade* decision and creating new hurdles for women seeking to end their pregnancies. Without question, these Supreme Court decisions signal a new era of abortion politics. For the first time since 1973, state legislatures were empowered to restrict women's access to abortion.

PORNOGRAPHY

Pornography includes pictures, films, literature, and objects that are designed to cause sexual excitement or arousal. The word *pornography* is derived from the Greek word *porna,* meaning "prostitute," and *graphos,* "writing." Originally pornography referred to the writings of prostitutes themselves or descriptions of their lives written by others. Although pornography has been around for many centuries, there is no consensus on exactly what it constitutes and whether to permit or restrict it.

What exactly constitutes pornography? Is all pornography illegal?

Many people mistakenly think that all pornography is illegal. Actually, pornography is not considered illegal unless it is found to be obscene. *Obscene* refers to anything that is offensive or disgusting to morality, modesty, or decency. Pornographic material in general is protected by the First Amendment, which prohibits the enactment of any law abridging the freedom of speech or of the press. In most instances, only if material is first judged obscene may it be prohibited. However, as law experts such as Daniel Moretti (1984) point out, defining obscenity has proved to be a difficult task. In fact, obscenity law has given rise to one of the longest and most arduous struggles in the history of American jurisprudence.

pornography Pictures, films, literature, and objects that are designed to cause sexual excitement or arousal.

Historical and Legal Perspectives

Explicit reference to sexual activity was common among classic Greek and Roman poets such as Aristophanes, Catullus, and Ovid. Statues and paintings of Priapus, the Greek god of fruitfulness, showed a greatly exaggerated penis. In Pompeii many brothels displayed depictions of intercourse as well as other forms of sexual activity. In Eastern cultures, as we saw in an earlier chapter, love manuals such as the *Kama Sutra* provided readers with explicit narratives and pictures of sexual techniques and pleasuring. During medieval times the writings of Chaucer, Dunbar, and others were sometimes sexually explicit.

So sexually explicit materials have been with us since the earliest civilizations. Efforts at defining obscenity have been with us almost as long. One of our earliest *legal* definitions is derived from the English case of *Regina* v. *Hicklin,* decided in 1868. Taking their cue from this case, U.S. courts deemed material to be obscene if it tended to "deprave" and corrupt those whose minds were open to such immoral influences. The custom in the nineteenth century was for courts to view isolated passages from books and judge whether these would have harmful effects upon susceptible individuals. Until well into the twentieth century, the *Hicklin* ruling was the foundation of American obscenity law.

The first serious challenge to the *Hicklin* precedent came in 1957, in *Roth* v. *United States*. Samuel Roth was accused of violating obscenity statutes because he sold books and magazines that government authorities deemed obscene. Roth, however, claimed that the material being sold was protected under the First Amendment. Up to this point, the U.S. Supreme Court had never dealt directly with the First Amendment issue. After extensive deliberations, it ruled that obscene material was not protected by the First Amendment.

However, the Court also rejected the *Hicklin* precedent and established three new criteria for determining whether material was obscene. First, the Court said that material was obscene if its dominant theme appealed to a prurient interest in sex— that is, if it had a tendency to excite lustful thoughts. Second, material was judged obscene if it was "patently offensive" to contemporary community standards regarding sexual matters. Finally, material was deemed obscene if it was "utterly without redeeming social value."

In time, the *Roth* decision was also challenged, particularly for its vague and subjective language. Many people questioned whether such phrases as *prurient interest, patently offensive*, and *utterly without redeeming social value* could be objectively applied. Prosecutors found it difficult to obtain obscenity convictions because of the ambiguity of these phrases. Most of those interested in the law thought that the obscenity standard in the United States needed to be more clearly defined.

The Supreme Court did just this in 1973, in *Miller* v. *California*. In this decision the Court stated that *local* community standards could be used in obscenity trials. The Court ruled that all three of the following conditions had to be met in order for something to be considered obscene:

1. The average person, applying contemporary community standards, finds that the work, taken as a whole, appears to be of prurient interest;
2. The work describes or depicts, in a patently offensive way, sexual conduct, specifically defined by the applicable state law.
3. The work, taken as a whole, lacks serious literary, artistic, political, or scientific value.

The *Miller* ruling was important for several reasons. First, it did not require that material be "utterly without redeeming social value" in order to be judged obscene. Rather, it only required that the material not have "serious value"—making it easier to establish a finding of obscenity. The *Miller* ruling also stated that obscenity is not to be judged by some national standard, but rather according to the prevailing standards of the community in which the trial is conducted. Finally, the *Miller* ruling also provided examples of what the Court regarded as "patently offensive," thus giving states guidelines for defining and prohibiting obscenity. These examples included: representations or descriptions of ultimate sexual acts, normal or perverted, actual or simulated; representations or descriptions of masturbation or excretory functions; and lewd or vulgar exhibitions of the genitalia. The *Miller* ruling did not make anyone liable to prosecution for the sale or exposure of obscene materials unless these materials depicted "hard-core" sexual conduct (i.e., persons engaged in sexual activity) specifically defined as such by the regulating state law.

Thus while the *Miller* decision reaffirmed the *Roth* ruling that obscene materials were not protected by the First Amendment, the Supreme Court substantially modified the standard for determining what constitutes obscenity. First, only "hard-core" pornography could be prohibited. Second, the material must not possess any "serious value." Third, material was to be judged on a community-by-community basis. Fourth, specific guidelines were established as to what material can be deemed "patently offensive." While many people feel that these terms are still vague and subjective, and that depictions and descriptions of sexual acts have different meanings for different people, the *Miller* criteria remain the constitutional test for obscenity (Moretti, 1984).

Pornography and Public Opinion

Public opinion on pornography is divided. Many Americans are vehemently opposed to pornography, believing that it is morally wrong. Others feel that pornography dehumanizes and debases women, depicting them as sex objects to be used, abused, and exploited by men. Some feminist activists have even launched strong antipornography campaigns—although other feminists see these campaigns as a dangerous assault on First Amendment rights. Very many Americans think that pornography depicting sadomasochism or sex with children serves as a "trigger" for sexual offenses.

Feminists have objected to pornography for several reasons. They feel that it debases women, particularly some hard-core pornography in which women are depicted in chains, being urinated upon, raped, or set upon by animals. The ability to purchase such depictions, they feel, engenders or reinforces negative male attitudes toward women. Worse, the violence in such pornography, many believe fosters rape and other violent crimes against women (see, for example, Demare, Briere, & Lips, 1988). Finally, feminists point out that pornography characteristically depicts women as subordinate to men.

Others who also oppose pornography believe that censorship is an even greater evil. They think that banning pornography is a violation of the First Amendment. Civil liberties organizations, in particular, see censorship as all of a piece—whether it be of pornography, serious literature, or schoolbooks.

Finally, there are those who defend pornography on the grounds that it provides an outlet for bottled-up sexual impulses, thus serving as a "safety valve" rather than a trigger. In their view, pornography gives people an opportunity to privately discharge or release their sexual fantasies without harming others. Used this way, they say, pornography is a harmless source of sexual pleasure and excitement. What do you think? Do you find this view consistent with the violence portrayed in so much contemporary pornography?

Investigations of Obscenity and Pornography

The preceding discussion illustrates the enormous variation in opinions on pornography. Can any of these opinions be supported by fact? What have social science researchers discovered about the effects of sexually explicit material? Does pornography serve as a "trigger" and inspire crimes of violence, particularly against women? Or is it a "safety valve," as others contend? These are important questions, and several investigations in recent decades have attempted to address them.

1970 COMMISSION ON OBSCENITY AND PORNOGRAPHY. In 1968 President Richard M. Nixon appointed a special commission to study pornography, including its effects upon the public, laws pertaining to its control, and the nature and volume of pornographic traffic. The 18-member commission, headed by William B. Lockhart, examined scientific research, viewed publications and films that might be considered pornographic, and listened to hours of expert testimony. In 1970 the commission issued its report, a 10-volume compilation of exhibits accompanied by the commission's findings.

The report's conclusions were not unanimously agreed to by the commissioners, several of whom also strongly disagreed with the methods used by the commission. In individual and group statements they claimed that the research used was flawed in that it relied on surveys and interviews rather than on experimental findings. Critics also pointed out that the commission had conducted no research on violent pornography, an omission that made its findings questionable.

Essentially, the commission report stated that there was no evidence that exposure to or use of explicit sexual materials played a significant role in crime, delinquency, sexual or nonsexual deviance, or severe emotional disturbance. Sex offenders,

Those who oppose the views of feminists and other antipornography activists argue that it is only the depiction of violent sexual acts that incites rape and other abusive behavior. Some feminists respond that any material that depicts sexual acts, no matter how nonviolent, panders to men for whom women are simply sexual objects.

the commission concluded, were not more heavily exposed to pornography than other people were. In addition, the commission found that explicit sexual materials were sought as a source of entertainment and information by substantial numbers of American adults. In fact, the report pointed out, the most frequent purchaser of explicit sexual materials was a college-educated married man in his 30s or 40s who was of above-average socioeconomic status. Even where materials were legally available to them, adolescents and young adults did not purchase such materials in large numbers. As a result of these findings, the commission recommended relaxing the state and federal regulations that prohibited the distribution of pornographic materials to consenting adults.

The findings of the 1970 commission did not settle the pornography issue, for many people did not accept the judgment that pornography appeared to be harmless. In fact, the report was immediately attacked for being too liberal. Opponents of pornography continued to believe that it had an eroding effect on public morals and that tighter government controls were needed to regulate it.

1986 COMMISSION ON OBSCENITY AND PORNOGRAPHY. By the early 1980s, the moral and political climate of the United States had become more conservative and there was a renewed interest in studying the effects of pornography. In 1985 President Ronald Reagan asked Attorney General Edwin Meese to appoint another commission to investigate the topic. This commission, consisting of 11 members and chaired by Henry E. Hudson, was asked to "determine the nature, extent, and impact on society of pornography in the United States, and to make specific recommendations concerning more effective ways in which the spread of pornography could be contained, consistent with constitutional guarantees."

The Meese Commission evaluated five categories of pornographic material: sexually violent material, sexually degrading material, nonviolent and nondegrading material, nudity, and child pornography. In addition to reviewing thousands of magazines, films, and books, the commission listened to both expert testimony and the testimony of women, men, and children who believed they had been harmed in some manner by or as a result of pornography. In 1986 the commission released its findings in an exhaustive two-volume 1960-page report.

The Meese Commission's conclusions contrasted sharply with those drawn by President Nixon's 1970 commission. The Meese Commission found that there was indeed a causal relationship between exposure to sexually violent materials and aggressive behavior toward women. Viewers' exposure to sexually violent material also tends, the commission said, to encourage the myth that women secretly want to be raped. Moreover, men exposed to sexually violent material become desensitized to the seriousness of rape, perceiving victims as less injured and worthy of sympathy than other men did. The commission also found that rapists were more likely than nonoffenders to have been exposed as children to hard-core pornography. Finally, the commission concluded that even the most nonviolent, nondegrading sexual material was harmful to children exposed to it.

The Meese Commission made 92 recommendations, including proposed changes to federal and state law that would make it easier for prosecutors to bring charges against producers and sellers of pornography. It also recommended stronger enforcement of existing criminal laws against the production, sale, and distribution of child pornography. These recommendations were welcomed by those who found the 1970 commission's report far too liberal.

Still, the Meese Commission report stirred considerable controversy. To begin with, critics felt that its methods lacked scientific objectivity. They also charged that the commission was biased from the start because six of its members had been involved in some type of opposition to pornography before their appointment, and therefore obviously were predisposed to perceive pornography as evil. Another criticism was that the commission ignored research that went contrary to the commissioners' preconceived notions about obscenity and pornography. The American Civil Liberties Union (1986) charged that the commission actually suppressed materials that presented alternative or opposing viewpoints. Criticism was also leveled against the commission's conclusion that there is a link between the viewing of sexually violent pornography and aggressive behavior toward women (we will explore this supposed connection in more detail shortly). Critics felt that such a conclusion was too simplistic and loosely drawn; that while the gathered evidence did indicate a trend toward a cause-effect relationship, there was a need for more methodical and substantive research before claims of definite causation could be made.

RESEARCH ON THE EFFECTS OF SEXUALLY EXPLICIT MATERIAL. There have been some important research studies investigating the effects of sexually explicit material, including the proposed link between violent pornography and aggression against women. One is a study done by Edward Donnerstein (1980) to examine the effects of aggressive-erotic stimuli on male aggression toward women. In Donnerstein's study 120 college men were either provoked or treated neutrally by a female confederate of the experimenter. Later the male subjects viewed neutral, erotic, or aggressive-erotic films. The aggressive-erotic films showed a man forcing himself into a woman's residency and then raping her. The male subjects were then given the opportunity to act aggressively against the female confederate of the experimenter through a fake-shock apparatus. The measure of aggression was the intensity of the shock selected. As anticipated, provoked subjects administered higher shock intensities. But nonprovoked men who saw the aggressive-erotic film demonstrated higher levels of aggression toward the female confederates. Provoked men who saw the aggressive-erotic film administered the strongest shocks to the female confederates.

Neil Malamuth (Malamuth 1981; Malamuth, Heim, & Feshback, 1980) found that both male and female college students usually reported greater levels of sexual arousal to stories about mutually desired sex than to those about rape. However, both men and women were more aroused if the rape victim had an orgasm during the assault than if she did not. Female subjects were most responsive when the victim in the story did not have pain during orgasms, while male subjects were most aroused by depictions of orgasm with pain. The researchers suggested that showing sexual arousal and resulting orgasm in a rape victim legitimized the violence in viewers' minds.

Later Malamuth joined forces with psychologists James Check and John Briere (Malamuth, Check, and Briere, 1986) to construct a two-part experiment designed to explore how levels of sexual arousal relate to aggression. In the first part 37 male and 42 female undergraduate students reported more sexual arousal in response to nonaggressiveness than to aggressive depictions when the depicted activity was sexually explicit. However, the opposite occurred when the depicted activity was nonsexual. In the second part of the experiment 367 males were classified into *no, moderate,* or *high* "arousal from force" groups on the basis of self-reports. To evaluate the self-reports penile tumescence (extent of erection) in response to various depictions was assessed. The findings generally matched those of the first half of the experiment and confirmed the accuracy of the "arousal from force" classification. The *no* and the *moderate* "arousal from force" subjects were less sexually aroused by aggressive than by nonaggressive portrayals, but the opposite was found for the *high* "arousal from force" subjects.

Certain research (e.g., Zillmann & Bryant, 1984; Malamuth & Donnerstein, 1984) shows that exposure to pornography tends to desensitize men to violence against women. Edward Donnerstein and Daniel Linz (1984) explored such desensitization and how it might spill over into decision-making about victims. In their study male subjects watched nearly 10 hours of R-rated and X-rated movies. They saw either R-rated, sexually violent films; X-rated movies that depicted sexual assault; or X-rated movies that showed only consenting sex. After a week of viewing, the men watched a reenactment of an actual rape trial. When it was over, the subjects were asked to

After a grand jury returned indictments of two first-degree misdemeanors—pandering obscenity and using a minor in nudity-displaying materials—Cincinnati police blocked the entrance to the exhibition of Robert Mapplethorpe's highly controversial photographs of children.

child pornography Books, magazines, photographs, and films that depict children in sexually explicit acts.

render judgments about how responsible the victim was for her rape and how much injury she had suffered.

Subjects who were exposed to depictions of sexual violence and assault were initially annoyed and anxious about what they saw, but over the course of the week, these feelings subsided. In addition, they judged fewer scenes and acts of violence offensive in each successive film. By the last day of viewing graphic violence against women, these men were rating the material as significantly less debasing and degrading to women, and more humorous and enjoyable, and were expressing a greater willingness to see this type of film again. The effects of desensitization were also evident in the subjects' reactions to the reenacted trial. The rape victim was perceived as significantly more worthless and her injury as significantly less severe by those men who had been exposed to films depicting sexual violence.

Putting the Findings into Perspective

What does all of this information mean? Today most experts agree that materials that depict sexual violence against women encourage male viewers to be aggressive toward women, although we still don't know why. On the other hand, research to date has *not* shown that sexually explicit material *without* violence encourages aggressive or violent behaviors. This prompts researchers such as Edward Donnerstein and Daniel Linz (1986) to remark that it is violent images, rather than sexual ones, that are an obscenity in our society.

Clearly, there is a need for more research concerning the effects of *all* forms of sexually explicit materials on behavior. This would include not only sexually violent materials, but also degrading and debasing forms of pornography, along with the other varieties. As James Henslin (1990) sees it, future explorations will illuminate the total picture of pornography in a systematic and methodical fashion. The truth about pornography's effects will become apparent as studies are done, scrutinized, repeated, and scrutinized again. At this point, we have to say that social science research cannot settle the questions of causation raised in this chapter. Absent any kind of irrefutable evidence, social activists on either side of the issue must continue to take their positions based on personal conviction.

Child Pornography

Child pornography, also referred to as "kiddie porn," includes books, magazines, photographs, and films that depict children in sexually explicit acts. Over the last 25 years child pornography has become a highly organized multimillion-dollar industry. While it is hard to determine the full extent of child pornography because of its secretive nature, it is believed that thousands of youngsters are being sexually exploited each year. Often there is a link between child pornography and child prostitution; many adults who hire a child prostitute also film their activities.

To protect youngsters from child pornography, Congress and 48 states have enacted statutes specifically prohibiting the *production* of child pornography. About half of the state statutes do not require that materials have to be legally obscene to be banned; as long as they contain child pornography, they can be banned. In addition, 20 states also prohibit the *distribution* of material depicting children in sexual conduct, again without requiring that the material be legally obscene. In adopting such broad statutes states hope to effectively eliminate the child pornography industry (Moretti, 1984).

Ruth and Henry Kempe (1984) tell us that the methods by which youngsters are recruited for child pornography vary. Some are persuaded by promises of money or gifts, while others are seduced by an adult and later introduced to the trade. Some children are deceived and told the acts will be "only pretend"—and then the sexual exploitation begins in front of the camera. Sometimes the child's services are sold by a parent or guardian. Some children become so greedy for the money they are paid that they perform eagerly. Others have to be given alcohol or drugs to make them willing.

The supply of children for the pornography industry seems inexhaustible. They come from every socioeconomic class, family background, and religion. A majority are exploited by someone who knows them, either by virtue of his or her occupation, or through a neighborhood, family, or community relationship. Many victims are too young to know what has happened to them; others are powerless to refuse the demands of an authority figure. Adolescents used in pornography are often runaways, homeless youths, or juvenile prostitutes who may feel they have little choice but to participate (U.S. Attorney General's Commission on Pornography, 1986).

Recruiting a child to the world of pornography generally follows a pattern. First, pornographic pictures are carefully left about where they will be seen, or perhaps are shown as part of a "sex education" lesson. Next, the child is encouraged to copy the depicted behavior. Often videotapes or movies are shown to convince the youngster that explicit sex is acceptable or that others routinely practice it. At this point, the child usually becomes less inhibited. Eventually, the child is enticed into engaging in the suggested sexual activity. Finally, the child is persuaded to perform the activity in front of a camera (Kempe & Kempe, 1984; U.S. Attorney General's Commission on Pornography, 1986). Figure 21–1 illustrates the cycle of child pornography.

The effects of such sexual exploitation on children are devastating. Howard Davidson (1981) writes that many children suffer physical harm as a result of the premature and inappropriate sexual demands placed on them. Even more serious, they are denied healthy emotional development. While the psychological problems of children who are sexually exploited through pornography have not been extensively investigated, there is ample evidence that they often suffer the same kinds of harmful

FIGURE 21–1
A Cycle of Child Pornography.
(Adapted from *Attorney General's Commission on Pornography, Final Report*, 1986)

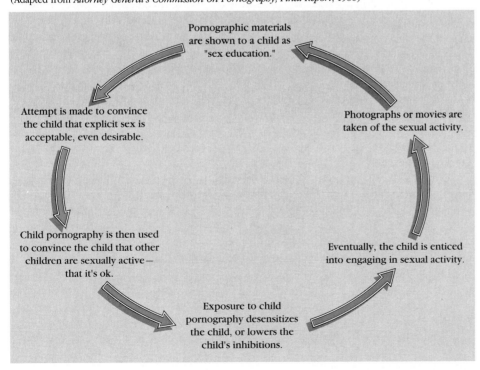

effects that incest victims do, including psychologically induced somatic disorders, depression, and guilt. Often these children grow up to lead a life ruled by drugs and prostitition. Some who are sexually abused turn around and abuse their own children. All of these negative effects signal the need for therapeutic intervention for victims of child pornography. Many of the treatment approaches presented in Chapter 19 are applicable, including individual, group, and play therapy.

Prostitution

prostitution The exchange of sexual services for money.

What's a gigolo? Is it the same as a pimp?

pimp A man who provides a prostitute with protection and basic necessities while living off her earnings.

madam A woman who heads a house of prostitution or brothel.

Prostitution is the provision of sexual activity in return for money. As we saw in Chapter 1, the practice is rooted in antiquity. In the most common form of prostitution, a woman, sometimes called a *whore* or a *hooker,* engages in sexual activity with a man for an agreed price. A male prostitute, called a *gigolo,* provides sexual services to female clients. Some male prostitutes, called *hustlers,* service other men. Least common of all are female prostitutes who provide sexual services to women.

Most prostitutes work for other people and do not get to keep all of the money paid by their clients (called *johns, scores, marks,* or *tricks*). A **pimp** is a man who provides a prostitute with protection and basic necessities while living off her earnings. When he has more than one prostitute working for him, the pimp is said to control a *stable*. A **madam** is a woman who heads a house of prostitution or brothel (also called a *whorehouse*) and makes her living from her employees' earnings.

Legal Status of Prostitution

In the United States prostitution is illegal in every state except Nevada. Nevada permits county autonomy on this issue, and prostitution is tolerated in 15 out of 17 counties, though solicitation in public and semipublic places is illegal. Prostitutes who work in Nevada must register with the state and receive monthly health examinations, including HIV antibody testing. In recent years the AIDS scare has created a significant decline in the Nevada sex-for-sale business (Chaze, Hawkins, & Lord, 1987).

Despite its illegal status, prostitution is a thriving business in all other states as well, and it is openly practiced in most major cities. It is difficult to determine how many prostitutes there are in the United States today, but one conservative estimate (Sheehy, 1983) places the figure between 200,000 to 250,000. Taking the lower estimate, and assuming six clients per day at the bottom price of $20 per "trick," prostitution generates between $7 billion and $9 billion a year—all of it untaxed. This is about 10 times the entire annual budget of the U.S. Department of Justice! One source (Elias, 1985) estimates that the average prostitute in the United States today earns $75,000 tax-free annually. However, as we'll see, few prostitutes pocket this kind of money because most of it is siphoned off by pimps and other figures who control this shadowy enterprise.

Should prostitution be legalized? Proponents of legalization point out that laws have failed to stamp out, or even repress, prostitution from time immemorial. Organizations such as COYOTE (Call Off Your Old Tired Ethics) and PUMA (Prostitutes' Union of Massachusetts) stress that prostitution is an activity between two consenting adults, and therefore shouldn't be defined as a crime. They claim that legalizing it would reduce police and court costs, thus allowing the legal system to focus on more pressing issues.

In other nations the legalization and regulation of prostitution have met with some degree of success. In European cities such as Stockholm, Amsterdam, and Hamburg, there are stipulated places where prostitution is tolerated by the police and the community. In Holland, for instance, prostitution is allowed in designated

In this New York City scene, a streetwalking prostitute negotiates with the driver of a passing car.

red-light districts to which prostitutes are confined. Informal controls limit the number of prostitutes, who must be 21 years of age or married (Carmen & Moody, 1985).

Opponents of legalization believe that prostitution is immoral and that the state has the obligation to protect society against it. They maintain that prostitution abuses, exploits, and degrades women, especially those who lack the job skills to compete in the legitimate labor force. Opponents also cite how prostitution and crime are interwoven and how random sexual encounters inevitably contain some aspect of squalor and violence. In recent years the escalating numbers of sexually transmitted diseases, particularly AIDS, have proved a powerful argument against the legalization of prostitution. Opponents believe that even tight medical scrutiny would not be able to stop the spread of sexually transmitted diseases since many prostitutes would probably not register with the authorities and undergo regular medical examinations. This is especially true of those who are infected, since most would fear being arrested (Horton, Leslie, & Larson, 1988).

Categories of Prostitutes

As in other times, prostitution today is characterized by different social levels, or classes. Prostitutes within these levels charge different fees for their services, serve different clienteles, and have different socioeconomic and educational backgrounds. Let's briefly examine five types.

STREETWALKER. A streetwalker occupies the lowest level of prostitution and is the most visible kind of prostitute. She walks the streets, or "works the block," in an effort to attract clients, often approaching men and attempting to initiate a conversation. Most streetwalkers are members of an ethnic or racial minority, poorly educated, and from low socioeconomic backgrounds. Streetwalkers are the most frequently arrested of all prostitutes, and their sexual services are usually the least expensive (anywhere from $20 to $75).

MASSAGE PARLOR PROSTITUTE. It is incorrect to think that all massage parlors are thinly veiled houses of prostitution. Many employ legitimate massage therapists and offer a range of other health and fitness services, including sauna baths and suntanning booths. Still, many are no more than fronts for paid sex. A massage parlor prostitute, often referred to as a *hand whore,* usually specializes in massage and masturbation (also called *M and M* or *local*). Fees usually range from $15 to $20 for a massage, with extra fees for additional services performed (for example, wearing no top, no bottom, or performing fellatio).

BAR GIRL. The bar girl, or B-girl, seeks clients in bars and nightclubs. Usually, she has some type of financial arrangement with the owner to use the establishment as her headquarters. She generally hustles drinks for the bar owner in addition to making her own arrangements for paid sex. Sometimes the bar or nightclub makes rooms available for the trick, the cost of which can range from $50 to $100.

HOUSE PROSTITUTE. An employee of a brothel, the house prostitute must accept any customer the madam assigns her and must split the fee (often $100 to $150) with the madam. In return, the madam provides her with room, board and, usually, medical examinations. Although her living conditions may be reasonably good, the house prostitute is often as exploited by her madam as the streetwalker is by her pimp. Most cities have brothels, but they are illegal in every state but Nevada.

CALL GIRL. A call girl is the aristocrat of prostitutes. Call girls are usually the most attractive, best educated, best dressed, and most socially skilled of all prostitutes. They also charge the highest fees (anywhere from $250 to $500), and many of their clients are referrals from other customers or personal references. The call girl usually makes an appointment with the client over the telephone and arranges to meet him in her residence or his. Sometimes call girls are hired as companions for social events. Most of the clients are from upper socioeconomic classes.

What Motivates Prostitutes?

Why do some women want to become prostitutes? Are all prostitutes the same?

There are many different reasons for becoming a prostitute. Many turn to prostitution because of the prospects for making fast money. While there are some from upper socioeconomic brackets, most people who become prostitutes are from lower socioeconomic backgrounds. In fact, most prostitutes are uneducated and unemployed and turn to prostitution as a quick and easy way to make a living. Consider the reflections of these two female prostitutes:

> . . . It all started when one of my girlfriends was working. We used to sit down and talk about what she was doing. She used to tell me about how much money she was making and the things she used to do, and I started thinking about the money I didn't have. . . . (Carmen & Moody, 1985, p. 102).

> I was all by myself, had nowhere to go. I was hungry, couldn't go home, and I had no money to eat or live. So I came on the streets and started working to make some money, and now I'm not hungry and have a place to live. No one had to put me on the streets. The money is cool, but at least I don't have to be hungry or sleep on the streets, or worry about where my next meal is coming from, or where I'm going to sleep." (pp. 102–103).

Researchers (e.g., Silbert & Pines, 1982; Williams & Kornblum, 1985) have found that many prostitutes grew up in an unfavorable home climate. In addition to poverty, they often experienced sexual abuse, physical battering, neglect, and emotional deprivation. Such experiences tended to create shame, loss of self-esteem, and a wide mixture of insecurities. A large number of prostitutes come from broken homes. During childhood, many tended to be disruptive or labeled "different" by teachers and friends. Many were also sexually active as teenagers. In her research on black, Hispanic, and white prostitutes, Eleanor Miller (1986) found that drugs were often milestones on the road to prostitution. Many of her subjects first used drugs and then turned to prostitution to obtain the money they needed to support their drug habit.

What Motivates Clients?

People have many different reasons for visiting a prostitute. Some men, such as servicemen and salesmen, are away from their partners for extended periods of time and turn to prostitutes for sexual release. Some clients are separated or divorced and seek a sexual partner. Some, such as those who use call girls, desire companionship for a social event such as dinner or a concert. Many men use prostitutes because they offer sexual novelty, experience, or nonconventional sex practices. Some men hire prostitutes because they have difficulty initiating and maintaining sexual relationships, perhaps because of physical deformities or psychological insecurities. Still others desire a brief, unattached relationship that meets their immediate needs. Men often use prostitutes because they want a relationship that is purely sexual, does not entail emotional commitment, and occurs in an anonymous setting.

Life-Style Problems and Adjustments

A popular misconception about prostitution is that it is a glamorous, intriguing, and exciting life style. While this may be true for a few high-earning call girls, the majority of prostitutes live in a tough and dangerous underworld and their lives are often characterized by gradual self-destruction. As Arlene Carmen and Howard Moody (1985) observe, it would be hard to find a group of people in our society whose rights are more violated, whose dignity is more denigrated, and whose work is made more miserable than streetwalking prostitutes.

Most prostitutes have an uneasy alliance with their pimps and feel used and intimidated by them. At best, they are servants; at worst, they are treated like slaves. Many are physically beaten by their pimps and exposed to a steady barrage of threats, insults, and humiliation. Additionally, most feel degraded by their clients and harassed by the police. And they are discriminated against: far more women are arrested for providing illegal sexual services than men are arrested for purchasing those same illegal services. There are hardly any advocates of the rights of prostitutes, not to mention their protection.

Because of such hardships, abuse, and inequalities, most prostitutes express gloom and dissatisfaction about "the life." They feel trapped, but reason that without occupational skills, prostitution offers the path of least resistance. Many resign themselves to thinking there is "no way out." Because they are financially exploited by others, most have little to show for their efforts. The average prostitute becomes old before her time in a profession that exalts youth and physical attractiveness. Many turn to drugs to ward off the stark realities of their everyday lives. The possibility of contracting AIDS or other sexually transmitted diseases further adds to the risks and drawbacks of being a prostitute. Similar to other victims of sexual exploitation, therapeutic intervention is needed for these individuals, including individual and group treatment approaches.

SEXUALITY IN THE NEWS

Mapplethorpe: Obscenity in Cincinnati

*T*his video deals with the censorship of materials deemed obscene. Or pornographic. Aired April 10, 1990, on ABC's "Nightline," the segment discusses Robert Mapplethorpe's controversial photographs of children, which include explicit sexual poses, at the Cincinnati Contemporary Arts Center. As Ted Koppel notes, the director of the Center was exposed to public outcry on both sides of the issue concerning First Amendment rights and the right of artistic expression. The issue of community values—in this case, Cincinnati's—came under scrutiny because of the media coverage of the controversy.

DISCUSSION QUESTIONS

1. Ted Koppel asks, "Who decides what is art and what is obscene and what you should and should not be allowed to see in a museum?" After viewing the video, do you believe this question was answered in Cincinnati? Defend your answer.

2. The photograph exhibit was shown in several cities without public uproar. Why do you believe Cincinnati authorities took such offense?

3. Did either Mark Snyder, spokesman for Citizens for Community Values, or Allen Brown, an attorney who has defended the First Amendment rights of a number of controversial artists, persuade you to his point of view? Which side of this issue do you find yourself on? How would you react if this photography exhibit came to your hometown?

LOOKING BACK

■ Laws pertaining to sexual behaviors exist at the federal, state, and municipal levels. Consensual sexual activities such as fornication or adultery involve sexual activities in which adults agree to participate. They are designated illegal because they are considered immoral in and of themselves or because they occur outside the institution of marriage. Laws against sodomy illustrate how certain specific sexual behaviors between consenting adults may be illegal. Nonconsensual sexual behaviors such as rape are those that involve the use or threat of force, violence, or exploitation in sexual relations.

■ Numerous legal efforts have been made to eliminate sex discrimination, which is the unfair or unequal treatment of a person on the basis of his or her sex. While there have been important gains in this area, sex discrimination persists: employed women generally earn far less than employed men; and women are underrepresented in virtually every job that is prestigious or well paid, while they are overrepresented in low-paid, dead-end jobs. Sexual harassment is defined as any unwanted sexual advance, verbal or physical, that occurs in the workplace or in an academic setting. Besides making the environment uncomfortable—even intolerable—for its victims, sexual harassment endangers their jobs, undermines their job performance and threatens their economic livelihood. Women are far

more frequent targets of sexual harassment than men are.

■ Over the years laws have been passed banning sexual activities, like fellatio and anal intercourse, that are preferred by some homosexuals, reflecting society's general disapproval of homosexuality. In addition, gay and lesbian couples cannot legally marry, which has numerous financial and medical consequences. The rights of gay and lesbian parents are also limited. Currently, gays and lesbians are ineligible for service in the armed forces, though the military's policy of discrimination is under challenge in the courts.

■ Important legal issues have evolved in the area of reproduction. While new reproductive technologies have provided hope for infertile couples, these innovative medical procedures have given rise to unprecedented legal and ethical controversies. The practice of surrogate motherhood, in particular calls for the establishment of some guiding principles to ensure the protection of children, the right of privacy, informed consent, the honoring of individuals' intentions, and access to reproductive technology. The legalization of abortion in *Roe* v. *Wade* also generated intense passions and legal challenges. The Supreme Court's landmark decisions in 1989 and 1992 allowed states to put significant restrictions on the right to abortion.

■ Pornography includes pictures, films, literature, and objects that are designed to cause sexual excitement or arousal. Pornography has existed for centuries, but there is still considerable disagreement over exactly what it constitutes and whether to permit or restrict it. Pornography is not considered illegal unless it is found to be obscene, but defining obscenity has been difficult. Most researchers believe that materials that depict sexual violence against women encourage male viewers to be aggressive toward women, but we have no hard evidence as yet that this is so.

■ Prostitution is the provision of sexual services in return for money. Different forms of prostitution exist, the most common of which involves heterosexual sexual activity for which the female prostitute is paid by a male client. Although prostitution is illegal in every state except Nevada, it is a thriving business in most states and is openly practiced in many major cities. Prostitutes may be streetwalkers or work in massage parlors, bars, or houses of prostitution; or they may work for a central agency, or out of their own homes, as call girls.

THINKING THINGS OVER

1. Some of the laws you have learned about here may regulate your own behavior. Which of these laws do you believe should be stricken from the books? Why?

2. A friend at work informs you that she thinks she is a victim of sexual harrassment. While her employer has not asked for sexual favors, he continually makes suggestive comments that make her feel uncomfortable and nervous. What kinds of information on sexual harassment can you supply your friend? What steps might she take to stop the unwanted behavior?

3. Which of the ethical and legal issues surrounding the reproductive technologies do you feel are the most pressing? Support your answer. Can you think of any other issues that we have not considered in this chapter?

4. React to the following statement: "Pornography is in the eyes of the beholder." Try to define pornography.

5. Why do you believe that prostitution is illegal throughout the United States except in Nevada? Choose a position on legalizing prostitution in all states and defend that position.

DISCOVER FOR YOURSELF

Donnerstein, E., Linz, D., & Penrod, S. (1987). *The question of pornography: Research findings and policy implications*. New York: Free Press. A comprehensive examination of research to date on pornography.

McNamara, D. E., & Sagarin, E. (1983). *Sex, crime, and the law*. New York: Free Press. An assortment of topics on the law, including the need to rethink and reform some laws.

Miller, E. M. (1986). *Street woman*. Philadelphia: Temple University Press. An intriguing and captivating account of the everyday life of street prostitutes.

Soble, A. (1986). *Pornography*. New Haven, CT: Yale University Press. Soble offers a good discussion of feminism, pornography, and erotica.

Shilling, D. (1985). *Redress for success: Using the law to enforce your rights as a woman*. New York: Penguin Books. A readable guide to how to take legal action to ensure women's rights. Topics range from sex discrimination in employment to reproductive rights.

Glossary

abortion The termination of a pregnancy by natural or artificially induced means.

abstinence The avoidance of sexual intercourse.

acquaintance rape Rape that occurs between people who know each other.

acquired immune deficiency syndrome (AIDS) A catastrophic illness in which the human immunodeficiency virus destroys the ability of the body to fight off invaders, rendering the person vulnerable to a host of diseases.

acrosomal cap The covering of the head of the spermatozoon that contains a special enzyme designed to penetrate the outer structure of the ovum.

adolescence The life stage between childhood and adulthood.

adolescent growth spurt The rapid gain in height, weight, and skeletal mass that precedes puberty. This growth continues at a slower rate throughout adolescence.

adultery Sexual intercourse with a person other than one's spouse.

agape love A gentle, altruistic form of love.

alveoli Milk-producing lobes in the breast that are separated from each other by fibrous and fatty walls and drained by the lactiferous ducts.

amniocentesis Removal of fluid from the amniotic sac for chromosomal analysis.

amniotic fluid Liquid that holds the embryo or fetus in suspension and protects it against jarring and from any pressure exerted by the mother's internal organs.

amniotic fluid replacement A type of induced abortion usually performed between the 16th and 20th weeks of pregnancy. Most often, the drug prostaglandin is used to cause contractions and fetal expulsion.

amniotic sac Transparent membrane completely enveloping the embryo or fetus, except where the umbilical cord passes through to the placenta.

amphetamines Drugs that act as central nervous system stimulants, generally causing accelerated bodily functions as well as heightened energy and mood changes.

ampulla In the female, the outer two-thirds of the fallopian tube; the portion of the tube in which fertilization of the ovum by a spermatozoon typically takes place. In the male, the enlarged portion of the vas deferens that combines with the seminal vesicle to form an ejaculatory duct.

amyl nitrite A vasodilator prescription drug used in the treatment of angina pectoris. As a recreational drug, it is used as a sexual stimulant.

anal intercourse The insertion of the penis into a partner's rectum.

anal stage The second stage of Freud's psychosexual development theory in which the child is focused on anal pleasure.

anaphrodisiac A substance that has the capacity to diminish or inhibit sexual arousal, desire, and satisfaction.

anatomical sex The physical characteristics and features that distinguish females from males.

androgens Hormones produced primarily by the interstitial (Leydig's) cells of the testes, and to a lesser extent by the adrenal glands of both males and females. Testosterone is the most common form of androgen.

androgyny The quality of having both masculine and feminine characteristics. Considered by some to be a desirable quality, inasmuch as both male and female traits and skills are useful and beneficial.

anger rapist A rapist who engages in unpremeditated savage attacks that are prompted by feelings of hatred and resentment.

angina pectoris A cardiac condition that occurs when the supply of blood to a part of the heart muscle is insufficient to meet its needs, causing severe pain in the chest and often the left shoulder and arm.

antiandrogens Drugs designed to temporarily reduce testosterone levels and, thus to moderate sexual aggressiveness.

antianxiety drugs Drugs used to reduce anxiety and induce relaxation and sometimes sleep.

antidepressants Drugs used to elevate mood and relieve depression.

antihistamines Medications used to relieve the symptoms of allergies and colds.

antihypertensive drugs Drugs used to treat hypertension (high blood pressure). One class of these drugs is the vasodilators, which open narrow blood vessels that contribute to hypertension by increasing resistance to flow.

antipsychotic drugs Substances that calm the activity of certain areas of the brain but allow the rest of the brain to function normally; used to treat such illnesses as schizophrenia and severe depression.

Apgar test An assessment of the newborn to check basic life processes. The test evaluates five life signs: heart rate, respiration, muscle tone, reflex irritability, and color.

aphrodisiac A substance that is supposed to heighten sexual desire, pleasure, or performance.

appetite suppressants Medications used to treat obesity.

areola A pigmented area of skin around the central portion of the nipple.

arthritis A disorder in which the joints become inflamed and painful.

artificial insemination A procedure in which sperm (fresh or frozen) are artificially injected into a woman's vagina, either on or near the cervix, at the time of ovulation.

ascetic orientation A value orientation advocating sexual self-denial, the avoidance of all sexual activity, and the implementation of spiritual self-discipline.

attachment The affectional bond between infant and caregiver that is a vital prerequisite of healthy sexual, emotional, personality, and social functioning.

autonomic nervous system   A set of regulatory centers that control the operation of many of the internal organs and glands of the body.

autonomy versus shame and doubt   Erikson's second psychosocial crisis, occurring between the ages of one and three, in which the child must achieve independence and self-control.

aversion therapy   A behavioral technique designed to reduce or extinguish inappropriate behavior by pairing it with a noxious or unpleasant stimulus.

Bartholin's glands   Two glands that open into the vaginal vestibule on either side of the vaginal opening and that are thought to provide some lubrication during sexual arousal.

B-cell   Type of lymphocyte that combats infectious diseases. It produces infection-fighting antibodies when stimulated.

barbiturates   Sedative drugs that often induce relaxation and sleep.

basal body temperature technique (BBT)   A birth control technique in which couples compile a record of the woman's basal body temperature to identify her periods of fertility.

basic trust versus basic mistrust   Erikson's first psychosocial crisis, occurring in the first year of life, in which the child must learn not only to trust others but to trust oneself.

behavioral model of sex therapy   A therapeutic approach to sexual dysfunctions that conceptualizes sexual disorders as forms of conditioned behavior.

behavioral theory of gender-role development   A theory proposing that gender-role behaviors are conditioned by the environment.

benign prostatic hypertrophy   Enlargement of the prostate gland that constricts the urethra and impedes the flow of urine.

biological perspective on human sexuality   A model of sexuality that focuses on its physical aspects: the anatomy and physiology of the body's sexual and reproductive systems, as well as their development and maturation.

birthing chair   A special chair that elevates a woman's body so that it is in a near-vertical position during delivery.

birthing room   Delivery room offering a homelike, relaxed atmosphere within the hospital's general delivery unit.

bisexuality   A sexual orientation in which the person is attracted both sexually and emotionally to persons of both sexes.

blended orgasm   Female orgasm proposed by Singer and Singer in which both vulval-clitoral and deeper, uterine contractions combine.

Braxton Hicks contractions   Intermittent uterine contractions prior to the onset of actual labor.

breasts   In the female, accessory organs of reproduction, composed of glandular tissue and fat, that are designed to suckle the newborn and that also play a role in female sexual arousal.

breech presentation   The appearance of the lower part of the fetus first during delivery.

carcinoma   Cancer arising from epithelial cells (skin, mucous membranes, etc.). Carcinomas tend to be solid tumors.

cardiovascular disease   A category of disorders that involve malfunctioning of the heart and circulatory system.

case study   A type of research methodology in which extensive information is gathered about one person only.

celibacy   Voluntary abstention from all forms of sexual activity.

central nervous system   The branch of the nervous system that consists of the brain, the spinal cord, and the nerves that extend out from both.

cerebral cortex   The outer covering of the cerebral hemispheres.

cerebral palsy   A disability characterized by defects in motor control and coordination.

cerebrovascular accident   Any interruption of the brain's arterial flow that results in a loss of body functions. Also called a *stroke*.

cervical cap   A barrier contraceptive that blocks sperm from passing from the vagina into the uterus. It resembles a miniature diaphragm with a tall dome and must be used with a spermicide.

cervicitis   Inflammation of the cervix.

cervix   The small, lower portion of the uterus that projects into the vagina.

cesarean delivery   A method of childbirth in which a baby is delivered not through the vaginal canal but through a surgical incision in the mother's abdomen and uterus. Also called *cesarean section* or *C-section*.

chastity belt   A device used during the Middle Ages to ensure the fidelity of wives as well as the virginity of unmarried women. Usually made of metal, the belt covered the vaginal and anal areas, leaving a small opening for the passage of urine and menstrual blood.

child pornography   Books, magazines, photographs, and films that depict children in sexually explicit acts.

child sexual abuse   Sexual contact between a child and an unrelated adult in which the child is used for the sexual stimulation and pleasure of the adult.

chlamydia   A sexually transmitted disease caused by the parasite *Chlamydia trachomatis*. Chlamydial infections in women often lead to pelvic inflammatory disease and cervicitis; in men the infection often develops into nongonococcal urethritis, epididymitis, and proctitis.

chromosomes   Thin rodlike structures located inside the cell's nucleus that contain the directions for the cell's activity.

cilia   Tiny hairlike projections that line the fallopian tubes and propel the ovum toward the uterus.

circumcision   A surgical procedure in which all or part of the prepuce, or foreskin, of the penis or clitoris is removed.

climacteric   The period of a woman's life from the onset of irregularity of the menses to their total cessation.

clitoral orgasm   A term used to refer to an orgasm that derives from stimulation of the clitoris or other noncoital activity.

clitoris   A small, highly sensitive organ located at the anterior juncture of the labia minora.

cocaine   An alkaloid that acts as a central nervous system stimulant.

cognitive model of sex therapy   A therapeutic approach that focuses on changing patterns of thought on the theory that faulty or distorted ways of thinking underlie sexual dysfunction.

cognitive-developmental theory of gender-role development   A theory proposing that gender-role development emerges through children's growing cognitive awareness of their identity.

cohabitation   The sharing of a residence by an unmarried woman and man who are sexually intimate.

coitus   Penile-vaginal intercourse.

colostrum   A thin yellowish fluid secreted by the breasts toward the end of pregnancy.

combination pills   Oral contraceptives that contain a synthetic estrogen combined with chemicals called *progestogens* or *progestins* (synthetic progesterone derivatives).

coming out   The public self-disclosure by a homosexual of his or her same-sex preferences.

communication   The exchange of information, signals, and messages between people.

concurrent bisexuality   Having both male and female sexual partners during a particular period of one's life.

condom   A thin sheath made usually of latex rubber that is placed over the erect penis before sexual intercourse. The condom is categorized as a barrier method of contraception because it contains the ejaculate, thereby preventing sperm from entering the vagina.

conflict   An interpersonal process that occurs whenever the actions of one person interfere with the actions of another.

congestive heart failure   A condition that interferes with the heart's ability to pump blood.

consensual extramarital relationship   Sexual activity with someone other than one's spouse, but with the knowledge of that spouse.

contraception   Any natural, barrier, chemical, hormonal, or surgical method used to prevent conception.

contraceptive implant   A female birth control device consisting of six small silicone rods implanted under the skin of the inner arm, just above the elbow. The rods contain the hormone levonorgestrel, which is released slowly over five years.

control   The stage in scientific research when the ability to explain and predict a phenomenon makes it possible to change or modify that phenomenon.

control group   In a research study, a group of subjects used primarily for comparison purposes.

coprophilia   Sexual excitement derived from contact with feces.

corona   A raised rim or ridge of tissue that separates the penile glans from the shaft.

coronary artery disease   A condition in which the accumulation of fatty deposits in the coronary arteries lessens the flow of blood to the heart.

corpora cavernosa   The two larger and uppermost cylindrical masses of penile tissue that lie side by side and are enclosed in separate fibrous coverings.

corpus luteum   A small body that develops within a ruptured ovarian follicle after the ovum is released; it secretes the hormone progesterone, which helps regulate the menstrual cycle.

corpus spongiosum   The lower, smaller cylindrical mass of penile tissue that contains the urethra.

Cowper's glands   A pair of small pea-shaped structures, located below the prostate gland, that contribute an alkaline fluid to the semen.

cross-sectional study   A research design in which comparative data are gathered from different groups of subjects at more or less the same point in time.

crowning   During childbirth, the encirclement of the largest diameter of the baby's head by the vulva.

crura   Tapering parts of the corpora cavernosa that help connect the penis to the pubic bone.

cultural anthropological perspective on human sexuality   A model that explores the sexual behavior of different ethnic groups in order to discover cross-cultural similarities and differences.

cultural role scripts   Preconceptions of how one should behave within a relationship setting, including expectations for one's partner.

cunnilingus   Oral stimulation of the female genitals.

cystectomy   The surgical excision of an ovarian cyst, leaving the ovary intact.

cystic disease of the breast   A condition in which noncancerous lumps form in the breast. Also referred to as *fibrocystic disease, mammary dysplasia, chronic cystic mastitis*, and *chronic cystic disease*.

cysts   Lumps that are either solid masses or fluid-filled sacs.

delayed puberty   Impeded puberty that results because of inadequate supplies of gonadotrophins.

dependent variable   In an experiment, the behavior affected by the independent variable.

description   In scientific research, the empirical process that often relies on counting, frequencies, percentages, and descriptive statistics.

desire phase   The first phase of Kaplan's sexual response cycle in which a specific neural system in the brain produces sexual desire, or libido, which leads a person to seek out or become responsive to sexual experiences.

developmental disability   Significantly below-average intellectual functioning, along with difficulty in adapting to everyday life.

diabetes mellitus   A chronic metabolic disease in which the body is unable to properly process carbohydrates.

diaphragm   A female method of contraception that provides a barrier between the sperm and the egg. It is a thin sheet of rubber or latex stretched over a collapsible spring rim that is inserted into the vagina so that it covers the cervix, the entrance to the uterus.

dilation   The enlargement of the cervix during labor.

dilation and curettage   A type of induced abortion used during the first trimester of pregnancy. The developing organism is removed from the uterus by dilating the cervix and scraping out the contents of the uterus.

dilation and evacuation   A type of induced abortion employed from the 13th to the 20th week of pregnancy. The technique involves the removal of the organism by an alternation of suction and curettage.

dysmenorrhea   Painful menstruation.

dyspareunia   Recurrent or persistent genital pain in either a man or a woman before, during, or after sexual intercourse.

eclampsia   A type of toxemia causing muscle spasms, rapid reflex movements, and eventually convulsions and seizures.

ectopic pregnancy   Pregnancy that results when the fertilized egg becomes lodged somewhere outside the uterus.

effacement   The shortening and thinning of the cervical canal during labor.

ego   According to Freud, the part of the personality that acts as a rational agent, mediating between the id and the superego.

ejaculation   The process by which semen is expelled through the penis.

ejaculatory ducts   Two short tubes that pass through the prostate gland and terminate in the urethra. The ejaculatory ducts serve as passageways for semen and fluid secreted by the seminal vesicles.

ELISA test   The enzyme-linked immunosorbent assay test, which can detect whether or not antibodies have been produced by the body in response to HIV.

embryo   The developing organism during the first eight weeks of prenatal life.

embryo transplant   A procedure in which a woman other than the prospective mother is impregnated with the husband's sperm. After several days, the fertilized egg is removed from her womb and placed within the mother's uterus.

endocrine system   A group of glands that release specific hormones into the bloodstream.

endometriosis   A condition in which endometrial cells that normally line the uterus detach themselves and grow elsewhere in the pelvic cavity.

endometrium   The innermost lining of the uterus that builds up a rich blood supply during ovulation in preparation for a fertilized egg and sloughs off this material each month as the menstrual flow if fertilization does not take place.

epididymis   A single, tightly coiled tube, lying along the top and behind each testis, that stores spermatozoa.

epididymitis An inflammation of the epididymis, causing pain and swelling of the testicle.

Equal Rights Amendment (ERA) An amendment to the U.S. Constitution that states, in essence, that the sexes have equal rights under the law. The deadline for ratification by the states has been exceeded, and the amendment must again pass both houses of Congress and be ratified by three-quarters of the states before it can become law.

equity Element of attraction stressing the importance of role stability and fairness in relation to responsibilities and expectations.

erectile dysfunction The inability to attain or maintain an erection during sexual activity, as well as a subjective lack of sexual excitement and pleasure.

erection The process by which body tissues like the penis or clitoris become engorged with blood and increase markedly in size and firmness.

erogenous zones Those parts of the body particularly sensitive to erotic stimulation.

eros love Love characterized by the desire for sexual intimacy.

estradiol An estrogen that affects the development and maintenance of the female reproductive organs as well as all female secondary sex characteristics.

estrogens Hormones produced primarily by follicle cells in the ovaries and by the testes in men. Several types of estrogens are estradiol, esteriol, and estrone.

ethnography A subfield of cultural anthropology that describes the lives and culture of people in particular social groups.

ethnology A subfield of cultural anthropology that develops generalizations about the social patterns and cultural practices of social groups.

ethnomethodology The study of methods people use to communicate in everyday, routine activities.

exchange An element of attraction proposing that people are drawn to those who provide the greatest relational rewards and require the fewest number of sacrifices.

excitement phase The first stage of Masters and Johnson's sexual response cycle, which develops from any source of somatogenic or psychogenic sexual stimulation. In Kaplan's model the second phase of sexual response, characterized primarily by vasocongestion.

exhibitionism The exposure by a man of his genitals to unsuspecting strangers, usually women and children.

experimental group A group of subjects in a research experiment who receive a special stimulus, or treatment.

experimental research Research designed to facilitate the determination of relationships between differing phenomena.

explanation In scientific research, the process by which one attempts to derive reasons for why something happens or is the way it is.

external validity The degree to which conclusions drawn from one set of observations can be generalized to other sets of observations.

facts In science, collected data that represent the findings of systematic observation or of experimental manipulations.

fallopian tubes Two thin, flexible, muscular structures that connect the uterus with the ovaries, providing a passageway for the ovum to travel toward the uterus.

fellatio Oral stimulation of the male genitals.

female nondemand position A position proposed by Masters and Johnson to reduce anxiety related to sexual performance. The man sits behind the woman in a slightly reclining fashion while she places her hand on his to indicate preferences for stimulative contact.

female sexual arousal disorder A sexual dysfunction characterized by difficulties in attaining or maintaining the lubrication-swelling response of sexual excitement, as well as a lack of subjective sexual excitement and pleasure.

fetal alcohol syndrome Condition among newborns caused by excessive alcohol consumption by the mother. Affected infants are often born undersized, mentally deficient, and with assorted physical deformities.

fetal distress Unusual changes in fetal activity, such as a slow, irregular heartbeat, indicating that the fetus is in jeopardy.

fetal period Prenatal life from approximately the third month of pregnancy until birth.

fetishism The use of an inanimate object (fetish) to produce sexual excitement or gratification. Sexual arousal is usually obtained by touching, fondling, or rubbing the fetish.

fetoscopy Technique that inserts a fetoscope, equipped with a light source and biopsy forceps, into the amniotic cavity to view the fetus directly and take blood and skin samples for chromosomal and biochemical studies.

fetus Term used to refer to the developing organism from the third month of prenatal life until birth.

fimbriae Fringelike projections of the infundibulum that reach out to the ovary to draw a released ovum into the fallopian tube.

follicle-stimulating hormone (FSH) A hormone released by the anterior lobe of the pituitary gland, FSH is necessary for the growth and maturation of the primary ovarian follicles. It also stimulates follicular cells to secrete estrogen.

forceps An obstetrical instrument designed to assist in the delivery of a baby.

frenulum The underside of the penis, between the shaft and the glans.

frotteurism Achieving sexual arousal by touching or rubbing against a nonconsenting person, often a stranger.

gay A term preferred by male, and some female homosexuals to describe themselves, though *lesbian* is preferred for gay women.

gay liberation movement A political movement seeking to reduce discrimination and ensure the civil rights of gay men and lesbians.

gender The social meanings attached to being a female or a male.

gender identity One's identity as male or female based on the psychological awareness of being either "masculine" or "feminine." See also *gender role*.

gender role A set of expectations that prescribes how females and males should behave.

gender-identity disorder A disorder characterized by an incongruence between one's sexual identity and one's gender identity.

gender-role stereotype A generalization that reflects our beliefs about females and males.

generativity versus self-absorption The seventh of eight psychosocial crises proposed by Erik Erikson. It occurs during middle adulthood.

genes Structures composed of deoxyribonucleic acid (DNA) that carry the instructions that determine the inheritance of characteristics.

genetic sex Biological maleness or femaleness as determined by our chromosomal makeup.

genital herpes A sexually transmitted disease caused by herpes simplex viruses. The virus itself lodges in the cell center of specific sensory nerves.

genital warts A sexually transmitted disease originating from the human papilloma virus and usually found on the penis, vulva, vagina, or rectum.

germ cells An organism's reproductive cells; the female ovum and the male sperm.

glans In the female, the tip of the clitoris. In the male, the enlarged conic structure at the top of the penis.

gonadal hormones Hormones secreted primarily by the gonads (testes in the male, ovaries in the female) beginning at puberty and involved in such processes as reproduction and the development of secondary sex characteristics.

gonadotrophin-releasing hormone A substance manufactured by the hypothalamus that stimulates the pituitary gland to secrete gonadotrophins.

gonadotrophins Gonad-stimulating hormones secreted by the pituitary gland.

gonorrhea A sexually transmitted disease caused by a bacterial infection and spread by sexual contact with an infected person. Gonorrhea is much more common in men than in women and is highly contagious.

graafian follicle A mature ovarian follicle.

Grafenberg spot A mass of erectile and glandular tissue that may surround the urethra just below the neck of the bladder. Some women report sexual arousal and orgasm when the G-spot is stimulated.

group model of sex therapy An approach to the treatment of sexual dysfunctions that usually involves six to eight people meeting with a qualified therapist to focus on a particular sexual problem.

hallucinogen A drug capable of producing a hallucination.

hedonistic orientation A value orientation emphasizing the importance of sexual pleasure and satisfaction rather than moral constraint.

hermaphroditism A condition in which a person has both ovarian and testicular tissue, and thus genital features of both sexes. See *true hermaphroditism* and *pseudo-hermaphroditism*.

heterosexism The belief that heterosexuality is the only acceptable and viable life option.

historical perspective on human sexuality A model that examines the way the past has influenced present-day sexual attitudes and behaviors.

homogamy Element of attraction suggesting that people are drawn to partners of similar age, education, and physical appearance.

homophobia A fear and dread of homosexuals as well as a fear of the possibility of homosexuality in oneself.

homosexuality Sexual attraction and emotional attachment to persons of the same gender as oneself.

hormones Chemical substances that are secreted by internal organs and carried in the blood stream to other organs or tissues whose structure or function they control.

human sexuality A field of study that encompasses all aspects of human beings that affect their gender-specific and sexual behaviors: their anatomy, physiology, thoughts, attitudes, beliefs, emotions, and social roles. Some of its many topics of study are sexual maturation and reproduction, gender identity, sexual drives and response cycles, sexual life styles, and sexual health and disease.

hydrocele A noncancerous collection of fluid around a testis that leads to swelling of the scrotum.

hydrocelectomy Surgical excision of the membrane covering the testis to treat hydrocele.

hymen A thin mucous membrane that partially covers the vaginal opening.

hypertension A condition characterized by persistently elevated pressure of blood within and against the walls of the arteries, which carry blood from the heart throughout the body. Also known as *high blood pressure*.

hyperventilation A greatly accelerated rate of respiration, sometimes occurring during orgasm.

hypothesis An educated guess as to the nature of some phenomenon or event and its relationship to other phenomena and events.

hypoxyphilia Sexual arousal by means of oxygen deprivation.

hysterectomy The surgical removal of the uterus.

hysterotomy A type of induced abortion usually performed between the 16th and 24th weeks of pregnancy; the fetus is surgically removed.

induced abortion Deliberate removal of the organism from the uterus.

identification theory of gender-role development A psychoanalytic theory that suggests a child develops a gender role by interacting closely with and emulating the behavior of the parent of the same sex.

identity versus role diffusion The fifth of eight psychosocial crises proposed by Erik Erikson. It encompasses the years of adolescence.

id According to Freud, the instinctive aspect of one's personality that contains the basic motivational drives for food, water, sex, and warmth.

in vitro fertilization A procedure in which one or more ova are surgically removed from the mother, fertilized by the father's sperm, and then placed back in the mother's uterus.

incest Sexual relations or intercourse between close blood relatives such as father and daughter, mother and son, or brother and sister.

independent variable The special treatment given to an experimental group.

industry versus inferiority The fourth of eight psychosocial crises proposed by Erik Erikson. It takes place during middle childhood.

infertility The inability to achieve a pregnancy after at least one year of regular, unprotected intercourse.

infundibulum The part of the fallopian tube that, opening into the peritoneal cavity, draws the ovum released by the ovary into the tube.

inguinal canal A tunnel-like passage in the abdominal cavity through which the testes descend during fetal development.

inguinal hernia A hernia that occurs when a loop of intestine passes through the abdominal inguinal ring and follows the course of the spermatic cord into the inguinal canal.

inhibited female orgasm A persistent or recurrent delay in, or absence of, orgasm following adequate sexual arousal and stimulation.

inhibited sexual desire A condition in which the person has sexual fantasies and desire for sexual activity only rarely or never has them at all.

initiative versus guilt The third of eight psychosocial crises proposed by Erik Erikson. It occurs during the years of early childhood.

integrity versus despair The eighth and final psychosocial crisis theorized by Erikson. It takes place during late adulthood.

internal validity The degree to which observed change can be attributed to an experimental treatment and not to some other, extraneous variable.

interstitial (Leydig's) cells Cells, located between the seminiferous tubules, that manufacture androgens.

intimacy versus isolation The sixth of eight psychosocial crises proposed by Erik Erikson. It occupies the young adulthood years.

intimate relationship A relationship in which two people come to know the innermost, subjective aspects of each other.

intrauterine device Small, plastic birth control device that is inserted into the uterus so that a fertilized egg cannot implant itself in the uterine lining. Also called an IUD.

intrauterine fetal surgery Microsurgery on the unborn child to correct problems diagnosed during the mother's pregnancy.

intromission Insertion of the penis into the vagina.

isthmus The portion of the fallopian tube nearest to the uterus.

Kaplan model of sex therapy An approach to the treatment of sexual dysfunctions developed by Helen Singer Kaplan. It seeks to explore both immediate and more deeply rooted and hidden causes of dysfunctions.

Kaposi's sarcoma A type of cancer that often afflicts AIDS patients.

Kegel exercises A set of exercises designed to restore the tone of the pubococcygeal muscles between the vagina and the anus.

Klinefelter syndrome A genetic disorder in which males have an extra X chromosome, making them XXY instead of XY.

labia majora Outer folds of skin and tissue that originate at the mons pubis and extend backward toward the perineum. The labia majora surround the labia minora.

labia minora Inner folds of skin and erectile tissue that enclose the vaginal and urethral openings.

labor The process of giving birth, including uterine contractions, actual delivery of the baby, and expulsion of the placenta.

lactation The secretion of milk from the mother's breasts.

lactiferous ducts Tubes that drain the lobes, or alveoli, of the breast, which produce milk. Each lobe has its own duct, and all ducts lead into the nipple.

Lamaze method A natural childbirth approach that emphasizes a conditioned learning technique in which the mother replaces one set of learned responses (fear, pain) with another (relaxation, muscle control).

latency stage The fourth stage of psychosexual development proposed by Sigmund Freud. It occupies the years of middle childhood.

Leboyer method Birthing technique emphasizing a gentle delivery of the baby as well as the establishment of a peaceful and soothing delivery room environment.

lesbian A woman who is attracted sexually and emotionally to other women.

leukemia Cancer developing in the hematological (blood) system.

libido Sexual desire. In Freudian psychoanalytic theory, the driving force of the id.

lightening Descent of the fetus into the pelvis during the early stages of labor.

limbic system An integrated network of brain structures that includes the cingulate gyrus, the hippocampus, the septal area, the amygdala, portions of the reticular activating system, and the hypothalamus.

lochia During the puerperium, the discharge of materials remaining after delivery.

longitudinal study A research design in which data are collected on the same group of individuals at intervals over an extended period of time.

LSD A potent synthetic hallucinogen (known technically as lysergic acid diethylamide) capable of changing the user's perception and creating extreme sensory distortions.

ludus love Love that is playful, flirtatious, and often self-centered.

lumpectomy Local excision of a cancerous lump in the breast, along with some of the surrounding breast tissue.

luteinizing hormone (LH) A hormone secreted by the anterior lobe of the pituitary gland, LH is important in the later stages of maturation of the ovarian follicle. It is also important for ovulation and for the transformation of the emptied follicle into a corpus luteum.

lymphocyte A type of white blood cell, manufactured primarily in the bone marrow, whose primary function is to protect the body from invasive foreign substances.

lymphoma Cancer originating in lymphoid tissues.

madam A woman who heads a house of prostitution or brothel.

male nondemand position A position proposed by Masters and Johnson to reduce anxiety related to sexual performance. The man lies on his back while his partner sits between his legs facing him.

mammography Low-dose X-ray examination designed to reveal breast tumors too small to be felt by palpation.

manic love Love that is intense and obsessive.

marijuana A hallucinogenic drug derived from the leaves of the hemp plant.

marital rape Sexual assault in which a wife is forced by her husband to engage in sexual intercourse or other forms of sexual activity against her will.

mastectomy The surgical removal of a breast or part of it.

Masters and Johnson model of sex therapy An intensive two-week treatment approach that includes, among other features, treatment of the couple rather than the individual, and use of a male-female co-therapy team.

masturbation Self-stimulation of the genitals or other parts of the body for sexual arousal and pleasure.

matrilineal descent Inheritance through the female side of the family.

maturity A state of psychological well-being that is instrumental in shaping psychological adjustment and competence.

medical perspective on human sexuality A model of sexuality that focuses on sexual health and its maintenance.

menarche The onset of menstruation.

menopause The normal cessation of the menstrual cycle.

menses The discharge of blood from the uterus during menstruation.

menstrual phase The last three days or so of the menstrual cycle.

menstruation The monthly shedding of endometrial tissue, blood, and other secretions from the uterus that occurs when the ovum is not fertilized by a sperm.

metamessage An intentional alteration of speech rhythm or pitch for emphasis, or the use of special verbal modifiers or body language. Metamessages add another level of meaning to a sentence, often an incongruent one.

metastasis The spread of cancer from an original site to another, new site.

mini-pill An oral contraceptive that contains progestin and no estrogen.

miscarriage The natural termination of a pregnancy before the embryo or fetus has the opportunity to fully develop.

monogamy The marriage of one man to one woman.

mons pubis The mound of fatty tissue over the pubic bone.

moral value A type of value representing a person's ethical standards of right and wrong.

Mullerian ducts One of two paired internal duct systems in the embryo that develop into the fallopian tubes, uterus, and inner parts of the vagina in the female.

Mullerian-inhibiting hormone (MIH) During prenatal life, a chemical secreted by the testes that inhibits the further development of the Mullerian ducts in the male embryo.

multiple orgasms More than one orgasmic experience within a relatively short period of time.

multiple sclerosis A chronic, progressive disease of the central nervous system.

myomectomy The surgical removal of uterine fibroids, leaving the muscle walls of the uterus in place.

myometrium The layers of smooth muscle that make up most of the body of the uterus.

myotonia A generalized increase in muscle tension.

narcotic A drug that in moderate doses depresses the central nervous system. Examples are morphine, heroin, and methadone.

National Gay and Lesbian Task Force An organization that promotes the acceptance by society of its homosexual members and that seeks to ensure that gays and lesbians have the same opportunities as heterosexual men and women to achieve and to contribute to society.

National Organization for Women (NOW) The chief organization of the women's movement, NOW has been particularly active in implementing reforms in education and in the workplace.

natural childbirth Method of childbirth that avoids the use of anesthesia and allows both husband and wife to play an active role in the delivery of their baby.

necrophilia Sexual pleasure from viewing or having sexual contact with a corpse.

needs Things that a person feels would help him or her. Statements of need are usually not judgmental or pejorative and, in themselves, do not blame or assign fault.

negative feedback loop A regulatory system that coordinates the production of gonadal hormones through the complex interaction of the gonads, the hypothalmus, and the pituitary gland.

nervous system A highly complex network of specialized tissue that regulates emotions, thoughts, sensations, behaviors, and bodily functions. The nervous system is subdivided into the central and peripheral systems, and the peripheral system is further divided into the autonomic and somatic systems.

nicotine A toxic alkaloid found in all parts of tobacco plants but especially the leaves.

nipple The protuberance in the breast through which, in the female, the lactiferous ducts discharge milk.

nocturnal emission The ejaculation of seminal fluid during sleep.

nonconsensual extramarital relationship Sexual activity with another person without the consent of one's spouse.

nongonococcal urethritis An infection of the urethra not caused by gonorrhea. It is transmitted primarily by direct sexual contact with an infected person, and is more common in men than in women.

nontranssexual gender-identity disorder A disorder in which people feel some discomfort about their sexual identity and cross-dress but do not feel compelled to alter their physical sex.

nonverbal communication Communication without words, in forms such as facial expressions, gestures, and posture.

nurse-midwife A trained delivery specialist who provides qualified medical care to expectant mothers. Usually the midwife has earned a bachelor's degree in nurse-midwifery and works on a medical team including a gynecologist and an obstetrician.

observations In research, reports of perceived stimuli, without speculations, inferences, or conclusions.

obstetrics The branch of medicine concerned with pregnancy, labor, and delivery.

oligospermia A condition in which there are very few or no sperm in a man's ejaculate or in which seminal fluid itself is absent.

oophorectomy The surgical removal of an ovary.

open marriage A marriage that is flexible and stresses the importance of continual self-growth for both partners.

oral contraceptive Birth control pill that prevents ovulation. It is a hormonal method of birth control.

oral stage The first stage in Freudian psychosexual development in which the infant focuses on oral pleasure.

oral-genital stimulation Stimulation of the genitals with the mouth, including kissing, licking, and sucking. Commonly referred to as *oral sex*.

orchiectomy The surgical removal of a testis.

orgasm disorders Sexual dysfunctions characterized by orgasm difficulties in both men and women. The basic categories are inhibited female orgasm, retarded ejaculation, and premature ejaculation.

orgasm phase The third phase of Masters and Johnson's sexual response cycle, in which the vasoconstriction and myotonia developed in response to sexual stimulation are released. In Kaplan's model of sexual response, this phase comprises reflex pelvic muscle contractions governed by specialized spinal nerve centers.

orgasmic platform Swelling of the walls of the outer portion of the vagina as a result of increased vasocongestion during the plateau phase of the sexual response cycle.

osteoarthritis A type of arthritis characterized by the gradual wearing away of cartilage in the joints.

outing The public disclosure, by someone else and without the individual's permission, of a public figure's homosexuality.

ovarian cyst An abnormal swelling or saclike growth on the ovary. The cyst may be fluid-filled, semifluid. solid, or semisolid.

ovaries The female gonads, located in the upper portion of the pelvic cavity, one on either side of the uterus.

ovulation The release of a mature ovum from the ovarian follicle.

ovum The female reproductive cell.

Papanicolaou (Pap) smear A test used primarily to screen for cervical cancer.

paralanguage The vocal component of speech, considered separate from its verbal content. Paralanguage includes volume, pitch, articulation, resonance, tempo, and rhythm.

paraphilia Sexual arousal in response to objects or situations that are not related to normal arousal-activity patterns. To varying degrees, a paraphilia interferes with the capacity for reciprocal, affectionate sexual activity.

paraplegia Paralysis of the legs and lower part of the body, including bowel and bladder tone loss.

parasympathetic nervous system A subdivision of the autonomic nervous system that stimulates processes that restore or conserve the body's energy.

patrilineal descent Inheritance through the male side of the family.

pediatrician A specialist in the treatment of children, including hygienic care and diseases particular to them.

pelvic inflammatory disease (PID) An infection of the pelvic organs in women, particularly the upper genital tract.

penile implant A prosthesis that is inserted into the penis to achieve erection.

penis The male organ of copulation. The urethra, which passes through the penis, provides a passageway for both semen and urine.

perineum   In both men and women, muscle tissue located between the genital area and the anal canal.

peripheral nervous system   A network of neural tissue that connects the brain and spinal cord, or central nervous system, with other parts of the body.

Peyronie's disease   A condition characterized by the formation of hard, fibrous plaques in the sheath of the corpus cavernosum.

phallic stage   The third stage in Freudian psychosexual development theory in which the child focuses on genital pleasure.

physical dependence   A physiological need for a drug.

pimp   A man who provides a prostitute with protection and basic necessities while living off her earnings.

placenta   An intrauterine membrane that allows nourishment to pass from mother to developing organism and for waste products to be channeled from organism to mother.

plateau phase   The second phase of Masters and Johnson's sexual response cycle. It is reached if effective sexual stimulation continues, and it is characterized by increases in sexual tension.

pleasure principle   The human tendency to seek pleasure and avoid discomfort. The id operates on this principle.

PLISSIT model   A framework for the treatment for sexual dysfunctions consisting of four progressive levels: permission, limited information, specific suggestions, and intensive therapy.

pneumocystis carinii pneumonia   A parasitic infection of the lungs that often afflicts AIDS patients.

polygamy   The marriage of one man to several women or of one woman to several men.

polygyny   The marriage of one man to more than one woman.

pornography   Pictures, films, literature, and objects that are designed to cause sexual excitement or arousal.

postpartum period   The first month or so after childbirth.

post-test   A test given after the experimental treatment to both the experimental and control groups to determine whether the treatment given the experimental group has had a significant effect.

power rapist   A rapist who uses intimidation and force as a means of achieving his victim's sexual submission.

pragma love   Love that is practical and realistic.

precocious puberty   A condition that results when excessive amounts of gonadotrophins are released during the early years of childhood.

prediction   In scientific endeavor, the process of telling in advance that something is going to occur or how it will occur.

preeclampsia   A type of toxemia characterized by the mother's retention of salt and water, which often leads to weight increases, swelling, and raised blood pressure.

premature ejaculation   Persistent or recurrent ejaculation with minimal sexual stimulation before, upon, or shortly after penetration and before the couple wish it to happen.

premenstrual syndrome (PMS)   The cyclic occurrence, between ovulation and the onset of menstruation, of symptoms that interfere substantially with some aspect of a woman's life.

prepuce   In women, the loose-fitting fold of skin that covers the clitoral glans, also called the clitoral hood. In men, the loose-fitting, retractable casing of skin that forms over the penile glans, also called the foreskin.

pre-test   A test given before the experimental procedure to establish a baseline for comparative purposes.

primary amenorrhea   The absence of menstruation.

primary follicle   Podlike structure containing immature ova.

primary sex characteristics   The fully developed sexual and reproductive organs, including the male penis and testes and the female clitoris and vagina.

procreational orientation   A value orientation emphasizing that coital activity is acceptable only within marriage and primarily for the purpose of having children.

proctitis   An inflammation of the mucous membranes of the rectum.

progesterone   A hormone manufactured by the corpus luteum, progesterone is most abundant during the secretory phase of the menstrual cycle. Small amounts of progesterone are also found in the male.

proliferative phase   A period of time between the 6th and 13th day of the menstrual cycle; also called the follicular phase.

propinquity   An element of attraction suggesting that people need to have continual contact with each other if their relationship is to endure.

prostate gland   A large structure that surrounds the portion of the urethra that is just below the bladder.

prostatectomy   Surgical removal of part or all of the prostate gland.

prostatitis   An infection or inflammation of the prostate gland.

prosthesis   A fabricated substitute for a missing body part.

prostitution   The exchange of sexual services for money.

pseudo-hermaphroditism   A condition that occurs when the person has either ovaries or testes (not both), but external genitals that are characteristic of the opposite sex.

psychiatric drugs   Drugs used to treat behavioral disturbances. Examples are the antipsychotic, antidepressant, and antianxiety drugs.

psychoanalysis   A school of psychology developed by Sigmund Freud, psychoanalysis suggests that one's past exerts an important role in determining one's present behavior.

psychological dependence   A psychological need for a drug.

psychological perspective on human sexuality   A model of sexuality that examines the ways sexuality is shaped by personality dynamics, motivation, emotions, attitudes, beliefs, and interpersonal behavior.

psychosexual development   The Freudian notion that early sexual experiences are important to personality development. The individual must successfully pass through a series of five sequential stages to reach psychosexual maturity.

psychosocial development   The Eriksonian notion that social interactions are critical to personality development. The individual must successfully resolve eight sequential crises to reach psychosocial maturity.

puberty   The stage of development during which physiological changes create sexual maturity, including reproductive capability.

puerperium   The time after childbirth in which the mother's reproductive organs return to their prepregnant condition.

quadriplegia   Paralysis of all four body limbs.

questionnaire   A type of survey that requires respondents to mark their own answers.

quickening   Fetal movements that can be felt by the mother. Quickening usually begins between 16 and 18 weeks.

rape   An act of a sexual nature that is forced upon an unwilling person or that an unwilling person is forced to perform on someone else.

rape trauma syndrome   The physical, psychological, social, and/or sexual disruption of a victim's life brought about by rape.

rational-emotive therapy   A therapeutic approach developed by Albert Ellis. It suggests that many psychological disorders, including those of a sexual nature, originate in irrational beliefs.

reality principle   The notion that human needs can be fulfilled in socially acceptable ways. The ego operates on this principle.

refractory period   A period of time after orgasm when a man is unresponsive to sexual stimulation. It is highly variable and may last for minutes or for hours.

relational orientation   A value orientation that views sexual intercourse as acceptable if accompanied by love and emotional attachment between partners.

resolution phase   The fourth stage of Masters and Johnson's sexual response cycle, when vasocongestion and myotonia rapidly dissipate and the person returns to an unstimulated state.

retarded ejaculation   A persistent or recurrent delay in, or absence of, intravaginal ejaculation following adequate sexual excitement.

retrograde ejaculation   A condition in which semen is passed back into the bladder rather than ejaculated externally through the urethra.

rheumatoid arthritis   A type of arthritis that inflames the membranes lining and lubricating the joints.

rhythm method   A type of birth control that involves abstaining from intercourse on days when pregnancy can occur. Also called *natural family planning*.

rooming-in hospital facilities   Facilities that allow the parents of newborns to care for their baby in the mother's hospital room.

sadistic rapist   A rapist who uses sexual assault as a pre-planned and aggressive ritual, frequently involving torture, bondage, and other forms of sexual abuse.

sadomasochism   The presence of both sexual sadism and sexual masochism in the same person.

sample   A group of people considered to be representative of a larger population.

sarcoma   Cancer developing from muscle, bone, fat, and other connective tissues.

scabies   A highly contagious parasitic disease caused by an organism called *Sarcoptes scabei*. The organism is a mite that lives, burrows, and lays eggs in the outer layers of the skin.

scientific method   An organized series of steps designed to promote maximum objectivity and consistency in gathering and interpreting observable evidence.

scrotal hernia   A hernia that descends into the scrotum.

scrotum   A skin-covered pouch suspended from the perineal area that contains the testes.

secondary amenorrhea   The cessation of menstruation in a female who has previously experienced menstruation.

secondary sex characteristics   Nongenital bodily features that usually develop during puberty and serve to distinguish a sexually mature man from a sexually mature woman.

secretory phase   The 15th to the 25th day of the menstrual cycle during which the corpus luteum develops, begins to secrete progesterone, and then, unless conception occurs, fades away.

self-actualization   A harmonious integration of the personality enabling people to make full use of their potentialities, capabilities, and talents.

self-disclosure   The process of letting oneself be known by another.

self-selection   A threat to the reliability of research studies wherein many members of a sample may choose not to participate, throwing off the balance the research hoped to achieve among various characteristics of subjects such as sex and age.

semen   The male ejaculate, which consists of spermatozoa and seminal fluid.

seminal fluid   Fluid made up of secretions from the seminal vesicles, prostate gland, Cowper's glands, and the epididymis.

seminal vesicles   A pair of secretory glands that lie close to the bladder and in front of the rectum.

seminiferous tubules   Tightly packed, convoluted structures located in the testicles, that produce sperm.

serial bisexuality   Alternating female and male sexual partners over time.

sex   A person's biological status as either a male or a female.

sex discrimination   Unfair and unequal treatment of a person on the basis of his or her sex.

sex flush   A superficial vasocongestive skin response to increasing sexual tension.

sex reassignment surgery   Surgery that alters the genitals and sometimes the secondary sex characteristics in order to conform to a person's felt, though not actual, sexual identity.

sexual addiction   An excessive or insatiable desire for sexual stimulation and gratification.

sexual aversion disorder   Persistent or extreme aversion to, and avoidance of, all or almost all genital sexual contact with a sexual partner.

sexual dysfunction   A problem in sexual responding that may occur at any phase of the sexual response cycle.

sexual fantasy   A mental image or series of images centering around erotic thoughts and desires.

sexual harassment   Any unwanted sexual advance, verbal or physical, that occurs in the workplace or in an academic setting.

sexual identity   One's identity as either female or male based on biological characteristics, both genetic and anatomical.

sexual masochism   Achieving sexual pleasure and gratification by being humiliated or made to suffer.

sexual orientation   A person's preference for sexual and affectional relationships with persons of the other sex, of the same sex, or of both sexes.

sexual revolution   Changes in thinking about human sexuality that occurred during the 1960s and 1970s and that focused on gender roles as well as specifically sexual behavior.

sexual sadism   Achieving sexual pleasure and gratification by inflicting pain on a sexual partner.

sexual value   A conceptual structure representing a person's *beliefs* about what is appropriate or inappropriate, desirable or undesirable, in sexual behavior.

sexual value system   A framework of values or set of assumptions that shapes a person's sexual life.

sexuality education   Intervention on the part of parents and teachers to provide children with age-appropriate sex-related information.

sexually transmitted disease   A contagious infection that, for the most part, is passed on by intimate sexual contact with others. The sexual contact can be through open-mouthed kissing, coitus, oral-genital sex, or anal intercourse.

short-term longitudinal method   A variation of the longitudinal research design that reduces the amount of time subjects are studied and investigates fewer behavioral phenomena.

simultaneous bisexuality   Having sex with at least one partner of the same sex and one of the opposite sex at the same time.

single life style   A life style in which persons choose not to marry.

situational orientation   A value orientation suggesting that sexual decision making should take place in the context of the particular situation and people involved.

Skene's glands   A group of small mucous glands that open into the vaginal vestibule near the urethral orifice.

smegma   Accumulation of secretions on the penile or clitoral glans from the glands of the foreskin.

social learning theory of gender-role development A theory suggesting that gender roles are learned through imitation of sex-typed behaviors.

sociobiology A science that combines the sociological and biological perspectives. Sociobiologists explore how social behavior, including sexuality, is shaped by evolutionary forces.

sociological perspective on human sexuality A model that focuses on the shaping of sexuality by the society in which one lives.

sodomy A broad legal term that refers to "unnatural sexual relations," including such noncoital sexual behaviors as anal-genital and oral-genital sex.

somatic cells The majority of the cells of an organism, which control all characteristics except those that are sexual.

somatic nervous system A system of sensory neurons that connects the central nervous system to voluntary muscles throughout the body.

sonography Technique used to explore the prenatal environment. Also called *ultrasound*, the technique utilizes sound waves to gather such information as fetal age, position, defects, and the presence of multiple fetuses.

sperm Reproductive cells produced in the testes.

spermarche The first ejaculation of seminal fluid.

spermatic cord The cord that suspends the testis in the scrotum. It contains arteries, nerves, veins, and the vas deferens.

spermatogenesis The process of sperm production.

spermatozoon The male reproductive cell.

spontaneous abortion Separation of the organism from the uterine wall, followed by expulsion by the uterus. Also referred to as a *miscarriage*.

squeeze technique A technique developed by Masters and Johnson to treat premature ejaculation and inhibited male orgasm. Pressure is applied to the penis just below the coronal ridge prior to ejaculation to cause a partial loss of erection and delayed orgasm.

statutory rape Sexual assault on a minor.

sterilization A family planning measure that permanently blocks a person's reproductive capacity.

storge love Calm and affectionate love that embodies companionship and the enjoyment of doing things with one's partner.

subject bias In research studies, a phenomenon in which inherent bias in the subject or some feature of the study's design interferes with the subject's response.

superego According to Freud, the part of personality that represents societal expectations and demands.

surrogate motherhood A procedure in which a chosen surrogate mother is artificially inseminated with the husband's sperm. The surrogate mother carries and bears the child, which is then given to the couple.

survey A technique of gathering information from people, a survey generally takes the form of a questionnaire or an interview.

swinging A relationship involving two or more married couples who decide to switch sexual partners or to engage in group sex. Also called *mate swapping*.

sympathetic nervous system A subdivision of the autonomic nervous system that prepares the body to use its energy and serves to increase activity levels such as heart rate and blood pressure.

sympto-thermal technique A birth control technique in which couples combine the woman's basal body temperature readings with observation of changes in the character of the woman's cervical mucus.

syphilis A highly infectious sexually transmitted disease. The syphilis bacterium can enter the body through any break in the mucous membrane, after which it burrows into the bloodstream.

systematic desensitization A therapeutic approach employed by behavioral practitioners. In the treatment of sexual dysfunctions, it is used to counteract the anxiety of a sexual situation by interposing and associating a relaxation response to that situation.

T-cell Type of lymphocyte that combats infectious diseases. In AIDS victims T-cells are significantly reduced in number.

teratogen Any substance that creates a change in normal genetic functioning and in turn produces an abnormality or malformation in the developing organism.

testes A pair of bilateral, oval, glandular organs contained in the scrotum. The testes produce sperm and secrete male sex hormones.

testicular torsion A rotation or kinking of the spermatic artery that causes severe pain, tenderness, and swelling of the testicle.

testosterone A male hormone produced by the testes. Testosterone is essential for the production of sperm, for the growth and development of male sex organs, and for the development of male secondary sex characteristics.

theory An explanation that unifies a set of facts or hypotheses, enabling us to understand their interrelationships.

tolerance A condition that results when greater dosages of a drug are needed to achieve the effects of that drug.

tort Harm or injury that one person inflicts on another.

toxemia The presence of a toxic substance in the blood.

toxic shock syndrome (TSS) A rare and sometimes fatal disease that develops rapidly when a bacterium called staphylococcus aureus enters the bloodstream. The bacterium manufactures a toxin that causes a breakdown of cell walls.

transsexualism A severe gender-identity disorder in which people experience persistent discomfort and a sense of inappropriateness about their sexual identity and often seek sex reassignment surgery.

transurethral resection (TUR) A surgical procedure used to treat benign prostate enlargement, in which the surgeon inserts an instrument through the urethra and scrapes out some or all of the tissue of the prostate gland.

transvestism Achieving sexual pleasure and gratification by dressing in the clothing of the other sex.

trimester Term referring to the duration of pregnancy. Pregnancy is divided into three trimesters, each lasting about three months.

triple X syndrome A genetic disorder in which females have an extra X chromosome, making them XXX instead of XX.

true hermaphroditism The possession of characteristics of the sexual anatomy of both sexes.

tubal ligation A form of sterilization in which the fallopian tubes are cut and tied.

tumor A benign or malignant mass of tissue created by the uncontrolled growth and spread of cells. Also called a *neoplasm*.

Turner syndrome A genetic disorder in which females are missing an X chromosome, making them XO instead of XX.

tunica albuginea A fibrous substance covering each testis.

umbilical cord A cord connecting the placenta to the developing organism. It contains three blood vessels: a vein carrying oxygenated blood from the placenta to the organism, and two arteries that carry blood and waste products from the organism to the placenta.

urethra A small tube that serves to transport both urine from the bladder and semen and seminal fluid from the reproductive system.

urophilia Sexual arousal derived from contact with urine.

uterine fibroids Solid noncancerous growths composed of smooth muscle fibers and connective tissue that develop in and on the uterus.

uterine orgasm According to Singer and Singer, an orgasm caused by deep intravaginal stimulation.

uterus A hollow, muscular organ located above the vagina whose primary function is to protect and nurture the developing fetus.

vacuum aspiration A form of induced abortion generally used during the first trimester of pregnancy. With this technique, the embryo is suctioned from the uterus.

vagina A tubular organ that connects the external genitals with the uterus.

vaginal orgasm A term used to refer to an orgasm that derives from coital activity alone, without further stimulation.

vaginal spermicides Agents that have sperm-killing properties. They come in a wide variety of forms, including aerosol foams, creams, jellies, tablets, and suppositories.

vaginal sponge A disposable spongelike device made of polyurethene that contains one gram of nonoxynol-9 spermicide.

vaginal vestibule The cleft, below the clitoris and between the labia, that contains the vaginal and urethral openings.

vaginismus A female sexual pain disorder characterized by recurrent or persistent involuntary constriction of the musculature surrounding the vaginal opening and the outer third of the vagina.

vaginitis Bacterial or fungal infections and inflammations of the vagina that are usually characterized by itching and burning of the external genital organs and a vaginal discharge.

vas deferens Paired structures that serve to transport spermatozoa from the testes to the urethra.

vasectomy A surgical procedure in which the vas deferens are severed, thus preventing sperm from passing from the epididymis into the ejaculate.

vasocongestion An increased amount of blood in body tissues that causes swelling and, in some cases erection, as in the penis and nipples.

viral hepatitis An infectious disease that attacks the liver and causes inflammation. The disease is caused by several viruses, including hepatitis A, hepatitis B, and non-A/non-B hepatitis.

voyeurism A disorder characterized by sexual arousal obtained from looking at unsuspecting people, usually strangers, who are either naked, in the process of disrobing, or engaging in sexual activity. Also called "peeping."

vulva The female external genitalia, including the mons pubis, labia majora, labia minora, clitoris, urethral and vaginal openings, and perineum.

vulval orgasm According to Singer and Singer, an orgasm that involves contractions of the outer third of the vagina and that can result either from stimulation of the clitoris or from penile-vaginal intercourse.

withdrawal method A birth control technique in which the man withdraws his penis from the woman's vagina when he is at the point of ejaculation, so as to prevent his ejaculate from entering her vagina. Also called *coitus interruptus*, the withdrawal method has a low effectiveness rate.

withdrawal The intense craving and physical pain that results in a heavy drug user when the drug becomes unavailable or the person decides to quit. Withdrawal is a sign of physical, and possibly psychological, dependence on a drug.

Wolffian ducts One of two paired internal duct systems in the embryo that develop into the epididymis, vas deferens, and seminal vesicles in the male.

XYY syndrome A genetic disorder in which males have an extra Y chromosome.

zoophilia The preference for sexual activity with an infrahuman animal.

References

Abbey, A., Cozzarelli, C., McLaughlin, K., & Harnish, R. J. (1987). The effects of clothing and dyad sex composition on perceptions of sexual intent: Do women and men evaluate these cues differently? *Journal of Applied Social Psychology, 17,* 108–126.

Abbey, A., & Melby, C. (1986). The effects of nonverbal cues on gender differences in perceptions of sexual intent. *Sex Roles, 15,* 283–298.

Abbey-Harris, N. (1984). *Family life education: Homework for parents and teens.* Santa Cruz, CA: Network Publications.

Abbott, J. T. (1989). Vaginal bleeding: Matching the cause and the cure. *Emergency Medicine, 21*(5), 84–96.

Abel, E. L. (1985). *Psychoactive drugs and sex.* New York: Plenum Press.

Abel, E. L. (1990). *New literature on fetal alcohol exposure and effects.* Westport, CT: Greenwood Press.

Abel G., Becker, J., & Skinner, L. (1983). Treatment of the violent sex offender. In L. Roth (Ed.), *Clinical treatment of the violent person: Crime and delinquency issues.* Bethesda, MD: National Institute of Mental Health.

Abel, G., Mittelman, M., & Becker, J. (1985, June). *The effects of erotica on paraphiliacs' behavior.* Paper presented at the 11th annual meeting of the International Academy of Sex Researchers, Seattle, WA.

Abrahamse, A. F., Morrison, P. A., & Waite, L. J. (1988a). *Beyond stereotypes: Who becomes a single mother?* Santa Monica, CA: Rand.

Abrahamse, A. F., Morrison, P. A., & Waite, L. J. (1988b). Teenagers willing to consider single parenthood: Who is at greatest risk? *Family Planning Perspectives, 20,* 13–19.

Abu-Laban, S. (1981). Women and aging: A futurist perspective. *Psychology of Women Quarterly, 6,* 85–98.

Ackerman, D. (1990). *A natural history of the senses.* New York: Random House.

Adams, G. R. (1980). The effects of physical attractiveness on the socialization process. In G. W. Lucker, K. A. Ribbins, & J. A. McNamara (Eds.), *Psychological aspects of facial form* (Monograph No. 11, Craniofacial Growth Series). Ann Arbor, MI: Center for Human Growth and Development.

Adams, G. R. (1981). The effects of physical attractiveness on the socialization process. In G. W. Lucker, K. A. Ribbins, & J. A. McNamara (Eds.), *Psychological aspects of facial form.* Ann Arbor, MI: Center for Human Growth and Development.

Adams, G. R. (1991). Physical attractiveness and adolescent development. In R. M. Lerner, A. C. Petersen, & J. Brooks-Gunn (Eds.), *Encyclopedia of adolescence.* New York: Garland.

Adams, R., Fliegelman, E., & Grieco, A. (1987). Cutting the risks for STD's. *Medical Aspects of Human Sexuality, 3,* 70ff.

Adams, R., Fleigelman, E., & Grieco, A. (1987). How to use a condom. *Medical Aspects of Human Sexuality, 7,* 1–2.

Adams, G. R., & Schvaneveldt, J. D. (1985). *Understanding research methods.* New York: Longman.

Adams, J. W., Kottke, J. L., & Padgett, J. S. (1983). Sexual harassment of college students. *Journal of College Student Personnel, 24,* 484–490.

Adams, P. L. (1984). Fathers absent and present. *Canadian Journal of Psychiatry, 29,* 228–233.

Adams-Tucker, C. (1981). A sociological overview of 28 abused children. *Child Abuse and Neglect, 5,* 361–367.

Adler, N. E. (1981). Sex roles and unwanted pregnancy in adolescent and adult women. *Professional Psychology, 12,* 56–66.

Aiken, L. R. (1982). *Later life* (2nd ed.). New York: Holt, Rinehart, & Winston.

Alan Guttmacher Institute. (1989). *Teenage pregnancy: The problem that hasn't gone away.* New York: Author.

Alan Guttmacher Institute. (1991). *Teenage sexual and reproductive behavior in the United States.* New York: Author.

Aldridge, S. A. (1982). Drug induced sexual dysfunction. *Clinical Pharmacy, 1,* 141–147.

Alexander, P. C. (1985). A systems theory conceptualization of incest. *Family Process, 24,* 79–87.

Allan, J. P., & Hauser, S. T. (1989, April). *Autonomy and relatedness in adolescent-family interactions as predictors of adolescent ego development.* Paper presented at the biennial meeting of the Society for Research in Child Development. Kansas City.

Allan, J. R., & Curran, J. W. (1985). AIDS: Epidemiology of the acquired immunodeficiency syndrome. In J. I. Gallin & A. S. Fauci (Eds.), *Acquired immunodeficiency syndrome (AIDS).* New York: Raven Press.

Allen, B. (1990). *Personality, social, and biological perspectives on personal adjustment.* Pacific Grove, CA: Brooks/Cole.

Alliance Against Sexual Coercion. Cambridge, MA, 1982.

Allport, G. W. (1961). *Pattern and growth in personality.* New York: Holt, Rinehart, & Winston.

Alston, J., & Tucker, F. (1973). The myth of sexual permissiveness. *Journal of Sex Research, 9,* 34–40.

Alter, J. (1989). Sexuality education for parents. In C. Cassell & P. M. Wilson (Eds.), *Sexuality education: A resource book.* New York: Garland.

Althof, S. E. (1989). Psychogenic impotence: Treatment of men and couples. In S. R. Leiblum & R. C. Rosen (Eds.), *Principles and practice of sex therapy,* 2nd ed. New York: Guilford.

Althof, S. E., Turner, L. A., Levine, S. B., Risen, C. B., Bodner, D., Kursh, D., & Resnick, M. I. (1988, April). *Why do so many people drop out from injection therapy for impotence? The view after two years.* Paper presented at the Society for Sex Therapy and Research, New York.

Alzate, H., & London, M. (1984). Vaginal etotic sensitivity. *Journal of Sex and Marital Therapy, 10,* 49.

American Academy of Pediatrics, Committee on Fetus and Newborn. (1989). Report of the Ad Hoc Task Force on Circumcision (1989). *Pediatrics, 83,* 388–397.

American Baby for the Mother-to-Be. (1973). July, 19–21.

American Cancer Society. (1990). *Cancer facts and figures.* New York: Author.

American Civil Liberties Union. (1986). *Polluting the censorship debate.* Washington, DC: Author.

American College Health Association. (1987). *Acquaintance rape: Is dating dangerous?* Washington, DC: Author.

American College Health Association. (1989). *Survey of AIDS on American college and university campuses.* Washington, DC: Author.

American Psychiatric Association. (1987). *Diagnostic and statistical manual of mental disorders* (3rd ed., rev.) (DSM-III-R). Washington, DC: Author.

Andersen, M. (1988). *Thinking about women.* New York: Macmillan.

Anderson, M. (1989). *Basic maternal nursing.* New York: Delmar.

Anderson, S. C., Bach, C., M., & Griffith, S. (1981, April). *Psychosocial sequelae in intrafamilial victims of sexual assault and abuse.* Paper presented at the Third International Conference on Child Abuse and Neglect, Washington, DC.

Annon, J. S. (1984). Simple behavioral treatment of sexual problems. In J. M. Swanson & K. A. Forrest (Eds.), *Men's reproductive health.* New York: Springer.

Anspaugh, D., Hamrick, M. H., & Rosato, F. (1991). *Wellness: Concepts and applications.* St. Louis: Mosby.

Apfelbaum, B. (1980). Why we should not accept sexual fantasies. In B. Apfelbaum (Ed.), *Expanding the boundaries of sex therapy.* Berkeley, CA: Berkeley Sex Therapy Group.

Apfelbaum, B. (1988). An ego-analytic perspective on desire disorders. In S. R. Leiblum & R. C. Rosen (Eds.), *Sexual desire disorders.* New York: Guilford.

Apfelbaum, B. (1989). Retarded ejaculation: A much-misunderstood syndrome. In S. R. Leiblum & R. C. Rosen (Eds.), *Principles and practice of sex therapy* (2nd ed.). New York: Guilford.

Aral, S. O., & Holmes, K. K. (1990). Epidemiology of sexual behavior and sexually transmitted diseases. In K. K. Holmes, P. A. Mardh, & F. P. Sparling (Eds.), *Sexually transmitted diseases.* New York: McGraw-Hill.

Archer, D. F. (1989). Effects of clomiphene citrate on episodic luteinizing hormone secretion throughout the menstrual cycle. *American Journal of Obstetrics and Gynecology, 161*(3), 581–593.

Archer, R. L., & Cook, C. E. (1986). Personalistic self-disclosure and attraction: Basis for relationship or scarce resource. *Social Psychology Quarterly, 49,* 268–272.

Archer, S. L. (1989). Gender differences in identity development: Issues of process, domain, and timing. *Journal of Adolescence, 12,* 117–138.

Arizona Association for Home Care. (1985). *Home care guidelines for patients with AIDS.* Tucson: Arizona Department of Health Services.

Aro, H., & Taipale, V. (1987). The impact of timing of puberty on psychosomatic symptoms among fourteen to sixteen-year-old Finnish girls. *Child Development, 58,* 261–268.

Astrachan, A. (1986). *How men feel.* New York: Doubleday.

Atwater, E. (1986). *Human relations.* Englewood Cliffs, NJ: Prentice Hall.

Atwater, L. (1982). *The extramarital connection: Sex, intimacy, and identity.* New York: Irvington.

Atwater, L. (1985). Long-term cohabitation without a legal ceremony is equally valid and desirable. In H. Feldman & M. Feldman (Eds.), *Current controversies in marriage and family.* Beverly Hills, CA: Sage.

Atwood, J. (1988). Sexually single again. In E. Weinstein & E. Rosen (Eds.), *Sexuality counseling: Issues and implications.* Monterey, CA: Brooks/Cole.

Atwood, J., & Gagnon, J. (1987). Masturbatory behavior in college youth. *Journal of Sex Education and Therapy, 13,* 35–42.

August, R. L., & Forman, B. D. (1989). A comparison of sexually abused and non-sexually abused children's behavior responses to anatomically correct dolls. *Child Psychiatry and Human Development, 20,* 39–47.

Awad, G., & Saunders, E. B. (1989). Adolescent child molesters: Clinical observations. *Child Psychiatry and Human Development, 19,* 195–206.

Bachmann, G., Leiblum, S., & Grill, J. (1989). Brief sexual inquiry in gynecologic practice. *Obstetrics and Gynecology, 73,* 425–427.

Backhouse, C., & Cohen, L. (1981). *Sexual harassment on the job.* Englewood Cliffs, NJ: Prentice Hall.

Backstrom, T., Sanders, D., Leask, R., Davidson, D., Warner, P., & Bancroft, J. (1983). Mood, sexuality, hormones, and the menstrual cycle: II. Hormone levels and their relationship to the premenstrual syndrome. *Psychosomatic Medicine, 45,* 503–507.

Badgley, R. (1984). *Sexual offenses against children: Report of the Committee on Sexual Offenses Against Children and Youths.* Ottawa: Government of Canada.

Bagley, C. (1985). Child sexual abuse: A child welfare perspective. In K. Levitt & B. Wharf (Eds.), *The challenge of child welfare.* Vancouver: University of British Columbia Press.

Bagley, C., & Ramsay, R. (1986). Disrupted childhood and vulnerability to sexual assault: Long-term sequels with implications for counseling. *Social Work and Human Sexuality, 4,* 33–48.

Bailey, N. & Pillard, R. (1991). Are some people born gay? *New York Times,* December 17, 13.

Baird, P. A. (1982). Children of incest. *Journal of Pediatrics, 101,* 854–857.

Baker, T. B. (1988). Models of addiction. *Journal of Abnormal Psychology, 97,* 115–117.

Baldwin, J., & Baldwin, J. (1988). Factors affecting AIDS related sexual risk-taking behavior among college students. *Journal of Sex Research, 25,* 181–196.

Ballard, D. T., Blair, G. D., Devereaux, L. K., Valentine, A. L., Horton, B., & Johnson, L. (1990). A comparative profile of the incest perpetrator: Background characteristics, abuse history, and use of social skills. In A. L. Horton, B. Johnson, L. M. Roundy, & D. Williams (Eds.), *The incest perpetrator: A family member no one wants to treat.* Newbury Park, CA: Sage.

Bancroft, J. (1983). *Human sexuality and its problems.* New York: Churchill Livingstone.

Bancroft, J. (1985). Hormones and human sexual behavior. *Journal of Sex and Marital Therapy, 10,* 3–21.

Bancroft, J., Sanders, D., Davidson, D., & Warner, P. (1983). Mood, sexuality, hormones, and the menstrual cycle: III. Sexuality and the role of androgens. *Psychosomatic Medicine, 45,* 509–516.

Banmen, J., & Vogel, N. A. (1985). The relationship between marital quality and interpersonal sexual communication. *Family Therapy, 12,* 45–58.

Baranowski, M. D., Schilmoeller, G. L., & Higgins, B. S. (1990). Parenting attitudes of adolescent and older mothers. *Adolescence, 25,* 781–790.

Barbach, L. (1980). Group treatment of anorgasmic women. In S. R. Leiblum & L. A. Pervin (Eds.), *Principles and practice of sex therapy.* New York: Guilford.

Barbach, L. (1984). *For each other: Sharing sexual intimacy.* New York: Signet.

Barbach, L., & Levine, L. (1981). *Shared intimacies.* New York: Bantam.

Bardwell, J. R., Cochran, S. W., & Walker, S. (1986). Relationship of parental education, race, and gender to sex role stereotyping in five-year-old kindergartners. *Sex Roles, 15,* 275–281.

Barlow, D. H. (1986). Causes of sexual dysfunction: The role of anxiety and cognitive interference. *Journal of Consulting and Clinical Psychology, 54,* 140–148.

Barnes, R. C., & Holmes, K. K. (1984). Epidemiology of gonorrhea: Current perspectives. *Epidemiology Review, 6,* 1–30.

Barr, H. M., Streissguth, A. P., Darby, B. L., & Sampson, P. D. (1990). Prenatal exposure to alcohol, caffeine, tobacco, and aspirin: Effects on fine and gross motor performance in four-year-old children. *Developmental Psychology, 26,* 339–348.

Barry, S. (1980). Spousal rape: The uncommon law. *American Bar Association Journal, 9,* 1088–1091.

Bartol, B. (1986). Cocaine babies: Hooked at birth. *Newsweek,* July 28, 56–57.

Basow, S. S. (1980). *Sex-role stereotypes: Traditions and alternatives.* Monterey, CA: Brooks/Cole.

Bateman, A. W. (1986). Rape: The forgotten victim. *British Medical Journal, 292,* 1306–1317.

Batterman, R. (1985, Winter). A comprehensive approach to treating infertility. *Health and Social Work,* 46–54.

Baumrind, D. (1982). Are androgynous individuals more effective persons and parents? *Child Development, 53,* 44–75.

Baus, R. D. (1987, May). *Indicators of relationship satisfaction in sexually intimate relationships.* Paper presented at the Iowa Conference on Personal Relationships, Iowa City.

Beatrice, J. (1985). A psychological comparison of heterosexuals, and post-operative transsexuals. *Journal of Nervous and Mental Disease, 173,* 358–365.

Beck, A. T. (1988). *Love is never enough.* New York: Harper & Row.

Beck, C. M., Rawlins, R. P., & Williams, S. R. (1984). *Mental health psychiatric nursing.* St Louis, MO: Mosby.

Becker, J. V. (1989). Impact of sexual abuse on sexual functioning. In S. R. Leiblum & R. C. Rosen (Eds.), *Principles and practice of sex therapy* (2nd ed.). New York: Guilford.

Becker, M., & Joseph, J. (1988). AIDS and behavioral change to reduce risk: A review. *American Journal of Public Health, 78,* 394–414.

Becker, T., & Larsen, S. A. (1984). Genital wart infections: Another sexual plague? *Diagnostic Medicine, 9,* 66–74.

Bedeian, A. G. (1986). *Management.* New York: Holt, Rinehart, & Winston.

Bedsworth, J. A., & Molen, M. T. (1982). Psychological stress in spouses of patients with myocardial infarction. *Heart and Lung, 11,* 450–456.

Begley, S., & Murr, A. (1987, November 23). All about twins. *Newsweek,* pp. 58–69.

Behrman, R. E., & Vaughn, V. C. (1987). *Nelson textbook of pediatrics.* Philadelphia: Saunders.

Belcastro, P. A. (1985). Sexual behavior differences between black and white students. *Journal of Sex Research, 21,* 56–67.

Bell, A. P., & Weinberg, M. S. (1978). *Homosexualities: A study of diversity among men and women.* New York: Simon & Schuster.

Bell, A. P., Weinberg, M. S., & Hammersmith, S. K. (1981). *Sexual preference: Its development in men and women.* Bloomington: Indiana University Press.

Bell, R. R. (1981). *World of friendship.* Beverly Hills, CA: Sage.

Bell, R. R. (1983). *Marriage and family interaction* (6th ed.). Homewood, IL: Dorsey Press.

Bell, R. R., & Coughey, K. (1980). Premarital sexual experience among college females: 1958, 1968, and 1978. *Family Relations, 7,* 353–357.

Bell, T. A., & Holmes, K. K. (1985). Age specific risks of syphilis, gonorrhea, and hospitalized pelvic inflammatory disease in sexually experienced U.S. women. *Sexually Transmitted Diseases, 7,* 291–295.

Bellinger, D. C., & Gleason, J. B. (1982). Sex differences in parental directives to young children. *Sex Roles, 8,* 1123–1139.

Belsky, J. (1985). Exploring individual differences in marital change across the transition to parenthood: The role of violated expectations. *Journal of Marriage and the Family, 47,* 1037–1044.

Belsky, J., Spanier, G. B., & Rovine, M. (1983). Stability and change in marriage across the transition to parenthood. *Journal of Marriage and the Family, 45,* 567–577.

Bem, S. L. (1981). Gender schema theory: A cognitive account of sex typing. *Psychological Review, 88,* 354–364.

Bender, S. D., & Kellerher, K. (1986). *PMS: A positive program to gain control.* Los Angeles, CA: Body Press.

Benedict, H. (1985). *Recovery.* New York: Doubleday.

Benesch, J., Kapp, J., & Peloquin, L. (1985). *Implementation of family life education curriculum: Teaching materials and strategies.* Washington, DC: Sex Education Coalition.

Benin, M. H., & Agostinelli, J. (1988). Husbands' and wives' satisfaction with the division of labor. *Journal of Marriage and the Family, 50,* 349–361.

Benin, M. H., & Nienstedt, B. C. (1985). Happiness in single- and dual-earner families: The effects of marital happiness, job satisfaction, and the life cycle. *Journal of Marriage and the Family, 47,* 975–984.

Bennett, S. (1984). Family environment for sexual learning as a function of father's involvement in family work and discipline. *Adolescence, 19,* 609–627.

Bentler, P. M., & Peeler, W. H. (1979). Models of female orgasm. *Archives of Sexual Behavior, 8,* 405–423.

Berg, J. H., & McQuinn, R. D. (1986). Attraction and exchange in continuing and noncontinuing dating relationships. *Journal of Personality and Social Psychology, 50,* 942–952.

Bergkrist, L. (1989). The risk of breast cancer after estrogen and estrogen-progestin replacement. *New England Journal of Medicine, 8,* 113–126.

Bergum, V. (1988). *Woman to mother: A transformation.* Westport, CT: Greenwood Press.

Berlin, F. S., & Meinecke, C. F. (1981). Treatment of sex offenders with antiandrogenic medication. *American Journal of Psychiatry, 138,* 601–607.

Berliner, L., & Ernst, E. (1984). Group work with preadolescent sexual assault victims. In I. R. Stuart & J. G. Greer (Eds.), *Victims of sexual aggression: Treatment of children, women, and men.* New York: Van Nostrand Reinhold.

Berndt, T. J. (1982). The features and effects of friendship in early adolescence. *Child Development, 53,* 1447–1460.

Berndt, T. J., & Ladd, G. W. (1989). *Peer relationships in child development.* New York: Wiley.

Berndt, T. J., & Perry, T. B. (1990). Distinctive features and effects of early adolescent friendships. In R. Montemayor (Ed.), *Advances in adolescent research.* Greenwich, CT: JAI Press.

Berne, E. (1964). *Games people play.* New York: Grove.

Berscheid, E. (1985). Interpersonal attraction. In G. Lindzey & E. Aronson (Eds.), *Handbook of social psychology* (Vol. 2). New York: Random House/Erlbaum.

Berscheid, E., & Peplau, L. A. (1983). The emerging science of relationships. In H. H. Kelly (Ed.), *Close relationships.* New York: Freeman.

Bert, D., Dusay, K., Haydock, A., Keel, S., Oei, M., Traina, D. S., & Yanehiro, J. (1984). *Having a baby.* New York: Dell.

Berzon, B. (1984). *Positively gay.* Studio City, CA: Mediamix Associates.

Bessell, H. (1984). *The love test.* New York: Warner Books.

Bieber, I. (1962). *Homosexuality: A psychoanalytic study.* New York: Basic Books.

Biglan, A., Metzler, C., Wirt, R., Ary, D., Noell, J., Ochs, L., French, C., & Hood, D. (1990). Social and behavioral factors associated with high-risk sexual behavior among adolescents. *Journal of Behavioral Medicine, 13,* 245–262.

Bignell, S. (1982). *Sex education: Teacher's guide and resource manual.* Santa Cruz, CA: Network Publications.

Bigner, J. J., & Bozett, J. J. (1990). Parenting gay fathers. In F. W. Bozett & M. B. Sussman (Eds.), *Homosexuality and family relations.* New York: Haworth Press.

Billstein, S. (1984). Human lice. In K. Holmes, P. Mardh, P. Sparling, & P. Wiesner (Eds.), *Sexually transmitted diseases.* New York: McGraw-Hill.

Bingham, C. R. (1989). AIDS and adolescents: Threat of infection and approaches for prevention. *Journal of Early Adolescence, 9,* 50–66.

Blair, C., & Lanyon, R. (1981). Exhibitionism: Etiology and treatment. *Psychological Bulletin, 89,* 439–463.

Blitchington, W. P. (1984). Traditional sex-roles result in healthier sexual relationships and healthier, more stable family life. In H. Feldman & A. Parrot (Eds.), *Human sexuality: Contemporary controversies.* Beverly Hills, CA: Sage.

Block, M. N., & Pellegrini, A. D. (1989). *The ecological context of children's play.* Norwood, NJ: Ablex.

Bloom, F. E., & Lazerson, A. (1988). *Brain, mind, and behavior* (2nd ed.). New York: Freeman.

Blumenfeld, W. J., & Raymond, D. (1988). *Looking at gay and lesbian life.* Boston: Beacon Press.

Blumstein, P., & Schwartz, P. (1983). *American couples.* New York: Simon & Schuster.

Blyth, D. A., & Foster-Clark, F. S. (1987). Gender differences in perceived intimacy with different members of adolescents' social networks. *Sex Roles, 17,* 689–718.

Blyth, D. A., Simmons, R. G., & Zakin, D. F. (1985). Satisfaction with body image for early adolescent females. *Journal of Youth and Adolescence, 14,* 207–225.

Blythe, M. J., & Orr, D. P. (1985). Childhood sexual abuse: Guidelines for evaluation. *Indiana Medicine, 1,* 11–18.

Bohlen, C. (1990, January 15). AIDS epidemic among Romanian babies. *New London Day,* p. 14.

Bolig, R., Stein, P. J., & McKenry, P. C. (1984). The self advertisement approach to dating: Male–female differences. *Family Relations, 33,* 587–592.

Boller, F., & Frank, E. (1982). *Sexual dysfunction in neurological disorders.* New York: Raven Press.

Bolton, F. G., Jr., Morris, L. A., & MacEachron, A. E. (1990). *Males at risk: The other side of child sexual abuse.* Beverly Hills, CA: Sage.

Booth, A., Johnson, D. R., White, L. K., & Edwards, J. N. (1986). Divorce and marital instability over the life course. *Journal of Family Issues, 7,* 421–442.

Booth-Butterfield, M. (1984). She hears . . . he hears: What they hear and why. *Personnel and Guidance Journal, 63,* 36–41.

Borgotta, L., Piening, S. L., & Cohen, W. R. (1989). Association of episiotomy and delivery position with deep perineal laceration during spontaneous delivery in nulliparous women. *American Journal of Obstetrical Gynecology, 160,* 1294–1298.

Borland, D. (1975). An alternative model of the wheel theory. *Family Coordinator, 24,* 289–292.

Boskin, W., Grof, G., & Kreisworth, V. (1990). *Health dynamics: Attitudes and behaviors.* Mountain View, CA: West.

Boston Woman's Health Book Collective. (1984). *The new our bodies, ourselves.* New York: Simon & Schuster.

Bowen, G. L. (1987). Changing gender-role preferences and marital adjustment: Implications for clinical practice. *Family Therapy, 14,* 17–29.

Bowen, G. S. (1990). Risk behaviors for HIV infection in clients of Pennsylvania family planning clinics. *Family Planning Perspectives, 22,* 62–64.

Bowlby, J. (1989). *Secure attachment.* New York: Basic Books.

Box, S. (1983). *Power, crime, and mystification.* London: Tavistock.

Boxer, A. M. (1988, August). *Developmental continuities of gay and lesbian youth.* Paper presented at the annual meeting of the American Psychological Association, Atlanta.

Boyer, C. B., & Hein, K. (1991). AIDS and HIV infection in adolescents: The role of education and antibody testing. In R. M. Lerner, A. C. Petersen, & J. Brooks-Gunn (Eds.), *Encyclopedia of adolescence.* New York: Garland.

Boyer, M. R. (1987). Counseling couples to deal with the sexual concerns of their children. In G. R. Weeks & L. Hof (Eds.), *Integrating sex and marital therapy: A clinical guide.* New York: Brunner/Mazel.

Bozet, F. W. (1984). Parenting concerns of gay fathers. *Topics in Clinical Nursing, 6,* 60–71.

Branden, N. (1981). *The psychology of romantic love.* Los Angeles: Tarcher.

Brannon, L., & Feist, J. (1992). *Health psychology* (2nd ed.). Belmont, CA: Wadsworth.

Bray, J. H. (1988). The effects of early remarriage on children's development: Preliminary analyses of the developmental issues in stepfamily research. In E. M. Hetherington & J. D. Arasteh (Eds.), *Impact of divorce, single-parenting, and step-parenting on children.* Hillsdale, NJ: Erlbaum.

Brazzell, J. F., & Acock, A. C. (1988). Influence of attitudes, significant others, and aspirations on how adolescents intend to resolve a premarital pregnancy. *Journal of Marriage and the Family, 50,* 413–425.

Brecher, E. M. (1984). *Love, sex, and aging*. Boston, Little, Brown.

Breckler, S. J., & Wiggins, E. C. (1989). On defining attitudes and attitude theory: Once more with feeling. In A. R. Pratkanis, S. J. Breckler, & A. C. Greenwald (Eds.), *Attitude structure and function*. Hillsdale, NJ: Erlbaum.

Brehm, S. S. (1985). *Intimate relationships*. New York: Random House.

Brendt, R. L., & Beckman, D. A. (1990). Teratology. In R. D. Eden, F. H. Boehm, & M. Haire (Eds.), *Assessment and care of the fetus: Physiological, clinical, and medico-legal principles*. Norwalk, CT: Appleton & Lange.

Breslin, E. (1988). Genital herpes simplex. *Nursing Clinics of North America, 23*, 907–916.

Breslow, N., Evans, L., & Langley, J. (1985). On the prevalence and roles of females in the sadomasochistic subculture: Report of an empirical study. *Archives of Sexual Behavior, 14*, 303–317.

Breslow, N., Evans, L., & Langley, J. (1986). Comparisons among heterosexual, bisexual and homosexual male sadomasochists. *Journal of Homosexuality, 15*, 83–107.

Brett, E. A., & Ostroff, R. (1985). Imagery and post-traumatic stress disorder: An overview. *American Journal of Psychiatry, 142*, 417–424.

Bretl, D., & Cantor, J. (1988). The portrayal of men and women in United States television commercials: A recent content analysis and trends over fifteen years. *Sex Roles, 18*, 595–609.

Bretschneider, J. G., & McCoy, N. L. (1988). Sexual interest and behavior in healthy 80- to 102-year-olds. *Archives of Sexual Behavior, 17*, 109–129.

Briere, J. (1984, April). *The effects of childhood sexual abuse on later psychological functioning: Defining a post-sexual abuse syndrome*. Paper presented at the annual meeting of the American Psychological Association, Los Angeles.

Briere, J., Evans, D., Runtz, M., & Wall, T. (1988). Symptomalogy in men who were molested as children: A comparison study. *American Journal of Orthopsychiatry, 58*, 457–461.

Briere, J., & Runtz, M. (1985, June). *Symptomatology associated with prior sexual abuse in a non-clinical sample*. Paper presented at the Third National Conference on Sexual Victimization of Children, Washington, DC.

Briere, J., & Runtz, M. (1988). Post-sexual abuse trauma. In G. Wyatt & G. Powell (Eds.), *The lasting effects of child sexual abuse*. Newbury Park, CA: Sage.

Briggs, G. C., Freeman, R. K., & Yaffe, S. J. (1986). *Drugs in pregnancy and lactation* (2nd ed.). Baltimore: Williams & Wilkins.

Bright, M., & Stockdale, D. F. (1984). Mothers', fathers', and preschool children's interactive behaviors in a play setting. *Journal of Genetic Psychology, 144*, 219–232.

Brindis, C. (1990). Reducing adolescent pregnancy: The next steps for program, research, and policy. *Family Life Educator, 9*, 3–60.

Brindis, C., & Jeremy, R. (1988). *Adolescent pregnancy and parenting in California: A strategic plan for action*. San Francisco: Center for Reproductive Health Policy Research, University of California.

Britton, B. (1982). *The love muscle: Every woman's guide to intensifying sexual pleasure*. New York: Signet.

Broadhurst, D. D. (1986). *Educators, schools, and child abuse*. Chicago: National Committee for Prevention of Child Abuse.

Broderick, C. B. (1989). *Marriage and the family* (3rd ed.). Englewood Cliffs, NJ: Prentice Hall.

Brody, C. H., & Steelman, L. C. (1985). Sibling structure and parental sex-typing of children's household tasks. *Journal of Marriage and the Family, 47*, 265–273.

Broering, J., Moscicki, B., Millstein, S., Policar, M., & Irwin, C. (1989, March). *Sexual practices among adolescents*. Paper presented at Society for Adolescent Medicine, San Francisco.

Broman, S. H. (1981). Long-term development of children born to teenagers. In K. G. Scott, T. Field, & E. Robertson (Eds.), *Teenage parents and their offspring*. New York: Grune & Stratton.

Brookins, G. B. (1991). Socialization of African-American adolescents. In R. M. Lerner, A. C. Petersen, & J. Brooks-Gunn (Eds.), *Encyclopedia of adolescence*. New York: Garland.

Brooks-Gunn, J. (1984). The psychological significance of different pubertal events to young girls. *Journal of Early Adolescence 4*, 315–327.

Brooks-Gunn, J. (1987). Pubertal processes: Their relevance to developmental research. In V. B. Van Hasselt & M. Hersen (Eds.), *Handbook of adolescent psychology*. New York: Pergamon.

Brooks-Gunn, J. (1988). Antecedents and consequences of variations in girls' maturational timing. In M. D. Levine & E. R. McAnarney (Eds.), *Early adolescent transitions*. Lexington, MA: Lexington Books.

Brooks-Gunn, J. (1991). Antecedents of maturational timing variation in adolescent girls. In R. M. Lerner, A. C. Petersen, & J. Brooks-Gunn (Eds.), *Encyclopedia of adolescence*. New York: Garland.

Brooks-Gunn, J., & Furstenberg, F. F., Jr. (1989). Adolescent sexual behavior. *American Psychologist, 44*, 249–257.

Brooks-Gunn, J., & Petersen, A. C. (Eds.). (1983). *Girls at puberty*. New York: Plenum.

Brooks-Gunn, J., & Reiter, E. O. (1990). The role of pubertal processes. In S. S. Feldman & G. R. Elliott (Eds.), *At the threshold: The developing adolescent*. Cambridge, MA: Harvard University Press.

Brooks-Gunn, J., & Ruble, D. N. (1983). The experience of menarche from a developmental perspective. In J. Brooks-Gunn & A. C. Petersen (Eds.), *Girls at puberty*. New York: Plenum.

Brooks-Gunn, J., & Warren, M. P. (1989, April). *How important are pubertal and social events for different problem behaviors and contexts*. Paper presented at the biennial meeting of the Society for Research in Child Development, Kansas City.

Brower, K. J., & Anglin, M. D. (1987). Adolescent cocaine use: Epidemiology, risk factors, and prevention. *Journal of Drug Education, 17*, 163–180.

Brown, M., & Auerback, A. (1981). Communication patterns in initiation of marital sex. *Medical Aspects of Human Sexuality, 15*, 107–117.

Brown, R. (1986). *Social psychology* (2nd ed.). New York: Free Press.

Browne, A., & Finkelhor, D. (1986). Impact of child sexual abuse: A review of the research. *Psychological Bulletin, 99*, 66–77.

Browning, C. (1984). Changing theories of lesbianism: Challenging the stereotypes. In T. Darty & S. Potter (Eds.), *Women-identified women*. Palo Alto, CA: Mayfield.

Bruess, C. E., & Richardson, G. E. (1989). *Decisions for health* (2nd ed.). Dubuque, IA: Wm. C. Brown.

Buffum, J. C. (1984). Sexual and reproductive effects of pharmacologic agents. In J. M. Swanson & K. A. Forrest (Eds.), *Men's reproductive health*. New York: Springer.

Bulcroft, K., & Bulcroft, R. (1985). Dating and courtship in later life: An exploratory study. In W. A. Peterson & J. Quadagno (Eds.), *Social bonds in later life*. Beverly Hills, CA: Sage.

Bullard, D. G. (1988). The treatment of desire disorders in the medically ill and physically disabled. In S. R. Leiblum & R. C. Rosen (Eds.), *Sexual desire disorders*. New York: Guilford.

Bullough, B. L. (1964). *The history of prostitution*. New York: University Books.

Bullough, V. L. (1981, Summer). Myths about teenage pregnancy. *Free Inquiry*, 16–20.

Bullough, V. L. (1988). Historical perspective. In D. M. Dailey (Ed.), *The sexually unusual: Guide to understanding and helping*. New York: Harrington Park Press.

Bullough, V. (1990). The Kinsey scale in historical perspective. In D. P. McWhirter, S. A. Sanders, & J. M. Reinisch (Eds.), *Homosexuality/heterosexuality: Concepts of sexual orientation*. New York: Oxford University Press.

Bullough, V. L., Bullough, B., & Smith, R. W. (1983). A comparative study of male transvestites, male to female transsexuals, and male homosexuals. *Journal of Sex Research, 3*, 19–25.

Bumpass, L. L. (1989, March). *Panel discussion of the results of a 1987 cohabitation survey by Larry L. Bumpass, James A. Sweet, and Andrew Cherlin*. Annual meeting of the Population Association of America, San Francisco.

Bumpass, L. L., & Martin T. C. (1989). Recent trends in marital disruption. *Demography, 2*, 26–41.

Bumpass, L. L., & Sweet, J. A. (1988, June 14). University of Wisconsin survey on cohabitation. *Wall Street Journal*, p. 37.

Burda, P. C., Jr., Vaux, A., & Schill, T. (1984). Social support resources: Variation across sex and sex-role. *Personality and Social Psychology Bulletin, 10*, 119–126.

Burge, S. K. (1983). Rape: Individual and family reactions. In C. R. Figley & H. I. McCubbin (Eds.), *Stress and the family*. New York: Brunner/Mazel.

Burger, J. M., & Burns, L. (1988). The illusion of unique invulnerability and the use of effective contraceptive. *Personality and Social Psychology Bulletin, 14*, 264–270.

Burgess, A. W., & Holmstrom, L. L. (1974). Rape trauma syndrome. *American Journal of Psychiatry, 131*, 981–986.

Burgess, A. W., & Holmstrom, L. L. (1980). Rape typology and the coping behavior of rape victims. In S. L. McCombie (Ed.), *The rape crisis intervention handbook*. New York: Plenum.

Burgess, A. W., & Holmstrom, L. L. (1985). Rape trauma syndrome and post traumatic stress response. In A. W. Burgess (Ed.), *Rape and sexual assault*. New York: Garland.

Burke, L. (1990). Cardiovascular disturbances and sexuality. In C. I. Fogel & D. Lauver (Eds.), *Sexual health promotion*. Philadelphia: W. B. Saunders.

Burns, D. B. (1985). *Intimate connections*. New York: Signet.

Burt, M. (1980). Cultural myths and supports for rape. *Journal of Personality and Social Psychology, 38*, 217–230.

Busch-Rossnagel, N. A., & Zayas, L. H. (1991). Hispanic adolescents. In R. M. Lerner, A. C. Petersen, & J. Brooks-Gunn (Eds.), *Encyclopedia of adolescence*. New York: Garland.

Buss, A. (1966). *Psychopathology*. New York: Wiley.

Buss, D. M., & Barnes, M. (1986). Preferences in human mate selection. *Journal of Personality and Social Psychology, 50*, 559–570.

Butler, R. N., & Lewis, M. I. (1988). *Love and sex after 60*. New York: Harper & Row.

Byrne, D. (1983). Sex with contraception. In D. Byrne & W. A. Fisher (Eds.), *Adolescents, sex, and contraception*. New York: McGraw-Hill.

Cado, S., & Leitenbert, H. (1990). Guilt reactions to sexual fantasies during intercourse. *Archives of Sexual Behavior, 19*, 49–56.

Cagen, R. (1986). The cervical cap as a barrier contraceptive. *Contraception, 33*, 487–496.

Caggiula, A. R., & Hoebel, B. G. (1966). Copulation reward site in the posterior hypothalamus. *Science, 153*, 1284–1285.

Calderone, M. (1983). Fetal erection and its message to us. *SIECUS Report, XI* (5/6), 9–10.

Calderone, M. S., & Johnson, E. W. (1989). *The family book about sexuality*. New York: Harper & Row.

Cameron, I. T., Michie, A. F., & Baird, D. T. (1986, November). Therapeutic abortion in early pregnancy with antiprogestogen RU 486 alone or in combination with prostaglandin analogue (gemeprost). *Contraception, 34*, 459–468.

Campbell, S. M. (1980). *The couple's journey: Intimacy as a path to wholeness*. San Luis Obispo, CA: Impact Publishers.

Cancellier, P. H., & Crews, K. A. (1986). *Women in the world: The women's decade and beyond*. Washington, DC: Population Reference Bureau.

Cancian, F. M. (1985). Gender politics: Love and power in the private and public sphere. In A. Rossi (Ed.), *Gender and the life course*. New York: Aldine.

Caplan, N., Choy, M. H., & Whitmore, J. K. (1992). Indochinese refugee families and academic achievement. *Scientific American, 266*(2), February.

Cargan, L. (1985). Gender and sexuality: Influences on intimate relationships. In L. Cargan (Ed.), *Marriage and family: Coping with change*. Belmont, CA: Wadsworth.

Cargan, L., & Melko, M. (1982). *Singles: Myths and realities*. Beverly Hills, CA: Sage.

Cargan, L., & Melko, M. (1985). Being single on Noah's ark. In L. Cargan (Ed.), *Marriage and family: Coping with change*. Belmont, CA.

Carmen, A., & Moody, H. (1985). *Working women: The subterranean world of street prostitution*. New York: Harper & Row.

Carnes, P. (1983). *Out of the shadows: Understanding sexual addiction*. Minneapolis: CompCare Publications.

Caron, S. L., & Bertran, R. M. (1988, April). What college students want to know about sex. *Medical Aspects of Human Sexuality*, 18–20, 22–25.

Carozza, P. M., & Hiersteiner, C. L. (1982). Young female incest victims in treatment: Stages of growth in a group art therapy model. *Clinical Social Work Journal, 10*, 165–167.

Carrera, M. (1988, July). *Testimony before the Presidential Commission on the Human Immunodeficiency Virus Epidemic*, Washington, DC.

Carrol, C. R. (1989). *Drugs in modern society* (2nd ed.). Dubuque, IA: Wm. C. Brown.

Carroll, C., & Miller, D. (1991). *Health: The science of human adaptation* (5th ed.). Dubuque, IA: Wm. C. Brown.

Carter, D. B. (1989, April). *Gender identity and gender constancy*. Paper presented at the biennial meeting of the Society for Research in Child Development, Kansas City.

Carter, M. (1990). Illness, chronic disease, and sexuality. In C. I. Fogel & D. Lauver (Eds.), *Sexual health promotion*. Philadelphia: W. B. Saunders.

Cash, T., & Janda, L. H. (1984). The eye of the beholder. *Psychology Today*, *18*, 46–52.

Cass, V. C. (1979). Homosexual identity formation: A theoretical model. *Journal of Homosexuality*, *4*, 32–39.

Cassata, M., Anderson, P. A., & Skill, T. (1983). Images of old age on day-time television. In M. Cassata & T. Skill (Eds.), *Life on daytime television*. Norwood, NJ: Ablex.

Cates, W., Jr. (1986). Priorities for sexually transmitted diseases in the late 1980's and beyond. *Sexually Transmitted Diseases*, *12*, 114–117.

Cates, W. Jr. (1990). The epidemiology and control of sexually transmitted diseases in adolescents. In M. Schydlower & M. A. Shafer (Eds.), *AIDS and the other sexually transmitted diseases*. Philadelphia: Hanley and Belfus.

Cates, W. Jr., & Holmes, K. K. (1986). Public health and preventative medicine. *Sexually Transmitted Diseases*, *12*, 257–295.

Cauhape, E. (1983). *Fresh starts: Men and women after divorce*. New York: Basic Books.

Centers for Disease Control. (1985a). Education and foster care of children infected with HTLV-III/LAV. *Morbidity and Mortality Weekly Report*, *34*, 613–615.

Centers for Disease Control. (1985b). Recommendations for preventing transmission of infection with HTLV-III/LAV in the workplace. *Mobidity and Mortality Weekly Report*, *34*, 682–695.

Centers for Disease Control. (1989). 1989 sexually transmitted diseases treatment guidelines. *Morbidity and Mortality Weekly Report*, *38*, S-8.

Centers for Disease Control. (1990). 1990 sexually transmitted diseases treatment guidelines. *Morbidity and Mortality Weekly Report*, *39*, J-3.

Centers for Disease Control. (1991). *HIV/AIDS Surveillance Report*. Division of HIV/AIDS Center for Infectious Diseases. Atlanta: Author.

Centers for Disease Control. (1991). HIV prevalence estimates and AIDS case projections for the United States. *Morbidity and Mortality Weekly Report*, *40*, RR-16.

Centers for Disease Control. (1992). The second 100,000 cases of acquired immunodeficiency syndrome. *Morbidity and Mortality Weekly Report*, *41*(2), 28–30.

Cerio, N. G. (1982). Counseling victims and perpetrators of campus violence. *Response to the Victimization of Women and Children*, *2*, 7–10.

Cervera, N. (1991). Unwed teenage pregnancy: Family relationships with the father of the baby. *Families in Society: The Journal of Contemporary Human Services*, *72*(1), 29–37.

Chalmers, I. (1988). *Love and loving*. Stamford, CT: Longmeadow Press.

Charlesworth, E., & Nathan, R. (1984). *Stress management*. New York: Ballantine Books.

Chasnoff, I. J. (1991, April). *Cocaine versus tobacco: Impact on infant and child outcome*. Paper presented at the Society for Research in Child Development, Seattle.

Chaze, W. L., Hawkins, S. L., & Lord, M. (1987, February 16). Fear of AIDS chills sex industry. *U.S. News & World Report*, p. 25.

Check, J., & Malamuth, N. (1983). Sex-role stereotyping and reactions to depictions of stranger versus acquaintance rape. *Journal of Personality and Social Psychology*, *45*, 344–356.

Cherlin, A., & Furstenberg, F. K., Jr. (1983). The American family in the year 2000. *The Futurist*, *17*, 7–14.

Cherry, S. H. (1990). *Understanding pregnancy and childbirth*. New York: Bantam Books.

Chelune, G. J., Robison, J. T., & Kommor, M. J. (1984). A cognitive interactional model of intimate relationships. In V. J. Derlega (Ed.), *Communication, intimacy, and close relationships*. New York: Academic Press.

Chez, R. A., & Chervenak, J. L. (1990). Nutrition in pregnancy. In R. D. Eden, F. H. Boehm, & M. Haire (Eds.), *Assessment and care of the fetus: Physiological, clinical, and medicolegal principles*. Norwalk, CT: Appleton & Lange.

Chhaya, M. (1987, July 16). Amniocentesis leads to abortion of female fetuses in India. *New London (CT) Day*.

Children's Defense Fund. (1988). *Teenage pregnancy: An advocate's guide to the numbers*. Washington, DC: Author.

Child's Protective Society. (1981). (OHDS) 81-30203. Washington, DC: U.S. Government Printing Office.

Chilman, C. S. (1980). Social and psychological research concerning adolescent childbearing: 1970–1980. *Journal of Marriage and the Family*, *42*, 793–806.

Chilman, C. S. (1988). Single adolescent parents. In C. Chilman, E. Nunnally, & F. Cox (Eds.), *Families in trouble*. Newbury Park, CA: Sage.

Chilman, C. S. (1990). Promoting healthy adolescent sexuality. *Family Relations*, *39*, 123–131.

Chin, J. (1987, September). *World Health Organization report on AIDS worldwide*. Presented at the Centers for Disease Control, New York.

Chin, J. (1991, June 18). AIDS from a worldwide perspective. *New York Times*, p. 12.

Chmiel, J. S., Detels, R., Kaslow, R. A., Van Raden, M., Kingsley, L. S., & Brookmeyer, R. (1987). Factors associated with prevalent human immunodeficiency virus (HIV) infection in the Multicenter AIDS Cohort Study. *American Journal of Epidemiology*, *126*, 568–577.

Christiansen, J. R., & Blake, R. H. (1990). The grooming process in father–daughter incest. In A. L. Horton, B. Johnson, L. M. Roundy, & D. Williams (Eds.), *The incest perpetrator: A family member no one wants to treat*. Newbury Park, CA: Sage.

Christopher, F. S. (1988). An initial investigation into a continuum of premarital sexual pressure. *Journal of Sex Research*, *25*, 255–266.

Christopher, F. S., & Cate, R. M. (1985). Premarital sexual pathways and relationship development. *Journal of Social and Personal Relationships*, *2*, 271–288.

Christopher, F. S., & Roosa, M. W. (1990). An evaluation of an adolescent pregnancy prevention program: Is "just say no" enough? *Family Relations*, *39*, 68–72.

Chumlea, W. C. (1982). Physical growth in adolescence. In B. B. Wolman (Ed.), *Handbook of developmental psychology*. Englewood Cliffs, NJ: Prentice Hall.

Cirese, S. (1985). *Quest: A search for self*. New York: Holt, Rinehart, & Winston.

Clark, A. (Ed.). (1981). *Culture and childrearing*. Philadelphia: Davis.

Clark, K. (1985). *Nongonococcal urethritis*. Santa Cruz, CA: Network.

Clark, L., & Lewis, D. (1977). *Rape: The price of coercive sexuality*. Toronto: Women's Press.

Clark, M. S., & Reis, H. T. (1988). Interpersonal processes in close relationships. *Annual Review of Psychology*, *39*, 609–672.

Clark, N., & Bennetts, A. (1982). Vital statistics and nonhospital births: A mortality study of infants born out of hospital in Oregon. *Research issues in the assessment of birth settings*. Washington, DC: National Academy Press.

Clayton, R. R., & Bokemeier, J. L. (1980). Premarital sex in the seventies. *Journal of Marriage and the Family, 42*, 759–775.

Clunis, D. M., & Green, G. D. (1988). *Lesbian couples*. Seattle, WA: Seal Press.

Cohen, N. W., & Estner, L. J. (1983). *Silent knife: Cesarean prevention and vaginal birth after cesarean*. South Hadley, MA: Bergin & Garvey.

Cohen, P. T., Sande, M. A., & Volberding, P. A. (Eds.). (1990). *The AIDS knowledge base*. Waltham, MA: The Medical Publishing Group.

Cohen, R. L. (1982). A comparison study of women choosing two different childbirth alternatives. *Birth, 9*, 13–19.

Cohen, T. (1983). The incestuous family revisited. *Social Casework, 64*, 154–161.

Colditz, G. (1988). Cigarette smoking and risk of stroke in middle-aged women. *New England Journal of Medicine, 318*, 937–941.

Cole, J., & Laibson, H. (1983). When parents argue (and kids listen). In O. Pocs & R. Walsh (Eds.), *Marriage and family 1983/84*. Guilford, CT: Dushkin.

Coleman, E. (1985). Developmental stages of the coming out process. In J. C. Gonsiorek (Ed.), *A guide to psychotherapy with gay and lesbian clients*. New York: Harrington Park Press.

Coleman, E. (1987). Sexual compulsion vs. sexual addiction: The debate continues. *SIECUS Report, 14*(6), 7–10.

Coleman, J. C. (1980). Friendship and the peer group in adolescence. In J. Adelson (Ed.), *Handbook of adolescent psychology*. New York: Wiley.

Coles, R., & Stokes, G. (1985). *Sex and the American teenager*. New York: Harper & Row.

Collins, J. L. (1982). Incest and child sexual abuse. *Journal of the National Medical Association, 72*, 513–517.

Comfort, A. (1986). *The joy of sex* (rev. ed.). New York: Crown.

Commission on Obscenity and Pornography. (1970). The Report of the Commission on Obscenity and Pornography. Washington, DC: U.S. Government Printing Office.

Conant, M., Hardy, D., Sernatinger, J., Spicer, D., & Levy, J. A. (1986). Condoms prevent transmission of AIDS-associated retrovirus. *Journal of the American Medical Association, 255*, 1706.

Condelli, L. (1986). Social and attitudinal determinants of contraceptive choice: Using the health belief model. *Journal of Sex Research, 22*, 478–491.

Condy, S. R., Templer, D. I., Brown, R., & Veaco, L. (1987). Parameters of sexual contacts of boys with women. *Archives of Sexual Behavior, 16*, 379–393.

Condry, J. C. (1989). *The psychology of television*. Hillsdale, NJ: Erlbaum.

Conger, J. J. (1988). Hostages to the future: Youth, values, and the public interest. *American Psychologist, 43*, 291–300.

Conkling, W. (1991). From infertility to fatherhood: New techniques can increase the odds for conception. *American Health, 10*, 10–13.

Connor-Greene, P. (1986). The role of counseling in the treatment of genital herpes. *Journal of American College Health, 34*, 286–287.

Conte, J. R. (1990). The incest offender: An overview and introduction. In A. L. Horton, B. Johnson, L. M. Roundy, & D. Williams (Eds.), *The incest perpetrator: A family member no one wants to treat*. Newbury Park, CA: Sage.

Conte, J. R., & Berliner, L. (1981). Prosecution of the offender in cases of sexual assault against children. *Victimology, 6*, 102–109.

Conte, J. R., & Berliner, L. (1987). The impact of sexual abuse on children: Empirical findings. In L. Walker (Ed.), *Handbook on sexual abuse of children: Assessment and treatment issues*. New York: Springer.

Conte, J. R., Rosen, C., Saperstein, L., & Shermack, R. (1985). An evaluation of a program to prevent sexual victimization of young children. *Child Abuse and Neglect, 9*, 319–328.

Cooper, A. J. (1985). Myocardial infarction and advice on sexual activity. *The Practitioner, 229*, 575–579.

Cooper, C. R., & Grotevant, H. D. (1989, April). *Individuality and connectedness in the family and adolescents' self and relational competence*. Paper presented at the biennial meeting of the Society for Research in Child Development. Kansas City.

Cooper, K., Chassin, L., & Zeiss, A. (1985). The relation of sex role self-concept and sex-role attitudes to the marital satisfaction and personal adjustment of dual-worker couples with preschool children. *Sex Roles, 12*, 227–241.

Cooperman, C., & Rhoades, C. (1983). *New methods for puberty education: Grades 4–9*. Morristown: Planned Parenthood of Northwest New Jersey.

Cordell, A. S., Parke, R. D., & Swain, D. B. (1980). Father's views on fatherhood with special reference to infancy. *Family Relations, 29*, 331–338.

Corey, G. (1990). *I never knew I had a choice* (4th ed.). Monterey, CA: Brooks/Cole.

Corey, L. (1982). The diagnosis and treatment of genital herpes. *Journal of the American Medical Association, 248*, 1041–1049.

Corey, L., & Holmes, K. K. (1983). Genital herpes simplex virus infections: Current concepts in diagnosis, therapy, and prevention. *Annals of Internal Medicine, 98*, 973–983.

Corless, I. B., & Pittman-Lindeman, M. (1988). *AIDS: Principles, practices, and politics*. New York: Hemisphere.

Corwin, D. (1985, September). *Sexually abused child's disorder*. Paper presented at the National Summit Conference on Diagnosing Child Sexual Abuse, Los Angeles.

Cotten-Huston, A. L., & Wheeler, K. A. (1983). Preorgasmic group treatment: Assertiveness, marital adjustment and sexual function in women. *Journal of Sex and Marital Therapy, 9*, 296–302.

Cotton, D. J., & Groth, A. N. (1982). Inmate rape: Prevention and intervention. *Journal of Prison and Jail Health, 2*, 47–57.

Court, J. H. (1984). Sex and violence: A ripple effect. In N. M. Malamuth & E. Donnerstein (Eds.), *Pornography and sexual aggression*. Orlando, FL: Academic Press.

Courtney, A. E., & Whipple, T. W. (1983). *Sex stereotyping in advertising*. Lexington, MA: Heath.

Coustan, D. R. (1990). Diabetes mellitus. In R. D. Eden, F. H. Boehm, & M. Haire (Eds.), *Assessment and care of the fetus: Physiological, clinical, and medicolegal principles*. Norwalk, CT: Appleton & Lange.

Couzinet, B., LeStrat, N., Ulmann, A., Baulieu, E. E., & Schaison, G. (1986). Termination of early pregnancy by the progesterone antagonist RU 496 (Mifepristone). *New England Journal of Medicine, 315*, 25, 1565–1570.

Covington, T. R., & McClendon, J. F. (1987). *Sex care*. New York: Pocket Books.

Cowan, C. P., Cowan, P. A., Heming, G., Garett, E., Coysh, W. S., Curtis-Boles, H., & Boles, A. J. (1985). Transitions to parenthood: His, hers, and theirs. *Journal of Family Issues, 6,* 451–481.

Cowan, W. M. (1986). The development of the brain. In R. Thompson (Ed.), *Progress in neuroscience.* New York: Freeman.

Coward, R. (1984). *Female desire.* London: Paladin.

Cox, F. D. (1984). *Human intimacy, marriage, and the family.* St. Paul, MN: West.

Creager, J. G., Black, J. G., & Davison, V. E. (1990). *Microbiology: Principles and applications.* Englewood Cliffs, NJ: Prentice Hall.

Crewdson, J. (1988). *By silence betrayed.* Boston: Little, Brown.

Crisci, G. A. (1983). *Personal safety curriculum: Prevention of child sexual abuse.* Hadley, MA: Personal Safety Programs.

Crissey, J. T. (1984). Scabies and pediculosis pubis. *Urologic Clinics of North America, 11,* 171–176.

Crosby, J. F. (1980). A critique of divorce statistics and their interpretation. *Family Relations, 1,* 51–56.

Croughan, J. L., Saghir, M., Cohen, R., & Robbins, E. (1981). A comparison of treated and untreated male cross-dressers. *Archives of Sexual Behavior, 10,* 515–528.

Crowe, L. C., & George, W. H. (1989). Alcohol and human sexuality: Review and integration. *Psychological Bulletin, 105,* 374–386.

Cruikshank, D. P. (1990). Cardiovascular, pulmonary, renal, and hematologic diseases in pregnancy. In J. R. Scott (Ed.), *Danforth's obstetrics and gynecology* (6th ed.). Philadelphia: Lippincott.

Crum, C., & Ellner, P. (1985). Chlamydia infections: Making the diagnosis. *Contemporary Obstetrics and Gynecology, 25,* 153–168.

Culp, R. E., Appelbaum, M. I., Osofsky, J. D., & Levy, J. A. (1988). Adolescent and older mothers: Comparison between prenatal maternal variables and newborn interaction measures. *Infant Behavior and Development, 11,* 353–362.

Cunningham, F. G., MacDonald, P. C., & Gant, N. F. (1989). *Williams obstetrics* (18th ed.). Norwalk, CT: Appleton & Lange.

Cunningham, J., & Strassberg, D. (1981). Neuroticism and disclosure reciprocity. *Journal of Counseling Psychology, 28,* 455–458.

Cupach, W. R., & Comstock, J. (1988). Satisfaction with sexual communication in marriage: Links to sexual satisfaction and dyadic adjustment. In D. O'Hair & B. Patterson (Eds.), *Advances in Interpersonal Communication Research: Proceedings of the WSCA Convention.* Las Cruces: Communication Resources Center of New Mexico State University.

Cvetkovich, G., & Grote, B. (1983). Adolescent development and teenage fertility. In D. Byrne & W. A. Fisher (Eds.), *Adolescents, sex, and contraception.* New York: McGraw-Hill.

Dacey, J. S. (1982). *Adult development.* Glenview, IL: Scott, Foresman.

Dalton, J. (1990). Chronic musculoskeletal symptoms and sexuality. In C. I. Fogel & D. Lauver (Eds.), *Sexual health promotion.* Philadelphia, PA: W. B. Saunders.

Dalton, H. L., & Burris, S. (Eds.). (1987). *AIDS and the law.* New Haven, CT: Yale University Press.

Daniel, H., O'Brien, K. F., McCabe, R. B., & Quinter, V. E. (1985). Values in mate selection: A 1984 campus survey. *College Student Journal, 19,* 44–50.

Danziger, S. K., & Wertz, D. C. (1989). Sociological and social psychological aspects of reproduction. In K. McKinney & S. Sprecher (Eds.), *Human sexuality: The societal and interpersonal context.* Norwood, NJ: Ablex.

Darling, C. A., & Davidson, J. K. (1986). Enhancing relationships: Understanding the feminine mystique of pretending orgasm. *Journal of Sex and Marital Therapy, 12,* 182–196.

Darling, C. A., & Mabe, A. R. (1989). Analyzing ethical issues in sexual relationships. *Journal of Sex Education and Therapy, 15,* 126–144.

Darrow, W. W., Echenberg, D. F., & Jaffe, H. W. (1977). Risk factors for human immunodeficiency virus infections in homosexual men. *American Journal of Public Health, 77,* 479–483.

Dash, L. (1989). *When children want children: The urban crisis of teenage childbearing.* New York: William Morrow.

Davidson, H. (1981). *Child sexual exploitation: Background and legal analysis.* Washington, DC: National Legal Resource Center for Child Advocacy and Protection.

Davidson, J. K. (1982). *A comparison of sexual fantasies between sexually experienced never-married males and females.* Paper presented at the annual meeting of the Southern Sociological Society. Memphis, TN.

Davidson, J. K., Sr., & Darling, C. A. (1989). Self-perceived differences in the female orgasmic response. *Family Practice Research Journal, 8,* 75–84.

Davidson, J. M., & Myers, L. S. (1988). Endocrine factors in sexual psychophysiology. In R. C. Rosen & J. G. Beck (Eds.), *Patterns of sexual arousal.* New York: Guilford.

Davis, G. E., & Leitenberg, H. (1987). Adolescent sex offenders. *Psychological Bulletin, 101,* 417–427.

Davis, J. A., & Smith. T. (1987). *General social surveys: 1982–1987: Cumulative data.* Storrs, CT: University of Connecticut, Roper Center for Public Opinion Research.

Davis, K. E., & Todd, M. J. (1985, February). Near and dear: Friendship and love compared. *Psychology Today,* pp. 22–30.

Davis, L. K., & Rosen, S. L. (1986). Cesarean section. In B. P. Sacks & D. Acker (Eds.), *Clinical obstetrics: A public health perspective.* Littleton, MA: PSG Publishing.

Davis, M. (1988). *Lovers, doctors and the law.* New York: Harper & Row.

Davis, R. A. (1989). Teenage pregnancy: A theoretical analysis of a social problem. *Adolescence, 24*(93), 19–28.

Dawson, D. A. (1986). The effects of sex education on adolescent behavior. *Family Planning Perspectives, 18,* 162–183.

Deaux, K., & Hanna, R. (1984). Courtship in the personals column: The influence of gender and sexual orientation. *Sex Roles, 11,* 363–375.

DeBuono, B. A. (1990). Sexual behavior of college women in 1975, 1986, and 1989. *New England Journal of Medicine, 322,* 821–825.

Dechesnay, M. (1983). Incest: A family triangle. *Nursing Times, 79,* 64–65.

de Krester, D. M., Simpson, R. W., Wilson, J. D., Rennie, G. C., Hudson, B., & Burger, H. G. (1983). Androgens and sexual behavior. In G. Burrows, L. Dennerstein, & I. Fraser (Eds.), *Obstetrics, gynecology, and psychiatry.* Melbourne: Australian Society of Psychosomatic Obstetrics and Gynecology.

DeLamater, J. (1981). The social control of sexuality. *Annual Review of Sociology, 7,* 76–89.

DeLamater, J. (1989). The social control of human sexuality. In K. McKinney & S. Sprecher (Eds.), *Human sexuality:*

The societal and interpersonal context. Norwood, NJ: Ablex.

Demare, D., Briere, J., & Lips, H. (1988). Violent pornography and self-reported likelihood of sexual aggression. *Journal of Research in Personality*, 22, 140–153.

DeMaris, A. (1987). The efficacy of a spouse abuse model in accounting for courtship violence. *Journal of Family Issues*, 8, 291–305.

D'Emillo, J. (1989). Gay politics and community in San Francisco since World War II. In M. B. Duberman, M. Vicinus, & G. Chauncey, Jr. (Eds.), *Hidden from history: Reclaiming the gay and lesbian past*. New York: New American Library.

D'Emillo, J., & Freedman, E. B. (1988). *Intimate matters: A history of sexuality in America*. New York: Harper & Row.

Denney, N. W., Field, J. K., & Quadagno, D. (1984). Sex differences in sexual needs and desires. *Archives of Sexual Behavior*, 13, 233–245.

Department of Health and Human Services. (1990). *America responds to AIDS*. Washington, DC: U.S. Government Printing Office.

Derlega, V. J. (1984). Self-disclosure and intimate relationships. In V. J. Derlega (Ed.), *Communication, intimacy, and close relationships*. New York: Academic Press.

DeVita, V. T., Hellman, S., & Rosenberg, S. A. (Eds.). (1988). *AIDS: Etiology, diagnosis, treatment, and prevention* (2nd ed.). Philadelphia: Lippincott.

Devroey, P. (1989). Zygote intrafallopian transfer as a successful treatment for unexplained infertility. *Fertility and Sterility*, 52(2), 246–256.

DeYoung, M. (1982). *The sexual victimization of children*. Jefferson, NC: McFarland.

Diamant, L. (Ed.). (1987). *Male and female homosexuality: Psychological approaches*. New York: Hemisphere.

Diamond, E. E. (1988). Women's occupational plans and decisions: An introduction. In B. A. Gutek (Ed.), *Applied psychology: An international review*. Beverly Hills, CA: Sage.

Dickinson, G. E., & Leming, M. R. (1990). *Understanding families: Diversity, continuity, and change*. Boston: Allyn & Bacon.

DiClemente, R. J. (1990). The emergence of adolescents as a risk group for human immunodeficiency virus infection. *Journal of Adolescent Research*, 5, 7–17.

DiClemente, R. J., Zorn, J., & Temoshok, L. (1987). Adolescents' knowledge of AIDS near an AIDS epicenter. *American Journal of Public Health*, 77, 876–877.

Dinkmeyer, D., & Carlson, J. (1984). *Time for a better marriage*. Circle Pines, MN: American Guidance Service.

Dion, K. K. (1985). Personality, gender, and the phenomenology of romantic love. In P. Shaver (Ed.), *Self, situations, and social behavior*. Beverly Hills, CA: Sage.

Dion, K. K. (1986). Stereotyping based on physical attractiveness: Issues and conceptual perspectives. In C. P. Herman, M. P. Zanna, & E. T. Higgings (Eds.), *Physical appearance, stigma, and social behavior: The Ontario symposium on personality and social psychology*. Hillsdale, NJ: Erlbaum.

DiPietro, J. (1981). Rough and tumble play: A function of gender. *Developmental Psychology*, 17, 50–58.

Dodge, K. (1990). Developmental psychopathology in children of depressed mothers. *Developmental Psychology*, 26(1), 3–6.

Dole, P. (1984). Sex development in adolescence. In J. M. Swanson & K. A. Forrest (Eds.), *Men's reproductive health*. New York: Springer.

Donaldson, M. A. (1983, November). *Incest victims years after*. Paper presented at the National Association of Social Workers Professional Symposium, Washington, DC.

Donaldson, P. J., & Tsui, A. O. (1990). *The international family planning movement*. Washington, DC: Population Reference Bureau.

Donnerstein, A. (1980). Aggressive erotica and violence against women. *Journal of Personality and Social Psychology*, 39, 269–277.

Donnerstein, E. I., & Linz, D. G. (1984a). Pornography may lead to sexual violence. In G. E. McCuen (Ed.), *Pornography and sexual violence*. Hudson, WI: G. M. Publications.

Donnerstein, E. I., & Linz, D. G. (1984b). Sexual violence in the media: A warning. *Psychology Today*, pp. 14–15.

Donnerstein, E. I., & Linz, D. G. (1986). The question of pornography. *Psychology Today*, pp. 56–60.

Dorner, G. (1976). *Hormones and brain differentiation*. Amsterdam: Elsevier.

Douglas, J. D., & Atwell, F. C. (1988). *Love, intimacy, and sex*. Beverly Hills, CA: Sage.

Douglas, P. H., & Pinsky, L. (1987). *The essential AIDS factbook*. New York: Pocket Books.

Downer, A. (1984). *The development and testing of an evaluation instrument for assessing the effectiveness of a child abuse prevention curriculum: Talking about touching*. Seattle, WA: Committee for Children.

Downs, A. C. (1981). Sex-role stereotyping on prime-time television. *Journal of Genetic Psychology*, 138, 253–258.

Downs, A. C., & Langlois, J. H. (1988). Sex typing: Construct and measurement issues. *Sex Roles*, 18, 87–100.

Doyle, J. (1985). *Sex and gender*. Dubuque, IA: Wm. C. Brown.

Doyle, J., & Paludi, M. A. (1991). *Sex and gender* (2nd ed.). Dubuque, IA: Wm. C. Brown.

Drass, K. (1986). The effect of gender identity on conversation. *Social Psychology Quarterly*, 49, 294–301.

Dreikurs, R. (1964). *Children: The challenge*. New York: Hawthorne.

Drenth, J. J. (1988). Vaginismus and the desire for a child. *Journal of Psychosomatic Obstetrics and Gynecology*, 9, 125–138.

Dreyer, P. H. (1982). Sexuality during adolescence. In B. B. Wolman (Ed.), *Handbook of developmental psychology*. Englewood Cliffs, NJ: Prentice Hall.

Dryfoos, J. (1988). *Putting the boys in the picture: A review of programs to promote sexual responsibility among young males*. Santa Cruz, CA: Network Publications.

Dryfoos, J. (1990). *Adolescents at risk: Prevalence and prevention*. New York: Oxford University Press.

Duck, S. (1989). *Relating to others*. Chicago: Dorsey Press.

Duncan, P., Ritter, P. L., Dornbusch, S. M., Gross, R. T., & Carlsmith, J. M. (1985). The effects of pubertal timing on body image, school behavior and deviance. *Journal of Youth and Adolescence*, 14, 227–235.

Dunn, L. J. (1990). Cesarean section and other obstetric operations. In J. R. Scott (Ed.), *Danforth's obstetrics and gynecology* (6th ed.). Philadelphia: Lippincott.

Dunn, P. C., Ryan, I. J., & O'Brien, K. (1988). College students' level of acceptability of the new medical science of conception and problems of infertility. *Journal of Sex Research*, 24, 282–287.

Durkin, K. (1984). Children's account of sex-role stereotypes in television. *Communication Research*, 11, 341–362.

Durkin, K. (1985). Television and sex-role acquisition. *British Journal of Social Psychology*, 24, 101–113.

Dwyer, M. (1988). Exhibitionism/voyeurism. In D. M. Dailey (Ed.), *The sexually unusual: Guide to understanding and helping*. New York: Harrington Park Press.

Dziech, B. W., & Weiner, L. (1984). *The lecherous professor: Sexual harassment*. Boston: Beacon.

Eagan, A. (1989, April). The X-rated office. *Working Mother*, pp. 86–90.

Eagly, A. H., Ashmore, R. D., Makhijani, M. G., & Kennedy, L. C. (1991). What is beautiful, but . . . : A meta-analytic review of research on the physical attractiveness stereotype. *Psychological Bulletin, 110*, 109–128.

Earle, R., & Crow, G. (1989). *Lonely all the time*. New York: Pocket Books.

Eccles, J. S., & Midgley, C. (1990). Changes in academic motivation and self-perception during early adolescence. In R. Montemayor, G. R. Adams, & T. P. Gullotta (Eds.), *From childhood to adolescence: A transitional period?* Newbury Park, CA: Sage.

Edelman, M. W. (1987). *Families in peril: An agenda for social change*. New York: Alan Guttmacher Institute.

Edlin, J., & Schanche, D. (1990, September 30). In Africa, a half million in jeopardy. *New London Day*, pp. 6–7.

Edwards, M., & Waldorf, M. (1984). *Reclaiming birth: History and heroines of American childbirth reform*. Trumansburg, NY: Crossing Press.

Edwards, S. R. (1986). A sex addict speaks. *SIECUS Report, 14*(6), 1–3.

Egeland, B. (1989, January 12). Secure attachment in infancy and competence in the third grade. Paper presented at the meeting of the American Association for the Advancement of Science, San Francisco.

Ehrhart, J., & Sandler, B. (1985). *Campus gang rape: Party games?* New York: Association of American Colleges, Project on the Status and Education of Women.

Eisenberg, A., & Eisenberg, H. (1983). *Alive and well: Decisions in health*. New York: McGraw-Hill.

Eisenberg, A., Murkoff, H. E., & Hathaway, S. E. (1991). *What to expect when you're expecting* (rev. ed.). New York: Workman.

Elias, M. (1990, March 12). Women weighing the benefits and risks of estrogen therapy. *Norwich Bulletin*, p. C5.

Elias, T. D. (1985, January 13). Survey: Hookers often love the life. *Atlanta Journal and Constitution*, p. 15A.

Ellis, A. (1980). Treatment of premature ejaculation. In S. R. Leiblum & L. A. Pervin (Eds.), *Principles and practice of sex therapy*. New York: Guilford.

Ellis, A. (1989). Rational-emotive therapy. In R. J. Corsini & D. Wedding (Eds.), *Current psychotherapies*. Itasca, IL: Peacock.

Ellis, H. H. (1936). *Studies in the psychology of sex, 1896–1928*. New York: Modern Library.

Ellis, L., & Ames, M. A. (1987). Neurohormonal functioning and sexual orientation: A theory of homosexuality-heterosexuality. *Psychological Bulletin, 101*, 233–258.

Elmer-DeWitt, P. (1990, February 26). A bitter pill to swallow. *Time*, p. 44.

Elster, A. B., & Panzarine, S. (1983). Adolescent fathers. In E. R. McAnarney (Ed.), *Premature adolescent pregnancy and parenthood*. New York: Grune & Stratton.

Entwisle, D. R. (1985). Becoming a parent. In L. L'Abate (Ed.), *The handbook of family psychology and therapy*. Homewood, IL: Dorsey Press.

Erikson, E. H. (1963). *Childhood and society* (2nd ed.). New York: Norton.

Erikson, E. H. (1982). *The life cycle completed: A review*. New York: Norton.

Erikson, E. H., Erikson, J. M., & Kivnick, H. Q. (1986). *Vital involvement in old age: The experience of old age in our time*. New York: Norton.

Eschenbach, D. (1986). Pelvic infections. In D. Danforth & J. Scott (Eds.), *Obstetrics and gynecology* (5th ed.). Philadelphia: Lippincott.

Eshleman, J. R. (1988). *The family: An introduction* (5th ed.). Boston: Allyn & Bacon.

Etaugh, C. (1980). Effects of nonmaternal care on children: Research evidence and popular reviews. *American Psychologist, 35*, 309–319.

Etaugh, C., Collins, G., & Gerson, A. (1975). Reinforcement of sex-typed behaviors of two-year-old children in a nursery school setting. *Developmental Psychology, 11*, 255–278.

Evaraerd, W., & Dekker, J. (1982). Treatment of secondary orgasmic dysfunction: A comparison of systematic desensitization and sex therapy. *Behaviour Research and Therapy, 20*, 269–274.

Eysenck, H., & Wilson, E. (1979). *The psychology of sex*. London: Dent.

Fagot, B. I., & Kronsberg, S. J. (1982). Sex differences: Biological and social factors influencing the behavior of young boys and girls. In S. G. Moore & S. G. Cooper (Eds.), *The young child: Reviews of research* (Vol. 3). Washington, DC: National Association for the Education of Young Children.

Faich, G., Pearson, K., Fleming, D., Sobel, S., & Anello, C. (1986). Toxic shock syndrome and the vaginal contraceptive sponge. *Journal of the American Medical Association, 255*, 216–218.

Falk, D. R., & Wagner, P. N. (1985). Intimacy of self-disclosure and response processes as factors affecting the development of interpersonal relationships. *Journal of Social Psychology, 124*, 557–570.

Faller, K. C. (1990). *Understanding child sexual maltreatment*. Newbury Park, CA: Sage.

Fallon, W. K. (1981). *Effective communication on the job* (3rd ed.). New York: AMACOM.

Family Sexual Abuse Project. (1987). Female sex offenders. *Innovation and Inquiry in Family Sexual Abuse Intervention, 1*, 1–6.

Farnsworth, C. H. (1991). Canada ending anti-gay army rules. *New York Times*, October 11, B-11.

Faulkenberry, J. R., Murray, V., Arnold, J., & Johnson, W. (1987). Coital behaviors, attitudes, and knowledge of students who experience early coitus. *Adolescence, 22*, 321–332.

Fay, R., Turner, C. E., Klasseu, A. D., & Gagnon, J. (1989). Prevalence and patterns of same-gender sexual contact among men. *Science, 243*, 338–348.

Feather, N. T. (1984). Masculinity, femininity, psychological androgyny, and the structure of values. *Journal of Personality and Social Psychology, 47*, 604–620.

Featherstone, M., & Hepworth, M. (1985). The male menopause: Lifestyle and sexuality. *Maturitas, 7*, 235–246.

Feeney, J. A., & Noller, P. (1990). Attachment style as a predictor of adult romantic relationships. *Journal of Personality and Social Psychology, 58*, 281–291.

Fein, R. (1980). Research on fathering. In A. Skolnick & J. Skolnick (Eds.), *The family transition*. Boston: Little, Brown.

Feinbloom, R. I., & Forman, B. Y. (1987). *Pregnancy, birth, and the early months*. Reading, MA: Addison-Wesley.

Feingold, A. (1988). Cognitive gender differences are disappearing. *American Psychologist, 43*, 95–103.

Feingold, A. (1988). Matching for attractiveness in romantic partners and same-sex friends: A meta-analysis and theoretical critique. *Psychological Bulletin, 104*, 226–235.

Feldstein, J. H., & Feldstein, S. (1982). Sex differences on televised toy commercials. *Sex Roles, 8*, 581–593.

Fendrich, M., Warner, V., & Weissman, M. M. (1990). Family risk factors, parental depression, and psychopathology in offspring. *Developmental Psychology, 26*(1), 40–50.

Ferenczy, A. (1984). Comparison of 5-fluorouracil and co2 laser for treatment of vaginal condylomata. *Obstetrics and Gynecology, 64*, 773–776.

Fichten, C. S., Libman, E., & Brender, W. (1986). Measurement of therapy outcome and maintenance of gains in the behavioral treatment of secondary orgasmic dysfunction. *Journal of Sex and Marital Therapy, 12*, 22–34.

Field, T., Healy, B. T., Goldstein, S., & Guthertz, M. (1990). Behavior-state matching and synchrony in mother-infant interactions of nondepressed versus depressed dyads. *Developmental Psychology, 26*(1), 7–14.

Fincham, F. D., & Bradbury, T. N. (Eds.). (1990). *The psychology of marriage: Basic issues and applications*. New York: Guilford.

Fineberg, H. V. (1988). The social dimensions of AIDS. *Scientific American, 259*, 128–134.

Fink, A., & Kosecoff, J. (1985). *How to conduct surveys*. Beverly Hills, CA: Sage.

Finkelhor, D. (1984). *Child sexual abuse: New theory and research*. New York: Free Press.

Finkelhor, D. (Ed.). (1986). *A sourcebook on child sexual abuse*. Beverly Hills, CA: Sage.

Finkelhor, D. (1988). The trauma of child sexual abuse. In G. E. Wyatt & G. J. Powell (Eds.), *Lasting effects of child sexual abuse*. Beverly Hills, CA: Sage.

Finkelhor, D. (1990). Sexual abuse in a national survey of adult men and women: Prevalence, characteristics, and risk factors. *Child Abuse and Neglect, 14*, 19–28.

Finkelhor, D., & Baron, L. (1986). High-risk children. In D. Finkelhor (Ed.), *A sourcebook on child sexual abuse*. Beverly Hills, CA: Sage.

Finkelhor, D., & Browne, A. (1985). The traumatic impact of child sexual abuse: A conceptualization. *American Journal of Orthopsychiatry, 55*, 530–541.

Finkelhor, D., & Yllo, K. (1988). Rape in marriage. In M. Strauss (Ed.), *Abuse and victimization across the lifespan*. Baltimore: Johns Hopkins University Press.

Fiorentine, R. (1988). Increasing similarity in the values and life plans of male and female college students? Evidence and implications. *Sex Roles, 18*, 143–158.

Fisher, M., & Stricker, G. (Eds.). (1982). *Intimacy*. New York: Plenum.

Fisher, S. (1972). *The female orgasm*. New York: Basic Books.

Fisher, S. (1973). *Understanding the female orgasm*. New York: Bantam.

Fisher, W. A. (1983). Adolescent contraception: Summary and recommendations. In D. Byrne & W. A. Fisher (Eds.), *Adolescents, sex, and contraception*. New York: McGraw-Hill.

Fisher, W. A. (1984). Predicting contraceptive behavior among university men: The role of emotions and behavioral intentions. *Journal of Applied Social Psychology, 14*, 104–123.

Fitzgerald, F. (1984). The classic venereal diseases: Syphilis and gonorrhea in the '80s. *Postgraduate Medicine, 75*, 91–101.

Fitzpatrick, M. (1988). *Between husbands and wives: Communication in marriage*. Newbury Park, CA: Sage.

Fleming, A. S., Ruble, D. N., Flett, G. L., & Van Wagner, V. (1990). Adjustment in first-time mothers: Changes in mood and mood content during the early postpartum months. *Developmental Psychology, 26*(1), 137–143.

Fletcher, J. (1966). *Situation ethics: The new morality*. Philadelphia: Westminister.

Flick, L. H. (1986). Paths to adolescent parenthood: Implications for prevention. *Public Health Reports, 102*, 132–147.

Fligiel, S. E. G., Venkat, H., Gong, H., & Tashkin, D. P. (1988). Bronchial pathology in chronic marijuana smokers: A light and electron microscopy study. *Journal of Psychoactive Drugs, 20*, 33–42.

Fogel, C. I. (1990). Human sexuality and health care. In C. I. Fogel & D. Lauver (Eds.), *Sexual health promotion*. Philadelphia: W. B. Saunders.

Fogel, C. I. (1990). Sexual health promotion. In C. I. Fogel & D. Lauver (Eds.), *Sexual health promotion*. Philadelphia: Saunders.

Fogel, C. I., & Lauver, D. (1990). *Sexual health promotion*. Philadelphia: Saunders.

Fogel, C. I., Forker, J., & Welch, M. B. (1990). Sexual health care. In C. I. Fogel & D. Lauver (Eds.), *Sexual health promotion*. Philadelphia: Saunders.

Forrest, J. (1986). *Women ever pregnant before age twenty*. New York: Alan Guttmacher Institute.

Forrest, J. D., & Silverman, J. (1989). What public school teachers teach about preventing pregnancy, AIDS and sexually transmitted diseases. *Family Planning Perspectives, 21*, 65–72.

Forsyth, C. J., & Fournet, L. (1987). A typology of office harlots: Mistresses, party girls, and career climbers. *Deviant Behavior, 8*, 319–324.

Fox, C. A., & Fox, B. A. (1969). Blood pressure and respiratory patterns during human coitus. *Journal of Reproduction and Fertility, 19*, 405–415.

Fox, N. A., Sutton, B., Aaron, N., & Luebering, A. (1989, April 26). Infant temperament and attachment: A new look at an old issue. Paper presented at the Society for Research in Child Development meeting, Kansas City.

Francis, D. (1984). Occurrences of hepatitis, A, B, non-A, non-B in the United States: CDC sentinel county hepatitis study. *American Journal of Medicine, 76*, 69–74.

Frank, D. I. (1984). Counseling the infertile couple. *Journal of Psychosocial Nursing, 22*, 17–23.

Frank, E., & Enos, S. (1983, February). The love life of the American wife. *Ladies' Home Journal*, pp. 71–72, 116–119.

Franklin, D. (1988). Race, class, and adolescent pregnancy. *American Journal of Orthopsychiatry, 58*, 339–354.

Freeman, R. K. (1990, April). Can we lower the cesarean birth rate? Tenth International Symposium on Perinatal Medicine and Obstetrical Ultrasound. Las Vegas, Nevada.

Freud, S. (1905). *Three essays on the theory of sexuality*. London: Hogarth Press.

Freud, S. (1938). *An outline of psychoanalysis*. London: Hogarth Press.

Freud, S. (1938). *The basic writings of Sigmund Freud*. New York: Modern Library.

Freud, S. (1946). *Group psychology and the analysis of the ego*. London: Hogarth Press.

Freud, S. (1948). *Collected letters*. London: Hogarth Press.

Freud, S. (1953). *A general introduction to psychoanalysis* (J. Riviere, trans.) New York: Permabooks.

Freudberg, F., & Emanuel, S. (1982). *Herpes: A complete guide to relief and reassurance*. Philadelphia: Running Press.

Frey, K. A. (1981). Middle-aged women's experience and perceptions of menopause. *Women and Health, 6,* 25–36.

Fribourg, S. (1982). Cigarette smoking and sudden infant death syndrome. *Journal of Obstetrics and Gynecology, 142,* 934–941.

Fried, P., & O'Connell, C. (1991, April). *Marijuana and tobacco as prenatal correlates of child behavior: Follow up to school age.* Paper presented at the Society for Research in Child Development, Seattle.

Friedan, B. (1963). *The feminine mystique.* New York: Dell.

Friedland, G. H., & Klein, R. S. (1987). Transmission of the human immunodeficiency virus. *New England Journal of Medicine, 317,* 1125–1135.

Friedrich, W. N., Urquiza, A. J., & Beilke, R. (1986). Behavioral problems in sexually abused young children. *Journal of Pediatric Psychology, 11,* 47–57.

Frieze, I. (1983). Causes and consequences of marital rape. *Signs, 8,* 532–553.

Fritz, G. S., Stoll, K., & Wagner, N. (1981). A comparison of males and females who were sexually molested as children. *Journal of Sex and Marital Therapy, 7,* 54–59.

Fromuth, M. E. (1986). The relationship of childhood sexual abuse with later psychological and sexual adjustment in a sample of college women. *Child Abuse and Neglect, 10,* 5–15.

Fu, V., & Leach, D. J. (1980). Sex-role preferences among elementary school children in rural America. *Psychological Reports, 46,* 555–560.

Furstenberg, F., Shea, J., Allison, P., Herceg-Baron, R., & Well, D. (1983). Contraceptive continuation among adolescents attending family planning clinics. *Family Planning Perspectives, 15,* 211–217.

Furstenberg, F. F., Jr. (1987). *Recycling the family: Remarriage after divorce* (Updated Edition). Beverly Hills, CA: Sage.

Furstenberg, F. F., Jr. (1988). Childcare after divorce and remarriage. In E. M. Hetherington & J. D. Arasteh (Eds.), *Impact of divorce, single-parenting, and step-parenting on children.* Hillsdale, NJ: Erlbaum.

Furstenberg, F. F. (1991). Pregnancy and childbearing: Effects on teen mothers. In R. M. Lerner, A. C. Petersen, & J. Brooks-Gunn (Eds.), *Encyclopedia of adolescence.* New York: Garland.

Furstenberg, F. F., Jr., Brooks-Gunn, J., & Chase-Lansdale, L. (1989). Teenage pregnancy and childbearing. *American Psychologist, 44,* 313–320.

Furstenberg, F. F., Jr., & Spanier, G. G. (1984). *Recycling the family: Remarriage after divorce.* Beverly Hills, CA: Sage.

Gabor, D. (1983). *How to start a conversation and make friends.* New York: Simon & Schuster.

Gagnon, J. (1977). *Human sexualities.* Glenview, IL: Scott, Foresman.

Gagnon, J., Rosen, R., & Leiblum, S. (1982). Cognitive and social aspects of sexual dysfunction: Sexual scripts in sex therapy. *Journal of Marriage and Marital Therapy, 8,* 44–56.

Gagnon, J., & Simon, N. (1987). The sexual scripting of oral genital contacts. *Archives of Sexual Behavior, 16,* 1–25.

Gale, J., Thompson, R., Miran, T., & Sach, W. (1988). Sexual abuse in young children: Its clinical presentation and characteristic patterns. *Child Abuse and Neglect, 12,* 163–170.

Gallup Poll Survey. (1983). Americans' attitudes toward gays. *Family Life Educator, 2,* 21.

Ganong, L. H., & Coleman, M. (1987). Sex, sex roles, and familial love. *Journal of Genetic Psychology, 148,* 45–52.

Garbarino, J. (1985). *Adolescent development: An ecological perspective.* Columbus, OH: Merrill.

Gargan, E. (1991). Coming out in India, with a nod from the Gods. *New York Times,* August 15, 22.

Gartrell, N. K. (1982). Hormones and homosexuality. In W. Paul (Ed.), *Homosexuality: Social, psychological, and biological issues.* Beverly Hills, CA: Sage.

Gastel, B., & Hecht, A. (1980). Estrogen: Another riddle for middle age. *FDA Consumer, 14,* 14–15.

Gayle, H. D., Keeling, R. P., Garcia-Tunon, M., Kilbourne, B. W., Narkunas, J. P., Ingram, F. R., Rogers, M. F., & Curran, J. W. (1990). Prevalence of the human immunodeficiency virus among university students. *New England Journal of Medicine, 323*(22), 1538–1541.

Geis, B. D., & Gerrard, M. (1984). Predicting male and female contraceptive behavior: A discriminant analysis of groups high, moderate, and low in contraceptive effectiveness. *Journal of Personality and Social Psychology, 46,* 669–680.

Geiser, R. L. (1982). Incest and psychological violence. *International Journal of Family Psychiatry, 2,* 291–300.

Gelinas, D. J. (1983). The persisting effects of incest. *Psychiatry, 46,* 312–332.

Gelles, R. J., & Cornell, C. P. (1990). *Intimate violence in families.* Newbury Park, CA: Sage.

Gelles, R. J., & Straus, M. A. (1988). *Intimate violence.* New York: Simon & Schuster.

Gelman, D. (1987, October 26). Not tonight, dear. *Newsweek,* pp. 64–66.

George, L. K. (1980). *Role transitions in later life.* Monterey, CA: Brooks/Cole.

George, L. K., & Weiler, S. J. (1981). Sexuality in middle and later life: The effects of age, cohort, and gender. *Archives of General Psychiatry, 38,* 919–923.

Gerrard, M. (1982). Sex, sex guilt, and contraceptive use. *Journal of Personality and Social Psychology, 42,* 153–158.

Geschwind, N., & Bahan, P. (1982). Left-handedness: Association with immune disease, migraine, and developmental learning disorder. *Proceedings of the National Academy of Science USA, 79,* 5097–5100.

Gesell, A. (1940). *The first five years of life.* New York: Harper.

Giaretto, H. (1982). *Integrated treatment of child sexual abuse.* Palo Alto, CA: Science & Behavior.

Gibbs, J. T. (1991). Black adolescents at risk: Approaches to prevention. In R. M. Lerner, A. C. Petersen, & J. Brooks-Gunn (Eds.), *Encyclopedia of adolescence.* New York: Garland.

Giblin, P. T., Poland, M. L., Waller, J. B. Jr., & Ager, J. W. (1989). Correlates of neonatal morbidity: Maternal characteristics and family resources. *Journal of Genetic Psychology, 149,* 527–533.

Gieringer, D. H. (1988). Marijuana, driving, and accident safety. *Journal of Psychoactive Drugs, 20,* 93–102.

Gilbert, A. L., & Davidson, S. (1989). Dual-career families at midlife. In S. Hunter & M. Sundell (Eds.), *Midlife myths: Issues, findings, and practical implications.* Beverly Hills, CA: Sage.

Gilbert, B., & Cunningham, G. (1986). Women's post-rape sexual functioning: Review and implications for counseling. *Journal of Counseling and Development, 65,* 71–73.

Gilgoff, A. (1988). *Home birth: An invitation and guide.* Westport, CT: Greenwood Press.

Gilgun, J. F., & Connor, T. M. (1990). Isolation and the adult male perpetrator of child sexual abuse: Clinical concerns. In A. L. Horton, B. Johnson, L. M. Roundy, & D. Williams (Eds.), *The incest perpetrator: A family member no one wants to treat.* Newbury Park, CA: Sage.

Gilgun, J. F., & Gordon, S. (1984). Sex education and the prevention of child sexual abuse. *Journal of Sex Education and Therapy, 11,* 46–52.

Gill, S., Stockard, J., Johnson, M., & Williams, S. (1987). Measuring gender differences: The expressive dimension and critique of the androgyny scales. *Sex Roles, 17,* 375–400.

Gilligan, C. (1982). *In a different voice.* Cambridge, MA: Harvard University Press.

Ginott, H. (1965). *Between parent and child.* New York: Avon.

Ginsburg, H., Wright, L. S., Harrell, P. M., & Hill, D. W. (1989). Childhood victimization: Desensitization effects in the later lifespan. *Child Psychiatry and Human Development, 20,* 59–71.

Giuliano, A. (1987). The breast. In M. Pernoll & R. Benson (Eds.), *Current obstetric and gynecologic diagnosis and treatment, 1987.* Los Altos, CA: Appleton & Lange.

Givens, D. B. (1983). *Love signals.* New York: Pinnacle Books.

Glasser, R., & Thorpe, J. (1986). Unethical intimacy: A survey of sexual contact and advances between psychology educators and female graduate students. *American Psychologist, 41,* 43–51.

Glenn, N. D. (1981). The well-being of persons remarried after divorce. *Journal of Family Issues, 2,* 61–75.

Glenn, N. D., & Supancic, M. (1984). The social and demographic correlates of divorce and separation in the United States: An update and reconstruction. *Journal of Marriage and the Family, 46,* 563–570.

Glick, P. C. (1984). Marriage, divorce, and living arrangements: Prospective changes. *Journal of Family Issues, 5,* 7–26.

Glick, P. C. (1988). Fifty years of family demography: A record of social change. *Journal of Marriage and the Family, 42,* 861–873.

Glick, P. C., & Spanier, G. (1980). Married and unmarried cohabitation in the United States. *Journal of Marriage and the Family, 42,* 19–30.

Gochros, J. S. (1985). Wives' reactions to learning that their husbands are bisexual. In F. Klein & T. J. Wolf (Eds.), *Two lives to lead: Bisexuality in men and women.* New York: Harrington Park Press.

Goedert, J. (1987). What is safe sex? Suggested standards linked to testing for HIV. *New England Journal of Medicine, 316,* 1339–1341.

Goetting, A. (1986). Parental satisfaction: A review of research. *Journal of Family Issues, 7,* 83–109.

Gold, S., & Chick, D. (1988). Sexual fantasy patterns as related to sexual attitude, experience, guilt, and sex. *Journal of Sex Education and Therapy, 14,* 18–23.

Goldberg, H. (1983). *The new male–female relationship.* New York: Signet.

Goldberg, W. A., Michaels, G. Y., & Lamb, M. E. (1985). Husbands' and wives' adjustment to pregnancy and first parenthood. *Journal of Family Issues, 6,* 483–503.

Golding, J., Siegel, J., Sorenson, S., Burnam, M., & Stein, J. (1989). Social support sources following sexual assault. *Journal of Community Psychology, 17,* 92–107.

Goldsmith, L. (1988). Treatment of sexual dysfunction. In E. Weinstein & E. Rosen (Eds.), *Sexuality counseling: Issues and implications.* Monterey, CA: Brooks/Cole.

Gomez-Schwartz B., Horowitz, J. M., & Cardarelli, A. P. (1990). *Child sexual abuse: The initial effects.* Beverly Hills, CA: Sage.

Goode, E. (1989). *Drugs in American society* (3rd ed.). New York: Knopf.

Goode, E., & Haber, L. (1977). Sexual correlates of homosexual experience: An exploratory study of college women. *Journal of Sex Research, 13,* 12–21.

Goodman, D. (1985). *Straight talk.* Oklahoma City: Planned Parenthood Association of Oklahoma City.

Goodman, S. H., & Brumley, H. E. (1990). Schizophrenic and depressed mothers: Relational deficits in parenting. *Developmental Psychology, 26*(1), 31–39.

Goodwin, J. (1982). *Sexual abuse: Incest victims and their families.* Boston: John Wright.

Gordon, D. E. (1990). Formal operational thinking: The role of cognitive-developmental processes in adolescent decision-making about pregnancy and contraception. *American Journal of Orthopsychiatry, 60*(3), 346–356.

Gordon, L., & O'Keefe, P. (1984). Incest as a form of family violence: Evidence from historical case records. *Journal of Marriage and the Family, 46,* 27–34.

Gordon, S. (1989). Sexual abuse prevention: Issues and answers. In C. Cassell & P. M. Wilson (Eds.), *Sexuality education: A resource book.* New York: Garland.

Gordon, S., & Gordon, J. (1989). *Raising a child conservatively in a sexually permissive world.* New York: Simon & Schuster.

Gordon, S., & Snyder, C. W. (1986). *Personal issues in human sexuality.* Newton, MA: Allyn & Bacon.

Gordon, T. (1978). *P.E.T. in action.* New York: Bantam.

Gottman, J. S. (1990). Children of gay and lesbian parents. In F. W. Bozett & M. B. Sussman (Eds.), *Homosexuality and family relations.* New York: Haworth Press.

Gramick, J. (1984). Developing a lesbian identity. In T. Darty & S. Potter (Eds.), *Women-identified women.* Palo Alto, CA: Mayfield.

Granberg, D., & Granberg, B. (1982). The sexual politics of the new right. *Sociology and Social Research, 65,* 424–429.

Grasha, A. F., & Kirschenbaum, D. S. (1986). *Adjustment and competence.* St. Paul, MN: West.

Grauerholz, E., & Solomon, J. C. (1989). Sexual coercion: Power and violence. In K. McKinney & S. Sprecher (Eds.), *Human sexuality: The societal and interpersonal context.* Norwood, NJ: Ablex.

Gray, M. (1981). *The changing years: Menopause without fear* (3rd ed.). New York: Signet Books.

Green, A. H. (1986). True and false allegations of sexual abuse in child custody disputes. *Journal of the American Academy of Child Psychiatry, 25,* 449–456.

Green, R. (1978). Sexual identity of 37 children raised by homosexual or transsexual parents. *American Journal of Psychiatry, 135,* 682–687.

Green, R. (1987). *The "sissy boy" syndrome and the development of homosexuality.* New Haven, CT: Yale University Press.

Green, S. K., Buchanan, D. R., & Heuer, S. K. (1984). Winners, losers, and choosers: A field investigation of dating initiation. *Personality and Social Psychology Bulletin, 10,* 502–512.

Greenblat, C. S. (1983). The salience of sexuality in the early years of marriage. *Journal of Marriage and the Family, 45,* 289–299.

Greenblatt, D. R. (1966). *Semantic differential analysis of the "triangular system" hypothesis in adjusted overt male homosexuals.* Unpublished doctoral dissertation, University of California.

Greenfeld, D., Diamond, M., Breslin, R., & DeCherney, A. (1986). Infertility and the new reproductive technology. *Social Work in Health Care, 12,* 71–81.

Greenough, W. T., Carter, C. S., Steerman, C., & DeVoogt, T. J. (1977). Sex differences in dendritic patterns in hamster preoptic area. *Brain Research, 126,* 63–72.

Greenspoon, J., & Lamal, P. A. (1987). A behavioristic approach. In L. Diamant (Ed.), *Male and female homosexuality: Psychological approaches.* New York: Hemisphere.

Gregersen, E. (1983). *Sexual practices.* New York: Franklin Watts.

Greif, E. B., & Ulman, K. (1982). The psychological impact of menarche on early adolescent females: A review. *Child Development, 53,* 1413–1430.

Grieco, A. (1987). Cutting the risks for STD's. *Medical Aspects of Human Sexuality, 3,* 70–84.

Grigsby, J. P., & Weatherley, D. (1983). Gender and sex-role differences in intimacy of self-disclosure. *Psychological Reports, 53,* 891–897.

Gross, R. T., & Duke, P. M. (1980). The effect of early vs. late maturation on adolescent behavior. *Pediatric Clinics of North America, 27,* 71–77.

Grossman, M. (1988). Children with AIDS. In I. C. Corless & M. Pittman-Lindeman (Eds.), *AIDS: Principles, practices, and politics.* New York: Hemisphere.

Groth, A. N. (1983). Treatment of the sexual offender in a correctional institution. In J. G. Greer & I. R. Stuart (Eds.), *The sexual aggressor: Current perspectives on treatment.* New York: Van Nostrand Reinhold.

Groth, A. N., & Hobson, W. F. (1983). The dynamics of sexual assault. In L. B. Schlesinger & E. Revitch (Eds.), *Sexual dynamics of anti-social behavior.* Springfield, IL: Chas. C. Thomas.

Groth, A. N., Hobson, W. F., & Gary, T. S. (1982). The child-molester: Clinical observations. In J. Conte & D. Shore (Eds.), *Social work and child sexual abuse.* New York: Haworth.

Guinan, M. (1986). Sexually transmitted diseases may reverse the revolution. *Journal of the American Medical Association, 255,* 16665.

Gutek, B. A. (1985). *Sex and the workplace.* San Francisco: Jossey-Bass.

Gutek, B. A. (1988). Sex segregation and women at work: A selective review. In B. A. Gutek (Ed.), *Applied psychology: An international review.* Beverly Hills, CA: Sage.

Gutek, B. A., & Nakumura, C. Y. (1983). Gender roles and sexuality in the world of work. In E. R. Allgeier & N. B. McCormick (Eds.), *Changing boundaries: Gender roles and sexual behavior.* Palo Alto, CA: Mayfield.

Gutek, B. A., Stromberg, A. H., & Larwood, L. (Eds.). (1988). *Women and work.* Beverly Hills, CA: Sage.

Guyton, A. C. (1981). *Textbook of physiology* (6th ed.). Philadelphia: Saunders.

Gyepi-Garbrah, B., Nichols, D. J., Gottlieb, M., & Kpedekpo, K. (1985). *Adolescent fertility in sub-Sahara Africa: An Overview.* Chestnut Hill, MA: Pathfinder Fund.

Hacker, H. M. (1981). Blabbermouths and clams: Sex differences in self-disclosure in same-sex and cross-sex friendship dyads. *Psychology of Women Quarterly, 5,* 385–401.

Haffner, D. W. (1989). The AIDS epidemic and sexuality education. In C. Cassell & P. M. Wilson (Eds.), *Sexuality education: A resource book.* New York: Garland.

Hales, D. (1989). *Pregnancy and birth.* New York: Chelsea House.

Hales, D., & Creasy, R. K. (1982). *New hope for problem pregnancies.* New York: Harper & Row.

Hales, D., & Hales, R. E. (1982, November/December). Testosterone: The bonding hormone. *American Health,* pp. 18–23.

Hall, J. A. (1984). *Nonverbal sex differences: Communication accuracy and expressive style.* Baltimore: Johns Hopkins University Press.

Hall, R. E. (1983). *Nine months reading.* New York: Bantam Books.

Hallberg, E. (1980). *The gray itch: The male metapause syndrome.* New York: Warner.

Hamilton, E. N., & Whitney, E. N. (1982). *Nutrition: Concepts and controversies.* St. Paul, MN: West.

Hammen, C., Burge, D., & Stansbury, K. (1990). Relationship of mother and child variables to child outcomes in a high-risk sample: A causal modeling analysis. *Developmental Psychology, 26*(1), 24–30.

Haney, D. Q. (1990, November 17). Test-tube fertilization works after menopause. *New London Day,* pp. 12–14.

Hans, S. (1989, April). *Infant behavioral effects of prenatal exposure to methadone.* Paper presented at the biennial meeting of the Society for Research in Child Development, Kansas City.

Hansen, C. E., & Evans, A. (1985). Bisexuality reconsidered: An idea in pursuit of a definition. In F. Klein & T. J. Wolf (Eds.), *Two lives to lead: Bisexuality in men and women.* New York: Harrington Park Press.

Hansen, S. L., & Hicks, M. W. (1980). Sex role attitudes and perceived dating-mating choices of youth. *Adolescence, 15,* 83–90.

Hansfield, H. H. (1963). Problems in the treatment of bacterial sexually transmitted diseases. *Sexually Transmitted Diseases, 13,* 179–184.

Hansfield, H. H. (1984). Gonorrhea and uncomplicated gonococcal infection. In K. Holmes, P. Mardh, P. Sparling, & P. Wiesner (Eds.), *Sexually transmitted diseases.* New York: McGraw-Hill.

Hanson, R. A. (1990). Initial parenting attitudes of pregnant adolescents and a comparison with the decision about adoption. *Adolescence, 25,* 629–643.

Hanson, S. M., & Bozett, F. W. (Eds.). (1985). *Dimensions of fatherhood.* Beverly Hills, CA: Sage.

Hare-Mustin, R., & Maracek, J. (1988). The meaning of difference: Gender theory, postmodernism, and psychology. *American Psychologist, 43,* 455–464.

Harlap, S., Kost, K., & Forrest, J. D. (1991). *Preventing pregnancy, protecting health: A new look at birth control choices in the United States.* New York: Alan Guttmacher Institute.

Harriman, L. C. (1983). Personal and marital changes accompanying parenthood. *Family Relations, 32,* 387–394.

Harriman, L. C. (1986). Marital adjustment as related to personal and marital changes accompanying parenthood. *Family Relations, 35,* 233–239.

Harris, A. (1988). *Sexual exercises for women.* New York: Carroll & Graf.

Harris, M. B., & Satter, B. J. (1981). Sex-role stereotypes of kindergarten children. *Journal of Genetic Psychology, 138,* 49–61.

Harry, J. (1990). A probability sample of gay males. *Journal of Homosexuality, 19,* 89–104.

Hart, L. E., Mader, L., Friffith, K., & DeMendonca, M. (1989). Effects of sexual and physical abuse: A comparison of adolescent inpatients. *Child Psychiatry and Human Development, 20,* 49–57.

Hartup, W. W. (1989). Social relationships and their developmental significance. *American Psychologist, 44,* 120–126.

Hasselbring, B. (1983, Summer). Every woman's guide to vaginal infections. *Medical Self-Care,* 45–49.

Hassitt, J. (1981, December 14). But that would be wrong. *Psychology Today,* pp. 34–53.

Hatcher, R. A., Stewart, F., Trussell, J., Kowal, D., Guest, F., Stewart, G. K. & Cates, W. (1990). *Contraceptive technology, 1990–1992* (15th ed.). New York: Irvington.

Hatfield, E. (1984). The dangers of intimacy. In V. J. Derlega (Ed.), *Communication, intimacy, and close relationships.* New York: Academic Press.

Hatfield, E., Traupmann, J., Sprecher, S., Utne, M., & Hay, J. (1985). Equity and intimate relationships: Recent research. In W. Ickes (Ed.), *Compatible and incompatible relationships.* New York: Springer-Verlag.

Hayden-Thomson, L., Rubin, K. H., & Hymel, S. (1987). Sex preferences in sociometric choices. *Developmental Psychology, 23,* 558–562.

Hayes, C. D. (Ed.). (1987). *Risking the future: Adolescent sexuality, pregnancy, and childbearing.* Washington, DC: National Academy Press.

Heath, D. (1984). An investigation into the origins of a copious vaginal discharge during intercourse—"enough to wet the bed"—that "is not urine." *Journal of Sex Research, 20,* 194–215.

Heilman, J. R. (1980). Menopause: Myths are unyielding to new scientific research. *Science Digest, 87,* 66–68.

Heiman, J. R., & Grafton-Becker, V. (1989). Orgasmic disorders in women. In S. R. Leiblum & R. C. Rosen (Eds.), *Principles and practice of sex therapy* (2nd ed.). New York: Guilford.

Heiman, J. R., & LoPiccolo, J. (1983). Clinical outcome of sex therapy: Effects of daily versus weekly treatment. *Archives of General Psychiatry, 40,* 443–449.

Hein, K. (1989a). Commentary on adolescent acquired immunodeficiency syndrome: The next wave of immunodeficiency virus epidemic. *Journal of Pediatrics, 114,* 144–149.

Hein, K. (1989b). AIDS in adolescence. *Journal of Adolescent Health Care, 10,* 105–135.

Heins, M., & Seiden, A. M. (1987). *Child care, parent care.* New York: Doubleday.

Helms, D. B., & Turner, J. S. (1986). *Exploring child behavior* (3rd ed.). Monterey, CA: Brooks/Cole.

Helsinga, K. (1974). *Not made of stone: The sexual problems of handicapped people.* Springfield, IL: Charles C Thomas.

Helson, R., Elliot, T., & Leigh, J. (1989). Adolescent antecedents of women's work patterns. In D. Stern & D. Eichorn (Eds.), *Adolescence and work.* Hillsdale, NJ: Erlbaum.

Henderson, J. (1983). Fifteen incest harmfuls. *Canadian Journal of Psychiatry, 28,* 34–39.

Hendrick, C. (Ed.). (1989). *Close relationships.* Newbury Park, CA: Sage.

Hendrick, C., & Hendrick, S. (1986). A theory and method of love. *Journal of Personality and Social Psychology, 50,* 392–402.

Hendrick, S., & Hendrick, C. (1992). *Liking, loving, and relating* (2nd ed.). Pacific Grove, CA: Brooks/Cole.

Hendrick, C., & Hendrick, S. S. (1988). Lovers wear rose colored glasses. *Journal of Social and Personal Relationships, 5,* 161–183.

Hendrick, J. (1988). *The whole child: Developmental education for the early years* (4th ed.). Columbus, OH: Merrill.

Henig, R. M. (1985). *How a woman ages.* New York: Ballantine.

Henry, A. K., & Feldhausen, J. (1989). *Drugs, vitamins, and minerals during pregnancy.* Tucson, AZ: Fisher Books.

Henshaw, S., Kenney, A., Somberg, D., & Van Vort, J. (1989). *Teenage pregnancy in the United States.* New York: Alan Guttmacher Institute.

Henshaw, S. K., Binkin, N., Blaine, E., & Smith, J. (1985). A portrait of American women who obtain abortions. *Family Planning Perspectives, 17,* 90–96.

Henshaw, S. K., Forrest, J. D., & Van Vort, J. (1987). Abortion services in the United States, 1984 and 1985. *Family Planning Perspectives, 19,* 63–70.

Henshaw, S. K., & Silverman, J. (1988). The characteristics and prior contraceptive use of U.S. abortion patients. *Family Planning Perspectives, 20,* 158–168.

Henshaw, S. K., & Van Vort, J. (1989). Teenage abortion, birth, and pregnancy statistics: An update. *Family Planning Perspectives, 21,* 85–88.

Henslin, J. M. (1985). Sex roles. In J. M. Henslin (Ed.), *Marriage and family in a changing society* (2nd ed.). New York: Free Press.

Henslin, J. M. (1990). *Social problems* (2nd ed.). Englewood Cliffs, NJ: Prentice Hall.

Herdt, G. H. (1988, August). *Coming out processes as an anthropological rite of passage.* Paper presented at the annual meeting of the American Psychological Association, Atlanta.

Herek, G. (1985). Beyond homophobia: A social psychological perspective on attitudes toward lesbians and gay men. In J. P. DeCecco (Ed.), *Bashers, baiters, and bigots: Homophobia in American society.* New York: Harrington Park Press.

Herek, G. (1988). Heterosexual's attitudes toward lesbians and gay men: Correlates and gender differences. *Journal of Sex Research, 25,* 451–477.

Herman, D. H. (1987). Torts: Private lawsuits about AIDS. In H. L. Dalton & S. Burris (Eds.). *AIDS and the law.* New Haven: Yale University Press.

Herman, J. (1981). *Father–daughter incest.* Cambridge, MA: Harvard University Press.

Herold, E. S. (1981). Measurement issues involved in examining contraceptive use among young single women. *Population and Environment, 4,* 128–144.

Herold, E. S., & McNamee, J. E. (1982). An exploratory model of contraceptive use among young single women. *Journal of Sex Research, 18,* 289–304.

Herold, E. S., & Samson, L. M. (1980). Differences between women who begin pill use before and after intercourse: Ontario, Canada. *Family Planning Perspectives, 12,* 304–305.

Herold, E. S., & Way, L. (1983). Oral-genital sexual behavior in a sample of university females. *Journal of Sex Research, 19,* 327–339.

Hess, D. J., & Grant, G. W. (1983). Prime-time television and gender role behavior. *Teaching Sociology, 10,* 371–388.

Heston, L., & Shields, J. (1968). Homosexuality in twins: A family study and a registry study. *Archives of General Psychiatry, 18,* 149–160.

Hetherington, E. M. (1989). Coping with family transitions: Winners, losers, and survivors. *Child Development, 60,* 1–14.

Hetherington, E. M., Hagan, M. S., & Anderson, E. R. (1989). Family transitions: A child's perspective. *American Psychologist, 44,* 303–312.

Hetrick, E. S., & Martin, A. D. (1987). The development of the gay and lesbian adolescent. *Journal of Homosexuality, 14,* 25–44.

Hewlett, S. (1986). *A lesser life: The myth of women's liberation in America.* New York: Morrow.

Heyl, B. S. (1989). Homosexuality: A social phenomenon. In K. McKinney & S. Sprecher (Eds.), *Human sexuality: The societal and interpersonal context.* Norwood, NJ: Ablex.

Heyward, W. L., & Curran, J. W. (1988). The epidemiology of AIDS in the United States. *Scientific American, 259,* 72–81.

Higgins, B. S. (1990). Couple infertility: From the perspective of the close-relationship model. *Family Relations, 39,* 81–86.

Higgins, L. P., & Hawkins, J. W. (1984). *Human sexuality across the life span: Implications for nursing practice.* Monterey, CA: Wadsworth.

Higham, E. (1980). Variations in adolescent psychohormonal development. In J. Adelson (Ed.), *Handbook of adolescent psychology.* New York: Wiley.

Hill, E. (1987). Premalignant and malignant disorders of the uterine cervix. In M. Pernoll & R. Benson (Eds.), *Current obstetric and gynecologic diagnosis and treatment, 1987.* Los Altos, CA: Appleton & Lange.

Hill, J., & Kassam, S. (1984). Sexual competence in multiple sclerosis. *Female Patient, 9,* 81–84.

Hillard, P. A., & Panter, G. G. (1985). *Pregnancy and childbirth.* New York: Ballantine.

Hilts, P. (1991). Fetus to fetus transplant blocks deadly genetic defect. *New York Times,* November 21, B14.

Hite, S. (1976). *The Hite report on female sexuality.* New York: Dell.

Hite, S. (1981). *The Hite report on male sexuality.* New York: Ballantine.

Hite, S. (1987). *Women and love: A cultural revolution in progress.* New York: Knopf.

Hock, E., & DeMeis, D. K. (1990). Depression in mothers of infants: The role of maternal employment. *Developmental Psychology, 26*(2), 285–291.

Hoenig, J. (1985). Etiology of transsexualism. In B. W. Steiner (Ed.), *Gender dysphoria: Development, research, and management.* New York: Plenum.

Hofferth, S. L., & Hayes, C. D. (Eds.). (1987). *Risking the future: Adolescent sexuality, pregnancy, and childbearing: Working Papers.* Washington, DC: National Academy Press.

Hofferth, S. L., & Miller, B. B. (1989). An overview of adolescent pregnancy prevention programs and their evaluations. In J. Card (Ed.), *Evaluating programs at preventing teenage pregnancies.* Palo Alto, CA: Sociometrics.

Hoffman, L. W. (1989). Effects of maternal employment in the two-parent family. *American Psychologist, 44,* 283–292.

Hogge, W., Schonberg, S., & Golbus, M. (1986). Chorionic villus sampling: Experience of the first 1,000 cases. *American Journal of Obstetrics and Gynecology, 154,* 1249–1252.

Holden, C. (1989). Koop finds abortion evidence "inconclusive." *Science, 243,* 730–731.

Holland, M. K. (1985). *Using psychology.* Boston: Little, Brown.

Holmbeck, G. N., Gasiewski, E., & Crossman, R. (1989, April). *Cognitive development, egocentrism, and adolescent contraceptive knowledge.* Paper presented at the biennial meeting of the Society for Research in Child Development, Kansas City.

Honer, W. G., Gewirtz, G., & Turey, M. (1987). Psychosis and violence in cocaine smokers. *Lancet, 4,* 451–466.

Honig, A. (1983). Research in review: Sex-role socialization in early childhood. *Young Children, 38,* 57–70.

Hood, K. E. (1991). Menstrual cycle. In R. M. Lerner, A. C. Petersen, & J. Brooks-Gunn (Eds.), *Encyclopedia of adolescence.* New York: Garland.

Hopson, J. (1979). *Scent signals.* New York: Morrow.

Horowitz, A. N. (1983). Guidelines for treating father–daughter incest. *Social Casework, 64,* 515–517.

Horton, A. L., Johnson, B. L., Roundy, L. M., & Williams, D. (Eds.). (1990). *The incest perpetrator: A family member no one wants to treat.* Beverly Hills, CA: Sage.

Horton, P. B., Leslie, G. R., & Larson, R. F. (1988). *The sociology of social problems* (9th ed.). Englewood Cliffs, NJ: Prentice Hall.

Hotchner, T. (1984). *Pregnancy and childbirth.* New York: Avon.

Hoult, T. F. (1984). Human sexuality in biological perspective: Theoretical and methodological considerations. *Journal of Homosexuality, 9,* 137–155.

Houseknecht, S. K., Vaughan, S., & Statham, A. (1987). The impact of singlehood on the career patterns of professional women. *Journal of Marriage and the Family, 49,* 353–366.

Howard, J. A., Blumstein, P., & Schwartz, P. (1986). Sex, power, and influence tactics in intimate relationships. *Journal of Personality and Social Psychology, 51,* 102–109.

Howard, M., & McCabe, J. (1990). Helping teenagers postpone sexual involvement. *Family Planning Perspectives, 22,* 21–26.

Howard, M., Mitchell, M., & Pollard, B. (1990). *Postponing sexual involvement: An educational series for young teens* (rev. ed.). Atlanta: Grady Memorial Hospital.

Howes, C. (1988). Peer interaction of young children. *Monographs of the Society for Research in Child Development, 53,* 94–104.

Howley, P. M. (1986). On human papillomavir. *New England Journal of Medicine, 315,* 1098–1090.

Hughes, J. O., & Sandler, B. R. (1987). *Friends raping friends: Could it happen to you?* Washington, DC: Association of American Colleges, Project on the Status and Education of Women.

Humphrey, F. G. (1987). Treating extramarital sexual relationships in sex and couples therapy. In G. R. Weeks & L. Hof (Eds.), *Integrating sex and marital therapy: A clinical guide.* New York: Brunner/Mazel.

Hunt, M. (1974). *Sexual behavior in the 1970's.* Chicago: Playboy Press.

Hunt, M. (1987). *Gay.* New York: Michael di Capua Books.

Hunter, J. (1982). *Human sexuality: A course for parents.* Rochester, NY: Genesee Region Family Planning Program.

Hunter, J., & Schaecher, R. (1987). Stresses on gay and lesbian adolescents in schools. *Social Work in Education, 9,* 180–190.

Hunter, L. J. (1989). Family life education in a public school system. In C. Cassell & P. M. Wilson (Eds.), *Sexuality education: A resource book.* New York: Garland.

Huston, A. C. (1983). Sex-typing. In P. H. Mussen (Ed.), *Handbook of child psychology* (4th ed.). New York: Wiley.

Huston, A. C., & Alvarez, M. (1990). The socialization context of gender role development in early adolescence. In R. Montemayor, G. R. Adams, & T. P. Gulotta (Eds.), *From childhood to adolescence: A transitional period?* Newbury Park, CA: Sage.

Hyde, J. S. (1991). *Half the Human Experience: The Psychology of Women*. Lexington, MA: D. C. Heath.

Hyde, J. S., Fennema, E., & Lamon, S. J. (1990). Gender differences in mathematics performance: A meta-analysis. *Psychological Bulletin, 107*, 139–155.

Hyden, P., & McCandless, N. J. (1983). Men and women as portrayed in the lyrics of contemporary music. *Popular Music and Society, 9*, 10–26.

Iams, J. D., & Zuspan, F. P. (1990). *Zuspan and Quilligan's manual of obstetrics and gynecology*. St. Louis: Mosby.

Imperato-McGinley, J. (1985). Disorders of sexual differentiation. In J. B. Wyngaarden & L. H. Smith, Jr. (Eds.), *Cecil textbook of medicine* (17th ed.). Philadelphia: Saunders.

Inazu, J. K., & Fox, G. L. (1980). Maternal influence on the sexual behavior of teenage daughters. *Journal of Family Issues, 3*, 81–102.

Insel, P. M., & Roth, W. T. (1991). *Core concepts in health* (6th ed.). Mountain View, CA: West.

Irvin, F. S. (1988, August). *Clinical perspectives on resilience among gay and lesbian youth*. Paper presented at the annual meeting of the American Psychological Association, Atlanta.

Isenberg, J., & Quisenberry, N. L. (1988). Play: A necessity for all children. *Childhood Education, 64*, 138–145.

Issacs, F. (1986, January). High-tech pregnancies. *Working Mother*, pp. 18–26.

Issacs, S. L., & Holt, R. J. (1987). Redefining procreation: Facing the issues. *Population Bulletin, 42*.

Jacklin, C. N. (1989). Female and male: Issues of gender. *American Psychologist, 44*, 127–133.

Jackson, S. (1982). *Childhood and sexuality: Understanding everyday experiences*. Oxford: Basil Blackwell.

Jaffee, H. W. (1982). Nongonococcal urethritis: Treatment of men and their sexual partners. *Review of Infectious Diseases, 4*, 5772–5777.

James, B. (1984). Orgasm via breast feeding. *Medical Aspects of Human Sexuality, 18*, 144, 16–32.

James, B., & Nasjleti, M. (1983). *Treating sexually abused children and their families*. Palo Alto, CA: Consulting Psychologists Press.

Jarrow, J. P. (1987). Vasectomy update: Effects on health and sexuality. *Medical Aspects of Human Sexuality, 12*, 64–67.

Jensen, L. C., & Kingston, M. (1986). *Parenting*. New York: Holt, Rinehart, & Winston.

Jensen, S. B. (1985). Sexual dysfunction in younger insulin-treated diabetic females. *Diabetes and Metabolism, 11*, 278–282.

Johnson, K. (1985). *If you are raped*. Holmes Beach, FL: Learning Publications.

Johnson, R. E., Nahmias, A., & Magder, L. S. (1989). A sero-epidemiologic survey of the prevalence of herpes simplex virus type 2 infection in the United States. *New England Journal of Medicine, 321*, 7–12.

Johnston, D. (1992). Survey shows number of rapes far higher than official figures. *New York Times*, April 24, K-6.

Jones, C. (1989). *Sharing birth: A father's guide to giving support during labor*. Westport, CT: Greenwood Press.

Jones, D. J., & Battle, S. F. (1990). *Teenage pregnancy: Developing strategies for change in the twenty-first century*. New Brunswick, NJ: Transaction.

Jones, E. F., & Forrest, J. K. (1989). Contraceptive failure in the United States: Revised estimates from the 1982 National Survey of Family Growth. *Family Planning Perspectives, 17*, 53–63.

Jones, E. F., Forrest, J., Goldman, N., Henshaw, S., Lincoln, R., Rossoff, J., Westoff, C., & Wulf, D. (1986). *Teenage pregnancy in industrialized countries*. New Haven: Yale University Press.

Jones, J. B., & Philliber, S. (1983). Sexually active but not pregnant: A comparison of teens who risk and teens who plan. *Journal of Youth and Adolescence, 12*, 235–251.

Jordan, J. (1985). *Empathy and self boundaries: Works in progress*, No. 16. Wellesley, MA: Stone Centers Working Papers Series.

Jorgensen, S. R. (1980). Contraceptive attitude-behavior consistency in adolescence. *Population and Environment, 3*, 174–194.

Jorgensen, S. R., & Sonstegard, J. (1984). Predicting adolescent sexual and contraceptive behavior: An application and test of the Fishbein model. *Journal of Marriage and the Family, 46*, 43–55.

Jose, P. E., & McCarthy, W. J. (1988). Perceived agentic and communal behavior in mixed-sex group interactions. *Personality and Social Psychology Bulletin, 14*, 57–67.

Judson, F. N. (1983). What practical advice can physicians give patients on avoiding genital herpes. *Medical Aspects of Human Sexuality, 17*, 7–15.

Judson, F. N. (1986). Treatment of uncomplicated gonorrhea with ceftriaxone: A review. *Sexually Transmitted Diseases, 13*, 199–201.

Julien, R. M. (1988). *A primer of drug action* (5th ed.). New York: Freeman.

Julius, M. (1986). Marital stress and suppressed anger linked to death of spouses. *Marriage and Divorce Today, 11*, 1–2.

Kahn, A. (1984). *Social psychology*. Dubuque, IA: Wm. C. Brown.

Kahn, J. R., Kalsbeek, W. D., & Hofferth, S. L. (1988). National estimates of teenage sexual activity: Evaluating the comparability of three national surveys. *Demography, 25*, 189–204.

Kahn, S. S. (1983). *The Kahn report on sexual preferences: What the opposite sex likes and dislikes—and why*. New York: St. Martin's Press.

Kalichman, S. C. (1989). Sex roles and sex differences in adult spatial performance. *Journal of Genetic Psychology, 150*, 93–100.

Kallman, F. J. (1952). Comparative twin study on the genetic aspects of male homosexuality. *Journal of Nervous and Mental Disease, 115*, 283–298.

Kamo, Y. (1988). Determinants of household division of labor. *Journal of Family Issues, 9*, 177–200.

Kanin, E. J. (1985). Date rapists: Selected socialization and relative deprivation. *Archives of Sexual Behavior, 14*, 219–232.

Kantner, J. F., & Zelnik, M. (1980). Sexual and contraceptive experience of young unmarried women, 1979. *Family Planning Perspectives, 16*, 17–24.

Kantor, D., & Okun, B. (Eds.). (1989). *Intimate environments: Sex, intimacy, and gender in families*. New York: Guilford.

Kaplan, H. S. (1974). *The new sex therapy*. New York: Brunner/Mazel.

Kaplan, H. S. (1979). *Disorders of sexual desire*. New York: Simon & Schuster.

Kaplan, H. S. (1983). *The Evaluation of Sexual Disorders*. New York: Brunner/Mazel.

Kaplan, H. S. (1989). *How to overcome premature ejaculation*. New York: Brunner/Mazel.

Kargan, M. W. (1985). *How to manage a marriage*. Boston: Foundation Books.

Kart, C. S. (1990). *The realities of aging* (3rd ed.). Boston: Allyn & Bacon.

Kasl, C. D. (1989). *Women, sex, and addiction*. New York: Ticknor and Fields.

Kassler, J. (1983). *Gay men's health*. New York: Harper & Row.

Kastner, L. (1984). Ecological factors predicting adolescent contraceptive use: Implications to intervention. *Journal of Adolescent Health Care, 5*, 79–86.

Kaus, D. S., & Reed, R. D. (1987). *Teaching about AIDS: A teacher's guide*. Saratoga, CA: R & E Publishers.

Kay, B., & Neely, J. N. (1982). Sexuality and aging: A review of the current literature. *Sexual Diseases, 5*, 38–46.

Kaye, C. (1981). Genetic counseling. *Medical Aspects of Human Sexuality, 15*, 164–180.

Kazak, A. E., & Repucci, D. N. (1980). *On love and loving*. San Francisco: Jossey-Bass.

Keen, S. (1985). Don't come any closer! The barriers that keep people from caring. In O. Pocs & R. Walsh (Eds.), *Marriage and family 85/86*. Guilford, CT: Dushkin.

Kegeles, S., Adler, N., & Irwin, C. (1988). Sexually active adolescents and condoms. *American Journal of Public Health, 78*, 460–466.

Kelly, J. A., & de Armas, A. (1989). Social relationships in adolescence: Skill development and training. In J. Worell & F. Danner (Eds.), *The adolescent as decision-maker*. San Diego: Academic Press.

Kelly, J. A., St. Lawrence, J. S. Brasfield, T. L., Lemke, A., Amidee, T., Roffman, R. E., Hood, H. V., Smith, J. E., Kilgore, H., & McNeill, C., Jr. (1990). Psychosocial factors that predict AIDS high-risk versus AIDS precautionary behavior. *Journal of Consulting and Clinical Psychology, 58*, 117–120.

Kelly, K. (1983). Adolescent sexuality: The first lessons. In D. Byrne & W. A. Fisher (Eds.), *Adolescents, sex, and contraception*. New York: McGraw-Hill.

Kempe, R. S., & Kempe, C. H. (1984). *The common secret: Sexual abuse of children and adolescents*. New York: Freeman.

Kendall-Tackett, K. A. (1988). Molestation and the onset of puberty: Data from 363 adults molested as children. *Child Abuse and Neglect, 12*, 73–81.

Kendrick, J., & Rubin, G. L. (1986). Vasectomies performed by private physicians, United States, 1980 to 1984. *Fertility and Sterility, 46*, 528–530.

Kent, C. A. (1982). *No easy answers: A sexual abuse prevention curriculum for junior and senior high students*. Minneapolis, MN: Illusion Theater.

Kernberg, O. F. (1987). Projection and projective identification: Developmental and clinical aspects. *Journal of the American Psychoanalytic Association, 35*, 795–819.

Kersey-Cantril, C., & McCarthy, P. K. (1987). AIDS: Meeting the challenge. *Current Concepts in Nursing, 1*, 2–7.

Keye, W. (1984). Psychosexual responses to infertility. *Clinical Obstetrics and Gynecology, 27*, 760–766.

Khan, M. (1983). Sexual abuse of young children. *Clinical Pediatrics, 22*, 363–372.

Khourg, M. J., Gomex-Farias, M., & Mulinare, J. (1989). Does maternal cigarette smoking during pregnancy cause cleft lip and palate in offspring? *American Journal of Diseases of Children, 143*, 333–338.

Kilby, D. (1986). *A manual of safe sex: Intimacy without fear*. Toronto: B. C. Decker.

Kilmann, P. R., Boland, J. P., Norton, S. P., Davidson, E., & Caid, C. (1986). Perspectives of sex therapy outcome: A survey of AASECT providers. *Journal of Sex and Marital Therapy, 12*, 116–138.

Kilmann, P. R., Milan, R., Boland, T., Nankin, H., Davidson, E., West, M., Sabalis, R., Caid, C., & Devine, J. (1987). Group treatment of secondary erectile dysfunction. *Journal of Sex and Marital Therapy, 13*, 168–182.

Kilmann, P. R., Sabalis, R. F., Gearing, M. L., Bukstel, L. H., & Scovein, A. W. (1982). The treatment of sexual paraphilias: A review of the outcome of research. *Journal of Sex Research, 18*, 193–252.

Kilpatrick, D. G., Best, C. L., Veronen, L. J., Amick, A. E., Villeponteaux, L. A., & Ruff, G. A. (1985). Mental health correlates of criminal victimization: A random community survey. *Journal of Consulting and Clinical Psychology, 53*, 866–873.

Kilpatrick, D. G., Resick, P., & Veronen, L. (1981). Effects of a rape experience: A longitudinal study. *Journal of Social Issues, 37*, 105–122.

Kimball, M. M. (1989). A new perspective on women's math achievement. *Psychological Bulletin, 105*, 198–214.

King, P. A., Caddy, G. M., & Cohen, S. H. (1989). Circumcision: Maternal attitudes. *Pediatric Surgical Intervention, 4*, 222–238.

Kinnaird, K. L., & Gerrard, M. (1986). Premarital sexual behavior and attitudes toward marriage and divorce among young women as a function of their mothers' marital status. *Journal of Marriage and the Family, 48*, 757–765.

Kinsey, A. C., Pomeroy, W. B., & Martin, C. E. (1948). *Sexual behavior in the human male*. Philadelphia: Saunders.

Kinsey, A. C., Pomeroy, W. B., & Martin, C. E. (1953). *Sexual behavior in the human female*. Philadelphia: Saunders.

Kirby, D., Peterson, L., & Brown, J. G. (1982). A joint parent–child sex education program. *Child Welfare, 61*, 105–114.

Kirkpatrick, M. (1982). Lesbian mother families. *Psychiatric Annals, 12*, 842–845.

Kitzinger, S. (1983). *Women's experience of sex*. New York: Penguin Books.

Klein, J. M. (1989, November 15). The fate of the frozen embryos. New London (CT) Day, C-7.

Klein, S. S. (1988). Using sex equity and research to improve education policies. *Theory into Practice, 27*, 152–160.

Kleinke, C. L., Meeker, F. B., & Staneski, R. A. (1986). Preference for opening lines: Comparing ratings by men and women. *Sex Roles, 15*, 585–600.

Knox, D., & Wilson, K. (1981). Dating behaviors of university students. *Family Relations, 4*, 255–258.

Koblinsky, S., & Behana, N. (1984). Child sexual abuse: The educator's role in prevention, detection, and intervention. *Young Children, 11*, 32–41.

Kochanek, K. (1989, April). Induced terminations of pregnancy: Reporting states, 1985 and 1986. *Monthly Vital Statistics Report*, U.S. Department of Health and Human Services, *37* (12), DHHS Pub. No. 89-1120.

Koff, E., & Riordan, J. (1991). Menarche and body image. In R. M. Lerner, A. C. Petersen, & J. Brooks-Gunn (Eds.), *Encyclopedia of adolescence*. New York: Garland.

Kohn, A. (1988, February). Girl talk, guy talk. *Psychology Today*, pp. 65–66.

Kolb, B., & Wishaw, I. (1988). *Fundamentals of human neuropsychology*. New York: Freeman.

Kolodny, R. C. (1980, November). *Adolescent sexuality*. Paper presented at the Annual Convention of the Michigan Personnel and Guidance Association. Detroit.

Kolodny, R. C., Masters, W. H., Hendry, J., & Toro, G. (1971). Plasma testosterone and semen analysis in male homosexuals. *New England Journal of Medicine, 285,* 1170–1174.

Koop, C. E. (1987). *Understanding AIDS: A message from the surgeon general.* Washington, DC: U.S. Public Health Service.

Koop, C. E., & Samuels, M. E. (1988). The surgeon general's report on AIDS. In I. C. Corless & M. Pittman-Lindeman (Eds.), *AIDS: Principles, practices, and politics.* New York: Hemisphere.

Korones, S. B. (1986). *High risk newborn infants.* St. Louis: Mosby.

Koss, M., Gidycz, P., & Wisniewski, N. (1987). The scope of rape: Incidence and prevalence of sexual aggression and victimization in a national sample of higher education students. *Journal of Consulting and Clinical Psychology, 55,* 162–170.

Krafft-Ebing, R. V. (1922). *Psychopathia sexualis.* New York: Physicians & Surgeons Book Co.

Krause, M. V. (1984). *Food, nutrition, and diet therapy* (7th ed.). Philadelphia: Saunders.

Krueger, D. W. (1982). Transvestites. *Medical Aspects of Human Sexuality, 16,* 17–18.

Krukofsky, B. (1988). Sexuality counseling of people with chronic illness. In E. Weinstein & E. Rosen (Eds.), *Sexuality counseling: Issues and implications* Monterey, CA: Brooks/Cole.

Kulin, H. E. (1991). Hypothalamic-pituitary changes of puberty. In R. M. Lerner, A. C. Petersen, & J. Brooks-Gunn (Eds.), *Encyclopedia of adolescence.* New York: Garland.

Kuriansky, J. B., & Sharpe, L. (1981). Clinical and research implications of the evaluation of women's group therapy for anorgasmia: A review. *Journal of Sex and Marital Therapy, 7,* 268–277.

Kuriansky, J. B., Sharpe, L., & O'Connor, D. (1982). The treatment of anorgasmia: Long-term effectiveness of a short-term behavioral group therapy. *Journal of Sex and Marital Therapy, 8,* 29–43.

Kurland, M. L. (1988). *Coping with AIDS: Facts and fears.* New York: Rosen.

Kus, R. J. (1988). Alcoholism and non-acceptance of gay self: The critical link. In M. W. Ross (Ed.), *The treatment of homosexuals with mental health disorders.* New York: Harrington Park Press.

Lacoste-Utamsing, D., & Holloway, R. (1982). Sexual dimorphism in the human corpus callosum. *Science, 216,* 1431–1432.

Ladas, A. K., Whipple, B., & Perry, J. D. (1982). *The G-spot and other recent discoveries about human sexuality.* New York: Holt, Rinehart, & Winston.

Lafferty, W. E., Coombs, R. W., Benedetti, J., Critchlow, C., & Corey, L. (1987). Recurrences after oral and genital herpes simplex virus infection: Influence of site of infection and viral type. *New England Journal of Medicine, 316,* 1444–1449.

Lamb, M. E. (Ed.). (1981). *The role of the father in child development* (2nd ed.). New York: Wiley.

Lamb, M. E. (1982). Paternal influences on early socio-emotional development. *Journal of Child Psychology and Psychiatry and Allied Disciplines, 23,* 185–190.

Lamb, M. E. (1983, June). *The changing role of the father.* Paper presented at the Greater New York Area Fatherhood Forum, Bank Street College of Education, New York.

Lamb, M. E., Easterbrooks, M. A., & Holden, G. W. (1980). Reinforcement and punishment among preschoolers: Characteristics, effects, and correlates. *Child Development, 51,* 1230–1236.

Lamb, M. E., Pleck, J. H., & Levine, J. A. (1986). Effects of increased paternal involvement in children in two-parent families. In R. A. Lewis & R. E. Salt (Eds.), *Men in families.* Beverly Hills, CA: Sage.

Landers, D. V., & Sweet, R. L. (1990). Perinatal infections. In J. R. Scott (Ed.), *Danforth's obstetrics and gynecology.* Philadelphia: Lippincott.

Landesman, S., & Ramey, C. (1989). Developmental psychology and mental retardation: Integrating scientific principles with treatment practices. *American Psychologist, 44,* 409–415.

Laner, M. R. (1989). *Dating: Delights, discontents, and dilemmas.* Salem, WI: Sheffield.

Laner, M. R., & Housker, S. L. (1990). Sexual permissiveness in younger and older adults. *Journal of Family Issues, 1,* 103–124.

Langfeldt, T. (1981). Sexual development in children. In M. Cook & K. Howells (Eds.), *Adult sexual interest in children.* London: Academic Press.

Langlois, J. H., & Down, A. C. (1980). Mothers, fathers, and peers as socialization agents of sex-typed play behaviors in young children. *Young Children, 51,* 1217–1247.

Langmade, C. J. (1983). The impact of pre- and postpubertal onset of incest experiences in adult women as measured by sex anxiety, sex guilt, sexual satisfaction, and sexual behavior. *Dissertation Abstracts International, 44,* 917B.

LaRossa, R., & LaRossa, M. M. (1981). *Transition to parenthood: How infants change families.* Beverly Hills, CA: Sage.

Larsen, K. S., Reed, M., & Hoffman, S. (1980). Attitudes of heterosexuals toward homosexuality: A Likert type scale and construct validity. *Journal of Sex Research, 16,* 245–257.

Lasker, J. N., & Borg, S. (1987). *In Search of parenthood: Coping with infertility.* Boston: Beacon Press.

Lauer, J. C., & Lauer, R. H. (1986). *'Til death do us part: How couples stay together.* New York: Haworth.

Lauer, R. H., & Lauer, J. C. (1991). *Marriage and family: The quest for intimacy.* Dubuque, IA: Wm. C. Brown.

Lauersen, N. (1983). *Childbirth with love.* New York: Berkley.

Lauersen, N., & Graves, Z. (1984). Pretended orgasm. *Medical Aspects of Human Sexuality, 18,* 74–81.

Lauwers, J., & Woessner, C. (1990). *Counseling the nursing mother* (2nd ed.). Wayne, NJ: Avery.

Lawrence, R. A. (1983). Early mothering by adolescents. In E. R. McAnarney (Ed.), *Premature adolescent pregnancy and parenthood.* New York: Grune & Stratton.

Lawrence, R. A. (1989). *Breastfeeding: A guide for the medical profession* (3rd ed.). St. Louis: Mosby.

Lawrence, R. A., McAnarney, E. R., Aten, M. J., Iker, H. P., Baldwin, C. P., & Baldwin, A. L. (1981). Aggressive behaviors in young mothers: Markers of future morbidity? *Pediatric Research, 15,* 443–451.

Lawson, C. (1989, June 15). Toys: Boys fight wars, girls still apply makeup. *New York Times,* p. C-1.

Lawson, J., & Hillix, W. A. (1985, February). Coercion and seduction in robbery and rape. *Psychology Today,* pp. 50–60.

Lay-Dopyera, M., & Dopyera, J. E. (1990). *Becoming a teacher of young children* (4th ed.). Lexington, MA: Heath.

Lazarus, A. A. (1980). Psychological treatment of dyspareunia. In S. R. Leiblum & L. A. Pervin (Eds.), *Principles and practice of sex therapy.* New York: Guilford.

Lazarus, A. A. (1989). Dyspareunia: A multimodal psycho-therapeutic perspective. In S. R. Leiblum & R. C. Rosen (Eds.), *Principles and practice of sex therapy* (2nd ed.). New York: Guilford.

Leary, M. R., & Dobbins, S. E. (1983). Social anxiety, sexual behavior, and contraceptive use. *Journal of Personality and Social Psychology, 45,* 1347–1354.

Leboyer, F. (1975). *Birth without violence.* New York: Knopf.

Ledray, L. E. (1986). *Recovering from rape.* New York: Henry Holt.

Lee, J. A. (1974). The styles of loving. *Psychology Today,* October, 43–52.

Lee, J. A. (1976). *The colors of love.* Englewood Cliffs, NJ: Prentice-Hall.

Lee, J. A. (1988). Love styles. In R. J. Sternberg & M. L. Barnes (Eds.), *The psychology of love.* New Haven, CT: Yale University Press.

Leiblum, S. R., & Bachmann, G. (1988a). The sexuality of the climactic woman. In B. Eskin (Ed.), *The menopause: Comprehensive management.* New York: Yearbook Medical Publications.

Leiblum, S. R., & Bachmann, G. (1988b). *Sexuality in sexagenarian women.* Paper presented at the Annual Meeting of the International Academy of Sex Research, Minneapolis, MN.

Leiblum, S. R., & Pervin, L. A. (1980). The development of sex therapy from a sociocultural perspective. In S. R. Leiblum & L. A. Pervin (Eds.), *Principles and practice of sex therapy.* New York: Guilford.

Leiblum, S. R., Pervin, L. A., & Campbell, E. N. (1989). The treatment of vaginismus: Success and failure. In S. R. Leiblum & R. C. Rosen (Eds.), *Principles and practice of sex therapy* (2nd ed.). New York: Guilford.

Leiblum, S. R., & Rosen, R. C. (Eds.). (1988). *Sexual desire disorders.* New York: Guilford Press.

Leiblum, S. R., & Segraves, R. T. (1989). Sex therapy with aging adults. In S. R. Leiblum & R. C. Rosen (Eds.), *Principles and practice of sex therapy* (2nd ed.). New York: Guilford.

Leibowitz, A., Eisen, M., & Chow, W. K. (1986). An economic model of teenage pregnancy decision-making. *Demography, 23,* 67–77.

LeMasters, E. E., & DeFrain, J. (1989). *Parents in contemporary America* (5th ed.). Homewood, IL: Dorsey Press.

Lemon, S. M. (1984). Viral hepatitis. In K. Holmes, P. Mardh, P. Sparling, & P. Wiesner (Eds.), *Sexually transmitted diseases.* New York: McGraw-Hill.

Lentz, S., & Zeiss, A. (1984). Fantasy and sexual arousal in college women: An empirical investigation. *Imagination, Cognition, and Personality, 3,* 185–202.

Leo, J. (1986, November 24). Sex and Schools. *Time,* pp. 54–60.

Leoung, G., & Mills, J. (Eds.). (1989). *Opportunistic infections in patients with the acquired immunodeficiency syndrome.* New York: Marcel Dekker.

Lerner, R. M., & Lerner, J. V. (1988). *Effects of physical attractiveness.* William T. Grant Foundation Annual Report, New York.

Lerner, R. M., Lerner, J. V., & Tubman, J. (1989). Organismic and contextual bases of development in adolescence: A developmental contextual view. In G. R. Adams, R. Montemayor, & T. P. Gullotta (Eds.), *Biology of adolescent behavior and development.* Newbury Park, CA: Sage.

Lesko, W., & Lesko, M. (1984). *Pregnancy and childbirth.* New York: Warner Books.

Levay, S. (1991). A difference in hypothalamic structure between heterosexual and homosexual men. *Science, 253,* 1034.

Levert, S. (1987). *AIDS: In search of a killer.* New York: Julian Messner.

Levi, J. (1987). Public health and the gay perspective: Creating a basis for trust. In V. Gong & N. Rudnick (Eds.), *AIDS: Facts and issues.* New Brunswick, NJ: Rutgers University Press.

Levin, I., & Stokes, J. P. (1986). An examination of the relation of individual difference variables to loneliness. *Journal of Personality, 54,* 727–733.

Levin, R. J., & Wagner, G. (1987). Self-reported central sexual arousal without vaginal arousal: Duplicity or veracity revealed by objective measurement. *Journal of Sex Research, 23,* 540–544.

Levine, M. P., & Troiden, R. R. (1988). The myth of sexual compulsivity. *Journal of Sex Research, 25,* 347–363.

Levinger, G. (1983). Development and change. In H. H. Kelly (Ed.), *Close relationships.* New York: Freeman.

Levinson, A. (1984). Home birth: Joy or jeopardy? In O. Pocs (Ed.), *Human sexuality, 1984/85.* Guilford, CT: Dushkin.

Levinthal, C. F. (1990). *Introduction to physiological psychology* (3rd ed.). Englewood Cliffs, NJ: Prentice Hall.

Lewin, M., & Tragos, L. M. (1987). Has the feminist movement influenced adolescent sex role attitudes? A reassessment after a quarter century. *Sex Roles, 16,* 125–135.

Lewis, C., & O'Brien, M. (Eds.). (1987). *Reassessing fatherhood.* Beverly Hills, CA: Sage.

Lewis, M. (1987). Early sex-role behavior and school age adjustment. In J. M. Reinisch, L. A. Rosenblum, & S. A. Sanders (Eds.), *Masculinity/femininity: Basic Perspectives.* New York: Oxford University Press.

Lewis, R. A., & Salt, R. E. (Eds.). (1986). *Men in families.* Beverly Hills, CA: Sage.

Lewis, R. W. (1988). Venous surgery for impotence. *Urologic Clinics of North America, 15,* 115–121.

Lightfoot-Klein, H. (1990). *Prisoners of ritual: An odyssey into female genital circumcision in Africa.* New York: Haworth Press.

Lindberg, L., & Swedlow, R. (1985). *Young children: Exploring and learning.* Boston: Allyn & Bacon.

Lindemalm, G., Korlin, D., & Uddenberg, N. (1986). Long-term follow-up of sex-change in 13 male to female transsexuals. *Archives of Sexual Behavior, 15,* 187–210.

Linn, M. C., & Hyde, J. S. (1991). Cognitive and psychosocial gender differences. In R. M. Lerner, A. C. Petersen, & J. Brooks-Gunn (Eds.), *Encyclopedia of adolescence.* New York: Garland.

Linton, S., & Rousso, H. (1988). Sexuality counseling for people with disabilities. In E. Weinstein & E. Rosen (Eds.), *Sexuality counseling: Issues and implications.* Monterey, CA: Brooks/Cole.

Linz, D. G., Donnerstein, E., & Penrod, S. (1988). Effects of long-term exposure to violent and sexually degrading depictions of women. *Journal of Personality and Social Psychology, 55,* 758–768.

Lipsitt, L. P. (1989). Fetal development in the drug age. *Brown University Child Behavior and Development Newsletter, 1,* 1–3.

Livson, N., & Peskin, H. (1980). Perspectives on adolescence from longitudinal research. In J. Adelson (Ed.), *Handbook of adolescent psychology.* New York: Wiley.

Lloyd, S. A., Cate, R. M., & Henton, J. M. (1984). Predicting premarital relationship stability: A methodological refinement. *Journal of Marriage and the Family, 46,* 71–76.

Lockhart, L. L., & Wodarski, J. S. (1990). Teenage pregnancy: Implications for social work practice. *Family Therapy, 17*(1), 29–47.

Londerville, S., & Main, M. (1981). Security of attachment, compliance and maternal training methods in the second year of life. *Developmental Psychology, 17,* 289–299.

London, K., Mosher, W., Pratt, W., & Williams, L. (1989, April). Preliminary findings from the NSFG, Cycle IV. Paper presented at the annual meeting of the Population Association of America, Baltimore, MD.

Long, J. (1984). Nontraditional roles of men and women strengthen the family and provide healthier sexual relationships. In H. Feldman & A. Parrot (Eds.), *Human sexuality: Contemporary controversies.* Beverly Hills, CA: Sage.

Lopez, N. (1987). *Hispanic teenage pregnancy.* Washington, DC: National Council of La Raza.

LoPiccolo, J. (1985). Diagnosis and treatment of male sexual dysfunction. *Journal of Sex and Marital Therapy, 11,* 215–232.

LoPiccolo, J., & Friedman, J. M. (1988). Blood-spectrum treatment of low sexual desire: Integration of cognitive, behavioral, and systematic therapy. In S. R. Leiblum & R. C. Rosen (Eds.), *Sexual desire disorders.* New York: Guilford.

Lorenzetti, P. (1991). AIDS-related knowledge and behaviors among teenagers in Italy, 1990. *Morbidity and Mortality Weekly Report, 40,* 214–221.

Los Angeles Commission on Assaults against Women. (1983). *Surviving sexual assault.* New York: Congdon & Weed.

Lossick, J. G. (1984). Sexually transmitted vaginitus. *Urological Clinics of North America, 11,* 141–153.

Lothstein, L. (1984). Psychological testing with transsexuals. A 30-year review. *Journal of Personality Assessment, 48,* 500–507.

Loudin, J. (1981). *The hoax of romance.* Englewood Cliffs, NJ: Prentice Hall.

Loulan, J. (1984). *Lesbian sex.* San Francisco: Spinsters Ink.

Lourea, D. N. (1985). Psycho-social issues related to counseling bisexuals. In F. Klein & T. J. Wolf (Eds.), *Two lives to lead: Bisexuality in men and women.* New York: Harrington Park Press.

Lowe, W., Kretchmer, A., Petersen, J. R., Nellis, B., Lever, J., & Hertz, R. (1983, July). The Playboy reader's sex survey (Part 4). *Playboy,* 130–134.

Lowrey, G. H. (1984). *Growth and development of children* (8th ed.). Chicago: Yearbook Medical Publishers.

Lubic, R. W., & Hawes, G. R. (1987). *Childbearing.* New York: McGraw-Hill.

Ludeman, K. (1981). The sexuality of the older person: Review of the literature. *The Gerontologist, 21,* 203–208.

Lund, M. M. (1990). Perspectives on newborn male circumcision. *Neonatal Network, 9*(3), 7–15.

Lutz, S. E., & Medway, J. P. (1984). Contextual family therapy with the victims of incest. *Journal of Adolescence, 7,* 319–327.

Lynch, M., & McKeon, V. A. (1990). Cocaine use during pregnancy. *Journal of Gynecological Nursing, 19,* 285–293.

Maccoby, E. E. (1980). *Social development.* New York: Harcourt Brace Jovanovich.

Maccoby, E. E. (1987). The varied meanings of "masculine" and "feminine." In J. M. Reinisch, L. A. Rosenblum, & S. A. Sanders (Eds.), *Masculinity/femininity: Basic perspectives.* New York: Oxford University Press.

Maccoby, E. E. (1988). Gender as a social category. *Developmental Psychology, 24,* 755–765.

Maccoby, E. E. (1989, August). *Gender and relationships: A developmental account.* Paper presented at the annual meeting of the American Psychological Association, New Orleans.

Maccoby, E. E. (1990). Gender and relationships: A developmental account. *American Psychologist, 45,* 513–520.

Maccoby, E. E., & Mnookin, R. (1989, April). *Custody, conflict, and family processes following divorce.* Paper presented at the biennial meeting of the Society for Research in Child Development, Kansas City.

MacCorquodale, P. (1984). Gender roles and premarital contraception. *Journal of Marriage and the Family, 46,* 57–63.

MacCorquodale, P. (1989). Gender and sexual behavior. In K. McKinney & S. Sprecher (Eds.), *Human sexuality: The societal and interpersonal context.* Norwood, NJ: Ablex.

MacFarlane, K. (1988, October 6). Promises, promises: A child's view of incest. *New London Day,* p. 6.

MacFarlane, K. (1989). Cindy's poem . . . A child's view of incest. In A. Horton, B. J. Johnson, L. M. Roundy, & D. Williams (Eds.), *The incest perpetrator: A family member no one wants to treat.* Newbury Park, CA: Sage.

MacFarlane, K., Waterman, J., Conerly, S., Damon, L., Durfee, M., & Long, S. (1988). *Sexual abuse of young children: Evaluation and treatment.* New York: Guilford.

MacGregor, S. N., Keith, L. G., Chasnoff, I. J., Rosner, M. A., Chisum, G. M., Shaw, P., & Minogue, J. P. (1987). Cocaine use during pregnancy: Adverse perinatal outcome. *American Journal of Obstetrics and Gynecology, 1,* 66–90.

MacKinnon, C. (1979). *Sexual harassment of working women.* New Haven: Yale University Press.

MacLean, P. D. (1976). Brain mechanisms of elemental sexual functions. In B. J. Adock, H. I. Kaplan, & A. M. Freedman (Eds.), *The sexual experience.* Baltimore: Williams & Wilkins.

Macklin, E. D. (1980). Nontraditional family forms: A decade of research. *Journal of Marriage and the Family, 42,* 905–922.

Macklin, E. D. (1988). Heterosexual couples who cohabit non-maritally: Some common problems and issues. In Catherine S. Chilman, E. W. Nunnally, & F. M. Cox (Eds.), *Variant family forms.* Newbury Park, CA: Sage.

MacLaury, S. C. (1982). *A comparison of three methods of teaching about human sexuality to determine their effectiveness in positively modifying attitudes about homosexuality.* Unpublished doctoral dissertation, New York University.

Macovsky, S. J. (1983). Coping with cohabitation. In O. Pocs & R. Walsh (Eds.), *Marriage and family 1983/84.* Guilford, CT: Dushkin.

Madaras, L., & Patterson, J. (1981). *Womancare.* New York: Avon.

Mahlstedt, P. P. (1987). The crisis of infertility: An opportunity for growth. In G. R. Weeks & L. Hof (Eds.), *Integrating sex and marital therapy: A clinical guide.* New York: Brunner/Mazel.

Malamuth, N. M. (1981). Rape fantasies as a function of exposure to violent sexual stimuli. *Archives of Sexual Behavior, 10,* 33–48.

Malamuth, N. M., & Briere, J. (1986). Sexual violence in the media: Indirect effects on aggression against women. *Journal of Social Issues, 42,* 75–92.

Malamuth, N. M., Check, J. V., & Briere, J. (1986). Sexual arousal in response to aggression: Ideological, aggressive, and sexual correlates. *Journal of Personality and Social Psychology, 50,* 330–340.

Malamuth, N. M., & Donnerstein, E. (Eds.). (1984). *Pornography and sexual aggression.* Orlando, FL: Academic Press.

Malamuth, N. M., Heim, N., & Feshbach, S. (1980). Sexual responsiveness of college students to rape depictions: Inhibitory or disinhibitory effects. *Journal of Personality and Social Psychology, 38,* 399–408.

Maletzky, B. M. (1990). *Treating the sexual offender.* Newbury Park, CA: Sage.

Maletzky, B., & Price, R. (1984). Public masturbation in men: Precursor to exhibitionism? *Journal of Sex Education and Therapy, 10,* 31–36.

Malina, R. M. (1991). Adolescent growth spurt. In R. M. Lerner, A. C. Petersen, & J. Brooks-Gunn (Eds.), *Encyclopedia of adolescence.* New York: Garland.

Mandel, B., & Mandel, R. (1986). *Play safe: How to avoid getting sexually transmitted diseases.* Foster City, CA: Center for Health Information.

Mandell, J. G., & Damon, L. (1989). *Group treatment of sexually abused children.* New York: Guilford.

Manley, G. (1990). Endocrine disturbances and sexuality. In C. I. Fogel & D. Lauver (Eds.), *Sexual health promotion.* Philadelphia, PA: W. B. Saunders.

Mann, J. M., Chin, J., Piot, P., & Quinn, T. (1988). The international epidemiology of AIDS. *Scientific American, 259,* 82–89.

Manning, M. L. (1983). Three myths concerning adolescence. *Adolescence, 18,* 823–829.

Maracek, J., Finn, S. E., & Cardell, M. (1988). Gender roles in the relationships of lesbians and gay men. In J. P. DeCecco (Ed.), *Gay relationships.* New York: Harrington Park Press.

Marcus, E. (1988). *The male couple's guide to living together.* New York: Harper & Row.

Margolis, S. (1982). Therapy for condyloma acuminatum: A review. *Review of Infectious Diseases, 4,* 5829–5836.

Marin, G. (1989). AIDS prevention among Hispanics: Needs, risk behaviors, and cultural values. *Public Health Reports, 104,* 411–415.

Marshall, D. S. (1971). Sexual behavior on Mangaia. In D. S. Marshall & R. C. Suggs (Eds.), *Human sexual behavior: Variation in the ethnographic spectrum.* New York: Basic Books.

Marshall, S. (1989). Evaluation and management of simple erectile dysfunction in office practice. *Medical Aspects of Human Sexuality,* April, 5–8.

Marsiglio, W., & Mott, F. L. (1986). The impact of sex education on sexual activity, contraceptive use, and premarital pregnancy among American teenagers. *Family Planning Perspectives, 18,* 151–162.

Martin, A. D. (1982). The minority question. *Journal of General Semantics, 39,* 22–42.

Martin, A. D., Hetrick, E. S. (1988). The stigmatization of the gay and lesbian adolescent. In G. Herdt (Ed.), *Gay and lesbian youth.* New York: Haworth Press.

Martin, C. E. (1981). Factors affecting sexual functioning in 60–79 year-old married males. *Archives of Sexual Behavior, 10,* 399–420.

Martin, C. L. (1989, April). *Beyond knowledge-based conceptions of gender schematic processing.* Paper presented at the biennial meeting of the Society for Research in Child Development, Kansas City.

Martin, M. J., & Walters, J. (1982). Familial correlates of selected types of child abuse and neglect. *Journal of Marriage and the Family, 44,* 267–276.

Martin, P., & Hummer, R. (1989). Fraternities and rape on campus. *Gender and Society, 3,* 457–473.

Martin, S. E. (1984). Sexual harassment: The link between gender stratification, sexuality, and women's economic status. In J. Freeman (Ed.), *Women: A feminist perspective.* Palo Alto, CA: Mayfield.

Martinson, F. M. (1981). Eroticism in infancy and childhood. In L. L. Constantine & F. M. Martinson (Eds.), *Children and sex: New findings, new perspectives.* Boston: Little, Brown.

Mash, E. J., & Barkley, R. A. (1989). *Treatment of childhood disorders.* New York: Guilford.

Maslow, A. H. (1968). *Toward a psychology of being* (2nd ed.). Princeton, NJ: Von Nostrand Reinhold.

Maslow, A. H. (1970). *Motivation and personality* (2nd ed.). New York: Harper & Row.

Masnick, G., & Bane, M. J. (1980). *The nation's families: 1960–1990.* Cambridge, MA: Joint Center for Urban Studies of MIT & Harvard University.

Mast, C. K. (1988). How to say "no" to sex. *Medical Aspects of Human Sexuality, 22*(9), 26–27, 30–32.

Masters, W. H., & Johnson, V. E. (1966). *Human sexual response.* Boston: Little, Brown.

Masters, W. H., & Johnson, V. E. (1970). *Human sexual inadequacy.* Boston: Little, Brown.

Masters, W. H., & Johnson, V. E. (1979). *Homosexuality in perspective.* Boston: Little, Brown.

Masters, W. H., & Johnson, V. E. (1988). *Crisis: Heterosexual behavior in the age of AIDS.* New York: Grove Press.

Masters, W. H., Johnson, V. E., & Kolodny, R. C. (1985). *Human sexuality* (2nd ed.). Boston: Little, Brown.

Masters, W. H., Johnson, V. E., & Kolodny, R. C. (1988). *Sex and human loving.* Boston: Little, Brown.

Matek, O. (1988). Obscene phone callers. In D. M. Dailey (Ed.), *The sexually unusual: Guide to understanding and helping.* New York: Harrington Park Press.

Matlin, M. W. (1987). *The psychology of women.* New York: Holt, Rinehart, & Winston.

Mayer, A. (1983). *Incest: A treatment manual for therapy with victims, spouses, and offenders.* Holmes Beach, FL: Learning Press.

Maziade, M., Boudreault, M., Copte, R., & Thivierge, J. (1986). Influence of gentle birth delivery procedures and other perinatal circumstances on infant temperament: Developmental and social implications. *Journal of Pediatrics, 108,* 134–136.

McBroom, W. H. (1987). Longitudinal change in sex role orientations: Differences between men and women. *Sex Roles, 16,* 439–452.

McCabe, M. P. (1987). Desired and experienced levels of premarital affection and sexual intercourse during dating. *Journal of Sex Research, 23,* 23–33.

McCandlish, B. M. (1985). Therapeutic issues with lesbian clients. In J. C. Gonsiorek (Ed.), *A guide to therapy with gay and lesbian clients.* New York: Harrington Park Press.

McCann, M. E. (1989). Sexual healing after a heart attack. *American Journal of Nursing, 89,* 1132–1140.

McCarthy, B. (1985). Use and misuse of behavioral homework exercises in sex therapy. *Journal of Sex and Marital Therapy, 11,* 185–191.

McCarthy, B. (1988). *Male sexual awareness.* New York: Carroll & Graf.

McCarthy, B. W. (1989). Cognitive-behavioral strategies and techniques in the treatment of early ejaculation. In S. R. Leiblum & R. C. Rosen (Eds.), *Principles and practice of sex therapy* (2nd ed.). New York: Guilford.

McCarthy, B., & McCarthy, E. (1989). *Female sexual awareness*. New York: Carroll & Graf.

McCarthy, B. W. (1992). Erectile dysfunction and inhibited sexual desire. *Journal of Sex Education and Therapy*, *18*(1), 22–34.

McCarty, L. M. (1986). Mother–child incest. *Child Welfare*, *65*, 447–458.

McCormack, A. (1985). Sexual harassment of students by teachers: The case of students in science. *Sex Roles*, *13*, 21–32.

McCormack, L., Rosner, B., McComb, D. E., & Zinner, S. H. (1985). Infection with chlamydia trachomatis in female college students. *American Journal of Obstetrical Gynecology*, *121*, 107–115.

McCown, D. E. (1981). Father/daughter incest: A family problem. *Pediatric Nursing*, *11*, 25–28.

McDonald, P. (1983). What percentages of Australian marriages end in divorce? *Institute of Family Studies Newsletter*, *8*, 4–8.

McElfresh, S. B. (1982, August). *Cojugal power and legitimating norms: A new perspective on resource therapy*. Paper presented at the annual meeting of the American Psychological Association, Washington, DC.

McGarrity, K. (1988). *Connecticut responds to AIDS*. Hartford, CT: Department of Health Services.

McGee, A. (1984). Gonococcal pelvic inflammatory disease. In K. Holmes, P. Mardh, P. Sparling, & P. Wiesner (Eds.), *Sexually transmitted diseases*. New York: McGraw-Hill.

McGolderick, M., & Carter, E. A. (1982). Remarriage and the family life cycle. In F. Walsh (Ed.), *Normal family processes*. New York: Guilford.

McHale, S. M., & Huston, T. L. (1985). The effect of the transition to parenthood on the marriage relationship. *Journal of Family Issues*, *6*, 409–433.

McKay, M., Davis, M., & Fanning, P. (1983). *Messages: The communication skills book*. Oakland, CA: New Harbinger Publications.

McKay, M., Rogers, P. D., Blades, J., & Goose, R. (1984). *The divorce book*. Oakland, CA: New Harbinger Publications.

McKinney, K. (1989). Social factors in contraceptive and abortion attitudes and behaviors. In K. McKinney & S. Sprecher (Eds.), *Human sexuality: The societal and interpersonal context*. Norwood, NJ: Ablex.

McKinney, K., & DeLamater, J. (1982). *College students' attitudes toward contraception: Analysis of the contraceptive attitude form*. Unpublished manuscript.

McKinney, K., Olson, C., & Satterfield, A. (1987). *Graduate students' perceptions and reactions to sexual harassment*. Unpublished manuscript.

McLaughlin, B., White, D., McDevitt, T., & Raskin, R. (1983). Mothers' and fathers' speech to their young children: Similar or different? *Journal of Child Language*, *10*, 245–252.

McMahon, F. B., & McMahon, J. W. (1982). *Psychology: The hybrid science*. Homewood, IL: Dorsey Press.

McWhirter, D. P., & Mattison, A. M. (1984). *The male couple: How relationships develop*. Englewood Cliffs, NJ: Prentice Hall.

McWhirter, D. P., & Mattison, A. M. (1985). Psychotherapy for gay male couples. In J. C. Gonsiorek (Ed.), *A guide to therapy with gay and lesbian clients*. New York: Harrington Park Press.

McWhirter, D. P., & Mattison, A. M. (1988). Stages in the development of gay relationships. In J. P. DeCecco (Ed.), *Gay relationships*. New York: Harrington Park Press.

Mead, M. (1950). *Sex and temperament in three primitive societies*. New York: Merton.

Mecklenburg, M. E., & Thompson, P. G. (1983). The adolescent family life program as a prevention measure. *Public Health Reports*, *98*, 21–29.

Melman, A., Tiefer, L., & Pedersen, R. (1988). Evaluation of the first 406 patients in a urology department based center for male sexual dysfunction. *Urology*, *32*, 6–10.

Meltzoff, A., & Kuhl, P. (1989). Infants' perceptions of faces and speech sounds: Challenges to developmental theory. In P. R. Zelazo & R. Barr (Eds.), *Challenges to developmental paradigms*. Hillsdale, NJ: Erlbaum.

Merit Systems Protection Board. (1981). *Sexual harassment in the federal workplace: Is it a problem?* Washington, DC: U.S. Government Printing Office.

Mertz, G. J. (1984). Double blind placebo-controlled trial of oral acyclovir in first episode genital herpes simplex virus infection. *Journal of the American Medical Association*, *254*, 1147–1151.

Messenger, J. C. (1971). Sex and repression in an Irish folk community. In D. S. Marshall & R. C. Suggs (Eds.), *Human sexual behavior: Variation in the ethnographic spectrum*. New York: Basic Books.

Metts, S., & Cupach, W. R. (1989). The role of communication in human sexuality. In K. McKinney & S. Sprecher (Eds.), *Human sexuality: The societal and interpersonal context*. Norwood, NJ: Ablex.

Meyer, J., & Dupkin, C. (1985). Gender disturbance in children. *Bulletin of the Menninger Clinic*, *49*, 236–269.

Meyer-Bahlburg, H. F. L. (1977). Sex hormones and male sexuality in comparative perspective. *Archives of Sexual Behavior*, *6*, 297–325.

Meyer-Bahlburg, H. F. L. (1979). Sex hormones and female homosexuality: A critical examination. *Archives of Sexual Behavior*, *8*, 101–119.

Meyer-Bahlburg, H. (1980). Homosexual orientation in women and men: A hormonal basis? In J. E. Parsons (Ed.), *The psychobiology of sex differences and sex roles*. New York: McGraw-Hill.

Michaelson, K. L. (1988). *Childbirth in America: Anthropological perspectives*. Westport, CT: Greenwood Press.

Midgley, R. (Ed.). (1981). *Sex: A user's manual*. New York: Berkley Books.

Milan, R. J., & Kilman, P. R. (1987). Interpersonal factors in premarital contraception. *Journal of Sex Research*, *23*, 289–321.

Miller, B., & Marshall, J. (1987). Coercive sex on the university campus. *Journal of College Students Personnel*, *1*, 38–47.

Miller, B. C. (1986). *Family research methods*. Beverly Hills, CA: Sage.

Miller, B. C., & Bowen, S. L. (1982). Father-to-newborn attachment behavior in relation to prenatal classes and presence at delivery. *Family Relations*, *31*, 71–78.

Miller, B. C., & Moore, K. A. (1990). Adolescent sexual behavior, pregnancy, and parenting: Research through the 1980's. *Journal of Marriage and the Family*, *52*, 1025–1044.

Miller, B. C., McCoy, K., Olson, T. D., & Wallace, C. M. (1986). Parental discipline and control attempts in relation to adolescent sexual attitudes and behavior. *Journal of Marriage and the Family*, *48*, 503–512.

Miller, B. C., & Olson, T. D. (1988). Sexual attitudes and behavior of high school students in relation to background and contextual factors. *Journal of Sex Research, 24*, 194–200.

Miller, B. C., & Sollie, D. L. (1980). Normal stress during the transition to parenthood. *Family Relations, 29*, 459–465.

Miller, E. M. (1986). *Street woman*. Philadelphia: Temple University Press.

Miller, S., Wackman, D., Nunnally, E., & Miller, P. (1988). *Connecting with self and others*. Littleton, CO: Interpersonal Communications.

Millet, K. (1969). *Sexual politics*. New York: Avon.

Millette, B. (1982). Menopause: A survey of attitudes and knowledge. *Issues of Health Care in Women, 3*, 263–276.

Millette, B., & Hawkins, J. (1983). *The passage through menopause: Women's lives in transition*. Reston, VA: Reston.

Mills, J., & Masur, H. (1990). AIDS-related infections. *Scientific American, 263*, 50–57.

Mills, K. H., & Kilmann, P. R. (1982). Group treatment of sexual dysfunctions: A methodological review of the outcome literature. *Journal of Sex and Marital Therapy, 8*, 259–296.

Mishell, D. R. (1989). Contraception. *New England Journal of Medicine, 320*, 777–787.

Mitchell, H., Drake, M., & Medley, G. (1986). Prospective evaluation of the risk of cervical cancer after cytological evidence of human papillomavirus infection. *Lancet, 1*, 573–575.

Mitchell, K. (1983). The price tag of responsibility: A comparison of divorced and remarried mothers. *Journal of Divorce, 6*, 33–42.

Moghissi, K. (1989). The technology of AID and surrogacy. In L. Whiteford & M. Polan (Eds.), *Approaches to human reproduction*. Boulder, CO: Westview.

Money, J. (1968). *Sex errors of the body: Dilemmas, education, counselling*. Baltimore: Johns Hopkins University Press.

Money, J. (1980). *Love and love sickness*. Baltimore: Johns Hopkins University Press.

Money, J. (1981). Phyletic origins of erotosexual dysfunction. *International Journal of Mental Health, 10*, 75–109.

Money, J. (1984). Paraphilias: Phenomenology and classification. *American Journal of Psychotherapy, 38*, 164–179.

Money, J. (1985). Pediatric sexology and hermaphroditism. *Journal of Marriage and Sex Therapy, 11*, 139–156.

Money, J. (1987a). Propaeduetics of diecious G-I/R: Theoretical foundations for understanding dimorphic gender-identity/role. In J. M. Reinisch, L. A. Rosenblum, & S. A. Sanders (Eds.), *Masculinity/femininity: Basic perspectives*. New York: Oxford University Press.

Money, J. (1987b). Sin, sickness, or status? Homosexual gender identity and psychoneuroendocronology. *American Psychologist, 42*, 384–399.

Money, J., & Bennett, R. (1981). Postadolescent paraphilic sex offenders: Antiandrogenic and counseling therapy follow-up. *International Journal of Mental Health, 10*, 122–133.

Money, J., & Ehrhardt, A. (1972). *Man and woman, boy and girl*. Baltimore: Johns Hopkins University Press.

Money, J., & Ogunro, D. (1974). Behavioral sexology: Ten cases of genetic male intersexuality with implied prenatal and pubertal androgenization. *Archives of Sexual Behavior, 3*, 181–205.

Monroe, R. (1980). Male transvestism and the couvade: A psychocultural analysis. *Ethos, 8*, 49–59.

Moore, K., & Peterson, J. (1989). *The consequences of teenage pregnancy: Final report*. Washington, DC: Child Trends.

Moore, K. A., Peterson, J. L., & Furstenberg, F. F. (1986). Parental attitudes and the occurrence of early sexual activity. *Journal of Marriage and the Family, 48*, 777–782.

Moore, K. L. (1988). *The developing human* (4th ed.). Philadelphia: Saunders.

Moore, M. M. (1985). Nonverbal courtship patterns in women: Context and consequences. *Ethology and Sciobiology, 6*, 237–247.

Moore, P. G. (1984). Assessment of the effects of menopause on individual women: A review of the literature. *Issues of Health Care in Women, 4*, 341–350.

Morales, A., Condra, M. S., Owen, J. E., Fenemore, J., & Surridge, D. M. (1988). Oral and transcutaneous pharmacologic agents in the treatment of impotence. *Urologic Clinics of North America, 15*, 87–93.

Morgan, P., Lye, D., & Condran, G. (1988). Sons help a marriage. *American Journal of Sociology, 93*, 60–64.

Moretti, D. S. (1984). *Obscenity and pornography*. New York: Oceana Publications.

Morin, J. (1981). *Anal pleasure and health*. Burlingame, CA: Down There Press.

Morrell, M., Dixen, J., Carter, S., & Davidson, J. (1984). The influence of age and cycling status on sexual arousability in women. *American Journal of Obstetrics and Gynecology, 148*, 66–71.

Morrison, D. M. (1985). Adolescent contraceptive behavior: A review. *Psychological Bulletin, 98*, 538–568.

Morrison, G. C. (1988). *Early childhood education today* (4th ed.). Columbus, OH: Merrill.

Moser, C. (1988). Sadomasochism. In D. M. Dailey (Ed.), *The sexually unusual: Guide to understanding and helping*. New York: Harrington Park Press.

Moses, A. E., & Hawkins, R. O. (1985). Two hour in-service training session in homophobia. In H. Hidalgo, T. Peterson, & N. J. Woodman (Eds.), *Lesbian and gay issues: A resource manual for social workers*. Silver Springs, MD: National Association of Social Workers.

Mosher, W. D., & Horn, M. C. (1989). First family planning visits by young women. *Family Planning Perspectives, 21*, 33–40.

Mosher, D. L., & Vonderheide, S. G. (1985). Contributions of sex guilt and masturbation guilt to women's contraceptive attitudes and use. *Journal of Sex Research, 21*, 24–39.

Moskal, B. S. (1989, July 3). Sexual harassment: 80's style. *Industry Week*, pp. 22–24, 27.

Mott, F. L., & Haurin, R. J. (1988). Linkages between sexual activity and alcohol and drug used among American adolescents. *Family Planning Perspectives, 20*, 129–136.

Moultrup, D. J. (1990). *Husbands, wives, and lovers: The emotional system of the extramarital affair*. New York: Guilford.

Moyse-Steinberg, D. (1990). A model for adolescent pregnancy prevention through the use of small groups. *Social Work with Groups, 13*(2), 57.

Muasher, S. J. (1987). Infertility. In Z. Rosenwaks, F. Benjamin, & M. Stone (Eds.), *Gynecology: Principles and practice*. New York: Macmillan.

Muehlenhard, C. L. (1988). Misinterpreted dating behaviors and the risk of date rape. *Journal of Social and Clinical Psychology, 6*, 20–37.

Mueller, G. O. (1980). *Sexual conduct and the law*. New York: Oceana Publications.

Mueller, S. C., & Lue, T. F. (1988). Evaluation of vasculogenic impotence. *Urologic Clinics of North America, 15,* 65–76.

Muller, R., & Goldberg, S. (1980). Why William doesn't want a doll. Preschooler's expectations of adult behavior toward boys and girls. *Merrill-Palmer Quarterly, 26,* 259–269.

Murphy, C. (1983). *Teaching kids to play.* New York: Leisure Press.

Murphy, F. K., & Patamasucon, P. (1984). Congenital syphilis. In K. Holmes, P. Mardh, P. Sparling, & P. Wiesner (Eds.), *Sexually transmitted diseases.* New York: McGraw-Hill.

Murphy, P. A. (1987). Parental death in childhood and loneliness in young adults. *Omega, 17,* 219–228.

Murstein, B. L. (1980). Mate selection in the 1979's. *Journal of Marriage and the Family, 42,* 777–792.

Murstein, B. L. (1986). *Paths to marriage.* Beverly Hills, CA: Sage.

Myers, D. G. (1989). *Psychology* (2nd ed.). New York: Worth.

Myers, L., & Morokoff, P. (1985, April). *Physiological and subjective sexual arousal in pre- and postmenopausal women.* Paper presented at the annual American Psychological Association Meeting, New York.

Naeye, R. I. (1981). Influence of maternal cigarette smoking during pregnancy on fetal and childhood growth. *Journal of Obstetrics and Gynecology, 57,* 18–21.

Nannarone, N. (1983). Career father. *Marriage and Family Living, 65,* 8–11.

Nathanson, C. A., & Kim, Y. J. (1989). Components of change in adolescent fertility, 1971–1979. *Demography, 26,* 85–98.

National Center for Health Statistics. (1990). *Monthly Vital Statistics Report, 39*(7). Washington, DC: U.S. Government Printing Office.

National Center for Health Statistics. (1991). *Health: United States, 1990.* Hyattsville, MD: Public Health Service.

National Center for Health Statistics. (1991, January). Premarital sexual experience among adolescent women. *Morbidity and Mortality Weekly Report, 39*(51/52), 929–932.

National Center on Child Abuse and Neglect. (1984). Everything you wanted to know about child abuse and neglect and never asked. In *Perspectives on child maltreatment in the 1980's.* Washington, DC: U.S. Government Printing Office.

National Gay and Lesbian Task Force. (1988). *National antigay lesbian victimization report.* New York: Author.

National Research Council. (1987). *Risking the future: Adolescent sexuality, pregnancy, and childbearing.* Washington, DC: National Academy Press.

Nelson, J. (1985). Male sexuality and masculine spirituality. *SIECUS Report, 13,* 1–4.

Nelson, M., & Clark, K. (Eds.). (1986). *The educator's guide to preventing child sexual abuse.* Santa Cruz, CA: Network Publications.

Nelson, N. M., Murray, W. E., Saroj, S., Bennet, K. J., Milner, R., & Sackett, D. L. (1980). A randomized clinical trial of the Leboyer approach to childbirth. *New England Journal of Medicine, 303,* 655–660.

Neumann, F., & Toppert, M. (1986). Pharmacology of anti-androgens. *Journal of Steroid Biochemistry, 25,* 885–895.

Newcomb, M. D., & Bentler, P. M. (1983). Dimensions of subjective female orgasmic responsiveness. *Journal of Personality and Social Psychology, 44,* 862–873.

Newcomer, S., & Udry, J. (1985). Oral sex in an adolescent population. *Archives of Sexual Behavior, 14,* 41–46.

Newman, A. S., & Bertelson, A. D. (1986). Sexual dysfunction in diabetic women. *Journal of Behavioral Medicine, 9,* 261–269.

Ney, P. G. (1988). Transgenerational child abuse. *Child Psychiatry and Human Development, 18,* 151–168.

Nichols, M. (1989). Sex therapy with lesbians, gay men, and bisexuals. In S. R. Leiblum & R. C. Rosen (Eds.), *Principles and practices of sex therapy* (2nd ed.). New York: Guilford.

Nielsen, T. (1983). Sexual abuse of boys: Current perspectives. *Personnel and Guidance Journal, 62,* 139–143.

Nordstrom, B. (1986). Why men get married: More and less traditional men compared. In R. A. Lewis & R. E. Salt (Eds.), *Men in families.* Beverly Hills, CA: Sage.

Norton, A. J., & Moorman, J. (1987). Current trends in marriage and divorce among American women. *Journal of Marriage and the Family, 49,* 3–14.

Norwood, C. (1987). *Advice for life: A woman's guide to AIDS risks and prevention.* New York: Pantheon.

Nottebhm, F., & Arnold, A. P. (1976). Sexual dimorphism in vocal control areas of the songbird brain. *Science, 194,* 211–213.

Nurnberg, H. G., & Levine, P. E. (1987). Spontaneous remission of MAO-I-induced anorgasmia. *American Journal of Psychiatry, 144,* 805–807.

Nye, I. F., & Lamberts, M. B. (1980). *School-age parenthood.* Pullman: Washington State University.

Oakland, T. (1984). *Divorced fathers: Reconstructing a quality life.* New York: Human Sciences Press.

Obler, M. (1982). A comparison of hypnoanalytic/behavior modification technique and a cotherapist-type treatment with primary orgasmic dysfunctional females: Some preliminary results. *Journal of Sex Research, 18,* 331–345.

O'Brien, M., & Huston, A. C. (1985). The development of sex-typed play behavior in toddlers. *Developmental Psychology, 21,* 866–871.

O'Brien, S. (1984). *Child abuse and neglect: Everyone's problem.* Wheaton, MD: Association for Childhood Education International.

O'Brien, S. F., & Bierman, K. L. (1988). Conceptions and perceived influence of peer groups: Interviews with pre-adolescents and adolescents. *Child Development, 59,* 1360–1365.

O'Carroll, R., Shapiro, C., & Bancroft, J. (1985). Androgens, behavior, and nocturnal erection in hypogonadal men: The effects of varying the replacement dose. *Clinical Endocrinology, 23,* 527–538.

O'Connell, M. A., Leberg, E., & Donaldson, C. R. (1990). *Working with sex offenders: Practical guidelines for therapist selection.* Beverly Hills, CA: Sage.

O'Connor, P. J. (1964). Etiological factors in homosexuality as seen in Royal Air Force psychiatric practice. *British Journal of Psychiatry, 110,* 381–391.

Offer, D., & Church, R. B. (1991). Turmoil in adolescence. In R. M. Lerner, A. C. Petersen, & J. Brooks-Gunn (Eds.), *Encyclopedia of adolescence.* New York: Garland.

Offer, D., Ostrov, E., Howard, K. I., & Atkinson, R. (1988). *The teenage world: Adolescents' self-image in ten countries.* New York: Plenum.

O'Hare, W. P., Pollard, K. M., Mann, T. L., & Kent, M. M. (1991). African Americans in the 1990's. *Population Bulletin, 46*(1). Washington, DC: Population Reference Bureau.

References

Olds, S. B., London, M. L., & Ladewig, P. W. (1992). *Maternal-newborn nursing* (4th ed.). Redwood Park, CA: Addison-Wesley Nursing.

Olds, S. W. (1985). *The eternal garden: Seasons of our sexuality*. New York: Times Books.

Oliver, D. (1982). Why do people live together? *Journal of Social Welfare, 7*, 209–222.

Oppenheim, J., Boegehold, B., & Breener, B. (1984). *Raising a confident child*. New York: Pantheon Books.

Orbuch, T. L. (1989). Human sexuality education. In K. McKinney & S. Sprecher (Eds.), *Human sexuality: The societal and interpersonal context*. Norwood, NJ: Ablex.

Oriel, J. D. (1981). Genital warts. *Sexually Transmitted Diseases, 8*, 326–329.

Orkin, M., & Maibach, H. (1984). Scabies. In K. Holmes, P. Mardh, P. Sparling, & P. Wiesner (Eds.), *Sexually transmitted diseases*. New York: McGraw-Hill.

Orthner, D. (1981). *Intimate relationships*. Reading, MA: Addison-Wesley.

O'Shaughnessy, M. E., & Palmer, C. (1990). *Sexually stressful events survey*. Office of the Dean of Students, University of Illinois at Urbana-Champaign, pp. 1–20.

Oskamp, S., & Mindick, B. (1983). Personality and attitudinal barriers to contraception. In D. Byrne & W. A. Fisher (Eds.), *Adolescents, sex, and contraception*. New York: McGraw-Hill.

Padesky, C. (1988). Attaining and maintaining positive lesbian identity: A cognitive therapy approach. *Women and Therapy, 8*, 145–156.

Page, D. C., Mosher, R., Simpson, E. M., Fisher, E. C., Mardon, G., Pollack, J., & Brown, L. G. (1987). The sex-determining region of the human Y chromosome encodes a finger protein. *Cell, 51*, 1091–1104.

Pagel, M. D., & Davidson, A. R. (1984). A comparison of three social-psychological models of attitude and behavioral plan: Prediction of contraceptive behavior. *Journal of Personality and Social Psychology, 47*, 517–533.

Paikoff, R. L. & Brooks-Gunn, J. (1991). Interventions to prevent adolescent pregnancy. In R. M. Lerner, A. C. Petersen, & J. Brooks-Gunn (Eds.), *Encyclopedia of adolescence*. New York: Garland.

Paikoff, R. L., Buchanan, C. M., & Brooks-Gunn, J. (1991). Methodological links in the study of hormone-behavior links at puberty. In R. M. Lerner, A. C. Petersen, & J. Brooks-Gunn (Eds.), *Encyclopedia of adolescence*. New York: Garland.

Palka, J. (1991). The sobering geography of AIDS. *Science, 252*, 372–373.

Palm, G. F., & Palkovitz, R. (1988). The challenge of working with new fathers: Implications for support providers. In R. Palkovitz & M. B. Sussman (Eds.), *Transitions to parenthood*. New York: Haworth Press.

Paludi, M. A., & Gullo, D. F. (1986). The effect of sex labels on adults' knowledge of infant development. *Sex Roles, 16*, 19–30.

Paluszny, M. J., Cullen, B. J., Funk, J., & Liu, P. Y. (1989). Child abuse disposition: Concurrences and differences between a hospital team, child protective agency, and the court. *Child Psychiatry and Human Development, 20*, 25–38.

Papini, D., Barnett, J., Clark, S., & Micka, J. C. (1989, April). *Family influences and individual concomitants of adolescent ego identity statuses*. Paper presented at the biennial meeting of the Society for Research in Child Development. Kansas City.

Parer, J. T. (1989). Fetal heart rate. In R. K. Creasy & R. Resnik (Eds.), *Maternal-fetal medicine: Principles and practice*. Philadelphia: Saunders.

Parer, J. T., & Livingston, E. G. (1991). What is fetal distress? *American Journal of Obstetrics and Gynecology, 162*, 1421–1433.

Parke, R. D. (1981). *Fathers*. Cambridge, MA: Harvard University Press.

Parker, H., & Parker, S. (1986). Father–daughter sexual abuse: An emerging perspective. *American Journal of Orthopsychiatry, 56*, 531–549.

Parker, J. G., & Gottman, J. M. (1989). Social and emotional development in a relational context: Friendship interaction from early childhood to adolescence. In T. J. Berndt & G. W. Ladd (Eds.), *Peer relationships in child development*. New York: Wiley.

Parrot, A. (1984). Sex education should occur outside the family in schools, youth groups, and agencies. In H. Feldman & A. Parrot (Eds.), *Human sexuality: Contemporary controversies*. Beverly Hills, CA: Sage.

Parrot, A. (1986, June). *Emotional impact of acquaintance rape on college women*. Paper presented at the mid-continent region convention of the Society for the Scientific Study of Sex, Madison, WI.

Parrot, A. (1988). *Coping with date and acquaintance rape*. New York: Rosen.

Parrot, A., & Ellis, M. J. (1985). Homosexuals should be allowed to marry and adopt and rear children. In H. Feldman & M. Feldman (Eds.), *Current controversies in marriage and family*. Beverly Hills, CA: Sage.

Pasley, K., & Ihinger-Tallman, M. (1989). *Remarriage and stepparenting: Current research and theory*. New York: Guilford.

Pasquale, S. (1984). Rationale for a triphasic oral contraceptive. *Journal of Reproductive Medicine, 29*, 560–567.

Payne, F. D. (1987). "Masculinity," "femininity," and the complex construct of adjustment. *Sex Roles, 17*, 359–372.

Pearlman, J., Cohen, J., & Coburn, K. (1981). *Hitting our stride*. New York: Delacorte Press.

Pearse, W. H. (1987). Parturition: Place and priorities. *American Journal of Public Health, 77*, 923–924.

Pearson, J. C. (1985). *Gender and communication*. Dubuque, IA: Wm. C. Brown.

Peck, D. (1986). Public health modeling and populations at risk to sexually transmitted diseases. *Archives of Sexual Behavior, 15*, 13–152.

Pedersen, B., Tiefer, L., Ruiz, M., & Melman, A. (1988). Evaluation of patients and partners one to four years following penile prosthesis surgery. *Journal of Urology, 139*, 956–958.

Pedersen, D. M., & Bond, B. L. (1985). Shifts in sex roles after a decade of cultural change. *Psychological Reports, 57*, 43–48.

Pederson, D. R., Moran, G., Sitko, C., Campbell, K., Ghesquire, K., & Acton, H. (1989, April). *Maternal sensitivity and the security of infant–mother attachment*. Paper presented at the biennial meeting of the Society for Research in Child Development, Kansas City.

Pelletier, G., & Handy, L. C. (1986). Family dysfunction and the psychological impact of child sexual abuse. *Canadian Journal of Psychiatry, 31*, 407–412.

Peo, R. E. (1988). Transvestism. In D. M. Dailey (Ed.), *The sexually unusual: A guide to understanding and helping*. New York: Harrington Park Press.

Pepe, M. V., & Byrne, T. J. (1991). Women's perceptions of immediate and long-term effects of failed infertility treatment on marital and sexual satisfaction. *Family Relations, 40,* 303–309

Peplau, L. A. (1981, March). What homosexuals want. *Psychology Today,* pp. 19–27.

Peplau, L. A. (1983). Roles and gender. In H. H. Kelley (Ed.), *Close relationships.* New York: Freeman.

Peplau, L. A., & Cochran, S. D. (1980). *Sex differences in values concerning love relationships.* Paper presented at the annual meeting of the American Psychological Association, Montreal.

Peplau, L. A., & Cochran, S. D. (1981). Value orientations in the intimate relationships of gay men. *Journal of Homosexuality, 6,* 1–19.

Peplau, L. A., & Gordon, S. L. (1983). The intimate relationships of lesbians and gay men. In E. R. Allgeier & N. B. McCormick (Eds.), *Changing Boundaries: Gender Roles and Sexual Behavior.* Palo Alto, CA: Mayfield.

Perelman, M. A. (1980). Treatment of premature ejaculation. In S. R. Leiblum & L. A. Pervin (Eds.), *Principles and practices of sex therapy.* New York: Guilford.

Perlman, D. S., & Abramson, P. R. (1982). Sexual satisfaction among married and cohabiting individuals. *Journal of Consulting and Clinical Psychology, 50,* 458–460.

Perlman, D. S., & Duck, S. (Eds.). (1986). *Intimate relationships: Development, dynamics, and deterioration.* Beverly Hills, CA: Sage.

Perlman, D. S., & Fehr, B. (1986). The development of intimate relationships. In D. S. Perlman & S. Duck (Eds.), *Intimate relationships: Development, dynamics, and deterioration.* Beverly Hills, CA: Sage.

Perry, J. D., & Whipple, B. (1981). Pelvic muscle strength of female ejaculators: Evidence in support of a new theory of orgasm. *Journal of Sex Research, 17,* 22–39.

Peters, S. D. (1988). Child sexual abuse and later psychological problems. In G. E. Wyatt & G. J. Powell (Eds.), *The lasting effects of child sexual abuse.* Newbury Park, CA: Sage.

Peters, S. D., Wyatt, G. E., & Finkelhor, D. (1986). Prevalence of child sexual abuse. In D. Finkelhor (Ed.), *A sourcebook of child sexual abuse.* Newbury Park, CA: Sage.

Petersen, A. C. (1983). Menarche: Meaning of measures and measuring meaning. In S. Golub (Ed.), *Menarche.* Lexington, MA: Lexington Books.

Petersen, A. C. (1987, June). Those gangly years. *Psychology Today,* pp. 28–34.

Petersen, A. C. (1988). Pubertal change and psychosocial development. In D. L. Baltes, R. M. Featherman, & R. M. Lerner (Eds.), *Lifespan development and behavior* (Vol. 9). New York: Academic Press.

Petersen, A. C., & Taylor, B. (1980). The biological approach to adolescence: Biological change and psychological adaptation. In J. Adelson (Ed.), *Handbook of adolescent psychology.* New York: Wiley.

Peterson, D. R. (1983). Conflict. In H. H. Kelly (Ed.), *Close relationships.* New York: Freeman.

Petersen, J. R., Kretchmer, A., Nellis, B., Lever J., & Hertz, R. (1983a, January). The Playboy reader's sex survey (Part 1). *Playboy,* pp. 76–88.

Petersen, J. R., Kretchmer, A., Nellis, B., Lever, J., & Hertz, R. (1983b, February). The Playboy reader's sex survey (Part 2). *Playboy,* pp. 108–110.

Petty, R. E., & Mirels, H. L. (1981). Intimacy and scarcity of self-disclosure: Effects on interpersonal attraction for males and females. *Personality and Social Psychology Bulletin, 7,* 493–503.

Pies, C. (1990). Lesbians and the choice to parent. In F. W. Bozett & M. B. Sussman (Eds.), *Homosexuality and family relations.* New York: Haworth Press.

Pietromonaco, P. R., Manis, J., & Markus, H. (1987). The relationship of employment to self-perception and well-being in women: A cognitive analysis. *Sex Roles, 17,* 467–477.

Pillard, R., Rose, R. M., & Sherwood, M. (1974). Plasma testosterone levels in homosexual men. *Archives of Sexual Behavior, 3,* 577–584.

Pinhas, V. (1988). Sexuality counseling of people with alcohol problems. In E. Weinstein & E. Rosen (Eds.), *Sexuality counseling: Issues and implications.* Monterey, CA: Brooks/Cole.

Pipes, P. (1989). *Nutrition in infancy and childhood* (4th ed.). St. Louis, MO: Mosby.

Pitcher, E. G., Feinberg, S. G., & Alexander, D. (1984). *Helping young children learn* (4th ed.). Columbus, OH: Merrill.

Pitcher, E. G., & Schultz, L. H. (1983). *Boys and girls at play: The development of sex roles.* New York: Praeger.

Pittman, F. (1989). *Private lies: Infidelity and the betrayal of intimacy.* New York: Norton.

Pittman, F. S. (1987). *Turning points: Treating families in transition and crisis.* New York: Norton.

Pizzo, P. A. (1990). Pediatric AIDS: Problems within problems. *Journal of Infectious Diseases, 161,* 316–324.

Planned Parenthood Federation of America. (1987). *Deciding on abortion.* New York: Author.

Platt, R., Rice, P., & McCormack, W. (1983). Risk of acquiring gonorrhea and prevalence of abnormal adnexal findings among women recently exposed to gonorrhea. *Journal of the American Medical Association, 250,* 3205–3209.

Pleck, J. H. (1985). *Working wives, working husbands.* Beverly Hills, CA: Sage.

Pleck, J. (1989). Correlates of black adolescent males' condom use. *Journal of Adolescent Research, 4,* 247–253.

Plomin, R., & Foch, T. T. (1981). Sex differences and individual differences. *Child Development, 52,* 383–385.

Plummer, C. (1985, August). *Preventing child abuse: What in-school programs teach children.* Paper presented at the Second National Conference for Family Violence Researchers, Durham, NH.

Pocs, O., & Walsh, R. (1985). *Marriage and family 85/86.* Guilford, CT: Dushkin.

Pohl, R. (1983). Anorgasmia caused by MAOIs. *American Journal of Psychiatry, 140,* 510.

Population Reference Bureau. (1985). *Population handbook* (2nd ed.). Washington, DC: Author.

Powell, G. J. (1988). Child sexual abuse research: The implications for clinical practice. In G. E. Wyatt & G. J. Powell (Eds.), *The lasting effects of child sexual abuse.* Newbury Park, CA: Sage.

Powell, M. G., Mears, J. B., Deber, R. B., & Ferguson, D. (1986). Contraception with the cervical cap: Effectiveness, safety, continuity of use, and user satisfaction. *Contraception, 33,* 215–232.

Powers, S. I., Hauser, S. T., & Kilmer, L. A. (1989). Adolescent mental health. *American Psychologist, 44,* 200–208.

Pratt, W. (1990, April). Premarital sexual behavior, multiple sexual partners, and marital experience. Paper presented at the annual meeting of the Population Association of America, Toronto.

Pratt, W., Mosher, W., Bachrach, C., & Horn, M. (1984). Understanding U.S. fertility: Findings from the National Survey of Family Growth, cycle III. *Population Bulletin, 39,* 1–42.

Preston, J., & Swann, G. (1987). *Safe sex: The ultimate erotic guide*. New York: New American Library.

Price, J. H., Desmond, S., & Kukulka, G. (1985). High school students' perceptions and misperceptions of AIDS. *Journal of School Health, 55*, 107–109.

Price, S. J., & McKenry, P. C. (1988). *Divorce*. Newbury Park, CA: Sage.

Price-Bonham, S., & Balswick, J. O. (1980). The non-institutions: Divorce, desertion, and remarriage. *Journal of Marriage and the Family, 42*, 959–972.

Pridjian, G. (1991). Cesarean: Changing the trends. *Obstetrics and Gynecology, 77*, 195–209.

Prothrow-Stith, D. (1989). Excerpts from address to the Massachusetts Department of Public Health. *Journal of Adolescent Health Care, 10*, 5–7.

Pruett, K. D. (1987). *The nurturing father*. New York: Warner.

Pugh, D. (1983). Bringing an end to mutilation. *New Statesman, 11*, 8–9.

Quinn, T. C. (1989). Heterosexuals with STD's face greater risk of HIV infection. *Medical Aspects of Human Sexuality, 23*, 101–102.

Quinsey, V., & Marshall, W. (1983). Procedures for reducing inappropriate sexual arousal: An evaluation review. In J. G. Greer & I. R. Stuart (Eds.), *The sexual aggressor: Current perspectives on treatment*. New York: Van Nostrand Reinhold.

Rabin, D. S., & Chrousos, G. P. (1991). Gonadal androgens. In R. M. Lerner, A. C. Petersen, & J. Brooks-Gunn (Eds.), *Encyclopedia of adolescence*. New York: Garland.

Radin, N. (1981). Childrearing fathers in intact families: Some antecedents and consequences. *Merrill-Palmer Quarterly, 27*, 489–514.

Ray, J. (1984, August). *Evaluation of the Child Abuse Prevention Project*. Paper presented at the Second National Conference for Family Violence Researchers, Durham, NH.

Reedy, M. N., Birren, J. K., & Schaie, K. W. (1981). Age and sex differences in satisfying love relationships across the adult life span. *Human Development, 24*, 52–66.

Reinisch, J. M., & Beasley, R. (1990). *The Kinsey Institute new report on sex: What you must know to be sexually literate*. New York: St. Martin's Press.

Reinisch, J. M., Rosenblum, L. A., & Sanders, S. A. (Eds.). (1987). *Masculinity/femininity: Basic Perspectives*. New York: Oxford University Press.

Reis, H. T. (1986). Gender effects in social participation: Intimacy, loneliness, and the conduct of social interaction. In R. Gilmour & S. Duck (Eds.), *The emerging field of personal relationships*. Hillsdale, NJ: Erlbaum.

Reis, H. T., Senchak, M., & Solomon, B. (1985). Sex differences in the intimacy of social interaction: Further examination of potential explanations. *Journal of Personality and Social Psychology, 48*, 1204–1217.

Reis, H. T., & Shaver, P. (1988). Intimacy as an interpersonal process. In S. Duck (Ed.), *Handbook of personal relationships: Theory, relationships, and interventions*. New York: Wiley.

Reis, H. T., & Wright, S. (1982). Knowledge of sex-role stereotypes in children aged 3–5. *Sex Roles, 8*, 10–49.

Reiss, I. L. (1960). *Premarital sexual standards in America*. New York: Free Press.

Reiss, I. L. (1981). Some observations on ideology and sexuality in America. *Journal of Marriage and the Family, 43*, 271–283.

Reiss, I. L. (1989). Society and sexuality: A sociological explanation. In K. McKinney & S. Sprecher (Eds.), *Human sexuality: The societal and interpersonal context*. Norwood, NJ: Ablex.

Reiss, I. L., & Lee, G. R. (1988). *Family systems in America* (4th ed.). New York: Holt, Rinehart, & Winston.

Reiss, I. L., & Reiss, H. M. (1990). *An end to shame: Shaping our next sexual revolution*. New York: Prometheus.

Reiss, I. R. (1960). Toward a sociology of the heterosexual love relationship. *Marriage and Family Living, 26*, 139–145.

Reiss, I. R. (1980). *Family systems in America* (3rd ed.). New York: Holt, Rinehart & Winston.

Reitmeijer, C., Krebs, J., Feorino, P., & Judson, F. (1988). Condoms as physical and chemical barriers against human immunodeficiency virus. *Journal of the American Medical Association, 259*, 1851–1853.

Remafedi, G. (1987). Adolescent homosexuality: Psychosocial and medical implications. *Pediatrics, 79*, 331–337.

Renfrew, M., Fisher, C., & Arms, S. (1990). *Breastfeeding: Getting breastfeeding right for you*. Berkeley: Celestial Arts.

Renshaw, D. C. (1983, February). Incest: Handling the disclosure. *Sexual Medicine Today*, pp. 2–5.

Renshaw, T. (1988). Sexuality in the later years. *Geriatric Sexual Counseling Medi-Guide to Aging, 3*, 1–6.

Report of President's Commission on Pornography and Obscenity. (1970). Washington, DC.

Resnick, R. R., & Resnick, E. B. (1984). Cocaine abuse and its treatment. *Psychiatric Clinics of North America, 7*, 713–738.

Rich, A. R., & Scovel, M. (1987). Causes of depression in college students: A cross-lagged panel correlational analysis. *Psychological Reports, 60*, 27–30.

Richardson, L. (1988). *The dynamics of sex and gender* (3rd ed.). New York: Harper & Row.

Richart, R. M. (1987). Causes and management of cervical intrepithelial neoplasis. *Cancer, 60*, 1951–1958.

Rickel, A. U. (1989). *Teen pregnancy and parenting*. New York: Hemisphere.

Ricketts, W. (1984). Biological research on homosexuality: Ansell's cow or Ocam's razor? *Journal of Homosexuality, 9*, 45–63.

Ricketts, W., & Achtenberg, R. (1990). Adoption and foster parenting for lesbians and gay men: Creating new traditions in family. In F. W. Bozett & M. B. Sussman (Eds.), *Homosexuality and family relations*. New York: Haworth Press.

Riesenberg, D. (1987). Treating a societal malignancy—rape. *Journal of the American Medical Association, 257*, 726–727.

Riggio, R. E., & Woll, S. B. (1984). The role of nonverbal cues and physical attractiveness in dating choice. *Journal of Social and Personal Relationships, 1*, 347–357.

Riggs, R. S. (1982). Incest: The school's role. *Journal of School Health, 52*, 365–370.

Riley, A. J., & Riley, E. J. (1986). Cyproheptadine and antidepressant-induced anorgasmia. *British Journal of Psychiatry, 148*, 217–218.

Riportella-Muller, R. (1989). Sexuality in the elderly: A review. In K. McKinney & S. Sprecher (Eds.), *Human sexuality: The societal and interpersonal context*. Norwood, NJ: Ablex.

Risen, L. I., & Koss, M. P. (1987). The sexual abuse of boys: Prevalence and descriptive characteristics of childhood victimizations. *Journal of Interpersonal Violence, 2*, 309–323.

Roark, M. (1989). Sexual violence. In J. M Sherrill & O. G. Siegel (Eds.), *Responding to violence on campus*. San Francisco: Jossey-Bass.

Robins, J. M., & DeLamater, J. D. (1985). Support from significant others and loneliness following induced abortion. *Social Psychiatry, 20*, 92–99.

Robinson, B. E., & Barret, R. L. (1986). *The developing father*. New York: Guilford.

Robinson, B. E., Skeen, P., Flake-Hobson, C., & Herrman, M. (1982). Gay men's and women's perceptions of early family life and their relationships with parents. *Family Relations: Journal of Applied Family and Child Studies, 31*, 79–83.

Robinson, I. E., & Jedlicka, D. (1982). Change in sexual attitudes and behavior of college students from 1965 to 1980: A research note. *Journal of Marriage and the Family, 2*, 237–240.

Robinson, P. K. (1983). The sociological perspective. In R. B. Weg (Ed.), *Sexuality in the later years: Roles and behavior*. New York: Academic Press.

Roche, J. P. (1986). Premarital sex: Attitudes and behavior by dating stage. *Adolescence, 21*, 107–121.

Rockner, G., Wahlberg, V., Olund, A. (1989). Episiotomy and perineal trauma during childbirth. *Journal of Advanced Nursing, 14*, 264–279.

Rodman, H., Sarvis, G., & Bonar, J. (1987). *The abortion question*. New York: Columbia University Press.

Roffman, D. M. (1989). Sexuality education in the independent school setting. In C. Cassell & P. M. Wilson (Eds.), *Sexuality education: A resource book*. New York: Garland.

Rogers, C., & Terry, T. (1984). Clinical intervention with boy victims of sexual abuse. In I. Stewart & J. Greer (Eds.), *Victims of sexual aggression*. New York: Van Nostrand Reinhold.

Rollins, J. (1986). Single men and women: Differences and similarities. *Family Perspective, 20*, 117–125.

Rook, K. S. (1987). Reciprocity of social exchange and social satisfaction among older women. *Journal of Personality and Social Psychology, 52*, 145–154.

Roopnarine, J. L., & Miller, B. C. (1985). Transitions to fatherhood. In S. Hanson & F. Bozett (Eds.), *Dimensions of fatherhood*. Beverly Hills, CA: Sage.

Roosa, M. W. (1991). Adolescent pregnancy programs collection: An introduction. *Family Relations, 40*, 370–372.

Roosa, W. M., & Christopher, S. F. (1990). Evaluation of an abstinence only adolescent pregnancy prevention program: A replication. *Family Relations, 39*, 363–367.

Roper, M. (1989). Sexuality education in senior high schools. In C. Cassell & P. M. Wilson (Eds.), *Sexuality education: A resource book*. New York: Garland.

Roscoe, B., Goodwin, M., Repp, S., & Rose, M. (1987). Sexual harassment of university students and student-employees: Findings and implications. *College Student Journal, 12*, 254–273.

Roscoe, B., Kennedy, D., & Pope, T. (1987). Adolescents' view of intimacy: Distinguishing intimate from nonintimate relationships. *Adolescence, 22*, 511–516.

Roscoe, B., & Kruger, T. L. (1990). AIDS: Late adolescent's knowledge and its influence on sexual behavior. *Adolescence, 25*, 39–48.

Rose, S., & Larwood, L. (Eds.). (1988). *Women's careers: Pathways and pitfalls*. Westport, CT: Greenwood Press.

Rosen, M. C. (1991). Vaginal birth after cesarean: A meta-analysis of morbidity and mortality. *Obstetrics and Gynecology, 77*, 211–220.

Rosen, E., & Weinstein, E. (1988). Introduction: Sexuality counseling. In E. Weinstein & E. Rosen (Eds.), *Sexuality counseling: Issues and implications*. Monterey, CA: Brooks/Cole.

Rosen, I. (1982). The psychoanalytic approach. *British Journal of Psychiatry, 140*, 85–93.

Rosen, R., & Ager, J. W. (1981). Self-concept and contraception: Preconception decision-making. *Population and Environment, 4*, 11–23.

Rosen, R. C., & Beck, J. G. (1988). *Patterns of sexual arousal*. New York: Guilford.

Rosen, R. C., & Leiblum, S. R. (1988). A sexual scripting approach to problems of desire. In S. R. Leiblum & R. C. Rosen (Eds.), *Sexual desire disorders*. New York: Guilford.

Rosen, R. C., & Leiblum, S. R. (1989). Assessment and treatment of desire disorders. In S. R. Leiblum & R. C. Rosen (Eds.), *Principles and practice of sex therapy* (2nd ed.). New York: Guilford.

Rosen, R. C., & Leiblum, S. R. (1992). *Erectile disorders: Assessment and treatment*. New York: Guilford Press.

Rosen, R. C., Leiblum, S. R., & Hall, K. S. (1987). *Etiological and predictive factors in sex therapy*. Unpublished manuscript.

Rosenberg, E. (1989). Beyond the facts: Sexuality education in junior/middle school. In C. Cassell & P. M. Wilson (Eds.), *Sexuality education: A resource book*. New York: Garland.

Rosenthal, E., & Keshet, H. F. (1980). *Fathers without partners*. New York: Rowman & Littlefield.

Ross, M. W., Paulsen, J. A., & Stalstrom, O. W. (1988). Homosexuality and mental health: A cross-cultural review. In M. W. Ross (Ed.), *The treatment of homosexuals with mental health disorders*. New York: Harrington Park Press.

Rothblum, E. (1988). Introduction: Lesbianism as a model of a positive lifestyle for women. *Women and Therapy, 8*, 1–12.

Rothenberg, E. P. S. (1988). *Racism and sexism: An integrated study*. New York: St. Martin's Press.

Rotheram-Borus, M. J., & Koopman, C. (1991). AIDS and adolescents. In R. M. Lerner, A. C. Petersen, & J. Brooks-Gunn (Eds.), *Encyclopedia of adolescence*. New York: Garland.

Ruan, F. F., & Bullough, V. L. (1989). Sex in China. *Medical Aspects of Human Sexuality, 6*, 59–62.

Rubenfeld, A. R. (1987). Legal aspects of AIDS. In V. Gong & N. Rudnick (Eds.), *AIDS: Facts and issues*. New Brunswick, NJ: Rutgers University Press.

Rubenstein, C. (1983). The modern art of courtly love. *Psychology Today*, July, pp. 40–49.

Rubenstein, C. (1988). Is there sex after baby? *Utne Reader*, September, pp. 66–67.

Rubenstein, E., Panzarine, S., & Lanning, P. (1990). Peer counseling with adolescent mothers: A pilot program. *Families in Society: The Journal of Contemporary Human Services, 71*(3), 136–141.

Rubin, R. Reinisch, J., & Haskett, R. (1981). Postnatal gonadal steroid effects on human behavior. *Science, 211*, 1318–1324.

Rubin, R. H. (1985). It is important that both men and women have premarital sex, especially with the person they are considering for marriage. In I. H. Feldman & M. Feldman (Eds.), *Current controversies in marriage and family*. Beverly Hills, CA: Sage.

Rubin, T. I. (1983). *One to one*. New York: Viking.

Rubin, Z. (1980). *Children's friendships*. Cambridge, MA: Harvard University Press.

Rubin, Z., Peplau, A., & Hill, C. T. (1981). Loving and leaving: Sex differences in romantic attachments. *Sex Roles, 7*, 821–834.

Rubinow, D. R., & Roy-Byrne, P. (1984). Premenstrual syndromes: Overview from a methodical perspective. *American Journal of Psychiatry, 141*, 163–169.

Rubinson, L., & Neutens, J. (1987). *Research techniques in the health sciences.* New York: Macmillan.

Ruble, D. N., Fleming, A. S., Hackel, L., & Stangor, C. (1988). Changes in the marital relationship during the transition to first-time motherhood: Effects of violated expectations concerning division of household labor. *Journal of Personality and Social Psychology, 55*, 78–87.

Russell, D. E. (1975). *The politics of rape: The victim's perspective.* New York: Stein & Day.

Russell, D. E. H. (1982). *Rape in marriage.* New York: Macmillan.

Russell, D. E. H. (1983). The incidence and prevalence of intrafamilial and extrafamilial sexual abuse of female children. *Child Abuse and Neglect, 7*, 133–146.

Russell, D. E. H. (1984). *Sexual exploitation: Rape, child sexual abuse, and sexual harassment.* Beverly Hills, CA: Sage.

Russell, D. E. H. (1986). *The secret trauma: Incest in the lives of girls and women.* New York: Basic Books.

Russell, G. (1983). *The changing role of fathers?* Lawrence, MA: Queensland University Press.

Ryan, A. S., Rush, D., & Krieger, F. W. (1991). Recent declines in breastfeeding in the United States, 1984–1989. *Pediatrics, 88*, 719–725.

Ryan, K., & Cooper, J. M. (1980). *Those who can, teach* (3rd ed.). Boston: Houghton Mifflin.

Sabatier, R. (1988). *Blaming others: Prejudice, race, and worldwide AIDS.* Philadelphia: New Society Publishers.

Sack, A. R., Billingham, R. E., & Howard, R. D. (1985). Premarital contraceptive use: A discriminant analysis approach. *Archives of Sexual Behavior, 14*, 165–182.

Sackett, C. (1990). Spinal cord conditions and sexuality. In C. I. Fogel & D. Lauver (Eds.), *Sexual health promotion.* Philadelphia: W. B. Saunders.

Sacks, S. L. (1983). Genital ulcers: Syphilis, herpes, and chancroid. *Journal of the American Medical Association, 2*, 526–527.

Sadker, M., & Sadker, D. (1986). Sexism in the classroom: From grade school to graduate school. *Phi Delta Kappan, 3*, 512–515.

Sadker, M., Sadker, D., & Klein, S. S. (1986). Abolishing misperceptions about sex equity in education. *Theory into Practice, 25*, 219–226.

Sager, C. J. (1983). *Treating the remarried family.* New York: Brunner/Mazel.

Saghir, M. T., & Robins, E. (1973). *Male and female homosexuality.* Baltimore: Williams & Wilkins.

Saliba, P. (1982). Research project on sexual orientation. *The Bi-Monthly Newsletter of the Bisexual Center of San Francisco, 6*, 3–6.

Salter, A. C. (1988). *Treating child sex offenders and victims.* Newbury Park, CA: Sage.

Sampson, E. E. (1985). The decentralization of identity: Toward a revised concept of personal and social order. *American Psychologist, 40*, 1203–1211.

Samuels, M., & Samuels, N. (1986). *The well pregnancy book.* New York: Summit Books.

Sanday, P. R. (1986). Rape and the silencing of the feminine. In S. Tomaselli & R. Porter (Eds.), *Rape.* London: Basil Blackwell.

Sanders, D., Warner, P., Backstrom, T., & Bancroft, J. (1983). Mood, sexuality, hormones, and the menstrual cycle: 1. Changes in mood and physical state. *Psychosomatic Medicine, 45*, 487–501.

Sanders, L. L. Jr. (1986). Treatment of sexually transmitted chlamydial infections. *Journal of the American Medical Association, 255*, 1750–1756.

Sanger, M. (1938). *Margaret Sanger.* New York: Norton.

Santrock, J. W. (1990). *Adolescence* (4th ed.). Dubuque, IA: Wm. C. Brown.

Sarason, I. G., & Sarason, B. R. (1989). *Abnormal psychology* (6th ed.). Englewood Cliffs, NJ: Prentice Hall.

Sargent, T. O. (1988). Fetishism. In D. M. Dailey (Ed.), *The sexually unusual: Guide to understanding and helping.* New York: Harrington Park Press.

Sarnoff, I., & Sarnoff, S. (1989). *Love-centered marriage in a self-centered world.* New York: Hemisphere.

Sarrel, L. J., & Sarrel, P. M. (1984). *Sexual turning points: The seven stages of adult sexuality.* New York: Macmillan.

Saslawsky, D. A., & Wurtele, S. K. (1986). Educating children about sexual abuse: Implications for pediatric intervention and possible prevention. *Journal of Pediatric Psychology, 11*, 235–245.

Satter, E. (1990). The feeding relationship: Problems and interventions. *Journal of Pediatrics, 117*(2), S181–S194.

Satterfield, S. B. (1988). Transsexualism. In D. M. Dailey (Ed.), *The sexually unusual: Guide to understanding and helping.* New York: Harrington Park Press.

Sattin, R. W., Rubin, G. L., Wingo, P. A., Webster, L. A., & Ory, H. W. (1986). Oral contraceptive use and the risk of breast cancer. *New England Journal of Medicine, 315*, 405–411.

Saul, S. C., & Scherman, A. (1984). Divorce grief and personal adjustment in divorced persons who remarry or remain single. *Journal of Divorce, 7*, 75–85.

Savin-Williams, R. C. (1990). Gay and lesbian adolescents. In F. W. Bozett & M. B. Sussman (Eds.), *Homosexuality and family relations.* New York: Haworth Press.

Savin-Williams, R. C., & Small, S. A. (1986). The timing of puberty and its relationship to adolescent and parent perceptions of family interactions. *Developmental Psychology, 32*, 342–347.

Sawley, L. (1989). Infant feeding. *Nursing, 39*, 18–25.

Saxton, L. (1990). *The individual, marriage, and the family* (7th ed.). Belmont, CA: Wadsworth.

Scales, P. (1982). Values' role in sexuality education. *Planned Parenthood Review, 12*, 6–8.

Scanzoni, J., & Fox, G. L. (1980). Sex roles, family, and society: The seventies and beyond. *Journal of Marriage and the Family, 11*, 88–96.

Scharff, D. E., & Scharff, J. S. (1987). Object relations theory and family therapy. In D. E. Scharff & J. S. Scharff (Eds.), *Object relations family therapy.* Northvale, NJ: Jason Aronson.

Scharli, A. F. (1989). Circumcision: An everlasting discussion. *Pediatric Surgical Intervention, 4*, 219–221.

Scheppele, K. L., & Bart, P. B. (1983). Through women's eyes: Defining danger in the wake of sexual assault. *Journal of Social Issues, 39*, 63–81.

Schiavi, R. C., & Fisher, C. (1982). Assessment of diabetic impotence: Measurement of nocturnal erections. *Clinics in Endocrinology and Metabolism, 11*, 769–784.

Schiavi, R. C., & Schreiner-Engel, P. (1988, April). *Healthy aging and male sexual arousal.* Paper presented at the annual meeting of the Society for Sex Therapy and Research, New York.

Schinke, S. P., Holden, G. W., & Moncher, M. S. (1989). Preventing HIV infection among black and Hispanic adolescents. *Journal of Social Work and Human Sexuality, 8,* 63–73.

Schmitt, E. (1991). Citing AIDS, judge backs service ban on gays. *New York Times.* December 10, B-28.

Schofield, M. (1965). *Sociological aspects of homosexuality.* Boston: Little, Brown.

Scholz, C. (1989). Elementary school sexuality education. In C. Cassell & P. M. Wilson (Eds.), *Sexuality education: A resource book.* New York: Garland.

Schover, L. R. (1984). *Prime time: Sexual health for men over fifty.* New York: Holt, Rinehart, & Winston.

Schover, L. R. (1989). Sexual problems in chronic illness. *Principles and practices of sex therapy* (2nd ed.). New York: Guilford.

Schover, L. R., & Jensen, S. B. (1988). *Sexuality and chronic illness.* New York: Guilford.

Schreiner-Engel, P., Schiavi, R. C., Veitorisz, D., & Smith, H. (1987). The differential impact on diabetes type on female sexuality. *Journal of Psychosomatic Research, 31,* 23–33.

Schultz, D. (1980). Estrogen replacement: A qualified okay. *Science Digest, 87,* 56–58.

Schur, E. M. (1988). *The Americanization of sex.* Philadelphia: Temple University Press.

Schwartz, M. F., & Brasted, W. S. (1985). Sexual addiction. *Medical Aspects of Human Sexuality, 19,* 103–107.

Schwartz, M. F., & Masters, W. H. (1983). Conceptual factors in the treatment of paraphilias: A preliminary report. *Journal of Sex and Marital Therapy, 9,* 3–18.

Scott, J. R. (Ed.). (1990). *Danforth's obstetrics and gynecology* (6th ed.). Philadelphia: Lippincott.

Scott, J. R. (1986). Spontaneous abortion. In D. Danforth & J. R. Scott (Eds.), *Obstetrics and gynecology* (5th ed.). Philadelphia: Lippincott.

Scotti, A. T., & Moore, T. A. (1987). *Safe sex.* Toronto: Paperjacks.

Scott-Jones, D., & White, A. B. (1990). Correlates of sexual activity in early adolescence. *Journal of Early Adolescence, 10*(2), 221–238.

Seagraves, K. B. (1989). Extramarital affairs. *Medical Aspects of Human Sexuality, 23,* 99–105.

Seaman, B. (1972). *Free and female.* New York: Coward, McGann, & Goghegan.

Sedaka, S. D., & O'Reilly, M. (1986). The financial implications of AIDS. *Caring, 5,* 38–46.

Sedney, M. A., & Brooks, B. (1984). Factors associated with a history of childhood sexual experiences in a nonclinical female population. *Journal of the American Academy of Child Psychiatry, 23,* 215–218.

Segal, J. (1984). *The sex lives of college students.* Wayne, PA: Miles Standish Press.

Segraves, R. T. (1985). Female orgasm and psychiatric drugs. *Journal of Sex Education and Therapy, 11,* 69–71.

Segraves, R. T. (1986). Implications of the behavioral sex therapies for psychoanalytic theory and practice: Intrapsychic sequelae of symptom removal in the patient and spouse. *Journal of the American Academy of Psychoanalysis, 14,* 485–493.

Segraves, R. T. (1988a). Hormones and libido. In S. R. Leiblum & R. C. Rosen (Eds.), *Sexual desire disorders.* New York: Guilford.

Segraves, R. T. (1988b). Drugs and desire. In S. R. Leiblum & R. C. Rosen (Eds.), *Sexual desire disorders.* New York: Guilford.

Seibel, M. M. (1990). *Infertility: A comprehensive text.* Norwalk, CT: Appleton & Lange.

Seibert, J. M., & Olson, R. A. (Eds.). (1989). *Children, adolescents, and AIDS.* Lincoln: University of Nebraska Press.

Selman, R. (1981). The child as friendship philosopher. In J. M. Gottman (Ed.), *The development of children's friendships.* Cambridge, Eng.: Cambridge University Press.

Sem-Jacobsen, C. W. (1968). *Depth-electrographic stimulation of the human brain and behavior.* Springfield, IL: Chas. C. Thomas.

Senderowitz, J., & Paxman, J. M. (1985). Adolescent fertility: Worldwide concerns. *Population Bulletin, 40,* 2–36.

Sgroi, S. (Ed.). (1982). *Handbook of clinical intervention in child sexual abuse.* Lexington, MA: Lexington Books.

Sgroi, S., Porter, F., & Blick, L. (1982). Validation of child sexual abuse. In S. Sgroi (Ed.), *Handbook of clinical intervention in child sexual abuse.* Lexington, MA: Lexington Books.

Shaevitz, M. H. (1984). *The superwoman syndrome.* New York: Warner Books.

Shaffer, M. (1982). *Life after stress.* New York: Plenum.

Shaffer, M., & Sweet, R. L. (1989). Pelvic inflammatory disease in adolescent females: Epidemiology, pathogenesis, diagnosis, treatment, and sequelae. *Pediatric Clinics of North America, 36,* 513–532.

Shakin, M., Sternglanz, S. H., & Shakin, D. (1985). Infant clothing: Sex labeling for strangers. *Sex Roles, 5,* 28–37.

Shapiro, H. I. (1983). *The pregnancy book for today's woman.* New York: Harper & Row.

Shapiro, S. (1986). Oral contraceptives—time to take stock. *New England Journal of Medicine, 315,* 450–451.

Sharabany, R., Gershoni, R., & Hofman, J. E. (1981). Girlfriend, boyfriend: Age and sex differences in intimate friendships. *Developmental Psychology, 17,* 800–808.

Sharlip, I. D. (1984). Diagnosis and management of organic male sexual dysfunction. In J. M. Swanson & K. A. Forrest (Eds.), *Men's reproductive health.* New York: Springer.

Shaver, P., Furman, W., & Buhrmester, D. (1985). Transition to college: Network changes, social skills, and loneliness. In S. Duck & D. Perlman (Eds.), *Understanding personal relationships.* Beverly Hills, CA: Sage.

Shea, V. (1990). Developmental disability and sexuality. In C. I. Fogel & D. Lauver (Eds.), *Sexual health promotion.* Philadelphia: W. B. Saunders.

Sheehy, G. (1983). Decriminalization of prostitution will support crime. In B. Leone & M. T. O'Neill (Eds.), *Sexual values.* St. Paul, MN: Greenhaven Press.

Shepard, J. M. (1987). *Sociology* (3rd ed.). St. Paul, MN: West.

Sherwin, B. B. (1986, May). *Effects on sexual behavior of the chronic administration of estrogen and/or androgen to postmenopausal women.* Paper presented at the 12th annual meeting of the International Academy of Sex Research, Amsterdam.

Sherwin, B. B., Gelfand, M. M., & Brender, W. (1985). Androgen enhances sexual motivation of females: A prospective cross-over study of sex steroid administration in the surgical menopause. *Psychosomatic Medicine, 47,* 339–351.

Shilling, D. (1985). *Redress for success: Using the law to enforce your rights as a woman.* New York: Penguin Books.

Shiono, P. H., Klebanoff, M. A., & Rhoads, G. G. (1986). Smoking and drinking during pregnancy: Their effects on preterm birth. *Journal of the American Medical Association*, *225*, 82–84.

Shornack, L. L., & Ahmed, F. (1989). Adolescent religiousness and pregnancy prevention. *Journal of Marriage and the Family*, *51*, 1083–1089.

Shostak, A. B., & McLouth, G. (1984). *Men and abortion: Lessons, losses, and love*. New York: Praeger.

Shotland, R., & Goodstein, L. (1983). Just because she doesn't want to doesn't mean it's rape: An experimentally-based causal model of the perception of rape in a dating situation. *Social Psychology Quarterly*, *46*, 220–232.

Shoupe, D., Mishell, D. R., Jr., Brenner, P. F., & Spitz, I. M. (1986, May). Pregnancy termination with a high and medium dosage regimen of RU 486. *Contraception*, *33*, 455–461.

Shuran, P. (1987). *Women, society, the state, and abortion: A structuralist analysis*. New York: Praeger.

Siegel, R. (1982). Cocaine and sexual dysfunction. *Journal of Psychoactive Drugs*, *14*, 71–74.

Siegel, R. (1990). *Intoxication*. New York: Pocket Books.

Siegelman, M. (1974). Parental background of male homosexuals and heterosexuals. *Archives of Sexual Behavior*, *3*, 3–18.

Sikorski, J. M. (1985). Knowledge, concerns, and questions of wives of convalescent coronary artery bypass graft surgery patients. *Journal of Cardiac Rehabilitation*, *5*, 74–85.

Silberman, B. O., & Hawkins, R. O. (1988). Lesbian women and gay men: Issues for counseling. In E. Weinstein & E. Rosen (Eds.), *Sexuality counseling: Issues and implications*. Monterey, CA: Brooks/Cole.

Silbert, M. H. (1984). Treatment of prostitute victims of sexual assault. In I. R. Stuart & J. G. Greer (Eds.), *Victims of sexual aggression: Treatment of children, women, and men*. New York: Van Nostrand Reinhold.

Silbert, M. H., & Pines, A. M. (1982). Entrance into prostitution. *Youth and Society*, *13*, 471–500.

Silver, R. L., Boon, C., & Stones, M. H. (1983). Searching for meaning in misfortune. *Journal of Social Issues*, *39*, 81–101.

Silverberg, E., Boring, C. C., & Squires, T. S. (1990). Cancer statistics, 1990. *Ca-A Cancer Journal for Clinicians*, *40*, 9–26.

Simenauer, J., & Carroll, D. (1982). *Singles: The new Americans*. New York: Simon & Schuster.

Simon, W., & Gagnon, J. H. (1987). A sexual scripts approach. In J. H. Geer & W. O'Donohue (Eds.), *Theories of human sexuality*. New York: Plenum.

Simons, R. G., & Blyth, D. A. (1988). *Moving into adolescence: The impact of pubertal change and school context*. New York: Aldine.

Simpson, J. A. (1990). Influence of attachment styles on romantic relationships. *Journal of Personality and Social Psychology*, *59*, 971–980.

Simpson, J. L. (1990). Genetic causes of spontaneous abortion. *Contemporary Obstetrics and Gynecology*, *35*, 25–34.

Singer, J., & Singer, I. (1972). Types of female orgasm. *Journal of Sex Research*, *8*, 255–267.

Sizer, F. S., Whitney, E. N. (1988). *Life choices*. St. Paul, MN: West.

Skalka, P. (1984). *The American Medical Association guide to health and well-being after fifty*. New York: Random House.

Skeen, P., & Robinson, B. E. (1985). Gay fathers and gay nonfathers relationships with their parents. *Journal of Sex Research*, *21*, 86–91.

Sloan, I. J. (1987). *Homosexual conduct and the law*. New York: Oceana Publications.

Sloan, I. J. (1988). *AIDS law: Implications for the individual and society*. New York: Oceana Publications.

Sloan, S. Z., & L'Abate, L. (1985). Intimacy. In L. L'Abate (Ed.), *The handbook of family psychology and therapy*. Homewood, IL: Free Press.

Sloane, E. (1985). *Biology of women* (2nd ed.). New York: Wiley.

Smith, E. A., & Udry, J. R. (1985). Coital and non-coital sexual behavior of white and black adolescents. *American Journal of Public Health*, *10*, 1200–1218.

Smith, L. S., Lauver, D., & Gray, P. A., Jr. (1990). Sexually transmitted diseases. In C. I. Fogel & D. Lauver (Eds.), *Sexual health promotion*. Philadelphia: Saunders.

Smith, P. B., & Kolenda, K. (1984). The male role in teenage pregnancy. In O. Pocs (Ed.), *Human sexuality 84/85*. Guilford, CT: Dushkin.

Smith, S. F., & Smith, C. M. (1990). *Personal health choices*. Boston: Jones & Bartlett.

Snell, W. E., Jr., Belk, S. S., Flowers, A., & Warren, J. (1988). Women's and men's willingness to self-disclose to therapists and friends: The moderating influence of instrumental, expressive, masculine, and feminine topics. *Sex Roles*, *18*, 59–73.

Snell, W. E., Jr., Miller, R. S., & Belk, S. S. (1988). Development of the emotional self-disclosure scale. *Sex Roles*, *18*, 59–73.

Snyder, M., Berscheid, E., & Glick, P. (1985). Focusing on the exterior and the interior: Two investigations on the initiation of personal relationships. *Journal of Personality and Social Psychology*, *48*, 1427–1439.

Snyder, M., & Simpson, J. A. (1986). Orientations toward romantic relationships. In D. S. Perlman & S. Duck (Eds.), *Intimate relationships: Development, dynamics, and deterioration*. Beverly Hills, CA: Sage.

Snyder, M., Simpson, J. A., & Gangestad, S. (1986). Personality and sexual relations. *Journal of Personality and Social Psychology*, *51*, 181–190.

Solie, L. J., & Fielder, L. J. (1988). The relationship between sex role identity and a widow's adjustment to the loss of a spouse. *Omega*, *18*, 33–40.

Sollie, D. L., & Fisher, J. L. (1985). Sex role orientation, intimacy of topic and target person differences in self-disclosure among women. *Sex Roles*, *12*, 917–929.

Solnick, R. E., & Corby, N. (1984). Human sexuality and aging. In D. S. Woodruff & J. E. Birren (Eds.), *Aging: Scientific perspectives and social issues* (2nd ed.). Monterey, CA: Brooks/Cole.

Somers, L., & Somers, B. C. (1989). *Talking to your children about love and sex*. New York: Penguin Books.

Sonenstein, F. L., Pleck, J. H., & Ku, L. C. (1989). Sexual activity, condom use, and AIDS awareness in a national sample of adolescent males. *Family Planning Perspectives*, *21*, 152–158.

Sophie, J. (1986). A critical examination of stage theories of lesbian identity development. *Journal of Homosexuality*, *12*, 39–51.

Sorenson, C. (1973). *Adolescent sexuality in contemporary America*. New York: Worth.

Sorochan, W. D. (1981). *Promoting your health*. New York: Wiley.

Sorrenti-Little, L., Bagley, C., & Robertson, S. (1984). An operational definition of the long-term harmfulness of sexual relations with peers and adults by young children. *Canadian Children: Journal of the Canadian Association for Young Children*, *9*, 26–33.

Soules, M. R. (1985). The in-vitro fertilization pregnancy rate: Let's be honest with one another. *Fertility and Sterility, 43*(4), 512.

Spanier, G. B., & Furstenberg, F. F., Jr. (1982). Remarriage after divorce: A longitudinal analysis of well-being. *Journal of Marriage and the Family, 44,* 709–720.

Spanier, G. B., & Thompson, L. (1984). *Parting: The aftermath of divorce and separation.* Beverly Hills, CA: Sage.

Spence, S. H. (1985). Group versus individual treatment of primary and secondary female orgasmic dysfunction. *Behaviour Research and Therapy, 23,* 539–548.

Spencer, M. B. (1991). Identity development and minority adolescents. In R. M. Lerner, A. C. Petersen, & J. Brooks-Gunn (Eds.), *Encyclopedia of adolescence.* New York: Garland.

Spencer, S., & Zeiss, A. (1987). Sex roles and sexual dysfunction in college students. *Journal of Sex Research, 23,* 338–347.

Speroff, L., Glass, R., & Kase, N. (1989). *Clinical gynecologic endocrinology and infertility* (4th ed.). Baltimore: Williams & Wilkins.

Sperry, R. W. (1982). Some effects of disconnecting the cerebral hemispheres. *Science, 217,* 1223–1226.

Spieler, S. (1982). Can fathers be nurturers? *Marriage and Divorce Today, 7,* 1.

Spitze, G. (1988). Work and family. *Journal of Marriage and the Family, 50,* 37–48.

Spitzer, P. G., & Weiner, N. J. (1989). Transmission of HIV infection from a woman to a man by oral sex. *New England Journal of Medicine, 320,* 251.

Spitzer, R. L., Skodol, A. E., Gibbon, M., & Williams, J. B. (1981). *DSM-III casebook.* Washington, DC: American Psychiatric Association.

Spock, B. (1945). *The common sense book of baby and child care.* New York: Duell, Sloan, & Pearce.

Sponaugle, G. C. (1989). Attitudes toward extramarital relations. In K. McKinney & S. Sprecher (Eds.), *Human sexuality: The societal and interpersonal context.* Norwood, NJ: Ablex.

Sprecher, S. (1986). The relation between inequity and emotions in close relationships. *Social Psychology Quarterly, 49,* 309–321.

Sprecher, S. (1989). Influences on choice of a partner and on sexual decision making in the relationship. In K. McKinney & S. Sprecher (Eds.), *Human sexuality: The societal and interpersonal context.* Norwood, NJ: Ablex.

Sprecher, S., & McKinney, K. (1987). Barriers in the initiation of intimate heterosexual relationships and strategies for intervention. In W. Ricketts & H. L. Gochros (Eds.), *Intimate relationships: Some social perspectives on love.* New York: Haworth Press.

Sprecher, S., McKinney, K., Walsh, R., & Anderson, C. (1988). A revision of the Reiss premarital sexual permissiveness scale. *Journal of Marriage and the Family, 47,* 121–136.

Springer, S. P., & Deutsch, G. (1986). *Left brain, right brain* (rev. ed.). San Francisco: Freeman.

Stadel, B. (1989). Oral contraceptives used in women with a family history of breast cancer. *Obstetrics and Gynecology, 73,* 977–983.

Stamm, W. E., & Holmes, J. (1984). Chlamydia trachomatis infections of the adult. In K. Holmes, P. Mardh, P. Sparling, & P. Wiesner (Eds.), *Sexually transmitted diseases.* New York: McGraw-Hill.

Stampfer, M. J. (1988). A prospective study of past uses of oral contraceptive agents and risk of cardiovascular diseases. *New England Journal of Medicine, 17,* 1313–1318.

Stanway, A. (1989). *The art of sensual loving.* New York: Carroll & Graf.

Stark, E. (1984, May). The unspeakable family secret. *Psychology Today,* pp. 38–46.

Stark, E. (1986, October). Young and pregnant. *Psychology Today,* pp. 28–35.

Starr, B., & Weiner, M. B. (1981). *Sex and sexuality in the mature years.* New York: Stein & Day.

Staver, S. (1989). Women found contracting HIV via unprotected sex. *American Medical News, 6,* 4.

Steele, B., & Alexander, H. (1981). Long-term effects of sexual abuse in childhood. In P. B. Mrazek & C. H. Kempe (Eds.), *Sexually abused children and their families.* Oxford: Pergamon.

Steele, C. M., & Josephs, R. A. (1990). Alcohol myopia: Its prized and dangerous effects. *American Psychologist, 45,* 921–933.

Stein, P. J. (1981). *Single life: Unmarried adults in a social context.* New York: St. Martin's Press.

Stein, P. J. (1989). The diverse world of the single adult. In J. M. Henslin (Ed.), *Marriage and family in a changing society* (3rd ed.). New York: Free Press.

Stein, P. J., & Fingrutd, M. (1985). The single life has more potential for happiness than marriage and parenthood for both men and women. In H. Feldman & M. Feldman (Eds.), *Current controversies in marriage and family.* Beverly Hills, CA: Sage.

Stein, R. A. (1980). Sexual counseling and coronary heart disease. In S. R. Leiblum & L. A. Pervin (Eds.), *Principles and practices of sex therapy.* New York: Guilford.

Stein, T. S. (1988). Theoretical considerations in psychotherapy with gay men and lesbian women. In M. W. Ross (Ed.), *The treatment of homosexuals with mental health disorders.* New York: Harrington Park Press.

Stephen, T. D., & Harrison, T. M. (1985). Gender, sex-role identity, and communication: A Q-sort analysis of behavioral differences. *Communication Research Reports, 2,* 53–61.

Sternberg, R. J. (1985). The measure of love. *Science Digest, 60,* 78–79.

Sternberg, R. J. (1986). A triangular theory of love. *Psychological Review, 93,* 119–135.

Sternberg, R. J. (1988). Liking versus loving: A comparative evaluation of theories. *Psychological Bulletin, 102,* 331–345.

Sternberg, R. J. (1988). Triangulating love. In R. J. Sternberg & M. L. Barnes (Eds.), *The psychology of love.* New Haven, CT: Yale University Press.

Stewart, D. E. (1983). *The television family: A content analysis of the portrayal of family life in prime time television.* Melbourne: Institute of Family Studies.

Stine, G. J. (1993). *Acquired immune deficiency syndrome: Biological, medical, social and legal issues.* Englewood Cliffs, NJ: Prentice Hall.

Stinnett, N., & DeFrain, J. (1985). *Secrets of strong families.* Boston: Little, Brown.

Stinnett, N., Walters, J., & Stinnett, N. (1991). *Relationships in marriage and the family* (3rd ed.). New York: Macmillan.

Stock, W., & Geer, J. A. (1982). A study of fantasy-based sexual arousal in women. *Archives of Sexual Behavior, 11,* 33–47.

Stoklosa, J. (1984). Counseling men about disability, illness, and aging. In J. M. Swanson & K. A. Forrest (Eds.), *Men's reproductive health.* New York: Springer.

Stone, J. D. (1987). Marital and sexual counseling of elderly couples. In G. R. Weeks & L. Hof (Eds.), *Integrating sex and marital therapy: A clinical guide*. New York: Brunner/Mazel.

Stone, K. M., Grimes, D. A., & Magder, L. S. (1986). Primary prevention of sexually transmitted diseases: A primer for clinicians. *Journal of the American Medical Association, 255*, 1763–1766.

Stone, S. (1989). Assessing oral contraceptive risks. *Medical Aspects of Human Sexuality, 23*, 112–122.

Stoppard, J. M., & Paisley, K. J. (1987). Masculinity, femininity, life stress, and depression. *Sex Roles, 16*, 489–496.

Storms, M. D. (1981). A theory of erotic orientation development. *Psychological Review, 88*, 340–353.

Strahle, W. M. (1983). A model of premarital coitus and contraceptive behavior among female adolescents. *Archives of Sexual Behavior, 12*, 67–94.

Straus, S., Seidlin, M., & Takiff, H. (1984). Management of mucocutaneous herpes simplex. *Drugs, 27*, 364–372.

Streissguth, A. P. (1984). Intrauterine alcohol and nicotine exposure: Attention and reaction time in four-year-old children. *Developmental Psychology, 20*, 533–541.

Streissguth, A. P., Barr, H. M., & Martin, D. C. (1983). Maternal alcohol use and neonatal habituation assessed with the Braezelton Scale. *Child Development, 54*, 1109–1118.

Streissguth, A. P., Barr, H. M., Sampson, P. D., & Darby, B. (1989). IQ at age four in relation to maternal alcohol use and smoking during pregnancy. *Developmental Psychology, 25*, 3–11.

Strouse, J. (1987). College bars as social settings for heterosexual contacts. *Journal of Sex Research, 23*, 374–382.

Strunin, L., & Hingston, R. (1987). Acquired immunodeficiency syndrome and adolescents: Knowledge, beliefs, and attitudes, and behaviors. *Pediatrics, 79*, 825–828.

Stuart, F., Hammond, C., & Pett, M. (1987). Inhibited sexual desire in women. *Archives of Sexual Behavior, 16*, 91–106.

Stubblefield, P. (1984). Fertility after induced abortion: A prospective follow-up study. *Obstetrics and Gynecology, 63*, 186–193.

Stubblefield, P., Fuller, A., & Foster, S. (1988). Ultra-sound guided intrauterine removal of intrauterine contraceptive devices in pregnancy. *Obstetrics and Gynecology, 72*, 961.

Sturkie, K. (1983). Structured group treatment for sexually abused children. *Health and Social Work, 8*, 299–308.

Sue, D. (1979). Erotic fantasies of college students during coitus. *Journal of Sex Research, 15*, 299–305.

Sullivan, D. A., & Weitz, R. (1988). *Labor pains: Modern midwives and home birth*. New Haven, CT: Yale University Press.

Sullivan, W. (1982, December 1). Reverence of the elderly: A factor of longevity in Caucasus. *New York Times*, pp. B-16-18.

Summit, R. (1983). The child sexual abuse accommodation syndrome. *Child Abuse and Neglect, 7*, 177–193.

Summit, R., & Kryso, J. (1981). Sexual abuse of children: A clinical spectrum. *American Journal of Orthopsychiatry, 48*, 237–251.

Surgeon general's workshop on pornography and public health. (1986). Washington, DC: U.S. Government Printing Office.

Surgeon general's report on acquired immune deficiency syndrome. (1987). Washington, DC: U.S. Department of Health and Human Services.

Suran, B. G., & Rizzo, J. V. (1983). *Special children: An integrative approach* (2nd ed.). Glenview, IL: Scott, Foresman.

Surra, C. A., & Huston, T. L. (1986). Mate selection as a social transition. In D. S. Perlman & S. Duck (Eds.), *Intimate relationships: Development, dynamics, and deterioration*. Beverly Hills, CA: Sage.

Surrey, J. (1983). *Self-in-relation: A theory of women's development*. Wellesley, MA: Stone Centers Working Papers Series.

Susman, E. J., & Dorn, L. D. (1991). Hormones and behavior in adolescence. In R. M. Lerner, A. C. Petersen, & J. Brooks-Gunn (Eds.), *Encyclopedia of adolescence*. New York: Garland.

Swanson, J. M., & Forrest, K. A. (Eds.). (1984). *Men's reproductive health*. New York: Springer.

Sweet, E. (1985, October). Date rape: The story of an epidemic and those who deny it. *Campus Times*, pp. 56–86.

Swensen, C. H. (1985). Love in the family. In L. L'Abate (Ed.), *The handbook of family psychology and therapy*. Homewood, IL: Dorsey.

Swensen, C. H., & Trahaug, G. (1985). Commitment and the long-term marriage. *Journal of Marriage and the Family, 47*, 939–945.

Swinkler, M. (1986). Chlamydia trachomatis genital infections in college women. *Journal of American College Health, 34*, 207–209.

Talmadge, W. C. (1985a). Premarital sexuality. In L. L'Abate (Ed.), *The handbook of family psychology and therapy*. Homewood, IL: Dorsey.

Talmadge, W. C. (1985b). Marital sexuality. In L. L'Abate (Ed.), *The handbook of family psychology and therapy*. Homewood, IL: Dorsey.

Talmadge, W. C., & Talmadge, L. D. (1985). A transactional perspective on the treatment of sexual dysfunctions. In L. L'Abate (Ed.), *The handbook of family psychology and therapy*. Homewood, IL: Dorsey.

Tanner, J. M. (1981). Growth and maturation during adolescence. *Nutrition Review, 39*, 43–55.

Tanner, J. M. (1991). Adolescent growth spurt. In R. M. Lerner, A. C. Petersen, & J. Brooks-Gunn (Eds.), *Encyclopedia of adolescence*. New York: Garland.

Tarver, J. D., & Miller, H. M. (1986). Women head Botswana's households. *Population Today, 14*, 4–9.

Task Force on Pediatric AIDS. (1989). Pediatric AIDS and human immunodeficiency virus infection. *American Psychologist, 44*, 248–264.

Tatum, M. L. (1989). Overview: A perspective on sexuality education school programs. In C. Cassell & P. M. Wilson (Eds.), *Sexuality Education*. New York: Garland.

Tavris, C., & Sadd, S. (1975). *The Redbook report on female sexuality*. New York: Delacorte Press.

Tavris, C., & Wade, C. (1984). *The longest war: Sex differences in perspective* (2nd ed.). New York: Harcourt Brace Jovanovich.

Taylor, D. (1985). *Women: A world review*. New York: Oxford University Press.

Taylor, D. (1988). *Red flower: Rethinking menstruation*. Freedom, CA: Crossing Press.

Taylor, R. L. (1984). Marital therapy in the treatment of incest. *Social Casework: The Journal of Contemporary Social Work, 65*, 195–202.

Taylor, S. E. (1983). Adjustment to life-threatening events: A theory of cognitive adaptation. *American Psychologist, 53*, 1161–1173.

Teti, D. M., & Lamb, M. E. (1989). Socioeconomic and marital outcomes of adolescent marriage, adolescent childbirth, and their co-occurrence. *Journal of Marriage and the Family, 51,* 203–212.

Thomas, D. B. (1989). Oral contraceptives and cancer risk: Comparing results from developing and developed countries. *Outlook, 7,* 2–7.

Thomas, E., Rickel, A. U., & Butler, C. (1990). Adolescent pregnancy and parenting. *Journal of Primary Prevention, 10*(3), 195–206.

Thompson, R. A. (1991). Construction and reconstruction of early attachments: Taking perspective on attachment theory and research. In D. P. Keating & H. G. Rosen (Eds.), *Constructivist perspectives on atypical development.* Hillsdale, NJ: Erlbaum.

Thornburg, H. (1981). Adolescent sources of information about sex. *Journal of School Health, 51,* 274–277.

Thorne, B., & Luria, Z. (1986). Sexuality and gender in children's daily worlds. *Social Problems, 33,* 176–190.

Thornton, A., & Camburn, D. (1987). The influence of the family on premarital sexual attitudes and behavior. *Demography, 24,* 323–340.

Thorp, J. M., & Bowes, W. A. (1989). Episiotomy: Can its routine use be defended? *American Journal of Obstetrical Gynecology, 160,* 1027–1033.

Tiefer, L., & Melman, A. (1989). Comprehensive evaluation of erectile dysfunction and medical treatments. In S. R. Leiblum & R. C. Rosen (Eds.), *Principles and practice of sex therapy* (2nd ed.). New York: Guilford.

Tiefer, L., Pedersen, B., & Melman, A. (1988). Psychosocial follow-up of penile prosthesis implant patients and partners. *Journal of Sex and Marital Therapy, 14,* 184–201.

Tietjen, A. M. (1982). The social networks of preadolescent children in Sweden. *International Journal of Behavioral Development, 5,* 111–130.

Tietze, C. (1983). *Induced abortion: A world review* (5th ed.). New York: Population Council.

Tietze, C., & Henshaw, S. K. (1986). *Induced abortion: A world review* (6th ed.). New York: Alan Guttmacher Institute.

Till, F. J. (1980). *Sexual harassment: A report on the sexual harassment of students.* Washington, DC: Report of the National Advisory Council of Women's Educational Programs.

Tittle, C. K. (1988). Validity, gender research, and studies of the effects of career development interventions. In B. A. Gutek (Ed.), *Applied psychology: An international review.* Beverly Hills, CA: Sage.

Toal, S. D. (1985). *Children's safety and protection training project: Three interrelated analyses.* Stockton, CA: Toal Consultation Services.

Torrington, J. (1985). Pelvic inflammatory disease. *Journal of Obstetric, Gynecologic, and Neonatal Nursing, 14,* 21–31.

Tourney, G., Petrilli, A. J., & Hatfield, L. N. (1975). Hormonal relationships in homosexual men. *American Journal of Psychiatry, 132,* 288–290.

Trainor, C. (1984, August). *Sexual maltreatment in the United States: A five-year perspective.* Paper presented at the International Congress on Child Abuse and Neglect, Montreal.

Traupmann, J., Hatfield, E., & Wexler, P. (1983). Equity and sexual satisfaction in dating couples. *British Journal of Social Psychology, 22,* 33–40.

Treboux, D. A., & Busch-Rossnagel, N. A. (1991). Age differences in adolescent sexual behavior, sexual attitudes, and contraceptive use. In R. M. Lerner, A. C. Petersen, & J. Brooks-Gunn (Eds.), *Encyclopedia of adolescence.* New York: Garland.

Trofatter, K. E., Jr. (1990). Fetal immunology. In R. D. Eden, F. H. Boehm, & M. Haire (Eds.), *Assessment and care of the fetus: Physiological, clinical, and medicolegal principles.* Norwalk, CT: Appleton & Lange.

Troiden, R. R. (1988). *Gay and lesbian identity: A sociological analysis.* Dix Hills, NY: General Hall.

Trussell, J., Hatcher, R. A., Cates, W., Stewart, F. H., & Kost, K. (1990). Contraceptive failure in the United States: An update. *Studies in Family Planning, 21,* 51–54.

Tufts New England Medical Center, Division of Child Psychiatry. (1984). *Sexually exploited children: Service and research project.* Washington, DC: U.S. Department of Justice.

Tuller, N. R. (1988). Couples: The hidden segment of the gay world. In J. P. DeCecco (Ed.), *Gay relationships.* New York: Harrington Park Press.

Turner, B. F., & Adams, C. G. (1988). Reported change in preferred sexual activity over the adult years. *Journal of Sex Research, 25,* 289–303.

Turner, J. S., & Helms, D. B. (1988). *Marriage and family: Traditions and transitions.* San Diego, CA: Harcourt Brace Jovanovich.

Turner, J. S., & Helms, D. B. (1989). *Contemporary adulthood* (4th ed.). Ft. Worth, TX: Holt, Rinehart, & Winston.

Turner, J. S., & Helms, D. B. (1991). *Lifespan development,* (4th ed.). Ft. Worth, TX: Holt, Rinehart, & Winston.

Ulene, A. (1987). *Safe sex in a dangerous world.* New York: Vintage Books.

U.S. Attorney General's Commission on Pornography. (1986). *Final report of the attorney general's commission on pornography.* Washington, DC: U.S. Justice Department.

U.S. Bureau of the Census. (1988). *Statistical abstract of the United States* (108th ed.). Washington, DC: U.S. Government Printing Office.

U.S. Bureau of the Census. (1989). *Statistical abstract of the United States* (109th ed.). Washington, DC: U.S. Government Printing Office.

U.S. Bureau of the Census. (1990). *Statistical abstract of the United States* (110th ed.). Washington, DC: U.S. Government Printing Office.

U.S. Department of Education. (1988). *AIDS and the education of our children.* Washington, DC: U.S. Government Printing Office.

U.S. Department of Health and Human Services. (1986). *Surgeon general's report on acquired immune deficiency syndrome.* Washington, DC: U.S. Government Printing Office.

U.S. Department of Health and Human Services. (1990). *Talking with young people about HIV infection and AIDS.* Washington, DC: U.S. Government Printing Office.

U.S. Federal Bureau of Investigation. (1988). *Uniform crime reports.* Washington, DC: U.S. Government Printing Office.

U.S. Federal Bureau of Investigation. (1990). *Population-at-risk rates and selected crime indicators.* Washington, DC: U.S. Government Printing Office.

U.S. Federal Bureau of Investigation. (1990). *Uniform crime reports.* Washington, DC: U.S. Department of Justice.

Uphold, C., & Susman, E. (1981). Self-reported climacteric symptoms. *Nursing Research, 30,* 84–88.

Vance, E. B., & Wagner, N. N. (1976). Written descriptions of orgasm: A study of sex differences. *Archives of Sexual Behavior, 5,* 87–98.

van de Kaa, D. (1987). Europe's second demographic transition. *Population Bulletin, 42,* 1–59.

Van de Loo, E. (1987). *Genital exposing behavior in adult human males: A clinical study of a coping mechanism.* Thesis, Rijksuniversiteit Leiden, the Netherlands.

Vander Mey, B. J., & Neff, R. L. (1982). Adult–child incest: A review of research and treatment. *Adolescence, 18,* 717–735.

Vander Mey, B. J., & Neff, R. L. (1986). *Incest as child abuse: Research and applications.* New York: Praeger.

Vaudeville, E., & Fisher, A. (1962). Male sexual behavior induced by intracranial electrical stimulation. *Science, 137,* 758–760.

Vaughn, D. (1986). *Uncoupling: How relationships come apart.* New York: Vintage Books.

Ventura, J. N. (1987). The stresses of parenthood reexamined. *Family Relations, 36,* 26–29.

Victor, J. B., Halverson, C. F., & Montague, R. B. (1985). Relations between reflection-impulsivity and behavioral impulsivity. *Developmental Psychology, 21,* 141–148.

Voeller, B. Quoted in Coffey, A. L. (1983). *Growing up: Some thoughts.* New York: National Gay and Lesbian Task Force Report Series.

Vorhees, C. V., & Mollnow, E. (1987). Behavioral teratogenesis: Long-term influences in behavior from early exposure to environmental agents. In J. D. Osofsky (Ed.), *Handbook of infant development.* New York: Wiley.

Voydanoff, P. (Ed.). (1984). *Work and family: Changing roles of men and women.* Palo Alto, CA: Mayfield.

Voydanoff, P. (1988). Work role characteristics, family structure demands, and work/family conflict. *Journal of Marriage and the Family, 50,* 749–761.

Voydanoff, P., & Donnelly, B. W. (1990). *Adolescent sexuality and pregnancy.* Newbury Park, CA: Sage.

Wachowiak, D., & Bragg, H. (1980). Open marriage and marital adjustment. *Journal of Marriage and the Family, 42,* 57–62.

Waldron, H., & Routh, D. K. (1981). The effect of the first child on the marital relationship. *Journal of Marriage and the Family, 43,* 785–788.

Walen, S. R., & Roth, D. (1987). A cognitive approach. In J. H. Geer & W. T. O'Donohue (Eds.), *Theories of human sexuality.* New York: Plenum.

Walker, P. S., Berger, O. C., Green, R., Laub, D. R., Reynolds, C. L., & Wollman, L. (1981). *Standards of care: The hormonal and surgical sex reassignment of gender dysphoric persons.* Chicago: Harry Benjamin International Gender Dysphoria Association.

Wallace, H. M., & Vienonen, M. (1989). Teenage pregnancy in Sweden and Finland: Implications for the United States. *Journal of Adolescent Health Care, 10,* 231–236.

Wallerstein, J., & Blakeslee, S. (1989). *Second chances: Men, women, and children a decade after divorce.* New York: Ticknor & Fields.

Wallis, C. (1985, December 9). Children having children. *Time,* pp. 76–90.

Walsh, R. H. (1989). Premarital sex among teenagers and young adults. In K. McKinney & S. Sprecher (Eds.), *Human sexuality: The societal and interpersonal context.* Norwood, NJ: Ablex.

Waring, E. M., & Chelune, G. J. (1983). Marital intimacy and self-disclosure. *Journal of Clinical Psychology, 39,* 183–190.

Waring, E. M., & Russell, L. (1980). Cognitive family therapy. *Journal of Sex and Marital Therapy, 6,* 258–273.

Waring, E. M., Tillman, M. P., Frelick, L., Russell, L., & Weisz, G. (1981). Concepts of intimacy in the general population. *Journal of Nervous and Mental Disease, 168,* 471–474.

Warshaw, R. (1988). *I never called it rape.* New York: Harper & Row.

Washington, A. E. (1982). Update on treatment recommendations for gonococcal infections. *Review of Infectious Diseases, 5758–5771.*

Washington, A. E., Amos, P. S., & Brooks, M. A. (1986). The economic cost of pelvic inflammatory disease. *Journal of the American Medical Association, 255,* 1735–1738.

Washington, A. E., Johnson, R. M., & Sanders, L. L. (1987). Chlamydia trachomatis infections in the United States. *Journal of the American Medical Association, 257,* 2070–2073.

Washington, A. E., Sweet, R. L., & Shafer, M. (1985). Pelvic inflammatory disease and its sequelae in adolescents. *Journal of Adolescent Health Care, 6,* 298–310.

Waters, H. (1980). Don't just talk. Communicate! *Marriage and Family Living, 62,* 18–21.

Watson, M. A. (1981). Sexually open marriages: Three perspectives. *Alternate Lifestyles, 4,* 3–21.

Watters, D. N. (1987). Teaching about homosexuality: A review of the literature. *Journal of Sex Education and Therapy, 13,* 63–66.

Wattleton, F. (1986). *How to talk with your child about sexuality.* New York: Doubleday.

Way, P. O., & Stanecki, K. (1991). *How bad will it be? Modeling the AIDS epidemic in eastern Africa.* Washington, DC: Center for Educational Research.

Weber, J. N., & Weiss, R. A. (1988). HIV infection: The cellular picture. *Scientific American, 259,* 101–109.

Weeks, J. (1985). *Sexuality and its discontents.* London: Routledge & Kegan Paul.

Weg, R. B. (1983). *Sexuality in the later years: Roles and behavior.* New York: Academic Press.

Wehren, A., & DeLisi, R. (1983). The development of gender understanding: Judgments and explanations. *Child Development, 54,* 1568–1578.

Weinberg, G. (1972). *Society and the healthy homosexual.* New York: St. Martin's Press.

Weinberg, M. S., Williams, C. J., & Moser, C. A. (1984). The social constituents of sadomasochism. *Social Problems, 31,* 379–389.

Weinberg, T. S. (1987). Sadomasochism in the United States: A review of the recent sociological literature. *Journal of Sex Research, 25,* 50–69.

Weingarten, H. (1980). Remarriage and well-being: National survey evidence of social and psychological effects. *Journal of Family Issues, 1,* 533–559.

Weinstein, E., & Rosen, E. (1988a). Counseling victims of sexual assault. In E. Weinstein & E. Rosen (Eds.), *Sexuality counseling: Issues and implications.* Monterey, CA: Brooks/Cole.

Weinstein, E., & Rosen, E. (1988b). Intrafamily sexual intimacy. In E. Weinstein & E. Rosen (Eds.), *Sexuality counseling: Issues and implications.* Monterey, CA: Brooks/Cole.

Weinstein, E., & Rosen, E. (1991). The development of adolescent sexual intimacy: Implications for counseling. *Adolescence, 26,* 331–339.

Weis, K., & Borges, S. (1973). Victimology and rape: The case of the legitimate victim. *Issues in Criminology, 8,* 71–115.

Weis, R. D., & Mirin, S. M. (1987). *Cocaine.* Washington, DC: American Psychiatric Press.

Weiss, L., & Meadow, R. (1983). Group treatment for female sexual dysfunction. *Arizona Medicine, 9,* 626–628.

Weller, R., & Halikas, J. (1982). Marijuana use and sexual pleasure. *Journal of Sex Research, 18,* 1–17.

Werner, P. D., & LaRussa, G. W. (1988). Persistence and change in sex-role stereotypes. *Sex Roles, 12,* 1089–1100.

Wertheimer, D. M. (1989). Victims of violence: A rising tide of anti-gay sentiment. In O. Pocs (Ed.), *Human sexuality 89/90.* Guilford, CT: Dushkin.

Wertz, D. C., & Fletcher, J. C. (1989). *Ethics and human genetics: A cross-cultural perspective.* Heidelberg: Springer-Verlag.

Wertz, R. W., & Wertz, D. C. (1989). *Lying-in: A history of childbirth in America.* New Haven, CT: Yale University Press.

Westoff, C. (1988). Contraceptive paths toward the reduction of unintended pregnancy and abortion. *Family Planning Perspectives, 20,* 4–6.

Westoff, C., Calot, G., & Foster, A. (1983). Teenage fertility in developed nations. *International Family Planning Perspectives, 9,* 45–50.

Westrom, L., & Mardh, P. A. (1982). Genital chlamydial infections in the female. In P. A. Mardh (Ed.), *Chlamydial infections.* Amsterdam: Elsevier Biomedical Press.

Wheeler, L, Reis, H., & Nezlek, J. (1983). Loneliness, social interaction, and sex-roles. *Journal of Personality and Social Psychology, 45,* 943–953.

Wheeler, R. J., & Berliner, L. (1988). Treating the effects of sexual abuse on children. In G. E. Wyatt & G. J. Powell (Eds.), *The lasting effects of child sexual abuse.* Newbury Park, CA: Sage.

Wheeless, I. R., Wheeless, V. E., & Baus, R. (1984). Sexual communication, communication satisfaction, and solidarity in the developmental stages of intimate relationships. *Western Journal of Speech Communication, 48,* 217–230.

Wheeless, V. E., Zakahi, W. R., & Chan, M. B. (1988). A test of self-disclosure based on perceptions of a target's loneliness and gender orientation. *Communication Quarterly, 36,* 109–121.

Whipple, B., & Ogden, G. (1989). *Safe encounters: How women can say yes to pleasure and no to unsafe sex.* New York: McGraw-Hill.

White, D. (1981, September 15). Pursuit of the ultimate aphrodisiac. *Psychology Today,* pp. 9–11.

White, G. L., & Knight, T. D. (1984). Misattribution of arousal and attraction: Effects of salience of explanations for arousal. *Journal of Experimental Social Psychology, 20,* 55–64.

White, P., Mascalo, A., Thomas, S., & Shoun, S. (1986). Husbands' and wives' perceptions of marital intimacy and wives' stresses in dual-career marriages. *Family Perspective, 20,* 27–35.

Whiteford, L. M. (1989). Commercial surrogacy: Social issues behind the controversy. In L. Whiteford & M. Polan (Eds.), *Approaches to human reproduction.* Boulder, CO: Westview.

Whitehurst, R. N. (1985). There are a number of equally valid forms of marriage, such as multiple marriage, swinging, adultery, and open marriage. In H. Feldman & M. Feldman (Eds.), *Current controversies in marriage and family.* Beverly Hills, CA: Sage.

Whiting, B. B., & Edwards, C. P. (1988). *Children of different worlds: The formation of social behavior.* Cambridge, MA: Harvard University Press.

Whitley, B. E., & Schofield, J. W. (1984, August). *Adolescent contraceptive use: Models, research, and directions.* Paper presented at the American Psychological Association annual meeting, Toronto.

Whitley, B. E., Jr. (1990). The relationships of heterosexuals' attributions for the causes of homosexuality to attitudes toward lesbians and gay men. *Personality and Social Psychology Bulletin, 16,* 369–377.

Wiest, W. (1977). Semantic differential profiles of orgasm and other experiences among men and women. *Sex Roles, 3,* 399–403.

Wiggins, J. S., & Holzmuller, A. (1981). Further evidence on androgyny and interpersonal flexibility. *Journal of Research in Personality, 15,* 67–80.

Wilbanks, G. D. (1987). Update on genital herpes. *Modern Medicine, 58,* 37–52.

Wilen, J. B., & Petersen, A. C. (1980, June). *Young adolescents' responses to the timing of pubertal changes.* Paper presented at the Psychology of Adolescence Conference, Chicago.

Williams, F., LaRose, R., & Frost, F. (1981). *Children, television, and sex-role stereotyping.* New York: Praeger.

Williams, G. J. (1984). Management and treatment of parental abuse and neglect of children: An overview. In G. J. Williams & J. Money (Eds.), *Traumatic abuse and neglect of children at home.* Baltimore: Johns Hopkins University Press.

Williams, J. A., Vernon, J. A., Williams, M. C., & Malecha, K. (1987). Sex role socialization in picture books: An update. *Social Science Quarterly, 68,* 148–156.

Williams, T. M., & Kornblum, W. (1985). *Growing up poor.* Lexington, MA: Lexington Books.

Willis, J. (1985). *Comparing contraceptives.* Publication No. 85-1123. Rockville, MD: Department of Health and Human Services.

Wilson, E. (1975). *Sociobiology: The new synthesis.* Cambridge, MA, & London: Belknap Press of Harvard University.

Wilson, M. N. (1989). Child development in the context of the extended family. *American Psychologist, 44,* 380–385.

Wilson, P., & Kirby, D. (1984). *Sexuality education: A curriculum for adolescents.* Santa Cruz, CA: Network Publications.

Wincze, J. P. (1989). Assessment and treatment of atypical sexual behavior. In S. R. Leiblum & R. C. Rosen (Eds.), *Principles and practice of sex therapy* (2nd ed.). New York: Guilford.

Wincze, J., Bansal, S., & Malamud, M. (1986). Effects of medroxyprogesterone acetate on subjective arousal, arousal to erotic stimulation, and nocturnal penile tumescence in male sex offenders. *Archives of Sexual Behavior, 4,* 293–306.

Wise, T. N. (1985). Fetishism-etiology and treatment: A review from multiple perspectives. *Comprehensive Psychiatry, 26,* 249–257.

Witherington, R. (1988). Suction device therapy in the management of erectile impotence. *Urologic Clinics of North America, 15,* 123–128.

Witkin, H., Mednick, S., Schulsinger, F., Bakkestrom, E., Christiansen, K., Goodenough, D., Hirschorn, K., Lundsteen, C., Owen, D., Philip, J., Rubin, D., & Stoking, M. (1976). Criminality in XYY and XXY men. *Science, 193,* 147–155.

Wolfe, L. (1971). *Love between women.* New York: St. Martin's Press.

Wolfe, L. (1982). *The Cosmo report*. New York: Bantam.

Wolfson, C. (1986). Midwives and home birth: Social, medical, and legal perspectives. *Hastings Law Journal, 37*, 909–967.

Wolhandler, J., & Weber, R. (1984). Physical and emotional aspects of abortion. *The new our bodies, ourselves*. New York: Simon & Schuster.

Wood, S. C., & Dean, K. S. (1984). *Final report: Sexual abuse of males research project*. Washington, DC: National Center on Child Abuse and Neglect.

World Health Organization. (1991, April 1). Update: AIDS cases reported to surveillance, forecasting, and impact assessment unit. Global Program on AIDS, Geneva.

Worthington-Roberts, B., & Williams, S. R. (1989). *Nutrition in pregnancy and lactation* (4th ed.). St. Louis, MO: Mosby.

Wright, M. R. (1989). Body image satisfaction in adolescent girls and boys. *Journal of Youth and Adolescence, 18*, 71–84.

Wroblewski, R., & Huston, A. C. (1987). Televised occupational stereotypes and their effects on early adolescents: Are they changing? *Journal of Early Adolescence, 7*, 283–297.

Wurtele, S. K. (1986). Teaching personal safety skills for potential prevention of sexual abuse: A comparison of treatments. *Journal of Consulting and Clinical Psychology, 54*, 688–692.

Wyatt, G. E., & Peters, S. D. (1986). Issues in the definition of child sexual abuse in prevalence research. *Child Abuse and Neglect, 10*, 231–240.

Wyatt, G. E., Peters, S. D., & Guthrie, D. (1988). Kinsey revisited: Part I. Comparisons of the sexual socialization and sexual behavior of white women over 35 years. *Archives of Sexual Behavior, 17*, 201–210.

Wyatt, G. E., & Powell, G. J. (Eds.). (1988). *The lasting effects of child sexual abuse*. Newbury Park, CA: Sage.

Yaffee, M., & Fenwick, E. (1988a). *Sexual happiness for women: A practical approach*. New York: Henry Holt.

Yaffee, M., & Fenwick, E. (1988b). *Sexual happiness for men: A practical approach*. New York: Henry Holt.

Yamaguchi, K., & Kandell, D. (1987). Drug use and other determinants of premarital pregnancy and its outcome: A dynamic analysis of competing life events. *Journal of Marriage and the Family, 49*, 257–270.

Yankelovich, D. (1981). *New rules in American life: Searching for self-fulfillment in a world turned upside down*. New York: Random House.

Yankelovich, D., Clancy, D., & Schulman, I. (1986, November 24). How the public feels about school sexuality education. *Time*, pp. 58–59.

Yarbrough, L. (1987). AIDS survival manual. Sacramento, CA: GIWC.

Yegidis, B. L. (1986). Date rape and other forced sexual encounters among college students. *Journal of Sex Education and Therapy, 12*, 51–54.

Yelsma, P. (1986). Marriage vs. cohabitation: Couples' communication practices and satisfaction. *Journal of Communication, 36*, 94–107.

Yelsma, P., & Athappilly, K. (1986, November 2). *Comparisons among Indian and American couples' communication practices and marital satisfaction*. Paper presented at the Speech Communication Association Convention, Chicago.

Yelsma, P., & Brown, C. T. (1985). Gender roles, biological sex, and predisposition to conflict management. *Sex Roles, 12*, 731–747.

Yllo, K., & Finkelhor, D. (1985). Marital rape. In A. W. Burgess (Ed.), *Rape and sexual assault: A research handbook*. New York: Garland.

Yoder, J. D., & Nichols, R. C. (1980). A life perspective comparison of married and divorced persons. *Journal of Marriage and the Family, 43*, 413–419.

Young, W. C. (1961). Hormones and mating behavior. In W. C. Young (Ed.), *Sex and internal secretions*. Baltimore: Williams & Wilkins.

Young, W. M. (1988). Structuring a response to child sexual abuse. In A. Salter (Ed.), *Treating child sex offenders and victims*. Newbury Park, CA: Sage.

Zabin, L. S., & Clark, S. D., Jr. (1981). Why the delay: A study of teenage family planning clinic patients. *Family Planning Perspectives, 13*, 205, 217.

Zabin, L. S., Hirsh, M. B., Smith, E. A., Street, R., & Hardy, J. B. (1986). Evaluation of a pregnancy prevention program for urban teenagers. *Family Planning Perspectives, 18*, 119–126.

Zahn-Waxler, C., Kochanska, G., Krupnick, J., & McKnew, D. (1990). Patterns of guilt in children of depressed and well mothers. *Developmental Psychology, 26*(1), 51–59.

Zehring, J. W. (1986). Are you a good listener? *Marriage and Family Living, 68*(3), 22–25.

Zelnick, M., Kantner, J. F., & Ford, K. (1981). *Sex and pregnancy in adolescence*. Beverly Hills, CA: Sage.

Zelnick, M., & Shah, T. (1983). First intercourse among young Americans. *Family Planning Perspectives, 15*, 64–70.

Zellman, G. L., & Goodchild, J. D. (1983). Becoming sexual in adolescence. In E. R. Allgeier & N. B. McCormick (Eds.), *Changing boundaries: Gender roles and sexual behavior*. Palo Alto, CA: Mayfield.

Zheng, S., & Colombo, J. (1989). Sibling configuration and gender differences in preschool social participation. *Journal of Genetic Psychology, 150*, 45–50.

Zilbergeld, B. (1978). *Male sexuality: A guide to sexual fulfillment*. Boston: Little, Brown.

Zill, N. (1988). Behavior, achievement, and health problems among children in stepfamilies: Findings from a national survey of child health. In E. M. Hetherington & J. D. Arasteh (Eds.), *Impact of divorce, single-parenting, and step-parenting on children*. Hillsdale, NJ: Erlbaum.

Zillman, D., & Bryant, J. (1983). Effects of massive exposure to pornography. In N. Malamuth & E. Donnerstein (Eds.), *Pornography and sexual aggression*. Orlando, FL: Academic Press.

Zimmer, D. (1983). Interaction patterns and communication skills in sexually distressed, maritally distressed, and normal couples: Two experimental studies. *Journal of Sex and Marital Therapy, 9*, 251–265.

Zimmer, D., Borchardt, E., & Fischle, C. (1983). Sexual fantasies of sexually distressed and non-distressed men and women: An empirical consideration. *Journal of Sex and Marital Therapy, 9*, 38–50.

Zimmerman, R. S. (1989). AIDS: Social causes, patterns, "cures," and problems. In K. McKinney & S. Sprecher (Eds.), *Human sexuality: The societal and interpersonal context*. Norwood, NJ: Ablex.

Zimmerman, R. S., & Olson, K. (1988, August 12). *AIDS-related risk behavior and behavior change in a heterosexual, sexually active sample: A test of three models of prevention*. Paper presented at the American Sociological Association meeting, Atlanta.

Zinik, G. (1983). *The relationship between sexual orientation and eroticism, cognitive flexibility, and negative affect*.

Unpublished doctoral dissertation, University of California, Santa Barbara.

Zinik, G. (1985). Identity conflict or adaptive flexibility? Bisexuality reconsidered. In F. Klein & T. J. Wolf (Eds.), *Two lives to lead: Bisexuality in men and women*. New York: Harrington Park Press.

Zinn, M. B., & Eitzen, D. S. (1990). *Diversity in families* (2nd ed.). New York: Harper & Row.

Zuckerman, D. M., & Sayre, D. H. (1982). Cultural role expectations and children's sex-role concepts. *Sex Roles, 8*, 453–462.

Zuckerman, E. J. Viral hepatitis. (1982). *Practical Gastroenterology, 6*, 21–27.

Credits and Acknowledgments

Photos

CHAPTER 1   page xviii Olive R. Pierce/Stock, Boston; 4 Bob Daemmrich/ The Image Works; 6 United Nations Photo/Ian Steele; 11 Culver Pictures; 16 New York Public Library Picture Collection; 18 Culver Pictures; 19 Topham/The Image Works; 22 The Bettmann Archive; 29 Jim Whitmer/Stock, Boston.

CHAPTER 2   page 32 Robert A. Isaacs/Photo Researchers, Inc.; 34 (top & bottom) Topham/The Image Works; 35 AP/Wide World Photos; 36 The Bettmann Archive; 38 UPI/Bettmann Newsphotos; 41 Joan Liftin.

CHAPTER 3   page 59 Charles Gatewood/The Image Works; 68 (left & right) W. Hill, Jr./The Image Works; 75 Sara Krulwich/N.Y.T. Pictures; 80 Hazel Hankin/Stock, Boston; 83 Stewart Smucker/Anthro Photo.

CHAPTER 4   page 87 Spencer Grant/Monkmeyer Press; 91 Joel Gordon; 100, 103 Farrall Instruments, Grand Island, Nebraska; 106 Wesley Bocxe/Photo Researchers, Inc.; 109 Courtesy of Helen Singer Kaplan, M.D., Ph.D.; 112 Bob Daemmrich/The Image Works.

CHAPTER 5   page 120 AP/Wide World Photos; 123 By permission of the Upjohn Company, Kalamazoo, Michigan and Margery Shaw, M.D.; 130 Laimute E. Druskis/Photo Researchers, Inc.; 134 Bob Daemmrich/ Stock, Boston; 135 Richard Hutchings/Photo Researchers, Inc.; 140 (top) The San Francisco Examiner; 140 (bottom) Bob McLeod/The San Francisco Examiner; 141 Joel Gordon.

CHAPTER 6   page 153 David M. Grossman/Photo Researchers; 155 Rhoda Sidney; 157 Harriet Ganx/The Image Works; 161 Arvind Garg/Photo Researchers, Inc.; 163 AP/Wide World Photos; 169 Ira Kirschenbaum/Stock, Boston; 173 Culver Pictures; 182 Michael Malyszko/Stock, Boston.

CHAPTER 7   page 190 Arlene Collins/Monkmeyer Press; 194 Spencer Grant/Photo Researchers, Inc.; 195 Joel Gordon; 198 M.B. Duda/ Photo Researchers, Inc.; 200 Don Roberts/Selznick International Pictures; 203 Spencer Grant/Stock, Boston; 207 Joel Gordon; 209 Hella Hammid/Photo Researchers, Inc.

CHAPTER 8   page 214 Barbara Alper/Stock, Boston; 216 George Holton/Photo Researchers, Inc.; 217 Topham/The Image Works; 222 Joel Gordon; 224 Beringer/Dratch/The Image Works; 243 Lily Solmssen/ Photo Researchers, Inc.

CHAPTER 9   page 250 Joel Gordon; 254 Jan Lukas/Photo Researchers, Inc.; 259 Ken Karp; 260 Barbara Rios/Photo Researchers, Inc.; 264 Ira Kirschenbaum/Stock, Boston; 267 Joel Gordon; 279 Richard Sobol/Stock, Boston.

CHAPTER 10   page 285 James Stevenson/Science Photo Library/Photo Researchers, Inc.; 286 Elizabeth Crews/Stock, Boston; 293 Erika Stone/ Photo Researchers, Inc.; 295 Joel Gordon; 297 Laimute E. Druskis/ Photo Researchers; 300 Hazel Hankin/Stock, Boston; 307 Alexander Tsiaras/Photo Researchers, Inc.; 317 Jeff Davis/New York Times Pictures.

CHAPTER 11   page 320 Renee Lyn/Photo Researchers, Inc.; 322 Culver Pictures, Inc.; 325 (left, right, & middle), 335 Joel Gordon; 338 Teri Stratford; 339 Peter Menzel/Stock, Boston; 344 Shirley Zeiberg; 346 Deborah Davis/Photo Edit.

CHAPTER 12   page 352 Joel Gordon; 355 UPI/Bettmann; 360, 361 Joel Gordon; 364 NYPL; 365 Teri Leigh Stratford, materials courtesy of Planned Parenthood, NYC; 368 Joel Gordon; 369 Teri Leigh Stratford; 382 Michael Dwyer/Stock, Boston.

CHAPTER 13   page 387 E. Mandelmann/WHO; 391 Teri Leigh Stratford; 394 John Coletti/Stock; 397 Steve Takatsuno; 400 Joel Gordon; 402 Michael Hayman/Stock, Boston; 403 (left) Laimute Druskis/Stock, Boston, (right) Blair Seitz/Photo Researchers.

CHAPTER 14   page 413 Randy Matusow; 417 Joseph Szabo/Photo Researchers, Inc.; 418 Anthro-Photo File; 423 Barbara Alper/Stock, Boston; 426 Spencer Grant/Monkmeyer Press Photo; 430 Francene Keery/ Stock, Boston; 437 Elizabeth Crews/The Image Works; 440 Morgan Gwenwald.

CHAPTER 15   page 443 Randy Matusow; 448 Teri Leigh Stratford; 452 AP/Wide World Photos; 453 Ken Karp; 455 Charles Gatewood; 463 Elizabeth Crews/Stock, Boston; 466 Joel Gordon.

CHAPTER 16   page 474 Randy Matusow; 477 John Liftin/Actuality Inc.; 479 Michael Siluk/The Image Works; 484 Joan Liftin/Actuality Inc.; 490 Nancy Durrell McKenna/Photo Researchers, Inc.; 493 Van Bucher/ Photo Researchers, Inc.

CHAPTER 17   page 502 Barbara Rios/Photo Researchers, Inc.; 505, 507, 509, 515 Centers for Disease Control, Atlanta; 526 Courtesy of Saul Hoffman, M.D.

CHAPTER 18   page 538 Barbara Alper/Stock, Boston; 543 Centers for Disease Control; 546 AP/Wide World Photos; 548 John Griffin/The Image Works; 550, 552 AP/Wide World Photos; 559 W. Campbell/ Sygma; 562 Bob Mahoney; 563 Joel Gordon.

CHAPTER 19   page 566 Mary Ellen Mark/Library; 570 Laimute E. Druskis; 576 Mary Allen Mark; 580 Charles Gatewood; 583 Barbara Rios/Photo Researchers; 584 Bettye Lane/Photo Researchers; 588 Mariette Pathy Allen.

CHAPTER 20   page 594 Marc Anderson; 598 Michael Grecco/Stock, Boston; 602 Chester Higgins, Jr./Photo Researchers; 604 Joseph Schuyler/Stock, Boston; 607 Bonnie Freer/Photo Researchers; 613, 614 Bettye Lane/Photo Researchers; 616 Ethan Hoffman/Picture Project.

CHAPTER 21   page 621 Michael Weisbrot/Stock, Boston; 627 AP/Wide World Photos; 634 Randy Matusow; 640 Joel Gordon; 643 Charles Gatewood; 646, 649 AP/Wide World Photos.

Inserts

CHAPTER 3   *Illustrations:* Figs. 3–5, 3–7, 3–10, and 3–12 Adapted from Martini, *Fundamentals of Anatomy and Physiology*, 2nd ed., Prentice Hall, Englewood Cliffs, New Jersey. Drawings by Craig Luce. Figs. 3–3, 3–4, 3–13, and 3–14 Adapted from Martini, *Fundamentals of Anatomy and Physiology*, 2nd ed., Prentice Hall, Englewood

707

Cliffs, New Jersey. Drawings by William C. Ober, M.D. and Claire W. Garrison, R.N. *Photos*: Figs. 3–2 and 3–11 Justine Hill; Fig. 3–7 Joel Gordon.

CHAPTER 10 *Illustrations:* Fig. 10–2 Adapted from Martini, *Fundamentals of Anatomy and Physiology,* 2nd ed., Prentice Hall, Englewood Cliffs, New Jersey. Drawing by William C. Ober, M.D. and Claire W. Garrison, R.N. *Photos:* Sperm penetrating egg, D.W. Fawcett/Science Source/Photo Researchers; all others, Petit Format/Nestle/Science Source/Photo Researchers.

Cartoons

Ch. 1: Drawing by Frascino; © 1991 The New Yorker Magazine, Inc.; **Ch. 2:** © 1993 by Sidney Harris; **Ch. 3:** Copyright © 1992 John Caldwell; **Ch. 4:** Reproduced by Special Permission of *Playboy* Magazine. Copyright © 1991 by *Playboy;* **Ch. 5:** Drawing by Weber; © 1990 The New Yorker Magazine, Inc.; **Ch. 6:** From *The Wall Street Journal*-Permission, Cartoon Features Syndicate; **Ch. 7:** Scott Arthur Masear; **Ch. 8:** Drawing by Mankoff; © 1991 The New Yorker Magazine, Inc.; **Ch. 9:** © 1993 by Sidney Harris; **Ch. 10:** © 1993 by Sidney Harris; **Ch. 11:** Silvio Redinger; **Ch. 12:** Reproduced by special permission of *Playboy Magazine*. Copyright © Fed. 1980 by Playboy; **Ch. 13:** Cartoon by John Jonik; **Ch. 14:** © 1993 by Sidney Harris; **Ch. 15:** Drawing by Cline; © 1991 The New Yorker Magazine, Inc.; **Ch. 16:** Scott Arthur Masear; **Ch. 17:** Stewart Slocum; **Ch. 18:** Chas. Almon; **Ch. 19:** Chas. Almon; **Ch. 21:** © 1993 by Sidney Harris.

Further Acknowledgments

Fig. 2–10 Reprinted with the permission of Macmillan Publishing Company from *Research Techniques for the Health Sciences* by L. Rubinson and J. Neutens. Copyright © 1987 by Macmillan Publishing Company, Inc. **Quiz, pp. 49–51**, Copyright © 1990 by The Kinsey Institute for Research in Sex, Gender, and Reproduction. From the book *The Kinsey Institute New Report on Sex* and reprinted through arrangement with St. Martin's Press, Inc., New York, NY. **Fig. 4–1** From Geer/Heiman/Lietenberg, *Human Sexuality*, © 1984 p.52. Reprinted by permission of Prentice Hall, Englewood Cliffs, New Jersey. **Fig. 4–3** Adapted from Martini, *Fundamentals of Anatomy and Physiology*, 2nd ed., Prentice Hall, Englewood Cliffs, New Jersey. Drawing by William C. Ober, M.D. and Claire W. Garrison, R.N. **Fig. 4–6** From *On Sex and Human Loving* by William H. Masters, M.D., Virginia E. Johnson and Robert C. Kolodny, M.D. Copyright © 1982, 1985, 1986, 1988 by William H. Masters, M.D., Virginia E. Johnson and Robert C. Kolodny, M.D. By permission of Little, Brown and Company. **Fig. 5–4** From *Human Sexuality* 4th Edition by William H. Masters, et al. Copyright © 1992 by William H. Masters, Virginia E. Johnson, Robert C. Kolodny. Reprinted by permission of HarperCollins Publishers. **Fig. 7–1** From *Management* by Arthur G. Bedeian, copyright © 1986 by The Dryden Press. Reprinted by permission of the publisher. **Quiz, p. 197,** From *Sexual Happiness: A Practical Approach* by Maurice Yaffe and Elizabeth Fenwick. Copyright © 1986 by Dorling Kindersley Ltd. Copyright © 1988 by Maurice Yaffe and Elizabeth Fenwick. Reprinted by permission of Henry Holt and Company, Inc. **Lyrics, p. 341,** From "My Blue Heaven," words and music by Leo Feist and Walter Donaldson. Copyright 1927 by MCA Music Publishing, a division of MCA Inc.; George Whiting Publishing Co.; and Donaldson Publishing Co. Copyright renewed. Used by permission. All rights reserved. **Fig. 12–11** From Kelley/Byrne, *Exploring Human Sexuality*, copyright © 1992, p. 121. Reprinted by permission of Prentice Hall, Englewood Cliffs, New Jersey.

Index